PLACESRATED
ALMANAC

The Classic Guide for Finding Your Best
Places to Live in America

7th Edition

DAVID SAVAGEAU

PlacesRated
Books

ACKNOWLEDGMENTS

This 7th (and 25th anniversary) edition of *Places Rated Almanac* could not have begun without insightful criticisms from hundreds of readers. Nor would the book have been finished minus the generous advice from experts whom we've come to know personally over the years.

PUBLISHER'S NOTE

This book is a creative work protected by applicable copyright laws. The publisher has added value to facts and statistics by original selection, coordination, expression, arrangement, and classification of the information. It is published for general reference and not as a substitute for independent verification by users when circumstances warrant. Care and diligence have been used in the preparation of this book. All data sources are explicitly cited. The interpretation of these data and the views expressed are solely the publisher's and not necessarily those of the persons and organizations that have furnished them.

PLACES RATED BOOKS LLC

Box 77464

National Capital Station

Washington, DC 20013

Find us online at www.placesratedbooks.com

Copyright © 2007 by Places Rated Books LLC

Maps copyright by Places Rated Partners

Digital Cartography

Gary Antonetti, Ortelius Design

Hillsboro, Wisconsin

Design & Layout

Brian Davis, Bombastic Graphics

www.bombasticgraphics.com

ISBN 978-0-9793199-07

ISSN 1526-517X

Special Sales

Places Rated Almanac is available at quantity discounts with bulk purchase for educational, business, or sales promotional use. For information, please write to: Special Sales Department, Places Rated Books LLC, Box 77464 National Capital Station, Washington, DC 20013.

Manufactured in the United States of America

Table of Contents

TRANSPORTATION 217

EDUCATION 279

HEALTH CARE 371

RECREATION 417

Table of Contents

Preface

eaders may wonder about differences in the final rankings in *Places Rated*'s previous (2000) edition and this one. There are five reasons:

New scoring methods. Scores in each chapter are expressed in percents where 50 marks the point where half of the areas are better and the other half worse. Using this scheme, a score of 30 means seven out of ten metro areas do better. A score of 75 means three out of four metro areas lag. In addition, the methods used to rate each area in Climate, Crime, Transportation, Education, Ambiance, Health Care, and Recreation have been fine tuned.

New scoring elements. The scoring has been further refined by new data elements. For example, the number of international nonstop flights originating from the local airport has been added to the Transportation chapter. For another example, the number of historic districts and contributing buildings are added to the Ambiance scoring mix.

The interval effect. A minor change in just a handful of the 379 metro areas has resulted in shifting ranks throughout. Some metro areas have nearly the same Crime figures as they had in previous editions, yet their rankings in this category slipped. They aren't necessarily getting more dangerous; it's just that other places are getting safer faster and have moved them to a lower ranking.

Time series data. Local population figures (for deriving per capita access to public golf courses, for example), prices (for measuring living costs), and household income have increased at varying rates since the 2000 edition was published.

New geography. In June 2003, the federal government announced wholesale changes in metropolitan area geography based on information from the 2000 Census. Not only were

nearly 50 new metro areas created, but most of the traditional ones grew larger in area thanks to longer commutes. Metro Atlanta, for example, took in three core counties and another fifteen suburban ones at the start of the 1990s. Now it embraces twenty-eight counties.

Places Rated, it is said later in this book, is like a snapshot of a moving target. Metro areas are dynamic and won't sit still for their numerical portraits. With so much in life that's changeable, you'd be wise to supplement this book with your own verification. For now, what follows are fresh facts and figures on nine factors most of us would agree influence livability in metropolitan America.

Introduction

O h, for San Francisco's cool ambience, the hot job market in Las Vegas, for Miami's winters and the safe streets of St. Cloud. Ah, for Salt Lake City skiing and Topeka's affordable homes, for Pittsburgh's Carnegie Museums, for Washington's convenient Metro. If you could snap your fingers and suddenly find yourself living somewhere else, would you?

Forget the usual constraints: Family ties, friendships, a good job, lack of cash, and a sentimental attachment to familiar turf can certainly snap you out of such a fantasy. Let's put the question in another way: What if there was a place somewhere in America that suited you better than the one you're living in now and you knew nothing about it?

Every so often people tell pollsters they would rather be somewhere else when asked whether they are satisfied with where they currently live. Most of us change our address eleven times in our lifetimes, but we do it by simply moving out of one house and into another within the same city. However, there are 7 million Americans who move to another state each year. They may have 7 million different reasons for relocating beyond their old city's limits, but they do have one thing in common - the need for information.

Like its predecessors, this 7th (and 25th anniversary) edition of *Places Rated Almanac* is meant for people thinking of moving as well as for anyone who enjoys learning about cities and towns and what they have to offer. As an almanac, it provides thousands of facts - found neither in standard guidebooks nor in chamber of commerce blandishments - about all of the 379 officially-defined metropolitan areas in which four out of five of us live.

Places Rated Almanac is more than a collection of interesting, odd, and useful information about metropolitan areas. It also rates and ranks the metro areas on nine factors that influence the quality of a place: ambience, housing, the local economy, transportation, education, health care, crime, recreation, and climate. *Places Rated Almanac* could be considered a self-help book with one difference: Instead of pointing the way toward inner peace or upward mobility as most self-help books do, it helps you decide whether geographical mobility could lead to a more satisfying life.

Where you live affects your happiness and personal success. It just may be that

Postal Abbreviations and Regions

The state abbreviations used after each metro area name come from the Post Office's standards for shortening state names to two characters. Here is a guide.

AK	Alaska	MS	Mississippi
AL	Alabama	MT	Montana
AR	Arkansas	NC	North Carolina
AZ	Arizona	ND	North Dakota
CA	California	NE	Nebraska
CO	Colorado	NH	New Hampshire
CT	Connecticut	NJ	New Jersey
DC	District of Columbia	NM	New Mexico
		NV	Nevada
DE	Delaware	NY	New York
FL	Florida	OH	Ohio
GA	Georgia	OK	Oklahoma
HI	Hawaii	OR	Oregon
IA	Iowa	PA	Pennsylvania
ID	Idaho	RI	Rhode Island
IL	Illinois	SC	South Carolina
IN	Indiana	SD	South Dakota
KS	Kansas	TN	Tennessee
KY	Kentucky	TX	Texas
LA	Louisiana	UT	Utah
MA	Massachusetts	VA	Virginia
MD	Maryland	VT	Vermont
ME	Maine	WA	Washington
MI	Michigan	WI	Wisconsin
MN	Minnesota	WV	West Virginia
MO	Missouri	WY	Wyoming

your present location doesn't fit your needs and preferences. After all, given the amazing variety that American cities offer, what are the odds that the place you happen to live is the right one for you?

After using *Places Rated Almanac*, you may very well confirm your hunch that you've never had it so good. But if you're part of the discontented majority identified by pollsters, you may find yourself asking: What am I waiting for?

RATING PLACES: AN AMERICAN TRADITION

"The tradition of hating New York started long before it began asking the rest of us to pay its bills while condescendingly viewing us as amusing rustics," the late Mike Royko once wrote in one of his wonderful *Chicago Sun-Times* columns. "Actually, I like New York," he continued. "There are better reasons to hate cities like Cleveland or Indianapolis or Detroit or Dallas. But I do dislike New Yorkers."

How times change. On 9/11/01, the Big Apple became America's most loved city and its firefighters, cops, and ordinary citizens became a new national ideal for true grit, compassion, and grace under pressure. *Money Magazine* even dropped its annual survey of best places to live and saluted New York for its own special livability.

It may seem the utmost of brass, this business of judging places. Yet everyone does it, privately. Some suspect that culture in Omaha or Des Moines or Pocatello is a contradiction. Others surmise that daily life in Miami consists of surviving drug-trade shoot-outs, that snowy and windy Fargo is no place for the seasonally depressed, that Waco has more than a few berserk evangelists walking about, and that people in Los Angeles spend most of their waking hours behind a steering wheel waiting for the Big Temblor.

Judging places from best to worst with numbers may seem the highest effrontery of all. Ultimately, how can intangible things like friendliness and optimism be measured with statistics? Yet numeracy is almost as strong an American character trait as literacy. When it comes to choosing where to live, people have been digesting statistics for a long, long time. To sell newcomers on settling in colonial Maryland instead of neighboring Virginia, 17th-century promoters put together figures showing heavier livestock, more plentiful game, and lower mortality from foul air and Indian attacks.

California for Health, Wealth, and Residence, just one volume in a library of post-Civil War guides touting the West's superior quality of life, compiled data to show the climate along the southern Pacific coast to be the world's best. Not so, countered the Union Pacific Railroad's land office in 1871; settlers will find the most "genial and healthy" seasons in western Kansas.

In this century, the statistical nets were flung even wider. "There are plenty of Americans who regard Kansas as almost barbaric," wrote H. L. Mencken, "just as there are other Americans who shudder whenever they think of Arkansas, Ohio, Indiana, Oklahoma, Texas, or California." Californians brag that their state burns more gasoline per capita, attracts more retired farmers, produces more movies, jails more labor agitators, and supports more "inventors of new religions" than anywhere else, he noted, "but everywhere else there are only scoffs."

Mencken wrote these words in a 1931 issue of his *American Mercury* magazine to introduce his formula for measuring the progress of civilization in each of the states. He mixed the numbers of Boy Scouts and *Atlantic Monthly* subscribers with lynchings and pellagra cases, added a dash of Who's Who listing along with rates for divorce and murder, threw in figures for rainfall and gasoline consumption, and found that, hands down, Mississippi was the worst American state.

Fast forward seven decades later. Delaware, the 21st Century's new worst state "is a rapacious parasite ... with a long history of disloyalty and avarice," according to *The New Republic.* It is bad enough that the tiny state was the last to ban public whipping (it flogged convicts until 1952) and the last Union state to ban slavery, it is now home to an "axis of evil" that takes in credit card companies and corporations that prefer lax regulation. And, it enjoys hustling money from non-residents, by means of its ubiquitous tollbooths on the state's turnpike.

So much for states. What about cities? A few years after Mencken's rant, well-known educator E.L. Thorndike joined the search for the best place in his 1939 book, *Your City.* Using numbers like Mencken did (but a lot more of them), several of his findings still surprise. For one, the numbers showed Los Angeles to be the country's most habitable city. For another, there was a strong connection between lax church attendance and livability, i.e., the more people sitting in pews on Sunday, the worse the city.

Let's fast forward again, this time to a book

Population Size

The metro area nearest the population midpoint is Waco, TX, with 225,340 people. Sixty-one metro areas have more than 1 million people, and together these giants have more people than the other 318 metro areas *combined.*

Smallest	2007 Population
Carson City, NV	58,500
Lewiston, ID-WA	59,879
Casper, WY	69,043
Hinesville-Fort Stewart, GA	71,824
Columbus, IN	74,189
Sandusky, OH	79,531
Great Falls, MT	79,801
Danville, IL	81,812
Corvallis, OR	81,891
Ames, IA	84,622
Cheyenne, WY	85,202
Pocatello, ID	85,766
Fairbanks, AK	87,193
Elmira, NY	89,467

Largest	2007 Population
New York-White Plains, NY-NJ	11,613,029
Los Angeles-Long Beach, CA	9,978,085
Chicago-Naperville-Joliet, IL	7,984,928
Houston-Sugar Land, TX	5,394,479
Atlanta-Sandy Springs, GA	4,945,063
Washington, DC-VA-MD-WV	4,194,418
Dallas-Plano-Irving, TX	3,986,718
Riverside-San Bernardino, CA	3,948,512
Phoenix-Mesa-Scottsdale, AZ	3,936,377
Philadelphia, PA	3,907,650
Minneapolis-St. Paul, MN-WI	3,252,803
San Diego-Carlsbad, CA	3,127,038
Santa Ana-Anaheim-Irvine, CA	3,122,879
Nassau-Suffolk, NY	2,854,015
St. Louis, MO-IL	2,809,316
Baltimore-Towson, MD	2,735,489
Tampa-St. Petersburg, FL	2,677,041
Oakland-Fremont, CA	2,590,972
Warren-Troy, MI	2,536,388
Seattle-Bellevue-Everett, WA	2,512,859

Source: Woods & Poole Economics, Inc.

from the Environmental Protection Agency that looked like nothing so much as a mainframe computer printout. *Quality of Life Indicators in U.S. Metropolitan Areas* (1974) used numbers, too, and pointed to any small metro area in the inner South as the country's worst. And the best possible place? La Crosse, Wisconsin.

METROPOLITAN AREAS

Places Rated Almanac is more useful than any system that considers just states because numbers for big areas of geography hide the smaller exceptions. Instead, *Places Rated Almanac* focuses on metropolitan areas, the smallest unit of urban geography for which there is the largest and freshest amount of comparable data.

The term metropolitan area simply means a large city including its suburbs. Since 1950, metro areas have taken on an official connotation defined by detailed federal standards. Simply put, an area qualifies as "metropolitan" if there is an urbanized area of at least 50,000 people (the "core") together with the surrounding county. Adjacent suburban and rural counties are added to the metro area based on how many persons commute to work into the core.

From Abilene, TX, to Yuma, AZ; from huge Los Angeles-Long Beach-Glendale to tiny Enid, OK; from foggy Portland, ME, to sunny San Diego, these 379 metro areas cover a lot of ground, indeed. There is one in every state. California has 25, Texas has 26, and Florida has 21. They cover just 2.3 percent of America's land area yet hold more than 80 percent of its population. Among them, you'll find agricultural centers and fashion markets, college towns and mill towns and cow towns, bedroom communities, financial centers, resorts and retirement colonies, and cultural havens right next to international gateways and industrial giants.

A metro area's boundaries coincide with those of the surrounding county or counties. (For a view of metro geography, see the eight pages of maps following this Introduction. The irregular dark areas within the colored counties are the densely-settled urbanized cores.) Most metropolitan areas are within single states. However, forty-four cross state lines. Washington includes not just the District of Columbia, but three counties in suburban Maryland, fifteen counties and independent cities in northern

Virginia, and even a county in West Virginia's eastern panhandle. Memphis takes in three counties in Tennessee, another across the Mississippi River in Arkansas, and another four over the border in Mississippi.

The idea for metro areas has been around a long time but the United States was one of a few countries that officially defined them in 1950. Today, most countries do so at least for their capital city, and several others from Asia (Bangladesh) to North America (Canada) define their metro areas with criteria and terminology borrowed from American practice.

There are ample reasons for focusing on metro areas rather than on individual cities, counties, or states. Thanks to the four-lane highway, cities, counties, and states are less relevant to our daily personal geography.

Commonly, we live in one community; commute to work in another; and eat at the restaurants, shop at the stores, and take advantage of the recreational assets of all the towns around us. We pay taxes or fees for water, sewer, parks, and school districts that often cross city lines. And every so often we keep or throw out of office our local representative whose district seems to encompass everything in sight.

The perimeters of metro areas supersede the anachronistic political boundaries of incorporated areas and include not just the troubled and depressed older city cores, but also the newer parts of suburbia with their sleek new malls, mirror-windowed office parks, low-rise factories, and choice neighborhoods. Greater Newark, for example, includes affluent Morris County. Buffalo-Niagara Falls includes quaint and toney Lewiston. Cleveland embraces Shaker Heights, and Boston, with its 129 cities and towns, takes in a wealthy fringe of high-tech industries. In the Appendix at the end of this book, a "Metro Area Place Finder" lists not only the principal cities after which metro areas are named, but suburban and rural towns within the area's boundaries as well.

The alphabetical list "379 Metropolitan Areas" on the following pages shows each metro area's population size and expected growth to the year 2015. It also counts the number of cities and towns and surrounding counties that make up each metro area's official definition in this edition of *Places Rated Almanac*.

The chances are good that you live in one of the official metropolitan areas profiled here.

Metro Area	Population 2007	Population 2015	Percent Growth
Abilene, TX 3 counties and 17 cites and towns	161,496	168,245	4.0
Akron, OH 2 counties and 64 cites and towns	709,002	727,095	2.5
Albany, GA 5 counties and 12 cites and towns	165,065	173,930	5.1
Albany-Schenectady, NY 5 counties and 130 cites and towns	852,564	880,573	3.2
Albuquerque, NM 4 counties and 17 cites and towns	845,579	957,897	11.7
Alexandria, LA 2 parishes and 15 cites and towns	147,719	151,395	2.4
Allentown, PA-NJ 4 counties and 103 cites and towns	792,276	844,636	6.2
Altoona, PA 1 county and 26 cites and towns	125,871	123,947	-1.6
Amarillo, TX 4 counties and 12 cites and towns	238,845	251,252	4.9
Ames, IA 1 county and 15 cites and towns	85,182	89,902	5.3
Anchorage, AK 2 boroughs and 4 cites and towns	356,758	393,410	9.3
Anderson, IN 1 county and 42 cites and towns	131,856	133,998	1.6
Anderson, SC 1 county and 11 cites and towns	179,205	195,422	8.3
Ann Arbor, MI 1 county and 37 cites and towns	353,121	383,640	8.0
Anniston, AL 1 county and 9 cites and towns	113,647	117,521	3.3
Appleton, WI 2 counties and 58 cites and towns	220,514	241,069	8.5
Asheville, NC 4 counties and 19 cites and towns	401,232	442,005	9.2
Athens, GA 4 counties and 17 cites and towns	183,345	206,501	11.2
Atlanta, GA 28 counties and 136 cites and towns	4,945,063	5,637,604	12.3
Atlantic City, NJ 1 county and 23 cites and towns	273,539	295,052	7.3
Auburn-Opelika, AL 1 county and 7 cites and towns	126,625	141,293	10.4

Metro Area	Population 2007	Population 2015	Percent Growth
Augusta, GA-SC 6 counties and 26 cites and towns	530,053	569,754	7.0
Austin-Round Rock, TX 5 counties and 47 cites and towns	1,530,344	1,841,823	16.9
Bakersfield, CA 1 county and 11 cites and towns	757,641	850,336	10.9
Baltimore-Towson, MD 6 counties, 1 independent city and 22 cites and towns	2,735,489	2,986,605	8.4
Bangor, ME 1 county and 67 cites and towns	149,782	156,118	4.1
Barnstable Town, MA 1 county and 15 cites and towns	241,234	265,648	9.2
Baton Rouge, LA 9 parishes and 35 cites and towns	755,352	824,370	8.4
Battle Creek, MI 1 county and 32 cites and towns	139,182	140,440	0.9
Bay City, MI 1 county and 20 cites and towns	108,352	106,677	-1.6
Beaumont, TX 3 counties and 20 cites and towns	389,019	403,709	3.6
Bellingham, WA 1 county and 7 cites and towns	188,175	212,340	11.4
Bend, OR 1 county and 3 cites and towns	145,826	179,152	18.6
Bethesda, MD 2 counties and 31 cites and towns	1,190,086	1,310,501	9.2
Billings, MT 2 counties and 8 cites and towns	147,880	158,537	6.7
Binghamton, NY 2 counties and 51 cites and towns	249,777	248,388	-0.6
Birmingham-Hoover, AL 7 counties and 91 cites and towns	1,110,529	1,191,606	6.8
Bismarck, ND 2 counties and 60 cites and towns	100,445	108,275	7.2
Blacksburg, VA 3 counties, 1 independent city and 10 cites and towns	156,339	164,600	5.0
Bloomington, IN 3 counties and 60 cites and towns	186,617	202,836	8.0
Bloomington-Normal, IL 1 county and 79 cites and towns	166,251	185,635	10.4
Boise City-Nampa, ID 5 counties and 22 cites and towns	552,942	639,447	13.5

Metro Area	Population 2007	Population 2015	Percent Growth
Boston-Quincy, MA 3 counties and 59 cites and towns	1,853,936	1,925,665	3.7
Boulder, CO 1 county and 10 cites and towns	321,369	360,838	10.9
Bowling Green, KY 2 counties and 6 cites and towns	112,738	123,485	8.7
Bremerton, WA 1 county and 4 cites and towns	254,068	282,055	9.9
Bridgeport, CT 1 county and 25 cites and towns	914,051	948,320	3.6
Brownsville, TX 1 county and 17 cites and towns	387,503	438,029	11.5
Brunswick, GA 3 counties and 4 cites and towns	101,618	112,810	9.9
Buffalo, NY 2 counties and 90 cites and towns	1,157,725	1,160,021	0.2
Burlington, NC 1 county and 10 cites and towns	141,621	151,921	6.8
Burlington, VT 3 counties and 46 cites and towns	210,872	226,652	7.0
Cambridge, MA 1 county and 54 cites and towns	1,476,416	1,493,127	1.1
Camden, NJ 3 counties and 100 cites and towns	1,259,822	1,334,911	5.6
Canton-Massillon, OH 2 counties and 76 cites and towns	408,687	413,856	1.2
Cape Coral, FL 1 county and 5 cites and towns	539,257	635,622	15.2
Carson City, NV 1 independent city	59,581	68,381	12.9
Casper, WY 1 county and 6 cites and towns	69,342	71,958	3.6
Cedar Rapids, IA 3 counties and 41 cites and towns	253,174	275,239	8.0
Champaign-Urbana, IL 3 counties and 139 cites and towns	218,960	223,340	2.0
Charleston, WV 5 counties and 30 cites and towns	306,918	308,755	0.6
Charleston, SC 3 counties and 26 cites and towns	606,100	677,640	10.6
Charlotte, NC-SC 6 counties and 57 cites and towns	1,534,002	1,733,714	11.5
Charlottesville, VA 4 counties, 1 independent city and 4 cities and towns	190,968	210,544	9.3

Metro Area	Population 2007	Population 2015	Percent Growth
Chattanooga, TN-GA 6 counties and 26 cites and towns	498,656	526,804	5.3
Cheyenne, WY 1 county and 4 cites and towns	85,607	89,049	3.9
Chicago-Naperville, IL 8 counties and 624 cites and towns	7,984,928	8,379,329	4.7
Chico, CA 1 county and 5 cites and towns	223,105	248,275	10.1
Cincinnati, OH-KY-IN 15 counties and 297 cites and towns	2,107,198	2,237,299	5.8
Clarksville, TN-KY 4 counties and 10 cites and towns	254,064	289,941	12.4
Cleveland, TN 2 counties and 5 cites and towns	110,849	120,254	7.8
Cleveland-Elyria, OH 5 counties and 186 cites and towns	2,145,324	2,167,672	1.0
Coeur d'Alene, ID 1 county and 14 cites and towns	131,595	160,538	18.0
College Station-Bryan, TX 3 counties and 12 cites and towns	205,581	232,634	11.6
Colorado Springs, CO 2 counties and 11 cites and towns	613,972	700,210	12.3
Columbia, MO 2 counties and 15 cites and towns	160,037	178,519	10.4
Columbia, SC 6 counties and 30 cites and towns	706,073	778,695	9.3
Columbus, GA-AL 5 counties and 10 cites and towns	291,048	300,450	3.1
Columbus, IN 1 county and 29 cites and towns	74,854	80,223	6.7
Columbus, OH 8 counties and 265 cites and towns	1,757,771	1,932,002	9.0
Corpus Christi, TX 3 counties and 21 cites and towns	418,930	445,099	5.9
Corvallis, OR 1 county and 5 cites and towns	82,826	90,193	8.2
Cumberland, MD-WV 2 counties and 12 cites and towns	101,002	101,845	0.8
Dallas-Plano-Irving, TX 8 counties and 140 cites and towns	3,986,718	4,499,064	11.4
Dalton, GA 2 counties and 6 cites and towns	132,413	143,284	7.6
Danville, IL 1 county and 59 cites and towns	81,528	79,452	-2.6

Continues on Page 15

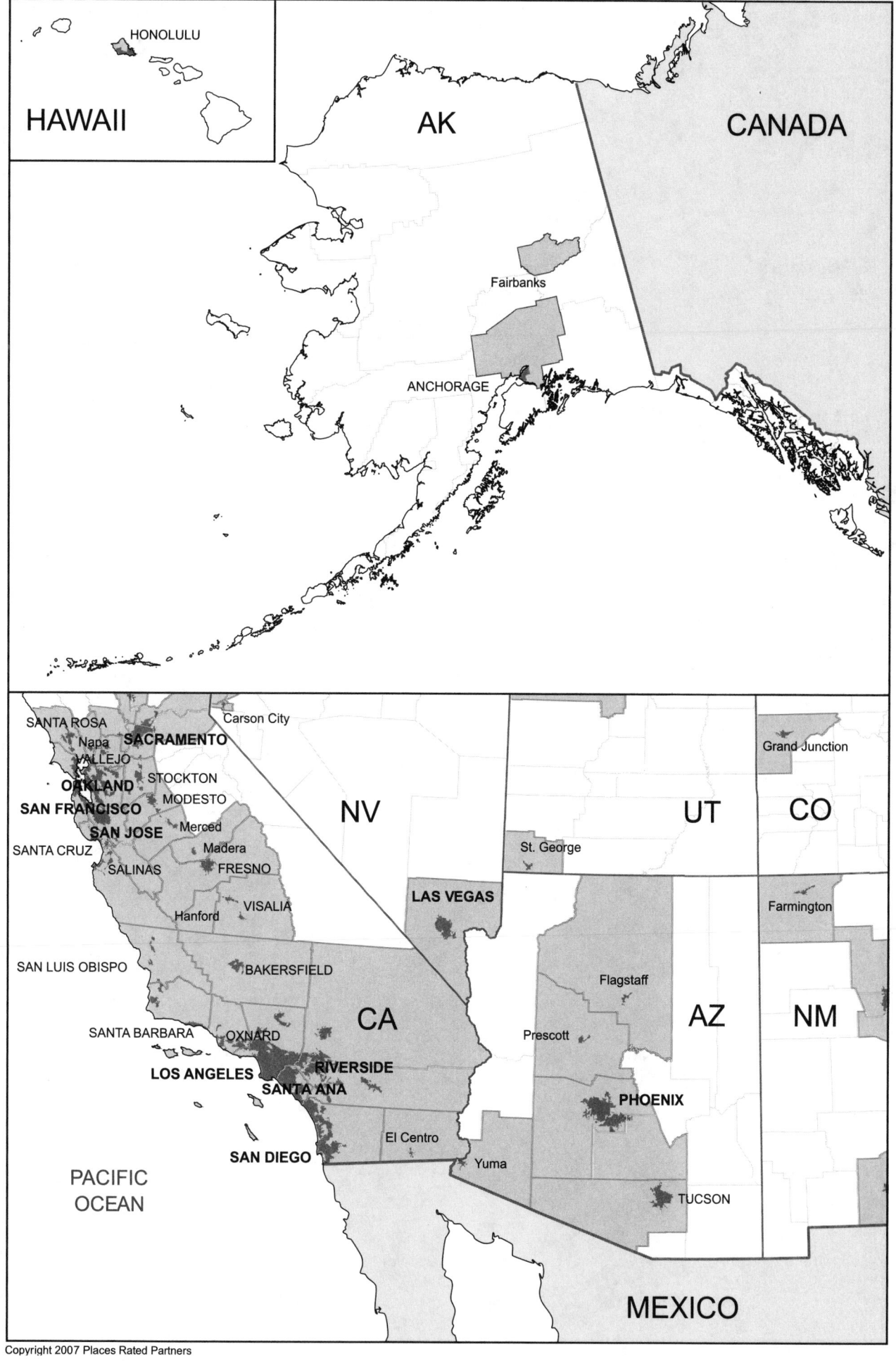

HAWAII

HONOLULU

AK

CANADA

Fairbanks

ANCHORAGE

SANTA ROSA
Napa
VALLEJO
SACRAMENTO
Carson City
OAKLAND
STOCKTON
SAN FRANCISCO
MODESTO
SAN JOSE
Merced
SANTA CRUZ
Madera
SALINAS
FRESNO
Hanford
VISALIA

NV

Grand Junction

UT

CO

St. George

LAS VEGAS

Farmington

SAN LUIS OBISPO

BAKERSFIELD

Flagstaff

CA

Prescott

AZ

NM

SANTA BARBARA
OXNARD

LOS ANGELES
RIVERSIDE
SANTA ANA

PHOENIX

SAN DIEGO

El Centro

Yuma

TUCSON

PACIFIC
OCEAN

MEXICO

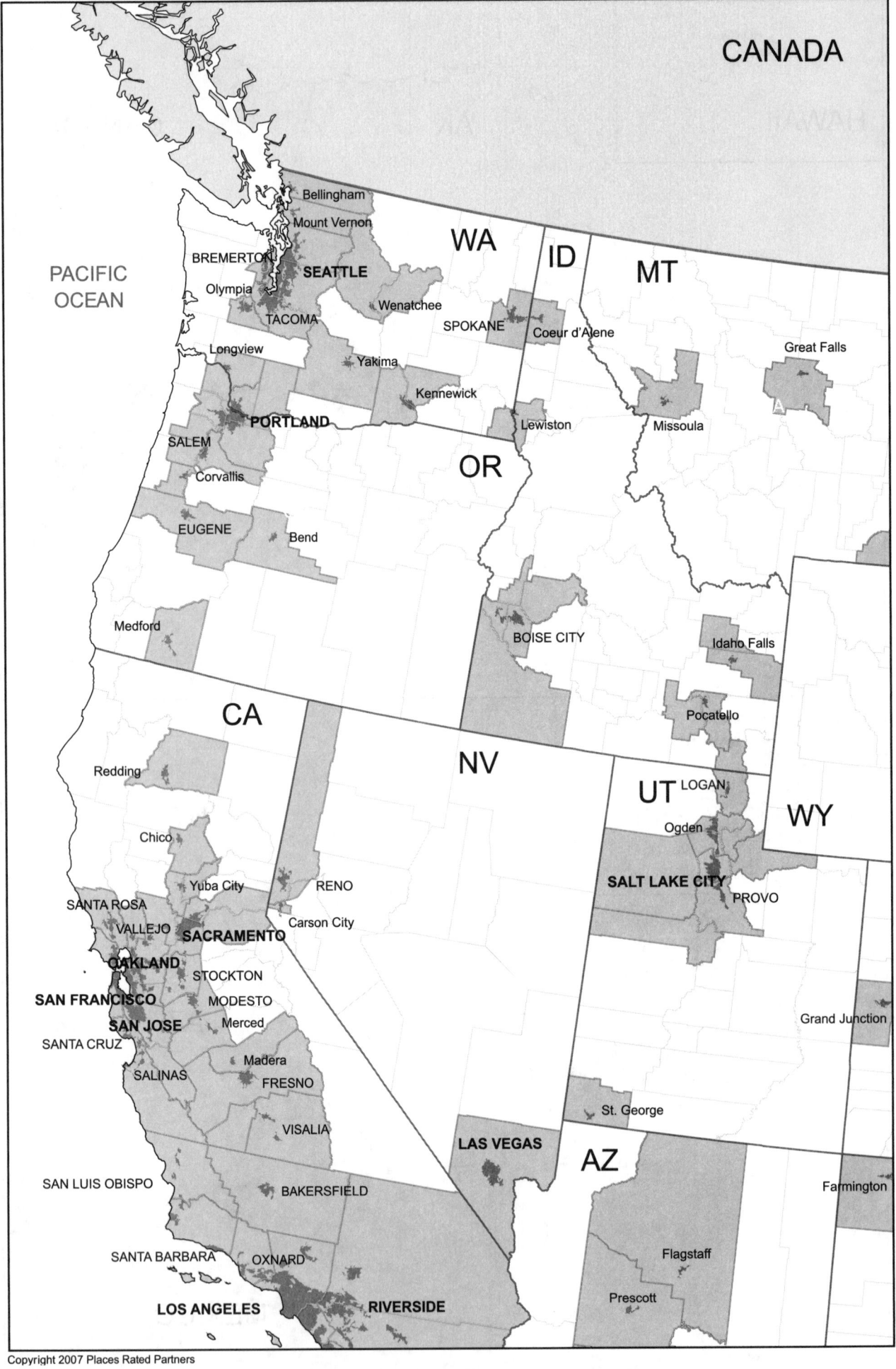

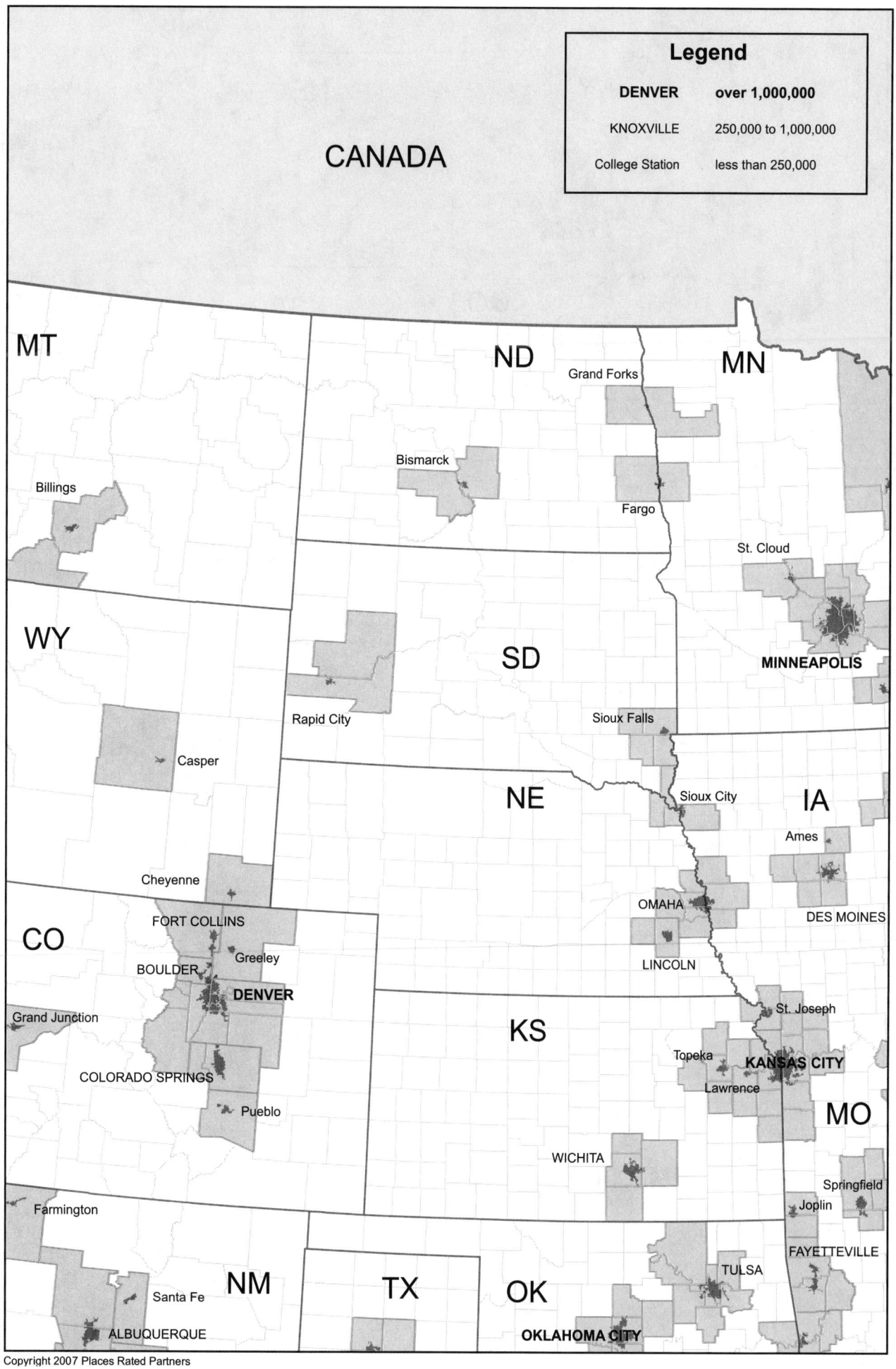

CANADA

Legend

DENVER **over 1,000,000**

KNOXVILLE 250,000 to 1,000,000

College Station less than 250,000

Metro Area Maps

MT

ND MN

Grand Forks

Bismarck

Fargo

St. Cloud

Billings

WY

SD

MINNEAPOLIS

Rapid City

Sioux Falls

Casper

NE

Sioux City

IA

Ames

OMAHA

DES MOINES

Cheyenne

LINCOLN

CO

FORT COLLINS

Greeley

BOULDER

St. Joseph

DENVER

Grand Junction

Topeka

KANSAS CITY

KS

Lawrence

COLORADO SPRINGS

MO

Pueblo

WICHITA

Springfield

Farmington

Joplin

FAYETTEVILLE

NM

TX

OK

TULSA

Santa Fe

ALBUQUERQUE

OKLAHOMA CITY

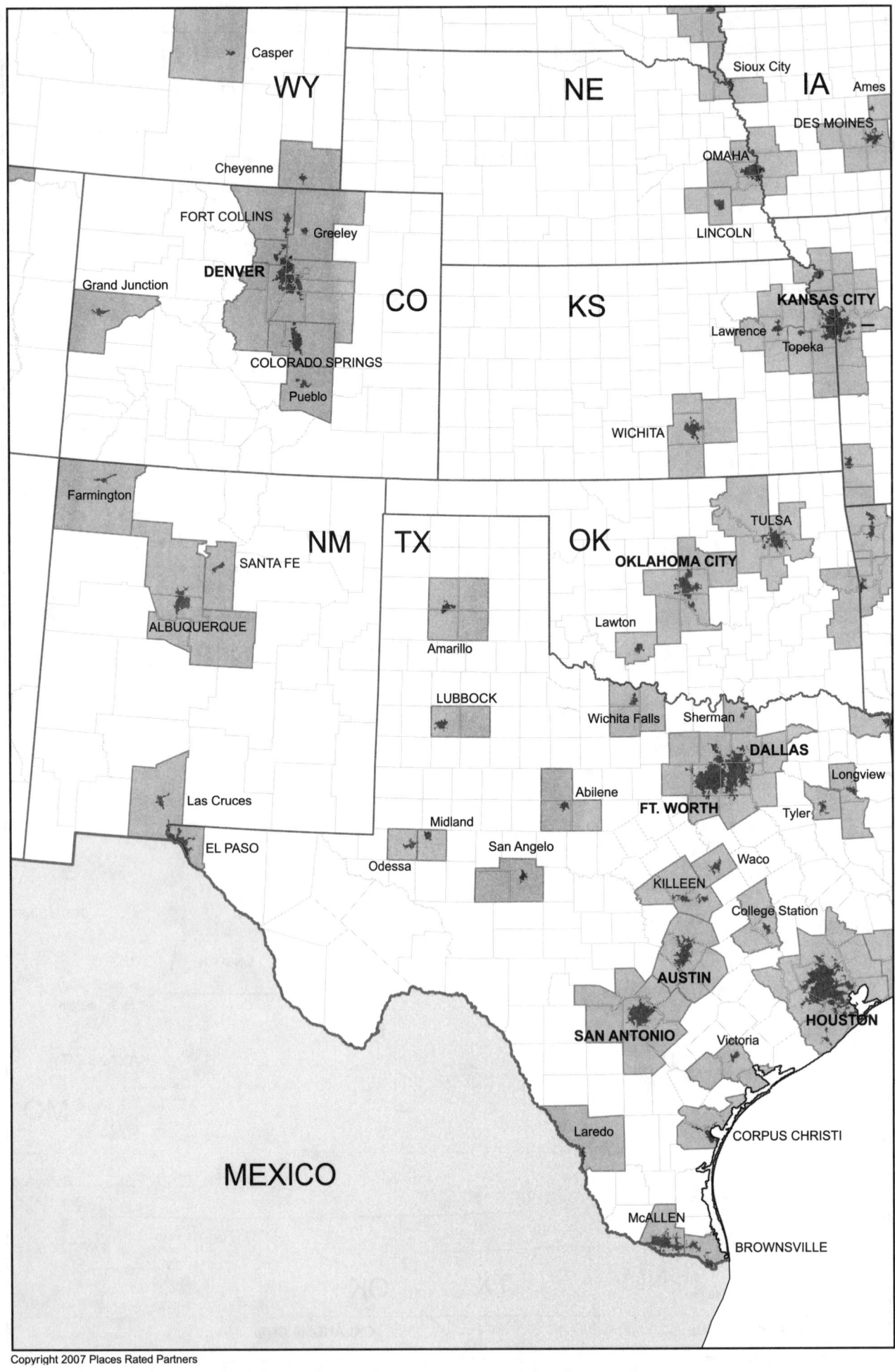

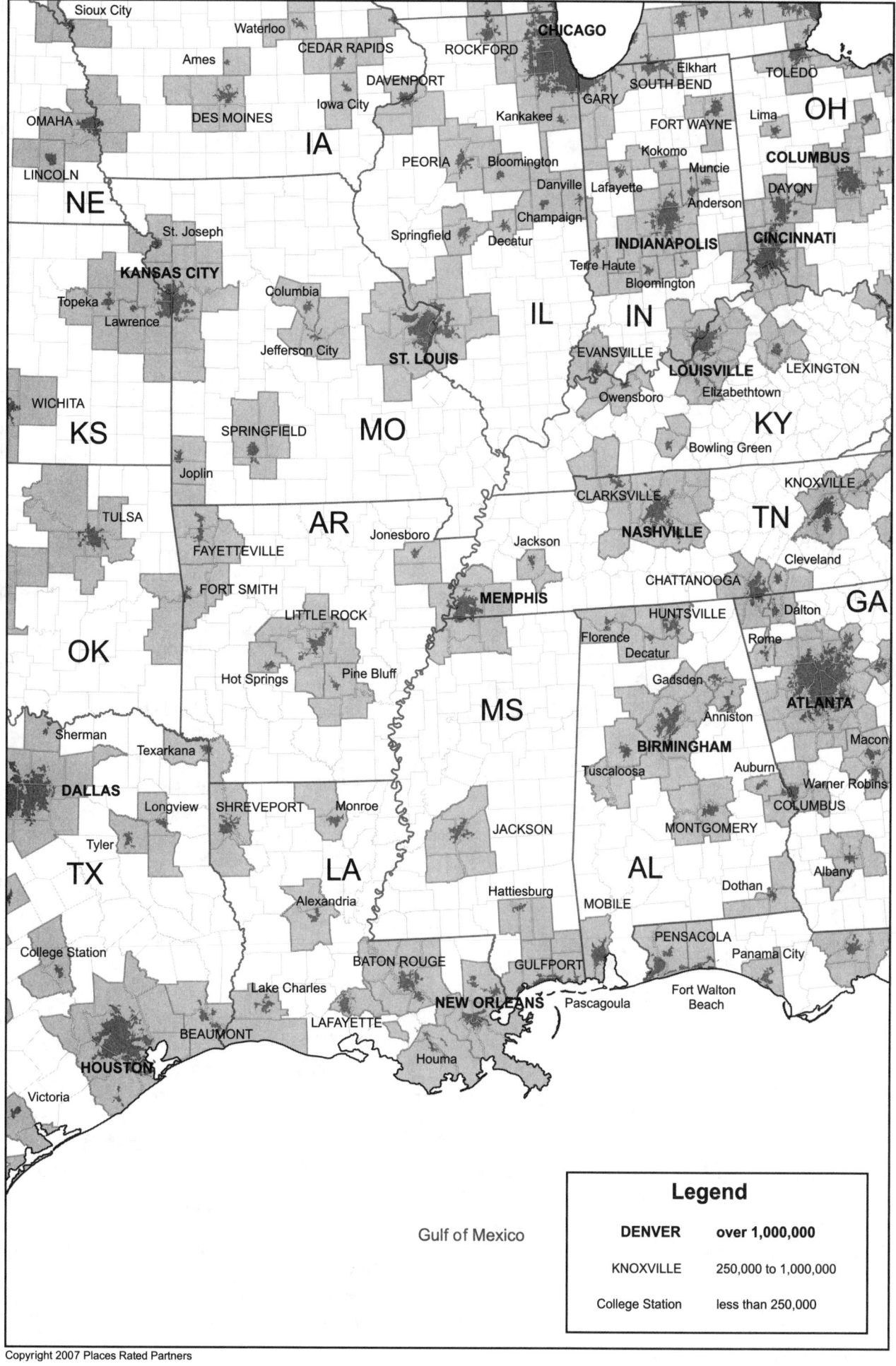

Sioux City, Waterloo, CEDAR RAPIDS, ROCKFORD, CHICAGO, DAVENPORT, Ames, Iowa City, TOLEDO, Elkhart, SOUTH BEND, GARY, OH, Kankakee, FORT WAYNE, Lima, OMAHA, DES MOINES, IA, Kokomo, COLUMBUS, PEORIA, Bloomington, Muncie, DAYON, LINCOLN, Danville, Lafayette, Anderson, Springfield, Champaign, INDIANAPOLIS, CINCINNATI, NE, Decatur, Terre Haute, St. Joseph, Bloomington, IL, IN, KANSAS CITY, EVANSVILLE, LOUISVILLE, LEXINGTON, Topeka, Columbia, Owensboro, Elizabethtown, Lawrence, Jefferson City, ST. LOUIS, KY, WICHITA, MO, Bowling Green, KS, SPRINGFIELD, CLARKSVILLE, KNOXVILLE, Joplin, NASHVILLE, TN, TULSA, AR, Jonesboro, Jackson, Cleveland, FAYETTEVILLE, CHATTANOOGA, Dalton, GA, FORT SMITH, MEMPHIS, HUNTSVILLE, Rome, LITTLE ROCK, Florence, OK, Decatur, Hot Springs, Pine Bluff, Gadsden, ATLANTA, MS, Anniston, Macon, Sherman, BIRMINGHAM, Texarkana, Tuscaloosa, Auburn, Warner Robins, DALLAS, SHREVEPORT, Monroe, COLUMBUS, Longview, MONTGOMERY, Albany, Tyler, JACKSON, AL, TX, LA, Dothan, Hattiesburg, Alexandria, MOBILE, PENSACOLA, College Station, Panama City, BATON ROUGE, GULFPORT, Fort Walton, Lake Charles, Pascagoula, Beach, NEW ORLEANS, BEAUMONT, LAFAYETTE, HOUSTON, Houma, Victoria

Gulf of Mexico

Legend	
DENVER	**over 1,000,000**
KNOXVILLE	250,000 to 1,000,000
College Station	less than 250,000

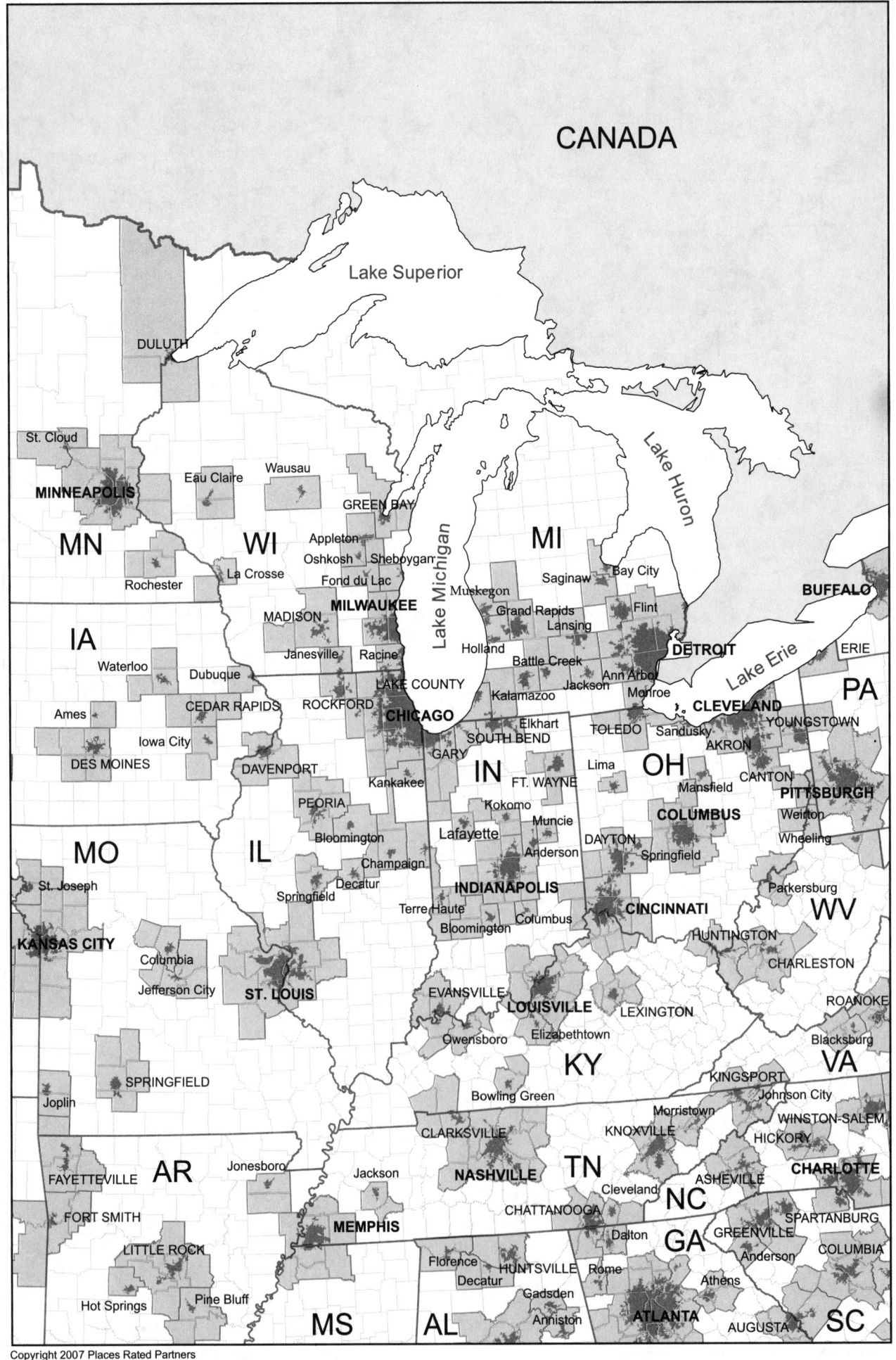

Copyright 2007 Places Rated Partners

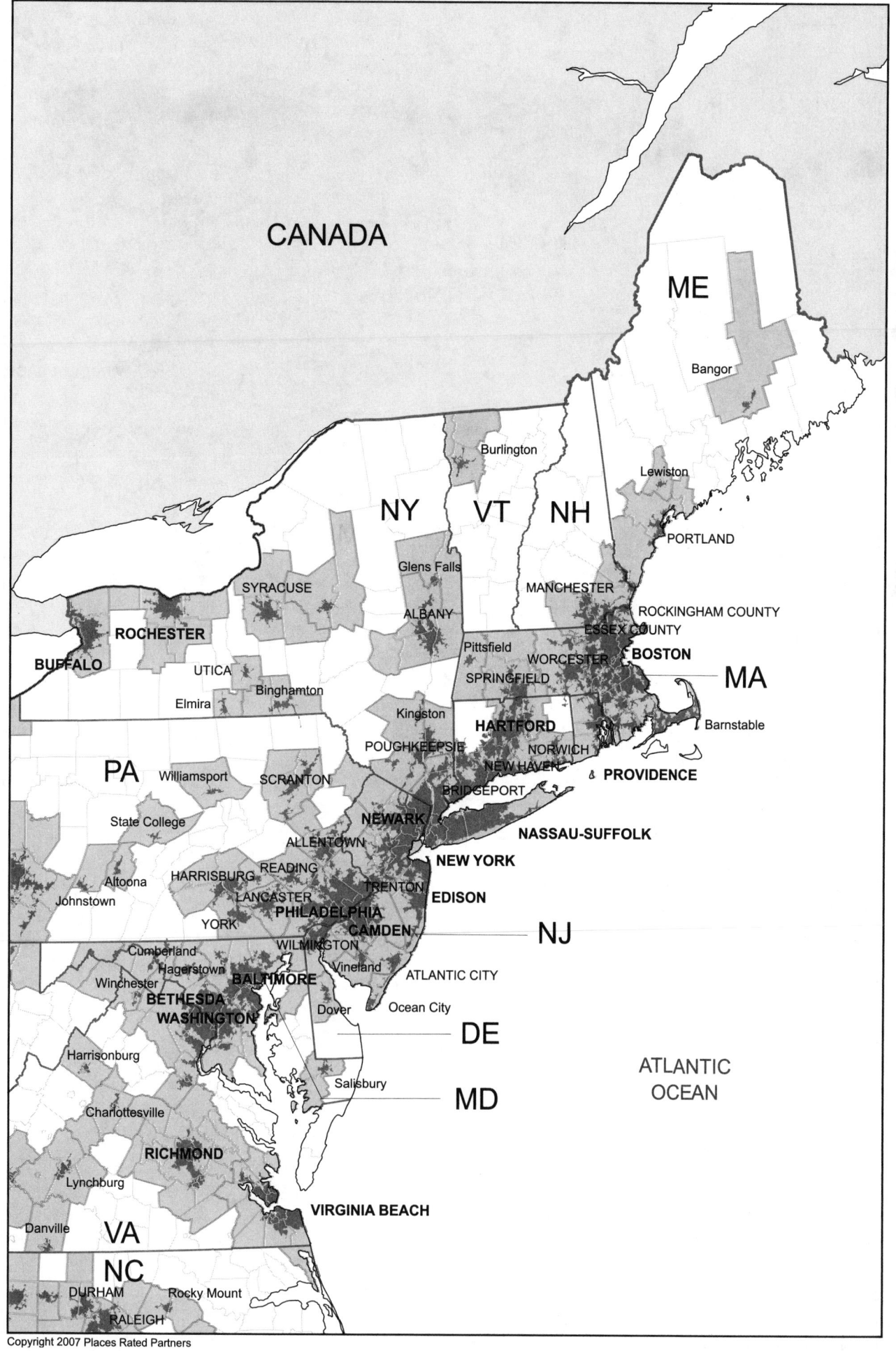

CANADA

ME

Bangor

Lewiston

Burlington

NY   VT   NH

PORTLAND

Glens Falls

MANCHESTER

SYRACUSE

ALBANY   ROCKINGHAM COUNTY

ESSEX COUNTY

ROCHESTER   Pittsfield   WORCESTER   BOSTON

BUFFALO   UTICA   SPRINGFIELD   MA

Binghamton   Barnstable

Elmira   Kingston   HARTFORD

NORWICH

POUGHKEEPSIE   NEW HAVEN   PROVIDENCE

PA   Williamsport   SCRANTON   BRIDGEPORT

NASSAU-SUFFOLK

State College   NEWARK

ALLENTOWN

Altoona   READING   NEW YORK

HARRISBURG   TRENTON

Johnstown   LANCASTER   EDISON

YORK   PHILADELPHIA   NJ

CAMDEN

WILMINGTON

Cumberland   Vineland

Hagerstown   ATLANTIC CITY

Winchester   BALTIMORE   Ocean City

BETHESDA   Dover   DE

WASHINGTON

Harrisonburg   ATLANTIC
OCEAN

Salisbury   MD

Charlottesville

RICHMOND

Lynchburg

Danville   VA

VIRGINIA BEACH

NC

DURHAM   Rocky Mount

RALEIGH

Copyright 2007 Places Rated Partners

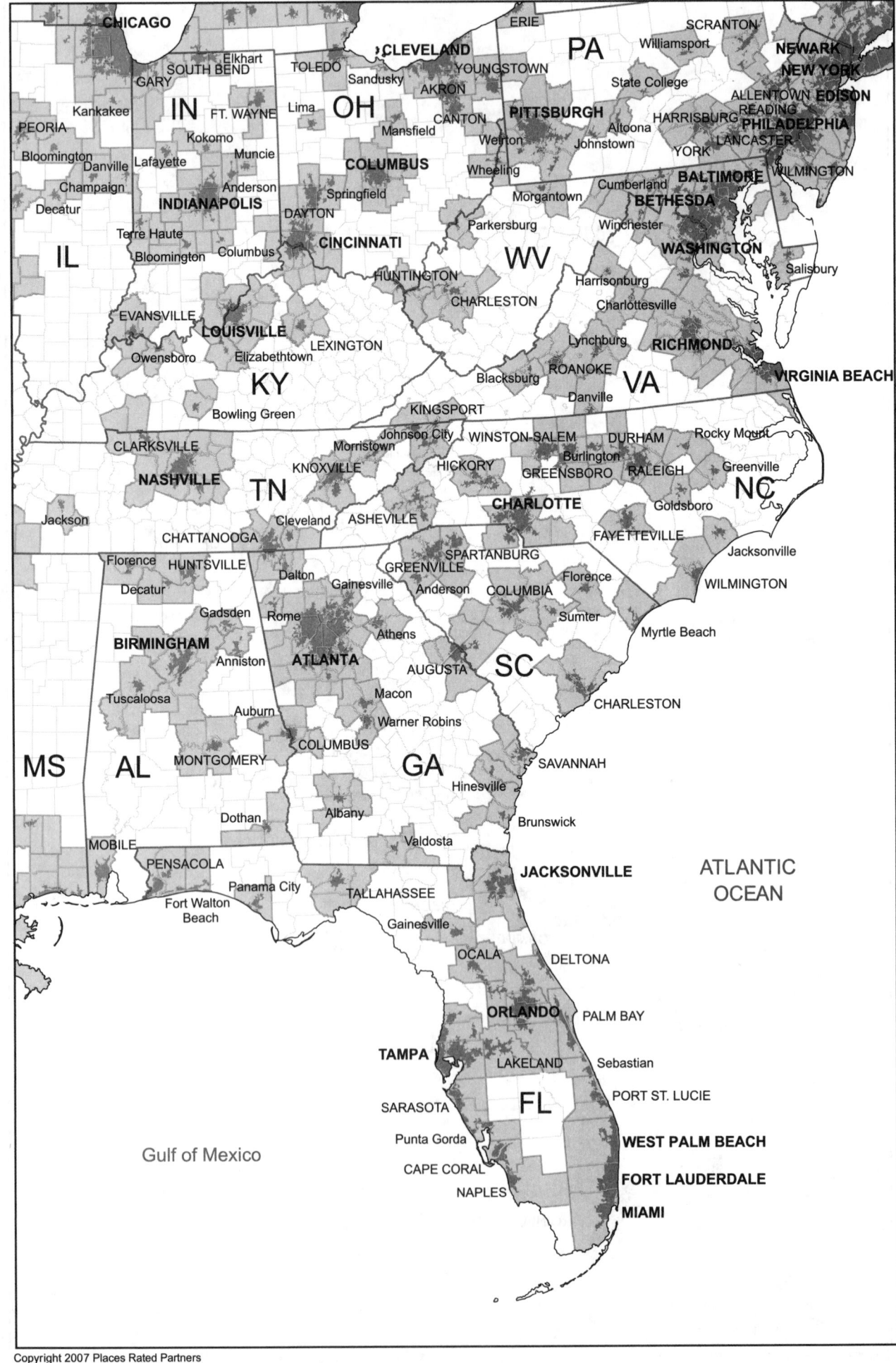

The 379 Metropolitan Areas

Metro Area	Population 2007	Population 2015	Percent Growth
Danville, VA 1 county, 1 independent city and 4 cities and towns	108,537	108,930	0.4
Davenport-Moline,.IA-IL 4 counties and 168 cites and towns	377,803	385,330	2.0
Dayton, OH 4 counties and 134 cites and towns	842,069	838,368	-0.4
Decatur, AL 2 counties and 12 cites and towns	152,704	164,420	7.1
Decatur, IL 1 county and 46 cites and towns	109,836	107,745	-1.9
Daytona Beach, FL 1 county and 17 cites and towns	490,730	537,243	8.7
Denver-Aurora, CO 10 counties and 45 cites and towns	2,444,425	2,790,225	12.4
Des Moines, IA 5 counties and 63 cites and towns	520,641	558,894	6.8
Detroit-Livonia, MI 1 county and 45 cites and towns	1,994,780	1,937,511	-3.0
Dothan, AL 3 counties and 24 cites and towns	137,102	145,394	5.7
Dover, DE 1 county and 20 cites and towns	140,036	151,956	7.8
Dubuque, IA 1 county and 21 cites and towns	91,193	93,983	3.0
Duluth, MN-WI 3 counties and 181 cites and towns	276,548	279,096	0.9
Durham, NC 4 counties and 12 cites and towns	475,131	533,347	10.9
Eau Claire, WI 2 counties and 51 cites and towns	155,616	165,562	6.0
Edison, NJ 4 counties and 131 cites and towns	2,386,255	2,627,864	9.2
El Centro, CA 1 county and 7 cites and towns	156,465	171,610	8.8
Elizabethtown, KY 2 counties and 8 cites and towns	112,513	119,061	5.5
Elkhart-Goshen, IN 1 county and 41 cites and towns	194,731	207,487	6.1
Elmira, NY 1 county and 23 cites and towns	89,205	87,305	-2.2
El Paso, TX 1 county and 6 cites and towns	745,885	830,077	10.1

Metro Area	Population 2007	Population 2015	Percent Growth
Erie, PA 1 county and 38 cites and towns	281,364	285,488	1.4
Essex County, MA 1 county and 34 cites and towns	751,425	782,163	3.9
Eugene-Springfield, OR 1 county and 12 cites and towns	346,695	380,606	8.9
Evansville, IN-KY 6 counties and 95 cites and towns	349,127	357,932	2.5
Fairbanks, AK 1 borough and 3 cites and towns	87,652	91,422	4.1
Fargo, ND-MN 2 counties and 121 cites and towns	186,442	201,968	7.7
Farmington, NM 1 county and 3 cites and towns	131,488	150,481	12.6
Fayetteville, NC 2 counties and 10 cites and towns	354,686	382,507	7.3
Fayetteville, AR-MO 4 counties and 40 cites and towns	419,311	503,753	16.8
Flagstaff, AZ 1 county and 5 cites and towns	131,083	151,251	13.3
Flint, MI 1 county and 38 cites and towns	442,000	443,712	0.4
Florence, SC 2 counties and 13 cites and towns	200,801	210,853	4.8
Florence, AL 2 counties and 13 cites and towns	143,828	149,227	3.6
Fond du Lac, WI 1 county and 36 cites and towns	100,156	105,247	4.8
Fort Collins, CO 1 county and 8 cites and towns	288,450	333,360	13.5
Fort Lauderdale, FL 1 county and 30 cites and towns	1,851,403	2,099,704	11.8
Fort Smith, AR-OK 5 counties and 52 cites and towns	294,436	325,275	9.5
Fort Walton Beach, FL 1 county and 9 cites and towns	194,394	227,887	14.7
Fort Wayne, IN 3 counties and 81 cites and towns	409,123	430,042	4.9
Fort Worth-Arlington, TX 4 counties and 75 cites and towns	2,007,503	2,331,722	13.9
Fresno, CA 1 county and 15 cites and towns	901,198	1,006,957	10.5

Metro Area	Population 2007	Population 2015	Percent Growth
Gadsden, AL 1 county and 13 cites and towns	104,062	106,633	2.4
Gainesville, FL 2 counties and 12 cites and towns	249,757	272,024	8.2
Gainesville, GA 1 county and 9 cites and towns	164,085	180,787	9.2
Gary, IN 4 counties and 117 cites and towns	700,201	732,933	4.5
Glens Falls, NY 2 counties and 53 cites and towns	128,465	132,940	3.4
Goldsboro, NC 1 county and 7 cites and towns	114,557	118,027	2.9
Grand Forks, ND-MN 2 counties and 123 cites and towns	96,712	99,466	2.8
Grand Junction, CO 1 county and 5 cites and towns	132,730	149,516	11.2
Grand Rapids, MI 4 counties and 131 cites and towns	796,720	869,858	8.4
Great Falls, MT 1 county and 4 cites and towns	79,934	81,098	1.4
Greeley, CO 1 county and 31 cites and towns	223,713	249,491	10.3
Green Bay, WI 3 counties and 69 cites and towns	301,900	324,658	7.0
Greensboro, NC 3 counties and 28 cites and towns	680,903	722,807	5.8
Greenville, NC 2 counties and 13 cites and towns	169,770	192,655	11.9
Greenville, SC 3 counties and 19 cites and towns	602,944	654,671	7.9
*Gulfport-Biloxi, MS 3 counties and 8 cites and towns	260,923	286,120	8.8
Hagerstown, MD-WV 3 counties and 13 cites and towns	246,431	265,552	7.2
Hanford-Corcoran, CA 1 county and 4 cites and towns	146,645	163,453	10.3
Harrisburg-Carlisle, PA 3 counties and 102 cites and towns	537,516	580,148	7.3
Harrisonburg, VA 1 county, 1 independent city and 8 cities and towns	117,026	130,490	10.3
Hartford, CT 3 counties and 59 cites and towns	1,193,039	1,229,247	2.9
Hattiesburg, MS 3 counties and 8 cites and towns	133,636	144,516	7.5
Hickory-Lenoir, NC 4 counties and 25 cites and towns	358,732	377,735	5.0
Hinesville, GA 2 counties and 8 cites and towns	72,556	78,596	7.7
Holland, MI 1 county and 26 cites and towns	263,929	294,197	10.3
Honolulu, HI 1 county and 1 cites and towns	923,836	969,472	4.7
Hot Springs, AR 1 county and 4 cites and towns	95,557	104,725	8.8
Houma-Bayou Cane, LA 2 parishes and 4 cites and towns	200,323	207,117	3.3
Houston, TX 10 counties and 125 cites and towns	5,394,479	6,056,093	10.9
Huntington, WV-KY-OH 5 counties and 47 cites and towns	285,298	284,507	-0.3
Huntsville, AL 2 counties and 12 cites and towns	374,266	408,733	8.4
Idaho Falls, ID 2 counties and 13 cites and towns	114,290	129,000	11.4
Indianapolis-Carmel, IN 10 counties and 194 cites and towns	1,676,061	1,845,417	9.2
Iowa City, IA 2 counties and 21 cites and towns	144,893	161,597	10.3
Ithaca, NY 1 county and 21 cites and towns	102,303	104,565	2.2
Jackson, MI 1 county and 35 cites and towns	163,030	165,350	1.4
Jackson, MS 5 counties and 28 cites and towns	533,095	581,764	8.4
Jackson, TN 2 counties and 8 cites and towns	115,469	127,518	9.4
Jacksonville, FL 5 counties and 18 cites and towns	1,279,919	1,439,914	11.1
Jacksonville, NC 1 county and 6 cites and towns	150,070	155,884	3.7
Janesville, WI 1 county and 31 cites and towns	157,527	163,739	3.8
Jefferson City, MO 4 counties and 28 cites and towns	150,188	165,852	9.4
Johnson City, TN 3 counties and 6 cites and towns	192,241	205,364	6.4
Johnstown, PA 1 county and 64 cites and towns	145,827	139,411	-4.6
Jonesboro, AR 2 counties and 18 cites and towns	113,406	120,807	6.1
Joplin, MO 2 counties and 42 cites and towns	170,679	188,649	9.5

Metro Area	Population 2007	Population 2015	Percent Growth
Kalamazoo-Portage, MI 2 counties and 69 cites and towns	326,581	340,602	4.1
Kankakee-Bradley, IL 1 county and 56 cites and towns	107,156	110,744	3.2
Kansas City, MO-KS 15 counties and 310 cites and towns	1,979,219	2,137,342	7.4
Kennewick-Richland, WA 2 counties and 9 cites and towns	224,087	253,469	11.6
Killeen-Temple, TX 3 counties and 21 cites and towns	363,315	404,769	10.2
Kingsport-Bristol, TN-VA 4 counties, 1 independent city and 19 cities and towns	303,879	313,834	3.2
Kingston, NY 1 county and 27 cites and towns	187,719	201,921	7.0
Knoxville, TN 5 counties and 21 cites and towns	671,810	744,842	9.8
Kokomo, IN 2 counties and 36 cites and towns	101,466	102,344	0.9
La Crosse, WI-MN 2 counties and 43 cites and towns	132,266	140,262	5.7
Lafayette, IN 3 counties and 71 cites and towns	190,746	204,129	6.6
Lafayette, LA 2 parishes and 11 cites and towns	253,896	274,591	7.5
Lake Charles, LA 2 parishes and 6 cites and towns	196,703	203,826	3.5
Lakeland-Kenosha, IL-WI 2 counties and 133 cites and towns	903,510	1,031,494	12.4
Lakeland, FL 1 county and 17 cites and towns	532,566	579,309	8.1
Lancaster, PA 1 county and 61 cites and towns	497,420	529,038	6.0
Lansing-East Lansing, MI 3 counties and 93 cites and towns	464,220	483,330	4.0
Laredo, TX 1 county and 3 cites and towns	242,331	300,561	19.4
Las Cruces, NM 1 county and 4 cites and towns	194,070	218,674	11.3
Las Vegas-Paradise, NV 1 county and 5 cites and towns	1,781,690	2,198,951	19.0
Lawrence, KS 1 county and 16 cites and towns	109,545	123,194	11.1
Lawton, OK 1 county and 10 cites and towns	113,935	114,655	0.6
Lebanon, PA 1 county and 26 cites and towns	125,032	130,419	4.1

Metro Area	Population 2007	Population 2015	Percent Growth
Lewiston, ID-WA 2 counties and 6 cites and towns	60,445	65,037	7.1
Lewiston-Auburn, ME 1 county and 14 cites and towns	107,963	112,243	3.8
Lexington-Fayette, KY 6 counties and 13 cites and towns	441,677	482,685	8.5
Lima, OH 1 county and 30 cites and towns	107,291	105,954	-1.3
Lincoln, NE 2 counties and 23 cites and towns	290,817	318,372	8.7
Little Rock, AR 6 counties and 48 cites and towns	658,223	721,190	8.7
Logan, UT-ID 2 counties and 25 cites and towns	114,386	128,604	11.1
Longview, TX 3 counties and 19 cites and towns	204,147	216,910	5.9
Longview, WA 1 county and 5 cites and towns	97,563	103,033	5.3
Los Angeles, CA 1 county and 88 cites and towns	9,978,085	10,235,909	2.5
Louisville, KY-IN 13 counties and 206 cites and towns	1,229,373	1,314,114	6.4
Lubbock, TX 2 counties and 12 cites and towns	262,200	273,409	4.1
Lynchburg, VA 4 counties, 2 independent cities and 7 cities and towns	238,314	254,173	6.2
Macon, GA 5 counties and 9 cites and towns	229,487	237,571	3.4
Madera, CA 1 county and 2 cites and towns	145,526	170,116	14.5
Madison, WI 3 counties and 136 cites and towns	559,068	626,266	10.7
Manchester-Nashua, NH 1 county and 31 cites and towns	409,744	441,847	7.3
Mansfield, OH 1 county and 46 cites and towns	128,119	128,482	0.3
McAllen-Edinburg, TX 1 county and 22 cites and towns	700,412	833,028	15.9
Medford, OR 1 county and 11 cites and towns	207,528	243,327	14.7
Memphis, TN-MS-AR 8 counties and 49 cites and towns	1,284,341	1,380,475	7.0
Merced, CA 1 county and 6 cites and towns	243,640	268,846	9.4
Miami-Miami Beach, FL 1 county and 33 cites and towns	2,447,206	2,670,515	8.4

Metro Area	Population 2007	Population 2015	Percent Growth
Michigan City, IN 1 county and 50 cites and towns	109,843	110,317	0.4
Midland, TX 1 county and 2 cites and towns	122,058	129,490	5.7
Milwaukee, WI 4 counties and 97 cites and towns	1,541,347	1,602,895	3.8
Minneapolis, MN-WI 13 counties and 349 cites and towns	3,252,803	3,605,356	9.8
Missoula, MT 1 county and 1 cites and towns	106,325	122,232	13.0
Mobile, AL 1 county and 10 cites and towns	404,003	414,518	2.5
Modesto, CA 1 county and 9 cites and towns	527,384	600,081	12.1
Monroe, LA 2 parishes and 11 cites and towns	173,926	180,875	3.8
Monroe, MI 1 county and 29 cites and towns	155,762	166,720	6.6
Montgomery, AL 4 counties and 19 cites and towns	365,037	391,818	6.8
Morgantown, WV 2 counties and 15 cites and towns	116,366	121,497	4.2
Morristown, TN 3 counties and 9 cites and towns	133,202	145,802	8.6
Mount Vernon, WA 1 county and 8 cites and towns	116,000	130,123	10.9
Muncie, IN 1 county and 30 cites and towns	116,346	114,695	-1.4
Muskegon, MI 1 county and 31 cites and towns	176,660	184,621	4.3
Myrtle Beach, SC 1 county and 8 cites and towns	232,270	276,293	15.9
Napa, CA 1 county and 5 cites and towns	138,654	153,417	9.6
Naples-Marco Island, FL 1 county and 3 cites and towns	319,979	388,007	17.5
Nashville-Davidson, TN 13 counties and 55 cites and towns	1,467,249	1,665,590	11.9
Nassau-Suffolk, NY 2 counties and 132 cites and towns	2,854,015	2,960,899	3.6
Newark-Union, NJ-PA 6 counties and 142 cites and towns	2,189,567	2,298,622	4.7
New Haven-Milford, CT 1 county and 30 cites and towns	851,171	873,907	2.6
*New Orleans, LA 7 parishes and 15 cites and towns	1,025,014	1,188,923	15.9

Metro Area	Population 2007	Population 2015	Percent Growth
New York, NY-NJ 11 counties and 196 cites and towns	11,613,029	12,051,482	3.6
Niles-Benton Harbor, MI 1 county and 51 cites and towns	162,170	161,801	-0.2
Norwich, CT 1 county and 27 cites and towns	267,798	276,691	3.2
Oakland-Fremont, CA 2 counties and 33 cites and towns	2,590,972	2,860,190	9.4
Ocala, FL 1 county and 5 cites and towns	297,127	332,324	10.6
Ocean City, NJ 1 county and 16 cites and towns	104,879	111,431	5.9
Odessa, TX 1 county and 2 cites and towns	124,130	127,611	2.7
Ogden-Clearfield, UT 3 counties and 31 cites and towns	503,572	574,952	12.4
Oklahoma City, OK 7 counties and 80 cites and towns	1,174,032	1,262,161	7.0
Olympia, WA 1 county and 7 cites and towns	236,331	266,152	11.2
Omaha, NE-IA 8 counties and 132 cites and towns	824,255	890,368	7.4
Orlando-Kissimmee, FL 4 counties and 36 cites and towns	1,972,017	2,318,275	14.9
Oshkosh-Neenah, WI 1 county and 24 cites and towns	164,027	175,845	6.7
Owensboro, KY 3 counties and 8 cites and towns	111,940	114,762	2.5
Oxnard, CA 1 county and 10 cites and towns	829,881	911,298	8.9
Palm Bay-Melbourne, FL 1 county and 15 cites and towns	527,507	573,684	8.0
Panama City, FL 1 county and 8 cites and towns	163,866	181,914	9.9
Parkersburg, WV-OH 4 counties and 41 cites and towns	162,995	163,622	0.4
*Pascagoula, MS 2 counties and 5 cites and towns	160,171	172,569	7.2
Pensacola-Ferry Pass, FL 2 counties and 5 cites and towns	458,531	519,665	11.8
Peoria, IL 5 counties and 202 cites and towns	368,221	374,607	1.7
Philadelphia, PA 5 counties and 231 cites and towns	3,907,650	3,992,131	2.1
Phoenix-Mesa, AZ 2 counties and 35 cites and towns	3,936,377	4,638,575	15.1

Metro Area	Population 2007	Population 2015	Percent Growth	Metro Area	Population 2007	Population 2015	Percent Growth
Pine Bluff, AR 3 counties and 12 cites and towns	106,229	107,279	1.0	**Rochester, NY** 5 counties and 168 cities and towns	1,047,821	1,066,340	1.7
Pittsburgh, PA 7 counties and 441 cites and towns	2,414,701	2,435,711	0.9	**Rockford, IL** 2 counties and 65 cities and towns	341,273	363,771	6.2
Pittsfield, MA 1 county and 32 cites and towns	133,089	133,386	0.2	**Rockingham County, NH** 2 counties and 50 cities and towns	434,605	490,161	11.3
Pocatello, ID 2 counties and 9 cites and towns	86,738	94,585	8.3	**Rocky Mount, NC** 2 counties and 18 cities and towns	147,379	153,624	4.1
Portland, ME 3 counties and 67 cites and towns	520,235	552,398	5.8	**Rome, GA** 1 county and 2 cites and towns	95,245	99,435	4.2
Portland, OR-WA 7 counties and 60 cites and towns	2,166,588	2,429,126	10.8	**Sacramento, CA** 4 counties and 19 cities and towns	2,139,196	2,476,884	13.6
Port St. Lucie, FL 2 counties and 7 cites and towns	379,823	444,143	14.5	**Saginaw, MI** 1 county and 43 cities and towns	207,467	204,824	-1.3
Poughkeepsie, NY 2 counties and 96 cites and towns	682,608	743,007	8.1	**St. Cloud, MN** 2 counties and 90 cities and towns	182,768	200,894	9.0
Prescott, AZ 1 county and 10 cites and towns	209,070	259,169	19.3	**St. George, UT** 1 county and 14 cities and towns	125,838	169,689	25.8
Providence, RI-MA 6 counties and 59 cites and towns	1,655,944	1,729,994	4.3	**St. Joseph, MO-KS** 4 counties and 61 cities and towns	124,129	127,155	2.4
Provo-Orem, UT 2 counties and 29 cites and towns	453,984	550,230	17.5	**St. Louis, MO-IL** 15 counties, 1 independent city and 507 cites and towns	2,809,316	2,922,754	3.9
Pueblo, CO 1 county and 3 cites and towns	152,301	160,104	4.9	**Salem, OR** 2 counties and 25 cities and towns	379,046	413,069	8.2
Punta Gorda, FL 1 county and 1 cites and towns	174,551	217,588	19.8	**Salinas, CA** 1 county and 12 cities and towns	439,833	492,543	10.7
Racine, WI 1 county and 19 cites and towns	194,389	199,554	2.6	**Salisbury, MD** 2 counties and 10 cities and towns	116,603	124,730	6.5
Raleigh-Cary, NC 3 counties and 28 cites and towns	961,231	1,118,663	14.1	**Salt Lake City, UT** 3 counties and 28 cities and towns	1,091,466	1,268,504	14.0
Rapid City, SD 2 counties and 48 cites and towns	121,120	130,748	7.4	**San Angelo, TX** 2 counties and 2 cites and towns	105,741	107,225	1.4
Reading, PA 1 county and 76 cites and towns	393,531	411,856	4.4	**San Antonio, TX** 8 counties and 51 cities and towns	1,933,054	2,166,546	10.8
Redding, CA 1 county and 3 cites and towns	187,489	211,973	11.6	**San Diego, CA** 1 county and 18 cities and towns	3,127,038	3,533,056	11.5
Reno-Sparks, NV 2 counties and 2 cites and towns	397,561	445,766	10.8	**Sandusky, OH** 1 county and 24 cities and towns	79,871	82,579	3.3
Richmond, VA 15 counties, 5 independent cities and 17 cities and towns	1,195,632	1,316,185	9.2	**San Francisco, CA** 3 counties and 32 cities and towns	1,718,124	1,772,203	3.1
Riverside, CA 2 counties and 48 cites and towns	3,948,512	4,580,163	13.8	**San Jose, CA** 2 counties and 17 cities and towns	1,794,068	1,921,109	6.6
Roanoke, VA 4 counties, 2 independent cities and 9 cities and towns	298,462	315,953	5.5	**San Luis Obispo, CA** 1 county and 7 cities and towns	272,149	311,537	12.6
Rochester, MN 3 counties and 79 cities and towns	182,098	202,275	10.0	**Santa Ana-Anaheim, CA** 1 county and 34 cities and towns	3,122,879	3,467,861	9.9

Metro Area	Population 2007	Population 2015	Percent Growth
Santa Barbara, CA 1 county and 8 cites and towns	415,714	442,784	6.1
Santa Cruz, CA 1 county and 4 cites and towns	261,405	282,254	7.4
Santa Fe, NM 1 county and 3 cites and towns	148,730	173,970	14.5
Santa Rosa-Petaluma, CA 1 county and 9 cites and towns	499,379	566,861	11.9
Sarasota-Bradenton, FL 2 counties and 9 cites and towns	692,099	812,091	14.8
Savannah, GA 3 counties and 13 cites and towns	313,961	334,797	6.2
Scranton, PA 3 counties and 138 cites and towns	548,518	544,377	-0.8
Seattle-Bellevue, WA 2 counties and 58 cites and towns	2,512,859	2,748,642	8.6
Sebastian-Vero Beach, FL 1 county and 5 cites and towns	130,746	151,892	13.9
Sheboygan, WI 1 county and 28 cites and towns	115,696	120,862	4.3
Sherman-Denison, TX 1 county and 16 cites and towns	119,284	128,061	6.9
Shreveport, LA 3 parishes and 23 cites and towns	384,575	398,904	3.6
Sioux City, IA-NE-SD 4 counties and 70 cites and towns	145,248	150,877	3.7
Sioux Falls, SD 4 counties and 104 cites and towns	210,435	235,301	10.6
South Bend, IN-MI 2 counties and 62 cites and towns	324,026	338,195	4.2
Spartanburg, SC 1 county and 14 cites and towns	268,891	285,334	5.8
Spokane, WA 1 county and 13 cites and towns	449,102	487,250	7.8
Springfield, IL 2 counties and 80 cites and towns	206,318	211,072	2.3
Springfield, MA 3 counties and 69 cites and towns	694,336	709,750	2.2
Springfield, MO 5 counties and 34 cites and towns	411,604	467,476	12.0
Springfield, OH 1 county and 29 cites and towns	141,125	137,398	-2.7
State College, PA 1 county and 36 cites and towns	146,176	155,916	6.2
Stockton, CA 1 county and 7 cites and towns	668,878	744,258	10.1

Metro Area	Population 2007	Population 2015	Percent Growth
Sumter, SC 1 county and 3 cites and towns	107,401	110,846	3.1
Syracuse, NY 3 counties and 130 cites and towns	654,738	659,189	0.7
Tacoma, WA 1 county and 24 cites and towns	782,374	868,695	9.9
Tallahassee, FL 4 counties and 10 cites and towns	349,923	395,570	11.5
Tampa-St. Petersburg, FL 4 counties and 35 cites and towns	2,677,041	2,979,449	10.1
Terre Haute, IN 4 counties and 84 cites and towns	169,060	168,638	-0.3
Texarkana, TX-AR 2 counties and 13 cites and towns	135,570	144,080	5.9
Toledo, OH 4 counties and 144 cites and towns	659,941	661,363	0.2
Topeka, KS 5 counties and 146 cites and towns	228,623	234,697	2.6
Trenton-Ewing, NJ 1 county and 13 cites and towns	370,957	390,637	5.0
Tucson, AZ 1 county and 5 cites and towns	959,655	1,097,512	12.6
Tulsa, OK 7 counties and 77 cites and towns	919,075	1,001,912	8.3
Tuscaloosa, AL 3 counties and 16 cites and towns	199,090	208,973	4.7
Tyler, TX 1 county and 11 cites and towns	191,870	208,382	7.9
Utica-Rome, NY 2 counties and 106 cites and towns	295,612	292,235	-1.2
Valdosta, GA 4 counties and 10 cites and towns	127,267	138,073	7.8
Vallejo-Fairfield, CA 1 county and 7 cites and towns	446,688	517,305	13.7
Victoria, TX 3 counties and 5 cites and towns	117,380	126,733	7.4
Vineland-Millville, NJ 1 county and 14 cites and towns	150,569	153,856	2.1
Virginia Beach, VA-NC 7 counties, 9 independent cities and 14 cities and towns	1,703,506	1,844,110	7.6
Visalia-Porterville, CA 1 county and 8 cites and towns	410,697	452,431	9.2
Waco, TX 1 county and 21 cites and towns	227,289	243,170	6.5
Warner Robins, GA 1 county and 4 cites and towns	126,729	139,936	9.4

Metro Area	Population 2007	Population 2015	Percent Growth
Warren-Troy, MI 5 counties and 200 cites and towns	2,536,388	2,710,547	6.4
Washington, DC-VA-MD 13 counties, 7 independent cites and 65 cities and towns	4,194,418	4,684,718	10.5
Waterloo-Cedar Falls, IA 3 counties and 27 cites and towns	162,350	163,679	0.8
Wausau, WI 1 county and 68 cites and towns	130,874	138,898	5.8
Weirton, WV-OH 3 counties and 58 cites and towns	126,684	123,686	-2.4
Wenatchee, WA 2 counties and 11 cites and towns	106,362	116,152	8.4
West Palm Beach, FL 1 county and 37 cites and towns	1,341,821	1,598,538	16.1
Wheeling, WV-OH 3 counties and 55 cites and towns	148,976	147,142	-1.2
Wichita, KS 4 counties and 206 cites and towns	599,604	635,825	5.7
Wichita Falls, TX 3 counties and 18 cites and towns	151,387	155,429	2.6
Williamsport, PA 1 county and 52 cites and towns	118,709	120,084	1.1
Wilmington, DE-MD-NJ 3 counties and 38 cites and towns	697,236	749,575	7.0

Metro Area	Population 2007	Population 2015	Percent Growth
Wilmington, NC 3 counties and 30 cites and towns	316,674	365,083	13.3
Winchester, VA-WV 2 counties, 1 independent city and 5 cities and towns	116,805	130,535	10.5
Winston-Salem, NC 4 counties and 19 cites and towns	457,613	499,910	8.5
Worcester, MA 1 county and 60 cites and towns	797,053	841,685	5.3
Yakima, WA 1 county and 14 cites and towns	238,110	261,985	9.1
York-Hanover, PA 1 county and 72 cites and towns	405,525	428,684	5.4
Youngstown, OH-PA 3 counties and 124 cites and towns	587,116	577,900	-1.6
Yuba City, CA 2 counties and 4 cites and towns	154,767	168,652	8.2
Yuma, AZ 1 county and 4 cites and towns	208,084	243,955	14.7

Source: Woods & Poole Economics, Inc., population forecasts. For a complete listing of each metro area's counties, cities and towns, see the "Metro Area Place Finder" in the Appendix at the end of this book.

* Population figures for three Gulf coast metro areas are based on pre- Hurricane Katrina trends.

The 379 Metropolitan Areas

Decisions, Decisions

More than 30 years ago a group of futurists, academics, and government scientists got together at a hotel outside Washington, DC, for a conference sponsored by the Environmental Protection Agency. Their job was to discover just what people mean by "quality of life" when they talk about places.

The players quickly split into three groups over the issue. One group argued that defining what's good for all people at all times is not only unfair, it's impossible and shouldn't be tried at all. "Quality of life for whom?" went their argument. The artist or the BMX biker who wants mountain vistas? The entrepreneur who wants low taxes and a minimum of red tape? The new college graduate looking to start a career? Retired workers in need of low-cost health care? Parents in search of alternatives to public schools?

Another group held that you can rate places for their relative livability but you shouldn't do it because measuring a touchy and fuzzy concept like livability makes places unwilling rivals of one another. When you claim your own turf is the most livable, you're implying that others are a lot less so. Look at the dumb jokes and occasional ill will that flow between neighbors like Dallas and Ft. Worth, Minneapolis and St. Paul, or San Francisco and Oakland. Rating places is an exercise unworthy of responsible citizens, according to this view. Every place is habitable—that's why people are *living* in them. Since we're all in this world together, then together we'll make our cities and towns even more livable.

The third group in effect said 'baloney' to the other two. All other things being equal, people prefer to live where the streets are safer, the costs of living are lower, the weather is milder, and the local economy is thriving. Of course you can measure livability. To urge cities to stop their unsavory competition is to ignore reality. Just try asking that of Atlanta or Denver or Seattle the next time those areas battle to be the site of a political convention or the new headquarters for a large white-collar employer. As long as you know who your audience is and make clear what your statistical yardsticks are and use them consistently,

you'll be doing what's done all the time by chambers of commerce and other city boosters from Miami to Puget Sound and from West Quoddy Head, Maine, to San Diego. More importantly, you'll be giving mobile people what they need most: information.

Although there is something to be said for viewpoints one and two, *Places Rated* sides with the third.

RATING PLACES: ONE WAY

This is a book of current statistics about America's metropolitan areas. Certainly it is a more objective source of information about urban livability than the hearsay that people share at a dinner party, a rest stop on the Interstate, an airport bar, or blogging on the Internet. All of the 379 metro areas in this book are rated by nine factors, each of which would be important to anyone considering a move.

• The chapter on *Ambience* compares cultural assets, among them art museums, opera and ballet companies, and symphony orchestras. Racial diversity, politics, historic districts, bookstores and good restaurants also go into the mix.

• *Housing* measures price appreciation since 2000, local prices for *starter* homes, *move-up* homes, and *elite* houses, plus property taxes, utilities and mortgage payments. We also consider how much typical rents are.

• The *Jobs* chapter looks at local risks for unemployment and weighs prospects for job growth to the year 2015 in nine basic industries, especially the higher-paying ones like manufacturing, transportation, communications, and government.

• A metro area's *Crime* rating is determined by the average annual number of violent and property crimes per 100,000 people over the past 5 years and whether the trend is upward, downward or unchanged.

• *Transportation* is rated by local commuting time, public transit, and how easy it is to get into and out of each metro area by air, rail, and interstate highway.

• Each metro area's public and private schools, its collection of colleges and universities, and its public libraries produce an *Education* rating.

• The supply of accredited hospitals and patient-treating physicians, plus special services like open-heart surgery and sports medicine, forms the basis for a metro area's *Health Care* rating.

• *Recreation* also rates assets, from public golf courses and movie theatres, to zoos, professional sports, ocean coastlines, and national parks, forests, and wildlife acreage.

• *Climate* is rated on mildness, that is, how close temperatures remain to 65° Fahrenheit throughout the year. Brightness and stability also are part of the rating.

Some readers may question *Places Rated*'s choice of criteria. Admittedly, its benchmarks for health care, transportation, higher education choices, and crowd pleasers all favor bigger places over smaller ones. On the other hand, the methods for judging safety from crime and calculating living costs favor smaller places over bigger ones. *Places Rated*'s standards for climate and outdoor recreation assets are certainly not everyone's, but they have nothing to do with population size.

Gathered here are the most up-to-date figures for all 379 metro areas. The sources, which are documented throughout, include federal and state agencies and a growing number of private organizations.

This 7th edition of *Places Rated Almanac* is as much a snapshot of a moving target as were each of its six predecessors over the past twenty-five years. Metro areas are dynamic and just don't sit still for statistical portraits. An economic rebound in many smaller metro areas draws native sons and daughters—some with families—back from the Big City. On the other hand, a taste for racial diversity, the performing arts, and the excitement of Big City life attracts newcomers from the smaller metro areas. Likewise, many of the thousands of Louisianans and Mississippians who fled Katrina's devastation have returned to find empty home turf that's down so low the only direction is up. So, life being unpredictable, you'd be wise to supplement *Places Rated Almanac* with your own independent confirmation.

RATING PLACES: YOUR WAY

At the end of this book, in *Putting It All Together*, ambience, housing, jobs, crime, transportation, education, health care, recreation and climate get

equal weight when identifying metro areas with across-the-board strengths.

You may not agree with this equal-weight system. You may give more importance to forecasted job growth than to a relative lack of crime or an outstanding calendar of performing arts events. For you, a place where living costs are low may be much more important than an ocean coastline, an abundance of medical specialists, or an active higher education scene. To identify which factors are more important and which factors are less, you may want to take stock of your preferences.

Your *Preference Inventory*
The following Preference Inventory has seventy-two pairs of statements. For each pair, decide which statement is more important to you when judging whether a place is livable. Even if both statements are equally important or neither is important, select one anyway. If you can't decide quickly, pass up the item, but return to it after you complete the rest of the inventory.

Don't worry about being consistent. The paired statements aren't repeated. There aren't any right or wrong answers, only those that are best for you. Although the inventory takes about 10 minutes to finish, there is no time limit. Before you start, you might want to photocopy the inventory and ask your spouse or a friend to take it independently. Or visit *www.placesrated.com* and try it out. Comparing your Preference Inventory with another person's can be an interesting exercise.

Directions
For each numbered item, decide which of the two statements is more important to you when choosing a place to live. Mark the box next to that statement. Be sure to make a choice for all items.

1. *I.* □ The number of days over 90 degrees.
   B. □ Typical property taxes.

2. *D.* □ The local robbery and murder rate.
   F. □ The choice of public school districts.

3. *G.* □ Variety of medical specialists.
   E. □ Local public transit.

4. *A.* □ Classical music broadcasting.
   I. □ Temperature and humidity.

5. *B.* □ The typical price of a starter home.
   E. □ How long it takes to commute to work.

6. *A.* □ Opera and professional theatre.
   H. □ Local college sports.

7. *G.* □ Good children's hospitals.
   I. □ Annual amount of rain and snow.

8. *B.* □ Recent home price appreciation.
   D. □ Local property crime rates.

9. *C.* □ Forecasted job growth.
   F. □ The pupil/teacher ratio in public schools.

10. *A.* □ Art museums and repertory theaters.
    D. □ The number of auto thefts in a year.

11. *H.* □ The number of public golf courses.
    E. □ Freeway traffic congestion.

12. *G.* □ Local emergency medical care.
    A. □ Good restaurants and bookstores.

13. *A.* □ Repertory theatre companies.
    B. □ The median apartment rent.

14. *B.* □ Property taxes and utilities costs.
    C. □ The outlook for job growth.

15. *G.* □ Family medical services.
    F. □ Books held in local libraries.

16. *A.* □ Performing arts facilities.
    C. □ Job opportunities in the service sector.

17. *C.* □ Local threat of unemployment.
    I. □ Annual number of clear days.

18. *H.* □ Accessible ski areas.
    F. □ Variety of public and private colleges.

19. *E.* □ Public transportation.
    B. □ Prices for elite homes.

20. *B.* □ Prices for starter houses.
    G. □ Medical schools and teaching hospitals.

21. *B.* □ Recent home price appreciation.
    H. □ Local professional sports teams.

22. *A.* □ Politica and racial diversity.
    E. □ Airlines and interstate highways.

23. *G.* □ Supply of family medical practitioners.
    H. □ Nearby national parks and forests.

24. *D.* □ The violent crime rate.
    I. □ Annual amounts of rain and snow.

25. *F.* □ Pupil/teacher ratio in public schools.
    I. □ Annual number of clear and cloudy days.

26. *H.* □ The supply of public golf courses.
    D. □ Number of robberies and assaults.

27. *G.* □ Hospitals affiliated with medical schools.
    D. □ Number of burglaries during the year.

28. *F.* □ Local support of public schools.
    A. □ Ballet companies and repertory theaters.

29. *H.* □ Beaches, fishing, and boating.
    C. □ Number of new jobs by 2010.

30. *H.* □ Nearby national parks and forests.
    I. □ Number of stormy days during the year.

31. *C.* □ The mix of white- and blue-collar jobs.
    D. □ Number of robberies in a year.

32. *E.* □ Airlines serving the local airport.
    D. □ Number of auto thefts in a year.

33. *E.* □ Available public transportation.
    F. □ Local colleges and universities.

34. *B.* □ Home property taxes and utility costs.
    G. □ General hospitals and family doctors.

35. *F.* □ Quality of public schools.
    B. □ Rent for a one-bedroom apartment.

36. *E.* □ Interstate highways and airline service.
    I. □ How cold the winters are.

37. *G.* □ Variety of medical specialists.
    I. □ Number of annual rainy and snowy days.

38. *D.* □ Local auto thefts and burglaries.
    B. □ Local property taxes and utilities.

39. *A.* □ Live theatres and concert halls.
    H. □ Zoos and family amusement parks.

40. *D.* □ Annual muggings per capita.
    F. □ Pupil/teacher ratio in public schools.

41. *C.* □ Outlook for job growth.
    E. □ Average daily commuting time.

42. *I.* □ Seasonal temperature variation.
    B. □ Typical property taxes.

43. *G.* □ Medical schools and teaching hospitals.
    A. □ Historic homes and buildings.

44. *H.* □ Opportunities for pari-mutuel wagering.
    E. □ Freeway traffic congestion.

45. *C.* □ Mix of white- and blue-collar jobs.
    F. □ Alternatives to public schools.

46. *I.* □ Seasonal temperature variation.
    C. □ Forecasted growth of jobs.

47. *D.* □ Auto thefts, muggings, and shootings.
    I. □ Annual number of freezing days.

48. *B.* □ Cost of heating a home.
    F. □ Variety of private K-12 schools.

49. *C.* □ Expected white-collar job growth.
    D. □ Annual property crime rate.

50. *C.* □ Forecasted number of good jobs.
    B. □ Prices for starter and elite houses.

51 *A.* □ Good bookstores and restaurants.
   E. □ Freeway traffic congestion.

52. *G.* □ Primary medical care.
    H. □ Nearby state parks and forests.

53. **F.** ☐ The quality of public libraries.
    I. ☐ Local wind speed and humidity.

54. **H.** ☐ Thoroughbred horse racing.
    C. ☐ Jobs in health and education services.

55. **I.** ☐ Number of days over 90 degrees.
    E. ☐ Supply of public transit.

56. **H.** ☐ Beaches, boating, and fishing.
    F. ☐ Variety of public and private colleges.

57. **A.** ☐ Opera and professional theatre.
    C. ☐ Local risk of unemployment.

58. **H.** ☐ Local professional sports teams.
    I. ☐ Annual amounts of rain and snow.

59. **A.** ☐ Repertory theatre and the symphony.
    I. ☐ How cold the winters are.

60. **B.** ☐ Median price of homes.
    A. ☐ Politics and racial diversity.

61. **D.** ☐ The odds of being burglarized.
    A. ☐ Local art museums and bookstores.

62. **D.** ☐ Burglaries and auto thefts.
    G. ☐ Specialized medical care.

63. **C.** ☐ Job outlook from now to the year 2010.
    E. ☐ Freeway traffic congestion.

64. **D.** ☐ The property crime rate.
    H. ☐ Nearby national parks and forests.

65. **G.** ☐ Surgeons and medical specialists.
    C. ☐ Forecast for white-collar job growth

66. **F.** ☐ Higher education opportunities.
    A. ☐ Opera and professional theatre.

67. **E.** ☐ Access to interstate highways.
    F. ☐ Private alternatives to public schools.

68. **H.** ☐ Local public golf courses.
    B. ☐ The median rent for an apartment.

69. **G.** ☐ Physicians in family practice.
    F. ☐ Variety of public school districts.

70. **E.** ☐ Airlines serving the area.
    D. ☐ Local burglaries and auto thefts.

71. **G.** ☐ Family doctors and children's hospitals.
    E. ☐ Quality of public transit.

72. **G.** ☐ Medical Specialists
    C. ☐ Prospects for white-collar job growth.

Plotting Your *Preference Profile*

It is important that you make a choice for each of the seventy-two items. Have you left any unchecked? If not, you're ready to draw your *Preference Profile*.

    First Step. Count all the marks you've made in the boxes next to the letter A. Then enter the number of "A" statements on the line next to the words "Ambience" on your Preference Profile. In the same way, count the number of statements for each of the other letters. Enter their totals in their respective places on your *Preference Profile*.

    Second Step. Now plot your totals on the blank chart. Place a dot on the appropriate line for each of the numbers and connect the dots to form a line graph of your results (see the Sample Preference Profile below).

Analyzing Your *Preference Profile*

Each of the factors in your Preference Profile—ambiance, costs of living, the economy, crime, transportation, education, health care, recreation, and climate—is not only a big concern when choosing a place to live, but it also has a complete chapter in this book. The purpose of the *Preference Inventory* is to help you decide the relative importance of each of these nine factors to you.

    If your scores are high for one or two of these factors, you may want to give extra attention to the chapters devoted to them. Likewise, if your scores are how for any of the nine factors, you may not need to give as much consideration to them as you would to those with high scores. Keep in mind that the inventory orders your preferences in a hierarchy, that each of the factors has some importance to you, and that none should be completely ignored.

Decisions, Decisions

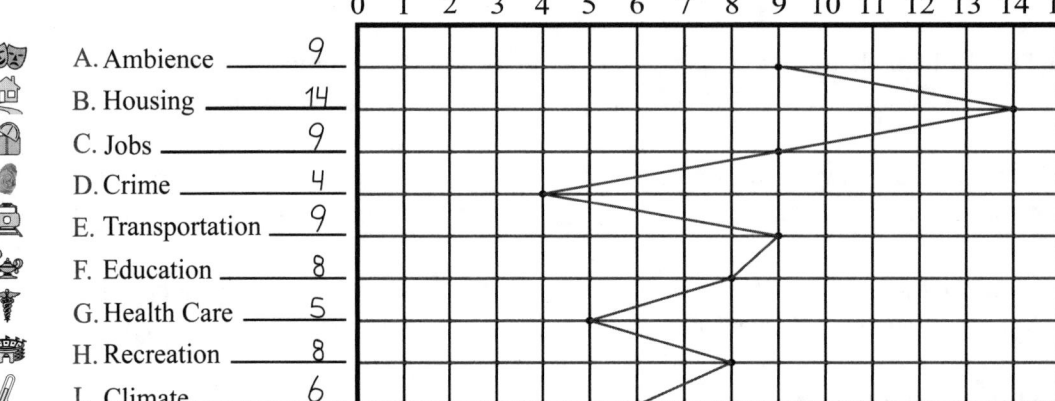

		0 1 2 3 4 5 6 7 8 9 10 11 12 13 14 15
	A. Ambience	9
	B. Housing	14
	C. Jobs	9
	D. Crime	4
	E. Transportation	9
	F. Education	8
	G. Health Care	5
	H. Recreation	8
	I. Climate	6

		0 1 2 3 4 5 6 7 8 9 10 11 12 13 14 15
	A. Ambience	
	B. Housing	
	C. Jobs	
	D. Crime	
	E. Transportation	
	F. Education	
	G. Health Care	
	H. Recreation	
	I. Climate	

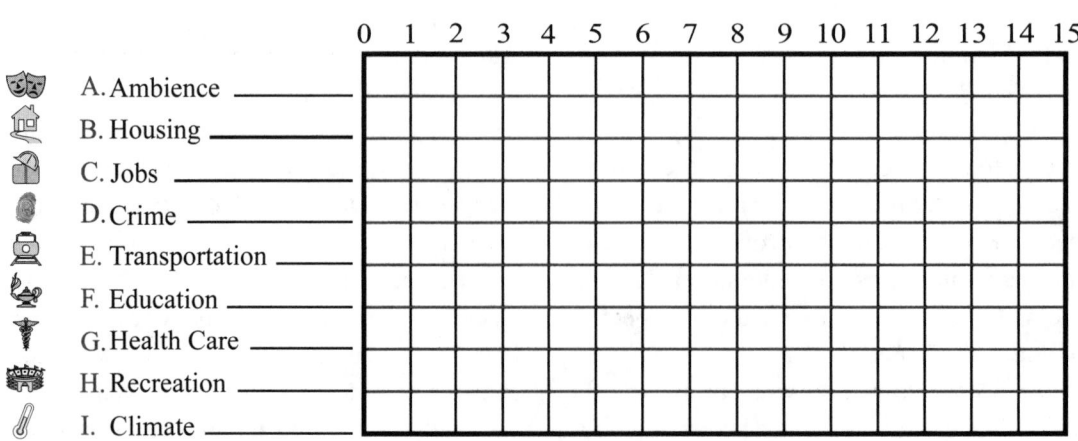

		0 1 2 3 4 5 6 7 8 9 10 11 12 13 14 15
	A. Ambience	
	B. Housing	
	C. Jobs	
	D. Crime	
	E. Transportation	
	F. Education	
	G. Health Care	
	H. Recreation	
	I. Climate	

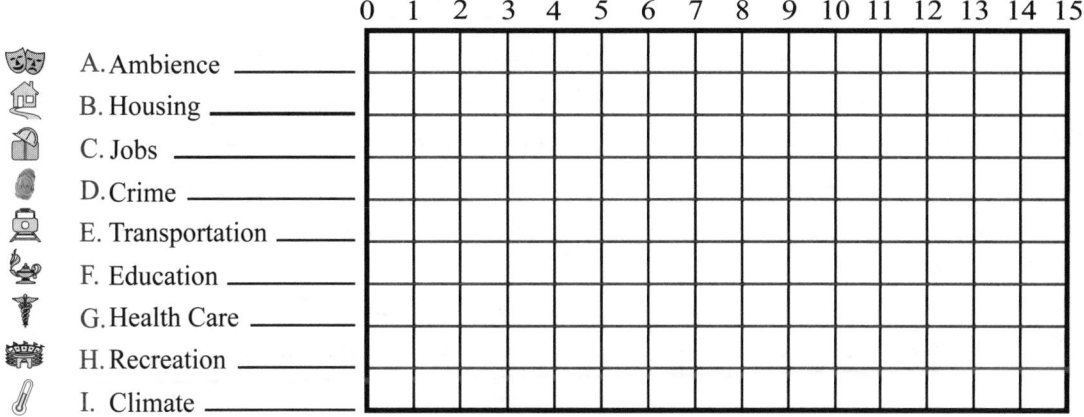

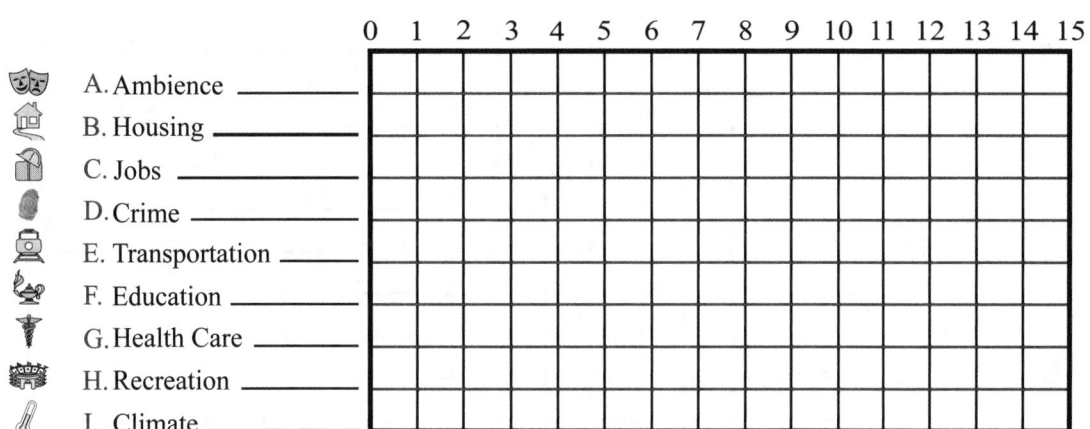

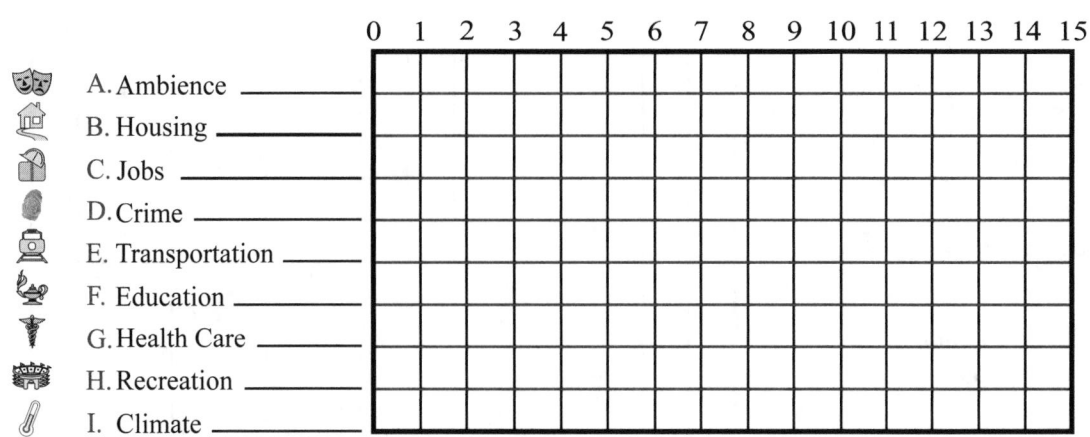

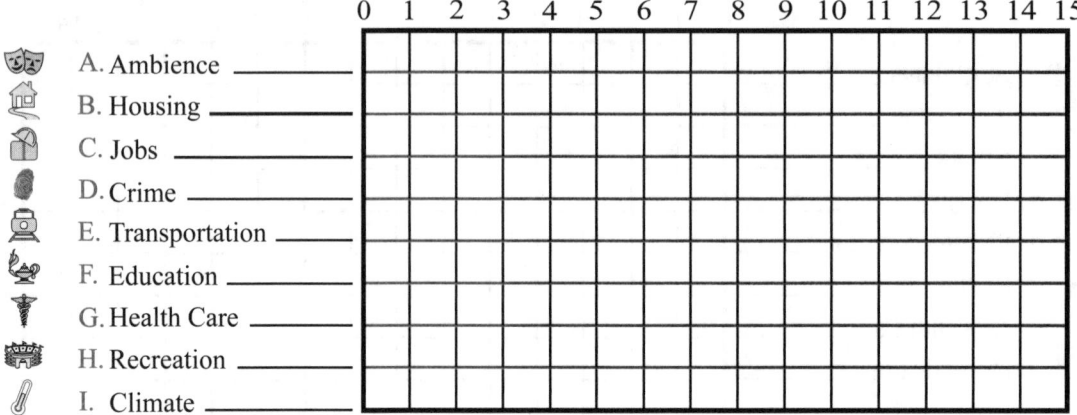

| | A. Ambience | B. Housing | C. Jobs | D. Crime | E. Transportation | F. Education | G. Health Care | H. Recreation | I. Climate |

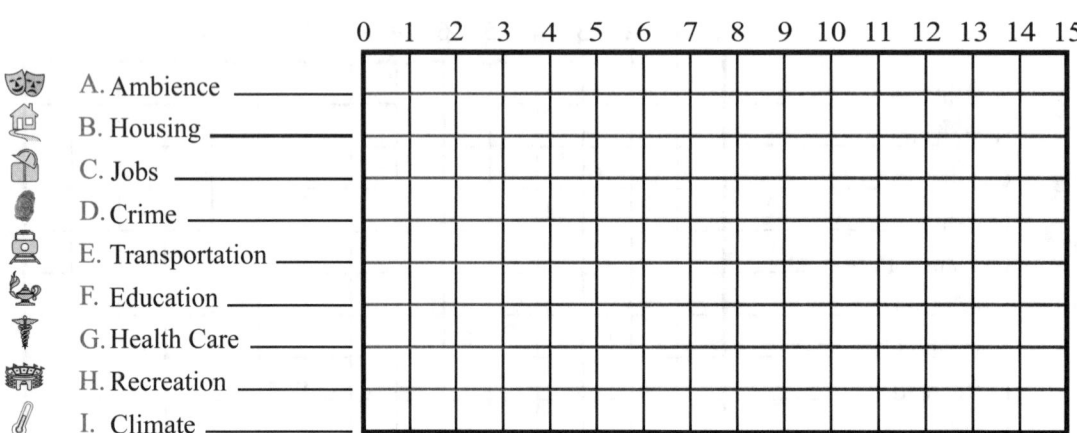

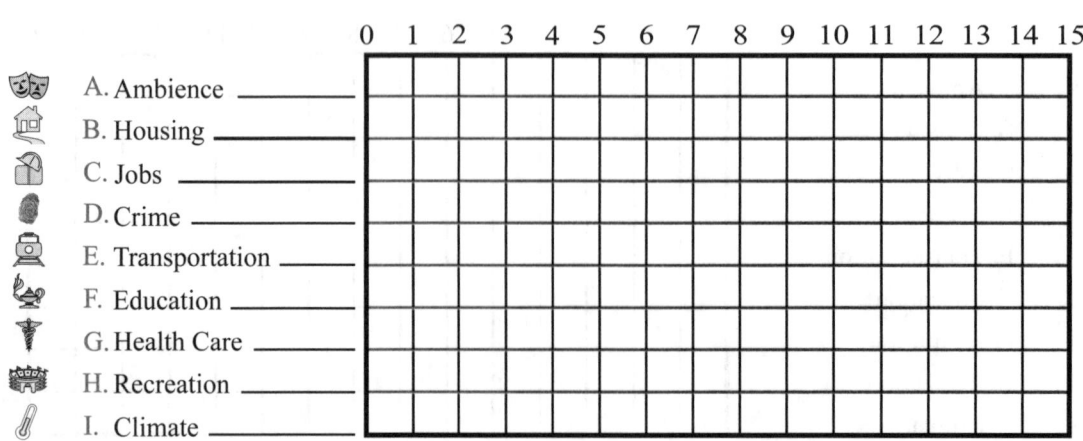

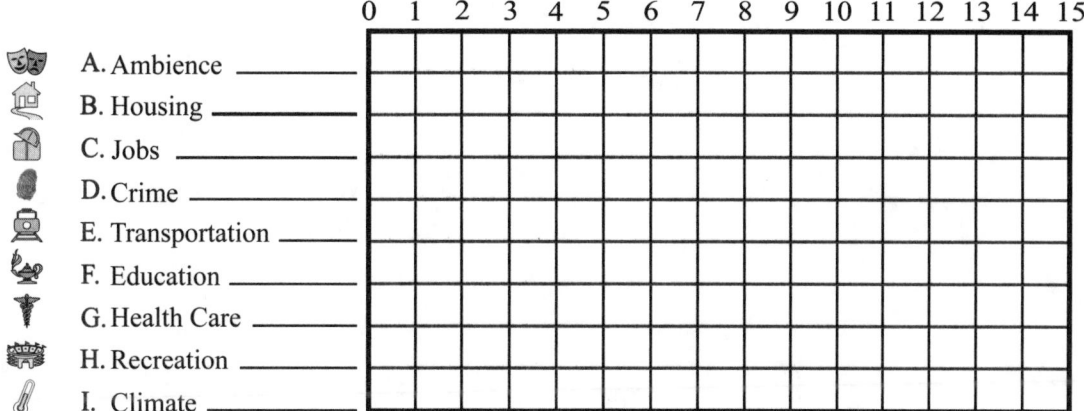

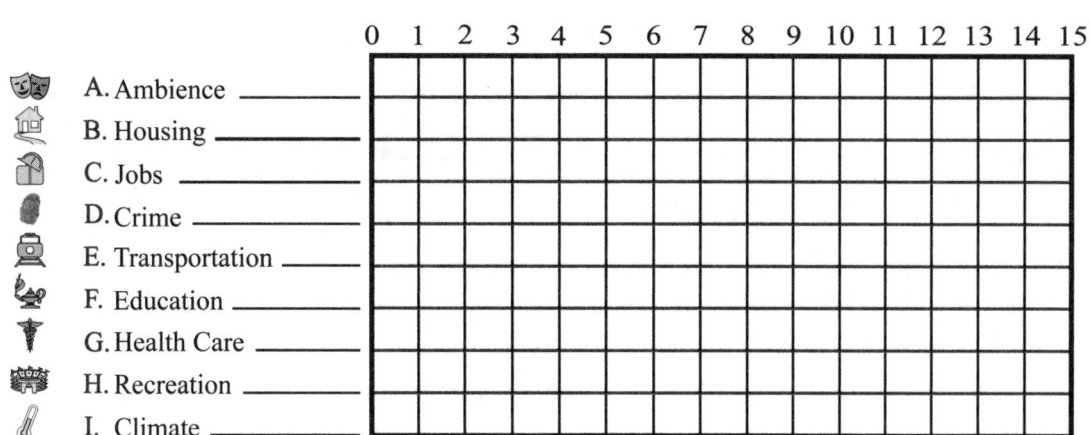

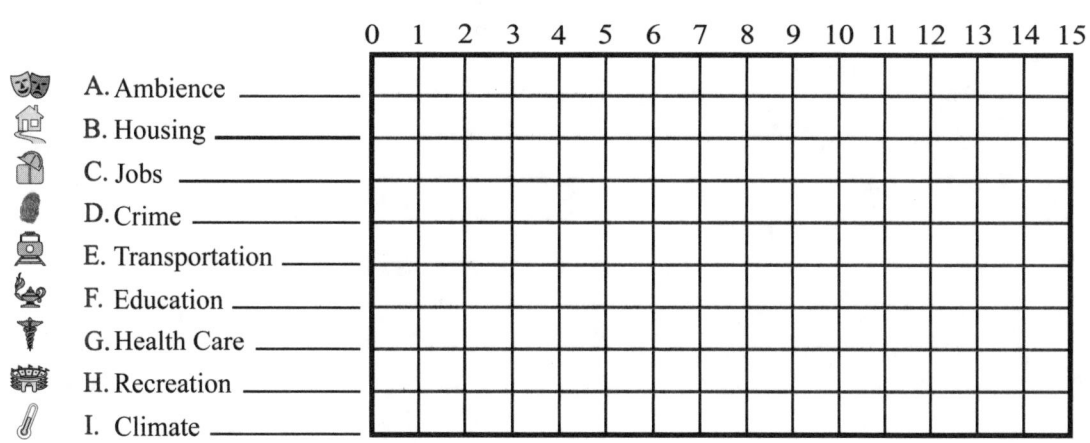

Ambience

In San Francisco, a recent civic uproar over clearing out the bums in the Tenderloin district wasn't about displacing human beings so much as it was about the loss of ambience. Ambience? Cleaning up derelict buildings and moving the street people into more comfortable shelter implied loss of ambience?

Ambience. Now there's a word that was uttered a lot by visitors to the older parts of pre-Katrina New Orleans. For many, the word sticks to older parts of San Antonio as it does Capitol Hill in Washington, DC, or the central West End in St. Louis. Oh, yeah? The arguments in favor of San Francisco's Telegraph Hill or Brooklyn's Park Slope are just around the corner.

We disagree about which city has it, but there's less disagreement on which cities don't. For a lot of people, the younger, sprawling Sunbelt boomtowns (Houston, Las Vegas, or Orlando) lack ambience. For others, so do no-growth, blue-collar metros (Buffalo, Cleveland, Detroit).

A STAB AT AMBIENCE

The word stems from *air* or *atmosphere* and like so many things cultural, has evolved to define something different: The special qualities of place - the air, the feel, the place's *genius loci*, even the way it makes you behave.

Places Rated will not claim here that it knows better than you which metro areas have more of that subtle quality than others. But it does attempt to measure a number of attributes that many of us think contribute to a place's ambience: Dining out, good bookstores, a visible past, the performing arts, and people.

Bricks and Mortar: Good Food

The most common service establishment is the one where you walk in, sit down, and order something to eat. If you enjoy a dinner splurge, you may as well go to a worthwhile eatery instead of a diner or a portion-controlled *Casa de la Maison House* where distantly prepared frozen packs of beef Wellington and veal cordon bleu are menued, microwaved, and plated at 10 times what the chef paid for them.

To learn which places have restaurants more than just a cut above average, *Places Rated* consulted all 23 of the *American Automobile Association (AAA) TourBooks*. In these volumes, about one out of nine of America's 224,000 full service establishments are rated from one to five diamonds.

One AAA diamond indicates a simple meal in clean, pleasant, and informal surroundings. The menu is limited to specialties: Fried chicken, pizza, tacos, or hamburgers. New York City's *Carnegie Delicatessen* ("A landmark since 1937") fits this description with its brisk service and takeout.

Epicenter in downtown Los Angeles, serving Asian and California cuisine in an earthquake-motif decor, is a two-diamond establishment. Eateries at this level focus on food presentation such as "common garnishes" and "styled dishware." They offer a more extensive menu. Service is attentive but informal and the decor is comfortable, or trendy and upbeat.

Three-diamond restaurants mark pricey adult dining. There is a specialty-beer and wine list and food is cooked to order and creatively prepared with quality ingredients. The wait staff is skilled and professional, and the ambience is inviting, trendy or formal. Oklahoma City's *Lotus*, specializing in Asian fusion cuisine, is an instance in this category.

The *Hill Country Dining Room*, in the Barton Creek Resort in Austin, Texas, is a four-diamond establishment. It's dressy, expensive, and has a view of the resort's golf course and the Texas Hill Country beyond. The service is formally attired and sophisticated; a wine steward runs the wine list; an executive chef runs the kitchen; the food is complex and creatively presented.

The five-diamond designation means the eatery is "renowned and provides a world-class" experience. Step into *Artisans* in the Ritz-Carlton Hotel in Naples, Florida: Semi-formal attire, whispering wait staff, grand piano and violin music. "Flawless" is the key word—in food preparation and presentation, in service, and in atmosphere.

Bricks and Mortar: Good Bookstores

The chain booksellers have won. At $9 billion in annual dollars from some 2,200 outlets, three chains—Barnes & Noble, Borders Group, and Books-A-Million—account for 70 percent all general bookstore sales.

Of course independent booksellers still operate. Several—Denver's Tattered Cover, Bookpeople in Austin, TX, Powell's in Portland, OR—operate superstores as big as the chains. To survive, though, some 2,000 other independent stores must specialize in religious, scientific and engineering, business, and childrens books.

All bookstores are good bookstores because they all are great third places—spots separate from home and work where you can spend time - which is what the chains are striving to be. Now you can sit at a Starbucks cafe, scan a Dummies book, sample a hip hop CD, and answer your email.

Bricks and Mortar: Visible Past

In demolishing an early 19th century orphanage in Charleston, South Carolina, in 1953, workmen lashed a heavy chain around a large marble angel atop the pediment and pulled it crashing down with a tow truck. That incident so outraged some citizens, that their campaign to save Charleston's historic buildings marked the start of civic historic preservation.

Preserving buildings recognizes the value of a community's culture and past. It draws people. It brings prestige and pride and value.

The Lively Arts Calendar

Most people would exchange any worn-out city for a serene place that's safer, cheaper, and less crowded. The escape to a smaller place is a sustaining dream for big-city residents, according to opinion polls.

You might even pack up and make your own break if the chance arrives in the form of a job transfer, a mid-life change, or retirement. You may be pleased to discover that towns with courthouse squares, angle parking, and kids riding two-wheelers on streets actually named Main still exist. You might write home that you'd finally found a sense of cohesion, of continuity and tradition, of community spirit and neighborliness that you thought had vanished. You're happier than you've been in years.

For about four months.

Because in your headlong rush to abandon the aggravations of big-city life, you abandoned the classic marble art museum you barely glanced at in passing twice each day in the crush of commuter traffic. You also turned your back on the local newspaper's arts section, the local public television station's earnest fundraising auctions, and your annual subscription to the repertory theatre's season.

Despite the competition, the audience's increasingly precious leisure time, rolling economic recessions, and the drop in government arts funding, the lively arts continue to endure.

For all their troubles, the lively arts still outdraw

professional sports. Unlike professional football or major league baseball, however, resident symphony orchestras, opera companies, professional theatre, and dance companies are urban assets that are all the more exceptional in a metro area because they are endangered.

Touring Artists Bookings

Long before the Brassissimo Vienna, Harlem Spiritual Ensemble, or Borealis Wind Quintet comes to town for a date at the local performing arts center, they are booked by a college or nonprofit community concert association.

Filling the concert halls with classical artists, big business for agents and presenters in former times, is getting tougher and less fun. In spite of marketing twists like rush-hour recitals, sound clips on the Internet, park concerts, tie-ins with art exhibits, celebrity narrators, and free kids admission, younger audiences are demanding more popular entertainment.

Opera

Opera fans boast that their passion embraces the greatest of the performing arts, since it combines a love for orchestral and vocal music, theatre, and dance. The first grand opera performed in this country was Rossini's *The Barber of Seville*, at New York's Park Theatre in 1825.

To this day, New York remains America's operatic capital. More than 30 companies with some kind of budget call New York home, including the grand New York City and the grand Metropolitan Opera where superstars Placido Domingo and Luciano Pavarotti celebrated 30 years of association.

Outside New York, opera has been diffused throughout the continent. From some 75 professional companies in the late 1970s, opera has expanded to more than 150, reaching an audience of 8 million during the 2005-2006 season.

These companies have typical annual budgets topping $1,000,000. Full-scale opera productions using professional orchestras and bringing the world's leading singers to the stage aren't cheap tickets, and most metro areas haven't the resources or audiences to support this singular form of the lively arts.

Symphony Orchestras

"The greatest instrument ever invented," Andre Previn once called the symphony. Of course, it is really a collection of many different instruments and musicians. The original definition—"to sound together," from the Greek—is just vague enough to embrace all the ensembles playing some type of symphonic music today in North America.

In all, there are some 1,500 groups, ranging in size and experience from youths playing before captive audiences of parents to accomplished and well-paid professionals working under the baton of Loren Maazel at the New York Philharmonic. Orchestras are far from uncommon in metro areas: 307 metro areas claim at least one. Forty-five of these places support four or more orchestras, and 18 metro areas support eight or more.

PEOPLE

How do you rate a metro area's population? Answer: You don't. *Places Rated* measures selected features of people on a scale that implies no progression from bad to good or good to bad.

From Younger to Older...

Since 1970, median age—a point where half the people are younger and the other half older—has advanced from 27.5 years to 36.6 years across America. The figure differs among metro areas mainly because of the local birth rate and also because of who moves in and out.

The two metro areas with the youngest populations are military posts: Jacksonville, North Carolina (home of the Marines' Camp Lejeune) and Hinesville-Fort Stewart, Georgia (site of the largest Army installation east of the Mississippi, Fort Stewart). Their residents' median age is under 25. The oldest metro area (median age: 54) is Punta Gorda, a retirement spot on Florida's gulf coast.

From Less Diverse to Diverse...

America's metropolitan area population is 63.8 percent White, 13.4 percent Black, 16.7 percent Latino, 5.5 percent Asian and Pacific Islander, and 0.6 percent Native American.

Sumter, South Carolina, and Albany, Georgia, are America's two metro areas with a Black majority according to Woods & Poole Economics estimates. Fifteen metro areas have Latino populations greater than 50 percent. Honolulu has a 67 percent Asian and Pacific Islander majority. The metro area with the highest portion of Native Americans—40 percent— is Farmington, New Mexico.

Which metro areas are the most diverse? Via the "chi-square test," a statistical technique used to

Searching for Normal People

Where might SONY test market a new eBook machine or Kraft sound out opinionson powdered hash brown potatoes for lunch? Why Albany or Jacksonville, of course. Below are the best and worst metropolitan test markets, according to market researcher Acxiom. The rankings are based on how closely people in 150 metropolitan areas mirror consumers nationwide.

Best

1. Albany-Schenectady-Troy, NY
2. Rochester, NY
3. Greensboro–Winston-Salem–High Point, NC
4. Birmingham, AL
5. Syracuse, NY
6. Charlotte-Gastonia-Rock Hill, NC-SC
7. Nashville, TN
8. Eugene-Springfield, OR
9. Wichita, KS
10. Richmond-Petersburg, VA
11. Davenport-Moline-Rock Island, IA-IL
12. Lexington, KY
13. Charleston-North Charleston, SC
14. Macon, GA
15. Jacksonville, FL

Worst

135. Miami, FL
136. Chicago, IL
137. Boston, MA-NH
138. Los Angeles-Long Beach, CA
139. Anchorage, AK
140. Philadelphia, PA-NJ
141. El Paso, TX
142. Columbia, MO
143. Tallahassee, FL
144. Brownsville-Harlingen-San Benito, TX
145. Provo-Orem, UT
146. Ocala, FL
147. McAllen-Edinburg-Mission, TX
148. Honolulu, HI
149. San Francisco, CA
150. New York, NY

Source: Acxiom - www.acxiom.com

compare observed data with expected data, metro areas are rated from more diverse to less diverse by how closely they match national diversity. West Palm Beach and College Station most approach the picture of national diversity. Other metro areas close behind are Atlantic City, Bridgeport, Newark, and Denver. At the other extreme, Altoona, with a population that is 97 percent White, and Laredo, that has a 96 percent Latino population, are among the least diverse.

From Less Affluent to Affluent...

Per capita income has rocketed from $4,000 in 1970 to $36,500 today. The metro areas with the highest figures are found among New York suburbs and the San Francisco Bay area. The poorest are smaller metro areas along the Rio Grande and in the inner South.

Although the United States is a high-income country, there's a lot of variation among metro areas because of local industries and worker skills. And there's more to per capita income than just earnings. There's income from dividends, interest, rent, and government welfare payments. The Woods & Poole Wealth Index weights income more positively for a relatively high proportion of income from dividends, interest, and rent and more negatively for a relatively high proportion of income from transfer payments. The Wealth Index average for the United States is 100, ranging from 186 in Bridgeport-Stamford-Norwalk, Connecticut, to 51 in McAllen-Edinburg-Mission, Texas.

From Less Educated to Educated...

In a moment sometime during 1967, the portion of adults with a high school diploma shifted from a minority to a majority. In the four decades since, high school has gone from being the mark of the educated person to the minimum education level for 4 out of 5 adults.

No region can claim the best-educated population. The Midwest has the highest portion of people with a high school diploma, but the Northeast has the highest portion of people with B.A.'s, M.A.'s and Ph.D's, while the West has the highest portion of people with at least some college.

But some metro areas certainly can lay claim to the best-educated people. The winners are smaller metro areas dominated by major universities. The Berkeleys, Boulders, Austins, and Madisons magazines label "smart."

Education after high school certainly makes a big difference in lifetime earnings. Adults with a bachelor's degree will make almost twice the income that adults with just a high school diploma will earn.

Advanced degree holders will do even better, more than triple the income of high school graduates only.

From Conservative to Liberal...

The notorious map that pinged about the Internet after the 2004 national elections showing red counties and blue counties is a cliché. Since *Places Rated* began tracking elections, the metro area total plurality has swung from center left to center right to center left again.

To rate metro areas for where they lie on the political spectrum, county-level pluralities for the last three congressional elections are weighted by the winner's National Journal Liberal Composite Rating. Pittsfield, in western Massachusetts, is the most liberal metro area. It congressman, Democrat John Olver, has a 96 Liberal rating and an average 86 percent plurality. Brunswick, in southeast Georgia, is the most conservative. It's representative, Republican Jack Kingston, has a 3 Liberal rating and an average 82 percent plurality.

JUDGING: AMBIENCE

Let's admit that ranking metro areas for ambience can't be done fairly. A cop on foot patrol in Boston's Back Bay, shaking off the snow, may care nothing about the number of performing artists bookings in suburban Quincy. A harried homemaker in Sacramento, concerned about the quality of the schools, may have no time for meetings scheduled to discuss historic preservation.

There are simply too many differences in taste for an ambience rating system to suit everyone. Still, it's possible to measure the supply of specific amenities. *Places Rated* tries the objective approach with five features of a place's atmosphere or ambience: Good Restaurants, Bookstores, a Visible Past, the Performing Arts, and People.

SCORING: AMBIENCE

• **Good Restaurants** are rated based on (1) the percent of a metro area's eateries rated by AAA, and (2) the number of rated eateries weighted by AAA diamonds. Dallas edges New York for the best score here. Seven smaller metro areas, with no eateries rated by AAA, do the worst.

• **Good Bookstores** are rated by the per capita sales as reported by the latest Census of Retail Trade.

Estimated sales figures for college textbooks are excluded. Of course, sales aren't entirely books but also music, newspapers, magazines, food and incidentals.

• *Visible History* takes into account (1) the number of historic landmarks and contributing buildings within residential historic districts and (2) the land area these official districts occupy.

• The ***Performing Arts Calendar*** simply counts the annual number of touring artist appearances in campus and civic auditoriums and adds the number of performance of resident symphony orchestras and opera companies.

• The various demographic descriptions under *People* are included for information and are not factors in a metro areas ambience ranking.

PLACE PROFILES: AMBIENCE

The following description are grouped into five headings to show each metro area's service and retail, historic, cultural and artistic, and demographic features that contribute to its ambience, its own look and feel, its *genius loci*.

The first figure to the right of the heading **Good Restaurants** is the total number of eateries the AAA rates one diamond ("basic management, cleanliness, and overall quality"), two diamonds ("enhanced food preparation, wide selection, family-oriented"), three diamonds ("professional chef, décor, efficient staff, wine and beer list"), four diamonds ("executive chef, wine steward, creative and complex menus") to five diamonds ("a world-class experience"). The second figure is the total number of full-service restaurants in the metro area. The stars indicate (1) the percent of AAA-rated eateries of all local eateries, and (2) their quality, weighted by the number of AAA diamonds. The stars represent equal breaks in percentiles: 0 to 20th, 21st to 40th, 41st to 60th, 61st to 80th, and 81st to 100th. The more stars, the better.

The stars to the right of **Bookstores and Reading** indicate the estimated sales per capita for books, magazines, and newspapers. The number of stars represent identical percentiles as with good restaurants; the more, the better. Under the heading are the metro area's number of Barnes & Noble, Borders, or Books-a-Million superstores and the area's total number of independent booksellers and

Ambience

www.placesrated.com

Ambience rankings, from 1 to 379, are in the *Place Profiles* section coming next. Ambience scores, from 100.0 to 0.0, are in Putting It All Together at the end of the book. Readers can view and print out these rankings and scores, from #1 New York-White Plains-Wayne, NY-NJ (score: 100.0) to #379 Brownsville-Harlingen, TX (score: 0.0), by visiting *Places Rated's* website.

Here are the top twenty:

Rank	Score
1. New York-White Plains, NY-NJ	100.0
2. Boston-Quincy, MA	99.7
3. Atlanta-Sandy Springs, GA	99.4
4. Chicago-Naperville-Joliet, IL	99.2
5. Hartford-West Hartford, CT	98.9
6. Philadelphia, PA	98.6
7. Austin-Round Rock, TX	98.4
8. Denver-Aurora, CO	98.1
9. Columbus, OH	97.8
10. San Francisco-San Mateo, CA	97.6
11. Portland-Vancouver, OR-WA	97.3
12. Virginia Beach-Norfolk, VA-NC	97.0
13. New Haven-Milford, CT	96.8
14. Albany-Schenectady-Troy, NY	96.5
15. Durham, NC	96.2
16. Dallas-Plano-Irving, TX	96.0
17. Los Angeles-Long Beach, CA	95.7
18. Madison, WI	95.5
19. Flagstaff, AZ	95.2
20. Salt Lake City, UT	94.9

At *www.placesrated.com* you'll also find more information on National Historic Landmarks, National Register Historic Districts, good restaurants, and the performing arts.

college bookstores.

The *Visible History* entry shows the number of state and federal historic sites and the number of residential historic districts and their "contributing buildings" within the metro area. Listed underneath are up to five historic districts that have the most contributing buildings.

The *Lively Arts Calendar* names the metro area's largest performance hall for touring artists and resident ensembles and enumerates their performances as reported by *Musical America*. Listed underneath are all symphony orchestras and opera companies above a specific budget figure.

The *People* entry comes last and shows six ways of looking at population on a continuum, from Younger to Older based on median age; from Less Diverse to Diverse based on how closely race and Hispanic origin matches the U.S. metro area average; from Less Affluent to Affluent based on the wealth index; from Less Educated to Educated based on the portion of people who've gone beyond high school; from Conservative to Liberal based on popular votes in congressional elections weighted by the National Journal's Composite Liberal Ratings; and from Catholic to Protestant based on the estimated population who attend a Catholic church or a Protestant church (see Appendix B for selected figures).

Information comes from these sources: American Automobile Association, *Tourbooks, 2006;* American Symphony Orchestra League, *Symphony* magazine, January-February 2006; Association of Religion Data Archives, unpublished county-level church membership (www.thearda.com); Barnes & Noble, "store locator" (www.storelocator.barnesandnoble.com); Books-a-Million, "store finder" (www.booksamillion.com); Borders, "store locator" (www.bordersstores.com); Elections Data Services, unpublished county-level election returns; Musical America, *International Directory of the Performing Arts*, 2006; National Journal, unpublished composite Liberal Score Ratings; Opera America, *Profile*, 2006; U.S. Department of Commerce, Bureau of the Census, 2005 American Community Survey; U.S. Department of the Interior, National Park Service, National Register of Historic Places (www.cr.nps.gov/nr) and National Historic Landmarks Program (www.cr.nps.gov/nhl); Woods & Poole Economics, Inc., unpublished race and Hispanic origin population forecasts;

A check mark (✓) in front of the metro area's name highlights it as one of the top 40 places for ambience.

Abilene, TX

Good Restaurants: 20/118 .... ☆☆☆☆

Bookstores and Reading: .... ☆☆
Chain Superstores: 1

Visible History
Registered Neighborhoods: 4
Contributing Buildings: 139
  Abilene Commercial District
  Parramore District
  Sayles Boulevard District

Lively Arts Calendar
Touring Artist Bookings: 3
  Abilene Civic Center
Dates, Resident Ensembles: 17
  Abilene Opera Association
  Abilene Philharmonic Association

People						
Younger		●				Older
Less Diverse				●		Diverse
Less Affluent	●					Affluent
Less Educated		●				Educated
Conservative	●					Liberal
Catholic				●		Protestant

Places Rated Rank: 288

Akron, OH

Good Restaurants: 52/697 .... ☆☆☆☆

Bookstores and Reading: .... ☆☆☆
Chain Superstores: 5
Independent Stores: 6

Visible History
National Landmarks and Sites: 2
Registered Neighborhoods: 29
Contributing Buildings: 649
  East Main Street District
  Hall Park Allotment District
  Hudson District
  Peninsula Village District

Lively Arts Calendar
Touring Artist Bookings: 58
  Thomas Performing Arts Hall
Dates, Resident Ensembles: 56
  Akron Symphony Orchestra

People						
Younger			●			Older
Less Diverse		●				Diverse
Less Affluent			●			Affluent
Less Educated			●			Educated
Conservative				●		Liberal
Catholic		●				Protestant

Places Rated Rank: 118

Albany, GA

Good Restaurants: 3/107 .... ☆

Bookstores and Reading: .... ☆☆☆
Chain Superstores: 2

Visible History
Registered Neighborhoods: 7
Contributing Buildings: 679
  Dawson District
  Parrott District

Lively Arts Calendar
Touring Artist Bookings: 11
  Municipal Auditorium
Dates, Resident Ensembles: 18
  Albany Symphony Orchestra

People						
Younger		●				Older
Less Diverse			●			Diverse
Less Affluent	●					Affluent
Less Educated		●				Educated
Conservative				●		Liberal
Catholic				●		Protestant

Places Rated Rank: 273

Albany-Schenectady-Troy, NY

Good Restaurants: 79/977 ..... ☆☆☆☆

Bookstores and Reading: ...... ☆☆☆☆☆
Chain Superstores: 9
Independent Stores: 8

Visible History
National Landmarks and Sites: 29
Registered Neighborhoods: 73
Contributing Buildings: 7,280
  Central Troy District
  Clinton Avenue District
  Mansion District
  South End-Groesbeckville District
  West Side District

Lively Arts Calendar
Touring Artist Bookings: 198
  Palace Theatre
  The Egg, Hart Theatre
Dates, Resident Ensembles: 49
  Albany Symphony Orchestra
  Lake George Opera Festival

People						
Younger					●	Older
Less Diverse		●				Diverse
Less Affluent			●			Affluent
Less Educated					●	Educated
Conservative			●			Liberal
Catholic	●					Protestant

Places Rated Rank: 14

✓ Albuquerque, NM

Good Restaurants: 155/594 ... ☆☆☆☆☆

Bookstores and Reading: .... ☆☆☆☆
Chain Superstores: 5
Independent Stores: 9

Visible History
National Landmarks and Sites: 12
Registered Neighborhoods: 23
Contributing Buildings: 2,159
  Huning Highlands District
  Manzano Court Addition District
  Monte Vista and College View District
  Silver Hill District
  Spruce Park District

Lively Arts Calendar
Touring Artist Bookings: 36
  KIMO Theatre
  Popejoy Hall
Dates, Resident Ensembles: 272
  Chamber Orchestra of Albuquerque
  New Mexico Symphony Orchestra
  Opera Southwest

People						
Younger		●				Older
Less Diverse	●					Diverse
Less Affluent			●			Affluent
Less Educated				●		Educated
Conservative			●			Liberal
Catholic	●					Protestant

Places Rated Rank: 28

Alexandria, LA

Good Restaurants: 8/69 .... ☆☆

Bookstores and Reading: .... ☆☆☆
Chain Superstores: 2

Visible History
National Landmarks and Sites: 1
Registered Neighborhoods: 4
Contributing Buildings: 317
  Alexandria Garden District
  Crowell Sawmill District
  Inglewood Plantation District
  McNutt Rural District

Lively Arts Calendar
Touring Artist Bookings: 2
  Guinn Auditorium
Dates, Resident Ensembles: 5

People						
Younger		●				Older
Less Diverse			●			Diverse
Less Affluent		●				Affluent
Less Educated	●					Educated
Conservative		●				Liberal
Catholic			●			Protestant

Places Rated Rank: 311

Allentown-Bethlehem, PA-NJ

Good Restaurants: 133/847 ... ☆☆☆☆☆

Bookstores and Reading: .... ☆☆
Chain Superstores: 7
Independent Stores: 2

Visible History
National Landmarks and Sites: 6
Registered Neighborhoods: 36
Contributing Buildings: 4,214

39

Ambience

College Hill Residential District
Easton District
Nazareth District
Oxford Industrial District
South Bethlehem Downtown District

Lively Arts Calendar
Touring Artist Bookings: 152
  Lehigh Zoellner Hall
  Symphony Hall
Dates, Resident Ensembles: 27
  Allentown Symphony
  The Pennsylvania Sinfonia Orchestra

People						
Younger				●		Older
Less Diverse		●				Diverse
Less Affluent			●			Affluent
Less Educated		●				Educated
Conservative		●				Liberal
Catholic	●					Protestant

Places Rated Rank: 80

Altoona, PA

Good Restaurants: 2/140 .... ☆

Bookstores and Reading: .... ☆☆
Chain Superstores: 2
Independent Stores: 2

Visible History
National Landmarks and Sites: 3
Registered Neighborhoods: 11
Contributing Buildings: 2,418
  Downtown Altoona District
  Hollidaysburg District
  Roaring Spring District
  Tyrone Borough District
  Williamsburg District

Lively Arts Calendar
Touring Artist Bookings: 5
  Roosevelt Auditorium
Dates, Resident Ensembles: 7
  Altoona Symphony Orchestra

People						
Younger				●		Older
Less Diverse	●					Diverse
Less Affluent	●					Affluent
Less Educated		●				Educated
Conservative	●					Liberal
Catholic	●					Protestant

Places Rated Rank: 295

Amarillo, TX

Good Restaurants: 30/208 .... ☆☆☆

Bookstores and Reading: .... ☆☆☆
Chain Superstores: 1
Independent Stores: 1

Visible History
National Landmarks and Sites: 1
Registered Neighborhoods: 6
Contributing Buildings: 828
  Plemons-Eakle Additions District
  US Route 66-Sixth Street District
  Wolflin District

Lively Arts Calendar
Touring Artist Bookings: 4
  Civic Center Auditorium
Dates, Resident Ensembles: 44
  Amarillo Opera
  Amarillo Symphony Orchestra

People						
Younger		●				Older
Less Diverse				●		Diverse
Less Affluent		●				Affluent
Less Educated		●				Educated
Conservative	●					Liberal
Catholic			●			Protestant

Places Rated Rank: 147

Ames, IA

Good Restaurants: 12/80 .... ☆☆☆

Bookstores and Reading: ...... ☆☆☆☆
Chain Superstores: 1
Independent Stores: 1

Visible History
National Landmarks and Sites: 1
Registered Neighborhoods: 3
Contributing Buildings: 229
  Old Town District

Lively Arts Calendar
Touring Artist Bookings: 22
  Ames City Auditorium
  ISU Stephens Auditorium
Dates, Resident Ensembles: 4

People						
Younger	●					Older
Less Diverse		●				Diverse
Less Affluent			●			Affluent
Less Educated				●		Educated
Conservative			●			Liberal
Catholic			●			Protestant

Places Rated Rank: 190

Anchorage, AK

Good Restaurants: 28/365 .... ☆☆☆
Bookstores and Reading: ...... ☆☆☆☆☆
Chain Superstores: 5
Independent Stores: 4

Visible History
National Landmarks and Sites: 1
Registered Neighborhoods: 6
Contributing Buildings: 45

Lively Arts Calendar
Touring Artist Bookings: 42
  Alaska Center
Dates, Resident Ensembles: 24
  Anchorage Opera

People						
Younger		●				Older
Less Diverse			●			Diverse
Less Affluent				●		Affluent
Less Educated			●			Educated
Conservative			●			Liberal
Catholic			●			Protestant

Places Rated Rank: 158

Anderson, IN

Good Restaurants: 9/125 .... ☆☆
Bookstores and Reading: .... ☆☆☆
Chain Superstores: 1

Visible History
National Landmarks and Sites: 1
Registered Neighborhoods: 5
Contributing Buildings: 671
  Pendleton District
  West Central District

Lively Arts Calendar
Touring Artist Bookings: 2
  AU Reardon Auditorium
Dates, Resident Ensembles: 35

People						
Younger				●		Older
Less Diverse		●				Diverse
Less Affluent		●				Affluent
Less Educated	●					Educated
Conservative	●					Liberal
Catholic				●		Protestant

Places Rated Rank: 263

Anderson, SC

Good Restaurants: 11/142 .... ☆☆☆
Bookstores and Reading: .... ☆
Chain Superstores: 1

Visible History
Registered Neighborhoods: 4
Contributing Buildings: 169
  Pendleton District

Lively Arts Calendar
Touring Artist Bookings: 5
Dates, Resident Ensembles: 6

People						
Younger				●		Older
Less Diverse			●			Diverse
Less Affluent		●				Affluent
Less Educated	●					Educated
Conservative	●					Liberal
Catholic					●	Protestant

Places Rated Rank: 294

✓ Ann Arbor, MI

Good Restaurants: 48/288 ..... ☆☆☆☆

Bookstores and Reading: ...... ☆☆☆☆
Chain Superstores: 3
Independent Stores: 5

Visible History
Registered Neighborhoods: 12
Contributing Buildings: 2,254
Main Street District
North Ann Arbor Street District
Old West Side District
Ypsilanti District

Lively Arts Calendar
Touring Artist Bookings: 51
UM Hill Auditorium
Michigan Theatre
Dates, Resident Ensembles: 52
Ann Arbor Symphony Orchestra
Comic Opera Guild

People					
Younger	●				Older
Less Diverse			●		Diverse
Less Affluent				●	Affluent
Less Educated				●	Educated
Conservative			●		Liberal
Catholic		●			Protestant

Places Rated Rank: 25

Anniston-Oxford, AL

Good Restaurants: 2/78 .... ☆

Bookstores and Reading: .... ☆☆
Chain Superstores: 1

Visible History
Registered Neighborhoods: 6
Contributing Buildings: 576
Downtown Jacksonville District
East Anniston Residential District

Lively Arts Calendar
Touring Artist Bookings: 6
Anniston Auditorium

People					
Younger			●		Older
Less Diverse		●			Diverse
Less Affluent	●				Affluent
Less Educated	●				Educated
Conservative	●				Liberal
Catholic			●		Protestant

Places Rated Rank: 343

Appleton, WI

Good Restaurants: 36/283 .... ☆☆☆☆

Bookstores and Reading: ...... ☆☆☆☆
Chain Superstores: 2

Visible History
Registered Neighborhoods: 10
Contributing Buildings: 205
Appleton City Park District

Lively Arts Calendar
Touring Artist Bookings: 9
Fox Cities Center
Dates, Resident Ensembles: 10
Fox Valley Symphony

People					
Younger		●			Older
Less Diverse	●				Diverse
Less Affluent			●		Affluent
Less Educated			●		Educated
Conservative		●			Liberal
Catholic	●				Protestant

Places Rated Rank: 172

✓ Asheville, NC

Good Restaurants: 79/390 ..... ☆☆☆☆

Bookstores and Reading: .... ☆☆☆
Chain Superstores: 6
Independent Stores: 5

Visible History
National Landmarks and Sites: 4
Registered Neighborhoods: 38
Contributing Buildings: 2,460
Chestnut Hill District
Grove Park District
Hyman Heights-Mt. Royal District
Montford Area District
West Side District

Lively Arts Calendar
Touring Artist Bookings: 23
Thomas Wolfe Auditorium
Dates, Resident Ensembles: 20
Asheville Lyric Opera
Asheville Symphony Orchestra

People					
Younger			●		Older
Less Diverse	●				Diverse
Less Affluent		●			Affluent
Less Educated			●		Educated
Conservative	●				Liberal
Catholic			●		Protestant

Places Rated Rank: 33

Athens-Clarke County, GA

Good Restaurants: 3/140 .... ☆

Bookstores and Reading: .... ☆☆☆☆
Chain Superstores: 2
Independent Stores: 1

Visible History
National Landmarks and Sites: 1
Registered Neighborhoods: 29
Contributing Buildings: 1,724
Bloomfield Street District
Boulevard District
Cobbham District
Comer District
West Hancock Avenue District

Lively Arts Calendar
Touring Artist Bookings: 11
Classic Center
UGA Performing Arts Center

People					
Younger	●				Older
Less Diverse			●		Diverse
Less Affluent		●			Affluent
Less Educated				●	Educated
Conservative	●				Liberal
Catholic			●		Protestant

Places Rated Rank: 212

✓ Atlanta-Sandy Springs, GA

Good Restaurants: 362/4037 . ☆☆☆☆

Bookstores and Reading: .... ☆☆☆
Chain Superstores: 40
Independent Stores: 25

Visible History
National Landmarks and Sites: 16
Registered Neighborhoods: 151
Contributing Buildings: 22,098
Candler Park District
College Park District
Grant Park District
Oakland City District
Virginia-Highland District

Lively Arts Calendar
Touring Artist Bookings: 633
Atlanta Civic Center
Fox Theatre
Rialto Center
Woodruff Arts Center
Dates, Resident Ensembles: 571
Atlanta Opera
Atlanta Symphony Orchestra

People					
Younger	●				Older
Less Diverse			●		Diverse
Less Affluent			●		Affluent
Less Educated			●		Educated
Conservative		●			Liberal
Catholic			●		Protestant

Places Rated Rank: 3

Atlantic City, NJ

Good Restaurants: 19/372 .... ☆☆☆

Bookstores and Reading: ...... ☆☆☆☆☆
Chain Superstores: 2

Visible History
National Landmarks and Sites: 4
Registered Neighborhoods: 7
Contributing Buildings: 824
Bay Front District
Linwood District

Marven Gardens District
Mays Landing District
Port Republic District

Lively Arts Calendar
Touring Artist Bookings: 50

People						
Younger			✱			Older
Less Diverse					✱	Diverse
Less Affluent				✱		Affluent
Less Educated		✱				Educated
Conservative			✱			Liberal
Catholic	✱					Protestant

Places Rated Rank: 140

Auburn-Opelika, AL

Good Restaurants: 7/75 .... ☆☆

Bookstores and Reading: .... ☆☆☆
Chain Superstores: 2
Independent Stores: 1

Visible History
Registered Neighborhoods: 7
Contributing Buildings: 397
 Geneva Street District
 Northside District
 Old Main & Church St. District

Lively Arts Calendar
Touring Artist Bookings: 5

People						
Younger	✱					Older
Less Diverse			✱			Diverse
Less Affluent	✱					Affluent
Less Educated			✱			Educated
Conservative	✱					Liberal
Catholic				✱		Protestant

Places Rated Rank: 244

Augusta-Richmond County, GA-SC

Good Restaurants: 21/347 .... ☆☆☆

Bookstores and Reading: .... ☆
Chain Superstores: 4
Independent Stores: 1

Visible History
National Landmarks and Sites: 8
Registered Neighborhoods: 31
Contributing Buildings: 6,341
 Bethlehem District
 Harrisburg-West End District
 Laney-Walker North District
 Pinched Gut District
 Summerville District

Lively Arts Calendar
Touring Artist Bookings: 14
 Imperial Theatre
 Maxwell Grover Theatre

Dates, Resident Ensembles: 24
 Augusta Opera Company
 Augusta Symphony Orchestra

People						
Younger		✱				Older
Less Diverse				✱		Diverse
Less Affluent		✱				Affluent
Less Educated			✱			Educated
Conservative	✱					Liberal
Catholic				✱		Protestant

Places Rated Rank: 203

✓ Austin-Round Rock, TX

Good Restaurants: 213/1210 .. ☆☆☆☆

Bookstores and Reading: ...... ☆☆☆☆
Chain Superstores: 11
Independent Stores: 10

Visible History
National Landmarks and Sites: 2
Registered Neighborhoods: 38
Contributing Buildings: 3,698
 Hyde Park District
 Old West Austin District
 Sixth Street District
 Smithville Residential District
 West Line District

Lively Arts Calendar
Touring Artist Bookings: 90
 Paramount Theatre
 UT Performing Arts Center
Dates, Resident Ensembles: 216
 Austin Lyric Opera
 Austin Symphony Orchestra

People						
Younger	✱					Older
Less Diverse					✱	Diverse
Less Affluent					✱	Affluent
Less Educated					✱	Educated
Conservative				✱		Liberal
Catholic			✱			Protestant

Places Rated Rank: 7

Bakersfield, CA

Good Restaurants: 9/413 .... ☆

Bookstores and Reading: .... ☆
Chain Superstores: 2
Independent Stores: 2

Visible History
National Landmarks and Sites: 3
Registered Neighborhoods: 2
Contributing Buildings: 8

Lively Arts Calendar
Touring Artist Bookings: 6
 Bakersfield Convention Center
Dates, Resident Ensembles: 50

People						
Younger	✱					Older
Less Diverse	✱					Diverse
Less Affluent	✱					Affluent
Less Educated	✱					Educated
Conservative			✱			Liberal
Catholic	✱					Protestant

Places Rated Rank: 341

✓ Baltimore-Towson, MD

Good Restaurants: 96/2135 .... ☆☆☆☆

Bookstores and Reading: .... ☆☆☆☆
Chain Superstores: 21
Independent Stores: 23

Visible History
National Landmarks and Sites: 75
Registered Neighborhoods: 202
Contributing Buildings: 108,753
 Baltimore East/South Clifton Park
 Canton District
 Hampden District
 Patterson Park-Highlandtown District
 Old West Baltimore District

Lively Arts Calendar
Touring Artist Bookings: 319
 Friedberg Concert Hall
 Lyric Opera House
 Meyerhoff Symphony Hall
Dates, Resident Ensembles: 277
 Annapolis Opera
 Annapolis Symphony Orchestra
 Baltimore Chamber Orchestra
 Baltimore Concert Artists
 Baltimore Opera Company
 Baltimore Symphony Orchestra
 Peabody Conservatory Symphony Orchestra

People						
Younger			✱			Older
Less Diverse				✱		Diverse
Less Affluent				✱		Affluent
Less Educated			✱			Educated
Conservative					✱	Liberal
Catholic		✱				Protestant

Places Rated Rank: 24

Bangor, ME

Good Restaurants: 16/139 .... ☆☆☆

Bookstores and Reading: ...... ☆☆☆☆
Chain Superstores: 1
Independent Stores: 1

Visible History
Registered Neighborhoods: 11
Contributing Buildings: 195
 Orono Main Street District
 Whitney Park District

Lively Arts Calendar

Touring Artist Bookings: 20
Maine Center for the Arts
Dates, Resident Ensembles: 20
Bangor Symphony Orchestra

People

	1	2	3	4	5	
Younger				●		Older
Less Diverse	●					Diverse
Less Affluent		●				Affluent
Less Educated			●			Educated
Conservative				●		Liberal
Catholic		●				Protestant

Places Rated Rank: 146

Barnstable Town, MA

Good Restaurants: 51/485 .... ☆☆☆

Bookstores and Reading: ...... ☆☆☆☆
Chain Superstores: 2
Independent Stores: 12

Visible History
National Landmarks and Sites: 3
Registered Neighborhoods: 35
Contributing Buildings: 4,202
Brewster Old King's Highway District
Northside District
Old King's Highway District
Provincetown District
South Yarmouth/Bass River District

Lively Arts Calendar
Touring Artist Bookings: 3
Dates, Resident Ensembles: 29
Cape Cod Symphony Orchestra

People

	1	2	3	4	5	
Younger				●		Older
Less Diverse	●					Diverse
Less Affluent				●		Affluent
Less Educated				●		Educated
Conservative				●		Liberal
Catholic	●					Protestant

Places Rated Rank: 68

Baton Rouge, LA

Good Restaurants: 21/471 .... ☆☆☆

Bookstores and Reading: .... ☆☆
Chain Superstores: 5

Visible History
National Landmarks and Sites: 14
Registered Neighborhoods: 21
Contributing Buildings: 2,302
Beauregard Town District
Donaldsonville District
Kleinert Terrace District
Roseland Terrace District
Spanish Town

Lively Arts Calendar

Touring Artist Bookings: 11
LSU Union Theatre
Riverside Centroplex
Dates, Resident Ensembles: 48
Baton Rouge Symphony Orchestra

People

	1	2	3	4	5	
Younger	●					Older
Less Diverse			●			Diverse
Less Affluent		●				Affluent
Less Educated		●				Educated
Conservative			●			Liberal
Catholic		●				Protestant

Places Rated Rank: 196

Battle Creek, MI

Good Restaurants: 8/152 .... ☆

Bookstores and Reading: .... ☆☆☆
Chain Superstores: 1
Independent Stores: 2

Visible History
National Landmarks and Sites: 1
Registered Neighborhoods: 9
Contributing Buildings: 1,314
Advent District
Homer Village District
Maple Street District
Marshall Michigan Landmark District

Lively Arts Calendar
Touring Artist Bookings: 35
Kellogg Auditorium
Dates, Resident Ensembles: 7
Battle Creek Symphony Orchestra

People

	1	2	3	4	5	
Younger			●			Older
Less Diverse		●				Diverse
Less Affluent		●				Affluent
Less Educated	●					Educated
Conservative		●				Liberal
Catholic			●			Protestant

Places Rated Rank: 250

Bay City, MI

Good Restaurants: 11/130 .... ☆☆☆

Bookstores and Reading: .... ☆☆☆
Chain Superstores: 1

Visible History
Registered Neighborhoods: 3
Contributing Buildings: 336
Center Avenue Residential District

Lively Arts Calendar
Touring Artist Bookings: 38
Dates, Resident Ensembles: 18
Midland Symphony Orchestra

People

	1	2	3	4	5	
Younger		●				Older
Less Diverse	●					Diverse
Less Affluent	●					Affluent
Less Educated	●					Educated
Conservative			●			Liberal
Catholic	●					Protestant

Places Rated Rank: 248

Beaumont-Port Arthur, TX

Good Restaurants: 5/232 .... ☆

Bookstores and Reading: .... ☆
Chain Superstores: 2

Visible History
National Landmarks and Sites: 2
Registered Neighborhoods: 3
Contributing Buildings: 220
Beaumont Commercial District
Navy Park District

Lively Arts Calendar
Touring Artist Bookings: 24
Julie Rogers Theatre
Dates, Resident Ensembles: 13
Symphony of Southeast Texas

People

	1	2	3	4	5	
Younger		●				Older
Less Diverse			●			Diverse
Less Affluent	●					Affluent
Less Educated	●					Educated
Conservative		●				Liberal
Catholic		●				Protestant

Places Rated Rank: 357

Bellingham, WA

Good Restaurants: 11/225 .... ☆☆

Bookstores and Reading: ...... ☆☆☆☆
Chain Superstores: 2
Independent Stores: 4

Visible History
National Landmarks and Sites: 1
Registered Neighborhoods: 6
Contributing Buildings: 881
Eldridge Avenue District
Sehome Hill District

Lively Arts Calendar
Touring Artist Bookings: 30
Mount Baker Theater
WWU Performing Arts Center
Dates, Resident Ensembles: 6

Ambience

(People chart — Bend, OR)

People	1	2	3	4	5	
Younger	●					Older
Less Diverse		●				Diverse
Less Affluent		●				Affluent
Less Educated				●		Educated
Conservative				●		Liberal
Catholic	●					Protestant

Places Rated Rank: 184

Bend, OR

Good Restaurants: 15/160 .... ☆☆☆

Bookstores and Reading: .... ☆☆
Chain Superstores: 1
Independent Stores: 3

Visible History
National Landmarks and Sites: 1
Registered Neighborhoods: 4
Contributing Buildings: 320
  Drake Park Neighborhood District
  Old Town District

Lively Arts Calendar
Touring Artist Bookings: 3
  Pickney Center for the Arts

(People chart — Bethesda-Gaithersburg, MD)

People	1	2	3	4	5	
Younger			●			Older
Less Diverse	●					Diverse
Less Affluent			●			Affluent
Less Educated			●			Educated
Conservative	●					Liberal
Catholic		●				Protestant

Places Rated Rank: 312

Bethesda-Gaithersburg, MD

Good Restaurants: 39/571 .... ☆☆☆☆

Bookstores and Reading: .... ☆☆☆
Chain Superstores: 13
Independent Stores: 8

Visible History
National Landmarks and Sites: 10
Registered Neighborhoods: 36
Contributing Buildings: 5,394
  Brunswick District
  Frederick District
  Garrett Park District
  Middletown District

Lively Arts Calendar
Touring Artist Bookings: 120
  Strathmore Center
Dates, Resident Ensembles: 33
  National Chamber Orchestra
  Victorian Lyric Opera Company

(People chart — Billings, MT)

People	1	2	3	4	5	
Younger		●				Older
Less Diverse				●		Diverse
Less Affluent				●		Affluent
Less Educated				●		Educated
Conservative				●		Liberal
Catholic	●					Protestant

Places Rated Rank: 96

Billings, MT

Good Restaurants: 17/201 .... ☆☆☆

Bookstores and Reading: ...... ☆☆☆☆☆
Chain Superstores: 2
Independent Stores: 2

Visible History
National Landmarks and Sites: 3
Registered Neighborhoods: 8
Contributing Buildings: 267
  Billings District
  Hi Bug District
  Joliet Residential District
  Red Lodge Commercial District

Lively Arts Calendar
Touring Artist Bookings: 40
  Alberta Bair Theatre
Dates, Resident Ensembles: 15
  Billings Symphony Orchestra
  Rimrock Opera Company

(People chart — Binghamton, NY)

People	1	2	3	4	5	
Younger				●		Older
Less Diverse	●					Diverse
Less Affluent			●			Affluent
Less Educated			●			Educated
Conservative	●					Liberal
Catholic			●			Protestant

Places Rated Rank: 165

Binghamton, NY

Good Restaurants: 24/344 .... ☆☆☆

Bookstores and Reading: .... ☆☆☆
Chain Superstores: 2
Independent Stores: 1

Visible History
National Landmarks and Sites: 1
Registered Neighborhoods: 8
Contributing Buildings: 596
  Berkshire Village District
  Owego Central District
  Windsor Village District

Lively Arts Calendar
Touring Artist Bookings: 4
  Anderson Center
Dates, Resident Ensembles: 36
  Binghamton Symphony & Choral
  Tri-Cities Opera

(People chart — Birmingham-Hoover, AL)

People	1	2	3	4	5	
Younger				●		Older
Less Diverse	●					Diverse
Less Affluent	●					Affluent
Less Educated			●			Educated
Conservative				●		Liberal
Catholic	●					Protestant

Places Rated Rank: 179

Birmingham-Hoover, AL

Good Restaurants: 53/731 .... ☆☆☆☆

Bookstores and Reading: .... ☆
Chain Superstores: 11
Independent Stores: 5

Visible History
National Landmarks and Sites: 3
Registered Neighborhoods: 71
Contributing Buildings: 7,468
  Avondale Park District
  Hollywood District
  Red Mountain Suburbs District
  South Highlands of East Lake
  Woodlawn District

Lively Arts Calendar
Touring Artist Bookings: 20
  Alys Stephens Center
  Birmingham-Jefferson Complex
Dates, Resident Ensembles: 145
  Alabama Operworks
  Opera Birmingham

(People chart — Bismarck, ND)

People	1	2	3	4	5	
Younger		●				Older
Less Diverse			●			Diverse
Less Affluent			●			Affluent
Less Educated		●				Educated
Conservative	●					Liberal
Catholic				●		Protestant

Places Rated Rank: 115

Bismarck, ND

Good Restaurants: 11/90 .... ☆☆☆

Bookstores and Reading: .... ☆☆☆
Chain Superstores: 2

Visible History
National Landmarks and Sites: 4
Registered Neighborhoods: 6
Contributing Buildings: 195
  Bismarck Cathedral Area District
  Downtown Bismarck District

Lively Arts Calendar
Touring Artist Bookings: 3
  Belle Mehus City Auditorium
Dates, Resident Ensembles: 15
  Bismarck-Mandan Symphony
  Orchestra

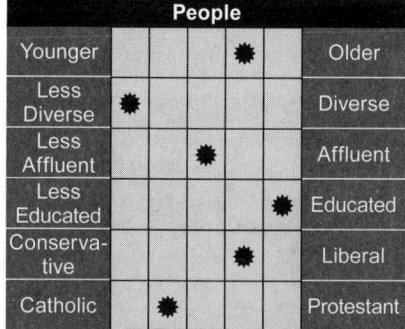

Places Rated Rank: 275

Blacksburg-Christiansburg, VA

Good Restaurants: 10/127 .... ☆☆☆

Bookstores and Reading: ...... ☆☆☆☆
Chain Superstores: 2

Visible History
Registered Neighborhoods: 24
Contributing Buildings: 2,572
 East Radford District
 Greater Newport Rural District
 Miller-Southside District
 Pulaski Residential District

Lively Arts Calendar
Touring Artist Bookings: 14
Dates, Resident Ensembles: 6

People						
Younger	✹					Older
Less Diverse	✹					Diverse
Less Affluent	✹					Affluent
Less Educated			✹			Educated
Conservative			✹			Liberal
Catholic				✹		Protestant

Places Rated Rank: 109

Bloomington, IN

Good Restaurants: 37/150 ...... ☆☆☆☆

Bookstores and Reading: .... ☆☆☆
Chain Superstores: 2
Independent Stores: 4

Visible History
Registered Neighborhoods: 10
Contributing Buildings: 810
 Bloomington West Side District
 Maple Grove Road Rural District
 North Indiana Avenue District
 University Courts District
 Vinegar Hill District

Lively Arts Calendar
Touring Artist Bookings: 20
 Creative Arts Auditorium
 Musical Arts Center
Dates, Resident Ensembles: 128

People						
Younger	✹					Older
Less Diverse		✹				Diverse
Less Affluent		✹				Affluent
Less Educated				✹		Educated
Conservative				✹		Liberal
Catholic				✹		Protestant

Places Rated Rank: 69

Bloomington-Normal, IL

Good Restaurants: 11/162 .... ☆☆

Bookstores and Reading: ...... ☆☆☆☆
Chain Superstores: 2

Visible History
National Landmarks and Sites: 1
Registered Neighborhoods: 5
Contributing Buildings: 403
 East Grove Street District
 Franklin Square
 White Place District

Lively Arts Calendar
Touring Artist Bookings: 15
 Braden Auditorium

People						
Younger	✹					Older
Less Diverse		✹				Diverse
Less Affluent					✹	Affluent
Less Educated					✹	Educated
Conservative			✹			Liberal
Catholic				✹		Protestant

Places Rated Rank: 208

Boise City-Nampa, ID

Good Restaurants: 20/507 .... ☆☆

Bookstores and Reading: .... ☆☆☆☆
Chain Superstores: 3
Independent Stores: 6

Visible History
National Landmarks and Sites: 1
Registered Neighborhoods: 23
Contributing Buildings: 1,061
 Boise District
 Fort Street District
 Harrison Boulevard District
 Placerville District
 Warm Springs Avenue District

Lively Arts Calendar
Touring Artist Bookings: 19
 Morrison Center
Dates, Resident Ensembles: 13
 Boise Philharmonic
 Opera Idaho!

Places Rated Rank: 98

✓ Boston-Quincy, MA

Good Restaurants: 110/2,340 ☆☆☆☆

Bookstores and Reading: ...... ☆☆☆☆
Chain Superstores: 14
Independent Stores: 15

Visible History
National Landmarks and Sites: 82
Registered Neighborhoods: 121
Contributing Buildings: 13,565
 Back Bay District
 Beacon Hill District
 Lincoln District
 Roxbury Highlands District
 South End District

Lively Arts Calendar
Touring Artist Bookings: 390
 Boston Opera House
 BU Tsai Performance Center
 Jordan Hall
 Symphony Hall
 Wang Center
Dates, Resident Ensembles: 412
 Boston Bel Canto Opera
 Boston Lyric Opera Company
 Boston Opera Association
 Boston Symphony Chamber Players
 Boston Symphony Orchestra
 Handel & Haydn Society
 Longwood Opera
 Opera Boston
 Plymouth Philharmonic Orchestra

People						
Younger	✹					Older
Less Diverse		✹				Diverse
Less Affluent			✹			Affluent
Less Educated		✹				Educated
Conservative	✹					Liberal
LDS		✹				Protestant

People						
Younger		✹				Older
Less Diverse				✹		Diverse
Less Affluent				✹		Affluent
Less Educated				✹		Educated
Conservative				✹		Liberal
Catholic	✹					Protestant

Places Rated Rank: 2

Boulder, CO

Good Restaurants: 36/356 .... ☆☆☆☆

Bookstores and Reading: ...... ☆☆☆☆
Chain Superstores: 3
Independent Stores: 7

Visible History
National Landmarks and Sites: 1
Registered Neighborhoods: 15
Contributing Buildings: 595

Ambience

Colorado Chautauqua
East Side District
Eldora District
Gold Hill District
West Side District

Lively Arts Calendar
Touring Artist Bookings: 75
  CU Macky Auditorium
Dates, Resident Ensembles: 107
  Boulder Philharmonic Orchestra
  Colorado Music Festival Orchestra
  Longmont Symphony Orchestra

People						
Younger	●					Older
Less Diverse			●			Diverse
Less Affluent				●		Affluent
Less Educated				●		Educated
Conservative		●				Liberal
Catholic	●					Protestant

Places Rated Rank: 45

Bowling Green, KY

Good Restaurants: 9/90 .... ☆☆☆

Bookstores and Reading: .... ☆☆☆
Chain Superstores: 2
Independent Stores: 1

Visible History
Registered Neighborhoods: 15
Contributing Buildings: 341
  College Hill District
  Magnolia Street District
  Oakland-Freeport District
  Shake Rag District
  St. Joseph's District

Lively Arts Calendar
Touring Artist Bookings: 9
  Capitol Arts Center
Dates, Resident Ensembles: 7

People						
Younger		●				Older
Less Diverse		●				Diverse
Less Affluent	●					Affluent
Less Educated			●			Educated
Conservative	●					Liberal
Catholic				●		Protestant

Places Rated Rank: 216

Bremerton-Silverdale, WA

Good Restaurants: 7/208 .... ☆

Bookstores and Reading: .... ☆☆
Chain Superstores: 2
Independent Stores: 6

Visible History
National Landmarks and Sites: 5
Registered Neighborhoods: 8
Contributing Buildings: 99

Lively Arts Calendar
Touring Artist Bookings: 2
  Admiral Theatre
Dates, Resident Ensembles: 9
  Bremerton Symphony Orchestra

People						
Younger		●				Older
Less Diverse		●				Diverse
Less Affluent				●		Affluent
Less Educated			●			Educated
Conservative				●		Liberal
Catholic		●				Protestant

Places Rated Rank: 337

✓ Bridgeport-Stamford, CT

Good Restaurants: 40/1,100 .... ☆☆☆

Bookstores and Reading: ...... ☆☆☆☆☆
Chain Superstores: 11
Independent Stores: 7

Visible History
National Landmarks and Sites: 13
Registered Neighborhoods: 79
Contributing Buildings: 5,032
  East Bridgeport District
  Ridgefield Center District
  South End District
  Stratfield District
  Stratford Center District

Lively Arts Calendar
Touring Artist Bookings: 237
  Charles Ives Center
  Klein Memorial Auditorium
  Norwalk Concert Hall
  Stamford Center
Dates, Resident Ensembles: 161
  Connecticut Grand Opera
  Fairfield Orchestra
  Greater Bridgeport Symphony
  Greenwich Symphony Orchestra
  Hat City Music Theatre
  New England Lyric Operetta
  Norwalk Symphony Orchestra
  Stamford Symphony Orchestra

People						
Younger				●		Older
Less Diverse				●		Diverse
Less Affluent				●		Affluent
Less Educated				●		Educated
Conservative				●		Liberal
Catholic	●					Protestant

Places Rated Rank: 26

Brownsville-Harlingen, TX

Good Restaurants: 5/276 .... ☆

Bookstores and Reading: .... ☆
Chain Superstores: 2

Visible History
National Landmarks and Sites: 6
Registered Neighborhoods: 1
Contributing Buildings: 15

Lively Arts Calendar
Touring Artist Bookings: 2
  UTB Fort Brown Memorial Center

People						
Younger	●					Older
Less Diverse	●					Diverse
Less Affluent	●					Affluent
Less Educated	●					Educated
Conservative			●			Liberal
Catholic	●					Protestant

Places Rated Rank: 379

Brunswick, GA

Good Restaurants: 8/121 .... ☆☆

Bookstores and Reading: .... ☆☆☆
Chain Superstores: 1
Independent Stores: 3

Visible History
National Landmarks and Sites: 3
Registered Neighborhoods: 9
Contributing Buildings: 618
  Brunswick Old Town District
  Hog Hammock District
  Vernon Square-Columbus Square District
  West Darien District

Lively Arts Calendar
Touring Artist Bookings: 3

People						
Younger			●			Older
Less Diverse			●			Diverse
Less Affluent		●				Affluent
Less Educated	●					Educated
Conservative	●					Liberal
Catholic				●		Protestant

Places Rated Rank: 297

Buffalo-Niagara Falls, NY

Good Restaurants: 97/1,505 ...... ☆☆☆☆

Bookstores and Reading: .... ☆☆☆☆
Chain Superstores: 7
Independent Stores: 5

Visible History
National Landmarks and Sites: 17
Registered Neighborhoods: 15
Contributing Buildings: 2,930
  Allentown District
  Lowertown District
  Parkside East District
  Parkside West District
  West Village District

Lively Arts Calendar
Touring Artist Bookings: 74
   Kleinhans Music Hall
Dates, Resident Ensembles: 183
   Buffalo Philharmonic Orchestra

People					
Younger				●	Older
Less Diverse		●			Diverse
Less Affluent		●			Affluent
Less Educated			●		Educated
Conservative			●		Liberal
Catholic	●				Protestant

Places Rated Rank: 43

Burlington, NC

Good Restaurants: 1/115 .... ☆

Bookstores and Reading: .... ☆☆
Chain Superstores: 1

Visible History
Registered Neighborhoods: 13
Contributing Buildings: 630
   Glencoe Mill Village District
   Graham District
   North Main Street District
   South Broad-East Fifth Streets District
   West Davis Street-Fountain Place District

Lively Arts Calendar
Touring Artist Bookings: 8

People					
Younger		●			Older
Less Diverse				●	Diverse
Less Affluent		●			Affluent
Less Educated	●				Educated
Conservative			●		Liberal
Catholic				●	Protestant

Places Rated Rank: 336

Burlington-South Burlington, VT

Good Restaurants: 25/258 .... ☆☆☆☆

Bookstores and Reading: ...... ☆☆☆☆☆
Chain Superstores: 3
Independent Stores: 3

Visible History
National Landmarks and Sites: 1
Registered Neighborhoods: 39
Contributing Buildings: 1,506
   Battery Street District
   Buell Street-Bradley Street District
   Fort Ethan Allen District
   South Union Street District
   South Willard Street District

Lively Arts Calendar
Touring Artist Bookings: 94
   Burlington Memorial Auditorium
   Flynn Theatre

Dates, Resident Ensembles: 40
   Vermont Symphony Orchestra

People					
Younger			●		Older
Less Diverse	●				Diverse
Less Affluent			●		Affluent
Less Educated			●		Educated
Conservative			●		Liberal
Catholic	●				Protestant

Places Rated Rank: 55

✓ Cambridge-Newton, MA

Good Restaurants: 67/1,621 ...... ☆☆☆☆

Bookstores and Reading: ...... ☆☆☆☆☆
Chain Superstores: 12
Independent Stores: 12

Visible History
National Landmarks and Sites: 46
Registered Neighborhoods: 185
Contributing Buildings: 7,368
   Forge Village District
   Old Cambridge District
   Rogers Fort Hill Park District
   Shirley Village District
   Tyler Park District

Lively Arts Calendar
Touring Artist Bookings: 96
Dates, Resident Ensembles: 113
   Boston Baroque
   Boston Modern Orchestra Project
   Boston Philharmonic
   Indian Hill Symphony Orchestra
   Pro Arte Chamber Orchestra Boston

People					
Younger			●		Older
Less Diverse		●			Diverse
Less Affluent			●		Affluent
Less Educated			●		Educated
Conservative			●		Liberal
Catholic	●				Protestant

Places Rated Rank: 30

Camden, NJ

Good Restaurants: 0/1,015 .... ☆

Bookstores and Reading: .... ☆☆☆
Chain Superstores: 10
Independent Stores: 2

Visible History
National Landmarks and Sites: 12
Registered Neighborhoods: 42
Contributing Buildings: 6,202
   Bordentown District
   Fairview District
   Haddonfield District
   Riverton District
   South Camden District

Lively Arts Calendar
Touring Artist Bookings: 165
Dates, Resident Ensembles: 10

People					
Younger			●		Older
Less Diverse				●	Diverse
Less Affluent			●		Affluent
Less Educated			●		Educated
Conservative			●		Liberal
Catholic	●				Protestant

Places Rated Rank: 181

Canton-Massillon, OH

Good Restaurants: 33/401 .... ☆☆☆

Bookstores and Reading: .... ☆
Chain Superstores: 3

Visible History
National Landmarks and Sites: 2
Registered Neighborhoods: 8
Contributing Buildings: 436
   Canal Fulton District
   Fourth Street District
   Ridgewood District
   Upper Downtown Canton District

Lively Arts Calendar
Touring Artist Bookings: 2
   Palace Theatre
Dates, Resident Ensembles: 110
   Canton Symphony Orchestra

People					
Younger				●	Older
Less Diverse	●				Diverse
Less Affluent		●			Affluent
Less Educated	●				Educated
Conservative		●			Liberal
Catholic		●			Protestant

Places Rated Rank: 206

Cape Coral-Fort Myers, FL

Good Restaurants: 49/504 .... ☆☆☆

Bookstores and Reading: .... ☆
Chain Superstores: 5
Independent Stores: 4

Visible History
National Landmarks and Sites: 1
Registered Neighborhoods: 3
Contributing Buildings: 90
   Fort Myers Downtown Commercial District

Lively Arts Calendar
Touring Artist Bookings: 87
   Harborside Event Center
   Mann Performing Arts Hall
Dates, Resident Ensembles: 17
   Southwest Florida Symphony Orchestra & Chorus

People						
Younger				●		Older
Less Diverse				●		Diverse
Less Affluent				●		Affluent
Less Educated			●			Educated
Conservative			●			Liberal
Catholic	●					Protestant

Places Rated Rank: 217

Carson City, NV

Good Restaurants: 9/50 .... ☆☆☆

Bookstores and Reading: .... ☆☆☆

Visible History
Registered Neighborhoods: 2
Contributing Buildings: 65

Lively Arts Calendar
Touring Artist Bookings: 42
Dates, Resident Ensembles: 6

People						
Younger				●		Older
Less Diverse				●		Diverse
Less Affluent				●		Affluent
Less Educated	●					Educated
Conservative	●					Liberal
Catholic		●				Protestant

Places Rated Rank: 242

Casper, WY

Good Restaurants: 3/80 .... ☆

Bookstores and Reading: .... ☆☆☆

Chain Superstores: 1
Independent Stores: 2

Visible History
National Landmarks and Sites: 3
Registered Neighborhoods: 2
Contributing Buildings: 245
South Wolcott Street District

Lively Arts Calendar
Touring Artist Bookings: 7
Casper Events Center
Dates, Resident Ensembles: 6
Wyoming Symphony Orchestra

People						
Younger			●			Older
Less Diverse		●				Diverse
Less Affluent				●		Affluent
Less Educated			●			Educated
Conservative	●					Liberal
Catholic			●			Protestant

Places Rated Rank: 324

Cedar Rapids, IA

Good Restaurants: 7/266 .... ☆

Bookstores and Reading: .... ☆☆☆

Chain Superstores: 2

Visible History
Registered Neighborhoods: 18
Contributing Buildings: 679
Bohemian Commercial District
Cornell College-Mount Vernon District
Pucker Street District
Redmond Park-Grande Avenue District
Second and Third Avenue District

Lively Arts Calendar
Touring Artist Bookings: 4
Paramount Theatre
Dates, Resident Ensembles: 37
Cedar Rapids Opera Theatre
Cedar Rapids Symphony Orchestra

People						
Younger			●			Older
Less Diverse	●					Diverse
Less Affluent			●			Affluent
Less Educated			●			Educated
Conservative			●			Liberal
Catholic		●				Protestant

Places Rated Rank: 254

Champaign-Urbana, IL

Good Restaurants: 17/245 .... ☆☆☆

Bookstores and Reading: ...... ☆☆☆☆

Chain Superstores: 3
Independent Stores: 1

Visible History
National Landmarks and Sites: 2
Registered Neighborhoods: 4
Contributing Buildings: 128
North State Street District
South Charter Street District

Lively Arts Calendar
Touring Artist Bookings: 30
Krannert Center
Dates, Resident Ensembles: 26
Champaign-Urbana Symphony
Sinfonia Da Camera

People						
Younger	●					Older
Less Diverse		●				Diverse
Less Affluent			●			Affluent
Less Educated					●	Educated
Conservative			●			Liberal
Catholic			●			Protestant

Places Rated Rank: 186

Charleston, WV

Good Restaurants: 8/207 .... ☆☆

Bookstores and Reading: .... ☆

Chain Superstores: 3
Independent Stores: 1

Visible History
National Landmarks and Sites: 1
Registered Neighborhoods: 13
Contributing Buildings: 1,057
Charleston Downtown District
East End District
Edgewood District
Malden District
Nellis District

Lively Arts Calendar
Touring Artist Bookings: 18
Charleston Civic Center
Clay Center
Geary Auditorium
Dates, Resident Ensembles: 30
West Virginia Symphony

People						
Younger				●		Older
Less Diverse	●					Diverse
Less Affluent			●			Affluent
Less Educated	●					Educated
Conservative				●		Liberal
Catholic					●	Protestant

Places Rated Rank: 264

Charleston-North Charleston, SC

Good Restaurants: 163/602 ... ☆☆☆☆

Bookstores and Reading: .... ☆☆

Chain Superstores: 7
Independent Stores: 2

Visible History
National Landmarks and Sites: 56
Registered Neighborhoods: 29
Contributing Buildings: 2,943
Charleston Old and District
Hampton Park Terrace District
Indian Fields Methodist Campground
McClellanville District
Summerville District

Lively Arts Calendar
Touring Artist Bookings: 8
Gaillard Municipal Auditorium
North Charleston PAC
Dates, Resident Ensembles: 180
Charleston Symphony Orchestra

People						
Younger	●					Older
Less Diverse				●		Diverse
Less Affluent		●				Affluent
Less Educated			●			Educated
Conservative		●				Liberal
Catholic		●				Protestant

Places Rated Rank: 46

Charlotte-Gastonia, NC-SC

Good Restaurants: 57/1,440 ...... ☆☆☆☆

Bookstores and Reading: .... ☆☆☆☆

Chain Superstores: 13
Independent Stores: 8

[Charlotte, NC]

Visible History
National Landmarks and Sites: 2
Registered Neighborhoods: 61
Contributing Buildings: 6,604
  Dilworth District
  Elizabeth District
  Monroe Residential District
  Myers Park District
  York-Chester District

Lively Arts Calendar
Touring Artist Bookings: 85
  Blumenthal Performing Arts Center
  Ovens Auditorium
  UNC Belk Theatre
Dates, Resident Ensembles: 246
  Charlotte Philharmonic Orchestra
  Charlotte Symphony Orchestra Society
  Opera Carolina

People						
Younger	✸					Older
Less Diverse				✸		Diverse
Less Affluent				✸		Affluent
Less Educated			✸			Educated
Conservative		✸				Liberal
Catholic			✸			Protestant

Places Rated Rank: 53

Charlottesville, VA

Good Restaurants: 21/215 .... ☆☆☆

Bookstores and Reading: ...... ☆☆☆☆

Chain Superstores: 2
Independent Stores: 4

Visible History
National Landmarks and Sites: 5
Registered Neighborhoods: 22
Contributing Buildings: 2,067
  Charlottesville and Albemarle County
    Courthouse
  Lovingston District
  Rugby Road-University Corner District
  Southwest Mountains Rural District
  Stanardsville District

Lively Arts Calendar
Touring Artist Bookings: 56
Cabell Hall Auditorium
  Martin Luther King Center
  Paramount Theatre
Dates, Resident Ensembles: 3
  Ash Lawn Opera Festival

People						
Younger		✸				Older
Less Diverse		✸				Diverse
Less Affluent				✸		Affluent
Less Educated				✸		Educated
Conservative	✸					Liberal
Catholic			✸			Protestant

Places Rated Rank: 58

Chattanooga, TN-GA

Good Restaurants: 46/369 .... ☆☆☆

Bookstores and Reading: .... ☆☆☆

Chain Superstores: 6
Independent Stores: 3

Visible History
National Landmarks and Sites: 2
Registered Neighborhoods: 23
Contributing Buildings: 1,968
  McLemore Cove District
  Missionary Ridge District
  Signal Mountain District
  South Pittsburg District
  St. Elmo District

Lively Arts Calendar
Touring Artist Bookings: 19
  Tivoli Theatre
Dates, Resident Ensembles: 103
  Chattanooga Opera
  Chattanooga Symphony & Opera
    Association

People						
Younger			✸			Older
Less Diverse	✸					Diverse
Less Affluent		✸				Affluent
Less Educated	✸					Educated
Conservative	✸					Liberal
Catholic				✸		Protestant

Places Rated Rank: 48

Cheyenne, WY

Good Restaurants: 8/71 .... ☆☆

Bookstores and Reading: .... ☆☆☆

Chain Superstores: 2
Independent Stores: 2

Visible History
National Landmarks and Sites: 3
Registered Neighborhoods: 12
Contributing Buildings: 613
  Capitol North District
  Downtown Cheyenne District
  Lakeview District
  Rainsford District

Lively Arts Calendar
Touring Artist Bookings: 10
  Civic Center
Dates, Resident Ensembles: 7
  Cheyenne Symphony Orchestra

People						
Younger		✸				Older
Less Diverse			✸			Diverse
Less Affluent			✸			Affluent
Less Educated		✸				Educated
Conservative	✸					Liberal
Catholic	✸					Protestant

Places Rated Rank: 265

✓ Chicago-Naperville-Joliet, IL

Good Restaurants: 1,047/7,105 ☆☆☆☆

Bookstores and Reading: .... ☆☆☆

Chain Superstores: 62
Independent Stores: 44

Visible History
National Landmarks and Sites: 56
Registered Neighborhoods: 98
Contributing Buildings: 24,162
  East Ravenswood District
  Hyde Park-Kenwood District
  Pilsen District
  Ridgeland-Oak Park District
  Sheffield District

Lively Arts Calendar
Touring Artist Bookings: 947
  Civic Opera House
  Orchestra Hall
Dates, Resident Ensembles: 1866
  Chicago Opera Theater
  Chicago Philharmonia
  Chicago Sinfonietta
  Chicago Symphony Orchestra
  Civic Orchestra of Chicago
  Classical Symphony Orchestra
    & Protégé Philharmoni
  da Corneto Opera
  Du Page Opera Theatre
  Elgin Symphony Orchestra
  Grant Park Symphony Orchestra
    & Chorus
  Illinois Philharmonic Orchestra
  Light Opera Works
  L'Opera Piccola
  Lyric Opera of Chicago
  Midwest Young Artists
  Music of the Baroque Chorus
    & Orchestra
  New Philharmonic
  Northbrook Symphony Orchestra
  Symphony II
  Symphony of the Shores
  The Chinese Classical Orchestra

People						
Younger	✸					Older
Less Diverse				✸		Diverse
Less Affluent				✸		Affluent
Less Educated				✸		Educated
Conservative				✸		Liberal
Catholic	✸					Protestant

Places Rated Rank: 4

Chico, CA

Good Restaurants: 14/159 .... ☆☆☆

Bookstores and Reading: ...... ☆☆☆☆☆

Chain Superstores: 1
Independent Stores: 1

Visible History
National Landmarks and Sites: 1
Registered Neighborhoods: 1
Contributing Buildings: 114
  South of Campus Neighborhood

Lively Arts Calendar
Touring Artist Bookings: 53
Dates, Resident Ensembles: 5

People

	Younger					Older
Younger		●				Older
Less Diverse				●		Diverse
Less Affluent	●					Affluent
Less Educated				●		Educated
Conservative	●					Liberal
Catholic			●			Protestant

Places Rated Rank: 156

Cincinnati-Middletown, OH-KY-IN

Good Restaurants: 176/1,961 ☆☆☆☆

Bookstores and Reading: .... ☆☆
Chain Superstores: 18
Independent Stores: 12

Visible History
National Landmarks and Sites: 28
Registered Neighborhoods: 122
Contributing Buildings: 15,722
 Austinberg District
 East Newport District
 Over-the-Rhine District
 Taylor's Daughters District
 West Side-Main Strasse District

Lively Arts Calendar
Touring Artist Bookings: 179
 Aronoff Center for the Arts
 Hamilton County Memorial Hall
 Music Hall
 Riverbend Music Center
Dates, Resident Ensembles: 262
 Cincinnati Chamber Orchestra
 Cincinnati Opera Association
 Cincinnati Symphony Orchestra
 Northern Kentucky Symphony
 Sorg Opera Company

People

	Younger					Older
Younger			●			Older
Less Diverse		●				Diverse
Less Affluent				●		Affluent
Less Educated			●			Educated
Conservative			●			Liberal
Catholic		●				Protestant

Places Rated Rank: 51

Clarksville, TN-KY

Good Restaurants: 3/180 .... ☆

Bookstores and Reading: .... ☆
Chain Superstores: 2
Independent Stores: 1

Visible History
National Landmarks and Sites: 2
Registered Neighborhoods: 15
Contributing Buildings: 394
 Alumni-Latham-Mooreland District
 Cadiz Main Street Residential District

Dog Hill Architectural District
Glenwood District
Madison Street District

Lively Arts Calendar
Touring Artist Bookings: 7

People

	Younger					Older
Younger	●					Older
Less Diverse			●			Diverse
Less Affluent		●				Affluent
Less Educated		●				Educated
Conservative		●				Liberal
Catholic				●		Protestant

Places Rated Rank: 345

Cleveland, TN

Good Restaurants: 1/60 .... ☆

Bookstores and Reading: .... ☆☆☆
Chain Superstores: 1

Visible History
National Landmarks and Sites: 1
Registered Neighborhoods: 10
Contributing Buildings: 420
 Buzzard's Roost District
 Centenary Avenue District
 Copperhill District
 Ducktown District
 Newtown District

Lively Arts Calendar
Touring Artist Bookings: 5

People

	Younger					Older
Younger			●			Older
Less Diverse	●					Diverse
Less Affluent	●					Affluent
Less Educated	●					Educated
Conservative		●				Liberal
Catholic				●		Protestant

Places Rated Rank: 351

Cleveland-Elyria-Mentor, OH

Good Restaurants: 127/2,364 ☆☆☆☆☆

Bookstores and Reading: .... ☆☆
Chain Superstores: 16
Independent Stores: 11

Visible History
National Landmarks and Sites: 11
Registered Neighborhoods: 75
Contributing Buildings: 19,454
 Brooklyn Centre District
 East Boulevard District
 Magnolia-Wade Park District
 Shaker Village District
 Tremont District

Lively Arts Calendar
Touring Artist Bookings: 633
 Cleveland Institute of Music

Playhouse Square
Severance Hall
Dates, Resident Ensembles: 265
 Cleveland Chamber Symphony
 Cleveland Opera
 Lyric Opera Cleveland
 Ohio Chamber Orchestra
 The Cleveland Orchestra

People

	Younger					Older
Younger				●		Older
Less Diverse			●			Diverse
Less Affluent				●		Affluent
Less Educated			●			Educated
Conservative				●		Liberal
Catholic	●					Protestant

Places Rated Rank: 49

Coeur d'Alene, ID

Good Restaurants: 10/153 .... ☆☆

Bookstores and Reading: .... ☆☆☆
Chain Superstores: 1

Visible History
National Landmarks and Sites: 2
Registered Neighborhoods: 5
Contributing Buildings: 79
 Sherman Park Addition

Lively Arts Calendar
Touring Artist Bookings: 28

People

	Younger					Older
Younger			●			Older
Less Diverse	●					Diverse
Less Affluent		●				Affluent
Less Educated			●			Educated
Conservative		●				Liberal
Catholic			●			Protestant

Places Rated Rank: 314

College Station-Bryan, TX

Good Restaurants: 10/149 .... ☆☆

Bookstores and Reading: ...... ☆☆☆☆☆
Chain Superstores: 2
Independent Stores: 1

Visible History
Registered Neighborhoods: 2
Contributing Buildings: 102
 Calvert District
 East Side District

Lively Arts Calendar
Touring Artist Bookings: 19
 Texas A & M Auditorium
Dates, Resident Ensembles: 7
 Brazos Valley Symphony Orchestra

People

	1	2	3	4	5	
Younger	✸					Older
Less Diverse				✸		Diverse
Less Affluent	✸					Affluent
Less Educated				✸		Educated
Conservative		✸				Liberal
Catholic		✸				Protestant

Places Rated Rank: 211

Colorado Springs, CO

Good Restaurants: 41/557 .... ☆☆☆☆

Bookstores and Reading: .... ☆☆☆☆
Chain Superstores: 4
Independent Stores: 2

Visible History
National Landmarks and Sites: 3
Registered Neighborhoods: 14
Contributing Buildings: 2,018
  Manitou Springs District
  North End District
  North Weber-Wasatch Avenue District

Lively Arts Calendar
Touring Artist Bookings: 22
  Colorado Springs Center
  Pikes Peak Center
  USAFA Arnold Hall Theatre
Dates, Resident Ensembles: 77
  Colorado Springs Symphony

People

	1	2	3	4	5	
Younger		✸				Older
Less Diverse				✸		Diverse
Less Affluent			✸			Affluent
Less Educated				✸		Educated
Conservative	✸					Liberal
Catholic		✸				Protestant

Places Rated Rank: 66

Columbia, MO

Good Restaurants: 18/179 .... ☆☆☆

Bookstores and Reading: .... ☆
Chain Superstores: 1

Visible History
National Landmarks and Sites: 3
Registered Neighborhoods: 9
Contributing Buildings: 474
  East Campus Neighborhood District
  Rocheport
  South Main Street District

Lively Arts Calendar
Touring Artist Bookings: 26
  Missouri Theatre
  UM Jesse Auditorium
Dates, Resident Ensembles: 23
  Missouri Symphony Society

People

	1	2	3	4	5	
Younger	✸					Older
Less Diverse		✸				Diverse
Less Affluent			✸			Affluent
Less Educated				✸		Educated
Conservative		✸				Liberal
Catholic			✸			Protestant

Places Rated Rank: 246

Columbia, SC

Good Restaurants: 36/574 .... ☆☆☆

Bookstores and Reading: .... ☆☆☆☆
Chain Superstores: 8
Independent Stores: 3

Visible History
National Landmarks and Sites: 8
Registered Neighborhoods: 30
Contributing Buildings: 1,451
  Bellevue District
  Elmwood Park District
  Kendall Mill District
  University Neighborhood District
  Waverly District

Lively Arts Calendar
Touring Artist Bookings: 32
  USC Koger Center for the Arts
Dates, Resident Ensembles: 76
  South Carolina Philharmonic Orchestra

People

	1	2	3	4	5	
Younger		✸				Older
Less Diverse			✸			Diverse
Less Affluent		✸				Affluent
Less Educated			✸			Educated
Conservative		✸				Liberal
Catholic				✸		Protestant

Places Rated Rank: 83

Columbus, GA-AL

Good Restaurants: 12/214 .... ☆☆

Bookstores and Reading: .... ☆
Chain Superstores: 3

Visible History
National Landmarks and Sites: 7
Registered Neighborhoods: 28
Contributing Buildings: 3,514
  Brownville-Summerville District
  Columbus District
  Fort Benning Main Post District
  Weracoba-St. Elmo District
  Wynnton Village District

Lively Arts Calendar
Touring Artist Bookings: 2
  RiverCenter
  State University
Dates, Resident Ensembles: 26
  Columbus Symphony Orchestra

People

	1	2	3	4	5	
Younger	✸					Older
Less Diverse			✸			Diverse
Less Affluent		✸				Affluent
Less Educated		✸				Educated
Conservative	✸					Liberal
Catholic				✸		Protestant

Places Rated Rank: 238

Columbus, IN

Good Restaurants: 6/47 .... ☆☆☆

Bookstores and Reading: .... ☆☆☆
Chain Superstores: 1
Independent Stores: 1

Visible History
National Landmarks and Sites: 4
Registered Neighborhoods: 3
Contributing Buildings: 785
  Columbus District
  Hope District

Lively Arts Calendar
Touring Artist Bookings: 114
Dates, Resident Ensembles: 30
  Columbus Indiana Philharmonic

People

	1	2	3	4	5	
Younger			✸			Older
Less Diverse		✸				Diverse
Less Affluent			✸			Affluent
Less Educated	✸					Educated
Conservative	✸					Liberal
Catholic			✸			Protestant

Places Rated Rank: 194

Columbus, OH

Good Restaurants: 466/1,551 ☆☆☆☆☆

Bookstores and Reading: .... ☆☆☆
Chain Superstores: 15
Independent Stores: 8

Visible History
National Landmarks and Sites: 16
Registered Neighborhoods: 48
Contributing Buildings: 8,198
  Columbus Near East Side District
  German Village
  Glen Echo District
  Historic Northwest District
  Upper Arlington District

Lively Arts Calendar
Touring Artist Bookings: 300
  Ohio Theatre
  OSU Wexner Center for the Arts
  Palace Theatre
Dates, Resident Ensembles: 766
  Columbus Symphony Orchestra
  Opera Columbus
  Chamber Orchestra of Columbus

People						
Younger	●					Older
Less Diverse		●				Diverse
Less Affluent				●		Affluent
Less Educated				●		Educated
Conservative	●					Liberal
Catholic			●			Protestant

Places Rated Rank: 9

Corpus Christi, TX

Good Restaurants: 79/425 ..... ☆☆☆☆

Bookstores and Reading: .... ☆☆☆
Chain Superstores: 2
Independent Stores: 1

Visible History
National Landmarks and Sites: 4
Registered Neighborhoods: 1
Contributing Buildings: 4

Lively Arts Calendar
Touring Artist Bookings: 24
American Bank Center
Bayfront Plaza Auditorium
Texas A & M Center
Dates, Resident Ensembles: 48
Corpus Christi Symphony

People						
Younger		●				Older
Less Diverse	●					Diverse
Less Affluent		●				Affluent
Less Educated		●				Educated
Conservative				●		Liberal
Catholic		●				Protestant

Places Rated Rank: 202

Corvallis, OR

Good Restaurants: 8/64 .... ☆☆☆

Bookstores and Reading: .... ☆☆☆
Chain Superstores: 1
Independent Stores: 3

Visible History
Registered Neighborhoods: 4
Contributing Buildings: 587
Avery-Helm District
College Hill West District
North College Hill District

Lively Arts Calendar
Touring Artist Bookings: 14

People						
Younger	●					Older
Less Diverse		●				Diverse
Less Affluent				●		Affluent
Less Educated				●		Educated
Conservative				●		Liberal
Catholic				●		Protestant

Places Rated Rank: 307

Cumberland, MD-WV

Good Restaurants: 4/123 .... ☆

Bookstores and Reading: .... ☆☆☆
Chain Superstores: 1
Independent Stores: 3

Visible History
National Landmarks and Sites: 2
Registered Neighborhoods: 14
Contributing Buildings: 2,339
Chapel Hill District
Decatur Heights District
Frostburg District
Lonaconing District
Mount Savage District

Lively Arts Calendar
Touring Artist Bookings: 6
Western Maryland Center
Dates, Resident Ensembles: 5

People						
Younger				●		Older
Less Diverse	●					Diverse
Less Affluent	●					Affluent
Less Educated	●					Educated
Conservative			●			Liberal
Catholic			●			Protestant

Places Rated Rank: 237

✓ Dallas-Plano-Irving, TX

Good Restaurants: 944/2,795 ☆☆☆☆☆

Bookstores and Reading: ....☆☆☆☆
Chain Superstores: 23
Independent Stores: 6

Visible History
National Landmarks and Sites: 4
Registered Neighborhoods: 40
Contributing Buildings: 3,799
Colonial Hill District
Kessler Park District
Peak's Suburban Addition District
Wheatley Place District
Winnetka Heights District

Lively Arts Calendar
Touring Artist Bookings: 66
Majestic Theatre
Meyerson Symphony Center
Music Hall at Fair Park
SMU Karuth Auditorium
Dates, Resident Ensembles: 1570
Dallas Bach Orchestra & Choir
Dallas Opera
Dallas Symphony Orchestra
Garland Symphony Orchestra
Irving Symphony Orchestra
Las Colinas Symphony Orchestra
Plano Chamber Orchestra

People						
Younger	●					Older
Less Diverse			●			Diverse
Less Affluent			●			Affluent
Less Educated			●			Educated
Conservative		●				Liberal
Catholic		●				Protestant

Places Rated Rank: 16

Dalton, GA

Good Restaurants: 5/82 .... ☆

Bookstores and Reading: .... ☆☆☆
Independent Stores: 1

Visible History
National Landmarks and Sites: 1
Registered Neighborhoods: 7
Contributing Buildings: 350
Chatsworth Downtown District
Crown Mill District
McCarty Subdivision District
Spring Place District
Thornton Avenue-Murray Hill District

People						
Younger		●				Older
Less Diverse				●		Diverse
Less Affluent			●			Affluent
Less Educated	●					Educated
Conservative	●					Liberal
Catholic				●		Protestant

Places Rated Rank: 339

Danville, IL

Good Restaurants: 3/99 .... ☆

Bookstores and Reading: .... ☆☆☆
Chain Superstores: 1
Independent Stores: 1

Visible History
Registered Neighborhoods: 1
Contributing Buildings: 47

Lively Arts Calendar
Touring Artist Bookings:
Dates, Resident Ensembles: 24
Danville Symphony Orchestra

People						
Younger			●			Older
Less Diverse		●				Diverse
Less Affluent	●					Affluent
Less Educated	●					Educated
Conservative			●			Liberal
Catholic			●			Protestant

Places Rated Rank: 342

Danville, VA

Good Restaurants: 5/82 ....☆

Bookstores and Reading: .... ☆☆☆
Chain Superstores: 1
Independent Stores: 1

Visible History
National Landmarks and Sites: 1
Registered Neighborhoods: 7
Contributing Buildings: 1,589
Chatham District
Danville District
Danville Tobacco Warehouse and Residential District

Holbrook-Ross Street District
North Danville District

Lively Arts Calendar
Touring Artist Bookings: 10

People							
Younger					●		Older
Less Diverse					●		Diverse
Less Affluent	●						Affluent
Less Educated	●						Educated
Conservative		●					Liberal
Catholic					●		Protestant

Places Rated Rank: 296

Davenport-Moline-Rock Island, IA-IL

Good Restaurants: 43/472 .... ☆☆☆

Bookstores and Reading: .... ☆
Chain Superstores: 3
Independent Stores: 1

Visible History
National Landmarks and Sites: 4
Registered Neighborhoods: 25
Contributing Buildings: 2,129
Broadway District
College Square District
Davenport Village
Hamburg District
McClellan Heights District

Lively Arts Calendar
Touring Artist Bookings: 27
Adler Theatre
Centennial Hall
Dates, Resident Ensembles: 46
Quad City Symphony Orchestra

People							
Younger				●			Older
Less Diverse		●					Diverse
Less Affluent			●				Affluent
Less Educated		●					Educated
Conservative				●			Liberal
Catholic			●				Protestant

Places Rated Rank: 174

Dayton, OH

Good Restaurants: 86/723 ..... ☆☆☆☆☆

Bookstores and Reading: .... ☆☆
Chain Superstores: 4
Independent Stores: 4

Visible History
National Landmarks and Sites: 14
Registered Neighborhoods: 37
Contributing Buildings: 4,829
Elizabeth Township Rural District
Huffman District
Saint Anne's Hill District
Schantz Park District
South Park District

Lively Arts Calendar
Touring Artist Bookings: 90
Montgomery County Memorial Hall
Victoria Theatre Association
Dates, Resident Ensembles: 53
Dayton Opera Association
Dayton Philharmonic Orchestra

People							
Younger				●			Older
Less Diverse			●				Diverse
Less Affluent				●			Affluent
Less Educated			●				Educated
Conservative		●					Liberal
Catholic			●				Protestant

Places Rated Rank: 85

Decatur, AL

Good Restaurants: 3/92 .... ☆

Bookstores and Reading: .... ☆☆☆
Chain Superstores: 1

Visible History
Registered Neighborhoods: 10
Contributing Buildings: 972
Albany Heritage Neighborhood District
Bank Street-Old Decatur District
Courtland District
New Decatur-Albany District
New Decatur-Albany Residential District

Lively Arts Calendar
Touring Artist Bookings: 20
Princess Theatre Center

People							
Younger				●			Older
Less Diverse			●				Diverse
Less Affluent		●					Affluent
Less Educated	●						Educated
Conservative		●					Liberal
Catholic					●		Protestant

Places Rated Rank: 303

Decatur, IL

Good Restaurants: 10/115 .... ☆☆☆

Bookstores and Reading: .... ☆☆☆
Chain Superstores: 1

Visible History
National Landmarks and Sites: 1
Registered Neighborhoods: 3
Contributing Buildings: 2,426
Decatur District
West End District

Lively Arts Calendar
Touring Artist Bookings: 26
Kirkland Fine Arts Center
Dates, Resident Ensembles: 36
Millikin-Decatur Symphony Orchestra

People							
Younger					●		Older
Less Diverse		●					Diverse
Less Affluent			●				Affluent
Less Educated		●					Educated
Conservative				●			Liberal
Catholic				●			Protestant

Places Rated Rank: 195

Deltona-Daytona Beach, FL

Good Restaurants: 58/450 .... ☆☆☆

Bookstores and Reading: .... ☆☆☆
Chain Superstores: 3
Independent Stores: 2

Visible History
National Landmarks and Sites: 5
Registered Neighborhoods: 22
Contributing Buildings: 3,502
Daytona Beach Surfside District
New Smyrna Beach District
Seabreeze District
South Peninsula District
West DeLand Residential District

Lively Arts Calendar
Touring Artist Bookings: 57
Ocean Center
Peabody Auditorium

People							
Younger					●		Older
Less Diverse			●				Diverse
Less Affluent		●					Affluent
Less Educated				●			Educated
Conservative		●					Liberal
Catholic			●				Protestant

Places Rated Rank: 137

✓ Denver-Aurora, CO

Good Restaurants: 143/2,355 ☆☆☆☆☆

Bookstores and Reading: ...... ☆☆☆☆☆
Chain Superstores: 23
Independent Stores: 13

Visible History
National Landmarks and Sites: 7
Registered Neighborhoods: 72
Contributing Buildings: 4,982
Curtis-Champa Streets District
Park Hill
Potter Highlands District
San Rafael District
South Side-Baker District

Lively Arts Calendar
Touring Artist Bookings: 219
Boettcher Concert Hall
Buell Theatre
Caulkins Opera House
Newman Center for the Arts
Red Rocks Amphitheatre

Dates, Resident Ensembles: 188
- Central City Opera House Association
- Colorado Opera Troupe
- Colorado Symphony Orchestra
- Jefferson Symphony Orchestra
- Opera Colorado

People						
Younger	●					Older
Less Diverse				●		Diverse
Less Affluent				●		Affluent
Less Educated				●		Educated
Conservative		●				Liberal
Catholic	●					Protestant

Places Rated Rank: 8

Des Moines-West Des Moines, IA

Good Restaurants: 36/556 .... ★★★

Bookstores and Reading: .... ★★
Chain Superstores: 4
Independent Stores: 4

Visible History
National Landmarks and Sites: 2
Registered Neighborhoods: 31
Contributing Buildings: 1,707
- Kingman Place District
- Linden Heights District
- Middlesex Plat District
- Sherman Hill District
- Woodland Place District

Lively Arts Calendar
Touring Artist Bookings: 25
- Civic Center
Dates, Resident Ensembles: 65
- Des Moines Metro Opera
- Des Moines Symphony

People						
Younger		●				Older
Less Diverse		●				Diverse
Less Affluent				●		Affluent
Less Educated				●		Educated
Conservative		●				Liberal
Catholic			●			Protestant

Places Rated Rank: 163

Detroit-Livonia-Dearborn, MI

Good Restaurants: 100/1,613 ..... ★★★★

Bookstores and Reading: .... ★
Chain Superstores: 11
Independent Stores: 4

Visible History
National Landmarks and Sites: 13
Registered Neighborhoods: 57
Contributing Buildings: 5,464
- Boston-Edison District
- Highland Heights-Stevens District
- Medbury's-Grove Lawn District
- St. Florian District
- Woodbridge Neighborhood District

Lively Arts Calendar
Touring Artist Bookings: 233
- Detroit Opera House
- Fisher Theatre
- Masonic Temple Theatre
- Symphony Orchestra Hall
Dates, Resident Ensembles: 233
- Detroit Symphony Orchestra
- Michigan Opera Theatre

People						
Younger			●			Older
Less Diverse			●			Diverse
Less Affluent		●				Affluent
Less Educated		●				Educated
Conservative					●	Liberal
Catholic	●					Protestant

Places Rated Rank: 104

Dothan, AL

Good Restaurants: 10/91 .... ★★

Bookstores and Reading: .... ★
Chain Superstores: 2

Visible History
Registered Neighborhoods: 1
Contributing Buildings: 49
- Main Street Commercial District

Lively Arts Calendar
Touring Artist Bookings: 3
- Dothan Civic Center

People						
Younger				●		Older
Less Diverse			●			Diverse
Less Affluent		●				Affluent
Less Educated		●				Educated
Conservative	●					Liberal
Catholic				●		Protestant

Places Rated Rank: 368

Dover, DE

Good Restaurants: 7/95 .... ★★

Bookstores and Reading: .... ★★
Chain Superstores: 1

Visible History
National Landmarks and Sites: 2
Registered Neighborhoods: 17
Contributing Buildings: 1,861
- Felton District
- Frederica District
- Smyrna District
- Victorian Dover District
- Wyoming District

Lively Arts Calendar
Touring Artist Bookings: 4
- Schwartz Center

People						
Younger		●				Older
Less Diverse			●			Diverse
Less Affluent	●					Affluent
Less Educated	●					Educated
Conservative				●		Liberal
Catholic		●				Protestant

Places Rated Rank: 269

Dubuque, IA

Good Restaurants: 8/133 .... ★★

Bookstores and Reading: .... ★★★
Chain Superstores: 1

Visible History
National Landmarks and Sites: 5
Registered Neighborhoods: 8
Contributing Buildings: 557
- Cathedral District
- Jackson Park District
- Langworthy District
- Old Main District
- West Eleventh Street District

Lively Arts Calendar
Touring Artist Bookings: 25
- Five Flags Theatre
Dates, Resident Ensembles: 28
- Dubuque Symphony Orchestra

People						
Younger			●			Older
Less Diverse	●					Diverse
Less Affluent			●			Affluent
Less Educated		●				Educated
Conservative		●				Liberal
Catholic	●					Protestant

Places Rated Rank: 261

Duluth, MN-WI

Good Restaurants: 28/461 .... ★★★

Bookstores and Reading: .... ★
Chain Superstores: 2
Independent Stores: 3

Visible History
National Landmarks and Sites: 5
Registered Neighborhoods: 22
Contributing Buildings: 210
- Virginia Commercial District

Lively Arts Calendar
Touring Artist Bookings: 14
- Marshall Performing Arts Center
- St. Louis County Arts Center

Dates, Resident Ensembles: 42
Duluth-Superior Symphony Orchestra

	1	2	3	4	5	
People						
Younger				✸		Older
Less Diverse	✸					Diverse
Less Affluent		✸				Affluent
Less Educated		✸				Educated
Conservative			✸			Liberal
Catholic	✸					Protestant

Places Rated Rank: 257

✓ Durham, NC

Good Restaurants: 108/420 ... ☆☆☆☆

Bookstores and Reading: .... ☆☆☆
Chain Superstores: 3
Independent Stores: 3

Visible History
National Landmarks and Sites: 6
Registered Neighborhoods: 42
Contributing Buildings: 4,063
East Durham District
Forest Hills District
Trinity District
Watts-Hillandale District
West Chapel Hill District

Lively Arts Calendar
Touring Artist Bookings: 23
Duke University Page Auditorium
Dates, Resident Ensembles: 235

	1	2	3	4	5	
People						
Younger	✸					Older
Less Diverse				✸		Diverse
Less Affluent			✸			Affluent
Less Educated				✸		Educated
Conservative				✸		Liberal
Catholic			✸			Protestant

Places Rated Rank: 15

Eau Claire, WI

Good Restaurants: 29/215 .... ☆☆☆

Bookstores and Reading: .... ☆☆
Chain Superstores: 1

Visible History
Registered Neighborhoods: 6
Contributing Buildings: 358
Eau Claire Park Company Addition District
Emery Street Bungalow District
Randall Park District
Third Ward District

Lively Arts Calendar
Touring Artist Bookings: 20
Gantner Concert Hall
Regional Arts Center
Dates, Resident Ensembles: 32

	1	2	3	4	5	
People						
Younger		✸				Older
Less Diverse	✸					Diverse
Less Affluent		✸				Affluent
Less Educated			✸			Educated
Conservative				✸		Liberal
Catholic		✸				Protestant

Places Rated Rank: 231

Edison, NJ

Good Restaurants: 25/2,238 .... ☆☆

Bookstores and Reading: .... ☆☆☆☆
Chain Superstores: 18
Independent Stores: 6

Visible History
National Landmarks and Sites: 24
Registered Neighborhoods: 56
Contributing Buildings: 4,719
Allentown District
Bay Head District
Island Heights District
Livingston Manor District
Ocean Grove Camp Mtg. Ass'n District

Lively Arts Calendar
Touring Artist Bookings: 420
Dates, Resident Ensembles: 25
Philharmonic Orchestra Of New Jersey

	1	2	3	4	5	
People						
Younger				✸		Older
Less Diverse				✸		Diverse
Less Affluent				✸		Affluent
Less Educated				✸		Educated
Conservative			✸			Liberal
Catholic	✸					Protestant

Places Rated Rank: 93

El Centro, CA

Good Restaurants: 3/90 .... ☆

Bookstores and Reading: .... ☆☆☆
Independent Stores: 1

Visible History
National Landmarks and Sites: 1
Registered Neighborhoods: 1
Contributing Buildings: 14

Lively Arts Calendar
Touring Artist Bookings: 3
Southwest Theatre

	1	2	3	4	5	
People						
Younger	✸					Older
Less Diverse	✸					Diverse
Less Affluent	✸					Affluent
Less Educated	✸					Educated
Conservative			✸			Liberal
Catholic	✸					Protestant

Places Rated Rank: 373

Elizabethtown, KY

Good Restaurants: 6/51 .... ☆☆

Bookstores and Reading: .... ☆☆☆
Chain Superstores: 2

Visible History
National Landmarks and Sites: 1
Registered Neighborhoods: 8
Contributing Buildings: 189
Glendale District
West Point District

Lively Arts Calendar
Touring Artist Bookings:

	1	2	3	4	5	
People						
Younger		✸				Older
Less Diverse		✸				Diverse
Less Affluent		✸				Affluent
Less Educated		✸				Educated
Conservative	✸					Liberal
Catholic			✸			Protestant

Places Rated Rank: 350

Elkhart-Goshen, IN

Good Restaurants: 17/176 .... ☆☆☆

Bookstores and Reading: .... ☆☆☆
Chain Superstores: 1
Independent Stores: 1

Visible History
Registered Neighborhoods: 7
Contributing Buildings: 1,096
Goshen District
Nappaness Eastside District
State Street-Division Street District

Lively Arts Calendar
Touring Artist Bookings:
Elco Performing Arts Center
Dates, Resident Ensembles: 21

	1	2	3	4	5	
People						
Younger	✸					Older
Less Diverse			✸			Diverse
Less Affluent		✸				Affluent
Less Educated	✸					Educated
Conservative	✸					Liberal
Catholic			✸			Protestant

Places Rated Rank: 245

Elmira, NY

Good Restaurants: 14/120 .... ☆☆☆

Bookstores and Reading: ...... ☆☆☆☆☆
Chain Superstores: 2

Visible History
National Landmarks and Sites: 2
Registered Neighborhoods: 6
Contributing Buildings: 557
Hanover Square District
Horseheads 1855 Extension District
Near Westside District

(continued)

Lively Arts Calendar
Touring Artist Bookings: 4
  Clenens Center
Dates, Resident Ensembles: 5

People						
Younger					●	Older
Less Diverse		●				Diverse
Less Affluent	●					Affluent
Less Educated			●			Educated
Conservative				●		Liberal
Catholic		●				Protestant

Places Rated Rank: 173

El Paso, TX

Good Restaurants: 23/570 .... ☆☆

Bookstores and Reading: .... ☆
Chain Superstores: 2
Independent Stores: 1

Visible History
National Landmarks and Sites: 2
Registered Neighborhoods: 8
Contributing Buildings: 1,473
  Fort Bliss Main Post District
  Manhattan Heights District
  Montana Avenue District
  Rio Grande Avenue District
  Sunset Heights District

Lively Arts Calendar
Touring Artist Bookings: 57
  El Paso Performing Arts Theater
Dates, Resident Ensembles: 47
  El Paso Opera
  El Paso Symphony Orchestra

People						
Younger	●					Older
Less Diverse	●					Diverse
Less Affluent	●					Affluent
Less Educated	●					Educated
Conservative			●			Liberal
Catholic	●					Protestant

Places Rated Rank: 223

Erie, PA

Good Restaurants: 18/354 .... ☆☆☆

Bookstores and Reading: .... ☆☆☆
Chain Superstores: 3
Independent Stores: 1

Visible History
Registered Neighborhoods: 7
Contributing Buildings: 407
  North East District
  Union City District
  Waterford Bourough District
  West 21st Street District
  West Sixth Street District

Lively Arts Calendar
Touring Artist Bookings: 24
  Civic Center Warner Theatre
Dates, Resident Ensembles: 18
  Erie Philharmonic

People						
Younger			●			Older
Less Diverse		●				Diverse
Less Affluent		●				Affluent
Less Educated			●			Educated
Conservative			●			Liberal
Catholic		●				Protestant

Places Rated Rank: 182

✓ Essex County, MA

Good Restaurants: 54/792 .... ☆☆☆☆

Bookstores and Reading: .... ☆☆☆☆
Chain Superstores: 7
Independent Stores: 8

Visible History
National Landmarks and Sites: 29
Registered Neighborhoods: 84
Contributing Buildings: 9,059
  Bridge Street Neck District
  Diamond District
  Marblehead District
  Newburyport District
  Olmsted Subdivision District

Lively Arts Calendar
Touring Artist Bookings: 32
Dates, Resident Ensembles: 14

People						
Younger			●			Older
Less Diverse				●		Diverse
Less Affluent				●		Affluent
Less Educated				●		Educated
Conservative				●		Liberal
Catholic	●					Protestant

Places Rated Rank: 35

Eugene-Springfield, OR

Good Restaurants: 19/342 .... ☆☆☆

Bookstores and Reading: ...... ☆☆☆☆☆
Chain Superstores: 3
Independent Stores: 3

Visible History
National Landmarks and Sites: 2
Registered Neighborhoods: 11
Contributing Buildings: 893
  Amazon Family Housing Complex
  Coburg District
  East Skinner Butte District
  South University District
  Washburne District

Lively Arts Calendar
Touring Artist Bookings: 396
  Hult Center
  UO Beall Concert Hall
Dates, Resident Ensembles: 33
  Eugene Symphony Orchestra
  Oregon Mozart Players

People						
Younger			●			Older
Less Diverse		●				Diverse
Less Affluent			●			Affluent
Less Educated			●			Educated
Conservative				●		Liberal
Catholic			●			Protestant

Places Rated Rank: 98

Evansville, IN-KY

Good Restaurants: 30/306 .... ☆☆☆

Bookstores and Reading: .... ☆
Chain Superstores: 3
Independent Stores: 1

Visible History
National Landmarks and Sites: 2
Registered Neighborhoods: 21
Contributing Buildings: 2,696
  Bayard Park District
  New Harmony District
  Riverside District
  Washington Avenue District
  Welborn District

Lively Arts Calendar
Touring Artist Bookings: 30
  Vanderburgh Auditorium
Dates, Resident Ensembles: 65
  Evansville Philharmonic Orchestra

People						
Younger			●			Older
Less Diverse	●					Diverse
Less Affluent			●			Affluent
Less Educated		●				Educated
Conservative		●				Liberal
Catholic			●			Protestant

Places Rated Rank: 160

Fairbanks, AK

Good Restaurants: 11/97 .... ☆☆☆

Bookstores and Reading: .... ☆☆☆
Chain Superstores: 2
Independent Stores: 2

Visible History
National Landmarks and Sites: 3
Registered Neighborhoods: 5
Contributing Buildings: 62

Lively Arts Calendar
Touring Artist Bookings: 8
  Davis Concert Hall UAF
Dates, Resident Ensembles: 22

People — (Rank 268)

	1	2	3	4	5	
Younger	☀					Older
Less Diverse		☀				Diverse
Less Affluent				☀		Affluent
Less Educated					☀	Educated
Conservative				☀		Liberal
Catholic			☀			Protestant

Places Rated Rank: 268

Fargo, ND-MN

Good Restaurants: 42/192 ..... ☆☆☆☆

Bookstores and Reading: .... ☆☆☆

Chain Superstores: 1
Independent Stores: 1

Visible History
Registered Neighborhoods: 8
Contributing Buildings: 519
  Fargo South Residential District
  North Side Residential District

Lively Arts Calendar
Touring Artist Bookings: 30
  NDSU Festival Concert Hall
Dates, Resident Ensembles: 34
  Fargo-Moorhead Civic Opera Company
  Fargo-Moorhead Symphony Orchestra

People

	1	2	3	4	5	
Younger	☀					Older
Less Diverse	☀					Diverse
Less Affluent			☀			Affluent
Less Educated				☀		Educated
Conservative			☀			Liberal
Catholic			☀			Protestant

Places Rated Rank: 171

Farmington, NM

Good Restaurants: 5/73 .... ☆☆

Bookstores and Reading: .... ☆☆

Chain Superstores: 1

Visible History
National Landmarks and Sites: 1
Registered Neighborhoods: 3
Contributing Buildings: 108
  Church Avenue-Lovers Lane District
  Farmington Downtown District

Lively Arts Calendar
Touring Artist Bookings: 5
  Civic Center

People

	1	2	3	4	5	
Younger	☀					Older
Less Diverse	☀					Diverse
Less Affluent	☀					Affluent
Less Educated	☀					Educated
Conservative				☀		Liberal
Catholic		☀				Protestant

Places Rated Rank: 360

Fayetteville, NC

Good Restaurants: 8/223 .... ☆

Bookstores and Reading: .... ☆

Chain Superstores: 2

Visible History
National Landmarks and Sites: 1
Registered Neighborhoods: 7
Contributing Buildings: 298
  Fayetteville Downtown District
  Haymount District
  Hope Mills District
  Long Valley Farm

Lively Arts Calendar
Touring Artist Bookings:
  Reeves Auditorium
Dates, Resident Ensembles: 13

People

	1	2	3	4	5	
Younger	☀					Older
Less Diverse			☀			Diverse
Less Affluent		☀				Affluent
Less Educated		☀				Educated
Conservative		☀				Liberal
Catholic				☀		Protestant

Places Rated Rank: 320

Fayetteville-Springdale, AR-MO

Good Restaurants: 18/305 .... ☆☆☆

Bookstores and Reading: .... ☆☆

Chain Superstores: 3
Independent Stores: 1

Visible History
National Landmarks and Sites: 1
Registered Neighborhoods: 16
Contributing Buildings: 347
  Rogers Commercial District
  Washington-Willow District
  Wilson Park District

Lively Arts Calendar
Touring Artist Bookings: 59
  Walton Arts Center
Dates, Resident Ensembles: 15

People

	1	2	3	4	5	
Younger	☀					Older
Less Diverse		☀				Diverse
Less Affluent		☀				Affluent
Less Educated			☀			Educated
Conservative	☀					Liberal
Catholic				☀		Protestant

Places Rated Rank: 180

✓ Flagstaff, AZ

Good Restaurants: 69/196 ..... ☆☆☆☆☆

Bookstores and Reading: ...... ☆☆☆☆☆

Chain Superstores: 2
Independent Stores: 2

Visible History
National Landmarks and Sites: 12
Registered Neighborhoods: 23
Contributing Buildings: 893
  Flagstaff Townsite District
  Grand Canyon Lodge
  Grand Canyon Village District
  North End Residential District
  Williams Residential District

Lively Arts Calendar
Touring Artist Bookings: 51
  NAU Ardrey Auditorium
Dates, Resident Ensembles: 26
  NAU Orchestra

People

	1	2	3	4	5	
Younger	☀					Older
Less Diverse	☀					Diverse
Less Affluent		☀				Affluent
Less Educated				☀		Educated
Conservative	☀					Liberal
LDS		☀				Protestant

Places Rated Rank: 19

Flint, MI

Good Restaurants: 22/356 .... ☆☆☆

Bookstores and Reading: .... ☆

Chain Superstores: 3
Independent Stores: 1

Visible History
National Landmarks and Sites: 1
Registered Neighborhoods: 8
Contributing Buildings: 1,242
  Bridge Street-Broad Street District
  Civic Park District
  Dibbleville-Fentonville District

Lively Arts Calendar
Touring Artist Bookings: 3
  The Whiting Auditorium
Dates, Resident Ensembles: 40

People

	1	2	3	4	5	
Younger		☀				Older
Less Diverse			☀			Diverse
Less Affluent		☀				Affluent
Less Educated		☀				Educated
Conservative				☀		Liberal
Catholic		☀				Protestant

Places Rated Rank: 256

Florence, SC

Good Restaurants: 8/146 .... ☆☆

Bookstores and Reading: .... ☆

Chain Superstores: 1
Independent Stores: 1

Visible History
National Landmarks and Sites: 2
Registered Neighborhoods: 14
Contributing Buildings: 568

East Home Avenue District
Lake City Downtown District
Oaklyn Plantation
St. John's District
Welsh Neck-Long Bluff-Society Hill District

Lively Arts Calendar
Touring Artist Bookings: 12
Dates, Resident Ensembles: 5

People							
Younger			✹				Older
Less Diverse				✹			Diverse
Less Affluent	✹						Affluent
Less Educated		✹					Educated
Conservative					✹		Liberal
Catholic					✹		Protestant

Places Rated Rank: 284

Florence-Muscle Shoals, AL

Good Restaurants: 1/115 .... ☆

Bookstores and Reading: .... ☆
Chain Superstores: 1

Visible History
National Landmarks and Sites: 3
Registered Neighborhoods: 20
Contributing Buildings: 1,915
Locust Street District
Nitrate Village District
Sheffield Downtown Commercial District
Sheffield Residential District
Tuscumbia District

Lively Arts Calendar
Touring Artist Bookings:

People							
Younger				✹			Older
Less Diverse		✹					Diverse
Less Affluent	✹						Affluent
Less Educated	✹						Educated
Conservative			✹				Liberal
Catholic				✹			Protestant

Places Rated Rank: 347

Fond du Lac, WI

Good Restaurants: 12/131 .... ☆ ☆

Bookstores and Reading: .... ☆ ☆
Chain Superstores: 1

Visible History
National Landmarks and Sites: 1
Registered Neighborhoods: 6
Contributing Buildings: 314
North Main Street District
Southwest District

Lively Arts Calendar
Touring Artist Bookings: 11

People							
Younger					✹		Older
Less Diverse	✹						Diverse
Less Affluent				✹			Affluent
Less Educated		✹					Educated
Conservative			✹				Liberal
Catholic	✹						Protestant

Places Rated Rank: 315

Fort Collins-Loveland, CO

Good Restaurants: 34/309 .... ☆ ☆ ☆

Bookstores and Reading: .... ☆ ☆ ☆
Chain Superstores: 3
Independent Stores: 7

Visible History
National Landmarks and Sites: 2
Registered Neighborhoods: 17
Contributing Buildings: 800
Laurel School District

Lively Arts Calendar
Touring Artist Bookings: 108
CSU Lory Student Center
Lincoln Center Auditorium
Rialto Theatre
Dates, Resident Ensembles: 17
Fort Collins Symphony Orchestra
Opera Fort Collins

People							
Younger		✹					Older
Less Diverse			✹				Diverse
Less Affluent					✹		Affluent
Less Educated					✹		Educated
Conservative	✹						Liberal
Catholic			✹				Protestant

Places Rated Rank: 90

Fort Lauderdale, FL

Good Restaurants: 121/1,704. ☆ ☆ ☆ ☆

Bookstores and Reading: .... ☆
Chain Superstores: 12
Independent Stores: 1

Visible History
National Landmarks and Sites: 1
Registered Neighborhoods: 1
Contributing Buildings: 34
Hollywood Boulevard District

Lively Arts Calendar
Touring Artist Bookings: 859
Dates, Resident Ensembles: 183
Florida Philharmonic Orchestra
Gold Coast Opera
Symphony of the Americas

People							
Younger				✹			Older
Less Diverse				✹			Diverse
Less Affluent					✹		Affluent
Less Educated				✹			Educated
Conservative					✹		Liberal
Jewish		✹					Protestant

Places Rated Rank: 178

Fort Smith, AR-OK

Good Restaurants: 12/186 .... ☆ ☆

Bookstores and Reading: .... ☆
Chain Superstores: 2

Visible History
National Landmarks and Sites: 8
Registered Neighborhoods: 6
Contributing Buildings: 129
West Garrison Avenue District

Lively Arts Calendar
Touring Artist Bookings: 5
Fort Smith Convention Center
UAFS Breedlove Auditorium
Dates, Resident Ensembles: 8

People							
Younger			✹				Older
Less Diverse		✹					Diverse
Less Affluent	✹						Affluent
Less Educated	✹						Educated
Conservative			✹				Liberal
Catholic					✹		Protestant

Places Rated Rank: 359

Fort Walton Beach-Crestview, FL

Good Restaurants: 23/220 .... ☆ ☆ ☆

Bookstores and Reading: .... ☆ ☆ ☆
Chain Superstores: 4
Independent Stores: 1

Visible History
National Landmarks and Sites: 1
Registered Neighborhoods: 3
Contributing Buildings: 44

Lively Arts Calendar
Touring Artist Bookings: 10
Civic Auditorium
Dates, Resident Ensembles: 4

People							
Younger			✹				Older
Less Diverse			✹				Diverse
Less Affluent				✹			Affluent
Less Educated					✹		Educated
Conservative		✹					Liberal
Catholic				✹			Protestant

Places Rated Rank: 233

Fort Wayne, IN

Good Restaurants: 50/408 .... ☆☆☆☆

Bookstores and Reading: .... ☆☆
Chain Superstores: 3

Visible History
National Landmarks and Sites: 1
Registered Neighborhoods: 12
Contributing Buildings: 1,618
Columbia City District
Oakdale District
South Wayne District
West End District
Williams-Woodland Park District

Lively Arts Calendar
Touring Artist Bookings: 9
Embassy Center
Dates, Resident Ensembles: 184
Fort Wayne Philharmonic Orchestra

People						
Younger		✸				Older
Less Diverse			✸			Diverse
Less Affluent				✸		Affluent
Less Educated			✸			Educated
Conservative	✸					Liberal
Catholic			✸			Protestant

Places Rated Rank: 132

Fort Worth-Arlington, TX

Good Restaurants: 161/1,226 .. ☆☆☆☆☆

Bookstores and Reading: .... ☆
Chain Superstores: 15
Independent Stores: 6

Visible History
Registered Neighborhoods: 18
Contributing Buildings: 1,678
Fairmount-Southside District
Grand Avenue District
Near Southeast District
Old Town District
Original Town Residential District

Lively Arts Calendar
Touring Artist Bookings: 20
Bass Performance Hall
Fort Worth Cenvention Center
Dates, Resident Ensembles: 543
Fort Worth Opera
Fort Worth Symphony & Chamber Orchestra

People						
Younger	✸					Older
Less Diverse					✸	Diverse
Less Affluent				✸		Affluent
Less Educated			✸			Educated
Conservative			✸			Liberal
Catholic				✸		Protestant

Places Rated Rank: 105

Fresno, CA

Good Restaurants: 13/558 .... ☆☆

Bookstores and Reading: .... ☆
Chain Superstores: 4
Independent Stores: 3

Visible History
National Landmarks and Sites: 1
Registered Neighborhoods: 2
Contributing Buildings: 6

Lively Arts Calendar
Touring Artist Bookings: 11
Tower Theatre for Performing Arts
Warmors Performing Arts Center
William Saroyan Theatre
Dates, Resident Ensembles: 21
Fresno Philharmonic Orchestra

People						
Younger	✸					Older
Less Diverse	✸					Diverse
Less Affluent	✸					Affluent
Less Educated			✸			Educated
Conservative				✸		Liberal
Catholic			✸			Protestant

Places Rated Rank: 348

Gadsden, AL

Good Restaurants: 2/71 .... ☆

Bookstores and Reading: .... ☆☆☆

Visible History
Registered Neighborhoods: 4
Contributing Buildings: 160
Gadsden Downtown District
Turrentine District

Lively Arts Calendar
Touring Artist Bookings: 2
Wallace Hall and Gadsden Amphitheatre
Dates, Resident Ensembles: 3

People						
Younger					✸	Older
Less Diverse				✸		Diverse
Less Affluent	✸					Affluent
Less Educated	✸					Educated
Conservative	✸					Liberal
Catholic					✸	Protestant

Places Rated Rank: 365

Gainesville, FL

Good Restaurants: 27/183 .... ☆☆☆☆

Bookstores and Reading: ...... ☆☆☆☆☆
Chain Superstores: 3
Independent Stores: 4

Visible History
National Landmarks and Sites: 3
Registered Neighborhoods: 12
Contributing Buildings: 1,141
City of Alachua Downtown District
High Springs District
Northeast Gainesville Residential District
Pleasant Street District
Southeast Gainesville Residential District

Lively Arts Calendar
Touring Artist Bookings: 12
UF Performing Arts Center
Dates, Resident Ensembles: 6

People						
Younger	✸					Older
Less Diverse				✸		Diverse
Less Affluent		✸				Affluent
Less Educated				✸		Educated
Conservative		✸				Liberal
Catholic			✸			Protestant

Places Rated Rank: 116

Gainesville, GA

Good Restaurants: 4/98 .... ☆

Bookstores and Reading: .... ☆
Chain Superstores: 1

Visible History
Registered Neighborhoods: 11
Contributing Buildings: 556
Chicopee Mill and Village District
Gainesville Commercial District
Gillsville District
Green Street District
Green Street-Brenau District

Lively Arts Calendar
Touring Artist Bookings: 3
Dates, Resident Ensembles: 4

People						
Younger	✸					Older
Less Diverse				✸		Diverse
Less Affluent		✸				Affluent
Less Educated	✸					Educated
Conservative	✸					Liberal
Catholic				✸		Protestant

Places Rated Rank: 349

Gary, IN

Good Restaurants: 15/633 .... ☆☆

Bookstores and Reading: .... ☆
Chain Superstores: 4

Visible History
National Landmarks and Sites: 2
Registered Neighborhoods: 12
Contributing Buildings: 477
Crown Point Courthouse Square District
Fountain Park Chautauqua
Gary City Center District
Marktown District
West Fifth Avenue Apartments District

Lively Arts Calendar
Touring Artist Bookings: 124
Dates, Resident Ensembles: 39
Northwest Indiana Symphony Orchestra

People						
Younger			●			Older
Less Diverse					●	Diverse
Less Affluent			●			Affluent
Less Educated		●				Educated
Conservative			●			Liberal
Catholic	●					Protestant

Places Rated Rank: 270

Glens Falls, NY

Good Restaurants: 35/235 .... ☆☆☆

Bookstores and Reading: .... ☆☆☆
Independent Stores: 3

Visible History
National Landmarks and Sites: 5
Registered Neighborhoods: 12
Contributing Buildings: 1,145
Cambridge District
Hamlet of Warrensburgh District
Hudson Falls District
Salem District
Village of Greenwich District

Lively Arts Calendar
Touring Artist Bookings:
Dates, Resident Ensembles: 4

People						
Younger					●	Older
Less Diverse	●					Diverse
Less Affluent		●				Affluent
Less Educated			●			Educated
Conservative			●			Liberal
Catholic		●				Protestant

Places Rated Rank: 227

Goldsboro, NC

Good Restaurants: 2/81 .... ☆

Bookstores and Reading: .... ☆☆☆
Chain Superstores: 1

Visible History
Registered Neighborhoods: 2
Contributing Buildings: 468
Mount Olive District

Lively Arts Calendar
Touring Artist Bookings:

People						
Younger		●				Older
Less Diverse				●		Diverse
Less Affluent		●				Affluent
Less Educated		●				Educated
Conservative		●				Liberal
Catholic					●	Protestant

Places Rated Rank: 354

Grand Forks, ND-MN

Good Restaurants: 14/106 .... ☆☆☆

Bookstores and Reading: ...... ☆☆☆☆
Chain Superstores: 2

Visible History
Registered Neighborhoods: 3
Contributing Buildings: 504
Grand Forks Near Southside District

Lively Arts Calendar
Touring Artist Bookings: 20
UND Fritz Auditorium
Dates, Resident Ensembles: 6
Greater Grand Forks Symphony

People						
Younger		●				Older
Less Diverse	●					Diverse
Less Affluent			●			Affluent
Less Educated					●	Educated
Conservative				●		Liberal
Catholic	●					Protestant

Places Rated Rank: 168

Grand Junction, CO

Good Restaurants: 7/116 .... ☆☆

Bookstores and Reading: ...... ☆☆☆☆
Chain Superstores: 2
Independent Stores: 1

Visible History
Registered Neighborhoods: 4
Contributing Buildings: 40
North Seventh Street District

Lively Arts Calendar
Touring Artist Bookings: 5
Grand Junction HS Auditorium
Dates, Resident Ensembles: 9
Grand Junction Symphony Orchestra

People						
Younger				●		Older
Less Diverse			●			Diverse
Less Affluent			●			Affluent
Less Educated			●			Educated
Conservative	●					Liberal
Catholic			●			Protestant

Places Rated Rank: 276

Grand Rapids-Wyoming, MI

Good Restaurants: 46/651 .... ☆☆☆

Bookstores and Reading: .... ☆☆☆
Chain Superstores: 3
Independent Stores: 9

Visible History
National Landmarks and Sites: 1
Registered Neighborhoods: 12
Contributing Buildings: 1,064
Chief Noonday Group Camp District
Downtown Lowell District
Heritage Hill District
Ionia District
Long Lake Group Camp District

Lively Arts Calendar
Touring Artist Bookings: 3
DeBos Performance Hall
Van Andel Arena
Dates, Resident Ensembles: 128
Grand Rapids Symphony Orchestra
Opera Grand Rapids

People						
Younger		●				Older
Less Diverse			●			Diverse
Less Affluent			●			Affluent
Less Educated			●			Educated
Conservative		●				Liberal
Catholic			●			Protestant

Places Rated Rank: 108

Great Falls, MT

Good Restaurants: 4/139 .... ☆

Bookstores and Reading: ...... ☆☆☆☆
Chain Superstores: 2

Visible History
National Landmarks and Sites: 3
Registered Neighborhoods: 14
Contributing Buildings: 493
Great Falls Central Business District
Great Falls Northside Residential District

Lively Arts Calendar
Touring Artist Bookings: 4
Mansfield Center
Dates, Resident Ensembles: 10
Great Falls Symphony

People						
Younger					●	Older
Less Diverse	●					Diverse
Less Affluent			●			Affluent
Less Educated			●			Educated
Conservative		●				Liberal
Catholic			●			Protestant

Places Rated Rank: 235

Greeley, CO

Good Restaurants: 19/176 .... ☆☆☆

Bookstores and Reading: .... ☆☆☆
Chain Superstores: 1
Independent Stores: 2

Visible History
National Landmarks and Sites: 1
Registered Neighborhoods: 5
Contributing Buildings: 46

Lively Arts Calendar
Touring Artist Bookings: 27
UNC Langworthy Theatre
Union Colony Civic Auditorium

Dates, Resident Ensembles: 35
Greeley Philharmonic Orchestra

People						
Younger	●					Older
Less Diverse				●		Diverse
Less Affluent		●				Affluent
Less Educated				●		Educated
Conservative			●			Liberal
Catholic			●			Protestant

Places Rated Rank: 161

Green Bay, WI

Good Restaurants: 45/444 .... ☆☆☆

Bookstores and Reading: .... ☆
Chain Superstores: 2
Independent Stores: 3

Visible History
National Landmarks and Sites: 3
Registered Neighborhoods: 10
Contributing Buildings: 616
Astor District
Marquette District
North Broadway Street District
West Main Street District

Lively Arts Calendar
Touring Artist Bookings: 34
Weidner Center for Performing Arts
Dates, Resident Ensembles: 20
Green Bay Symphony Orchestra

People						
Younger			●			Older
Less Diverse		●				Diverse
Less Affluent				●		Affluent
Less Educated			●			Educated
Conservative		●				Liberal
Catholic	●					Protestant

Places Rated Rank: 236

Greensboro-High Point, NC

Good Restaurants: 25/664 .... ☆☆☆

Bookstores and Reading: .... ☆☆
Chain Superstores: 5
Independent Stores: 1

Visible History
National Landmarks and Sites: 1
Registered Neighborhoods: 34
Contributing Buildings: 2,916
College Hill District
Fisher Park District
Reidsville District
South Greensboro District
Summit Avenue District

Lively Arts Calendar
Touring Artist Bookings: 37
Aycock Auditorium
Carolina Theatre
High Point Theatre
War Memorial Auditorium

Dates, Resident Ensembles: 43
Greensboro Opera Company
Greensboro Symphony Orchestra

People						
Younger			●			Older
Less Diverse					●	Diverse
Less Affluent			●			Affluent
Less Educated			●			Educated
Conservative				●		Liberal
Catholic					●	Protestant

Places Rated Rank: 167

Greenville, NC

Good Restaurants: 7/116 .... ☆☆

Bookstores and Reading: ...... ☆☆☆☆
Chain Superstores: 1

Visible History
Registered Neighborhoods: 9
Contributing Buildings: 1,627
Ayden District
College View District
Farmville District
Skinnerville-Greenville Heights District
Snow Hill District

Lively Arts Calendar
Touring Artist Bookings: 25
ECU Wright Auditorium

People						
Younger	●					Older
Less Diverse			●			Diverse
Less Affluent		●				Affluent
Less Educated			●			Educated
Conservative		●				Liberal
Catholic					●	Protestant

Places Rated Rank: 170

Greenville, SC

Good Restaurants: 37/500 .... ☆☆☆☆

Bookstores and Reading: .... ☆☆
Chain Superstores: 3
Independent Stores: 2

Visible History
National Landmarks and Sites: 4
Registered Neighborhoods: 17
Contributing Buildings: 931
Earle, Col. Elias, District
East Park District
Laurens District
Pettigru Street District
Woodside Cotton Mill Village District

Lively Arts Calendar
Touring Artist Bookings: 41
Bob Jones Performing Arts Center
Peace Center for Performing Arts
Dates, Resident Ensembles: 35
Greenville Symphony Orchestra

People						
Younger		●				Older
Less Diverse			●			Diverse
Less Affluent		●				Affluent
Less Educated			●			Educated
Conservative	●					Liberal
Catholic				●		Protestant

People						
Younger		●				Older
Less Diverse			●			Diverse
Less Affluent		●				Affluent
Less Educated		●				Educated
Conservative	●					Liberal
Catholic				●		Protestant

Places Rated Rank: 125

Gulfport-Biloxi, MS

Good Restaurants: 24/231 .... ☆☆☆

Bookstores and Reading: .... ☆
Chain Superstores: 3
Independent Stores: 3

Visible History
National Landmarks and Sites: 2
Registered Neighborhoods: 10
Contributing Buildings: 682
Beach Boulevard District
Scenic Drive District
West Beach District
West Central District

Lively Arts Calendar
Touring Artist Bookings:
Saenger Theater
Dates, Resident Ensembles: 8
Gulf Coast Opera Theatre

People						
Younger			●			Older
Less Diverse				●		Diverse
Less Affluent	●					Affluent
Less Educated	●					Educated
Conservative			●			Liberal
Catholic		●				Protestant

Places Rated Rank: 284

Hagerstown-Martinsburg, MD-WV

Good Restaurants: 12/206 .... ☆☆☆

Bookstores and Reading: .... ☆
Chain Superstores: 3
Independent Stores: 2

Visible History
National Landmarks and Sites: 10
Registered Neighborhoods: 44
Contributing Buildings: 5,330
Downtown Martinsburg District
Funkstown District
Hagerstown District
Martinsburg, Mining, Manufacturing &
Improvement Co.
Williamsport District

Lively Arts Calendar
Touring Artist Bookings: 9
Maryland Theatre
Dates, Resident Ensembles: 16
Maryland Symphony Orchestra

People						
Younger				●		Older
Less Diverse	●					Diverse
Less Affluent	●					Affluent
Less Educated	●					Educated
Conservative			●			Liberal
Catholic				●		Protestant

Places Rated Rank: 150

Hanford-Corcoran, CA

Good Restaurants: 0/58 .... ☆

Bookstores and Reading: .... ☆☆☆
Chain Superstores: 1

People						
Younger	●					Older
Less Diverse	●					Diverse
Less Affluent	●					Affluent
Less Educated	●					Educated
Conservative				●		Liberal
Catholic	●					Protestant

Places Rated Rank: 377

Harrisburg-Carlisle, PA

Good Restaurants: 14/587 .... ☆☆

Bookstores and Reading: ...... ☆☆☆☆
Chain Superstores: 6
Independent Stores: 1

Visible History
National Landmarks and Sites: 6
Registered Neighborhoods: 19
Contributing Buildings: 5,804
 Carlisle District
 Midtown Harrisburg District
 Mount Pleasant District
 Newport District
 Old Uptown Harrisburg District

Lively Arts Calendar
Touring Artist Bookings: 75
 The Forum
Dates, Resident Ensembles: 44
 Harrisburg Opera Association
 Harrisburg Symphony Orchestra

People						
Younger				●		Older
Less Diverse		●				Diverse
Less Affluent			●			Affluent
Less Educated			●			Educated
Conservative		●				Liberal
Catholic		●				Protestant

Places Rated Rank: 110

Harrisonburg, VA

Good Restaurants: 12/100 .... ☆☆

Bookstores and Reading: ...... ☆☆☆☆
Chain Superstores: 2
Independent Stores: 2

Visible History
Registered Neighborhoods: 7
Contributing Buildings: 593
 Bridgewater District
 Dayton District
 Harrisonburg Downtown District
 Port Republic District
 Singers Glen District

Lively Arts Calendar
Touring Artist Bookings: 9
 JMU Wilson Auditorium

People						
Younger	●					Older
Less Diverse		●				Diverse
Less Affluent		●				Affluent
Less Educated		●				Educated
Conservative	●					Liberal
Catholic				●		Protestant

Places Rated Rank: 164

✓ Hartford-West Hartford, CT

Good Restaurants: 82/1,331 ...... ☆☆☆☆

Bookstores and Reading: ...... ☆☆☆☆☆
Chain Superstores: 10
Independent Stores: 7

Visible History
National Landmarks and Sites: 25
Registered Neighborhoods: 146
Contributing Buildings: 14,917
 Frog Hollow
 Manchester District
 Old Wethersfield District
 Rockville District

Lively Arts Calendar
Touring Artist Bookings: 293
 Lincoln Theater
 The Bushnell Center
Dates, Resident Ensembles: 147
 Connecticut Concert Opera
 Connecticut Opera Association
 Goodspeed Opera House
 Hartford Symphony Orchestra

People						
Younger					●	Older
Less Diverse					●	Diverse
Less Affluent					●	Affluent
Less Educated					●	Educated
Conservative					●	Liberal
Catholic	●					Protestant

Places Rated Rank: 5

Hattiesburg, MS

Good Restaurants: 8/78 .... ☆☆☆

Bookstores and Reading: .... ☆
Chain Superstores: 1

Visible History
Registered Neighborhoods: 6
Contributing Buildings: 859
 Hattiesburg Historic District
 North Main Street District
 Oaks District
 Parkhaven District

Lively Arts Calendar
Touring Artist Bookings: 20
 Bennett Performing Arts Center
Dates, Resident Ensembles: 24

People						
Younger	●					Older
Less Diverse		●				Diverse
Less Affluent	●					Affluent
Less Educated		●				Educated
Conservative		●				Liberal
Catholic				●		Protestant

Places Rated Rank: 255

Hickory-Lenoir-Morganton, NC

Good Restaurants: 27/299 .... ☆☆☆

Bookstores and Reading: .... ☆
Chain Superstores: 2
Independent Stores: 1

Visible History
Registered Neighborhoods: 36
Contributing Buildings: 1,022
 Avery Avenue District
 Balls Creek Campground
 Broughton Hospital District
 North Main Avenue District
 West Union Street District

Lively Arts Calendar
Touring Artist Bookings: 132
 Monroe Auditorium
 Municipal Auditorium
Dates, Resident Ensembles: 24
 Western Piedmont Symphony

People						
Younger			●			Older
Less Diverse		●				Diverse
Less Affluent	●					Affluent
Less Educated	●					Educated
Conservative	●					Liberal
Catholic				●		Protestant

Places Rated Rank: 166

Hinesville-Fort Stewart, GA

Good Restaurants: 1/34 .... ☆

Bookstores and Reading: .... ☆
Independent Stores: 1

Visible History
National Landmarks and Sites: 2

Registered Neighborhoods: 1
Contributing Buildings: 20
St. Catherine's Island

People						
Younger	✸					Older
Less Diverse			✸			Diverse
Less Affluent	✸					Affluent
Less Educated	✸					Educated
Conservative	✸					Liberal
Catholic				✸		Protestant

Places Rated Rank: 331

Holland-Grand Haven, MI

Good Restaurants: 14/158 .... ☆☆☆

Bookstores and Reading: .... ☆
Chain Superstores: 2
Independent Stores: 4

Visible History
Registered Neighborhoods: 4
Contributing Buildings: 388
Holland District
Ottawa Beach District

Lively Arts Calendar
Touring Artist Bookings: 56
Dates, Resident Ensembles: 9

People						
Younger	✸					Older
Less Diverse		✸				Diverse
Less Affluent			✸			Affluent
Less Educated			✸			Educated
Conservative	✸					Liberal
Catholic			✸			Protestant

Places Rated Rank: 267

Honolulu, HI

Good Restaurants: 55/997 .... ☆☆☆☆

Bookstores and Reading: ...... ☆☆☆☆☆
Chain Superstores: 8
Independent Stores: 1

Visible History
National Landmarks and Sites: 20
Registered Neighborhoods: 8
Contributing Buildings: 633
`Ewa Sugar Plantation Villages
Palm Circle District
Schofield Barracks District

Lively Arts Calendar
Touring Artist Bookings: 58
Blaisdell Concert Hall
Dates, Resident Ensembles: 79
Hawaii Opera Theatre
Honolulu Symphony Orchestra

People						
Younger			✸			Older
Less Diverse	✸					Diverse
Less Affluent			✸			Affluent
Less Educated			✸			Educated
Conservative				✸		Liberal
Catholic		✸				Protestant

Places Rated Rank: 91

Hot Springs, AR

Good Restaurants: 12/123 .... ☆☆☆

Bookstores and Reading: .... ☆☆☆
Chain Superstores: 2

Visible History
National Landmarks and Sites: 2
Registered Neighborhoods: 15
Contributing Buildings: 306
Hot Springs Central Avenue District
Klein, George, Tourist Court District
Pleasant Street District
Quapaw-Prospect District

Lively Arts Calendar
Touring Artist Bookings: 20

People						
Younger				✸		Older
Less Diverse		✸				Diverse
Less Affluent			✸			Affluent
Less Educated		✸				Educated
Conservative			✸			Liberal
Catholic					✸	Protestant

Places Rated Rank: 289

Houma-Bayou Cane-Thibodaux, LA

Good Restaurants: 5/174 .... ☆

Bookstores and Reading: .... ☆
Chain Superstores: 2

Visible History
National Landmarks and Sites: 3
Registered Neighborhoods: 3
Contributing Buildings: 170
Houma District
Laurel Valley Sugar Plantation

Lively Arts Calendar
Touring Artist Bookings: 4
Houma Terrebonne Civic Center

People						
Younger		✸				Older
Less Diverse			✸			Diverse
Less Affluent	✸					Affluent
Less Educated	✸					Educated
Conservative			✸			Liberal
Catholic	✸					Protestant

Places Rated Rank: 369

Houston-Sugar Land-Baytown, TX

Good Restaurants: 663/3,471 ☆☆☆☆

Bookstores and Reading: .... ☆☆☆
Chain Superstores: 30
Independent Stores: 19

Visible History
National Landmarks and Sites: 10
Registered Neighborhoods: 21
Contributing Buildings: 2,521
Denver Court District
East End District
Freedmen's Town District
Old Sixth Ward District
Silk Stocking Residential District

Lively Arts Calendar
Touring Artist Bookings: 450
1894 Grand Opera House
Hobby Center
Jones Hall for Performing Arts
Rice University Brown Hall
Dates, Resident Ensembles: 590
Houston Grand Opera Association
Houston Symphony

People						
Younger	✸					Older
Less Diverse		✸				Diverse
Less Affluent			✸			Affluent
Less Educated		✸				Educated
Conservative		✸				Liberal
Catholic		✸				Protestant

Places Rated Rank: 61

Huntington-Ashland, WV-KY-OH

Good Restaurants: 17/187 .... ☆☆☆

Bookstores and Reading: .... ☆☆
Chain Superstores: 3
Independent Stores: 2

Visible History
National Landmarks and Sites: 1
Registered Neighborhoods: 11
Contributing Buildings: 409
Bath Avenue District
Fifth and Lawrence Streets Residential District
Mortimer Place District
Rankin District
Ritter Park District

Lively Arts Calendar
Touring Artist Bookings: 94
Big Sandy Superstore Arena
Paramount Arts Center
Dates, Resident Ensembles: 28
Huntington Chamber Orchestra

People						
Younger				✸		Older
Less Diverse	✸					Diverse
Less Affluent	✸					Affluent
Less Educated	✸					Educated
Conservative				✸		Liberal
Catholic			✸			Protestant

Places Rated Rank: 214

Huntsville, AL

Good Restaurants: 21/265 .... ☆☆☆

Bookstores and Reading: .... ☆☆☆
Chain Superstores: 7

Visible History
National Landmarks and Sites: 6
Registered Neighborhoods: 11
Contributing Buildings: 860
 Houston, George S., District
 Madison Station District
 Old Town District
 Robert Beaty District
 Twickenham District

Lively Arts Calendar
Touring Artist Bookings: 35
 Von Braun Civic Center Concert Hall
Dates, Resident Ensembles: 40

People						
Younger		✸				Older
Less Diverse			✸			Diverse
Less Affluent			✸			Affluent
Less Educated				✸		Educated
Conservative			✸			Liberal
Catholic				✸		Protestant

Places Rated Rank: 136

Idaho Falls, ID

Good Restaurants: 9/109 .... ☆☆

Bookstores and Reading: ...... ☆☆☆☆
Chain Superstores: 1
Independent Stores: 2

Visible History
Registered Neighborhoods: 5
Contributing Buildings: 182
 Eleventh Street District
 Ridge Avenue District

Lively Arts Calendar
Touring Artist Bookings: 3
 Civic Auditorium
Dates, Resident Ensembles: 7

People						
Younger	✸					Older
Less Diverse			✸			Diverse
Less Affluent		✸				Affluent
Less Educated			✸			Educated
Conservative		✸				Liberal
Catholic		✸				Protestant

Places Rated Rank: 251

Indianapolis-Carmel, IN

Good Restaurants: 105/1,356 ☆☆☆☆☆

Bookstores and Reading: .... ☆
Chain Superstores: 16
Independent Stores: 12

Visible History
National Landmarks and Sites: 9
Registered Neighborhoods: 70
Contributing Buildings: 8,475
 Herron-Morton Place District
 Irvington District
 Meridian Park District
 Northside District
 West Side District

Lively Arts Calendar
Touring Artist Bookings: 33
 Clowes Memorial Hall
 De Haan Fine Arts Center
 Hilbert Circle Theatre
 Opike Performing Arts Center
 Warren Performing Arts Center
Dates, Resident Ensembles: 343
 Indiana Opera Theatre
 Indianapolis Chamber Orchestra
 Indianapolis Opera
 Indianapolis Symphony Orchestra
 Marion Philharmonic Orchestra

People						
Younger	✸					Older
Less Diverse		✸				Diverse
Less Affluent				✸		Affluent
Less Educated			✸			Educated
Conservative	✸					Liberal
Catholic			✸			Protestant

Places Rated Rank: 77

Iowa City, IA

Good Restaurants: 7/164 .... ☆☆

Bookstores and Reading: ...... ☆☆☆☆
Chain Superstores: 2
Independent Stores: 3

Visible History
National Landmarks and Sites: 1
Registered Neighborhoods: 14
Contributing Buildings: 785
 Brown Street District
 Gilbert-Linn Street District
 Longfellow District
 Melrose District

Lively Arts Calendar
Touring Artist Bookings: 35
 UI Hancher Auditorium

People						
Younger	✸					Older
Less Diverse		✸				Diverse
Less Affluent			✸			Affluent
Less Educated				✸		Educated
Conservative			✸			Liberal
Catholic		✸				Protestant

Places Rated Rank: 192

Ithaca, NY

Good Restaurants: 38/161 ..... ☆☆☆☆

Bookstores and Reading: .... ☆☆☆☆
Chain Superstores: 2
Independent Stores: 2

Visible History
National Landmarks and Sites: 1
Registered Neighborhoods: 7
Contributing Buildings: 719
 Cornell Heights District
 Dryden District
 East Hill District
 Forest Home District
 Ithaca Downtown District

Lively Arts Calendar
Touring Artist Bookings: 19
 IC Whalen Center for Music
Dates, Resident Ensembles: 55

People						
Younger	✸					Older
Less Diverse			✸			Diverse
Less Affluent			✸			Affluent
Less Educated				✸		Educated
Conservative				✸		Liberal
Catholic		✸				Protestant

Places Rated Rank: 106

Jackson, MI

Good Restaurants: 3/146 .... ☆

Bookstores and Reading: .... ☆
Chain Superstores: 1
Independent Stores: 1

Visible History
Registered Neighborhoods: 2
Contributing Buildings: 108
 Concord Village District

Lively Arts Calendar
Touring Artist Bookings: 20
 Potter Center Music Hall
Dates, Resident Ensembles: 10
 Jackson Symphony Orchestra

People						
Younger			✸			Older
Less Diverse	✸					Diverse
Less Affluent	✸					Affluent
Less Educated	✸					Educated
Conservative	✸					Liberal
Catholic	✸					Protestant

Places Rated Rank: 363

Jackson, MS

Good Restaurants: 81/305 ..... ☆☆☆☆☆

Bookstores and Reading: .... ☆☆
Chain Superstores: 4
Independent Stores: 2

Visible History
National Landmarks and Sites: 3
Registered Neighborhoods: 21

Contributing Buildings: 1,821
- *Belhaven Heights District*
- *Crystal Springs District*
- *Farish Street Neighborhood District*
- *Hazlehurst District*
- *Poindexter Park District*

Lively Arts Calendar
Touring Artist Bookings: 12
- *Belhaven College Center*
- *Thalia Mara Hall*
Dates, Resident Ensembles: 167
- *Mississippi Opera*
- *Mississippi Symphony Orchestra*

People							
Younger	✸						Older
Less Diverse		✸					Diverse
Less Affluent		✸					Affluent
Less Educated				✸			Educated
Conservative			✸				Liberal
Catholic					✸		Protestant

Places Rated Rank: 89

Jackson, TN

Good Restaurants: 7/79 .... ☆☆

Bookstores and Reading: ...... ☆☆☆☆
Chain Superstores: 1
Independent Stores: 1

Visible History
National Landmarks and Sites: 2
Registered Neighborhoods: 4
Contributing Buildings: 581
- *Bemis District*
- *East Main Street District*
- *Northwood Avenue District*

Lively Arts Calendar
Touring Artist Bookings: 2
- *Civic Center*
Dates, Resident Ensembles: 14
- *Jackson Symphony Orchestra*

People							
Younger	✸						Older
Less Diverse			✸				Diverse
Less Affluent		✸					Affluent
Less Educated		✸					Educated
Conservative			✸				Liberal
Catholic					✸		Protestant

Places Rated Rank: 215

Jacksonville, FL

Good Restaurants: 109/1,006 ✪✪✪✪✪

Bookstores and Reading: .... ☆☆
Chain Superstores: 9
Independent Stores: 5

Visible History
National Landmarks and Sites: 12
Registered Neighborhoods: 16

Contributing Buildings: 6,861
- *Avondale District*
- *Lincolnville District*
- *Old Ortega District*
- *Riverside District*
- *Springfield District*

Lively Arts Calendar
Touring Artist Bookings: 94
- *The Florida Theatre*
- *Times-Union Center for Performing Arts*
- *UNF Lazzara Performance Hall*
Dates, Resident Ensembles: 184
- *First Coast Opera*
- *Jacksonville Symphony Orchestra*

People							
Younger			✸				Older
Less Diverse				✸			Diverse
Less Affluent			✸				Affluent
Less Educated			✸				Educated
Conservative	✸						Liberal
Catholic			✸				Protestant

Places Rated Rank: 76

Jacksonville, NC

Good Restaurants: 5/112 .... ☆

Bookstores and Reading: .... ☆☆☆
Chain Superstores: 2

Visible History
Registered Neighborhoods: 8
Contributing Buildings: 247
- *Mill Avenue District*
- *Richlands District*
- *Swansboro District*
- *Venters Farm District*

Lively Arts Calendar
Touring Artist Bookings: 4

People							
Younger	✸						Older
Less Diverse			✸				Diverse
Less Affluent		✸					Affluent
Less Educated	✸						Educated
Conservative		✸					Liberal
Catholic			✸				Protestant

Places Rated Rank: 330

Janesville, WI

Good Restaurants: 24/211 .... ☆☆☆

Bookstores and Reading: .... ☆
Chain Superstores: 1
Independent Stores: 1

Visible History
National Landmarks and Sites: 2
Registered Neighborhoods: 21
Contributing Buildings: 2,965
- *Courthouse Hill District*
- *Evansville District*

- *Look West District*
- *Near East Side District*
- *Old Fourth Ward District*

Lively Arts Calendar
Touring Artist Bookings: 8
Dates, Resident Ensembles: 28
- *Beloit Janesville Symphony Orchestra*

People							
Younger			✸				Older
Less Diverse		✸					Diverse
Less Affluent			✸				Affluent
Less Educated	✸						Educated
Conservative			✸				Liberal
Catholic		✸					Protestant

Places Rated Rank: 209

Jefferson City, MO

Good Restaurants: 13/113 .... ☆☆☆

Bookstores and Reading: .... ☆
Chain Superstores: 1

Visible History
National Landmarks and Sites: 3
Registered Neighborhoods: 13
Contributing Buildings: 391
- *Bonnots Mill District*
- *Broadway-Dunklin District*
- *Capitol Avenue District*
- *Missouri State Capitol District*

Lively Arts Calendar
Touring Artist Bookings:

People							
Younger		✸					Older
Less Diverse	✸						Diverse
Less Affluent			✸				Affluent
Less Educated	✸						Educated
Conservative		✸					Liberal
Catholic		✸					Protestant

Places Rated Rank: 322

Johnson City, TN

Good Restaurants: 14/135 .... ☆☆☆

Bookstores and Reading: .... ☆☆☆☆
Chain Superstores: 2

Visible History
National Landmarks and Sites: 2
Registered Neighborhoods: 10
Contributing Buildings: 808
- *Johnson City Commercial District*
- *Jonesboro District*
- *Tree Streets District*

Lively Arts Calendar
Touring Artist Bookings: 2
- *Seeger Hall*
Dates, Resident Ensembles: 18
- *Johnson City Symphony Orchestra*

Ambience

People

	1	2	3	4	
Younger				●	Older
Less Diverse	●				Diverse
Less Affluent	●				Affluent
Less Educated		●			Educated
Conservative	●				Liberal
Catholic				●	Protestant

Places Rated Rank: 193

Johnstown, PA

Good Restaurants: 6/160 .... ☆

Bookstores and Reading: .... ☆☆☆
Chain Superstores: 1

Visible History
National Landmarks and Sites: 3
Registered Neighborhoods: 14
Contributing Buildings: 3,803
   Colver District
   Moxham District
   Portage District
   Westmont District
   Windber District

Lively Arts Calendar
Touring Artist Bookings: 20
   Pasquerilla Preforming Arts Center
Dates, Resident Ensembles: 20
   Johnstown Symphony & Chamber Orch.

People

	1	2	3	4	
Younger				●	Older
Less Diverse	●				Diverse
Less Affluent	●				Affluent
Less Educated	●				Educated
Conservative		●			Liberal
Catholic	●				Protestant

Places Rated Rank: 222

Jonesboro, AR

Good Restaurants: 3/64 .... ☆

Bookstores and Reading: ...... ☆☆☆☆☆
Chain Superstores: 2

Visible History
Registered Neighborhoods: 2
Contributing Buildings: 16

Lively Arts Calendar
Touring Artist Bookings: 8
   Jonesboro Forum
Dates, Resident Ensembles: 4

People

	1	2	3	4	
Younger		●			Older
Less Diverse		●			Diverse
Less Affluent	●				Affluent
Less Educated	●				Educated
Conservative			●		Liberal
Catholic				●	Protestant

Places Rated Rank: 286

Joplin, MO

Good Restaurants: 10/133 .... ☆☆

Bookstores and Reading: .... ☆☆☆
Chain Superstores: 2

Visible History
National Landmarks and Sites: 1
Registered Neighborhoods: 6
Contributing Buildings: 622
   Carthage South District

Lively Arts Calendar
Touring Artist Bookings: 7

People

	1	2	3	4	
Younger		●			Older
Less Diverse		●			Diverse
Less Affluent	●				Affluent
Less Educated	●				Educated
Conservative	●				Liberal
Catholic				●	Protestant

Places Rated Rank: 326

Kalamazoo-Portage, MI

Good Restaurants: 45/303 .... ☆☆☆☆

Bookstores and Reading: .... ☆☆☆☆
Chain Superstores: 2
Independent Stores: 1

Visible History
Registered Neighborhoods: 15
Contributing Buildings: 949
Henderson Park-West Main Hill District
   Richland District
   South Street District
   Stuart Area District
   Vine Area District

Lively Arts Calendar
Touring Artist Bookings: 4
   Chenery Auditorium
   Kalamazoo Civic Theatre
   WMU Miller Auditorium
Dates, Resident Ensembles: 60
   Kalamazoo Symphony Orchestra

People

	1	2	3	4	
Younger	●				Older
Less Diverse		●			Diverse
Less Affluent		●			Affluent
Less Educated			●		Educated
Conservative		●			Liberal
Catholic			●		Protestant

Places Rated Rank: 124

Kankakee-Bradley, IL

Good Restaurants: 3/113 .... ☆

Bookstores and Reading: .... ☆☆☆☆
Chain Superstores: 1

Visible History
Registered Neighborhoods: 2

Contributing Buildings: 136
   Riverview District

Lively Arts Calendar
Touring Artist Bookings: 5
   Larsen Fine Arts Center
Dates, Resident Ensembles: 21

People

	1	2	3	4	
Younger		●			Older
Less Diverse			●		Diverse
Less Affluent		●			Affluent
Less Educated	●				Educated
Conservative			●		Liberal
Catholic			●		Protestant

Places Rated Rank: 280

Kansas City, MO-KS

Good Restaurants: 229/1,675 ☆☆☆☆

Bookstores and Reading: .... ☆
Chain Superstores: 16
Independent Stores: 7

Visible History
National Landmarks and Sites: 13
Registered Neighborhoods: 69
Contributing Buildings: 4,047
   Hyde Park District
   Hyde Park West District, Old
   Old Neighborhoods District
   Santa Fe Place District
   Simpson-Yeomans-Country Side District

Lively Arts Calendar
Touring Artist Bookings: 110
   Folly Theatre
   Lyric Theatre
   Music Hall
   UMKC White Recital Hall
Dates, Resident Ensembles: 772
   Kansas City Camerata
   Kansas City Symphony
   Lyric Opera of Kansas City

People

	1	2	3	4	
Younger		●			Older
Less Diverse			●		Diverse
Less Affluent				●	Affluent
Less Educated			●		Educated
Conservative			●		Liberal
Catholic		●			Protestant

Places Rated Rank: 60

Kennewick-Richland-Pasco, WA

Good Restaurants: 8/190 .... ☆☆

Bookstores and Reading: .... ☆☆☆☆
Chain Superstores: 1

Visible History
National Landmarks and Sites: 2
Registered Neighborhoods: 1
Contributing Buildings: 117

Gold Coast District

Lively Arts Calendar
Touring Artist Bookings:
Dates, Resident Ensembles: 8
Mid-Columbia Symphony
Washington East Opera

People						
Younger	●					Older
Less Diverse				●		Diverse
Less Affluent		●				Affluent
Less Educated			●			Educated
Conservative	●					Liberal
Catholic		●				Protestant

Places Rated Rank: 281

Killeen-Temple-Fort Hood, TX

Good Restaurants: 5/194 .... ☆

Bookstores and Reading: .... ☆
Chain Superstores: 2

Visible History
Registered Neighborhoods: 5
Contributing Buildings: 254
Lampasas Downtown District
Temple Commercial District

Lively Arts Calendar
Touring Artist Bookings: 2
Cultural Activities Center

People						
Younger	●					Older
Less Diverse				●		Diverse
Less Affluent	●					Affluent
Less Educated			●			Educated
Conservative	●					Liberal
Catholic			●			Protestant

Places Rated Rank: 344

Kingsport-Bristol-Bristol, TN-VA

Good Restaurants: 21/130.......... ☆ ☆ ☆

Bookstores and Reading: .... ☆
Chain Superstores: 3
Independent Stores: 1

Visible History
National Landmarks and Sites: 1
Registered Neighborhoods: 13
Contributing Buildings: 640
Abingdon District
Bulls Gap District
Rogersville District
Solar Hill District
Virginia Hill District

Lively Arts Calendar
Touring Artist Bookings: 4
Paramount Center for Arts
Dates, Resident Ensembles: 29
Kingsport Symphony Orchestra

People						
Younger				●		Older
Less Diverse	●					Diverse
Less Affluent	●					Affluent
Less Educated	●					Educated
Conservative			●			Liberal
Catholic					●	Protestant

Places Rated Rank: 243

Kingston, NY

Good Restaurants: 20/257 .... ☆ ☆ ☆

Bookstores and Reading: .... ☆ ☆
Chain Superstores: 2
Independent Stores: 3

Visible History
National Landmarks and Sites: 8
Registered Neighborhoods: 24
Contributing Buildings: 1,254
Cragsmoor District
Kingston Stockade District
Lake Mohonk Mountain House Complex
Main Street District
Rondout-West Strand District

Lively Arts Calendar
Touring Artist Bookings: 17
Ulster Performing Arts Center
Dates, Resident Ensembles: 210

People						
Younger				●		Older
Less Diverse		●				Diverse
Less Affluent		●				Affluent
Less Educated			●			Educated
Conservative				●		Liberal
Catholic	●					Protestant

Places Rated Rank: 121

✓ Knoxville, TN

Good Restaurants: 44/484 .... ☆ ☆ ☆

Bookstores and Reading: ...... ☆ ☆ ☆ ☆ ☆
Chain Superstores: 6
Independent Stores: 6

Visible History
National Landmarks and Sites: 1
Registered Neighborhoods: 37
Contributing Buildings: 7,513
Fort Sanders District
Oak Ridge District
Old North Knoxville District
Park City District
Woodland-Scarboro District

Lively Arts Calendar
Touring Artist Bookings: 83
Tennessee Theatre
UT Clarence Brown Theatre
Dates, Resident Ensembles: 210
Knoxville Opera Company
Knoxville Symphony Orchestra
Oak Ridge Symphony Orchestra

People						
Younger			●			Older
Less Diverse	●					Diverse
Less Affluent			●			Affluent
Less Educated				●		Educated
Conservative		●				Liberal
Catholic					●	Protestant

Places Rated Rank: 21

Kokomo, IN

Good Restaurants: 9/103 .... ☆ ☆

Bookstores and Reading: .... ☆ ☆ ☆
Chain Superstores: 1

Lively Arts Calendar
Touring Artist Bookings: 2
Havens Auditorium
Dates, Resident Ensembles: 16
Kokomo Symphony Orchestra

People						
Younger			●			Older
Less Diverse		●				Diverse
Less Affluent			●			Affluent
Less Educated	●					Educated
Conservative	●					Liberal
Catholic			●			Protestant

Places Rated Rank: 334

La Crosse, WI-MN

Good Restaurants: 4/201 .... ☆

Bookstores and Reading: .... ☆ ☆ ☆ ☆
Chain Superstores: 2

Visible History
National Landmarks and Sites: 1
Registered Neighborhoods: 5
Contributing Buildings: 355
10th and Cass Streets Neighborhood District
Cass and King Street Residential District

Lively Arts Calendar
Touring Artist Bookings: 32
Viterbo Fine Arts Center
Dates, Resident Ensembles: 6
La Crosse Symphony Orchestra

People						
Younger		●				Older
Less Diverse	●					Diverse
Less Affluent				●		Affluent
Less Educated					●	Educated
Conservative			●			Liberal
Catholic		●				Protestant

Places Rated Rank: 266

Lafayette, IN

Good Restaurants: 23/177 .... ☆☆☆

Bookstores and Reading: ...... ☆☆☆☆

Chain Superstores: 3
Independent Stores: 2

Visible History

National Landmarks and Sites: 1
Registered Neighborhoods: 17
Contributing Buildings: 2,373
  Centennial Neighborhood District
  Chauncey-Stadium Avenues District
  Highland Park Neighborhood District
  Jefferson District
  Perrin District

Lively Arts Calendar

Touring Artist Bookings: 20
Long Center for Performing Arts
Dates, Resident Ensembles: 28
  Lafayette Symphony Orchestra

People						
Younger	✹					Older
Less Diverse			✹			Diverse
Less Affluent			✹			Affluent
Less Educated				✹		Educated
Conservative		✹				Liberal
Catholic			✹			Protestant

Places Rated Rank: 78

Lafayette, LA

Good Restaurants: 16/223 .... ☆☆☆

Bookstores and Reading: .... ☆☆☆☆

Chain Superstores: 1
Independent Stores: 2

Visible History

National Landmarks and Sites: 3
Registered Neighborhoods: 4
Contributing Buildings: 104
  Breaux Bridge District
  St. Martinville District
  Sterling Grove District

Lively Arts Calendar

Touring Artist Bookings: 21
Heymann Center for Performing Arts
Dates, Resident Ensembles: 9
  Arcadiana Symphony

People						
Younger		✹				Older
Less Diverse				✹		Diverse
Less Affluent			✹			Affluent
Less Educated		✹				Educated
Conservative				✹		Liberal
Catholic	✹					Protestant

Places Rated Rank: 240

Lake Charles, LA

Good Restaurants: 6/128 .... ☆

Bookstores and Reading: .... ☆☆☆

Chain Superstores: 2

Visible History

Registered Neighborhoods: 1
Contributing Buildings: 280
Lake Charles District

Lively Arts Calendar

Touring Artist Bookings: 3
  Lake Charles Civic Centre
Dates, Resident Ensembles: 8
  Lake Charles Symphony

People						
Younger		✹				Older
Less Diverse				✹		Diverse
Less Affluent		✹				Affluent
Less Educated	✹					Educated
Conservative				✹		Liberal
Catholic		✹				Protestant

Places Rated Rank: 340

Lake County-Kenosha County, IL-WI

Good Restaurants: 54/855 .... ☆☆☆

Bookstores and Reading: .... ☆☆☆

Chain Superstores: 7
Independent Stores: 4

Visible History

National Landmarks and Sites: 1
Registered Neighborhoods: 21
Contributing Buildings: 1,370
  Barrington District
  Great Lakes Naval Training Station
  Green Bay Road District
  Lake Forest District
  Near North District

Lively Arts Calendar

Touring Artist Bookings: 37
Dates, Resident Ensembles: 100
  Lake Forest Symphony
  Sinfonetta Americana, Sinfonia Americana

People						
Younger		✹				Older
Less Diverse				✹		Diverse
Less Affluent				✹		Affluent
Less Educated				✹		Educated
Conservative		✹				Liberal
Catholic	✹					Protestant

Places Rated Rank: 87

Lakeland, FL

Good Restaurants: 8/316 .... ☆

Bookstores and Reading: .... ☆

Chain Superstores: 4

Visible History

National Landmarks and Sites: 1
Registered Neighborhoods: 23
Contributing Buildings: 2,836
  Dixieland District
  East Lake Morton Residential District
  Lake Wales Residential District
  South Bartow Residential District
  South Lake Morton District

Lively Arts Calendar

Touring Artist Bookings: 51
  Lakeland Center
Dates, Resident Ensembles: 16
  Imperial Symphony Orchestra

People						
Younger			✹			Older
Less Diverse					✹	Diverse
Less Affluent		✹				Affluent
Less Educated	✹					Educated
Conservative	✹					Liberal
Catholic			✹			Protestant

Places Rated Rank: 249

Lancaster, PA

Good Restaurants: 57/391 ..... ☆☆☆☆

Bookstores and Reading: .... ☆☆☆

Chain Superstores: 3

Visible History

National Landmarks and Sites: 5
Registered Neighborhoods: 36
Contributing Buildings: 16,709
  Columbia District
  Lancaster City District
  Lancaster District
  Manheim Borough District
  Marietta District

Lively Arts Calendar

Touring Artist Bookings: 8
  Barshinger Auditorium
  Fulton Opera House
Dates, Resident Ensembles: 2
  Opera Lancaster

People						
Younger			✹			Older
Less Diverse		✹				Diverse
Less Affluent			✹			Affluent
Less Educated		✹				Educated
Conservative	✹					Liberal
Catholic				✹		Protestant

Places Rated Rank: 117

Lansing-East Lansing, MI

Good Restaurants: 63/394 ..... ☆☆☆☆☆

Bookstores and Reading: ...... ☆☆☆☆☆

Chain Superstores: 3
Independent Stores: 7

Visible History

National Landmarks and Sites: 2
Registered Neighborhoods: 5

Contributing Buildings: 485
Courthouse Square District
River Ledge District
Westside Neighborhood District

Lively Arts Calendar
Touring Artist Bookings: 55
Wharton Center
Dates, Resident Ensembles: 12
Greater Lansing Symphony

People							
Younger	●						Older
Less Diverse		●					Diverse
Less Affluent		●					Affluent
Less Educated			●				Educated
Conservative		●					Liberal
Catholic		●					Protestant

Places Rated Rank: 120

Laredo, TX

Good Restaurants: 4/130 ....☆

Bookstores and Reading: ....☆☆☆
Chain Superstores: 1

Visible History
Registered Neighborhoods: 4
Contributing Buildings: 337
Barrio Azteca District
Lively Arts Calendar
Touring Artist Bookings: 2
Civic Center
Dates, Resident Ensembles: 30
Chamber Orchestra of the Two Laredos
Laredo Philharmonic Orchestra

People							
Younger	●						Older
Less Diverse	●						Diverse
Less Affluent	●						Affluent
Less Educated	●						Educated
Conservative				●			Liberal
Catholic	●						Protestant

Places Rated Rank: 306

Las Cruces, NM

Good Restaurants: 15/107 ....☆☆☆

Bookstores and Reading: ....☆
Chain Superstores: 1
Independent Stores: 2

Visible History
National Landmarks and Sites: 3
Registered Neighborhoods: 6
Contributing Buildings: 500
Alameda-Depot District
Dona Ana Village District
La Mesilla District
Mesquite St. Original TownsitenDistrict

Lively Arts Calendar
Touring Artist Bookings: 12
NMSU Performance Center
Dates, Resident Ensembles: 12
Las Cruces Symphony

People							
Younger	●						Older
Less Diverse	●						Diverse
Less Affluent	●						Affluent
Less Educated		●					Educated
Conservative		●					Liberal
Catholic	●						Protestant

Places Rated Rank: 226

Las Vegas-Paradise, NV

Good Restaurants: 151/1,199 . ☆☆☆☆

Bookstores and Reading: .... ☆☆
Chain Superstores: 12
Independent Stores: 6

Visible History
National Landmarks and Sites: 2
Registered Neighborhoods: 6
Contributing Buildings: 707
Boulder City District
John Park Historic Park
Las Vegas High School District

Lively Arts Calendar
Touring Artist Bookings: 84
Artemus Ham Concert Hall
Sammy Davis Jr. Festival Plaza
Wipple Cultural Center
Dates, Resident Ensembles: 14
Nevada Opera Theatre
Nevada Symphony Orchestra

People							
Younger		●					Older
Less Diverse						●	Diverse
Less Affluent			●				Affluent
Less Educated		●					Educated
Conservative			●				Liberal
Catholic	●						Protestant

Places Rated Rank: 135

Lawrence, KS

Good Restaurants: 6/108 .... ☆☆

Bookstores and Reading: ...... ☆☆☆☆
Chain Superstores: 1
Independent Stores: 5

Visible History
National Landmarks and Sites: 2
Registered Neighborhoods: 8
Contributing Buildings: 333
Lawrence's Downtown District
North Rhode Island District
Old West Lawrence District
Pinckney I District
South Rhode Island District

Lively Arts Calendar
Touring Artist Bookings: 33
Leid Centre of Kansas
Dates, Resident Ensembles: 8

People							
Younger	●						Older
Less Diverse		●					Diverse
Less Affluent			●				Affluent
Less Educated				●			Educated
Conservative			●				Liberal
Catholic				●			Protestant

Places Rated Rank: 187

Lawton, OK

Good Restaurants: 0/98 ....☆

Bookstores and Reading: ....☆☆☆
Chain Superstores: 1

Visible History
National Landmarks and Sites: 1
Registered Neighborhoods: 1
Contributing Buildings: 28
Fort Sill

Lively Arts Calendar
Touring Artist Bookings: 4
McMahon Auditorium
Dates, Resident Ensembles: 12
Lawton Philharmonic Orchestra

People							
Younger	●						Older
Less Diverse					●		Diverse
Less Affluent	●						Affluent
Less Educated	●						Educated
Conservative	●						Liberal
Catholic					●		Protestant

Places Rated Rank: 318

Lebanon, PA

Good Restaurants: 2/99 ....☆

Bookstores and Reading: .... ☆☆☆
Chain Superstores: 1

Visible History
National Landmarks and Sites: 3
Registered Neighborhoods: 2
Contributing Buildings: 330
Annville District
Cornwall Iron Furnace

Lively Arts Calendar
Touring Artist Bookings: 33

People							
Younger					●		Older
Less Diverse		●					Diverse
Less Affluent			●				Affluent
Less Educated	●						Educated
Conservative				●			Liberal
Catholic			●				Protestant

Places Rated Rank: 316

Lewiston, ID-WA

Good Restaurants: 8/70 .... ☆☆

Bookstores and Reading: .... ☆☆☆

Visible History
National Landmarks and Sites: 1
Registered Neighborhoods: 3
Contributing Buildings: 52
Hells Canyon Archeological District

Lively Arts Calendar
Touring Artist Bookings: 6

People					
Younger				✸	Older
Less Diverse	✸				Diverse
Less Affluent		✸			Affluent
Less Educated		✸			Educated
Conservative		✸			Liberal
Catholic			✸		Protestant

Places Rated Rank: 282

Lewiston-Auburn, ME

Good Restaurants: 3/101 .... ☆

Bookstores and Reading: .... ☆☆☆
Chain Superstores: 1
Independent Stores: 2

Visible History
National Landmarks and Sites: 1
Registered Neighborhoods: 5
Contributing Buildings: 53

Lively Arts Calendar
Touring Artist Bookings: 10

People					
Younger				✸	Older
Less Diverse	✸				Diverse
Less Affluent		✸			Affluent
Less Educated		✸			Educated
Conservative				✸	Liberal
Catholic	✸				Protestant

Places Rated Rank: 338

Lexington-Fayette, KY

Good Restaurants: 16/393 .... ☆☆

Bookstores and Reading: ...... ☆☆☆☆
Chain Superstores: 3
Independent Stores: 3

Visible History
National Landmarks and Sites: 5
Registered Neighborhoods: 81
Contributing Buildings: 5,754
Ashland Park District
Downtown Paris District
Southeast Lexington Residential and
Commercial District
Stoner Creek Rural District
Thomson Neighborhood District

Lively Arts Calendar
Touring Artist Bookings: 56
Lexington Opera House
UK Singletary Center
Dates, Resident Ensembles: 98
Lexington Philharmonic Orchestra

People					
Younger	✸				Older
Less Diverse		✸			Diverse
Less Affluent			✸		Affluent
Less Educated			✸		Educated
Conservative		✸			Liberal
Catholic		✸			Protestant

Places Rated Rank: 70

Lima, OH

Good Restaurants: 10/102 .... ☆☆

Bookstores and Reading: .... ☆☆☆
Chain Superstores: 1
Independent Stores: 1
Visible History
National Landmarks and Sites: 1
Registered Neighborhoods: 1
Contributing Buildings: 35
West Market Street Boulevard District

Lively Arts Calendar
Touring Artist Bookings: 26
Veterans Civic Center
Dates, Resident Ensembles: 13
Lima Symphony Orchestra

People					
Younger		✸			Older
Less Diverse	✸				Diverse
Less Affluent	✸				Affluent
Less Educated	✸				Educated
Conservative	✸				Liberal
Catholic		✸			Protestant

Places Rated Rank: 304

Lincoln, NE

Good Restaurants: 25/244 .... ☆☆☆

Bookstores and Reading: ...... ☆☆☆☆☆
Chain Superstores: 3
Independent Stores: 4

Visible History
National Landmarks and Sites: 2
Registered Neighborhoods: 6
Contributing Buildings: 1,473
Greek Row District
Mount Emerald & Capitol Additions HD
South Bottoms District
University Place Residential District

Lively Arts Calendar
Touring Artist Bookings: 37
Lied Center for Performing Arts
Pershing Auditorium
Dates, Resident Ensembles: 25
Lincoln Symphony Orchestra

People					
Younger	✸				Older
Less Diverse	✸				Diverse
Less Affluent			✸		Affluent
Less Educated				✸	Educated
Conservative		✸			Liberal
Catholic			✸		Protestant

Places Rated Rank: 95

Little Rock-North Little Rock, AR

Good Restaurants: 35/455 .... ☆☆☆

Bookstores and Reading: .... ☆☆
Chain Superstores: 4
Independent Stores: 2

Visible History
National Landmarks and Sites: 9
Registered Neighborhoods: 23
Contributing Buildings: 3,217
Capitol View Neighborhood District
Central High School Neighborhood
District
Governor's Mansion District
Hillcrest District
Park Hill District

Lively Arts Calendar
Touring Artist Bookings: 15
Robinson Center Music Hall
Wildwood Park for Performing Arts
Dates, Resident Ensembles: 55
Arkansas Symphony
Conway Orchestra
Opera Theatre at Wildwood

People					
Younger		✸			Older
Less Diverse			✸		Diverse
Less Affluent		✸			Affluent
Less Educated		✸			Educated
Conservative			✸		Liberal
Catholic				✸	Protestant

Places Rated Rank: 149

Logan, UT-ID

Good Restaurants: 5/52 .... ☆☆

Bookstores and Reading: .... ☆☆☆
Chain Superstores: 1
Independent Stores: 2

Visible History
National Landmarks and Sites: 1
Registered Neighborhoods: 2
Contributing Buildings: 361
Logan Center Street District

Lively Arts Calendar
Touring Artist Bookings: 31
Chase Fine Arts Center
Dates, Resident Ensembles: 3
Utah Festival Opera Company

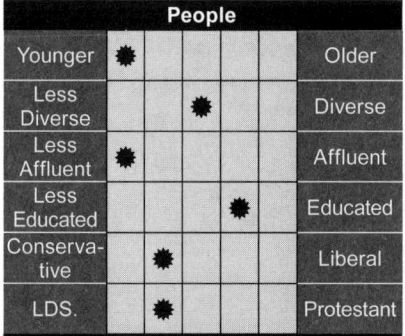

People						
Younger	●					Older
Less Diverse			●			Diverse
Less Affluent	●					Affluent
Less Educated				●		Educated
Conservative		●				Liberal
LDS.		●				Protestant

Places Rated Rank: 272

Longview, TX

Good Restaurants: 6/134 .... ☆

Bookstores and Reading: .... ☆☆☆
Chain Superstores: 2
Independent Stores: 1

Visible History
Registered Neighborhoods: 2
Contributing Buildings: 84
Nuggett Hill District

Lively Arts Calendar
Touring Artist Bookings: 4
Civic Center and Auditorium
Dates, Resident Ensembles: 7
Longview Symphony Orchestra
Opera East Texas

People						
Younger			●			Older
Less Diverse				●		Diverse
Less Affluent		●				Affluent
Less Educated	●					Educated
Conservative				●		Liberal
Catholic				●		Protestant

Places Rated Rank: 283

Longview, WA

Good Restaurants: 6/96 .... ☆☆

Bookstores and Reading: .... ☆☆☆
Chain Superstores: 1

Visible History
Registered Neighborhoods: 1
Contributing Buildings: 3

Lively Arts Calendar
Touring Artist Bookings: 2
Columbia Theatre for Performing Arts

People						
Younger			●			Older
Less Diverse		●				Diverse
Less Affluent		●				Affluent
Less Educated	●					Educated
Conservative				●		Liberal
Catholic			●			Protestant

Places Rated Rank: 364

✓ Los Angeles-Long Beach, CA

Good Restaurants: 270/7,662 ☆☆☆☆

Bookstores and Reading: .... ☆☆☆
Chain Superstores: 51
Independent Stores: 60

Visible History
National Landmarks and Sites: 23
Registered Neighborhoods: 59
Contributing Buildings: 2,311
Baldwin Hills Village
Lincoln Park District
Prospect District
St. James Park District
Whitley Heights District

Lively Arts Calendar
Touring Artist Bookings: 2,282
Alex Theatre
Carpenter Performing Arts Center
Disney Concert Hall
Dorothy Chandler Pavillion
Hollywood Bowl
Terrace Theatre
Wilshire-Ebell Theatre
Dates, Resident Ensembles: 367
American Jazz Philharmonic
American Youth Symphony
Asia America Symphony
California Festival Opera
Casa Itallana Opera Company
Contemporary Opera of Los Angeles
Glendale Symphony Orchestra
Long Beach Opera
Los Angeles Mozart Orchestra
Los Angeles Opera

People						
Younger		●				Older
Less Diverse	●					Diverse
Less Affluent				●		Affluent
Less Educated				●		Educated
Conservative					●	Liberal
Catholic	●					Protestant

Places Rated Rank: 17

Louisville-Jefferson County, KY-IN

Good Restaurants: 80/932 .... ☆☆☆☆

Bookstores and Reading: .... ☆
Chain Superstores: 11
Independent Stores: 5

Visible History
National Landmarks and Sites: 11
Registered Neighborhoods: 97
Contributing Buildings: 14,017
Audubon Park District
Cherokee Triangle Area Residential District
Highlands District
Old Louisville Residential District
Russell District

Lively Arts Calendar
Touring Artist Bookings: 311
Brown Theatre
Kentucky Center for the Arts

Dates, Resident Ensembles: 136
Kentucky Opera
The Louisville Orchestra

People						
Younger			●			Older
Less Diverse		●				Diverse
Less Affluent			●			Affluent
Less Educated	●					Educated
Conservative		●				Liberal
Catholic		●				Protestant

Places Rated Rank: 75

Lubbock, TX

Good Restaurants: 12/204 .... ☆☆

Bookstores and Reading: ...... ☆☆☆☆
Chain Superstores: 2
Independent Stores: 1

Visible History
National Landmarks and Sites: 2
Registered Neighborhoods: 3
Contributing Buildings: 427
South Overton Residential District

Lively Arts Calendar
Touring Artist Bookings: 21
Lubbock Memorial Civic Center
Dates, Resident Ensembles: 12
Lubbock Symphony Orchestra

People						
Younger	●					Older
Less Diverse			●			Diverse
Less Affluent		●				Affluent
Less Educated			●			Educated
Conservative	●					Liberal
Catholic			●			Protestant

Places Rated Rank: 129

Lynchburg, VA

Good Restaurants: 21/166............ ☆☆☆

Bookstores and Reading: .... ☆☆
Chain Superstores: 2
Independent Stores: 4

Visible History
National Landmarks and Sites: 4
Registered Neighborhoods: 17
Contributing Buildings: 1,870
Appomattox District
Bedford District
Daniel's Hill District
Diamond Hill District
Rivermont District

Lively Arts Calendar
Touring Artist Bookings: 7
Dates, Resident Ensembles: 5

People						
Younger				●		Older
Less Diverse			●			Diverse
Less Affluent		●				Affluent
Less Educated			●			Educated
Conservative	●					Liberal
Catholic				●		Protestant

Places Rated Rank: 213

Macon, GA

Good Restaurants: 30/159 ....☆☆☆

Bookstores and Reading: ....☆☆☆
Chain Superstores: 3

Visible History
National Landmarks and Sites: 3
Registered Neighborhoods: 22
Contributing Buildings: 5,751
 Fort Hill District
 Macon District
 Pleasant Hill District
 Tindall Heights District
 Vineville District

Lively Arts Calendar
Touring Artist Bookings: 10
 Mercer University Opera House
Dates, Resident Ensembles: 30
 Macon Symphony Orchestra

People						
Younger	●					Older
Less Diverse				●		Diverse
Less Affluent			●			Affluent
Less Educated		●				Educated
Conservative		●				Liberal
Catholic				●		Protestant

Places Rated Rank: 84

Madera, CA

Good Restaurants: 1/69 ....☆

Bookstores and Reading: ....☆☆☆
Independent Stores: 1

Visible History
National Landmarks and Sites: 1

People						
Younger	●					Older
Less Diverse	●					Diverse
Less Affluent	●					Affluent
Less Educated	●					Educated
Conservative			●			Liberal
Catholic	●					Protestant

Places Rated Rank: 376

✓ Madison, WI

Good Restaurants: 107/694 ... ☆☆☆☆☆

Bookstores and Reading: ...... ☆☆☆☆
Chain Superstores: 5
Independent Stores: 8

Visible History
National Landmarks and Sites: 12
Registered Neighborhoods: 50
Contributing Buildings: 4,443
 Mineral Point District
 Nakoma District
 University Heights District
 West Lawn Heights District
 Wingra Park District

Lively Arts Calendar
Touring Artist Bookings: 97
 Oscar Mayer Theatre
 Overture Center for the Arts
 UW Union Theatre
Dates, Resident Ensembles: 73
 Madison Opera
 Madison Symphony Orchestra
 Wisconsin Chamber Orchestra

People						
Younger		●				Older
Less Diverse			●			Diverse
Less Affluent				●		Affluent
Less Educated				●		Educated
Conservative				●		Liberal
Catholic		●				Protestant

Places Rated Rank: 18

Manchester-Nashua, NH

Good Restaurants: 56/373 ..... ☆☆☆☆☆

Bookstores and Reading: ...... ☆☆☆☆☆
Chain Superstores: 3
Independent Stores: 2

Visible History
National Landmarks and Sites: 6
Registered Neighborhoods: 18
Contributing Buildings: 675
 Amherst Village District
 Hollis Village District
 MacDowell Colony
 Nashville District
 New Ipswich Center Village District

Lively Arts Calendar
Touring Artist Bookings: 75
 Palace Theatre
Dates, Resident Ensembles: 46
 Nashua Symphony Orchestra & Choral
 New Hampshire Philharmonic Orchestra
 New Hampshire Symphony Orchestra
 Opera New Hampshire

People						
Younger			●			Older
Less Diverse		●				Diverse
Less Affluent				●		Affluent
Less Educated				●		Educated
Conservative			●			Liberal
Catholic	●					Protestant

Places Rated Rank: 44

Mansfield, OH

Good Restaurants: 44/140 ..... ☆☆☆☆☆

Bookstores and Reading: .... ☆☆☆
Chain Superstores: 2

Visible History
National Landmarks and Sites: 1
Registered Neighborhoods: 5
Contributing Buildings: 60

Lively Arts Calendar
Touring Artist Bookings: 4
 Renaissance Theatre
Dates, Resident Ensembles: 39
 Mansfield Symphony Orchestra

People						
Younger				●		Older
Less Diverse		●				Diverse
Less Affluent		●				Affluent
Less Educated	●					Educated
Conservative	●					Liberal
Catholic			●			Protestant

Places Rated Rank: 162

McAllen-Edinburg-Mission, TX

Good Restaurants: 2/330 .... ☆

Bookstores and Reading: .... ☆☆☆
Chain Superstores: 1

Visible History
Registered Neighborhoods: 2
Contributing Buildings: 220
 Oblate Park District

Lively Arts Calendar
Touring Artist Bookings: 4
 UTPA Fine Arts Auditorium
Dates, Resident Ensembles: 6

People						
Younger	●					Older
Less Diverse	●					Diverse
Less Affluent	●					Affluent
Less Educated	●					Educated
Conservative				●		Liberal
Catholic	●					Protestant

Places Rated Rank: 353

Medford, OR

Good Restaurants: 19/260 .... ☆☆☆

Bookstores and Reading: .... ☆☆
Chain Superstores: 2
Independent Stores: 4

Visible History
National Landmarks and Sites: 1
Registered Neighborhoods: 12
Contributing Buildings: 1,243
 Ashland Railroad Addition District
 Medford Downtown District
 Siskiyou-Hargandine District

Skidmore Academy District
Union Creek District

Lively Arts Calendar
Touring Artist Bookings: 4
  Britt Festivals Pavilion
Dates, Resident Ensembles: 37
  Britt Festival Orchestra
  Rogue Opera
  Rogue Valley Symphony

People						
Younger					●	Older
Less Diverse		●				Diverse
Less Affluent			●			Affluent
Less Educated			●			Educated
Conservative		●				Liberal
Catholic			●			Protestant

Places Rated Rank: 188

Memphis, TN-MS-AR

Good Restaurants: 46/790 .... ☆☆☆

Bookstores and Reading: .... ☆☆
Chain Superstores: 6
Independent Stores: 4

Visible History
National Landmarks and Sites: 4
Registered Neighborhoods: 81
Contributing Buildings: 17,331
  Central Gardens District
  Cooper-Young District
  Evergreen District
  Glenview District
  Vollintine Evergreen District

Lively Arts Calendar
Touring Artist Bookings: 30
  Buckman Performing Arts Center
  Harris Concert Hall
  Orpheum Theatre
Dates, Resident Ensembles: 78
  Memphis Symphony Orchestra
  Opera Memphis

People						
Younger		●				Older
Less Diverse			●			Diverse
Less Affluent				●		Affluent
Less Educated		●				Educated
Conservative				●		Liberal
Catholic					●	Protestant

Places Rated Rank: 113

Merced, CA

Good Restaurants: 4/127 .... ☆
Bookstores and Reading: .... ☆☆☆
Chain Superstores: 1

People						
Younger	●					Older
Less Diverse	●					Diverse
Less Affluent	●					Affluent
Less Educated	●					Educated
Conservative				●		Liberal
Catholic	●					Protestant

Places Rated Rank: 370

Miami-Miami Beach-Kendall, FL

Good Restaurants: 214/1,925 ☆☆☆☆

Bookstores and Reading: .... ☆☆☆
Chain Superstores: 10
Independent Stores: 5

Visible History
National Landmarks and Sites: 2
Registered Neighborhoods: 14
Contributing Buildings: 1,378
  Bay Shore District
  Downtown Miami District
  Lummus Park District
  MacFarlane Homestead District
  Miami Beach Architectural District

Lively Arts Calendar
Touring Artist Bookings:
  Byron Carlyle Theatre
  Colony Theatre
  Dade County Auditorium
  Gusman Center for Performing Arts
  Jackie Gleason Center
  Knight International Center
  Littman Theatre
  Miami Performing Arts Center
Dates, Resident Ensembles: 90
  Florida Grand Opera
  Miami Lyric Opera Company
  The New World Symphony

People						
Younger				●		Older
Less Diverse	●					Diverse
Less Affluent		●				Affluent
Less Educated			●			Educated
Conservative				●		Liberal
Catholic	●					Protestant

Places Rated Rank: 54

Michigan City-La Porte, IN

Good Restaurants: 4/128 .... ☆

Bookstores and Reading: .... ☆☆☆

Visible History
Registered Neighborhoods: 2
Contributing Buildings: 83
  Downtown LaPorte District

People						
Younger		●				Older
Less Diverse		●				Diverse
Less Affluent		●				Affluent
Less Educated	●					Educated
Conservative	●					Liberal
Catholic		●				Protestant

Places Rated Rank: 366

Midland, TX

Good Restaurants: 10/118 .... ☆☆☆

Bookstores and Reading: .... ☆☆☆
Chain Superstores: 1

Lively Arts Calendar
Touring Artist Bookings:
  Midland Center
Dates, Resident Ensembles: 35
  Midland-Odessa Symphony & Chorale

People						
Younger	●					Older
Less Diverse			●			Diverse
Less Affluent				●		Affluent
Less Educated		●				Educated
Conservative	●					Liberal
Catholic			●			Protestant

Places Rated Rank: 239

Milwaukee-Waukesha-West Allis, WI

Good Restaurants: 215/1,714 . ☆☆☆☆

Bookstores and Reading: .... ☆☆
Chain Superstores: 7
Independent Stores: 14

Visible History
National Landmarks and Sites: 9
Registered Neighborhoods: 74
Contributing Buildings: 5,970
  Bay View District
  Greendale District
  Kenwood Park-Prospect Hill District
  Walker's Point District
  Washington Highlands District

Lively Arts Calendar
Touring Artist Bookings: 156
  Macus Performing Arts Center
  Pabst Theatre
Dates, Resident Ensembles: 1075
  Florentine Opera Company
  Milwaukee Symphony Orchestra
  Skylight Opera Theatre
  Waukesha Symphony Orchestra

People — Minneapolis-St. Paul

	1	2	3	4	
Younger		✹			Older
Less Diverse				✹	Diverse
Less Affluent				✹	Affluent
Less Educated			✹		Educated
Conservative			✹		Liberal
Catholic	✹				Protestant

Places Rated Rank: 57

Minneapolis-St. Paul, MN-WI

Good Restaurants: 294/2,715 ✮✮✮✮✩

Bookstores and Reading: .... ✮✮
Chain Superstores: 27
Independent Stores: 31

Visible History
National Landmarks and Sites: 12
Registered Neighborhoods: 48
Contributing Buildings: 3,002
  Carver District
  Country Club District
  Historic Hill District
  Nokomis Knoll Residential District
  West Summit Avenue District

Lively Arts Calendar
Touring Artist Bookings: 837
  Fitzgerald Theatre
  Northrup Memorial Auditorium
  Orchestra Hall
  Ordway Music Theatre
  O'Shaughnessy Center'
  Walker Art Center
Dates, Resident Ensembles: 543
  Greater Twin Cities' Youth Symphonies
  Minnesota Opera
  Minnesota Orchestra
  Minnesota Youth Symphonies
  Minnetonka Symphony Orchestra
  St Paul Chamber Orchestra

People — Missoula

	1	2	3	4	
Younger		✹			Older
Less Diverse		✹			Diverse
Less Affluent			✹		Affluent
Less Educated			✹		Educated
Conservative			✹		Liberal
Catholic		✹			Protestant

Places Rated Rank: 47

Missoula, MT

Good Restaurants: 12/159 .... ✮✮✮

Bookstores and Reading: ...... ✮✮✮✮✮
Chain Superstores: 2
Independent Stores: 3

Visible History
National Landmarks and Sites: 3
Registered Neighborhoods: 10
Contributing Buildings: 1,709
  Lower Rattlesnake District

McCormick Neighborhood District
Missoula Southside District
Northside Missoula Railroad District
University Area District

Lively Arts Calendar
Touring Artist Bookings: 7
  University of Montana Theatre
Dates, Resident Ensembles: 10

People — Mobile

	1	2	3	4	
Younger		✹			Older
Less Diverse	✹				Diverse
Less Affluent			✹		Affluent
Less Educated				✹	Educated
Conservative		✹			Liberal
Catholic			✹		Protestant

Places Rated Rank: 147

Mobile, AL

Good Restaurants: 19/293 .... ✮✮✮

Bookstores and Reading: .... ✮
Chain Superstores: 3
Independent Stores: 1

Visible History
National Landmarks and Sites: 4
Registered Neighborhoods: 22
Contributing Buildings: 3,235
  Chickasaw Shipyard Village District
  Leinkauf District
  Oakleigh Garden District
  Old Dauphin Way District
  The Campground

Lively Arts Calendar
Touring Artist Bookings: 22
  Mobile Civic Center Concert Hall
Dates, Resident Ensembles: 2

People — Modesto

	1	2	3	4	
Younger		✹			Older
Less Diverse			✹		Diverse
Less Affluent	✹				Affluent
Less Educated		✹			Educated
Conservative	✹				Liberal
Catholic			✹		Protestant

Places Rated Rank: 157

Modesto, CA

Good Restaurants: 0/333 .... ✮

Bookstores and Reading: .... ✮
Chain Superstores: 3

Visible History
Registered Neighborhoods: 1
Contributing Buildings: 12

Lively Arts Calendar
Touring Artist Bookings: 5
  Gallo Performing Arts Center
Dates, Resident Ensembles: 33
  Townsend Opera Players

People — (Monroe, LA top)

	1	2	3	4	
Younger	✹				Older
Less Diverse		✹			Diverse
Less Affluent	✹				Affluent
Less Educated	✹				Educated
Conservative			✹		Liberal
Catholic	✹				Protestant

Places Rated Rank: 366

Monroe, LA

Good Restaurants: 12/109 .... ✮✮

Bookstores and Reading: .... ✮
Chain Superstores: 1
Independent Stores: 2

Visible History
Registered Neighborhoods: 2
Contributing Buildings: 534
  Monroe Residential District

Lively Arts Calendar
Touring Artist Bookings: 5
  Monroe Civic Center Theatre
Dates, Resident Ensembles: 12
  Monroe Symphony Orchestra

People — (Monroe, LA second)

	1	2	3	4	
Younger		✹			Older
Less Diverse				✹	Diverse
Less Affluent	✹				Affluent
Less Educated		✹			Educated
Conservative			✹		Liberal
Catholic				✹	Protestant

Places Rated Rank: 310

Monroe, MI

Good Restaurants: 10/130 .... ✮✮

Bookstores and Reading: .... ✮✮✮
Chain Superstores: 1
Independent Stores: 1

Visible History
Registered Neighborhoods: 5
Contributing Buildings: 753
  East Elm-North Macomb Street District
  Old Village District

People — Monroe, MI

	1	2	3	4	
Younger			✹		Older
Less Diverse	✹				Diverse
Less Affluent			✹		Affluent
Less Educated		✹			Educated
Conservative				✹	Liberal
Catholic		✹			Protestant

Places Rated Rank: 325

Montgomery, AL

Good Restaurants: 13/237 .... ☆☆

Bookstores and Reading: .... ☆
Chain Superstores: 3
Independent Stores: 2

Visible History
National Landmarks and Sites: 5
Registered Neighborhoods: 21
Contributing Buildings: 1,795
  Cloverdale District
  Cottage Hill District
  Daniel Pratt District
  Garden District
  Maxwell Air Force Base Senior
    Officer's Quarters

Lively Arts Calendar
Touring Artist Bookings: 5
  Davis Theatre
Dates, Resident Ensembles: 10
  Montgomery Symphony Orchestra

People	1	2	3	4	5	
Younger		●				Older
Less Diverse			●			Diverse
Less Affluent		●				Affluent
Less Educated		●				Educated
Conservative	●					Liberal
Catholic				●		Protestant

Places Rated Rank: 258

Morgantown, WV

Good Restaurants: 8/106 .... ☆☆

Bookstores and Reading: ...... ☆☆☆☆
Chain Superstores: 3

Visible History
National Landmarks and Sites: 2
Registered Neighborhoods: 10
Contributing Buildings: 1,440
  Arthurdale District
  Chancery Hill District
  Downtown Morgantown District
  Greenmont District
  South Park District

Lively Arts Calendar
Touring Artist Bookings: 11
  WVU Creative Arts Center

People	1	2	3	4	5	
Younger		●				Older
Less Diverse	●					Diverse
Less Affluent		●				Affluent
Less Educated			●			Educated
Conservative				●		Liberal
Catholic				●		Protestant

Places Rated Rank: 169

Morristown, TN

Good Restaurants: 3/57 .... ☆

Bookstores and Reading: .... ☆☆☆

Visible History
Registered Neighborhoods: 2
Contributing Buildings: 40
  Dandridge District
Lively Arts Calendar
Touring Artist Bookings: 8

People	1	2	3	4	5	
Younger			●			Older
Less Diverse		●				Diverse
Less Affluent	●					Affluent
Less Educated	●					Educated
Conservative		●				Liberal
Catholic				●		Protestant

Places Rated Rank: 356

Mount Vernon-Anacortes, WA

Good Restaurants: 15/137 .... ☆☆☆

Bookstores and Reading: .... ☆☆☆
Chain Superstores: 1
Independent Stores: 2

Visible History
National Landmarks and Sites: 1
Registered Neighborhoods: 1
Contributing Buildings: 29

People	1	2	3	4	5	
Younger			●			Older
Less Diverse			●			Diverse
Less Affluent			●			Affluent
Less Educated		●				Educated
Conservative				●		Liberal
Catholic		●				Protestant

Places Rated Rank: 329

Muncie, IN

Good Restaurants: 0/122 .... ☆

Bookstores and Reading: ...... ☆☆☆☆
Chain Superstores: 1
Independent Stores: 1

Visible History
Registered Neighborhoods: 10
Contributing Buildings: 945
  Gilbert District
  Kimbrough District
  Old West End District
  Westwood District

Lively Arts Calendar
Touring Artist Bookings: 3
  Emens Auditorium
Dates, Resident Ensembles: 22
  Muncie Symphony Orchestra

People	1	2	3	4	5	
Younger		●				Older
Less Diverse		●				Diverse
Less Affluent		●				Affluent
Less Educated			●			Educated
Conservative				●		Liberal
Catholic				●		Protestant

Places Rated Rank: 232

Muskegon-Norton Shores, MI

Good Restaurants: 8/164 .... ☆

Bookstores and Reading: .... ☆☆☆
Chain Superstores: 1
Independent Stores: 1

Visible History
Registered Neighborhoods: 1
Contributing Buildings: 17

Lively Arts Calendar
Touring Artist Bookings: 15
  Frauenthal Theatre
Dates, Resident Ensembles: 40
  West Shore Symphony Orchestra

People	1	2	3	4	5	
Younger		●				Older
Less Diverse		●				Diverse
Less Affluent	●					Affluent
Less Educated		●				Educated
Conservative	●					Liberal
Catholic		●				Protestant

Places Rated Rank: 309

Myrtle Beach-Conway, SC

Good Restaurants: 91/484 ..... ☆☆☆☆☆

Bookstores and Reading: .... ☆☆☆☆
Chain Superstores: 5

Visible History
Registered Neighborhoods: 5
Contributing Buildings: 147
  Galivants Ferry District
  Myrtle Heights-Oak Park District

Lively Arts Calendar
Touring Artist Bookings: 5
  Myrtle Beach Auditorium
Dates, Resident Ensembles: 15
  Long Bay Symphony Orchestra

People	1	2	3	4	5	
Younger				●		Older
Less Diverse		●				Diverse
Less Affluent		●				Affluent
Less Educated			●			Educated
Conservative	●					Liberal
Catholic				●		Protestant

Places Rated Rank: 143

(Minneapolis, MN — top sidebar People grid)

People	1	2	3	4	5	
Younger		●				Older
Less Diverse		●				Diverse
Less Affluent		●				Affluent
Less Educated		●				Educated
Conservative	●					Liberal
Catholic				●		Protestant

Places Rated Rank: 232

Napa, CA

Good Restaurants: 10/158 .... ☆☆☆

Bookstores and Reading: .... ☆☆☆
Independent Stores: 5

Visible History
National Landmarks and Sites: 2
Registered Neighborhoods: 6
Contributing Buildings: 370
  Aetna Springs Resort
  Napa Abajo-Fuller Park District

Lively Arts Calendar
Touring Artist Bookings: 13
Dates, Resident Ensembles: 17

People						
Younger			●			Older
Less Diverse					●	Diverse
Less Affluent				●		Affluent
Less Educated				●		Educated
Conservative				●		Liberal
Catholic	●					Protestant

Places Rated Rank: 229

Naples-Marco Island, FL

Good Restaurants: 50/341 ..... ☆☆☆☆

Bookstores and Reading: .... ☆☆☆
Chain Superstores: 3
Independent Stores: 1

Visible History
Registered Neighborhoods: 2
Contributing Buildings: 75
  Naples District

Lively Arts Calendar
Touring Artist Bookings: 100
  Philharmonic Center for the Arts
Dates, Resident Ensembles: 80
  Naples Philharmonic

People						
Younger					●	Older
Less Diverse					●	Diverse
Less Affluent					●	Affluent
Less Educated			●			Educated
Conservative		●				Liberal
Catholic		●				Protestant

Places Rated Rank: 134

✓ Nashville-Davidson, TN

Good Restaurants: 98/1,137 ... ☆☆☆☆

Bookstores and Reading: ...... ☆☆☆☆☆
Chain Superstores: 10
Independent Stores: 5

Visible History
National Landmarks and Sites: 11
Registered Neighborhoods: 74
Contributing Buildings: 4,566
  Belmont-Hillsboro District
  Buena Vista District
  East Nashville District
  Hillsboro-West End District
  Old Hickory District

Lively Arts Calendar
Touring Artist Bookings: 114
  Schermerhorn Symphony Center
  Tennessee Performing Arts Center
Dates, Resident Ensembles: 144
  Nashville Opera
  Nashville Symphony Orchestra

People						
Younger		●				Older
Less Diverse			●			Diverse
Less Affluent			●			Affluent
Less Educated			●			Educated
Conservative			●			Liberal
Catholic				●		Protestant

Places Rated Rank: 22

✓ Nassau-Suffolk, NY

Good Restaurants: 38/2,205 .... ☆☆

Bookstores and Reading: .... ☆☆☆
Chain Superstores: 21
Independent Stores: 9

Visible History
National Landmarks and Sites: 15
Registered Neighborhoods: 65
Contributing Buildings: 3,349
  East Hampton Village District
  Greenport Village District
  Sag Harbor Village District
  Shelter Island Heights District
  Southampton Village District

Lively Arts Calendar
Touring Artist Bookings: 818
Dates, Resident Ensembles: 3

People						
Younger				●		Older
Less Diverse				●		Diverse
Less Affluent				●		Affluent
Less Educated				●		Educated
Conservative				●		Liberal
Jewish	●					Protestant

Places Rated Rank: 111

Newark-Union, NJ-PA

Good Restaurants: 65/2,277 ...... ☆☆☆☆

Bookstores and Reading: .... ☆☆☆☆
Chain Superstores: 11
Independent Stores: 16

Visible History
National Landmarks and Sites: 17
Registered Neighborhoods: 122
Contributing Buildings: 13,382
  Forest Hill District
  Glen Ridge District
  Montrose Park District
  Mountain Lakes District
  Weequahic Park District

Lively Arts Calendar
Touring Artist Bookings: 182
  Kean University Wilkins Theatre
  New Jersey Performing Arts Center
  Newark Symphony Hall
Dates, Resident Ensembles: 208
  Community Opera Incorporated
  Coro Lirico
  New Jersey State Opera
  New Jersey Symphony Orchestra
  New Philharmonic of New Jersey
  New Sussex Symphony
  Riverside Symphonia
  Westfield Symphony Orchestra

People						
Younger			●			Older
Less Diverse				●		Diverse
Less Affluent				●		Affluent
Less Educated				●		Educated
Conservative			●			Liberal
Catholic	●					Protestant

Places Rated Rank: 41

✓ New Haven-Milford, CT

Good Restaurants: 60/918 .... ☆☆☆☆

Bookstores and Reading: ...... ☆☆☆☆☆
Chain Superstores: 8
Independent Stores: 7

Visible History
National Landmarks and Sites: 12
Registered Neighborhoods: 65
Contributing Buildings: 9,010
  Branford Center District
  Dwight Street District
  Orange Street District
  Whitney Avenue District
  Winchester Repeating Arms Company District

Lively Arts Calendar
Touring Artist Bookings: 223
  Lyman Center for the Arts
  Palace Theatre
  Shubert Performing Arts Center
  Sprague Memorial Hall
Dates, Resident Ensembles: 242
  New Haven Symphony Orchestra Inc
  Waterbury Symphony Orchestra

People						
Younger			●			Older
Less Diverse				●		Diverse
Less Affluent				●		Affluent
Less Educated			●			Educated
Conservative				●		Liberal
Catholic	●					Protestant

Places Rated Rank: 13

New Orleans-Metairie-Kenner, LA

Good Restaurants: 160/1,588 ★★★★★

Bookstores and Reading: .... ★★
Chain Superstores: 6
Independent Stores: 14

Visible History
National Landmarks and Sites: 39
Registered Neighborhoods: 35
Contributing Buildings: 39,378
   Carrollton District
   Central City District
   Esplanade Ridge District
   Mid-City District
   Uptown New Orleans District

Lively Arts Calendar
Touring Artist Bookings: 47
   Mahalia Jackson Theatre
   Orpheum Theater
   Saenger Performing Arts Center
   Tulane University Dixon Hall'
Dates, Resident Ensembles: 141
   Louisiana Philharmonic Orchestra
   New Orleans Opera Association

People					
Younger		✹			Older
Less Diverse			✹		Diverse
Less Affluent		✹			Affluent
Less Educated		✹			Educated
Conservative		✹			Liberal
Catholic	✹				Protestant

Places Rated Rank: 56

✓ New York-White Plains, NY-NJ

Good Restaurants: 1,503/12,224 ★★★★★

Bookstores and Reading: ...... ★★★★★
Chain Superstores: 49
Independent Stores: 57

Visible History
National Landmarks and Sites: 151
Registered Neighborhoods: 185
Contributing Buildings: 28,431
   Clinton Hill District
   Cobble Hill District
   Jackson Heights District
   Park Slope District
   Sunset Park District

Lively Arts Calendar
Touring Artist Bookings: 3,087
   Alice Tully Hall
   Avery Fisher Hall
   Carnegie Hall
   Lincoln Center
   Shea Auditorium
   Town Hall
Dates, Resident Ensembles: 3415
   Amato Opera Theatre
   American Chamber Opera
   American Composers Orchestra
   American International Lyric Theatre
   American Opera Music Theater
   American Opera Projects
   American Symphony Orchestra
   Bronx Opera Company
   Center For Contemporary Opera
   Chelsea Opera
   Concert Royal

The Concordia Orchestra
Dicapo Opera Theatre
Downtown Chamber & Opera Players
Encompass New Opera Theatre
Eos Music
Gotham Chamber Opera
ISO Symphony
Juilliard Opera Center
La Gran Scena Opera Company
Liederkranz Opera Theatre
The Little Orchestra Society of New York
Long Island Opera Company
L'Opera Francais de New York
Magic Circle Opera Repertory Ensemble
Manhattan Opera Association
Manhattan Philharmonic
Metropolitan Opera Association
New Rochelle Opera
New York Chamber Opera
New York Chamber Symphony
New York City Opera
New York City Symphony
New York Gilbert & Sullivan Players
New York Grand Opera
New York Opera Project
New York Orchestral Society
New York Philharmonic
New York Pops Orchestra
New York Youth Symphony
Opera Company of Brooklyn
Opera New York
Opera Northeast
Opera Orchestra of New York
Orchestra of St. Luke's
Orpheus Chamber Orchestra
P A L A Opera Association
Philharmonia Virtuosi
The Riverside Symphony
Rockland Opera
Symphony For United Nations
Taconic Opera
Teatro Grattacielo
Theato Rococco
Wayne Chamber Orchestra
West End Symphony
Westchester Symphony Orchestra

People					
Younger		✹			Older
Less Diverse	✹				Diverse
Less Affluent				✹	Affluent
Less Educated				✹	Educated
Conservative				✹	Liberal
Jewish	✹				Protestant

Places Rated Rank: 1

Niles-Benton Harbor, MI

Good Restaurants: 14/212 .... ★★

Bookstores and Reading: .... ★★
Chain Superstores: 1
Independent Stores: 1

Visible History
Registered Neighborhoods: 3
Contributing Buildings: 21

Lively Arts Calendar
Touring Artist Bookings: 30
Dates, Resident Ensembles: 10
   Southwest Michigan Symphony
    Orchestra

People					
Younger			✹		Older
Less Diverse			✹		Diverse
Less Affluent	✹				Affluent
Less Educated		✹			Educated
Conservative		✹			Liberal
Catholic		✹			Protestant

Places Rated Rank: 301

Norwich-New London, CT

Good Restaurants: 18/300 .... ★★★

Bookstores and Reading: .... ★★★
Chain Superstores: 2
Independent Stores: 3

Visible History
National Landmarks and Sites: 16
Registered Neighborhoods: 52
Contributing Buildings: 5,877
   Chelsea Parade District
   Greeneville District
   Mechanic Street District
   Mystic Bridge District
   Mystic River District

Lively Arts Calendar
Touring Artist Bookings: 66
   Garde Arts Center
   Palmer Auditorium
Dates, Resident Ensembles: 13
   Eastern Connecticut Symphony
    Orchestra
   Salt Marsh Opera

People					
Younger				✹	Older
Less Diverse		✹			Diverse
Less Affluent				✹	Affluent
Less Educated			✹		Educated
Conservative				✹	Liberal
Catholic	✹				Protestant

Places Rated Rank: 92

Oakland-Fremont-Hayward, CA

Good Restaurants: 35/2,209 .... ★★

Bookstores and Reading: ...... ★★★★★
Chain Superstores: 20
Independent Stores: 30

Visible History
National Landmarks and Sites: 13
Registered Neighborhoods: 20
Contributing Buildings: 855
   Atchison Village Defense Housing
    Project, Cal. 4171-x
   Hercules Village
   Panoramic Hill
   Point Richmond District

Lively Arts Calendar
Touring Artist Bookings: 211
   Kaiser Events Center

Paramount Theatre
Dates, Resident Ensembles: 108
  Berkeley Opera
  California Chamber Orchestra & Chamber Opera Co.
  California Symphony Orchestra
  Classical Philharmonic of Northern California
  Festival Opera Association
  Oakland East Bay Symphony
  Oakland Lyric Opera

People						
Younger			●			Older
Less Diverse	●					Diverse
Less Affluent				●		Affluent
Less Educated				●		Educated
Conservative				●		Liberal
Catholic	●					Protestant

Places Rated Rank: 88

Ocala, FL

Good Restaurants: 19/158 .... ☆☆☆

Bookstores and Reading: .... ☆
Chain Superstores: 2
Independent Stores: 2

Visible History
National Landmarks and Sites: 1
Registered Neighborhoods: 9
Contributing Buildings: 590
  Dunnellon Boomtown District
  Lake Lillian Neighborhood District
  McIntosh District
  Ocala District
  West Ocala District

Lively Arts Calendar
Touring Artist Bookings:
Dates, Resident Ensembles: 10

People						
Younger				●		Older
Less Diverse			●			Diverse
Less Affluent		●				Affluent
Less Educated	●					Educated
Conservative		●				Liberal
Catholic			●			Protestant

Places Rated Rank: 299

Ocean City, NJ

Good Restaurants: 31/341.......... ☆☆☆☆

Bookstores and Reading: .... ☆☆☆
Independent Stores: 2

Visible History
National Landmarks and Sites: 1
Registered Neighborhoods: 5
Contributing Buildings: 878
  Cape May District
  Dennisville District
  Ocean City Residential District
  South Tuckahoe District

Lively Arts Calendar

Touring Artist Bookings: 145
Dates, Resident Ensembles: 40
  Ocean City Pops

People						
Younger				●		Older
Less Diverse	●					Diverse
Less Affluent				●		Affluent
Less Educated			●			Educated
Conservative			●			Liberal
Catholic	●					Protestant

Places Rated Rank: 144

Odessa, TX

Good Restaurants: 5/84 .... ☆☆

Bookstores and Reading: .... ☆☆
Chain Superstores: 1

People						
Younger	●					Older
Less Diverse	●					Diverse
Less Affluent	●					Affluent
Less Educated	●					Educated
Conservative	●					Liberal
Catholic			●			Protestant

Places Rated Rank: 374

Ogden-Clearfield, UT

Good Restaurants: 7/258 .... ☆

Bookstores and Reading: .... ☆☆☆
Chain Superstores: 2
Independent Stores: 6

Visible History
National Landmarks and Sites: 1
Registered Neighborhoods: 9
Contributing Buildings: 3,042
  Bountiful District
  Jefferson Avenue District
  Ogden Central Bench District

Lively Arts Calendar
Touring Artist Bookings: 79
Weber State Browning Center
  West Bountiful District
Dates, Resident Ensembles: 6

People						
Younger	●					Older
Less Diverse		●				Diverse
Less Affluent		●				Affluent
Less Educated			●			Educated
Conservative	●					Liberal
Catholic		●				Protestant

Places Rated Rank: 130

✓ Oklahoma City, OK

Good Restaurants: 110/954 ... ☆☆☆☆☆

Bookstores and Reading: .... ☆☆☆
Chain Superstores: 10
Independent Stores: 1

Visible History
National Landmarks and Sites: 4
Registered Neighborhoods: 30
Contributing Buildings: 4,195
  Crown Heights District
  Gatewood East District
  Gatewood West District
  Heritage Hills Historic District
  Jefferson Park District

Lively Arts Calendar
Touring Artist Bookings: 20
  Civic Center Music Hall
Dates, Resident Ensembles: 172
  Oklahoma City Philharmonic Orchestra

People						
Younger		●				Older
Less Diverse			●			Diverse
Less Affluent			●			Affluent
Less Educated			●			Educated
Conservative	●					Liberal
Catholic				●		Protestant

Places Rated Rank: 36

Olympia, WA

Good Restaurants: 5/183 .... ☆

Bookstores and Reading: .... ☆☆☆
Chain Superstores: 2

Visible History
Registered Neighborhoods: 6
Contributing Buildings: 582
  Olympia Downtown District
  South Capitol Neighborhood District
  Tumwater District

Lively Arts Calendar
Touring Artist Bookings: 43
  Washington Center for Performing Arts
Dates, Resident Ensembles: 10

People						
Younger			●			Older
Less Diverse		●				Diverse
Less Affluent			●			Affluent
Less Educated				●		Educated
Conservative				●		Liberal
Catholic		●				Protestant

Places Rated Rank: 221

Omaha-Council Bluffs, NE-IA

Good Restaurants: 43/874 .... ☆☆☆

Bookstores and Reading: .... ☆☆
Chain Superstores: 7
Independent Stores: 4

Visible History

National Landmarks and Sites: 6
Registered Neighborhoods: 21
Contributing Buildings: 3,429
   Country Club District
   Dundee-Happy Hollow District
   Father Flanagan's Boys' Home
   Gold Coast District
   Willow-Bluff-3rd Street District

Lively Arts Calendar

Touring Artist Bookings: 56
   Orpheum Theater
   UNO Performing Arts Cente
   Witherspoon Concert Hall
Dates, Resident Ensembles: 385
   Omaha Symphony Chamber Orchestra
   Omaha Symphony Orchestra
   Opera Omaha

People						
Younger		●				Older
Less Diverse			●			Diverse
Less Affluent				●		Affluent
Less Educated				●		Educated
Conservative	●					Liberal
Catholic		●				Protestant

Places Rated Rank: 102

Orlando-Kissimmee, FL

Good Restaurants: 300/1,203 ☆☆☆☆

Bookstores and Reading: ....☆☆☆
Chain Superstores: 22
Independent Stores: 3

Visible History

Registered Neighborhoods: 14
Contributing Buildings: 1,381
   Eatonville District
   Kissimmee District
   Lake Eola Heights District
   Sanford Residential District

Lively Arts Calendar

Touring Artist Bookings: 15
   Carr Performing Arts Center
   Winter Garden Residential District
Dates, Resident Ensembles: 97
   Orlando Opera Company
   Orlando Philharmonic

People						
Younger			●			Older
Less Diverse				●		Diverse
Less Affluent			●			Affluent
Less Educated				●		Educated
Conservative	●					Liberal
Catholic			●			Protestant

Places Rated Rank: 71

Oshkosh-Neenah, WI

Good Restaurants: 33/226 ....☆☆☆☆

Bookstores and Reading: ....☆☆☆
Independent Stores: 7

Visible History

Registered Neighborhoods: 11
Contributing Buildings: 465
   Algoma Boulevard District
   Irving Church District
   Washington Avenue District

Lively Arts Calendar

Touring Artist Bookings: 7
   Grand Opera House
Dates, Resident Ensembles: 25
   Fox Valley Symphony
   Oshkosh Symphony Orchestra

People						
Younger			●			Older
Less Diverse	●					Diverse
Less Affluent				●		Affluent
Less Educated				●		Educated
Conservative			●			Liberal
Catholic		●				Protestant

Places Rated Rank: 185

Owensboro, KY

Good Restaurants: 3/80 ....☆

Bookstores and Reading: ....☆☆☆
Chain Superstores: 1

Visible History

Registered Neighborhoods: 6
Contributing Buildings: 193
   Hawesville District
   Moore, J. Z., District
   Phillip's Court District

Lively Arts Calendar

Touring Artist Bookings: 5
   RiverPark Center
Dates, Resident Ensembles: 15
   Owensboro Symphony Orchestra

People						
Younger				●		Older
Less Diverse	●					Diverse
Less Affluent		●				Affluent
Less Educated	●					Educated
Conservative		●				Liberal
Catholic				●		Protestant

Places Rated Rank: 290

Oxnard-Thousand Oaks, CA

Good Restaurants: 18/590 ....☆☆

Bookstores and Reading: ....☆☆
Chain Superstores: 5
Independent Stores: 4

Visible History

National Landmarks and Sites: 1
Registered Neighborhoods: 6
Contributing Buildings: 179
   Oxnard, Henry T., District

Lively Arts Calendar

Touring Artist Bookings: 138
   Oxnard Convention Center
Dates, Resident Ensembles: 12

People						
Younger		●				Older
Less Diverse		●				Diverse
Less Affluent			●			Affluent
Less Educated				●		Educated
Conservative					●	Liberal
Catholic	●					Protestant

Places Rated Rank: 247

Palm Bay-Melbourne-Titusville, FL

Good Restaurants: 34/443 .... ☆☆☆

Bookstores and Reading: .... ☆☆
Chain Superstores: 6
Independent Stores: 1

Visible History

National Landmarks and Sites: 2
Registered Neighborhoods: 6
Contributing Buildings: 234
   Barton Avenue Residential District
   Rockledge Drive Residential District
   Valencia Subdivision Residential District

Lively Arts Calendar

Touring Artist Bookings: 73
Dates, Resident Ensembles: 29
   Brevard Symphony Orchestra
   King Center for Performing Arts

People						
Younger				●		Older
Less Diverse		●				Diverse
Less Affluent		●				Affluent
Less Educated			●			Educated
Conservative	●					Liberal
Catholic		●				Protestant

Places Rated Rank: 220

Panama City-Lynn Haven, FL

Good Restaurants: 1/195......................☆

Bookstores and Reading: ....☆
Chain Superstores: 2

Lively Arts Calendar

Touring Artist Bookings: 10
   Marina Civic Center

People						
Younger				●		Older
Less Diverse	●					Diverse
Less Affluent	●					Affluent
Less Educated	●					Educated
Conservative			●			Liberal
Catholic				●		Protestant

Places Rated Rank: 378

Ambience

Parkersburg-Marietta, WV-OH

Good Restaurants: 23/147.........☆☆☆

Bookstores and Reading: ....☆☆☆
Chain Superstores: 1
Independent Stores: 1

Visible History
National Landmarks and Sites: 4
Registered Neighborhoods: 12
Contributing Buildings: 3,088
  Avery Street District
  Harmar District
  Julia-Ann Square District
  Marietta District
  Parkersburg High School District

Lively Arts Calendar
Touring Artist Bookings: 4

People						
Younger				✦		Older
Less Diverse	✦					Diverse
Less Affluent	✦					Affluent
Less Educated	✦					Educated
Conservative				✦		Liberal
Catholic			✦			Protestant

Places Rated Rank: 204

Pascagoula, MS

Good Restaurants: 11/99..............☆☆☆

Bookstores and Reading: ....☆☆☆
Chain Superstores: 1

Visible History
Registered Neighborhoods: 9
Contributing Buildings: 137
  Old Ocean Springs District

People						
Younger		✦				Older
Less Diverse			✦			Diverse
Less Affluent	✦					Affluent
Less Educated		✦				Educated
Conservative			✦			Liberal
Catholic				✦		Protestant

Places Rated Rank: 317

Pensacola-Ferry Pass-Brent, FL

Good Restaurants: 11/290 ....☆☆

Bookstores and Reading: ....☆
Chain Superstores: 3
Independent Stores: 1

Visible History
National Landmarks and Sites: 3
Registered Neighborhoods: 6
Contributing Buildings: 792
  Alger-Sullivan Company District
  Bagdad Village District
  Milton District
  North Hill Preservation District
  Pensacola District

(Pensacola, continued)

Lively Arts Calendar
Touring Artist Bookings: 15
  Saenger Theater
  UWF Center for Performing Arts
Dates, Resident Ensembles: 10
  Greater Pensacola Symphony Orchestra
  Pensacola Opera

People						
Younger			✦			Older
Less Diverse				✦		Diverse
Less Affluent		✦				Affluent
Less Educated			✦			Educated
Conservative	✦					Liberal
Catholic				✦		Protestant

Places Rated Rank: 228

Peoria, IL

Good Restaurants: 18/504 ....☆☆

Bookstores and Reading: ....☆
Chain Superstores: 3
Independent Stores: 1

Visible History
National Landmarks and Sites: 2
Registered Neighborhoods: 8
Contributing Buildings: 273
  North Side District
  West Bluff District

Lively Arts Calendar
Touring Artist Bookings: 107
  Dingeldine Music Center
  Illinois Central Center
  Peoria Civic Center
Dates, Resident Ensembles: 21
  Opera Illinois
  Peoria Symphony Orchestra

People						
Younger			✦			Older
Less Diverse		✦				Diverse
Less Affluent			✦			Affluent
Less Educated		✦				Educated
Conservative		✦				Liberal
Catholic		✦				Protestant

Places Rated Rank: 271

✓ Philadelphia, PA

Good Restaurants: 161/4,259 ☆☆☆☆☆

Bookstores and Reading: ...... ☆☆☆☆☆
Chain Superstores: 28
Independent Stores: 29

Visible History
National Landmarks and Sites: 101
Registered Neighborhoods: 213
Contributing Buildings: 30,999
  Chestnut Hill District
  Cobbs Creek Automobile Suburb District
  Doylestown District
  Rittenhouse District
  West Philadelphia Streetcar Suburb District

Lively Arts Calendar
Touring Artist Bookings: 409
  Academy of Music
  Annenburg Center
  Kimmel Center for Performing Arts
  Mann Center for Performing Arts
  Merriam Theatre
  Walnut Street Theatre
Dates, Resident Ensembles: 285
  AVA Opera Theater
  ConcertOPERA
  Lyric Opera Theatre
  Opera Company of Philadelphia
  Orchestra of the Pennsylvania Ballet
  Philadelphia Orchestra

People						
Younger		✦				Older
Less Diverse				✦		Diverse
Less Affluent				✦		Affluent
Less Educated			✦			Educated
Conservative			✦			Liberal
Catholic	✦					Protestant

Places Rated Rank: 6

Phoenix-Mesa-Scottsdale, AZ

Good Restaurants: 219/2,659 ☆☆☆☆☆

Bookstores and Reading: .... ☆☆
Chain Superstores: 28
Independent Stores: 15

Visible History
National Landmarks and Sites: 6
Registered Neighborhoods: 48
Contributing Buildings: 4,750
  Coronado Neighborhood District
  Encanto-Palmcroft District
  Fairview Place District
  Story, F. Q., Neighborhood District
  Willo District

Lively Arts Calendar
Touring Artist Bookings: 660
  ASU Gammage Auditorium
  Dodge Theatre
  Mesa Convention Amphitheatre
  Phoenix Symphony Hall
  Scottsdale Center
Dates, Resident Ensembles: 158
  Arizona Opera Company
  Scottsdale Symphony Orchestra

People						
Younger	✦					Older
Less Diverse				✦		Diverse
Less Affluent			✦			Affluent
Less Educated			✦			Educated
Conservative		✦				Liberal
Catholic	✦					Protestant

Places Rated Rank: 62

Pine Bluff, AR

Good Restaurants: 3/52 .... ☆

Bookstores and Reading: .... ☆☆☆
Chain Superstores: 1

Visible History
National Landmarks and Sites: 2
Registered Neighborhoods: 5
Contributing Buildings: 112
 Lake Dick
 Plum Bayou Homesteads

Lively Arts Calendar
Touring Artist Bookings: 10
 Pine Bluff Auditorium
Dates, Resident Ensembles: 4

People					
Younger			✹		Older
Less Diverse			✹		Diverse
Less Affluent	✹				Affluent
Less Educated	✹				Educated
Conservative				✹	Liberal
Catholic				✹	Protestant

Places Rated Rank: 305

Pittsburgh, PA

Good Restaurants: 178/2,911. ☆☆☆☆☆

Bookstores and Reading: .... ☆☆
Chain Superstores: 21
Independent Stores: 19

Visible History
National Landmarks and Sites: 25
Registered Neighborhoods: 73
Contributing Buildings: 9,020
 Beaver District
 Deutschtown District
 Homestead District
 Manchester District
 Vandergrift District

Lively Arts Calendar
Touring Artist Bookings: 226
Benedum Center for Performing Arts
 Carneige Music Hall
 Heinz Hall for Performing Arts
Dates, Resident Ensembles: 379
 American Wind Symphony Orchestra
 Opera Theater of Pittsburgh
 Pittsburgh Opera
 Pittsburgh Symphony Orchestra
 River City Brass Band
Westmoreland Symphony Orchestra

People					
Younger				✹	Older
Less Diverse	✹				Diverse
Less Affluent			✹		Affluent
Less Educated			✹		Educated
Conservative		✹			Liberal
Catholic	✹				Protestant

Places Rated Rank: 50

Pittsfield, MA

Good Restaurants: 40/273 ..... ☆☆☆☆

Bookstores and Reading: .... ☆☆☆
Chain Superstores: 3
Independent Stores: 3

Visible History
National Landmarks and Sites: 9
Registered Neighborhoods: 46
Contributing Buildings: 1,806
 Church Street-Caddy Hill District
 Cranesville District
 Freeman's Grove District
 Sheffield Center District
 Taconic and West Avenues District

Lively Arts Calendar
Touring Artist Bookings: 47
 Colonial Theatre
Dates, Resident Ensembles: 3
 Berkshire Opera Company

People					
Younger				✹	Older
Less Diverse	✹				Diverse
Less Affluent				✹	Affluent
Less Educated				✹	Educated
Conservative				✹	Liberal
Catholic	✹				Protestant

Places Rated Rank: 67

Pocatello, ID

Good Restaurants: 6/96 .... ☆☆

Bookstores and Reading: .... ☆☆☆
Chain Superstores: 1
Independent Stores: 2

Visible History
National Landmarks and Sites: 2
Registered Neighborhoods: 6
Contributing Buildings: 688
 Idaho State University Neighborhood District
 Lincoln-Johnson Avenues Residential District
 Pocatello District
 Pocatello Westside Residential District

Lively Arts Calendar
Touring Artist Bookings: 10
 Goranson Hall
Dates, Resident Ensembles: 22

People					
Younger	✹				Older
Less Diverse		✹			Diverse
Less Affluent	✹				Affluent
Less Educated			✹		Educated
Conservative		✹			Liberal
Catholic			✹		Protestant

Places Rated Rank: 219

Portland-South Portland, ME

Good Restaurants: 143/685 ... ☆☆☆☆

Bookstores and Reading: .... ☆☆
Chain Superstores: 2
Independent Stores: 10

Visible History
National Landmarks and Sites: 24
Registered Neighborhoods: 65
Contributing Buildings: 2,189
 Federal Street District
 Kennebunk District
 Kennebunkport District
 Saco District
 Western Promenade District

Lively Arts Calendar
Touring Artist Bookings: 58
 Merrill Auditorium at City Hall
Dates, Resident Ensembles: 53
 Portland Symphony
 PORTopera

People					
Younger				✹	Older
Less Diverse	✹				Diverse
Less Affluent			✹		Affluent
Less Educated				✹	Educated
Conservative				✹	Liberal
Catholic	✹				Protestant

Places Rated Rank: 72

✓ Portland-Vancouver, OR-WA

Good Restaurants: 322/2,258 ☆☆☆☆

Bookstores and Reading: ...... ☆☆☆☆☆
Chain Superstores: 13
Independent Stores: 29

Visible History
National Landmarks and Sites: 9
Registered Neighborhoods: 27
Contributing Buildings: 2,014
 Alphabet District
 Clark District
 King's Hill District
 Ladd's Addition District
 South Portland District

Lively Arts Calendar
Touring Artist Bookings: 333
 Schnitzer Concert Hall
Dates, Resident Ensembles: 471
 Oregon Symphony Orchestra
 Portland Baroque Orchestra
 Portland Opera Association

People					
Younger		✹			Older
Less Diverse			✹		Diverse
Less Affluent					Affluent
Less Educated				✹	Educated
Conservative			✹		Liberal
Catholic		✹			Protestant

Places Rated Rank: 11

Port St. Lucie-Fort Pierce, FL

Good Restaurants: 13/299 .... ★★

Bookstores and Reading: .... ★
Chain Superstores: 2

Visible History
National Landmarks and Sites: 1
Registered Neighborhoods: 1
Contributing Buildings: 34
St. Lucie Village District

Lively Arts Calendar
Touring Artist Bookings: 4
St. Lucie County Civic Center
Dates, Resident Ensembles: 4

People						
Younger				●		Older
Less Diverse			●			Diverse
Less Affluent				●		Affluent
Less Educated		●				Educated
Conservative				●		Liberal
Catholic	●					Protestant

Places Rated Rank: 372

✓ Poughkeepsie-Newburgh, NY

Good Restaurants: 37/719 .... ★★★

Bookstores and Reading: .... ★★★
Chain Superstores: 6
Independent Stores: 7

Visible History
National Landmarks and Sites: 28
Registered Neighborhoods: 45
Contributing Buildings: 6,042
East End District
Hudson River Heritage District
Montgomery-Grand-Liberty Streets District
Rhinebeck Village District
Sixteen Mile District

Lively Arts Calendar
Touring Artist Bookings: 223
Bardavon 1896 Opera House
Mid-Hudson Civic Center
Dates, Resident Ensembles: 68
Hudson Opera Company
Hudson Valley Philharmonic Socity

People						
Younger		●				Older
Less Diverse				●		Diverse
Less Affluent			●			Affluent
Less Educated			●			Educated
Conservative			●			Liberal
Catholic	●					Protestant

Places Rated Rank: 34

Prescott, AZ

Good Restaurants: 55/240 ..... ★★★★

Bookstores and Reading: .... ★
Chain Superstores: 1
Independent Stores: 3

Visible History
National Landmarks and Sites: 3
Registered Neighborhoods: 24
Contributing Buildings: 1,137
Clarkdale District
East Prescott District
Joslin and Whipple District
South Prescott Townsite
West Prescott District

Lively Arts Calendar
Touring Artist Bookings: 26

People						
Younger				●		Older
Less Diverse			●			Diverse
Less Affluent		●				Affluent
Less Educated			●			Educated
Conservative		●				Liberal
Catholic			●			Protestant

Places Rated Rank: 189

✓ Providence-New Bedford, RI-MA

Good Restaurants: 135/2,063 ★★★★★

Bookstores and Reading: .... ★★★★
Chain Superstores: 11
Independent Stores: 10

Visible History
National Landmarks and Sites: 54
Registered Neighborhoods: 201
Contributing Buildings: 17,529
Broadway-Amory District
College Hill District
County Street District
Warren Waterfron District
Wayland District
Lively Arts Calendar
Touring Artist Bookings: 119
Veterans Memorial Auditorium
Zeiterion Theatre
Dates, Resident Ensembles: 49
Opera Providence
Rhode Island Philharmonic Orchestra

People						
Younger				●		Older
Less Diverse				●		Diverse
Less Affluent				●		Affluent
Less Educated				●		Educated
Conservative					●	Liberal
Catholic	●					Protestant

Places Rated Rank: 32

Provo-Orem, UT

Good Restaurants: 8/160 .... ★★

Bookstores and Reading: .... ★★★
Chain Superstores: 3
Independent Stores: 6

Visible History
National Landmarks and Sites: 3
Registered Neighborhoods: 11
Contributing Buildings: 2,251
American Fork District
Eureka District
Pleasant Grove District
Provo East Central District
Springville District

Lively Arts Calendar
Touring Artist Bookings: 10
Harris Center Concert Hall

People						
Younger	●					Older
Less Diverse		●				Diverse
Less Affluent	●					Affluent
Less Educated				●		Educated
Conservative		●				Liberal
LDS	●					Protestant

Places Rated Rank: 207

Pueblo, CO

Good Restaurants: 8/195 .... ★★

Bookstores and Reading: .... ★★
Chain Superstores: 2

Visible History
National Landmarks and Sites: 1
Registered Neighborhoods: 5
Contributing Buildings: 90

Lively Arts Calendar
Touring Artist Bookings: 8
Hoag Hall
Sangre de Christo Arts Center
Dates, Resident Ensembles: 6
Pueblo Symphony

People						
Younger		●				Older
Less Diverse		●				Diverse
Less Affluent	●					Affluent
Less Educated		●				Educated
Conservative	●					Liberal
Catholic	●					Protestant

Places Rated Rank: 300

Punta Gorda, FL

Good Restaurants: 3/117 .... ★

Bookstores and Reading: .... ★★★
Chain Superstores: 2

Visible History
Registered Neighborhoods: 1
Contributing Buildings: 126
Punta Gorda Residential District

Lively Arts Calendar
Touring Artist Bookings: 21
Dates, Resident Ensembles: 6

People

Younger				★		Older
Less Diverse		★				Diverse
Less Affluent			★			Affluent
Less Educated	★					Educated
Conservative		★				Liberal
Catholic		★				Protestant

Places Rated Rank: 335

Racine, WI

Good Restaurants: 6/216 .... ☆

Bookstores and Reading: .... ☆
Chain Superstores: 2

Visible History
National Landmarks and Sites: 2
Registered Neighborhoods: 6
Contributing Buildings: 839
Burlington Downtown District
 Northside District of Cream Brick Workers'
 Old Main Street District
 Southside District

Lively Arts Calendar
Touring Artist Bookings: 6
 Memorial Hall
Dates, Resident Ensembles: 15
 Racine Symphony Orchestra

People

Younger			★		Older
Less Diverse			★		Diverse
Less Affluent			★		Affluent
Less Educated		★			Educated
Conservative		★			Liberal
Catholic		★			Protestant

Places Rated Rank: 323

✓ Raleigh-Cary, NC

Good Restaurants: 79/714 ..... ☆☆☆☆☆

Bookstores and Reading: .... ☆☆☆☆
Chain Superstores: 7
Independent Stores: 9

Visible History
National Landmarks and Sites: 4
Registered Neighborhoods: 53
Contributing Buildings: 6,389
 Bloomsbury District
 East Raleigh-South Park District
 Hayes Barton District
 Roanoke Park District
 West Raleigh District

Lively Arts Calendar
Touring Artist Bookings: 32
 Civic Center Complex Theatre
 Raleigh Memorial Auditorium

Dates, Resident Ensembles: 227
 North Carolina Symphony Orchestra
 Opera Company of North Carolina
 Raleigh Symphony Orchestra

People

Younger	★				Older
Less Diverse				★	Diverse
Less Affluent				★	Affluent
Less Educated				★	Educated
Conservative				★	Liberal
Catholic			★		Protestant

Places Rated Rank: 27

Rapid City, SD

Good Restaurants: 33/141 .... ☆☆☆☆

Bookstores and Reading: .... ☆☆☆☆
Chain Superstores: 1
Independent Stores: 1

Visible History
National Landmarks and Sites: 1
Registered Neighborhoods: 15
Contributing Buildings: 774
 Rapid City Commercial District
 Rapid City West Boulevard District

Lively Arts Calendar
Touring Artist Bookings: 30
 Rushmore Plaza Civic Center
Dates, Resident Ensembles: 6
 Black Hills Symphony Orchestra

People

Younger		★			Older
Less Diverse	★				Diverse
Less Affluent			★		Affluent
Less Educated			★		Educated
Conservative			★		Liberal
Catholic	★				Protestant

Places Rated Rank: 127

Reading, PA

Good Restaurants: 18/379 .... ☆☆

Bookstores and Reading: .... ☆
Chain Superstores: 3
Independent Stores: 2

Visible History
National Landmarks and Sites: 3
Registered Neighborhoods: 30
Contributing Buildings: 3,754
 Morgantown District
 Oley Township District
 Queen Anne District
 Tulpehocken Creek District
 Womelsdorf District

Lively Arts Calendar
Touring Artist Bookings: 22
 Sovereign Center for Performing Arts

Dates, Resident Ensembles: 12
 Reading Symphony Orchestra

People

Younger		★			Older
Less Diverse			★		Diverse
Less Affluent			★		Affluent
Less Educated	★				Educated
Conservative	★				Liberal
Catholic		★			Protestant

Places Rated Rank: 199

Redding, CA

Good Restaurants: 6/148 .... ☆

Bookstores and Reading: .... ☆☆
Chain Superstores: 1

Visible History
National Landmarks and Sites: 1
Registered Neighborhoods: 10
Contributing Buildings: 106

Lively Arts Calendar
Touring Artist Bookings: 8
 Redding Civic Auditorium
Dates, Resident Ensembles: 4

People

Younger				★	Older
Less Diverse		★			Diverse
Less Affluent	★				Affluent
Less Educated	★				Educated
Conservative	★				Liberal
Catholic			★		Protestant

Places Rated Rank: 361

Reno-Sparks, NV

Good Restaurants: 26/381 .... ☆☆☆

Bookstores and Reading: .... ☆☆☆☆
Chain Superstores: 2
Independent Stores: 3

Visible History
National Landmarks and Sites: 3
Registered Neighborhoods: 8
Contributing Buildings: 435
 Virginia City District

Lively Arts Calendar
Touring Artist Bookings: 10
 Pioneer Center for Performing Arts
Dates, Resident Ensembles: 46
 Nevada Opera Association
 Reno Chamber Orchestra
 Reno Philharmonic

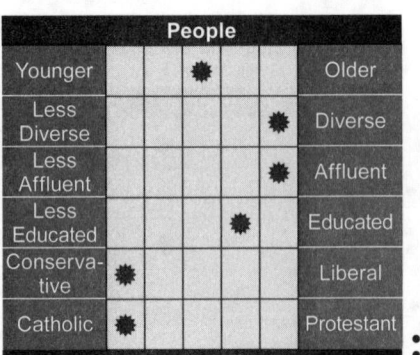

Ambience

People

	1	2	3	4	5	
Younger		●				Older
Less Diverse				●		Diverse
Less Affluent				●		Affluent
Less Educated			●			Educated
Conservative	●					Liberal
Catholic	●					Protestant

Places Rated Rank: 74

✓ Richmond, VA

Good Restaurants: 102/930 ... ☆☆☆☆

Bookstores and Reading: .... ☆☆☆
Chain Superstores: 12
Independent Stores: 9

Visible History
National Landmarks and Sites: 46
Registered Neighborhoods: 96
Contributing Buildings: 18,880
    Brookland Park District
    Fan Area District
    Highland Park Plaza District
    Oakwood-Chimborazo District
    West of Boulevard District

Lively Arts Calendar
Touring Artist Bookings: 34
    Carpenter Center for Performing Arts
    University of Richmond Modlin Hall
    VCU Singleton Center
Dates, Resident Ensembles: 200
    Richmond Symphony

People

	1	2	3	4	5	
Younger		●				Older
Less Diverse				●		Diverse
Less Affluent				●		Affluent
Less Educated			●			Educated
Conservative		●				Liberal
Catholic			●			Protestant

Places Rated Rank: 23

Riverside-San Bernardino, CA

Good Restaurants: 96/1,926 ...... ☆☆☆☆

Bookstores and Reading: .... ☆
Chain Superstores: 19
Independent Stores: 4

Visible History
National Landmarks and Sites: 4
Registered Neighborhoods: 15
Contributing Buildings: 756
    Highland District
    Russian Village District
    Smiley Park District
Lively Arts Calendar
Touring Artist Bookings: 284
    California Theatre for the Arts
    Coussoulis Arena
    Riverside Municipal Auditorium

    University of California Theatre
Dates, Resident Ensembles: 42
    Redlands Symphony Orchestra
    San Bernardino Symphony Orchestra
    West Coast Opera Theatre

People

	1	2	3	4	5	
Younger	●					Older
Less Diverse	●					Diverse
Less Affluent	●					Affluent
Less Educated		●				Educated
Conservative		●				Liberal
Catholic	●					Protestant

Places Rated Rank: 145

Roanoke, VA

Good Restaurants: 28/282 .... ☆☆☆☆

Bookstores and Reading: .... ☆☆
Chain Superstores: 4

Visible History
Registered Neighborhoods: 28
Contributing Buildings: 4,471
    Franklin District
    Gainsboro District
    New Castle District
    Rocky Mount District
    Southwest District

Lively Arts Calendar
Touring Artist Bookings: 6
    Civic Center
    Shaftman Performance Hall
Dates, Resident Ensembles: 20
    Opera Roanoke
    Roanoke Symphony & Choral Society

People

	1	2	3	4	5	
Younger				●		Older
Less Diverse		●				Diverse
Less Affluent				●		Affluent
Less Educated			●			Educated
Conservative		●				Liberal
Catholic				●		Protestant

Places Rated Rank: 177

Rochester, MN

Good Restaurants: 34/157 ..... ☆☆☆☆☆

Bookstores and Reading: .... ☆
Chain Superstores: 1

Visible History
National Landmarks and Sites: 1
Registered Neighborhoods: 6
Contributing Buildings: 223
    Mantorville District
    Pill Hill Residential District
    Wabasha Commercial District

Lively Arts Calendar
Touring Artist Bookings: 10
    Mayo Civic Center

People

	1	2	3	4	5	
Younger		●				Older
Less Diverse		●				Diverse
Less Affluent				●		Affluent
Less Educated				●		Educated
Conservative	●					Liberal
Catholic		●				Protestant

Places Rated Rank: 262

✓ Rochester, NY

Good Restaurants: 65/1,147 .... ☆☆☆

Bookstores and Reading: .... ☆☆☆
Chain Superstores: 6
Independent Stores: 6

Visible History
National Landmarks and Sites: 10
Registered Neighborhoods: 49
Contributing Buildings: 3,966
    Browncroft District
    Canandaigua District
    East Avenue District
    Main Street District
    Maplewood District

Lively Arts Calendar
Touring Artist Bookings: 85
    Auditorium Theatre
    Eastman Theater
Dates, Resident Ensembles: 205
    Mercury Opera Rochester
    Rochester Philharmonic Orchestra

People

	1	2	3	4	5	
Younger			●			Older
Less Diverse			●			Diverse
Less Affluent			●			Affluent
Less Educated				●		Educated
Conservative			●			Liberal
Catholic	●					Protestant

Places Rated Rank: 39

Rockford, IL

Good Restaurants: 26/322 .... ☆☆☆☆

Bookstores and Reading: .... ☆☆☆☆
Chain Superstores: 3
Independent Stores: 1

Visible History
Registered Neighborhoods: 6
Contributing Buildings: 366
    Haight Village District
    Rockton District

Lively Arts Calendar
Touring Artist Bookings: 19
    Midway Theatre
Dates, Resident Ensembles: 36
    Rockford Symphony Orchestra

People

Younger		●				Older
Less Diverse			●			Diverse
Less Affluent		●				Affluent
Less Educated	●					Educated
Conservative	●					Liberal
Catholic		●				Protestant

Places Rated Rank: 152

Rockingham County, NH

Good Restaurants: 60/421 ..... ☆☆☆☆☆

Bookstores and Reading: ...... ☆☆☆☆☆
Chain Superstores: 4
Independent Stores: 4

Visible History
National Landmarks and Sites: 18
Registered Neighborhoods: 20
Contributing Buildings: 673
  Durham District
  Exeter Waterfront Commercial District
  Little Boar's Head District
  Newmarket Industrial and Commercial District
  Rochester Commercial and Industrial District

Lively Arts Calendar
Touring Artist Bookings: 42
Dates, Resident Ensembles: 3
  Granite State Opera

People

Younger				●		Older
Less Diverse	●					Diverse
Less Affluent				●		Affluent
Less Educated				●		Educated
Conservative			●			Liberal
Catholic	●					Protestant

Places Rated Rank: 79

Rocky Mount, NC

Good Restaurants: 6/98 .... ☆

Bookstores and Reading: .... ☆☆
Independent Stores: 1

Visible History
National Landmarks and Sites: 1
Registered Neighborhoods: 16
Contributing Buildings: 2,127
  Spring Hope District
  Tarboro District
  Villa Place District
  West Haven District

Lively Arts Calendar
Touring Artist Bookings: 3
  Wesleyan College Dunn Center
Dates, Resident Ensembles: 12

People

Younger			●			Older
Less Diverse		●				Diverse
Less Affluent	●					Affluent
Less Educated	●					Educated
Conservative		●				Liberal
Catholic				●		Protestant

Places Rated Rank: 260

Rome, GA

Good Restaurants: 1/81........................ ☆

Bookstores and Reading: .... ☆☆
Chain Superstores: 1

Visible History
National Landmarks and Sites: 2
Registered Neighborhoods: 14
Contributing Buildings: 661
  Between the Rivers District
  East Rome District
  Oakdene Place
  South Broad Street District
  Upper Avenue A District

Lively Arts Calendar
Touring Artist Bookings: 4
Dates, Resident Ensembles: 9

People

Younger		●				Older
Less Diverse			●			Diverse
Less Affluent		●				Affluent
Less Educated	●					Educated
Conservative	●					Liberal
Catholic				●		Protestant

Places Rated Rank: 291

Sacramento–Arden-Arcade, CA

Good Restaurants: 27/1,607............. ☆☆

Bookstores and Reading: ....☆☆☆☆
Chain Superstores: 15
Independent Stores: 9

Visible History
National Landmarks and Sites: 19
Registered Neighborhoods: 24
Contributing Buildings: 607
  Alkali Flat Central District
  Dutch Flat District
  Elk Grove District
  Locke District
  Tahoe Meadows

Lively Arts Calendar
Touring Artist Bookings: 54
  Sacramento Community Center Theatre
Dates, Resident Ensembles: 31
  Capitol Opera
  Sacramento Opera Company

People

Younger	●					Older
Less Diverse			●			Diverse
Less Affluent			●			Affluent
Less Educated			●			Educated
Conservative			●			Liberal
Catholic	●					Protestant

Places Rated Rank: 175

Saginaw, MI

Good Restaurants: 19/209 .... ☆☆☆

Bookstores and Reading: ....☆☆☆
Chain Superstores: 3

Visible History
Registered Neighborhoods: 10
Contributing Buildings: 1,004
  Saginaw Central City Expansion District
  Saginaw Central City District
  South Jefferson Avenue District
  South Michigan Avenue District
  West Side Residential District

Lively Arts Calendar
Touring Artist Bookings: 3
  Dow Event Center'
Dates, Resident Ensembles: 15
  Saginaw Symphony Orchestra

People

Younger		●				Older
Less Diverse			●			Diverse
Less Affluent	●					Affluent
Less Educated	●					Educated
Conservative			●			Liberal
Catholic		●				Protestant

Places Rated Rank: 197

St. Cloud, MN

Good Restaurants: 38/205 ..... ☆☆☆☆☆

Bookstores and Reading: ...... ☆☆☆☆☆
Chain Superstores: 2
Independent Stores: 2

Visible History
National Landmarks and Sites: 1
Registered Neighborhoods: 5
Contributing Buildings: 174
  Original Main Street District

Lively Arts Calendar
Touring Artist Bookings: 28
  Benedicta Arts Center
  Paramount Theatre
Dates, Resident Ensembles: 36

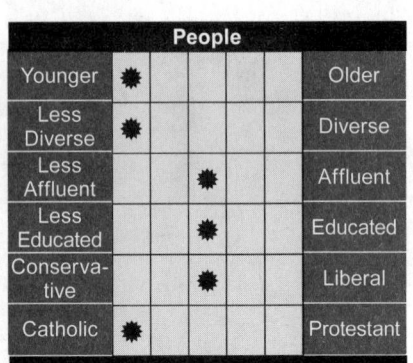

People						
Younger	●					Older
Less Diverse	●					Diverse
Less Affluent		●				Affluent
Less Educated		●				Educated
Conservative		●				Liberal
Catholic	●					Protestant

Places Rated Rank: 113

St. George, UT

Good Restaurants: 11/56..........☆☆☆

Bookstores and Reading: ....☆☆
Chain Superstores: 1
Independent Stores: 1

Visible History
Registered Neighborhoods: 7
Contributing Buildings: 188
  Hurricane District
  Zion Lodge District

Lively Arts Calendar
Touring Artist Bookings: 10
Dates, Resident Ensembles: 6

People						
Younger	●					Older
Less Diverse		●				Diverse
Less Affluent	●					Affluent
Less Educated			●			Educated
Conservative				●		Liberal
Catholic		●				Protestant

Places Rated Rank: 274

St. Joseph, MO-KS

Good Restaurants: 13/115.............☆☆☆

Bookstores and Reading: ....☆☆
Chain Superstores: 1

Visible History
National Landmarks and Sites: 1
Registered Neighborhoods: 23
Contributing Buildings: 1,405
  Cathedral Hill District
  Harris Addition District
  Kemper Addition District
  Museum Hill District
  Patee Town District

Lively Arts Calendar
Touring Artist Bookings: 17
  Missouri Theatre
Dates, Resident Ensembles: 5
  St. Joseph Symphony Orchestra

People						
Younger			●			Older
Less Diverse	●					Diverse
Less Affluent	●					Affluent
Less Educated	●					Educated
Conservative	●					Liberal
Catholic			●			Protestant

Places Rated Rank: 225

St. Louis, MO-IL

Good Restaurants: 160/2,700 ☆☆☆☆☆

Bookstores and Reading: ....☆☆
Chain Superstores: 25
Independent Stores: 15

Visible History
National Landmarks and Sites: 44
Registered Neighborhoods: 245
Contributing Buildings: 43,337
  Benton Park District
  Gravois-Jefferson District
  Mount Cabanne-Raymond Place District
  Tower Grove Heights District

Lively Arts Calendar
Touring Artist Bookings: 457
  Fox Theatre
  Powell Symphony Hall
  Sheldon Concert Hall
Dates, Resident Ensembles: 274
  Bellville Philharmonic Society
  Opera Theatre of St Louis
  St Louis Symphony Orchestra

People						
Younger			●			Older
Less Diverse		●				Diverse
Less Affluent				●		Affluent
Less Educated			●			Educated
Conservative			●			Liberal
Catholic		●				Protestant

Places Rated Rank: 42

Salem, OR

Good Restaurants: 15/331 ....☆☆

Bookstores and Reading: ....☆
Chain Superstores: 2
Independent Stores: 1

Visible History
National Landmarks and Sites: 1
Registered Neighborhoods: 11
Contributing Buildings: 577
  Aurora Colony District
  Court Street-Chemeketa Street District
  Gaiety Hill-Bush's Pasture Park District
  Independence District
  St. Paul District

Lively Arts Calendar
Touring Artist Bookings: 5
  Historic Elsinor Theatre
  Smith Auditorium

People						
Younger		●				Older
Less Diverse				●		Diverse
Less Affluent		●				Affluent
Less Educated		●				Educated
Conservative				●		Liberal
Catholic		●				Protestant

Places Rated Rank: 319

Salinas, CA

Good Restaurants: 44/434 ....☆☆☆

Bookstores and Reading: ....☆☆☆
Chain Superstores: 4
Independent Stores: 1

Visible History
National Landmarks and Sites: 8
Registered Neighborhoods: 6
Contributing Buildings: 48

Lively Arts Calendar
Touring Artist Bookings: 15

People						
Younger	●					Older
Less Diverse	●					Diverse
Less Affluent				●		Affluent
Less Educated		●				Educated
Conservative				●		Liberal
Catholic	●					Protestant

Places Rated Rank: 200

Salisbury, MD

Good Restaurants: 5/83 ....☆

Bookstores and Reading: ....☆☆☆☆
Chain Superstores: 1

Visible History
Registered Neighborhoods: 7
Contributing Buildings: 578
  Crisfield District
  Manokin District
  Princess Anne District
  Upper Fairmount District
  Whitehaven District

Lively Arts Calendar
Touring Artist Bookings: 12

People						
Younger		●				Older
Less Diverse			●			Diverse
Less Affluent	●					Affluent
Less Educated	●					Educated
Conservative			●			Liberal
Catholic			●			Protestant

Places Rated Rank: 218

✓ Salt Lake City, UT

Good Restaurants: 66/802 ..... ☆☆☆☆☆

Bookstores and Reading: ...... ☆☆☆☆☆
Chain Superstores: 8
Independent Stores: 14

Visible History
National Landmarks and Sites: 10
Registered Neighborhoods: 24
Contributing Buildings: 4,690
  Central City District
  Copperton District
  Highland Park District
  Salt Lake Northwest District
  University Neighborhood District

Lively Arts Calendar
Touring Artist Bookings: 380
  Salt Lake County Center
  University of Utah Kingsbury Hall
Dates, Resident Ensembles: 264
  Utah Opera
  Utah Symphony Orchestra

People						
Younger	✸					Older
Less Diverse				✸		Diverse
Less Affluent			✸			Affluent
Less Educated			✸			Educated
Conservative		✸				Liberal
LDS	✸					Protestant

Places Rated Rank: 20

San Angelo, TX

Good Restaurants: 5/97 .... ☆

Bookstores and Reading: ...... ☆☆☆☆☆
Chain Superstores: 1

Visible History
National Landmarks and Sites: 1
Registered Neighborhoods: 2
Contributing Buildings: 54
  Angelo Heights District

Lively Arts Calendar
Touring Artist Bookings: 4
  City Auditorium
Dates, Resident Ensembles: 12
  San Angelo Symphony Orchestra

People						
Younger		✸				Older
Less Diverse				✸		Diverse
Less Affluent			✸			Affluent
Less Educated		✸				Educated
Conservative	✸					Liberal
Catholic				✸		Protestant

Places Rated Rank: 279

San Antonio, TX

Good Restaurants: 225/1,580 ☆☆☆☆☆

Bookstores and Reading: .... ☆☆
Chain Superstores: 11
Independent Stores: 9

Visible History
National Landmarks and Sites: 13
Registered Neighborhoods: 28
Contributing Buildings: 3,294
  Comfort District
  King William District
  Lavaca District
  Monte Vista Residential District
  South Alamo-South Mary's District

Lively Arts Calendar
Touring Artist Bookings: 62
  Lauri Auditorium
  Lila Cockrell Theatre
  Majestic Theater
  Municipal Auditorium
Dates, Resident Ensembles: 208
  San Antonio Symphony

People						
Younger		✸				Older
Less Diverse	✸					Diverse
Less Affluent			✸			Affluent
Less Educated			✸			Educated
Conservative			✸			Liberal
Catholic	✸					Protestant

Places Rated Rank: 65

San Diego-Carlsbad, CA

Good Restaurants: 92/2,417 ...... ☆☆☆☆

Bookstores and Reading: .... ☆☆☆☆
Chain Superstores: 23
Independent Stores: 13

Visible History
National Landmarks and Sites: 18
Registered Neighborhoods: 12
Contributing Buildings: 262
  Gaslamp Quarter District

Lively Arts Calendar
Touring Artist Bookings: 246
  Copley Symphony Hall
  Old Globe Theatre
  San Diego Concourse
Dates, Resident Ensembles: 25
  Lyric Opera San Diego
  San Dieg Civic Light Opera
  San Diego Opera

People						
Younger		✸				Older
Less Diverse			✸			Diverse
Less Affluent					✸	Affluent
Less Educated					✸	Educated
Conservative			✸			Liberal
Catholic	✸					Protestant

Places Rated Rank: 82

Sandusky, OH

Good Restaurants: 32/132 .... ☆☆☆☆

Bookstores and Reading: ...... ☆☆☆☆☆
Chain Superstores: 1
Independent Stores: 1

Visible History
National Landmarks and Sites: 5
Registered Neighborhoods: 7
Contributing Buildings: 397
  Cable Park District
  Kelleys Island District
  Kelleys Island South Shore District

Lively Arts Calendar
Touring Artist Bookings: 57
  Sandusky State Theatre

People						
Younger					✸	Older
Less Diverse		✸				Diverse
Less Affluent			✸			Affluent
Less Educated	✸					Educated
Conservative				✸		Liberal
Catholic		✸				Protestant

Places Rated Rank: 80

✓ San Francisco-San Mateo, CA

Good Restaurants: 198/3,082 ☆☆☆☆☆

Bookstores and Reading: ...... ☆☆☆☆☆
Chain Superstores: 16
Independent Stores: 47

Visible History
National Landmarks and Sites: 30
Registered Neighborhoods: 33
Contributing Buildings: 817
  Fort Mason District
  Hamilton Army Air Fld. Discontiguous Dist.
  Larkspur Downtown District
  Liberty Street District
  Lower Nob Hill Apartment Hotel District

Lively Arts Calendar
Touring Artist Bookings: 326
Graham Civic Auditorium
  Nob Hill Masonic Center
  War Memorial & Performing Arts Center
  Yerba Buena Center for the Arts
Dates, Resident Ensembles: 389
  City Concert Opera
  Golden Gate Opera
  Marin Symphony Orchestra
  New Century Chamber Orchestra
  Peninsula Symphony Orchestra
  Philharmonia Baroque Orchestra
  San Francisco Opera
  San Francisco Opera Center

People						
Younger				✸		Older
Less Diverse		✸				Diverse
Less Affluent				✸		Affluent
Less Educated				✸		Educated
Conservative				✸		Liberal
Catholic	✸					Protestant

Places Rated Rank: 10

✓ San Jose-Sunnyvale, CA

Good Restaurants: 52/1,920 .... ☆☆

Bookstores and Reading: ...... ☆☆☆☆☆
Chain Superstores: 14
Independent Stores: 14

Visible History
National Landmarks and Sites: 9
Registered Neighborhoods: 20
Contributing Buildings: 1,030
  Green Gables
  Greenmeadow
  Hensley District
  Monterey Street District
  Professorville District

Lively Arts Calendar
Touring Artist Bookings: 524
  Center for Performing Arts
  Flint Center for Performing Arts
Dates, Resident Ensembles: 123
  American Musical Theatre of San Jose
  California Youth Symphony
  El Camino Youth Symphony
  Opera San Jose
  West Bay Opera

People						
Younger			●			Older
Less Diverse	●					Diverse
Less Affluent				●		Affluent
Less Educated				●		Educated
Conservative				●		Liberal
Catholic	●					Protestant

Places Rated Rank: 40

San Luis Obispo-Paso Robles, CA

Good Restaurants: 30/333 .... ☆☆☆☆

Bookstores and Reading: .... ☆☆☆
Chain Superstores: 2
Independent Stores: 4

Visible History
National Landmarks and Sites: 2
Registered Neighborhoods: 2
Contributing Buildings: 6

Lively Arts Calendar
Touring Artist Bookings: 105
  Performing Arts Center
Dates, Resident Ensembles: 13
  Pacific Repertory Opera

People						
Younger			●			Older
Less Diverse				●		Diverse
Less Affluent				●		Affluent
Less Educated				●		Educated
Conservative			●			Liberal
Catholic	●					Protestant

Places Rated Rank: 154

Santa Ana-Anaheim-Irvine, CA

Good Restaurants: 127/2,496 ☆☆☆☆

Bookstores and Reading: .... ☆☆☆
Chain Superstores: 20
Independent Stores: 21

Visible History
National Landmarks and Sites: 2
Registered Neighborhoods: 10
Contributing Buildings: 1,600
  Crystal Cove District
  Downtown Santa Ana Districts
  French Park District
  Kroger-Melrose District
  Old Towne Orange District

Lively Arts Calendar
Touring Artist Bookings: 150
  Irvine Barclay Theatre
  Spreckels Performing Arts Center
  UC Bren Events Center
Dates, Resident Ensembles: 136
  Capistrano Valley Symphony
  Fullerton Civic Light Opera
  Mozart Camerata
  Opera Pacific

People						
Younger		●				Older
Less Diverse		●				Diverse
Less Affluent				●		Affluent
Less Educated				●		Educated
Conservative		●				Liberal
Catholic	●					Protestant

Places Rated Rank: 63

Santa Barbara-Santa Maria, CA

Good Restaurants: 47/444 .... ☆☆☆☆

Bookstores and Reading: ...... ☆☆☆☆☆
Chain Superstores: 5
Independent Stores: 8

Visible History
National Landmarks and Sites: 10
Registered Neighborhoods: 3
Contributing Buildings: 12

Lively Arts Calendar
Touring Artist Bookings: 44
  Grenada Theatre
  Lobero Theatre
Dates, Resident Ensembles: 44
  Music Academy of the West Summer Festival Orchestr
  Opera Santa Barbara
  Santa Barbara Chamber Orchestra

People						
Younger		●				Older
Less Diverse			●			Diverse
Less Affluent				●		Affluent
Less Educated				●		Educated
Conservative			●			Liberal
Catholic	●					Protestant

Places Rated Rank: 141

Santa Cruz-Watsonville, CA

Good Restaurants: 10/290 .... ☆☆

Bookstores and Reading: ...... ☆☆☆☆☆
Chain Superstores: 2
Independent Stores: 9

Visible History
National Landmarks and Sites: 2
Registered Neighborhoods: 8
Contributing Buildings: 339
  Mission Hill Area District
  Old Riverview District
  Santa Cruz Downtown District
  Venetian Court Apartments

Lively Arts Calendar
Touring Artist Bookings: 78
  Santa Cruz Civic Auditorium

People						
Younger		●				Older
Less Diverse				●		Diverse
Less Affluent				●		Affluent
Less Educated				●		Educated
Conservative				●		Liberal
Catholic	●					Protestant

Places Rated Rank: 191

Santa Fe, NM

Good Restaurants: 64/168 ..... ☆☆☆☆☆

Bookstores and Reading: ...... ☆☆☆☆☆
Chain Superstores: 2
Independent Stores: 4

Visible History
National Landmarks and Sites: 8
Registered Neighborhoods: 11
Contributing Buildings: 596
Camino del Monte Sol District
  Don Gaspar District
  Madrid District
Lively Arts Calendar
Touring Artist Bookings: 22
  Lensic Performing Arts Center
  Santa Fe District
Dates, Resident Ensembles: 26
  Santa Fe Opera
  Santa Fe Pro Musica

People						
Younger				●		Older
Less Diverse	●					Diverse
Less Affluent				●		Affluent
Less Educated			●			Educated
Conservative				●		Liberal
Catholic	●					Protestant

Places Rated Rank: 59

Santa Rosa-Petaluma, CA

Good Restaurants: 19/531 .... ☆☆

Bookstores and Reading: ...... ☆☆☆☆☆
Chain Superstores: 3
Independent Stores: 9

Visible History
National Landmarks and Sites: 10
Registered Neighborhoods: 7
Contributing Buildings: 129
  Sonoma Plaza

Lively Arts Calendar
Touring Artist Bookings: 23
  Burbank Center for the Arts
Dates, Resident Ensembles: 51

People						
Younger			●			Older
Less Diverse				●		Diverse
Less Affluent				●		Affluent
Less Educated			●			Educated
Conservative				●		Liberal
Catholic	●					Protestant

Places Rated Rank: 176

Sarasota-Bradenton-Venice, FL

Good Restaurants: 74/624 ..... ☆☆☆☆

Bookstores and Reading: .... ☆
Chain Superstores: 7
Independent Stores: 7

Visible History
National Landmarks and Sites: 3
Registered Neighborhoods: 17
Contributing Buildings: 892
  Braden Castle Park District
  Central-Cocoanut District
  Edgewood District
  Palmetto District
  Venezia Park District

Lively Arts Calendar
Touring Artist Bookings: 116
  Glenridge Performing Arts Center
  Sarasota Opera House
  Van Wezel Performing Arts Hall
Dates, Resident Ensembles: 61
  Florida West Coast Symphony Orchestra
  Sarasota Opera Association
  Venice Symphony

People						
Younger				●		Older
Less Diverse		●				Diverse
Less Affluent				●		Affluent
Less Educated			●			Educated
Conservative		●				Liberal
Catholic		●				Protestant

Places Rated Rank: 139

Savannah, GA

Good Restaurants: 36/342 .... ☆☆☆

Bookstores and Reading: .... ☆☆
Chain Superstores: 3
Independent Stores: 1

Visible History
National Landmarks and Sites: 12
Registered Neighborhoods: 22
Contributing Buildings: 6,259
  Ardsley Park-Chatham Crescent District
  Cuyler-Brownville District
  Daffin Park-Parkside Place District
  Savannah District
  Thomas Square Streetcar District

Lively Arts Calendar
Touring Artist Bookings: 6
  Johnny Mercer Theatre
Dates, Resident Ensembles: 75
  Savannah Symphony Orchestra

People						
Younger	●					Older
Less Diverse				●		Diverse
Less Affluent		●				Affluent
Less Educated		●				Educated
Conservative	●					Liberal
Catholic			●			Protestant

Places Rated Rank: 97

Scranton-Wilkes-Barre, PA

Good Restaurants: 44/813 .... ☆☆☆

Bookstores and Reading: .... ☆☆
Chain Superstores: 4
Independent Stores: 2

Visible History
National Landmarks and Sites: 2
Registered Neighborhoods: 8
Contributing Buildings: 785
  Bear Creek Village District
  Eckley District
  River Street District
  Tunkhannock District
  Waverly District

Lively Arts Calendar
Touring Artist Bookings: 147
  Cultural Center at Masonic Temple
  Kirby Center for Performing Arts

People						
Younger				●		Older
Less Diverse	●					Diverse
Less Affluent			●			Affluent
Less Educated		●				Educated
Conservative				●		Liberal
Catholic	●					Protestant

Places Rated Rank: 152

✓ Seattle-Bellevue-Everett, WA

Good Restaurants: 230/2,916 ☆☆☆☆☆

Bookstores and Reading: ...... ☆☆☆☆
Chain Superstores: 20
Independent Stores: 48

Visible History
National Landmarks and Sites: 9
Registered Neighborhoods: 26
Contributing Buildings: 625
  Ballard Avenue District
  Harvard-Belmont District
  Pioneer Square-Skid Road District
  Rucker Hill District
  Snohomish District

Lively Arts Calendar
Touring Artist Bookings: 163
  UW Meany Hall
  Seattle Center
Dates, Resident Ensembles: 191
  Bellevue Philharmonic Orchestra
  Everett Symphony Orchestra
  Federal Way Philharmonic
  Northwest Chamber Orchestra
  Orchestra Seattle
  Seattle Opera Association
  Seattle Symphony

People						
Younger			●			Older
Less Diverse			●			Diverse
Less Affluent				●		Affluent
Less Educated				●		Educated
Conservative				●		Liberal
Catholic	●					Protestant

Places Rated Rank: 31

Sebastian-Vero Beach, FL

Good Restaurants: 6/113 .... ☆☆

Bookstores and Reading: .... ☆☆
Chain Superstores: 1
Independent Stores: 1

Visible History
National Landmarks and Sites: 1
Registered Neighborhoods: 2
Contributing Buildings: 28

Lively Arts Calendar
Touring Artist Bookings: 4

People						
Younger				●		Older
Less Diverse		●				Diverse
Less Affluent				●		Affluent
Less Educated		●				Educated
Conservative	●					Liberal
Catholic		●				Protestant

Places Rated Rank: 362

Sheboygan, WI

Good Restaurants: 13/150 .... ☆☆☆

Bookstores and Reading: .... ☆☆
Chain Superstores: 1
Independent Stores: 1

Visible History
National Landmarks and Sites: 1
Registered Neighborhoods: 3
Contributing Buildings: 45

Ambience

Lively Arts Calendar
Touring Artist Bookings: 14
Kohler Memorial Theatre
Weill Center
Dates, Resident Ensembles: 18

People					
Younger				●	Older
Less Diverse	●				Diverse
Less Affluent			●		Affluent
Less Educated		●			Educated
Conservative		●			Liberal
Catholic		●			Protestant

Places Rated Rank: 286

Sherman-Denison, TX

Good Restaurants: 2/85 .... ☆

Bookstores and Reading: .... ☆ ☆
Chain Superstores: 2

Visible History
National Landmarks and Sites: 1
Registered Neighborhoods: 1
Contributing Buildings: 67

Lively Arts Calendar
Touring Artist Bookings: 33
Dates, Resident Ensembles: 6

People					
Younger		●			Older
Less Diverse		●			Diverse
Less Affluent	●				Affluent
Less Educated		●			Educated
Conservative		●			Liberal
Catholic				●	Protestant

Places Rated Rank: 333

Shreveport-Bossier City, LA

Good Restaurants: 35/249 .... ☆ ☆ ☆ ☆

Bookstores and Reading: .... ☆
Chain Superstores: 4

Visible History
National Landmarks and Sites: 2
Registered Neighborhoods: 12
Contributing Buildings: 2,817
Fairfield District
Highland District
South Highlands District
St. Paul's Bottoms

Lively Arts Calendar
Touring Artist Bookings: 48
Shreveport Civic Center
Strand Theatre of Shreveport
Dates, Resident Ensembles: 143
Shreveport Opera
Shreveport Symphony Orchestra

People					
Younger	●				Older
Less Diverse			●		Diverse
Less Affluent		●			Affluent
Less Educated	●				Educated
Conservative	●				Liberal
Catholic			●		Protestant

Places Rated Rank: 133

Sioux City, IA-NE-SD

Good Restaurants: 4/171 .... ☆

Bookstores and Reading: .... ☆ ☆
Chain Superstores: 1
Independent Stores: 1

Visible History
National Landmarks and Sites: 2
Registered Neighborhoods: 7
Contributing Buildings: 201
Ponca District
Rose Hill District

Lively Arts Calendar
Touring Artist Bookings: 5
Eppley Auditorium
Dates, Resident Ensembles: 12
Sioux City Symphony Orchestra

People					
Younger	●				Older
Less Diverse			●		Diverse
Less Affluent		●			Affluent
Less Educated	●				Educated
Conservative	●				Liberal
Catholic			●		Protestant

Places Rated Rank: 327

Sioux Falls, SD

Good Restaurants: 67/230 ..... ☆ ☆ ☆ ☆ ☆

Bookstores and Reading: .... ☆ ☆ ☆
Chain Superstores: 2

Visible History
National Landmarks and Sites: 1
Registered Neighborhoods: 17
Contributing Buildings: 1,193
All Saints District
Hayes District
McKennan Park District
Sherman District
Sioux Falls District

Lively Arts Calendar
Touring Artist Bookings: 4
Convention Center Grand Ballroom
Dates, Resident Ensembles: 40
South Dakota Symphony

People					
Younger	●				Older
Less Diverse	●				Diverse
Less Affluent				●	Affluent
Less Educated			●		Educated
Conservative			●		Liberal
Catholic		●			Protestant

Places Rated Rank: 112

South Bend-Mishawaka, IN-MI

Good Restaurants: 24/338 .... ☆ ☆ ☆

Bookstores and Reading: ...... ☆ ☆ ☆ ☆
Chain Superstores: 2
Independent Stores: 3

Visible History
National Landmarks and Sites: 1
Registered Neighborhoods: 15
Contributing Buildings: 1,387
Chapin Park District
New Carlisle District
Normain Heights District
St. Casimir Parish District
West Washington District

Lively Arts Calendar
Touring Artist Bookings: 56
Century Center
De Bartolo Center
Morris Performing Arts Center
Dates, Resident Ensembles: 50
South Bend Symphony Orchestra

People					
Younger	●				Older
Less Diverse		●			Diverse
Less Affluent		●			Affluent
Less Educated		●			Educated
Conservative	●				Liberal
Catholic	●				Protestant

Places Rated Rank: 86

Spartanburg, SC

Good Restaurants: 4/277 .... ☆

Bookstores and Reading: .... ☆
Chain Superstores: 1

Visible History
National Landmarks and Sites: 1
Registered Neighborhoods: 7
Contributing Buildings: 213
Hampton Heights District
Hurricane Tavern

Lively Arts Calendar
Touring Artist Bookings: 20
Twitchell Auditorium
Dates, Resident Ensembles: 5
Greater Spartanburg Philharmonic

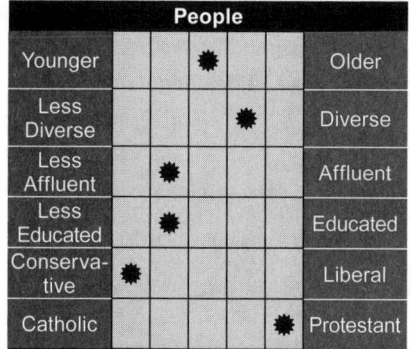

People						
Younger		●				Older
Less Diverse		●				Diverse
Less Affluent		●				Affluent
Less Educated		●				Educated
Conservative	●					Liberal
Catholic				●		Protestant

Places Rated Rank: 352

Spokane, WA

Good Restaurants: 30/407 .... ☆☆☆

Bookstores and Reading: .... ☆☆☆☆
Chain Superstores: 3
Independent Stores: 3

Visible History
National Landmarks and Sites: 1
Registered Neighborhoods: 22
Contributing Buildings: 2,328
Browne's Addition District
Nettleton's Addition District
Ninth Avenue District
Peaceful Valley District
Rockwood District

Lively Arts Calendar
Touring Artist Bookings: 24
Metropolitan Performing Arts Center
Opera House
Dates, Resident Ensembles: 43
Spokane Symphony Orchestra

People						
Younger		●				Older
Less Diverse	●					Diverse
Less Affluent		●				Affluent
Less Educated			●			Educated
Conservative		●				Liberal
Catholic		●				Protestant

Places Rated Rank: 123

Springfield, IL

Good Restaurants: 24/284 .... ☆☆☆

Bookstores and Reading: .... ☆☆☆
Chain Superstores: 2
Independent Stores: 2

Visible History
National Landmarks and Sites: 6
Registered Neighborhoods: 7
Contributing Buildings: 178
Lincoln's New Salem Village

Lively Arts Calendar
Touring Artist Bookings: 40
UI Sangamon Auditorium
Petersburg District
Dates, Resident Ensembles: 87
Illinois Symphony Orchestra

People						
Younger			●			Older
Less Diverse	●					Diverse
Less Affluent				●		Affluent
Less Educated				●		Educated
Conservative				●		Liberal
Catholic			●			Protestant

Places Rated Rank: 155

Springfield, MA

Good Restaurants: 20/804 .... ☆☆

Bookstores and Reading: .... ☆☆☆☆
Chain Superstores: 4
Independent Stores: 17

Visible History
National Landmarks and Sites: 8
Registered Neighborhoods: 96
Contributing Buildings: 6,685
Forest Park Heights District
Hadley Center District
McKnight District
Turner Falls District

Lively Arts Calendar
Touring Artist Bookings: 53
Paramount Theatre
Symphony Hall
Dates, Resident Ensembles: 46
Commonwealth Opera
Springfield Symphony Orchestra
Western Mass Young People's
Symphony & Philharmoni

People						
Younger			●			Older
Less Diverse				●		Diverse
Less Affluent			●			Affluent
Less Educated			●			Educated
Conservative				●		Liberal
Catholic	●					Protestant

Places Rated Rank: 103

Springfield, MO

Good Restaurants: 57/361 ..... ☆☆☆☆☆

Bookstores and Reading: .... ☆☆☆
Chain Superstores: 2
Independent Stores: 2

Visible History
National Landmarks and Sites: 3
Registered Neighborhoods: 16
Contributing Buildings: 798
Mid-Town District
Walnut Street District

Lively Arts Calendar
Touring Artist Bookings: 38
Hammons Hall for Performing Arts

Dates, Resident Ensembles: 32
Springfield Regional Opera
Springfield Symphony Orchestra

People						
Younger			●			Older
Less Diverse	●					Diverse
Less Affluent		●				Affluent
Less Educated		●				Educated
Conservative			●			Liberal
Catholic				●		Protestant

Places Rated Rank: 131

Springfield, OH

Good Restaurants: 16/110 .... ☆☆☆

Bookstores and Reading: .... ☆☆
Chain Superstores: 2

Visible History
Registered Neighborhoods: 3
Contributing Buildings: 292
South Charleston District
South Fountain Avenue District

Lively Arts Calendar
Touring Artist Bookings: 24
Dates, Resident Ensembles: 19
Ohio Lyric Theatre of Springfield
Springfield Symphony Orchestra

People						
Younger			●			Older
Less Diverse		●				Diverse
Less Affluent		●				Affluent
Less Educated	●					Educated
Conservative		●				Liberal
Catholic			●			Protestant

Places Rated Rank: 253

State College, PA

Good Restaurants: 7/131 .... ☆☆

Bookstores and Reading: ...... ☆☆☆☆☆
Chain Superstores: 1

Visible History
Registered Neighborhoods: 18
Contributing Buildings: 2,734
Aaronsburg District
Bellefonte District
College Heights District
Holmes-Foster-Highlands District
Philipsburg District

Lively Arts Calendar
Touring Artist Bookings: 35
PSU Center for Performing Arts
Dates, Resident Ensembles: 11

Ambience

People

	1	2	3	4	5	
Younger	✸					Older
Less Diverse		✸				Diverse
Less Affluent			✸			Affluent
Less Educated				✸		Educated
Conservative		✸				Liberal
Catholic			✸			Protestant

Places Rated Rank: 126

Stockton, CA

Good Restaurants: 3/433 .... ☆

Bookstores and Reading: .... ☆
Chain Superstores: 3
Independent Stores: 2

Lively Arts Calendar
Touring Artist Bookings: 9
Atherton Auditorium
Faye Spanos Concert Hall
Dates, Resident Ensembles: 20

People

	1	2	3	4	5	
Younger	✸					Older
Less Diverse	✸					Diverse
Less Affluent	✸					Affluent
Less Educated		✸				Educated
Conservative			✸			Liberal
Catholic	✸					Protestant

Places Rated Rank: 375

Sumter, SC

Good Restaurants: 0/58 .... ☆

Bookstores and Reading: .... ☆ ☆
Chain Superstores: 1

Visible History
National Landmarks and Sites: 4
Registered Neighborhoods: 5
Contributing Buildings: 157
Mayesville District
Sumter District

Lively Arts Calendar
Touring Artist Bookings: 3
Patriot Hall

People

	1	2	3	4	5	
Younger		✸				Older
Less Diverse			✸			Diverse
Less Affluent	✸					Affluent
Less Educated		✸				Educated
Conservative				✸		Liberal
Catholic				✸		Protestant

Places Rated Rank: 332

Syracuse, NY

Good Restaurants: 68/822 .... ☆ ☆ ☆

Bookstores and Reading: .... ☆ ☆ ☆
Chain Superstores: 5
Independent Stores: 7

Visible History
National Landmarks and Sites: 4
Registered Neighborhoods: 42
Contributing Buildings: 1,997
Berkeley Park Subdivision District
Cazenovia Village District
Earlville District
Hamilton Village District
Main-Broad-Grove Streets District

Lively Arts Calendar
Touring Artist Bookings: 86
Landmark Theater
Mulroy Civic Center
Dates, Resident Ensembles: 213
Syracuse Opera Company
Syracuse Symphony Orchestra

People

	1	2	3	4	5	
Younger				✸		Older
Less Diverse		✸				Diverse
Less Affluent			✸			Affluent
Less Educated				✸		Educated
Conservative			✸			Liberal
Catholic	✸					Protestant

Places Rated Rank: 52

Tacoma, WA

Good Restaurants: 22/581 .... ☆ ☆ ☆

Bookstores and Reading: .... ☆
Chain Superstores: 3
Independent Stores: 6

Visible History
National Landmarks and Sites: 6
Registered Neighborhoods: 21
Contributing Buildings: 1,501
DuPont Village District
Longmire District
Mount Rainier National Park
North Slope District
Stadium-Seminary District

Lively Arts Calendar
Touring Artist Bookings: 47
Broadway Center for Performing Arts
Dates, Resident Ensembles: 38
Tacoma Opera
Tacoma Symphony Orchestra

People

	1	2	3	4	5	
Younger	✸					Older
Less Diverse			✸			Diverse
Less Affluent			✸			Affluent
Less Educated		✸				Educated
Conservative			✸			Liberal
Catholic		✸				Protestant

Places Rated Rank: 200

Tallahassee, FL

Good Restaurants: 18/240 .... ☆ ☆

Bookstores and Reading: ...... ☆ ☆ ☆ ☆
Chain Superstores: 3
Independent Stores: 3

Visible History
National Landmarks and Sites: 7
Registered Neighborhoods: 13
Contributing Buildings: 361
Magnolia Heights District
Monticello District
Park Avenue District
Quincy District

Lively Arts Calendar
Touring Artist Bookings: 42
Tallahassee-Leon County Civic Center
Dates, Resident Ensembles: 21
Tallahassee Symphony

People

	1	2	3	4	5	
Younger	✸					Older
Less Diverse				✸		Diverse
Less Affluent		✸				Affluent
Less Educated				✸		Educated
Conservative		✸				Liberal
Catholic				✸		Protestant

Places Rated Rank: 100

Tampa-St. Petersburg, FL

Good Restaurants: 236/2,221 ☆ ☆ ☆ ☆

Bookstores and Reading: .... ☆
Chain Superstores: 16
Independent Stores: 6

Visible History
National Landmarks and Sites: 5
Registered Neighborhoods: 23
Contributing Buildings: 11,898
Hyde Park Districts
Kenwood District
North Shore District
Round Lake District
West Tampa District

Lively Arts Calendar
Touring Artist Bookings: 578
Baumgardner Center for Performing Arts
Bayfront Center/Mahaffey Theatre
Tampa Bay Performing Arts Center
Tampa Theatre
Dates, Resident Ensembles: 177
Florida Lyric Opera
Opera Tampa
Spanish Lyric Theatre
The Florida Orchestra

People

	1	2	3	4	5	
Younger				✸		Older
Less Diverse				✸		Diverse
Less Affluent			✸			Affluent
Less Educated		✸				Educated
Conservative	✸					Liberal
Catholic		✸				Protestant

Places Rated Rank: 72

Terre Haute, IN

Good Restaurants: 10/201 .... ✩✩

Bookstores and Reading: .... ✩✩
Chain Superstores: 2

Visible History
National Landmarks and Sites: 1
Registered Neighborhoods: 13
Contributing Buildings: 1,832
  Clinton Downtown District
  Collett Park Neighborhood District
  Farington's Grove District
  Meridian-Forest District
  Ohio Boulevard-Demming Park District

Lively Arts Calendar
Touring Artist Bookings: 9
  Tilson Music Hall
Dates, Resident Ensembles: 16
  Terre Haute Symphony Orchestra

People						
Younger		●				Older
Less Diverse	●					Diverse
Less Affluent	●					Affluent
Less Educated		●				Educated
Conservative		●				Liberal
Catholic				●		Protestant

Places Rated Rank: 234

Texarkana, TX-Texarkana, AR

Good Restaurants: 4/80 .... ✩

Bookstores and Reading: .... ✩✩
Chain Superstores: 2

Visible History
Registered Neighborhoods: 1
Contributing Buildings: 2

Lively Arts Calendar
Touring Artist Bookings: 5
  Perot Theatre

People						
Younger		●				Older
Less Diverse			●			Diverse
Less Affluent	●					Affluent
Less Educated	●					Educated
Conservative		●				Liberal
Catholic				●		Protestant

Places Rated Rank: 321

✓ **Toledo, OH**

Good Restaurants: 74/793 .... ✩✩✩✩

Bookstores and Reading: .... ✩✩✩
Chain Superstores: 4
Independent Stores: 3

Visible History
National Landmarks and Sites: 7
Registered Neighborhoods: 36
Contributing Buildings: 7,297
  Birmingham District
  East Toledo District
  Lakeside District
  Toledo Olde Towne District
  Yondota District

Lively Arts Calendar
Touring Artist Bookings: 78
  Stranahan Theatre
Dates, Resident Ensembles: 98
  Toledo Opera
  Toledo Symphony Orchestra

People						
Younger		●				Older
Less Diverse		●				Diverse
Less Affluent		●				Affluent
Less Educated		●				Educated
Conservative			●			Liberal
Catholic	●					Protestant

Places Rated Rank: 37

Topeka, KS

Good Restaurants: 18/205 .... ✩✩✩

Bookstores and Reading: .... ✩✩✩
Chain Superstores: 1

Visible History
National Landmarks and Sites: 2
Registered Neighborhoods: 6
Contributing Buildings: 236
  Holliday Park District I
  Potwin Place District

Lively Arts Calendar
Touring Artist Bookings: 20
  Topeka Performing Arts Center
  WU White Concert Hall
Dates, Resident Ensembles: 14
  Topeka Symphony

People						
Younger			●			Older
Less Diverse		●				Diverse
Less Affluent		●				Affluent
Less Educated	●					Educated
Conservative	●					Liberal
Catholic		●				Protestant

Places Rated Rank: 205

Trenton-Ewing, NJ

Good Restaurants: 11/407 .... ✩✩

Bookstores and Reading: ...... ✩✩✩✩✩
Chain Superstores: 5
Independent Stores: 3

Visible History
National Landmarks and Sites: 20
Registered Neighborhoods: 17
Contributing Buildings: 884
  Berkeley Square District
  Mill Hill District
  Stockton Street District
  Titusville District
  Windsor District

Lively Arts Calendar
Touring Artist Bookings: 98
  War Memorial Auditorium
Dates, Resident Ensembles: 24
  Boheme Opera New Jersey
  Greater Trenton Symphony Orchestra
  New Jersey Opera Theatre
  Princeton Chamber Symphony

People						
Younger		●				Older
Less Diverse				●		Diverse
Less Affluent				●		Affluent
Less Educated				●		Educated
Conservative				●		Liberal
Catholic	●					Protestant

Places Rated Rank: 94

Tucson, AZ

Good Restaurants: 103/709 ... ✩✩✩✩

Bookstores and Reading: .... ✩✩
Chain Superstores: 4
Independent Stores: 6

Visible History
National Landmarks and Sites: 4
Registered Neighborhoods: 30
Contributing Buildings: 5,604
  Armory Park Residential District
  Blenman-Elm District
  Sam Hughes Neighborhood District
  West University District

Lively Arts Calendar
Touring Artist Bookings: 111
  Tucson Convention Center Music Hall
  University of Arizona Centennial Hall
Dates, Resident Ensembles: 88
  Arizona Opera Company

People						
Younger		●				Older
Less Diverse		●				Diverse
Less Affluent		●				Affluent
Less Educated				●		Educated
Conservative			●			Liberal
Catholic	●					Protestant

Places Rated Rank: 64

Tulsa, OK

Good Restaurants: 106/720 ... ✩✩✩✩✩

Bookstores and Reading: ....✩
Chain Superstores: 5
Independent Stores: 4

Visible History
National Landmarks and Sites: 4

Registered Neighborhoods: 17
Contributing Buildings: 2,907
Maple Ridge District
Owen Park District
Swan Lake District
White City District
Yorktown District

Lively Arts Calendar
Touring Artist Bookings: 240
Tulsa Performing Arts Center
Dates, Resident Ensembles: 303
Bartlesville Symphony Orchestra
Sinfonia
Tulsa Opera
Tulsa Philharmonic Orchestra

People						
Younger		●				Older
Less Diverse		●				Diverse
Less Affluent				●		Affluent
Less Educated		●				Educated
Conservative	●					Liberal
Catholic					●	Protestant

Places Rated Rank: 101

Tuscaloosa, AL

Good Restaurants: 7/140 .... ☆☆

Bookstores and Reading: .... ☆☆
Chain Superstores: 1
Independent Stores: 1

Visible History
National Landmarks and Sites: 3
Registered Neighborhoods: 22
Contributing Buildings: 879
Capitol Park District
Druid City District
East Northport District
Northport District

Lively Arts Calendar
Touring Artist Bookings: 20
Bama Performing Arts Center
Dates, Resident Ensembles: 6

People						
Younger	●					Older
Less Diverse			●			Diverse
Less Affluent	●					Affluent
Less Educated	●					Educated
Conservative		●				Liberal
Catholic				●		Protestant

Places Rated Rank: 258

Tyler, TX

Good Restaurants: 7/104 .... ☆☆

Bookstores and Reading: .... ☆☆
Chain Superstores: 1
Independent Stores: 2

Visible History
National Landmarks and Sites: 2
Registered Neighborhoods: 6
Contributing Buildings: 1,582
Azalea Residential District
Brick Streets Neighborhood District
Charnwood Residential District
Donnybrook Duplex Residential District

Lively Arts Calendar
Touring Artist Bookings: 10
UTT Cowan Fine Arts Center
Vaughn Auditorium
Dates, Resident Ensembles: 11
East Texas Symphony Orchestra

People						
Younger		●				Older
Less Diverse				●		Diverse
Less Affluent			●			Affluent
Less Educated			●			Educated
Conservative			●			Liberal
Catholic			●			Protestant

Places Rated Rank: 277

Utica-Rome, NY

Good Restaurants: 43/396 .... ☆☆☆☆

Bookstores and Reading: .... ☆
Chain Superstores: 1
Independent Stores: 1

Visible History
National Landmarks and Sites: 13
Registered Neighborhoods: 11
Contributing Buildings: 521
Boonville District
Clinton Village District
Lower Genesee Street District
Rutger-Steuben Park District
Waterville Triangle District

Lively Arts Calendar
Touring Artist Bookings: 95
Capitol Theatre
Stanley Performing Arts Center
Dates, Resident Ensembles: 9
Utica Symphony Orchestra

People						
Younger				●		Older
Less Diverse		●				Diverse
Less Affluent	●					Affluent
Less Educated			●			Educated
Conservative			●			Liberal
Catholic	●					Protestant

Places Rated Rank: 183

Valdosta, GA

Good Restaurants: 5/87 .... ☆

Bookstores and Reading: .... ☆
Chain Superstores: 2

Visible History
Registered Neighborhoods: 8
Contributing Buildings: 1,720
Brookwood North District
East End District
Fairview District
Quitman District

Lively Arts Calendar
Touring Artist Bookings: 4
Dates, Resident Ensembles: 6

People						
Younger	●					Older
Less Diverse				●		Diverse
Less Affluent	●					Affluent
Less Educated		●				Educated
Conservative		●				Liberal
Catholic				●		Protestant

Places Rated Rank: 313

Vallejo-Fairfield, CA

Good Restaurants: 2/288 .... ☆

Bookstores and Reading: .... ☆
Chain Superstores: 2
Independent Stores: 1

Visible History
National Landmarks and Sites: 2
Registered Neighborhoods: 4
Contributing Buildings: 1,098
Mare Island District
Saint Vincent's Hill District

Lively Arts Calendar
Touring Artist Bookings: 32
Dates, Resident Ensembles: 10
Vallejo Symphony

People						
Younger	●					Older
Less Diverse		●				Diverse
Less Affluent			●			Affluent
Less Educated		●				Educated
Conservative				●		Liberal
Catholic	●					Protestant

Places Rated Rank: 302

Victoria, TX

Good Restaurants: 3/110 .... ☆

Bookstores and Reading: .... ☆☆
Chain Superstores: 1

Visible History
National Landmarks and Sites: 3
Registered Neighborhoods: 4
Contributing Buildings: 83
San Antonio River Valley (West of Goliad) Rural

Lively Arts Calendar
Touring Artist Bookings: 7
Victoria College Auditorium

Dates, Resident Ensembles: 5
Victoria Symphony Orchestra

People					
Younger	●				Older
Less Diverse	●				Diverse
Less Affluent			●		Affluent
Less Educated	●				Educated
Conservative				●	Liberal
Catholic		●			Protestant

Places Rated Rank: 293

Vineland-Millville-Bridgeton, NJ

Good Restaurants: 0/102 .... ☆

Bookstores and Reading: .... ☆☆
Independent Stores: 2

Visible History
Registered Neighborhoods: 2
Contributing Buildings: 2,019
Bridgeton District

Lively Arts Calendar
Dates, Resident Ensembles: 17
Bridgeton Symphony

People					
Younger		●			Older
Less Diverse			●		Diverse
Less Affluent	●				Affluent
Less Educated	●				Educated
Conservative		●			Liberal
Catholic		●			Protestant

Places Rated Rank: 298

✓ Virginia Beach-Norfolk, VA-NC

Good Restaurants: 341/1,371. ☆☆☆☆

Bookstores and Reading: .... ☆☆☆
Chain Superstores: 17
Independent Stores: 7

Visible History
National Landmarks and Sites: 26
Registered Neighborhoods: 54
Contributing Buildings: 10,502
Ballentine Place District
Colonial Place
Craddock District
Park Place District
South Norfolk District

Lively Arts Calendar
Touring Artist Bookings: 60
Chrysler Hall
Ferguson Center for the Arts
Pavillion
Willett Hall
Dates, Resident Ensembles: 124
Virginia Opera

Virginia Symphony
Williamsburg Symphonia

People					
Younger	●				Older
Less Diverse				●	Diverse
Less Affluent			●		Affluent
Less Educated			●		Educated
Conservative		●			Liberal
Catholic			●		Protestant

Places Rated Rank: 12

Visalia-Porterville, CA

Good Restaurants: 9/209 .... ☆☆

Bookstores and Reading: .... ☆
Chain Superstores: 1
Independent Stores: 1

Visible History
National Landmarks and Sites: 1
Registered Neighborhoods: 7
Contributing Buildings: 318
Allensworth District
Giant Forest Lodge District
Giant Forest Village-Camp Kaweah District
Mineral King Road Cultural Landscape
Wilsonia District

Lively Arts Calendar
Touring Artist Bookings: 12
Visalia Convention Center
Dates, Resident Ensembles: 30
Tulare County Symphony

People					
Younger	●				Older
Less Diverse	●				Diverse
Less Affluent	●				Affluent
Less Educated	●				Educated
Conservative		●			Liberal
Catholic		●			Protestant

Places Rated Rank: 308

Waco, TX

Good Restaurants: 13/157 .... ☆☆

Bookstores and Reading: ...... ☆☆☆☆
Chain Superstores: 1

Visible History
Registered Neighborhoods: 2
Contributing Buildings: 31

Lively Arts Calendar
Touring Artist Bookings: 18
Waco Hall
Waco Hippodrome Theatre
Dates, Resident Ensembles: 8
Waco Symphony Orchestra

People					
Younger	●				Older
Less Diverse			●		Diverse
Less Affluent			●		Affluent
Less Educated			●		Educated
Conservative	●				Liberal
Catholic			●		Protestant

Places Rated Rank: 230

Warner Robins, GA

Good Restaurants: 8/77 .... ☆☆

Bookstores and Reading: .... ☆☆
Chain Superstores: 1

Visible History
Registered Neighborhoods: 1
Contributing Buildings: 6

People					
Younger	●				Older
Less Diverse			●		Diverse
Less Affluent		●			Affluent
Less Educated		●			Educated
Conservative	●				Liberal
Catholic				●	Protestant

Places Rated Rank: 346

✓ Warren-Troy-Farmington Hills, MI

Good Restaurants: 163/2,318 ☆☆☆☆☆

Bookstores and Reading: .... ☆☆☆☆
Chain Superstores: 23
Independent Stores: 8

Visible History
National Landmarks and Sites: 2
Registered Neighborhoods: 32
Contributing Buildings: 2,514
Clarkston Village District
Lathrup Village District
Modern Housing Corp. Addition District
North Milford Village District
Pleasant Ridge District

Lively Arts Calendar
Touring Artist Bookings: 282
Dates, Resident Ensembles: 53
Farmington Area Philharmonic
National Sinfonietta

People					
Younger			●		Older
Less Diverse		●			Diverse
Less Affluent				●	Affluent
Less Educated			●		Educated
Conservative		●			Liberal
Catholic	●				Protestant

Places Rated Rank: 38

✓ Washington, DC-VA-MD-WV

Good Restaurants: 338/4,301 ☆☆☆☆

Bookstores and Reading: .... ☆☆
Chain Superstores: 49
Independent Stores: 47

Visible History
National Landmarks and Sites: 124
Registered Neighborhoods: 180
Contributing Buildings: 47,433
  Capitol Hill District
  Dupont Circle District
  Georgetown District
  Greenbelt District
  Hyattsville District

Lively Arts Calendar
Touring Artist Bookings: 4,370
  DAR Constitution Hall
  GWU Lisner Auditorium
  Kenmore Auditorium
  Kennedy Center for Performing Arts
  Schlesinger Concert Hall
Dates, Resident Ensembles: 539
  Alexandria Symphony Orchestra
  American Chamber Orchestra
  Arlington Symphony
  Kennedy Cener Opera House Orchestra
  National Lyric Opera Company
  National Symphony Orchestra
  Opera Bel Canto
  Opera Lafayette
  Opera Theatre of Northern Virginia
  Summer Opera Theatre Company
  The Washington National Opera
  Washington Bach Consort
  Washington Chamber Symphony
  Washington Concert Opera
  Washington DC Youth Orchestra
    Program
  Washington Philharmonic
  Washington Symphony Orchestra
  Wolf Trap Opera Company

People						
Younger		●				Older
Less Diverse				●		Diverse
Less Affluent				●		Affluent
Less Educated				●		Educated
Conservative			●			Liberal
Catholic		●				Protestant

Places Rated Rank: 29

Waterloo-Cedar Falls, IA

Good Restaurants: 12/207 .... ☆☆

Bookstores and Reading: ...... ☆☆☆☆
Chain Superstores: 3
Independent Stores: 1

Visible History
National Landmarks and Sites: 1
Registered Neighborhoods: 3
Contributing Buildings: 335
  Highland District

Lively Arts Calendar
Touring Artist Bookings: 10
  Kersenbrock Auditorium
  University Northern Iowa Lang Hall
Dates, Resident Ensembles: 27
  Waterloo-Cedar Falls Symphony

People						
Younger		●				Older
Less Diverse	●					Diverse
Less Affluent		●				Affluent
Less Educated			●			Educated
Conservative			●			Liberal
Catholic			●			Protestant

Places Rated Rank: 198

Wausau, WI

Good Restaurants: 16/169 .... ☆☆☆

Bookstores and Reading: .... ☆☆
Chain Superstores: 2

Visible History
Registered Neighborhoods: 2
Contributing Buildings: 197
  Andrew Warren District
  East Hill Residential District

Lively Arts Calendar
Touring Artist Bookings: 45
  Grand Theatre
Dates, Resident Ensembles: 12

People						
Younger			●			Older
Less Diverse	●					Diverse
Less Affluent			●			Affluent
Less Educated		●				Educated
Conservative				●		Liberal
Catholic	●					Protestant

Places Rated Rank: 252

Weirton-Steubenville, WV-OH

Good Restaurants: 23/175 .... ☆☆☆

Bookstores and Reading: .... ☆☆
Chain Superstores: 1

Visible History
National Landmarks and Sites: 5
Registered Neighborhoods: 10
Contributing Buildings: 999
  Bethany District
  North End Neighborhood District
  North Hill District
  Wellsburg District

Lively Arts Calendar
Touring Artist Bookings: 12
Dates, Resident Ensembles: 11

People						
Younger				●		Older
Less Diverse	●					Diverse
Less Affluent	●					Affluent
Less Educated	●					Educated
Conservative				●		Liberal
Catholic		●				Protestant

Places Rated Rank: 210

Wenatchee, WA

Good Restaurants: 18/109 .... ☆☆☆☆

Bookstores and Reading: .... ☆☆
Chain Superstores: 1
Independent Stores: 2

Visible History
National Landmarks and Sites: 3
Registered Neighborhoods: 6
Contributing Buildings: 97
  Cottage Avenue District

Lively Arts Calendar
Touring Artist Bookings:
  Bank of America Performing Arts Center
Dates, Resident Ensembles: 4

People						
Younger				●		Older
Less Diverse				●		Diverse
Less Affluent		●				Affluent
Less Educated		●				Educated
Conservative	●					Liberal
Catholic		●				Protestant

Places Rated Rank: 292

West Palm Beach-Boca Raton, FL

Good Restaurants: 95/1,287 .. ☆☆☆☆☆

Bookstores and Reading: .... ☆☆
Chain Superstores: 13
Independent Stores: 3

Visible History
National Landmarks and Sites: 2
Registered Neighborhoods: 12
Contributing Buildings: 2,300
  El Cid District
  Flamingo Park District
  Grandview Heights District
  Northwest District
  Northwood, Old, District

Lively Arts Calendar
Touring Artist Bookings: 599
  Kravis Center for Performing Arts
Dates, Resident Ensembles: 75
  Boca Pops
  Palm Beach Opera
  Palm Beach Pops

People						
Younger				●		Older
Less Diverse				●		Diverse
Less Affluent				●		Affluent
Less Educated			●			Educated
Conservative			●			Liberal
Catholic	●					Protestant

Places Rated Rank: 107

Wheeling, WV-OH

Good Restaurants: 30/170 .... ☆☆☆☆

Bookstores and Reading: .... ☆
Chain Superstores: 1

Visible History

National Landmarks and Sites: 4
Registered Neighborhoods: 28
Contributing Buildings: 3,621
- *Barnesville District*
- *Centre Market Square District*
- *East Wheeling District*
- *Wheeling Island District*
- *Woodsdale-Edgewood Neighborhood District*

Lively Arts Calendar

Touring Artist Bookings: 95
- *Capitol Music Hall*

Dates, Resident Ensembles: 66
- *Wheeling Symphony Orchestra*

People							
Younger					●		Older
Less Diverse	●						Diverse
Less Affluent		●					Affluent
Less Educated	●						Educated
Conservative				●			Liberal
Catholic		●					Protestant

Places Rated Rank: 138

Wichita, KS

Good Restaurants: 26/537 .... ☆☆☆

Bookstores and Reading: .... ☆☆
Chain Superstores: 6
Independent Stores: 2

Visible History

National Landmarks and Sites: 1
Registered Neighborhoods: 10
Contributing Buildings: 475
- *Bitting District*
- *East Douglas Avenue District*
- *Park Place-Fairview District*
- *Topeka-Emporia District*

Lively Arts Calendar

Touring Artist Bookings: 22
- *Alexander Auditorium*
- *Century II Concert Hall*
- *WSU Duerksen Fine Arts Center*

Dates, Resident Ensembles: 81
- *Wichita Grand Opera*
- *Wichita Symphony Orchestra*

People							
Younger	●						Older
Less Diverse			●				Diverse
Less Affluent			●				Affluent
Less Educated			●				Educated
Conservative	●						Liberal
Catholic				●			Protestant

Places Rated Rank: 224

Wichita Falls, TX

Good Restaurants: 4/128 .... ☆

Bookstores and Reading: .... ☆☆
Chain Superstores: 1

Visible History

Registered Neighborhoods: 2
Contributing Buildings: 100
- *Depot Square District*
- *Morningside District*

Lively Arts Calendar

Touring Artist Bookings: 4
- *Memorial Auditorium*

Dates, Resident Ensembles: 8
- *Wichita Falls Symphony Orchestra*

People							
Younger	●						Older
Less Diverse					●		Diverse
Less Affluent			●				Affluent
Less Educated		●					Educated
Conservative	●						Liberal
Catholic			●				Protestant

Places Rated Rank: 358

Williamsport, PA

Good Restaurants: 10/144 .... ☆☆

Bookstores and Reading: .... ☆☆
Chain Superstores: 1
Independent Stores: 3

Visible History

Registered Neighborhoods: 3
Contributing Buildings: 847
- *Jersey Shore District*
- *Millionaire's Row District*
- *Muncy District*

Lively Arts Calendar

Touring Artist Bookings: 35
- *Community Arts Center*

Dates, Resident Ensembles: 5
- *Williamsport Symphony Orchestra*

People							
Younger				●			Older
Less Diverse	●						Diverse
Less Affluent	●						Affluent
Less Educated	●						Educated
Conservative			●				Liberal
Catholic			●				Protestant

Places Rated Rank: 240

Wilmington, DE-MD-NJ

Good Restaurants: 27/599 .... ☆☆☆

Bookstores and Reading: .... ☆☆
Chain Superstores: 4
Independent Stores: 3

Visible History

National Landmarks and Sites: 17
Registered Neighborhoods: 63
Contributing Buildings: 5,063

- *Ardens District*
- *Cool Spring Park District*
- *New Castle District*
- *Shipley Run District*
- *Wawaset Park District*

Lively Arts Calendar

Touring Artist Bookings: 154
- *Christina Cultural Arts Center*
- *DuPont Theatre*
- *Grand Opera House*
- *Playhouse Theatre*

Dates, Resident Ensembles: 73
- *Delaware Symphony Orchestra*
- *OperaDelaware*

People							
Younger		●					Older
Less Diverse			●				Diverse
Less Affluent				●			Affluent
Less Educated			●				Educated
Conservative			●				Liberal
Catholic	●						Protestant

Places Rated Rank: 121

Wilmington, NC

Good Restaurants: 37/363 .... ☆☆☆☆

Bookstores and Reading: .... ☆
Chain Superstores: 3
Independent Stores: 4

Visible History

National Landmarks and Sites: 3
Registered Neighborhoods: 11
Contributing Buildings: 2,779
- *Carolina Heights District*
- *Carolina Place District*
- *Southport District*
- *Sunset Park District*
- *Wilmington District*

Lively Arts Calendar

Touring Artist Bookings: 74
- *UNC Kenan Memorial Auditorium*

Dates, Resident Ensembles: 5

People							
Younger			●				Older
Less Diverse		●					Diverse
Less Affluent		●					Affluent
Less Educated			●				Educated
Conservative			●				Liberal
Catholic		●					Protestant

Places Rated Rank: 151

Winchester, VA-WV

Good Restaurants: 8/83 .... ☆☆

Bookstores and Reading: .... ☆☆
Chain Superstores: 2
Independent Stores: 1

Visible History
National Landmarks and Sites: 2
Registered Neighborhoods: 7
Contributing Buildings: 1,535
   Middletown District
   Newtown-Stephensburg District
   Opequon District
   Winchester District

Lively Arts Calendar
Touring Artist Bookings:
   Shenandoah University Auditorium

People							
Younger				✦			Older
Less Diverse		✦					Diverse
Less Affluent			✦				Affluent
Less Educated		✦					Educated
Conservative			✦				Liberal
Catholic				✦			Protestant

Places Rated Rank: 278

Winston-Salem, NC

Good Restaurants: 27/393 .... ☆☆☆

Bookstores and Reading: .... ☆☆
Chain Superstores: 2
Independent Stores: 3

Visible History
National Landmarks and Sites: 7
Registered Neighborhoods: 25
Contributing Buildings: 5,459
   Ardmore District
   Washington Park District
   Waughtown-Belview District
   West End District
   West Salem District

Lively Arts Calendar
Touring Artist Bookings: 143
   Stevens Center for Performing Arts
Dates, Resident Ensembles: 57
   Piedmont Triad Symphony

People							
Younger		✦					Older
Less Diverse				✦			Diverse
Less Affluent				✦			Affluent
Less Educated			✦				Educated
Conservative					✦		Liberal
Catholic					✦		Protestant

Places Rated Rank: 128

Worcester, MA

Good Restaurants: 32/823 .... ☆☆☆

Bookstores and Reading: .... ☆☆☆
Chain Superstores: 7
Independent Stores: 10

Visible History
National Landmarks and Sites: 9
Registered Neighborhoods: 128

Contributing Buildings: 6,144
   Farnumsville District
   Holden Center District
   Hopedale Village District
   West Brookfield Center District
   Whitinsville District

Lively Arts Calendar
Touring Artist Bookings: 24
   Mechanics Hall
Dates, Resident Ensembles: 14
   Central Massachusetts Symphony Orchestra
   Thayer Symphony Orchestra

People							
Younger			✦				Older
Less Diverse			✦				Diverse
Less Affluent			✦				Affluent
Less Educated					✦		Educated
Conservative					✦		Liberal
Catholic	✦						Protestant

Places Rated Rank: 119

Yakima, WA

Good Restaurants: 8/179 .... ☆☆

Bookstores and Reading: .... ☆
Chain Superstores: 1
Independent Stores: 1

Visible History
National Landmarks and Sites: 1
Registered Neighborhoods: 3
Contributing Buildings: 24

Lively Arts Calendar
Touring Artist Bookings: 20
   Capitol Theatre
Dates, Resident Ensembles: 10
   Yakima Symphony Orchestra

People							
Younger	✦						Older
Less Diverse		✦					Diverse
Less Affluent	✦						Affluent
Less Educated	✦						Educated
Conservative	✦						Liberal
Catholic		✦					Protestant

Places Rated Rank: 355

York-Hanover, PA

Good Restaurants: 27/330 .... ☆☆☆☆

Bookstores and Reading: .... ☆
Chain Superstores: 4
Independent Stores: 2

Visible History
Registered Neighborhoods: 21
Contributing Buildings: 10,101
   Hanover District
   Northwest York District
   Red Lion Borough District

Wrightsville District
York District

Lively Arts Calendar
Touring Artist Bookings: 25
   Strand-Capitol Performing Arts Center
Dates, Resident Ensembles: 20
   York Symphony

People							
Younger					✦		Older
Less Diverse		✦					Diverse
Less Affluent			✦				Affluent
Less Educated		✦					Educated
Conservative		✦					Liberal
Catholic				✦			Protestant

Places Rated Rank: 159

Youngstown-Warren, OH-PA

Good Restaurants: 59/623 .... ☆☆☆☆

Bookstores and Reading: .... ☆
Chain Superstores: 5

Visible History
National Landmarks and Sites: 3
Registered Neighborhoods: 21
Contributing Buildings: 881
   Crandall Park-Fifth Avenue District
   Forest Glen Estates District
   Warren Commercial District
   Wick Park District
   Youngstown Sheet and Tube Company Housing

Lively Arts Calendar
Touring Artist Bookings: 185
   Packard Music Hall
   Stambaugh Auditorium
   Youngstown Symphony Center
Dates, Resident Ensembles: 103
   Youngstown Symphony Orchestra

People							
Younger					✦		Older
Less Diverse		✦					Diverse
Less Affluent		✦					Affluent
Less Educated	✦						Educated
Conservative				✦			Liberal
Catholic		✦					Protestant

Places Rated Rank: 142

Yuba City, CA

Good Restaurants: 2/97 .... ☆

Bookstores and Reading: .... ☆☆
Chain Superstores: 1
Independent Stores: 1

Visible History
Registered Neighborhoods: 2
Contributing Buildings: 67
   Marysville Commercial District

Lively Arts Calendar
Touring Artist Bookings: 5

People					
Younger ✸					Older
Less Diverse				✸	Diverse
Less Affluent ✸					Affluent
Less Educated	✸				Educated
Conservative ✸					Liberal
Catholic	✸				Protestant

Places Rated Rank: 370

Yuma, AZ

Good Restaurants: 11/117 .... ☆☆☆

Bookstores and Reading: .... ☆
Chain Superstores: 1

Visible History
National Landmarks and Sites: 2
Registered Neighborhoods: 4
Contributing Buildings: 155
 Brinley Avenue District
 Yuma Century Heights District

Lively Arts Calendar
Touring Artist Bookings: 20

People					
Younger	✸				Older
Less Diverse ✸					Diverse
Less Affluent ✸					Affluent
Less Educated ✸					Educated
Conservative			✸		Liberal
Catholic ✸					Protestant

Places Rated Rank: 327

Ambience

THE DAVID AND GOLIATH PROPOSITION

Aside from New York, show you other big metro areas and you'll be shown the best places to live for the arts: Chicago, Los Angeles, Washington, and San Francisco. The consistent relationship between a metro area's size and its performing arts assets might make you think places such as Little Rock and Louisville and Peoria—all with populations under 1,000,000—must resign themselves to being cultural underdogs. Think again.

Pick on Someone Your Own Size

What would happen if Little Rock, Louisville, and Peoria (remembering the old playground cliché) were to say to New York, "Go pick on someone your own size"? By grouping metro areas into those with more than 1 million people and those with less, we are able to explore which have a large supply of cultural assets relative to their size and which might be considered cultural backwaters because they don't.

Sure, it's intuitive that *Big Winners* will be the largest metro areas. The top four in the arts are the top four in population. New York, Washington, Los Angeles, and Chicago each have critical masses to support ballet, opera, professional theatre, and the symphony. They also tend to have older central cities with long-established arts facilities and a tradition of philanthropy.

What isn't intuitive are the *Big Loser*. These are metro areas with populations over 1 million where people ought to enjoy a full calendar of professional, non-profit ballet, opera, theatre, and symphony—but don't. Three—Bethesda in Maryland, Cambridge in Massachusetts, and Camden in New Jersey—are suburbs to cultural meccas. Getting a performing arts fix in these places means a long evening commute to the central city. Others like Las Vegas or Orlando have grown so fast there's either no lively arts tradition in town, or the arts have withered in the face of tourist attractions, or both.

But Small Winners show where the 'isolation-proximity' principle in geography is at play.

AMBIENCE: BIG LOSERS

According to this notion, sizeable locations that are somewhat removed get more than their share of scarce amenities. Though smaller than the giants, they nevertheless are the only game for miles around. Little Rock is the biggest spot on the 450-mile stretch between Memphis and Dallas. Omaha is a minor culture oasis roughly midway on an 18-hour drive between Chicago and Denver.

ART MUSEUMS AND GALLERIES

In ancient Greece, it wasn't just the devoutly religious who visited temples; uninvited tourists also stole in to admire the statues and paintings. In Revolutionary France, artists had their daily exclusive run of the Louvre in order to copy the great works of the past. But on infrequent public days, the peasants, prostitutes, soldiers, and common laborers came in great numbers. To this day, going to an art museum has something of the democratic, the sacred, and the carnival to it.

The American Association of Museums' requirements are as solid as any: "an organized and permanent nonprofit institution, essentially educational or aesthetic in purpose, with professional staff, which owns and utilizes tangible objects, cares for them, and exhibits them to the public on some regular schedule."

The first great North American art museums were founded in Montreal in 1860, and in Boston and New York 10 years later. New York now has more art museums than any other city on the continent, and the Metropolitan Museum, with five million visitors a year, is the city's most popular tourist attraction.

Museums count visitors religously. New York's Metropolitan counts each tin button it hands out, reconciles that number with an electronic eye at the museum's front door, and records the weather, too—all for comparing each day's visitors with those on the previous year's date.

The number of visitors to art museums is impressive. Combining regular tickets sales with those from traveling special exhibitions make art museums and non-profit exhibit spaces more popular than professional theatre and opera. "Picasso: The Early Years" packed in nearly 1 million people when it ran in Boston's Museum of Fine Arts and Washington's National Gallery. In fact, the National Gallery's recent Van Gogh exhibit drew crowds bigger than all of the Redskins's home games.

Housing

Have you heard the story about the two tract-house developers who bumped into each other at a Florida real estate auction after the market went south? It might be retold in other parts of the country in the coming months.

"Congratulate me, Ralph," one of them says. "I've just sold my first $350,000 house!"

"Whoa! Earl, last time we talked you were building half a million dollar houses."

"I still am, but now I get $350,000 for them."

Yes, prices are coming down according the National Association of Realtors. In October of 2006, the median price of existing homes had fallen to $221,000, down 3.5 percent from their historic, $229,000 peak a year earlier.

Except in scattered pockets of appreciation—mainly in the West—real estate brokers are coaching sellers to cut their price to encourage the sale. Some sellers are even offering cash at closing, even a vacation or car in addition to a discount.

The six-year party may be over, but depending on where you look there is a wide range in prices and how they got there. At 13 percent appreciation, homes in greater Lafayette, IN, seemed to sit in a time warp while in Naples, FL, prices rocketed 223 percent. In Brownsville, TX, an "elite" house priced at the 90th percentile is $111,300, half the U.S. median. In San Francisco, a "starter" house is a shade under $1 million. If your move is from an expensive area to a cheaper one, can you be better housed for less money? If you're coming from an inexpensive area to a costly one, what are the rent vs. buy options.

LIFE STAGE SHELTER STRATEGIES

Most of us change our address 11 times during our lives according to an old AT&T company rule of thumb. In most metro areas the options are an apartment, a detached single-family home, a condo, or a mobile home. The choices often fall within common life stages and

WHERE TO BUY

These metro areas (1) are ranked among the top ten percent in *Places Rated*'s JOBS chapter, (2) they experienced more modest runups in home price appreciation since 2000, and (3) median home prices are way below 6.0 times per capita personal income. In other words, they're showing promising signs of price appreciation.

income levels. Here are several possibilities:

• *You are eighteen to twenty-one*, carefully looking at a college or graduate school in Big Ten Country. Unless you take a room in a dormitory, the odds are you'll rent an apartment. Small metro areas dominated by a major university tend to have an oversupply of structures with five or more rental units.

• *You are twenty to twenty-five*, single, with a minimum of responsibilities, diligently working at your first job but willing to change employers and move anywhere for a better opportunity. If moving in with Mom and Dad is not your preference, you could take the common tack of renting a studio or one-bedroom apartment; your commitment lasts only as long as the term of the lease.

• *You are twenty-five to thirty-five*, married, with two small children and an offer for a better job in a

distant and unfamiliar metro area. Renting a house for a year or so may give you an opportunity to become thoroughly acquainted with the new area before you invest in a home of your own. You might also consider buying an inexpensive starter home that can easily be resold or rented once you find a house and neighborhood that are right for you.

• *You are thirty-five to forty-five*, married, with children, and have recently taken a promotion in another city with a fat relocation bonus and corresponding pay increase. If you're selling a home, the odds are you'll move up for a larger house in the suburbs.

• *You are well into your sixth decade*, your children have scattered like tumbleweeds in the wind, and you have an ark of a home that you plan to sell. Your options are wider than those of other age groups: You can rent an apartment or buy a smaller home, condo, or mobile home in town or in another metro

area, perhaps one with a milder climate and a lower cost of living.

MAJOR HOUSING CHOICES

If you're thinking of moving to a metro area hundreds of miles distant, it would help to know what the average costs would be for renting, and—because two thirds of us eventually end up buying a single-family home—what are typical homeowner costs you'll encounter there.

Single Houses

If you walk through the front door of the typical American home, you'll find yourself in a structure that was built in 1973 and has a single-level, 2,000-square foot floor plan enclosing five rooms (three bedrooms, one and one-half baths, a complete kitchen, a living room and a dining room), no basement, an attached garage, and an insulated attic and storm windows to conserve the heat from its gas-fired, warm-air furnace. This house is kept cool during hot spells by a central air-conditioning unit. It is also connected to city water and sewerage lines.

So much for national composites. Among the 76 million single houses in the United States (and particularly among the newer suburban homes), a buyer can choose from many building styles—Cape Cods and Cape Anns, mountain A-frames, cabins of peeled pine log, desert adobes, Greek revivals, American and Dutch colonials, Puget Sounds, catslides, exotic glass solaria, futuristic earth berms, Victorian revivals, plantation cottages, and ubiquitous split-levels and California bungalows.

Apartments

Looking for digs close to work, with reasonable rent, tenants similar to yourself, a pleasant landlord, off-street parking, ambience, and all the other items on your checklist might turn out to be a quest that stops when the lease is signed but starts up again on the lease's anniversary. Still, for most newcomers to a metro area, renting is the main style of housing tenure.

As a renter you remain flexible, since you need not stay in an apartment beyond the term of the lease should your income slump or your job take you to another part of the country. You don't need to come up with a down payment; taxes, insurance, repairs, and sometimes utilities are the landlord's headaches.

One Sign of a Bargain Rental Market

Buy or rent?

The standard answer: It depends on how long you plan to stay in the locale.

If you're trying out the area and don't plan to stay more than two years, it makes sense to sign a lease. If you buy a home, it may take a longer time for the home's price appreciation to offset taxes, mortgage interest points and closing fees, all of which totals 5 to 10 percent of a home's sales price.

Is there a way of distance learning whether a metro area is good for renting? Consider the M/R or Mortgage to Rent Ratio.

Just like stocks have Price/Earnings (P/E) multiples, metro areas have M/R multiples—the ratio of twelve months of mortgage payments to one month's rent. A look at the Housing Place Profiles section shows the annual mortgage on Atlanta's median-priced Starter Home is 19.6 times the area's median monthly rent ($13,344 to $680). East on I-20 in Augusta, Georgia, its 16.8 ($7,932 to $470). Further east into Florence, South Carolina, its 15.7 ($6,456 to $410).

In normal times the M/R ratio is 11 to 12 nationwide, but we've just lived through seven inflationary years in house prices. Atlanta's high M/R is a sign it has seen a faster runup in house prices than Augusta and Florence. It also means that rents haven't caught up and that you can rent a median-price home in the Georgia capital for a lot less money than you can buy it.

Even better bargains can be found in metro areas where investors bought homes and condos for flipping, i.e., immediate resale. Owing to a deflating market these properties can only be sold at a big loss or they can rented until the market turns. Phoenix, with an M/R of 35.6 thanks to two years of frothy home inflation, is one of the best rental bargains in the country.

But you also miss out on such ownership benefits as growing equity, property appreciation, and tax deductions for mortgage interest, while being subject to condo conversion or arbitrary rent hikes in times of low vacancy rates.

Many of us tend to think that apartments are available only in blocks of large, high-rise tower complexes near a large metro area's central business district. In fact, only one out of 50 apartments is in a building of 13 stories or more, and only one out of ten is in a building higher than three stories. Moreover, apartments make up as large a part of occupied housing in smaller metro areas dominated by state universities as they do in metro areas that are much larger in population.

Buying That Single-Family Home...

Where are the best markets for prospective buyers? You might guess that a consequence of the country's west-by-south population shift would be dramatically inflated home prices in the same direction. But some of the highest prices estimated for 2007 are found in places where homes have always been expensive: Anchorage, Honolulu, New York City and its suburbs in Connecticut and New Jersey, the District of Columbia and its environs, and, for more than three decades, California metro areas. This doesn't mean that the U.S. median $220,000 house can't be found for half that much. It can, in smaller metro areas of Alabama, Indiana, Missouri, and Texas.

One way of figuring how much house you can afford is to use the conservative 20/28 lending requirements set by the Federal National Mortgage Association, a major purchaser of mortgages in the secondary mortgage market. According to this rule, a family making a 20 percent down payment can finance the rest as long as no more than 28 percent of their gross income (income before taxes) covers the annual principal and interest.

For example, at a mortgage rate of 6.0 percent, a family would need a gross income of $60,000 to handle the $1,275 monthly principal and interest payments on that $220,000 median-priced house after a $22,000 down payment.

That's one way of looking at it. A far more conservative way is to recall the long-standing rule of thumb handed down from parents to children which states that, if you buy a house that costs much more than two and a half times your gross income, you're headed for trouble. For example, if your gross annual income is $75,000, the range of mortgages to shop for is $150,000 to $187,500; if your income is $90,000, you can afford a house costing between $180,000 and $225,000.

...And Rebuying it with Property Taxes

During the 1970s, homeowners who banded together to protest confiscatory property taxes likened them to a ransom that they were forced to pay to keep their shelter off the local tax assessor's auction block. Using this analogy, homeowners in Islip, New York, bought their homes back from the town every 22 years, since the then effective tax rate (a tax on the home's full value) was 4.63 percent. Down in Mobile County, Alabama, on the other hand, the "ransom" period was 526 years because of an extremely low effective rate of 0.19 percent. The difference in these figures illustrated the wide variation in property taxes around the country.

Today, local property taxes can vary enormously and be madly confusing to homeowners. In California, two houses on the same block with identical price tags and physical characteristics can have substantially different, yet legally impeccable tax bills if one of them was sold before the approval of Proposition 13 and the other after. In Texas, a home's value can be assessed at different levels at different times of the year by different assessors.

HOME ENERGY REQUIREMENTS

Along with mortgage interest rates, fuel and electricity for the home have been an increasingly expensive major item on the Consumer Price Index. What was once a minor and predictable expense, averaging less than 1 percent of a household's budget 40 years ago, can now approach the cost of medical care or clothing.

There are three reasons for the $1,740 difference between the annual average residential utility bills in Olympia, WA, and Manchester-Nashua, NH: climate, the form of energy used to maintain comfortable temperatures in the house, and the source of this energy.

Counting the Hours

Texans say that their Gulf Coast, from Brownsville to Corpus Christi and beyond that to Beaumont-Port Arthur, is a place where air-conditioning is a necessity like food and water, without which all mankind becomes delirious, withers and dies.

WHERE NOT TO BUY

These metro areas (1) are ranked in the bottom third in *Places Rated's* JOBS chapter, (2) they experienced rapid runups in home price appreciation since 2000, and (3) median home prices are now more than 6.8 times per capita personal income. In other words, they're showing signs the home price bubble is about to burst.

Here, a meteorologist measuring humidity with a psychrometer whenever the temperature climbs over 80 degrees Fahrenheit will count nearly 2,500 hours every year when the instrument's bulb stays wet from moist air. New Delhi records similar numbers, and so does Kinshasa, capital of the Democratic Republic of the Congo. These 2,500-odd hours are the equivalent of more than 200 days per year with uncomfortable, sweaty, 12-hour periods of high humidity.

Among *Places Rated* metro areas, it's over 80 degrees outside an average of 911 hours a year, and ranges from 0 in Anchorage, Alaska, to 4,046 in Yuma in Arizona's Sonoran Desert. The hours were measured by Defense Department building engineers in the 1940s and again in 1978 for a worldwide inventory of military bases, supply depots, and weather stations and are now the official design standard for America's heating, ventilation, and air conditioning (HVAC) contractors.

Not only are these A/C hours useful for gauging how hot a given place is over time, they are also a good indicator of how fast the readout on your home's electric meter may be spinning along.

Counting the Days

In 1915, Eugene P. Milener, an engineer with the Gas Company of Baltimore, made a discovery for which he received little recognition outside of his industry: The amount of natural gas needed to keep buildings warm can be accurately predicted for every degree that the outdoor temperature falls below 65 degrees. Natural gas utilities still use this measurement, called a degree day, to estimate consumption patterns among their customers.

A heating-degree day is the number of degrees the daily average temperature is below 65. Heating a home isn't critical when the temperature outdoors is more than 65, but most people fire up the furnace when the outdoor temperature falls below that mark. Thus, a heating-degree day indicates the number of degrees of heating required to keep a house at 65. If the temperature on a winter day is 35, that day has 30 heating-degree days, meaning that 30 degrees of

heating are called for.

The average for annual heating-degree days (total heating-degree days over one year) among *Places Rated* metro areas is 4,497, ranging from 0 in Honolulu, Hawaii, to 13,980 in Fairbanks, Alaska. The number of annual degree days in a given place tells you how cold it gets and also how often you'll need to run a home's heating system to keep the indoors comfortable.

Household Energy Geography

In the early 1950s, the rumbling of coal trucks along their delivery routes was a familiar urban street sound. Three-dollar-a-ton black anthracite was the dominant home heating fuel everywhere east of the Mississippi except for Florida and New England. The blue flame of piped-in natural gas, the major heating fuel today, was just starting to burn in new refrigerators, stoves, clothes dryers, and in furnaces in new homes. Electric utilities were just beginning to encourage construction of total-electric homes.

Today, coal has virtually disappeared from the home energy scene. In spite of the heavy marketing of airtight coal stoves as an auxiliary means of heating houses, the number of homes burning this fuel declined by more than one million over the past decade. The major options now, from most expensive to least, are electric power, residual fuel oil or kerosene, and piped-in natural gas. And, in some timber country metro areas, there's wood.

• *Electricity.* Electric homes were so rare in 1940 that Census Bureau statisticians didn't bother to tally usage. In 1950, the only place where most of the homes were all-electric was the small desert town of Las Vegas, seat of Nevada's Clark County. The power there was the cheapest in the country, because it was generated by falling water at the new Boulder Canyon hydroelectric project some 25 miles southeast. It still is cheap, relative to nuclear-generated or fossil fuel–generated power that homeowners pay for elsewhere in the country. So is the power that heats and lights homes in the Pacific Northwest and in certain Alabama and Tennessee metro areas close to TVA projects.

Although most American homes are heated with natural gas, electricity is gaining fast. The reason: It costs much less to wire a new house for electric resistance heat than to install a gas or oil furnace with piping and sheet-metal hot-air conduits. All-electric homes now predominate in 113 of the 379 metro areas.

• *Oil and Kerosene.* Fuel oil has had a roller coaster ride from 1940 to 2007. It, like gas, was used by only 10 percent of American homes in 1940. By 1960, it had risen to 33 percent. Then, it has declined ever since. You won't find the price varying greatly by location, but you will find these distillates of imported crude to be the most common heating fuel in 61 metro areas, most of them in New England and Mid-Atlantic states.

• *Natural Gas.* In 237 metro areas, the major source for heating a house is a by-product of oil drilling that for many years flamed at the wellhead for lack of a market. Natural gas, a fossil fuel, meant inexpensive heat for most householders before the 1990s, mainly because the federal government has regulated its interstate price.

Natural gas has never been cheap to homeowners at the end of the continental transmission lines that begin in Louisiana and Texas gas fields, however. This explains why natural gas isn't preferred in New England or Mid-Atlantic homes, where oil is the least expensive of fuels; or in the Pacific Northwest, where hydroelectric power costs the least.

• *Wood.* Anyone who feeds a wood stove has heard the proverb about this fuel: it warms you twice, first when you cut and stack it, and second when you watch it burn. From Rocky Mountain pinion to hickory and ash from Ozark forests, it is the main heating fuel in 1.8 million homes. Among metro areas today, only a small percentage of homes—10 percent or so— in Maine, Oregon, and Vermont burn wood exclusively.

JUDGING: HOUSING

Are homes more expensive in Danbury, Dayton, or Duluth? When it comes to paying property taxes, might you be better off in Birmingham than Boston? Would relocation in February to the Texas Gulf haunt you in August when you realize how much air-conditioning costs?

To help you answer these questions, *Places Rated* tallies the three biggest monthly expenses of owning the single-family Starter Home: utility bills, local property taxes, and mortgage payments. The sum of these items is the amount you can expect to pay each month for the basics of homeownership. The sum is also used to derive each metro area's score. As

in Crime, the lower the score the better.

SCORING: HOUSING

Each metro area starts with a base score of zero. Points are added according to the following indicators:

1. Utilities. Monthly utility bills are estimated for a home using natural gas for space heating, water heating, and cooking, because this fuel is available everywhere and is the most frequently chosen in most of the metro areas. Also included are electricity bills for lighting, running appliances, and air-conditioning based on typical 750 kilowatt-hours per month of consumption. In metro areas where total-electric homes predominate, utility bills are estimates of annual residential all-electric costs.

2. Property taxes. Property taxes are calculated by multiplying the local value of a starter house by the state's average effective tax rate for residential property. For example, Ann Arbor's $341 monthly tax bill is derived from a Starter Home value of $222,400 multiplied by Michigan's effective tax rate of 1.838 percent.

3. Mortgage. Monthly mortgage payments are based on a 6 percent, 25-year loan on the Starter House, after a ten percent down payment.

Scoring Examples
A small metro area in the rice-growing Arkansas Delta and a gentrifying Connecticut county just outside New York City illustrate how places are rated for Housing.

Almost the Priciest: Bridgeport-Stamford-Norwalk, CT
Does anyone recall J. Blandings? Cary Grant played him in the 1948 movie "Mr. Blandings Builds His Dream House." The film tells the story of a New York City couple, tired of living in a crowded apartment, who one day discover a rambling old house for sale on 50 bucolic acres in nearby Connecticut. They fall in love with the place and take a $10,000 plunge to join the suburban gentry.

The ensuing comedy of Mr. Blandings and his trials with country carpenters, stonemasons, and well-diggers may be familiar to homeowners today who buy a fixer-upper and then get into money trouble. At the end of the film, Mr. Blandings adds up what he spent to "put the place in shape" and learns that he is out more than $50,000. He might have been better off with a new Cape Cod-style home then being built on the potato patches of Long Island in a place called Levittown.

Or would he? Today, 50 residential-zoned acres close to New York City would be worth millions and a restored farmhouse in a good location would bring millions all by itself. Nowhere is this more apparent than in Fairfield County (Bridgeport-Stamford-Norwalk), a metro area that mixes white-collar Greenwich, Darien, and New Canaan with blue-collar Bridgeport and Norwalk.

Starter homes here go for close to $600,000. Utilities average $200 a month, property taxes $916, and mortgage payments another $3,293, all of which adds up to a rather steep $4,409 per month or $52,916 per year. Just eleven metro areas, all in California, show higher costs for basic homeownership than Bridgeport-Stamford-Norwalk, CT.

The Cheapest: Pine Bluff, AR
In contrast to Bridgeport-Stamford-Norwalk, the lowest basic homeowner costs in metropolitan America are found some 1,135 miles west southwest in the environs of Pine Bluff, a small city in Arkansas some thirty minutes south of Little Rock. As in Bridgeport-Stamford-Norwalk, many of the homes were built before World War II, and most are owned by the people living in them.

But unlike the pricey suburban Connecticut, Pine Bluff can boast a median market value for homes of $66,500. The housing stock here is old (median age: 35 years) for a Sun Belt location. Existing houses range from nineteenth-century farmhouses in rural sections to some fine Victorian homes near downtown and newer brick-and-frame bi-levels and ranches out on Dollarway Road to suburban White Hall. Estimated utility bills in Pine Bluff amount to $127 a month, property taxes $63, and mortgage payments $386, the lowest homeowner costs among *Places Rated*'s 379 metro areas.

PLACE PROFILES: HOUSING

The pages following are snapshots of housing costs in America's 379 metro areas. *Home Prices*, the first entry under the metro area's name, shows the percent increase in home prices from 1st quarter

www.placesrated.com

Housing rankings, from 1 to 379, are in the *Place Profiles* section coming next. Housing scores, from 100.0 to 0.0, are in *Putting It All Together* at the end of the book. Readers can print out homeowner cost rankings and scores, from #1 Pine Bluff, AR (score: 100.0) to #379 San Francisco-San Mateo-Redwood City, CA (score: 0.0), by visiting *Places Rated's* website.

Here are the top twenty:

Rank	Score
1. Pine Bluff, AR	100.0
2. Brownsville-Harlingen, TX	99.8
3. McAllen-Edinburg-Mission, TX	99.5
4. Texarkana, TX-Texarkana, AR	99.3
5. Danville, IL	99.0
6. Odessa, TX	98.7
7. Fort Smith, AR-OK	98.5
8. Danville, VA	98.2
9. Abilene, TX	97.9
10. Monroe, LA	97.7
11. Weirton-Steubenville, WV-OH	97.4
12. Victoria, TX	97.1
13. Florence-Muscle Shoals, AL	96.9
14. Gadsden, AL	96.6
15. Decatur, AL	96.3
16. Decatur, IL	96.1
17. Wheeling, WV-OH	95.8
18. Joplin, MO	95.6
19. Alexandria, LA	95.3
20. Albany, GA	95.0

At *www.placesrated.com*, you'll also find more information on current price changes, rates of new home construction, property tax changes, and rental costs.

2000 to the 4th quarter of 2006. "Starter" prices are medians, marking a point where half of all homes in the area are cheaper and half are more expensive. "Move Up" prices are the 75th percentile, marking a point where three out of four homes in the area are cheaper. "Elite" prices are the 90th percentile; just one of ten homes in the area costs more than this figure.

Under *Energy Requirements:* (1) the area's number of degree days, or annual number of degrees the temperature falls below 65° F, (2) the annual hours the outside temperature exceeds 80° F - the air conditioning design standards for the area, and (3) the major heating source—fuel oil, utility gas, or all-electric—prevailing in the area.

Monthly Costs are (1) mortgage payments you would make on the Starter Home based on a 25-year loan at 6 percent interest, after a ten percent down payment, (2) monthly average utility bills, and (3) monthly property taxes on the Starter Home's value.

Rental Options compare renter-occupied apartments and renter-occupied houses and duplexes against the U.S. metro area average of 100. Finding a one-bedroom apartment to rent in Farmington, NM, for instance, with an apartment index of 24 might be more difficult than finding one in New York City with an apartment index of 253. Rent figures show the range between the low median monthly rent and the higher estimated fair market rent for a one-bedroom apartment,

Figures are derived from these sources: American Society of Heating, Refrigeration, and Air Conditioning Engineers, *ASHRAE Handbook* (www.ashrae.org); National Association of Realtors, *Existing Homes Sales Rise in October, Market Stabilizing* (www.realtor.org); U.S. Department of Commerce, Bureau of the Census, *2005 American Community Survey* (www. census.gov), and National Climatic Data Center, *1971-2000 U.S. Climate Normals* (www.ncdc. noaa.gov); U.S. Department of Energy, Energy Information Administration, various reports (www.eia.doe.gov); U.S. Department of Housing and Urban Development, Office of Federal Housing Enterprise Oversight, *Housing Price Index 3rd Quarter* 2006 (www.ofhoe.gov), and Office of the Secretary, *2007 Fair Market Rents for the Housing Choice Voucher Program.*

✓ Abilene, TX
Places Rated Rank: 9

Home Prices
36%
Starter: $70,300
Move Up: $109,800
Elite: $139,200

Energy Requirements
Heat: 2,659 degree days
A/C: 1,842 hours
Source: Utility gas, Electricity

Monthly Costs
Mortgage: $408
Utilities: $157
Taxes: $166

Rental Options US = 100
Apartments: 47
Houses/Duplexes: 135
Rent: $440 to $540

Akron, OH
Places Rated Rank: 188

Home Prices
30%
Starter: $144,000
Move Up: $201,300
Elite: $255,000

Energy Requirements
Heat: 6,154 degree days
A/C: 324 hours
Source: Utility gas, Electricity

Monthly Costs
Mortgage: $835
Utilities: $174
Taxes: $216

Rental Options US = 100
Apartments: 74
Houses/Duplexes: 78
Rent: $550 to $680

✓ Albany, GA
Places Rated Rank: 20

Home Prices
38%
Starter: $95,400
Move Up: $153,800
Elite: $194,800

Energy Requirements
Heat: 2,108 degree days
A/C: 1,632 hours
Source: All-Electric

Monthly Costs
Mortgage: $553
Utilities: $107
Taxes: $115

Rental Options US = 100
Apartments: 47
Houses/Duplexes: 161
Rent: $400 to $510

Albany-Schenectady-Troy, NY
Places Rated Rank: 257

Home Prices
89%
Starter: $181,800
Move Up: $262,500
Elite: $332,600

Energy Requirements
Heat: 6,860 degree days
A/C: 247 hours
Source: Utility gas, Electricity

Monthly Costs
Mortgage: $1,054
Utilities: $211
Taxes: $259

Rental Options US = 100
Apartments: 73
Houses/Duplexes: 87
Rent: $590 to $720

Albuquerque, NM
Places Rated Rank: 210

Home Prices
61%
Starter: $184,800
Move Up: $260,800
Elite: $330,400

Energy Requirements
Heat: 4,281 degree days
A/C: 838 hours
Source: Utility gas, Electricity

Monthly Costs
Mortgage: $1,072
Utilities: $111
Taxes: $138

Rental Options US = 100
Apartments: 84
Houses/Duplexes: 72
Rent: $560 to $710

✓ Alexandria, LA
Places Rated Rank: 19

Home Prices
45%
Starter: $95,400
Move Up: $150,500
Elite: $190,700

Energy Requirements
Heat: 1,908 degree days
A/C: 1,976 hours
Source: All-Electric

Monthly Costs
Mortgage: $553
Utilities: $123
Taxes: $94

Rental Options US = 100
Apartments: 52
Houses/Duplexes: 97
Rent: $380 to $510

Allentown-Bethlehem-Easton, PA-NJ
Places Rated Rank: 277

Home Prices
90%
Starter: $216,700
Move Up: $336,500
Elite: $426,300

Energy Requirements
Heat: 5,830 degree days
A/C: 454 hours
Source: Fuel oil, Electricity

Monthly Costs
Mortgage: $1,257
Utilities: $177
Taxes: $322

Rental Options US = 100
Apartments: 67
Houses/Duplexes: 70
Rent: $620 to $760

Altoona, PA
Places Rated Rank: 51

Home Prices
42%
Starter: $93,700
Move Up: $140,900
Elite: $178,500

Energy Requirements
Heat: 5,952 degree days
A/C: 271 hours
Source: Utility gas, Electricity

Monthly Costs
Mortgage: $543
Utilities: $185
Taxes: $152

Rental Options US = 100
Apartments: 50
Houses/Duplexes: 94
Rent: $400 to $480

Amarillo, TX
Places Rated Rank: 116

Home Prices
35%
Starter: $101,200
Move Up: $150,900
Elite: $191,200

Energy Requirements
Heat: 4,318 degree days
A/C: 890 hours
Source: Utility gas, Electricity

Monthly Costs
Mortgage: $587
Utilities: $183
Taxes: $238

Rental Options US = 100
Apartments: 73
Houses/Duplexes: 95
Rent: $460 to $570

Ames, IA
Places Rated Rank: 234

Home Prices
37%
Starter: $155,200
Move Up: $209,200
Elite: $265,000

Energy Requirements
Heat: 6,791 degree days
A/C: 464 hours
Source: Utility gas, Electricity

Monthly Costs
Mortgage: $900
Utilities: $178
Taxes: $328

Rental Options US = 100
Apartments: 162
Houses/Duplexes: 74
Rent: $570 to $720

Anchorage, AK
Places Rated Rank: 302

Home Prices
81%
Starter: $269,700
Move Up: $361,700
Elite: $458,200

Energy Requirements
Heat: 10,470 degree days
A/C: 0 hours
Source: Utility gas, Electricity

Monthly Costs
Mortgage: $1,564
Utilities: $160
Taxes: $368

Rental Options US = 100
Apartments: 89
Houses/Duplexes: 75
Rent: $800 to $1,020

Housing

Anderson, IN

Home Prices

Starter: $96,000
Move Up: $132,400
19%   Elite: $167,700

Energy Requirements
Heat: 5,807 degree days
A/C: 491 hours
Source: Utility gas, Electricity

Monthly Costs

Mortgage: $557
Utilities: $159
Taxes: $160

Rental Options US = 100
Apartments: 35
Houses/Duplexes: 90
Rent: $470 to $540

Anderson, SC
Places Rated Rank: 75

Home Prices

Starter: $112,000
Move Up: $176,000
37%   Elite: $222,900

Energy Requirements
Heat: 3,360 degree days
A/C: 994 hours
Source: All-Electric

Monthly Costs

Mortgage: $649
Utilities: $120
Taxes: $163

Rental Options US = 100
Apartments: 32
Houses/Duplexes: 87
Rent: $430 to $550

Ann Arbor, MI
Places Rated Rank: 279

Home Prices

Starter: $222,400
Move Up: $341,700
46%   Elite: $432,900

Energy Requirements
Heat: 6,503 degree days
A/C: 343 hours
Source: Utility gas, Electricity

Monthly Costs

Mortgage: $1,290
Utilities: $139
Taxes: $341

Rental Options US = 100

Apartments: 149
Houses/Duplexes: 50
Rent: $740 to $920

✓ Anniston-Oxford, AL
Places Rated Rank: 24

Home Prices

Starter: $97,800
Move Up: $154,800
51%   Elite: $196,100

Energy Requirements
Heat: 2,763 degree days
A/C: 1,283 hours
Source: Utility gas, Electricity

Monthly Costs
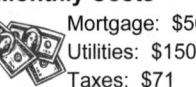
Mortgage: $567
Utilities: $150
Taxes: $71

Rental Options US = 100

Apartments: 47
Houses/Duplexes: 77
Rent: $370 to $490

Appleton, WI
Places Rated Rank: 204

Home Prices

Starter: $146,300
Move Up: $194,200
36%   Elite: $246,100

Energy Requirements
Heat: 7,639 degree days
A/C: 295 hours
Source: Utility gas, Electricity

Monthly Costs
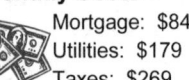
Mortgage: $848
Utilities: $179
Taxes: $269

Rental Options US = 100

Apartments: 73
Houses/Duplexes: 53
Rent: $520 to $610

Asheville, NC
Places Rated Rank: 231

Home Prices

Starter: $186,100
Move Up: $279,300
82%   Elite: $353,800

Energy Requirements
Heat: 4,326 degree days
A/C: 392 hours
Source: All-Electric

Monthly Costs
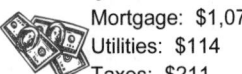
Mortgage: $1,079
Utilities: $114
Taxes: $211

Rental Options US = 100

Apartments: 40
Houses/Duplexes: 82
Rent: $500 to $670

Athens-Clarke County, GA
Places Rated Rank: 166

Home Prices

Starter: $148,100
Move Up: $213,200
45%   Elite: $270,100

Energy Requirements
Heat: 2,861 degree days
A/C: 1,226 hours
Source: All-Electric

Monthly Costs

Mortgage: $859
Utilities: $107
Taxes: $178

Rental Options US = 100

Apartments: 91
Houses/Duplexes: 117
Rent: $530 to $690

Atlanta-Sandy Springs-Marietta, GA
Places Rated Rank: 249

Home Prices

Starter: $191,800
Move Up: $296,300
50%   Elite: $375,400

Energy Requirements
Heat: 2,827 degree days
A/C: 1,240 hours
Source: Utility gas, Electricity

Monthly Costs

Mortgage: $1,112
Utilities: $150
Taxes: $231

Rental Options US = 100

Apartments: 105
Houses/Duplexes: 67
Rent: $680 to $830

Atlantic City, NJ
Places Rated Rank: 321

Home Prices

Starter: $301,300
Move Up: $447,800
153%   Elite: $567,300

Energy Requirements
Heat: 5,113 degree days
A/C: 551 hours
Source: Utility gas, Electricity

Monthly Costs

Mortgage: $1,747
Utilities: $160
Taxes: $407

Rental Options US = 100
Apartments: 94
Houses/Duplexes: 78
Rent: $750 to $890

Auburn-Opelika, AL
Places Rated Rank: 86

Home Prices

Starter: $124,600
Move Up: $187,700
55%   Elite: $237,900

Energy Requirements
Heat: 2,507 degree days
A/C: 1,345 hours
Source: Utility gas, Electricity

Monthly Costs

Mortgage: $723
Utilities: $145
Taxes: $91

Rental Options US = 100

Apartments: 83
Houses/Duplexes: 102
Rent: $440 to $630

Augusta-Richmond County, GA-SC
Places Rated Rank: 72

Home Prices

Starter: $114,000
Move Up: $184,900
45%   Elite: $234,300

Energy Requirements
Heat: 2,525 degree days
A/C: 1,440 hours
Source: All-Electric

Monthly Costs

Mortgage: $661
Utilities: $113
Taxes: $151

Rental Options US = 100

Apartments: 45
Houses/Duplexes: 95
Rent: $470 to $590

Austin-Round Rock, TX

Home Prices

Starter: $183,100
Move Up: $266,600
46% Elite: $337,700

Energy Requirements
Heat: 1,648 degree days
A/C: 2,330 hours
Source: All-Electric

Monthly Costs

Mortgage: $1,062
Utilities: $137
Taxes: $431

Rental Options US = 100

Apartments: 143
Houses/Duplexes: 72
Rent: $630 to $790

Bakersfield, CA
Places Rated Rank: 301

Home Prices
Starter: $316,500
Move Up: $482,100
172% Elite: $610,700

Energy Requirements
Heat: 2,120 degree days
A/C: 1,775 hours
Source: Utility gas, Electricity

Monthly Costs
Mortgage: $1,835
Utilities: $104
Taxes: $146

Rental Options US = 100
Apartments: 45
Houses/Duplexes: 135
Rent: $560 to $720

Baltimore-Towson, MD
Places Rated Rank: 327

Home Prices
Starter: $327,400
Move Up: $537,400
134% Elite: $680,800

Energy Requirements
Heat: 3,807 degree days
A/C: 1,286 hours
Source: Utility gas, Electricity

Monthly Costs
Mortgage: $1,898
Utilities: $158
Taxes: $307

Rental Options US = 100
Apartments: 97
Houses/Duplexes: 77
Rent: $690 to $910

Bangor, ME
Places Rated Rank: 184

Home Prices
Starter: $125,500
Move Up: $185,300
76% Elite: $234,800

Energy Requirements
Heat: 7,676 degree days
A/C: 102 hours
Source: Fuel oil, Electricity

Monthly Costs
Mortgage: $728
Utilities: $221
Taxes: $262

Rental Options US = 100
Apartments: 63
Houses/Duplexes: 57
Rent: $510 to $630

Barnstable Town, MA
Places Rated Rank: 354

Home Prices
Starter: $460,100
Move Up: $661,100
170% Elite: $837,400

Energy Requirements
Heat: 5,931 degree days
A/C: 64 hours
Source: Utility gas, Electricity

Monthly Costs
Mortgage: $2,668
Utilities: $190
Taxes: $399

Rental Options US = 100
Apartments: 24
Houses/Duplexes: 81
Rent: $890 to $1,140

Baton Rouge, LA
Places Rated Rank: 133

Home Prices

Starter: $136,500
Move Up: $204,900
48% Elite: $259,500

Energy Requirements
Heat: 1,689 degree days
A/C: 1,966 hours
Source: All-Electric

Monthly Costs
Mortgage: $792
Utilities: $123
Taxes: $134

Rental Options US = 100

Apartments: 68
Houses/Duplexes: 74
Rent: $470 to $610

Battle Creek, MI
Places Rated Rank: 98

Home Prices

Starter: $113,600
Move Up: $168,900
45% Elite: $214,000

Energy Requirements
Heat: 6,742 degree days
A/C: 264 hours
Source: Utility gas, Electricity

Monthly Costs
Mortgage: $659
Utilities: $142
Taxes: $174

Rental Options US = 100

Apartments: 67
Houses/Duplexes: 61
Rent: $460 to $560

Bay City, MI
Places Rated Rank: 78

Home Prices

Starter: $108,400
Move Up: $155,400
43% Elite: $196,900

Energy Requirements
Heat: 6,645 degree days
A/C: 350 hours
Source: Utility gas, Electricity

Monthly Costs

Mortgage: $629
Utilities: $140
Taxes: $166

Rental Options US = 100

Apartments: 37
Houses/Duplexes: 59
Rent: $440 to $560

✓ Beaumont-Port Arthur, TX
Places Rated Rank: 31

Home Prices
Starter: $81,900
Move Up: $129,900
35% Elite: $164,600

Energy Requirements
Heat: 1,447 degree days
A/C: 2,120 hours
Source: All-Electric

Monthly Costs

Mortgage: $475
Utilities: $137
Taxes: $193

Rental Options US = 100

Apartments: 62
Houses/Duplexes: 102
Rent: $420 to $540

Bellingham, WA
Places Rated Rank: 322

Home Prices

Starter: $322,600
Move Up: $486,100
109% Elite: $615,800

Energy Requirements
Heat: 5,400 degree days
A/C: 6 hours
Source: Utility gas, Electricity

Monthly Costs

Mortgage: $1,871
Utilities: $146
Taxes: $304

Rental Options US = 100

Apartments: 94
Houses/Duplexes: 102
Rent: $650 to $800

Bend, OR
Places Rated Rank: 342

Home Prices
Starter: $415,600
Move Up: $656,700
154% Elite: $831,900

Energy Requirements
Heat: 7,042 degree days
A/C: 43 hours
Source: All-Electric

Monthly Costs

Mortgage: $2,410
Utilities: $85
Taxes: $413

Rental Options US = 100

Apartments: 44
Houses/Duplexes: 111
Rent: $690 to $840

Bethesda-Gaithersburg-Frederick, MD
Places Rated Rank: 361

Home Prices
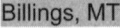
Starter: $565,800
Move Up: $834,200
147% Elite: $1,056,800

Energy Requirements
Heat: 4,430 degree days
A/C: 804 hours
Source: Utility gas, Electricity

Monthly Costs

Mortgage: $3,281
Utilities: $169
Taxes: $530

Rental Options US = 100
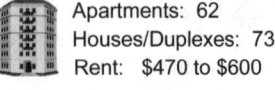
Apartments: 124
Houses/Duplexes: 47
Rent: $1,080 to $1,350

Billings, MT
Places Rated Rank: 202

Home Prices
Starter: $153,100
Move Up: $215,300
68% Elite: $272,700

Energy Requirements
Heat: 7,006 degree days
A/C: 307 hours
Source: Utility gas, Electricity

Monthly Costs
Mortgage: $888
Utilities: $154
Taxes: $249

Rental Options US = 100
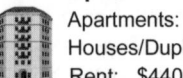
Apartments: 62
Houses/Duplexes: 73
Rent: $470 to $600

Binghamton, NY
Places Rated Rank: 69

Home Prices
Starter: $97,300
Move Up: $144,100
52% Elite: $182,600

Energy Requirements
Heat: 7,237 degree days
A/C: 157 hours
Source: Utility gas, Electricity

Monthly Costs
Mortgage: $564
Utilities: $218
Taxes: $138

Rental Options US = 100

Apartments: 57
Houses/Duplexes: 81
Rent: $440 to $530

Birmingham-Hoover, AL
Places Rated Rank: 117

Home Prices
Starter: $131,800
Move Up: $212,900
50% Elite: $269,800

Energy Requirements
Heat: 2,823 degree days
A/C: 1,321 hours
Source: Utility gas, Electricity

Monthly Costs
Mortgage: $764
Utilities: $151
Taxes: $96

Rental Options US = 100
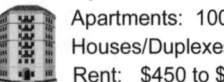
Apartments: 80
Houses/Duplexes: 64
Rent: $480 to $650

Bismarck, ND
Places Rated Rank: 169

Home Prices

Starter: $122,500
Move Up: $177,800
54% Elite: $225,200

Energy Requirements
Heat: 8,802 degree days
A/C: 234 hours
Source: Utility gas, Electricity

Monthly Costs

Mortgage: $710
Utilities: $194
Taxes: $250

Rental Options US = 100
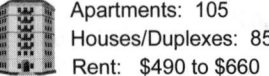
Apartments: 100
Houses/Duplexes: 42
Rent: $450 to $560

Blacksburg-Christiansburg-Radford, VA
Places Rated Rank: 126

Home Prices

Starter: $133,700
Move Up: $199,800
65% Elite: $253,200

Energy Requirements
Heat: 5,559 degree days
A/C: 216 hours
Source: All-Electric

Monthly Costs

Mortgage: $775
Utilities: $114
Taxes: $144

Rental Options US = 100
Apartments: 105
Houses/Duplexes: 85
Rent: $490 to $660

Bloomington, IN
Places Rated Rank: 122

Home Prices

Starter: $116,800
Move Up: $173,800
39% Elite: $220,200

Energy Requirements
Heat: 5,348 degree days
A/C: 606 hours
Source: Utility gas, Electricity

Monthly Costs
Mortgage: $677
Utilities: $152
Taxes: $194

Rental Options US = 100
Apartments: 118
Houses/Duplexes: 73
Rent: $520 to $650

Bloomington-Normal, IL
Places Rated Rank: 183

Home Prices

Starter: $143,200
Move Up: $190,100
29% Elite: $240,900

Energy Requirements
Heat: 6,190 degree days
A/C: 601 hours
Source: Utility gas, Electricity

Monthly Costs
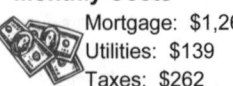
Mortgage: $830
Utilities: $151
Taxes: $225

Rental Options US = 100

Apartments: 92
Houses/Duplexes: 65
Rent: $550 to $700

Boise City-Nampa, ID
Places Rated Rank: 269

Home Prices

Starter: $217,600
Move Up: $323,800
86% Elite: $410,200

Energy Requirements
Heat: 5,727 degree days
A/C: 463 hours
Source: Utility gas, Electricity

Monthly Costs

Mortgage: $1,262
Utilities: $139
Taxes: $262

Rental Options US = 100
Apartments: 61
Houses/Duplexes: 75
Rent: $570 to $720

Boston-Quincy, MA
Places Rated Rank: 349

Home Prices
Starter: $431,900
Move Up: $606,500
128% Elite: $768,300

Energy Requirements
Heat: 5,630 degree days
A/C: 432 hours
Source: Utility gas, Electricity

Monthly Costs
Mortgage: $2,504
Utilities: $184
Taxes: $375

Rental Options US = 100
Apartments: 121
Houses/Duplexes: 63
Rent: $960 to $1,260

Boulder, CO
Places Rated Rank: 334

Home Prices

Starter: $367,800
Move Up: $562,000
56% Elite: $711,900

Energy Requirements
Heat: 5,687 degree days
A/C: 248 hours
Source: Utility gas, Electricity

Monthly Costs
Mortgage: $2,133
Utilities: $128
Taxes: $334

Rental Options US = 100
Apartments: 100
Houses/Duplexes: 86
Rent: $870 to $1,150

Bowling Green, KY
Places Rated Rank: 125

Home Prices
Starter: $132,000
Move Up: $173,600
31% Elite: $220,000

Energy Requirements
Heat: 4,243 degree days
A/C: 947 hours
Source: Utility gas, Electricity

Monthly Costs
Mortgage: $765
Utilities: $138
Taxes: $130

Rental Options US = 100
Apartments: 77
Houses/Duplexes: 69
Rent: $440 to $530

Bremerton-Silverdale, WA
Places Rated Rank: 314

Home Prices
Starter: $320,200
Move Up: $492,600
112% Elite: $624,000

Energy Requirements
Heat: 4,994 degree days
A/C: 29 hours
Source: All-Electric

Monthly Costs
Mortgage: $1,857
Utilities: $79
Taxes: $302

Rental Options US = 100
Apartments: 84
Houses/Duplexes: 67
Rent: $690 to $840

Bridgeport-Stamford-Norwalk, CT
Places Rated Rank: 367

Home Prices
Starter: $567,800
Move Up: $891,900
115% Elite: $1,129,800

Energy Requirements
Heat: 5,466 degree days
A/C: 416 hours
Source: Fuel oil, Electricity

Monthly Costs
Mortgage: $3,293
Utilities: $201
Taxes: $875

Rental Options US = 100
Apartments: 69
Houses/Duplexes: 65
Rent: $920 to $1,280

✓Brownsville-Harlingen, TX
Places Rated Rank: 2

Home Prices
Starter: $59,500
Move Up: $87,800
28% Elite: $111,300

Energy Requirements
Heat: 644 degree days
A/C: 3,085 hours
Source: Utility gas, Electricity

Monthly Costs
Mortgage: $345
Utilities: $124
Taxes: $140

Rental Options US = 100
Apartments: 52
Houses/Duplexes: 107
Rent: $370 to $510

Brunswick, GA
Places Rated Rank: 177

Home Prices
Starter: $152,400
Move Up: $312,500
84% Elite: $395,900

Energy Requirements
Heat: 1,308 degree days
A/C: 2,245 hours
Source: Utility gas, Electricity

Monthly Costs
Mortgage: $884
Utilities: $118
Taxes: $184

Rental Options US = 100
Apartments: 49
Houses/Duplexes: 115
Rent: $450 to $620

Buffalo-Niagara Falls, NY
Places Rated Rank: 92

Home Prices
Starter: $105,400
Move Up: $157,600
37% Elite: $199,600

Energy Requirements
Heat: 6,692 degree days
A/C: 242 hours
Source: Utility gas, Electricity

Monthly Costs
Mortgage: $611
Utilities: $208
Taxes: $150

Rental Options US = 100
Apartments: 58
Houses/Duplexes: 110
Rent: $460 to $590

Burlington, NC
Places Rated Rank: 147

Home Prices
Starter: $131,800
Move Up: $190,800
27% Elite: $241,800

Energy Requirements
Heat: 3,588 degree days
A/C: 996 hours
Source: Utility gas, Electricity

Monthly Costs
Mortgage: $764
Utilities: $163
Taxes: $150

Rental Options US = 100
Apartments: 48
Houses/Duplexes: 96
Rent: $490 to $630

Burlington-South Burlington, VT
Places Rated Rank: 304

Home Prices
Starter: $249,200
Move Up: $348,200
93% Elite: $441,100

Energy Requirements
Heat: 7,665 degree days
A/C: 226 hours
Source: Utility gas, Electricity

Monthly Costs
Mortgage: $1,445
Utilities: $194
Taxes: $464

Rental Options US = 100
Apartments: 66
Houses/Duplexes: 66
Rent: $700 to $900

Cambridge-Newton-Framingham, MA
Places Rated Rank: 352

Home Prices
Starter: $451,600
Move Up: $638,500
100% Elite: $808,900

Energy Requirements
Heat: 6,060 degree days
A/C: 306 hours
Source: Utility gas, Electricity

Monthly Costs
Mortgage: $2,619
Utilities: $192
Taxes: $392

Rental Options US = 100
Apartments: 101
Houses/Duplexes: 75
Rent: $980 to $1,330

Camden, NJ
Places Rated Rank: 293

Home Prices
Starter: $260,600
Move Up: $389,100
112% Elite: $492,900

Energy Requirements
Heat: 4,759 degree days
A/C: 794 hours
Source: Utility gas, Electricity

Monthly Costs
Mortgage: $1,511
Utilities: $154
Taxes: $352

Rental Options US = 100
Apartments: 76
Houses/Duplexes: 56
Rent: $710 to $880

Canton-Massillon, OH
Places Rated Rank: 156

Home Prices
Starter: $129,800
Move Up: $176,300
32% Elite: $223,400

Energy Requirements
Heat: 6,154 degree days
A/C: 324 hours
Source: Utility gas, Electricity

Monthly Costs
Mortgage: $753
Utilities: $174
Taxes: $195

Rental Options US = 100
Apartments: 49
Houses/Duplexes: 97
Rent: $450 to $550

Cape Coral-Fort Myers, FL
Places Rated Rank: 337

Home Prices

- Starter: $364,700
- Move Up: $605,800
- **200%** Elite: $767,400

Energy Requirements
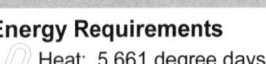
- Heat: 302 degree days
- A/C: 2,938 hours
- Source: All-Electric

Monthly Costs

- Mortgage: $2,115
- Utilities: $128
- Taxes: $487

Rental Options US = 100
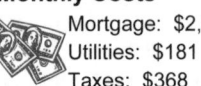
- Apartments: 66
- Houses/Duplexes: 76
- Rent: $740 to $900

Carson City, NV
Places Rated Rank: 348

Home Prices

- Starter: $433,100
- Move Up: $577,500
- **138%** Elite: $731,500

Energy Requirements
- Heat: 5,661 degree days
- A/C: 163 hours
- Source: Utility gas, Electricity

Monthly Costs

- Mortgage: $2,511
- Utilities: $181
- Taxes: $368

Rental Options US = 100
- Apartments: 98
- Houses/Duplexes: 87
- Rent: $700 to $880

Casper, WY
Places Rated Rank: 240

Home Prices

- Starter: $163,200
- Move Up: $217,100
- **102%** Elite: $275,100

Energy Requirements
- Heat: 7,571 degree days
- A/C: 179 hours
- Source: Utility gas, Electricity

Monthly Costs

- Mortgage: $946
- Utilities: $157
- Taxes: $346

Rental Options US = 100
- Apartments: 45
- Houses/Duplexes: 71
- Rent: $440 to $550

Cedar Rapids, IA
Places Rated Rank: 172

Home Prices

- Starter: $123,600
- Move Up: $178,000
- **29%** Elite: $225,500

Energy Requirements
- Heat: 6,837 degree days
- A/C: 510 hours
- Source: Utility gas, Electricity

Monthly Costs

- Mortgage: $717
- Utilities: $179
- Taxes: $261

Rental Options US = 100
- Apartments: 69
- Houses/Duplexes: 61
- Rent: $470 to $580

Champaign-Urbana, IL
Places Rated Rank: 158

Home Prices

- Starter: $132,300
- Move Up: $184,300
- **49%** Elite: $233,500

Energy Requirements
- Heat: 5,916 degree days
- A/C: 578 hours
- Source: Utility gas, Electricity

Monthly Costs

- Mortgage: $767
- Utilities: $147
- Taxes: $208

Rental Options US = 100
- Apartments: 126
- Houses/Duplexes: 92
- Rent: $550 to $720

✓ Charleston, WV
Places Rated Rank: 36

Home Prices

- Starter: $97,300
- Move Up: $150,500
- **31%** Elite: $190,600

Energy Requirements
- Heat: 4,644 degree days
- A/C: 586 hours
- Source: Utility gas, Electricity

Monthly Costs

- Mortgage: $564
- Utilities: $142
- Taxes: $120

Rental Options US = 100

- Apartments: 30
- Houses/Duplexes: 86
- Rent: $410 to $530

Charleston-North Charleston, SC
Places Rated Rank: 272

Home Prices

- Starter: $217,200
- Move Up: $343,200
- **114%** Elite: $434,800

Energy Requirements
- Heat: 1,755 degree days
- A/C: 1,825 hours
- Source: All-Electric

Monthly Costs

- Mortgage: $1,259
- Utilities: $120
- Taxes: $315

Rental Options US = 100

- Apartments: 79
- Houses/Duplexes: 81
- Rent: $620 to $810

Charlotte-Gastonia-Concord, NC-SC
Places Rated Rank: 222

Home Prices

- Starter: $169,700
- Move Up: $253,900
- **38%** Elite: $321,600

Energy Requirements
- Heat: 3,162 degree days
- A/C: 1,093 hours
- Source: Utility gas, Electricity

Monthly Costs

- Mortgage: $984
- Utilities: $157
- Taxes: $220

Rental Options US = 100

- Apartments: 92
- Houses/Duplexes: 74
- Rent: $570 to $710

Charlottesville, VA
Places Rated Rank: 307

Home Prices

- Starter: $293,800
- Move Up: $468,400
- **120%** Elite: $593,300

Energy Requirements
- Heat: 4,103 degree days
- A/C: 740 hours
- Source: All-Electric

Monthly Costs

- Mortgage: $1,704
- Utilities: $114
- Taxes: $317

Rental Options US = 100

- Apartments: 97
- Houses/Duplexes: 93
- Rent: $700 to $860

Chattanooga, TN-GA
Places Rated Rank: 114

Home Prices
- Starter: $129,400
- Move Up: $186,500
- **52%** Elite: $236,300

Energy Requirements
- Heat: 3,427 degree days
- A/C: 1,092 hours
- Source: All-Electric

Monthly Costs
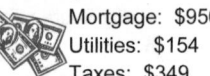
- Mortgage: $750
- Utilities: $106
- Taxes: $145

Rental Options US = 100

- Apartments: 53
- Houses/Duplexes: 89
- Rent: $460 to $600

Cheyenne, WY
Places Rated Rank: 243

Home Prices
- Starter: $164,900
- Move Up: $229,000
- **62%** Elite: $290,200

Energy Requirements
- Heat: 7,388 degree days
- A/C: 83 hours
- Source: Utility gas, Electricity

Monthly Costs
- Mortgage: $956
- Utilities: $154
- Taxes: $349

Rental Options US = 100
- Apartments: 40
- Houses/Duplexes: 60
- Rent: $510 to $630

Chicago-Naperville-Joliet, IL

Home Prices

Starter: $284,500
Move Up: $433,200
79% Elite: $548,800

Energy Requirements
Heat: 6,083 degree days
A/C: 618 hours
Source: Utility gas, Electricity

Monthly Costs

Mortgage: $1,650
Utilities: $150
Taxes: $448

Rental Options US = 100

Apartments: 106
Houses/Duplexes: 55
Rent: $720 to $900

Chico, CA
Places Rated Rank: 319

Home Prices

Starter: $347,400
Move Up: $509,200
166% Elite: $645,100

Energy Requirements
Heat: 2,945 degree days
A/C: 817 hours
Source: Utility gas, Electricity

Monthly Costs

Mortgage: $2,014
Utilities: $116
Taxes: $160

Rental Options US = 100

Apartments: 83
Houses/Duplexes: 113
Rent: $660 to $830

Cincinnati-Middletown, OH-KY-IN
Places Rated Rank: 187

Home Prices

Starter: $149,000
Move Up: $215,900
35% Elite: $273,600

Energy Requirements
Heat: 5,148 degree days
A/C: 605 hours
Source: Utility gas, Electricity

Monthly Costs

Mortgage: $864
Utilities: $153
Taxes: $206

Rental Options US = 100

Apartments: 90
Houses/Duplexes: 69
Rent: $520 to $660

✓ Clarksville, TN-KY
Places Rated Rank: 34

Home Prices

Starter: $105,500
Move Up: $151,100
40% Elite: $191,400

Energy Requirements
Heat: 4,058 degree days
A/C: 1,039 hours
Source: All-Electric

Monthly Costs
Mortgage: $612
Utilities: $94
Taxes: $106

Rental Options US = 100

Apartments: 43
Houses/Duplexes: 122
Rent: $500 to $610

Cleveland, TN
Places Rated Rank: 85

Home Prices

Starter: $124,400
Move Up: $181,800
46% Elite: $230,400

Energy Requirements
Heat: 3,782 degree days
A/C: 835 hours
Source: All-Electric

Monthly Costs
Mortgage: $721
Utilities: $105
Taxes: $129

Rental Options US = 100

Apartments: 27
Houses/Duplexes: 89
Rent: $420 to $510

Cleveland-Elyria-Mentor, OH
Places Rated Rank: 197

Home Prices

Starter: $151,200
Move Up: $214,700
31% Elite: $271,900

Energy Requirements
Heat: 6,121 degree days
A/C: 362 hours
Source: Utility gas, Electricity

Monthly Costs
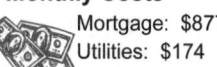
Mortgage: $877
Utilities: $174
Taxes: $227

Rental Options US = 100

Apartments: 93
Houses/Duplexes: 82
Rent: $540 to $680

Coeur d'Alene, ID
Places Rated Rank: 282

Home Prices

Starter: $244,200
Move Up: $341,200
108% Elite: $432,300

Energy Requirements
Heat: 6,540 degree days
A/C: 222 hours
Source: Utility gas, Electricity

Monthly Costs

Mortgage: $1,416
Utilities: $150
Taxes: $294

Rental Options US = 100

Apartments: 46
Houses/Duplexes: 106
Rent: $590 to $740

College Station-Bryan, TX
Places Rated Rank: 131

Home Prices

Starter: $110,700
Move Up: $174,400
36% Elite: $221,000

Energy Requirements
Heat: 1,616 degree days
A/C: 2,291 hours
Source: All-Electric

Monthly Costs

Mortgage: $642
Utilities: $137
Taxes: $261

Rental Options US = 100

Apartments: 112
Houses/Duplexes: 119
Rent: $530 to $670

Colorado Springs, CO
Places Rated Rank: 259

Home Prices
Starter: $211,100
Move Up: $300,000
54% Elite: $380,100

Energy Requirements
Heat: 6,480 degree days
A/C: 162 hours
Source: Utility gas, Electricity

Monthly Costs
Mortgage: $1,224
Utilities: $138
Taxes: $192

Rental Options US = 100

Apartments: 98
Houses/Duplexes: 78
Rent: $650 to $880

Columbia, MO
Places Rated Rank: 159

Home Prices
Starter: $138,900
Move Up: $210,600
40% Elite: $266,800

Energy Requirements
Heat: 5,177 degree days
A/C: 809 hours
Source: Utility gas, Electricity

Monthly Costs

Mortgage: $805
Utilities: $153
Taxes: $166

Rental Options US = 100
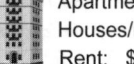
Apartments: 75
Houses/Duplexes: 115
Rent: $500 to $630

Columbia, SC
Places Rated Rank: 141

Home Prices
Starter: $130,700
Move Up: $194,300
44% Elite: $246,200

Energy Requirements
Heat: 2,594 degree days
A/C: 1,487 hours
Source: All-Electric

Monthly Costs

Mortgage: $758
Utilities: $120
Taxes: $190

Rental Options US = 100
Apartments: 69
Houses/Duplexes: 73
Rent: $520 to $640

Housing

Columbus, GA-AL

Home Prices

Starter: $128,600
Move Up: $206,800
54% Elite: $262,000

Energy Requirements
Heat: 2,154 degree days
A/C: 1,690 hours
Source: All-Electric

Monthly Costs
Mortgage: $746
Utilities: $111
Taxes: $124

Rental Options US = 100
Apartments: 96
Houses/Duplexes: 110
Rent: $450 to $590

Columbus, IN
Places Rated Rank: 129

Home Prices

Starter: $118,700
Move Up: $170,000
21% Elite: $215,400

Energy Requirements
Heat: 5,367 degree days
A/C: 641 hours
Source: Utility gas, Electricity

Monthly Costs
Mortgage: $688
Utilities: $153
Taxes: $197

Rental Options US = 100
Apartments: 47
Houses/Duplexes: 84
Rent: $550 to $640

Columbus, OH
Places Rated Rank: 219

Home Prices

Starter: $162,900
Move Up: $232,700
37% Elite: $294,800

Energy Requirements
Heat: 5,492 degree days
A/C: 514 hours
Source: Utility gas, Electricity

Monthly Costs
Mortgage: $945
Utilities: $163
Taxes: $245

Rental Options US = 100
Apartments: 92
Houses/Duplexes: 77
Rent: $560 to $680

Corpus Christi, TX
Places Rated Rank: 74

Home Prices

Starter: $98,000
Move Up: $153,700
54% Elite: $194,800

Energy Requirements
Heat: 950 degree days
A/C: 2,712 hours
Source: Utility gas, Electricity

Monthly Costs
Mortgage: $568
Utilities: $129
Taxes: $231

Rental Options US = 100
Apartments: 87
Houses/Duplexes: 85
Rent: $530 to $670

Corvallis, OR
Places Rated Rank: 281

Home Prices

Starter: $261,300
Move Up: $376,500
59% Elite: $476,900

Energy Requirements
Heat: 4,715 degree days
A/C: 64 hours
Source: All-Electric

Monthly Costs
Mortgage: $1,515
Utilities: $85
Taxes: $260

Rental Options US = 100
Apartments: 126
Houses/Duplexes: 81
Rent: $590 to $740

Cumberland, MD-WV
Places Rated Rank: 61

Home Prices

Starter: $107,700
Move Up: $162,300
68% Elite: $205,600

Energy Requirements
Heat: 5,191 degree days
A/C: 486 hours
Source: Utility gas, Electricity

Monthly Costs
Mortgage: $625
Utilities: $167
Taxes: $117

Rental Options US = 100
Apartments: 42
Houses/Duplexes: 93
Rent: $360 to $430

Dallas-Plano-Irving, TX
Places Rated Rank: 221

Home Prices

Starter: $149,700
Move Up: $219,700
34% Elite: $278,300

Energy Requirements
Heat: 2,219 degree days
A/C: 2,297 hours
Source: All-Electric

Monthly Costs
Mortgage: $868
Utilities: $137
Taxes: $352

Rental Options US = 100
Apartments: 152
Houses/Duplexes: 56
Rent: $630 to $800

Dalton, GA
Places Rated Rank: 71

Home Prices

Starter: $116,600
Move Up: $169,200
54% Elite: $214,300

Energy Requirements
Heat: 3,377 degree days
A/C: 1,109 hours
Source: All-Electric

Monthly Costs
Mortgage: $676
Utilities: $107
Taxes: $141

Rental Options US = 100
Apartments: 39
Houses/Duplexes: 87
Rent: $460 to $550

✓ Danville, IL
Places Rated Rank: 5

Home Prices

Starter: $72,700
Move Up: $108,400
46% Elite: $137,300

Energy Requirements
Heat: 5,555 degree days
A/C: 612 hours
Source: Utility gas, Electricity

Monthly Costs
Mortgage: $422
Utilities: $142
Taxes: $114

Rental Options US = 100
Apartments: 47
Houses/Duplexes: 104
Rent: $380 to $460

✓ Danville, VA
Places Rated Rank: 8

Home Prices

Starter: $89,100
Move Up: $127,900
35% Elite: $162,000

Energy Requirements
Heat: 3,970 degree days
A/C: 938 hours
Source: All-Electric

Monthly Costs
Mortgage: $517
Utilities: $114
Taxes: $96

Rental Options US = 100
Apartments: 36
Houses/Duplexes: 105
Rent: $350 to $460

Davenport-Moline-Rock Island, IA-IL
Places Rated Rank: 127

Home Prices
Starter: $114,200
Move Up: $170,800
40% Elite: $216,400

Energy Requirements
Heat: 6,246 degree days
A/C: 668 hours
Source: Utility gas, Electricity

Monthly Costs
Mortgage: $662
Utilities: $161
Taxes: $210

Rental Options US = 100
Apartments: 63
Houses/Duplexes: 68
Rent: $450 to $550

Dayton, OH

Home Prices

Starter: $127,900
Move Up: $177,900
26% Elite: $225,400

Energy Requirements
Heat: 5,942 degree days
A/C: 406 hours
Source: Utility gas, Electricity

Monthly Costs

Mortgage: $742
Utilities: $171
Taxes: $192

Rental Options US = 100
Apartments: 73
Houses/Duplexes: 84
Rent: $500 to $630

✓ Decatur, AL

Home Prices

Starter: $98,900
Move Up: $148,200
28% Elite: $187,800

Energy Requirements
Heat: 3,236 degree days
A/C: 1,276 hours
Source: All-Electric

Monthly Costs

Mortgage: $573
Utilities: $114
Taxes: $72

Rental Options US = 100

Apartments: 43
Houses/Duplexes: 62
Rent: $390 to $480

✓ Decatur, IL

Home Prices

Starter: $84,000
Move Up: $124,600
29% Elite: $157,900

Energy Requirements
Heat: 5,458 degree days
A/C: 713 hours
Source: Utility gas, Electricity

Monthly Costs

Mortgage: $487
Utilities: $141
Taxes: $132

Rental Options US = 100
Apartments: 68
Houses/Duplexes: 84
Rent: $400 to $520

Deltona-Daytona Beach-Ormond Beach, FL

Home Prices
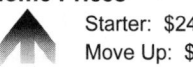
Starter: $246,400
Move Up: $368,100
171% Elite: $466,300

Energy Requirements
Heat: 815 degree days
A/C: 2,083 hours
Source: All-Electric

Monthly Costs
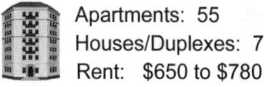
Mortgage: $1,429
Utilities: $128
Taxes: $329

Rental Options US = 100
Apartments: 55
Houses/Duplexes: 71
Rent: $650 to $780

Denver-Aurora, CO

Home Prices
Starter: $251,900
Move Up: $360,200
54% Elite: $456,300

Energy Requirements
Heat: 6,128 degree days
A/C: 356 hours
Source: Utility gas, Electricity

Monthly Costs
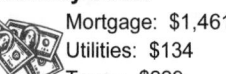
Mortgage: $1,461
Utilities: $134
Taxes: $229

Rental Options US = 100
Apartments: 117
Houses/Duplexes: 63
Rent: $690 to $900

Des Moines-West Des Moines, IA

Home Prices

Starter: $146,000
Move Up: $207,800
43% Elite: $263,300

Energy Requirements
Heat: 6,436 degree days
A/C: 648 hours
Source: Utility gas, Electricity

Monthly Costs

Mortgage: $847
Utilities: $173
Taxes: $308

Rental Options US = 100
Apartments: 92
Houses/Duplexes: 61
Rent: $570 to $690

Detroit-Livonia-Dearborn, MI

Home Prices

Starter: $134,300
Move Up: $193,200
38% Elite: $244,800

Energy Requirements
Heat: 6,422 degree days
A/C: 377 hours
Source: Utility gas, Electricity

Monthly Costs

Mortgage: $779
Utilities: $138
Taxes: $206

Rental Options US = 100
Apartments: 79
Houses/Duplexes: 105
Rent: $550 to $690

✓ Dothan, AL

Home Prices

Starter: $102,000
Move Up: $167,300
48% Elite: $211,900

Energy Requirements
Heat: 2,340 degree days
A/C: 1,342 hours
Source: All-Electric

Monthly Costs

Mortgage: $591
Utilities: $114
Taxes: $74

Rental Options US = 100

Apartments: 29
Houses/Duplexes: 97
Rent: $350 to $460

Dover, DE

Home Prices

Starter: $192,500
Move Up: $281,000
89% Elite: $356,000

Energy Requirements
Heat: 4,212 degree days
A/C: 790 hours
Source: Utility gas, Electricity

Monthly Costs

Mortgage: $1,116
Utilities: $150
Taxes: $115

Rental Options US = 100
Apartments: 44
Houses/Duplexes: 82
Rent: $560 to $740

Dubuque, IA

Home Prices

Starter: $127,200
Move Up: $182,500
41% Elite: $231,200

Energy Requirements
Heat: 7,270 degree days
A/C: 324 hours
Source: Utility gas, Electricity

Monthly Costs

Mortgage: $738
Utilities: $186
Taxes: $269

Rental Options US = 100
Apartments: 50
Houses/Duplexes: 55
Rent: $410 to $510

Duluth, MN-WI

Home Prices
Starter: $137,600
Move Up: $202,100
95% Elite: $256,000

Energy Requirements
Heat: 9,724 degree days
A/C: 61 hours
Source: Utility gas, Electricity

Monthly Costs

Mortgage: $798
Utilities: $204
Taxes: $195

Rental Options US = 100
Apartments: 60
Houses/Duplexes: 63
Rent: $470 to $640

Housing

Durham, NC
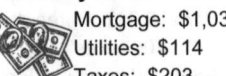 Places Rated Rank: 220

Home Prices

Starter: $179,200
Move Up: $266,500
42% Elite: $337,700

Energy Requirements

Heat: 3,650 degree days
A/C: 996 hours
Source: All-Electric

Monthly Costs
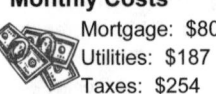
Mortgage: $1,039
Utilities: $114
Taxes: $203

Rental Options US = 100

Apartments: 117
Houses/Duplexes: 82
Rent: $600 to $740

Eau Claire, WI
Places Rated Rank: 190

Home Prices

Starter: $138,300
Move Up: $185,200
51% Elite: $234,700

Energy Requirements
Heat: 8,196 degree days
A/C: 281 hours
Source: Utility gas, Electricity

Monthly Costs
Mortgage: $802
Utilities: $187
Taxes: $254

Rental Options US = 100

Apartments: 66
Houses/Duplexes: 81
Rent: $480 to $580

Edison, NJ
Places Rated Rank: 357

Home Prices

Starter: $450,000
Move Up: $621,900
146% Elite: $787,800

Energy Requirements
Heat: 5,346 degree days
A/C: 426 hours
Source: Utility gas, Electricity

Monthly Costs

Mortgage: $2,609
Utilities: $163
Taxes: $608

Rental Options US = 100
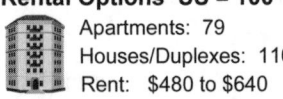
Apartments: 74
Houses/Duplexes: 53
Rent: $920 to $1,170

El Centro, CA
Places Rated Rank: 270

Home Prices

Starter: $252,100
Move Up: $356,900
140% Elite: $452,100

Energy Requirements
Heat: 1,080 degree days
A/C: 3,449 hours
Source: Utility gas, Electricity

Monthly Costs

Mortgage: $1,462
Utilities: $88
Taxes: $116

Rental Options US = 100
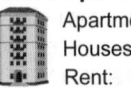
Apartments: 79
Houses/Duplexes: 116
Rent: $480 to $640

Elizabethtown, KY
Places Rated Rank: 99

Home Prices

Starter: $131,500
Move Up: $178,100
48% Elite: $225,600

Energy Requirements
Heat: 4,897 degree days
A/C: 648 hours
Source: All-Electric

Monthly Costs
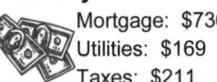
Mortgage: $763
Utilities: $83
Taxes: $129

Rental Options US = 100

Apartments: 40
Houses/Duplexes: 72
Rent: $410 to $540

Elkhart-Goshen, IN
Places Rated Rank: 154

Home Prices

Starter: $127,000
Move Up: $173,900
33% Elite: $220,300

Energy Requirements
Heat: 6,474 degree days
A/C: 350 hours
Source: Utility gas, Electricity

Monthly Costs
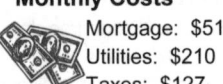
Mortgage: $736
Utilities: $169
Taxes: $211

Rental Options US = 100

Apartments: 63
Houses/Duplexes: 78
Rent: $540 to $640

Elmira, NY
Places Rated Rank: 42

Home Prices

Starter: $89,300
Move Up: $134,400
39% Elite: $170,400

Energy Requirements
Heat: 6,806 degree days
A/C: 191 hours
Source: Utility gas, Electricity

Monthly Costs

Mortgage: $518
Utilities: $210
Taxes: $127

Rental Options US = 100

Apartments: 54
Houses/Duplexes: 105
Rent: $440 to $530

El Paso, TX
Places Rated Rank: 79

Home Prices

Starter: $97,100
Move Up: $135,500
54% Elite: $171,700

Energy Requirements
Heat: 2,543 degree days
A/C: 1,632 hours
Source: Utility gas, Electricity

Monthly Costs
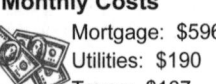
Mortgage: $563
Utilities: $155
Taxes: $229

Rental Options US = 100

Apartments: 97
Houses/Duplexes: 77
Rent: $440 to $560

Erie, PA
Places Rated Rank: 83

Home Prices

Starter: $102,700
Move Up: $154,000
32% Elite: $195,100

Energy Requirements
Heat: 6,243 degree days
A/C: 266 hours
Source: Utility gas, Electricity

Monthly Costs
Mortgage: $596
Utilities: $190
Taxes: $167

Rental Options US = 100

Apartments: 48
Houses/Duplexes: 92
Rent: $430 to $540

Essex County, MA
Places Rated Rank: 341

Home Prices

Starter: $403,700
Move Up: $541,300
112% Elite: $685,600

Energy Requirements
Heat: 6,435 degree days
A/C: 266 hours
Source: Utility gas, Electricity

Monthly Costs
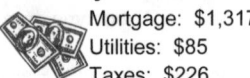
Mortgage: $2,341
Utilities: $199
Taxes: $350

Rental Options US = 100

Apartments: 88
Houses/Duplexes: 70
Rent: $820 to $1,010

Eugene-Springfield, OR
Places Rated Rank: 264

Home Prices
Starter: $227,200
Move Up: $325,000
83% Elite: $411,700

Energy Requirements
Heat: 4,786 degree days
A/C: 79 hours
Source: All-Electric

Monthly Costs
Mortgage: $1,317
Utilities: $85
Taxes: $226

Rental Options US = 100
Apartments: 86
Houses/Duplexes: 109
Rent: $600 to $730

Evansville, IN-KY

Home Prices

33%
Starter: $110,200
Move Up: $168,100
Elite: $212,900

Energy Requirements
Heat: 4,617 degree days
A/C: 943 hours
Source: Utility gas, Electricity

Monthly Costs

Mortgage: $639
Utilities: $143
Taxes: $146

Rental Options US = 100

Apartments: 74
Houses/Duplexes: 64
Rent: $430 to $550

Fairbanks, AK
Places Rated Rank: 260

Home Prices
56%
Starter: $192,400
Move Up: $252,200
Elite: $319,600

Energy Requirements
Heat: 13,980 degree days
A/C: 14 hours
Source: Fuel oil, Electricity

Monthly Costs

Mortgage: $1,116
Utilities: $185
Taxes: $263

Rental Options US = 100

Apartments: 91
Houses/Duplexes: 118
Rent: $760 to $920

Fargo, ND-MN
Places Rated Rank: 143

Home Prices
61%
Starter: $135,300
Move Up: $185,500
Elite: $235,000

Energy Requirements
Heat: 9,092 degree days
A/C: 266 hours
Source: All-Electric

Monthly Costs

Mortgage: $785
Utilities: $78
Taxes: $206

Rental Options US = 100
Apartments: 168
Houses/Duplexes: 42
Rent: $500 to $630

Farmington, NM
Places Rated Rank: 76

Home Prices

87%
Starter: $122,900
Move Up: $203,800
Elite: $258,200

Energy Requirements
Heat: 5,508 degree days
A/C: 412 hours
Source: Utility gas, Electricity

Monthly Costs
Mortgage: $713
Utilities: $128
Taxes: $92

Rental Options US = 100
Apartments: 24
Houses/Duplexes: 70
Rent: $500 to $650

Fayetteville, NC
Places Rated Rank: 45

Home Prices
34%
Starter: $107,700
Move Up: $158,600
Elite: $200,900

Energy Requirements
Heat: 3,097 degree days
A/C: 1,193 hours
Source: All-Electric

Monthly Costs

Mortgage: $625
Utilities: $114
Taxes: $122

Rental Options US = 100
Apartments: 54
Houses/Duplexes: 134
Rent: $560 to $670

Fayetteville-Springdale-Rogers, AR-MO
Places Rated Rank: 185

Home Prices
64%
Starter: $155,600
Move Up: $232,300
Elite: $294,300

Energy Requirements
Heat: 4,166 degree days
A/C: 1,002 hours
Source: Utility gas, Electricity

Monthly Costs

Mortgage: $902
Utilities: $143
Taxes: $167

Rental Options US = 100
Apartments: 69
Houses/Duplexes: 111
Rent: $490 to $610

Flagstaff, AZ-UT
Places Rated Rank: 330

Home Prices

138%
Starter: $330,200
Move Up: $526,900
Elite: $667,400

Energy Requirements
Heat: 6,999 degree days
A/C: 19 hours
Source: Utility gas, Electricity

Monthly Costs

Mortgage: $1,915
Utilities: $209
Taxes: $360

Rental Options US = 100
Apartments: 77
Houses/Duplexes: 100
Rent: $670 to $870

Flint, MI
Places Rated Rank: 148

Home Prices

34%
Starter: $127,400
Move Up: $177,000
Elite: $224,300

Energy Requirements
Heat: 7,005 degree days
A/C: 264 hours
Source: Utility gas, Electricity

Monthly Costs

Mortgage: $739
Utilities: $145
Taxes: $195

Rental Options US = 100

Apartments: 66
Houses/Duplexes: 82
Rent: $460 to $570

✓ Florence, SC
Places Rated Rank: 26

Home Prices

38%
Starter: $92,700
Move Up: $151,500
Elite: $191,900

Energy Requirements
Heat: 2,524 degree days
A/C: 1,446 hours
Source: All-Electric

Monthly Costs

Mortgage: $538
Utilities: $120
Taxes: $135

Rental Options US = 100

Apartments: 32
Houses/Duplexes: 91
Rent: $410 to $500

✓ Florence-Muscle Shoals, AL
Places Rated Rank: 13

Home Prices

31%
Starter: $90,900
Move Up: $147,700
Elite: $187,200

Energy Requirements
Heat: 3,236 degree days
A/C: 1,276 hours
Source: Utility gas, Electricity

Monthly Costs

Mortgage: $527
Utilities: $159
Taxes: $66

Rental Options US = 100

Apartments: 33
Houses/Duplexes: 92
Rent: $330 to $410

Fond du Lac, WI
Places Rated Rank: 192

Home Prices

44%
Starter: $139,700
Move Up: $202,500
Elite: $256,500

Energy Requirements
Heat: 7,534 degree days
A/C: 292 hours
Source: Utility gas, Electricity

Monthly Costs

Mortgage: $810
Utilities: $177
Taxes: $257

Rental Options US = 100

Apartments: 77
Houses/Duplexes: 68
Rent: $480 to $590

Durham, NC–Fond du Lac, WI

Fort Collins-Loveland, CO
Places Rated Rank: 273

Home Prices
Starter: $236,000
Move Up: $329,200
46% Elite: $417,000

Energy Requirements
Heat: 6,238 degree days
A/C: 205 hours
Source: Utility gas, Electricity

Monthly Costs

Mortgage: $1,368
Utilities: $135
Taxes: $214

Rental Options US = 100
Apartments: 83
Houses/Duplexes: 90
Rent: $690 to $910

Fort Lauderdale-Pompano Beach-Deerfield Beach, FL
Places Rated Rank: 340

Home Prices
Starter: $381,400
Move Up: $609,500
203% Elite: $772,100

Energy Requirements
Heat: 178 degree days
A/C: 3,119 hours
Source: All-Electric

Monthly Costs

Mortgage: $2,212
Utilities: $128
Taxes: $510

Rental Options US = 100
Apartments: 107
Houses/Duplexes: 48
Rent: $840 to $1,090

✓ Fort Smith, AR-OK
Places Rated Rank: 7

Home Prices
Starter: $85,200
Move Up: $130,900
39% Elite: $165,800

Energy Requirements
Heat: 3,437 degree days
A/C: 1,418 hours
Source: Utility gas, Electricity

Monthly Costs
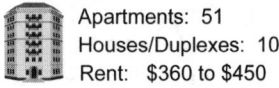
Mortgage: $494
Utilities: $133
Taxes: $84

Rental Options US = 100
Apartments: 51
Houses/Duplexes: 109
Rent: $360 to $450

Fort Walton Beach-Crestview-Destin, FL
Places Rated Rank: 290

Home Prices
Starter: $257,100
Move Up: $425,800
152% Elite: $539,400

Energy Requirements
Heat: 1,920 degree days
A/C: 1,628 hours
Source: Utility gas, Electricity

Monthly Costs
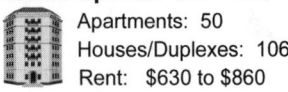
Mortgage: $1,491
Utilities: $157
Taxes: $344

Rental Options US = 100
Apartments: 50
Houses/Duplexes: 106
Rent: $630 to $860

Fort Wayne, IN
Places Rated Rank: 84

Home Prices
Starter: $105,500
Move Up: $160,900
23% Elite: $203,800

Energy Requirements
Heat: 6,205 degree days
A/C: 449 hours
Source: Utility gas, Electricity

Monthly Costs
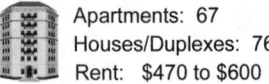
Mortgage: $612
Utilities: $165
Taxes: $175

Rental Options US = 100
Apartments: 67
Houses/Duplexes: 76
Rent: $470 to $600

Fort Worth-Arlington, TX
Places Rated Rank: 170

Home Prices
Starter: $124,800
Move Up: $182,000
33% Elite: $230,600

Energy Requirements
Heat: 2,219 degree days
A/C: 2,297 hours
Source: All-Electric

Monthly Costs
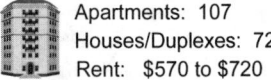
Mortgage: $724
Utilities: $137
Taxes: $294

Rental Options US = 100
Apartments: 107
Houses/Duplexes: 72
Rent: $570 to $720

Fresno, CA
Places Rated Rank: 325

Home Prices
Starter: $355,500
Move Up: $524,700
178% Elite: $664,600

Energy Requirements
Heat: 2,447 degree days
A/C: 1,471 hours
Source: Utility gas, Electricity

Monthly Costs
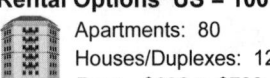
Mortgage: $2,061
Utilities: $109
Taxes: $164

Rental Options US = 100
Apartments: 80
Houses/Duplexes: 120
Rent: $600 to $760

✓ Gadsden, AL
Places Rated Rank: 14

Home Prices
Starter: $91,700
Move Up: $147,800
48% Elite: $187,300

Energy Requirements
Heat: 3,220 degree days
A/C: 1,193 hours
Source: Utility gas, Electricity

Monthly Costs

Mortgage: $532
Utilities: $159
Taxes: $67

Rental Options US = 100
Apartments: 38
Houses/Duplexes: 93
Rent: $350 to $440

Gainesville, FL
Places Rated Rank: 251

Home Prices
Starter: $193,900
Move Up: $297,100
120% Elite: $376,400

Energy Requirements
Heat: 1,143 degree days
A/C: 1,871 hours
Source: All-Electric

Monthly Costs

Mortgage: $1,124
Utilities: $128
Taxes: $259

Rental Options US = 100
Apartments: 137
Houses/Duplexes: 89
Rent: $570 to $830

Gainesville, GA
Places Rated Rank: 214

Home Prices

Starter: $175,100
Move Up: $266,100
52% Elite: $337,100

Energy Requirements
Heat: 3,099 degree days
A/C: 998 hours
Source: All-Electric

Monthly Costs

Mortgage: $1,015
Utilities: $107
Taxes: $211

Rental Options US = 100
Apartments: 48
Houses/Duplexes: 79
Rent: $630 to $740

Gary, IN
Places Rated Rank: 186

Home Prices

Starter: $139,800
Move Up: $195,300
40% Elite: $247,400

Energy Requirements
Heat: 6,497 degree days
A/C: 434 hours
Source: Utility gas, Electricity

Monthly Costs

Mortgage: $811
Utilities: $170
Taxes: $232

Rental Options US = 100

Apartments: 63
Houses/Duplexes: 89
Rent: $560 to $670

Glens Falls, NY
Places Rated Rank: 215

Home Prices
Starter: $153,800
Move Up: $228,900
98% Elite: $290,000

Energy Requirements

Heat: 7,486 degree days
A/C: 142 hours
Source: Fuel oil, Electricity

Monthly Costs
Mortgage: $892
Utilities: $223
Taxes: $219

Rental Options US = 100

Apartments: 43
Houses/Duplexes: 83
Rent: $540 to $630

✓ Goldsboro, NC
Places Rated Rank: 40

Home Prices
Starter: $103,900
Move Up: $158,600
33% Elite: $200,900

Energy Requirements

Heat: 2,771 degree days
A/C: 1,372 hours
Source: All-Electric

Monthly Costs
Mortgage: $602
Utilities: $114
Taxes: $118

Rental Options US = 100
Apartments: 23
Houses/Duplexes: 125
Rent: $380 to $500

Grand Forks, ND-MN
Places Rated Rank: 139

Home Prices
Starter: $118,500
Move Up: $171,800
55% Elite: $217,700

Energy Requirements
Heat: 9,489 degree days
A/C: 184 hours
Source: Utility gas, Electricity

Monthly Costs
Mortgage: $687
Utilities: $199
Taxes: $180

Rental Options US = 100
Apartments: 146
Houses/Duplexes: 57
Rent: $470 to $600

Grand Junction, CO
Places Rated Rank: 255

Home Prices
Starter: $207,600
Move Up: $288,500
85% Elite: $365,500

Energy Requirements
Heat: 5,700 degree days
A/C: 778 hours
Source: Utility gas, Electricity

Monthly Costs
Mortgage: $1,204
Utilities: $128
Taxes: $189

Rental Options US = 100
Apartments: 42
Houses/Duplexes: 87
Rent: $560 to $700

Grand Rapids-Wyoming, MI
Places Rated Rank: 176

Home Prices
Starter: $141,900
Move Up: $195,400
35% Elite: $247,600

Energy Requirements
Heat: 6,896 degree days
A/C: 295 hours
Source: Utility gas, Electricity

Monthly Costs
Mortgage: $823
Utilities: $144
Taxes: $217

Rental Options US = 100

Apartments: 71
Houses/Duplexes: 56
Rent: $540 to $660

Great Falls, MT
Places Rated Rank: 150

Home Prices
Starter: $124,200
Move Up: $164,100
50% Elite: $207,900

Energy Requirements
Heat: 7,828 degree days
A/C: 134 hours
Source: Utility gas, Electricity

Monthly Costs
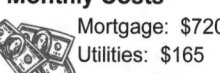
Mortgage: $720
Utilities: $165
Taxes: $202

Rental Options US = 100

Apartments: 59
Houses/Duplexes: 82
Rent: $420 to $530

Greeley, CO
Places Rated Rank: 237

Home Prices
Starter: $194,200
Move Up: $261,900
44% Elite: $331,700

Energy Requirements
Heat: 5,980 degree days
A/C: 403 hours
Source: Utility gas, Electricity

Monthly Costs

Mortgage: $1,126
Utilities: $132
Taxes: $176

Rental Options US = 100

Apartments: 59
Houses/Duplexes: 77
Rent: $590 to $840

Green Bay, WI
Places Rated Rank: 225

Home Prices
Starter: $157,100
Move Up: $211,600
42% Elite: $268,100

Energy Requirements

Heat: 7,963 degree days
A/C: 204 hours
Source: Utility gas, Electricity

Monthly Costs
Mortgage: $911
Utilities: $184
Taxes: $289

Rental Options US = 100

Apartments: 80
Houses/Duplexes: 88
Rent: $540 to $650

Greensboro-High Point, NC
Places Rated Rank: 124

Home Prices
Starter: $132,200
Move Up: $195,600
28% Elite: $247,800

Energy Requirements
Heat: 3,848 degree days
A/C: 832 hours
Source: All-Electric

Monthly Costs

Mortgage: $767
Utilities: $114
Taxes: $150

Rental Options US = 100

Apartments: 79
Houses/Duplexes: 87
Rent: $520 to $640

Greenville, NC
Places Rated Rank: 64

Home Prices
Starter: $115,200
Move Up: $179,200
35% Elite: $227,000

Energy Requirements
Heat: 3,112 degree days
A/C: 1,099 hours
Source: All-Electric

Monthly Costs

Mortgage: $668
Utilities: $114
Taxes: $131

Rental Options US = 100

Apartments: 98
Houses/Duplexes: 112
Rent: $410 to $510

Greenville, SC
Places Rated Rank: 132

Home Prices
Starter: $126,900
Move Up: $188,200
34% Elite: $238,500

Energy Requirements
Heat: 3,272 degree days
A/C: 1,000 hours
Source: All-Electric

Monthly Costs

Mortgage: $736
Utilities: $120
Taxes: $184

Rental Options US = 100

Apartments: 78
Houses/Duplexes: 73
Rent: $460 to $600

Gulfport-Biloxi, MS

Home Prices
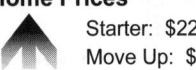
Starter: $136,500
Move Up: $208,400
67% Elite: $264,000

Energy Requirements
Heat: 1,645 degree days
A/C: 1,844 hours
Source: Utility gas, Electricity

Monthly Costs
Mortgage: $792
Utilities: $128
Taxes: $208

Rental Options US = 100

Apartments: 62
Houses/Duplexes: 102
Rent: $510 to $640

Hagerstown-Martinsburg, MD-WV
Places Rated Rank: 263

Home Prices

Starter: $220,600
Move Up: $335,500
125% Elite: $425,000

Energy Requirements
Heat: 5,249 degree days
A/C: 498 hours
Source: All-Electric

Monthly Costs
Mortgage: $1,279
Utilities: $92
Taxes: $240

Rental Options US = 100

Apartments: 62
Houses/Duplexes: 79
Rent: $530 to $670

Hanford-Corcoran, CA
Places Rated Rank: 276

Home Prices

Starter: $261,300
Move Up: $352,000
140% Elite: $445,900

Energy Requirements
Heat: 2,749 degree days
A/C: 1,174 hours
Source: Utility gas, Electricity

Monthly Costs
Mortgage: $1,515
Utilities: $113
Taxes: $121

Rental Options US = 100

Apartments: 71
Houses/Duplexes: 168
Rent: $560 to $710

Harrisburg-Carlisle, PA
Places Rated Rank: 193

Home Prices

Starter: $155,800
Move Up: $217,400
50% Elite: $275,500

Energy Requirements
Heat: 5,201 degree days
A/C: 586 hours
Source: All-Electric

Monthly Costs
Mortgage: $903
Utilities: $95
Taxes: $253

Rental Options US = 100

Apartments: 63
Houses/Duplexes: 81
Rent: $540 to $680

Harrisonburg, VA
Places Rated Rank: 246

Home Prices

Starter: $198,000
Move Up: $281,100
84% Elite: $356,100

Energy Requirements
Heat: 5,447 degree days
A/C: 281 hours
Source: All-Electric

Monthly Costs
Mortgage: $1,148
Utilities: $114
Taxes: $214

Rental Options US = 100

Apartments: 86
Houses/Duplexes: 101
Rent: $510 to $650

Hartford-West Hartford-East Hartford, CT
Places Rated Rank: 309

Home Prices

Starter: $262,300
Move Up: $382,600
82% Elite: $484,700

Energy Requirements
Heat: 6,104 degree days
A/C: 406 hours
Source: Fuel oil, Electricity

Monthly Costs
Mortgage: $1,521
Utilities: $214
Taxes: $404

Rental Options US = 100

Apartments: 91
Houses/Duplexes: 53
Rent: $680 to $850

Hattiesburg, MS
Places Rated Rank: 52

Home Prices

Starter: $102,600
Move Up: $162,400
47% Elite: $205,800

Energy Requirements
Heat: 2,024 degree days
A/C: 1,697 hours
Source: Utility gas, Electricity

Monthly Costs
Mortgage: $595
Utilities: $134
Taxes: $156

Rental Options US = 100

Apartments: 85
Houses/Duplexes: 80
Rent: $430 to $540

Hickory-Lenoir-Morganton, NC
Places Rated Rank: 77

Home Prices

Starter: $118,300
Move Up: $173,900
34% Elite: $220,400

Energy Requirements
Heat: 3,608 degree days
A/C: 835 hours
Source: All-Electric

Monthly Costs
Mortgage: $686
Utilities: $114
Taxes: $134

Rental Options US = 100

Apartments: 27
Houses/Duplexes: 82
Rent: $420 to $500

Hinesville-Fort Stewart, GA
Places Rated Rank: 96

Home Prices

Starter: $121,300
Move Up: $136,200
30% Elite: $172,600

Energy Requirements
Heat: 1,552 degree days
A/C: 1,854 hours
Source: Utility gas, Electricity

Monthly Costs
Mortgage: $703
Utilities: $123
Taxes: $146

Rental Options US = 100

Apartments: 35
Houses/Duplexes: 106
Rent: $550 to $670

Holland-Grand Haven, MI
Places Rated Rank: 211

Home Prices

Starter: $161,900
Move Up: $217,500
32% Elite: $275,600

Energy Requirements
Heat: 6,589 degree days
A/C: 328 hours
Source: Utility gas, Electricity

Monthly Costs
Mortgage: $939
Utilities: $140
Taxes: $248

Rental Options US = 100

Apartments: 30
Houses/Duplexes: 59
Rent: $620 to $700

Honolulu, HI
Places Rated Rank: 359

Home Prices
Starter: $588,600
Move Up: $859,600
102% Elite: $1,088,800

Energy Requirements
Heat: 0 degree days
A/C: 3,320 hours
Source: All-Electric

Monthly Costs
Mortgage: $3,413
Utilities: $147
Taxes: $173

Rental Options US = 100
Apartments: 140
Houses/Duplexes: 93
Rent: $940 to $1,410

Hot Springs, AR

Home Prices

Starter: $136,700
Move Up: $218,300
59% Elite: $276,600

Energy Requirements
Heat: 3,133 degree days
A/C: 1,511 hours
Source: Utility gas, Electricity

Monthly Costs
Mortgage: $793
Utilities: $131
Taxes: $130

Rental Options US = 100
Apartments: 61
Houses/Duplexes: 93
Rent: $420 to $530

Houma-Bayou Cane-Thibodaux, LA
Places Rated Rank: 47

Home Prices

Starter: $110,600
Move Up: $172,700
56% Elite: $218,800

Energy Requirements
Heat: 1,349 degree days
A/C: 2,088 hours
Source: All-Electric

Monthly Costs
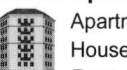
Mortgage: $641
Utilities: $123
Taxes: $109

Rental Options US = 100
Apartments: 29
Houses/Duplexes: 82
Rent: $410 to $510

Houston-Sugar Land-Baytown, TX
Places Rated Rank: 194

Home Prices

Starter: $137,000
Move Up: $203,100
45% Elite: $257,300

Energy Requirements
Heat: 1,174 degree days
A/C: 2,480 hours
Source: All-Electric

Monthly Costs

Mortgage: $794
Utilities: $137
Taxes: $323

Rental Options US = 100
Apartments: 138
Houses/Duplexes: 60
Rent: $580 to $730

✓ Huntington-Ashland, WV-KY-OH
Places Rated Rank: 27

Home Prices
Starter: $92,300
Move Up: $141,600
46% Elite: $179,400

Energy Requirements
Heat: 4,583 degree days
A/C: 650 hours
Source: Utility gas, Electricity

Monthly Costs
Mortgage: $535
Utilities: $144
Taxes: $115

Rental Options US = 100
Apartments: 42
Houses/Duplexes: 89
Rent: $380 to $470

Huntsville, AL
Places Rated Rank: 134

Home Prices
Starter: $143,200
Move Up: $214,700
38% Elite: $272,000

Energy Requirements
Heat: 3,262 degree days
A/C: 1,135 hours
Source: All-Electric

Monthly Costs

Mortgage: $830
Utilities: $114
Taxes: $104

Rental Options US = 100
Apartments: 84
Houses/Duplexes: 68
Rent: $450 to $570

Idaho Falls, ID
Places Rated Rank: 155

Home Prices
Starter: $136,400
Move Up: $199,700
50% Elite: $253,000

Energy Requirements
Heat: 7,604 degree days
A/C: 172 hours
Source: Utility gas, Electricity

Monthly Costs

Mortgage: $791
Utilities: $164
Taxes: $164

Rental Options US = 100
Apartments: 36
Houses/Duplexes: 72
Rent: $460 to $590

Indianapolis-Carmel, IN
Places Rated Rank: 181

Home Prices
Starter: $139,100
Move Up: $198,200
27% Elite: $251,000

Energy Requirements
Heat: 5,521 degree days
A/C: 610 hours
Source: Utility gas, Electricity

Monthly Costs
Mortgage: $807
Utilities: $155
Taxes: $231

Rental Options US = 100
Apartments: 87
Houses/Duplexes: 71
Rent: $550 to $680

Iowa City, IA
Places Rated Rank: 235

Home Prices
Starter: $159,500
Move Up: $234,800
40% Elite: $297,500

Energy Requirements
Heat: 6,052 degree days
A/C: 726 hours
Source: Utility gas, Electricity

Monthly Costs

Mortgage: $925
Utilities: $167
Taxes: $337

Rental Options US = 100
Apartments: 144
Houses/Duplexes: 67
Rent: $570 to $750

Ithaca, NY
Places Rated Rank: 230

Home Prices
Starter: $163,800
Move Up: $233,000
78% Elite: $295,200

Energy Requirements
Heat: 7,182 degree days
A/C: 96 hours
Source: Utility gas, Electricity

Monthly Costs

Mortgage: $950
Utilities: $217
Taxes: $233

Rental Options US = 100
Apartments: 116
Houses/Duplexes: 101
Rent: $680 to $900

Jackson, MI
Places Rated Rank: 161

Home Prices
Starter: $134,500
Move Up: $195,700
42% Elite: $248,000

Energy Requirements
Heat: 6,873 degree days
A/C: 275 hours
Source: Utility gas, Electricity

Monthly Costs

Mortgage: $780
Utilities: $143
Taxes: $206

Rental Options US = 100
Apartments: 44
Houses/Duplexes: 70
Rent: $550 to $650

Jackson, MS
Places Rated Rank: 110

Home Prices

Starter: $116,900
Move Up: $184,700
40% Elite: $234,000

Energy Requirements
Heat: 2,401 degree days
A/C: 1,684 hours
Source: Utility gas, Electricity

Monthly Costs

Mortgage: $678
Utilities: $140
Taxes: $178

Rental Options US = 100
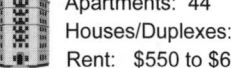
Apartments: 77
Houses/Duplexes: 80
Rent: $520 to $650

Housing

Jackson, TN

Home Prices

25%
- Starter: $111,500
- Move Up: $163,600
- Elite: $207,300

Energy Requirements
- Heat: 3,504 degree days
- A/C: 1,224 hours
- Source: Utility gas, Electricity

Monthly Costs
- Mortgage: $647
- Utilities: $147
- Taxes: $115

Rental Options US = 100
- Apartments: 46
- Houses/Duplexes: 110
- Rent: $420 to $550

Jacksonville, FL
Places Rated Rank: 275

Home Prices
131%
- Starter: $226,200
- Move Up: $345,600
- Elite: $437,800

Energy Requirements
- Heat: 1,354 degree days
- A/C: 1,889 hours
- Source: All-Electric

Monthly Costs
- Mortgage: $1,312
- Utilities: $128
- Taxes: $302

Rental Options US = 100
- Apartments: 82
- Houses/Duplexes: 73
- Rent: $650 to $820

Jacksonville, NC
Places Rated Rank: 101

Home Prices
65%
- Starter: $124,600
- Move Up: $186,200
- Elite: $235,900

Energy Requirements
- Heat: 2,545 degree days
- A/C: 1,240 hours
- Source: All-Electric

Monthly Costs
- Mortgage: $723
- Utilities: $114
- Taxes: $141

Rental Options US = 100
- Apartments: 26
- Houses/Duplexes: 135
- Rent: $530 to $660

Janesville, WI
Places Rated Rank: 175

Home Prices
42%
- Starter: $132,900
- Move Up: $182,300
- Elite: $230,900

Energy Requirements
- Heat: 6,969 degree days
- A/C: 347 hours
- Source: Utility gas, Electricity

Monthly Costs
- Mortgage: $771
- Utilities: $169
- Taxes: $244

Rental Options US = 100
- Apartments: 58
- Houses/Duplexes: 81
- Rent: $520 to $590

Jefferson City, MO
Places Rated Rank: 68

Home Prices
35%
- Starter: $119,000
- Move Up: $176,700
- Elite: $223,800

Energy Requirements
- Heat: 5,158 degree days
- A/C: 842 hours
- Source: All-Electric

Monthly Costs
- Mortgage: $690
- Utilities: $85
- Taxes: $142

Rental Options US = 100
- Apartments: 38
- Houses/Duplexes: 80
- Rent: $390 to $500

Johnson City, TN
Places Rated Rank: 48

Home Prices
46%
- Starter: $112,500
- Move Up: $171,800
- Elite: $217,700

Energy Requirements
- Heat: 4,178 degree days
- A/C: 646 hours
- Source: All-Electric

Monthly Costs
- Mortgage: $652
- Utilities: $105
- Taxes: $116

Rental Options US = 100
- Apartments: 56
- Houses/Duplexes: 68
- Rent: $400 to $500

✓ Johnstown, PA
Places Rated Rank: 21

Home Prices
44%
- Starter: $81,200
- Move Up: $123,600
- Elite: $156,600

Energy Requirements
- Heat: 5,455 degree days
- A/C: 412 hours
- Source: Utility gas, Electricity

Monthly Costs
- Mortgage: $471
- Utilities: $176
- Taxes: $132

Rental Options US = 100
- Apartments: 43
- Houses/Duplexes: 88
- Rent: $330 to $420

✓ Jonesboro, AR
Places Rated Rank: 29

Home Prices
23%
- Starter: $98,100
- Move Up: $155,900
- Elite: $197,600

Energy Requirements
- Heat: 3,737 degree days
- A/C: 1,374 hours
- Source: Utility gas, Electricity

Monthly Costs
- Mortgage: $569
- Utilities: $141
- Taxes: $93

Rental Options US = 100
- Apartments: 68
- Houses/Duplexes: 126
- Rent: $410 to $540

✓ Joplin, MO
Places Rated Rank: 18

Home Prices
38%
- Starter: $89,900
- Move Up: $139,100
- Elite: $176,200

Energy Requirements
- Heat: 4,253 degree days
- A/C: 1,128 hours
- Source: Utility gas, Electricity

Monthly Costs
- Mortgage: $521
- Utilities: $139
- Taxes: $108

Rental Options US = 100
- Apartments: 24
- Houses/Duplexes: 128
- Rent: $390 to $500

Kalamazoo-Portage, MI
Places Rated Rank: 168

Home Prices
40%
- Starter: $137,900
- Move Up: $200,000
- Elite: $253,400

Energy Requirements
- Heat: 6,235 degree days
- A/C: 416 hours
- Source: Utility gas, Electricity

Monthly Costs
- Mortgage: $800
- Utilities: $135
- Taxes: $211

Rental Options US = 100
- Apartments: 97
- Houses/Duplexes: 67
- Rent: $550 to $670

Kankakee-Bradley, IL
Places Rated Rank: 165

Home Prices
44%
- Starter: $134,000
- Move Up: $187,400
- Elite: $237,400

Energy Requirements
- Heat: 6,355 degree days
- A/C: 493 hours
- Source: Utility gas, Electricity

Monthly Costs
- Mortgage: $777
- Utilities: $154
- Taxes: $211

Rental Options US = 100
- Apartments: 39
- Houses/Duplexes: 94
- Rent: $520 to $610

Kansas City, MO-KS

Home Prices
47% Starter: $154,600
Move Up: $219,400
Elite: $278,000

Energy Requirements
Heat: 5,249 degree days
A/C: 890 hours
Source: Utility gas, Electricity

Monthly Costs
Mortgage: $896
Utilities: $151
Taxes: $260

Rental Options US = 100
Apartments: 78
Houses/Duplexes: 77
Rent: $560 to $700

Kennewick-Richland-Pasco, WA
Places Rated Rank: 136

Home Prices
35% Starter: $144,800
Move Up: $201,700
Elite: $255,600

Energy Requirements
Heat: 5,133 degree days
A/C: 414 hours
Source: All-Electric

Monthly Costs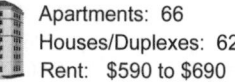
Mortgage: $840
Utilities: $79
Taxes: $136

Rental Options US = 100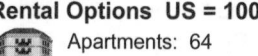
Apartments: 66
Houses/Duplexes: 62
Rent: $590 to $690

Killeen-Temple-Fort Hood, TX
Places Rated Rank: 82

Home Prices
33% Starter: $99,500
Move Up: $145,400
Elite: $184,200

Energy Requirements
Heat: 2,191 degree days
A/C: 1,963 hours
Source: All-Electric

Monthly Costs
Mortgage: $577
Utilities: $137
Taxes: $234

Rental Options US = 100
Apartments: 64
Houses/Duplexes: 149
Rent: $540 to $710

✓ Kingsport-Bristol-Bristol, TN-VA
Places Rated Rank: 35

Home Prices
48% Starter: $102,600
Move Up: $156,000
Elite: $197,700

Energy Requirements
Heat: 4,178 degree days
A/C: 646 hours
Source: All-Electric

Monthly Costs
Mortgage: $595
Utilities: $109
Taxes: $108

Rental Options US = 100
Apartments: 40
Houses/Duplexes: 78
Rent: $360 to $460

Kingston, NY
Places Rated Rank: 312

Home Prices
148% Starter: $278,800
Move Up: $403,300
Elite: $510,900

Energy Requirements
Heat: 6,438 degree days
A/C: 250 hours
Source: Fuel oil, Electricity

Monthly Costs
Mortgage: $1,617
Utilities: $204
Taxes: $397

Rental Options US = 100
Apartments: 65
Houses/Duplexes: 95
Rent: $730 to $930

Knoxville, TN
Places Rated Rank: 144

Home Prices
52% Starter: $141,500
Move Up: $210,900
Elite: $267,100

Energy Requirements
Heat: 3,690 degree days
A/C: 919 hours
Source: All-Electric

Monthly Costs
Mortgage: $821
Utilities: $105
Taxes: $146

Rental Options US = 100
Apartments: 76
Houses/Duplexes: 79
Rent: $470 to $610

Kokomo, IN
Places Rated Rank: 81

Home Prices
18% Starter: $105,100
Move Up: $142,700
Elite: $180,900

Energy Requirements
Heat: 6,041 degree days
A/C: 462 hours
Source: Utility gas, Electricity

Monthly Costs
Mortgage: $609
Utilities: $163
Taxes: $175

Rental Options US = 100
Apartments: 52
Houses/Duplexes: 89
Rent: $490 to $590

La Crosse, WI-MN
Places Rated Rank: 179

Home Prices
54% Starter: $141,700
Move Up: $198,400
Elite: $251,400

Energy Requirements
Heat: 7,340 degree days
A/C: 433 hours
Source: Utility gas, Electricity

Monthly Costs
Mortgage: $822
Utilities: $169
Taxes: $201

Rental Options US = 100
Apartments: 73
Houses/Duplexes: 77
Rent: $470 to $620

Lafayette, IN
Places Rated Rank: 146

Home Prices
13% Starter: $122,300
Move Up: $171,100
Elite: $216,700

Energy Requirements
Heat: 6,132 degree days
A/C: 488 hours
Source: Utility gas, Electricity

Monthly Costs
Mortgage: $709
Utilities: $164
Taxes: $203

Rental Options US = 100
Apartments: 119
Houses/Duplexes: 99
Rent: $550 to $690

Lafayette, LA
Places Rated Rank: 112

Home Prices
54% Starter: $128,800
Move Up: $189,600
Elite: $240,100

Energy Requirements
Heat: 1,493 degree days
A/C: 2,004 hours
Source: Utility gas, Electricity

Monthly Costs
Mortgage: $747
Utilities: $127
Taxes: $126

Rental Options US = 100
Apartments: 67
Houses/Duplexes: 72
Rent: $430 to $530

✓ Lake Charles, LA
Places Rated Rank: 33

Home Prices
47% Starter: $101,600
Move Up: $166,000
Elite: $210,300

Energy Requirements
Heat: 1,546 degree days
A/C: 2,009 hours
Source: All-Electric

Monthly Costs
Mortgage: $589
Utilities: $123
Taxes: $100

Rental Options US = 100
Apartments: 24
Houses/Duplexes: 108
Rent: $410 to $490

Lake County-Kenosha County, IL-WI

Home Prices

Starter: $262,500
Move Up: $441,300
Elite: $559,000
61%

Energy Requirements

Heat: 6,999 degree days
A/C: 281 hours
Source: Utility gas, Electricity

Monthly Costs
Mortgage: $1,522
Utilities: $166
Taxes: $448

Rental Options US = 100

Apartments: 71
Houses/Duplexes: 57
Rent: $720 to $940

Lakeland, FL

Home Prices

Starter: $161,300
Move Up: $265,200
Elite: $336,000
123%

Energy Requirements
Heat: 489 degree days
A/C: 3,018 hours
Source: All-Electric

Monthly Costs
Mortgage: $935
Utilities: $128
Taxes: $216

Rental Options US = 100

Apartments: 44
Houses/Duplexes: 76
Rent: $540 to $690

Lancaster, PA

Home Prices

Starter: $185,200
Move Up: $254,000
Elite: $321,800
61%

Energy Requirements

Heat: 5,448 degree days
A/C: 420 hours
Source: All-Electric

Monthly Costs
Mortgage: $1,074
Utilities: $95
Taxes: $301

Rental Options US = 100

Apartments: 61
Houses/Duplexes: 91
Rent: $600 to $740

Lansing-East Lansing, MI

Home Prices

Starter: $156,300
Move Up: $214,000
Elite: $271,100
45%

Energy Requirements

Heat: 7,098 degree days
A/C: 268 hours
Source: Utility gas, Electricity

Monthly Costs
Mortgage: $906
Utilities: $146
Taxes: $239

Rental Options US = 100

Apartments: 116
Houses/Duplexes: 56
Rent: $590 to $730

Laredo, TX

Home Prices

Starter: $95,100
Move Up: $135,600
Elite: $171,800
33%

Energy Requirements
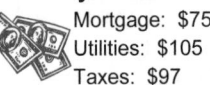
Heat: 931 degree days
A/C: 3,547 hours
Source: All-Electric

Monthly Costs
Mortgage: $551
Utilities: $137
Taxes: $224

Rental Options US = 100

Apartments: 73
Houses/Duplexes: 105
Rent: $440 to $600

Las Cruces, NM

Home Prices

Starter: $130,600
Move Up: $206,100
Elite: $261,100
67%

Energy Requirements
Heat: 3,818 degree days
A/C: 904 hours
Source: Utility gas, Electricity

Monthly Costs
Mortgage: $757
Utilities: $105
Taxes: $97

Rental Options US = 100

Apartments: 52
Houses/Duplexes: 87
Rent: $440 to $630

Las Vegas-Paradise, NV

Home Prices

Starter: $367,600
Move Up: $511,200
Elite: $647,600
141%

Energy Requirements

Heat: 2,239 degree days
A/C: 2,754 hours
Source: Utility gas, Electricity

Monthly Costs
Mortgage: $2,132
Utilities: $127
Taxes: $312

Rental Options US = 100

Apartments: 130
Houses/Duplexes: 73
Rent: $770 to $960

Lawrence, KS

Home Prices

Starter: $173,400
Move Up: $240,100
Elite: $304,200
52%

Energy Requirements

Heat: 4,685 degree days
A/C: 1,156 hours
Source: Utility gas, Electricity

Monthly Costs
Mortgage: $1,005
Utilities: $139
Taxes: $377

Rental Options US = 100

Apartments: 116
Houses/Duplexes: 109
Rent: $590 to $770

✓ Lawton, OK

Home Prices

Starter: $98,800
Move Up: $149,200
Elite: $189,000
49%

Energy Requirements

Heat: 3,326 degree days
A/C: 1,734 hours
Source: Utility gas, Electricity

Monthly Costs
Mortgage: $573
Utilities: $129
Taxes: $101

Rental Options US = 100

Apartments: 52
Houses/Duplexes: 170
Rent: $430 to $520

Lebanon, PA

Home Prices
Starter: $161,800
Move Up: $226,700
Elite: $287,300
58%

Energy Requirements
Heat: 5,960 degree days
A/C: 260 hours
Source: Fuel oil, Electricity

Monthly Costs
Mortgage: $938
Utilities: $185
Taxes: $263

Rental Options US = 100
Apartments: 57
Houses/Duplexes: 93
Rent: $480 to $610

Lewiston, ID-WA

Home Prices

Starter: $183,300
Move Up: $272,200
Elite: $344,900
63%

Energy Requirements
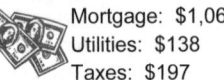
Heat: 5,220 degree days
A/C: 478 hours
Source: Utility gas, Electricity

Monthly Costs
Mortgage: $1,063
Utilities: $138
Taxes: $197

Rental Options US = 100

Apartments: 44
Houses/Duplexes: 101
Rent: $500 to $630

Lewiston-Auburn, ME
Places Rated Rank: 241

Home Prices

88%
Starter: $157,800
Move Up: $210,900
Elite: $267,100

Energy Requirements

Heat: 7,107 degree days
A/C: 194 hours
Source: Fuel oil, Electricity

Monthly Costs
Mortgage: $915
Utilities: $210
Taxes: $330

Rental Options US = 100
Apartments: 71
Houses/Duplexes: 57
Rent: $550 to $660

Lexington-Fayette, KY
Places Rated Rank: 178

Home Prices

44%
Starter: $153,900
Move Up: $231,700
Elite: $293,600

Energy Requirements

Heat: 4,713 degree days
A/C: 683 hours
Source: Utility gas, Electricity

Monthly Costs

Mortgage: $892
Utilities: $145
Taxes: $151

Rental Options US = 100
Apartments: 91
Houses/Duplexes: 103
Rent: $500 to $670

Lima, OH
Places Rated Rank: 65

Home Prices

39%
Starter: $101,900
Move Up: $154,900
Elite: $196,300

Energy Requirements
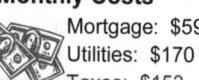
Heat: 5,932 degree days
A/C: 449 hours
Source: Utility gas, Electricity

Monthly Costs
Mortgage: $591
Utilities: $170
Taxes: $153

Rental Options US = 100
Apartments: 44
Houses/Duplexes: 113
Rent: $410 to $490

Lincoln, NE
Places Rated Rank: 198

Home Prices
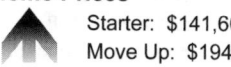
35%
Starter: $141,600
Move Up: $194,200
Elite: $246,000

Energy Requirements
Heat: 6,242 degree days
A/C: 775 hours
Source: Utility gas, Electricity

Monthly Costs

Mortgage: $821
Utilities: $171
Taxes: $286

Rental Options US = 100
Apartments: 122
Houses/Duplexes: 83
Rent: $510 to $680

Little Rock-North Little Rock, AR
Places Rated Rank: 80

Home Prices

43%
Starter: $121,100
Move Up: $186,300
Elite: $236,000

Energy Requirements
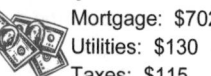
Heat: 3,084 degree days
A/C: 1,558 hours
Source: Utility gas, Electricity

Monthly Costs
Mortgage: $702
Utilities: $130
Taxes: $115

Rental Options US = 100

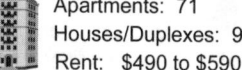
Apartments: 71
Houses/Duplexes: 90
Rent: $490 to $590

Logan, UT-ID
Places Rated Rank: 200

Home Prices

37%
Starter: $166,800
Move Up: $221,700
Elite: $280,800

Energy Requirements
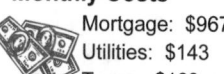
Heat: 6,723 degree days
A/C: 392 hours
Source: Utility gas, Electricity

Monthly Costs

Mortgage: $967
Utilities: $143
Taxes: $169

Rental Options US = 100
Apartments: 60
Houses/Duplexes: 79
Rent: $480 to $590

Longview, TX
Places Rated Rank: 102

Home Prices

46%
Starter: $101,100
Move Up: $148,100
Elite: $187,700

Energy Requirements

Heat: 2,574 degree days
A/C: 1,568 hours
Source: Utility gas, Electricity

Monthly Costs

Mortgage: $586
Utilities: $155
Taxes: $238

Rental Options US = 100
Apartments: 54
Houses/Duplexes: 84
Rent: $440 to $530

Longview, WA
Places Rated Rank: 236

Home Prices

65%
Starter: $200,800
Move Up: $273,900
Elite: $347,000

Energy Requirements

Heat: 4,900 degree days
A/C: 26 hours
Source: All-Electric

Monthly Costs

Mortgage: $1,164
Utilities: $79
Taxes: $189

Rental Options US = 100
Apartments: 57
Houses/Duplexes: 104
Rent: $500 to $620

Los Angeles-Long Beach-Glendale, CA
Places Rated Rank: 369

Home Prices

205%
Starter: $736,200
Move Up: $1,074,600
Elite: $1,361,200

Energy Requirements

Heat: 1,274 degree days
A/C: 203 hours
Source: Utility gas, Electricity

Monthly Costs

Mortgage: $4,269
Utilities: $91
Taxes: $340

Rental Options US = 100
Apartments: 178
Houses/Duplexes: 94
Rent: $850 to $1,140

Louisville-Jefferson County, KY-IN
Places Rated Rank: 167

Home Prices

40%
Starter: $141,300
Move Up: $206,000
Elite: $261,000

Energy Requirements

Heat: 4,352 degree days
A/C: 956 hours
Source: Utility gas, Electricity

Monthly Costs
Mortgage: $819
Utilities: $138
Taxes: $187

Rental Options US = 100
Apartments: 76
Houses/Duplexes: 71
Rent: $490 to $600

Lubbock, TX
Places Rated Rank: 55

Home Prices

35%
Starter: $89,200
Move Up: $130,100
Elite: $164,800

Energy Requirements

Heat: 3,508 degree days
A/C: 1,264 hours
Source: Utility gas, Electricity

Monthly Costs

Mortgage: $517
Utilities: $170
Taxes: $210

Rental Options US = 100
Apartments: 70
Houses/Duplexes: 141
Rent: $530 to $700

Lynchburg, VA

Home Prices

58%
Starter: $141,300
Move Up: $205,600
Elite: $260,500

Energy Requirements

Heat: 4,354 degree days
A/C: 648 hours
Source: All-Electric

Monthly Costs

Mortgage: $819
Utilities: $114
Taxes: $152

Rental Options US = 100

Apartments: 51
Houses/Duplexes: 64
Rent: $410 to $510

Macon, GA
Places Rated Rank: 53

Home Prices

36%
Starter: $112,100
Move Up: $178,500
Elite: $226,100

Energy Requirements

Heat: 2,364 degree days
A/C: 1,610 hours
Source: All-Electric

Monthly Costs

Mortgage: $650
Utilities: $107
Taxes: $135

Rental Options US = 100
Apartments: 58
Houses/Duplexes: 121
Rent: $410 to $570

Madera, CA
Places Rated Rank: 344

Home Prices

173%
Starter: $456,700
Move Up: $631,200
Elite: $799,600

Energy Requirements
Heat: 2,670 degree days
A/C: 1,172 hours
Source: Utility gas, Electricity

Monthly Costs

Mortgage: $2,648
Utilities: $112
Taxes: $211

Rental Options US = 100
Apartments: 34
Houses/Duplexes: 110
Rent: $550 to $670

Madison, WI
Places Rated Rank: 284

Home Prices

57%
Starter: $221,600
Move Up: $303,300
Elite: $384,300

Energy Requirements

Heat: 7,493 degree days
A/C: 290 hours
Source: Utility gas, Electricity

Monthly Costs

Mortgage: $1,285
Utilities: $176
Taxes: $407

Rental Options US = 100
Apartments: 138
Houses/Duplexes: 59
Rent: $670 to $820

Manchester-Nashua, NH
Places Rated Rank: 329

Home Prices

121%
Starter: $297,800
Move Up: $404,200
Elite: $512,000

Energy Requirements

Heat: 7,742 degree days
A/C: 70 hours
Source: Fuel oil, Electricity

Monthly Costs

Mortgage: $1,727
Utilities: $223
Taxes: $500

Rental Options US = 100
Apartments: 90
Houses/Duplexes: 50
Rent: $840 to $1,040

Mansfield, OH
Places Rated Rank: 118

Home Prices

35%
Starter: $114,200
Move Up: $158,300
Elite: $200,500

Energy Requirements

Heat: 6,364 degree days
A/C: 320 hours
Source: Utility gas, Electricity

Monthly Costs

Mortgage: $662
Utilities: $178
Taxes: $172

Rental Options US = 100
Apartments: 54
Houses/Duplexes: 88
Rent: $390 to $460

✓ McAllen-Edinburg-Mission, TX
Places Rated Rank: 3

Home Prices

31%
Starter: $63,500
Move Up: $98,700
Elite: $125,100

Energy Requirements

Heat: 625 degree days
A/C: 3,386 hours
Source: All-Electric

Monthly Costs

Mortgage: $368
Utilities: $137
Taxes: $150

Rental Options US = 100
Apartments: 42
Houses/Duplexes: 101
Rent: $390 to $510

Medford, OR
Places Rated Rank: 324

Home Prices

154%
Starter: $330,700
Move Up: $511,000
Elite: $647,300

Energy Requirements

Heat: 4,539 degree days
A/C: 383 hours
Source: All-Electric

Monthly Costs

Mortgage: $1,918
Utilities: $85
Taxes: $329

Rental Options US = 100
Apartments: 52
Houses/Duplexes: 111
Rent: $620 to $760

Memphis, TN-MS-AR
Places Rated Rank: 119

Home Prices

30%
Starter: $125,600
Move Up: $197,700
Elite: $250,500

Energy Requirements

Heat: 3,041 degree days
A/C: 1,655 hours
Source: Utility gas, Electricity

Monthly Costs

Mortgage: $728
Utilities: $140
Taxes: $147

Rental Options US = 100
Apartments: 88
Houses/Duplexes: 84
Rent: $520 to $670

Merced, CA
Places Rated Rank: 343

Home Prices

210%
Starter: $451,300
Move Up: $611,600
Elite: $774,800

Energy Requirements

Heat: 2,602 degree days
A/C: 1,034 hours
Source: Utility gas, Electricity

Monthly Costs
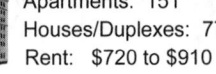
Mortgage: $2,617
Utilities: $111
Taxes: $208

Rental Options US = 100
Apartments: 47
Houses/Duplexes: 152
Rent: $610 to $840

Miami-Miami Beach-Kendall, FL
Places Rated Rank: 347

Home Prices
204%
Starter: $408,700
Move Up: $627,700
Elite: $795,100

Energy Requirements
Heat: 149 degree days
A/C: 3,332 hours
Source: All-Electric

Monthly Costs
Mortgage: $2,370
Utilities: $128
Taxes: $546

Rental Options US = 100
Apartments: 151
Houses/Duplexes: 77
Rent: $720 to $910

Michigan City-La Porte, IN
Places Rated Rank: 163

 Home Prices
Starter: $129,800
Move Up: $184,800
46% Elite: $234,100

 Energy Requirements
Heat: 6,338 degree days
A/C: 444 hours
Source: Utility gas, Electricity

 Monthly Costs
Mortgage: $753
Utilities: $167
Taxes: $216

Rental Options US = 100
Apartments: 34
Houses/Duplexes: 83
Rent: $460 to $550

Midland, TX
Places Rated Rank: 130

 Home Prices
Starter: $108,100
Move Up: $174,200
57% Elite: $220,800

 **Energy Requirements**
Heat: 2,716 degree days
A/C: 1,600 hours
Source: Utility gas, Electricity

 Monthly Costs
Mortgage: $627
Utilities: $158
Taxes: $255

Rental Options US = 100
Apartments: 86
Houses/Duplexes: 75
Rent: $420 to $560

Milwaukee-Waukesha-West Allis, WI
Places Rated Rank: 274

 **Home Prices**
Starter: $204,500
Move Up: $280,400
65% Elite: $355,300

Energy Requirements
Heat: 7,087 degree days
A/C: 322 hours
Source: Utility gas, Electricity

Monthly Costs
Mortgage: $1,186
Utilities: $170
Taxes: $376

Rental Options US = 100
Apartments: 109
Houses/Duplexes: 85
Rent: $590 to $730

Minneapolis-St. Paul-Bloomington, MN-WI
Places Rated Rank: 297

 Home Prices
Starter: $260,800
Move Up: $377,500
96% Elite: $478,200

Energy Requirements
Heat: 7,876 degree days
A/C: 378 hours
Source: Utility gas, Electricity

 Monthly Costs
Mortgage: $1,512
Utilities: $177
Taxes: $370

Rental Options US = 100
Apartments: 103
Houses/Duplexes: 42
Rent: $710 to $890

Missoula, MT
Places Rated Rank: 291

Home Prices
Starter: $247,200
Move Up: $351,900
93% Elite: $445,800

Energy Requirements
Heat: 7,562 degree days
A/C: 137 hours
Source: Utility gas, Electricity

 Monthly Costs
Mortgage: $1,433
Utilities: $161
Taxes: $402

Rental Options US = 100
Apartments: 69
Houses/Duplexes: 106
Rent: $550 to $680

Mobile, AL
Places Rated Rank: 56

 Home Prices
Starter: $120,200
Move Up: $183,600
51% Elite: $232,600

 **Energy Requirements**
Heat: 1,681 degree days
A/C: 1,865 hours
Source: All-Electric

Monthly Costs
Mortgage: $697
Utilities: $114
Taxes: $87

Rental Options US = 100
Apartments: 74
Houses/Duplexes: 90
Rent: $430 to $530

Modesto, CA
Places Rated Rank: 350

 Home Prices
Starter: $477,600
Move Up: $620,900
198% Elite: $786,500

 **Energy Requirements**
Heat: 2,358 degree days
A/C: 1,001 hours
Source: Utility gas, Electricity

 Monthly Costs
Mortgage: $2,769
Utilities: $107
Taxes: $220

Rental Options US = 100
Apartments: 53
Houses/Duplexes: 137
Rent: $700 to $900

✓ Monroe, LA
Places Rated Rank: 10

 Home Prices
Starter: $91,900
Move Up: $156,900
41% Elite: $198,900

 Energy Requirements
Heat: 2,190 degree days
A/C: 1,934 hours
Source: All-Electric

 Monthly Costs
Mortgage: $533
Utilities: $123
Taxes: $90

Rental Options US = 100
Apartments: 57
Houses/Duplexes: 114
Rent: $380 to $520

Monroe, MI
Places Rated Rank: 223

 Home Prices
Starter: $168,300
Move Up: $232,800
42% Elite: $295,000

 Energy Requirements
Heat: 6,529 degree days
A/C: 360 hours
Source: Utility gas, Electricity

 Monthly Costs
Mortgage: $976
Utilities: $139
Taxes: $258

Rental Options US = 100
Apartments: 55
Houses/Duplexes: 44
Rent: $530 to $680

Montgomery, AL
Places Rated Rank: 44

Home Prices
Starter: $110,500
Move Up: $183,400
34% Elite: $232,400

 Energy Requirements
Heat: 2,194 degree days
A/C: 1,640 hours
Source: Utility gas, Electricity

 Monthly Costs
Mortgage: $641
Utilities: $138
Taxes: $80

Rental Options US = 100
Apartments: 68
Houses/Duplexes: 87
Rent: $460 to $620

Morgantown, WV
Places Rated Rank: 66

 Home Prices
Starter: $108,300
Move Up: $180,700
57% Elite: $229,000

 Energy Requirements
Heat: 5,312 degree days
A/C: 398 hours
Source: Utility gas, Electricity

 Monthly Costs
Mortgage: $628
Utilities: $153
Taxes: $134

Rental Options US = 100
Apartments: 74
Houses/Duplexes: 77
Rent: $450 to $600

Morristown, TN
Places Rated Rank: 100

Home Prices

Starter: $127,600
Move Up: $184,600
51% Elite: $233,800

Energy Requirements
Heat: 4,214 degree days
A/C: 703 hours
Source: All-Electric

Monthly Costs
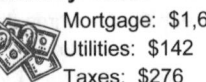
Mortgage: $740
Utilities: $105
Taxes: $132

Rental Options US = 100

Apartments: 29
Houses/Duplexes: 90
Rent: $380 to $490

Mount Vernon-Anacortes, WA
Places Rated Rank: 306

Home Prices
Starter: $293,000
Move Up: $427,400
95% Elite: $541,400

Energy Requirements
Heat: 5,138 degree days
A/C: 2 hours
Source: Utility gas, Electricity

Monthly Costs
Mortgage: $1,699
Utilities: $142
Taxes: $276

Rental Options US = 100
Apartments: 44
Houses/Duplexes: 107
Rent: $690 to $860

✓ Muncie, IN
Places Rated Rank: 37

Home Prices

Starter: $89,600
Move Up: $133,200
28% Elite: $168,800

Energy Requirements
Heat: 5,807 degree days
A/C: 491 hours
Source: Utility gas, Electricity

Monthly Costs

Mortgage: $520
Utilities: $159
Taxes: $149

Rental Options US = 100

Apartments: 60
Houses/Duplexes: 102
Rent: $470 to $590

Muskegon-North Shores, MI
Places Rated Rank: 97

Home Prices

Starter: $113,200
Move Up: $160,700
36% Elite: $203,600

Energy Requirements
Heat: 6,943 degree days
A/C: 205 hours
Source: Utility gas, Electricity

Monthly Costs
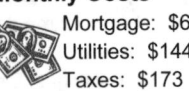
Mortgage: $656
Utilities: $144
Taxes: $173

Rental Options US = 100

Apartments: 43
Houses/Duplexes: 51
Rent: $430 to $570

Myrtle Beach-Conway-North Myrtle Beach, SC
Places Rated Rank: 250

Home Prices

Starter: $191,700
Move Up: $294,500
89% Elite: $373,000

Energy Requirements
Heat: 2,704 degree days
A/C: 1,208 hours
Source: All-Electric

Monthly Costs
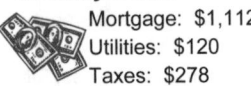
Mortgage: $1,112
Utilities: $120
Taxes: $278

Rental Options US = 100

Apartments: 85
Houses/Duplexes: 50
Rent: $580 to $720

Napa, CA
Places Rated Rank: 372

Home Prices

Starter: $787,500
Move Up: $1,053,200
185% Elite: $1,334,200

Energy Requirements
Heat: 2,689 degree days
A/C: 154 hours
Source: Utility gas, Electricity

Monthly Costs
Mortgage: $4,566
Utilities: $112
Taxes: $364

Rental Options US = 100

Apartments: 59
Houses/Duplexes: 103
Rent: $990 to $1,320

Naples-Marco Island, FL
Places Rated Rank: 368

Home Prices

Starter: $632,600
Move Up: $1,051,500
224% Elite: $1,332,000

Energy Requirements
Heat: 329 degree days
A/C: 2,694 hours
Source: All-Electric

Monthly Costs
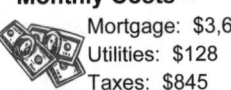
Mortgage: $3,668
Utilities: $128
Taxes: $845

Rental Options US = 100

Apartments: 72
Houses/Duplexes: 61
Rent: $880 to $1,150

Nashville-Davidson-Murfreesboro, TN
Places Rated Rank: 196

Home Prices

Starter: $171,300
Move Up: $260,300
48% Elite: $329,700

Energy Requirements
Heat: 3,677 degree days
A/C: 1,134 hours
Source: All-Electric

Monthly Costs
Mortgage: $993
Utilities: $105
Taxes: $177

Rental Options US = 100

Apartments: 96
Houses/Duplexes: 75
Rent: $560 to $690

Nassau-Suffolk, NY
Places Rated Rank: 365

Home Prices

Starter: $565,300
Move Up: $785,600
165% Elite: $995,200

Energy Requirements
Heat: 5,231 degree days
A/C: 474 hours
Source: Utility gas, Electricity

Monthly Costs
Mortgage: $3,278
Utilities: $181
Taxes: $804

Rental Options US = 100

Apartments: 39
Houses/Duplexes: 54
Rent: $1,150 to $1,51

Newark-Union, NJ-PA
Places Rated Rank: 358

Home Prices

Starter: $482,200
Move Up: $698,300
125% Elite: $884,600

Energy Requirements
Heat: 4,843 degree days
A/C: 808 hours
Source: Utility gas, Electricity

Monthly Costs
Mortgage: $2,796
Utilities: $160
Taxes: $718

Rental Options US = 100

Apartments: 108
Houses/Duplexes: 68
Rent: $820 to $1,040

New Haven-Milford, CT
Places Rated Rank: 326

Home Prices

Starter: $292,300
Move Up: $436,500
104% Elite: $552,900

Energy Requirements
Heat: 5,466 degree days
A/C: 416 hours
Source: Fuel oil, Electricity

Monthly Costs
Mortgage: $1,695
Utilities: $201
Taxes: $450

Rental Options US = 100
Apartments: 91
Houses/Duplexes: 66
Rent: $720 to $900

New Orleans-Metairie-Kenner, LA
Places Rated Rank: 213

Home Prices

76% Starter: $177,900
Move Up: $263,400
Elite: $333,600

Energy Requirements
Heat: 1,417 degree days
A/C: 2,062 hours
Source: All-Electric

Monthly Costs
Mortgage: $1,032
Utilities: $123
Taxes: $175

Rental Options US = 100
Apartments: 81
Houses/Duplexes: 103
Rent: $510 to $650

New York-White Plains-Wayne, NY-NJ
Places Rated Rank: 366

Home Prices

142% Starter: $578,600
Move Up: $852,200
Elite: $1,079,500

Energy Requirements
Heat: 4,754 degree days
A/C: 725 hours
Source: Utility gas, Electricity

Monthly Costs
Mortgage: $3,355
Utilities: $163
Taxes: $803

Rental Options US = 100
Apartments: 254
Houses/Duplexes: 62
Rent: $840 to $1,160

Niles-Benton Harbor, MI
Places Rated Rank: 164

Home Prices
51% Starter: $136,000
Move Up: $207,800
Elite: $263,300

Energy Requirements
Heat: 6,675 degree days
A/C: 326 hours
Source: Utility gas, Electricity

Monthly Costs
Mortgage: $789
Utilities: $141
Taxes: $208

Rental Options US = 100
Apartments: 51
Houses/Duplexes: 90
Rent: $440 to $540

Norwich-New London, CT
Places Rated Rank: 317

Home Prices
108% Starter: $277,700
Move Up: $412,300
Elite: $522,300

Energy Requirements
Heat: 5,916 degree days
A/C: 287 hours
Source: Fuel oil, Electricity

Monthly Costs
Mortgage: $1,610
Utilities: $211
Taxes: $428

Rental Options US = 100
Apartments: 80
Houses/Duplexes: 79
Rent: $730 to $920

Oakland-Fremont-Hayward, CA
Places Rated Rank: 371

Home Prices

180% Starter: $786,900
Move Up: $1,023,500
Elite: $1,296,500

Energy Requirements
Heat: 2,720 degree days
A/C: 26 hours
Source: Utility gas, Electricity

Monthly Costs
Mortgage: $4,563
Utilities: $113
Taxes: $363

Rental Options US = 100
Apartments: 111
Houses/Duplexes: 83
Rent: $1,010 to $1,290

Ocala, FL
Places Rated Rank: 227

Home Prices

137% Starter: $176,800
Move Up: $273,100
Elite: $345,900

Energy Requirements
Heat: 910 degree days
A/C: 2,160 hours
Source: All-Electric

Monthly Costs
Mortgage: $1,025
Utilities: $128
Taxes: $236

Rental Options US = 100
Apartments: 25
Houses/Duplexes: 48
Rent: $520 to $630

Ocean City, NJ
Places Rated Rank: 353

Home Prices

200% Starter: $428,900
Move Up: $741,200
Elite: $938,900

Energy Requirements
Heat: 4,480 degree days
A/C: 518 hours
Source: Utility gas, Electricity

Monthly Costs
Mortgage: $2,487
Utilities: $150
Taxes: $579

Rental Options US = 100
Apartments: 16
Houses/Duplexes: 104
Rent: $710 to $930

✓ Odessa, TX
Places Rated Rank: 6

Home Prices

49% Starter: $65,100
Move Up: $98,000
Elite: $124,200

Energy Requirements
Heat: 2,716 degree days
A/C: 1,600 hours
Source: Utility gas, Electricity

Monthly Costs

Mortgage: $377
Utilities: $158
Taxes: $153

Rental Options US = 100
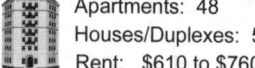
Apartments: 78
Houses/Duplexes: 64
Rent: $390 to $510

Ogden-Clearfield, UT
Places Rated Rank: 217

Home Prices

36% Starter: $183,700
Move Up: $252,100
Elite: $319,300

Energy Requirements
Heat: 5,868 degree days
A/C: 625 hours
Source: Utility gas, Electricity

Monthly Costs

Mortgage: $1,065
Utilities: $124
Taxes: $151

Rental Options US = 100

Apartments: 48
Houses/Duplexes: 58
Rent: $610 to $760

Oklahoma City, OK
Places Rated Rank: 62

Home Prices
48% Starter: $113,900
Move Up: $166,000
Elite: $210,300

Energy Requirements
Heat: 3,663 degree days
A/C: 1,422 hours
Source: Utility gas, Electricity

Monthly Costs
Mortgage: $660
Utilities: $134
Taxes: $117

Rental Options US = 100
Apartments: 82
Houses/Duplexes: 103
Rent: $460 to $590

Olympia, WA
Places Rated Rank: 283

Home Prices
92% Starter: $265,000
Move Up: $381,000
Elite: $482,600

Energy Requirements
Heat: 5,531 degree days
A/C: 23 hours
Source: All-Electric

Monthly Costs

Mortgage: $1,537
Utilities: $79
Taxes: $250

Rental Options US = 100
Apartments: 65
Houses/Duplexes: 99
Rent: $680 to $860

Housing

Omaha-Council Bluffs, NE-IA

Home Prices
38%
Starter: $143,400
Move Up: $204,000
Elite: $258,400

Energy Requirements
Heat: 6,311 degree days
A/C: 708 hours
Source: Utility gas, Electricity

Monthly Costs
Mortgage: $832
Utilities: $171
Taxes: $296

Rental Options US = 100
Apartments: 105
Houses/Duplexes: 81
Rent: $540 to $680

Orlando-Kissimmee, FL

Home Prices
155%
Starter: $304,200
Move Up: $465,300
Elite: $589,500

Energy Requirements
Heat: 580 degree days
A/C: 2,495 hours
Source: All-Electric

Monthly Costs
Mortgage: $1,764
Utilities: $128
Taxes: $407

Rental Options US = 100
Apartments: 112
Houses/Duplexes: 72
Rent: $720 to $870

Oshkosh-Neenah, WI

Home Prices
37%
Starter: $138,600
Move Up: $188,800
Elite: $239,200

Energy Requirements
Heat: 7,639 degree days
A/C: 295 hours
Source: Utility gas, Electricity

Monthly Costs
Mortgage: $804
Utilities: $179
Taxes: $255

Rental Options US = 100
Apartments: 95
Houses/Duplexes: 88
Rent: $490 to $600

✓ Owensboro, KY

Home Prices
27%
Starter: $96,200
Move Up: $145,000
Elite: $183,700

Energy Requirements
Heat: 4,159 degree days
A/C: 1,090 hours
Source: Utility gas, Electricity

Monthly Costs
Mortgage: $558
Utilities: $136
Taxes: $95

Rental Options US = 100
Apartments: 57
Houses/Duplexes: 88
Rent: $360 to $430

Oxnard-Thousand Oaks-Ventura, CA

Home Prices
193%
Starter: $837,100
Move Up: $1,028,800
Elite: $1,303,100

Energy Requirements
Heat: 1,904 degree days
A/C: 222 hours
Source: Utility gas, Electricity

Monthly Costs
Mortgage: $4,854
Utilities: $101
Taxes: $386

Rental Options US = 100
Apartments: 75
Houses/Duplexes: 88
Rent: $1,100 to $1,460

Palm Bay-Melbourne-Titusville, FL

Home Prices
172%
Starter: $272,600
Move Up: $424,800
Elite: $538,100

Energy Requirements
Heat: 610 degree days
A/C: 2,296 hours
Source: All-Electric

Monthly Costs
Mortgage: $1,581
Utilities: $128
Taxes: $364

Rental Options US = 100
Apartments: 71
Houses/Duplexes: 60
Rent: $640 to $790

Panama City-Lynn Haven, FL

Home Prices
145%
Starter: $212,600
Move Up: $362,400
Elite: $459,100

Energy Requirements
Heat: 1,817 degree days
A/C: 1,498 hours
Source: All-Electric

Monthly Costs
Mortgage: $1,233
Utilities: $128
Taxes: $284

Rental Options US = 100
Apartments: 53
Houses/Duplexes: 94
Rent: $570 to $700

Parkersburg-Marietta-Vienna, WV-OH

Home Prices
38%
Starter: $97,700
Move Up: $146,700
Elite: $185,800

Energy Requirements
Heat: 4,966 degree days
A/C: 539 hours
Source: Utility gas, Electricity

Monthly Costs
Mortgage: $567
Utilities: $151
Taxes: $134

Rental Options US = 100
Apartments: 32
Houses/Duplexes: 84
Rent: $370 to $450

Pascagoula, MS

Home Prices
64%
Starter: $121,100
Move Up: $190,200
Elite: $241,000

Energy Requirements
Heat: 1,870 degree days
A/C: 1,633 hours
Source: All-Electric

Monthly Costs
Mortgage: $702
Utilities: $120
Taxes: $184

Rental Options US = 100
Apartments: 38
Houses/Duplexes: 76
Rent: $440 to $580

Pensacola-Ferry Pass-Brent, FL

Home Prices
107%
Starter: $170,700
Move Up: $269,300
Elite: $341,200

Energy Requirements
Heat: 1,498 degree days
A/C: 1,961 hours
Source: All-Electric

Monthly Costs
Mortgage: $990
Utilities: $128
Taxes: $228

Rental Options US = 100
Apartments: 47
Houses/Duplexes: 89
Rent: $540 to $750

Peoria, IL

Home Prices
38%
Starter: $120,200
Move Up: $174,000
Elite: $220,400

Energy Requirements
Heat: 6,097 degree days
A/C: 592 hours
Source: Utility gas, Electricity

Monthly Costs
Mortgage: $697
Utilities: $150
Taxes: $189

Rental Options US = 100
Apartments: 58
Houses/Duplexes: 77
Rent: $470 to $580

Philadelphia, PA

Home Prices

- Starter: $258,800
- Move Up: $423,800
- **106%** Elite: $536,900

Energy Requirements

- Heat: 4,759 degree days
- A/C: 794 hours
- Source: Utility gas, Electricity

Monthly Costs

- Mortgage: $1,501
- Utilities: $163
- Taxes: $421

Rental Options US = 100
- Apartments: 80
- Houses/Duplexes: 88
- Rent: $660 to $870

Phoenix-Mesa-Scottdale, AZ

Home Prices

- Starter: $332,400
- Move Up: $543,300
- **157%** Elite: $688,200

Energy Requirements

- Heat: 1,125 degree days
- A/C: 3,913 hours
- Source: All-Electric

Monthly Costs

- Mortgage: $1,927
- Utilities: $108
- Taxes: $363

Rental Options US = 100
- Apartments: 105
- Houses/Duplexes: 60
- Rent: $650 to $850

✓ Pine Bluff, AR

Home Prices

- Starter: $66,500
- Move Up: $104,100
- **38%** Elite: $131,900

Energy Requirements
- Heat: 2,935 degree days
- A/C: 1,559 hours
- Source: Utility gas, Electricity

Monthly Costs
- Mortgage: $386
- Utilities: $127
- Taxes: $63

Rental Options US = 100

- Apartments: 45
- Houses/Duplexes: 125
- Rent: $340 to $470

Pittsburgh, PA

Home Prices

- Starter: $110,100
- Move Up: $169,500
- **43%** Elite: $214,700

Energy Requirements
- Heat: 5,829 degree days
- A/C: 350 hours
- Source: Utility gas, Electricity

Monthly Costs
- Mortgage: $638
- Utilities: $182
- Taxes: $179

Rental Options US = 100

- Apartments: 62
- Houses/Duplexes: 80
- Rent: $460 to $610

Pittsfield, MA

Home Prices

- Starter: $199,300
- Move Up: $312,200
- **88%** Elite: $395,500

Energy Requirements
- Heat: 7,406 degree days
- A/C: 95 hours
- Source: Fuel oil, Electricity

Monthly Costs
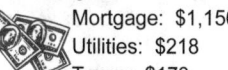
- Mortgage: $1,156
- Utilities: $218
- Taxes: $173

Rental Options US = 100

- Apartments: 63
- Houses/Duplexes: 68
- Rent: $480 to $630

Pocatello, ID

Home Prices

- Starter: $114,700
- Move Up: $160,900
- **45%** Elite: $203,800

Energy Requirements
- Heat: 7,109 degree days
- A/C: 146 hours
- Source: Utility gas, Electricity

Monthly Costs
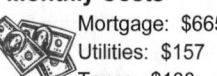
- Mortgage: $665
- Utilities: $157
- Taxes: $138

Rental Options US = 100
- Apartments: 35
- Houses/Duplexes: 91
- Rent: $500 to $600

Portland-South Portland-Biddeford, ME

Home Prices

- Starter: $252,600
- Move Up: $365,400
- **110%** Elite: $462,900

Energy Requirements
- Heat: 7,318 degree days
- A/C: 136 hours
- Source: Fuel oil, Electricity

Monthly Costs

- Mortgage: $1,465
- Utilities: $214
- Taxes: $528

Rental Options US = 100

- Apartments: 67
- Houses/Duplexes: 76
- Rent: $690 to $850

Portland-Vancouver-Beaverton, OR-WA

Home Prices

- Starter: $316,200
- Move Up: $468,300
- **96%** Elite: $593,200

Energy Requirements
- Heat: 4,400 degree days
- A/C: 151 hours
- Source: All-Electric

Monthly Costs
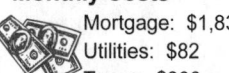
- Mortgage: $1,834
- Utilities: $82
- Taxes: $306

Rental Options US = 100

- Apartments: 117
- Houses/Duplexes: 76
- Rent: $650 to $810

Port St. Lucie-Fort Pierce, FL

Home Prices
- Starter: $302,300
- Move Up: $478,200
- **182%** Elite: $605,700

Energy Requirements

- Heat: 483 degree days
- A/C: 2,497 hours
- Source: All-Electric

Monthly Costs
- Mortgage: $1,753
- Utilities: $128
- Taxes: $404

Rental Options US = 100

- Apartments: 37
- Houses/Duplexes: 88
- Rent: $730 to $980

Poughkeepsie-Newburgh-Middletown, NY

Home Prices

- Starter: $357,800
- Move Up: $467,400
- **130%** Elite: $592,000

Energy Requirements

- Heat: 5,809 degree days
- A/C: 294 hours
- Source: Fuel oil, Electricity

Monthly Costs
- Mortgage: $2,075
- Utilities: $192
- Taxes: $509

Rental Options US = 100

- Apartments: 72
- Houses/Duplexes: 77
- Rent: $810 to $980

Prescott, AZ

Home Prices

- Starter: $269,600
- Move Up: $441,900
- **128%** Elite: $559,800

Energy Requirements

- Heat: 4,849 degree days
- A/C: 365 hours
- Source: Utility gas, Electricity

Monthly Costs
- Mortgage: $1,563
- Utilities: $173
- Taxes: $294

Rental Options US = 100

- Apartments: 30
- Houses/Duplexes: 93
- Rent: $630 to $750

Housing

Providence-New Bedford-Fall River, RI-MA
Places Rated Rank: 331

Home Prices
Starter: $339,300
Move Up: $456,100
140% Elite: $577,800

Energy Requirements
Heat: 5,754 degree days
A/C: 374 hours
Source: Utility gas, Electricity

Monthly Costs
Mortgage: $1,968
Utilities: $182
Taxes: $363

Rental Options US = 100
Apartments: 87
Houses/Duplexes: 71
Rent: $650 to $830

Provo-Orem, UT
Places Rated Rank: 252

Home Prices
Starter: $210,100
Move Up: $281,400
41% Elite: $356,500

Energy Requirements
Heat: 5,663 degree days
A/C: 530 hours
Source: Utility gas, Electricity

Monthly Costs
Mortgage: $1,218
Utilities: $121
Taxes: $173

Rental Options US = 100
Apartments: 70
Houses/Duplexes: 100
Rent: $590 to $790

Pueblo, CO
Places Rated Rank: 106

Home Prices
Starter: $129,100
Move Up: $175,100
42% Elite: $221,800

Energy Requirements
Heat: 5,598 degree days
A/C: 541 hours
Source: Utility gas, Electricity

Monthly Costs
Mortgage: $749
Utilities: $127
Taxes: $117

Rental Options US = 100
Apartments: 56
Houses/Duplexes: 114
Rent: $480 to $630

Punta Gorda, FL
Places Rated Rank: 296

Home Prices
Starter: $269,900
Move Up: $445,900
173% Elite: $564,900

Energy Requirements
Heat: 409 degree days
A/C: 2,720 hours
Source: Utility gas, Electricity

Monthly Costs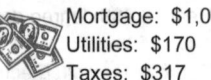
Mortgage: $1,565
Utilities: $117
Taxes: $361

Rental Options US = 100
Apartments: 23
Houses/Duplexes: 56
Rent: $700 to $1,020

Racine, WI
Places Rated Rank: 247

Home Prices
Starter: $172,600
Move Up: $248,000
62% Elite: $314,200

Energy Requirements
Heat: 7,032 degree days
A/C: 276 hours
Source: Utility gas, Electricity

Monthly Costs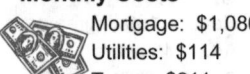
Mortgage: $1,001
Utilities: $170
Taxes: $317

Rental Options US = 100
Apartments: 62
Houses/Duplexes: 89
Rent: $550 to $670

Raleigh-Cary, NC
Places Rated Rank: 233

Home Prices
Starter: $186,300
Move Up: $277,900
32% Elite: $352,000

Energy Requirements
Heat: 3,465 degree days
A/C: 994 hours
Source: All-Electric

Monthly Costs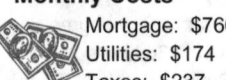
Mortgage: $1,080
Utilities: $114
Taxes: $211

Rental Options US = 100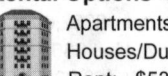
Apartments: 96
Houses/Duplexes: 63
Rent: $610 to $750

Rapid City, SD
Places Rated Rank: 174

Home Prices
Starter: $132,100
Move Up: $187,700
66% Elite: $237,800

Energy Requirements
Heat: 7,211 degree days
A/C: 319 hours
Source: Utility gas, Electricity

Monthly Costs
Mortgage: $766
Utilities: $174
Taxes: $237

Rental Options US = 100
Apartments: 76
Houses/Duplexes: 86
Rent: $530 to $720

Reading, PA
Places Rated Rank: 232

Home Prices
Starter: $165,600
Move Up: $238,800
68% Elite: $302,600

Energy Requirements
Heat: 5,395 degree days
A/C: 444 hours
Source: Fuel oil, Electricity

Monthly Costs
Mortgage: $960
Utilities: $175
Taxes: $269

Rental Options US = 100
Apartments: 51
Houses/Duplexes: 82
Rent: $530 to $650

Redding, CA
Places Rated Rank: 305

Home Prices
Starter: $319,000
Move Up: $478,300
156% Elite: $606,000

Energy Requirements
Heat: 2,961 degree days
A/C: 1,314 hours
Source: Utility gas, Electricity

Monthly Costs
Mortgage: $1,850
Utilities: $116
Taxes: $147

Rental Options US = 100
Apartments: 66
Houses/Duplexes: 97
Rent: $610 to $780

Reno-Sparks, NV
Places Rated Rank: 339

Home Prices
Starter: $401,300
Move Up: $577,500
136% Elite: $731,600

Energy Requirements
Heat: 5,600 degree days
A/C: 222 hours
Source: Utility gas, Electricity

Monthly Costs
Mortgage: $2,327
Utilities: $180
Taxes: $341

Rental Options US = 100
Apartments: 126
Houses/Duplexes: 83
Rent: $720 to $930

Richmond, VA
Places Rated Rank: 267

Home Prices
Starter: $221,300
Move Up: $326,600
91% Elite: $413,800

Energy Requirements
Heat: 3,919 degree days
A/C: 961 hours
Source: All-Electric

Monthly Costs
Mortgage: $1,283
Utilities: $114
Taxes: $239

Rental Options US = 100
Apartments: 81
Houses/Duplexes: 74
Rent: $620 to $770

Riverside-San Bernardino-Ontario, CA

Home Prices

Starter: $519,400
Move Up: $703,500
206% Elite: $891,100

Energy Requirements

Heat: 1,475 degree days
A/C: 1,268 hours
Source: Utility gas, Electricity

Monthly Costs

Mortgage: $3,012
Utilities: $94
Taxes: $240

Rental Options US = 100
Apartments: 74
Houses/Duplexes: 87
Rent: $820 to $1,070

Roanoke, VA
Places Rated Rank: 205

Home Prices

Starter: $162,800
Move Up: $233,600
63% Elite: $295,900

Energy Requirements

Heat: 4,284 degree days
A/C: 667 hours
Source: Utility gas, Electricity

Monthly Costs
Mortgage: $944
Utilities: $177
Taxes: $176

Rental Options US = 100
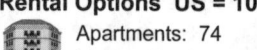
Apartments: 74
Houses/Duplexes: 63
Rent: $480 to $590

Rochester, MN
Places Rated Rank: 206

Home Prices

Starter: $164,800
Move Up: $227,900
50% Elite: $288,700

Energy Requirements
Heat: 8,308 degree days
A/C: 239 hours
Source: Utility gas, Electricity

Monthly Costs

Mortgage: $956
Utilities: $178
Taxes: $165

Rental Options US = 100
Apartments: 59
Houses/Duplexes: 42
Rent: $590 to $760

Rochester, NY
Places Rated Rank: 142

Home Prices

Starter: $118,900
Move Up: $168,100
31% Elite: $213,000

Energy Requirements
Heat: 6,728 degree days
A/C: 275 hours
Source: Utility gas, Electricity

Monthly Costs

Mortgage: $689
Utilities: $209
Taxes: $169

Rental Options US = 100
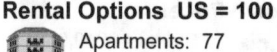
Apartments: 77
Houses/Duplexes: 75
Rent: $570 to $690

Rockford, IL
Places Rated Rank: 162

Home Prices

Starter: $131,600
Move Up: $174,300
39% Elite: $220,800

Energy Requirements
Heat: 6,933 degree days
A/C: 410 hours
Source: Utility gas, Electricity

Monthly Costs
Mortgage: $763
Utilities: $162
Taxes: $207

Rental Options US = 100
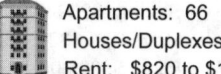
Apartments: 48
Houses/Duplexes: 79
Rent: $500 to $640

Rockingham County-Strafford County, NH
Places Rated Rank: 332

Home Prices

Starter: $316,900
Move Up: $431,300
118% Elite: $546,300

Energy Requirements
Heat: 6,593 degree days
A/C: 157 hours
Source: Fuel oil, Electricity

Monthly Costs

Mortgage: $1,838
Utilities: $202
Taxes: $532

Rental Options US = 100
Apartments: 66
Houses/Duplexes: 52
Rent: $820 to $1,050

✓ Rocky Mount, NC
Places Rated Rank: 28

Home Prices

Starter: $99,200
Move Up: $151,400
27% Elite: $191,800

Energy Requirements

Heat: 3,215 degree days
A/C: 997 hours
Source: All-Electric

Monthly Costs

Mortgage: $575
Utilities: $114
Taxes: $113

Rental Options US = 100
Apartments: 53
Houses/Duplexes: 129
Rent: $380 to $460

Rome, GA
Places Rated Rank: 54

Home Prices

Starter: $104,500
Move Up: $172,000
44% Elite: $217,900

Energy Requirements

Heat: 3,510 degree days
A/C: 860 hours
Source: Utility gas, Electricity

Monthly Costs

Mortgage: $606
Utilities: $165
Taxes: $126

Rental Options US = 100
Apartments: 43
Houses/Duplexes: 119
Rent: $380 to $500

Sacramento-Arden-Arcade-Roseville, CA
Places Rated Rank: 346

Home Prices

Starter: $467,400
Move Up: $646,400
171% Elite: $818,900

Energy Requirements

Heat: 2,666 degree days
A/C: 694 hours
Source: Utility gas, Electricity

Monthly Costs

Mortgage: $2,710
Utilities: $112
Taxes: $216

Rental Options US = 100
Apartments: 95
Houses/Duplexes: 96
Rent: $810 to $1,040

Saginaw-Saginaw Township North, MI
Places Rated Rank: 87

Home Prices

Starter: $111,500
Move Up: $163,600
30% Elite: $207,200

Energy Requirements

Heat: 6,645 degree days
A/C: 350 hours
Source: Utility gas, Electricity

Monthly Costs

Mortgage: $647
Utilities: $140
Taxes: $171

Rental Options US = 100
Apartments: 59
Houses/Duplexes: 63
Rent: $470 to $570

St. Cloud, MN
Places Rated Rank: 239

Home Prices
Starter: $185,800
Move Up: $248,400
84% Elite: $314,600

Energy Requirements
Heat: 8,815 degree days
A/C: 193 hours
Source: Utility gas, Electricity

Monthly Costs
Mortgage: $1,077
Utilities: $185
Taxes: $186

Rental Options US = 100
Apartments: 114
Houses/Duplexes: 42
Rent: $580 to $690

Housing

St. George, UT
 Places Rated Rank: 292

Home Prices
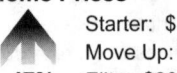
Starter: $289,100
Move Up: $459,200
98% Elite: $581,700

Energy Requirements
Heat: 3,103 degree days
A/C: 2,021 hours
Source: Utility gas, Electricity

Monthly Costs
Mortgage: $1,676
Utilities: $90
Taxes: $237

Rental Options US = 100
Apartments: 46
Houses/Duplexes: 119
Rent: $620 to $800

St. Joseph, MO-KS
Places Rated Rank: 70

Home Prices
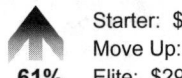
Starter: $103,100
Move Up: $158,300
47% Elite: $200,600

Energy Requirements
Heat: 5,271 degree days
A/C: 838 hours
Source: Utility gas, Electricity

Monthly Costs
Mortgage: $598
Utilities: $151
Taxes: $174

Rental Options US = 100
Apartments: 55
Houses/Duplexes: 89
Rent: $390 to $490

St. Louis, MO-IL
Places Rated Rank: 195

Home Prices

Starter: $155,800
Move Up: $230,900
61% Elite: $292,600

Energy Requirements
Heat: 4,758 degree days
A/C: 1,097 hours
Source: Utility gas, Electricity

Monthly Costs
Mortgage: $903
Utilities: $139
Taxes: $216

Rental Options US = 100
Apartments: 60
Houses/Duplexes: 63
Rent: $500 to $650

Salem, OR
Places Rated Rank: 254

Home Prices

Starter: $210,900
Move Up: $298,600
66% Elite: $378,300

Energy Requirements
Heat: 4,784 degree days
A/C: 86 hours
Source: All-Electric

Monthly Costs
Mortgage: $1,223
Utilities: $85
Taxes: $210

Rental Options US = 100
Apartments: 79
Houses/Duplexes: 96
Rent: $550 to $680

Salinas, CA
Places Rated Rank: 377

Home Prices

Starter: $912,000
Move Up: $1,251,000
221% Elite: $1,584,600

Energy Requirements
Heat: 3,080 degree days
A/C: 7 hours
Source: Utility gas, Electricity

Monthly Costs
Mortgage: $5,288
Utilities: $118
Taxes: $421

Rental Options US = 100
Apartments: 96
Houses/Duplexes: 140
Rent: $950 to $1,300

Salisbury, MD
Places Rated Rank: 253

Home Prices

Starter: $209,700
Move Up: $320,200
112% Elite: $405,600

Energy Requirements
Heat: 3,936 degree days
A/C: 764 hours
Source: All-Electric

Monthly Costs
Mortgage: $1,216
Utilities: $105
Taxes: $196

Rental Options US = 100
Apartments: 77
Houses/Duplexes: 108
Rent: $580 to $700

Salt Lake City, UT
Places Rated Rank: 265

Home Prices

Starter: $227,800
Move Up: $319,600
58% Elite: $404,900

Energy Requirements
Heat: 5,631 degree days
A/C: 726 hours
Source: Utility gas, Electricity

Monthly Costs
Mortgage: $1,321
Utilities: $121
Taxes: $187

Rental Options US = 100
Apartments: 97
Houses/Duplexes: 66
Rent: $610 to $730

San Angelo, TX
Places Rated Rank: 50

Home Prices

Starter: $90,700
Move Up: $131,200
48% Elite: $166,200

Energy Requirements
Heat: 2,396 degree days
A/C: 1,830 hours
Source: All-Electric

Monthly Costs
Mortgage: $526
Utilities: $137
Taxes: $214

Rental Options US = 100
Apartments: 100
Houses/Duplexes: 78
Rent: $450 to $580

San Antonio, TX
Places Rated Rank: 123

Home Prices

Starter: $109,000
Move Up: $172,700
46% Elite: $218,800

Energy Requirements
Heat: 1,573 degree days
A/C: 2,384 hours
Source: All-Electric

Monthly Costs
Mortgage: $632
Utilities: $137
Taxes: $257

Rental Options US = 100
Apartments: 91
Houses/Duplexes: 80
Rent: $540 to $690

San Diego-Carlsbad-San Marcos, CA
Places Rated Rank: 363

Home Prices
Starter: $647,200
Move Up: $849,900
188% Elite: $1,076,600

Energy Requirements
Heat: 1,063 degree days
A/C: 306 hours
Source: Utility gas, Electricity

Monthly Costs
Mortgage: $3,753
Utilities: $88
Taxes: $299

Rental Options US = 100
Apartments: 131
Houses/Duplexes: 93
Rent: $1,000 to $1,350

Sandusky, OH
Places Rated Rank: 140

Home Prices
Starter: $122,400
Move Up: $164,400
28% Elite: $208,300

Energy Requirements
Heat: 6,065 degree days
A/C: 407 hours
Source: Utility gas, Electricity

Monthly Costs
Mortgage: $710
Utilities: $173
Taxes: $184

Rental Options US = 100
Apartments: 47
Houses/Duplexes: 118
Rent: $490 to $610

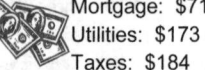

San Francisco-San Mateo-Redwood City, CA
Places Rated Rank: 379

Home Prices

Starter: $964,700
Move Up: $1,255,100
144% Elite: $1,589,800

Energy Requirements
Heat: 2,589 degree days
A/C: 20 hours
Source: Utility gas, Electricity

Monthly Costs
Mortgage: $5,594
Utilities: $111
Taxes: $445

Rental Options US = 100
Apartments: 171
Houses/Duplexes: 84
Rent: $1,150 to $1,600

San Jose-Sunnyvale-Santa Clara, CA
Places Rated Rank: 375

Home Prices
Starter: $878,600
Move Up: $1,184,300
144% Elite: $1,500,200

Energy Requirements
Heat: 2,171 degree days
A/C: 308 hours
Source: Utility gas, Electricity

Monthly Costs
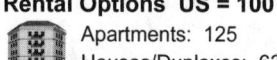
Mortgage: $5,095
Utilities: $105
Taxes: $406

Rental Options US = 100
Apartments: 128
Houses/Duplexes: 78
Rent: $1,140 to $1,490

San Luis Obispo-Paso Robles, CA
Places Rated Rank: 364

Home Prices
Starter: $660,900
Move Up: $928,200
185% Elite: $1,175,800

Energy Requirements
Heat: 2,129 degree days
A/C: 133 hours
Source: Utility gas, Electricity

Monthly Costs
Mortgage: $3,832
Utilities: $104
Taxes: $305

Rental Options US = 100
Apartments: 55
Houses/Duplexes: 132
Rent: $940 to $1,300

Santa Ana-Anaheim-Irvine, CA
Places Rated Rank: 376

Home Prices

Starter: $908,900
Move Up: $1,208,100
206% Elite: $1,530,300

Energy Requirements
Heat: 1,153 degree days
A/C: 656 hours
Source: Utility gas, Electricity

Monthly Costs
Mortgage: $5,270
Utilities: $89
Taxes: $420

Rental Options US = 100
Apartments: 125
Houses/Duplexes: 63
Rent: $1,160 to $1,460

Santa Barbara-Santa Maria, CA
Places Rated Rank: 373

Home Prices

Starter: $795,300
Move Up: $1,217,600
210% Elite: $1,542,300

Energy Requirements
Heat: 2,121 degree days
A/C: 156 hours
Source: Utility gas, Electricity

Monthly Costs
Mortgage: $4,612
Utilities: $104
Taxes: $367

Rental Options US = 100
Apartments: 101
Houses/Duplexes: 120
Rent: $1,050 to $1,470

Santa Cruz-Watsonville, CA
Places Rated Rank: 378

Home Prices
Starter: $929,700
Move Up: $1,228,500
161% Elite: $1,556,100

Energy Requirements
Heat: 2,836 degree days
A/C: 18 hours
Source: Utility gas, Electricity

Monthly Costs

Mortgage: $5,391
Utilities: $115
Taxes: $429

Rental Options US = 100
Apartments: 59
Houses/Duplexes: 140
Rent: $1,110 to $1,470

Santa Fe, NM
Places Rated Rank: 311

Home Prices
Starter: $316,800
Move Up: $531,700
81% Elite: $673,500

Energy Requirements
Heat: 6,613 degree days
A/C: 48 hours
Source: Utility gas, Electricity

Monthly Costs
Mortgage: $1,837
Utilities: $143
Taxes: $236

Rental Options US = 100
Apartments: 52
Houses/Duplexes: 93
Rent: $720 to $960

Santa Rosa-Petaluma, CA
Places Rated Rank: 370

Home Prices
Starter: $757,700
Move Up: $984,900
164% Elite: $1,247,600

Energy Requirements

Heat: 2,694 degree days
A/C: 192 hours
Source: Utility gas, Electricity

Monthly Costs

Mortgage: $4,394
Utilities: $112
Taxes: $350

Rental Options US = 100
Apartments: 72
Houses/Duplexes: 115
Rent: $970 to $1,350

Sarasota-Bradenton-Venice, FL
Places Rated Rank: 336

Home Prices
Starter: $347,600
Move Up: $570,900
190% Elite: $723,200

Energy Requirements
Heat: 556 degree days
A/C: 2,450 hours
Source: All-Electric

Monthly Costs
Mortgage: $2,016
Utilities: $128
Taxes: $465

Rental Options US = 100
Apartments: 63
Houses/Duplexes: 68
Rent: $730 to $940

Savannah, GA
Places Rated Rank: 201

Home Prices
Starter: $168,200
Move Up: $279,800
88% Elite: $354,400

Energy Requirements
Heat: 1,799 degree days
A/C: 1,798 hours
Source: All-Electric

Monthly Costs
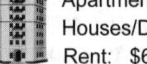
Mortgage: $975
Utilities: $107
Taxes: $203

Rental Options US = 100
Apartments: 65
Houses/Duplexes: 97
Rent: $600 to $780

Scranton-Wilkes-Barre, PA
Places Rated Rank: 145

Home Prices
Starter: $119,300
Move Up: $177,000
54% Elite: $224,300

Energy Requirements
Heat: 6,234 degree days
A/C: 278 hours
Source: Utility gas, Electricity

Monthly Costs

Mortgage: $692
Utilities: $190
Taxes: $194

Rental Options US = 100
Apartments: 41
Houses/Duplexes: 108
Rent: $430 to $520

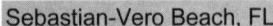
Housing

Seattle-Bellevue-Everett, WA
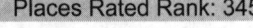Places Rated Rank: 345

Home Prices
Starter: $431,400
Move Up: $613,800
101% Elite: $777,600

Energy Requirements
Heat: 4,615 degree days
A/C: 42 hours
Source: All-Electric

Monthly Costs
Mortgage: $2,502
Utilities: $79
Taxes: $407

Rental Options US = 100
Apartments: 141
Houses/Duplexes: 60
Rent: $750 to $970

Sebastian-Vero Beach, FL
Places Rated Rank: 299

Home Prices
Starter: $274,800
Move Up: $501,900
167% Elite: $635,700

Energy Requirements
Heat: 455 degree days
A/C: 2,497 hours
Source: Utility gas, Electricity

Monthly Costs
Mortgage: $1,593
Utilities: $119
Taxes: $367

Rental Options US = 100
Apartments: 55
Houses/Duplexes: 73
Rent: $740 to $960

Sheboygan, WI
Places Rated Rank: 209

Home Prices
Starter: $150,200
Move Up: $209,800
49% Elite: $265,700

Energy Requirements
Heat: 7,056 degree days
A/C: 281 hours
Source: Utility gas, Electricity

Monthly Costs
Mortgage: $871
Utilities: $170
Taxes: $276

Rental Options US = 100
Apartments: 50
Houses/Duplexes: 90
Rent: $480 to $560

Sherman-Denison, TX
Places Rated Rank: 104

Home Prices
Starter: $101,600
Move Up: $153,700
44% Elite: $194,700

Energy Requirements
Heat: 2,850 degree days
A/C: 1,619 hours
Source: Utility gas, Electricity

Monthly Costs
Mortgage: $589
Utilities: $160
Taxes: $239

Rental Options US = 100
Apartments: 40
Houses/Duplexes: 98
Rent: $480 to $650

✓ Shreveport-Bossier City, LA
Places Rated Rank: 39

Home Prices
Starter: $102,300
Move Up: $162,600
48% Elite: $206,000

Energy Requirements
Heat: 2,251 degree days
A/C: 1,801 hours
Source: Utility gas, Electricity

Monthly Costs
Mortgage: $593
Utilities: $139
Taxes: $100

Rental Options US = 100
Apartments: 71
Houses/Duplexes: 91
Rent: $420 to $550

Sioux City, IA-NE-SD
Places Rated Rank: 67

Home Prices
Starter: $95,400
Move Up: $145,000
27% Elite: $183,800

Energy Requirements
Heat: 6,900 degree days
A/C: 542 hours
Source: Utility gas, Electricity

Monthly Costs
Mortgage: $553
Utilities: $175
Taxes: $188

Rental Options US = 100
Apartments: 75
Houses/Duplexes: 86
Rent: $420 to $540

Sioux Falls, SD
Places Rated Rank: 191

Home Prices
Starter: $139,700
Move Up: $193,500
40% Elite: $245,100

Energy Requirements
Heat: 7,812 degree days
A/C: 436 hours
Source: Utility gas, Electricity

Monthly Costs
Mortgage: $810
Utilities: $183
Taxes: $251

Rental Options US = 100
Apartments: 99
Houses/Duplexes: 63
Rent: $520 to $640

South Bend-Mishawaka, IN-MI
Places Rated Rank: 108

Home Prices
Starter: $114,000
Move Up: $167,000
33% Elite: $211,600

Energy Requirements
Heat: 6,294 degree days
A/C: 446 hours
Source: Utility gas, Electricity

Monthly Costs
Mortgage: $661
Utilities: $151
Taxes: $182

Rental Options US = 100
Apartments: 71
Houses/Duplexes: 77
Rent: $540 to $680

Spartanburg, SC
Places Rated Rank: 46

Home Prices
Starter: $102,500
Move Up: $153,300
25% Elite: $194,300

Energy Requirements
Heat: 3,080 degree days
A/C: 1,063 hours
Source: All-Electric

Monthly Costs
Mortgage: $594
Utilities: $120
Taxes: $149

Rental Options US = 100
Apartments: 43
Houses/Duplexes: 102
Rent: $450 to $550

Spokane, WA
Places Rated Rank: 238

Home Prices
Starter: $188,900
Move Up: $264,700
71% Elite: $335,300

Energy Requirements
Heat: 6,820 degree days
A/C: 185 hours
Source: Utility gas, Electricity

Monthly Costs
Mortgage: $1,095
Utilities: $167
Taxes: $178

Rental Options US = 100
Apartments: 94
Houses/Duplexes: 96
Rent: $520 to $650

Springfield, IL
Places Rated Rank: 93

Home Prices
Starter: $112,200
Move Up: $167,200
24% Elite: $211,800

Energy Requirements
Heat: 5,596 degree days
A/C: 728 hours
Source: Utility gas, Electricity

Monthly Costs
Mortgage: $651
Utilities: $143
Taxes: $176

Rental Options US = 100
Apartments: 51
Houses/Duplexes: 91
Rent: $440 to $550

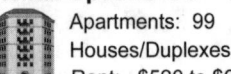

Springfield, MA
Places Rated Rank: 271

Home Prices

94%
- Starter: $220,000
- Move Up: $298,600
- Elite: $378,200

Energy Requirements

- Heat: 6,856 degree days
- A/C: 175 hours
- Source: Fuel oil, Electricity

Monthly Costs

- Mortgage: $1,276
- Utilities: $207
- Taxes: $191

Rental Options US = 100
- Apartments: 101
- Houses/Duplexes: 83
- Rent: $580 to $720

Springfield, MO
Places Rated Rank: 120

Home Prices

40%
- Starter: $125,400
- Move Up: $187,100
- Elite: $237,000

Energy Requirements

- Heat: 4,602 degree days
- A/C: 911 hours
- Source: Utility gas, Electricity

Monthly Costs

- Mortgage: $727
- Utilities: $144
- Taxes: $150

Rental Options US = 100
- Apartments: 62
- Houses/Duplexes: 108
- Rent: $450 to $580

Springfield, OH
Places Rated Rank: 88

Home Prices
29%
- Starter: $108,000
- Move Up: $150,100
- Elite: $190,200

Energy Requirements
- Heat: 5,921 degree days
- A/C: 425 hours
- Source: Utility gas, Electricity

Monthly Costs

- Mortgage: $626
- Utilities: $170
- Taxes: $162

Rental Options US = 100
- Apartments: 54
- Houses/Duplexes: 99
- Rent: $430 to $560

State College, PA
Places Rated Rank: 216

Home Prices

59%
- Starter: $167,100
- Move Up: $256,500
- Elite: $325,000

Energy Requirements
- Heat: 6,345 degree days
- A/C: 242 hours
- Source: All-Electric

Monthly Costs
- Mortgage: $969
- Utilities: $95
- Taxes: $272

Rental Options US = 100
- Apartments: 166
- Houses/Duplexes: 60
- Rent: $650 to $870

Stockton, CA
Places Rated Rank: 356

Home Prices

192%
- Starter: $520,200
- Move Up: $676,800
- Elite: $857,300

Energy Requirements
- Heat: 2,710 degree days
- A/C: 557 hours
- Source: Utility gas, Electricity

Monthly Costs

- Mortgage: $3,016
- Utilities: $113
- Taxes: $240

Rental Options US = 100
- Apartments: 75
- Houses/Duplexes: 120
- Rent: $760 to $940

✓ Sumter, SC
Places Rated Rank: 32

Home Prices

46%
- Starter: $95,200
- Move Up: $141,100
- Elite: $178,800

Energy Requirements

- Heat: 2,577 degree days
- A/C: 1,326 hours
- Source: All-Electric

Monthly Costs

- Mortgage: $552
- Utilities: $120
- Taxes: $138

Rental Options US = 100
- Apartments: 37
- Houses/Duplexes: 82
- Rent: $390 to $510

Syracuse, NY
Places Rated Rank: 95

Home Prices

52%
- Starter: $105,500
- Move Up: $160,800
- Elite: $203,700

Energy Requirements
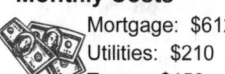
- Heat: 6,803 degree days
- A/C: 234 hours
- Source: Utility gas, Electricity

Monthly Costs

- Mortgage: $612
- Utilities: $210
- Taxes: $150

Rental Options US = 100
- Apartments: 83
- Houses/Duplexes: 81
- Rent: $520 to $620

Tacoma, WA
Places Rated Rank: 294

Home Prices

103%
- Starter: $289,000
- Move Up: $397,300
- Elite: $503,300

Energy Requirements
- Heat: 4,991 degree days
- A/C: 29 hours
- Source: All-Electric

Monthly Costs

- Mortgage: $1,676
- Utilities: $79
- Taxes: $272

Rental Options US = 100
- Apartments: 104
- Houses/Duplexes: 86
- Rent: $680 to $850

Tallahassee, FL
Places Rated Rank: 242

Home Prices

96%
- Starter: $186,400
- Move Up: $281,200
- Elite: $356,200

Energy Requirements
- Heat: 1,604 degree days
- A/C: 1,832 hours
- Source: All-Electric

Monthly Costs

- Mortgage: $1,081
- Utilities: $128
- Taxes: $249

Rental Options US = 100
- Apartments: 79
- Houses/Duplexes: 84
- Rent: $560 to $750

Tampa-St. Petersburg-Clearwater, FL
Places Rated Rank: 289

Home Prices

163%
- Starter: $251,300
- Move Up: $381,600
- Elite: $483,400

Energy Requirements
- Heat: 591 degree days
- A/C: 2,579 hours
- Source: All-Electric

Monthly Costs

- Mortgage: $1,457
- Utilities: $128
- Taxes: $336

Rental Options US = 100
- Apartments: 85
- Houses/Duplexes: 61
- Rent: $640 to $810

✓ Terre Haute, IN
Places Rated Rank: 38

Home Prices
36%
- Starter: $90,600
- Move Up: $138,000
- Elite: $174,900

Energy Requirements
- Heat: 5,433 degree days
- A/C: 690 hours
- Source: Utility gas, Electricity

Monthly Costs

- Mortgage: $525
- Utilities: $154
- Taxes: $151

Rental Options US = 100
- Apartments: 42
- Houses/Duplexes: 96
- Rent: $390 to $490

✓ Texarkana, TX-Texarkana, AR 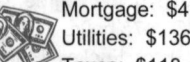 Places Rated Rank: 4

Home Prices
Starter: $71,300
Move Up: $109,400
31% Elite: $138,700

Energy Requirements
Heat: 2,421 degree days
A/C: 1,720 hours
Source: Utility gas, Electricity

Monthly Costs
Mortgage: $413
Utilities: $136
Taxes: $118

Rental Options US = 100
Apartments: 47
Houses/Duplexes: 97
Rent: $390 to $520

Toledo, OH   Places Rated Rank: 152

Home Prices
Starter: $126,300
Move Up: $177,100
34% Elite: $224,300

Energy Requirements
Heat: 6,460 degree days
A/C: 373 hours
Source: Utility gas, Electricity

Monthly Costs
Mortgage: $732
Utilities: $179
Taxes: $190

Rental Options US = 100
Apartments: 77
Houses/Duplexes: 86
Rent: $470 to $590

Topeka, KS   Places Rated Rank: 113

Home Prices
Starter: $107,000
Move Up: $154,600
42% Elite: $195,900

Energy Requirements
Heat: 5,225 degree days
A/C: 937 hours
Source: Utility gas, Electricity

Monthly Costs
Mortgage: $620
Utilities: $147
Taxes: $232

Rental Options US = 100
Apartments: 63
Houses/Duplexes: 87
Rent: $450 to $580

Trenton-Ewing, NJ   Places Rated Rank: 335

Home Prices
Starter: $340,300
Move Up: $525,900
118% Elite: $666,200

Energy Requirements
Heat: 5,357 degree days
A/C: 370 hours
Source: Utility gas, Electricity

Monthly Costs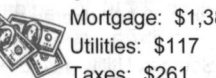
Mortgage: $1,973
Utilities: $163
Taxes: $460

Rental Options US = 100
Apartments: 91
Houses/Duplexes: 75
Rent: $810 to $980

Tucson, AZ   Places Rated Rank: 278

Home Prices
Starter: $239,600
Move Up: $355,900
121% Elite: $450,800

Energy Requirements
Heat: 1,578 degree days
A/C: 2,479 hours
Source: Utility gas, Electricity

Monthly Costs
Mortgage: $1,389
Utilities: $117
Taxes: $261

Rental Options US = 100
Apartments: 106
Houses/Duplexes: 70
Rent: $550 to $710

Tulsa, OK   Places Rated Rank: 58

Home Prices
Starter: $112,400
Move Up: $164,800
34% Elite: $208,700

Energy Requirements
Heat: 3,642 degree days
A/C: 1,570 hours
Source: Utility gas, Electricity

Monthly Costs
Mortgage: $652
Utilities: $134
Taxes: $115

Rental Options US = 100
Apartments: 74
Houses/Duplexes: 89
Rent: $480 to $600

Tuscaloosa, AL   Places Rated Rank: 107

Home Prices
Starter: $130,600
Move Up: $190,100
47% Elite: $240,800

Energy Requirements
Heat: 2,371 degree days
A/C: 1,664 hours
Source: Utility gas, Electricity

Monthly Costs
Mortgage: $757
Utilities: $142
Taxes: $95

Rental Options US = 100
Apartments: 106
Houses/Duplexes: 83
Rent: $450 to $600

Tyler, TX   Places Rated Rank: 138

Home Prices
Starter: $113,300
Move Up: $183,300
47% Elite: $232,200

Energy Requirements
Heat: 2,228 degree days
A/C: 1,801 hours
Source: All-Electric

Monthly Costs
Mortgage: $657
Utilities: $137
Taxes: $267

Rental Options US = 100
Apartments: 74
Houses/Duplexes: 96
Rent: $510 to $650

Utica-Rome, NY   Places Rated Rank: 59

Home Prices
Starter: $94,800
Move Up: $140,000
56% Elite: $177,400

Energy Requirements
Heat: 7,164 degree days
A/C: 181 hours
Source: Utility gas, Electricity

Monthly Costs
Mortgage: $550
Utilities: $217
Taxes: $135

Rental Options US = 100
Apartments: 60
Houses/Duplexes: 92
Rent: $420 to $510

Valdosta, GA   Places Rated Rank: 43

Home Prices
Starter: $107,100
Move Up: $163,900
45% Elite: $207,600

Energy Requirements
Heat: 1,757 degree days
A/C: 1,613 hours
Source: All-Electric

Monthly Costs
Mortgage: $621
Utilities: $107
Taxes: $129

Rental Options US = 100
Apartments: 57
Houses/Duplexes: 121
Rent: $450 to $590

Vallejo-Fairfield, CA   Places Rated Rank: 360

Home Prices
Starter: $603,800
Move Up: $804,400
190% Elite: $1,019,000

Energy Requirements
Heat: 2,649 degree days
A/C: 457 hours
Source: Utility gas, Electricity

Monthly Costs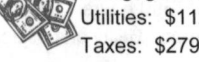
Mortgage: $3,501
Utilities: $112
Taxes: $279

Rental Options US = 100
Apartments: 83
Houses/Duplexes: 92
Rent: $990 to $1,280

✓ Victoria, TX
Places Rated Rank: 12

Home Prices

29%
Starter: $75,200
Move Up: $118,600
Elite: $150,300

Energy Requirements
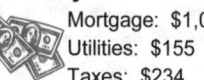
Heat: 1,248 degree days
A/C: 2,483 hours
Source: All-Electric

Monthly Costs
Mortgage: $436
Utilities: $137
Taxes: $177

Rental Options US = 100

Apartments: 33
Houses/Duplexes: 107
Rent: $450 to $540

Vineland-Millville
Places Rated Rank: 228

Home Prices

98%
Starter: $173,100
Move Up: $241,600
Elite: $306,000

Energy Requirements
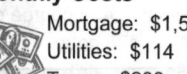
Heat: 4,835 degree days
A/C: 571 hours
Source: Utility gas, Electricity

Monthly Costs
Mortgage: $1,004
Utilities: $155
Taxes: $234

Rental Options US = 100
Apartments: 69
Houses/Duplexes: 91
Rent: $580 to $710

Virginia Beach-Norfolk-Newport News, VA-NC
Places Rated Rank: 286

Home Prices

130%
Starter: $260,100
Move Up: $397,100
Elite: $503,100

Energy Requirements
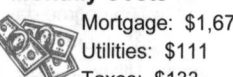
Heat: 3,368 degree days
A/C: 1,104 hours
Source: All-Electric

Monthly Costs
Mortgage: $1,508
Utilities: $114
Taxes: $288

Rental Options US = 100

Apartments: 90
Houses/Duplexes: 93
Rent: $670 to $850

Visalia-Porterville, CA
Places Rated Rank: 287

Home Prices

141%
Starter: $288,100
Move Up: $421,500
Elite: $533,900

Energy Requirements
Heat: 2,588 degree days
A/C: 1,130 hours
Source: Utility gas, Electricity

Monthly Costs
Mortgage: $1,671
Utilities: $111
Taxes: $133

Rental Options US = 100

Apartments: 31
Houses/Duplexes: 159
Rent: $510 to $670

Waco, TX
Places Rated Rank: 94

Home Prices

46%
Starter: $102,200
Move Up: $160,700
Elite: $203,600

Energy Requirements
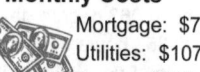
Heat: 2,164 degree days
A/C: 2,272 hours
Source: All-Electric

Monthly Costs
Mortgage: $593
Utilities: $137
Taxes: $241

Rental Options US = 100

Apartments: 94
Houses/Duplexes: 113
Rent: $470 to $610

Warner Robins, GA
Places Rated Rank: 91

Home Prices

35%
Starter: $122,000
Move Up: $177,400
Elite: $224,800

Energy Requirements

Heat: 2,364 degree days
A/C: 1,610 hours
Source: All-Electric

Monthly Costs
Mortgage: $707
Utilities: $107
Taxes: $147

Rental Options US = 100

Apartments: 62
Houses/Duplexes: 119
Rent: $550 to $700

Warren-Troy-Farmington Hills, MI
Places Rated Rank: 262

Home Prices

37%
Starter: $199,800
Move Up: $298,800
Elite: $378,500

Energy Requirements
Heat: 6,680 degree days
A/C: 301 hours
Source: Utility gas, Electricity

Monthly Costs

Mortgage: $1,159
Utilities: $141
Taxes: $306

Rental Options US = 100

Apartments: 75
Houses/Duplexes: 40
Rent: $650 to $840

Washington-Arlington-Alexandria, DC-VA-MD-WV
Places Rated Rank: 362

Home Prices

165%
Starter: $558,600
Move Up: $834,000
Elite: $1,056,500

Energy Requirements
Heat: 4,055 degree days
A/C: 1,078 hours
Source: Utility gas, Electricity

Monthly Costs

Mortgage: $3,239
Utilities: $156
Taxes: $599

Rental Options US = 100

Apartments: 138
Houses/Duplexes: 54
Rent: $980 to $1,260

Waterloo-Cedar Falls, IA
Places Rated Rank: 137

Home Prices

55%
Starter: $109,900
Move Up: $160,700
Elite: $203,600

Energy Requirements
Heat: 7,348 degree days
A/C: 415 hours
Source: Utility gas, Electricity

Monthly Costs

Mortgage: $637
Utilities: $187
Taxes: $232

Rental Options US = 100
Apartments: 70
Houses/Duplexes: 75
Rent: $460 to $570

Wausau, WI
Places Rated Rank: 173

Home Prices
46%
Starter: $129,200
Move Up: $183,100
Elite: $232,000

Energy Requirements
Heat: 8,237 degree days
A/C: 217 hours
Source: Utility gas, Electricity

Monthly Costs

Mortgage: $749
Utilities: $188
Taxes: $237

Rental Options US = 100

Apartments: 55
Houses/Duplexes: 66
Rent: $480 to $610

✓ Weirton-Steubenville, WV-OH
Places Rated Rank: 11

Home Prices
37%
Starter: $82,000
Move Up: $117,400
Elite: $148,800

Energy Requirements
Heat: 5,620 degree days
A/C: 376 hours
Source: Utility gas, Electricity

Monthly Costs
Mortgage: $475
Utilities: $162
Taxes: $112

Rental Options US = 100
Apartments: 35
Houses/Duplexes: 95
Rent: $350 to $460

Wenatchee, WA

Home Prices

Starter: $199,000
Move Up: $285,100
54% Elite: $361,200

Energy Requirements

Heat: 5,533 degree days
A/C: 500 hours
Source: Utility gas, Electricity

Monthly Costs
Mortgage: $1,154
Utilities: $148
Taxes: $188

Rental Options US = 100
Apartments: 41
Houses/Duplexes: 106
Rent: $500 to $610

West Palm Beach-Boca Raton-Boynton Beach, FL
Places Rated Rank: 351

Home Prices

Starter: $417,800
Move Up: $659,200
201% Elite: $835,000

Energy Requirements
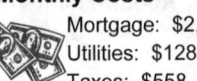
Heat: 246 degree days
A/C: 2,959 hours
Source: All-Electric

Monthly Costs

Mortgage: $2,423
Utilities: $128
Taxes: $558

Rental Options US = 100
Apartments: 86
Houses/Duplexes: 52
Rent: $810 to $1,060

✓ Wheeling, WV-OH
Places Rated Rank: 17

Home Prices

Starter: $84,600
Move Up: $130,800
41% Elite: $165,700

Energy Requirements

Heat: 5,428 degree days
A/C: 478 hours
Source: Utility gas, Electricity

Monthly Costs
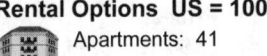
Mortgage: $491
Utilities: $159
Taxes: $116

Rental Options US = 100
Apartments: 41
Houses/Duplexes: 81
Rent: $350 to $430

Wichita, KS
Places Rated Rank: 105

Home Prices

Starter: $106,700
Move Up: $156,000
30% Elite: $197,600

Energy Requirements

Heat: 4,765 degree days
A/C: 1,235 hours
Source: Utility gas, Electricity

Monthly Costs

Mortgage: $619
Utilities: $140
Taxes: $232

Rental Options US = 100
Apartments: 66
Houses/Duplexes: 102
Rent: $450 to $580

✓ Wichita Falls, TX
Places Rated Rank: 23

Home Prices

Starter: $76,600
Move Up: $117,900
32% Elite: $149,300

Energy Requirements
Heat: 3,024 degree days
A/C: 1,909 hours
Source: Utility gas, Electricity

Monthly Costs

Mortgage: $444
Utilities: $163
Taxes: $180

Rental Options US = 100
Apartments: 61
Houses/Duplexes: 111
Rent: $460 to $560

Williamsport, PA
Places Rated Rank: 121

Home Prices

Starter: $112,500
Move Up: $163,900
45% Elite: $207,700

Energy Requirements
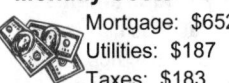
Heat: 6,063 degree days
A/C: 353 hours
Source: Fuel oil, Electricity

Monthly Costs
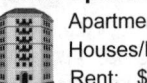
Mortgage: $652
Utilities: $187
Taxes: $183

Rental Options US = 100
Apartments: 55
Houses/Duplexes: 112
Rent: $440 to $520

Wilmington, DE-MD-NJ
Places Rated Rank: 288

Home Prices

Starter: $259,300
Move Up: $384,900
97% Elite: $487,500

Energy Requirements
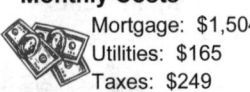
Heat: 4,888 degree days
A/C: 695 hours
Source: Utility gas, Electricity

Monthly Costs

Mortgage: $1,504
Utilities: $165
Taxes: $249

Rental Options US = 100
Apartments: 85
Houses/Duplexes: 72
Rent: $720 to $860

Wilmington, NC
Places Rated Rank: 261

Home Prices

Starter: $213,600
Move Up: $353,900
94% Elite: $448,400

Energy Requirements

Heat: 2,429 degree days
A/C: 1,408 hours
Source: All-Electric

Monthly Costs

Mortgage: $1,239
Utilities: $114
Taxes: $242

Rental Options US = 100
Apartments: 60
Houses/Duplexes: 84
Rent: $580 to $750

Winchester, VA-WV
Places Rated Rank: 303

Home Prices

Starter: $286,900
Move Up: $446,100
148% Elite: $565,100

Energy Requirements

Heat: 5,204 degree days
A/C: 462 hours
Source: All-Electric

Monthly Costs

Mortgage: $1,664
Utilities: $97
Taxes: $332

Rental Options US = 100
Apartments: 35
Houses/Duplexes: 111
Rent: $640 to $780

Winston-Salem, NC
Places Rated Rank: 151

Home Prices

Starter: $140,400
Move Up: $197,500
35% Elite: $250,200

Energy Requirements

Heat: 3,399 degree days
A/C: 910 hours
Source: All-Electric

Monthly Costs

Mortgage: $814
Utilities: $114
Taxes: $159

Rental Options US = 100
Apartments: 67
Houses/Duplexes: 82
Rent: $490 to $620

Worcester, MA
Places Rated Rank: 323

Home Prices

Starter: $317,600
Move Up: $425,100
116% Elite: $538,500

Energy Requirements
Heat: 6,831 degree days
A/C: 182 hours
Source: Fuel oil, Electricity

Monthly Costs
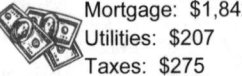
Mortgage: $1,842
Utilities: $207
Taxes: $275

Rental Options US = 100
Apartments: 85
Houses/Duplexes: 57
Rent: $680 to $880

Yakima, WA

Home Prices

38%
Starter: $135,800
Move Up: $184,600
Elite: $233,800

Energy Requirements
Heat: 6,104 degree days
A/C: 222 hours
Source: All-Electric

Monthly Costs
Mortgage: $787
Utilities: $79
Taxes: $128

Rental Options US = 100
Apartments: 61
Houses/Duplexes: 108
Rent: $470 to $590

York-Hanover, PA

Home Prices

72%
Starter: $174,400
Move Up: $243,200
Elite: $308,100

Energy Requirements
Heat: 5,233 degree days
A/C: 457 hours
Source: Utility gas, Electricity

Monthly Costs
Mortgage: $1,011
Utilities: $172
Taxes: $283

Rental Options US = 100
Apartments: 45
Houses/Duplexes: 68
Rent: $510 to $640

Youngstown-Warren-Boardman, OH-PA

Home Prices
30%
Starter: $97,000
Move Up: $144,600
Elite: $183,200

Energy Requirements
Heat: 6,451 degree days
A/C: 248 hours
Source: Utility gas, Electricity

Monthly Costs
Mortgage: $562
Utilities: $186
Taxes: $152

Rental Options US = 100
Apartments: 52
Houses/Duplexes: 81
Rent: $420 to $510

Yuba City, CA

Home Prices
175%
Starter: $340,600
Move Up: $471,600
Elite: $597,400

Energy Requirements
Heat: 2,488 degree days
A/C: 1,142 hours
Source: Utility gas, Electricity

Monthly Costs
Mortgage: $1,975
Utilities: $109
Taxes: $157

Rental Options US = 100
Apartments: 66
Houses/Duplexes: 131
Rent: $630 to $790

Yuma, AZ

Home Prices

126%
Starter: $152,000
Move Up: $233,100
Elite: $295,300

Energy Requirements
Heat: 782 degree days
A/C: 4,046 hours
Source: All-Electric

Monthly Costs
Mortgage: $881
Utilities: $108
Taxes: $166

Rental Options US = 100
Apartments: 42
Houses/Duplexes: 72
Rent: $530 to $720

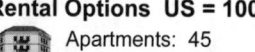

A GEOGRAPHY OF NEW HOME FEATURES

For decades, housing experts at the Census Bureau have followed regional trends in new single-family home construction. Here's a look at regional differences in certain home features.

Stories. The use of the word "story" to refer to flights of buildings may have originated with tiers of stained-glass or painted windows that described a special event. The common definition today is the space between the floor and the ceiling, roof, or the floor above, in the case of a multistory home. It has nothing to do with the height of a house; a house that appears from the outside to be two stories may actually be a single-story with a cathedral ceiling.

A generation ago, more than 75 percent of new houses were either one story or split level, i.e., having floors on more than one level when the difference in floor levels was less then one story. Today, new split level homes have disappeared from the American scene. Countrywide, four out of ten new homes are built on a single level; the rest are two or more stories.

Construction and Exterior. In frame construction, the wood frame supports the floors and roof; in masonry construction, the exterior masonry wall serves as the support. Masonry construction using local stone has virtually disappeared in new houses. Concrete block construction, however, is a common technique in Arizona (40 percent of new homes have it) and Florida (85 percent), where the exterior is either spray-painted or stuccoed. Everywhere else, the majority of new houses are of frame construction.

Aluminum siding has disappeared thanks to tougher and more easily maintained vinyl siding. The exterior's biggest market is in the Midwest, where two-thirds of new homes have it, and in the Northeast, where ninety-percent of new homes have it. The majority (86 percent) of all homes being built with brick exteriors in the United States are in the South. Stucco over cinder block is the predominant choice in the West, especially in California and Nevada.

Basements. The basement is an area of full-story height below the first floor that is not meant for year-round living. Only a third of new houses have basements because they are expensive to excavate. In six states, however, two out of three new houses come with some kind of basement, reflecting a pattern of locating the furnace below grade and a preference for extra living space. These states are Illinois, Iowa, Michigan, Minnesota, New York, and Pennsylvania.

Most new houses without basements either have a crawl space (an unfinished, accessible space below the first floor that is usually less than full-story height) or are simply resting on a concrete slab poured on the ground. In the United States, crawl spaces are preferred only in the Pacific Northwest and the Carolinas. Concrete slab footings support almost all new houses in the Sun Belt states of Arizona, Arkansas, Georgia, Louisiana, Mississippi, Oklahoma, and Texas.

Floor Area. New homes have gotten much larger over the past twenty-five years—from 1,660 square feet to 2,434 square feet on average, or enough difference to equal the size of a small condo. Interestingly, during that time, the floor area of new homes in the Northeast went from smallest to largest in the country. Why the expansion there and in other regions? More bedrooms plus a bathroom for every bedroom.

Bedrooms. A bedroom is a finished room with closet specifically designed for sleeping. A den, a space in the attic, or a convertible basement aren't counted as bedrooms. A one-room house is considered to have one bedroom. The portion of new homes with two bedrooms or less hasn't changed in decades, but the portion of new homes with four bedrooms or more has almost doubled.

Bathrooms. Bathrooms are either full (a tub or shower stall, a sink, and a toilet) or half (just a sink and a toilet). A generation ago, one-quarter of new houses had one and a half baths or less. Today, one-quarter of new homes have three baths or more. In the West, the figure approaches one-third.

Fireplaces. Flueless imitation fireplaces like dinettes and rumpus rooms are memories of the 1950s. Most new homes twenty-five years ago had no working fireplace. Today, half of all new American homes now are built with working fireplaces and chimneys. Unfortunately, many fireplaces in these new homes aren't used because of smoke problems caused by short chimneys. For a good fireplace draft, the chimney cap should be at least 20 feet above the hearth.

Homes with two fireplaces can be found more frequently in the northern timber states of Idaho, Minnesota, Montana, Oregon, and Washington, and also in North Carolina and Pennsylvania.

Porches, Patios, and Decks. A porch is a covered addition or recessed space elevated above the ground at the home's entrance. These Main Street lookouts almost disappeared after World War II, but are fast returning in new home markets. You'll find an enclosed porch attached to half of new homes in this country, and more than that in the South and West.

A patio is a floored area with or without a roof that sits directly on the ground. They predominate in the South and West, where the climate allows longer use. Decks, on the other hand, are roofless floored areas not sitting directly on the ground and are more preferred in the Northeast than any other region.

Garages and Carports. Garages, as everyone knows, are completely enclosed shelters for automobiles; carports are roofed shelters that aren't completely enclosed. Detached garages are a feature of older homes and were typically built behind the home, invisible from the street. Attached two-car garages, which became a popular feature on new homes during the 1950s, now are a standard feature on two-thirds of all newly built homes. And the carport? Except on older homes in the South and West, it has disappeared along with the once popular split level design.

Swimming Pools. You won't find new tract houses anywhere with in-ground swimming pools. Builders have learned that few buyers shop for shelter and a swimming pool at the same time. Moreover, local ordinances can require expensive liability insurance and a four-foot-high fence around the pool's perimeter to prevent accidents.

A RENTER'S MISCELLANY

The kind of apartment building you choose to live in definitely makes a difference in your monthly costs, according to the latest Institute of Real Estate Management survey. Rents for a typical four-room, 850-square-foot unit are much higher in high-rise elevator buildings (U.S. median rent $950) than in garden apartments (U.S. median rent $715), defined by the institute as a group of low-rise apartment buildings on a large landscaped lot under one manager. The least expensive kind of building is the low-rise or walk up building with fewer than 24 units (U.S. median rent $675).

You'll find that the annual turnover rate, defined as newly occupied apartments as a percent of all the apartments in the building in a year's time, also varies by the kind of building. Around the country, high-rise elevator buildings have the lowest turnover rate (U.S. median 22 percent), whereas the turnover rate in walk-ups and elevator buildings of three or fewer stories is twice this (U.S. median 49 percent). The kind of apartment building with the most transient population is the garden apartment, in which 62 percent of tenants moved in within the previous 12 months.

The Rule of 156

One useful way of determining the rent for a house is to divide its market value by 156. This rule of 156 was developed by the city of San Francisco as a way of specifying the fair value of an apartment being converted into a condo for a tenant who had been renting it. As the landlord might put it, the price equals 156 times your monthly rent, take it or leave it.

What the rule implies in reverse is that landlords can expect a 156-month (or 13-year) payback on houses they rent. Using this rule plus the prices of starter houses given in the Place Profiles, it isn't difficult to figure roughly what it would cost you to rent a house in a given metro area, assuming that the landlord has realistic expectations for the rate of return on property.

In Miami, the rent would be $2,600; in San Francisco, $6,200; in Pine Bluff, Arkansas, $430. The rule of 156 may seem unfair to landlords, since there is only an 8 percent return from which maintenance and taxes must be paid. Bear in mind, however, that landlords rarely buy houses for the rental income they may bring; rather, they buy them for their ultimate market appreciation and rent them during the interim to cover expenses and generate a modest cash flow.

Renters' Rights

In some states with large renter populations, laws concerning relations between landlords and tenants give rights to the landlord while imposing obligations on the tenant.

Seventeen states, however, have passed landlord-tenant laws based on the Uniform Residential Landlord and Tenant Act (1972), a model law drawn up by the National Conference of Commissioners on Uniform State Laws. The act removes the landlord and tenant relationship from property law and establishes it on the basis of contract law with all the rights and

Housing

The Renter Majority

Some 60 percent of American households live in urbanized areas, which make up only 1.5 percent of U.S. land area. Renter households are even more concentrated. One in four or America's 36 million rental units are located in just 23 counties, taking in just 0.5 percent of the country's land area.

County	% Renter Households
Alameda County (Oakland), CA	45%
Bronx County (New York), NY	80
Clark County (Las Vegas), NV	41
Cook County (Chicago), IL	42
Cuyahoga County (Cleveland), OH	37
Dallas County (Dallas), TX	47
Harris County (Houston), TX	45
King County (Seattle), WA	40
Kings County (New York), NY	73
Los Angeles County, CA	52
Maricopa County (Phoenix), AZ	33
Miami-Dade County (Miami), FL	42
Middlesex County (suburban Boston), MA	38
New York County (New York), NY	80
Orange County (Santa Ana-Anaheim), CA	39
Philadelphia County, PA	41
Queens County (New York), NY	57
San Diego County, CA	45
San Francisco County, CA	65
Santa Clara County (San Jose), CA	40
Tarrant County (Ft. Worth), TX	39
Wayne County (Detroit), MI	33

Source: Census Bureau, 2005 American Community Survey

remedies. These states are Alaska, Arizona, Florida, Hawaii, Iowa, Kansas, Kentucky, Montana, Nebraska, New Mexico, Oregon, Rhode Island, South Carolina, Tennessee, and Virginia.

This law defines rights and obligations of both parties to a lease on an apartment or house, and it also specifies the way disputes can be resolved. Among its provisions are:

• The landlord cannot demand a security deposit greater than the amount of one months rent.

• The landlord may enter the dwelling unit without consent of the tenant in case of emergency. In all other cases, the tenant may not unreasonably withhold consent to enter the dwelling unit for purposes of inspection, repair, and improvement.

• If your dispute with a landlord leads you to complain to the local housing board, to join a tenants' group, or to sue your landlord, the landlord cannot retaliate by cutting services, raising your rent, or evicting you.

• If the landlord doesn't make needed repairs, and the cost of the repairs is no more than $100 or half the rent (whichever is greater), you may make the repairs and deduct the expense from your monthly rent.

• After you vacate the apartment or house, any money you've deposited as security must be returned. If there are any deductions from the deposit for damages or other reasons, these deductions must be itemized.

• If your landlord doesn't live up to the lease's terms, you can recover damages in small claims court.

NUCLEAR HOT SPOTS: A NATIONWIDE LOCATOR

Would you mind living near a nuclear power plant? Given the record of the industry after thousands of reactor-years of commercial operation in the United States, even an opponent of nuclear power would admit that arguments against a *Chernobyl–China Syndrome* meltdown or low-level environmental contamination aren't convincing.

Still, thanks to a stable demand for electricity, construction and regulatory delays, skyrocketing costs, and concerns about reactor safety after the 1979 Three Mile Island incident, the growth of nuclear power has slowed considerably from the 1970s. Utility planners aren't willing to take the risk of investing billions in a 12- to 14-year process of building a nuclear plant and then face the possibility of not being allowed to operate it. As a result, plans for 97 power plants have been canceled over the years.

There are 104 commercial nuclear generating units that are fully licensed by the U.S. Nuclear Regulatory Commission (NRC) to operate in the United States. Of these 104 reactors, 69 are categorized as pressurized water reactors (PWRs) totaling 65,100 net megawatts (electric) and 35 units are boiling water reactors (BWR) totaling 32,300 net megawatts (electric). Although the United States has the most nuclear capacity of any nation, no new commercial reactor has come on line since May 1996.

During 2005, the 782 billion kilowatt-hours produced by nuclear reactors accounted for about 20 percent of total U.S. electrical output. In Vermont, 73 percent of electricity consumed comes from nuclear power; in Connecticut, 46 percent; in Arkansas, 31 percent; and Nebraska, 25 percent or more. The state with the greatest generating capacity, however, is Illinois, partly because Chicago-based Commonwealth Edison has built more nuclear power plants than any other utility in the country.

The following list shows the 31 states in which nuclear power plants are found. The generating capacity, or power output, for a typical reactor is 1,000 megawatts (1 million kilowatts) of electricity, or enough to supply the needs of a city of 600,000 people. Because operating licenses are granted for 40 years, the startup date is also given for each unit, along with its location. The first operating license expires in 2009, and by 2015, some forty other licenses will expire.

Alabama: 5,008 megawatts total capacity

10 miles NW of Decatur (*Browns Ferry 1, 2,* and *3*) 1973, 1974, 1976; 18 miles SE of Dothan (*Joseph M. Farley 1* and *2*) 1977, 1977

Arizona: 3,804 megawatts total capacity

36 miles W of Phoenix (*Palo Verde 1, 2* and *3*) 1984, 1985, 1986

Arkansas: 1,837 megawatts total capacity

6 miles WNW of Russellville (*Arkansas Nuclear One 1* and *2*) 1974, 1978

California: 4,324 megawatts total capacity

12 miles WSW of San Luis Obispo (*Diablo Canyon 1* and *2*) 1984, 1985; 4 miles SE of San Clemente (*San Onofre 2* and *3*) 1983, 1984

Connecticut: 2,037 megawatts total capacity

3.2 miles WSW of New London (*Millstone 2* and *3*) 1975, 1986

Florida: 3,902 megawatts total capacity

7 miles NW of Crystal River (*Crystal River 3*) 1977; 12 miles SE of Ft. Pierce (*St. Lucie 1* and *2*) 1976, 1983; 25 miles S of Miami (*Turkey Point 3* and *4*) 1972, 1973

Georgia: 4,053 megawatts total capacity

11 miles N of Baxley (*Hatch 1* and *2*) 1977, 1981; 26 miles SE of Augusta (*Vogtle 1* and *2*) 1987, 1988

Illinois: 11,379 megawatts total capacity

24 miles SSW of Joilet (*Braidwood 1* and *2*) 1987, 1988; 17 miles SW of Rockford (*Byron 1* and *2*) 1985, 1987; 6 miles E of Clinton (*Clinton*) 1987; 9 miles E of Morris (*Dresden 2* and *3*) 1991, 1971; 11 miles SE of Ottawa (*LaSalle 1* and *2*) 1982, 1983; 20 miles NE of Moline (*Quad Cities 1* and *2*) 1972, 1972

Iowa: 563 megawatts total capacity

8 miles NW of Cedar Rapids (*Duane Arnold*) 1974

Kansas: 1,166 megawatts total capacity

3.5 miles NE of Burlington (*Wolf Creek 1*) 1985

Louisiana: 2,055 megawatts total capacity

24 miles NNW of Baton Rouge (*River Bend 1*) 1985; 20 miles W of New Orleans (*Waterford 3*) 1984

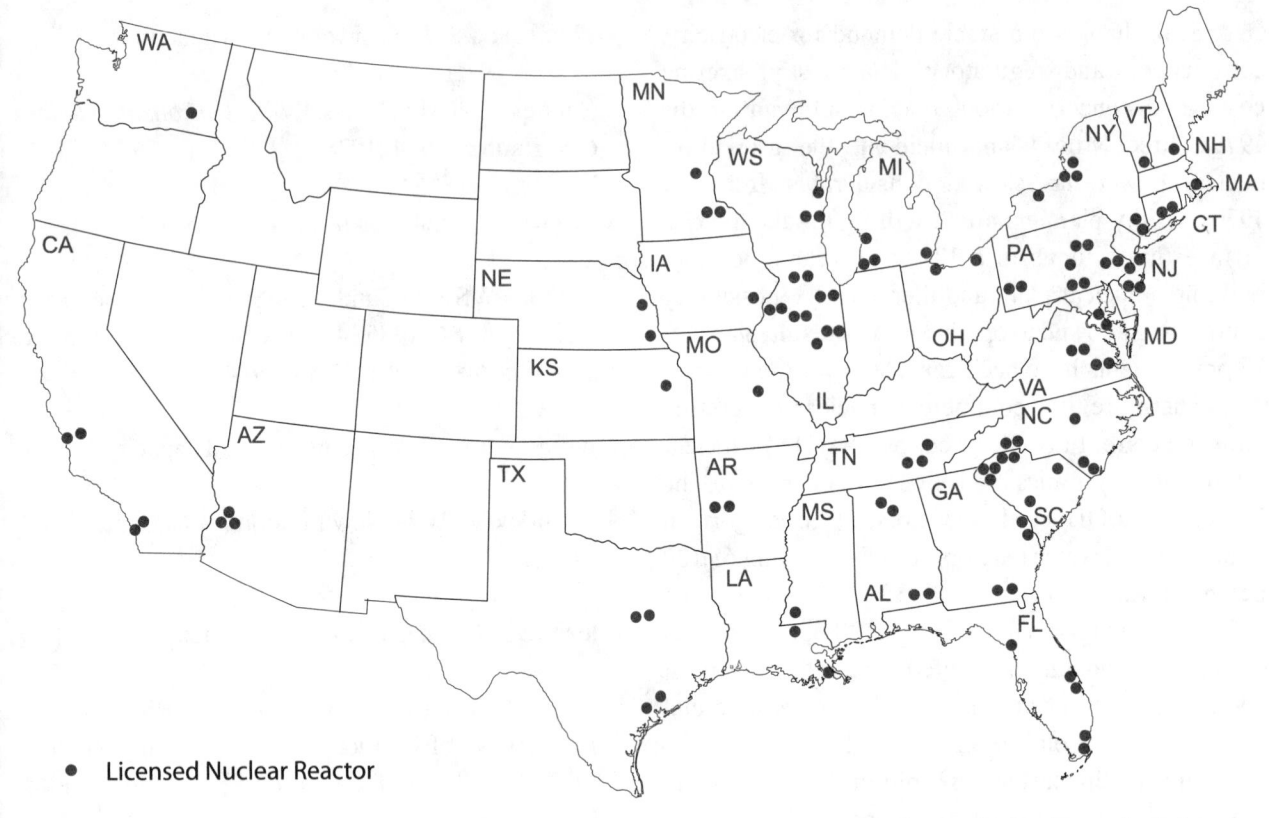

WA
MN
WS
MI
NY VT
NH
MA
CT
IA
NE
PA
NJ
CA
OH
MD
MO
KS
VA
NC
IL
AZ
TN
AR
GA
SC
TX
MS
LA
AL
FL

• Licensed Nuclear Reactor

Source: Nuclear Energy Institute

US NUCLEAR POWER PLANTS

Some 104 licensed reactors produce 20 percent of the nation'selectricity. During 2007, applications for 30 new reactors, located mainlyin the south, are expected to flood into the U.S. Nuclear RegulatoryCommission.

Maryland: 1,735 megawatts total capacity

40 miles S of Annapolis (*Calvert Cliffs 1* and *2*) 1974, 1976

Massachusetts: 685 megawatts total capacity

4 miles SE of Plymouth (*Pilgrim 1*) 1972

Michigan: 3,971 megawatts total capacity

11 miles S of Benton Harbor (*Cook 1* and *2*) 1974, 1977; 25 miles NE of Toledo (*Fermi 2*) 1985; 5 miles S of South Haven (*Palisades*) 1971

Minnesota: 1,613 megawatts total capacity

30 miles NW of Minneapolis (*Monticello*) 1971; 28 miles SE of Minneapolis (*Prairie Island 1* and *2*) 1973, 1974

Mississippi: 1,270 megawatts total capacity

25 miles S of Vicksburg (*Grand Gulf 1*) 1982

Missouri: 1,137 megawatts total capacity

10 miles SE of Fulton (*Callaway*) 1984

Nebraska: 1,232 megawatts total capacity

23 miles S of Nebraska City (*Cooper*) 1974; 19 miles N of Omaha (*Fort Calhoun*) 1973

New Hampshire: 1,159 megawatts total capacity

13 miles S of Portsmouth (*Seabrook 1*) 1985

New Jersey: 3,972 megawatts total capacity

18 miles SE of Wilmington (*Hope Creek 1*) 1986; 9 miles S of Toms River (*Oyster Creek 1*) 1969; 18 miles S of Wilmington (*Salem 1* and *2*) 1977, 1981

New York: 5,068 megawatts total capacity

20 miles NE of Rochester (*Ginna*) 1970; 24 miles N of New York City (*Indian Point 2* and *3*) 1973, 1976; 8 miles NE of Oswego (*James Fitzpatrick*) 1975; 6 miles NE of Oswego (*Nine Mile Point 1* and *2*) 1969, 1986

North Carolina: 4,938 megawatts total capacity

2 miles N of Southport (*Brunswick 1* and *2*) 1976, 1974; 17 miles NW of Charlotte (*McGuire 1* and *2*) 1981, 1984; 20 miles SW of Raleigh (*Harris 1*) 1986

Ohio: 2,108 megawatts total capacity

21 miles ESE of Toledo (*Davis-Besse*) 1977; 7 miles NE of Painesville (*Perry 1*) 1984

Pennsylvania: 9,229 megawatts total capacity

17 miles W of McCandles (*Beaver Valley 1* and *2*) 1976, 1987; 21 miles NW of Philadelphia (*Limerick 1* and *2*) 1985, 1988; 18 miles S of Lancaster (*Peach Bottom 2* and *3*) 1974, 1974; 7 miles NE of Berwick (*Susquehanna 1* and *2*) 1982, 1984; 10 miles SE of Harrisburg (*Three Mile Island 1*) 1974

South Carolina: 6,472 megawatts total capacity

6 miles NNW of Rock Hill (*Catawba 1* and *2*) 1985, 1986; 26 miles from Florence (*H.B. Robinson 2*) 1971; 30 miles W of Greenville (*Oconee 1, 2* and *3*) 1973, 1974, 1974; 26 miles NW of Columbia (*Summer*) 1984

Tennessee: 3,398 megawatts total capacity

9.5 miles NE of Chattanooga (*Sequoyah 1* and *2*) 1981, 1982; 10 miles S of Spring City (*Watts Bar 1*) 1984

Texas: 4,860 megawatts total capacity

4 miles N of Glen Rose (*Comanche Peak 1* and *2*) 1990, 1993; 12 miles SSW of Bay City (*South Texas Project 1* and *2*) 1989, 1987

Vermont: 506 megawatts total capacity

5 miles S of Battleboro (*Vermont Yankee 1*) 1972

Virginia: 3,440 megawatts total capacity

40 miles NW of Richmond (*North Anna 1* and *2*) 1978, 1980; 17 miles NW of Newport News (*Surry 1* and *2*) 1972, 1973

Washington: 1,122 megawatts total capacity

12 miles NW of Richland (*Columbia Generating Station*)

Wisconsin: 1,586 megawatts total capacity

27 miles E of Green Bay (*Kewaunee*) 1974; 13 miles NNW of Manitowoc (*Point Beach 1* and *2*) 1970, 1972

Source: U.S. Nuclear Regulatory Commission, Operating Nuclear Reactors

Jobs

We're all human resources on the lookout for our highest valued use, say economists. That explains why we change employers and even careers if the money is right.

We also pack up our things and move if we're underpaid or jobless and can't find work at all. This was true for the sailor who quit maritime Boston to take up farming in Ohio in the early 1800s, by the young entrepreneur who left New York for the Alaska goldfields in 1900, by the children of poor sharecroppers who left the South to work in Detroit automobile factories in the 1940s, or by *their* children who left Detroit (and Flint, Kalamazoo, Youngstown, and Erie) for jobs in the New South, where their grandparents remained.

The economy—meaning jobs—is a big issue. Among the factors behind relocating in *Places Rated Almanac*, it is the most important. For some people, it is the only factor. While we don't see boomtowns, we do see Casper, WY, Lafayette, LA, Fargo-Moorhead, ND-MN, and Sioux Falls, SD, where unemployment rates have fallen down to 2 percent in recent years. And we also see other metro areas sensing a whiff of the dark times they endured more than a decade ago.

WHERE WILL THE NEW WORK BE?

Economists who follow employment trends have an old joke: If you take each local planner's numbers for job growth in his or her area and add them all together, the total jobs forecasted would require that every man, woman, and child hold down one day job and moonlight two others.

Fortunately, economists with a national view have a better perspective. Although no one can predict the future with certainty, forecasting where jobs will be plentiful over the next few years isn't merely a matter of gazing into a crystal ball.

Start by asking the perennial question: Do people move to where the jobs are, or do jobs come to where the people are? While this is a good topic to argue about over beers at an academic convention, most economists think jobs come to where the people are. In other words, any growing place that has a concentration of people with a variety of worker skills will be a jobs Mecca.

But there's more to it than that. Some metro areas are saddled with sunset industries—shipbuilding, textiles, sawmills, and steel, for example—while others have sunrise industries - health care, higher education, and software. Most metro areas have varying mixes of both. Forecasting which ones will gain the jobs is as much a matter of determining the prospects for certain industries as it is predicting population shifts.

The great American jobs machine has churned out record numbers of jobs for decades and, depending on which expert is talking, the machine is either showing wear and tear or has shifted into a new and different gear. Still, millions of new jobs will be added to the U.S. economy by 2015. Although employment increases will occur at half the pace of the 1990s, the prospects for certain occupations look quite rosy.

The biggest continuing trend—one that's several decades old—is massive growth in service-producing sectors and marked decline in goods-producing industries. In other words, opportunities for highly trained white-collar workers are growing rapidly, with the blue-collar shade of many metro areas fading to white.

BLUE-COLLAR BLUES...

Shortly after World War II, white-collar jobs passed blue-collar jobs in number for the first time in history. White-collar workers as a group earn somewhat less than blue-collar workers because so many white-collar jobs are low-pay clerical and retail positions and so many blue-collar jobs are skilled occupations protected by union contracts. But white-collar jobs, although paying less, provide a ladder of opportunity that blue-collar jobs don't.

And the work is steadier. One of the biggest union issues now is security against layoffs and plant closings rather than higher wages. Blue-collar workers are beginning to want what's best in the white-collar world, and they are willing to sacrifice

higher wage demands.

The shrinking world of blue-collar work is divided into five basic industries. For the most part, job opportunities in four are expected to drop or merely hold steady past the year 2015.

Farming, Forestry, and Fishing

In 1850, half of America found work on a farm or ranch. Today, it's fewer than one in fifty. From Mississippi to Minnesota, the family farm is disappearing as mechanized agribusiness rounds up more acreage and concentrates on fewer crops. Thanks to competition abroad, farm exports won't ever regain the world dominance they enjoyed up to the 1980s. Between now and 2015, agriculture will see the largest jobs decline of any major sector. A bright spot: booming ethanol production in the Plains States from common field corn.

Some metro areas - those in California's Central Valley (Stockton, Merced, Bakersfield, Fresno) - have large numbers of farming jobs. Agriculture has a significant portion of self-employed workers, and the rising demand for organic farm produce may save many family farms.

One portion of the agricultural sector—agricultural services, such as veterinarian services, crop and livestock management, and even landscaping and lawn services—has been growing rapidly, and the growth will continue. Here is yet another indication of the shift toward a service economy.

Mining—A Hard Place

Jobs in mining, once a bedrock-stable employer in the West, are in a deep hole and likely to remain there. Half of these jobs are in hard-hatted oil and natural gas production and high-tech oil field services, disaster industries for the Southwest and Rockies. The simple reason is that foreign oil is cheaper.

Coal mining isn't as dangerous now, but it's still as dirty as depicted in *October Sky*, a film about growing up in a West Virginia company town. Output should increase to fuel the demand for more electricity. But companies aren't hiring, thanks to productivity boosts.

Metal mining isn't expected to recover any of the deep cuts experienced over the past decade, either. Exports of raw ores are expected to rise, but slow growth in basic steel, as well as iron and steel foundries will limit increases in demand. And while coal is getting more important as alternative energy,

the number of jobs in coal mines won't grow. Instead, new production methods will mean continued shrinking of employment.

Construction—Rebuilding Rather Than Building

Here's a footloose industry if there ever was one. Building contracts run out? Move on to another location. Why else do you think many itinerant general contractors have southwestern drawls? This industry, which thinks that half of North America's bridges, highways, and public buildings must be rebuilt within the next decade, is expected to provide most of the blue-collar jobs to 2015 and beyond. Whenever you see a place forecast to gain a large number of blue-collar jobs, you'll be seeing hammers, bulldozers, bricks, and lumber.

Slow population growth won't slow homebuilding. Aging baby-boomers want upgraded houses, second homes, and assisted-living facilities. Their children will boost the demand for houses of their own. The glut of 1990s office and commercial space is past, but technology will dampen demand for new commercial construction as nontraditional work and retail environments such as teleconferencing, home offices, telecommuting, and electronic shopping proliferate.

Manufacturing—Anything but Durable

Here is another job sector that's predicted to grow glacially or not at all. Smokestacks, low-rise buildings near rail tracks, even high-tech assembly work—we can tell it good-bye over time. Much of it is moving offshore or to third-world countries.

Although manufacturing will lose hundreds of thousands of jobs over the next decade, output is expected to almost keep pace with total GNP growth. At the same time, the occupational composition of the remaining manufacturing jobs will change. In general, following the trend of the disappearing blue-collar job, manufacturing employment will shift from production and assembly-line jobs toward professional, managerial, and technical occupations. The shift is more pronounced in industries where imports play a significant role. In some of those cases, design and engineering are done domestically, but much of the actual assembly is performed overseas.

Computer manufacturing, as we all might have guessed, has been one of the fastest-growing

Seven Million Steps Forward...

Occupations that will see the most new openings are large rather than fast growing and, with exceptions in health care and education, require the least education and training and offer the lowest pay.

Occupation	New Jobs
Retail salespersons	736,000
Registered nurses	703,000
Postsecondary teachers	524,000
Customer service reps	471,000
Janitors and cleaners	440,000
Waiters and waitresses	376,000
Fast food workers	367,000
Home health aides	350,000
Nursing aides	325,000
General and operations managers	308,000
Personal and home care aides	287,000
Elementary school teachers	265,000
Accountants and auditors	264,000
Office clerks, general	263,000
Laborers and freight movers	248,000
Receptionists	246,000
Landscapers and groundskeepers	230,000
Tractor-trailer drivers	223,000
Computer software engineers	222,000
Maintenance and repair workers	202,000

...And a Million Steps Back

Jobs on the decline are hit by technology and societal change. Bank tellers are elbowed aside by ATM machines. "Do Not Call" laws push telemarketers out into the street. Door-to-door sales workers aren't finding anyone at home because everyone is either in school or working.

Occupation	Lost Jobs
Farmers and ranchers	155,000
Stock clerks and order fillers	115,000
Sewing machine operators	93,000
File clerks	93,000
Order clerks	63,000
Mail clerks (not USPS)	59,000
Textile machine	50,000
Computer operators	49,000
Secretaries (not legal or medical)	48,000
Machine operators	43,000
Telemarketers	42,000
Word processors and typists	30,000
Credit authorizers and clerks	27,000
Machine feeders and offbearers	27,000
Meter readers	22,000
Office machine operators	22,000
Switchboard operators	19,000
Door-to-door sales workers	18,000
Photographic processors	17,000

Source: U.S. Department of Labor. Listed first are occupations that together will add 7 million jobs over the next eight years. Listed next are occupations that together will shrink by 1 million positions during the same period.

industries during the past 30 years. The nature of work in this industry, however, is uncharacteristic of manufacturing industries. It employs a high concentration of scientific personnel and a relatively low concentration of production workers. Employment in computer manufacturing is expected to expand beyond the year 2015, with even more of a shift at that time from production to research and development occupations.

The printing and publishing business is one of the manufacturing sectors to have registered consistent job gains in the past few years. Even during the recession, both output and employment increased steadily. And the introduction of electronic composition systems and other new technologies has not put a damper on this trend. As elsewhere, however, occupational shifts are occurring within the printing trades, from fewer typesetters and other craftspeople to more front-office personnel such as writers, editors, managers, and salesworkers.

Transportation, Communications, and Public Utilities

This catchall industry classification embraces electric power generation, 18-wheel trucking, airline food and baggage handlers, cable television, and much more. In recent years, deregulation has boosted employment in the air transportation industry, as many smaller firms entered the market and price competition stimulated demand. But, in the long run, consolidation and takeovers are expected to dampen the rate of job growth.

Overall, employment in this group is expected to decrease over the rest of the decade due to declining industry employment and technological changes. The railroad industry, for example, is expected to lose tens of thousands of jobs; likewise, the number of water transportation workers is expected to decline. Greater efficiency in scheduling, marketing, and cost control in the trucking industry is expected to produce greater gains in output than in employment.

... AND A WHITE-COLLAR CHORUS

White-collar work, which corresponds roughly with service-oriented occupations, is divided into four basic industry categories. With some variations within categories, this is where the real action is expected to occur through the early years of the 21st century.

Trade

Retail jobs outnumber wholesale positions by five to one and are expected to gain by nearly 1 million by the end of the decade. Unfortunately, retail trade jobs (counter help, merchandising, shoe fitting, aisle sweeping, cashiering) aren't worth having if your cash needs are immediate and above average. These jobs do, however, provide rapid advancement to managerial slots, which are still lower-paid despite the title. BJ's Wholesale Club, Home Depot, Circuit City, and Best Buy are the most ubiquitous establishments in North America, and heavy opportunity in this sector goes hand in hand with a local area that is swelling with people.

Finance, Insurance, and Real Estate

Referred to in regional developers' shorthand as FIRE, this is the purest of the white-collar industrial classifications. Here the compensation is greater than in the retail trade, and potentially greater by far than in any other industry. It is a briefcase and tie industry—an office-with-a-capital-O environment. It has both heavier government regulation than other industries and more unreported crime.

Banking, credit agencies, and investment offices—a big part of the FIRE industries—should enjoy substantial rates of business growth in the next decade, but not necessarily such growth in numbers of jobs. Consolidation and technological advances in automatic banking and other financial transactions will actually slow rates of employment gain. This doesn't mean no new jobs in these fields; there will be some growth—for example, thousands more in credit agencies and investment offices by the year 2015. But the rate of employment growth will be slower than in the past and will not match the growth in business output.

Similarly, greater efficiency in the insurance industry—computerized underwriting, for example means that job gains will be limited for insurance carriers and for independent agents and brokers. Not zero growth, but slower growth. Rapid projected growth in the real estate industry is expected to have a favorable impact on employment for brokers (increasing by 44 percent) and appraisers (increasing by 41 percent).

Service—What the World is Coming To

Think of high-rise marble and glass office buildings and medical centers with piped-in music. Think of

white smocks and clipboards and shaded college campuses. These are the most desirable kinds of developments—the kinds city fathers and mothers dream of. If the landscape is full of these buildings, you've got a well-educated work force, higher incomes, and a stable, service-oriented economy.

The service division includes careers in business, health, recreation, the professions, and education—an increasing proportion of which will require formal education and certification. Health and education, typically underwritten by government or third-party payers, lead the way in this division. It makes sense if you think about it; the numbers of educational staff are rising with the numbers of children of the baby-boom generation, and the health-care industry is growing as the population ages and needs more medical attention. Overall, this category has been and is projected to be the fastest-growing for new jobs well into the next century.

The big story in services is, as expected, computer and data processing, systems design, programming, and software development. Another big story in business services, with a very large projected increase in unemployment, is the personnel supply business, especially the temporary help industry. No longer limited to placing office workers, temporary personnel service businesses are beginning to place workers from industrial, medical, managerial, engineering, and technical occupations as well. The employers like the lower fringe benefits and the access to added help during peak times, and the temporary workers like the flexibility, variety, and experience.

With the trend toward development of new service businesses, the demand is growing for research, management, and consulting services. Independent laboratories for research and development, market researchers, personnel training or management consultants, economic researchers, efficiency experts, lobbyists, and other business consultants will be in increasing demand.

In the professions, the legal services industry has been growing, taking a place among the top ten fastest-growing employment industries. If you thought the legal profession was filled to capacity, think again. Increasing liability litigation, corporate mergers and acquisitions, high divorce levels, geographic expansion of law firms, a greater degree of legal specialization within firms, and an increase in litigation in general keep things moving.

In health care, too, important shifts are taking place. Cost-containment policies have halted the expansion of hospitals and hospital employment, with health-care delivery moving from the hospital to outpatient-care centers. Look for employment growth in the emergency care clinics, surgicenters, and walk-in treatment centers that are popping up all around us.

Government

If you're considering a job in the federal government, you might reconsider. The country's largest single employer will definitely be shrinking thanks to budgetary constraints, the growing use of private contractors, and the transfer of some functions to state and local governments.

Total public employment will rise over the next decade, however, with most of the increase hitting municipal workers such as teachers, firefighters, and police. On the other hand, count on a decline of jobs among clerical and administrative support workers and among government hospital workers.

For government jobs, though, some places—Austin, Columbus, Madison, Tallahassee and Atlanta, GA—are in enviable positions. They are state capitals with large bureaucracies that face little unemployment threat. That they are all higher education centers doesn't hurt, either.

JUDGING: JOBS

If you were out of work or looking for a better job, would the odds of tracking one down be better in Dallas, Denver, or Duluth? What about Honolulu, Houston, or Huntsville? To help you answer these questions, *Places Rated* compares each metro area's rate of job growth forecast between now and the year 2015, its number of new jobs that will be created during this period, the quality of these new jobs, and the area's historic resistance to unemployment.

Growth Rate

Twenty metro areas have 8-year job growth forecasts greater than 20%. Certainly a rosy forecast—such as St. George's 34.7 percent, Laredo's 27.3 percent, or the 22.8 percent seen for Coeur d'Alene, a resort and retirement area just east of the Idaho/Washington border from Spokane—always looks good at first view. For these smaller areas, however, a high rate translates to just 2,000 to 3,000 new jobs a year.

Jobs

The Jobs rankings, from 1 to 379, are in the *Place Profiles* section coming next. Jobs scores, from 100.0 to 0.0, are in *Putting It All Together* at the end of this book. Readers can view and print out Jobs rankings and scores, from #1 Austin-Round Rock, TX (score: 100.0) to #379 Danville, VA (score: 0.0), at *Places Rated's* website.

Here are the top twenty:

Rank	Score
1. Austin-Round Rock, TX	100.0
2. Phoenix-Mesa-Scottsdale, AZ	99.7
3. Las Vegas-Paradise, NV	99.4
4. Denver-Aurora, CO	99.2
5. Houston-Sugar Land-Baytown, TX	98.9
6. Sacramento--Arden-Arcade, CA	98.1
7. San Diego-Carlsbad-San Marcos, CA	98.1
8. Santa Ana-Anaheim-Irvine, CA	98.1
9. Lake County-Kenosha County, IL-WI	97.8
10. Dallas-Plano-Irving, TX	97.6
11. Atlanta-Sandy Springs-Marietta, GA	97.3
12. Fort Worth-Arlington, TX	97.0
13. West Palm Beach-Boca Raton, FL	96.8
14. Washington-Arlington, DC-VA-MD-WV	96.5
15. Charlotte-Gastonia-Concord, NC-SC	96.2
16. Warren-Troy-Farmington Hills, MI	96.0
17. Raleigh-Cary, NC	95.7
18. Seattle-Bellevue-Everett, WA	95.5
19. Orlando-Kissimmee, FL	95.2
20. Boulder, CO	94.9

At *www.placesrated.com*, you'll also find more information on each metro areas current unemployment rates, industrial mix and hiring trends.

Number of New Jobs

In contrast, Chicago's modest 9.1 percent forecast results in over 442,000 new jobs between now and the year 2015 and Washington, DC's expected 12.9 percent means nearly 378,000 new jobs over the same period. Because it is more likely that choice executive, professional, and managerial jobs in growth industries will be found in metro areas with larger numbers of newly created jobs, this factor may be the single most important of all.

New Job Quality

Most new jobs will be in the low-paying retail trade and modestly paying service industries. High-paying jobs are found there, too, but in fewer numbers. The biggest paychecks per worker are in manufacturing, government, transportation, communications, and public utilities. To gauge job quality, *Places Rated* uses the forecasted average earnings per worker (a quick measure of productivity, incidentally). Winners include San Jose, New York, and San Francisco.

SCORING: JOBS

To derive a score for the local economy, each area's forecasted *number* of new jobs gets twice the weight as the percent *rate* of new job growth and twice the weight of how many of the expected jobs are higher paying ones. A metro area's final score is a percentile on a scale of 0 to 100 corresponding to its rank.

Austin, the capital of Texas and the home of the University of Texas and companies like Dell Computer and Freescale Semiconductor, gets 100.0. St. Cloud, upriver from Minnesota's thriving Twin Cities, gets 50.0. Danville, VA, an aging textile city within commuting distance of North Carolina's Triad (Greensboro-Winston-Salem-High Point) gets 0.0. They are respectively the best, average, and worst American metro areas for jobs between now and into the new millennium.

PLACE PROFILES: JOBS

The following profiles show job forecasts for each metro area between the years 2007 and 2015. *Unemployment Risk* is an arrow indicating how prone the metro area is to cyclical recession based on too many jobs in vulnerable industries. Vulnerable

industries include construction, manufacturing, seasonal agriculture, and the military.

Sixty-seven metro areas show an arrow pointing downward (⬇), meaning the risk of unemployment is lower than average. Another 197 metro areas show a pair of arrows (⬅ ➡), indicating that the threat of unemployment is average. Finally, 119 metro areas show an arrow pointing up (⬆), indicating that the threat is higher than average.

Job Quality refers to forecasted earnings per worker, and is really another word for productivity. Arrow symbols indicate high (⬆), average (⬅ ➡), and low (⬇) job quality. Next comes the number of new jobs in industries where a worker's pay is *High* (government, manufacturing, transportation, and public utilities); those in industries where pay is *Average* (construction, services, finance, insurance, and real estate); and those in industries where pay is *Low* (retail trade, wholesale trade, farming, and mining).

Next are the forecasted numbers of new jobs in predominantly blue-collar industries (farming, forestry, fishing, mining, construction, manufacturing, transportation, and public utilities) and in predominantly white-collar industries (trade, finance, insurance, real estate, service and government other than military). *Total Growth Rate* is the forecasted percent increase in all jobs between 2007 and 2015.

Growth forecasts for U.S. metro areas are from July 1, 2007, to July 1, 2015 and are derived from employment forecasts from Woods & Poole Economics, Inc., of Washington, DC. The projections are based on historical data from the U.S. Department of Commerce; all data 2007-2015 is projected by Woods & Poole, and employment in number of jobs includes proprietors and part-time jobs. Projections are uncertain, and future data may differ substantially from Woods & Poole projections. Woods & Poole does not guarantee the accuracy of these data and projections. The use of these data and projections, and the conclusions drawn from them, are solely the responsibility of the author.

A check mark (✓) in front of a metro area's name highlights it as one of the top forty places for job growth between now and the year 2015.

Abilene, TX

Forecast 2007-2015

Earnings	New Jobs	Growth
High	299	2.0%
Average	1,820	7.4%
Low	5,017	9.6%

New Jobs in . .
   Blue-collar industries: 783
   White-collar industries: 6,353
Total Growth Rate: 7.8%
Unemployment Risk: ⬇
Job Quality: ⬇

Places Rated Rank: 357

Akron, OH

Forecast 2007-2015

Earnings	New Jobs	Growth
High	7,828	7.2%
Average	13,188	12.5%
Low	24,579	11.6%

New Jobs in . .
   Blue-collar industries: 12,249
   White-collar industries: 33,346
Total Growth Rate: 10.7%
Unemployment Risk: ⬇
Job Quality: ⬇

Places Rated Rank: 106

Albany, GA

Forecast 2007-2015

Earnings	New Jobs	Growth
High	313	1.6%
Average	1,682	8.2%
Low	5,674	13.2%

New Jobs in . .
   Blue-collar industries: 769
   White-collar industries: 6,900
Total Growth Rate: 9.3%
Unemployment Risk: ⬇
Job Quality: ⬇

Places Rated Rank: 288

Albany-Schenectady-Troy, NY

Forecast 2007-2015

Earnings	New Jobs	Growth
High	2,723	3.2%
Average	11,774	6.7%
Low	31,800	10.8%

New Jobs in . .
   Blue-collar industries: 4,836
   White-collar industries: 41,461
Total Growth Rate: 8.3%
Unemployment Risk: ⬇
Job Quality: ⬇

Places Rated Rank: 110

Albuquerque, NM

Forecast 2007-2015

Earnings	New Jobs	Growth
High	6,183	6.9%
Average	18,292	13.1%
Low	50,111	18.2%

New Jobs in . .
  Blue-collar industries: 10,128
  White-collar industries: 64,458
Total Growth Rate: 14.8%
Unemployment Risk: ⬇
Job Quality: ⬇

Places Rated Rank: 51

Alexandria, LA

Forecast 2007-2015

Earnings	New Jobs	Growth
High	907	6.4%
Average	2,990	12.4%
Low	5,442	13.2%

New Jobs in . .
  Blue-collar industries: 1,891
  White-collar industries: 7,448
Total Growth Rate: 11.7%
Unemployment Risk: ⬇
Job Quality: ⬇

Places Rated Rank: 250

Allentown-Bethlehem-Easton, PA-NJ

Forecast 2007-2015

Earnings	New Jobs	Growth
High	2,310	6.4%
Average	7,391	12.4%
Low	27,369	12.1%

New Jobs in . .
  Blue-collar industries: 4,371
  White-collar industries: 32,699
Total Growth Rate: 8.9%
Unemployment Risk: ⬇
Job Quality: ⬇

Places Rated Rank: 123

Altoona, PA

Forecast 2007-2015

Earnings	New Jobs	Growth
High	615	3.0%
Average	1,821	10.8%
Low	4,671	11.6%

New Jobs in . .
  Blue-collar industries: 1,270
  White-collar industries: 5,837
Total Growth Rate: 9.1%
Unemployment Risk: ⬇
Job Quality: ⬇

Places Rated Rank: 315

Amarillo, TX

Forecast 2007-2015

Earnings	New Jobs	Growth
High	155	0.5%
Average	3,871	9.4%
Low	10,605	13.1%

New Jobs in . .
  Blue-collar industries: 1,277
  White-collar industries: 13,354
Total Growth Rate: 9.7%
Unemployment Risk: ⬇
Job Quality: ⬇

Places Rated Rank: 299

Ames, IA

Forecast 2007-2015

Earnings	New Jobs	Growth
High	441	5.4%
Average	1,850	7.8%
Low	2,530	10.3%

New Jobs in . .
  Blue-collar industries: 840
  White-collar industries: 3,981
Total Growth Rate: 8.5%
Unemployment Risk: ⬇
Job Quality: ⬇

Places Rated Rank: 337

Anchorage, AK

Forecast 2007-2015

Earnings	New Jobs	Growth
High	4,474	10.0%
Average	4,704	8.6%
Low	15,734	13.5%

New Jobs in . .
  Blue-collar industries: 6,541
  White-collar industries: 18,371
Total Growth Rate: 11.5%
Unemployment Risk: ⬆
Job Quality: ⬆

Places Rated Rank: 71

Anderson, IN

Forecast 2007-2015

Earnings	New Jobs	Growth
High	-565	-4.1%
Average	843	6.2%
Low	1,777	5.6%

New Jobs in . .
  Blue-collar industries: -189
  White-collar industries: 2,244
Total Growth Rate: 3.5%
Unemployment Risk: ⬅➡
Job Quality: ⬅➡

Places Rated Rank: 354

Anderson, SC

Forecast 2007-2015

Earnings	New Jobs	Growth
High	1,024	4.3%
Average	2,849	12.5%
Low	5,127	12.3%

New Jobs in . .
  Blue-collar industries: 1,690
  White-collar industries: 7,310
Total Growth Rate: 10.2%
Unemployment Risk: ⬅➡
Job Quality: ⬇

Places Rated Rank: 304

Ann Arbor, MI

Forecast 2007-2015

Earnings	New Jobs	Growth
High	584	1.2%
Average	9,479	10.4%
Low	14,535	12.4%

New Jobs in . .
  Blue-collar industries: 1,936
  White-collar industries: 22,662
Total Growth Rate: 9.5%
Unemployment Risk: ⬇
Job Quality: ⬆

Places Rated Rank: 104

Anniston-Oxford, AL

Forecast 2007-2015

Earnings	New Jobs	Growth
High	16	0.1%
Average	1,312	9.6%
Low	3,379	11.0%

New Jobs in . .
  Blue-collar industries: 853
  White-collar industries: 3,854
Total Growth Rate: 7.5%
Unemployment Risk: ⬅➡
Job Quality: ⬇

Places Rated Rank: 363

Appleton, WI

Forecast 2007-2015

Earnings	New Jobs	Growth
High	2,861	7.1%
Average	4,174	11.7%
Low	8,702	12.5%

New Jobs in . .
  Blue-collar industries: 4,835
  White-collar industries: 10,902
Total Growth Rate: 10.8%
Unemployment Risk: ⬇
Job Quality: ⬅➡

Places Rated Rank: 172

Asheville, NC

Forecast 2007-2015

Earnings	New Jobs	Growth
High	3,214	6.9%
Average	7,239	12.5%
Low	18,710	14.3%

New Jobs in . .
  Blue-collar industries: 5,848
  White-collar industries: 23,315
Total Growth Rate: 12.4%
Unemployment Risk: ⬅➡
Job Quality: ⬇

Places Rated Rank: 201

Athens-Clarke County, GA

Forecast 2007-2015

Earnings	New Jobs	Growth
High	1,624	8.6%
Average	4,260	12.8%
Low	6,712	13.0%

New Jobs in . .
  Blue-collar industries: 2,660
  White-collar industries: 9,946
Total Growth Rate: 12.1%
Unemployment Risk: ⬇
Job Quality: ⬅➡

Places Rated Rank: 216

✓ Atlanta-Sandy Springs, GA

Forecast 2007-2015

Earnings	New Jobs	Growth
High	83,024	11.6%
Average	90,212	12.1%
Low	271,138	17.2%

New Jobs in . .
  Blue-collar industries: 118,200
  White-collar industries: 326,174
Total Growth Rate: 14.6%
Unemployment Risk: ⬅➡
Job Quality: ⬆

Places Rated Rank: 11

Atlantic City, NJ

Forecast 2007-2015

Earnings	New Jobs	Growth
High	1,028	5.6%
Average	2,178	5.5%
Low	13,459	10.5%

New Jobs in . .
  Blue-collar industries: 1,098
  White-collar industries: 15,567
Total Growth Rate: 9.0%
Unemployment Risk: ↑
Job Quality: ↑

Places Rated Rank: 151

Auburn-Opelika, AL

Forecast 2007-2015

Earnings	New Jobs	Growth
High	421	4.3%
Average	2,799	13.2%
Low	4,474	15.4%

New Jobs in . .
  Blue-collar industries: 1,020
  White-collar industries: 6,674
Total Growth Rate: 12.8%
Unemployment Risk: ↓
Job Quality: ↓

Places Rated Rank: 291

Augusta-Richmond County, GA-SC

Forecast 2007-2015

Earnings	New Jobs	Growth
High	6,102	8.9%
Average	5,454	7.5%
Low	17,452	12.8%

New Jobs in . .
  Blue-collar industries: 7,671
  White-collar industries: 21,337
Total Growth Rate: 10.5%
Unemployment Risk: ↑
Job Quality: ← ➡

Places Rated Rank: 148

✓ Austin-Round Rock, TX

Forecast 2007-2015

Earnings	New Jobs	Growth
High	31,239	17.8%
Average	49,623	16.6%
Low	157,717	30.0%

New Jobs in . .
  Blue-collar industries: 44,645
  White-collar industries: 193,934
Total Growth Rate: 23.9%
Unemployment Risk: ← ➡
Job Quality: ↑

Places Rated Rank: 1

Bakersfield, CA

Forecast 2007-2015

Earnings	New Jobs	Growth
High	3,421	6.0%
Average	11,931	13.5%
Low	28,695	14.2%

New Jobs in . .
  Blue-collar industries: 13,144
  White-collar industries: 30,903
Total Growth Rate: 12.7%
Unemployment Risk: ↑
Job Quality: ← ➡

Places Rated Rank: 82

✓ Baltimore-Towson, MD

Forecast 2007-2015

Earnings	New Jobs	Growth
High	9,622	3.2%
Average	41,890	9.7%
Low	139,378	15.0%

New Jobs in . .
  Blue-collar industries: 23,521
  White-collar industries: 167,369
Total Growth Rate: 11.5%
Unemployment Risk: ← ➡
Job Quality: ↑

Places Rated Rank: 32

Bangor, ME

Forecast 2007-2015

Earnings	New Jobs	Growth
High	572	2.9%
Average	2,011	8.4%
Low	4,830	9.2%

New Jobs in . .
  Blue-collar industries: 1,073
  White-collar industries: 6,340
Total Growth Rate: 7.7%
Unemployment Risk: ← ➡
Job Quality: ← ➡

Places Rated Rank: 325

Barnstable Town, MA

Forecast 2007-2015

Earnings	New Jobs	Growth
High	1,253	8.7%
Average	4,034	9.6%
Low	10,818	12.0%

New Jobs in . .
  Blue-collar industries: 2,564
  White-collar industries: 13,541
Total Growth Rate: 11.0%
Unemployment Risk: ← ➡
Job Quality: ← ➡

Places Rated Rank: 220

Baton Rouge, LA

Forecast 2007-2015

Earnings	New Jobs	Growth
High	3,864	5.3%
Average	12,473	8.2%
Low	38,605	17.7%

New Jobs in . .
  Blue-collar industries: 9,894
  White-collar industries: 45,048
Total Growth Rate: 12.4%
Unemployment Risk: ← ➡
Job Quality: ← ➡

Places Rated Rank: 96

Battle Creek, MI

Forecast 2007-2015

Earnings	New Jobs	Growth
High	106	0.5%
Average	618	4.0%
Low	4,025	10.4%

New Jobs in . .
  Blue-collar industries: 522
  White-collar industries: 4,227
Total Growth Rate: 6.1%
Unemployment Risk: ← ➡
Job Quality: ↑

Places Rated Rank: 292

Bay City, MI

Forecast 2007-2015

Earnings	New Jobs	Growth
High	-28	-0.3%
Average	1,350	10.2%
Low	2,473	8.3%

New Jobs in . .
  Blue-collar industries: 407
  White-collar industries: 3,388
Total Growth Rate: 7.0%
Unemployment Risk: ↑
Job Quality: ← ➡

Places Rated Rank: 347

Beaumont-Port Arthur, TX

Forecast 2007-2015

Earnings	New Jobs	Growth
High	400	1.0%
Average	6,818	11.5%
Low	11,346	10.9%

New Jobs in . .
  Blue-collar industries: 3,931
  White-collar industries: 14,633
Total Growth Rate: 9.1%
Unemployment Risk: ↑
Job Quality: ↑

Places Rated Rank: 176

Bellingham, WA

Forecast 2007-2015

Earnings	New Jobs	Growth
High	968	10.3%
Average	3,949	13.0%
Low	8,133	14.3%

New Jobs in . .
  Blue-collar industries: 3,063
  White-collar industries: 10,987
Total Growth Rate: 13.2%
Unemployment Risk: ↑
Job Quality: ↓

Places Rated Rank: 211

Bend, OR

Forecast 2007-2015

Earnings	New Jobs	Growth
High	1,240	9.8%
Average	4,287	16.9%
Low	12,979	25.0%

New Jobs in . .
  Blue-collar industries: 3,788
  White-collar industries: 14,718
Total Growth Rate: 20.6%
Unemployment Risk: ↑
Job Quality: ↓

Places Rated Rank: 159

Bethesda-Gaithersburg, MD

Forecast 2007-2015

Earnings	New Jobs	Growth
High	5,004	4.3%
Average	16,315	8.6%
Low	56,815	12.3%

New Jobs in . .
  Blue-collar industries: 13,345
  White-collar industries: 64,789
Total Growth Rate: 10.2%
Unemployment Risk: ↓
Job Quality: ↑

Places Rated Rank: 49

Jobs

Billings, MT

Forecast 2007-2015

Earnings	New Jobs	Growth
High	297	1.5%
Average	837	3.9%
Low	8,468	13.6%

New Jobs in . .
    Blue-collar industries: 519
    White-collar industries: 9,083
Total Growth Rate: 9.3%
Unemployment Risk: ← →
Job Quality: ↓

Places Rated Rank: 308

Binghamton, NY

Forecast 2007-2015

Earnings	New Jobs	Growth
High	752	2.1%
Average	2,067	5.7%
Low	5,212	7.4%

New Jobs in . .
    Blue-collar industries: 788
    White-collar industries: 7,243
Total Growth Rate: 5.6%
Unemployment Risk: ← →
Job Quality: ← →

Places Rated Rank: 319

Birmingham-Hoover, AL

Forecast 2007-2015

Earnings	New Jobs	Growth
High	7,567	5.3%
Average	20,290	11.0%
Low	46,476	13.8%

New Jobs in . .
    Blue-collar industries: 14,247
    White-collar industries: 60,086
Total Growth Rate: 11.2%
Unemployment Risk: ← →
Job Quality: ↑

Places Rated Rank: 53

Bismarck, ND

Forecast 2007-2015

Earnings	New Jobs	Growth
High	657	5.9%
Average	1,578	7.9%
Low	6,448	15.0%

New Jobs in . .
    Blue-collar industries: 786
    White-collar industries: 7,897
Total Growth Rate: 11.7%
Unemployment Risk: ↓
Job Quality: ↓

Places Rated Rank: 293

Blacksburg-Christiansburg, VA

Forecast 2007-2015

Earnings	New Jobs	Growth
High	412	2.0%
Average	2,728	9.9%
Low	3,841	10.6%

New Jobs in . .
    Blue-collar industries: 1,090
    White-collar industries: 5,891
Total Growth Rate: 8.3%
Unemployment Risk: ← →
Job Quality: ↓

Places Rated Rank: 327

Bloomington, IN

Forecast 2007-2015

Earnings	New Jobs	Growth
High	626	3.5%
Average	4,682	13.0%
Low	8.551	16.3%

New Jobs in . .
    Blue-collar industries: 1,776
    White-collar industries: 12,083
Total Growth Rate: 13.0%
Unemployment Risk: ← →
Job Quality: ↓

Places Rated Rank: 245

Bloomington-Normal, IL

Forecast 2007-2015

Earnings	New Jobs	Growth
High	616	3.9%
Average	10,441	21.5%
Low	9,538	15.7%

New Jobs in . .
    Blue-collar industries: 2,183
    White-collar industries: 18,412
Total Growth Rate: 16.5%
Unemployment Risk: ↓
Job Quality: ↑

Places Rated Rank: 50

✓ Boise City-Nampa, ID

Forecast 2007-2015

Earnings	New Jobs	Growth
High	9,044	11.7%
Average	13,027	14.3%
Low	43,587	23.5%

New Jobs in . .
    Blue-collar industries: 15,945
    White-collar industries: 49,713
Total Growth Rate: 18.6%
Unemployment Risk: ← →
Job Quality: ← →

Places Rated Rank: 39

Boston-Quincy, MA

Forecast 2007-2015

Earnings	New Jobs	Growth
High	12,767	5.8%
Average	31,841	8.1%
Low	75,867	9.5%

New Jobs in . .
    Blue-collar industries: 20,490
    White-collar industries: 99,985
Total Growth Rate: 8.5%
Unemployment Risk: ← →
Job Quality: ↑

Places Rated Rank: 70

✓ Boulder, CO

Forecast 2007-2015

Earnings	New Jobs	Growth
High	4,795	9.8%
Average	11,593	17.5%
Low	28,868	19.6%

New Jobs in . .
    Blue-collar industries: 9,818
    White-collar industries: 35,438
Total Growth Rate: 17.3%
Unemployment Risk: ← →
Job Quality: ↑

Places Rated Rank: 20

Bowling Green, KY

Forecast 2007-2015

Earnings	New Jobs	Growth
High	1,020	6.0%
Average	1,903	10.9%
Low	4,864	13.7%

New Jobs in . .
    Blue-collar industries: 1,466
    White-collar industries: 6,321
Total Growth Rate: 11.2%
Unemployment Risk: ← →
Job Quality: ↓

Places Rated Rank: 286

Bremerton-Silverdale, WA

Forecast 2007-2015

Earnings	New Jobs	Growth
High	-14	-0.1%
Average	3,140	10.7%
Low	11,103	17.9%

New Jobs in . .
    Blue-collar industries: 1,753
    White-collar industries: 12,476
Total Growth Rate: 12.5%
Unemployment Risk: ↑
Job Quality: ↑

Places Rated Rank: 115

Bridgeport-Stamford-Norwalk, CT

Forecast 2007-2015

Earnings	New Jobs	Growth
High	554	0.5%
Average	19,866	11.5%
Low	35,411	10.9%

New Jobs in . .
    Blue-collar industries: 2,901
    White-collar industries: 52,930
Total Growth Rate: 9.1%
Unemployment Risk: ← →
Job Quality: ↑

Places Rated Rank: 68

Brownsville-Harlingen, TX

Forecast 2007-2015

Earnings	New Jobs	Growth
High	3,116	11.5%
Average	7,822	17.6%
Low	12,422	13.7%

New Jobs in . .
    Blue-collar industries: 3,294
    White-collar industries: 20,066
Total Growth Rate: 14.4%
Unemployment Risk: ↑
Job Quality: ↓

Places Rated Rank: 207

Brunswick, GA

Forecast 2007-2015

Earnings	New Jobs	Growth
High	198	2.0%
Average	1,275	8.7%
Low	6,549	20.0%

New Jobs in . .
    Blue-collar industries: 911
    White-collar industries: 7,111
Total Growth Rate: 14.0%
Unemployment Risk: ← →
Job Quality: ↓

Places Rated Rank: 262

Buffalo-Niagara Falls, NY

Forecast 2007-2015

Earnings	New Jobs	Growth
High	1,814	1.2%
Average	5,674	3.4%
Low	24,215	7.0%

New Jobs in . .
    Blue-collar industries: 1,901
    White-collar industries: 29,802
Total Growth Rate: 4.8%
Unemployment Risk: ← →
Job Quality: ↑

Places Rated Rank: 206

Burlington, NC

Forecast 2007-2015

Earnings	New Jobs	Growth
High	694	3.0%
Average	2,315	12.8%
Low	5,034	11.9%

New Jobs in . .
    Blue-collar industries: 2,029
    White-collar industries: 6,014
Total Growth Rate: 9.7%
Unemployment Risk: ← →
Job Quality: ↓

Places Rated Rank: 305

Burlington-South Burlington, VT

Forecast 2007-2015

Earnings	New Jobs	Growth
High	1,245	3.7%
Average	3,496	10.1%
Low	10.550	12.4%

New Jobs in . .
    Blue-collar industries: 2,439
    White-collar industries: 12,852
Total Growth Rate: 9.9%
Unemployment Risk: ↓
Job Quality: ↑

Places Rated Rank: 174

Cambridge-Newton, MA

Forecast 2007-2015

Earnings	New Jobs	Growth
High	7,488	3.4%
Average	11,291	5.6%
Low	71,071	10.4%

New Jobs in . .
    Blue-collar industries: 11,901
    White-collar industries: 77,949
Total Growth Rate: 8.1%
Unemployment Risk: ← →
Job Quality: ↑

Places Rated Rank: 77

Camden, NJ

Forecast 2007-2015

Earnings	New Jobs	Growth
High	6,371	4.8%
Average	11,906	7.1%
Low	42,314	12.1%

New Jobs in . .
    Blue-collar industries: 8,038
    White-collar industries: 52,553
Total Growth Rate: 9.3%
Unemployment Risk: ← →
Job Quality: ↑

Places Rated Rank: 83

Canton-Massillon, OH

Forecast 2007-2015

Earnings	New Jobs	Growth
High	2,679	4.2%
Average	6,625	12.0%
Low	11,909	9.7%

New Jobs in . .
    Blue-collar industries: 5,178
    White-collar industries: 16,035
Total Growth Rate: 8.8%
Unemployment Risk: ← →
Job Quality: ↓

Places Rated Rank: 249

Cape Coral-Fort Myers, FL

Forecast 2007-2015

Earnings	New Jobs	Growth
High	4,255	14.8%
Average	15,108	17.6%
Low	39,511	24.4%

New Jobs in . .
    Blue-collar industries: 9,627
    White-collar industries: 49,247
Total Growth Rate: 21.3%
Unemployment Risk: ↓
Job Quality: ← →

Places Rated Rank: 60

Carson City, NV

Forecast 2007-2015

Earnings	New Jobs	Growth
High	1,246	18.4%
Average	2,498	13.7%
Low	2,631	14.6%

New Jobs in . .
    Blue-collar industries: 1,564
    White-collar industries: 4,811
Total Growth Rate: 14.8%
Unemployment Risk: ↑
Job Quality: ← →

Places Rated Rank: 162

Casper, WY

Forecast 2007-2015

Earnings	New Jobs	Growth
High	407	4.0%
Average	441	3.6%
Low	3,311	12.7%

New Jobs in . .
    Blue-collar industries: 443
    White-collar industries: 3,716
Total Growth Rate: 8.6%
Unemployment Risk: ← →
Job Quality: ↓

Places Rated Rank: 329

Cedar Rapids, IA

Forecast 2007-2015

Earnings	New Jobs	Growth
High	3,410	7.3%
Average	2,597	6.9%
Low	14,355	16.1%

New Jobs in . .
    Blue-collar industries: 4,523
    White-collar industries: 15,839
Total Growth Rate: 11.7%
Unemployment Risk: ↓
Job Quality: ← →

Places Rated Rank: 128

Champaign-Urbana, IL

Forecast 2007-2015

Earnings	New Jobs	Growth
High	2,253	8.7%
Average	2,921	5.8%
Low	6,973	9.8%

New Jobs in . .
    Blue-collar industries: 3,632
    White-collar industries: 8,335
Total Growth Rate: 8.2%
Unemployment Risk: ↓
Job Quality: ← →

Places Rated Rank: 297

Charleston, WV

Forecast 2007-2015

Earnings	New Jobs	Growth
High	2,338	6.0%
Average	3,944	7.9%
Low	11,815	12.2%

New Jobs in . .
    Blue-collar industries: 2,859
    White-collar industries: 15,238
Total Growth Rate: 9.7%
Unemployment Risk: ↑
Job Quality: ↑

Places Rated Rank: 140

Charleston-North Charleston, SC

Forecast 2007-2015

Earnings	New Jobs	Growth
High	7,078	11.1%
Average	9.920	10.0%
Low	38,472	20.1%

New Jobs in . .
    Blue-collar industries: 10,965
    White-collar industries: 44,505
Total Growth Rate: 15.7%
Unemployment Risk: ← →
Job Quality: ← →

Places Rated Rank: 64

✓ Charlotte-Gastonia, NC-SC

Forecast 2007-2015

Earnings	New Jobs	Growth
High	12,823	5.3%
Average	52,214	16.7%
Low	92,310	19.4%

New Jobs in . .
    Blue-collar industries: 20,822
    White-collar industries: 136,525
Total Growth Rate: 15.2%
Unemployment Risk: ← →
Job Quality: ↑

Places Rated Rank: 15

Charlottesville, VA

Forecast 2007-2015

Earnings	New Jobs	Growth
High	476	3.1%
Average	6,501	12.9%
Low	9,440	15.0%

New Jobs in . .
    Blue-collar industries: 2,337
    White-collar industries: 14,080
Total Growth Rate: 12.8%
Unemployment Risk: ↓
Job Quality: ← →

Places Rated Rank: 146

Chattanooga, TN-GA

Forecast 2007-2015

Earnings	New Jobs	Growth
High	6,795	7.4%
Average	6,040	8.0%
Low	17,209	11.7%

New Jobs in . .
    Blue-collar industries: 8,721
    White-collar industries: 21,323
Total Growth Rate: 9.6%
Unemployment Risk: ← →
Job Quality: ← →

Places Rated Rank: 166

Cheyenne, WY

Forecast 2007-2015

Earnings	New Jobs	Growth
High	462	5.0%
Average	984	5.4%
Low	2,564	9.5%

New Jobs in . .
    Blue-collar industries: 609
    White-collar industries: 3,401
Total Growth Rate: 7.3%
Unemployment Risk: ↓
Job Quality: ← →

Places Rated Rank: 334

Chicago-Naperville-Joliet, IL

Forecast 2007-2015

Earnings	New Jobs	Growth
High	38,807	3.5%
Average	105,880	8.6%
Low	298,228	11.8%

New Jobs in . .
    Blue-collar industries: 69,109
    White-collar industries: 373,806
Total Growth Rate: 9.1%
Unemployment Risk: ↑
Job Quality: ↑

Places Rated Rank: 48

Chico, CA

Forecast 2007-2015

Earnings	New Jobs	Growth
High	643	4.7%
Average	3,490	10.8%
Low	8,504	13.1%

New Jobs in . .
    Blue-collar industries: 1,688
    White-collar industries: 10,949
Total Growth Rate: 11.4%
Unemployment Risk: ↑
Job Quality: ↓

Places Rated Rank: 265

Cincinnati-Middletown, OH-KY-IN

Forecast 2007-2015

Earnings	New Jobs	Growth
High	14,314	4.6%
Average	31,856	10.1%
Low	87,070	12.7%

New Jobs in . .
    Blue-collar industries: 25,676
    White-collar industries: 107,564
Total Growth Rate: 10.2%
Unemployment Risk: ← →
Job Quality: ↑

Places Rated Rank: 63

Clarksville, TN-KY

Forecast 2007-2015

Earnings	New Jobs	Growth
High	1,303	5.0%
Average	3,649	13.8%
Low	13,258	21.4%

New Jobs in . .
    Blue-collar industries: 2,645
    White-collar industries: 15,565
Total Growth Rate: 15.9%
Unemployment Risk: ← →
Job Quality: ← →

Places Rated Rank: 115

Cleveland, TN

Forecast 2007-2015

Earnings	New Jobs	Growth
High	226	1.3%
Average	1,400	11.0%
Low	3,054	12.3%

New Jobs in . .
    Blue-collar industries: 465
    White-collar industries: 4,215
Total Growth Rate: 8.6%
Unemployment Risk: ← →
Job Quality: ↑

Places Rated Rank: 284

Cleveland-Elyria-Mentor, OH

Forecast 2007-2015

Earnings	New Jobs	Growth
High	12,723	3.8%
Average	40,287	11.7%
Low	70,406	10.1%

New Jobs in . .
    Blue-collar industries: 22,906
    White-collar industries: 100,510
Total Growth Rate: 9.0%
Unemployment Risk: ← →
Job Quality: ↑

Places Rated Rank: 76

Coeur d'Alene, ID

Forecast 2007-2015

Earnings	New Jobs	Growth
High	1,624	14.3%
Average	4,870	22.4%
Low	10,288	25.6%

New Jobs in . .
    Blue-collar industries: 3,523
    White-collar industries: 13,259
Total Growth Rate: 22.9%
Unemployment Risk: ↑
Job Quality: ↓

Places Rated Rank: 185

College Station-Bryan, TX

Forecast 2007-2015

Earnings	New Jobs	Growth
High	2,674	17.2%
Average	6,897	14.7%
Low	9,602	17.0%

New Jobs in . .
    Blue-collar industries: 3,499
    White-collar industries: 15,674
Total Growth Rate: 16.1%
Unemployment Risk: ↓
Job Quality: ↓

Places Rated Rank: 188

✓ Colorado Springs, CO

Forecast 2007-2015

Earnings	New Jobs	Growth
High	6,359	9.8%
Average	19,182	18.4%
Low	38,766	20.1%

New Jobs in . .
    Blue-collar industries: 14,087
    White-collar industries: 50,220
Total Growth Rate: 17.8%
Unemployment Risk: ← →
Job Quality: ↑

Places Rated Rank: 29

Columbia, MO

Forecast 2007-2015

Earnings	New Jobs	Growth
High	1,898	11.3%
Average	5,843	12.4%
Low	7,426	14.1%

New Jobs in . .
    Blue-collar industries: 2,418
    White-collar industries: 12,749
Total Growth Rate: 13.0%
Unemployment Risk: ↓
Job Quality: ↓

Places Rated Rank: 212

Columbia, SC

Forecast 2007-2015

Earnings	New Jobs	Growth
High	5,025	5.8%
Average	13,004	9.2%
Low	33,613	16.0%

New Jobs in . .
    Blue-collar industries: 7,970
    White-collar industries: 43,672
Total Growth Rate: 11.8%
Unemployment Risk: ← →
Job Quality: ← →

Places Rated Rank: 102

Columbus, GA-AL

Forecast 2007-2015

Earnings	New Jobs	Growth
High	1,432	4.2%
Average	3,646	9.1%
Low	10,098	13.0%

New Jobs in . .
    Blue-collar industries: 2,220
    White-collar industries: 12,956
Total Growth Rate: 10.0%
Unemployment Risk: ← →
Job Quality: ← →

Places Rated Rank: 189

Columbus, IN

Forecast 2007-2015

Earnings	New Jobs	Growth
High	1,620	8.1%
Average	1,258	11.2%
Low	3,997	16.7%

New Jobs in . .
    Blue-collar industries: 2,020
    White-collar industries: 4,855
Total Growth Rate: 12.4%
Unemployment Risk: ↓
Job Quality: ↑

Places Rated Rank: 171

 Columbus, OH

Forecast 2007-2015

Earnings	New Jobs	Growth
High	13,529	6.0%
Average	35,646	10.5%
Low	114,321	17.5%

New Jobs in . .
  Blue-collar industries: 21,467
  White-collar industries: 142,029
Total Growth Rate: 13.4%
Unemployment Risk: ← →
Job Quality: ↑

Places Rated Rank: 29

Corpus Christi, TX

Forecast 2007-2015

Earnings	New Jobs	Growth
High	377	1.0%
Average	6,620	9.7%
Low	15,756	12.9%

New Jobs in . .
  Blue-collar industries: 3,297
  White-collar industries: 19,456
Total Growth Rate: 9.9%
Unemployment Risk: ↑
Job Quality: ← →

Places Rated Rank: 196

Corvallis, OR

Forecast 2007-2015

Earnings	New Jobs	Growth
High	682	7.1%
Average	663	3.8%
Low	4,428	15.1%

New Jobs in . .
  Blue-collar industries: 1,469
  White-collar industries: 4,304
Total Growth Rate: 10.3%
Unemployment Risk: ← →
Job Quality: ← →

Places Rated Rank: 272

Cumberland, MD-WV

Forecast 2007-2015

Earnings	New Jobs	Growth
High	-313	-3.4%
Average	843	6.6%
Low	2,876	10.3%

New Jobs in . .
  Blue-collar industries: -150
  White-collar industries: 3,556
Total Growth Rate: 6.8%
Unemployment Risk: ↑
Job Quality: ↓

Places Rated Rank: 373

✓ Dallas-Plano-Irving, TX

Forecast 2007-2015

Earnings	New Jobs	Growth
High	56,274	9.0%
Average	72,516	11.0%
Low	244,041	18.1%

New Jobs in . .
  Blue-collar industries: 82,623
  White-collar industries: 290,208
Total Growth Rate: 14.1%
Unemployment Risk: ← →
Job Quality: ↑

Places Rated Rank: 10

Dalton, GA

Forecast 2007-2015

Earnings	New Jobs	Growth
High	3,147	6.2%
Average	1,274	10.0%
Low	3,074	11.8%

New Jobs in . .
  Blue-collar industries: 3,522
  White-collar industries: 3,973
Total Growth Rate: 8.4%
Unemployment Risk: ← →
Job Quality: ← →

Places Rated Rank: 283

Danville, IL

Forecast 2007-2015

Earnings	New Jobs	Growth
High	-779	-7.2%
Average	-357	-3.9%
Low	81	0.4%

New Jobs in . .
  Blue-collar industries: -847
  White-collar industries: -208
Total Growth Rate: -2.7%
Unemployment Risk: ↑
Job Quality: ↓

Places Rated Rank: 376

Danville, VA

Forecast 2007-2015

Earnings	New Jobs	Growth
High	244	1.4%
Average	626	5.2%
Low	973	3.6%

New Jobs in . .
  Blue-collar industries: 350
  White-collar industries: 1,493
Total Growth Rate: 3.3%
Unemployment Risk: ↑
Job Quality: ↓

Places Rated Rank: 379

Davenport-Moline-Rock Island, IA-IL

Forecast 2007-2015

Earnings	New Jobs	Growth
High	2,380	4.0%
Average	4,530	8.6%
Low	14,934	11.6%

New Jobs in . .
  Blue-collar industries: 4,816
  White-collar industries: 17,028
Total Growth Rate: 9.0%
Unemployment Risk: ← →
Job Quality: ← →

Places Rated Rank: 205

Dayton, OH

Forecast 2007-2015

Earnings	New Jobs	Growth
High	2,406	1.7%
Average	8,720	7.7%
Low	25,792	9.3%

New Jobs in . .
  Blue-collar industries: 5,931
  White-collar industries: 30,987
Total Growth Rate: 7.0%
Unemployment Risk: ← →
Job Quality: ↑

Places Rated Rank: 160

Decatur, AL

Forecast 2007-2015

Earnings	New Jobs	Growth
High	240	1.1%
Average	1,559	8.2%
Low	5,089	13.8%

New Jobs in . .
  Blue-collar industries: 1,146
  White-collar industries: 5,742
Total Growth Rate: 8.9%
Unemployment Risk: ← →
Job Quality: ↓

Places Rated Rank: 318

Decatur, IL

Forecast 2007-2015

Earnings	New Jobs	Growth
High	-289	-1.5%
Average	237	1.7%
Low	3,258	9.1%

New Jobs in . .
  Blue-collar industries: -117
  White-collar industries: 3,323
Total Growth Rate: 4.7%
Unemployment Risk: ↑
Job Quality: ← →

Places Rated Rank: 330

Deltona-Daytona Beach, FL

Forecast 2007-2015

Earnings	New Jobs	Growth
High	1,755	6.5%
Average	1,231	2.7%
Low	14,418	11.8%

New Jobs in . .
  Blue-collar industries: 2,823
  White-collar industries: 14,581
Total Growth Rate: 8.9%
Unemployment Risk: ← →
Job Quality: ↓

Places Rated Rank: 287

✓ Denver-Aurora, CO

Forecast 2007-2015

Earnings	New Jobs	Growth
High	33,925	10.5%
Average	86,470	17.3%
Low	146,622	17.0%

New Jobs in . .
  Blue-collar industries: 71,670
  White-collar industries: 195,347
Total Growth Rate: 15.8%
Unemployment Risk: ← →
Job Quality: ↑

Places Rated Rank: 4

Des Moines-West Des Moines, IA

Forecast 2007-2015

Earnings	New Jobs	Growth
High	1,182	1.7%
Average	11,018	9.5%
Low	25,941	13.0%

New Jobs in . .
  Blue-collar industries: 3,136
  White-collar industries: 35,005
Total Growth Rate: 9.9%
Unemployment Risk: ↓
Job Quality: ↑

Places Rated Rank: 100

Jobs

Detroit-Livonia-Dearborn, MI

Forecast 2007-2015

Earnings	New Jobs	Growth
High	-9,600	-3.4%
Average	-2,907	-1.4%
Low	19,603	3.9%

New Jobs in . .
  Blue-collar industries: -8,634
  White-collar industries: 15,730
Total Growth Rate: 0.7%
Unemployment Risk: ↑
Job Quality: ↑

Places Rated Rank: 253

Dothan, AL

Forecast 2007-2015

Earnings	New Jobs	Growth
High	1,206	6.5%
Average	1,588	8.1%
Low	5,009	12.3%

New Jobs in . .
  Blue-collar industries: 2,011
  White-collar industries: 5,792
Total Growth Rate: 9.9%
Unemployment Risk: ←→
Job Quality: ↓

Places Rated Rank: 324

Dover, DE

Forecast 2007-2015

Earnings	New Jobs	Growth
High	145	1.2%
Average	2,830	11.3%
Low	4,757	12.7%

New Jobs in . .
  Blue-collar industries: 350
  White-collar industries: 7,382
Total Growth Rate: 10.3%
Unemployment Risk: ↓
Job Quality: ←→

Places Rated Rank: 267

Dubuque, IA

Forecast 2007-2015

Earnings	New Jobs	Growth
High	816	4.9%
Average	414	3.9%
Low	5,622	14.5%

New Jobs in . .
  Blue-collar industries: 894
  White-collar industries: 5,958
Total Growth Rate: 10.3%
Unemployment Risk: ←→
Job Quality: ↓

Places Rated Rank: 301

Duluth, MN-WI

Forecast 2007-2015

Earnings	New Jobs	Growth
High	1,012	3.1%
Average	1,917	4.5%
Low	9,566	10.8%

New Jobs in . .
  Blue-collar industries: 1,923
  White-collar industries: 10,572
Total Growth Rate: 7.6%
Unemployment Risk: ←→
Job Quality: ←→

Places Rated Rank: 273

✓ Durham, NC

Forecast 2007-2015

Earnings	New Jobs	Growth
High	6,458	8.7%
Average	8,780	10.3%
Low	31,051	16.5%

New Jobs in . .
  Blue-collar industries: 7,589
  White-collar industries: 38,700
Total Growth Rate: 13.3%
Unemployment Risk: ←→
Job Quality: ↑

Places Rated Rank: 34

Eau Claire, WI

Forecast 2007-2015

Earnings	New Jobs	Growth
High	447	2.0%
Average	1,862	8.1%
Low	8,157	14.3%

New Jobs in . .
  Blue-collar industries: 989
  White-collar industries: 9,477
Total Growth Rate: 10.2%
Unemployment Risk: ←→
Job Quality: ↓

Places Rated Rank: 288

✓ Edison, NJ

Forecast 2007-2015

Earnings	New Jobs	Growth
High	15,307	5.6%
Average	35,036	10.5%
Low	109,391	15.5%

New Jobs in . .
  Blue-collar industries: 19,799
  White-collar industries: 139,935
Total Growth Rate: 12.2%
Unemployment Risk: ←→
Job Quality: ↑

Places Rated Rank: 27

El Centro, CA

Forecast 2007-2015

Earnings	New Jobs	Growth
High	776	7.1%
Average	2,888	13.8%
Low	2,391	6.7%

New Jobs in . .
  Blue-collar industries: 384
  White-collar industries: 5,671
Total Growth Rate: 9.0%
Unemployment Risk: ↑
Job Quality: ←→

Places Rated Rank: 300

Elizabethtown, KY

Forecast 2007-2015

Earnings	New Jobs	Growth
High	1,866	11.1%
Average	2,048	13.6%
Low	2,681	9.5%

New Jobs in . .
  Blue-collar industries: 2,286
  White-collar industries: 4,309
Total Growth Rate: 11.0%
Unemployment Risk: ←→
Job Quality: ←→

Places Rated Rank: 241

Elkhart-Goshen, IN

Forecast 2007-2015

Earnings	New Jobs	Growth
High	4,047	5.3%
Average	1,688	8.2%
Low	6,020	11.7%

New Jobs in . .
  Blue-collar industries: 4,495
  White-collar industries: 7,260
Total Growth Rate: 7.9%
Unemployment Risk: ↓
Job Quality: ↑

Places Rated Rank: 232

Elmira, NY

Forecast 2007-2015

Earnings	New Jobs	Growth
High	-361	-3.1%
Average	743	5.8%
Low	1,588	5.8%

New Jobs in . .
  Blue-collar industries: 22
  White-collar industries: 1,948
Total Growth Rate: 3.8%
Unemployment Risk: ←→
Job Quality: ↓

Places Rated Rank: 374

El Paso, TX

Forecast 2007-2015

Earnings	New Jobs	Growth
High	6,439	8.0%
Average	14,700	15.0%
Low	20,770	12.6%

New Jobs in . .
  Blue-collar industries: 8,768
  White-collar industries: 33,141
Total Growth Rate: 12.2%
Unemployment Risk: ↑
Job Quality: ←→

Places Rated Rank: 120

Erie, PA

Forecast 2007-2015

Earnings	New Jobs	Growth
High	96	0.2%
Average	3,681	10.1%
Low	9,715	10.7%

New Jobs in . .
  Blue-collar industries: 1,532
  White-collar industries: 11,960
Total Growth Rate: 8.0%
Unemployment Risk: ↑
Job Quality: ←→

Places Rated Rank: 294

Essex County, MA

Forecast 2007-2015

Earnings	New Jobs	Growth
High	2,154	2.4%
Average	6,842	7.1%
Low	21,803	9.7%

New Jobs in . .
  Blue-collar industries: 3,976
  White-collar industries: 26,823
Total Growth Rate: 7.5%
Unemployment Risk: ←→
Job Quality: ↑

Places Rated Rank: 141

Eugene-Springfield, OR

Forecast 2007-2015

Earnings	New Jobs	Growth
High	1,533	3.9%
Average	3,826	7.5%
Low	18,023	16.1%

New Jobs in . .
    Blue-collar industries: 2,419
    White-collar industries: 20,963
Total Growth Rate: 11.6%
Unemployment Risk: ↑
Job Quality: ↓

Places Rated Rank: 199

Evansville, IN-KY

Forecast 2007-2015

Earnings	New Jobs	Growth
High	783	1.3%
Average	5,073	10.6%
Low	10,789	9.5%

New Jobs in . .
    Blue-collar industries: 2,956
    White-collar industries: 13,689
Total Growth Rate: 7.5%
Unemployment Risk: ←→
Job Quality: ←→

Places Rated Rank: 218

Fairbanks, AK

Forecast 2007-2015

Earnings	New Jobs	Growth
High	1,082	10.0%
Average	657	4.7%
Low	2,437	10.2%

New Jobs in . .
    Blue-collar industries: 1,079
    White-collar industries: 3,097
Total Growth Rate: 8.6%
Unemployment Risk: ↑
Job Quality: ↑

Places Rated Rank: 254

Fargo, ND-MN

Forecast 2007-2015

Earnings	New Jobs	Growth
High	2,598	9.5%
Average	2,537	7.2%
Low	12,152	15.7%

New Jobs in . .
    Blue-collar industries: 3,246
    White-collar industries: 14,041
Total Growth Rate: 12.4%
Unemployment Risk: ↓
Job Quality: ←→

Places Rated Rank: 178

Farmington, NM

Forecast 2007-2015

Earnings	New Jobs	Growth
High	1,769	12.3%
Average	3,610	19.7%
Low	7,056	22.0%

New Jobs in . .
    Blue-collar industries: 2,078
    White-collar industries: 10,357
Total Growth Rate: 19.2%
Unemployment Risk: ↑
Job Quality: ←→

Places Rated Rank: 134

Fayetteville, NC

Forecast 2007-2015

Earnings	New Jobs	Growth
High	2,259	6.6%
Average	4,939	11.0%
Low	9,512	12.0%

New Jobs in . .
    Blue-collar industries: 2,828
    White-collar industries: 13,882
Total Growth Rate: 10.6%
Unemployment Risk: ↑
Job Quality: ←→

Places Rated Rank: 154

Fayetteville-Springdale, AR-MO

Forecast 2007-2015

Earnings	New Jobs	Growth
High	11,264	15.3%
Average	7,334	13.9%
Low	37,875	28.1%

New Jobs in . .
    Blue-collar industries: 14,733
    White-collar industries: 41,740
Total Growth Rate: 21.6%
Unemployment Risk: ↓
Job Quality: ←→

Places Rated Rank: 66

Flagstaff, AZ

Forecast 2007-2015

Earnings	New Jobs	Growth
High	481	4.7%
Average	5,309	20.6%
Low	11,958	25.2%

New Jobs in . .
    Blue-collar industries: 1,381
    White-collar industries: 16,367
Total Growth Rate: 21.3%
Unemployment Risk: ↑
Job Quality: ↓

Places Rated Rank: 183

Flint, MI

Forecast 2007-2015

Earnings	New Jobs	Growth
High	-2,611	-6.3%
Average	4,452	8.4%
Low	12,857	10.5%

New Jobs in . .
    Blue-collar industries: -1,019
    White-collar industries: 15,717
Total Growth Rate: 6.8%
Unemployment Risk: ↑
Job Quality: ↑

Places Rated Rank: 226

Florence, SC

Forecast 2007-2015

Earnings	New Jobs	Growth
High	528	1.9%
Average	6,421	18.2%
Low	4,563	8.7%

New Jobs in . .
    Blue-collar industries: 1,299
    White-collar industries: 10,213
Total Growth Rate: 10.0%
Unemployment Risk: ↑
Job Quality: ←→

Places Rated Rank: 234

Florence-Muscle Shoals, AL

Forecast 2007-2015

Earnings	New Jobs	Growth
High	95	0.6%
Average	1,732	8.4%
Low	3,358	10.0%

New Jobs in . .
    Blue-collar industries: 704
    White-collar industries: 4,481
Total Growth Rate: 7.3%
Unemployment Risk: ↑
Job Quality: ↓

Places Rated Rank: 369

Fond du Lac, WI

Forecast 2007-2015

Earnings	New Jobs	Growth
High	352	1.8%
Average	1,361	10.0%
Low	3,268	10.7%

New Jobs in . .
    Blue-collar industries: 1,095
    White-collar industries: 3,886
Total Growth Rate: 7.8%
Unemployment Risk: ↓
Job Quality: ←→

Places Rated Rank: 328

Fort Collins-Loveland, CO

Forecast 2007-2015

Earnings	New Jobs	Growth
High	3,321	11.1%
Average	10,047	16.5%
Low	20,032	20.0%

New Jobs in . .
    Blue-collar industries: 8,135
    White-collar industries: 25,265
Total Growth Rate: 17.5%
Unemployment Risk: ←→
Job Quality: ←→

Places Rated Rank: 60

✓ Fort Lauderdale, FL

Forecast 2007-2015

Earnings	New Jobs	Growth
High	23,035	15.3%
Average	34,582	12.9%
Low	75,138	13.6%

New Jobs in . .
    Blue-collar industries: 31,819
    White-collar industries: 100,936
Total Growth Rate: 13.7%
Unemployment Risk: ←→
Job Quality: ↑

Places Rated Rank: 40

Fort Smith, AR-OK

Forecast 2007-2015

Earnings	New Jobs	Growth
High	3,970	8.0%
Average	3,479	10.6%
Low	12,845	15.8%

New Jobs in . .
    Blue-collar industries: 5,253
    White-collar industries: 15,041
Total Growth Rate: 12.4%
Unemployment Risk: ←→
Job Quality: ↓

Places Rated Rank: 212

Jobs

Fort Walton Beach-Crestview, FL

Forecast 2007-2015

Earnings	New Jobs	Growth
High	2,407	13.5%
Average	3,521	13.2%
Low	21,352	28.1%

New Jobs in . .
    Blue-collar industries: 3,008
    White-collar industries: 24,272
Total Growth Rate: 22.6%
Unemployment Risk: ⬇
Job Quality: ⬅➡

Places Rated Rank: 75

Fort Wayne, IN

Forecast 2007-2015

Earnings	New Jobs	Growth
High	95	0.1%
Average	5,062	8.7%
Low	14,852	11.0%

New Jobs in . .
    Blue-collar industries: 2,263
    White-collar industries: 17,746
Total Growth Rate: 7.5%
Unemployment Risk: ⬅➡
Job Quality: ⬅➡

Places Rated Rank: 210

✓ Fort Worth-Arlington, TX

Forecast 2007-2015

Earnings	New Jobs	Growth
High	43,737	15.2%
Average	43,205	15.7%
Low	101,774	18.3%

New Jobs in . .
    Blue-collar industries: 60,287
    White-collar industries: 128,429
Total Growth Rate: 16.9%
Unemployment Risk: ⬅➡
Job Quality: ⬆

Places Rated Rank: 12

Fresno, CA

Forecast 2007-2015

Earnings	New Jobs	Growth
High	3,439	4.6%
Average	9,401	8.1%
Low	42,895	15.8%

New Jobs in . .
    Blue-collar industries: 14,297
    White-collar industries: 41,438
Total Growth Rate: 12.1%
Unemployment Risk: ⬆
Job Quality: ⬅➡

Places Rated Rank: 108

Gadsden, AL

Forecast 2007-2015

Earnings	New Jobs	Growth
High	-551	-5.2%
Average	644	6.0%
Low	3,360	11.4%

New Jobs in . .
    Blue-collar industries: -224
    White-collar industries: 3,677
Total Growth Rate: 6.8%
Unemployment Risk: ⬆
Job Quality: ⬇

Places Rated Rank: 377

Gainesville, FL

Forecast 2007-2015

Earnings	New Jobs	Growth
High	642	3.7%
Average	3,487	5.8%
Low	12,975	15.3%

New Jobs in . .
    Blue-collar industries: 1,318
    White-collar industries: 15,786
Total Growth Rate: 10.5%
Unemployment Risk: ⬇
Job Quality: ⬇

Places Rated Rank: 246

Gainesville, GA

Forecast 2007-2015

Earnings	New Jobs	Growth
High	2,708	9.8%
Average	2,503	11.7%
Low	4,754	12.3%

New Jobs in . .
    Blue-collar industries: 3,167
    White-collar industries: 6,798
Total Growth Rate: 11.3%
Unemployment Risk: ⬇
Job Quality: ⬅➡

Places Rated Rank: 192

Gary, IN

Forecast 2007-2015

Earnings	New Jobs	Growth
High	2,788	3.6%
Average	7,853	9.3%
Low	20,602	11.2%

New Jobs in . .
    Blue-collar industries: 4,920
    White-collar industries: 26,323
Total Growth Rate: 9.0%
Unemployment Risk: ⬅➡
Job Quality: ⬅➡

Places Rated Rank: 170

Glens Falls, NY

Forecast 2007-2015

Earnings	New Jobs	Growth
High	-77	-0.6%
Average	1,251	6.8%
Low	3,215	9.0%

New Jobs in . .
    Blue-collar industries: 351
    White-collar industries: 4,038
Total Growth Rate: 6.6%
Unemployment Risk: ⬅➡
Job Quality: ⬇

Places Rated Rank: 367

Goldsboro, NC

Forecast 2007-2015

Earnings	New Jobs	Growth
High	267	2.1%
Average	399	2.5%
Low	2,679	9.4%

New Jobs in . .
    Blue-collar industries: 393
    White-collar industries: 2,952
Total Growth Rate: 5.8%
Unemployment Risk: ⬅➡
Job Quality: ⬇

Places Rated Rank: 372

Grand Forks, ND-MN

Forecast 2007-2015

Earnings	New Jobs	Growth
High	585	5.4%
Average	863	4.9%
Low	3,766	10.1%

New Jobs in . .
    Blue-collar industries: 1,097
    White-collar industries: 4,117
Total Growth Rate: 7.9%
Unemployment Risk: ⬇
Job Quality: ⬇

Places Rated Rank: 361

Grand Junction, CO

Forecast 2007-2015

Earnings	New Jobs	Growth
High	461	3.7%
Average	4,158	17.7%
Low	6,832	15.4%

New Jobs in . .
    Blue-collar industries: 2,636
    White-collar industries: 8,815
Total Growth Rate: 14.3%
Unemployment Risk: ⬅➡
Job Quality: ⬇

Places Rated Rank: 239

Grand Rapids-Wyoming, MI

Forecast 2007-2015

Earnings	New Jobs	Growth
High	10,389	7.4%
Average	7,566	7.4%
Low	44,967	16.8%

New Jobs in . .
    Blue-collar industries: 13,389
    White-collar industries: 49,533
Total Growth Rate: 12.3%
Unemployment Risk: ⬅➡
Job Quality: ⬆

Places Rated Rank: 52

Great Falls, MT

Forecast 2007-2015

Earnings	New Jobs	Growth
High	-90	-1.3%
Average	680	6.0%
Low	2,352	8.1%

New Jobs in . .
    Blue-collar industries: 133
    White-collar industries: 2,809
Total Growth Rate: 6.3%
Unemployment Risk: ⬅➡
Job Quality: ⬇

Places Rated Rank: 375

Greeley, CO

Forecast 2007-2015

Earnings	New Jobs	Growth
High	1,512	6.5%
Average	4,984	15.2%
Low	9,846	17.9%

New Jobs in . .
    Blue-collar industries: 3,606
    White-collar industries: 12,736
Total Growth Rate: 14.7%
Unemployment Risk: ⬅➡
Job Quality: ⬅➡

Places Rated Rank: 138

Green Bay, WI

Forecast 2007-2015

Earnings	New Jobs	Growth
High	3,802	6.3%
Average	7,493	14.2%
Low	12,280	12.6%

New Jobs in . .
  Blue-collar industries: 5,584
  White-collar industries: 17,971
Total Growth Rate: 11.2%
Unemployment Risk: ← →
Job Quality: ← →

Places Rated Rank: 122

Greensboro-High Point, NC

Forecast 2007-2015

Earnings	New Jobs	Growth
High	6,563	4.8%
Average	6,164	6.3%
Low	24,119	11.3%

New Jobs in . .
  Blue-collar industries: 8,529
  White-collar industries: 28,317
Total Growth Rate: 8.2%
Unemployment Risk: ← →
Job Quality: ← →

Places Rated Rank: 167

Greenville, NC

Forecast 2007-2015

Earnings	New Jobs	Growth
High	958	6.2%
Average	4,610	14.4%
Low	9,430	18.8%

New Jobs in . .
  Blue-collar industries: 1,606
  White-collar industries: 13,392
Total Growth Rate: 15.3%
Unemployment Risk: ← →
Job Quality: ↓

Places Rated Rank: 181

Greenville, SC

Forecast 2007-2015

Earnings	New Jobs	Growth
High	7,192	7.3%
Average	6,444	7.6%
Low	27,575	14.5%

New Jobs in . .
  Blue-collar industries: 9,414
  White-collar industries: 31,797
Total Growth Rate: 11.1%
Unemployment Risk: ← →
Job Quality: ← →

Places Rated Rank: 109

Gulfport-Biloxi, MS

Unemployment Risk: ← →
Job Quality: ← →
Forecast 2007-2015

Earnings	New Jobs	Growth
High	1,807	6.7%
Average	4,680	13.3%
Low	17,330	19.0%

New Jobs in . .
  Blue-collar industries: 3,381
  White-collar industries: 20,436
Total Growth Rate: 15.5%

Places Rated Rank: 119

Hagerstown-Martinsburg, MD-WV

Forecast 2007-2015

Earnings	New Jobs	Growth
High	1,234	4.2%
Average	3,376	11.5%
Low	8,623	13.3%

New Jobs in . .
  Blue-collar industries: 2,039
  White-collar industries: 11,194
Total Growth Rate: 10.7%
Unemployment Risk: ← →
Job Quality: ← →

Places Rated Rank: 218

Hanford-Corcoran, CA

Forecast 2007-2015

Earnings	New Jobs	Growth
High	-16	-0.2%
Average	2,389	14.4%
Low	4,702	16.8%

New Jobs in . .
  Blue-collar industries: 1,468
  White-collar industries: 5,607
Total Growth Rate: 13.7%
Unemployment Risk: ↑
Job Quality: ← →

Places Rated Rank: 197

Harrisburg-Carlisle, PA

Forecast 2007-2015

Earnings	New Jobs	Growth
High	5,338	6.1%
Average	13,352	11.1%
Low	29,251	14.3%

New Jobs in . .
  Blue-collar industries: 8,824
  White-collar industries: 39,117
Total Growth Rate: 11.6%
Unemployment Risk: ↓
Job Quality: ↑

Places Rated Rank: 64

Harrisonburg, VA

Forecast 2007-2015

Earnings	New Jobs	Growth
High	1,127	5.1%
Average	2,365	13.0%
Low	4,928	13.4%

New Jobs in . .
  Blue-collar industries: 1,886
  White-collar industries: 6,534
Total Growth Rate: 10.9%
Unemployment Risk: ↓
Job Quality: ↓

Places Rated Rank: 297

Hartford-West Hartford, CT

Forecast 2007-2015

Earnings	New Jobs	Growth
High	3,124	1.9%
Average	12,239	5.1%
Low	34,056	8.8%

New Jobs in . .
  Blue-collar industries: 6,639
  White-collar industries: 42,780
Total Growth Rate: 6.3%
Unemployment Risk: ← →
Job Quality: ↑

Places Rated Rank: 124

Hattiesburg, MS

Forecast 2007-2015

Earnings	New Jobs	Growth
High	380	3.1%
Average	2,736	11.1%
Low	6,659	16.8%

New Jobs in . .
  Blue-collar industries: 877
  White-collar industries: 8,898
Total Growth Rate: 12.8%
Unemployment Risk: ← →
Job Quality: ↓

Places Rated Rank: 280

Hickory-Lenoir-Morganton, NC

Forecast 2007-2015

Earnings	New Jobs	Growth
High	2,046	2.3%
Average	3,782	9.1%
Low	11,026	13.0%

New Jobs in . .
  Blue-collar industries: 3,338
  White-collar industries: 13,516
Total Growth Rate: 7.8%
Unemployment Risk: ↑
Job Quality: ↓

Places Rated Rank: 285

Hinesville-Fort Stewart, GA

Forecast 2007-2015

Earnings	New Jobs	Growth
High	124	2.4%
Average	830	12.9%
Low	1,348	14.2%

New Jobs in . .
  Blue-collar industries: 172
  White-collar industries: 2,130
Total Growth Rate: 10.9%
Unemployment Risk: ↑
Job Quality: ↑

Places Rated Rank: 215

Holland-Grand Haven, MI

Forecast 2007-2015

Earnings	New Jobs	Growth
High	6,089	11.0%
Average	2,892	9.3%
Low	11,143	17.3%

New Jobs in . .
  Blue-collar industries: 7,474
  White-collar industries: 12,650
Total Growth Rate: 13.3%
Unemployment Risk: ← →
Job Quality: ↑

Places Rated Rank: 91

Honolulu, HI

Forecast 2007-2015

Earnings	New Jobs	Growth
High	2,292	2.3%
Average	2,074	1.5%
Low	20,660	6.9%

New Jobs in . .
  Blue-collar industries: 2,932
  White-collar industries: 22,094
Total Growth Rate: 4.7%
Unemployment Risk: ← →
Job Quality: ↑

Places Rated Rank: 193

Hot Springs, AR

Forecast 2007-2015

Earnings	New Jobs	Growth
High	473	5.6%
Average	1,559	11.5%
Low	4,000	13.1%

New Jobs in . .
        Blue-collar industries: 1,271
        White-collar industries: 4,761
Total Growth Rate: 11.5%
Unemployment Risk: ← →
Job Quality: ↓

Places Rated Rank: 326

Houma-Bayou Cane-Thibodaux, LA

Forecast 2007-2015

Earnings	New Jobs	Growth
High	2,483	7.9%
Average	1,821	7.0%
Low	5,722	11.1%

New Jobs in . .
        Blue-collar industries: 2,758
        White-collar industries: 7,268
Total Growth Rate: 9.2%
Unemployment Risk: ← →
Job Quality: ← →

Places Rated Rank: 278

✓ Houston-Sugar Land, TX

Forecast 2007-2015

Earnings	New Jobs	Growth
High	77,307	10.8%
Average	108,559	12.6%
Low	270,247	16.9%

New Jobs in . .
        Blue-collar industries: 104,788
        White-collar industries: 351,325
Total Growth Rate: 14.4%
Unemployment Risk: ↑
Job Quality: ↑

Places Rated Rank: 5

Huntington-Ashland, WV-KY-OH

Forecast 2007-2015

Earnings	New Jobs	Growth
High	25	0.1%
Average	3,588	10.3%
Low	10,372	12.6%

New Jobs in . .
        Blue-collar industries: 681
        White-collar industries: 13,304
Total Growth Rate: 9.5%
Unemployment Risk: ↑
Job Quality: ↓

Places Rated Rank: 270

Huntsville, AL

Forecast 2007-2015

Earnings	New Jobs	Growth
High	1,041	1.6%
Average	5,477	10.8%
Low	17,109	13.9%

New Jobs in . .
        Blue-collar industries: 2,793
        White-collar industries: 20,834
Total Growth Rate: 10.0%
Unemployment Risk: ↓
Job Quality: ↑

Places Rated Rank: 105

Idaho Falls, ID

Forecast 2007-2015

Earnings	New Jobs	Growth
High	713	6.1%
Average	1,951	11.2%
Low	7,764	18.7%

New Jobs in . .
        Blue-collar industries: 1,694
        White-collar industries: 8,734
Total Growth Rate: 15.0%
Unemployment Risk: ↓
Job Quality: ↓

Places Rated Rank: 227

✓ Indianapolis-Carmel, IN

Forecast 2007-2015

Earnings	New Jobs	Growth
High	15,579	6.1%
Average	28,196	10.1%
Low	95,903	16.4%

New Jobs in . .
        Blue-collar industries: 27,374
        White-collar industries: 112,304
Total Growth Rate: 12.5%
Unemployment Risk: ↓
Job Quality: ↑

Places Rated Rank: 31

Iowa City, IA

Forecast 2007-2015

Earnings	New Jobs	Growth
High	1,371	8.5%
Average	5,305	12.4%
Low	8,506	16.2%

New Jobs in . .
        Blue-collar industries: 1,965
        White-collar industries: 13,217
Total Growth Rate: 13.6%
Unemployment Risk: ↓
Job Quality: ← →

Places Rated Rank: 169

Ithaca, NY

Forecast 2007-2015

Earnings	New Jobs	Growth
High	494	6.2%
Average	488	4.6%
Low	4,489	9.3%

New Jobs in . .
        Blue-collar industries: 585
        White-collar industries: 4,886
Total Growth Rate: 8.2%
Unemployment Risk: ↓
Job Quality: ← →

Places Rated Rank: 312

Jackson, MI

Forecast 2007-2015

Earnings	New Jobs	Growth
High	-89	-0.5%
Average	1,532	7.7%
Low	3,376	8.2%

New Jobs in . .
        Blue-collar industries: 559
        White-collar industries: 4,260
Total Growth Rate: 6.1%
Unemployment Risk: ↑
Job Quality: ← →

Places Rated Rank: 336

Jackson, MS

Forecast 2007-2015

Earnings	New Jobs	Growth
High	5,261	7.8%
Average	12,804	12.4%
Low	28,451	17.5%

New Jobs in . .
        Blue-collar industries: 8,348
        White-collar industries: 38,168
Total Growth Rate: 13.9%
Unemployment Risk: ← →
Job Quality: ← →

Places Rated Rank: 87

Jackson, TN

Forecast 2007-2015

Earnings	New Jobs	Growth
High	2,328	10.5%
Average	2,192	10.2%
Low	4,634	13.6%

New Jobs in . .
        Blue-collar industries: 3,051
        White-collar industries: 6,103
Total Growth Rate: 11.8%
Unemployment Risk: ← →
Job Quality: ← →

Places Rated Rank: 202

Jacksonville, FL

Forecast 2007-2015

Earnings	New Jobs	Growth
High	7,694	5.5%
Average	19,522	9.9%
Low	76,408	17.8%

New Jobs in . .
        Blue-collar industries: 15,222
        White-collar industries: 88,402
Total Growth Rate: 13.5%
Unemployment Risk: ← →
Job Quality: ↑

Places Rated Rank: 44

Jacksonville, NC

Forecast 2007-2015

Earnings	New Jobs	Growth
High	456	4.1%
Average	1,653	10.5%
Low	3,625	12.6%

New Jobs in . .
        Blue-collar industries: 1,114
        White-collar industries: 4,620
Total Growth Rate: 10.3%
Unemployment Risk: ← →
Job Quality: ← →

Places Rated Rank: 252

Janesville, WI

Forecast 2007-2015

Earnings	New Jobs	Growth
High	505	2.0%
Average	1,860	10.2%
Low	3,701	8.6%

New Jobs in . .
        Blue-collar industries: 1,163
        White-collar industries: 4,903
Total Growth Rate: 7.0%
Unemployment Risk: ← →
Job Quality: ← →

Places Rated Rank: 310

Jefferson City, MO

Forecast 2007-2015

Earnings	New Jobs	Growth
High	1,013	6.1%
Average	4,999	12.1%
Low	7,284	15.5%

New Jobs in . .
    Blue-collar industries: 1,583
    White-collar industries: 11,713
Total Growth Rate: 12.6%
Unemployment Risk: ⬇
Job Quality: ⬇

Places Rated Rank: 229

Johnson City, TN

Forecast 2007-2015

Earnings	New Jobs	Growth
High	697	3.2%
Average	3,125	11.1%
Low	10,526	18.9%

New Jobs in . .
    Blue-collar industries: 2,120
    White-collar industries: 12,228
Total Growth Rate: 13.6%
Unemployment Risk: ⬅➡
Job Quality: ⬇

Places Rated Rank: 230

Johnstown, PA

Forecast 2007-2015

Earnings	New Jobs	Growth
High	-36	-0.2%
Average	1,534	8.3%
Low	4,688	10.6%

New Jobs in . .
    Blue-collar industries: 605
    White-collar industries: 5,581
Total Growth Rate: 8.0%
Unemployment Risk: ⬆
Job Quality: ⬇

Places Rated Rank: 358

Jonesboro, AR

Forecast 2007-2015

Earnings	New Jobs	Growth
High	1,120	9.9%
Average	1,496	9.4%
Low	4,015	11.9%

New Jobs in . .
    Blue-collar industries: 1,557
    White-collar industries: 5,074
Total Growth Rate: 10.1%
Unemployment Risk: ⬅➡
Job Quality: ⬇

Places Rated Rank: 335

Joplin, MO

Forecast 2007-2015

Earnings	New Jobs	Growth
High	2,512	7.9%
Average	2,203	10.8%
Low	8,790	16.0%

New Jobs in . .
    Blue-collar industries: 3,116
    White-collar industries: 10,389
Total Growth Rate: 12.6%
Unemployment Risk: ⬅➡
Job Quality: ⬇

Places Rated Rank: 256

Kalamazoo-Portage, MI

Forecast 2007-2015

Earnings	New Jobs	Growth
High	1,040	2.4%
Average	2,628	5.9%
Low	7,171	7.4%

New Jobs in . .
    Blue-collar industries: 1,676
    White-collar industries: 9,163
Total Growth Rate: 5.9%
Unemployment Risk: ⬅➡
Job Quality: ⬅➡

Places Rated Rank: 281

Kankakee-Bradley, IL

Forecast 2007-2015

Earnings	New Jobs	Growth
High	928	7.6%
Average	1,574	11.2%
Low	3,250	10.5%

New Jobs in . .
    Blue-collar industries: 1,504
    White-collar industries: 4,248
Total Growth Rate: 10.1%
Unemployment Risk: ⬆
Job Quality: ⬇

Places Rated Rank: 317

Kansas City, MO-KS

Forecast 2007-2015

Earnings	New Jobs	Growth
High	21,896	7.1%
Average	34,522	10.4%
Low	83,389	12.6%

New Jobs in . .
    Blue-collar industries: 32,687
    White-collar industries: 107,120
Total Growth Rate: 10.7%
Unemployment Risk: ⬅➡
Job Quality: ⬆

Places Rated Rank: 47

Kennewick-Richland-Pasco, WA

Forecast 2007-2015

Earnings	New Jobs	Growth
High	3,179	14.6%
Average	3,789	13.6%
Low	11,782	16.3%

New Jobs in . .
    Blue-collar industries: 5,313
    White-collar industries: 13,437
Total Growth Rate: 15.4%
Unemployment Risk: ⬆
Job Quality: ⬆

Places Rated Rank: 66

Killeen-Temple-Fort Hood, TX

UForecast 2007-2015

Earnings	New Jobs	Growth
High	2,571	8.7%
Average	6,755	14.5%
Low	13,945	17.1%

New Jobs in . .
    Blue-collar industries: 4,197
    White-collar industries: 19,074
Total Growth Rate: 14.8%
nemployment Risk: ⬅➡
Job Quality: ⬅➡

Places Rated Rank: 101

Kingsport-Bristol-Bristol, TN-VA

Forecast 2007-2015

Earnings	New Jobs	Growth
High	2,066	4.4%
Average	1,493	4.5%
Low	8,619	9.9%

New Jobs in . .
    Blue-collar industries: 3,018
    White-collar industries: 9,160
Total Growth Rate: 7.3%
Unemployment Risk: ⬅➡
Job Quality: ⬇

Places Rated Rank: 320

Kingston, NY

Forecast 2007-2015

Earnings	New Jobs	Growth
High	299	2.4%
Average	1,907	7.7%
Low	4,863	9.5%

New Jobs in . .
    Blue-collar industries: 726
    White-collar industries: 6,343
Total Growth Rate: 8.0%
Unemployment Risk: ⬅➡
Job Quality: ⬇

Places Rated Rank: 355

Knoxville, TN

Forecast 2007-2015

Earnings	New Jobs	Growth
High	6,431	7.1%
Average	10,306	9.4%
Low	43,286	18.1%

New Jobs in . .
    Blue-collar industries: 11,228
    White-collar industries: 48,795
Total Growth Rate: 13.7%
Unemployment Risk: ⬇
Job Quality: ⬅➡

Places Rated Rank: 62

Kokomo, IN

Forecast 2007-2015

Earnings	New Jobs	Growth
High	98	0.4%
Average	1,270	9.3%
Low	3,682	13.0%

New Jobs in . .
    Blue-collar industries: 477
    White-collar industries: 4,573
Total Growth Rate: 7.9%
Unemployment Risk: ⬅➡
Job Quality: ⬆

Places Rated Rank: 236

La Crosse, WI-MN

Forecast 2007-2015

Earnings	New Jobs	Growth
High	583	2.8%
Average	1,741	8.2%
Low	6,193	11.7%

New Jobs in . .
    Blue-collar industries: 1,216
    White-collar industries: 7,301
Total Growth Rate: 9.0%
Unemployment Risk: ⬇
Job Quality: ⬅➡

Places Rated Rank: 302

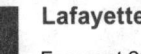

Lafayette, IN

Forecast 2007-2015

Earnings	New Jobs	Growth
High	1,700	6.1%
Average	4,094	10.8%
Low	7,874	14.2%

New Jobs in . .
Blue-collar industries: 2,622
White-collar industries: 11,046
Total Growth Rate: 11.3%
Unemployment Risk: ⬇
Job Quality: ⬅➡

Places Rated Rank: 204

Lafayette, LA

Forecast 2007-2015

Earnings	New Jobs	Growth
High	6,050	13.2%
Average	1,914	5.7%
Low	15,195	15.7%

New Jobs in . .
Blue-collar industries: 6,577
White-collar industries: 16,582
Total Growth Rate: 13.1%
Unemployment Risk: ⬅➡
Job Quality: ⬅➡

Places Rated Rank: 113

Lake Charles, LA

Forecast 2007-2015

Earnings	New Jobs	Growth
High	479	2.1%
Average	3,058	9.4%
Low	7,780	13.2%

New Jobs in . .
Blue-collar industries: 1,853
White-collar industries: 9,464
Total Growth Rate: 10.0%
Unemployment Risk: ⬅➡
Job Quality: ⬅➡

Places Rated Rank: 242

✓ Lake County, IL-WI

Forecast 2007-2015

Earnings	New Jobs	Growth
High	18,206	13.8%
Average	30,569	22.7%
Low	50,163	18.6%

New Jobs in . .
Blue-collar industries: 27,019
White-collar industries: 72,009
Total Growth Rate: 18.4%
Unemployment Risk: ⬅➡
Job Quality: ⬆

Places Rated Rank: 9

Lakeland, FL

Forecast 2007-2015

Earnings	New Jobs	Growth
High	1,948	3.9%
Average	4,922	7.9%
Low	19,836	13.6%

New Jobs in . .
Blue-collar industries: 2,962
White-collar industries: 23,744
Total Growth Rate: 10.4%
Unemployment Risk: ⬆
Job Quality: ⬅➡

Places Rated Rank: 177

Lancaster, PA

Forecast 2007-2015

Earnings	New Jobs	Growth
High	-705	-0.8%
Average	4,289	7.0%
Low	16,330	10.6%

New Jobs in . .
Blue-collar industries: 317
White-collar industries: 19,597
Total Growth Rate: 6.6%
Unemployment Risk: ⬇
Job Quality: ⬅➡

Places Rated Rank: 240

Lansing-East Lansing, MI

Forecast 2007-2015

Earnings	New Jobs	Growth
High	2,321	4.7%
Average	11,442	11.0%
Low	15,966	11.0%

New Jobs in . .
Blue-collar industries: 4,974
White-collar industries: 24,755
Total Growth Rate: 10.0%
Unemployment Risk: ⬅➡
Job Quality: ⬆

Places Rated Rank: 125

Laredo, TX

Forecast 2007-2015

Earnings	New Jobs	Growth
High	7,874	28.3%
Average	9,751	30.5%
Low	12,409	24.8%

New Jobs in . .
Blue-collar industries: 8,805
White-collar industries: 21,229
Total Growth Rate: 27.3%
Unemployment Risk: ⬆
Job Quality: ⬇

Places Rated Rank: 130

Las Cruces, NM

Forecast 2007-2015

Earnings	New Jobs	Growth
High	909	7.4%
Average	2,849	10.5%
Low	8,417	17.9%

New Jobs in . .
Blue-collar industries: 2,050
White-collar industries: 10,125
Total Growth Rate: 14.1%
Unemployment Risk: ⬆
Job Quality: ⬇

Places Rated Rank: 247

✓ Las Vegas-Paradise, NV

Forecast 2007-2015

Earnings	New Jobs	Growth
High	31,672	26.0%
Average	94,531	31.4%
Low	162,316	25.4%

New Jobs in . .
Blue-collar industries: 58,629
White-collar industries: 229,890
Total Growth Rate: 27.2%
Unemployment Risk: ⬅➡
Job Quality: ⬆

Places Rated Rank: 3

Lawrence, KS

Forecast 2007-2015

Earnings	New Jobs	Growth
High	232	3.3%
Average	3,018	12.0%
Low	6,079	16.6%

New Jobs in . .
Blue-collar industries: 593
White-collar industries: 8,827
Total Growth Rate: 13.2%
Unemployment Risk: ⬅➡
Job Quality: ⬇

Places Rated Rank: 274

Lawton, OK

Forecast 2007-2015

Earnings	New Jobs	Growth
High	202	2.0%
Average	1,031	6.7%
Low	2,611	9.8%

New Jobs in . .
Blue-collar industries: 607
White-collar industries: 3,237
Total Growth Rate: 7.3%
Unemployment Risk: ⬅➡
Job Quality: ⬅➡

Places Rated Rank: 351

Lebanon, PA

Forecast 2007-2015

Earnings	New Jobs	Growth
High	625	3.5%
Average	871	8.0%
Low	3,020	10.1%

New Jobs in . .
Blue-collar industries: 1,152
White-collar industries: 3,364
Total Growth Rate: 7.7%
Unemployment Risk: ⬇
Job Quality: ⬅➡

Places Rated Rank: 341

Lewiston, ID-WA

Forecast 2007-2015

Earnings	New Jobs	Growth
High	381	5.0%
Average	1,356	13.4%
Low	2,579	13.5%

New Jobs in . .
Blue-collar industries: 636
White-collar industries: 3,680
Total Growth Rate: 11.7%
Unemployment Risk: ⬅➡
Job Quality: ⬇

Places Rated Rank: 313

Lewiston-Auburn, ME

Forecast 2007-2015

Earnings	New Jobs	Growth
High	537	3.9%
Average	1,517	10.3%
Low	3,600	9.8%

New Jobs in . .
Blue-collar industries: 833
White-collar industries: 4,821
Total Growth Rate: 8.7%
Unemployment Risk: ⬅➡
Job Quality: ⬇

Places Rated Rank: 342

Lexington-Fayette, KY

Forecast 2007-2015

Earnings	New Jobs	Growth
High	5,072	7.1%
Average	9,302	11.7%
Low	19,752	11.8%

New Jobs in . .
 Blue-collar industries: 9,009
 White-collar industries: 25,117
Total Growth Rate: 10.8%
Unemployment Risk: ↓
Job Quality: ↑

Places Rated Rank: 95

Lima, OH

Forecast 2007-2015

Earnings	New Jobs	Growth
High	-508	-2.9%
Average	899	5.9%
Low	3,788	9.3%

New Jobs in . .
 Blue-collar industries: -165
 White-collar industries: 4,344
Total Growth Rate: 5.7%
Unemployment Risk: ↑
Job Quality: ←→

Places Rated Rank: 356

Lincoln, NE

Forecast 2007-2015

Earnings	New Jobs	Growth
High	3,758	9.3%
Average	5,429	8.6%
Low	14,563	13.4%

New Jobs in . .
 Blue-collar industries: 5,608
 White-collar industries: 18,142
Total Growth Rate: 11.2%
Unemployment Risk: ↓
Job Quality: ←→

Places Rated Rank: 158

Little Rock-North Little Rock, AR

Forecast 2007-2015

Earnings	New Jobs	Growth
High	5,012	5.6%
Average	12,056	10.4%
Low	32,253	15.3%

New Jobs in . .
 Blue-collar industries: 8,539
 White-collar industries: 40,782
Total Growth Rate: 11.8%
Unemployment Risk: ←→
Job Quality: ←→

Places Rated Rank: 84

Logan, UT-ID

Forecast 2007-2015

Earnings	New Jobs	Growth
High	2,357	15.5%
Average	1,761	9.5%
Low	5,987	18.7%

New Jobs in . .
 Blue-collar industries: 2,852
 White-collar industries: 7,253
Total Growth Rate: 15.4%
Unemployment Risk: ↓
Job Quality: ↓

Places Rated Rank: 251

Longview, TX

Forecast 2007-2015

Earnings	New Jobs	Growth
High	1,552	5.4%
Average	2,481	8.5%
Low	8,885	13.9%

New Jobs in . .
 Blue-collar industries: 2,642
 White-collar industries: 10,276
Total Growth Rate: 10.6%
Unemployment Risk: ↑
Job Quality: ↓

Places Rated Rank: 271

Longview, WA

Forecast 2007-2015

Earnings	New Jobs	Growth
High	353	2.9%
Average	729	6.5%
Low	2,464	10.0%

New Jobs in . .
 Blue-collar industries: 726
 White-collar industries: 2,820
Total Growth Rate: 7.4%
Unemployment Risk: ↑
Job Quality: ←→

Places Rated Rank: 314

Los Angeles-Long Beach, CA

Forecast 2007-2015

Earnings	New Jobs	Growth
High	10,765	0.8%
Average	89,961	6.5%
Low	264,139	8.5%

New Jobs in . .
 Blue-collar industries: 22,406
 White-collar industries: 342,459
Total Growth Rate: 6.3%
Unemployment Risk: ↑
Job Quality: ↑

Places Rated Rank: 92

Louisville-Jefferson County, KY-IN

Forecast 2007-2015

Earnings	New Jobs	Growth
High	16,287	8.4%
Average	20,914	11.1%
Low	50,189	12.6%

New Jobs in . .
 Blue-collar industries: 22,291
 White-collar industries: 65,099
Total Growth Rate: 11.2%
Unemployment Risk: ←→
Job Quality: ↑

Places Rated Rank: 69

Lubbock, TX

Forecast 2007-2015

Earnings	New Jobs	Growth
High	1,086	4.2%
Average	4,320	9.1%
Low	11,035	11.8%

New Jobs in . .
 Blue-collar industries: 940
 White-collar industries: 15,501
Total Growth Rate: 9.9%
Unemployment Risk: ←→
Job Quality: ↓

Places Rated Rank: 263

Lynchburg, VA

Forecast 2007-2015

Earnings	New Jobs	Growth
High	700	2.2%
Average	3,166	9.5%
Low	7,546	11.1%

New Jobs in . .
 Blue-collar industries: 2,112
 White-collar industries: 9,300
Total Growth Rate: 8.6%
Unemployment Risk: ↓
Job Quality: ↓

Places Rated Rank: 311

Macon, GA

Forecast 2007-2015

Earnings	New Jobs	Growth
High	456	1.7%
Average	1,994	5.9%
Low	6,825	10.0%

New Jobs in . .
 Blue-collar industries: 689
 White-collar industries: 8,586
Total Growth Rate: 7.2%
Unemployment Risk: ←→
Job Quality: ←→

Places Rated Rank: 290

Madera, CA

Forecast 2007-2015

Earnings	New Jobs	Growth
High	417	6.3%
Average	2,403	16.3%
Low	8,310	21.7%

New Jobs in . .
 Blue-collar industries: 1,981
 White-collar industries: 9,149
Total Growth Rate: 18.6%
Unemployment Risk: ↑
Job Quality: ↓

Places Rated Rank: 208

Madison, WI

Forecast 2007-2015

Earnings	New Jobs	Growth
High	6,515	8.6%
Average	14,342	10.1%
Low	38,574	17.5%

New Jobs in . .
 Blue-collar industries: 9,214
 White-collar industries: 50,217
Total Growth Rate: 13.6%
Unemployment Risk: ↓
Job Quality: ↑

Places Rated Rank: 45

Manchester-Nashua, NH

Forecast 2007-2015

Earnings	New Jobs	Growth
High	3,064	4.8%
Average	4,677	8.2%
Low	16,193	11.7%

New Jobs in . .
 Blue-collar industries: 4,281
 White-collar industries: 19,653
Total Growth Rate: 9.2%
Unemployment Risk: ↓
Job Quality: ↑

Places Rated Rank: 110

Jobs

Mansfield, OH

Forecast 2007-2015

Earnings	New Jobs	Growth
High	6	0.0%
Average	1,405	8.2%
Low	3,541	9.4%

New Jobs in . .
    Blue-collar industries: 464
    White-collar industries: 4,488
Total Growth Rate: 6.5%
Unemployment Risk: ↑
Job Quality: ←→

Places Rated Rank: 345

McAllen-Edinburg-Mission, TX

Forecast 2007-2015

Earnings	New Jobs	Growth
High	4,961	14.2%
Average	19,992	24.3%
Low	26,498	18.8%

New Jobs in . .
    Blue-collar industries: 9,876
    White-collar industries: 41,575
Total Growth Rate: 19.9%
Unemployment Risk: ↑
Job Quality: ↓

Places Rated Rank: 133

Medford, OR

Forecast 2007-2015

Earnings	New Jobs	Growth
High	1,463	7.2%
Average	2,567	9.6%
Low	14,883	21.1%

New Jobs in . .
    Blue-collar industries: 2,196
    White-collar industries: 16,717
Total Growth Rate: 16.1%
Unemployment Risk: ↑
Job Quality: ↓

Places Rated Rank: 175

✓ Memphis, TN-MS-AR

Forecast 2007-2015

Earnings	New Jobs	Growth
High	26,646	12.3%
Average	18,460	10.1%
Low	57,706	13.8%

New Jobs in . .
    Blue-collar industries: 32,127
    White-collar industries: 70,685
Total Growth Rate: 12.6%
Unemployment Risk: ←→
Job Quality: ↑

Places Rated Rank: 33

Merced, CA

Forecast 2007-2015

Earnings	New Jobs	Growth
High	278	1.5%
Average	1,862	2.1%
Low	5,723	10.9%

New Jobs in . .
    Blue-collar industries: 922
    White-collar industries: 6,941
Total Growth Rate: 8.4%
Unemployment Risk: ↑
Job Quality: ↓

Places Rated Rank: 332

Miami-Miami Beach-Kendall, FL

Forecast 2007-2015

Earnings	New Jobs	Growth
High	278	1.5%
Average	1,862	8.1%
Low	5,723	10.9%

New Jobs in . .
    Blue-collar industries: 21,131
    White-collar industries: 110,025
Total Growth Rate: 9.6%
Unemployment Risk: ↑
Job Quality: ↑

Places Rated Rank: 79

Michigan City-La Porte, IN

Forecast 2007-2015

Earnings	New Jobs	Growth
High	40	0.3%
Average	1,590	10.4%
Low	3,142	9.7%

New Jobs in . .
    Blue-collar industries: 635
    White-collar industries: 4,137
Total Growth Rate: 7.6%
Unemployment Risk: ←→
Job Quality: ↓

Places Rated Rank: 360

Midland, TX

Forecast 2007-2015

Earnings	New Jobs	Growth
High	1,800	8.0%
Average	1,878	9.0%
Low	4,601	11.6%

New Jobs in . .
    Blue-collar industries: 2,214
    White-collar industries: 6,065
Total Growth Rate: 10.0%
Unemployment Risk: ←→
Job Quality: ↑

Places Rated Rank: 203

Milwaukee-Waukesha-West Allis, WI

Forecast 2007-2015

Earnings	New Jobs	Growth
High	7,364	2.7%
Average	16,583	7.6%
Low	63,072	11.5%

New Jobs in . .
    Blue-collar industries: 13,023
    White-collar industries: 73,996
Total Growth Rate: 8.4%
Unemployment Risk: ←→
Job Quality: ↑

Places Rated Rank: 89

✓ Minneapolis-St. Paul, MN-WI

Forecast 2007-2015

Earnings	New Jobs	Growth
High	39,882	7.6%
Average	60,905	10.8%
Low	191,231	15.8%

New Jobs in . .
    Blue-collar industries: 55,125
    White-collar industries: 236,893
Total Growth Rate: 12.7%
Unemployment Risk: ↓
Job Quality: ↑

Places Rated Rank: 21

Missoula, MT

Forecast 2007-2015

Earnings	New Jobs	Growth
High	617	5.0%
Average	1,699	9.1%
Low	11,903	24.8%

New Jobs in . .
    Blue-collar industries: 1,166
    White-collar industries: 13,053
Total Growth Rate: 18.0%
Unemployment Risk: ←→
Job Quality: ↓

Places Rated Rank: 186

Mobile, AL

Forecast 2007-2015

Earnings	New Jobs	Growth
High	1,641	3.7%
Average	4,593	7.5%
Low	9,658	8.4%

New Jobs in . .
    Blue-collar industries: 4,919
    White-collar industries: 10,973
Total Growth Rate: 7.2%
Unemployment Risk: ←→
Job Quality: ←→

Places Rated Rank: 279

Modesto, CA

Forecast 2007-2015

Earnings	New Jobs	Growth
High	3,522	7.5%
Average	5,813	10.3%
Low	19,061	14.5%

New Jobs in . .
    Blue-collar industries: 6,552
    White-collar industries: 21,844
Total Growth Rate: 12.1%
Unemployment Risk: ↑
Job Quality: ←→

Places Rated Rank: 129

Monroe, LA

Forecast 2007-2015

Earnings	New Jobs	Growth
High	1,055	5.2%
Average	2,666	8.8%
Low	6,520	12.5%

New Jobs in . .
    Blue-collar industries: 1,312
    White-collar industries: 8,929
Total Growth Rate: 10.0%
Unemployment Risk: ←→
Job Quality: ↓

Places Rated Rank: 275

Monroe, MI

Forecast 2007-2015

Earnings	New Jobs	Growth
High	1,394	7.7%
Average	1,119	7.2%
Low	3,593	12.1%

New Jobs in . .
    Blue-collar industries: 1,886
    White-collar industries: 4,220
Total Growth Rate: 9.6%
Unemployment Risk: ←→
Job Quality: ↑

Places Rated Rank: 223

Montgomery, AL

Forecast 2007-2015

Earnings	New Jobs	Growth
High	1,502	3.5%
Average	6,864	10.4%
Low	16,095	15.0%

New Jobs in . .
    Blue-collar industries: 3,189
    White-collar industries: 21,272
Total Growth Rate: 11.3%
Unemployment Risk: ← →
Job Quality: ← →

Places Rated Rank: 121

Morgantown, WV

Forecast 2007-2015

Earnings	New Jobs	Growth
High	862	7.8%
Average	2,372	9.8%
Low	6,693	18.6%

New Jobs in . .
    Blue-collar industries: 862
    White-collar industries: 9,065
Total Growth Rate: 13.9%
Unemployment Risk: ← →
Job Quality: ← →

Places Rated Rank: 200

Morristown, TN

Forecast 2007-2015

Earnings	New Jobs	Growth
High	1,944	7.6%
Average	1,621	10.8%
Low	4,267	14.0%

New Jobs in . .
    Blue-collar industries: 2,803
    White-collar industries: 5,029
Total Growth Rate: 11.0%
Unemployment Risk: ↑
Job Quality: ↓

Places Rated Rank: 306

Mount Vernon-Anacortes, WA

Forecast 2007-2015

Earnings	New Jobs	Growth
High	931	8.4%
Average	1,999	10.3%
Low	6,080	17.2%

New Jobs in . .
    Blue-collar industries: 1,878
    White-collar industries: 7,132
Total Growth Rate: 13.7%
Unemployment Risk: ↑
Job Quality: ← →

Places Rated Rank: 195

Muncie, IN

Forecast 2007-2015

Earnings	New Jobs	Growth
High	30	0.2%
Average	1,058	5.9%
Low	4,389	11.4%

New Jobs in . .
    Blue-collar industries: 274
    White-collar industries: 5,203
Total Growth Rate: 7.7%
Unemployment Risk: ← →
Job Quality: ↓

Places Rated Rank: 346

Muskegon-Norton Shores, MI

Forecast 2007-2015

Earnings	New Jobs	Growth
High	1,658	7.9%
Average	1,431	7.6%
Low	5,632	12.2%

New Jobs in . .
    Blue-collar industries: 2,273
    White-collar industries: 6,448
Total Growth Rate: 10.1%
Unemployment Risk: ↑
Job Quality: ← →

Places Rated Rank: 255

Myrtle Beach-Conway, SC

Forecast 2007-2015

Earnings	New Jobs	Growth
High	2,571	17.9%
Average	9,821	22.8%
Low	18,814	21.3%

New Jobs in . .
    Blue-collar industries: 6,224
    White-collar industries: 24,982
Total Growth Rate: 21.4%
Unemployment Risk: ← →
Job Quality: ↓

Places Rated Rank: 152

Napa, CA

Forecast 2007-2015

Earnings	New Jobs	Growth
High	2,062	11.9%
Average	2,310	9.7%
Low	7,392	13.6%

New Jobs in . .
    Blue-collar industries: 3,553
    White-collar industries: 8,211
Total Growth Rate: 12.3%
Unemployment Risk: ← →
Job Quality: ↑

Places Rated Rank: 136

Naples-Marco Island, FL

Forecast 2007-2015

Earnings	New Jobs	Growth
High	2,875	19.6%
Average	9,431	16.8%
Low	33,571	28.5%

New Jobs in . .
    Blue-collar industries: 8,366
    White-collar industries: 37,511
Total Growth Rate: 24.3%
Unemployment Risk: ← →
Job Quality: ↑

Places Rated Rank: 41

✓ Nashville-Davidson, TN

Forecast 2007-2015

Earnings	New Jobs	Growth
High	14,740	7.3%
Average	21,888	9.7%
Low	113,558	19.7%

New Jobs in . .
    Blue-collar industries: 22,169
    White-collar industries: 128,017
Total Growth Rate: 14.9%
Unemployment Risk: ↓
Job Quality: ↑

Places Rated Rank: 26

Nassau-Suffolk, NY

Forecast 2007-2015

Earnings	New Jobs	Growth
High	17,997	6.1%
Average	21,870	4.9%
Low	57,012	6.7%

New Jobs in . .
    Blue-collar industries: 23,208
    White-collar industries: 73,671
Total Growth Rate: 6.1%
Unemployment Risk: ← →
Job Quality: ↑

Places Rated Rank: 118

Newark-Union, NJ-PA

Forecast 2007-2015

Earnings	New Jobs	Growth
High	7,406	2.5%
Average	20,507	5.9%
Low	61,478	9.4%

New Jobs in . .
    Blue-collar industries: 11,579
    White-collar industries: 77,812
Total Growth Rate: 6.9%
Unemployment Risk: ↑
Job Quality: ↑

Places Rated Rank: 97

New Haven-Milford, CT

Forecast 2007-2015

Earnings	New Jobs	Growth
High	848	0.8%
Average	7,541	6.8%
Low	26,000	9.3%

New Jobs in . .
    Blue-collar industries: 2,336
    White-collar industries: 32,053
Total Growth Rate: 7.0%
Unemployment Risk: ← →
Job Quality: ↑

Places Rated Rank: 139

New Orleans-Metairie-Kenner, LA

Forecast 2007-2015

Earnings	New Jobs	Growth
High	5,322	3.4%
Average	16,887	8.3%
Low	47,949	10.9%

New Jobs in . .
    Blue-collar industries: 9,330
    White-collar industries: 60,828
Total Growth Rate: 8.8%
Unemployment Risk: ↑
Job Quality: ↑

Places Rated Rank: 114

New York-White Plains, NY-NJ

Forecast 2007-2015

Earnings	New Jobs	Growth
High	-2,153	-0.2%
Average	81,219	4.6%
Low	257,192	7.3%

New Jobs in . .
    Blue-collar industries: 24,667
    White-collar industries: 311,591
Total Growth Rate: 5.2%
Unemployment Risk: ↑
Job Quality: ↑

Places Rated Rank: 93

Niles-Benton Harbor, MI

Forecast 2007-2015

Earnings	New Jobs	Growth
High	-406	-1.7%
Average	524	3.0%
Low	4,539	9.6%

New Jobs in . .
    Blue-collar industries: -190
    White-collar industries: 4,847
Total Growth Rate: 5.3%
Unemployment Risk: ⬆
Job Quality: ⬅➡

Places Rated Rank: 339

Norwich-New London, CT

Forecast 2007-2015

Earnings	New Jobs	Growth
High	-765	-2.6%
Average	4,358	7.9%
Low	11,878	14.2%

New Jobs in . .
    Blue-collar industries: 91
    White-collar industries: 15,380
Total Growth Rate: 9.2%
Unemployment Risk: ⬅➡
Job Quality: ⬆

Places Rated Rank: 143

✓ Oakland-Fremont-Hayward, CA

Forecast 2007-2015

Earnings	New Jobs	Growth
High	25,630	8.7%
Average	41,968	10.5%
Low	119,538	15.0%

New Jobs in . .
    Blue-collar industries: 38,545
    White-collar industries: 148,591
Total Growth Rate: 12.5%
Unemployment Risk: ⬅➡
Job Quality: ⬆

Places Rated Rank: 23

Ocala, FL

Forecast 2007-2015

Earnings	New Jobs	Growth
High	1,853	8.8%
Average	4,637	12.8%
Low	9,381	14.0%

New Jobs in . .
    Blue-collar industries: 3,157
    White-collar industries: 12,714
Total Growth Rate: 12.8%
Unemployment Risk: ⬅➡
Job Quality: ⬇

Places Rated Rank: 238

Ocean City, NJ

Forecast 2007-2015

Earnings	New Jobs	Growth
High	-15	-0.4%
Average	1,618	8.0%
Low	2,813	8.2%

New Jobs in . .
    Blue-collar industries: 151
    White-collar industries: 4,265
Total Growth Rate: 7.6%
Unemployment Risk: ⬆
Job Quality: ⬇

Places Rated Rank: 364

Odessa, TX

Forecast 2007-2015

Earnings	New Jobs	Growth
High	504	3.3%
Average	1,075	5.7%
Low	3,286	10.0%

New Jobs in . .
    Blue-collar industries: 550
    White-collar industries: 4,315
Total Growth Rate: 7.3%
Unemployment Risk: ⬆
Job Quality: ⬇

Places Rated Rank: 349

Ogden-Clearfield, UT

Forecast 2007-2015

Earnings	New Jobs	Growth
High	3,101	5.2%
Average	12,436	17.5%
Low	27,202	21.2%

New Jobs in . .
    Blue-collar industries: 8,881
    White-collar industries: 33,858
Total Growth Rate: 16.5%
Unemployment Risk: ⬅➡
Job Quality: ⬇

Places Rated Rank: 99

Oklahoma City, OK

Forecast 2007-2015

Earnings	New Jobs	Growth
High	7,349	4.7%
Average	15,250	8.3%
Low	51,883	13.1%

New Jobs in . .
    Blue-collar industries: 14,035
    White-collar industries: 60,447
Total Growth Rate: 10.1%
Unemployment Risk: ⬇
Job Quality: ⬅➡

Places Rated Rank: 126

Olympia, WA

Forecast 2007-2015

Earnings	New Jobs	Growth
High	885	7.0%
Average	5,934	11.3%
Low	9,882	16.5%

New Jobs in . .
    Blue-collar industries: 2,016
    White-collar industries: 14,685
Total Growth Rate: 13.4%
Unemployment Risk: ⬆
Job Quality: ⬅➡

Places Rated Rank: 117

Omaha-Council Bluffs, NE-IA

Forecast 2007-2015

Earnings	New Jobs	Growth
High	9,241	7.7%
Average	13,094	9.5%
Low	39,432	12.8%

New Jobs in . .
    Blue-collar industries: 14,070
    White-collar industries: 47,697
Total Growth Rate: 10.9%
Unemployment Risk: ⬇
Job Quality: ⬆

Places Rated Rank: 72

✓ Orlando-Kissimmee, FL

Forecast 2007-2015

Earnings	New Jobs	Growth
High	26,983	15.2%
Average	44,163	15.8%
Low	189,565	24.1%

New Jobs in . .
    Blue-collar industries: 36,593
    White-collar industries: 224,118
Total Growth Rate: 21.0%
Unemployment Risk: ⬅➡
Job Quality: ⬆

Places Rated Rank: 19

Oshkosh-Neenah, WI

Forecast 2007-2015

Earnings	New Jobs	Growth
High	3,181	7.8%
Average	1,351	5.8%
Low	5,875	12.4%

New Jobs in . .
    Blue-collar industries: 3,918
    White-collar industries: 6,489
Total Growth Rate: 9.3%
Unemployment Risk: ⬇
Job Quality: ⬆

Places Rated Rank: 181

Owensboro, KY

Forecast 2007-2015

Earnings	New Jobs	Growth
High	800	4.9%
Average	3,140	16.4%
Low	3,121	9.8%

New Jobs in . .
    Blue-collar industries: 1,935
    White-collar industries: 5,126
Total Growth Rate: 10.5%
Unemployment Risk: ⬆
Job Quality: ⬇

Places Rated Rank: 295

Oxnard-Thousand Oaks-Ventura, CA

Forecast 2007-2015

Earnings	New Jobs	Growth
High	2,384	2.8%
Average	12,520	11.2%
Low	32,835	13.1%

New Jobs in . .
    Blue-collar industries: 7,225
    White-collar industries: 40,514
Total Growth Rate: 10.7%
Unemployment Risk: ⬆
Job Quality: ⬆

Places Rated Rank: 73

Palm Bay-Melbourne-Titusville, FL

Forecast 2007-2015

Earnings	New Jobs	Growth
High	2,768	6.0%
Average	5,743	9.4%
Low	18,142	11.7%

New Jobs in . .
    Blue-collar industries: 4,771
    White-collar industries: 21,882
Total Growth Rate: 10.2%
Unemployment Risk: ⬅➡
Job Quality: ⬆

Places Rated Rank: 137

Panama City-Lynn Haven, FL

Forecast 2007-2015

Earnings	New Jobs	Growth
High	627	4.7%
Average	2,505	11.0%
Low	11,408	20.8%

New Jobs in . .
  Blue-collar industries: 2,116
  White-collar industries: 12,424
Total Growth Rate: 16.0%
Unemployment Risk: ⬆
Job Quality: ⬇

Places Rated Rank: 186

Parkersburg-Marietta, WV-OH

Forecast 2007-2015

Earnings	New Jobs	Growth
High	354	1.6%
Average	497	2.3%
Low	4,867	9.9%

New Jobs in . .
  Blue-collar industries: 87
  White-collar industries: 5,631
Total Growth Rate: 6.2%
Unemployment Risk: ⬆
Job Quality: ⬅➡

Places Rated Rank: 349

Pascagoula, MS

Forecast 2007-2015

Earnings	New Jobs	Growth
High	454	2.3%
Average	2,120	9.8%
Low	2,891	10.5%

New Jobs in . .
  Blue-collar industries: 907
  White-collar industries: 4,558
Total Growth Rate: 7.9%
Unemployment Risk: ⬆
Job Quality: ⬇

Places Rated Rank: 338

Pensacola-Ferry Pass-Brent, FL

Forecast 2007-2015

Earnings	New Jobs	Growth
High	2,072	6.3%
Average	4,976	9.3%
Low	30,051	23.0%

New Jobs in . .
  Blue-collar industries: 4,395
  White-collar industries: 32,704
Total Growth Rate: 17.1%
Unemployment Risk: ⬅➡
Job Quality: ⬅➡

Places Rated Rank: 94

Peoria, IL

Forecast 2007-2015

Earnings	New Jobs	Growth
High	1,716	3.1%
Average	4,219	8.5%
Low	14,636	11.7%

New Jobs in . .
  Blue-collar industries: 3,482
  White-collar industries: 17,089
Total Growth Rate: 9.0%
Unemployment Risk: ⬅➡
Job Quality: ⬅➡

Places Rated Rank: 184

Philadelphia, PA

Forecast 2007-2015

Earnings	New Jobs	Growth
High	1,289	0.3%
Average	31,277	6.0%
Low	135,241	9.8%

New Jobs in . .
  Blue-collar industries: 11,191
  White-collar industries: 156,616
Total Growth Rate: 7.1%
Unemployment Risk: ⬅➡
Job Quality: ⬆

Places Rated Rank: 88

✓ Phoenix-Mesa-Scottsdale, AZ

Forecast 2007-2015

Earnings	New Jobs	Growth
High	61,399	15.4%
Average	130,749	19.8%
Low	268,606	22.6%

New Jobs in . .
  Blue-collar industries: 91,302
  White-collar industries: 369,452
Total Growth Rate: 20.5%
Unemployment Risk: ⬅➡
Job Quality: ⬆

Places Rated Rank: 2

Pine Bluff, AR

Forecast 2007-2015

Earnings	New Jobs	Growth
High	381	2.7%
Average	1,191	8.9%
Low	1,879	8.0%

New Jobs in . .
  Blue-collar industries: 650
  White-collar industries: 2,801
Total Growth Rate: 6.8%
Unemployment Risk: ⬆
Job Quality: ⬇

Places Rated Rank: 362

Pittsburgh, PA

Forecast 2007-2015

Earnings	New Jobs	Growth
High	13,929	4.5%
Average	27,820	8.3%
Low	76,814	9.3%

New Jobs in . .
  Blue-collar industries: 23,363
  White-collar industries: 95,200
Total Growth Rate: 8.1%
Unemployment Risk: ⬅➡
Job Quality: ⬆

Places Rated Rank: 90

Pittsfield, MA

Forecast 2007-2015

Earnings	New Jobs	Growth
High	-385	-2.9%
Average	870	4.6%
Low	4,421	8.3%

New Jobs in . .
  Blue-collar industries: 158
  White-collar industries: 4,748
Total Growth Rate: 5.7%
Unemployment Risk: ⬅➡
Job Quality: ⬅➡

Places Rated Rank: 344

Pocatello, ID

Forecast 2007-2015

Earnings	New Jobs	Growth
High	-2	0.0%
Average	2,149	13.3%
Low	4,350	16.6%

New Jobs in . .
  Blue-collar industries: 464
  White-collar industries: 6,033
Total Growth Rate: 12.7%
Unemployment Risk: ⬅➡
Job Quality: ⬇

Places Rated Rank: 303

Portland-South Portland, ME

Forecast 2007-2015

Earnings	New Jobs	Growth
High	2,476	3.7%
Average	8,243	9.9%
Low	24,975	12.5%

New Jobs in . .
  Blue-collar industries: 5,006
  White-collar industries: 30,688
Total Growth Rate: 10.2%
Unemployment Risk: ⬇
Job Quality: ⬅➡

Places Rated Rank: 135

✓ Portland-Vancouver, OR-WA

Forecast 2007-2015

Earnings	New Jobs	Growth
High	24,017	7.9%
Average	26,572	8.3%
Low	130,175	18.2%

New Jobs in . .
  Blue-collar industries: 37,924
  White-collar industries: 142,840
Total Growth Rate: 13.5%
Unemployment Risk: ⬆
Job Quality: ⬆

Places Rated Rank: 25

Port St. Lucie-Fort Pierce, FL

Forecast 2007-2015

Earnings	New Jobs	Growth
High	3,446	15.6%
Average	6,956	14.9%
Low	22,404	21.2%

New Jobs in . .
  Blue-collar industries: 7,767
  White-collar industries: 25,039
Total Growth Rate: 18.8%
Unemployment Risk: ⬆
Job Quality: ⬇

Places Rated Rank: 142

Poughkeepsie-Newburgh, NY

Forecast 2007-2015

Earnings	New Jobs	Growth
High	-1,012	-1.5%
Average	5,311	6.2%
Low	24,856	14.5%

New Jobs in . .
  Blue-collar industries: 892
  White-collar industries: 28,263
Total Growth Rate: 9.0%
Unemployment Risk: ⬅➡
Job Quality: ⬆

Places Rated Rank: 150

Prescott, AZ

Forecast 2007-2015

Earnings	New Jobs	Growth
High	637	6.0%
Average	4,840	17.3%
Low	13,510	28.5%

New Jobs in . .
  Blue-collar industries: 2,772
  White-collar industries: 16,215
Total Growth Rate: 22.1%
Unemployment Risk: ← →
Job Quality: ↓

Places Rated Rank: 180

Providence-New Bedford, RI-MA

Forecast 2007-2015

Earnings	New Jobs	Growth
High	1,077	0.6%
Average	14,096	6.9%
Low	56,107	11.2%

New Jobs in . .
  Blue-collar industries: 5,432
  White-collar industries: 65,848
Total Growth Rate: 7.9%
Unemployment Risk: ↑
Job Quality: ↑

Places Rated Rank: 132

Provo-Orem, UT

Forecast 2007-2015

Earnings	New Jobs	Growth
High	5,072	16.2%
Average	17,544	26.2%
Low	34,701	24.7%

New Jobs in . .
  Blue-collar industries: 11,687
  White-collar industries: 45,630
Total Growth Rate: 24.0%
Unemployment Risk: ← →
Job Quality: ↓

Places Rated Rank: 103

Pueblo, CO

Forecast 2007-2015

Earnings	New Jobs	Growth
High	185	1.9%
Average	3,061	12.9%
Low	6,293	14.6%

New Jobs in . .
  Blue-collar industries: 1,682
  White-collar industries: 7,857
Total Growth Rate: 12.5%
Unemployment Risk: ↑
Job Quality: ↓

Places Rated Rank: 256

Punta Gorda, FL

Forecast 2007-2015

Earnings	New Jobs	Growth
High	568	11.8%
Average	3,415	17.6%
Low	12,584	25.4%

New Jobs in . .
  Blue-collar industries: 2,018
  White-collar industries: 14,549
Total Growth Rate: 22.5%
Unemployment Risk: ← →
Job Quality: ↓

Places Rated Rank: 191

Racine, WI

Forecast 2007-2015

Earnings	New Jobs	Growth
High	-196	-0.7%
Average	1,800	9.2%
Low	4,049	8.5%

New Jobs in . .
  Blue-collar industries: 584
  White-collar industries: 5,069
Total Growth Rate: 5.9%
Unemployment Risk: ← →
Job Quality: ↑

Places Rated Rank: 296

✓ Raleigh-Cary, NC

Forecast 2007-2015

Earnings	New Jobs	Growth
High	16,158	15.3%
Average	25,479	14.4%
Low	68,968	21.3%

New Jobs in . .
  Blue-collar industries: 24,967
  White-collar industries: 85,638
Total Growth Rate: 18.3%
Unemployment Risk: ↓
Job Quality: ↑

Places Rated Rank: 17

Rapid City, SD

Forecast 2007-2015

Earnings	New Jobs	Growth
High	1,562	10.5%
Average	2,501	12.3%
Low	6,542	13.8%

New Jobs in . .
  Blue-collar industries: 2,624
  White-collar industries: 7,981
Total Growth Rate: 12.8%
Unemployment Risk: ↓
Job Quality: ↓

Places Rated Rank: 259

Reading, PA

Forecast 2007-2015

Earnings	New Jobs	Growth
High	-69	-0.1%
Average	3,593	7.3%
Low	10,907	9.3%

New Jobs in . .
  Blue-collar industries: 1,482
  White-collar industries: 12,949
Total Growth Rate: 6.5%
Unemployment Risk: ← →
Job Quality: ← →

Places Rated Rank: 258

Redding, CA

Forecast 2007-2015

Earnings	New Jobs	Growth
High	582	4.3%
Average	1,774	6.6%
Low	9,753	17.1%

New Jobs in . .
  Blue-collar industries: 1,111
  White-collar industries: 10,998
Total Growth Rate: 12.4%
Unemployment Risk: ↑
Job Quality: ← →

Places Rated Rank: 214

Reno-Sparks, NV

Forecast 2007-2015

Earnings	New Jobs	Growth
High	6,834	13.4%
Average	7,158	10.1%
Low	24,289	16.7%

New Jobs in . .
  Blue-collar industries: 9,549
  White-collar industries: 28,732
Total Growth Rate: 14.3%
Unemployment Risk: ← →
Job Quality: ↑

Places Rated Rank: 42

Richmond, VA

Forecast 2007-2015

Earnings	New Jobs	Growth
High	8,013	5.4%
Average	22,754	9.3%
Low	51,638	14.3%

New Jobs in . .
  Blue-collar industries: 14,587
  White-collar industries: 67,818
Total Growth Rate: 10.9%
Unemployment Risk: ↓
Job Quality: ↑

Places Rated Rank: 54

✓ Riverside-San Bernardino, CA

Forecast 2007-2015

Earnings	New Jobs	Growth
High	41,449	13.8%
Average	78,990	16.5%
Low	141,027	16.7%

New Jobs in . .
  Blue-collar industries: 70,955
  White-collar industries: 190,511
Total Growth Rate: 16.1%
Unemployment Risk: ↑
Job Quality: ← →

Places Rated Rank: 36

Roanoke, VA

Forecast 2007-2015

Earnings	New Jobs	Growth
High	2,010	4.3%
Average	6,174	11.5%
Low	13,896	13.4%

New Jobs in . .
  Blue-collar industries: 3,865
  White-collar industries: 18,215
Total Growth Rate: 10.8%
Unemployment Risk: ↓
Job Quality: ← →

Places Rated Rank: 157

Rochester, MN

Forecast 2007-2015

Earnings	New Jobs	Growth
High	2,060	8.7%
Average	2,028	8.4%
Low	13,163	15.2%

New Jobs in . .
  Blue-collar industries: 2,960
  White-collar industries: 14,291
Total Growth Rate: 12.9%
Unemployment Risk: ↓
Job Quality: ↑

Places Rated Rank: 80

Rochester, NY

Forecast 2007-2015

Earnings	New Jobs	Growth
High	1,837	1.2%
Average	8,610	5.9%
Low	33,151	9.4%

New Jobs in . .
    Blue-collar industries: 3,497
    White-collar industries: 40,101
Total Growth Rate: 6.8%
Unemployment Risk: ← →
Job Quality: ↑

Places Rated Rank: 161

Rockford, IL

Forecast 2007-2015

Earnings	New Jobs	Growth
High	1,241	2.3%
Average	5,569	12.6%
Low	14,650	14.1%

New Jobs in . .
    Blue-collar industries: 3,366
    White-collar industries: 18,094
Total Growth Rate: 10.6%
Unemployment Risk: ↑
Job Quality: ← →

Places Rated Rank: 155

✓ Rockingham County, NH

Forecast 2007-2015

Earnings	New Jobs	Growth
High	10,325	18.8%
Average	5,143	8.4%
Low	25,634	17.4%

New Jobs in . .
    Blue-collar industries: 11,799
    White-collar industries: 29,303
Total Growth Rate: 15.6%
Unemployment Risk: ← →
Job Quality: ↑

Places Rated Rank: 38

Rocky Mount, NC

Forecast 2007-2015

Earnings	New Jobs	Growth
High	473	1.9%
Average	1,540	7.3%
Low	4,043	11.1%

New Jobs in . .
    Blue-collar industries: 1,329
    White-collar industries: 4,727
Total Growth Rate: 7.4%
Unemployment Risk: ↑
Job Quality: ← →

Places Rated Rank: 333

Rome, GA

Forecast 2007-2015

Earnings	New Jobs	Growth
High	534	3.8%
Average	481	4.1%
Low	3,056	11.1%

New Jobs in . .
    Blue-collar industries: 850
    White-collar industries: 3,221
Total Growth Rate: 7.6%
Unemployment Risk: ← →
Job Quality: ← →

Places Rated Rank: 340

✓ Sacramento-Arden-Arcade, CA

Forecast 2007-2015

Earnings	New Jobs	Growth
High	14,972	9.2%
Average	77,731	16.9%
Low	136,218	22.0%

New Jobs in . .
    Blue-collar industries: 32,658
    White-collar industries: 196,263
Total Growth Rate: 18.4%
Unemployment Risk: ← →
Job Quality: ↑

Places Rated Rank: 6

Saginaw, MI

Forecast 2007-2015

Earnings	New Jobs	Growth
High	83	0.3%
Average	2,206	8.6%
Low	6,446	9.8%

New Jobs in . .
    Blue-collar industries: 885
    White-collar industries: 7,850
Total Growth Rate: 7.3%
Unemployment Risk: ↑
Job Quality: ↑

Places Rated Rank: 248

St. Cloud, MN

Forecast 2007-2015

Earnings	New Jobs	Growth
High	4,380	13.3%
Average	2,306	8.8%
Low	9,823	14.1%

New Jobs in . .
    Blue-collar industries: 5,162
    White-collar industries: 11,347
Total Growth Rate: 12.8%
Unemployment Risk: ← →
Job Quality: ← →

Places Rated Rank: 189

St. George, UT

Forecast 2007-2015

Earnings	New Jobs	Growth
High	2,811	34.3%
Average	7,169	34.6%
Low	12,370	35.2%

New Jobs in . .
    Blue-collar industries: 6,134
    White-collar industries: 16,216
Total Growth Rate: 34.9%
Unemployment Risk: ← →
Job Quality: ↓

Places Rated Rank: 168

St. Joseph, MO-KS

Forecast 2007-2015

Earnings	New Jobs	Growth
High	-24	-0.2%
Average	1,815	9.3%
Low	2,387	6.7%

New Jobs in . .
    Blue-collar industries: 531
    White-collar industries: 3,647
Total Growth Rate: 5.9%
Unemployment Risk: ↑
Job Quality: ↓

Places Rated Rank: 371

St. Louis, MO-IL

Forecast 2007-2015

Earnings	New Jobs	Growth
High	14,715	3.7%
Average	38,803	9.2%
Low	102,678	11.1%

New Jobs in . .
    Blue-collar industries: 28,846
    White-collar industries: 127,350
Total Growth Rate: 8.9%
Unemployment Risk: ← →
Job Quality: ↑

Places Rated Rank: 81

Salem, OR

Forecast 2007-2015

Earnings	New Jobs	Growth
High	1,182	3.9%
Average	4,849	7.6%
Low	12,535	12.0%

New Jobs in . .
    Blue-collar industries: 3,151
    White-collar industries: 15,415
Total Growth Rate: 9.4%
Unemployment Risk: ↑
Job Quality: ← →

Places Rated Rank: 235

Salinas, CA

Forecast 2007-2015

Earnings	New Jobs	Growth
High	2,117	7.2%
Average	13,122	21.1%
Low	20,377	12.7%

New Jobs in . .
    Blue-collar industries: 10,098
    White-collar industries: 25,518
Total Growth Rate: 14.2%
Unemployment Risk: ↑
Job Quality: ↑

Places Rated Rank: 46

Salisbury, MD

Forecast 2007-2015

Earnings	New Jobs	Growth
High	495	3.8%
Average	1,746	9.7%
Low	3,742	10.6%

New Jobs in . .
    Blue-collar industries: 666
    White-collar industries: 5,317
Total Growth Rate: 9.0%
Unemployment Risk: ↑
Job Quality: ↓

Places Rated Rank: 331

✓ Salt Lake City, UT

Forecast 2007-2015

Earnings	New Jobs	Growth
High	12,354	8.0%
Average	36,437	15.6%
Low	104,207	25.7%

New Jobs in . .
    Blue-collar industries: 22,994
    White-collar industries: 130,004
Total Growth Rate: 19.3%
Unemployment Risk: ← →
Job Quality: ↑

Places Rated Rank: 22

San Angelo, TX

Forecast 2007-2015

Earnings	New Jobs	Growth
High	49	0.4%
Average	1,043	6.1%
Low	2,660	7.9%

New Jobs in . .
    Blue-collar industries: 662
    White-collar industries: 3,090
Total Growth Rate: 5.9%
Unemployment Risk: ←→
Job Quality: ↓

Places Rated Rank: 378

✓ San Antonio, TX

Forecast 2007-2015

Earnings	New Jobs	Growth
High	25,040	13.4%
Average	50,706	16.3%
Low	108,117	18.4%

New Jobs in . .
    Blue-collar industries: 41,914
    White-collar industries: 141,949
Total Growth Rate: 17.0%
Unemployment Risk: ←→
Job Quality: ↑

Places Rated Rank: 24

✓ San Diego-Carlsbad, CA

Forecast 2007-2015

Earnings	New Jobs	Growth
High	35,478	11.2%
Average	61,576	12.2%
Low	213,081	20.0%

New Jobs in . .
    Blue-collar industries: 51,135
    White-collar industries: 259,000
Total Growth Rate: 16.5%
Unemployment Risk: ←→
Job Quality: ↑

Places Rated Rank: 6

Sandusky, OH

Forecast 2007-2015

Earnings	New Jobs	Growth
High	590	4.4%
Average	1,420	11.8%
Low	2,774	9.8%

New Jobs in . .
    Blue-collar industries: 979
    White-collar industries: 3,805
Total Growth Rate: 8.9%
Unemployment Risk: ←→
Job Quality: ←→

Places Rated Rank: 307

✓ San Francisco-San Mateo, CA

Forecast 2007-2015

Earnings	New Jobs	Growth
High	4,784	2.2%
Average	26,316	7.0%
Low	122,384	14.0%

New Jobs in . .
    Blue-collar industries: 13,989
    White-collar industries: 139,495
Total Growth Rate: 10.4%
Unemployment Risk: ←→
Job Quality: ↑

Places Rated Rank: 37

✓ San Jose-Sunnyvale, CA

Forecast 2007-2015

Earnings	New Jobs	Growth
High	20,685	6.1%
Average	21,755	8.6%
Low	108,398	15.8%

New Jobs in . .
    Blue-collar industries: 30,246
    White-collar industries: 120,772
Total Growth Rate: 11.8%
Unemployment Risk: ↑
Job Quality: ↑

Places Rated Rank: 28

San Luis Obispo-Paso Robles, CA

Forecast 2007-2015

Earnings	New Jobs	Growth
High	2,979	14.3%
Average	5,193	10.3%
Low	16,784	18.4%

New Jobs in . .
    Blue-collar industries: 5,760
    White-collar industries: 19,196
Total Growth Rate: 15.3%
Unemployment Risk: ←→
Job Quality: ←→

Places Rated Rank: 127

✓ Santa Ana-Anaheim-Irvine, CA

Forecast 2007-2015

Earnings	New Jobs	Growth
High	60,332	13.6%
Average	78,103	14.2%
Low	183,905	16.7%

New Jobs in . .
    Blue-collar industries: 78,041
    White-collar industries: 244,299
Total Growth Rate: 15.4%
Unemployment Risk: ←→
Job Quality: ↑

Places Rated Rank: 6

Santa Barbara-Santa Maria, CA

Forecast 2007-2015

Earnings	New Jobs	Growth
High	2,119	6.3%
Average	8,063	11.5%
Low	16,328	10.0%

New Jobs in . .
    Blue-collar industries: 4,654
    White-collar industries: 21,856
Total Growth Rate: 9.9%
Unemployment Risk: ←→
Job Quality: ↑

Places Rated Rank: 144

Santa Cruz-Watsonville, CA

Forecast 2007-2015

Earnings	New Jobs	Growth
High	1,077	5.2%
Average	3,939	9.3%
Low	11,399	11.9%

New Jobs in . .
    Blue-collar industries: 2,367
    White-collar industries: 14,048
Total Growth Rate: 10.3%
Unemployment Risk: ↑
Job Quality: ↑

Places Rated Rank: 163

Santa Fe, NM

Forecast 2007-2015

Earnings	New Jobs	Growth
High	488	6.7%
Average	4,437	13.9%
Low	9,562	18.4%

New Jobs in . .
    Blue-collar industries: 2,065
    White-collar industries: 12,422
Total Growth Rate: 15.9%
Unemployment Risk: ←→
Job Quality: ←→

Places Rated Rank: 153

Santa Rosa-Petaluma, CA

Forecast 2007-2015

Earnings	New Jobs	Growth
High	5,659	10.6%
Average	10,127	12.3%
Low	25,915	15.5%

New Jobs in . .
    Blue-collar industries: 10,276
    White-collar industries: 31,425
Total Growth Rate: 13.8%
Unemployment Risk: ←→
Job Quality: ↑

Places Rated Rank: 55

Sarasota-Bradenton-Venice, FL

Forecast 2007-2015

Earnings	New Jobs	Growth
High	5,591	11.7%
Average	9,392	10.4%
Low	89,669	29.7%

New Jobs in . .
    Blue-collar industries: 9,190
    White-collar industries: 95,462
Total Growth Rate: 23.8%
Unemployment Risk: ↓
Job Quality: ←→

Places Rated Rank: 74

Savannah, GA

Forecast 2007-2015

Earnings	New Jobs	Growth
High	664	1.9%
Average	1,975	4.8%
Low	13,350	13.1%

New Jobs in . .
    Blue-collar industries: 1,290
    White-collar industries: 14,699
Total Growth Rate: 8.9%
Unemployment Risk: ←→
Job Quality: ←→

Places Rated Rank: 232

Scranton--Wilkes-Barre, PA

Forecast 2007-2015

Earnings	New Jobs	Growth
High	1,859	2.2%
Average	2,549	3.9%
Low	17,056	10.0%

New Jobs in . .
    Blue-collar industries: 2,345
    White-collar industries: 19,119
Total Growth Rate: 6.7%
Unemployment Risk: ↑
Job Quality: ←→

Places Rated Rank: 261

✓ Seattle-Bellevue-Everett, WA

Forecast 2007-2015

Earnings	New Jobs	Growth
High	26,241	6.5%
Average	45,820	9.9%
Low	157,091	16.5%

New Jobs in . .
    Blue-collar industries: 43,417
    White-collar industries: 185,735
Total Growth Rate: 12.6%
Unemployment Risk: ← →
Job Quality: ↑

Places Rated Rank: 18

Sebastian-Vero Beach, FL

Forecast 2007-2015

Earnings	New Jobs	Growth
High	1,092	15.6%
Average	2,303	14.3%
Low	7,266	17.4%

New Jobs in . .
    Blue-collar industries: 2,267
    White-collar industries: 8,394
Total Growth Rate: 16.4%
Unemployment Risk: ↑
Job Quality: ↓

Places Rated Rank: 194

Sheboygan, WI

Forecast 2007-2015

Earnings	New Jobs	Growth
High	1,183	3.9%
Average	1,289	8.5%
Low	3,839	11.7%

New Jobs in . .
    Blue-collar industries: 1,777
    White-collar industries: 4,534
Total Growth Rate: 8.1%
Unemployment Risk: ↓
Job Quality: ← →

Places Rated Rank: 277

Sherman-Denison, TX

Forecast 2007-2015

Earnings	New Jobs	Growth
High	172	1.4%
Average	1,958	12.8%
Low	4,024	12.5%

New Jobs in . .
    Blue-collar industries: 974
    White-collar industries: 5,180
Total Growth Rate: 10.3%
Unemployment Risk: ← →
Job Quality: ↓

Places Rated Rank: 316

Shreveport-Bossier City, LA

Forecast 2007-2015

Earnings	New Jobs	Growth
High	1,452	3.2%
Average	5,594	10.1%
Low	16,582	14.3%

New Jobs in . .
    Blue-collar industries: 3,051
    White-collar industries: 20,847
Total Growth Rate: 10.9%
Unemployment Risk: ↑
Job Quality: ← →

Places Rated Rank: 164

Sioux City, IA-NE-SD

Forecast 2007-2015

Earnings	New Jobs	Growth
High	2,320	7.6%
Average	1,548	8.1%
Low	5,012	10.3%

New Jobs in . .
    Blue-collar industries: 2,780
    White-collar industries: 6,100
Total Growth Rate: 9.0%
Unemployment Risk: ↓
Job Quality: ← →

Places Rated Rank: 282

Sioux Falls, SD

Forecast 2007-2015

Earnings	New Jobs	Growth
High	2,588	7.7%
Average	5,219	12.9%
Low	17,019	18.9%

New Jobs in . .
    Blue-collar industries: 4,168
    White-collar industries: 20,658
Total Growth Rate: 15.2%
Unemployment Risk: ↓
Job Quality: ← →

Places Rated Rank: 85

South Bend-Mishawaka, IN-MI

Forecast 2007-2015

Earnings	New Jobs	Growth
High	201	0.5%
Average	2,797	7.2%
Low	10,861	10.7%

New Jobs in . .
    Blue-collar industries: 83
    White-collar industries: 13,776
Total Growth Rate: 7.7%
Unemployment Risk: ← →
Job Quality: ↑

Places Rated Rank: 225

Spartanburg, SC

Forecast 2007-2015

Earnings	New Jobs	Growth
High	1,744	3.5%
Average	2,113	6.1%
Low	6,725	10.2%

New Jobs in . .
    Blue-collar industries: 2,346
    White-collar industries: 8,236
Total Growth Rate: 7.1%
Unemployment Risk: ← →
Job Quality: ← →

Places Rated Rank: 260

Spokane, WA

Forecast 2007-2015

Earnings	New Jobs	Growth
High	2,482	5.1%
Average	5,800	8.3%
Low	16,907	11.9%

New Jobs in . .
    Blue-collar industries: 3,995
    White-collar industries: 21,194
Total Growth Rate: 9.7%
Unemployment Risk: ↑
Job Quality: ← →

Places Rated Rank: 173

Springfield, IL

Forecast 2007-2015

Earnings	New Jobs	Growth
High	-434	-2.6%
Average	3,128	6.0%
Low	9,162	11.8%

New Jobs in . .
    Blue-collar industries: 369
    White-collar industries: 11,487
Total Growth Rate: 8.1%
Unemployment Risk: ← →
Job Quality: ↑

Places Rated Rank: 222

Springfield, MA

Forecast 2007-2015

Earnings	New Jobs	Growth
High	212	0.3%
Average	5,713	5.8%
Low	22,182	10.3%

New Jobs in . .
    Blue-collar industries: 1,286
    White-collar industries: 26,821
Total Growth Rate: 7.2%
Unemployment Risk: ← →
Job Quality: ← →

Places Rated Rank: 221

Springfield, MO

Forecast 2007-2015

Earnings	New Jobs	Growth
High	3,311	5.9%
Average	5,779	9.8%
Low	27,807	19.1%

New Jobs in . .
    Blue-collar industries: 5,307
    White-collar industries: 31,590
Total Growth Rate: 14.2%
Unemployment Risk: ↓
Job Quality: ↓

Places Rated Rank: 148

Springfield, OH

Forecast 2007-2015

Earnings	New Jobs	Growth
High	349	2.0%
Average	897	5.8%
Low	2,700	7.3%

New Jobs in . .
    Blue-collar industries: 683
    White-collar industries: 3,263
Total Growth Rate: 5.6%
Unemployment Risk: ↑
Job Quality: ↓

Places Rated Rank: 365

State College, PA

Forecast 2007-2015

Earnings	New Jobs	Growth
High	873	6.4%
Average	7,027	13.5%
Low	5,738	13.4%

New Jobs in . .
    Blue-collar industries: 1,258
    White-collar industries: 12,380
Total Growth Rate: 12.5%
Unemployment Risk: ↓
Job Quality: ↓

Places Rated Rank: 244

Jobs

Stockton, CA

Forecast 2007-2015

Earnings	New Jobs	Growth
High	3,131	5.3%
Average	8,703	11.3%
Low	16,831	11.2%

New Jobs in . .
  Blue-collar industries: 6,448
  White-collar industries: 22,217
Total Growth Rate: 10.0%
Unemployment Risk: ↑
Job Quality: ←➡

Places Rated Rank: 145

Sumter, SC

Forecast 2007-2015

Earnings	New Jobs	Growth
High	338	2.2%
Average	1,147	9.1%
Low	1,657	7.4%

New Jobs in . .
  Blue-collar industries: 647
  White-collar industries: 2,495
Total Growth Rate: 6.3%
Unemployment Risk: ↑
Job Quality: ↓

Places Rated Rank: 368

Syracuse, NY

Forecast 2007-2015

Earnings	New Jobs	Growth
High	3,231	3.7%
Average	3,641	3.7%
Low	17,778	8.7%

New Jobs in . .
  Blue-collar industries: 3,389
  White-collar industries: 21,261
Total Growth Rate: 6.3%
Unemployment Risk: ←➡
Job Quality: ↑

Places Rated Rank: 198

Tacoma, WA

Forecast 2007-2015

Earnings	New Jobs	Growth
High	4,085	7.0%
Average	11,065	11.1%
Low	35,616	19.0%

New Jobs in . .
  Blue-collar industries: 7,546
  White-collar industries: 43,220
Total Growth Rate: 14.7%
Unemployment Risk: ↑
Job Quality: ↑

Places Rated Rank: 43

Tallahassee, FL

Forecast 2007-2015

Earnings	New Jobs	Growth
High	1,696	9.5%
Average	7,952	8.9%
Low	23,026	20.0%

New Jobs in . .
  Blue-collar industries: 1,650
  White-collar industries: 31,024
Total Growth Rate: 14.7%
Unemployment Risk: ↓
Job Quality: ←➡

Places Rated Rank: 107

✓ Tampa-St. Petersburg

Forecast 2007-2015

Earnings	New Jobs	Growth
High	23,417	9.2%
Average	48,525	12.8%
Low	182,100	18.2%

New Jobs in . .
  Blue-collar industries: 37,276
  White-collar industries: 216,766
Total Growth Rate: 15.6%
Unemployment Risk: ←➡
Job Quality: ←➡

Places Rated Rank: 35

Terre Haute, IN

Forecast 2007-2015

Earnings	New Jobs	Growth
High	227	1.1%
Average	1,687	7.4%
Low	5,039	10.0%

New Jobs in . .
  Blue-collar industries: 672
  White-collar industries: 6,281
Total Growth Rate: 7.4%
Unemployment Risk: ↑
Job Quality: ↓

Places Rated Rank: 348

Texarkana, TX-Texarkana, AR

Forecast 2007-2015

Earnings	New Jobs	Growth
High	1,523	8.8%
Average	1,722	10.4%
Low	3,826	10.1%

New Jobs in . .
  Blue-collar industries: 2,323
  White-collar industries: 4,748
Total Growth Rate: 9.9%
Unemployment Risk: ↑
Job Quality: ↓

Places Rated Rank: 322

Toledo, OH

Forecast 2007-2015

Earnings	New Jobs	Growth
High	1,468	1.5%
Average	8,789	8.6%
Low	20,893	9.6%

New Jobs in . .
  Blue-collar industries: 5,013
  White-collar industries: 26,137
Total Growth Rate: 7.4%
Unemployment Risk: ↑
Job Quality: ↑

Places Rated Rank: 179

Topeka, KS

Forecast 2007-2015

Earnings	New Jobs	Growth
High	-34	-0.1%
Average	3,950	8.5%
Low	9,363	11.6%

New Jobs in . .
  Blue-collar industries: 706
  White-collar industries: 12,573
Total Growth Rate: 8.7%
Unemployment Risk: ←➡
Job Quality: ←➡

Places Rated Rank: 267

Trenton-Ewing, NJ

Forecast 2007-2015

Earnings	New Jobs	Growth
High	488	1.3%
Average	5,317	6.3%
Low	11,640	8.4%

New Jobs in . .
  Blue-collar industries: 1,137
  White-collar industries: 16,308
Total Growth Rate: 6.7%
Unemployment Risk: ←➡
Job Quality: ↑

Places Rated Rank: 164

Tucson, AZ

Forecast 2007-2015

Earnings	New Jobs	Growth
High	8,793	12.1%
Average	17,004	11.7%
Low	56,181	20.5%

New Jobs in . .
  Blue-collar industries: 10,657
  White-collar industries: 71,321
Total Growth Rate: 16.7%
Unemployment Risk: ←➡
Job Quality: ←➡

Places Rated Rank: 78

Tulsa, OK

Forecast 2007-2015

Earnings	New Jobs	Growth
High	7,434	5.5%
Average	12,536	10.0%
Low	48,999	15.7%

New Jobs in . .
  Blue-collar industries: 12,425
  White-collar industries: 56,544
Total Growth Rate: 12.0%
Unemployment Risk: ←➡
Job Quality: ↑

Places Rated Rank: 56

Tuscaloosa, AL

Forecast 2007-2015

Earnings	New Jobs	Growth
High	1,818	7.2%
Average	3,310	8.9%
Low	4,577	9.7%

New Jobs in . .
  Blue-collar industries: 2,294
  White-collar industries: 7,411
Total Growth Rate: 8.9%
Unemployment Risk: ←➡
Job Quality: ←➡

Places Rated Rank: 265

Tyler, TX

Forecast 2007-2015

Earnings	New Jobs	Growth
High	1,583	6.6%
Average	2,405	8.4%
Low	11,458	16.8%

New Jobs in . .
  Blue-collar industries: 2,399
  White-collar industries: 13,047
Total Growth Rate: 12.8%
Unemployment Risk: ←➡
Job Quality: ←➡

Places Rated Rank: 146

Utica-Rome, NY

Forecast 2007-2015

Earnings	New Jobs	Growth
High	-221	-0.7%
Average	1,444	3.3%
Low	8,902	9.8%

New Jobs in . .
Blue-collar industries: -23
White-collar industries: 10,148
Total Growth Rate: 6.2%
Unemployment Risk: ← →
Job Quality: ↓

Places Rated Rank: 343

Valdosta, GA

Forecast 2007-2015

Earnings	New Jobs	Growth
High	12	0.1%
Average	2,090	10.9%
Low	4,524	13.0%

New Jobs in . .
Blue-collar industries: 877
White-collar industries: 5,749
Total Growth Rate: 10.1%
Unemployment Risk: ↓
Job Quality: ↓

Places Rated Rank: 323

Vallejo-Fairfield, CA

Forecast 2007-2015

Earnings	New Jobs	Growth
High	1,559	5.8%
Average	10,865	19.1%
Low	14,496	15.5%

New Jobs in . .
Blue-collar industries: 5,831
White-collar industries: 21,089
Total Growth Rate: 15.2%
Unemployment Risk: ↑
Job Quality: ↑

Places Rated Rank: 57

Victoria, TX

Forecast 2007-2015

Earnings	New Jobs	Growth
High	1,619	10.8%
Average	2,350	11.5%
Low	4,868	14.1%

New Jobs in . .
Blue-collar industries: 2,527
White-collar industries: 6,310
Total Growth Rate: 12.7%
Unemployment Risk: ↑
Job Quality: ← →

Places Rated Rank: 217

Vineland-Millville-Bridgeton, NJ

Forecast 2007-2015

Earnings	New Jobs	Growth
High	-201	-1.1%
Average	402	1.9%
Low	2,181	6.6%

New Jobs in . .
Blue-collar industries: -192
White-collar industries: 2,574
Total Growth Rate: 3.3%
Unemployment Risk: ↑
Job Quality: ↑

Places Rated Rank: 321

Virginia Beach-Norfolk, VA-NC

Forecast 2007-2015

Earnings	New Jobs	Growth
High	7,213	3.8%
Average	29,830	12.0%
Low	76,278	15.4%

New Jobs in . .
Blue-collar industries: 14,962
White-collar industries: 98,359
Total Growth Rate: 12.1%
Unemployment Risk: ← →
Job Quality: ↑

Places Rated Rank: 58

Visalia-Porterville, CA

Forecast 2007-2015

Earnings	New Jobs	Growth
High	1,639	6.2%
Average	3,755	7.5%
Low	16,413	13.6%

New Jobs in . .
Blue-collar industries: 6,366
White-collar industries: 15,441
Total Growth Rate: 11.0%
Unemployment Risk: ↑
Job Quality: ↓

Places Rated Rank: 237

Waco, TX

Forecast 2007-2015

Earnings	New Jobs	Growth
High	2,168	7.2%
Average	3,108	8.8%
Low	9,235	13.7%

New Jobs in . .
Blue-collar industries: 3,154
White-collar industries: 11,357
Total Growth Rate: 10.9%
Unemployment Risk: ← →
Job Quality: ← →

Places Rated Rank: 228

Warner Robins, GA

Forecast 2007-2015

Earnings	New Jobs	Growth
High	322	1.7%
Average	1,799	12.4%
Low	7,644	23.5%

New Jobs in . .
Blue-collar industries: 1,369
White-collar industries: 8,396
Total Growth Rate: 14.9%
Unemployment Risk: ↓
Job Quality: ↑

Places Rated Rank: 98

✓ Warren-Troy-Farmington Hills, MI

Forecast 2007-2015

Earnings	New Jobs	Growth
High	34,953	8.6%
Average	48,849	13.2%
Low	133,019	15.4%

New Jobs in . .
Blue-collar industries: 48,735
White-collar industries: 168,086
Total Growth Rate: 13.2%
Unemployment Risk: ← →
Job Quality: ↑

Places Rated Rank: 16

✓ Washington, DC-VA-MD-WV

Forecast 2007-2015

Earnings	New Jobs	Growth
High	44,631	7.3%
Average	59,961	9.6%
Low	274,102	16.1%

New Jobs in . .
Blue-collar industries: 65,449
White-collar industries: 313,245
Total Growth Rate: 12.9%
Unemployment Risk: ← →
Job Quality: ↑

Places Rated Rank: 14

Waterloo-Cedar Falls, IA

Forecast 2007-2015

Earnings	New Jobs	Growth
High	32	0.1%
Average	1,899	7.0%
Low	5,046	8.8%

New Jobs in . .
Blue-collar industries: 318
White-collar industries: 6,659
Total Growth Rate: 6.3%
Unemployment Risk: ↓
Job Quality: ↓

Places Rated Rank: 353

Wausau, WI

Forecast 2007-2015

Earnings	New Jobs	Growth
High	3,040	9.2%
Average	1,694	8.3%
Low	4,041	10.4%

New Jobs in . .
Blue-collar industries: 3,534
White-collar industries: 5,241
Total Growth Rate: 9.5%
Unemployment Risk: ← →
Job Quality: ← →

Places Rated Rank: 264

Weirton-Steubenville, WV-OH

Forecast 2007-2015

Earnings	New Jobs	Growth
High	-645	-3.7%
Average	668	5.4%
Low	2,371	7.6%

New Jobs in . .
Blue-collar industries: -560
White-collar industries: 2,954
Total Growth Rate: 3.9%
Unemployment Risk: ↑
Job Quality: ↓

Places Rated Rank: 366

Wenatchee, WA

Forecast 2007-2015

Earnings	New Jobs	Growth
High	357	4.2%
Average	1,174	7.5%
Low	5,822	14.2%

New Jobs in . .
Blue-collar industries: 1,699
White-collar industries: 5,654
Total Growth Rate: 11.3%
Unemployment Risk: ↑
Job Quality: ↓

Places Rated Rank: 309

Jobs

✓ West Palm Beach-Boca Raton, FL

Forecast 2007-2015

Earnings	New Jobs	Growth
High	16,803	17.4%
Average	38,444	18.5%
Low	89,645	19.2%

New Jobs in . .
  Blue-collar industries: 28,517
  White-collar industries: 116,575
Total Growth Rate: 18.8%
Unemployment Risk: ↑
Job Quality: ↑

Places Rated Rank: 13

Wheeling, WV-OH

Forecast 2007-2015

Earnings	New Jobs	Growth
High	30	0.2%
Average	1,787	9.2%
Low	4,930	9.8%

New Jobs in . .
  Blue-collar industries: 495
  White-collar industries: 6,252
Total Growth Rate: 8.0%
Unemployment Risk: ↑
Job Quality: ↓

Places Rated Rank: 352

Wichita, KS

Forecast 2007-2015

Earnings	New Jobs	Growth
High	5,129	4.8%
Average	8,002	9.5%
Low	20,055	10.6%

New Jobs in . .
  Blue-collar industries: 6,872
  White-collar industries: 26,314
Total Growth Rate: 8.7%
Unemployment Risk: ←→
Job Quality: ↑

Places Rated Rank: 155

Wichita Falls, TX

Forecast 2007-2015

Earnings	New Jobs	Growth
High	-2	0.0%
Average	967	4.5%
Low	3,632	8.2%

New Jobs in . .
  Blue-collar industries: 522
  White-collar industries: 4,075
Total Growth Rate: 5.4%
Unemployment Risk: ←→
Job Quality: ↓

Places Rated Rank: 370

Williamsport, PA

Forecast 2007-2015

Earnings	New Jobs	Growth
High	144	0.7%
Average	284	1.9%
Low	4,298	12.3%

New Jobs in . .
  Blue-collar industries: 541
  White-collar industries: 4,185
Total Growth Rate: 6.7%
Unemployment Risk: ↑
Job Quality: ↓

Places Rated Rank: 359

Wilmington, DE-MD-NJ

Forecast 2007-2015

Earnings	New Jobs	Growth
High	1,324	1.6%
Average	20,990	14.7%
Low	22,732	11.1%

New Jobs in . .
  Blue-collar industries: 1,368
  White-collar industries: 43,678
Total Growth Rate: 10.5%
Unemployment Risk: ←→
Job Quality: ↑

Places Rated Rank: 59

Wilmington, NC

Forecast 2007-2015

Earnings	New Jobs	Growth
High	1,229	4.8%
Average	13,787	23.4%
Low	18,787	19.5%

New Jobs in . .
  Blue-collar industries: 6,899
  White-collar industries: 26,904
Total Growth Rate: 18.7%
Unemployment Risk: ←→
Job Quality: ↓

Places Rated Rank: 112

Winchester, VA-WV

Forecast 2007-2015

Earnings	New Jobs	Growth
High	1,297	7.3%
Average	1,410	9.1%
Low	5,296	13.8%

New Jobs in . .
  Blue-collar industries: 1,854
  White-collar industries: 6,149
Total Growth Rate: 11.2%
Unemployment Risk: ↓
Job Quality: ←→

Places Rated Rank: 242

Winston-Salem, NC

Forecast 2007-2015

Earnings	New Jobs	Growth
High	2,294	3.7%
Average	7,868	12.5%
Low	24,656	15.7%

New Jobs in . .
  Blue-collar industries: 4,775
  White-collar industries: 30,043
Total Growth Rate: 12.4%
Unemployment Risk: ←→
Job Quality: ↑

Places Rated Rank: 86

Worcester, MA

Forecast 2007-2015

Earnings	New Jobs	Growth
High	1,764	1.9%
Average	9,502	9.1%
Low	23,757	10.4%

New Jobs in . .
  Blue-collar industries: 4,211
  White-collar industries: 30,812
Total Growth Rate: 8.2%
Unemployment Risk: ←→
Job Quality: ↑

Places Rated Rank: 131

Yakima, WA

Forecast 2007-2015

Earnings	New Jobs	Growth
High	1,533	6.3%
Average	3,068	11.3%
Low	9,563	12.6%

New Jobs in . .
  Blue-collar industries: 3,788
  White-collar industries: 10,376
Total Growth Rate: 11.1%
Unemployment Risk: ↑
Job Quality: ↓

Places Rated Rank: 269

York-Hanover, PA

Forecast 2007-2015

Earnings	New Jobs	Growth
High	647	1.0%
Average	4,305	10.3%
Low	12,249	11.1%

New Jobs in . .
  Blue-collar industries: 2,790
  White-collar industries: 14,411
Total Growth Rate: 7.9%
Unemployment Risk: ←→
Job Quality: ←→

Places Rated Rank: 224

Youngstown-Warren, OH-PA

Forecast 2007-2015

Earnings	New Jobs	Growth
High	835	1.1%
Average	6,864	9.6%
Low	14,704	8.5%

New Jobs in . .
  Blue-collar industries: 3,348
  White-collar industries: 19,055
Total Growth Rate: 7.0%
Unemployment Risk: ↑
Job Quality: ↓

Places Rated Rank: 276

Yuba City, CA

Forecast 2007-2015

Earnings	New Jobs	Growth
High	743	7.2%
Average	2,730	14.3%
Low	7,009	16.8%

New Jobs in . .
  Blue-collar industries: 1,889
  White-collar industries: 8,593
Total Growth Rate: 14.8%
Unemployment Risk: ↑
Job Quality: ↓

Places Rated Rank: 209

Yuma, AZ

Forecast 2007-2015

Earnings	New Jobs	Growth
High	1,047	9.2%
Average	3,585	16.0%
Low	8,146	15.4%

New Jobs in . .
  Blue-collar industries: 2,223
  White-collar industries: 10,555
Total Growth Rate: 14.7%
Unemployment Risk: ↑
Job Quality: ↓

Places Rated Rank: 231

ET CETERA: JOBS

LIFE IN A BOOM TOWN

If you could live anywhere you choose, would you choose a boom town? The advantages include rising personal income; real estate appreciation; expanding personal employment opportunities; improved infrastructures; somewhat lower violent crime; increasing amenities; and high-quality health care and education.

The disadvantages of living in a boom town include rising costs of living, increased property crime rates, environmental pollution, and noticeable loss of personal time. But if you stay in a no-growth area, you face possible job loss, depreciating value of real estate, boarded-up businesses, and backwater schools and health care. Any advantages? Try declining living costs, increased personal time, and lower crime rates.

Unemployment opportunities are the single most important factor behind geographic mobility. No job or a lousy one can push a settled person to become a mobile. Consider, for example, that in 1980 you moved from withering Chicago or Detroit to booming Los Angeles. It's 1990 and you're thinking about your next move. Who would have guessed during the 1980 job boom that California would later be grabbing the ropes or that the Great Lakes would make a comeback? Now its 2005, and neither area is as promising as the sparsely settled states in the energy sector: the Dakotas and Wyoming!

We've seen some surprising shifts in regional economic growth. So the big question remains: Will a move to Anaheim or San Jose or Raleigh or Cheyenne be the answer? If there is any trend to be spotted from the past, it is that boom times and slumps aren't permanent in any metro area.

UNEMPLOYMENT CHECKS

Unemployment insurance provides workers who lose their jobs through no fault of their own with payments for a specific period of time or until the worker finds a new job. To receive benefits, you must meet the requirements for wages earned or time worked during the previous 12 months. Benefits are typically paid for a maximum of 26 weeks. In many states, the compensation will be half your earnings, up to a maximum amount. For example, in New York State you're entitled to collect up to a maximum of $405, which is half the state's average weekly wage. While in Arizona, the highest benefit rate is $205. Benefits are subject to Federal income taxes.

MINIMUM WAGES

The $5.15 per hour Federal minimum wage is now nine years old and shows definite signs of rising to $7.25 or beyond by early 2007. Over those nine years, states have passed their own minimum wage increases. Today 29 states, including six that passed referendums on the issue in November of 2006, have boosted their minimum wages past $5.15. Some cities have gone further; Santa Fe, NM, for instance, has a city minimum wage of $8.50 an hour which will gradually increase to $10.50 an hour by 2008.

LEGAL HOLIDAYS

The United States has no national holidays. A day off on Independence Day, Thanksgiving, or Christmas comes by the grace of local state legislatures rather than by presidential proclamations or acts of Congress.

The only thing *national* about the U.S. holiday calendar are the 10 days off given to everyone who works for the federal government: five fixed dates —Christmas, Independence Day, Labor Day, New Year's Day, and November's fourth Thursday, Thanksgiving—and five Mondays—Columbus Day, Memorial Day, Veterans Day, Washington's Birthday, and Martin Luther King Day.

The first four holiday Mondays were approved in 1968 to create predictable long weekends. The fifth, approved in 1986, honors Martin Luther King, Jr., on the third Monday of January.

If any of the fixed dates fall on Saturday, the Friday before is the holiday; if any fall on Sunday, the next day, Monday, is the holiday.

Most states observe federal legal holidays, and, depending on where you are, they commemorate many local ones as well. The Civil War era produced more events and heroes to honor with days off than any other

UNEMPLOYMENT BENEFITS AND MINIMUM WAGE

State	Maximum Benefits	Minimum Wage
ALABAMA	$230 week	$5.15 hour
ALASKA	248-320*	7.15
ARIZONA	240	6.75
ARKANSAS	395	6.25
CALIFORNIA	450	6.75
COLORADO	435	6.85
CONNECTICUT	465-540*	7.65
DELAWARE	330	6.65
FLORIDA	275	6.67
GEORGIA	320	5.15
HAWAII	459	7.25
IDAHO	322	5.15
ILLINOIS	350-475*	6.50
INDIANA	390	5.15
IOWA	334-410*	5.15
KANSAS	386	5.15
KENTUCKY	401	5.15
LOUISIANA	258	
MAINE	320-480*	7.00
MARYLAND	340	6.15
MASSACHUSETTS	551-826*	7.50
MICHIGAN	362	7.15
MINNESOTA	350-515*	6.15
MISSISSIPPI	210	
MISSOURI	270	6.50
MONTANA	362	6.15
NEBRASKA	288	5.15
NEVADA	362	6.15
NEW HAMPSHIRE	372	5.15
NEW JERSEY	521	7.15
NEW MEXICO	312-360*	5.15
NEW YORK	405	7.15
NORTH CAROLINA	457	5.15
NORTH DAKOTA	351	5.15
OHIO	343-462*	6.85
OKLAHOMA	317	5.15
OREGON	445	7.80
PENNSYLVANIA	497-505*	7.15
RHODE ISLAND	492-615*	7.15
SOUTH CAROLINA	303	5.15
SOUTH DAKOTA	274	5.15
TENNESSEE	275	
TEXAS	350	5.15
UTAH	383	5.15
VERMONT	394	7.25
VIRGINIA	347	5.15
WASHINGTON	496	7.93
WASHINGTON, DC	359	7.00
WEST VIRGINIA	391	6.55
WISCONSIN	341	6.50
WYOMING	349	5.15

Source: U.S. Department of Labor. * Eleven states base unemployment payments on the worker's number of dependents. Alabama, Louisiana, Mississippi, and Tennessee have no minimum wage laws.

GOOD ECONOMY, NOT SO GOOD CLIMATE

Twelve metro areas rank in the top 15 percent in JOBS and in the bottom 15 percent in CLIMATE.

period in American history. However, they aren't all celebrated nationwide. Just as no former secessionist state takes notice of Lincoln's birthday, so none of the Union states honor Robert E. Lee's birthday.

In contrast, the Canadian provinces celebrate ten national holidays in harmony with the terms of Canada's Holidays Act. Four days—Christmas, Labour Day, New Year's Day, and Remembrance Day (formerly Armistice Day, as was the U.S.'s Veterans Day)—may be said to be North American holidays since they are celebrated on the same date for the same reason throughout the United States.

AN AMERICAN LIST OF DAYS

January

Fixed Dates

January 1, *New Year's Day* (Federal)

January 2, Day after New Year's: Kentucky, Michigan, Louisiana

January 19, *Robert E. Lee's Birthday*: Florida

January 19, *Confederate Heroes Day*: Texas

January 20 (every four years), *Inauguration Day*: District of Columbia, Maryland (Montgomery and Prince Georges Counties), Virginia (Arlington and Fairfax Counties and Alexandria and Falls Church cities)

January 30, *F. D. Roosevelt's Birthday*: Kentucky

Moveable Feasts

Friday before Third Monday, *Lee-Jackson-King Day*: Virginia

Third Monday, *Martin Luther King Birthday* (Federal)

Third Monday, *Robert E. Lee's Birthday*: Alabama, Arkansas, Mississippi

Third Monday, *Equality Day*: Wyoming

Third Monday, *Civil Rights Day*: New Hampshire

February

Fixed Dates

February 12, *Lincoln's Birthday*: California,

187

Connecticut, Illinois, Missouri, New Jersey, and New York

February 15, *Susan B. Anthony's Birthday*: Florida

Moveable Feasts

Third Monday, *President's Day/Washington's Birthday* (Federal);

Third Monday, *George Washington's Birthday/ Gaston Bates Day*: Arkansas

Third Monday, *George Washington/Thomas Jefferson Birthdays*: Alabama

Tuesday before Ash Wednesday, *Mardi Gras*: Alabama, Florida (some counties), Louisiana (some parishes), Missouri

March

Fixed Dates

March 2, *Texas Independence Day*: Texas

March 17, *Evacuation Day*: Massachusetts (Suffolk County)

March 26, *Prince Jonah Kuhio Kalanianaole Day*: Hawaii

March 31, *Cesar Chavez Day*: California, Texas (Arizona and Colorado, optional)

Moveable Feasts

First Monday, *Casimir Pulaski's Birthday*: Illinois

First Tuesday, *Town Meeting Day*: Vermont

Last Monday, *Seward's Day*: Alaska

April

Fixed Dates

April 2, *Pascua Florida Day*: Florida

April 13, *Thomas Jefferson's Birthday*, Alabama, Oklahoma

April 15, *Federal Income Taxes are due*

April 21, *San Jacinto Day*: Texas

April 26, *Confederate Memorial Day*: Alabama, Florida, Georgia

Moveable Feasts

First Sunday, *Daylight Saving Time begins*

Two days before Easter, Good Friday: Connecticut, Delaware, Hawaii, Indiana, Kentucky, Louisiana, New Jersey, North Carolina, North Dakota, Tennessee

Third Monday, *Patriots' Day*: Maine, Massachusetts

Fourth/Last Monday, *Confederate Memorial Day*:

Alabama and Mississippi

Last Friday, *Arbor Day*: Delaware, Nebraska, Utah, Washington D.C., Wisconsin

May

Fixed Dates

May 4, *Rhode Island Independence Day*: Rhode Island

May 8, *Truman Day*: Missouri

May 10, *Confederate Memorial Day*: North Carolina, South Carolina

May 11, *Minnesota Day*: Minnesota

May 20, *Mecklenburg Independence Day*: North Carolina

Moveable Feasts

Tuesday on or after May 2, *Primary Election Day*: Indiana

Last Monday, *Jefferson Davis's Birthday*: Mississippi

Fourth Monday, *Memorial Day* (Federal)

June

Fixed Dates

June 3, *Jefferson Davis's Birthday*: Kentucky, Louisiana, Tennessee

June 11, *King Kamehameha I Day*: Hawaii

June 14, *Flag Day*

June 15, *Admission Day*: Arkansas

June 15, *Separation Day*: Delaware

June 17, *Bunker Hill Day*: Massachusetts (Suffolk County)

June 19, *Emancipation Day*: Texas

June 20, *West Virginia Day*: West Virginia

Moveable Feasts

First Monday, *Jefferson Davis's Birthday*: Alabama

July

Fixed Dates

July 4, *Independence Day* (Federal)

July 24, *Pioneer Day*: Utah

August

Fixed Dates

August 16, *Bennington Battle Day*: Vermont

August 26, *Susan B. Anthony Day*: Massachusetts

August 27, *Lyndon B. Johnson's Day*: Texas
August 30, *Huey P. Long Day*: Louisiana

Moveable Feasts
Second Monday, Victory Day: Rhode Island
Third Friday, *Admission Day*: Hawaii

September

Fixed Dates
September 9, *Admission Day*: California
September 12, *Defenders' Day*: Maryland
September 17, *Citizenship Day*

Moveable Feasts
First Monday, *Labor Day (Federal)*
Second Friday, *Native American Day,* Wyoming
Sunday on or before 17 September, Constitution Commeration Week

October

Fixed Dates
October 18, *Alaska Day*: Alaska

Moveable Feasts
Second Monday, *Columbus Day* (Federal)
Second Monday, *Native American Day*: South Dakota
Last Friday, *Nevada Day*: Nevada
Last Sunday, *Daylight Saving Time ends*

November

Fixed Dates
November 11, *Veterans Day* (Federal)
November 11, *Washington Admission Day*: Washington
November 24, *Lincoln's Birthday:* Indiana

Moveable Feasts
First Tuesday, *Election Day*, occurs every two years, in even numbered years: Delaware, Florida, Hawaii, Illinois, Indiana, Louisiana, Maryland, Montana, New Hampshire, New Jersey, New York, Rhode Island, Tennessee, and South Carolina.
Thursday after Election Day, *Return Day*: Delaware
Fourth Thursday, *Thanksgiving Day* (Federal)
Friday after Thanksgiving, *Second Day of Thanksgiving*: Delaware, Florida, Iowa, Michigan, Minnesota, Nebraska, New Hampshire, South Carolina, Texas
Friday after Thanksgiving, *Family Day*: Nevada

December

Fixed Dates
December 7, *Delaware Day*: Delaware
December 24, *Christmas Eve*: Kentucky, Michigan, North Carolina, Texas, West Virginia
December 25, *Christmas Day* (Federal)
December 26, *Boxing Day*: Arkansas, Indiana, Kentucky, Michigan, Missouri, North Carolina, West Virginia, South Carolina, Texas
December 31, *New Year's Eve*: West Virginia

THE *FORTUNE 500*

Arkansas is home to few large companies but it does have America's second biggest: Wal-Mart Stores. The retailer, ranked #2 in the current *Fortune 500*, opened its first store in the northwest part of the state in 1962. That same year, General Motors ranked #1 on *Fortune's* list of the country's largest corporations.

A quick comparison of the rankings on that list with any from the early years of the new millennium shows the dramatic shift the American economy has taken from a muscle-bound, goods-producing machine to a light-on-its-feet, service and information-producing one.   It also shows the remarkable westward and southward march of corporate headquarters away from the larger and older cites in the Northeast and Great Lakes.

The following are the 106 metro areas that are headquarters of one or more of *Fortune's* companies. The number in bold is the company's rank in the latest list, while the company's principle industry is detailed in parentheses. Exxon Mobil (Petroleum Refining) in Dallas is ranked first; Wal-Mart Stores (General Merchandisers) in Fayetteville, Arkansas is ranked second; LandAmerica Financial (Insurance: Personal & Casualty Insurance, stock) in Richmond is ranked 500.

Akron, OH
112 Goodyear Tire (Motor Vehicle Parts)
184 FirstEnergy (Gas & Electric Utilities)

Allentown-Bethlehem-Easton, PA-NJ
282 Air Products & Chemicals (Chemicals)
350 PPL (Gas & Electric Utilities)

Jobs

Ann Arbor, MI
490 Borders Group (Specialty Retailers)

Atlanta-Sandy Springs-Marietta, GA
14 Home Depot (Specialty Retailers)
44 United Parcel Service (Package Delivery)
89 Coca-Cola (Beverages)
106 BellSouth (Telecommunications)
120 Coca-Cola Enterprises (Beverages)
135 Delta Air Lines (Airlines)
165 Southern (Gas & Electric Utilities)
217 SunTrust Banks (Commercial Banking)
245 Genuine Parts (Diversified Wholesalers)
316 Cox Communications (Telecommunications)
332 Newell Rubbermaid (Home Equipment)
387 BlueLinx Holdings (Diversified Wholesalers)
399 AGCO (Industrial & Farm Equipment)
429 Beazer Homes USA (Homebuilders)
479 Mirant (Energy)

Austin-Round Rock, TX
25 Dell (Office Equipment)
368 Freescale Semiconductor (Semiconductors)
433 Temple-Inland (Packaging & Containers)
449 Whole Foods Market (Food & Drug Stores)

Baltimore-Towson, MD
125 Constellation Energy (Energy)
330 Black & Decker (Industrial Equipment)

Battle Creek, MI
233 Kellogg (Food Consumer Products)

Bay City, MI
36 Dow Chemical (Chemicals)

Bethesda-Gaithersburg-Frederick, MD
52 Lockheed Martin (Aerospace & Defense)
203 Marriott (Hotels & Resorts)
328 Coventry (Health Care Insurance & Managed Care)

Birmingham-Hoover, AL
354 Regions Financial (Commercial Banking)
362 Saks (General Merchandise)

Bloomington-Normal, IL
22 State Farm Insurance Companies (Insurance)

Boise City-Nampa, ID
47 Albertson's (Food & Drug Stores)
438 Micron Technology (Semiconductors)

Boston-Quincy, MA
102 Liberty Mutual Insurance (Insurance)
307 State Street (Commercial Banking)

Bridgeport-Stamford-Norwalk, CT
7 General Electric (Diversified Financial)

142 Xerox (Office Equipment)
297 Praxair (Chemicals)
322 MeadWestvaco (Packaging & Containers)
355 Terex (Industrial & Farm Equipment)
394 Pitney Bowes (Office Equipment)
428 W.R. Berkley (Insurance)
448 Emcor Group (Engineering & Construction)

Cambridge-Newton-Framingham, MA
97 Raytheon (Aerospace & Defense)
137 Staples (Specialty Retailers)
138 TJX (Specialty Retailers)
249 EMC (Computer Peripherals)
288 BJ's Wholesale (Specialty Retailers)
346 Boston Scientific (Medical Products)

Camden, NJ
302 Campbell Soup (Food Consumer Products)

Canton-Massillon, OH
417 Timken (Industrial & Farm Equipment)

Charlotte-Gastonia-Concord, NC-SC
12 Bank of America (Commercial Banking)
57 Wachovia (Commercial Banking)
117 Duke Energy (Gas & Electric Utilities)
177 Nucor (Metals)
276 Sonic (Automotive Services)
369 Family Dollar (General Merchandise)
402 Goodrich (Aerospace & Defense)
446 SPX (Electronics)

Chattanooga, TN-GA
229 UnumProvident (Insurance)

Chicago-Naperville-Joliet, IL
26 Boeing (Aerospace & Defense)
33 Sears (General Merchandise)
45 Walgreen (Food & Drug Stores)
54 Motorola (Communications Equipment)
58 Allstate (Insurance)
109 McDonald's (Food Services)
111 Sara Lee (Food Consumer Products)
124 UAL (Airlines)
144 Exelon (Gas & Electric Utilities)
173 Illinois Tool Works (Industrial Equipment)
201 Navistar (Motor Vehicles)
237 Aon (Diversified Financial)
258 OfficeMax (Specialty Retailers)
265 R.R. Donnelley (Publishing & Printing)
274 Smurfit-Stone Container (Packaging)
371 Ryerson (Diversified Wholesalers)
388 Tribune (Publishing & Printing)
420 USG (Building Materials, Glass)
468 United Stationers (Office Wholesalers)
482 William Wrigley (Food Consumer Products)
494 ServiceMaster (Diversified Outsourcing)

Cincinnati-Middletown, OH-KY-IN
21 Kroger (Food & Drug Stores)
24 Procter & Gamble (Household Products)

87 Federated Stores (General Merchandise)
239 Ashland (Chemicals)
308 Fifth Third Bancorp (Commercial Banking)
385 AK Steel Holding (Metals)
398 Cinergy (Gas & Electric Utilities)
406 Omnicare (Health Care: Pharmacy)
473 Western & Southern Financial (Insurance)
492 American Financial Group (Insurance)

Cleveland-Elyria-Mentor, OH

153 Progressive (Insurance)
210 Eaton (Industrial & Farm Equipment)
213 National City Corp (Commercial Banking)
279 Parker Hannifin (Industrial Equipment)
311 Sherwin-Williams (Chemicals)
325 KeyCorp (Commercial Banking)
486 Lubrizol (Chemicals)

Columbia, SC

447 SCANA (Gas & Electric Utilities)

Columbus, GA-AL

151 AFLAC (Insurance)

Columbus, IN

238 Cummins (Industrial Equipment)

Columbus, OH

19 Cardinal Health (Health Care Wholesalers)
98 Nationwide (Insurance)
185 American Electric Power (Energy)
246 Limited Brands (Specialty Retailers)
462 Hexion Specialty Chemicals (Chemicals)
465 Big Lots (Specialty Retailers)

Dallas-Plano-Irving, TX

1 Exxon Mobil (Petroleum Refining)
105 AMR (Airlines)
108 Electronic Data Systems (IT Services)
118 J.C. Penney (General Merchandise)
140 Kimberly-Clark (Household Products)
167 Texas Instruments (Electronic Components)
169 Fluor (Engineering & Construction)
175 Centex (Homebuilders)
216 Dean Foods (Food Consumer Products)
228 TXU (Energy)
236 Tenet Healthcare (Medical Facilities)
300 Southwest Airlines (Airlines)
329 Commercial Metals (Metals)
347 Energy Transfer Partners (Energy)
356 Celanese (Chemicals)
366 Blockbuster (Specialty Retailers)
430 Atmos Energy (Gas & Electric Utilities)
432 Triad Hospitals (Health Care)
471 Affiliated Computer Services (IT Services)

Davenport-Moline-Rock Island, IA-IL

96 Deere (Industrial & Farm Equipment)

Dayton, OH

357 NCR (Office Equipment)

Top *Fortune* Metros

When Boeing announced it would move its headquarters from Seattle to one of three cities the firm identified as more central to its aerospace business—Chicago, Dallas, and Denver—the keen competition among the three (Chicago won) shows how badly cities want to be company towns.

A city's name on a corporate letterhead confers prestige. A company headquarters boosts white-collar employment, business and legal services and the local real estate market. Another benefit: Companies are deep-pocketed citizens, bankrolling the arts and other civic events. The eighteen metro areas below are headquarters for more than half of all *Fortune 500* firms.

Metro Area	Fortune 500 Headquarters
New York-White Plains-Wayne, NY-NJ	53
Houston-Sugar Land-Baytown, TX	24
Chicago-Naperville-Joliet, IL	21
Dallas-Plano-Irving, TX	19
Minneapolis-St. Paul, MN-WI	17
Atlanta-Sandy Springs-Marietta, GA	15
Philadelphia, PA	15
Los Angeles-Long Beach, CA	15
San Jose-Sunnyvale-Santa Clara, CA	14
Cincinnati-Middletown, OH-KY-IN	10
Denver-Aurora, CO	10
San Francisco-San Mateo, CA	9
Seattle-Bellevue-Everett, WA	9
Bridgeport-Stamford-Norwalk, CT	8
Charlotte-Gastonia-Concord, NC-SC	8
Milwaukee-Waukesha-West Allis, WI	8
St. Louis, MO-IL	8
Warren-Farmington Hills-Troy, MI	8

Fortune 500 headquarters are found in 106 of the 379 metro areas,

Source: Fortune magazine

Jobs

Decatur, IL
56 Archer Daniels Midland (Food Production)

Denver-Aurora, CO
160 Qwest (Telecommunications)
224 First Data (Financial Data Services)
269 TransMontaigne (Pipelines)
273 Echostar (Telecommunications)
277 Liberty Media (Specialty Retailers)
373 Molson Coors Brewing (Beverages)
374 Ball (Packaging & Containers)
408 Liberty Global (Telecommunications)
437 MDC Holdings (Homebuilders)
461 Newmont (Mining & Crude Oil Production)

Des Moines, IA
261 Principal Financial (Insurance)

Detroit-Livonia-Dearborn, MI
3 General Motors (Motor Vehicles)
5 Ford Motor (Motor Vehicles)
128 Visteon (Motor Vehicle Parts)
174 Masco (Home Equipment Furnishings)
179 TRW Automotive (Motor Vehicle Parts)
259 DTE Energy (Gas & Electric Utilities)

Edison, NJ
32 Johnson & Johnson (Pharmaceuticals)
156 Chubb (Insurance)
230 American Standard (Industrial Equipment)
403 Hovnanian Enterprises (Homebuilders)
434 Avaya (Network & Communications Equipment)
454 Engelhard (Chemicals)
497 Pathmark Stores (Food & Drug Stores)

Erie, PA
421 Erie Insurance Group (Insurance)

Fayetteville-Springdale-Rogers, AR-MO
2 Wal-Mart Stores (General Merchandise)
80 Tyson Foods (Food Production)

Fort Lauderdale-Pompano Beach, FL
115 AutoNation (Automotive Retailing)

Fort Worth-Arlington, TX
162 D.R. Horton (Homebuilders)
171 Burlington Northern Santa Fe (Railroads)
423 RadioShack (Specialty Retailers)

Gary, IN
289 NiSource (Gas & Electric Utilities)

Green Bay, WI
318 WPS Resources (Energy)

Greensboro-High Point, NC
333 VF (Clothing)
478 Jefferson-Pilot (Insurance)

Harrisburg-Carlisle, PA
442 Hershey (Food Consumer Products)

Hartford-West Hartford-East Hartford, CT
43 United Technologies (Aerospace & Defense)
78 Hartford Financial Services (Insurance)
91 Aetna (Health Care Insurance)
304 Northeast Utilities (Gas & Electric Utilities)

Houston-Sugar Land-Baytown, TX
6 ConocoPhillips (Petroleum Refining)
23 Marathon Oil (Petroleum Refining)
65 Plains All America Pipeline (Pipelines)
68 Sysco (Food & Grocery Wholesalers)
103 Halliburton (Oil & Gas Equipment Services)
121 Lyondell Chemical (Chemicals)
170 Waste Management (Waste Management)
183 Enterprise Products (Pipelines)
207 Continental Airlines (Airlines)
220 Reliant Energy (Energy)
243 Kinder Morgan Energy (Pipelines)
244 CenterPoint (Gas & Electric Utilities)
267 TEPPCO Partners (Pipelines)
298 Burlington Resources (Crude Oil Production)
299 Apache (Mining & Crude Oil Production)
310 Baker Hughes (Oil & Gas Equipment Services)
314 Anadarko Petroleum (Crude Oil Production)
335 Enbridge Energy Partners (Pipelines)
337 Dynegy (Energy)
361 Group 1 Automotive (Automotive Retailing & Services)
390 Smith International (Oil & Gas Equipment Services)
452 National Oilwell Varco (Oil & Gas Equipment Services)
455 El Paso (Pipelines)
496 Frontier Oil (Petroleum Refining)

Indianapolis, IN
38 Wellpoint (Health Care Insurance & Managed Care)
148 Eli Lilly (Pharmaceuticals)
472 Conseco (Insurance)

Jackson, MI
344 CMS Energy (Gas & Electric Utilities)

Jacksonville, FL
231 Winn-Dixie Stores (Food & Drug Stores)
248 Fidelity National Financial (Insurance)
266 CSX (Railroads)

Joplin, MO
404 Leggett & Platt (Furniture)

Kalamazoo-Portage, MI
439 Stryker (Medical Products & Equipment)

Kansas City, MO-KS
263 YRC Worldwide (Trucking & Truck Leasing)

Kingsport-Bristol-Bristol, TN-VA
315 Eastman Chemical (Chemicals)

Lake County-Kenosha County, IL-WI
93 Abbott Laboratories (Pharmaceuticals)

240 Baxter International (Medical Products)
305 Fortune Brands (Home Equipment Furnishings)
343 CDW (Specialty Retailers)
363 Brunswick (Transportation & Logistics)
391 W.W. Grainger (Diversified Wholesalers)
463 Tenneco (Motor Vehicle Parts)

Lakeland, FL

104 Publix Super Markets (Food & Drug Stores)
Lansing-East Lansing, MI
426 Auto-Owners Insurance (Insurance)

Las Vegas-Paradise, NV

309 Harrah's Entertainment (Casinos)
334 MGM Mirage (Casinos)

Lexington-Fayette, KY

415 Lexmark International (Computer Peripherals)

Little Rock-North Little Rock, AR

251 Alltel (Telecommunications)
294 Dillard's (General Merchandise)

Los Angeles-Long Beach-Glendale, CA

63 Walt Disney (Entertainment)
67 Northrop Grumman (Aerospace & Defense)
122 Countrywide Financial (Diversified Financial)
133 Occidental Petroleum (Crude Oil Production)
141 Computer Sciences (IT Services)
168 DIRECTV Group (Telecommunications)
191 Health Net (Health Care Insurance)
194 Edison International (Gas & Electric Utilities)
254 KB Home (Homebuilders)
365 Dole Food (Food Consumer Products)
386 Jacobs Engineering (Engineering & Construction)
393 Avery Dennison (Chemicals)
416 Mattel (Toys & Sporting Goods)
444 Ryland Group (Homebuilders)
464 Hilton Hotels (Hotels, Casinos & Resorts)

Louisville, KY-IN

150 Humana (Health Care Insurance & Managed Care)
257 Yum Brands (Food Services)
498 Kindred Healthcare (Health Care: Medical Facilities)

Madison, WI

323 American Family Insurance (Insurance)

Memphis, TN-MS-AR

70 FedEx (Package Delivery)
378 AutoZone (Specialty Retailers)

Miami-Miami Beach-Kendall, FL

161 Lennar (Homebuilders)
264 World Fuel Services (Diversified Wholesalers)
375 Ryder System (Trucking & Truck Leasing)

Milwaukee-Waukesha-West Allis, WI

75 Johnson Controls (Motor Vehicle Parts)
116 Northwestern Mutual (Insurance)
136 Manpower (Temporary Help)

166 Kohl's (General Merchandise)
380 Harley-Davidson (Transportation & Logistics)
427 Rockwell Automation (Electronics)
488 Fiserv (Financial Data Services)
499 Marshall & Ilsley (Commercial Banking)

Minneapolis-St. Paul-Bloomington, MN-WI

29 Target (General Merchandise)
37 UnitedHealth Group (Health Care Insurance & Managed Care)
76 Best Buy (Specialty Retailers)
85 St. Paul Travelers Companies (Insurance)
113 Supervalu (Food & Grocery Wholesalers)
131 U.S. Bancorp (Commercial Banking)
182 Northwest Airlines (Airlines)
188 CHS (Food & Grocery Wholesalers)
206 General Mills (Food Consumer Products)
235 Medtronic (Medical Products & Equipment)
247 Xcel Energy (Gas & Electric Utilities)
301 Land O'Lakes (Food Consumer Products)
352 Thrivent Financial for Lutherans (Insurance)
379 C.H. Robinson (Transportation Equipment)
457 Nash Finch (Food & Grocery Wholesalers)
459 Ecolab (Chemicals)
470 Mosaic (Chemicals)

Nashville-Davidson--Murfreesboro, TN

60 Caremark Rx (Health Care: Pharmacy)
84 HCA (Health Care: Medical Facilities)
268 Dollar General (General Merchandise)

Nassau-Suffolk, NY

209 Arrow Electronics (Electronics Wholesalers)
414 Cablevision Systems (Telecommunications)
445 Henry Schein (Health Care Wholesalers)

Newark-Union, NJ-PA

64 Prudential Financial (Insurance)
71 Honeywell (Aerospace & Defense)
95 Merck (Pharmaceuticals)
119 Wyeth (Pharmaceuticals)
178 Public Service (Gas & Electric Utilities)
250 Schering-Plough (Pharmaceuticals)
255 Lucent (Communications Equipment)
271 ADP (Payroll Services)
419 Bed Bath & Beyond (Specialty Retailers)

New Orleans-Metairie-Kenner, LA

218 Entergy (Gas & Electric Utilities)
480 Freeport-McMoRan (Mining)

New York-White Plains-Wayne, NY-NJ

8 Citigroup (Commercial Banking)
9 American International (Insurance)
10 IBM (Office Equipment)
17 J.P. Morgan Chase (Commercial Banking)
18 Verizon (Telecommunications)
20 Altria Group (Tobacco)
30 Morgan Stanley (Securities)
31 Pfizer (Pharmaceuticals)
34 Merrill Lynch (Securities)
35 MetLife (Insurance)
40 Time Warner (Entertainment)

Jobs

41 Goldman Sachs Group (Securities)
51 Medco Health Solutions (Health Care: Pharmacy)
61 PepsiCo (Food Consumer Products)
62 Lehman Brothers (Securities)
69 American Express (Diversified Financial)
74 New York Life (Insurance)
79 Alcoa (Metals)
81 TIAA-CREF (Insurance)
86 News Corporation (Entertainment)
88 Amerada Hess (Petroleum Refining)
110 Bristol-Myers Squibb (Pharmaceuticals)
114 Cendant (Real Estate)
145 Loews (Insurance)
149 CBS (Entertainment)
186 Marsh & McLennan (Diversified Financial)
192 Pepsi Bottling (Beverages)
199 Consolidated Edison (Gas & Electric Utilities)
202 Bear Stearns (Securities)
204 Colgate (Household & Personal Products)
208 Toys "R" Us (Specialty Retailers)
225 Omnicom Group (Advertising & Marketing)
241 Viacom (Entertainment)
253 L-3 Communications (Aerospace & Defense)
256 Guardian Life of America (Insurance)
278 Bank of New York (Commercial Banking)
281 Avon Products (Household & Personal Products)
291 ITT Industries (Industrial & Farm Equipment)
295 KeySpan (Gas & Electric Utilities)
306 Assurant (Insurance)
313 IAC/InterActive (Internet Services)
340 Estee Lauder (Household & Personal Products)
342 Dover (Industrial & Farm Equipment)
348 Interpublic Group (Advertising & Marketing)
359 McGraw-Hill (Publishing & Printing)
360 Starwood Hotels & Resorts (Hotels, Casinos & Resorts)
364 Asbury Automotive Group (Automotive Retailing & Services)
383 Foot Locker (Specialty Retailers)
384 CIT Group (Diversified Financial)
392 Quest Diagnostics (Health Care: Pharmacy)
397 Becton Dickinson (Medical Products & Equipment)
422 Barnes & Noble (Specialty Retailers)
440 Liz Claiborne (Clothing)
489 Sealed Air (Packaging & Containers)

Niles-Benton Harbor, MI

152 Whirlpool (Electronics)

Oakland-Fremont-Hayward, CA

4 Chevron (Petroleum Refining)
50 Safeway (Food & Drug Stores)
326 Golden West Financial (Savings Institutions)
431 Ross Stores (Specialty Retailers)
450 Longs Drug Stores (Food & Drug Stores)
460 Clorox (Household & Personal Products)

Ogden-Clearfield, UT

351 Autoliv (Motor Vehicle Parts)

Oklahoma City, OK

219 Devon Energy (Mining & Crude Oil Production)

320 Kerr-McGee (Mining & Crude Oil Production)
358 OGE Energy (Gas & Electric Utilities)
451 Chesapeake Energy (Mining & Crude Oil Production)

Omaha-Council Bluffs, NE-IA

13 Berkshire Hathaway (Insurance)
143 ConAgra Foods (Food Consumer Products)
164 Union Pacific (Railroads)
483 Peter Kiewit Sons (Engineering & Construction)
491 Mutual of Omaha (Insurance)

Orlando-Kissimmee, FL

400 Hughes Supply (Diversified Wholesalers)
409 Darden Restaurants (Food Services)

Oxnard-Thousand Oaks-Ventura, CA

181 Amgen (Pharmaceuticals)

Peoria, IL

55 Caterpillar (Industrial & Farm Equipment)

Philadelphia, PA

27 Amerisource Bergen (Health Care Wholesalers)
66 Sunoco (Petroleum Refining)
94 Comcast (Telecommunications)
130 Cigna (Health Care Insurance & Managed Care)
215 Aramark (Diversified Outsourcing)
286 Rohm & Haas (Chemicals)
321 Crown Holdings (Packaging & Containers)
370 Toll Brothers (Homebuilders)
372 Unisys (IT Services)
396 Lincoln National (Insurance)
425 Jones Apparel Group (Clothing)
436 UGI (Energy)
443 Owens & Minor (Health Care Wholesalers)
485 Universal Health Services (Health Care: Medical Facilities)
495 SunGard Data Systems (Financial Data Services)

Phoenix-Mesa-Scottsdale, AZ

212 Avnet (Electronics & Office Equipment Wholesalers)
260 Phelps Dodge (Metals)
376 Allied Waste Industries (Waste Management)
424 US Airways Group (Airlines)

Pittsburgh, PA

129 Rite Aid (Food & Drug Stores)
158 United States Steel (Metals)
232 PPG Industries (Chemicals)
262 H.J. Heinz (Food Consumer Products)
290 PNC Financial Services Group (Commercial Banking)
377 Mellon Financial (Commercial Banking)
466 Wesco International (Diversified Wholesalers)

Portland-South Portland-Biddeford, ME

405 Energy East (Gas & Electric Utilities)

Portland-Vancouver-Beaverton, OR-WA

163 Nike (Clothing)

Providence-New Bedford-Fall River, RI-MA

53 CVS (Food & Drug Stores)
190 Textron (Aerospace & Defense)

Raleigh-Cary, NC

222 Progress Energy* (Gas & Electric Utilities)

Richmond, VA

123 Dominion Resources (Gas & Electric Utilities)
223 Genworth Financial (Insurance)
226 Circuit City Stores (Specialty Retailers)
349 Performance Food Group (Food & Grocery Wholesalers)
395 Brink's (Diversified Outsourcing)
411 CarMax (Automotive Retailing & Services)
500 LandAmerica Financial (Insurance)

Roanoke, VA

477 Advance Auto Parts (Specialty Retailers)

Rochester, NY

155 Eastman Kodak (Scientific & Photo Equipment)
487 Constellation Brands (Beverages)

Rockingham County-Strafford County, NH

389 Fisher Scientific (Diversified Wholesalers)

St. Louis, MO-IL

126 Emerson Electric (Electronics)
134 Express Scripts (Health Care: Pharmacy)
146 Anheuser-Busch (Beverages)
324 Ameren (Gas & Electric Utilities)
336 Monsanto (Chemicals)
413 Charter Communications (Telecommunications)
453 Peabody Energy (Mining & Crude Oil Production)
476 Graybar Electric (Diversified Wholesalers)

Salt Lake City, UT

172 Huntsman (Chemicals)

San Antonio, TX

15 Valero Energy (Petroleum Refining)
39 AT&T (Telecommunications)
132 Tesoro (Petroleum Refining)
189 USAA (Insurance)
252 Clear Channel Communications (Entertainment)

San Diego-Carlsbad-San Marcos, CA

197 Sempra Energy (Gas & Electric Utilities)
285 Science Applications International (IT Services)
381 Qualcomm (Network & Communications Equipment)

San Francisco-San Mateo-Redwood City, CA

16 McKesson (Health Care Wholesalers)
46 Wells Fargo (Commercial Banking)
139 Gap (Specialty Retailers)
196 Oracle (Computer Software)
200 PG&E Corporation (Gas & Electric Utilities)
418 Charles Schwab (Securities)
474 Franklin Resources (Securities)
481 CNF (Transportation Equipment)
484 Levi Strauss (Clothing)

San Jose-Sunnyvale-Santa Clara, CA

11 Hewlett-Packard (Office Equipment)
49 Intel (Semiconductors)
83 Cisco Systems (Network Equipment)
159 Apple Computer (Office Equipment)
198 Sanmina-SCI (Electronic Components)
211 Sun Microsystems (Office Equipment)
227 Solectron (Electronic Components)
275 Calpine (Energy)
317 Applied Materials (Electronic Components)
319 Agilent Technologies (Scientific Equipment)
353 Google (Internet Services & Retailing)
367 Advanced Micro Devices (Semiconductors)
412 Yahoo (Internet Services & Retailing)
458 eBay (Internet Services & Retailing)

Santa Ana-Anaheim-Irvine, CA

72 Ingram Micro (Electronics & Office Equipment Wholesalers)
284 First American Corporation (Insurance)
441 Pacific Life (Insurance)
493 Standard Pacific (Homebuilders)

Seattle-Bellevue-Everett, WA

28 Costco Wholesale (Specialty Retailers)
48 Microsoft (Computer Software)
90 Weyerhaeuser (Forest & Paper Products)
99 Washington Mutual (Savings Institutions)
157 Paccar (Motor Vehicle Parts)
272 Amazon.com (Internet Services & Retailing)
293 Nordstrom (General Merchandise)
338 Starbucks (Food Services)
339 Safeco (Insurance)

Springfield, MA

92 Mass. Mutual Life Insurance (Insurance)

Tampa-St. Petersburg-Clearwater, FL

107 Tech Data (Electronics & Office Equipment Wholesalers)
303 Jabil Circuit (Electronic Components)

Toledo, OH

234 Dana (Motor Vehicle Parts)
312 Owens-Illinois (Packaging & Containers)
341 Owens Corning (Building Materials, Glass)

Tulsa, OK

176 ONEOK (Energy)
180 Williams (Energy)

Virginia Beach-Norfolk-Newport News, VA-NC

205 Smithfield Foods (Food Production)
270 Norfolk Southern (Railroads)

Warren-Farmington Hills-Troy, MI

77 Delphi (Motor Vehicle Parts)
127 Lear (Motor Vehicle Parts)
147 Pulte Homes (Homebuilders)
214 United Auto Group (Automotive Retailing & Services)
242 ArvinMeritor (Motor Vehicle Parts)
345 Federal-Mogul (Motor Vehicle Parts)

407 Kelly Services (Temporary Help)
475 BorgWarner (Motor Vehicle Parts)

Washington-Arlington-Alexandria, DC-VA

59 Sprint Nextel (Telecommunications)
100 General Dynamics (Aerospace & Defense)
187 Capital One Financial (Commercial Banking)
221 AES (Gas & Electric Utilities)
283 Pepco Holdings (Gas & Electric Utilities)
287 Danaher (Scientific Equipment)
296 Gannett (Publishing & Printing)
331 SLM (Diversified Financial)

410 NVR (Homebuilders)

West Palm Beach-Boca Raton, FL

154 Office Depot (Specialty Retailers)
195 FPL Group (Gas & Electric Utilities)

Wilmington, DE-MD-NJ

73 DuPont (Chemicals)

Winston-Salem, NC

280 Reynolds American (Tobacco)
292 BB&T Corporation (Commercial Banking)

Crime

In 1993, violent crime rates started declining to a point where they were at their lowest level in decades. Police chiefs and mayors celebrated in front of TV cameras and declared strategies like community policing, zero tolerance, reclaiming public spaces, rapid deployment, accurate intelligence, and relentless follow-up were working. In most regions of the country, for the rest of the decade and into the new millennium, each year was safer than the one before.

Two Tales of Two Cities

Domestic violence on the farm and pushers developing a base for their illegal pharmaceutical trade aren't uncommon items in Duluth's *News Tribune*. Down I-35 in the Twin Cities, stories of convenience store stickups and drug-related drive-by shootings aren't uncommon in the Minneapolis *Star Tribune*, either. If you were passing through either metro area and heard of these crimes, you might wonder whether you were any safer on the northern prairie than you'd be in East Los Angeles or in the Bronx.

But neither Duluth nor Minneapolis-St. Paul experience crime rates above the metro area average. Among the metro areas profiled in *Places Rated Almanac*, reporters working the police beat in some have so few violent crime stories to write up that a reader of the paper may wonder whether anything interesting goes on there at all. In the inner cities of other metro areas, day-to-day existence seems just plain dangerous.

If you decide to live in Wausau, WI, for instance, the odds of your being a violent crime victim are less than 750 to 1. On the other hand, should you choose Miami the odds increase to 100 to 1. One could say that life in exciting, rapidly growing south Florida is nearly 8 times as dangerous as it is in a rather boring middle-class insurance town in central Wisconsin.

IS IT THE WEATHER?

These fifteen metro areas—with their rock-bottom violent crime and average property crime—most closely resemble the crime patterns of metro areas north of the border, in Canada.

Everyone's a Victim

But quoting odds distorts the local crime picture. Violence doesn't lurk in every metro area neighborhood. Veteran cops tell you that most murders occur within the same few square miles or even blocks. Sailors going ashore in an unfamiliar port get the word from commanders on which streets to avoid because of high risk for robberies and aggravated assaults.

Moreover, if you're young, white, and female and if you earn enough money, your chances of meeting up with crime are much less than those of an older, poor male. Why a chapter on crime if a combination of factors such as age, sex, race, income, and a wise selection of neighborhood can statistically remove you from danger?

The simple answer is that you are a different kind of crime victim depending on whether you have to trim back shrubbery along your home's foundation to restrict a crook's potential hiding places, or get rid of the mailbox and install a mail slot in your front door, or press down your car's door locks when driving down a darkened avenue, or keep feeling for your wallet at street festivals, or use only empty elevators, or stay indoors evenings more than you really care to. In some metro areas such tactics are advised, in others they are merely prudent,

and in still others they may not be necessary at all.

CRIME RISK: SEVERAL CONNECTIONS

Why some metro areas are safer than others incites arguments among citizens, politicians, police, and social scientists. Conservatives blame the criminal, the criminal's parents, and lenient courts. Liberals indict an oppressive society as the real offender. With all the debate, experts do agree on several factors.

Climate

Temperature has a striking connection with lawbreaking. Sultry 'bread knife weather," as some cops call it, seems to tip some people over the edge given the increased rates for murder, rape, and assault in the summer and in hot locations. In fact, police respond to more domestic disturbance calls on days immediately after summer temperatures are highest than on any other days of the year. Burglary and vandalism have been shown to increase with ambient temperature up to 85°F.

Indeed, in the Sun Belt and in the Frost Belt, cops and criminals are busiest throughout July and

August when all crimes except robbery are the likeliest to happen. Since people spend more time outdoors during these months, they are more exposed. Homes, too, are more unprotected during this time of year because they are left with open windows and unlocked doors. Robbery is *the* cold-weather exception. It is highest in December when shoppers and retail stores doing brisk holiday business make tempting targets in the early dark.

Population Size

Size matters in crime rates. Metro areas with lower crime rates—Grand Forks, ND, or Wausau, WI, for example—are small places. Metro areas with the high rates—Los Angeles-Long Beach or New York are two extreme examples—have large, overcrowded populations. There are exceptions, certainly. Pittsburgh's crime rate is lower than Ann Arbor's. Gainesville's, Jacksonville's, and Tallahassee's crime rates resemble New York's.

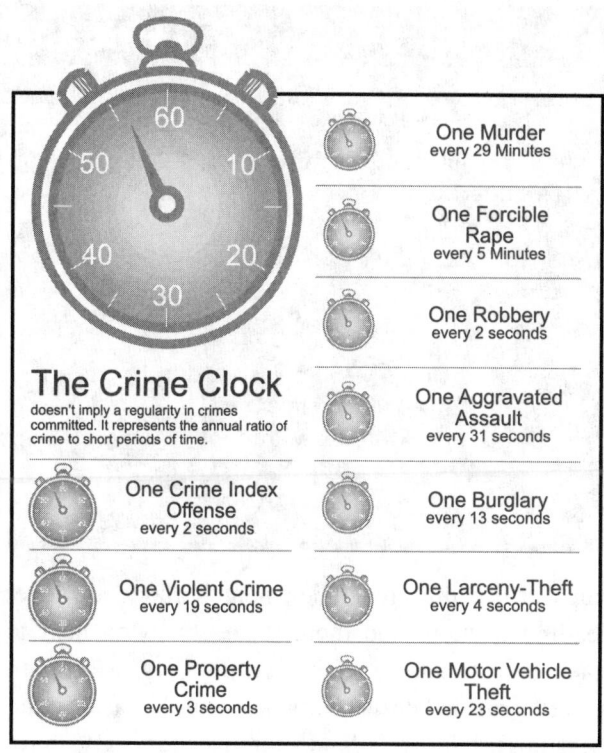

The Crime Clock doesn't imply a regularity in crimes committed. It represents the annual ratio of crime to short periods of time.

One Murder	every 29 Minutes
One Forcible Rape	every 5 Minutes
One Robbery	every 2 seconds
One Aggravated Assault	every 31 seconds
One Crime Index Offense	every 2 seconds
One Burglary	every 13 seconds
One Violent Crime	every 19 seconds
One Larceny-Theft	every 4 seconds
One Property Crime	every 3 seconds
One Motor Vehicle Theft	every 23 seconds

Time of Day and Photoperiod

December has the fewest hours of sunlight. After sundown is the time most cars are stolen, most persons and businesses are robbed, most persons are assaulted, and most thefts are committed. Burglaries, purse-snatchings, and pocket pickings, on the other hand, happen more often during daylight hours. Indeed, some veteran police dispatchers contend that the number of daylight minutes is a predictor of the kind of 911 calls they handle.

Local Traffic

Complain all you want about gridlock, but it does cut crime. The ease with which a criminal can drive off down the street, escape onto an arterial road, and merge onto the Interstate and disappear among commuters is an encouragement. Neighborhoods near Houston's I-610 Beltway urged the city to turn their streets into cul-de-sacs, and in Elizabeth, NJ, cops a while ago took the drastic step of erecting barricades at the corner of Madison Avenue and Fanny Street to stop neighboring Newark lawbreakers from fleeing into their jurisdiction.

Age and Sex

Some 5 million Americans have arrest records for misdeeds other than traffic violations. The proportion of suspects who are male is much higher than their proportion in the general population. The decades-old pattern continues to hold true: Half the persons picked up by police for violent and property crimes are under 20 years of age and four-fifths are male.

None of this should be taken to mean that persons hold up convenience stores, boost Cadillac Escalades or duke it out in dance club parking lots because they are young and male, but these characteristics are associated with other factors in crime. Like hearing distantly rolling thunder, some criminologists have warned that falling crime rates may well be short-lived once a huge group of pre-teen males grows up and takes to the streets.

The Economy

In most metro areas, each time unemployment goes up the police make more arrests. But joblessness and loss of income won't automatically make a place unsafe. Metro areas in the Ohio Valley and in the Northern Plains suffer job losses during business slumps but continue to experience low crime rates.

More affluent areas, given similar sets of circumstances, aren't nearly as safe as they seem. Rich offenders are arrested less often than poor ones, especially on suspicion. Once arrested, they are convicted with less frequency. This is especially true in juvenile cases involving thefts and break-ins.

Transience

Crooks are uncomfortable in a stable neighborhood where people know one another and look out for one another's safety and property, no matter how many

Hot and Cold Cars

Last year, one of every 200 BMW M-Series Roadsters manufactured in 2001 was stolen according to an industry group that tracks theft and vehicle damage. Six of the top 10 hot cars were models of the Acura Integra, which has a powerful engine that easily can be swapped into a lighter Honda Civic, making it a quick street racer.

An Insurance industry group notes that Buicks dominate the list of cars professional thieves pass up.

Hot Cars	Cold Cars
BMW M-Series Roadster	Buick LeSabre
Acura Integra	Buick Park Avenue
Mercury Marauder	Ford Taurus
Audi S4	Buick Rendezvous
Jaguar XJR	Saturn LW

cops cruise the area. High neighborhood turnover leading to more and more strangers living next to each other leads to higher crime rates. Moreover, resort areas that draw transients—Las Vegas, Miami, Myrtle Beach, or Orlando for instance—also have serious crime problems. When visitors are added to the year round residents, the higher population raises the odds that victim and crook will meet.

Police Strength

Most metro areas have between one and three uniformed police for every 1,000 residents. In Manhattan, there are 1,300 officers per square mile. In empty parts of Alaska and the Rocky Mountains there are police officers, but they drive Crown Vic cruisers with 200 gallon fuel tanks and need hours to respond to calls.

It's natural to think personal safety in a metro area rises or falls with to the size of the local police force, but it just isn't so. Police enforce traffic codes, investigate accidents, find lost children, and calm down fighting spouses. They battle crime, too, but most of what they do is after the fact. They respond to complaints; they interview victims and fill out reports; they follow up on tips; and they collar suspects and book them.

Criminologists still recount the famous Kansas City experiment conducted in 1972. Three precincts of the city, each with similar crime rates, were selected. In one area, the number of police cruisers was doubled. In the control neighborhood, the police maintained their usual strength and visibility. But in the third area, the police carefully but furtively pulled their uniformed officers out, entering only to respond to calls. All areas were carefully monitored for a year. The difference in crime rates? Practically none.

A large number of police usually means a high-crime area rather than an area where crime is being foiled. Among big cities, Washington, DC, has the most men and women in blue per capita and it has long experienced one of the highest crime rates in the country, too.

Other Factors

The street smarts and professional practices of local prosecutors, tough judges, conscientious juries, and dedicated parole boards have their own impact on criminal activity. Another critical factor: How willing are ordinary citizens to have their antennae up on the streets and pick up the phone and dial 911 whenever they see a crime?

CRIME INDEXES

Each year, the Federal Bureau of Investigation in Washington report crime figures from police departments. Eight crimes, because of their seriousness, frequency, and likelihood of being reported to police, make up a Crime Index for measuring local wrongdoing. Four are violent crimes; the other four are property crimes.

Violent Crime

City hall news releases during the 1990s announcing dramatic drops in homicide were just a local part of the national trend. By the end of the decade, the murder rate reached its lowest in more than thirty years. According to one study, the big reason isn't astute police work or a citizenry with cooler heads; it is the development of 911 services, rapid stabilization of trauma victims, and better training of people in the

hospital emergency room. Without those advances, some 50,000 assault victims would have ended up under sheets with tags on their toes.

But 2001 saw a 3 percent increase in the rate of people killing one another, not counting the deaths from 9/11's World Trade Center collapse. If those were counted as murders, the FBI said, the national rate would have increased by 26 percent.

• *Murder* is the most reported of all crimes, the crime with the fewest incidences, the crime with the highest rate of charges being brought, and the crime where the offender is most likely to have no criminal record. Victims are male in three of four cases, and most were slain in single-victim, single-killer set-tos. Half of all victims knew their killers, perhaps even sat across from them at the breakfast table the morning of the crime, or loaned them money the week before, or dissed them at a club the previous evening.

Victims and killers are becoming less connected, however. One murder in eight involves a victim and a stranger, one in twenty a juvenile gang killing. Based on the number of unsolved homicides each year and an increase in slayings involving strangers, the FBI estimates at least 35 unidentified serial killers are on the loose in the United States.

• *Rape*, too, frequently involves acquainted victims and aggressors. It is the most under-reported violent crime and also has the highest proportion of "unfounded" complaints. Except in Illinois, Michigan, and Minnesota victims are always female by current FBI crime reporting standards.

• *Robbery* is the violent crime most often involving more than one criminal and is the one violent crime committed less out of impulsive anger than as a way of earning a living. It is different from common theft because it requires force or threat of violence, thereby placing the victim in fear. The robbery rate is highest in large cities where half of the holdups take place on the street and a quarter occur in commercial establishments and banks. Except for some rural sections, the robbery rate is declining everywhere.

• *Assault* is simply an attempt, successful or not, to injure another person severely. Assault is usually accompanied by the use of a weapon. Its rate is highest in August, lowest in February, higher in the West than in other parts of the country and higher in areas with resort or military economies. With more than one million incidents, it is the most frequently reported violent crime.

Property Crime

Last year, some 10.2 million property crimes were reported nationwide. The good news: The figure means a drop of 14 percent from ten years ago.

• *Burglary* is either forcible entry, unlawful entry where no force is used, or attempted forcible entry, all to commit a felony or theft. Two of every three targets are a home or apartment. Nearly half of the incidents involve walking in rather than breaking in. The usual time is between 9 and 11 in the morning or between 1 and 3 in the afternoon, when you're least likely to be inside. The typical householder's dollar loss is $1,300.

Most burglaries take days to plan and minutes to pull off. A skilled burglar is a careful long-term practitioner, cruising residential streets for signs of affluence and stupidity. "They know more about your routine than you do," a veteran burglary detective once claimed.

• *Larceny-theft*, after drunk driving and drug offenses, is the most common crime in North America. Skipping out of a self-serve gas station is one example. Shoplifting a Russian sable coat is another. Except for purse snatches and picked pockets, in almost all of the larceny-theft cases, the victim never sees the offender.

• *Auto theft*, it's been said, is a victimless crime because you get over your loss with a check from the insurance company. About one in ten stolen luxury vehicles shows up in third-world showrooms, where a market for used Mercedes, Lexuses, Ford Explorers, and even Harley-Davidson motorcycles flourishes.

Miami is generally regarded as an American auto-theft capital. Cops in Miami report an increase in persons arrested who recently arrived from California and New York, where auto insurance fraud and packing a ship container with automobiles are underground arts. In fact, nearly every metro area with a high auto theft rate is on either coast or near the Mexican border, where a Porsche Boxster can be in another country before the owner finds it gone.

In the continent's interior, though, cars are infrequently stolen for export. In areas like Omaha,

Neighborhood Crime Watches

It is possible to see a crime in progress without recognizing it as such. Here are some situations that might be observed in any neighborhood. These are situations a trained police officer would investigate if he or she were making the observation.

Situations	Possible Significance
Situations Involving Vehicles	
Moving vehicles, especially if moving slowly without lights, following an aimless or repetitive course	Casing for a place to rob or burglarize; drug pusher, sex offender, or vandal
Parked, occupied vehicle, especially at an unusual hour (sometimes two people masquerading as lovers)	Lookout for burglary in progress
Vehicle parked in neighbor's drive being loaded with valuables, even if the vehicle looks legitimate, i.e., moving van or commercial van	Burglary or larceny in progress
Abandoned vehicle with or without license plate	Stolen or abandoned after being used in a crime
Persons loitering around parked cars	Burglary of vehicle contents, theft of accessories, vandalism
Persons detaching accessories and mechanical parts	Theft or vandalism
Apparent business transactions from a vehicle near school, park, or quiet residential neighborhood	Drug sales
Persons being forced into vehicle	Kidnapping, rape, robbery
Objects thrown from a moving vehicle	Disposal of contraband
Situations Involving Property	
Property in homes, garages, or storage areas, especially if several items of the same kind such as TVs and bicycles	Storage of stolen property
Property in vehicles, especially meaningful at night or if property is household goods, appliances, unmounted tape decks, stereo equipment	Stolen property, burglary in progress
Property being removed from a house or building; meaningful if residents are at work, on vacation, or are known to be absent	Burglary or larceny in progress
Open doors, broken doors or windows, or other signs of a forced entry	Burglary in progress or the scene of a recent burglary
Situations Involving Persons	
Door-to-door solicitors especially significant if one goes to the back of the house and one stays in front. Can be men or women, clean-cut and well dressed	Casing for burglary, burglary in progress, soliciting violation
Waiting in front of a house	Lookout for burglary in progress
Forced entry or entry through window	Burglary, vandalism, theft
Persons short-cutting through yards	Fleeing the scene of a crime
Persons running, especially if carrying items of value	Fleeing the scene of a crime
Person carrying property, especially if property isn't boxed or wrapped	Offender leaving the scene of a burglary, robbery, or larceny
High volume of human traffic in and out of residence	Drug sales, vice activities, "fence" operation

Source: Miami-Dade Police Department

Indianapolis, and Kansas City, choice vehicles are taken to chop shops and plundered for their air bags, seats, halogen headlamps, and fenders. These high-price components end up on eBay or at crooked auto repairers for resale as if they were new, legal parts.

• *Arson* was added to the Crime Index in 1979 following a Congressional mandate. It includes any willful or malicious burning or attempt to burn, with or with out the intent to defraud, a house, building, car, airplane, or the personal property of someone else. It doesn't include fires of suspicious or unknown origin.

CAVEATS

Metro areas are rated for personal safety based on the number of crimes actually reported to local police. This can work against a city's record. A classic story from the Boston Police Department came out of District 6, the infamous Southie. In one year, dispatchers took some 1,300 calls from an elderly resident complaining of gangs drinking and hanging out below his apartment window. The police would send a two-man sector car, shoo the youths away, notify the dispatcher, and leave. Within a few hours, the gangs returned...1,300 times.

More than 60 percent of all crime goes unreported according to national victim surveys and that percentage can vary from one metro area to another. Victims in the inner city may think it futile to file complaints on each missing garden hose, slashed tire, or domestic disturbance, while suburban victims may report every single incident. Even if a complaint is filed, the investigating officer's definition of the crime may change the numbers. Purse-snatching, for instance, is either a robbery or a larceny depending on the jurisdiction. Likewise, a slap in the face is either an aggravated or simple assault depending on motive.

In the past, too, some police departments have either padded the figures to oust a judge considered soft on crime or to persuade the city council to increase the department's budget, or they have fudged the number of crimes to create an image of effective law enforcement.

JUDGING: CRIME

One problem with understanding crime statistics is the confusion between crime *incidence* and the crime *rate*. Incidence is simply how many crimes are reported in a given place. The more people living in a place, the greater the crime incidence will be. In Boise City-Nampa, ID, police investigate some 150 street robberies a year. In southeast Georgia, police in Brunswick handle a similar number. From these figures, you might think that Brunswick resembles Boise City-Nampa. But more than a half million people live in Boise-Nampa while just 100,000 live in greater Brunswick.

Another problem to understanding crime statistics comes from lumping all crimes together. The single offense most often reported to local cops is larceny-theft: a stolen bike, a necklace missing from a jewelry retailer's display case, hubcaps gone from a used-car lot, a customer bolting from a fast-food restaurant. Yet these heists are counted as heavily as homicides to determine an area's crime rate. When it comes to comparing places, this method doesn't realistically show relative danger.

SCORING: CRIME

The realistic way to judge metro areas for personal safety is simple. For each place, *Places Rated* averages the rates for violent and property crime for the latest 5 years but since property crimes are much less serious than crimes against people, they get one-tenth the weight of violent crimes. The results for each metro area are then scaled into percentile scores where 0 is worst, 50 is average, and 100 is best. The higher the score, the safer the metro area.

A small location in Wisconsin, a much larger one in southeast Florida, and a sunny Old West spot

	Murder	Rape	Robbery	Assault	Burglary	Theft	Auto Theft	Rank
Metro Area Average	6.5	33.5	177.6	346.1	781	2,643	501	-
Wausau	1.3	18.9	17.0	91.5	423	1,630	101	19
Yuma	2.6	24.6	39.4	439.6	740	2,160	384	187
Miami-Miami Beach-Kendall	9.1	37.6	324.8	649.0	1,029	3,859	796	355

www.placesrated.com

Crime rankings, from 1 to 379, are in the *Place Profiles* section coming next. Crime scores, from 100.0 to 0.0, are in *Putting It All Together* at the end of the book. Readers can view and print out these rankings and scores, from #1 Appleton, WI (score: 100.0) to #379 Memphis, TN-MS-AR (score: 0.0), at *Places Rated*'s website.

Here are the top twenty:

Rank	Score
1. Appleton, WI	100.0
2. Logan, UT-ID	99.8
3. Fond du Lac, WI	99.5
4. Wheeling, WV-OH	99.3
5. Rockingham County, NH	99.0
6. State College, PA	98.7
7. Harrisonburg, VA	98.5
8. Bismarck, ND	98.2
9. La Crosse, WI-MN	97.9
10. St. Cloud, MN	97.7
11. Oshkosh-Neenah, WI	97.4
12. St. George, UT	97.1
13. York-Hanover, PA	96.9
14. Nassau-Suffolk, NY	96.6
15. Sheboygan, WI	96.3
16. Manchester-Nashua, NH	96.1
17. Weirton-Steubenville, WV-OH	95.8
18. Lynchburg, VA	95.6
19. Wausau, WI	95.3
20. Fargo, ND-MN	95.0

At *www.placesrated.com* you'll also find five-year average crime figures and trends for each of the thousands of cities and towns that are part of America's 379 metropolitan areas.

in southwestern Arizona are among the best, worst, and average metro areas by *Places Rated*'s scoring method for personal safety.

Always with the Best: Wausau, WI

The only connection Americans might make with this small metro area in north central Wisconsin is the engraved picture of a small-town railroad depot with '*Wausau*' on the sign. The picture is the logo of the city's largest employer, Wausau Insurance Companies. The depot, depicted decades ago in advertising with the city's modest skyline in the background, still stands at 720 Grant Street.

Wausau has another distinction: Violent and property crime per 100,000 residents here is a fraction of the metro area average, as it is for a handful of other post-industrial metro areas in the upper Ohio River valley and northern Great Lakes. A murder is reported here perhaps once every other year. An infrequent assortment of break-ins, bar fights, and garage thefts are all that seem to keep the cops in town and in surrounding Marathon County busy. This combination of some of the country's lowest violent and property crime rates produces Wausau's personal safety rank of 19, among the best of all metro areas in America.

In the Middle: Yuma, AZ

Scan the police blotter in the Yuma *Daily Sun* and you may have doubts about whether the desert is safe.

An Aug. 8 trial date has been for the Yuma man who allegedly used a machete to attack another man who was walking in front of his home.

A presentencing hearing for a man convicted of stabbing a retired Arizona Western College professor with a screwdriver is on hold pending a mental exam of the defendant.

Two juveniles and one adult have been arrested and charged after one of the minors allegedly threatened a clerk with a knife while stealing two cases of beer from a Barney's gas station early Sunday morning.

Border Patrol agents seized nearly 2,000 pounds of marijuana and arrested two smuggling suspects after stopping two vehicles traveling together on Interstate 8 west of Yuma Sunday afternoon.

In fact, Yuma (rank 187) is closest to the middle of the crime scale than any other metro area. Except for robbery, criminal activity here is well below the national average. The clips cited above are newsworthy in an area with 200,000 people, but wouldn't get space in the Miami *Herald*.

Among the Worst (but Getting Much Better): Miami, FL

When a European reporter once commented to former San Francisco Mayor Willie Brown that he felt unsafe on his last visit to the City by the Bay, the mayor retorted: "I think you have us confused with Miami."

Most metro areas in Florida rank near the bottom in personal safety. Of all the states, Florida owns the highest rates for violent crime and property crime. Miami, its best-known city, was the tropical backdrop for *Miami Vice*, a Friday-night television series in the 1980s where hip undercover narcs and drug lords brandished locally-made TEC 9 machine pistols at each other.

The city is the natural setting for Edna Buchanan's, Carl Hiaasen's, and Elmore Leonard's thrillers. Special Crime Tour buses leave the Dade Cultural Center for sightseeing excursions to the sites of Gianni Versace's Murder, the FDR Assassination Attempt, the Candy Mossler Murder case, and the Barbara Mackle Kidnapping. A standard item in hotel and rental car packets is a bulletin on guerrilla tactics for staying out of harm's way.

To its credit, this metro area—rated dead last in each of *Places Rated*'s six previous editions—has gotten dramatically better. It remains the car-theft capital of the South and burglary and theft rates are double what they are elsewhere in metropolitan America. But Miami-Dade County now outranks 25 other metro areas in freedom from crime.

PLACE PROFILES: CRIME

The *Place Profiles* following are a table headed at the top of each page by America's metro area average annual rates for seven crimes: murder, rape, robbery, aggravated assault, burglary, larceny-theft, and motor vehicle theft for the last 5 years. Underneath are the 379 metro area average annual rates for comparison.

Note: Although figures for rape are shown for metro areas, they aren't included in the scoring because many jurisdictions—notably those in Illinois, Michigan, and Minnesota—define this violent crime differently than does the FBI.

Figures are derived from the FBI's *Crime in the United States* for the last 5 years and from the Bureau's unpublished "Crime by County" reports for each of these years. For metro areas not included in either of the FBI's sources, figures are derived from the Places Rated Partnership survey of state Uniform Crime Reporting programs.

A check mark (✓) to the left of a metro area's name identifies it as one of the top 40 places for personal safety.

Metro Area	Murder	Rape	Robbery	Assault	Burglary	Theft	Auto Theft	Rank
Metro Area Average	*6.5*	*33.5*	*177.6*	*346.1*	*781*	*2,643*	*501*	*-*
Abilene, TX	3.7	40.1	72.0	208.8	911	2,377	177	186
Akron, OH	2.6	41.8	108.1	94.6	715	2,529	287	123
Albany, GA	5.9	27.7	164.5	239.2	1,138	2,889	269	272
Albany-Schenectady-Troy, NY	2.7	23.5	102.1	205.9	602	2,098	161	104
Albuquerque, NM	9.1	50.0	241.1	668.5	1,228	3,970	754	368
Alexandria, LA	9.6	32.0	142.9	612.8	1,600	3,459	250	375
Allentown-Bethlehem-Easton, PA-NJ	3.2	21.7	86.9	152.1	464	1,941	192	59
Altoona, PA	1.9	29.9	74.6	137.6	597	1,797	141	81
Amarillo, TX	5.9	43.8	131.1	472.1	1,075	4,206	407	319
✓ Ames, IA	0.8	32.0	14.4	161.9	385	2,541	117	36
Anchorage, AK	5.5	78.8	137.5	434.7	588	3,532	450	207
Anderson, IN	5.3	27.3	53.0	80.3	520	1,939	132	45
Anderson, SC	8.1	37.9	97.8	504.6	1,124	2,875	345	297
Ann Arbor, MI	3.2	38.9	85.1	212.3	688	2,427	292	129
Anniston-Oxford, AL	8.4	48.9	186.5	477.3	1,418	3,508	325	360
✓ Appleton, WI	0.7	17.3	8.8	65.3	228	1,738	80	1
Asheville, NC	4.1	22.7	81.4	185.2	803	1,991	243	139
Athens-Clarke County, GA	5.6	31.1	110.3	208.5	878	3,885	322	224
Atlanta-Sandy Springs-Marietta, GA	8.1	26.6	218.0	299.3	890	2,869	618	253
Atlantic City, NJ	5.5	26.3	191.7	290.5	775	3,988	207	233
Auburn-Opelika, AL	6.8	42.6	105.6	464.7	1,162	3,309	201	308
Augusta-Richmond County, GA-SC	6.0	45.5	122.4	231.1	877	2,923	365	213
Austin-Round Rock, TX	3.4	36.1	103.0	222.5	836	3,235	298	197
Bakersfield, CA	6.7	27.5	110.4	363.4	942	2,294	470	237
Baltimore-Towson, MD	10.9	26.8	291.1	601.1	816	2,842	490	292
✓ Bangor, ME	2.3	16.6	19.7	49.8	514	2,242	116	37
Barnstable Town, MA	1.6	29.8	24.2	437.9	654	1,696	135	137
Baton Rouge, LA	11.7	31.0	216.5	460.5	1,278	4,126	464	351
Battle Creek, MI	4.4	94.4	143.1	638.3	1,160	3,657	373	345
Bay City, MI	1.6	56.1	38.3	187.4	598	2,150	208	88
Beaumont-Port Arthur, TX	5.3	67.7	162.0	330.3	1,103	3,134	364	280
Bellingham, WA	1.7	59.1	50.1	133.0	974	3,565	270	212
Bend, OR	2.4	27.7	34.2	112.2	761	3,445	260	135
Bethesda-Gaithersburg-Frederick, MD	2.2	18.3	94.6	147.6	433	2,058	329	54
Billings, MT	2.4	18.2	47.1	161.4	484	3,774	289	93
✓ Binghamton, NY	1.8	22.4	44.2	111.8	358	1,982	69	21
Birmingham-Hoover, AL	10.8	39.8	184.0	312.5	914	2,781	403	249
✓ Bismarck, ND	1.1	18.6	11.9	43.1	332	2,033	162	8
✓ Blacksburg-Christiansburg-Radford, VA	2.5	25.1	20.2	139.7	389	1,682	108	24
Bloomington, IN	4.0	36.4	30.6	142.9	589	2,443	167	83
Bloomington-Normal, IL	2.6	72.1	78.6	356.4	735	2,264	108	169
Boise City-Nampa, ID	2.0	45.0	26.8	221.7	686	2,657	235	126
Boston-Quincy, MA	3.6	32.4	194.4	455.5	477	1,953	610	155
Boulder, CO	1.1	34.0	25.1	162.4	486	2,096	153	52
Bowling Green, KY	4.5	77.7	147.7	481.1	1,231	4,259	356	342
Bremerton-Silverdale, WA	1.9	75.7	49.4	270.6	849	2,362	250	181
Bridgeport-Stamford-Norwalk, CT	3.0	16.7	120.4	198.0	451	1,683	393	72
Brownsville-Harlingen, TX	3.7	27.9	79.8	342.4	989	4,433	247	273
Brunswick, GA	4.8	30.3	138.1	578.4	1,017	5,052	312	335
Buffalo-Niagara Falls, NY	5.0	27.6	176.9	251.7	657	2,177	348	149
Burlington, NC	6.6	19.7	99.0	234.3	1,053	2,967	210	245
Burlington-South Burlington, VT	2.7	20.1	18.4	113.0	619	2,312	167	80
✓ Cambridge-Newton-Framingham, MA	1.1	14.1	50.7	175.6	339	1,336	244	22
Camden, NJ	4.2	21.9	141.5	209.6	576	1,984	302	108
Canton-Massillon, OH	2.4	29.2	98.1	172.7	757	2,057	205	130

Metro Area	Murder	Rape	Robbery	Assault	Burglary	Theft	Auto Theft	Rank
Metro Area Average	*6.5*	*33.5*	*177.6*	*346.1*	*781*	*2,643*	*501*	*-*
Cape Coral-Fort Myers, FL	5.8	34.3	171.2	403.5	1,020	2,529	538	275
Carson City, NV	0.4	34.2	47.1	393.6	722	2,109	213	165
Casper, WY	4.8	33.5	30.2	223.1	912	3,191	274	200
Cedar Rapids, IA	1.5	24.6	45.5	134.6	661	2,681	176	103
Champaign-Urbana, IL	2.8	63.3	96.6	478.6	910	2,085	118	239
Charleston, WV	4.9	25.0	78.1	315.6	780	2,172	322	177
Charleston-North Charleston, SC	7.9	53.3	182.2	591.4	958	3,386	584	314
Charlotte-Gastonia-Concord, NC-SC	8.0	36.8	272.0	543.4	1,303	3,567	508	365
Charlottesville, VA	4.0	34.1	59.9	244.0	401	2,008	151	58
Chattanooga, TN-GA	6.9	35.1	157.2	539.3	1,035	3,390	535	316
Cheyenne, WY	2.0	47.0	32.8	126.4	404	3,021	133	47
Chicago-Naperville-Joliet, IL	20.3	n.a.	592.2	828.5	894	3,375	868	372
Chico, CA	3.6	38.9	65.4	224.6	958	2,047	502	196
Cincinnati-Middletown, OH-KY-IN	4.6	43.9	168.7	174.9	794	2,831	325	184
Clarksville, TN-KY	5.4	45.2	81.0	361.5	814	2,915	209	214
Cleveland, TN	5.8	31.7	41.1	387.7	727	2,279	239	170
Cleveland-Elyria-Mentor, OH	5.6	49.5	235.9	200.4	749	1,845	484	176
Coeur d'Alene, ID	2.4	48.2	28.8	272.5	740	2,633	210	144
College Station-Bryan, TX	4.1	65.1	53.7	299.8	865	3,284	188	215
Colorado Springs, CO	4.8	47.5	88.0	258.3	744	2,751	309	166
Columbia, MO	3.9	19.9	80.8	238.6	499	2,679	168	97
Columbia, SC	7.2	43.9	186.8	576.8	949	3,265	435	299
Columbus, GA-AL	8.7	13.9	161.5	230.9	852	3,500	440	228
✓ Columbus, IN	2.0	13.8	16.6	99.9	375	2,899	129	28
Columbus, OH	6.7	57.5	260.4	183.2	1,362	3,689	622	337
Corpus Christi, TX	5.4	64.3	133.7	445.1	1,213	4,282	401	338
Corvallis, OR	0.5	22.0	35.4	141.2	681	2,973	182	114
Cumberland, MD-WV	1.9	28.0	32.7	299.3	610	2,037	136	110
Dallas-Plano-Irving, TX	8.1	36.3	265.2	369.9	1,087	3,298	757	318
Dalton, GA	4.8	18.8	57.8	240.3	864	2,881	344	191
Danville, IL	3.5	91.6	86.9	485.1	1,051	3,364	112	282
Danville, VA	8.6	25.5	81.3	206.0	460	1,711	173	66
Davenport-Moline-Rock Island, IA-IL	3.0	46.8	123.1	710.9	958	3,625	264	326
Dayton, OH	5.4	52.3	190.7	136.1	971	2,962	605	232
Decatur, AL	3.3	12.4	68.1	87.7	685	2,072	142	92
Decatur, IL	6.9	63.6	152.1	318.8	1,480	2,727	173	340
Deltona-Daytona Beach-Ormond Beach, FL	4.8	48.5	154.4	501.2	1,126	2,655	399	307
Denver-Aurora, CO	4.9	41.6	106.9	216.0	716	2,672	685	161
Des Moines-West Des Moines, IA	3.0	28.8	72.6	147.6	599	3,229	289	111
Detroit-Livonia-Dearborn, MI	21.2	52.8	389.2	754.9	1,058	2,637	1,571	369
Dothan, AL	7.1	38.6	90.3	188.2	747	2,265	177	133
Dover, DE	1.9	37.4	97.7	529.7	637	2,646	197	202
Dubuque, IA	1.1	26.7	12.1	192.0	541	1,655	126	62
Duluth, MN-WI	2.7	48.2	35.9	133.6	680	2,607	236	105
Durham, NC	7.9	27.9	278.6	299.1	1,413	3,806	406	353
Eau Claire, WI	0.9	18.7	15.9	101.9	475	2,255	141	41
✓ Edison, NJ	1.6	10.9	64.0	122.1	402	1,589	170	26
El Centro, CA	3.6	18.4	93.8	387.0	1,348	1,697	581	302
Elizabethtown, KY	1.9	67.6	94.4	211.1	791	2,513	94	157
Elkhart-Goshen, IN	4.8	26.4	115.2	168.6	943	3,070	352	218
Elmira, NY	2.0	30.8	44.4	213.3	415	2,314	65	53
El Paso, TX	3.0	36.2	102.0	503.8	405	3,464	330	153
Erie, PA	2.5	37.7	91.6	124.5	500	1,796	130	55
Essex County, MA	1.5	20.4	70.3	332.5	497	1,478	564	96
Eugene-Springfield, OR	1.7	32.2	81.0	177.3	903	3,747	472	219

Metro Area	Murder	Rape	Robbery	Assault	Burglary	Theft	Auto Theft	Rank
Metro Area Average	*6.5*	*33.5*	*177.6*	*346.1*	*781*	*2,643*	*501*	*-*
Evansville, IN-KY	3.6	25.0	57.9	345.8	549	2,344	187	121
Fairbanks, AK	9.1	153.7	124.5	574.7	707	3,695	591	261
✓ Fargo, ND-MN	0.7	45.3	15.4	67.7	388	2,204	190	20
Farmington, NM	4.4	81.5	47.0	482.2	659	1,997	192	167
Fayetteville, NC	9.4	28.5	211.8	325.8	1,672	3,461	359	370
Fayetteville-Springdale-Rogers, AR-MO	2.2	34.0	28.9	186.9	479	2,080	144	60
Flagstaff, AZ	2.9	49.7	55.8	380.4	785	4,318	252	234
Flint, MI	10.5	58.9	168.8	465.6	1,157	2,848	687	323
Florence, SC	8.8	46.8	163.4	753.7	1,357	3,932	406	373
Florence-Muscle Shoals, AL	2.7	16.3	39.5	143.0	570	2,074	85	73
✓ Fond du Lac, WI	0.4	15.4	9.8	47.0	280	1,978	90	3
Fort Collins-Loveland, CO	1.5	54.9	22.8	166.6	525	2,643	163	77
Fort Lauderdale-Pompano Beach, FL	4.6	29.4	180.1	366.9	792	2,711	548	231
Fort Smith, AR-OK	5.7	35.3	52.0	373.0	774	2,663	258	189
Fort Walton Beach-Crestview-Destin, FL	2.5	34.7	64.4	246.6	591	1,992	147	98
Fort Wayne, IN	6.2	34.4	145.1	100.8	703	2,876	370	132
Fort Worth-Arlington, TX	5.5	40.1	141.9	283.9	998	3,425	473	263
Fresno, CA	6.5	34.1	200.6	472.5	929	3,240	1,023	291
Gadsden, AL	6.1	31.3	74.3	446.4	817	2,701	284	225
Gainesville, FL	3.3	62.7	162.5	654.8	1,254	3,562	422	358
Gainesville, GA	6.1	33.4	56.5	221.3	662	2,506	338	127
Gary, IN	16.6	23.7	159.3	260.5	686	2,452	583	174
✓ Glens Falls, NY	1.1	22.6	12.0	221.7	413	1,580	54	34
Goldsboro, NC	7.3	12.2	119.5	367.1	1,262	2,865	286	304
Grand Forks, ND-MN	2.3	48.9	14.4	89.4	543	2,674	259	67
Grand Junction, CO	3.0	22.5	22.0	175.0	642	2,941	190	109
Grand Rapids-Wyoming, MI	2.6	49.0	95.4	317.5	784	2,337	224	183
Great Falls, MT	4.0	24.3	51.8	378.9	508	4,900	227	178
Greeley, CO	3.1	48.5	37.9	232.2	730	2,974	302	145
✓ Green Bay, WI	1.6	24.7	24.4	120.3	471	1,965	135	38
Greensboro-High Point, NC	6.9	27.4	196.4	279.5	1,243	3,253	353	309
Greenville, NC	6.4	27.0	168.0	439.9	1,606	3,706	323	371
Greenville, SC	6.6	43.1	118.3	546.2	889	2,611	278	267
Gulfport-Biloxi, MS	7.9	49.0	147.7	138.8	1,327	4,455	418	317
Hagerstown-Martinsburg, MD-WV	5.4	17.5	66.5	261.0	591	1,798	223	100
Hanford-Corcoran, CA	2.1	24.4	54.2	219.3	582	1,540	334	85
Harrisburg-Carlisle, PA	3.4	30.8	110.6	147.6	417	1,851	134	46
✓ Harrisonburg, VA	1.5	26.6	27.1	110.3	305	1,374	113	7
Hartford-West Hartford-East Hartford, CT	4.0	20.8	152.3	172.6	574	2,355	435	113
Hattiesburg, MS	8.3	40.1	121.2	93.0	1,160	3,198	261	252
Hickory-Lenoir-Morganton, NC	4.5	19.7	59.9	173.4	955	2,298	196	185
Hinesville-Fort Stewart, GA	7.8	26.0	90.5	199.5	756	2,612	164	147
✓ Holland-Grand Haven, MI	0.7	52.1	11.8	122.9	412	1,635	105	23
Honolulu, HI	2.5	30.2	111.7	129.9	841	3,721	711	201
Hot Springs, AR	5.7	27.8	102.6	347.1	1,121	3,508	299	281
Houma-Bayou Cane-Thibodaux, LA	3.5	37.1	81.6	441.0	941	3,032	230	257
Houston-Sugar Land-Baytown, TX	7.8	36.3	261.9	418.0	985	2,747	648	287
Huntington-Ashland, WV-KY-OH	3.2	27.6	79.8	190.7	786	2,658	307	156
Huntsville, AL	4.9	34.4	109.2	275.6	801	2,985	330	199
Idaho Falls, ID	2.5	41.6	9.8	175.6	505	2,205	169	64
Indianapolis-Carmel, IN	9.2	40.6	230.9	371.3	881	2,384	569	256
Iowa City, IA	1.6	41.5	40.4	321.7	491	2,003	124	86
✓ Ithaca, NY	2.5	21.7	35.6	74.8	480	2,160	37	35
Jackson, MI	4.6	63.9	68.3	331.2	723	2,566	269	168
Jackson, MS	14.7	65.7	292.0	199.5	1,515	3,258	875	356

Metro Area	Murder	Rape	Robbery	Assault	Burglary	Theft	Auto Theft	Rank
Metro Area Average	**6.5**	**33.5**	**177.6**	**346.1**	**781**	**2,643**	**501**	**-**
Jackson, TN	7.3	48.4	190.5	671.6	1,227	3,220	470	357
Jacksonville, FL	8.8	38.9	205.8	593.1	1,065	3,362	514	333
Jacksonville, NC	4.8	34.3	56.2	155.7	764	1,971	218	124
Janesville, WI	1.6	27.2	59.6	135.9	673	3,012	174	118
Jefferson City, MO	3.2	29.5	33.2	245.2	477	1,708	110	65
Johnson City, TN	3.0	25.5	52.6	331.2	736	2,699	236	172
✓ Johnstown, PA	2.5	17.7	43.5	210.4	412	1,168	123	30
Jonesboro, AR	3.7	24.3	75.0	262.6	1,012	2,796	285	235
Joplin, MO	3.5	34.0	47.2	281.0	908	3,296	311	221
Kalamazoo-Portage, MI	4.8	60.7	81.7	334.8	894	3,045	326	229
Kankakee-Bradley, IL	5.7	67.4	94.9	220.2	548	2,463	122	99
Kansas City, MO-KS	7.7	37.4	178.3	419.4	883	3,347	647	271
Kennewick-Richland-Pasco, WA	2.6	33.5	42.6	178.1	654	2,684	243	112
Killeen-Temple-Fort Hood, TX	3.8	36.5	74.5	262.1	918	2,464	201	204
Kingsport-Bristol-Bristol, TN-VA	3.7	31.0	30.9	305.9	575	1,989	164	101
✓ Kingston, NY	1.9	15.0	41.2	204.7	387	1,557	110	31
Knoxville, TN	5.5	34.9	118.7	388.1	810	2,452	391	220
Kokomo, IN	5.0	22.7	59.4	235.1	705	2,866	182	140
✓ La Crosse, WI-MN	1.8	17.6	21.3	97.5	267	2,260	114	9
Lafayette, IN	2.4	32.6	41.3	114.9	564	2,630	144	79
Lafayette, LA	4.6	47.1	102.0	450.3	922	3,155	312	262
Lake Charles, LA	5.8	52.5	142.3	414.3	1,530	3,570	333	361
Lake County-Kenosha County, IL-WI	1.2	28.4	52.4	232.7	465	2,063	182	71
Lakeland, FL	4.5	50.1	136.5	401.6	1,291	3,175	418	330
✓ Lancaster, PA	2.4	20.4	92.6	109.6	429	1,809	187	40
Lansing-East Lansing, MI	3.5	69.5	75.4	306.6	622	2,547	209	131
Laredo, TX	7.0	29.2	102.7	426.5	1,007	4,969	498	301
Las Cruces, NM	5.0	73.5	96.4	353.1	1,181	4,503	236	313
Las Vegas-Paradise, NV	10.3	45.4	295.8	318.9	993	2,203	982	277
Lawrence, KS	1.5	25.8	28.0	171.6	547	2,200	124	74
Lawton, OK	5.6	47.2	113.1	417.0	1,153	2,972	252	290
✓ Lebanon, PA	2.1	31.7	64.5	182.3	370	1,831	124	32
Lewiston, ID-WA	1.7	24.5	20.4	125.6	744	2,857	174	122
Lewiston-Auburn, ME	2.1	46.0	36.8	65.4	698	2,419	140	91
Lexington-Fayette, KY	6.7	45.5	218.5	331.6	918	3,276	287	265
Lima, OH	5.0	76.2	129.4	254.5	997	3,109	199	246
Lincoln, NE	2.2	37.0	61.4	372.3	832	4,411	212	244
Little Rock-North Little Rock, AR	9.0	42.2	165.0	386.1	1,170	4,050	436	327
✓ Logan, UT-ID	1.0	29.2	3.5	51.6	285	1,789	67	2
Longview, TX	6.8	67.8	98.5	312.4	1,047	3,251	366	266
Longview, WA	3.2	43.9	65.1	268.3	1,295	4,183	534	315
Los Angeles-Long Beach-Glendale, CA	10.7	28.1	300.9	570.0	624	1,742	696	243
Louisville-Jefferson County, KY-IN	6.6	21.5	195.3	327.3	1,015	2,769	495	270
Lubbock, TX	5.4	54.3	119.4	844.8	1,221	3,769	296	367
✓ Lynchburg, VA	4.2	28.4	43.4	143.7	352	1,528	147	18
Macon, GA	10.3	33.4	158.5	252.5	1,494	4,166	762	352
Madera, CA	7.0	35.4	120.0	446.2	922	1,799	566	247
Madison, WI	1.5	25.7	71.6	129.8	487	2,397	199	68
✓ Manchester-Nashua, NH	1.5	31.2	64.7	58.1	394	1,635	199	16
Mansfield, OH	3.9	40.1	84.7	46.7	1,047	3,287	193	209
McAllen-Edinburg-Mission, TX	6.3	23.2	91.0	374.6	1,246	3,776	419	321
Medford, OR	1.6	27.2	34.1	197.8	609	3,329	222	119
Memphis, TN-MS-AR	14.5	59.3	403.7	574.9	1,722	3,426	928	379
Merced, CA	5.5	31.8	95.3	523.2	1,119	2,425	499	295
Miami-Miami Beach-Kendall, FL	9.1	37.6	324.8	649.0	1,029	3,859	796	355

Metro Area	Murder	Rape	Robbery	Assault	Burglary	Theft	Auto Theft	Rank
Metro Area Average	*6.5*	*33.5*	*177.6*	*346.1*	*781*	*2,643*	*501*	*-*
Michigan City-La Porte, IN	4.3	30.1	79.5	137.3	744	3,243	421	146
Midland, TX	2.8	60.8	54.5	297.6	781	2,301	175	163
Milwaukee-Waukesha-West Allis, WI	8.4	26.7	227.7	181.1	621	2,930	573	160
Minneapolis-St. Paul-Bloomington, MN-WI	3.0	43.8	120.0	177.9	582	2,788	357	117
Missoula, MT	2.7	59.1	60.4	296.7	576	5,006	203	180
Mobile, AL	11.8	36.1	275.3	284.1	1,543	3,806	518	366
Modesto, CA	5.1	38.5	135.5	464.8	1,009	3,206	792	289
Monroe, LA	7.3	43.4	92.3	577.5	1,174	3,715	284	334
Monroe, MI	2.9	52.2	33.2	183.0	627	1,886	237	89
Montgomery, AL	10.6	49.2	225.1	300.7	1,402	3,935	526	350
Morgantown, WV	1.1	21.2	27.8	249.0	532	1,583	157	75
Morristown, TN	5.2	25.2	42.4	358.2	756	2,437	300	179
Mount Vernon-Anacortes, WA	2.7	49.0	39.6	81.4	1,090	4,687	332	248
Muncie, IN	1.1	49.3	60.3	170.0	572	2,428	202	90
Muskegon-Norton Shores, MI	2.8	70.4	93.3	386.3	849	3,715	514	250
Myrtle Beach-Conway-North Myrtle Beach, SC	9.1	70.4	196.8	736.7	1,484	5,393	666	378
Napa, CA	1.6	26.2	37.6	209.7	429	1,661	202	44
Naples-Marco Island, FL	3.8	39.6	97.5	418.4	886	2,286	216	230
Nashville-Davidson--Murfreesboro, TN	6.5	47.6	192.7	655.4	900	3,275	504	312
✓ Nassau-Suffolk, NY	2.1	10.2	82.8	135.8	305	1,450	221	14
Newark-Union, NJ-PA	6.8	17.7	256.6	242.3	574	1,677	761	142
New Haven-Milford, CT	3.5	26.0	166.1	225.7	666	2,705	448	159
New Orleans-Metairie-Kenner, LA	21.5	33.2	271.0	413.6	896	3,060	894	284
New York-White Plains-Wayne, NY-NJ	11.5	17.5	311.1	385.1	421	1,654	384	138
Niles-Benton Harbor, MI	5.4	71.1	53.5	365.7	793	2,625	256	192
Norwich-New London, CT	3.0	59.1	105.8	202.5	547	2,182	206	94
Oakland-Fremont-Hayward, CA	7.2	30.1	221.2	324.0	731	2,665	777	223
Ocala, FL	4.7	55.4	93.1	616.3	984	2,299	215	278
Ocean City, NJ	1.8	33.1	77.3	227.0	865	3,462	144	205
Odessa, TX	3.4	20.2	69.5	436.1	988	3,743	220	274
Ogden-Clearfield, UT	2.6	38.1	37.4	140.6	588	2,710	221	87
Oklahoma City, OK	5.8	53.9	126.3	357.8	1,141	4,078	450	306
Olympia, WA	1.7	52.6	47.5	172.5	841	2,599	277	154
Omaha-Council Bluffs, NE-IA	5.1	37.4	137.4	351.9	691	3,429	687	217
Orlando-Kissimmee, FL	4.8	42.8	193.5	619.9	1,187	3,362	549	349
✓ Oshkosh-Neenah, WI	0.4	18.0	12.6	101.6	319	2,094	82	11
Owensboro, KY	2.0	20.4	57.1	125.6	727	2,481	137	115
Oxnard-Thousand Oaks-Ventura, CA	3.3	17.5	86.0	162.0	444	1,389	191	43
Palm Bay-Melbourne-Titusville, FL	3.7	47.3	113.4	590.7	922	2,670	259	276
Panama City-Lynn Haven, FL	5.0	70.0	108.1	482.7	1,054	3,808	249	296
Parkersburg-Marietta-Vienna, WV-OH	1.7	43.2	16.9	175.1	482	1,496	131	42
Pascagoula, MS	7.4	52.2	130.0	321.9	1,441	3,158	348	339
Pensacola-Ferry Pass-Brent, FL	4.0	45.4	116.3	439.0	903	2,377	193	242
Peoria, IL	4.9	n.a.	1008.3	358.6	776	2,229	246	346
Philadelphia, PA	9.6	36.7	303.8	374.6	493	2,129	534	175
Phoenix-Mesa-Scottsdale, AZ	8.6	29.0	176.5	343.6	1,137	3,579	1,157	320
Pine Bluff, AR	12.1	58.6	213.7	634.7	1,497	3,106	434	374
Pittsburgh, PA	4.5	22.9	117.6	209.5	432	1,681	263	69
Pittsfield, MA	1.3	30.6	28.6	314.0	509	1,340	179	78
Pocatello, ID	1.2	30.9	13.9	243.4	427	2,403	116	63
✓ Portland-South Portland-Biddeford, ME	1.0	28.4	28.7	61.3	519	2,024	114	39
Portland-Vancouver-Beaverton, OR-WA	2.3	42.4	110.6	259.3	766	3,472	540	203
Port St. Lucie-Fort Pierce, FL	6.2	34.5	130.3	449.3	945	2,438	249	258
✓ Poughkeepsie-Newburgh-Middletown, NY	3.0	18.4	70.0	184.2	362	1,690	106	29
Prescott, AZ	5.0	17.9	25.8	353.7	864	2,761	259	211

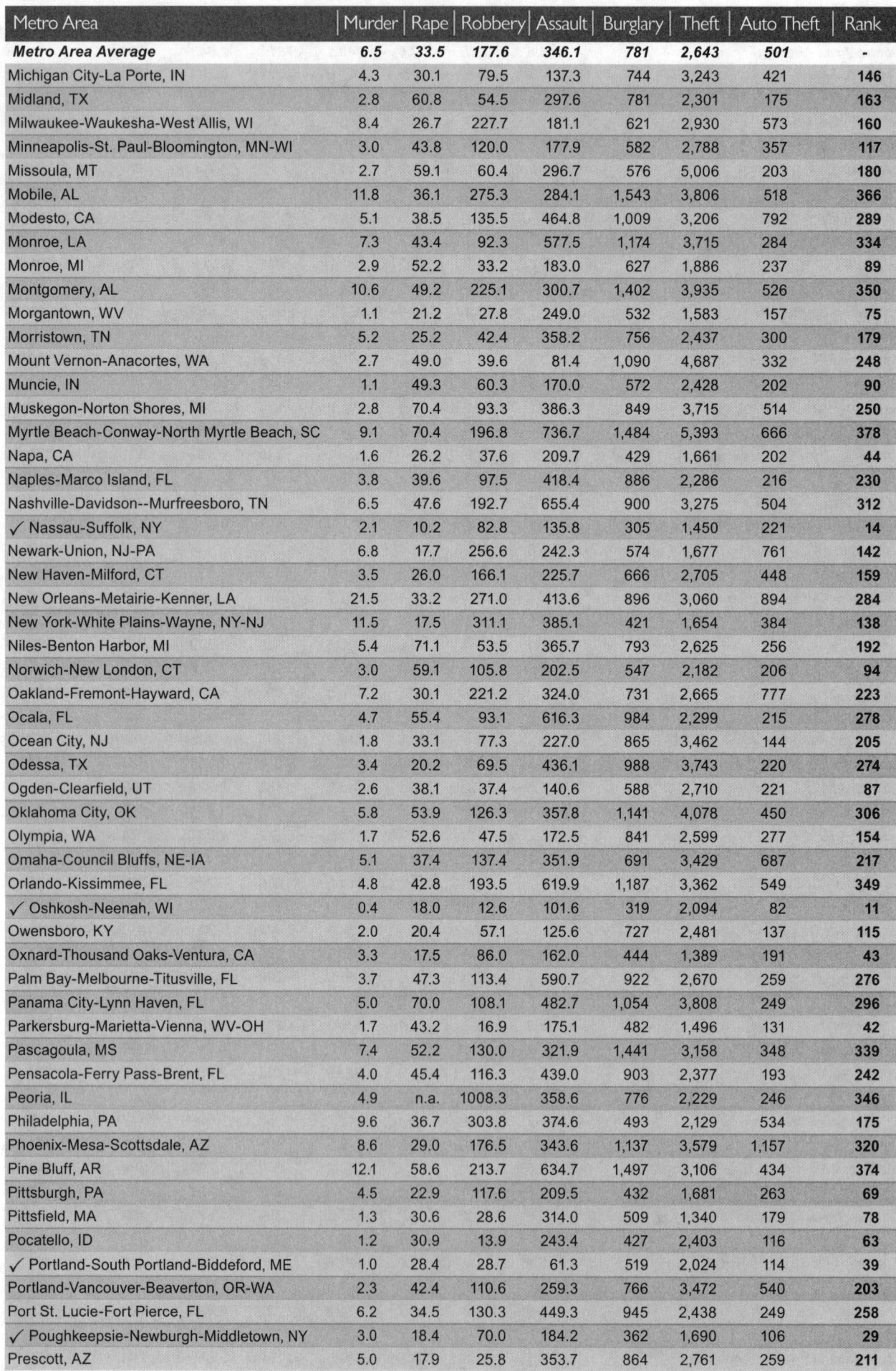

Metro Area	Murder	Rape	Robbery	Assault	Burglary	Theft	Auto Theft	Rank
Metro Area Average	*6.5*	*33.5*	*177.6*	*346.1*	*781*	*2,643*	*501*	*-*
Providence-New Bedford-Fall River, RI-MA	3.1	38.4	89.4	243.9	614	2,022	409	116
Provo-Orem, UT	0.7	28.0	13.5	63.3	542	2,726	179	56
Pueblo, CO	4.6	42.6	110.4	482.6	915	3,287	267	269
Punta Gorda, FL	2.2	14.7	30.3	199.1	660	1,775	176	95
Racine, WI	2.6	15.7	145.4	119.2	714	2,707	308	134
Raleigh-Cary, NC	4.1	20.5	135.3	242.8	1,009	2,715	301	238
Rapid City, SD	2.8	98.5	33.3	174.5	635	3,314	194	120
Reading, PA	6.7	23.5	159.3	214.2	626	1,936	302	125
Redding, CA	3.6	62.6	56.0	358.0	783	1,780	319	171
Reno-Sparks, NV	4.3	47.7	147.8	290.6	773	3,010	415	210
Richmond, VA	11.7	28.8	173.8	219.2	651	2,780	413	158
Riverside-San Bernardino-Ontario, CA	6.9	30.3	149.9	387.3	891	1,956	657	236
Roanoke, VA	4.8	29.6	64.0	228.5	366	2,087	184	49
✓ Rochester, MN	1.6	38.1	32.6	111.8	403	1,782	154	25
Rochester, NY	4.9	19.5	119.0	110.3	527	2,498	353	84
Rockford, IL	7.0	n.a.	246.2	449.2	1,699	5,278	620	377
✓ Rockingham County-Strafford County, NH	1.2	43.5	22.3	75.7	313	1,513	150	5
Rocky Mount, NC	9.7	21.4	188.2	310.2	1,442	3,386	269	343
Rome, GA	5.0	16.3	81.1	488.9	932	3,216	288	268
Sacramento--Arden-Arcade--Roseville, CA	5.1	33.4	164.0	315.6	845	2,419	754	227
Saginaw-Saginaw Township North, MI	7.7	71.9	126.6	680.0	898	2,803	316	288
✓ St. Cloud, MN	2.6	46.4	21.6	90.9	315	2,039	152	10
✓ St. George, UT	1.1	40.2	4.6	146.9	356	1,555	131	12
St. Joseph, MO-KS	0.9	21.1	45.4	168.3	766	3,300	227	150
St. Louis, MO-IL	7.8	19.1	191.3	386.6	751	3,264	677	241
Salem, OR	2.2	37.8	65.1	140.2	806	4,240	571	190
Salinas, CA	6.7	33.6	153.0	340.8	585	2,078	330	143
Salisbury, MD	3.8	46.0	159.7	623.7	1,007	2,700	209	300
Salt Lake City, UT	3.5	49.0	96.4	217.5	837	4,383	505	226
San Angelo, TX	2.1	72.8	45.6	287.5	1,005	3,944	191	254
San Antonio, TX	6.7	39.7	123.2	393.6	964	4,345	395	279
San Diego-Carlsbad-San Marcos, CA	3.6	28.5	118.2	342.0	591	1,796	675	136
Sandusky, OH	2.3	27.3	52.3	166.9	707	3,072	148	128
San Francisco-San Mateo-Redwood City, CA	4.9	24.3	239.3	249.8	571	2,389	525	152
San Jose-Sunnyvale-Santa Clara, CA	2.3	28.8	68.5	303.7	369	1,706	276	61
San Luis Obispo-Paso Robles, CA	1.9	34.4	26.7	212.4	573	1,881	173	82
Santa Ana-Anaheim-Irvine, CA	2.4	16.4	98.9	176.2	443	1,630	367	57
Santa Barbara-Santa Maria, CA	2.0	30.6	59.9	251.3	463	1,653	149	70
Santa Cruz-Watsonville, CA	3.4	38.5	81.8	330.3	631	2,497	213	141
Santa Fe, NM	5.8	54.1	57.0	478.7	1,721	1,850	326	363
Santa Rosa-Petaluma, CA	2.6	38.7	54.8	235.6	607	2,040	255	102
Sarasota-Bradenton-Venice, FL	3.9	33.2	132.4	471.0	1,053	2,966	303	285
Savannah, GA	14.1	32.7	281.7	333.9	1,103	3,608	682	324
✓ Scranton--Wilkes-Barre, PA	3.0	22.8	57.9	162.9	381	1,566	167	27
Seattle-Bellevue-Everett, WA	3.3	42.7	127.9	200.9	829	3,222	930	216
Sebastian-Vero Beach, FL	3.9	52.2	57.3	293.9	864	2,723	191	194
✓ Sheboygan, WI	1.1	27.5	14.4	65.2	367	2,336	114	15
Sherman-Denison, TX	2.7	22.0	61.0	220.9	837	2,972	224	182
Shreveport-Bossier City, LA	13.8	45.7	192.6	558.5	1,318	4,013	461	364
Sioux City, IA-NE-SD	2.6	49.2	44.6	330.9	898	3,007	285	222
Sioux Falls, SD	1.5	59.1	27.7	160.6	491	1,955	151	51
South Bend-Mishawaka, IN-MI	7.2	43.1	155.8	197.5	1,063	3,545	366	264
Spartanburg, SC	6.5	39.9	161.0	645.8	990	3,244	400	322
Spokane, WA	3.5	33.0	120.5	277.9	1,172	4,007	516	294
Springfield, IL	5.4	n.a.	149.7	715.5	1,114	3,419	243	344

Metro Area	Murder	Rape	Robbery	Assault	Burglary	Theft	Auto Theft	Rank
Metro Area Average	*6.5*	*33.5*	*177.6*	*346.1*	*781*	*2,643*	*501*	*-*
Springfield, MA	3.3	47.3	130.5	699.6	948	2,169	505	**293**
Springfield, MO	2.6	28.6	63.9	259.3	831	3,273	296	**193**
Springfield, OH	4.3	58.6	176.8	266.1	1,248	3,508	398	**310**
✓ State College, PA	2.4	27.5	13.4	85.7	290	1,871	60	**6**
Stockton, CA	8.4	37.9	236.0	573.0	978	3,272	844	**328**
Sumter, SC	7.4	41.0	221.0	712.4	1,539	2,724	550	**376**
Syracuse, NY	3.6	17.3	99.6	210.8	616	2,041	208	**107**
Tacoma, WA	4.0	49.8	163.7	373.9	1,096	3,638	859	**303**
Tallahassee, FL	4.2	72.2	179.8	651.8	1,275	3,347	384	**359**
Tampa-St. Petersburg-Clearwater, FL	5.2	47.7	220.8	620.8	1,130	3,282	643	**347**
Terre Haute, IN	5.2	30.5	88.8	285.3	1,367	4,507	441	**336**
Texarkana, TX-Texarkana, AR	7.0	43.9	92.7	445.7	894	3,087	262	**255**
Toledo, OH	3.6	38.2	219.6	270.4	1,180	3,614	605	**311**
Topeka, KS	9.0	46.4	196.2	372.0	1,294	4,603	422	**348**
Trenton-Ewing, NJ	4.7	25.2	243.3	258.6	714	2,097	526	**188**
Tucson, AZ	8.2	47.5	192.7	403.3	1,040	4,723	955	**329**
Tulsa, OK	6.4	43.8	111.7	497.8	1,038	2,690	532	**283**
Tuscaloosa, AL	7.5	48.8	148.6	469.6	1,155	4,364	319	**332**
Tyler, TX	6.0	55.5	94.8	385.7	986	3,103	294	**260**
Utica-Rome, NY	3.0	29.4	74.6	169.2	548	1,790	103	**76**
Valdosta, GA	4.9	30.3	82.1	326.5	711	2,782	196	**173**
Vallejo-Fairfield, CA	4.1	31.5	169.0	375.5	687	2,458	525	**198**
Victoria, TX	10.2	51.2	82.3	389.1	947	2,966	201	**251**
Vineland-Millville-Bridgeton, NJ	4.9	35.3	252.1	436.0	1,095	2,716	288	**305**
Virginia Beach-Norfolk-Newport News, VA-NC	7.3	34.0	174.7	239.0	645	2,900	373	**162**
Visalia-Porterville, CA	6.7	32.7	89.2	514.9	1,084	2,407	568	**286**
Waco, TX	7.3	59.7	130.5	373.2	1,242	4,074	473	**331**
Warner Robins, GA	4.4	22.1	86.7	224.1	863	3,296	265	**206**
Warren-Troy-Farmington Hills, MI	1.8	33.8	52.1	214.3	419	1,779	308	**50**
Washington-Arlington, DC-VA-MD-WV	10.7	23.2	226.6	301.3	504	2,460	704	**151**
Waterloo-Cedar Falls, IA	2.0	35.5	56.4	203.4	854	2,437	196	**164**
✓ Wausau, WI	1.3	18.9	17.0	91.5	423	1,630	101	**19**
✓ Weirton-Steubenville, WV-OH	1.9	19.4	47.0	190.8	334	1,262	110	**17**
Wenatchee, WA	2.4	42.7	28.7	122.6	821	3,304	204	**148**
West Palm Beach-Boca Raton, FL	4.8	40.7	218.3	490.4	1,291	3,721	674	**354**
✓ Wheeling, WV-OH	2.9	20.0	21.5	94.0	323	1,043	102	**4**
Wichita, KS	5.3	46.7	137.5	308.7	972	3,475	368	**259**
Wichita Falls, TX	5.0	32.2	132.9	431.1	1,106	3,482	365	**298**
✓ Williamsport, PA	1.3	17.6	60.3	93.6	473	1,646	117	**33**
Wilmington, DE-MD-NJ	3.4	25.1	183.9	388.4	689	2,486	433	**208**
Wilmington, NC	4.9	32.2	156.5	272.7	1,676	3,271	401	**362**
Winchester, VA-WV	3.8	30.0	32.3	127.7	486	2,085	157	**48**
Winston-Salem, NC	5.4	39.1	174.4	390.7	1,322	3,444	349	**341**
Worcester, MA	2.0	34.9	71.8	394.8	511	1,543	278	**106**
Yakima, WA	4.9	52.0	75.1	152.7	1,457	3,814	566	**325**
✓ York-Hanover, PA	1.5	20.8	39.0	134.4	319	1,819	112	**13**
Youngstown-Warren-Boardman, OH-PA	9.2	27.3	130.3	240.5	889	2,068	336	**195**
Yuba City, CA	4.9	39.3	71.9	336.0	1,014	2,199	548	**240**
Yuma, AZ	2.6	24.6	39.4	439.6	740	2,160	384	**187**

NATIONAL AND REGIONAL CRIME

Although criminal activity varies from place to place and from year to year, regional patterns haven't changed much since the FBI first began rounding up annual statistics in the 1930s from county sheriffs and police department chiefs.

The murder rate in the Southeast, where the frequency of people killing one another has traditionally been the country's highest, is nearly three times that of New England. Armed robbery, a big-city crime, is highest in the Mid-Atlantic states and lowest out in the Plains.

But the Mid-Atlantic states together see the lowest theft rate; meanwhile, thanks to Texas, the Southwest experiences the highest. One more disparity: auto theft is highest in the thriving Pacific coast and lowest on the lagging Plains.

Criminologists recognize the geographic pattern of crime-ridden places immediately. The continent's more dangerous places are located on the East Coast south of Delaware Bay. This area is growing, and the resulting conditions of strangers living close together are strongly associated with crime.

There are other reasons for high crime in this area. Professional crooks travel to where the living is easy and the pickings bountiful; they don't stay in the industrial towns of the North but head South to warm weather and popular resorts. This is one factor behind Miami's decades-old crime image.

Finally, most of the more dangerous places are hot much of the year. Knowing what we do about climate's influence on crime, it isn't surprising that large southern cities going through a steamy summer are America's most violent. Persons bidding farewell to Cedar Rapids, Milwaukee, Pittsburgh, or Syracuse to make their new homes in Palm Beach, Orlando, Phoenix, or Las Vegas may need time not only for acclimatizing to warm weather but also for getting used to crime's share in the local evening news.

DRUNK DRIVING

By the end of this year, 1.6 million people will have been arrested for DUI/DWI. Drunk driving is the most common single cause of arrest in the United States, and the penalties for the crime have gotten more severe. Most states and all provinces in Canada mandate license suspensions for first offenses and license revocations and jail terms for repeat offenses. Three other ways of controlling the drunk driver come by means of legislation.

Blood-Alcohol Exceptions

The American Medical Association (AMA) says that anyone with a blood alcohol (BAC) level of 0.05 percent is too drunk to drive. Above that threshold, the probability of a crash rises dramatically. Since 2002, a uniform 0.08 standard has been in force in every state. Canadian federal law sets the threshold at 0.08 percent, but most of the provinces have gone further, lowering it to 0.05 percent. Countries reported to have limited blood alcohol concentration to 0.00 percent are the Czech Republic, Croatia, Hungary, Japan, Malaysia, Romania, and Saudi Arabia.

Some states also include a lesser charge—known as *driving while impaired*—at a BAC of around 0.05 percent. In all states, drivers under the drinking age of 21 have committed a drunk driving offence if they have any alcohol in their blood (set at 0.01 percent or 0.02 percent in most states, 0.00 percent in nine states).

Open Container and Anti-Consumption Laws

Presumably in Connecticut and Mississippi, you can reach into a cooler on the front seat of your car, pop the top of a premixed can of Daiquiri and sip it as you continue on your way. Thirty-four states prohibit the possession of any open alcoholic beverage container and the consumption of any alcoholic beverage in the passenger area of a motor vehicle. Since every state has laws to prevent and punish impaired driving, police consider open container laws to be an important tool in their crusade against impaired driving.

Dram Shop Laws

All but seven states allow the last person and establishment to serve a drink to an intoxicated patron to be held responsible for the patron's actions immediately afterward. Victims of drunk drivers may sue not just the driver but also the bar owner, bartender, or party host who served the driver.

HANDGUNS

Handgun control isn't a subject to be lightly entered into in conversation unless you have the time and are ready for a prolonged discussion. On talk radio, the controversy continues. Changes in regulations occur frequently from state to state and even from city to city.

The National Rifle Association, the fiercest defender of gun enthusiasts, attempts to keep its members informed of regulation changes with a regular publication of state-by-state gun purchase and carrying laws, but even this comes with a disclaimer warning of the constant changes. The variations in different states' restrictions can be immense, reflecting how well those who vehemently defend their weapons and those who would take them away have done their jobs in state legislatures.

In Georgia and South Carolina, for example, there are few constraints. You can walk into a store,

buy a pistol, and walk out. There's not even a record of the sale. In Illinois, on the other hand, a prospective gun buyer has to apply for a permit, and then wait 30 days for a check of criminal records. A gun must then be registered and the sale reported. However, carrying a handgun, either openly or concealed, is unlawful in the state. You may store it at home or business, or broken and unloaded in a car.

In Chicago, the same rules apply, but only to guns purchased before a new law went into effect that prohibits any newly purchased handgun from being brought into the city. In the suburbs of Evanston, Oak Park, and Morton Grove, there are no handguns at all; they're prohibited.

Most of the states fall somewhere between these extremes, but the penalties for not knowing the law or for violating the law can be severe. Massachusetts, for example, has a law requiring a mandatory 1-year jail term for anyone caught with an unlicensed gun.

STATE RESTRICTIONS ON BUYING AND CARRYING HANDGUNS

State	Sale Reported to State	PURCHASE OF HANDGUNS			PROHIBITED		
		Waiting Period (Days)	Permit to Purchase	Owner ID Card	Open Carry	Assault Weapons	Concealed Carry
ALABAMA	●	2			●		
ALASKA							
ARIZONA							
ARKANSAS					●		
CALIFORNIA	●	10			●	●	L
COLORADO							L
CONNECTICUT	●	14	●		●	●	
DELAWARE							L
DISTRICT OF COLUMBIA	●		●	●	●	●	X
FLORIDA		3			●		
GEORGIA					●		
HAWAII	●		●		●	●	L
IDAHO							
ILLINOIS	●	3	●	●	●		X
INDIANA	●				●		
IOWA	●		●		●		L
KANSAS							X
KENTUCKY							
LOUISIANA							
MAINE							
MARYLAND	●	7			●	●	L
MASSACHUSETTS	●	7	●	●	●	●	L
MICHIGAN	●		●		●		L
MINNESOTA	●	7	●		●		L
MISSISSIPPI							
MISSOURI	●	7	●				X
MONTANA							
NEBRASKA			●				X

Happy Hour Prohibitions

A new form of server responsibility law means that drinking establishments cannot encourage excessive or immoderate consumption. Prohibitions against bars advertising a Happy Hour, selling two drinks for the price of one, or changing their prices at any time during the day make up the law in 21 states.

STATE	Lower BAC for Youth	Open Container Prohibited	Anti-Consumption	Happy Hours Prohibited	Dram Shop Law
ALABAMA	0.02%	●		●	●
ALASKA	0.00%		●	●	●
ARIZONA	0.00%	●	●	●	●
ARKANSAS	0.02%		●		●
CALIFORNIA	0.01%	●	●		
COLORADO	0.02%		●		●
CONNECTICUT	0.02%				●
DELAWARE	0.02%		●		
DIST. OF COLUMBIA	0.00%	●	●		●
FLORIDA	0.02%	●	●		●
GEORGIA	0.02%	●	●		●
HAWAII	0.02%	●	●	●	●
IDAHO	0.02%	●	●		●
ILLINOIS	0.00%	●	●	●	●
INDIANA	0.02%	●	●	●	●
IOWA	0.02%	●	●		●
KANSAS	0.02%	●	●	●	
KENTUCKY	0.02%	●	●		●
LOUISIANA	0.02%		●	●	●
MAINE	0.00%	●	●	●	●
MARYLAND	0.02%	●	●		
MASSACHUSETTS	0.02%	●		●	●
MICHIGAN	0.02%	●	●	●	●
MINNESOTA	0.00%	●	●		●
MISSISSIPPI	0.02%				●
MISSOURI	0.02%		●		●
MONTANA	0.02%	●			●
NEBRASKA	0.02%	●	●	●	
NEVADA	0.02%	●	●		
NEW HAMPSHIRE	0.02%	●			●
NEW JERSEY	0.01%	●	●	●	●
NEW MEXICO	0.02%	●	●		●
NEW YORK	0.02%	●	●		●
NORTH CAROLINA	0.00%	●	●	●	●
NORTH DAKOTA	0.02%	●	●		●
OHIO	0.02%	●	●	●	●
OKLAHOMA	0.00%	●	●	●	●
OREGON	0.00%	●	●		●
PENNSYLVANIA	0.02%	●	●		●
RHODE ISLAND	0.02%	●		●	●
SOUTH CAROLINA	0.02%	●	●	●	●
SOUTH DAKOTA	0.02%	●	●		
TENNESSEE	0.02%		●		●
TEXAS	0.00%	●	●	●	●
UTAH	0.00%	●	●	●	●
VERMONT	0.02%	●	●		●
VIRGINIA	0.02%		●	●	
WASHINGTON	0.02%	●	●		●
WEST VIRGINIA	0.02%		●		●
WISCONSIN	0.00%	●	●		●
WYOMING	0.02%		●		●

STATE RESTRICTIONS ON BUYING AND CARRYING HANDGUNS (CONT.)

State	Sale Reported to State	PURCHASE OF HANDGUNS			PROHIBITED		
		Waiting Period (Days)	Permit to Purchase	Owner ID Card	Open Carry	Assault Weapons	Concealed Carry
NEVADA							
NEW HAMPSHIRE	●						
NEW JERSEY	●		●	●	●	●	L
NEW MEXICO							X
NEW YORK	●		●	●	●		L
NORTH CAROLINA	●		●				
NORTH DAKOTA	●				●		
OHIO							X
OKLAHOMA					●		
OREGON	●						
PENNSYLVANIA	●	2			●		
RHODE ISLAND	●	7			●		L
SOUTH CAROLINA	●				●		
SOUTH DAKOTA	●	2			●		
TENNESSEE	●				●		
TEXAS					●		
UTAH							
VERMONT					●		
VIRGINIA						●	
WASHINGTON	●	5			●		
WEST VIRGINIA							
WISCONSIN	●	2					X
WYOMING							

Key: X-Regulation Applies; X-Action Prohibited L-Limited Restrictions
Source: National Rifle Association

REGIONAL CRIME RATES

	Murder	Rape	Robbery	Assault	Burglary	Theft	Auto Theft
United States Average	5.7	32.3	142.5	295.4	741.0	2,416.5	433.7
New England: CT, ME, MA NH, RI, VT	2.4	26.5	93.3	203.5	493.0	1,702.8	287.8
Middle Atlantic: NJ, NY, PA	4.8	21.0	161.3	226.6	412.0	1,649.3	253.6
Great Lakes: IL, IN MI, OH, WI	5.2	37.6	134.3	234.8	658.9	2,229.5	356.8
Plains: IA, KS, MN MO, NE, ND, SD	3.6	33.6	75.8	229.5	617.2	2,441.3	306.1
South Atlantic: DE, DC, FL GA, MD, NC, SC, VA, WV	6.5	30.9	155.4	372.4	869.3	2,603.1	421.8
East South Central: AL, KY MS, TN	6.1	36.4	118.2	291.7	906.4	2,453.1	317.1
West South Central: AR, LA OK, TX	6.9	38.2	143.8	357.3	994.0	3,021.9	400.3
Mountain: AZ, CO, ID MT, NV, NM, UT, WY	5.4	39.1	102.1	290.5	818.5	2,833.9	619.7
Pacific: AK, CA, HI OR, WA	5.8	30.8	150.8	311.6	737.7	2,312.0	683.1

Source: FBI, *Crime in the United States*

Transportation

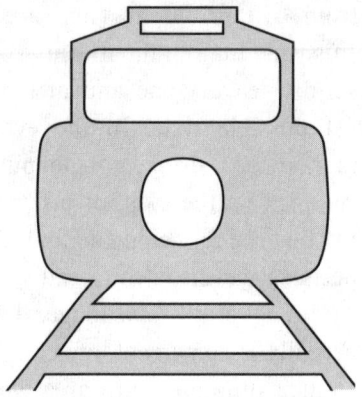

I f you travel often enough, you might take for granted all the expressway networks, airline routes, and passenger rails that lace up America's different cities. But spreading out a map would show you certain metro areas are transportation hubs with highway, rail, and air-route spokes, while others appear as lesser intersections, removed from the mainstream of inter-city travel.

Population size has something to do with an area's transportation assets, but so does the luck of geography and the accidents of culture. There are twenty-one metro areas bigger than Denver, but because the Mile-High City is plunked down at the edge of the Rocky Mountains halfway between Chicago and Los Angeles, and midway from Houston to Seattle, only five other airports in North America are busier than DEN, Denver International Airport. Las Vegas is smaller than thirty-seven other metro areas, but McCarran International Airport (LAS) south of the city is even busier than DEN, thanks to mainly to vacations and conventions.

Inter-city travel is only part of the picture. Some metro areas have clean and efficient public transit fleets relied on by hundreds of thousands of commuters each working day. In other metro areas, aging diesel buses with optimistic schedules lurch along routes that rarely reach any neighborhoods except those close to downtown. Still other metro areas have no public transit at all.

If you are moving to Atlanta, might your family get by without a second car if MARTA's routes reach your new neighborhood? If you are being transferred to company headquarters in downtown Cleveland, will it be more convenient to carpool or ride the RTA rails if you settle in Shaker Heights? How much time should you expect to spend each day getting to and from work? Becoming familiar with the local transportation features of a particular metro area will help you answer some of these questions.

THE SPRAWL AND CRAWL LIFE

Each weekday morning, in cities and towns all over, traffic trickles out of suburban streets, flows into arterial roads and floods freeways to capacity with people bound for work. The morning rush hour lasts 118 minutes, between 7:01 and 8:59am, transportation experts say. Most workers drive alone. One of five belongs to a car pool, and just one of fifteen boards public transit.

The evening rush hour lasts longer: 150 minutes, from 4:30 to 7:00pm. There are more traffic delays at this time than in the morning when people so purposefully leave home and arrive at work in the shortest possible time. In the evening, many commuters stop for a drink, go shopping at a mall, run errands, pick up the kids, or just dawdle. After all, you can't be fired for being late for supper. In fact, traffic experts say, even if you head straight home, the evening trip not only seems longer than the trip to work but actually is 20 percent longer.

How much time do metro-area workers spend going to and from the job each day? To allow for the longer trip home in the evening, *Places Rated* multiplies the average journey-to-work figure by 2.2 to estimate the round-trip time in each of the metro areas.

Daily commuting time increases with city size. Workers in Grand Forks, ND, for instance, putting in 220 working days a year, spend about 117 hours commuting. Workers from Staten Island spend 355 hours taking the ferry to and from their Manhattan jobs. So the contrast between Bismarck and Staten Island is more than one between a prairie state capital and a borough in the North America's largest city. Based on commuting time alone, Grand Forks workers have more free time than Staten Island workers, the equivalent of six 40-hour weeks each year.

PUBLIC TRANSIT

One reason for the long commute in big cities is the often exhausting job of making linked transit trips to get to work. The average duration of an unlinked transit trip—a direct route, with no transfers—is about 15 minutes. But many big-city commuters have to make *linked* trips: driving to a park-and-ride or kiss-and-ride lot; boarding a train, ferry, or bus; and sometimes switching again before finally getting to work.

Still, in larger cities where the tab for daily parking in a downtown garage nears $50, where rush-hour traffic approaches gridlock, and where distances are long and time always seems short, public transit really counts. In many a large city—Houston and Phoenix, for example—daily driving over long distances is a way of life unrelieved by rapid public transit; taking the bus is the only alternative. In other places, such as Atlanta, Washington, and San Francisco, large local bus fleets are complemented by rapid transit rail systems.

Depending on where they want to go, New York City commuters can choose from bus, heavy rail, light rail, commuter railroad, ferryboat, and even aerial tramway service. New York straphangers may not always enjoy their subway ride to work, but few among the jostled riders aboard a rocking, grimy subway car would ever envy a Houston driver who has missed his exit off Loop 610 at rush hour.

By Bus

In most cities, public transit is simply a roaring fleet of diesel-powered buses. Unlike rapid rail and trolley networks, a bus system requires no expensive construction, routes are easily changed to meet demand and cities can buy the service from private contractors.

The typical transit bus has front and center doors, low-back seating and no luggage racks or restrooms. The most common buses are 40-foot Orion, New Flyer, or Gillig vehicles designed for frequent stopping. Transit buses are powered by rear-mounted diesel or compressed natural gas engines.

Each of the country's 1,500 transit systems with fixed-route service puts buses on the street, but these systems vary in size and operation. Several large systems—Chicago's CTA, Washington's WMATA, and New York's NYCTA, for example—operate thousands around the clock with less than 2 minutes' wait between buses on the heaviest routes during morning and evening rush hours. At the other extreme are the one- and two-bus shoppers' specials that run loops in the central business district of smaller metro areas.

By Commuter Railroads

Since the 19th century, locomotive-hauled and self-propelled passenger cars have been an important form of transportation between distant suburbs to the downtowns of major cities. The service is marked by multi-trip tickets, station-to-station fares, railroad employment practices, and usually only one or two

stations in the central business district.

A typical passenger trip covers 24 miles at over 32 miles per hour. Twenty-four commuter railroads in fifteen metro areas ferry nearly 1.5 million commuters to and from work. The largest commuter railroad network, made up of seven firms, is found in the huge New York–New Jersey urbanized area and uses 3,200 cars to move 525,000 riders in a typical weekday. In Chicago, the next largest commuter railroad center, nine carriers operating 850 cars transport 300,000 workers in a typical day. New commuter railroads are under construction in Albuquerque, Boston, Salt Lake City, and Seattle.

By Heavy Rail

Known in local vernacular as metros, subways, rapid rail, elevated rail, or Els, these systems have high-level platform stations. The cars are individually powered through the third rail, and are hitched together to form longer trains during rush hours. Thanks to their exclusive rights-of-way, they are unaffected by traffic jams. Their trains and trams carry thousands of people quickly. The average speed of buses during peak rush hour, nationwide, is 13 miles per hour. Rapid rail systems average more than 22 miles per hour.

New York City's heavy rail system, composed of two separate networks, is the world's largest, with 6,248 cars traveling more than 450 miles of track. Philadelphia also has two systems. Sixteen other metro areas have heavy rail systems.

By Light Rail

In 1978, Edmonton, Alberta, imported a *Siemens–Duewag U2* system from Germany to create North America's first light rail transit system. Within three years, Calgary and San Diego followed with their own systems. Because tracks are laid above ground, light rail is less expensive to build and consequently is the fastest-growing form of mass transit. The lines include multi-car trains that can only be accessed at stations spaced from a few blocks to a mile or more apart. Some systems operate within roadways alongside automobile traffic, and others operate on their own separate right-of-way.

By Trolley Coach

Trolleys, or trolleybuses, are rubber-tired buses powered by overhead electric wires running on city streets with semiprivate or exclusive rights-of-way. They are a less efficient form of travel than rapid rail and are at the

Light Rail: A Desire Named Streetcar

Light Rail is a term invented in 1978 by American transit specialists to describe how a British-like tram or American-like trolley system could be reinvented for the new century. Three decades later, the transit mode is found in 22 cities, and in 26 other cities light rail lines are proposed or are in planning.

Future Light Rail Cities

Albuquerque, NM

Atlanta, GA

Austin, TX

Birmingham, AL

Cincinnati, OH

Columbus, OH

Fort Lauderdale, FL

Honolulu, HI

Indianapolis, IN

Kansas City, KS

Las Vegas, NV

Louisville, KY

Madison, WI

Memphis, TN

Milwaukee, WI

Minneapolis, MN

New York, NY

Norfolk, VA

Orange County, CA

Orlando, FL

Rochester, NY

San Antonio, TX

Spokane, WA

Tampa, FL

Tucson, AZ

Washington, DC

Source: lightrailnow.com

219

Getting to Work and Back

For thousands of years, the longest any city dweller had for a morning commute was 45 minutes. From ancient Athens and Rome to medieval Paris and London, that was the amount of time it took to walk the 3 miles from the edge of a typical large city to its center. According to a recent Census Bureau survey: What are the most minutes most persons will put up with commuting? Forty-five minutes.

Shortest Commutes
(minutes and seconds)

Grand Forks, ND-MN	31:51
Dubuque, IA	32:44
Great Falls, MT	33:44
Bismarck, ND	33:51
Fargo, ND-MN	34:21
Lewiston, ID-WA	34:27
Cheyenne, WY	34:39
Waterloo-Cedar Falls, IA	34:55
Casper, WY	35:29
Ames, IA	35:58
Sheboygan, WI	36:01
St. George, UT	36:02
Bloomington-Normal, IL	36:08
Lawton, OK	36:25
Logan, UT-ID	36:27
Pocatello, ID	36:39

Harvard professor Robert Putnam, author of *Bowling Alone: The Collapse and Revival of American Community*, estimates that, for every 10 additional minutes of commuting time, your social connections get cut by 10%.

Longest Commutes
(hours, minutes, and seconds)

New York-White Plains, NY-NJ	1:19:23
Nassau-Suffolk, NY	1:10:36
Washington, DC-VA-MD	1:09:53
Edison, NJ	1:09:22
Bethesda-Gaithersburg, MD	1:08:28
Bremerton-Silverdale, WA	1:08:13
Oakland-Fremont-Hayward, CA	1:08:08
Vallejo-Fairfield, CA	1:07:40
Chicago-Naperville-Joliet, IL	1:07:34
Poughkeepsie-Newburgh, NY	1:06:47
Atlanta-Sandy Springs, GA	1:06:20
Newark-Union, NJ-PA	1:06:18
Riverside-San Bernardino, CA	1:05:59
Boston-Quincy, MA	1:04:36
Miami-Miami Beach-Kendall, FL	1:04:30

Source: Bureau of the Census. Figures are average "Journey-to-Work" minutes multiplied by 2.2 for a round-trip total.

mercy of automobile traffic and, in some cities, even have to stop for traffic lights. Another disadvantage is that their routes cannot be altered. During the 1940s, nearly one hundred urban trolley coach systems ran in the United States. They have been largely replaced by buses. Today, only six metro areas still have trolley coach operations: Boston, Cambridge, Dayton, Philadelphia, San Francisco, and Seattle.

INTERSTATE HIGHWAYS

"You can't get there from here" is the punch line of the old joke about the lost city sharper who asked directions of a bemused farmer. The line has little meaning in today's metropolitan areas, given the networks of well-traveled highways that connect them.

Or does it? Obviously, you can't ramp onto the Interstate in the Lower 48 if your destination is Anchorage or Honolulu. For that matter, you can't get to Bakersfield, Bend, Bloomington, or Bremerton by the same means. When it comes to inter-city travel options, some metro areas are better off than others.

Back in 1938, when President Franklin Roosevelt idly penciled three east-west and five north-south lines on a U.S. map as part of a proposed national highway system, he had no idea that his drawing would become so important in determining whether some towns would grow and others would decline. He was thinking originally of a 34,000-mile network of multilane toll roads.

Although the Bureau of Public Roads soon dropped the concept of collecting tolls, the basic routes on Roosevelt's map foresaw the Interstate Highway System, a river of economic life to cities and towns along the way and possibly a cause of stagnation for those that were bypassed.

The Interstate System is a complete 46,700-mile road network, at least four traffic lanes wide, linking nearly every American city with a population of more than 50,000. Even though interstate routes account for only 1 percent of all road and street mileage in the United States, they carry 25 percent of all the traffic. Yet one in six U.S. metro areas isn't on the network.

AIRPORTS

It's getting to be a tired old saying in the South that when you die and are en route to heaven or hell, you'll have to make connections in Atlanta. For years,

Decoding the Interstate

The numbers in the middle of the red, white, and blue shield-shaped signs along the interstate system were developed in 1957 by American Association of State Highway Transportation officials. There are 35 odd-numbered routes running north and south and 27 even-numbered routes running east and west. The lowest-numbered routes are in the West and the South; I-5, for example, lies along the nation's West Coast and I-10 runs along the southern border.

In cities, these one- or two-digit numbers don't change as long as they are part of the major traffic stream. Beltways around the city, on the other hand, carry three numbers; the main route number with an even-numbered prefix. For example, I-495, an 88-mile long route around Boston, and I-287, a 94-mile long loop skirting New York City, are the two longest beltways in the interstate system. If a main route carries an odd-numbered prefix (such as I-195 in Miami or I-780 in San Francisco), the route is a spur that connects with the main route at only one end.

Three-digit route numbers are never used twice in the same state. In New York, I-90 runs through Schenectady, Syracuse, Rochester, and Buffalo, and the beltways off this main route in those cities are numbered, respectively, I-890, I-690, I-490 and I-290. This rule isn't carried across state lines, however. Two cities on I-10 but in different states, Houston and New Orleans, have the identical beltway number of I-610.

Empty and Congested Interstates

According to the Federal Highway Administration, the busiest stretches on the interstate carry 300,000 to 600,000 vehicles every 24 hours. The loneliest carry fewer than 2,500.

Busiest Stretches

I-5, I-20, I-405 and I-605 in Los Angeles
I-5 in Seattle
I-10, I-45, I-59 and I-610 in Houston
I-25 in Denver
I-35E and I-635 in Dallas
I-75 in Atlanta
I-80 and I-580 in Oakland
I-80 and I-380 in San Francisco
I-90 and I-94, I-290 in Chicago
I-95 in New York
I-280 in San Jose
I-395 in Washington, DC

Loneliest Stretches

I-15 Idaho Falls, ID to Butte, MT

I-25 Buffalo to Casper, WY

I-29 Grand Forks, ND, and Canada

I-29 Sioux Falls, SD, to Fargo, ND

I-70 Cove Fort, UT, to Colorado border

I-90 Buffalo to Gillette, WY

I-91 Derby Line to St. Johnsbury, VT

I-94 between Billings, MT, and North Dakota

Heavy Interstate Traffic

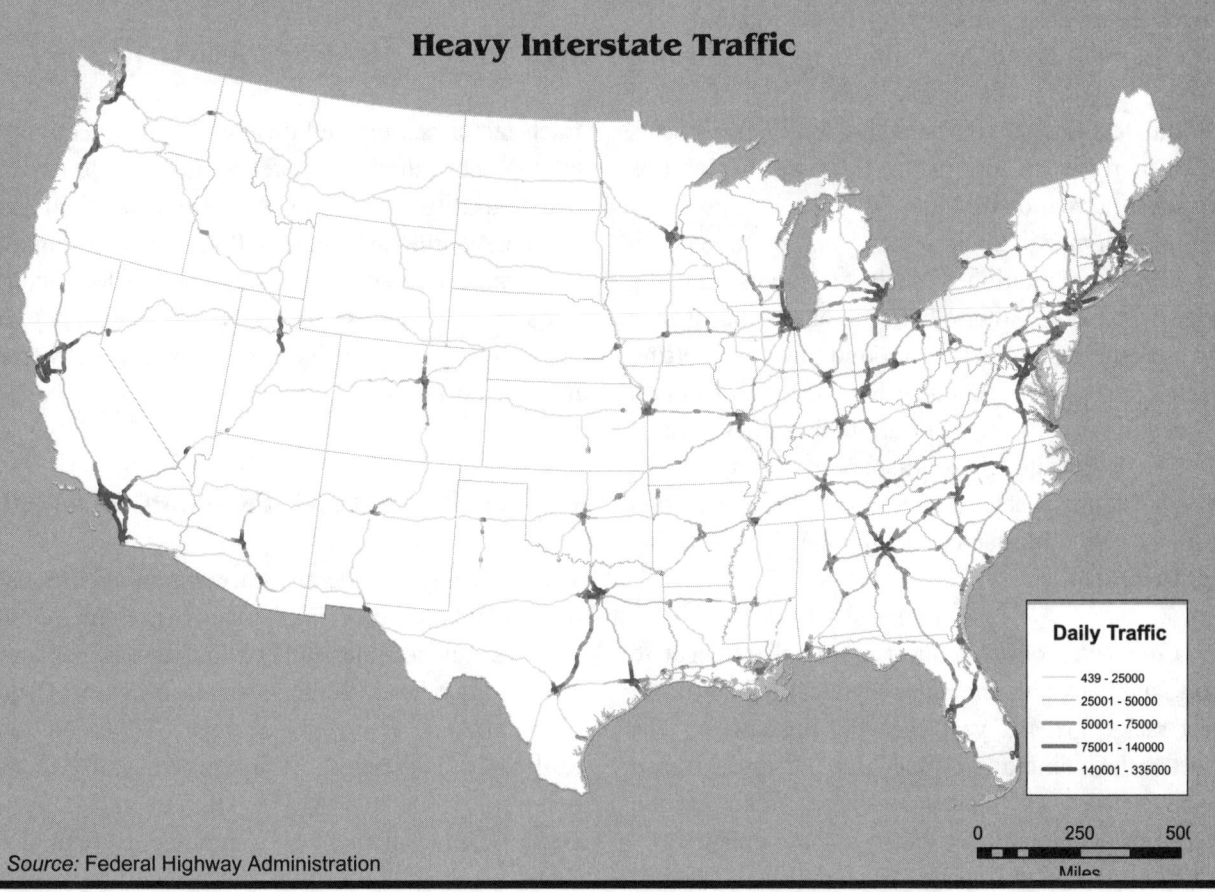

Daily Traffic

439 - 25000
25001 - 50000
50001 - 75000
75001 - 140000
140001 - 335000

0   250   50(

Miles

Source: Federal Highway Administration

Hartsfield–Jackson Atlanta International has been the world's busiest airport.

Like other airports reached by scheduled airlines Hartsfield is a 21st-century urban landmark in the same way the railroad station was a sign of the times in the late 19th century. Most of the 296 airports served by major airlines in the United States and Canada are quiet even desolate places.

But some resemble self-contained cities with 24-hour restaurants, health clubs, chapels, a weekly newspaper, free Internet connection, daycare, and office-based physicians and dentists. Of the nearly 700 million people who board domestic flights, one in ten travels between thirty of these airports in the continent's large hubs. Both Hartsfield–Jackson airport and Chicago's O'Hare International airport board more passengers than the 200 smallest airport combined.

JUDGING: TRANSPORTATION

Would a shopper in Syracuse or San Angelo have a better chance of finding a seat on a bus? Which airport—Phoenix's or Denver's—has departures to more nonstop destinations? Which metro area at opposite ends of the nation, Seattle or New York, is nearer the greatest number of other metro areas?

Transportation, let's admit, means differing things to the first 100 people walking out of Grand Central Terminal or to passengers finding their seats between rows 25 and 15 on a United 737 at Los Angeles International.

For some, it takes in the waiting time for a subway, the sanitation of seats and floors, and the price of a ticket. Fine, others might say, but it also includes the ease of getting around town and getting around the rest of the country. Do you have to make a connection every time you want to fly somewhere?

To reconcile these disparate views, *Places Rated* groups each metro area's transportation features into three factors: Commute, Connectivity, and Centrality.

• *Commute* considers the time it takes to get to work and back plus the miles the local public transit fleet racks up each year carrying passengers. The shorter the commuting time and the more transit revenue miles, the better. Both get equal weight. Winners include smaller metro areas dominated by a major university: Eugene OR; Lafayette, IN; State

College, PA; Ithaca, NY; Ames, IA. Losers are small southern metro areas without public transit.

• *Connectivity* combines Interstate Highways, passenger rail departures, and nonstop airline destinations. Passenger rail departures get the least weight. Except in dense urban corridors, riding the rails plays no part in inter-city travel. National highways get more weight, but are counted only if a metro area is a junction of more than one. A metro area's nonstop commuter, domestic jet, and international airline destinations are weighted equally. Connectivity winners are New York, Chicago, and Los Angeles.

• *Centrality* measures how near a metro area is to all other metro areas. Quick: In America, which two airports ship the most freight each year? Answer: Louisville's Standiford Field and Memphis International. Not for nothing is one the hub for United Parcel Service and the other for FedEx. Both airports are near a geographic point where every other metro area airport is nearest. Centrality winners include Louisville and Memphis, and Chicago, Cincinnati and Indianapolis as well. Losers are Anchorage, Fairbanks, Honolulu, Seattle.

SCORING: TRANSPORTATION

Each factor is weighted differently—connectivity is 60 percent of the final score, commute is 30 percent, and centrality, 10 percent. A metro area's final score is its percentile on a scale of 0 to 100 corresponding to its rank. Chicago's final score is 100.00, Victoria, TX's is 50.00; and Camden, NJ's is 0.00. They are, respectively, the best, average, and worst metro areas for transportation.

PLACE PROFILES: TRANSPORTATION

The following pages detail local commuting time, mass transit, and inter-city travel assets in each metro area. Sources include American Public Transit Association, *Transit Fact Book*, 2006; Jane's Information Group, *Jane's Urban Transport Systems*, 2006; National Railroad Passenger Corporation, *AMTRAK's America*, 2006, and AMTRAK Timetable, Spring 2006; U.S. Department of Commerce, Bureau of the Census, unpublished 2000 Census journey-to-work

minutes; U.S. Department of Transportation, Federal Aviation Administration, unpublished Form 41 T-100 nonstop destination data for commuter, domestic jet and international carriers, quarter ending May 2006; Federal Highway Administration, *Highway Statistics*, latest, and unpublished "Interstate System Log and Finder List," 2006; and Federal Transit Administration, *National Transit Database for 2004*, 2005.

• The first entry, ***Daily commute***, is the average minutes and seconds metro area workers spend getting to and from the job, regardless of the mode of transportation. These figures are derived from a metro area's total *journey-to work minutes* divided by the number of workers who do not work at home. The result is multiplied by 2.2 to represent a round-trip whose return half takes slightly longer than the first half.

• The next entry, ***Peak freeway traffic***, uses a term—Congested, Very Heavy, Heavy, Moderate, Light, or None—that a TV traffic reporter aboard a helicopter might use to describe traffic at rush hour. The terms are derived from the Federal Highway Administration's latest Highway Performance Monitoring System figures for each urban area. HOV, or High-Occupancy Vehicle, indicates the presence of *carpool lanes* or *diamond lanes* restricted during rush hours to vehicles with a driver and one or more passengers.

• Next to the heading ***Public transit*** is the name of the local transit agency (or the name of the largest agency if there is more than one). Next to the heading is the VOMS, or "vehicles operated in maximum service" in industry jargon, from all local agencies on the street at rush hour.

• A major part of a metro area's freeways is the heavily traveled routes of the country's ***Interstate highway***s. These highways are inter-city travel assets, too. Accordingly, each main route in the system that reaches the metro area is listed.

• Next to the heading ***Airline service*** is the FAA's hub classification for the metro area: Large Hub, Medium Hub, Small Hub, or Nonhub. The airport's name comes next. Thanks to local boosterism, airports like the ones in Great Falls, Montana and Midland, Texas have the word international in their names, but

Hubs and Hubs

Airports aren't hubs, but metro areas are - according to the Federal Aviation Administration (FAA) which rates each metro area for its share of airline service.

A metro area is a . . .	If passengers departing its airports total . . .
Large Hub	1% or more
Medium Hub	0.25% to 0.99%
Small Hub	0.05% to 0.24%
Nonhub	less than 0.005%

. . . of all U.S. airline passengers in a year.

Metro areas aren't hubs, but airports are – according to the airlines. An aiport is a hub if an airline uses it as a transfer point to get passengers to another destination. Some big airlines have fortress hubs: Airports dominated by a single airline which might fly 70 percent of an airport's traffic. Examples include Northwest Airlines hub in Minneapolis-Saint Paul, Delta Air Lines hub in Atlanta, and American Airlines hub in Dallas/Fort Worth.

Major Airline Hubs

Alaska Airlines
Seattle-Tacoma International (SEA)
Portland International (PDX)
Ted Stevens Anchorage International (ANC)

American Airlines
Dallas-Fort Worth International (DFW)
Chicago O'Hare International (ORD)
Lambert-St. Louis International (STL)
Miami International (MIA)

Continental Airlines
Newark Liberty International (EWR)
George Bush Houston Intercontinental (IAH)
Cleveland Hopkins International (CLE)

Delta Air Lines
Hartsfield-Jackson Atlanta International (ATL)
Cincinnati-Northern Kentucky International (CVG)
Salt Lake City International (SLC)
New York Kennedy International (JFK)

Midwest Airlines
Milwaukee Mitchell International (MKE)
Kansas City International (MCI).

Northwest Airlines
Minneapolis-Saint Paul International (MSP)
Detroit Metropolitan Wayne County (DTW)
Memphis International (MEM)

United Airlines
O'Hare International (ORD)
San Francisco International (SFO)
Washington Dulles International (IAD)
Denver International (DEN)
Los Angeles International (LAX)

US Airways
Charlotte/Douglas International (CLT)
Philadelphia International (PHL)
Phoenix Sky Harbor International (PHX)
Las Vegas's McCarran International (LAS)

www.placesrated.com

Transportation rankings, from 1 to 379, are in the *Place Profiles* section coming next. Transportation scores, from 100.0 to 0.0, are in Putting It All Together at the end of the book. Readers can view and print out these rankings and scores, from #1 Chicago-Naperville-Joliet, IL (score: 100.0) to #379 Camden, NJ (score: 0.0), by visiting *Places Rated*'s website.

Here are the top twenty:

Rank	Score
1. Chicago-Naperville-Joliet, IL	100.0
2. Milwaukee-Waukesha-West Allis, WI	99.7
3. Dallas-Plano-Irving, TX	99.4
4. Terre Haute, IN	99.2
5. Minneapolis-St. Paul, MN-WI	98.9
6. Houston-Sugar Land-Baytown, TX	98.6
7. Madison, WI	98.4
8. Atlanta-Sandy Springs-Marietta, GA	98.1
9. Reno-Sparks, NV	97.8
10. Cincinnati-Middletown, OH-KY-IN	97.6
11. Fort Worth-Arlington, TX	97.3
12. Lubbock, TX	97.0
13. St. Louis, MO-IL	96.8
14. Cleveland-Elyria-Mentor, OH	96.5
15. New York-White Plains-Wayne, NY-NJ	96.2
16. Washington-Arlington, DC-VA-MD-WV	96.0
17. Davenport-Moline-Rock Island, IA-IL	95.7
18. Kansas City, MO-KS	95.5
19. Springfield, IL	95.2
20. Detroit-Livonia-Dearborn, MI	94.9

At *www.placesrated.com* you'll also find more information on commuting, public transit, and air travel as well as useful links to transportation websites.

offer no customs and immigration services for aircraft arriving from abroad—the practical definition of an international airport.

Next to the airport's name is its three-letter identifier enclosed in parentheses. Every scheduled-service airport in the world has a unique identifier. When Baltimore's Friendship Airport (BAL) changed its name to Baltimore-Washington International, it could not get the identifier BWI until Bewani, a small airfield in the Papua New Guinea bush, agreed to take another identifier (BWP).

After the airport's identifier comes its distance and direction from the central business district. For instance, "3 miles N" means the airport is 3 miles north of downtown. Such distances range from 1 mile between downtown Boston or Cheyenne and their airports to more than 30 miles from downtown Denver to the new Denver International out east on the plains.

Below the airport's name are the number of nonstop jet destinations with more than 1,000 outbound passengers per year and the top destination by passengers emplaned. A similar listing is given for commuter airline (aircraft with fewer than sixty seats) destinations and for international airline destinations.

For areas that neither have airports nor share them, the location of the nearest airport is given along with its distance and direction.

A check mark (✓) preceding a metro area's name highlights it as one of America's top forty areas for transportation assets.

Abilene, TX

Daily commute: 37:34
Peak freeway traffic: ....Light

Public transit: .... *CityLink*
Service: .... 21 city buses, 1,087 miles/day

Interstate highway: I-20

Airline service: .... Nonhub
Airport: .... Abilene Regional (ABI) 3 miles SE

Service	Passengers	Carriers	Cities	Top Market
Commuter	37,937	3	2	Dallas (DFW)
Jet	41,351	2	1	Dallas (DFW)

Places Rated Rank: 159

Akron, OH

Daily commute: 49:23
Peak freeway traffic: .... Heavy

Public transit: .... *METRO*
Service: .... 169 city buses, 10,216 miles/day

Interstate highways: I-76, I-77

Airline service: .... Small Hub
Airport: .... Akron-Canton Regional (CAK) 10 miles SE

Service	Passengers	Carriers	Cities	Top Market
Commuter	40,832	1	1	Detroit
Jet	664,027	9	13	Atlanta

Places Rated Rank: 111

Albany, GA

Daily commute: 44:31
Peak freeway traffic: .... Moderate

Public transit: .... *ATS*
Service: ....7 city buses, 1,484 miles/day

Airline service: .... Nonhub
Airport: ... Southwest Georgia Regional (ABY) 3 miles SW

Service	Passengers	Carriers	Cities	Top Market
Jet	38,449	1	1	Atlanta

Places Rated Rank: 205

Albany-Schenectady-Troy, NY

Daily commute: 48:22
Peak freeway traffic: .... Heavy

Public transit: .... *CDTA*
Service: .... 194 city buses, 20,181 miles/day

AMTRAK corridor rail: .... Empire Service

Interstate highways: I-87, I-88, I-90

Airline service: .... Small Hub
Airport: .... Albany Int'l (ALB) 6 miles NW

Service	Passengers	Carriers	Cities	Top Market
Commuter	66,077	7	11	Buffalo
Jet	1,461,455	20	18	Baltimore
International	5,536	3	1	Toronto

Places Rated Rank: 53

Albuquerque, NM

Daily commute: 48:51
Peak freeway traffic: .... Heavy

Public transit: .... *SunTran*
Service: .... 134 city buses, 11,948 miles/day

Railrunner commuter rail to Belen

Interstate highways: I-25, I-40

Airline service: .... Medium Hub
Airport .... Albuquerque Int'l Sunport (ABQ) 3 miles SE

Service	Passengers	Carriers	Cities	Top Market
Commuter	31,292	2	6	Roswell
Jet	3,387,237	16	30	Phoenix

Places Rated Rank: 78

Alexandria, LA

Daily commute: 54:38
Peak freeway traffic: .... Light

Public transit: .... *ATRANS*
Service: ....8 city buses, 1,149 miles/day

Interstate highway: I-49

Airline service: .... Nonhub
Airport: .... Alexandria Int'l (AEX) 3 miles W

Service	Passengers	Carriers	Cities	Top Market
Commuter	31,168	2	2	Memphis
Jet	88,372	2	3	Houston

Places Rated Rank: 215

Allentown-Bethlehem-Easton, PA-NJ

Daily commute: 53:33
Peak freeway traffic: .... Heavy

Public transit: .... *LANTA*
Service: ....56 city buses, 7,645 miles/day

Interstate highways: I-476, I-78

Airline service: .... Small Hub
Airport: .... Lehigh Valley Int'l (ABE) 3 miles NE

Service	Passengers	Carriers	Cities	Top Market
Commuter	67,467	10	6	Washington (IAD)
Jet	300,791	13	12	Atlanta
International	5,171	1	1	Toronto

Places Rated Rank: 193

Altoona, PA

Daily commute: 43:22
Peak freeway traffic: .... Light

Public transit: .... *AMTRAN*
Service: ....27 city buses, 1,557 miles/day

Interstate highway: I-99

Airline service: .... Nonhub
Airport: .... Altoona-Blair County (AOO) 12 miles S

Service	Passengers	Carriers	Cities	Top Market
Commuter	6,721	1	2	Pittsburgh

Places Rated Rank: 234

Amarillo, TX

Daily commute: 39:41
Peak freeway traffic: .... Moderate

Public transit: .... *ACT*
Service: ....12 city buses, 1,860 miles/day

Interstate highways: I-27, I-40

✈ Airline service: .... Small Hub
✈ Airport: ....Rick Husband Amarillo Int'l (AMA) 6 miles E

Service	Passengers	Carriers	Cities	Top Market
Commuter	10,677	1	1	Denver
Jet	437,497	5	6	Dallas (DAL)

Places Rated Rank: 100

Ames, IA

🚗 Daily commute: 35:58
Peak freeway traffic:.. Light

🚌 Public transit: .... CyRide
Service:............................54 city buses, 3,033 miles/day

🛡 Interstate highway: I-35

✈ Nearest airport: ....Des Moines (DSM) 30 miles S

Places Rated Rank: 152

Anchorage, AK

🚗 Daily commute: 47:59
Peak freeway traffic:... Moderate

🚌 Public transit: .... People Mover
Service:............................46 city buses, 6,322 miles/day

🚂 Alaska RR service to Fairbanks

🛡 Interstate highways:................................. A-1, A-3, A-4

✈ Airline service:... Medium Hub
✈ Airport: ...Ted Stevens Anchorage Int'l (ANC) 4 miles SW

Service	Passengers	Carriers	Cities	Top Market
Commuter	287,931	6	19	Kenai
Jet	2,249,436	20	37	Seattle
International	364,473	13	9	Toronto

Places Rated Rank: 69

Anderson, IN

🚗 Daily commute: 49:55
Peak freeway traffic:... None

🚌 Public transit:... CATS
Service:..................................7 city buses, 728 miles/day

🛡 Interstate highway: I-89

✈ Nearest airport: .... Indianapolis (IND) 45 miles SE

Places Rated Rank: 315

Anderson, SC

🚗 Daily commute: 51:13
Peak freeway traffic:... Moderate

🚌 Public transit:.................................... Electric City Transit

🛡 Interstate highway: I-85

✈ Nearest airport: ....Greenville (GSP) 30 miles NE

Places Rated Rank: 368

Ann Arbor, MI

🚗 Daily commute: 47:00
Peak freeway traffic:....................................... Very Heavy

🚌 Public transit: .... AATA
Service:..........................87 city buses, 12,638 miles/day

🛡 Interstate highways:...................................... I-94, I-96

✈ Nearest airport: .... Detroit (DTW) 25 miles E

Places Rated Rank: 210

Anniston-Oxford, AL

🚗 Daily commute: 50:43
Peak freeway traffic:... Moderate

🛡 Interstate highway: I-20

✈ Nearest airport: .... Birmingham (BHM) 45 miles W

Places Rated Rank: 361

Appleton, WI

🚗 Daily commute: 38:56
Peak freeway traffic:.. Heavy

🚌 Public transit:.. Valley Transit
Service:..............................27 city buses, 2,442 miles/day

✈ Airline service: .... Nonhub
✈ Airport: .... Outagamie County Regional (ATW) 3 miles W

Service	Passengers	Carriers	Cities	Top Market
Commuter	29,309	2	3	Minneapolis
Jet	267,499	9	9	Chicago

Places Rated Rank: 95

Asheville, NC

🚗 Daily commute: 46:50
Peak freeway traffic:.. Heavy

🚌 Public transit:.. Asheville Transit
Service:..............................16 city buses, 2,359 miles/day

🛡 Interstate highways:..................................... I-26, I-40

✈ Airline service: .... Nonhub
✈ Airport: ....Asheville Regional (AVL) 9 miles S

Service	Passengers	Carriers	Cities	Top Market
Commuter	107,134	4	2	Atlanta
Jet	206,697	7	9	Charlotte

Places Rated Rank: 147

Athens-Clarke County, GA

🚗 Daily commute: 46:55
Peak freeway traffic:... Moderate

🚌 Public transit:............................... Athens Transit System
Service:............................... 19 city buses, 2,088 miles/day

🚂 GDOT commuter rail to Atlanta (proposed)

✈ Airline service:.. Nonhub
✈ Airport: ....Athens Ben Epps Field (AHN) 3 miles E

Service	Passengers	Carriers	Cities	Top Market
Commuter	6,848	1	1	Charlotte

Places Rated Rank: 246

✓Atlanta-Sandy Springs-Marietta, GA

🚗 Daily commute: 1:06:20
Peak freeway traffic:...................................... Congested
HOV lanes, certain routes

🚌 Public transit: .... MARTA
Service:........................804 city buses, 182,166 miles/day
184 heavy rail, 13,150 miles/day

🚂 GDOT commuter rail to Athens (proposed)

🛡 Interstate highways:............................... I-20, I-75, I-85

✈ Airline service: .... Large Hub
Airport: ... Hartsfield-Jackson Atlanta Int'l (ATL) 7 miles S

Service	Passengers	Carriers	Cities	Top Market
Commuter	616,984	2	17	Panama City
Jet	41,305,035	36	223	Orlando
International	3,007,707	15	51	Paris

Places Rated Rank: 8

Atlantic City, NJ

🚗 Daily commute: 51:04
Peak freeway traffic: .... Heavy

🚌 Public transit: .... *NJ TRANSIT*
Service: .... 115 city buses, 3,400 miles/day

🛤 NJ TRANSIT commuter rail to Philadelphia

✈ Airline service: .... Small Hub
Airport: .... Atlantic City Int'l (ACY) 9 miles NW

Service	Passengers	Carriers	Cities	Top Market
Jet	387,430	2	8	Orlando

Places Rated Rank: 227

Auburn-Opelika, AL

🚗 Daily commute: 44:27
Peak freeway traffic: .... Heavy

🚌 Public transit: .... *LETA*
Service: .... 3 city buses, 513 miles/day

🛡 Interstate highway: I-85

✈ Nearest airport: Columbus, GA (CSG) 25 miles E

Places Rated Rank: 284

Augusta-Richmond County, GA-SC

🚗 Daily commute: 52:08
Peak freeway traffic: .... Moderate

🚌 Public transit: .... *Augusta Public transit*
Service: .... 22 city buses, 1,915 miles/day

🛡 Interstate highway: I-20

✈ Airline service: .... Nonhub
Airport: .... Augusta Bush Field (AGS) 6 miles S

Service	Passengers	Carriers	Cities	Top Market
Commuter	138,729	3	2	Atlanta
Jet	19,202	2	1	Atlanta

Places Rated Rank: 230

✓Austin-Round Rock, TX

🚗 Daily commute: 54:08
Peak freeway traffic: .... Very Heavy

🚌 Public transit: .... *Capital Metro*
Service: .... 325 city buses, 32,955 miles/day

🛤 ASA commuter rail to San Antonio (proposed)

🛡 Interstate highway: I-35

✈ Airline service: .... Medium Hub
Airport: .... Austin Bergstrom Int'l (AUS) 3 miles NE

Service	Passengers	Carriers	Cities	Top Market
Jet	3,810,649	20	36	Dallas (DFW)

Places Rated Rank: 21

Bakersfield, CA

🚗 Daily commute: 49:45
Peak freeway traffic: .... Heavy

🚌 Public transit: .... *Golden Empire Transit*
Service: .... 65 city buses, 10,026 miles/day

🛤 AMTRAK corridor rail: .... San Joaquins

✈ Airline service: .... Nonhub
Airport: .... Meadows Field (BFL) 3 miles NW

Service	Passengers	Carriers	Cities	Top Market
Commuter	47,188	1	2	Los Angeles
Jet	95,839	3	4	Phoenix

Places Rated Rank: 195

✓Baltimore-Towson, MD

🚗 Daily commute: 1:03:25
Peak freeway traffic: .... Congested

🚌 Public transit: .... *MTA*
Service: .... 54 heavy rail, 2,779 miles/day
813 city buses, 62,392 miles/day
49 light rail, 3,354 miles/day

🛤 MARC commuter rail to Washington, DC
AMTRAK corridor rail: .... Acela Express

🛡 Interstate highways: I-70, I-83, I-95, I-97

✈ Airline service: .... Large Hub
Airport: ... Baltimore-Washington Thurgood Marshall Int'l (BWI)

Service	Passengers	Carriers	Cities	Top Market
Commuter	125,113	6	8	New York
Jet	10,023,164	27	68	Atlanta
International	227,620	11	9	London

Places Rated Rank: 39

Bangor, ME

🚗 Daily commute: 43:53
Peak freeway traffic: .... Moderate

🚌 Public transit: .... *BAT*
Service: .... 12 city buses, 1,490 miles/day

🛡 Interstate highway: I-95

✈ Airline service: .... Nonhub
Airport: .... Bangor Int'l (BGR) 3 miles W

Service	Passengers	Carriers	Cities	Top Market
Jet	240,062	9	8	Boston

Places Rated Rank: 139

Barnstable Town, MA

🚗 Daily commute: 50:11
Peak freeway traffic: .... Moderate

🚌 Public transit: .... *Cape Cod RTA*
Service: .... 20 city buses, 2,245 miles/day

✈ Airline service: .... Nonhub
Airport: .... Barnstable Municipal Field (HYA) 1 miles N

Service	Passengers	Carriers	Cities	Top Market
Commuter	114,961	2	4	Nantucket

Places Rated Rank: 261

Baton Rouge, LA

🚗 Daily commute: 55:02
Peak freeway traffic: .... Heavy

Public transit: .... *CATS*
Service:................................ 71 city buses, 8,712 miles/day

Interstate highways:... I-10, I-12

Airline service:... Small Hub
Airport: ....Baton Rouge Metropolitan (BTR) 4 miles N

Service	Passengers	Carriers	Cities	Top Market
Jet	510,099	13	14	Atlanta

Places Rated Rank: 155

Battle Creek, MI

Daily commute: 42:55
Peak freeway traffic:.. Heavy

Public transit: .... *BCT*
Service: .... 10 city buses, 1,379 miles/day

Interstate highway: I-94

Nearest airport: .... Kalamazoo (AZO) 30 miles W

Places Rated Rank: 232

Bay City, MI

Daily commute: 46:37
Peak freeway traffic:... Light

Public transit: .... *Bay Metro*
Service: .... 32 city buses, 2,124 miles/day

Interstate highway: I-75

Nearest airport: .... Saginaw (MBS) 20 miles S

Places Rated Rank: 273

Beaumont-Port Arthur, TX

Daily commute: 47:30
Peak freeway traffic:.. Heavy

Public transit: .... *BMT & PAT*
Service:.............................18 city buses, 2,066 miles/day

Interstate highway: I-10

Airline service:... Nonhub
Airport: ..... Southeast Texas Regional (BPT) 10 miles SE

Service	Passengers	Carriers	Cities	Top Market
Commuter	25,950	2	1	Houston
Jet	21,316	2	2	Houston

Places Rated Rank: 208

Bellingham, WA

Daily commute: 43:24
Peak freeway traffic:.. Heavy

Public transit: .... *Whatcom TA*
Service:.............................33 city buses, 3,882 miles/day

AMTRAK corridor rail:................................... Cascades

Interstate highway: I-5

Airline service:... Nonhub
Airport: ....Bellingham Int'l (BLI) 4 miles NW

Service	Passengers	Carriers	Cities	Top Market
Commuter	69,838	2	2	Seattle
Jet	26,247	1	1	Las Vegas

Places Rated Rank: 173

Bend, OR

Daily commute: 38:31
Peak freeway traffic:... None

Airline service:... Nonhub
Airport: .... Roberts Field (RDM) 17 miles N

Service	Passengers	Carriers	Cities	Top Market
Commuter	155,153	2	3	Portland
Jet	24,491	1	1	Salt Lake City

Places Rated Rank: 209

Bethesda-Gaithersburg-Frederick, MD

Daily commute: 1:08:28
Peak freeway traffic:....................................... Congested
HOV lanes, certain routes

Public transit: .... *WMATA METRO*
Service:............................ 45 heavy rail, 2,000 miles/day
19 city buses, 1,554 miles/day

MARC commuter rail to Washington, DC

Interstate highway: I-270

Nearest airport: .... Washington (IAD) 20 miles W

Places Rated Rank: 343

Billings, MT

Daily commute: 38:54
Peak freeway traffic:... Light

Public transit: .... *Billings MET*
Service:............................ 20 city buses, 1,795 miles/day

Interstate highways:.. I-90, I-94

Airline service:... Small Hub
Airport: ....Billings Logan Int'l (BIL) 2 miles NW

Service	Passengers	Carriers	Cities	Top Market
Commuter	82,879	2	10	Seattle
Jet	332,001	7	9	Denver

Places Rated Rank: 112

Binghamton, NY

Daily commute: 43:10
Peak freeway traffic:.. Moderate

Public transit: .... *Broome County Transit*
Service:............................39 city buses, 4,286 miles/day

Interstate highways:.. I-81, I-88

Airline service:... Nonhub
Airport: ....Binghamton Link Field (BGM) 7 miles N

Service	Passengers	Carriers	Cities	Top Market
Commuter	42,744	5	3	Philadelphia
Jet	78,538	5	4	Philadelphia

Places Rated Rank: 153

Birmingham-Hoover, AL

Daily commute: 57:58
Peak freeway traffic:.. Heavy

Public transit: .... *MAX*
Service:............................72 city buses, 9,117 miles/day

Interstate highways:................................. I-20, I-59, I-65

Airline service:... Small Hub
Airport: .... Birmingham Int'l (BHM) 4 miles NE

Service	Passengers	Carriers	Cities	Top Market
Jet	1,747,497	17	30	Atlanta

Places Rated Rank: 142

Bismarck, ND

🚗 Daily commute: 33:51
Peak freeway traffic: .... Light

🚌 Public transit: .... CAT
Service: .... 8 city buses, 487 miles/day

🛡 Interstate highway: I-94

✈ Airline service: .... Nonhub
Airport: ....Bismarck Municipal (BIS) 3 miles SE

Service	Passengers	Carriers	Cities	Top Market
Jet	173,028	5	3	Minneapolis

Places Rated Rank: 168

Blacksburg-Christiansburg-Radford, VA

🚗 Daily commute: 43:39
Peak freeway traffic: .... Light

🚌 Public transit: .... Blacksburg Transit
Service: .... 4 city buses, 1,200 miles/day

🛡 Interstate highway: I-81

✈ Nearest airport: .... Roanoke (ROA) 20 miles ENE

Places Rated Rank: 316

Bloomington, IN

🚗 Daily commute: 46:45
Peak freeway traffic: .... Moderate

🚌 Public transit: .... Bloomington Transit
Service: .... 29 city buses, 2,415 miles/day

✈ Nearest airport: .... Indianapolis (IND) 50 miles NNE

Places Rated Rank: 217

Bloomington-Normal, IL

🚗 Daily commute: 36:08
Peak freeway traffic: .... Moderate

🚌 Public transit: .... BN PTS
Service: .... 16 city buses, 2,259 miles/day

🛡 Interstate highways: I-39, I-55, I-74

✈ Airline service: .... Nonhub
Airport: .... Central Illinois Regional (BMI) 3 miles E

Service	Passengers	Carriers	Cities	Top Market
Commuter	37,420	2	2	Detroit
Jet	190,356	5	3	Atlanta

Places Rated Rank: 73

Boise City-Nampa, ID

🚗 Daily commute: 43:32
Peak freeway traffic: .... Heavy

🚌 Public transit: .... ValleyRide
Service: .... 35 city buses, 3,058 miles/day

🛡 Interstate highway: I-84

✈ Airline service: .... Small Hub
Airport: .... Boise Air Terminal (BOI) 4 miles SW

Service	Passengers	Carriers	Cities	Top Market
Commuter	289,581	2	12	Portland
Jet	1,424,119	11	17	Salt Lake City

Places Rated Rank: 84

Boston-Quincy, MA

🚗 Daily commute: 1:04:36
Peak freeway traffic: .... Very heavy
HOV lanes, certain routes

🚌 Public transit: .... MBTA
Service: .... 24 trollies, 1,871 miles/day
320 heavy rail, 12,618 miles/day
150 light rail, 11,465 miles/day
838 city buses, 68,694 miles/day

🚆 MBTA commuter rail hub
AMTRAK corridor rail: .... Acela Express
AMTRAK corridor rail: .... Downeaster

🛡 Interstate highways: I-90, I-93, I-95

✈ Airline service: .... Large Hub
Airport: .... Boston Logan Int'l (BOS) 1 miles E

Service	Passengers	Carriers	Cities	Top Market
Commuter	233,920	7	24	Nantucket
Jet	12,626,233	40	92	Chicago
International	1,594,103	25	29	London

Places Rated Rank: 42

Boulder, CO

🚗 Daily commute: 46:08
Peak freeway traffic: .... Heavy

🚌 Public transit: .... RTD
Service: .... 87 city buses, 12,000 miles/day

✈ Nearest airport: .... Denver (DEN) 50 miles ESE

Places Rated Rank: 220

Bowling Green, KY

🚗 Daily commute: 44:41
Peak freeway traffic: .... Light

🚌 Public transit: .... CART
Service: .... 6 city buses, 1,500 miles/day

🛡 Interstate highway: I-65

✈ Nearest airport: .... Nashville, TN (BNA) 50 miles SSW

Places Rated Rank: 317

Bremerton-Silverdale, WA

🚗 Daily commute: 1:08:13
Peak freeway traffic: .... Heavy

🚌 Public transit: .... Kitsap Transit
Service: .... 88 city buses, 7,804 miles/day
2 ferries, 123 miles/day

✈ Nearest airport: .... Seattle (SEA) 20 miles E

Places Rated Rank: 330

Bridgeport-Stamford-Norwalk, CT

🚗 Daily commute: 58:55
Peak freeway traffic: .... Very heavy

🚌 Public transit: .... GBTA
Service: .... 44 city buses, 5,895 miles/day

🚆 METRO NORTH commuter rail to New York City
AMTRAK corridor rail: .... Acela Express

🛡 Interstate highway: I-95

✈ Nearest airport: .... White Plains (HPN) 20 miles SE

Places Rated Rank: 301

Brownsville-Harlingen, TX

🚗 Daily commute: 44:18
Peak freeway traffic: .... Heavy

🚌 Public transit: .... *BUS*
Service: .... 14 city buses, 1,919 miles/day

✈ Airline service: .... Small Hub
Airports: ... Brownsville S. Padre Island Int'l (BRO) 4 miles E

Service	Passengers	Carriers	Cities	Top Market
Jet	76,071	1	1	Houston

Harlingen Valley Int'l (HRL) 3 miles NE

Service	Passengers	Carriers	Cities	Top Market
Jet	427,021	3	5	Houston

Places Rated Rank: 51

Brunswick, GA

🚗 Daily commute: 48:40
Peak freeway traffic: .... Heavy

🛣 Interstate highway: I-95

✈ Airline service: .... Nonhub
Airport: .... Brunswick Golden Isles (BQK) 5 miles N

Service	Passengers	Carriers	Cities	Top Market
Jet	37,101	1	1	Atlanta

Places Rated Rank: 325

✓Buffalo-Niagara Falls, NY

🚗 Daily commute: 45:28
Peak freeway traffic: .... Heavy

🚌 Public transit: .... *NFT METRO*
Service: .... 23 light rail, 1,056 miles/day
272 city buses, 27,403 miles/day

🚆 AMTRAK corridor rail: .... Empire Service

🛣 Interstate highway: I-90

✈ Airline service: .... Medium Hub
Airport: .... Buffalo Niagara Int'l (BUF) 5 miles E

Service	Passengers	Carriers	Cities	Top Market
Commuter	84,263	5	5	Pittsburgh
Jet	2,325,585	23	25	New York
International	1,132	10	1	Cancun

Places Rated Rank: 30

Burlington, NC

🚗 Daily commute: 46:40
Peak freeway traffic: .... Heavy

🚆 PART commuter rail to Greensboro (proposed)

✈ Nearest airport: .... Greensboro (GSO) 25 miles W

Places Rated Rank: 338

Burlington-South Burlington, VT

🚗 Daily commute: 45:00
Peak freeway traffic: .... Moderate

🚌 Public transit: .... *CCTA*
Service: .... 36 city buses, 3,126 miles/day

🛣 Interstate highways: I-40, I-85

✈ Airline service: .... Small Hub
Airport: .... Burlington Int'l (BTV) 3 miles E

Service	Passengers	Carriers	Cities	Top Market
Commuter	45,015	4	3	New York
Jet	644,557	16	13	New York

Places Rated Rank: 68

Cambridge-Newton-Framingham, MA

🚗 Daily commute: 58:06
Peak freeway traffic: .... Very heavy

🚌 Public transit: .... *MBTA*
Service: .... 37 city buses, 2,730 miles/day

🚆 MBTA commuter rail to Boston

🛣 Interstate highways: I-90, I-95

✈ Airline service: .... Nonhub
Airport: .... Laurence Hanscom Field (BED)

Service	Passengers	Carriers	Cities	Top Market
Commuter	8,620	1	1	Trenton

Places Rated Rank: 348

Camden, NJ

🚗 Daily commute: 1:00:07
Peak freeway traffic: .... Heavy

🚌 Public transit: .... *NJT*
Service: .... 42 city buses, 4,800 miles/day

🚆 NJT commuter rail to Trenton
PATCO commuter rail to Philadelphia

🛣 Interstate highways: I-76, I-95

✈ Nearest airport: .... Philadelphia (PHL) 10 miles SE

Places Rated Rank: 379

Canton-Massillon, OH

🚗 Daily commute: 46:41
Peak freeway traffic: .... Moderate

🚌 Public transit: .... *SARTA*
Service: .... 40 city buses, 7,503 miles/day

🛣 Interstate highway: I-77

✈ Airline service: .... Small Hub
Airport: .... Akron-Canton Regional (CAK) 12 miles N

Service	Passengers	Carriers	Cities	Top Market
Commuter	40,832	1	1	Detroit
Jet	664,027	9	13	Atlanta

Places Rated Rank: 115

Cape Coral-Fort Myers, FL

🚗 Daily commute: 53:08
Peak freeway traffic: .... Heavy

🚌 Public transit: .... *LeeTran*
Service: .... 44 city buses, 8,203 miles/day

🛣 Interstate highway: I-75

✈ Airline service: .... Medium Hub
Airport: .... Southwest Florida Int'l (RSW) 10 miles SE

Service	Passengers	Carriers	Cities	Top Market
Commuter	68,042	2	3	Miami
Jet	3,668,285	23	40	Atlanta
International	64,923	5	5	Dusseldorf

Places Rated Rank: 122

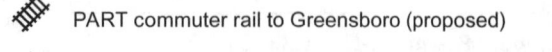

Carson City, NV

🚗 Daily commute: 37:43
Peak freeway traffic:.. Light

🚌 Public transit:................................... *Jump Around Carson*
Service:...............................3 city buses, 1,500 miles/day

✈ Nearest airport: .... Reno (RNO) 20 miles N

Places Rated Rank: 303

Casper, WY

🚗 Daily commute: 35:29
Peak freeway traffic:.. Light

🛡 Interstate highway: I-25

✈ Airline service:.. Nonhub
Airport: ....Natrona County Int'l (CPR) 7 miles NW

Service	Passengers	Carriers	Cities	Top Market
Commuter	68,899	1	2	Denver
Jet	17,788	1	1	Minneapolis

Places Rated Rank: 219

Cedar Rapids, IA

🚗 Daily commute: 40:16
Peak freeway traffic:... Moderate

🚌 Public transit:....................................... *Five Seasons TP*
Service:...............................33 city buses, 2,851 miles/day

🛡 Interstate highway: I-380

✈ Airline service:.. Small Hub
Airport: .... The Eastern Iowa Airport (CID) 5 miles SW

Service	Passengers	Carriers	Cities	Top Market
Commuter	41,929	2	2	Minneapolis
Jet	453,826	11	10	Chicago

Places Rated Rank: 52

Champaign-Urbana, IL

🚗 Daily commute: 37:14
Peak freeway traffic:... Moderate

🚌 Public transit:.. *CU MTD*
Service:........................ 73 city buses, 7,310 miles/day

🛡 Interstate highways:................................. I-57, I-72, I-74

✈ Airline service:.. Nonhub
Airport: ..... University of Illinois-Willard (CMI) 6 miles SW

Service	Passengers	Carriers	Cities	Top Market
Commuter	29,159	2	2	Detroit
Jet	101,049	2	3	Chicago

Places Rated Rank: 66

Charleston, WV

🚗 Daily commute: 54:05
Peak freeway traffic:.. Heavy

🚌 Public transit:.. *KVRTA*
Service:...........................47 city buses, 7,138 miles/day

🛡 Interstate highways:................................. I-64, I-77, I-79

✈ Airline service:.. Nonhub
Airport: ....Charleston Yeager (CRW) 3 miles E

Service	Passengers	Carriers	Cities	Top Market
Commuter	81,625	9	6	Detroit
Jet	233,876	8	7	Atlanta

Places Rated Rank: 134

Charleston-North Charleston, SC

🚗 Daily commute: 52:48
Peak freeway traffic:.. Heavy

🚌 Public transit:.. *CARTA*
Service:...............................43 city buses, 2,063 miles/day

🛡 Interstate highway: I-26

✈ Airline service:.. Small Hub
Airport:....................Charleston Int'l (CHS) 9 miles NW

Service	Passengers	Carriers	Cities	Top Market
Commuter	6,531	1	1	Raleigh/Durham
Jet	1,061,578	15	20	Atlanta

Places Rated Rank: 118

✓ Charlotte-Gastonia-Concord, NC-SC

🚗 Daily commute: 56:17
Peak freeway traffic:... Very heavy

🚌 Public transit:.. *CATS*
Service:........................243 city buses, 28,758 miles/day

🛤 CATS commuter rail to suburbs (proposed)

🛡 Interstate highways:................................. I-77, I-85

✈ Airline service:.. Large Hub
Airport: ....Charlotte Douglas Int'l (CLT) 4 miles W

Service	Passengers	Carriers	Cities	Top Market
Commuter	652,064	3	27	???
Jet	13,489,624	21	117	Atlanta
International	830,797	7	24	Cancun

Places Rated Rank: 33

Charlottesville, VA

🚗 Daily commute: 49:19
Peak freeway traffic:... Moderate

🚌 Public transit:.. *CTS*
Service:...............................23 city buses, 2,625 miles/day

🛡 Interstate highway: I-64

✈ Airline service:.. Nonhub
Airport: .... Charlottesville-Albemarle (CHO) 7 miles N

Service	Passengers	Carriers	Cities	Top Market
Commuter	95,117	6	5	Charlotte
Jet	99,588	4	4	Atlanta

Places Rated Rank: 170

Chattanooga, TN-GA

🚗 Daily commute: 51:12
Peak freeway traffic:.. Heavy

🚌 Public transit:.. *CARTA*
Service: ....49 city buses, 5,588 miles/day

🛡 Interstate highways:................................. I-24, I-75

✈ Airline service:.. Nonhub
Airport: .... Lovell Field (CHA) 5 miles E

Service	Passengers	Carriers	Cities	Top Market
Commuter	80,725	4	3	Atlanta
Jet	172,978	9	8	Cincinnati

Places Rated Rank: 184

Cheyenne, WY

🚗 Daily commute: 34:39
Peak freeway traffic:.. Light

Public transit: .... *CTP*
Service: .... 11 city buses, 945 miles/day

Interstate highways: I-25, I-80

Airline service: .... Nonhub
Airport: .... Cheyenne Olson Field (CYS) 1 miles N

Service	Passengers	Carriers	Cities	Top Market
Commuter	15,404	1	1	Denver
Jet	3,233	1	1	Denver

Places Rated Rank: 222

✓Chicago-Naperville-Joliet, IL

Daily commute: 1:07:34
Peak freeway traffic: .... Congested
HOV lanes, certain routes

Public transit: .... *CTA*
Service: .... 1,710 city buses, 185,707 miles/day
1,008 heavy rail, 32,581 miles/day

METRA suburban commuter rail
SOUTH SHORE commuter rail to South Bend
AMTRAK corridor rail: .... Hiawatha Line

Interstate highways: I-55, I-57, I-80, I-88, I-90, I-94

Airline service: .... Large Hub
Airports: .... Chicago Midway Int'l (MDW) 9 miles SW

Service	Passengers	Carriers	Cities	Top Market
Commuter	36,774	1	6	Indianapolis
Jet	8,753,048	15	65	Minneapolis
International	76,663	2	6	Guadalajara

Chicago O'Hare Int'l (ORD) 14 miles NW

Service	Passengers	Carriers	Cities	Top Market
Commuter	5,643	1	3	Indianapolis
Jet	36,061,312	64	234	New York
International	4,505,406	38	59	London

Places Rated Rank: 1

Chico, CA

Daily commute: 44:05
Peak freeway traffic: .... Heavy

Public transit: .... *CATS*
Service: .... 20 city buses, 1,595 miles/day

Airline service: .... Nonhub
Airport: .... Chico Municipal (CIC) 4 miles N

Service	Passengers	Carriers	Cities	Top Market
Commuter	17,759	1	1	San Francisco

Places Rated Rank: 245

✓Cincinnati-Middletown, OH-KY-IN

Daily commute: 52:14
Peak freeway traffic: .... Very heavy

Public transit: .... *SORTA/METRO*
Service: .... 344 city buses, 36,511 miles/day

Eastern Corridor suburban commuter rail (proposed)

Interstate highways: I-71, I-74, I-75

Airline service: .... Large Hub
Airport: .Cincinnati Northern Kentucky Int'l (CVG) 13 miles SW

Service	Passengers	Carriers	Cities	Top Market
Commuter	9,080	3	2	Cleveland
Jet	11,265,096	18	148	Salt Lake City
International	469,762	6	11	Paris

Places Rated Rank: 10

Clarksville, TN-KY

Daily commute: 51:16
Peak freeway traffic: .... Moderate

Public transit: .... *CTS*
Service: .... 11 city buses, 2,024 miles/day

Interstate highway: I-24

Nearest airport: .... Nashville (BNA) 35 miles SE

Places Rated Rank: 296

Cleveland, TN

Daily commute: 47:17
Peak freeway traffic: .... Light

Interstate highway: I-75

Nearest airport: .... Chatanooga (CHA) 20 miles SW

Places Rated Rank: 337

✓Cleveland-Elyria-Mentor, OH

Daily commute: 51:59
Peak freeway traffic: .... Heavy

Public transit: .... *GCRTA*
Service: .... 544 city buses, 67,264 miles/day
17 light rail, 2,809 miles/day
22 heavy rail, 4,756 miles/day

NEORail suburban commuter rail (proposed)

Interstate highway: I-71, I-77, I-80, I-90

Airline service: .... Medium Hub
Airport: .... Cleveland Hopkins Int'l (CLE) 9 miles SW

Service	Passengers	Carriers	Cities	Top Market
Commuter	138,324	4	12	Detroit
Jet	5,364,866	22	82	Chicago
International	104,543	8	8	Toronto

Places Rated Rank: 14

Coeur d'Alene, ID

Daily commute: 45:43
Peak freeway traffic: .... Moderate

Interstate highway: I-90

Nearest airport: .... Spokane, WA (GEG) 30 miles W

Places Rated Rank: 347

College Station-Bryan, TX

Daily commute: 39:48
Peak freeway traffic: .... Moderate

Public transit: .... *The District*
Service: .... 23 city buses, 2,139 miles/day

Airline service: .... Nonhub
Airport: .... Easterwood Field (CLL) 3 miles SW

Service	Passengers	Carriers	Cities	Top Market
Commuter	72,484	3	2	Dallas/Ft. Worth
Jet	15,766	2	2	Houston

Places Rated Rank: 166

Colorado Springs, CO

Daily commute: 47:37
Peak freeway traffic: .... Heavy

Public transit: .... *Mountain Metro*
Service: .... 54 city buses, 6,692 miles/day

Interstate highway: I-25

Airline service: .... Small Hub
Airport: .... Colorado Springs Municipal (COS) 6 miles SE

Service	Passengers	Carriers	Cities	Top Market
Commuter	21,208	2	2	Denver
Jet	995,578	13	14	Dallas (DFW)

Places Rated Rank: 99

Columbia, MO

Daily commute: 38:46
Peak freeway traffic:... Heavy

Public transit:.. Columbia Transit
Service:.............................. 11 city buses, 1,250 miles/day

Interstate highway: I-70

Airline service: .... Nonhub
Airport: ....Columbia Regional (COU) 12 miles S

Service	Passengers	Carriers	Cities	Top Market
Commuter	20,024	1	1	St. Louis

Places Rated Rank: 167

Columbia, SC

Daily commute: 52:23
Peak freeway traffic:... Heavy

Public transit:............................... *Central Midlands RTA*
Service:..............................49 city buses, 5,141 miles/day

Interstate highways:........................... I-20, I-26, I-77

Airline service: .... Small Hub
Airport: ....Columbia Metropolitan (CAE) 5 miles SW

Service	Passengers	Carriers	Cities	Top Market
Commuter	14,497	2	1	Charlotte
Jet	709,184	12	15	Atlanta

Places Rated Rank: 128

Columbus, GA-AL

Daily commute: 46:31
Peak freeway traffic:... Moderate

Public transit:... *METRA*
Service:.............................. 17 city buses, 2,642 miles/day

Interstate highway: I-185

Airline service:... Nonhub
Airport: .... Columbus Metropolitan (CSG) 3 miles NE

Service	Passengers	Carriers	Cities	Top Market
Commuter	44,896	1	1	Atlanta
Jet	8,085	2	1	Atlanta

Places Rated Rank: 229

Columbus, IN

Daily commute: 40:27
Peak freeway traffic:.. Light

Public transit:... *ColumBUS*
Service:...............................6 city buses, 1,800 miles/day

Interstate highway: I-65

Nearest airport: .... Indianapolis (IND) 47 miles N

Places Rated Rank: 282

Columbus, OH

Daily commute: 49:44
Peak freeway traffic:.. Very heavy

Public transit: .... *COTA*
Service:........................234 city buses, 27,452 miles/day

COTA suburban commuter rail (proposed)

Interstate highways:................................... I-70, I-71

Airline service: .... Medium Hub
Airport: .... Port Columbus Int'l (CMH) 6 miles E

Service	Passengers	Carriers	Cities	Top Market
Commuter	46,163	6	4	Pittsburgh
Jet	3,264,023	23	38	Chicago
International	20,538	4	2	Toronto

Places Rated Rank: 67

Corpus Christi, TX

Daily commute: 44:45
Peak freeway traffic:... Heavy

Public transit: .... The B
Service:.............................. 65 city buses, 9,170 miles/day

Interstate highway: I-37

Airline service:... Small Hub
Airport: ....Corpus Christi Int'l (CRP) 5 miles W

Service	Passengers	Carriers	Cities	Top Market
Jet	419,823	5	4	Houston

Places Rated Rank: 63

Corvallis, OR

Daily commute: 37:24
Peak freeway traffic:.. None

Public transit:.. *CTS*
Service:..............................9 city buses, 4,012 miles/day

Interstate highway: I-5

Nearest airport: .... Eugene (EUG) 30 miles SSE

Places Rated Rank: 307

Cumberland, MD-WV

Daily commute: 52:58
Peak freeway traffic:.. Light

Public transit:.. *Alltrans*
Service:.............................. 11 city buses, 4,200 miles/day

Interstate highway: I-68

Nearest airport: .....Morgantown, WV (MGW) 50 miles W

Places Rated Rank: 371

✓Dallas-Plano-Irving, TX

Daily commute: 59:08
Peak freeway traffic:... Very heavy
HOV lanes, certain routes

Public transit: .... *DART*
Service:........................798 city buses, 93,284 miles/day
82 light rail, 7,788 miles/day

TRE commuter rail to Ft. Worth

Interstate highways:...................... I-20, I-30, I-35E, I-45

Airline service:... Large Hub
Airports: ....Dallas Love Field (DAL) 5 miles NW

Service	Passengers	Carriers	Cities	Top Market
Jet	3,271,338	2	15	Houston

Dallas/Fort Worth Int'l (DFW) 12 miles NW

Service	Passengers	Carriers	Cities	Top Market
Commuter	323,186	2	14	Waco
Jet	27,461,954	34	170	Atlanta
International	1,984,505	16	36	Cancun

Places Rated Rank: 3

Dalton, GA

Daily commute: 47:31
Peak freeway traffic:................................... Light

Interstate highway: I-75

Nearest airport: . Chattanooga, TN (CHA) 35 miles NNW

Places Rated Rank: 340

Danville, IL

Daily commute: 43:36
Peak freeway traffic:................................... Light

Public transit:.............................. Danville Mass Transit
Service:.........................9 city buses, 2,400 miles/day

Interstate highway: i-74

Nearest airport: .... Champaign (CMI) 30 miles W

Places Rated Rank: 290

Danville, VA

Daily commute: 49:21
Peak freeway traffic:................................... Light

Public transit:.. Danville Transit
Service:.................................. 7 city buses, 741 miles/day

Nearest airport: ....Greensboro, NC (GSO) 40 miles S

Places Rated Rank: 326

✓Davenport-Moline-Rock Island, IA-IL

Daily commute: 41:21
Peak freeway traffic:................................... Moderate

Public transit:................................ CITIBUS & MetroLink
Service:...........................83 city buses, 8,217 miles/day

Interstate highways:.......................... I-74, I-80, I-88

Airline service:... Small Hub
Airport: .... Quad City Int'l (MLI) 3 miles S

Service	Passengers	Carriers	Cities	Top Market
Commuter	20,098	1	2	Detroit
Jet	410,041	12	11	Chicago

Places Rated Rank: 17

✓Dayton, OH

Daily commute: 45:24
Peak freeway traffic:................................... Heavy

Public transit:.. GDRTA
Service:........................ 115 city buses, 16,259 miles/day
43 trolleys, 4,548 miles/day

Interstate highways:.. I-70, I-75

Airline service:... Small Hub
Airport: .... Dayton Cox Int'l (DAY) 9 miles N

Service	Passengers	Carriers	Cities	Top Market
Commuter	57,420	5	5	Detroit
Jet	1,158,449	19	25	Atlanta

Places Rated Rank: 31

Decatur, AL

Daily commute: 52:09
Peak freeway traffic:................................... None

Interstate highway: I-65

Nearest airport: .... Huntsville (HSV) 20 ENE

Places Rated Rank: 364

Decatur, IL

Daily commute: 39:00
Peak freeway traffic:................................... Light

Public transit:.. DPTS
Service:............................20 city buses, 2,802 miles/day

Interstate highway: I-72

Airline service:... Nonhub
Airport: ....Decatur Regional (DEC) 4 miles E

Service	Passengers	Carriers	Cities	Top Market
Jet	11,642	1	1	St. Louis

Places Rated Rank: 191

Deltona-Daytona Beach-Ormond Beach, FL

Daily commute: 54:13
Peak freeway traffic:................................... Heavy

Public transit:.. VOTRAN
Service:............................48 city buses, 7,432 miles/day

Interstate highways:.................................... I-4, I-95

Airline service:... Nonhub
Airport: ....Daytona Beach Int'l (DAB) 3 miles SW

Service	Passengers	Carriers	Cities	Top Market
Commuter	7.155	1	3	Orlando
Jet	287,034	5	4	Atlanta
International	6,057	1	2	Marsh Harbour

Places Rated Rank: 185

✓Denver-Aurora, CO

Daily commute: 56:20
Peak freeway traffic:................................... Heavy
HOV lanes, certain routes

Public transit:.. RTD
Service:..................................47 light rail, 4,558 miles/day
769 city buses, 64,437 miles/day

CDOT commuter rail to Ft. Collins (proposed)

Interstate highways:.................................. I-25, I-70, I-76

Airline service:... Large Hub
Airport: .... Denver Int'l (DEN) 4 miles E

Service	Passengers	Carriers	Cities	Top Market
Commuter	662,054	6	39	Durango
Jet	20,206,827	32	125	Chicago
International	615,556	9	13	Frankfurt

Places Rated Rank: 28

Des Moines-West Des Moines, IA

Daily commute: 41:40
Peak freeway traffic:................................... Heavy

Public transit:.. MTA
Service:............................94 city buses, 6,792 miles/day

Interstate highways:.................................. I-35, I-80

✈ Airline service: .... Small Hub
✈ Airport: .... Des Moines Int'l (DSM) 3 miles SW

Service	Passengers	Carriers	Cities	Top Market
Commuter	34,100	3	3	Minneapolis
Jet	881,795	18	21	Chicago

Places Rated Rank: 45

✓Detroit-Livonia-Dearborn, MI

🚗 Daily commute: 55:39
Peak freeway traffic:.. Congested

🚌 Public transit:.. DDOT
Service:.......................... 617 city buses, 55,612 miles/day

🛡 Interstate highways:................................... I-75, I-94, I-96

✈ Airline service: .... Large Hub
Airport: ....Detroit Metropolitan (DTW) 15 miles S

Service	Passengers	Carriers	Cities	Top Market
Commuter	616,059	4	38	Akron/Canton
Jet	16,726,510	34	196	Chicago
International	1,532,788	15	30	Amsterdam

Places Rated Rank: 20

Dothan, AL

🚗 Daily commute: 47:18
Peak freeway traffic:... None

✈ Airline service: .... Nonhub
Airport: ....Dothan Regional (DHN) 5 miles NW

Service	Passengers	Carriers	Cities	Top Market
Commuter	28,270	1	1	Atlanta
Jet	39,735	1	1	Atlanta

Places Rated Rank: 276

Dover, DE

🚗 Daily commute: 48:24
Peak freeway traffic:.. Light

🚌 Public transit:.. DTC
Service:........................166 city buses, 13,969 miles/day

✈ Nearest airport: .... Philadelphia, PA (PHL) 60 miles NNE

Places Rated Rank: 251

Dubuque, IA

🚗 Daily commute: 32:44
Peak freeway traffic:... None

🚌 Public transit:.. KeyLine
Service:.............................8 city buses, 765 miles/day

✈ Airline service: .... Nonhub
Airport: ....Dubuque Regional (DBQ) 7 miles SW

Service	Passengers	Carriers	Cities	Top Market
Jet	40,129	1	1	Chicago

Places Rated Rank: 161

Duluth, MN-WI

🚗 Daily commute: 42:15
Peak freeway traffic:.. Moderate

🚌 Public transit:.. DTA
Service:...................44 city buses, 4,931 miles/day

🛡 Interstate highway: I-35

✈ Airline service: .... Nonhub
✈ Airport: .... Duluth Int'l (DLH) 5 miles NW

Service	Passengers	Carriers	Cities	Top Market
Commuter	11,703	1	1	Minneapolis
Jet	134,864	4	3	Minneapolis

Places Rated Rank: 130

Durham, NC

🚗 Daily commute: 48:26
Peak freeway traffic:.. Heavy

🚌 Public transit:.. DATA
Service:.............................35 city buses, 6,616 miles/day

🛡 Interstate highways:.................................... I-40, I-85

✈ Airline service: .... Medium Hub
Airport: .... Raleigh-Durham Int'l (RDU) 9 miles NW

Service	Passengers	Carriers	Cities	Top Market
Commuter	36,498	4	5	Pittsburgh
Jet	4,683,712	27	40	Atlanta
International	74,702	4	2	London

Places Rated Rank: 81

Eau Claire, WI

🚗 Daily commute: 39:27
Peak freeway traffic:.. Light

🚌 Public transit:.. ECT
Service:........................... 15 city buses, 1,928 miles/day

🛡 Interstate highway: I-94

✈ Airline service:.. Nonhub
Airport: .... Chippewa Valley Regional (EAU) 3 miles N

Service	Passengers	Carriers	Cities	Top Market
Jet	31,279	1	2	Minneapolis

Places Rated Rank: 172

Edison, NJ

🚗 Daily commute: 1:09:22
Peak freeway traffic:.. Heavy
HOV lanes, certain routes

🚌 Public transit: .... NJT
Service:........................ 130 city buses, 19,981 miles/day

🚃 NJT commuter rail to New York and Trenton
AMTRAK corridor rail: .... Acela Express
AMTRAK corridor rail:.......................... Keystone Service

🛡 Interstate highways:... I-287, I-95

✈ Nearest airport: .... Newark (EWR) 20 miles N

Places Rated Rank: 354

El Centro, CA

🚗 Daily commute: 43:16
Peak freeway traffic:.. Light

🚌 Public transit: .... IVT
Service:..............................5 city buses, 2,500 miles/day

🛡 Interstate highway: I-8

✈ Nearest airport: ....San Diego (SAN) 70 miles W

Places Rated Rank: 322

Elizabethtown, KY

Daily commute: 49:56
Peak freeway traffic:..................................... Light

Public transit: .... *TACK*
Service:.....................5 city buses, 3,000 miles/day

Interstate highway: I-65

Nearest airport: ....Louisville (SDF) 35 miles N

Places Rated Rank: 352

Elkhart-Goshen, IN

Daily commute: 39:07
Peak freeway traffic:..................................... Light

Public transit: .... *The BUS*
Service:.....................5 city buses, 2,400 miles/day

Interstate highway: I-80

Nearest airport: ....South Bend (SBN) 30 miles W

Places Rated Rank: 270

Elmira, NY

Daily commute: 41:27
Peak freeway traffic:..................................... Light

Public transit: .... *CCTS*
Service:.....................18 city buses, 2,542 miles/day

Interstate highway: I-86

Airline service:.. Nonhub
Airport: ...... Elmira-Corning Regional (ELM) 11 miles NW

Service	Passengers	Carriers	Cities	Top Market
Commuter	28,382	5	3	Philadelphia
Jet	57,256	3	2	Detroit

Places Rated Rank: 180

El Paso, TX

Daily commute: 48:49
Peak freeway traffic:................................ Very heavy

Public transit: .... *Sun Metro*
Service:.....................121 city buses, 19,349 miles/day

Interstate highways:................................ I-10, I-25

Airline service:....................................... Small Hub
Airport: ....El Paso Int'l (ELP) 4 miles NE

Service	Passengers	Carriers	Cities	Top Market
Commuter	2,693	1	1	???
Jet	1,801,636	11	18	Phoenix
International	2,722	2	1	Chihuahua

Places Rated Rank: 49

Erie, PA

Daily commute: 39:47
Peak freeway traffic:.................................. Moderate

Public transit: .... *EMTA*
Service:.....................52 city buses, 4,071 miles/day

Interstate highways:................................ I-79, I-90

Airline service:.. Nonhub
Airport: ....Tom Ridge Erie Int'l (ERI) 5 miles SW

Service	Passengers	Carriers	Cities	Top Market
Commuter	48,087	5	3	Detroit
Jet	138,689	7	5	Cincinnati

Places Rated Rank: 120

Essex County, MA

Daily commute: 57:34
Peak freeway traffic:..................................... Heavy

Public transit: .... CATA & MVRTA
Service:.....................48 city buses, 4,651 miles/day

MBTA commuter rail to Boston
AMTRAK corridor rail:.............................. Downeaster

Interstate highways:................................ I-93, I-95

Nearest airport: ....Boston (BOS) 30 miles S

Places Rated Rank: 332

Eugene-Springfield, OR

Daily commute: 41:34
Peak freeway traffic:..................................... Heavy

Public transit: .... Lane *TD*
Service:.....................85 city buses, 10,875 miles/day

AMTRAK corridor rail:.................................. Cascades

Interstate highway: I-5

Airline service:.. Nonhub
Airport: ....Mahlon Sweet Field (EUG) 7 miles NW

Service	Passengers	Carriers	Cities	Top Market
Commuter	135,773	2	3	Seattle
Jet	229,351	2	5	San Francisco

Places Rated Rank: 149

Evansville, IN-KY

Daily commute: 44:44
Peak freeway traffic:..................................... Light

Public transit: .... *METS*
Service:.....................24 city buses, 3,151 miles/day

Interstate highway: I-64

Airline service:.. Nonhub
Airport: ....Evansville Regional (EVV) 3 miles N

Service	Passengers	Carriers	Cities	Top Market
Commuter	28,548	3	3	Memphis
Jet	214,777	4	6	Chicago

Places Rated Rank: 80

Fairbanks, AK

Daily commute: 36:42
Peak freeway traffic:..................................... Light

Public transit: .... *MACS Transit*
Service:.....................7 city buses, 900 miles/day

Interstate highways:................................ A-2, A-4

Airline service:....................................... Small Hub
Airport: ....Fairbanks Int'l (FAI) 3 miles SW

Service	Passengers	Carriers	Cities	Top Market
Commuter	47,646	4	14	Anchorage
Jet	389,392	4	6	Anchorage
International	3,548	2	1	Frankfurt

Places Rated Rank: 103

Fargo, ND-MN

Daily commute: 34:21
Peak freeway traffic:..................................... Light

Public transit: .... *MATBUS*
Service:.....................20 city buses, 2,300 miles/day
8 city buses, 864 miles/day

🛡 Interstate highways:...I-29, I-94

✈ Airline service:... Nonhub
Airport: ....Hector Int'l (FAR) 3 miles NW

Service	Passengers	Carriers	Cities	Top Market
Commuter	3,902	1	1	Minneapolis
Jet	278,791	7	5	Minneapolis

Places Rated Rank: 105

Farmington, NM

🚗 Daily commute: 50:48
Peak freeway traffic:.. None

🚌 Public transit:.. Red Apple Transit
Service:............................... 5 city buses, 1,100 miles/day

✈ Airline service:.. Nonhub
Airport: ....Four Corners Regional (FMN) 1 miles NW

Service	Passengers	Carriers	Cities	Top Market
Commuter	28,688	2	3	Denver

Places Rated Rank: 346

Fayetteville, NC

🚗 Daily commute: 48:00
Peak freeway traffic:... Moderate

🚌 Public transit:... FAST
Service:............................... 16 city buses, 2,124 miles/day

🛡 Interstate highway: I-95

✈ Airline service:.. Nonhub
Airport: .....Fayetteville Grannis Regional (FAY) 3 miles S

Service	Passengers	Carriers	Cities	Top Market
Commuter	33,709	2	1	Charlotte
Jet	116,631	3	3	Charlotte

Places Rated Rank: 207

Fayetteville-Springdale-Rogers, AR-MO

🚗 Daily commute: 43:28
Peak freeway traffic:.. Heavy

🚌 Public transit:........................... ORT & Razorback Transit
Service:...............................20 city buses, 900 miles/day

🛡 Interstate highway: I-540

✈ Airline service:... Small Hub
Airport: Northwest Arkansas Regional (XNA) 15 miles NW

Service	Passengers	Carriers	Cities	Top Market
Commuter	13,339	1	1	St. Louis
Jet	544,618	11	16	Dallas (DFW)

Places Rated Rank: 92

Flagstaff, AZ

🚗 Daily commute: 40:17
Peak freeway traffic:... Moderate

🚌 Public transit:............................... Mountain Line Transit
Service:............................... 7 city buses, 1,023 miles/day

🛡 Interstate highways:...I-17, I-40

✈ Airline service:.. Nonhub
Airport: ....Flagstaff Pulliam (FLG) 5 miles S

Service	Passengers	Carriers	Cities	Top Market
Commuter	40,114	1	1	Phoenix

Places Rated Rank: 225

Flint, MI

🚗 Daily commute: 55:08
Peak freeway traffic:... Heavy

🚌 Public transit:... MTA
Service:................85 city buses, 7,380 miles/day

🛡 Interstate highways:...........................I-69, I-75, I-20, I-95

✈ Airline service:.. Small Hub
Airport: ....Bishop Int'l (FNT) 3 miles SW

Service	Passengers	Carriers	Cities	Top Market
Commuter	41,332	5	5	Milwaukee
Jet	510,994	7	12	Atlanta

Places Rated Rank: 154

Florence, SC

🚗 Daily commute: 50:59
Peak freeway traffic:... Moderate

🚌 Public transit:.. Pee Dee RTA
Service:.................................4 city buses, 304 miles/day

✈ Airline service:.. Nonhub
Airport: ....Florence Regional (FLO) 3 miles E

Service	Passengers	Carriers	Cities	Top Market
Commuter	33,000	2	1	Charlotte
Jet	21,162	1	1	Atlanta

Places Rated Rank: 288

Florence-Muscle Shoals, AL

🚗 Daily commute: 51:18
Peak freeway traffic:.. None

✈ Nearest airport: ....Huntsville (HSV) 50 miles E

Places Rated Rank: 360

Fond du Lac, WI

🚗 Daily commute: 39:40
Peak freeway traffic:.. Light

🚌 Public transit:... FDLAT
Service:.................................4 city buses, 500 miles/day

✈ Nearest airport: ....Milwaukee (MKE) 45 miles SSE

Places Rated Rank: 162

Fort Collins-Loveland, CO

🚗 Daily commute: 44:35
Peak freeway traffic:... Moderate

🚌 Public transit:... TRANSFORT
Service:...............................21 city buses, 2,486 miles/day

🚈 CDOT commuter rail to Denver (proposed)

🛡 Interstate highway: I-25

✈ Airline service:... Nonhub
Airport: Fort Collins-Loveland Municipal (FNL) 9 miles SE

Service	Passengers	Carriers	Cities	Top Market
Jet	33,076	1	1	Las Vegas

Places Rated Rank: 224

Fort Lauderdale-Pompano Beach-Deerfield Beach, FL

🚗 Daily commute: 58:28
Peak freeway traffic:... Congested
HOV lanes, certain routes

Public transit: .... *BCT*
Service:........................278 city buses, 38,947 miles/day
8 ferries, 409 miles/day

TRI-RAIL commuter rail to Miami

Interstate highway: I-95

Airline service: .... Large Hub
Airport: .Fort Lauderdale Hollywood Int'l (FLL) 3 miles SW

Service	Passengers	Carriers	Cities	Top Market
Commuter	239,319	5	13	Key West
Jet	10,406,492	26	82	New York
International	839,593	20	29	Nassau

Places Rated Rank: 85

Fort Smith, AR-OK

Daily commute: 48:11
Peak freeway traffic:............................... Moderate

Public transit: .... *FST*
Service:........................8 city buses, 924 miles/day

Interstate highway: I-40

Airline service: .... Nonhub
Airport: ....Fort Smith Regional (FSM) 3 miles SE

Service	Passengers	Carriers	Cities	Top Market
Commuter	3,404	1	1	Memphis
Jet	95,869	2	2	Dallas (DFW)

Places Rated Rank: 212

Fort Walton Beach-Crestview-Destin, FL

Daily commute: 47:08
Peak freeway traffic:............................... None

Public transit:.. *The Wave*
Service:............................... 12 city buses, 918 miles/day

Airline service:.. Small Hub
Airport: .... Okaloosa Regional (VPS) 2 miles NE

Service	Passengers	Carriers	Cities	Top Market
Commuter	11,843	2	2	Tampa
Jet	374,821	6	6	Atlanta

Places Rated Rank: 171

Fort Wayne, IN

Daily commute: 44:40
Peak freeway traffic:............................... Heavy

Public transit:.. *Citilink*
Service:........................27 city buses, 3,986 miles/day

Interstate highway: I-69

Airline service:.. Nonhub
Airport: ....Fort Wayne Int'l (FWA) 7 miles SW

Service	Passengers	Carriers	Cities	Top Market
Commuter	37,103	4	3	Detroit
Jet	269,069	7	5	Chicago

Places Rated Rank: 126

✓Fort Worth-Arlington, TX

Daily commute: 57:19
Peak freeway traffic:............................... Very heavy

Public transit:.. *The T*
Service:........................134 city buses, 11,791 miles/day

TRE commuter rail to Dallas

Interstate highways:............................... I-20, I-35W

Airline service:... Large Hub
Airport: ....Dallas-Fort Worth Int'l (DFW) 20 miles NE

Service	Passengers	Carriers	Cities	Top Market
Commuter	323,186	2	14	Waco
Jet	27,461,954	34	170	Atlanta
International	1,984,505	16	36	Cancun

Places Rated Rank: 11

Fresno, CA

Daily commute: 47:16
Peak freeway traffic:............................... Heavy

Public transit: .... *FAX*
Service:........................84 city buses, 11,838 miles/day

AMTRAK corridor rail:............................... San Joaquins

Airline service:.. Small Hub
Airport: ....Fresno Yosemite Int'l (FAT) 5 miles NE

Service	Passengers	Carriers	Cities	Top Market
Commuter	165,725	2	3	Los Angeles
Jet	402,203	5	9	Dallas (DFW)

Places Rated Rank: 109

Gadsden, AL

Daily commute: 52:53
Peak freeway traffic:............................... Light

Public transit: .... *Gadsden Trolley Company*
Service:...............................3 city buses, 600 miles/day

Interstate highway: I-59

Nearest airport: .... Birmingham (BHM) 50 miles SE

Places Rated Rank: 370

Gainesville, FL

Daily commute: 46:21
Peak freeway traffic:............................... Moderate

Public transit: .... *RTS*
Service:........................88 city buses, 7,690 miles/day

Interstate highway: I-75

Airline service:.. Nonhub
Airport: .... Gainesville Regional (GNV) 3 miles NE

Service	Passengers	Carriers	Cities	Top Market
Commuter	53,278	2	3	Atlanta
Jet	114,428	3	3	Atlanta

Places Rated Rank: 141

Gainesville, GA

Daily commute: 56:10
Peak freeway traffic:............................... Moderate

Interstate highway: I-985

Nearest airport: .... Atlanta (ATL) 60 miles SW

Places Rated Rank: 295

Gary, IN

Daily commute: 57:50
Peak freeway traffic:............................... Heavy

Public transit: .... *GPTC*
Service:........................30 city buses, 2,570 miles/day

South Shore Line commuter rail to Chicago

Interstate highways:............................... I-65, I-80/90, I-94

✈ Airline service: .... Nonhub
Nearest Airport: .. Chicago Midway (MDW) 20 miles NNW

Places Rated Rank: 266

Glens Falls, NY

🚗 Daily commute: 48:16
Peak freeway traffic:.. Light

🚌 Public transit: .... GGFT
Service:.................................... 5 city buses, 820 miles/day

🛡 Interstate highway: I-87

✈ Nearest airport: .... Albany (ALB) 30 miles N

Places Rated Rank: 306

Goldsboro, NC

🚗 Daily commute: 46:23
Peak freeway traffic:.. None

🚌 Public transit: .... GATEWAY
Service:.................................... 4 city buses, 800 miles/day

✈ Nearest airport: .... Raleigh (RDU) 35 miles NW

Places Rated Rank: 339

Grand Forks, ND-MN

🚗 Daily commute: 31:51
Peak freeway traffic:.. Light

🚌 Public transit: .... CAT
Service:.................................... 7 city buses, 929 miles/day

🛡 Interstate highway: I-29

✈ Airline service: .... Nonhub
Airport: .... Grand Forks Int'l (GFK) 5 miles NW

Service	Passengers	Carriers	Cities	Top Market
Commuter	11,199	1	2	Minneapolis
Jet	77,484	3	2	Minneapolis

Places Rated Rank: 182

Grand Junction, CO

🚗 Daily commute: 38:27
Peak freeway traffic:.. Light

🚌 Public transit: .... GRAND VALLEY TRANSIT
Service: .... 11 city buses, 1,723 miles/day

🛡 Interstate highway: I-70

✈ Airline service: .... Nonhub
Airport: ....Walker Field (GJT) 3 miles NE

Service	Passengers	Carriers	Cities	Top Market
Commuter	128,253	3	3	Denver
Jet	29,556	3	3	Denver

Places Rated Rank: 160

Grand Rapids-Wyoming, MI

🚗 Daily commute: 47:26
Peak freeway traffic:.. Heavy

🚌 Public transit: .... The Rapid
Service:................................ 74 city buses, 9,372 miles/day

🛡 Interstate highway: I-96

✈ Airline service: .... Small Hub
Airport: .... Gerald R. Ford Int'l (GRR) 6 miles SE

Service	Passengers	Carriers	Cities	Top Market
Commuter	21,878	2	2	Milwaukee
Jet	1,019,694	17	21	Detroit

Places Rated Rank: 74

Great Falls, MT

🚗 Daily commute: 33:44
Peak freeway traffic:.. Light

🚌 Public transit: .... GFTD
Service:.................................... 7 city buses, 864 miles/day

🛡 Interstate highway: I-15

✈ Airline service: .... Nonhub
Airport: .... Great Falls Int'l (GTF) 3 miles SW

Service	Passengers	Carriers	Cities	Top Market
Commuter	53,178	2	5	Helena
Jet	169,185	3	4	Salt Lake City

Places Rated Rank: 72

Greeley, CO

🚗 Daily commute: 49:59
Peak freeway traffic:.. Light

🚌 Public transit: .... The Bus
Service:................................ 10 city buses, 980 miles/day

🛡 Interstate highway: I-25

✈ Nearest airport: .... Denver (DEN) 50 miles SSE

Places Rated Rank: 327

Green Bay, WI

🚗 Daily commute: 39:56
Peak freeway traffic:.. Heavy

🚌 Public transit: .... Green Bay Metro
Service:........................... 30 city buses, 3,663 miles/day

🛡 Interstate highway: I-43

✈ Airline service: .... Small Hub
Airport: .... Austin Straubel Int'l (GRB) 7 miles SW

Service	Passengers	Carriers	Cities	Top Market
Commuter	18,894	1	1	Milwaukee
Jet	397,857	8	9	Chicago

Places Rated Rank: 96

Greensboro-High Point, NC

🚗 Daily commute: 48:13
Peak freeway traffic:.. Heavy

🚌 Public transit: .... GTA & HITRAN
Service:........................... 22 city buses, 3,642 miles/day

🛤 PART commuter rail to Burlington (proposed)

🛡 Interstate highways:.. I-40, I-85

✈ Airline service: .... Small Hub
Airport: .... Piedmont Triad Int'l (GSO) 7 miles W

Service	Passengers	Carriers	Cities	Top Market
Commuter	29,742	3	3	Baltimore
Jet	1,275,579	18	22	Atlanta

Places Rated Rank: 97

239

Greenville, NC

Daily commute: 46:14
Peak freeway traffic: .... None

Public transit: .... *GREAT*
Service: .... 4 city buses, 975 miles/day

Airline service: .... Nonhub
Airport: .... Pitt-Greenville (PGV) 2 miles N

Service	Passengers	Carriers	Cities	Top Market
Commuter	48,040	2	1	Charlotte

Places Rated Rank: 287

Greenville, SC

Daily commute: 48:01
Peak freeway traffic: .... Heavy

Public transit: .... *GTA*
Service: .... 9 city buses, 1,564 miles/day

Interstate highways: I-26, I-85

Airline service: .... Small Hub
Airport: .... Greenville Spartanburg Int'l (GSP) 3 miles S

Service	Passengers	Carriers	Cities	Top Market
Commuter	19,244	3	2	Charlotte
Jet	876,410	13	17	Atlanta

Places Rated Rank: 138

Gulfport-Biloxi, MS

Daily commute: 51:47
Peak freeway traffic: .... Heavy

Public transit: .... *CTA*
Service: .... 18 city buses, 2,259 miles/day

Interstate highway: I-10

Airline service: .... Small Hub
Airport: .... Gulfport-Biloxi Int'l (GPT) 3 miles NE

Service	Passengers	Carriers	Cities	Top Market
Jet	368,479	10	8	Atlanta

Places Rated Rank: 181

Hagerstown-Martinsburg, MD-WV

Daily commute: 58:02
Peak freeway traffic: .... Heavy

Public transit: .... *County Commuter*
Service: .... 9 city buses, 1,189 miles/day

MARC commuter rail to Washington, DC

Interstate highways: I-70, I-81

Airline service: .... Nonhub
Airport: .... Hagerstown Regional (HGR) 5 miles N

Service	Passengers	Carriers	Cities	Top Market
Commuter	5,019	1	1	Pittsburgh

Places Rated Rank: 268

Hanford-Corcoran, CA

Daily commute: 44:30
Peak freeway traffic: .... Light

Public transit: .... *KART*
Service: .... 5 city buses, 813 miles/day

Nearest airport: .... Fresno (FAT) 35 miles N

Places Rated Rank: 335

Harrisburg-Carlisle, PA

Daily commute: 47:00
Peak freeway traffic: .... Heavy

Public transit: .... *CAT*
Service: .... 56 city buses, 4,407 miles/day

Corridor One commuter rail hub
AMTRAK corridor rail: .... Keystone Service

Interstate highways: I-76, I-81, I-83

Airline service: .... Small Hub
Airport: .... Harrisburg Int'l (MDT) 8 miles SE

Service	Passengers	Carriers	Cities	Top Market
Commuter	103,610	3	4	Philadelphia
Jet	525,695	14	13	Chicago
International	5,723	2	1	Toronto

Places Rated Rank: 143

Harrisonburg, VA

Daily commute: 41:51
Peak freeway traffic: .... Light

Public transit: .... *HDPT*
Service: .... 7 city buses, 1,800 miles/day

Interstate highway: I-81

Nearest airport: .... Charlottesville (CHO) 45 miles SE

Places Rated Rank: 304

✓Hartford-West Hartford-East Hartford, CT

Daily commute: 48:44
Peak freeway traffic: .... Heavy
HOV lanes, certain routes

Public transit: .... *CTTransit*
Service: .... 321 city buses, 30,496 miles/day

CDOT commuter rail to New Haven (proposed)

Interstate highways: I-84, I-91

Airline service: .... Medium Hub
Airport: .... Bradley Int'l (BDL) 10 miles N

Service	Passengers	Carriers	Cities	Top Market
Commuter	49,031	4	5	Buffalo
Jet	3,555,021	22	37	Chicago
International	35,272	7	4	Toronto

Places Rated Rank: 38

Hattiesburg, MS

Daily commute: 51:34
Peak freeway traffic: .... Moderate

Interstate highway: I-59

Nearest airport: .... Jackson (JAN) 65 miles NW

Places Rated Rank: 363

Hickory-Lenoir-Morganton, NC

Daily commute: 45:48
Peak freeway traffic: .... Heavy

Public transit: .... PIEDMONT WAGON
Service: .... 7 city buses, 2,100 miles/day

Interstate highway: I-40

Nearest airport: .... Charlotte (CLT) 50 miles SE

Places Rated Rank: 328

Hinesville-Fort Stewart, GA

🚗 Daily commute: 48:41
Peak freeway traffic:.. None

✈ Nearest airport: .... Savannah (SAV) 30 miles NE

Places Rated Rank: 358

Holland-Grand Haven, MI

🚗 Daily commute: 41:20
Peak freeway traffic:... Light

🚌 Public transit: .... MAX
Service:.................................6 city buses, 806 miles/day

🛡 Interstate highway: I-196

✈ Nearest airport: .... Grand Rapids (GRR) 20 miles NE

Places Rated Rank: 244

Honolulu, HI

🚗 Daily commute: 58:23
Peak freeway traffic:... Heavy
HOV lanes, certain routes

🚌 Public transit:... *TheBus*
Service:.........................425 city buses, 53,097 miles/day

🛡 Interstate highway: I-1

✈ Airline service:... Large Hub
Airport: .... Honolulu Int'l (HNL) 3 miles NW

Service	Passengers	Carriers	Cities	Top Market
Commuter	196,329	1	7	Kapalua
Jet	9,424,167	32	56	Los Angeles
International	1,933,411	18	15	Tokyo

Places Rated Rank: 56

Hot Springs, AR

🚗 Daily commute: 45:04
Peak freeway traffic:... Moderate

🚌 Public transit:... *HSIT*
Service:............................12 city buses, 2,500 miles/day

🛡 Interstate highway: I-30

✈ Airline service:... Nonhub
Airport: .... Memorial Field (HOT) 3 miles SW

Service	Passengers	Carriers	Cities	Top Market
Commuter	8,174	1	2	Dallas (DFW)

Places Rated Rank: 293

Houma-Bayou Cane-Thibodaux, LA

🚗 Daily commute: 55:54
Peak freeway traffic:... Light

✈ Nearest airport: New Orleans (MSY) 25 miles NE

Places Rated Rank: 376

✓Houston-Sugar Land-Baytown, TX

🚗 Daily commute: 1:01:48
Peak freeway traffic:....................................... Congested
HOV lanes, certain routes

🚌 Public transit:... *METRO*
Service:.....................1,232 city buses, 118,115 miles/day
17 light rail, 1,309 miles/day

🛡 Interstate highways:................................... I-10, I-45

Airline service:.. Large Hub
Airports: .... Houston Intercontinental (IAH) 15 miles N

Service	Passengers	Carriers	Cities	Top Market
Commuter	206,899	3	15	College Station
Jet	18,315,849	34	182	Los Angeles
International	2,732,906	17	64	Mexico City

William P. Hobby Field (HOU) 8 miles SE

Service	Passengers	Carriers	Cities	Top Market
Jet	4,562,249	11	36	Dallas (DAL)

Places Rated Rank: 6

Huntington-Ashland, WV-KY-OH

🚗 Daily commute: 50:27
Peak freeway traffic:... Moderate

🚌 Public transit: .... *TTA*
Service:.............................18 city buses, 2,225 miles/day

🛡 Interstate highway: I-64

✈ Airline service: .... Nonhub
Airport: ....Tri-State Ferguson Field (HTS) 3 miles S

Service	Passengers	Carriers	Cities	Top Market
Commuter	25,975	2	1	Charlotte
Jet	22,910	2	1	Cincinnati

Places Rated Rank: 233

Huntsville, AL

🚗 Daily commute: 47:06
Peak freeway traffic:... Heavy

🚌 Public transit: .... *Huntsville SHUTTLE*
Service:.............................11 city buses, 1,782 miles/day

🛡 Interstate highway: I-65

✈ Airline service: .... Small Hub
Airport: ......Huntsville Int'l-Jones Field (HSV) 9 miles SW

Service	Passengers	Carriers	Cities	Top Market
Commuter	2,461	1	1	Memphis
Jet	624,209	12	13	Atlanta

Places Rated Rank: 137

Idaho Falls, ID

🚗 Daily commute: 42:59
Peak freeway traffic:... Light

🚌 Public transit: .... *PTA*
Service:...................................4 city buses, 900 miles/day

🛡 Interstate highway: I-15

✈ Airline service:... Nonhub
Airport: ....Idaho Falls Regional (IDA) 2 miles NW

Service	Passengers	Carriers	Cities	Top Market
Commuter	39,793	2	3	Boise
Jet	102,964	3	3	Salt Lake City

Places Rated Rank: 235

✓Indianapolis-Carmel, IN

🚗 Daily commute: 51:17
Peak freeway traffic:....................................... Very heavy

🚌 Public transit: .... *IndyGo*
Service:.........................124 city buses, 18,838 miles/day

🛡 Interstate highways:........................... I-65, I-69, I-70, I-74

✈ Airline service: .... Medium Hub
✈ Airport: ....Indianapolis Int'l (IND) 7 miles SW

Service	Passengers	Carriers	Cities	Top Market
Commuter	63,468	4	10	St. Louis
Jet	4,208,208	27	43	Chicago
International	16,418	3	2	Toronto

Places Rated Rank: 26

Iowa City, IA

🚗 Daily commute: 38:33
Peak freeway traffic:............................... Moderate

🚌 Public transit:.................................... CamBus & ICT
Service:................41 city buses, 3,600 miles/day

🛡 Interstate highway: I-80

✈ Nearest airport: Cedar Rapids Municipal (CID) 15 miles N

Places Rated Rank: 175

Ithaca, NY

🚗 Daily commute: 37:06
Peak freeway traffic:..................................... None

🚌 Public transit:.. TCAT
Service:................38 city buses, 3,541 miles/day

✈ Airline service:.. Nonhub
Airport: ....Ithaca Tompkins Regional (ITH) 3 miles NE

Service	Passengers	Carriers	Cities	Top Market
Commuter	54,090	4	3	Philadelphia
Jet	25,206	2	1	Philadelphia

Places Rated Rank: 108

Jackson, MI

🚗 Daily commute: 49:30
Peak freeway traffic:............................... Moderate

🚌 Public transit:... JTA
Service:..................8 city buses, 948 miles/day

🛡 Interstate highway: I-94

✈ Nearest airport: .... Lansing (LAN) 25 miles N

Places Rated Rank: 302

Jackson, MS

🚗 Daily commute: 51:33
Peak freeway traffic:..................................... Heavy

🚌 Public transit:.. JATRAN
Service:..................27 city buses, 2,822 miles/day

🛡 Interstate highways:............................... I-20, I-55

✈ Airline service:.. Small Hub
Airport: ....Jackson Int'l (JAN) 5 miles E

Service	Passengers	Carriers	Cities	Top Market
Jet	772,475	11	14	Atlanta

Places Rated Rank: 157

Jackson, TN

🚗 Daily commute: 43:08
Peak freeway traffic:..................................... Heavy

🚌 Public transit:... JTA
Service:................8 city buses, 1,576 miles/day

🛡 Interstate highway: I-40

✈ Airline service:... Nonhub
Airport: ....McKellar-Sipes Regional (MKL) 7 miles W

Service	Passengers	Carriers	Cities	Top Market
Commuter	2,670	1	1	St. Louis

Places Rated Rank: 183

Jacksonville, FL

🚗 Daily commute: 57:22
Peak freeway traffic:..................................... Heavy

🚌 Public transit:.. JTA
Service:................144 city buses, 27,949 miles/day

🛡 Interstate highways:.............................. I-10, I-95

✈ Airline service:...................................... Medium Hub
Airport: ....Jacksonville Int'l (JAX) 9 miles N

Service	Passengers	Carriers	Cities	Top Market
Commuter	72,636	2	2	Miami
Jet	2,954,947	20	29	Atlanta

Places Rated Rank: 106

Jacksonville, NC

🚗 Daily commute: 45:25
Peak freeway traffic:..................................... None

🚌 Public transit:.. The LOOP
Service:..................4 city buses, 840 miles/day

✈ Airline service:... Nonhub
Airport: .... Albert Ellis Airport (OAJ) 10 miles NW

Service	Passengers	Carriers	Cities	Top Market
Commuter	22,521	2	1	Charlotte
Jet	69,519	2	2	Charlotte

Places Rated Rank: 254

Janesville, WI

🚗 Daily commute: 43:24
Peak freeway traffic:..................................... Heavy

🚌 Public transit:....................................... BTS & JTS
Service:................23 city buses, 2,100 miles/day

🛡 Interstate highway: I-39/90

✈ Nearest airport: .... Madison (MSN) 30 miles NNW

Places Rated Rank: 243

Jefferson City, MO

🚗 Daily commute: 44:01
Peak freeway traffic:..................................... None

🚌 Public transit:....................................... JEFFTRAN
Service:................7 city buses, 1,450 miles/day

✈ Nearest airport: ....Columbia (COU) 30 miles N

Places Rated Rank: 294

Johnson City, TN

🚗 Daily commute: 46:45
Peak freeway traffic:............................... Moderate

🚌 Public transit:.. JCT
Service:..................8 city buses, 871 miles/day

🛡 Interstate highway: I-81

Airline service:...Nonhub
✈ Airport: ....Tri-Cities Regional (TRI) 12 miles SW

Service	Passengers	Carriers	Cities	Top Market
Commuter	107,285	5	5	Atlanta
Jet	136,044	7	4	Cincinnati

Places Rated Rank: 164

Johnstown, PA

🚗 Daily commute: 47:00
Peak freeway traffic:...Light

🚌 Public transit:...CamTran
Service:..............................23 city buses, 1,940 miles/day

✈ Airline service:...Nonhub
Airport: .....Johnstown-Cambria County (JST) 3 miles NE

Service	Passengers	Carriers	Cities	Top Market
Commuter	11,910	1	1	Pittsburgh

Places Rated Rank: 226

Jonesboro, AR

🚗 Daily commute: 41:26
Peak freeway traffic:...Light

🚌 Public transit:...JETS
Service:..............................5 city buses, 1,300 miles/day

✈ Airline service:...Nonhub
Airport: ....Jonesboro Municipal Airport (JBR) 3 miles E

Service	Passengers	Carriers	Cities	Top Market
Commuter	3,035	1	1	El Dorado

Places Rated Rank: 281

Joplin, MO

🚗 Daily commute: 40:50
Peak freeway traffic:...Moderate

🛡 Interstate highway: I-44

✈ Airline service:...Nonhub
Airport: ....Joplin Regional (JLN) 5 miles E

Service	Passengers	Carriers	Cities	Top Market
Commuter	9,882	1	1	St. Louis

Places Rated Rank: 264

Kalamazoo-Portage, MI

🚗 Daily commute: 44:01
Peak freeway traffic:...Heavy

🚌 Public transit:...Metro Transit
Service:..............................33 city buses, 4,630 miles/day

🛡 Interstate highway: I-94

✈ Airline service:...Nonhub
Airport: ...Kalamazoo Battle Creek Int'l (AZO) 3 miles SE

Service	Passengers	Carriers	Cities	Top Market
Commuter	20,178	1	1	Detroit
Jet	215,104	8	7	Chicago

Places Rated Rank: 107

Kankakee-Bradley, IL

🚗 Daily commute: 50:41
Peak freeway traffic:...Light

🚌 Public transit:...River Valley METRO
Service:..............................11 city buses, 2,000 miles/day

🛡 Interstate highway: I-57

✈ Nearest airport: ....Chicago (MWD) 45 miles N

Places Rated Rank: 344

✓Kansas City, MO-KS

🚗 Daily commute: 49:05
Peak freeway traffic:...Heavy

🚌 Public transit:...KCATA
Service:.........................260 city buses, 24,655 miles/day

🚃 The JO suburban commuter rail (proposed)

🛡 Interstate highways:.................................I-29, I-35, I-70

✈ Airline service:...Medium Hub
Airport: ....Kansas City Int'l (MCI) 15 miles NW

Service	Passengers	Carriers	Cities	Top Market
Commuter	26,434	1	5	Manhattan
Jet	5,449,846	23	49	Atlanta
International	26,572	3	2	Cancun

Places Rated Rank: 18

Kennewick-Richland-Pasco, WA

🚗 Daily commute: 45:16
Peak freeway traffic:...Light

🚌 Public transit:...BFT
Service:..............................13 city buses, 2,456 miles/day

🛡 Interstate highway: I-82

✈ Airline service:...Nonhub
Airport: ....Tri-Cities (PSC) 2 miles NW

Service	Passengers	Carriers	Cities	Top Market
Commuter	95,713	2	3	Seattle
Jet	149,323	3	3	Salt Lake City

Places Rated Rank: 223

Killeen-Temple-Fort Hood, TX

🚗 Daily commute: 46:04
Peak freeway traffic:...Heavy

🚌 Public transit:...The HOP
Service:..............................13 city buses, 2,870 miles/day

🛡 Interstate highway: I-35

✈ Airline service:...Nonhub
Airport: ....Killeen-Fort Hood Regional (GRK) 6 miles SW

Service	Passengers	Carriers	Cities	Top Market
Commuter	49,671	1	2	Dallas (DFW)
Jet	108,757	1	2	Dallas (DFW)

Places Rated Rank: 314

Kingsport-Bristol-Bristol, TN-VA

🚗 Daily commute: 49:07
Peak freeway traffic:...Moderate

🚌 Public transit:...KATS
Service:..............................4 city buses, 409 miles/day

🛡 Interstate highway: I-81

✈ Airline service:...Nonhub
Airport: ....Tri-Cities Regional (TRI) 12 miles SW

Service	Passengers	Carriers	Cities	Top Market
Commuter	107,285	5	5	Atlanta
Jet	136,044	7	4	Cincinnati

Places Rated Rank: 204

Kingston, NY

🚗 Daily commute: 56:19
Peak freeway traffic:... Light

🚌 Public transit: .... *CITIBUS & UCAT*
Service:........................... 15 city buses, 1,699 miles/day

🚆 AMTRAK corridor rail: .... Empire Service

✈ Nearest airport: .... Albany (ALB) 50 miles N

Places Rated Rank: 359

Knoxville, TN

🚗 Daily commute: 49:13
Peak freeway traffic:.. Heavy

🚌 Public transit:.. KAT
Service:........................... 71 city buses, 7,569 miles/day

🛡 Interstate highways:.. I-40, I-75

✈ Airline service:.................................... Small Hub
Airport: ....McGhee Tyson (TYS) 10 miles S

Service	Passengers	Carriers	Cities	Top Market
Commuter	29,222	5	3	Charlotte
Jet	876,443	16	18	Atlanta

Places Rated Rank: 101

Kokomo, IN

🚗 Daily commute: 39:06
Peak freeway traffic:... Light

✈ Nearest airport: ....Indianapolis (IND) 50 miles S

Places Rated Rank: 272

La Crosse, WI-MN

🚗 Daily commute: 37:38
Peak freeway traffic:.. Light

🚌 Public transit:... *La Crosse MTU*
Service:........................... 16 city buses, 2,135 miles/day

🛡 Interstate highway: I-90

✈ Airline service:.................................... Nonhub
Airport: ....La Crosse Municipal (LSE) 4 miles NW

Service	Passengers	Carriers	Cities	Top Market
Commuter	27,827	2	2	Minneapolis
Jet	94,555	5	3	Minneapolis

Places Rated Rank: 117

Lafayette, IN

🚗 Daily commute: 39:09
Peak freeway traffic:.. Heavy

🚌 Public transit:.. *CityBus*
Service:...........................54 city buses, 4,464 miles/day

🛡 Interstate highway: I-65

✈ Nearest airport: ....Indianapolis (IND) 60 miles SSE

Places Rated Rank: 158

Lafayette, LA

🚗 Daily commute: 53:26
Peak freeway traffic:.. Heavy

🚌 Public transit: .... *LTS*
Service:........................... 13 city buses, 1,601 miles/day

🛡 Interstate highways:.. I-10, I-49

✈ Airline service:.................................... Nonhub
Airport: ....Lafayette Regional (LFT) 2 miles SE

Service	Passengers	Carriers	Cities	Top Market
Commuter	26,321	1	1	Memphis
Jet	150,503	3	2	Houston

Places Rated Rank: 206

Lake Charles, LA

🚗 Daily commute: 44:40
Peak freeway traffic:.. Heavy

🚌 Public transit:.. LCTS
Service:...........................4 city buses, 700 miles/day

🛡 Interstate highway: I-10

✈ Airline service:.................................... Nonhub
Airport: .... Lake Charles Regional (LCH) 5 miles S

Service	Passengers	Carriers	Cities	Top Market
Commuter	6,491	1	1	Houston
Jet	41,463	1	1	Houston

Places Rated Rank: 253

Lake County-Kenosha County, IL-WI

🚗 Daily commute: 1:01:42
Peak freeway traffic:.. Heavy

🚌 Public transit:... *KT*
Service:.......................................1 light rail, 58 miles/day
48 city buses, 3,157 miles/day

🚆 METRA commuter rail to Chicago
WiseRide commuter rail (proposed)
AMTRAK corridor rail: .... Hiawatha Line

🛡 Interstate highway: I-94

✈ Nearest airport: ....Milwaukee, WI (MKE) 35 miles N

Places Rated Rank: 289

Lakeland, FL

🚗 Daily commute: 54:44
Peak freeway traffic:.. Moderate

🚌 Public transit:... *Citrus Connection*
Service:............................29 city buses, 3,986 miles/day

🛡 Interstate highway: I-4

✈ Nearest airport: .... Tampa (TPA) 35 miles W

Places Rated Rank: 297

Lancaster, PA

🚗 Daily commute: 45:30
Peak freeway traffic:.. Heavy

🚌 Public transit:... RRTA
Service:............................35 city buses, 4,298 miles/day

🚆 Corridor One commuter rail to Harrisburg
AMTRAK corridor rail: .... Keystone Service

✈ Airline service:.................................... Nonhub
Airport: ....Lancaster Municipal (LNS) 4 miles N

Service	Passengers	Carriers	Cities	Top Market
Commuter	5,847	1	1	Pittsburgh

Places Rated Rank: 267

Lansing-East Lansing, MI

🚗 Daily commute: 45:08
Peak freeway traffic:.. Moderate

Public transit:...*CATA*
Service:.............................85 city buses, 8,805 miles/day

Interstate highways:..I-69, I-96

Airline service:...Nonhub
Airport:.................Capital City Airport (LAN) 3 miles NW

Service	Passengers	Carriers	Cities	Top Market
Commuter	3,515	1	1	Milwaukee
Jet	307,757	8	9	Detroit

Places Rated Rank: 88

Laredo, TX

Daily commute: 46:25
Peak freeway traffic:.. Light

Public transit:..*El Metro*
Service:...............................35 city buses, 5,013 miles/day

Interstate highway: I-35

Airline service:..Nonhub
Airport: ....Laredo Int'l (LRD) 3 miles NE

Service	Passengers	Carriers	Cities	Top Market
Jet	88,770	3	3	Dallas (DFW)
International	5,571	3	1	Mexico City

Places Rated Rank: 146

Las Cruces, NM

Daily commute: 45:15
Peak freeway traffic:.. Light

Public transit:..*RoadRunner*
Service:.............................9 city buses, 1,093 miles/day

Interstate highways:..I-10, I-25

Nearest airport: ....El Paso, TX (ELP) 35 miles S

Places Rated Rank: 255

✓Las Vegas-Paradise, NV

Daily commute: 52:15
Peak freeway traffic:.. Congested

Public transit:..*RTC*
Service:..........................251 city buses, 44,032 miles/day

RTC suburban monorail (planned)

Interstate highway: I-15

Airline service:..Large Hub
Airport: ....McCarran Int'l (LAS) 5 miles S

Service	Passengers	Carriers	Cities	Top Market
Commuter	37,058	2	2	Palm Springs
Jet	21,140,751	35	124	Los Angeles
International	600,617	15	16	Vancouver

Places Rated Rank: 25

Lawrence, KS

Daily commute: 41:11
Peak freeway traffic:.. Light

Public transit:..............................*KU on Wheels & LTS*
Service:..............................20 city buses, 2,613 miles/day

Interstate highway: I-70

Nearest airport: ....Topeka (FOE) 31 miles W

Places Rated Rank: 241

Lawton, OK

Daily commute: 36:25
Peak freeway traffic:.. Light

Public transit:..*LATS*
Service:...............................10 city buses, 1,587 miles/day

Interstate highway: I-44

Airline service:..Nonhub
Airport: ....Lawton-Fort Sill Regional (LAW) 2 miles S

Service	Passengers	Carriers	Cities	Top Market
Commuter	44,623	1	1	Dallas (DFW)

Places Rated Rank: 104

Lebanon, PA

Daily commute: 45:57
Peak freeway traffic:.. Moderate

Public transit:..*COLT*
Service:...............................4 city buses, 850 miles/day

Interstate highway: I-81

Nearest airport: ....Harrisburg (MDT) 25 miles W

Places Rated Rank: 318

Lewiston, ID-WA

Daily commute: 34:27
Peak freeway traffic:.. Light

Public transit:..*Valley Transit*
Service:...............................5 city buses, 975 miles/day

Airline service:..Nonhub
Airport:.......Lewiston Nez Perce County (LWS) 2 miles S

Service	Passengers	Carriers	Cities	Top Market
Commuter	54,150	1	3	Seattle
Jet	22,517	1	1	Salt Lake City

Places Rated Rank: 228

Lewiston-Auburn, ME

Daily commute: 49:59
Peak freeway traffic:.. Light

Public transit:..CitiLink
Service:...............................5 city buses, 1,200 miles/day

Interstate highway: I-495

Nearest airport: ....Portland (PWM) 35 miles S

Places Rated Rank: 366

Lexington-Fayette, KY

Daily commute: 44:32
Peak freeway traffic:.. Heavy

Public transit:..*LexTran*
Service:...............................38 city buses, 4,349 miles/day

Interstate highways:..I-64, I-75

Airline service:..Small Hub
Airport: ....Blue Grass Field (LEX) 4 miles W

Service	Passengers	Carriers	Cities	Top Market
Commuter	25,844	3	4	Memphis
Jet	507,814	12	16	Atlanta

Places Rated Rank: 75

Lima, OH

Daily commute: 39:44
Peak freeway traffic:.. Heavy

Public transit:..*ACRTA*
Service: ....8 city buses, 1,300 miles/day

Interstate highway: I-75

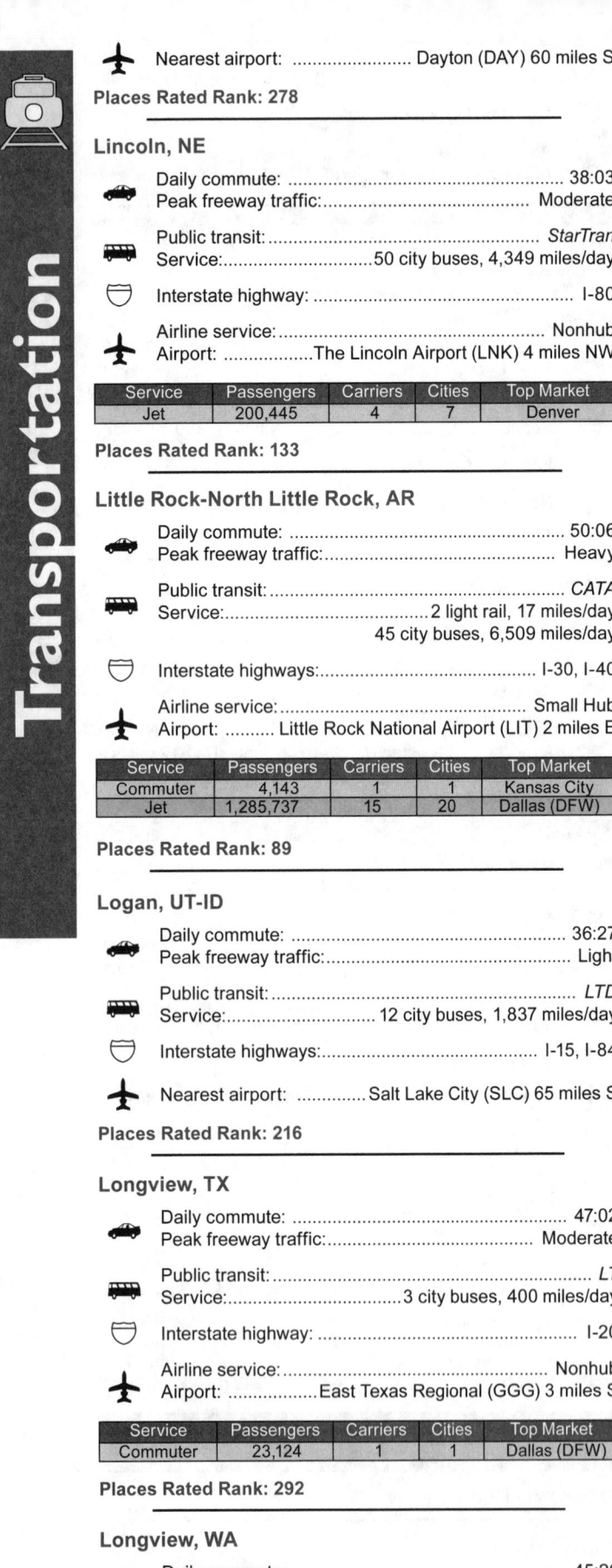

✈ Nearest airport: .... Dayton (DAY) 60 miles S

Places Rated Rank: 278

Lincoln, NE

🚗 Daily commute: 38:03
Peak freeway traffic: .... Moderate

🚌 Public transit: .... *StarTran*
Service: ....50 city buses, 4,349 miles/day

🛡 Interstate highway: I-80

✈ Airline service: .... Nonhub
Airport: ....The Lincoln Airport (LNK) 4 miles NW

Service	Passengers	Carriers	Cities	Top Market
Jet	200,445	4	7	Denver

Places Rated Rank: 133

Little Rock-North Little Rock, AR

🚗 Daily commute: 50:06
Peak freeway traffic: .... Heavy

🚌 Public transit: .... *CATA*
Service: ....2 light rail, 17 miles/day
45 city buses, 6,509 miles/day

🛡 Interstate highways: I-30, I-40

✈ Airline service: .... Small Hub
Airport: .... Little Rock National Airport (LIT) 2 miles E

Service	Passengers	Carriers	Cities	Top Market
Commuter	4,143	1	1	Kansas City
Jet	1,285,737	15	20	Dallas (DFW)

Places Rated Rank: 89

Logan, UT-ID

🚗 Daily commute: 36:27
Peak freeway traffic: .... Light

🚌 Public transit: .... *LTD*
Service: .... 12 city buses, 1,837 miles/day

🛡 Interstate highways: I-15, I-84

✈ Nearest airport: .... Salt Lake City (SLC) 65 miles S

Places Rated Rank: 216

Longview, TX

🚗 Daily commute: 47:02
Peak freeway traffic: .... Moderate

🚌 Public transit: .... *LT*
Service: ....3 city buses, 400 miles/day

🛡 Interstate highway: I-20

✈ Airline service: .... Nonhub
Airport: ....East Texas Regional (GGG) 3 miles S

Service	Passengers	Carriers	Cities	Top Market
Commuter	23,124	1	1	Dallas (DFW)

Places Rated Rank: 292

Longview, WA

🚗 Daily commute: 45:26
Peak freeway traffic: .... Moderate

🚌 Public transit: .... *CUBS*
Service: ....5 city buses, 593 miles/day

🚃 AMTRAK corridor rail: .... Cascades

🛡 Interstate highway: I-5

✈ Nearest airport: ....Portland, OR (PDX) 40 miles SSE

Places Rated Rank: 280

✓Los Angeles-Long Beach-Glendale, CA

🚗 Daily commute: 1:02:22
Peak freeway traffic: .... Congested
HOV lanes, certain routes

🚌 Public transit: .... *LACMTA*
Service: .... 70 heavy rail, 3,389 miles/day
2,172 city buses, 245,965 miles/day
96 light rail, 9,798 miles/day

🚃 METROLINK commuter rail hub
AMTRAK corridor rail: .... Pacific Surfliner

🛡 Interstate highways: I-10, I-5

✈ Airline service: .... Medium Hub
Airports: .... Burbank Bob Hope (BUR) 3 miles NW

Service	Passengers	Carriers	Cities	Top Market
Commuter	1,774	1	1	Portland
Jet	2,813,521	11	17	Oakland

Long Beach Daugherty Field (LGB) 3 miles NE

Service	Passengers	Carriers	Cities	Top Market
Jet	1,481,304	5	10	New York

Los Angeles Int'l (LAX) 9 miles SW

Service	Passengers	Carriers	Cities	Top Market
Commuter	1,172,710	4	24	San Diego
Jet	27,620,560	75	141	Las Vegas
International	7,109,722	53	63	London

Places Rated Rank: 22

Louisville-Jefferson County, KY-IN

🚗 Daily commute: 50:12
Peak freeway traffic: .... Very heavy

🚌 Public transit: .... *River City TA*
Service: .... 199 city buses, 22,151 miles/day

🛡 Interstate highways: I-64, I-65, I-71

✈ Airline service: .... Small Hub
Airport: ....Louisville Standiford Int'l (SDF) 4 miles S

Service	Passengers	Carriers	Cities	Top Market
Commuter	12,330	3	3	Milwaukee
Jet	1,906,871	20	31	Atlanta

Places Rated Rank: 48

✓Lubbock, TX

🚗 Daily commute: 36:57
Peak freeway traffic: .... Light

🚌 Public transit: .... *Citibus*
Service: ....50 city buses, 4,060 miles/day

🛡 Interstate highway: I-27

✈ Airline service: .... Small Hub
Airport: ....Lubbock Preston Smith Int'l (LBB) 4 miles N

Service	Passengers	Carriers	Cities	Top Market
Jet	576,832	5	7	Dallas (DAL)

Places Rated Rank: 12

Lynchburg, VA

🚗 Daily commute: 49:37
Peak freeway traffic: .... Moderate

Public transit:...GLTC
Service:..........................18 city buses, 2,878 miles/day

Airline service:.. Nonhub
Airport: .Lynchburg Preston Glenn Field (LYH) 5 miles SW

Service	Passengers	Carriers	Cities	Top Market
Commuter	36,246	2	1	Charlotte
Jet	28,082	1	1	Atlanta

Places Rated Rank: 203

Macon, GA

Daily commute: 52:31
Peak freeway traffic:.................................. Heavy

Public transit:...................................... MBTA-MAC
Service:............................19 city buses, 3,053 miles/day

Interstate highways:...................................... I-16, I-75

Airline service:.. Nonhub
Airport: ....Middle Georgia Regional (MCN) 9 miles S

Service	Passengers	Carriers	Cities	Top Market
Commuter	2,877	1	1	Atlanta
Jet	14,870	1	1	Atlanta

Places Rated Rank: 291

Madera, CA

Daily commute: 55:27
Peak freeway traffic:.................................. Light

Public transit:... MAX
Service:..................................4 city buses, 400 miles/day

Nearest airport: .... Fresno (FAT) 20 miles SE

Places Rated Rank: 378

✓Madison, WI

Daily commute: 43:21
Peak freeway traffic:.................................. Heavy

Public transit:.. Metro Transit
Service:.........................167 city buses, 15,240 miles/day

DANE COUNTY suburban commuter rail (proposed)

Interstate highways:.................................. I-39/90, I-94

Airline service:.. Small Hub
Airport: .... Dane County Truax Field (MSN) 5 miles NE

Service	Passengers	Carriers	Cities	Top Market
Commuter	19,296	2	2	St. Louis
Jet	782,176	12	19	Chicago

Places Rated Rank: 7

Manchester-Nashua, NH

Daily commute: 54:06
Peak freeway traffic:.................................. Heavy

Public transit:.. MTA & NTS
Service:..............................18 city buses, 2,000 miles/day

Interstate highways:.................................. I-89, I-93

Airline service:.. Medium Hub
Airport: .... Manchester Airport (MHT) 3 miles S

Service	Passengers	Carriers	Cities	Top Market
Commuter	48,388	4	3	New York
Jet	2,093,609	16	19	Baltimore
International	7,595	2	1	Toronto

Places Rated Rank: 145

Mansfield, OH

Daily commute: 43:13
Peak freeway traffic:.................................. Light

Public transit:... RCT
Service:..............................8 city buses, 592 miles/day

Interstate highway: I-71

Nearest airport: .... Columbus (LCK) 45 miles SSW

Places Rated Rank: 252

McAllen-Edinburg-Mission, TX

Daily commute: 44:55
Peak freeway traffic:.................................. Heavy

Public transit:.. LRGVDC
Service:............................11 city buses, 1,280 miles/day

Airline service:.. Nonhub
Airport: ....McAllen Miller Int'l (MFE) 2 miles S

Service	Passengers	Carriers	Cities	Top Market
Jet	349,974	4	4	Houston
International	6,731	2	1	Mexico City

Places Rated Rank: 149

Medford, OR

Daily commute: 39:10
Peak freeway traffic:.................................. Moderate

Public transit:.. Rogue Valley TD
Service:............................21 city buses, 2,093 miles/day

Interstate highway: I-5

Airline service:.. Nonhub
Airport: ....Medford Rogue Valley Int'l (MFR) 3 miles N

Service	Passengers	Carriers	Cities	Top Market
Commuter	205,431	2	5	Portland
Jet	111,870	3	5	Phoenix

Places Rated Rank: 140

Memphis, TN-MS-AR

Daily commute: 53:20
Peak freeway traffic:.................................. Very heavy
HOV lanes, certain routes

Public transit:... MATA
Service:..........................164 city buses, 22,474 miles/day
15 light rail, 882 miles/day

Interstate highways:.................................. I-40, I-55

Airline service:.. Medium Hub
Airport: .... Memphis Int'l (MEM) 3 miles S

Service	Passengers	Carriers	Cities	Top Market
Commuter	222,753	2	16	Lafayette
Jet	5,433,986	18	114	Atlanta
International	154,820	2	6	Amsterdam

Places Rated Rank: 41

Merced, CA

Daily commute: 55:19
Peak freeway traffic:.................................. Heavy

Public transit:... The Bus
Service:............................21 city buses, 2,776 miles/day

AMTRAK corridor rail:.............................. San Joaquins

Nearest airport: .... Modesto (MOD) 40 miles NW

Places Rated Rank: 353

Miami-Miami Beach-Kendall, FL

Daily commute: 1:04:30
Peak freeway traffic: .... Congested
HOV lanes, certain routes

Public transit: .... MDT
Service: .... 103 heavy rail, 4,805 miles/day
663 city buses, 98,733 miles/day

TRI-RAIL commuter rail to Ft. Lauderdale

Interstate highway: I-95

Airline service: .... Large Hub
Airport: .... Miami Int'l (MIA) 8 miles NW

Service	Passengers	Carriers	Cities	Top Market
Commuter	496,597	4	14	Key West
Jet	13,132,178	52	126	Atlanta
International	5,788,697	38	76	London

Places Rated Rank: 58

Michigan City-La Porte, IN

Daily commute: 47:13
Peak freeway traffic: .... Heavy

Public transit: .... Municipal Coach
Service: .... 4 city buses, 512 miles/day

South Shore Line commuter rail to Chicago

Interstate highway: I-94

Nearest airport: .... South Bend (SBN) 30 miles E

Places Rated Rank: 321

Midland, TX

Daily commute: 39:40
Peak freeway traffic: .... Light

Public transit: .... EZ RIDER
Service: .... 7 city buses, 840 miles/day

Interstate highway: I-20

Airline service: .... Small Hub
Airport: .... Midland Int'l (MAF) 8 miles SW

Service	Passengers	Carriers	Cities	Top Market
Jet	480,089	3	8	Dallas (DAL)

Places Rated Rank: 136

✓Milwaukee-Waukesha-West Allis, WI

Daily commute: 47:20
Peak freeway traffic: .... Heavy

Public transit: .... MCTS
Service: .... 411 city buses, 52,990 miles/day

WiseRide commuter rail (proposed)
AMTRAK corridor rail: .... Hiawatha Line

Interstate highways: I-43, I-94

Airline service: .... Medium Hub
Airport: .... General Mitchell Int'l (MKE) 5 miles S

Service	Passengers	Carriers	Cities	Top Market
Commuter	182,749	2	21	Green Bay
Jet	3,404,822	24	45	Minneapolis
International	34,623	7	2	Toronto

Places Rated Rank: 2

✓Minneapolis-St. Paul-Bloomington, MN-WI

Daily commute: 50:04
Peak freeway traffic: .... Congested
HOV lanes, certain routes

Public transit: .... Metro Transit
Service: .... 22 light rail, 980 miles/day
922 city buses, 74,282 miles/day

NORTHSTAR commuter rail (proposed)

Interstate highways: I-35, I-94

Airline service: .... Large Hub
Airport: .... Minneapolis-St Paul Int'l (MSP) 6 miles SW

Service	Passengers	Carriers	Cities	Top Market
Commuter	533,713	1	30	Wausau
Jet	17,231,748	31	207	Chicago
International	1,037,277	9	25	Amsterdam

Places Rated Rank: 5

Missoula, MT

Daily commute: 36:49
Peak freeway traffic: .... Light

Public transit: .... Mountain Line
Service: .... 16 city buses, 1,694 miles/day

Interstate highway: I-90

Airline service: .... Nonhub
Airport: .... Missoula Int'l (MSO) 4 miles SE

Service	Passengers	Carriers	Cities	Top Market
Commuter	80,132	2	5	Seattle
Jet	217,699	4	4	Salt Lake City

Places Rated Rank: 61

Mobile, AL

Daily commute: 54:23
Peak freeway traffic: .... Heavy

Public transit: .... MTS
Service: .... 26 city buses, 4,003 miles/day

Interstate highways: I-10, I-65

Airline service: .... Nonhub
Airport: .... Mobile Regional (MOB) 11 miles W

Service	Passengers	Carriers	Cities	Top Market
Jet	320,604	10	9	Atanta

Places Rated Rank: 196

Modesto, CA

Daily commute: 57:09
Peak freeway traffic: .... Congested

Public transit: .... MAX
Service: .... 36 city buses, 4,503 miles/day

AMTRAK corridor rail: .... San Joaquins

Airline service: .... Nonhub
Airport: .... Modesto Sham Field (MOD) 3 miles E

Service	Passengers	Carriers	Cities	Top Market
Commuter	17,721	1	1	San Francisco

Places Rated Rank: 305

Monroe, LA

Daily commute: 46:57
Peak freeway traffic: .... Light

Public transit: .... MTS
Service: .... 14 city buses, 1,875 miles/day

Interstate highway: I-20

✈ Airline service: .... Nonhub
Airport: .... Monroe Regional (MLU) 3 miles E

Service	Passengers	Carriers	Cities	Top Market
Commuter	50,953	3	2	Memphis
Jet	58,148	2	2	Atlanta

Places Rated Rank: 135

Monroe, MI

🚗 Daily commute: 51:47
Peak freeway traffic:... Moderate

🚌 Public transit:.. *Lake Erie Transit*
Service:.............................8 city buses, 630 miles/day

🛡 Interstate highway: I-75

✈ Nearest airport: .... Toledo, OH (TOL) 25 miles SSW

Places Rated Rank: 356

Montgomery, AL

🚗 Daily commute: 49:52
Peak freeway traffic:... Heavy

🚌 Public transit:.. *MATS*
Service:...........................19 city buses, 2,149 miles/day

🛡 Interstate highways:.. I-65, I-85

✈ Airline service: .... Nonhub
Airport: .. Montgomery Dannelly Field (MGM) 6 miles SW

Service	Passengers	Carriers	Cities	Top Market
Commuter	64,412	1	1	Atlanta
Jet	139,988	5	6	Memphis

Places Rated Rank: 211

Morgantown, WV

🚗 Daily commute: 48:49
Peak freeway traffic:... Moderate

🚌 Public transit:...................................... *Mountain Line TA*
Service:...........................8 city buses, 2,437 miles/day

🚞 PRT between downtown and WVU

🛡 Interstate highways:.. I-68, I-79

✈ Airline service: .... Nonhub
Airport: ....Morgantown Hart Field (MGW) 3 miles E

Service	Passengers	Carriers	Cities	Top Market
Commuter	16,776	1	2	Pittsburgh

Places Rated Rank: 329

Morristown, TN

🚗 Daily commute: 50:35
Peak freeway traffic:... Light

🛡 Interstate highway: I-81

✈ Nearest airport: ....Knoxville (TYS) 35 miles WSW

Places Rated Rank: 357

Mount Vernon-Anacortes, WA

🚗 Daily commute: 52:42
Peak freeway traffic:... None

🚌 Public transit:.. *SKAT*
Service:...........................8 city buses, 1,092 miles/day

🚞 AMTRAK corridor rail:...................................... Cascades

🛡 Interstate highway: I-5

✈ Nearest airport: ....Seattle (SEA) 45 miles S

Places Rated Rank: 275

Muncie, IN

🚗 Daily commute: 42:22
Peak freeway traffic:... Light

🚌 Public transit:.. MITS
Service:...........................26 city buses, 2,598 miles/day

🛡 Interstate highway: I-69

✈ Nearest airport: .... Indianapolis (IND) 60 miles SW

Places Rated Rank: 202

Muskegon-Norton Shores, MI

🚗 Daily commute: 44:26
Peak freeway traffic:... Moderate

🚌 Public transit:.. *MATS Shore Line*
Service:...........................13 city buses, 1,174 miles/day

🛡 Interstate highway: I-96

✈ Airline service: .... Nonhub
Airport: ....Muskegon County (MKG) 4 miles S

Service	Passengers	Carriers	Cities	Top Market
Commuter	38,506	2	3	Detroit

Places Rated Rank: 201

Myrtle Beach-Conway-North Myrtle Beach, SC

🚗 Daily commute: 50:44
Peak freeway traffic:... Heavy

🚌 Public transit:.. *Lymo*
Service:...........................29 city buses, 4,127 miles/day

✈ Airline service: .... Small Hub
Airport: ....Myrtle Beach Int'l (MYR) 3 miles SW

Service	Passengers	Carriers	Cities	Top Market
Commuter	53,582	1	1	Atlanta
Jet	649,055	15	15	Charlotte

Places Rated Rank: 174

Napa, CA

🚗 Daily commute: 50:41
Peak freeway traffic:... Heavy

🚌 Public transit:.. *NCTPA*
Service:...........................18 city buses, 2,240 miles/day

✈ Nearest airport: ....Oakland (OAK) 50 miles S

Places Rated Rank: 260

Naples-Marco Island, FL

🚗 Daily commute: 50:21
Peak freeway traffic:... Heavy

🚌 Public transit:.. *CAT*
Service:...........................9 city buses, 815 miles/day

🛡 Interstate highway: I-75

✈ Airline service: .... Nonhub
Airport: ....Naples Municipal (APF) 2 miles NE

Service	Passengers	Carriers	Cities	Top Market
Commuter	3,754	1	2	Key West
Jet	27,781	1	1	Atlanta

Places Rated Rank: 345

Nashville-Davidson--Murfreesboro, TN

Daily commute: 55:39
Peak freeway traffic:.. Heavy
HOV lanes, certain routes

Public transit: .... *MTA*
Service:........................... 113 city buses, 13,346 miles/day

Interstate highways:................................. I-24, I-40, I-65

Airline service: .... Medium Hub
Airport: ....Nashville Int'l (BNA) 5 miles SE

Service	Passengers	Carriers	Cities	Top Market
Commuter	17,850	2	3	St. Louis
Jet	4,934,351	23	52	Atlanta
International	16,347	4	2	Toronto

Places Rated Rank: 83

Nassau-Suffolk, NY

Daily commute: 1:10:36
Peak freeway traffic:.. Heavy

Public transit:............................... *MTA Long Island Bus*
Service:..........................443 city buses, 54,219 miles/day

LIRR commuter rail to New York City

Interstate highway: I-495

Airline service:.. Small Hub
Airport: ....Long Island MacArthur (ISP) 7 miles NE

Service	Passengers	Carriers	Cities	Top Market
Commuter	60,679	5	3	Philadelphia
Jet	992,878	4	12	Baltimore

Places Rated Rank: 121

✓Newark-Union, NJ-PA

Daily commute: 1:06:18
Peak freeway traffic:....................................... Very heavy
HOV lanes, certain routes

Public transit: .... *NJT*
Service:........................ 917 city buses, 232,157 miles/day
51 light rail, 2,658 miles/day

NJT suburban commuter rail to New York
AMTRAK corridor rail:.............................. Acela Express
AMTRAK corridor rail: .... Keystone Service

Interstate highways:................................. I-280, I-78, I-95

Airline service:.. Large Hub
Airport: ....Newark Liberty Int'l (EWR) 3 miles S

Service	Passengers	Carriers	Cities	Top Market
Jet	15,766,570	49	185	Atlanta
International	3,883,402	23	79	London

Places Rated Rank: 24

New Haven-Milford, CT

Daily commute: 49:47
Peak freeway traffic:.. Heavy

Public transit: .... *GNHTD*
Service:........................... 31 city buses, 2,551 miles/day

CDOT commuter rail to Hartford (proposed)
METRO NORTH commuter rail to New York City
SHORE LINE EAST commuter rail to New London
AMTRAK corridor rail: .... Acela Express

Interstate highways:... I-91, I-95

Airline service: .... Nonhub
Airport: ....Tweed New Haven (HVN) 3 miles SE

Service	Passengers	Carriers	Cities	Top Market
Commuter	39,381	2	1	Philadelphia
Jet	25,537	1	1	Cincinnati

Places Rated Rank: 259

New Orleans-Metairie-Kenner, LA

Daily commute: 57:19
Peak freeway traffic:.. Heavy

Public transit: .... *NORTA*
Service:.........................306 city buses, 31,053 miles/day
66 light rail, 2,863 miles/day

Interstate highways:................................. I-10, I-55, I-59

Airline service:.. Medium Hub
Airport: ....Louis Armstrong Int'l (MSY) 10 miles W

Service	Passengers	Carriers	Cities	Top Market
Jet	4,059,238	23	44	Atlanta
International	21,697	6	2	San Pedro Sula

Places Rated Rank: 65

✓New York-White Plains-Wayne, NY-NJ

Daily commute: 1:19:23
Peak freeway traffic:....................................... Very heavy
HOV lanes, certain routes

Public transit: .... *NYCT*
Service:..................... 5,191 heavy rail, 107,433 miles/day
3,849 city buses, 333,805 miles/day

LIRR commuter rail hub
METRO NORTH commuter rail hub
AMTRAK corridor rail:.............................. Acela Express
AMTRAK corridor rail:............................. Empire Service
AMTRAK corridor rail: .... Keystone Service

Interstate highways:........................ I-280, I-78, I-87, I-95

Airline service: .... Large Hub
Airports: ....John F. Kennedy Int'l (JFK) 13 miles SE

Service	Passengers	Carriers	Cities	Top Market
Jet	18,706,833	90	170	Los Angeles
International	7,720,032	72	89	London

La Guardia (LGA) 4 miles E

Service	Passengers	Carriers	Cities	Top Market
Commuter	388,284	3	18	Manchester
Jet	12,481,088	26	70	Chicago
International	615,737	8	7	Toronto

Westchester County (HPN) 25 miles NNE

Service	Passengers	Carriers	Cities	Top Market
Commuter	69,497	9	11	Washington
Jet	387,455	14	12	Chicago
International	7,553	1	1	Toronto

Places Rated Rank: 15

Niles-Benton Harbor, MI

Daily commute: 42:38
Peak freeway traffic:... Moderate

Public transit: .... *TCATA*
Service:...................................2 city buses, 148 miles/day

Interstate highways:.. I-196, I-94

Nearest airport: ....South Bend (SBN) 20 miles S

Places Rated Rank: 248

Norwich-New London, CT

- Daily commute: 47:36
  Peak freeway traffic:.. Heavy

- Public transit: .... *SEAT*
  Service:.............................. 19 city buses, 2,661 miles/day

- Shore Line East commuter rail: New Haven
  AMTRAK corridor rail:............................... Acela Express

- Interstate highway: I-95

- Nearest airport: ....Providence (PVD) 40 miles NE

Places Rated Rank: 231

Oakland-Fremont-Hayward, CA

- Daily commute: 1:08:08
  Peak freeway traffic:.. Congested
  HOV lanes, certain routes

- Public transit:..................................... *AC Transit & BART*
  Service:.........................633 city buses, 70,235 miles/day
  3 ferries, 246 miles/day
  522 heavy rail, 23,789 miles/day

- AMTRAK corridor rail:............................ Capitol Corridor
  AMTRAK corridor rail:................................. San Joaquins

- Interstate highway: I-80

- Airline service:.. Medium Hub
  Airport: .... Metropolitan Oakland Int'l (OAK) 4 miles S

Service	Passengers	Carriers	Cities	Top Market
Commuter	3,167	1	1	???
Jet	7,208,904	15	39	Los Angeles
International	85,663	3	5	Guadalajara

Places Rated Rank: 62

Ocala, FL

- Daily commute: 54:54
  Peak freeway traffic:... Heavy

- Public transit:... *SunTran*
  Service:............................... 6 city buses, 1,039 miles/day

- Interstate highway: I-75

- Nearest airport: .... Orlando (MCO) 50 miles SE

Places Rated Rank: 349

Ocean City, NJ

- Daily commute: 49:40
  Peak freeway traffic:... Heavy

- Public transit:.. *NJ TRANSIT*
  Service:.............................34 city buses, 2,900 miles/day

- NJ TRANSIT commuter rail to Newark

- Nearest airport: .... Atlantic City (ACY) 15 miles NE

Places Rated Rank: 365

Odessa, TX

- Daily commute: 40:00
  Peak freeway traffic:.. Light

- Public transit:.. *EZ RIDER*
  Service:................................. 7 city buses, 797 miles/day

- Interstate highway: I-20

- Nearest airport: ....Midland (MAF) 25 miles ENE

Places Rated Rank: 169

Ogden-Clearfield, UT

- Daily commute: 46:49
  Peak freeway traffic:... Heavy

- Public transit: .... *UTA*
  Service:..................30 city buses, 4,500 miles/day

- UTA commuter rail to SLC(proposed)

- Interstate highways:.. I-15, I-84

- Nearest airport: ....Salt Lake City (SLC) 30 miles S

Places Rated Rank: 350

Oklahoma City, OK

- Daily commute: 47:29
  Peak freeway traffic:... Heavy

- Public transit:.. *COTPA*
  Service:..........................80 city buses, 10,679 miles/day

- Interstate highways:.............................. I-35, I-40, I-44

- Airline service:.. Small Hub
  Airport: .... Will Rogers World (OKC) 6 miles SW

Service	Passengers	Carriers	Cities	Top Market
Jet	1,783,617	19	22	Dallas (DFW)

Places Rated Rank: 86

Olympia, WA

- Daily commute: 51:41
  Peak freeway traffic:... Heavy

- Public transit: .... *I.T.*
  Service:..........................44 city buses, 5,773 miles/day

- AMTRAK corridor rail:..................................... Cascades

- Interstate highway: I-5

- Nearest airport: .... Seattle (SEA) 45 miles NE

Places Rated Rank: 269

✓Omaha-Council Bluffs, NE-IA

- Daily commute: 41:59
  Peak freeway traffic:... Heavy

- Public transit:.. *MAT*
  Service:..........................107 city buses, 11,752 miles/day

- Interstate highway: I-80

- Airline service:.. Medium Hub
  Airport: ....Omaha Eppley Airfield (OMA) 3 miles NE

Service	Passengers	Carriers	Cities	Top Market
Commuter	4,141	1	2	Brookings
Jet	2,098,763	22	23	Denver

Places Rated Rank: 32

Orlando-Kissimmee, FL

- Daily commute: 57:36
  Peak freeway traffic:... Heavy
  HOV lanes, certain routes

- Public transit:.. *LYNX*
  Service:........................195 city buses, 38,580 miles/day

- CFRail commuter rail (proposed)

- Interstate highway: I-4

251

✈ Airline service: .... Large Hub
Airports: ....Orlando Int'l (MCO) 6 miles SE

Service	Passengers	Carriers	Cities	Top Market
Commuter	63,068	4	4	Miami
Jet	16,392,357	40	110	Atlanta
International	835,813	26	20	London

Orlando Sanford Int'l (MCO) 18 miles NE

Service	Passengers	Carriers	Cities	Top Market
Jet	76,287	2	15	San Juan

Places Rated Rank: 50

Oshkosh-Neenah, WI

🚗 Daily commute: 38:08
Peak freeway traffic: .... Heavy

🚌 Public transit: .... OTS
Service: .... 13 city buses, 1,313 miles/day

✈ Airline service: .... Nonhub
Airport: .... Outagamie County Regional (ATW) 3 miles W

Service	Passengers	Carriers	Cities	Top Market
Commuter	29,309	2	3	Minneapolis
Jet	267,499	9	9	Chicago

Places Rated Rank: 66

Owensboro, KY

🚗 Daily commute: 44:26
Peak freeway traffic: .... Light

🚌 Public transit: .... OTS
Service: .... 6 city buses, 900 miles/day

✈ Nearest airport: ....Evansville (EVV) 30 miles NW

Places Rated Rank: 299

Oxnard-Thousand Oaks-Ventura, CA

🚗 Daily commute: 53:28
Peak freeway traffic: .... Congested

🚌 Public transit: .... SCAT & VISTA
Service: .... 68 city buses, 4,262 miles/day

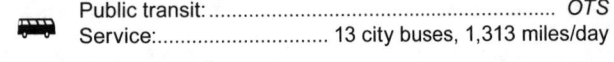 METROLINK commuter rail to Los Angeles
AMTRAK corridor rail: .... Pacific Surfliner

✈ Airline service: .... Nonhub
Airport: .... The Oxnard Airport (OXR) 1 miles W

Service	Passengers	Carriers	Cities	Top Market
Commuter	22,778	1	1	Los Angeles

Places Rated Rank: 270

Palm Bay-Melbourne-Titusville, FL

🚗 Daily commute: 52:23
Peak freeway traffic: .... Heavy

🚌 Public transit: .... SCAT
Service: .... 20 city buses, 2,854 miles/day

🛡 Interstate highway: I-95

✈ Airline service: .... Nonhub
Airport: .... Melbourne Int'l (MLB) 2 miles NW

Service	Passengers	Carriers	Cities	Top Market
Jet	222,720	3	4	Atlanta

Places Rated Rank: 237

Panama City-Lynn Haven, FL

🚗 Daily commute: 46:25
Peak freeway traffic: .... None

🚌 Public transit: .... BCCOA
Service: .... 7 city buses, 975 miles/day

✈ Airline service: .... Nonhub
Airport: .Panama City Bay County Int'l (PFN) 3 miles NW

Service	Passengers	Carriers	Cities	Top Market
Commuter	107,996	1	1	Atlanta
Jet	79,768	4	4	Memphis

Places Rated Rank: 198

Parkersburg-Marietta-Vienna, WV-OH

🚗 Daily commute: 46:08
Peak freeway traffic: .... Moderate

🚌 Public transit: .... EZ RIDER
Service: .... 7 city buses, 1,300 miles/day

🛡 Interstate highway: I-77

✈ Airline service: .... Nonhub
Airport: .... Mid-Ohio Valley Regional (PKB) 6 miles NE

Service	Passengers	Carriers	Cities	Top Market
Commuter	15,750	1	1	Pittsburgh

Places Rated Rank: 308

Pascagoula, MS

🚗 Daily commute: 54:06
Peak freeway traffic: .... Heavy

🚌 Public transit: .... COAST
Service: .... 18 city buses, 2,259 miles/day

🛡 Interstate highway: I-10

✈ Nearest airport: ....Mobile, AL (MOB) 35 miles ENE

Places Rated Rank: 373

Pensacola-Ferry Pass-Brent, FL

🚗 Daily commute: 53:09
Peak freeway traffic: .... Heavy

🚌 Public transit: .... ECAT
Service: .... 32 city buses, 4,068 miles/day

🛡 Interstate highway: I-10

✈ Airline service: .... Small Hub
Airport: ....Pensacola Regional (PNS) 3 miles NE

Service	Passengers	Carriers	Cities	Top Market
Commuter	10,360	1	1	Tampa
Jet	803,336	13	13	Atlanta

Places Rated Rank: 156

Peoria, IL

🚗 Daily commute: 42:49
Peak freeway traffic: .... Moderate

🚌 Public transit: .... CityLink
Service: .... 43 city buses, 4,778 miles/day

🛡 Interstate highway: I-74

✈ Airline service: .... Nonhub
Airport: .... Greater Peoria Regional (PIA) 4 miles W

Service	Passengers	Carriers	Cities	Top Market
Commuter	36,027	2	2	Minneapolis
Jet	219,164	6	5	Chicago

Places Rated Rank: 87

✓Philadelphia, PA

🚗 Daily commute: 1:01:43
Peak freeway traffic: .... Very heavy

🚌 Public transit: .... *SEPTA & PATCO*
Service: .... 1,169 city buses, 126,461 miles/day
276 heavy rail, 8,872 miles/day
117 light rail, 9,174 miles/day

🚆 ....SEPTA commuter rail hub
AMTRAK corridor rail: .... Acela Express
AMTRAK corridor rail: .... Keystone Service

🛡 Interstate highways: I-76, I-95

✈ Airline service: .... Large Hub
Airport: .... Philadelphia Int'l (PHL) 5 miles SW

Service	Passengers	Carriers	Cities	Top Market
Commuter	592,493	2	27	Harrisburg
Jet	14,856,893	31	127	Orlando
International	1,596,209	16	34	Frankfurt

Places Rated Rank: 27

Phoenix-Mesa-Scottsdale, AZ

🚗 Daily commute: 55:23
Peak freeway traffic: .... Congested
HOV lanes, certain routes

🚌 Public transit: .... *RPTA, TIM & Valley Metro*
Service: .... 510 city buses, 86,214 miles/day

🛡 Interstate highways: I-10, I-17

✈ Airline service: .... Large Hub
Airport: ....Phoenix Sky Harbor Int'l (PHX) 3 miles E

Service	Passengers	Carriers	Cities	Top Market
Commuter	193,801	3	16	Flagstaff
Jet	20,863,741	23	101	Las Vegas
International	732,657	6	17	San Jose del Cabo

Places Rated Rank: 46

Pine Bluff, AR

🚗 Daily commute: 49:30
Peak freeway traffic: .... Light

🚌 Public transit: .... PB Transit
Service: ....6 city buses, 985 miles/day

✈ Nearest airport: ....Little Rock (LIT) 5 miles NNW

Places Rated Rank: 341

✓Pittsburgh, PA

🚗 Daily commute: 54:25
Peak freeway traffic: .... Heavy
HOV lanes, certain routes

🚌 Public transit: .... *Port Authority of Allegheny County*
Service: .... 997 city buses, 100,192 miles/day
55 light rail, 3,462 miles/day

🛡 Interstate highways: I-70, I-76, I-79

✈ Airline service: .... Medium Hub
Airport: .... Pittsburgh Int'l (PIT) 12 miles NW

Service	Passengers	Carriers	Cities	Top Market
Commuter	460,659	10	34	Washington
Jet	4,766,804	27	66	Atlanta
International	73,994	9	4	Toronto

Places Rated Rank: 35

Pittsfield, MA

🚗 Daily commute: 40:46
Peak freeway traffic: .... Light

🚌 Public transit: .... *BRTA*
Service: .... 17 city buses, 2,345 miles/day

---

✈ Nearest airport: .... Albany, NY (ALB) 40 miles WNW

Places Rated Rank: 262

Pocatello, ID

🚗 Daily commute: 36:39
Peak freeway traffic: .... Light

🚌 Public transit: .... *PRT*
Service: ....8 city buses, 730 miles/day

🛡 Interstate highways: I-15, I-86

✈ Airline service: .... Nonhub
Airport: .... Pocatello Regional (PIH) 7 miles NW

Service	Passengers	Carriers	Cities	Top Market
Commuter	46,390	2	3	Salt Lake City
Jet	1,272	1	1	Salt Lake City

Places Rated Rank: 187

Portland-South Portland-Biddeford, ME

🚗 Daily commute: 49:21
Peak freeway traffic: .... Heavy

🚌 Public transit: .... *Metro CBITD*
Service: ....24 city buses, 2,252 miles/day
4 ferries, 201 miles/day

🚆 AMTRAK corridor rail: .... Downeaster

🛡 Interstate highway: I-95

✈ Airline service: .... Small Hub
Airport: ....Portland Int'l Jetport (PWM) 2 miles W

Service	Passengers	Carriers	Cities	Top Market
Commuter	9,794	4	3	New York
Jet	721,795	15	15	Washington

Places Rated Rank: 199

✓Portland-Vancouver-Beaverton, OR-WA

🚗 Daily commute: 51:27
Peak freeway traffic: .... Congested
HOV lanes, certain routes

🚌 Public transit: .... *TriMet*
Service: ....546 city buses, 75,047 miles/day
69 light rail, 9,842 miles/day

🚆 AMTRAK corridor rail: .... Cascades

🛡 Interstate highways: I-5, I-84

✈ Airline service: .... Medium Hub
Airport: ....Portland Int'l (PDX) 4 miles NE

Service	Passengers	Carriers	Cities	Top Market
Commuter	942,181	4	20	Seattle
Jet	5,914,787	17	39	Denver
International	202,256	8	4	Vancouver

Places Rated Rank: 29

Port St. Lucie-Fort Pierce, FL

🚗 Daily commute: 54:45
Peak freeway traffic: .... Moderate

🚌 Public transit: .... *CT*
Service: .... 3 city buses, 370 miles/day

🛡 Interstate highway: I-95

✈ Nearest airport: .... Melbourne (MLB) 40 miles N

Places Rated Rank: 369

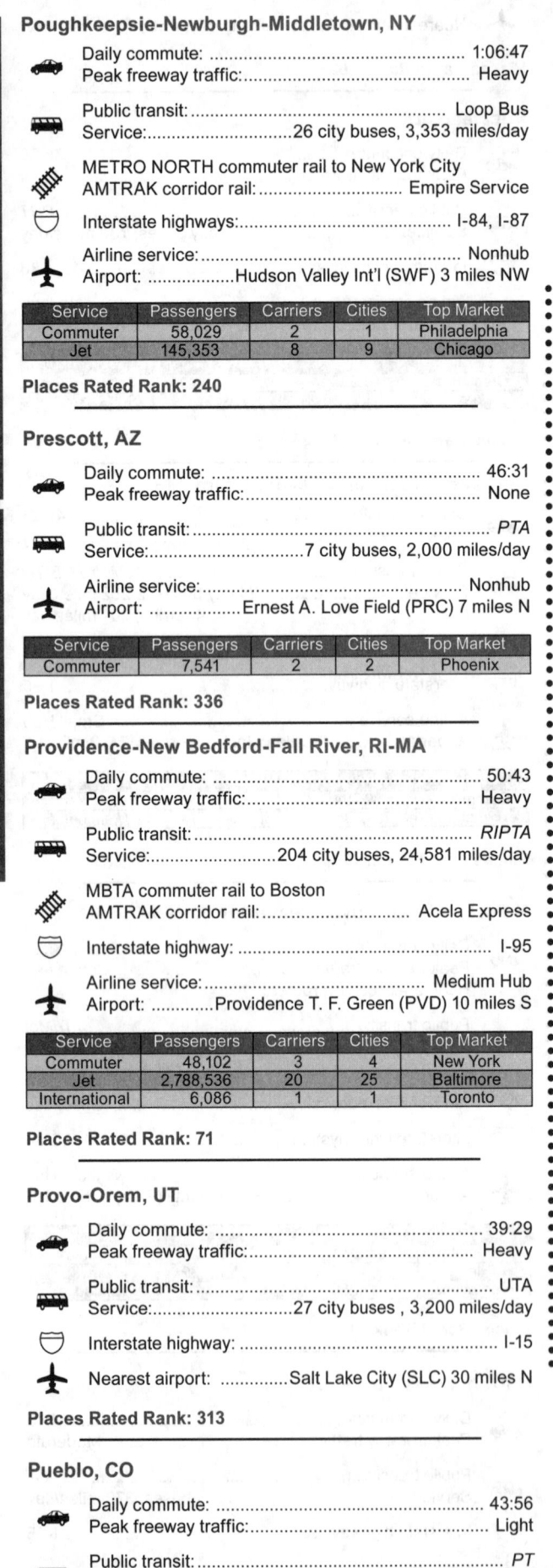

Poughkeepsie-Newburgh-Middletown, NY

Daily commute: 1:06:47
Peak freeway traffic:.. Heavy

Public transit:.. Loop Bus
Service:..........................26 city buses, 3,353 miles/day

METRO NORTH commuter rail to New York City
AMTRAK corridor rail:.............................. Empire Service

Interstate highways:.. I-84, I-87

Airline service:... Nonhub
Airport: ....Hudson Valley Int'l (SWF) 3 miles NW

Service	Passengers	Carriers	Cities	Top Market
Commuter	58,029	2	1	Philadelphia
Jet	145,353	8	9	Chicago

Places Rated Rank: 240

Prescott, AZ

Daily commute: 46:31
Peak freeway traffic:.. None

Public transit:... *PTA*
Service:............................7 city buses, 2,000 miles/day

Airline service:... Nonhub
Airport: ....Ernest A. Love Field (PRC) 7 miles N

Service	Passengers	Carriers	Cities	Top Market
Commuter	7,541	2	2	Phoenix

Places Rated Rank: 336

Providence-New Bedford-Fall River, RI-MA

Daily commute: 50:43
Peak freeway traffic:.. Heavy

Public transit:.. *RIPTA*
Service:.........................204 city buses, 24,581 miles/day

MBTA commuter rail to Boston
AMTRAK corridor rail:.............................. Acela Express

Interstate highway: I-95

Airline service:.. Medium Hub
Airport: ....Providence T. F. Green (PVD) 10 miles S

Service	Passengers	Carriers	Cities	Top Market
Commuter	48,102	3	4	New York
Jet	2,788,536	20	25	Baltimore
International	6,086	1	1	Toronto

Places Rated Rank: 71

Provo-Orem, UT

Daily commute: 39:29
Peak freeway traffic:.. Heavy

Public transit: .... UTA
Service:..........................27 city buses , 3,200 miles/day

Interstate highway: I-15

Nearest airport: ....Salt Lake City (SLC) 30 miles N

Places Rated Rank: 313

Pueblo, CO

Daily commute: 43:56
Peak freeway traffic:.. Light

Public transit: .... *PT*
Service:............................ 11 city buses, 1,462 miles/day

Interstate highway: I-25

Pueblo, CO (continued)

Airline service: .... Nonhub
Airport: ....Pueblo Memorial Field (PUB) 5 miles E

Service	Passengers	Carriers	Cities	Top Market
Commuter	1,763	1	1	Denver
Jet	1,364	1	1	Denver

Places Rated Rank: 250

Punta Gorda, FL

Daily commute: 50:19
Peak freeway traffic:.. Heavy

Interstate highway: I-75

Nearest airport: .... Fort Myers (RSW) 30 miles S

Places Rated Rank: 372

Racine, WI

Daily commute: 47:22
Peak freeway traffic:.. Heavy

Public transit:... *The Bus*
Service:............................25 city buses, 3,443 miles/day

Interstate highway: I-94

Nearest airport: ....Milwaukee (MKE) 20 miles N

Places Rated Rank: 200

Raleigh-Cary, NC

Daily commute: 55:29
Peak freeway traffic:.. Heavy

Public transit:... *CAT*
Service:............................46 city buses, 5,843 miles/day

Interstate highways:.. I-40, I-85

Airline service:.. Medium Hub
Airport: .... Raleigh-Durham Int'l (RDU) 9 miles NW

Service	Passengers	Carriers	Cities	Top Market
Commuter	36,498	4	5	Pittsburgh
Jet	4,683,712	27	40	Atlanta
International	74,702	4	2	London

Places Rated Rank: 110

Rapid City, SD

Daily commute: 36:57
Peak freeway traffic:.. Light

Public transit:............................. *Rapid Transit System*
Service:................................4 city buses, 456 miles/day

Interstate highway: I-90

Airline service: .... Nonhub
Airport: ....Rapid City Regional (RAP) 8 miles SE

Service	Passengers	Carriers	Cities	Top Market
Commuter	62,817	2	1	Denver
Jet	180,041	4	6	Minneapolis

Places Rated Rank: 148

Reading, PA

Daily commute: 47:45
Peak freeway traffic:.. Heavy

Public transit: .... BARTA
Service:............................43 city buses, 4,367 miles/day

Interstate highway: I-76

Places Rated Rank: 309

Redding, CA

🚗 Daily commute: 44:09
Peak freeway traffic:.. Moderate

🚌 Public transit: .... *RABA*
Service:............................. 13 city buses, 2,255 miles/day

🛡 Interstate highway: I-5

✈ Airline service: .... Nonhub
Airport: .... Redding Municipal (RDD) 6 miles SE

Service	Passengers	Carriers	Cities	Top Market
Commuter	91,094	2	4	San Francisco

Places Rated Rank: 194

✓Reno-Sparks, NV

🚗 Daily commute: 41:16
Peak freeway traffic:.. Very heavy

🚌 Public transit:.. *RTC*
Service:............................. 57 city buses, 9,101 miles/day

🛡 Interstate highway: I-80

✈ Airline service:... Medium Hub
Airport: .... Reno Tahoe Int'l (RNO) 3 miles SE

Service	Passengers	Carriers	Cities	Top Market
Commuter	85,218	4	4	Los Angeles
Jet	2,545,645	15	21	Las Vegas

Places Rated Rank: 9

Richmond, VA

🚗 Daily commute: 54:06
Peak freeway traffic:.. Heavy

🚌 Public transit:.. GRTC
Service:........................ 148 city buses, 14,384 miles/day

🛡 Interstate highways:............................. I-64, I-85, I-95

✈ Airline service:... Small Hub
Airport: .... Richmond Int'l (RIC) 6 miles E

Service	Passengers	Carriers	Cities	Top Market
Commuter	17,889	3	4	Pittsburgh
Jet	1,435,668	20	25	Atlanta

Places Rated Rank: 127

Riverside-San Bernardino-Ontario, CA

🚗 Daily commute: 1:05:59
Peak freeway traffic:.. Congested
HOV lanes, certain routes

🚌 Public transit: .... *RTA & SunLine*
Service:........................ 173 city buses, 19,384 miles/day

🚃 METROLINK commuter rail to Los Angeles

🛡 Interstate highways:... I-10, I-15

✈ Airline service:... Medium Hub
Airports: .... Ontario Int'l (ONT) 2 miles E

Service	Passengers	Carriers	Cities	Top Market
Commuter	57,749	1	1	Los Angeles
Jet	3,476,017	16	21	Phoenix
International	50,052	4	3	Guadalajara

Service	Passengers	Carriers	Cities	Top Market
Commuter	124,568	4	4	Los Angeles
Jet	578,068	14	14	San Francisco
International	16,993	3	2	Vancouver

Places Rated Rank: 93

Roanoke, VA

🚗 Daily commute: 47:36
Peak freeway traffic:.. Heavy

🚌 Public transit:................................... Valley Metro
Service:........................ 31 city buses, 3,594 miles/day

🛡 Interstate highway: I-81

✈ Airline service:... Nonhub
Airport:.................. Roanoke Woodrum (ROA) 3 miles NW

Service	Passengers	Carriers	Cities	Top Market
Commuter	102,787	5	5	Charlotte
Jet	218,902	8	7	Atlanta

Places Rated Rank: 116

Rochester, MN

🚗 Daily commute: 37:33
Peak freeway traffic:.. Moderate

🚌 Public transit:................................. *Rochester City Lines*
Service:........................ 27 city buses, 2,593 miles/day

🛡 Interstate highway: I-90

✈ Airline service:... Nonhub
Airport: .... Rochester Int'l (RST) 7 miles SW

Service	Passengers	Carriers	Cities	Top Market
Commuter	24,697	1	1	Minneapolis
Jet	118,602	5	5	Chicago

Places Rated Rank: 119

✓Rochester, NY

🚗 Daily commute: 44:53
Peak freeway traffic:.. Heavy

🚌 Public transit:... R-GRTA
Service:........................ 208 city buses, 18,461 miles/day

🚃 AMTRAK corridor rail:............................. Empire Service

🛡 Interstate highway: I-90

✈ Airline service:... Small Hub
Airport: .... Greater Rochester Int'l (ROC) 3 miles SW

Service	Passengers	Carriers	Cities	Top Market
Commuter	83,578	6	8	New York
Jet	1,360,712	19	23	New York
International	3,488	4	1	Toronto

Places Rated Rank: 37

Rockford, IL

🚗 Daily commute: 46:39
Peak freeway traffic:.. Moderate

🚌 Public transit: .... RMTD
Service:............................ 24 city buses, 3,432 miles/day

🛡 Interstate highways:... I-39, I-90

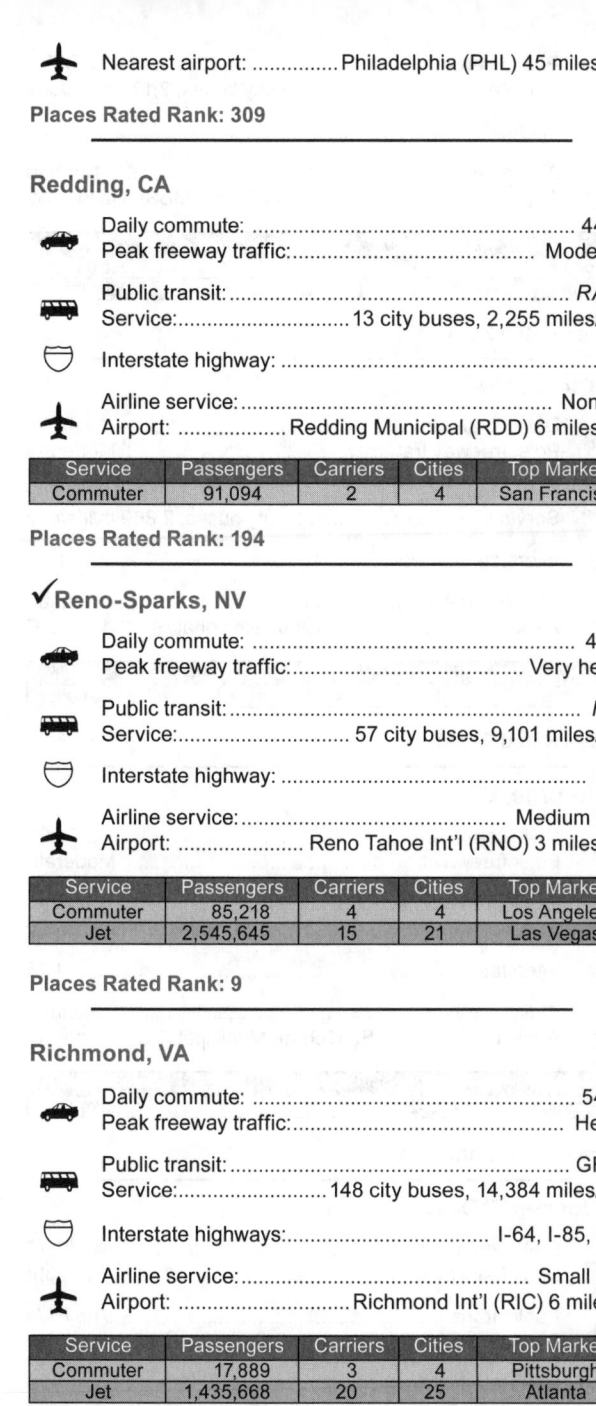

Poughkeepsie, FL – Rockford, IL

Airline service: .... Nonhub
Airport: ....Chicago-Rockford Int'l (RFD) 4 miles S

Service	Passengers	Carriers	Cities	Top Market
Jet	19,315	3	4	Detroit

Places Rated Rank: 236

Rockingham County-Strafford County, NH

Daily commute: 57:50
Peak freeway traffic:... Heavy

Public transit:.. COAST
Service:............................ 15 city buses, 1,584 miles/day

AMTRAK corridor rail: .... Downeaster

Interstate highway: I-95

Airline service: .... Nonhub
Airport: ....Pease Int'l Tradeport (PSM)

Service	Passengers	Carriers	Cities	Top Market
Jet	3,783	2	1	Sanford

Places Rated Rank: 324

Rocky Mount, NC

Daily commute: 47:39
Peak freeway traffic:... Light

Public transit:... Tar River Transit
Service:.............................9 city buses, 1,500 miles/day

Interstate highway: I-95

Nearest airport: ....Raleigh (RDU) 35 miles SW

Places Rated Rank: 351

Rome, GA

Daily commute: 51:00
Peak freeway traffic:... Moderate

Public transit:.. RTD
Service:............................22 city buses, 1,275 miles/day

Nearest airport: .... Atlanta (ATL) 45 miles SE

Places Rated Rank: 242

Sacramento–Arden-Arcade–Roseville, CA

Daily commute: 54:05
Peak freeway traffic:................................... Congested
HOV lanes, certain routes

Public transit:... Sacramento RT
Service:........................ 235 city buses, 27,821 miles/day
52 light rail, 3,491 miles/day

AMTRAK corridor rail:............................. Capitol Corridor
AMTRAK corridor rail:................................ San Joaquins

Interstate highways:..I-5, I-80

Airline service:.. Medium Hub
Airport: ....Sacramento Int'l (SMF) 10 miles NW

Service	Passengers	Carriers	Cities	Top Market
Commuter	94,333	2	5	Boise
Jet	5,100,814	17	28	Los Angeles
International	45,524	2	3	Guadalajara

Places Rated Rank: 77

Saginaw-Saginaw Township North, MI

Daily commute: 46:10
Peak freeway traffic:.. Moderate

Public transit:.. STARS
Service:............................ 29 city buses, 2,127 miles/day

Interstate highway: I-75

Airline service: .... Nonhub
Airport: .... MBS Int'l (MBS) 9 miles NW

Service	Passengers	Carriers	Cities	Top Market
Commuter	4,310	1	1	Detroit
Jet	201,932	6	5	Detroit

Places Rated Rank: 91

St. Cloud, MN

Daily commute: 40:57
Peak freeway traffic:... Moderate

Public transit:.. Metro Bus
Service:............................23 city buses, 2,869 miles/day

Interstate highway: I-94

Airline service:.. Nonhub
Airport: ....St. Cloud Regional (STC) 4 miles E

Service	Passengers	Carriers	Cities	Top Market
Commuter	24,570	1	1	Minneapolis

Places Rated Rank: 186

St. George, UT

Daily commute: 36:02
Peak freeway traffic:... Moderate

Public transit:.. SunTran
Service:............................4 city buses, 800 miles/day

Interstate highway: I-15

Airline service:.. Nonhub
Airport: .... St. George Municipal (SGU) 1 mile W

Service	Passengers	Carriers	Cities	Top Market
Commuter	49,526	1	2	Salt Lake City

Places Rated Rank: 238

St. Joseph, MO-KS

Daily commute: 42:48
Peak freeway traffic:... Light

Public transit:.. The Ride
Service:............................ 18 city buses, 2,120 miles/day

Interstate highway: I-29

Nearest airport: .... Kansas City (MCI) 45 miles S

Places Rated Rank: 239

✓ St. Louis, MO-IL

Daily commute: 54:48
Peak freeway traffic:... Heavy

Public transit:.. METRO
Service:........................ 348 city buses, 54,390 miles/day
34 light rail, 7,162 miles/day

Interstate highways:.......................... I-44, I-55, I-64, I-70

Airline service:.. Medium Hub
Airport: ....Lambert St. Louis Int'l (STL) 10 miles NW

Service	Passengers	Carriers	Cities	Top Market
Commuter	275,623	3	27	Springfield
Jet	6,823,294	23	70	Chicago
International	36,246	7	4	Toronto

Places Rated Rank: 13

Salem, OR

🚗 Daily commute: 49:14
Peak freeway traffic:.. Heavy

🚌 Public transit: .... *Cherriots*
Service:............................60 city buses, 7,464 miles/day

🚆 AMTRAK corridor rail: .... Cascades

🛡 Interstate highway: I-5

✈ Nearest airport: ....Portland (PDX) 45 miles N

Places Rated Rank: 277

Salinas, CA

🚗 Daily commute: 49:11
Peak freeway traffic:.. Heavy

🚌 Public transit: .... *MST*
Service:........................... 87 city buses, 7,676 miles/day

✈ Airline service:.. Nonhub
Airport: ....Monterey Peninsula (MRY) 3 miles SE

Service	Passengers	Carriers	Cities	Top Market
Commuter	121,925	2	2	Los Angeles
Jet	69,089	2	5	Phoenix

Places Rated Rank: 165

Salisbury, MD

🚗 Daily commute: 45:57
Peak freeway traffic:.. Light

🚌 Public transit: .... *Shore Transit*
Service:..............................3 city buses, 550 miles/day

✈ Airline service: .... Nonhub
Airport: .... Salisbury Ocean City (SBY) 4 miles SE

Service	Passengers	Carriers	Cities	Top Market
Commuter	63,581	2	2	Philadelphia

Places Rated Rank: 274

✓ Salt Lake City, UT

🚗 Daily commute: 48:31
Peak freeway traffic:.. Heavy

🚌 Public transit: .... *UTA*
Service:.............................. 37 light rail, 3,125 miles/day
350 city buses, 53,865 miles/day

🚆 UTA commuter rail to Ogden (proposed)

🛡 Interstate highways:............................... I-15, I-80, I-84

✈ Airline service:... Large Hub
Airport: .... Salt Lake City Int'l (SLC) 3 miles W

Service	Passengers	Carriers	Cities	Top Market
Commuter	307,025	2	11	???
Jet	10,472,545	19	93	Phoenix
International	145,883	7	5	Calgary

Places Rated Rank: 36

San Angelo, TX

🚗 Daily commute: 38:34
Peak freeway traffic:.. Light

🚌 Public transit: .... SAMPO
Service:................................5 city buses, 675 miles/day

✈ Airline service:.. Nonhub
Airport: ....San Angelo Mathis Field (SJT) 7 miles SW

Service	Passengers	Carriers	Cities	Top Market
Commuter	15,375	3	2	Houston
Jet	48,272	1	1	Dallas (DFW)

Places Rated Rank: 178

San Antonio, TX

🚗 Daily commute: 53:27
Peak freeway traffic:.. Very heavy

🚌 Public transit: .... VIA
Service:........................357 city buses, 52,507 miles/day

🚆 ASA commuter rail to Austin (proposed)

🛡 Interstate highways:................................. I-10, I-35, I-37

✈ Airline service:... Medium Hub
Airport: ....San Antonio Int'l (SAT) 7 miles N

Service	Passengers	Carriers	Cities	Top Market
Commuter	7,944	1	1	???
Jet	3,677,077	18	31	Dallas (DFW)
International	57,894	7	2	Mexico City

Places Rated Rank: 44

San Diego-Carlsbad-San Marcos, CA

🚗 Daily commute: 53:15
Peak freeway traffic:....................................... Congested
HOV lanes, certain routes

🚌 Public transit: .... *MTDB & NCTD*
Service:...................................83 light rail, 7,321 miles/day
598 city buses, 82,617 miles/day

🚆 NCTD COASTER suburban commuter rail
AMTRAK corridor rail: .... Pacific Surfliner

🛡 Interstate highways:.................................... I-15, I-5, I-8

✈ Airline service:... Large Hub
Airport: .... San Diego Int'l (SAN) 2 miles W

Service	Passengers	Carriers	Cities	Top Market
Commuter	338,592	2	2	Los Angeles
Jet	8,417,477	22	47	Phoenix
International	144,873	4	6	San Jose del Cabo

Places Rated Rank: 43

Sandusky, OH

🚗 Daily commute: 40:24
Peak freeway traffic:.. Light

🛡 Interstate highway: I-80/90

✈ Nearest airport: .... Cleveland (CLE) 40 miles E

Places Rated Rank: 283

San Francisco-San Mateo-Redwood City, CA

🚗 Daily commute: 1:01:37
Peak freeway traffic:....................................... Congested
HOV lanes, certain routes

🚌 Public transit: .... *MUNI*
Service:............................ 26 cable cars, 1,256 miles/day
400 city buses, 41,115 miles/day
5 ferries, 513 miles/day
130 light rail, 15,497 miles/day
259 trollies, 20,658 miles/day

🚆 CALTRAIN commuter rail to San Jose

🛡 Interstate highway: I-80

Airline service: .... Large Hub
Airport: ....San Francisco Int'l (SFO) 8 miles SE

Service	Passengers	Carriers	Cities	Top Market
Commuter	422,344	1	14	Santa Barbara
Jet	15,327,993	45	93	Chicago
International	3,295,102	26	31	London

Places Rated Rank: 57

San Jose-Sunnyvale-Santa Clara, CA

Daily commute: 56:06
Peak freeway traffic:.................................. Congested
HOV lanes, certain routes

Public transit: .... VTA
Service:...............................26 light rail, 4,009 miles/day
368 city buses, 50,825 miles/day

ACE commuter rail to Stockton
CALTRAIN commuter rail to San Francisco
AMTRAK corridor rail: .... Capitol Corridor

Interstate highway: I-80

Airline service:.. Medium Hub
Airport: ....Mineta San Jose Int'l (SJC) 2 miles NW

Service	Passengers	Carriers	Cities	Top Market
Commuter	29,775	3	4	Santa Barbara
Jet	5,373,761	18	31	Los Angeles
International	109,581	3	3	Tokyo

Places Rated Rank: 76

San Luis Obispo-Paso Robles, CA

Daily commute: 43:55
Peak freeway traffic:.................................... Light

Public transit: .... SLO Transit
Service:...............................11 city buses, 1,134 miles/day

AMTRAK corridor rail: .... Pacific Surfliner

Airline service: .... Nonhub
Airport: ....San Luis County Regional (SBP) 3 miles S

Service	Passengers	Carriers	Cities	Top Market
Commuter	110,535	2	2	Los Angeles
Jet	62,618	2	3	Phoenix

Places Rated Rank: 129

Santa Ana-Anaheim-Irvine, CA

Daily commute: 57:33
Peak freeway traffic:.................................. Congested

Public transit: .... OCTA
Service:......................... 402 city buses, 21,129 miles/day

METROLINK commuter rail to Los Angeles
AMTRAK corridor rail: .... Pacific Surfliner

Interstate highways:.................................. I-15, I-5

Airline service:... Medium Hub
Airport: ......John Wayne Orange County (SNA) 4 miles S

Service	Passengers	Carriers	Cities	Top Market
Commuter	40,020	1	1	Los Angeles
Jet	4,776,936	15	25	Phoenix

Places Rated Rank: 151

Santa Barbara-Santa Maria, CA

Daily commute: 40:27
Peak freeway traffic:.................................. Congested

Public transit: .... SBMTD
Service:...........................72 city buses, 7,355 miles/day

AMTRAK corridor rail: .... Pacific Surfliner

Airline service:.. Small Hub
Airport: ....Santa Barbara Municipal (SBA) 7 miles W

Service	Passengers	Carriers	Cities	Top Market
Commuter	147,630	2	3	Los Angeles
Jet	282,751	4	9	Phoenix

Places Rated Rank: 55

Santa Cruz-Watsonville, CA

Daily commute: 57:52
Peak freeway traffic:.................................. Congested

Public transit: .... SCMTD
Service:........................... 89 city buses, 10,841 miles/day

Nearest airport: .... San Jose (SJC) 40 miles N

Places Rated Rank: 312

Santa Fe, NM

Daily commute: 45:03
Peak freeway traffic:.................................. Moderate

Public transit: .... SFT
Service:............................20 city buses, 2,325 miles/day

Interstate highway: I-25

Airline service:.. Nonhub
Airport: ....Santa Fe Municipal (SAF) 10 miles SW

Service	Passengers	Carriers	Cities	Top Market
Commuter	10,295	1	1	Denver

Places Rated Rank: 249

Santa Rosa-Petaluma, CA

Daily commute: 55:50
Peak freeway traffic:.................................. Congested

Public transit: .... CityBus & SCT
Service:...........................61 city buses, 8,400 miles/day

Nearest airport: ....San Francisco (SFO) 35 miles S

Places Rated Rank: 334

Sarasota-Bradenton-Venice, FL

Daily commute: 47:25
Peak freeway traffic:.................................. Heavy

Public transit: .... MCAT & SCAT
Service:........................... 42 city buses, 7,300 miles/day

Interstate highway: I-75

Airline service:.. Small Hub
Airport: .... Sarasota Bradenton Int'l (SRQ) 3 miles N

Service	Passengers	Carriers	Cities	Top Market
Commuter	6,784	1	1	Tampa
Jet	642,329	10	12	Atlanta

Places Rated Rank: 131

Savannah, GA

Daily commute: 51:57
Peak freeway traffic:.................................. Heavy

Public transit: .... CAT
Service:...........................52 city buses, 6,891 miles/day
2 ferries, 23 miles/day

Left Column

🛡 Interstate highways:............................ I-16, I-95

✈ Airline service:............................ Small Hub
Airport: ..... Savannah Hilton Head Int'l (SAV) 7 miles NW

Service	Passengers	Carriers	Cities	Top Market
Commuter	3,332	1	1	Charlotte
Jet	1,027,640	17	18	Atlanta

Places Rated Rank: 124

Scranton-Wilkes-Barre, PA

🚗 Daily commute: 45:04
Peak freeway traffic:............................ Moderate

🚌 Public transit:............................ LCTA
Service:............................ 58 city buses, 5,600 miles/day

🛡 Interstate highways:............................ I-81, I-84

✈ Airline service:............................ Nonhub
Airport: ..... Wilkes-Barre Scranton Int'l (AVP) 5 miles SW

Service	Passengers	Carriers	Cities	Top Market
Commuter	56,514	8	6	Pittsburgh
Jet	157,091	8	6	Atlanta

Places Rated Rank: 132

Seattle-Bellevue-Everett, WA

🚗 Daily commute: 57:25
Peak freeway traffic:............................ Very heavy
HOV lanes, certain routes

🚌 Public transit:............................ KC METRO & WSF
Service:............................ 1,245 city buses, 119,132 miles/day
23 ferries, 2,677 miles/day
3 light rail, 118 miles/day
157 trollies, 9,700 miles/day

🚆 SOUNDER commuter rail to Tacoma
AMTRAK corridor rail:............................ Cascades

🛡 Interstate highways:............................ I-5, I-90

✈ Airline service:............................ Large Hub
Airports: ....Boeing King County Int'l (BFI) 4 miles S

Service	Passengers	Carriers	Cities	Top Market
Commuter	18,933	4	4	Los Angeles
International	1,820	1	1	Campbell River

Seattle Tacoma Int'l (SEA) 10 miles S

Service	Passengers	Carriers	Cities	Top Market
Commuter	1,608,727	3	26	Portland
Jet	12,837,836	29	75	Los Angeles
International	1,016,178	20	19	Vancouver

Places Rated Rank: 47

Sebastian-Vero Beach, FL

🚗 Daily commute: 42:56
Peak freeway traffic:............................ Moderate

🚌 Public transit:............................ Indian River Transit
Service:............................ 9 city buses, 681 miles/day

🛡 Interstate highway: I-95

✈ Nearest airport: ....West Palm Beach (PBI) 60 miles S

Places Rated Rank: 230

Sheboygan, WI

🚗 Daily commute: 36:01
Peak freeway traffic:............................ Light

Right Column

🚌 Public transit:............................ STS
Service:............................ 19 city buses, 1,714 miles/day

🛡 Interstate highway: I-43

✈ Nearest airport: .... Milwaukee (MKE) 40 miles S

Places Rated Rank: 257

Sherman-Denison, TX

🚗 Daily commute: 53:09
Peak freeway traffic:............................ Moderate

🚌 Public transit:............................ TCOG
Service:............................ 2 city buses, 971 miles/day

✈ Nearest airport: ....Dallas (DFW) 60 miles S

Places Rated Rank: 300

Shreveport-Bossier City, LA

🚗 Daily commute: 47:23
Peak freeway traffic:............................ Heavy

🚌 Public transit:............................ SporTran
Service:............................ 37 city buses, 5,869 miles/day

🛡 Interstate highways:............................ I-20, I-49

✈ Airline service:............................ Nonhub
Airport: ....Shreveport Regional (SHV) 4 miles SW

Service	Passengers	Carriers	Cities	Top Market
Commuter	18,855	2	2	Dallas (DFW)
Jet	301,806	7	7	Dallas (DFW)

Places Rated Rank: 286

Sioux City, IA-NE-SD

🚗 Daily commute: 37:47
Peak freeway traffic:............................ Light

🚌 Public transit:............................ SCTS
Service:............................ 12 city buses, 1,540 miles/day

🛡 Interstate highway: I-29

✈ Airline service:............................ Nonhub
Airport: ... Sioux Gateway-Bud Day Field (SUX) 6 miles S

Service	Passengers	Carriers	Cities	Top Market
Commuter	21,888	1	1	Minneapolis
Jet	19,620	1	1	Minneapolis

Places Rated Rank: 59

Sioux Falls, SD

🚗 Daily commute: 37:33
Peak freeway traffic:............................ Light

🚌 Public transit:............................ Sioux Falls Transit
Service:............................ 23 city buses, 1,964 miles/day

🛡 Interstate highways:............................ I-29, I-90

✈ Airline service:............................ Nonhub
Airport: ....Joe Foss Field (FSD) 3 miles NW

Service	Passengers	Carriers	Cities	Top Market
Commuter	13,528	1	1	Minneapolis
Jet	345,228	9	9	Minneapolis

Places Rated Rank: 188

South Bend-Mishawaka, IN-MI

🚗 Daily commute: 44:36
Peak freeway traffic:............................ Light

Public transit: .... *Transpo*
Service:.............................47 city buses, 4,439 miles/day

South Shore Line commuter rail to Chicago

Interstate highway: I-80/90

Airline service:.. Small Hub
Airport: South Bend Michiana Regional (SBN) 3 miles NW

Service	Passengers	Carriers	Cities	Top Market
Commuter	67,071	4	5	Detroit
Jet	278,385	12	9	Chicago

Places Rated Rank: 64

Spartanburg, SC

Daily commute: 48:30
Peak freeway traffic:.. Moderate

Public transit: .... *SPARTA*
Service:................................ 11 city buses, 702 miles/day

Interstate highways:.. I-26, I-85

Airline service:... Small Hub
Airport: .... Greenville Spartanburg Int'l (GSP) 3 miles S

Service	Passengers	Carriers	Cities	Top Market
Commuter	19,244	3	2	Charlotte
Jet	876,410	13	17	Atlanta

Places Rated Rank: 113

Spokane, WA

Daily commute: 44:43
Peak freeway traffic:.. Heavy

Public transit: .... *STA*
Service:...........................104 city buses, 14,428 miles/day

Interstate highway: I-90

Airline service:... Small Hub
Airport: .... Spokane Int'l (GEG) 5 miles SW

Service	Passengers	Carriers	Cities	Top Market
Commuter	357,072	3	5	Seattle
Jet	1,233,530	11	11	Seattle

Places Rated Rank: 82

✓Springfield, IL

Daily commute: 41:47
Peak freeway traffic:.. Moderate

Public transit: .... *SMTD*
Service:...........................37 city buses, 3,356 miles/day

Interstate highways:.. I-55, I-72

Airline service:.. Nonhub
Airport: .... Abraham Lincoln Capital (SPI) 3 miles NW

Service	Passengers	Carriers	Cities	Top Market
Commuter	27,542	1	1	St. Louis
Jet	53,222	2	1	Chicago

Places Rated Rank: 19

Springfield, MA

Daily commute: 47:04
Peak freeway traffic:.. Heavy

Public transit: .... *Pioneer Valley TA*
Service:........................187 city buses, 12,934 miles/day

CDOT commuter rail to Hartford (proposed)

Interstate highways:.. I-90, I-91

Airline service:...................................... Medium Hub
Airport: .... Bradley Int'l (BDL) 10 miles S

Service	Passengers	Carriers	Cities	Top Market
Commuter	49,031	4	5	Buffalo
Jet	3,555,021	22	37	Chicago
International	35,272	7	4	Toronto

Places Rated Rank: 189

✓Springfield, MO

Daily commute: 45:51
Peak freeway traffic:.. Heavy

Public transit: .... *The Bus*
Service:...........................19 city buses, 2,864 miles/day

Interstate highway: I-44

Airline service:... Small Hub
Airport: .Springfield Branson Regional (SGF) 5 miles NW

Service	Passengers	Carriers	Cities	Top Market
Commuter	12,862	1	1	St. Louis
Jet	418,187	10	14	Dallas (DFW)

Places Rated Rank: 23

Springfield, OH

Daily commute: 46:30
Peak freeway traffic:.. Heavy

Public transit: .... SCAT
Service:................................14 city buses, 739 miles/day

Nearest airport: ....Dayton (DAY) 15 miles W

Places Rated Rank: 98

State College, PA

Daily commute: 41:22
Peak freeway traffic:.. Light

Public transit: .... *CATA*
Service:...........................48 city buses, 3,768 miles/day

Interstate highway: I-80

Airline service:.. Nonhub
Airport: .... University Park (SCE) 4 miles N

Service	Passengers	Carriers	Cities	Top Market
Commuter	79,132	6	2	Philadelphia
Jet	60,934	5	4	Cincinnati

Places Rated Rank: 176

Stockton, CA

Daily commute: 1:02:19
Peak freeway traffic:.. Congested

Public transit: .... *SJRTD*
Service:...........................85 city buses, 13,494 miles/day

ACE commuter rail to San Jose
AMTRAK corridor rail:................................. San Joaquins

Interstate highway: I-5

Nearest airport: ....Oakland (OAK) 35 miles W

Places Rated Rank: 285

Sumter, SC

Daily commute: 46:26
Peak freeway traffic:.. Light

Public transit: .... *SWRTA*
Service:...........................23 city buses, 1,341 miles/day

Nearest airport: .... Columbia (CAE) 40 miles W

Places Rated Rank: 310

Syracuse, NY

🚗 Daily commute: 43:59
Peak freeway traffic:.................................. Moderate

🚌 Public transit: .... *CNY Centro*
Service:........................129 city buses, 10,556 miles/day

🚃 ONTRACK commuter rail hub
AMTRAK corridor rail: .... Empire Service

🛡 Interstate highways:.. I-81, I-90

✈ Airline service: .... Small Hub
Airport: .... Syracuse Hancock Int'l (SYR) 4 miles NE

Service	Passengers	Carriers	Cities	Top Market
Commuter	99,214	6	6	New York
Jet	1,091,823	18	16	Chicago

Places Rated Rank: 199

Tacoma, WA

🚗 Daily commute: 1:00:21
Peak freeway traffic:.................................. Very heavy

🚌 Public transit: .... *Pierce/Sound Transit*
Service:........................201 city buses, 33,223 miles/day
22 light rail, 300 miles/day

🚃 SOUNDER commuter rail to Seattle
AMTRAK corridor rail: .... Cascades

🛡 Interstate highway: I-5

✈ Airline service: .... Large Hub
Airport: ....Seattle Tacoma Int'l (SEA) 10 miles N

Service	Passengers	Carriers	Cities	Top Market
Commuter	1,608,727	3	26	Portland
Jet	12,837,836	29	75	Los Angeles
International	1,016,178	20	19	Vancouver

Places Rated Rank: 123

✓Tallahassee, FL

🚗 Daily commute: 50:56
Peak freeway traffic:.................................. Moderate

🚌 Public transit: .... *TalTran*
Service:........................49 city buses, 4,947 miles/day

🛡 Interstate highway: I-10

✈ Airline service: .... Small Hub
Airport: .... Tallahassee Regional (TLH) 4 miles SW

Service	Passengers	Carriers	Cities	Top Market
Commuter	16,855	1	2	Tampa
Jet	553,088	8	11	Atlanta

Places Rated Rank: 34

Tampa-St. Petersburg-Clearwater, FL

🚗 Daily commute: 54:31
Peak freeway traffic:.................................. Very heavy

🚌 Public transit: .... *HART & PSTA*
Service:........................290 city buses, 42,593 miles/day
4 light rail, 231 miles/day

🛡 Interstate highways:.. I-4, I-75

✈ Airline service: .... Small Hub
Airports: ....St Petersburg Clearwater Int'l (PIE) 8 miles N

Service	Passengers	Carriers	Cities	Top Market
Jet	244,565	3	11	Indianapolis

Tampa Int'l (TPA) 3 miles W

Service	Passengers	Carriers	Cities	Top Market
Commuter	156,411	3	12	Miami
Jet	9,256,238	23	75	Atlanta
International	143,383	10	5	Toronto

Places Rated Rank: 150

✓Terre Haute, IN

🚗 Daily commute: 45:28
Peak freeway traffic:.................................. Moderate

🚌 Public transit: .... *THTU*
Service:........................6 city buses, 596 miles/day

🛡 Interstate highway: I-70

✈ Nearest airport: ....Indianapolis (IND) 70 miles E

Places Rated Rank: 4

Texarkana, TX-Texarkana, AR

🚗 Daily commute: 43:43
Peak freeway traffic:.................................. Light

🚌 Public transit: .... *T Line*
Service:........................4 city buses, 475 miles/day

🛡 Interstate highway: I-30

✈ Airline service: .... Nonhub
Airport: .... Texarkana Webb Field (TXK) 4 miles NE

Service	Passengers	Carriers	Cities	Top Market
Commuter	17,814	3	2	Houston
Jet	16,386	1	1	Dallas (DFW)

Places Rated Rank: 258

Toledo, OH

🚗 Daily commute: 44:18
Peak freeway traffic:.................................. Heavy

🚌 Public transit: .... *TARTA*
Service:........................156 city buses, 13,341 miles/day

🛡 Interstate highways:.. I-75, I-80/90

✈ Airline service: .... Nonhub
Airport: .... Toledo Express (TOL) 10 miles W

Service	Passengers	Carriers	Cities	Top Market
Commuter	51,117	3	2	Detroit
Jet	160,304	5	7	Cincinnati

Places Rated Rank: 256

Topeka, KS

🚗 Daily commute: 44:01
Peak freeway traffic:.................................. Moderate

🚌 Public transit: .... *Topeka Transit*
Service:........................23 city buses, 2,406 miles/day

🛡 Interstate highways:.. I-35, I-70

✈ Nearest airport: .... Kansas City (MCI) 45 miles ENE

Places Rated Rank: 114

Trenton-Ewing, NJ

🚗 Daily commute: 57:42
Peak freeway traffic:.................................. Heavy

🚌 Public transit: .... *NJT*
Service:........................167 city buses, 12,900 miles/day

261

NJT commuter rail to Camden
SEPTA commuter rail to Philadelphia
AMTRAK corridor rail: .... Acela Express
AMTRAK corridor rail: .... Keystone Service

Interstate highway: I-95

Airline service:.. Nonhub
Airport: ....Trenton Mercer (TTN) 4 miles NW

Service	Passengers	Carriers	Cities	Top Market
Commuter	8,572	1	1	Bedford

Places Rated Rank: 320

Tucson, AZ

Daily commute: 50:41
Peak freeway traffic:.. Heavy

Public transit: .... COT
Service:................... 155 city buses, 21,454 miles/day

Interstate highways:.. I-10, I-19

Airline service:... Medium Hub
Airport:........................Tucson Int'l (TUS) 6 miles S

Service	Passengers	Carriers	Cities	Top Market
Commuter	5,239	1	1	???
Jet	2,031,297	13	17	Dallas (DFW)
International	11,672	3	1	Hermosillo

Places Rated Rank: 355

✓ Tulsa, OK

Daily commute: 46:33
Peak freeway traffic:.. Moderate

Public transit:... MTTA
Service:............................52 city buses, 5,790 miles/day

Interstate highway: I-44

Airline service:.. Small Hub
Airport: .... Tulsa Int'l (TUL) 5 miles NE

Service	Passengers	Carriers	Cities	Top Market
Jet	1,636,687	16	20	Dallas (DFW)

Places Rated Rank: 40

Tuscaloosa, AL

Daily commute: 47:26
Peak freeway traffic:.. Moderate

Public transit: .... TMT
Service:........................... 9 city buses, 714 miles/day

Interstate highways:.. I-20, I-59

Nearest airport: .... Birmingham (BHM) 40 miles NE

Places Rated Rank: 54

Tyler, TX

Daily commute: 47:39
Peak freeway traffic:.. Light

Public transit:.. Tyler Transit
Service:............................4 city buses, 385 miles/day

Interstate highway: I-20

Airline service:... Nonhub
Airport: .... Tyler Pounds Regional (TYR) 3 miles W

Service	Passengers	Carriers	Cities	Top Market
Commuter	68,538	3	2	Dallas (DFW)
Jet	18,317	2	2	Dallas (DFW)

Places Rated Rank: 311

Utica-Rome, NY

Daily commute: 43:59
Peak freeway traffic:.. Light

Public transit:... UTA
Service:...................25 city buses, 2,555 miles/day

AMTRAK corridor rail:............................ Empire Service

Interstate highway: I-90

Nearest airport: ....Syracuse (SYR) 40 miles W

Places Rated Rank: 221

Valdosta, GA

Daily commute: 43:30
Peak freeway traffic:.. Moderate

Public transit:....................................... Lowndes Transit
Service: ....3 city buses, 300 miles/day

Interstate highway: I-75

Airline service:... Nonhub
Airport:......................Valdosta Regional (VLD) 3 miles W

Service	Passengers	Carriers	Cities	Top Market
Commuter	15,313	1	1	Atlanta
Jet	26,430	1	1	Atlanta

Places Rated Rank: 247

Vallejo-Fairfield, CA

Daily commute: 1:07:40
Peak freeway traffic:.. Heavy

Public transit: .... Vallejo Transit & Baylink
Service:............................44 city buses, 6,952 miles/day
2 ferries, 662 miles/day

Interstate highway: I-80

Nearest airport: ....Oakland (OAK) 25 miles S

Places Rated Rank: 367

Victoria, TX

Daily commute: 46:35
Peak freeway traffic:.. Light

Public transit: .... VICTORIA TRANSIT
Service:.......................... 6 city buses, 712 miles/day

Airline service:... Nonhub
Airport: ....Victoria Regional (VCT) 5 miles NE

Service	Passengers	Carriers	Cities	Top Market
Commuter	10,909	2	1	Houston

Places Rated Rank: 190

Vineland-Millville-Bridgeton, NJ

Daily commute: 49:41
Peak freeway traffic:.. Light

Public transit:... NJTC
Service:................... 13 city buses, 1.005 miles/day

Nearest airport: ....Philadelphia, PA (PHL) 40 miles N

Places Rated Rank: 362

Virginia Beach-Norfolk-Newport News, VA-NC

Daily commute: 51:49
Peak freeway traffic:.. Heavy
HOV lanes, certain routes

🚌 Public transit: .... *HRT*
Service:.................287 city buses, 28,695 miles/day
3 ferries, 34 miles/day

🛡 Interstate highway: I-64

✈ Airline service:.................................... Medium Hub
Airports: ....Newport News Int'l (PHF) 9 miles NW

Service	Passengers	Carriers	Cities	Top Market
Commuter	41,337	2	2	Philadelphia
Jet	486,020	8	8	Atlanta

Norfolk Int'l (ORF) 3 miles NE

Service	Passengers	Carriers	Cities	Top Market
Commuter	84,596	6	7	New York
Jet	1,898,468	21	30	Atlanta

Places Rated Rank: 94

Visalia-Porterville, CA

🚗 Daily commute: 46:25
Peak freeway traffic:................................. Heavy

🚌 Public transit: .... *VCC*
Service:.............................19 city buses, 2,282 miles/day

✈ Nearest airport: ....Fresno (FAT) 40 miles NW

Places Rated Rank: 263

Waco, TX

🚗 Daily commute: 42:52
Peak freeway traffic:................................. Heavy

🚌 Public transit: .... *WTS*
Service:.............................15 city buses, 1,661 miles/day

🛡 Interstate highway: I-35

✈ Airline service:.. Nonhub
Airport: ....Waco Regional (ACT) 5 miles NW

Service	Passengers	Carriers	Cities	Top Market
Commuter	67,400	3	2	Dallas (DFW)
Jet	4,712	2	1	Dallas (DFW)

Places Rated Rank: 162

Warner Robins, GA

🚗 Daily commute: 43:45
Peak freeway traffic:.......................... Moderate

🛡 Interstate highway: I-75

✈ Nearest airport: ....Atlanta (ATL) 50 miles NW

Places Rated Rank: 319

Warren-Troy-Farmington Hills, MI

🚗 Daily commute: 58:13
Peak freeway traffic:.. Congested

🚌 Public transit:... *SMART Bus*
Service:............................32 city buses, 11,000 miles/day

🛡 Interstate highway: I-75

✈ Nearest airport: ....Detroit (DTW) 10 miles S

Places Rated Rank: 375

✓ Washington-Arlington-Alexandria, DC-VA-MD-WV

🚗 Daily commute: 1:09:53
Peak freeway traffic:.. Congested

🚌 Public transit: .... *WMATA*
Service:......................1,236 city buses, 130,863 miles/day
750 heavy rail, 33,487 miles/day

🚆 MARC commuter rail to Baltimore
VRE commuter rail to suburban Virginia
AMTRAK corridor rail: .... Acela Express

🛡 Interstate highways:............................... I-66, I-95

✈ Airline service:.................................... Large Hub
Airport: ....Ronald Reagan National (DCA) 3 miles S

Service	Passengers	Carriers	Cities	Top Market
Commuter	12,982	3	4	Charleston
Jet	8,692,954	26	81	Atlanta
International	137,603	4	4	Toronto

Washington Dulles Int'l (IAD) 20 miles W

Service	Passengers	Carriers	Cities	Top Market
Commuter	214,832	3	17	Pittsburgh
Jet	12,505,672	50	123	Atlanta
International	1,994,495	24	31	London

Places Rated Rank: 16

Waterloo-Cedar Falls, IA

🚗 Daily commute: 34:55
Peak freeway traffic:................................. Light

🚌 Public transit: .... *MET*
Service:.............................11 city buses, 1,435 miles/day

🛡 Interstate highway: I-380

✈ Airline service:.. Nonhub
Airport: ....Waterloo Municipal (ALO) 4 miles NW

Service	Passengers	Carriers	Cities	Top Market
Commuter	27,604	1	1	Minneapolis
Jet	9,377	1	1	Minneapolis

Places Rated Rank: 197

Wausau, WI

🚗 Daily commute: 38:25
Peak freeway traffic:................................. Light

🚌 Public transit: .... *WATS*
Service:.............................21 city buses, 1,580 miles/day

🛡 Interstate highway: I-39

✈ Airline service:.. Nonhub
Airport: ....Central Wisconsin (CWA) 11 miles S

Service	Passengers	Carriers	Cities	Top Market
Commuter	70,611	2	4	Minneapolis
Jet	89,657	5	3	Chicago

Places Rated Rank: 102

Weirton-Steubenville, WV-OH

🚗 Daily commute: 48:18
Peak freeway traffic:................................. Light

🚌 Public transit: .... *WTS* & *Steel Valley TS*
Service:.....................7 city buses, 350 miles/day

✈ Nearest airport: .... Pittsburgh, PA (PIT) 35 miles E

Places Rated Rank: 342

Wenatchee, WA

🚗 Daily commute: 37:59
Peak freeway traffic:................................. None

🚌 Public transit: .... Link
Service:.............................23 city buses, 3,717 miles/day

✈ Airline service:.. Nonhub
Airport: .... Pangborn Memorial (EAT) 4 miles E

Service	Passengers	Carriers	Cities	Top Market
Commuter	38,374	1	1	Seattle

Places Rated Rank: 177

West Palm Beach-Boca Raton-Boynton Beach, FL

Daily commute: 54:15
Peak freeway traffic:................................ Congested

Public transit: .... PalmTran
Service: .... 113 city buses, 20,001 miles/day

TRI-RAIL commuter rail to Miami

Interstate highway: I-95

Airline service:.. Medium Hub
Airport: .... Palm Beach Int'l (PBI) 3 miles W

Service	Passengers	Carriers	Cities	Top Market
Commuter	42,264	2	4	Tampa
Jet	3,442,944	15	26	Atlanta
International	50,310	5	5	Nassau

Places Rated Rank: 90

Wheeling, WV-OH

Daily commute: 48:56
Peak freeway traffic:................................ Moderate

Public transit: .... OVRTA
Service: .... 14 city buses, 2,004 miles/day

Interstate highway: I-70

Nearest airport: .... Pittsburgh (PIT) 40 miles NE

Places Rated Rank: 279

Wichita, KS

Daily commute: 41:10
Peak freeway traffic:................................ Moderate

Public transit:.. Wichita Transit
Service: .... 42 city buses, 4,765 miles/day

Interstate highway: I-35

Airline service:.. Small Hub
Airport: .... Wichita Mid-Continent (ICT) 5 miles SW

Service	Passengers	Carriers	Cities	Top Market
Jet	714,721	15	17	Dallas (DFW)

Places Rated Rank: 70

Wichita Falls, TX

Daily commute: 38:57
Peak freeway traffic:................................ Light

Interstate highway: I-44

Airline service:.. Nonhub
Airport: .... Wichita Falls Municipal (SPS) 6 miles N

Service	Passengers	Carriers	Cities	Top Market
Commuter	46,264	1	1	Dallas (DFW)
Jet	2,970	1	1	Dallas (DFW)

Places Rated Rank: 218

Williamsport, PA

Daily commute: 42:07
Peak freeway traffic:................................ Moderate

Public transit: .... CityBus
Service: .... 19 city buses, 2,160 miles/day

Interstate highway: I-180

Airline service:.. Nonhub
Airport: .... Williamsport Regional (IPT) 4 miles E

Service	Passengers	Carriers	Cities	Top Market
Commuter	30,771	2	1	Philadelphia

Places Rated Rank: 179

Wilmington, DE-MD-NJ

Daily commute: 53:12
Peak freeway traffic:................................ Very heavy

Public transit: .... DART
Service: .... 123 city buses, 12,344 miles/day

SEPTA commuter rail to Philadelphia
AMTRAK corridor rail: .... Acela Express

Interstate highway: I-95

Nearest airport: Philadelphia, PA (PHL) 25 miles NE

Places Rated Rank: 374

Wilmington, NC

Daily commute: 48:40
Peak freeway traffic:................................ Moderate

Public transit: .... Wave
Service: .... 19 city buses, 1,946 miles/day

Interstate highway: I-40

Airline service:.. Nonhub
Airport: .... Wilmington Int'l (ILM) 3 miles NE

Service	Passengers	Carriers	Cities	Top Market
Commuter	1,165	1	1	Charlotte
Jet	336,347	7	6	Charlotte

Places Rated Rank: 144

Winchester, VA-WV

Daily commute: 59:06
Peak freeway traffic:................................ Light

Interstate highway: I-81

Nearest airport: .... Washington, DC (IAD) 50 miles E

Places Rated Rank: 377

Winston-Salem, NC

Daily commute: 49:16
Peak freeway traffic:................................ Heavy

Public transit: .... WSTA
Service: .... 33 city buses, 4,146 miles/day

Interstate highway: I-40

Nearest airport: .... Greensboro (GSO) 15 miles E

Places Rated Rank: 298

Worcester, MA

Daily commute: 55:19
Peak freeway traffic:................................ Heavy

Public transit: .... WRTA
Service: .... 65 city buses, 8,000 miles/day

MBTA commuter rail to Boston

Interstate highway: I-90

Nearest airport: .... Bedford, MA (BED) 30 miles E

Places Rated Rank: 323

Yakima, WA

🚗 Daily commute: 41:16
Peak freeway traffic:... Light

🚌 Public transit: .... *YT*
Service:............................. 14 city buses, 1,884 miles/day

🛡 Interstate highway: I-82

✈ Airline service:... Nonhub
Airport: .... Yakima Air Terminal (YKM) 3 miles S

Service	Passengers	Carriers	Cities	Top Market
Commuter	56,410	1	1	Seattle

Places Rated Rank: 192

York-Hanover, PA

🚗 Daily commute: 51:16
Peak freeway traffic:... Heavy

🚌 Public transit: .... *rabbittransit*
Service:.............................34 city buses, 3,657 miles/day

🛡 Interstate highway: I-83

✈ Nearest airport: .... Harrisburg (MDT) 25 miles NNW

Places Rated Rank: 331

Youngstown-Warren-Boardman, OH-PA

🚗 Daily commute: 44:59
Peak freeway traffic:.. Moderate

🚌 Public transit: .... *WRTA*
Service:............................. 38 city buses, 3,748 miles/day

🛡 Interstate highways:... I-76, I-80

✈ Airline service:... Nonhub
Airport: . Youngstown Warren Regional (YNG) 10 miles N

Places Rated Rank: 265

Yuba City, CA

🚗 Daily commute: 54:37
Peak freeway traffic:... Light

🚌 Public transit: .... *YSTA*
Service:............................. 18 city buses, 1,863 miles/day

✈ Nearest airport: .... Sacramento (SMF) 30 miles S

Places Rated Rank: 333

Yuma, AZ

🚗 Daily commute: 40:14
Peak freeway traffic:... Light

🚌 Public transit:... *YMPO*
Service:.................................5 city buses, 533 miles/day

🛡 Interstate highway: I-8

✈ Airline service:... Nonhub
Airport: .... Yuma Int'l (YUM) 3 miles S

Service	Passengers	Carriers	Cities	Top Market
Commuter	51,395	2	2	Phoenix
Jet	9,830	1	1	Phoenix

Places Rated Rank: 214

ET CETERA: TRANSPORTATION

FERRYBOATS, CABLE CARS, MONORAILS, AERIAL TRAMS AND INCLINES

Besides the common bus and the unique rail systems in larger cities, transit systems operate other types of vehicles. Although these modes have little impact on total mass transit, they are by far the most fun to watch and ride, undeniably adding to a city's flavor.

• San Francisco has the continent's only *cable car* system. In operation since the 19th century, the MUNI's forty-one cars on Powell and on California Streets and the handsome 80-year-old dark olive Perley Thomas Company cars on New Orleans's Charles Street system are the only transit properties in the National Register of Historic Places.

• *Aerial trams* are passenger gondolas suspended from a system of aerial cables and propelled by separate cables attached to the vehicle suspension system. The cable system is powered by engines or motors at a central location, not on board the vehicle. New York operates the nation's only aerial commuter tram, traveling between Roosevelt Island and Manhattan some 250 feet above the East River. "The most exciting view in New York City", says the *New York Times*.

• *Automated guideways*, the newest public transit mode, includes personal rapid transit, group rapid transit, and people-mover systems. These electric vehicles run over fixed guideways and are without operators. Service may be on a fixed schedule or in response to a passenger-activated call button. You can catch one in eight locations:

Detroit, MI .... *Detroit People Mover*
Jacksonville, FL .... *Jacksonville TA*
Las Colinas, TX .... *Las Colinas RTA*
Las Vegas, NV .... *Las Vegas Monorail*
Miami, FL .... *Metro-Dade TA*
Morgantown, WV .... *West Virginia University*
Newark, NJ .... *AirTrain Newark*
Tampa, FL .... *Hillsborough Area RTA*

• *Ferryboats* are the largest transit vehicles, ranging in size up to 380 feet and carrying as many as 2,500 commuters per trip. Public transit ferries provide frequent bridge service over a fixed route and on a published schedule between two or more points. Hong Kong's Star Ferries and New York's Staten Island Ferries are the world's busiest. Washington State Ferries, the nation's largest system, operates 28 vessels between some 20 ports on Puget Sound.

Balboa, CA	Miami, FL
Baytown, TX	New Orleans, LA
Boston, MA	New York, NY
Bremerton, WA	Norfolk, VA
Chicago, IL	Philadelphia, PA
Cincinnati, OH	Port Huron, MI
Corpus Christi, TX	Portland, ME
Fort Lauderdale, FL	Providence, RI
Galveston, TX	Rock Island, IL
Glastonbury, CT	San Diego, CA
Harrisburg, IL	San Francisco, CA
Jersey City, NJ	Savannah, GA
Long Beach, CA	Seattle, WA
Mayport, FL	Tacoma, WA

• *Cog* or *cable incline cars* operate up and down steep slopes on rails via a cable mechanism so that passenger seats remain horizontal while the undercarriage (truck) is angled parallel to the slope. Called *funiculars* in Europe, these special tramway vehicles survive from the late 19th-century in five metro areas.

Chattanooga, TN-GA .... *Lookout Mountain*
Dubuque, IA .... *Fenelon Place Elevator*
Johnstown, PA .... *Johnstown-Westmont Incline*
Los Angeles, CA .... *Angels Flight Railway*
Pittsburgh, PA .... *Monongahela & Duquesne Hgts*

RIDING AMTRAK'S RAILS

Eighty-five years ago, anyone who had to get from one North American city to another did so aboard a train. There were 20,000 different routes from which to choose if you didn't care where you were going. *The Twentieth Century Limited, El Capitan, Blue Streak* —each had a unique, trademarked name. They still do—*Downeaster, Wolverine, Bay State, California Zephyr, Pacific Surfliner, Hiawatha, Sunset Limited, Empire Builder, Texas Eagle*, and *Yankee Clipper* - but today there are just 292 of them. Over the years,

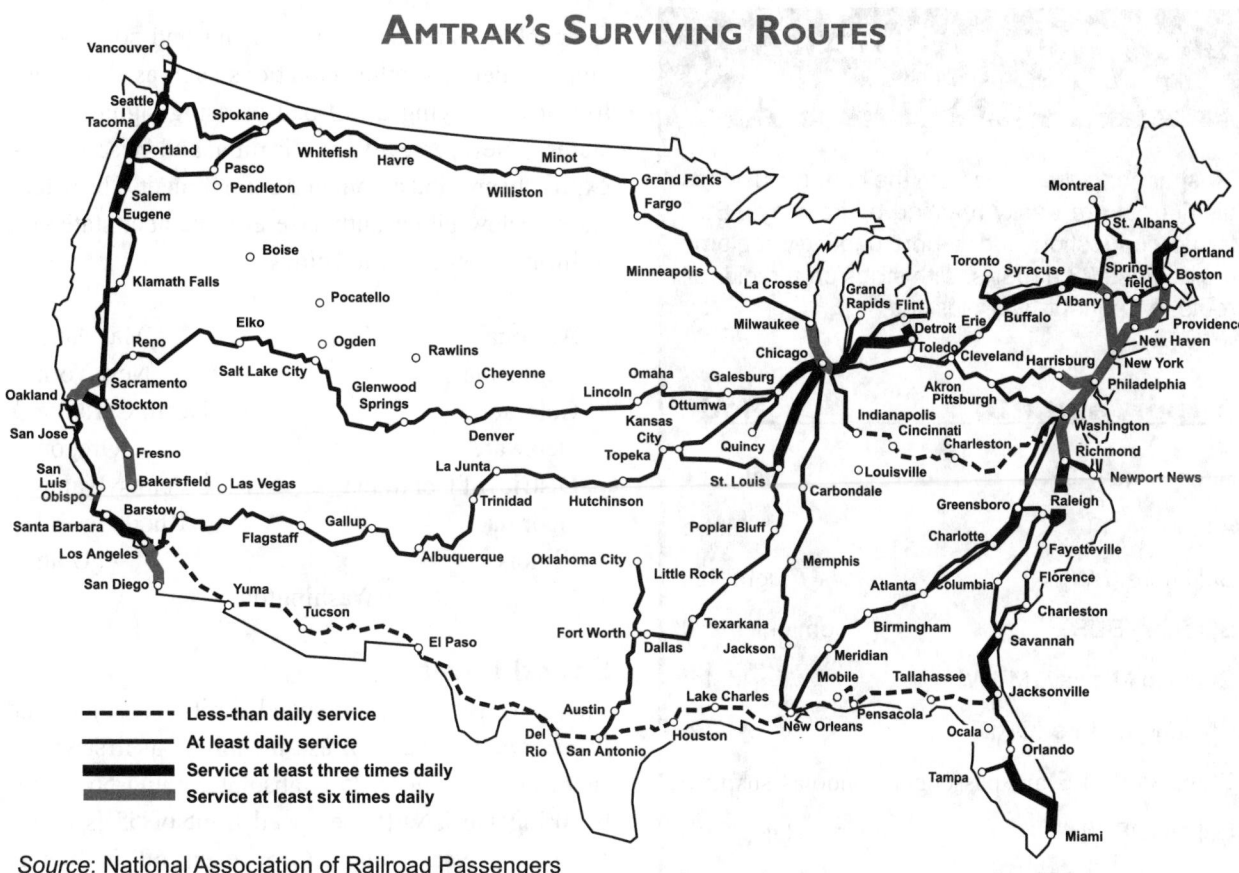

Source: National Association of Railroad Passengers

their share of the commercial inter-city passenger traffic has dwindled to less than 0.1 percent.

If passenger trains are ever to rise again, the renaissance will be caused not by high gasoline prices and spot fuel shortages, but by intolerable congestion on inter city highways. Railroads have two priceless assets: existing tracks and rights-of-way into the continent's population centers.

The National Railroad Passenger Corporation, a profit-making body, was created by Congress to subsidize the passenger business of its member railroads. Better known as AMTRAK, it started operation in 1971. Today it carries virtually all of the 25 million passengers who board U.S. inter-city trains each year.

The passenger rails don't reach everywhere, however. Although AMTRAK's and VIA's timetables boast of stops at hundreds of cities and towns from New York to San Diego, 157 of the 379 metro areas aren't on the route system. The metro areas bypassed include such large places as Phoenix, Tulsa, Las Vegas, Louisville, and Des Moines.

The most popular routes are on the Northeast Corridor, which include the *Acela Express*, *Metroliner*, and *Regional*. These routes serve Boston, New York, Philadelphia, Baltimore, Washington, and many other smaller cities and towns between Boston

and Newport News.

The fastest-growing routes are in California, particularly the *Pacific Surfliner*s between San Luis Obispo, Santa Barbara, Los Angeles, and San Diego, the *San Joaquins* between Oakland, Stockton, and Bakersfield and between Sacramento, Stockton, and Bakersfield, and the *Capitol Corridor* between Sacramento, Oakland, and San Jose. In the Northwest, another increasingly popular route is the *Cascade* between Seattle, Portland, and Eugene, Oregon.

OUR CONTRADICTORY RULES OF THE ROAD

Driving across political boundaries can mean a brush with contradictory traffic codes. Here are examples, with one caveat: The information comes from the American Automobile Association's latest *Digest of Motor Laws*, but it may not reflect recent changes in the law.

Automated Enforcement
A growing trend is the use of photo-imaging technology to enforce traffic safety laws. Most automated enforcement programs are for identifying red light runners. However, using automated cameras

Trains to Planes: Commuting to the Airport

Most airports are miles from the central business district but are easily reached by freeways. Still, traffic congestion and airport parking problems make these 23 airports, with stops on a rapid rail route, a frequent-flyer blessing.

Airport and (ID)	Mode
Anchorage (ACK)	Intercity
Atlanta (ATL)	Metro
Baltimore (BWI)	Light Rail
Burbank (BUR)	Commuter Rail
Chicago Midway (MDW)	Metro
Chicago O'Hare (ORD)	Metro
Cleveland (CLE)	Metro
Dallas (DFW)	Light Rail (2010)
Harrisburg (MDT)	Intercity
Milwaukee (MKE)	Intercity
Minneapolis (MSP)	Light Rail
New York JFK	Light Rail
Newark (EWR)	Commuter Rail
Oakland (OAK)	Intercity
Philadelphia (PHL)	Commuter Rail
Phoenix (PHX)	Light Rail (2006)
Portland (PDX)	Light Rail
St. Louis (STL)	Light Rail
San Francisco (SFO)	Metro
Seattle-Tacoma (SEA)	Light Rail (2009)
South Bend (SBN)	Commuter Rail
Washington Dulles (IAD)	Metro (2010)
Washington Reagan (DCA)	Metro

Source: National Association of Railroad Passengers. The list does not include airports that require a bus ride between the train station and terminal and airports that only have rail circulation systems.

for nabbing speeders is increasing and some states employ them for other violations such as skipping a toll or disobeying a railroad crossing signal. Three states—New Jersey, West Virginia, and Wisconsin—expressly prohibit automated enforcement. The fifteen states below either authorize enforcement statewide or limit its use specified cities.

Arizona	Maryland
California	New York
Colorado	North Carolina
Delaware	Oregon
District of Columbia	Pennsylvania
Georgia	Rhode Island
Illinois	Utah
Washington	

Speed Limits

There are two kinds of speed limits—absolute and *prima facie*, a legal phrase meaning "at first view." If the speed limit of 55 is absolute, going 56 means breaking the law. If the speed limit of 55 is *prima facie*, however, going 56 or even 60 is merely apparent evidence of unreasonable and imprudent speed. Drivers may escape a fine if they can convince the traffic court that their speed was reasonable and safe in light of the highway's condition, traffic, and visibility. States where all or some speed limits are prima facie are:

Arizona	Montana
Connecticut	New Hampshire
District of Columbia	New Jersey
Hawaii	New York
Idaho	Oregon
Indiana	Rhode Island
Louisiana	Utah
Maryland	West Virginia
Massachusetts	Wisconsin

Studded Tires

States allow drivers to mount studded snow tires on their automobiles for better traction during an icy winter. Because the carbide-tipped studs damage road surfaces, five states allow only hard rubber studs, and another nine states prohibit their use altogether:

Georgia	Minnesota
Hawaii	Mississippi
Illinois	New Mexico
Louisiana	Wisconsin
Maryland (except western counties)	

Glass Tinting

Tinted automobile window glass is a frequently chosen factory option. Over the past 10 years, however, aftermarket application of black and gunmetal-gray plastic sheeting to the inside of the windshield has become extremely popular. Because it interferes with night vision, it is restricted in varying degrees everywhere.

Audio Headsets

The issue here is whether the ears are as necessary for safe driving as the eyes. When you don't hear an ambulance siren, a ticket for failing to yield the right-of-way to an emergency vehicle is the likely consequence. But when you can't hear a train whistle or the air horn of an oncoming 18-wheeler, the result could be far more serious. Accordingly, several jurisdictions prohibit the driver from wearing an audio headset:

Alaska	Massachusetts
California	Minnesota
Colorado	Ohio
Florida	Pennsylvania
Georgia	Rhode Island
Illinois	Virginia
Louisiana	Washington
Maryland	

Motorcycle Helmets

The mileage fatality rate (deaths per 100 million miles) for motorcycle travel is five times that for auto travel and the major cause is head injuries. Consequently, nearly every state and all Canadian provinces require motorcycle riders to wear helmets. Motorcyclists have challenged the law, but state courts have generally upheld it because it affects the biker's right to receive insurance compensation for injuries. Only Colorado, Illinois, and Iowa do not require protective headgear of any kind for motorcyclists and passengers.

Bicycle Helmets

Bike riders without helmets are spotted less and less on the street. Still, there is an ongoing argument between libertarian cyclists and hospital emergency room staff about bicycle helmets. The latter holds that protective headgear prevents injury and death and its use should be as mandatory as seat belts. The former argues helmet use is everyone's own call.

No state requires adults to wear bicycle helmets, but most states have state-wide laws requiring children to wear helmets, especially children riding as passengers on bicycles. In addition to the states, cities often require helmets for adults and/or children. Up north, only British Columbia and Nova Scotia have passed mandatory helmet laws for all bike riders. Twenty-one states have no bicycle helmet laws.

Alabama	Massachusetts
California	New Hampshire
Connecticut	New Jersey
Delaware	New York
District of Columbia	North Carolina
Florida	Oregon
Georgia	Pennsylvania
Hawaii	Rhode Island
Louisiana	Tennessee
Maine	West Virginia
Maryland	

Mandatory Seat Belt Use

Because automobile accidents are the leading cause of death among young children, all states require the use of special vehicle restraints for children who are less than preschool age. Most jurisdictions also require the use of seat belts by the driver and all front seat passengers. Only New Hampshire does not.

Radar Detectors

All states use radar in speed enforcement programs and all but two—The District of Columbia and Virginia—permit automobile drivers to install radar detectors for advance warning. However, federal law makes radar detectors illegal in every state for trucks weighing more than 10,000 pounds.

DRIVER LICENSING

When you settle in a new state, you have to surrender your old driver's license and get a new one. The time permitted to do this ranges from immediately in twelve states, to 30 days in twenty-one jurisdictions and up to 6 months in Vermont. Hawaii lets you keep your license until it expires.

Required Tests

For a new resident with a valid driver's license, the requirements for getting a license in a new jurisdiction vary considerably. All states now require a vision test, but thirty states will waive all other tests. The written or road sign test is required in fourteen states. California, Florida, Illinois, and Ohio require getting

behind the wheel with a license examiner for a road test; in forty-seven other states, a road test may be waived at the discretion of the examiner.

Problem Drivers

If your license has been revoked, you won't get a new one simply by moving to another state. Every license application is checked with the National Driver Registry, a federal data file of persons whose license to drive has been denied or withdrawn. Moreover, forty-five states belong to the National Driver License Compact, an agreement among states to share information on drivers who accumulate tickets in one jurisdiction and try to escape control in another.

AFTER YOU MOVE DEADLINES

State	DRIVER LICENSING				VEHICLE REGISTRATION	
	Time Limit	Written Test	Road Test	NDL Compact	Time Limit	Inspection Required
ALABAMA	30 days	●		●	30 days	
ALASKA	90 days	●		●	10 days	E
ARIZONA	immediately			●	immediately	E
ARKANSAS	30 days			●	30 days	
CALIFORNIA	10 days	●	●		30 days	E
COLORADO	90 days			●	30 days	E
CONNECTICUT	30 days			●	60 days	S/E
DELAWARE	60 days			●	60 days	S/E
DISTRICT OF COLUMBIA	30 days			●	30 days	S/E
FLORIDA	30 days		●		10 days	
GEORGIA	30 days				30 days	E
HAWAII	*	●		●	*	S
IDAHO	30 days			●	90 days	
ILLINOIS	90 days	●	●		30 days	
INDIANA	60 days	●		●	60 days	
IOWA	30 days			●	30 days	
KANSAS	90 days			●	90 days	
KENTUCKY	30 days			●	30 days	
LOUISIANA	30 days			●	30 days	E
MAINE	30 days			●	30 days	
MARYLAND	60 days			●	60 days	S
MASSACHUSETTS	30 days				30 days	S/E
MICHIGAN	immediately				immediately	
MINNESOTA	60 days	●		●	60 days	
MISSISSIPPI	30 days	●		●	30 days	
MISSOURI	immediately			●	30 days	S/E
MONTANA	60 days			●	60 days	
NEBRASKA	30 days			●	30 days	
NEVADA	30 days	●		●	30 days	E
NEW HAMPSHIRE	60 days	●		●	60 days	
NEW JERSEY	60 days			●	60 days	S/E
NEW MEXICO	30 days			●	30 days	E
NEW YORK	30 days			●	30 days	E
NORTH CAROLINA	30 days			●	30 days	E
NORTH DAKOTA	90 days	●		●	90 days	
OHIO	immediately	●	●	●	immediately	
OKLAHOMA	immediately			●	immediately	S
OREGON	immediately			●	60 days	E
PENNSYLVANIA	60 days			●	20 days	S/E
RHODE ISLAND	30 days	●		●	30 days	S/E
SOUTH CAROLINA	90 days			●	45 days	

| | DRIVER LICENSING | | | | VEHICLE REGISTRATION | |
State	Time Limit	Written Test	Road Test	NDL Compact	Time Limit	Inspection Required
SOUTH DAKOTA	90 days			•	90 days	
TENNESSEE	30 days				30 days	E
TEXAS	30 days			•	30 days	S/E
UTAH	immediately			•	immediately	S/E
VERMONT	180 days			•	60 days	E
VIRGINIA	60 days			•	30 days	S/E
WASHINGTON	30 days			•	30 days	E
WEST VIRGINIA	30 days	•		•	30 days	S
WISCONSIN	60 days				2 days	
WYOMING	10 days			•	10 days	

The Interstate System: A Route Log and Finder List

4	132	FLORIDA	132	Daytona Beach, Lakeland, Orlando, Tampa, Winter Haven
5	1,382	CALIFORNIA	797	Anaheim, Los Angeles, Redding, Sacramento, San Diego, Santa Ana, Stockton
		OREGON	308	Eugene, Medford, Portland, Salem
		WASHINGTON	277	Bellingham, Olympia, Seattle, Tacoma, Vancouver
8	348	CALIFORNIA	170	El Centro, San Diego
		ARIZONA	178	Casa Grande, Yuma
10	2,460	CALIFORNIA	243	Los Angeles, Riverside, San Bernardino
		ARIZONA	392	Phoenix, Tucson
		NEW MEXICO	164	Deming, Las Cruces
		TEXAS	881	Beaumont, El Paso, Houston, San Antonio
		LOUISIANA	274	Baton Rouge, Lafayette, Lake Charles, New Orleans
		MISSISSIPPI	77	Biloxi, Gulfport, Pascagoula
		ALABAMA	66	Mobile
		FLORIDA	363	Jacksonville, Pensacola, Tallahassee
12	86	LOUISIANA	86	Baton Rouge, Slidell
15	1,434	CALIFORNIA	287	Riverside, San Bernardino, San Diego
		NEVADA	124	Las Vegas
		ARIZONA	29	
		UTAH	401	Brigham City, Ogden, Orem, Provo, Salt Lake City, St. George
		IDAHO	196	Blackfoot, Idaho Falls, Pocatello
		MONTANA	395	Butte, Great Falls, Helena, Sweetgrass
16	165	GEORGIA	165	Macon, Savannah
17	145	ARIZONA	145	Flagstaff, Phoenix
19	63	ARIZONA	63	Nogales, Tucson, Augusta

Transportation

The Interstate System: A Route Log and Finder List (Cont.)

20 1,540	TEXAS	636	Abilene, Arlington, Dallas, Fort Worth, Longview, Marshall, Midland, Odessa, Tyler	
	LOUISIANA	190	Monroe, Shreveport	
	MISSISSIPPI	155	Jackson, Meridian, Vicksburg	
	ALABAMA	215	Anniston, Birmingham, Tuscaloosa	
	GEORGIA	202	Atlanta	
	S. CAROLINA	142	Columbia, Florence	
24 316	ILLINOIS	39	Metropolis	
	KENTUCKY	93	Hopkinsville, Paducah	
	TENNESSEE	180	Chattanooga, Clarksville, Nashville	
	GEORGIA	4		
25 1,063	NEW MEXICO	463	Albuquerque, Las Cruces, Santa Fe	
	COLORADO	299	Colorado Springs, Denver, Fort Collins, Longmont, Pueblo	
	WYOMING	301	Casper, Cheyenne	
26 261	N. CAROLINA	40	Asheville, Hendersonville	
	S. CAROLINA	221	Charleston, Columbia, Spartanburg	
27 124	TEXAS	124	Amarillo, Lubbock	
29 753	MISSOURI	130	Kansas City, St. Joseph	
	IOWA	152	Council Bluffs, Sioux City	
	SOUTH DAKOTA	253	Sioux Falls	
	NORTH DAKOTA	218	Fargo, Grand Forks	
30 367	TEXAS	224	Dallas, Fort Worth, Texarkana	
	ARKANSAS	143	Little Rock, Texarkana	
35 1,569	TEXAS	504	Arlington, Austin, Dallas, Fort Worth, Laredo, San Antonio, Temple, Waco	
	OKLAHOMA	236	Norman, Oklahoma City	
	KANSAS	236	Kansas City, Lawrence, Topeka, Wichita	

FINDING YOUR WAY ON THE INTERSTATE

The Interstate's mid-1950s geometric and construction standards were meant to accommodate traffic expected by 1975: full control of access, design speeds of 50 to 70 miles per hour, a minimum of two travel lanes in each direction, 12-foot lane widths, 10-foot right paved shoulder, and 4-foot left paved shoulder. Today, the design is evolving for even heavier traffic expected by 2015.

By staying with a combination of interstate routes, it is possible for you to drive from one metro area in the United States to almost any other without stopping for a traffic light.

Five of the routes are more than 2,000 miles long. The longest, I-90, stretches 3,082 miles between downtown Boston and Seattle's waterfront. The next longest routes are I-80 (2,907 miles, from San Francisco to Hackensack, New Jersey), I-10 (2,460 miles along the nation's southern border, from Los Angeles to Jacksonville, Florida), I-40 (2,461 miles, from Barstow, California to

Route	Total	State	Miles	Cities
35	1,569	MISSOURI	115	Kansas City
		IOWA	218	Ames, Des Moines
		MINNESOTA	260	Albert Lea, Duluth, Minneapolis, St. Paul
37	143	TEXAS	143	Corpus Christi, San Antonio
39	131	ILLINOIS	131	Bloomington, Rockford
40	2,460	CALIFORNIA	155	Barstow, Needles
		ARIZONA	359	Flagstaff, Kingman
		NEW MEXICO	371	Albuquerque, Gallup, Tucumcari
		TEXAS	177	Amarillo
		OKLAHOMA	331	Clinton, Oklahoma City
		ARKANSAS	285	Fort Smith, Little Rock
		TENNESSEE	455	Jackson, Knoxville, Memphis, Nashville
		N. CAROLINA	327	Asheville, Burlington, Durham, Greensboro, Hickory, Raleigh, Winston-Salem
43	183	WISCONSIN	183	Green Bay, Milwaukee, Sheboygan
44	635	TEXAS	15	Wichita Falls
		MISSOURI	291	Joplin, Springfield, St. Louis
		OKLAHOMA	329	Oklahoma City, Tulsa
45	285	TEXAS	285	Dallas, Galveston, Houston, Texas City
49	207	LOUISIANA	207	Alexandria, Lafayette, Nachitoches, Opelousas, Shreveport
55	943	LOUISIANA	66	Hammond, LaPlace
		MISSISSIPPI	290	Grenada, Jackson, McComb
		TENNESSEE	12	Memphis
		ARKANSAS	72	Blytheville, West Memphis
		MISSOURI	209	Cape Girardeau, St. Louis
		ILLINOIS	294	Bloomington, Chicago, East St. Louis, Joliet, Springfield

Smithfield, North Carolina), and I-70 (2,175 miles from Cove Fort, Utah, to Baltimore). Three of these routes, I-10, I-80, and I-90, cross the country from coast to coast, and I-40 nearly makes it.

Seven interstate routes span the nation in a north-south direction: I-5 (1,382 miles, from San Diego to Bellingham, Washington), I-15 (1,437 miles, from San Diego to the Montana-Canada border), I-35 (1,568 miles, from suburban New Orleans to Chicago), I-65 (888 miles, from Mobile, Alabama, to Gary-Hammond, Indiana), I-75 (1,787 miles, from Naples, Florida, to the Michigan-Canada border), and I-95 (1,894 miles, from the city of Miami to the Maine-Canada border).

Certainly there are shorter 2-digit routes. I-97 connects Baltimore with Maryland's capital at Annapolis, a distance of 18 miles. I-19 in Arizona is a 63-mile fast route between Tucson and Nogales, and I-66 heads down out of the Virginia mountains 75 miles into Washington, DC

Transportation

The Interstate System: A Route Log and Finder List (Cont.)

57	381	MISSOURI	22	Charleston, Sikeston
		ILLINOIS	359	Champaign, Chicago, Kankakee, Rantoul, Urbana
59	443	LOUISIANA	11	New Orleans, Slidell
		MISSISSIPPI	171	Hattiesburg, Laurel, Meridian
		ALABAMA	241	Birmingham, Gadsden, Tuscaloosa
		GEORGIA	20	
64	937	MISSOURI	15	St. Louis
		ILLINOIS	128	Belleville, East St. Louis
		INDIANA	124	Evansville, New Albany
64		KENTUCKY	185	Frankfort, Lexington, Louisville
		WEST VIRGINIA	188	Charleston, Huntington, White Sulpher Springs
		VIRGINIA	298	Charlottesville, Newport News, Norfolk, Richmond
65	888	ALABAMA	367	Birmingham, Decatur, Mobile, Montgomery
		TENNESSEE	121	Nashville
		KENTUCKY	138	Bowling Green, Elizabethtown, Louisville
		INDIANA	262	Gary, Indianapolis, Lafayette
66	76	VIRGINIA	75	Arlington, Fairfax, Falls Church, Front Royal, Vienna
		WASH., DC	1	Washington
68	113	WEST VIRGINIA	32	Morgantown
		MARYLAND	81	Cumberland
69	356	INDIANA	158	Anderson, Fort Wayne, Indianapolis, Muncie
		MICHIGAN	198	Battle Creek, Flint, Lansing
70	2,175	UTAH	232	Cove Fort, Green River, Richfield
		COLORADO	451	Denver, Grand Junction
		KANSAS	424	Kansas City, Lawrence, Topeka
		MISSOURI	252	Columbia, Kansas City, St. Louis
		ILLINOIS	136	East St. Louis, Effingham, Vandalia
		INDIANA	154	Indianapolis, Richmond, Terre Haute
		OHIO	226	Columbus, Dayton, Springfield, Zanesville
		WEST VIRGINIA	14	Wheeling
		PENNSYLVANIA	167	Pittsburgh
		MARYLAND	93	Baltimore, Hagerstown
71	346	KENTUCKY	98	Covington, Louisville
		OHIO	248	Cincinnati, Cleveland, Columbus, Mansfield
72	79	ILLINOIS	79	Champaign, Decatur, Springfield
		MISSOURI	2	
73	12	N. CAROLINA	12	Greensboro
74	416	IOWA	5	Davenport
		ILLINOIS	220	Bloomington, Champaign, Moline, Peoria, Rock Island, Urbana
		INDIANA	172	Crawfordsville, Indianapolis, Shelbyville

(74)	416	OHIO	19	Cincinnati
(75)	1,788	FLORIDA	472	Bradenton, Fort Myers, Gainesville, Lakeland, Naples, Ocala, Sarasota, St. Petersburg, Tampa
		GEORGIA	355	Atlanta, Macon, Valdosta
		TENNESSEE	162	Chattanooga, Knoxville
		KENTUCKY	192	Covington, Lexington, Richmond
		OHIO	212	Cincinnati, Dayton, Lima, Middletown, Toledo
		MICHIGAN	395	Bay City, Detroit, Flint, Saginaw
(76)	618	COLORADO	184	Denver, Fort Morgan, Sterling
		NEBRASKA	2	
		OHIO	78	Akron, Youngstown
		PENNSYLVANIA	351	Harrisburg, Lancaster, Philadelphia, Pittsburgh, Reading
		NEW JERSEY	3	Camden
(77)	610	S. CAROLINA	91	Columbia, Rock Hill
		VIRGINIA	69	Bluefield, Wytheville
		WEST VIRGINIA	187	Beckley, Bluefield, Charleston, Parkersburg
		OHIO	160	Akron, Canton, Cleveland, Dover, Marietta
(78)	143	PENNSYLVANIA	75	Allentown, Bethlehem, Easton
		NEW JERSEY	68	Irvington, Jersey City, Newark, Plainfield
		NEW YORK	1	New York City
(79)	345	WEST VIRGINIA	161	Charleston, Fairmont, Morgantown
		PENNSYLVANIA	184	Erie, Meadville, Pittsburgh, Washington
(80)	2,908	CALIFORNIA	202	Davis, Fairfield, Oakland, Sacramento, San Francisco, Vallejo
		NEVADA	411	Elko, Reno, Sparks, Winnemucca
		UTAH	198	Salt Lake City
		WYOMING	403	Cheyenne, Evanston, Laramie, Rawlings, Rock Springs
		NEBRASKA	455	Grand Island, Kearney, Lincoln, Omaha
		IOWA	307	Davenport, Des Moines, Iowa City
		ILLINOIS	164	Chicago, Joliet, Moline, Rock Island,
		INDIANA	152	Elkhart, Gary, Hammond, Mishawaka, South Bend
		OHIO	237	Cleveland, Elyria, Toledo, Warren, Youngstown
		PENNSYLVANIA	311	Du Bois, Milton, Sharon, Stroudsburg
		NEW JERSEY	68	Bergen-Passaic
(81)	855	TENNESSEE	75	Bristol, Johnson City, Kingsport, Knoxville
		VIRGINIA	324	Bristol, Roanoke
		WEST VIRGINIA	26	Martinsburg
		MARYLAND	12	Hagerstown
		PENNSYLVANIA	234	Harrisburg, Scranton, Wilkes-Barre
		NEW YORK	184	Binghamton, Syracuse
(82)	143	WASHINGTON	132	Kennewick, Pasco, Richland, Yakima

Transportation

82	143	OREGON	11	Hermiston
83	84	MARYLAND	34	Baltimore
		PENNSYLVANIA	50	Harrisburg, York
84	767	OREGON	375	Baker, Pendleton, Portland
		IDAHO	275	Boise, Twin Falls
		UTAH	117	Ogden
84	230	PENNSYLVANIA	50	Scranton
		NEW YORK	72	Newburgh
		CONNECTICUT	99	Bristol, Danbury, Hartford, New Britain, Waterbury
		MASS.	8	
85	667	ALABAMA	80	Auburn, Montgomery, Opelika
		GEORGIA	179	Atlanta
		S. CAROLINA	106	Anderson, Greenville, Spartanburg
		N. CAROLINA	233	Burlington, Charlotte, Durham, Gastonia, Greensboro, High Point
		VIRGINIA	69	Petersburg
86	63	IDAHO	63	American Falls, Pocatello
86	183	NEW YORK	177	
		PENNSYLVANIA	7	
87	333	NEW YORK	333	Albany, Glens Falls, New York City, Newburgh, Poughkeepsie, Troy
88	173	ILLINOIS	173	Chicago, Moline
88	118	NEW YORK	118	Binghamton, Oneonta, Schenectady
89	191	N. HAMPSHIRE	61	Concord, Lebanon
		VERMONT	130	Burlington, Montpelier
90	2,983	WASHINGTON	297	Seattle, Spokane
		IDAHO	74	Coeur d'Alene, Kellogg
		MONTANA	550	Billings, Bozeman, Butte, Missoula
		WYOMING	209	Buffalo, Sheridan
		SOUTH DAKOTA	413	Rapid City, Sioux Falls
		MINNESOTA	276	Albert Lea, Austin, Rochester
		WISCONSIN	187	Beloit, Janesville, La Crosse, Madison
		ILLINOIS	108	Chicago, Elgin, Rockford
		INDIANA	157	Elkhart, Gary, Hammond, Mishawaka, South Bend
		OHIO	244	Cleveland, Elyria, Lorain, Toledo
		PENNSYLVANIA	47	Erie
		NEW YORK	287	Albany, Buffalo, Rochester, Rome, Schenectady, Syracuse, Troy, Utica

Route	Total	State	Miles	Cities
90	2,983	MASS.	134	Boston, Pittsfield, Springfield, Worcester
91	291	CONNECTICUT	58	Hartford, Hew Haven, Meriden
		MASS.	55	Springfield
		VERMONT	178	Brattleboro, St. Johnsbury
93	189	MASS.	46	Boston, Lawrence, Lowell
		N. HAMPSHIRE	132	Concord, Manchester
		VERMONT	11	St. Johnsbury
94	1,608	MONTANA	248	Billings, Glendive, Miles City
		NORTH DAKOTA	353	Bismarck, Fargo
		MINNESOTA	260	Minneapolis, Moorehead, St. Cloud, St. Paul
		WISCONSIN	348	Eau Claire, Kenosha, Madison, Milwaukee, Racine
		ILLINOIS	77	Chicago
		INDIANA	46	Gary, Hammond, Michigan City, Portage
		MICHIGAN	276	Ann Arbor, Battle Creek, Benton Harbor, Detroit, Jackson, Kalamazoo
95	1,894	FLORIDA	382	Boca Raton, Daytona Beach, Fort Lauderdale, Fort Pierce, Hialeah, Hollywood, Jacksonville, Melbourne, Miami, Palm Beach, Pompano Beach
		GEORGIA	112	Brunswick, Savannah
		S. CAROLINA	199	Florence
		N. CAROLINA	181	Fayetteville
		VIRGINIA	175	Arlington, Petersburg, Richmond
		WASH., DC	0	Washington
		MARYLAND	109	Baltimore
		DELAWARE	23	Wilmington
		PENNSYLVANIA	52	Philadelphia
		NEW JERSEY	79	Elizabeth, Newark, Trenton
		NEW YORK	23	New York City
		CONNECTICUT	112	Bridgeport, Milford, New Haven, New London, Norwalk, Stamford
		RHODE ISLAND	43	Cranston, Pawtucket, Providence, Warwick
		MASS.	90	Attleboro, Boston
		N. HAMPSHIRE	16	Portsmouth
		MAINE	298	Augusta, Bangor, Portland
96	193	MICHIGAN	193	Detroit, Grand Rapids, Lansing, Muskegon
97	18	MARYLAND	18	Annapolis, Baltimore
99	58	PENNSYLVANIA	58	Altoona

Source: Federal Highway Administration, The Dwight D. Eisenhower National System of Interstate and Defense Highways Route Log and Finder List

Education

N ine months of the year, three of every ten of us either work in an educational institution or learn in one. Education eats up 7.5 percent of the Gross National Product. Keeping the enterprise going is the biggest item on city budgets. Whether the results are worth it is an excuse for teachers, administrators, parents, politicians, and taxpayers to raise their voices with one another occasionally.

Education is certainly not the sacred cow it once was. The scores of high school students on most standardized tests aren't much better today than they were in 1960. Among high school seniors, a surprising portion can't draw inferences from written material, write a persuasive essay, or solve a math problem requiring several steps.

Parents and teachers blame each other. Although parents trust teachers more than they do politicians, journalists, or business people, the grades they award teachers hasn't risen above C+ over the past three decades. For their part, teachers are even stingier graders of parents—a C minus. Most parents, they say, are too tired and uninterested to get involved in their child's schooling.

PUBLIC SCHOOLS

Economists comparing homes among neighborhoods know price differences have less to do with a well-designed, well-built house and a lot to do with how good the schools are. The quality of the schools usually tips the balance when a relocating family weighs a neighborhood's good and bad points. Often their choice is influenced by a real estate agent's hearsay that the schools are great or ought to be because the local tax rate is high. Are there ways to compare districts and schools more objectively?

Shopping for a District

A sign of the times: In some of Long Island's school districts, local cops check the addresses of children and discover imposters who live in New York City taking up seats in suburban schools. To meet residency requirements, parents register their kids under the addresses of

America's 70 Largest School Districts

Representing less than 1 percent of all school districts, these systems educate one of every six public school students. While they are large enough to offer specialized courses and activities, two other items stand out: They operate larger schools (700 students compared to 500 in the average district) and they have a higher pupil/teacher ration (19 to 1 compared to 16.5 to 1).

District	Students	District	Students
New York City Public Schools	1,023,674	Austin (TX) Independent District	79,950
Los Angeles Unified District	741,367	Fort Worth (TX) Independent District	79,769
City of Chicago Schools	426,812	Cypress-Fairbanks (TX) District	79,314
Dade County (Miami) Schools	368,933	Fulton County (Atlanta) Schools	75,891
Clark County (NV) Schools	283,221	Jordan (Sandy, UT) District	75,548
Broward County (FL) Schools	274,591	Virginia Beach City Public Schools	75,515
Houston Independent District	208,945	Mesa (AZ) Unified District	75,471
Hillsborough County (Tampa) Schools	189,469	Brevard County (FL) School District	74,824
Philadelphia City School District	187,547	Northside (San Antonio) District	74,649
Hawaii Department of Education	183,185	Anne Arundel County (MD) Schools	73,991
Palm Beach County (FL) District	175,076	Nashville-Davidson (TN) County Schools	72,807
Orange County (FL) Schools	173,331	Denver County (CO) Schools	72,410
Fairfax County (VA) Public Schools	164,765	Lee County (Fl) Schools	71,210
Dallas Independent School District	158,027	Granite (Salt Lake City) District	68,783
Detroit City School District	141,461	Guilford County (NC) Schools	68,220
Montgomery County (MD) Schools	139,393	Seminole County (FL) Schools	66,692
Prince George`s (MD) Schools	136,095	Prince William County (VA) Schools	66,298
Gwinnett County (GA) Schools	135,392	Volusia County (FL) Schools	65,281
San Diego Unified District	134,709	Greenville County (SC) Schools	65,265
Duval County (FL) Schools	129,486	Orleans Parish (LA) School Board	64,920
Memphis City School District	121,028	Cleveland (OH) Municipal Schools	64,670
Charlotte-Mecklenburg (NC) Schools	118,765	Mobile County (AL) Schools	63,987
Wake County (Raleigh) Schools	114,568	Washoe County (Reno, NV) Schools	63,322
Pinellas County (FL) Schools	113,651	El Paso (TX) Independent District	63,216
Baltimore County Public Schools	107,701	Fort Bend (TX) Independent District	62,853
Cobb County (GA) Schools	103,935	District of Columbia Public Schools	62,306
DeKalb County (GA) Schools	99,986	Arlington (TX) Independent District	62,267
Jefferson County (KY) Schools	97,976	Santa Ana (CA)	61,693
Long Beach (CA) Unified District	96,319	Tucson (AZ) Unified District	61,204
Milwaukee School District	93,654	Pasco County (FL) School District	60,846
Albuquerque Public Schools	93,341	Columbus (OH) Public Schools	60,668
Baltimore City Public Schools	88,401	San Bernardino (CA) City Unified	59,105
Jefferson County (CO) Schools	86,868	Davis CA) District Schools	58,953
Polk County (FL) School District	86,292	Elk Grove (CA) Unified	58,670
Fresno Unified District	80,760	Boston (MA) Schools	57,742

Source: U.S. Department of Education, Core of Common Data.

relatives or friends.

Elsewhere, a new Illinois law makes fudging school registration to get children into a better district a misdemeanor punishable by 30 days in jail, a fine, and tuition restitution. In eastern Pennsylvania, districts routinely require parents to re-enroll their children to weed out interlopers from over the border in New Jersey.

In the 1930s, the United States was fragmented into 130,000 school districts. After decades of consolidation, there are fewer than 15,000. They range in size from hundreds that don't actually operate schools—but bus children to other districts—to the giants.

Moving into an unfamiliar area means stepping into a thicket of school districts, each with its own politics, funding, mission statement, standards, curricula, and results. Since your taxes support the district, you'll want to find out their differences with a consumer's eye. Visit the district principal or superintendent's office and consider several factors:

• A good district can give you a written philosophy or a statement of educational objectives approved within the past 5 years by the state board of education. If educational philosophy and objectives are explicit and under constant examination and review, then a district takes its mission seriously.

• The classroom teachers in the district should have not only a standard certificate but also (in 50 percent of the cases or better) at least a master's degree or equivalent in the subject they teach.

• A district's holding power—that is, the percentage of its ninth-grade pupils who stay in school and finish—should be at least 90 percent. If 95 percent of a district's enrollment is in average daily attendance, that's a good indication of how closely parents and schools keep tabs on children.

• Beware of the professional revolving door. A high number of eligible teachers not getting tenure might mean that the district has tough standards, but it could also be a sign that the district cuts costs by hiring beginners and then refusing them tenure at the end of their probationary period. Under this scheme, it is possible for a child to progress from kindergarten through high school and have inexperienced, unfamiliar teachers each year.

Shopping for a School

Outside Washington, DC, in late summer, days before the Prince Georges County school district throws open a single window, parents bring lawn chairs, paperbacks, and blankets to register children in choice magnet schools on a first-come, first-served basis.

Moving into a good school district doesn't necessarily mean you'll find quality education in all its schools. Get a district map of neighborhood boundaries for the schools as well as a list of Parent-Teacher Association (PTA) contacts. Talking with a local parent will save you time. Don't listen to administrators and guidance counselors who claim it's the curriculum that counts, not the teacher. Find out who the best teachers are and where they teach. Then make an appointment with their school's principal or the head guidance counselor to get specific information. Note the following:

• A good high school should have one guidance counselor for every 200 students, and it should have at least one full-time career counselor.

• Classroom size in high school should average no more than 30 students. The size of the senior class shouldn't be smaller than 300 students. If the enrollment is much less than that, many specialized or advance placement courses won't be offered.

• A quality high school should offer 4 years of English, 3 years of mathematics, 3 years of science, 3 years of social studies, and 2 years of foreign languages; second-year courses in biology, astronomy, chemistry, and physics; college-preparatory courses in the humanities; at least 1 year of computer literacy; and Advanced Placement (AP) courses for college credit.

• Because one of five 4-year public colleges must accept every high school graduate within the state, regardless of program followed or grades earned, it is no longer noteworthy that most of a high school's graduating seniors go on to college. The question to ask is: Which colleges are accepting them—top schools with tough admissions standards, or open-admission institutions with no requirements but that the check be good and the diploma in hand?

Don't cross a high school off your list if it doesn't measure up on all these points. A school can have all but one or two and still be a good one. Relocation experts advise clients that the stability of a town is reflected best

America's 15 Largest Community Colleges

About one in four people going on to college after high school attends a community college. Almost all institutions are publicly supported. Most of the ones below have several campuses.

Community College	Students
Houston Community College (TX)	80,331
City College of San Francisco (CA)	61,627
Northern Virginia Community College	59,707
Tarrant County Community College (TX)	55,053
College of DuPage (IL)	54,825
North Harris Montgomery College (TX)	53,070
Pima Community College (AZ)	52,967
Austin Community College (TX)	52,693
Broward Community College (FL)	49,134
American River College (CA)	47,363
Macomb Community College (MI)	46,983
Riverside Community College (CA)	45,192
Santa Ana College (CA)	44,255
Mesa Community College	43,931
Valencia Community College (FL)	42,961

America's 15 Largest Public Universities

Some 5 million people attend doctoral-level institutions in the United States. In a dramatic shift from the past, more women than men enroll in them and a good many more women than men graduate from them.

University	Students
University of Minnesota, Twin Cities	62,525
Ohio State University, Main Campus	60,294
Arizona State University, Tempe	57,138
University of Florida, Gainesville	56,217
The University of Texas, Austin	55,819
University of Arizona, Tucson	51,814
University of South Florida, Tampa	50,819
University of Central Florida	50,076
Temple University	49,768
Michigan State University	49,095
Texas A & M University	47,366
Pennsylvania State University	46,281
University of Wisconsin, Madison	46,153
Indiana University, Bloomington	45,955
University of Washington, Seattle	45,923

in its schools. If the high school is good, chances are that the schools at the lower levels will also be good.

In choosing an elementary school or a junior high, again ask questions of principals and other parents.

• Class size in elementary schools should average no more than 20 pupils. Reading should be emphasized over all other subjects, but writing,problem solving in math, hands-on work in science, and the social studies curriculum should get their due.

• In elementary schools, there should be a full-time librarian and a classroom-size library. There should also be one large room or auditorium for school meetings, arts performances, and special guest presentations.

• In junior high or middle schools-grades 7, 8, and 9-there should be special provisions for both bright students and slow learners.

PRIVATE SCHOOLS

One statistic about elementary and secondary education in the United States since 1930 is the 100 percent growth in the number of private schools, in contrast to the 75 percent decline in the number of public schools. This isn't to say that public schools are collapsing, though many literally are in older urban centers. Most of the schools that have closed were rural, one room buildings. But it does show that private schools are a thriving alternative.

Today, one of nine school-age children attends a private or parochial (parish) school. In spite of the decline in school enrollments during the 1980s, private schools held on to more of their enrollment than did public schools. Today, enrollment is on the rise in both sectors.

Recent research from the Department of Education shows that students in private high schools take more courses in smaller classes than do their public school counterparts. Critics of public education point out that because private institutions forego the smorgasbord of electives that public schools offer their students, graduates of private high schools have tougher basic courses on their transcripts and are better prepared for college study.

In most Canadian provinces, Catholic schools are publicly funded and run by separate school boards. In the United States, Catholic schools are the

private school alternative with the biggest enrollment (2.5 million pupils). Although half of all private school pupils sit in Catholic school classrooms, two of every three private schools are non-Catholic. Some 1.7 million pupils attend schools run by groups such as the Evangelical Lutheran Church, the Seventh-Day Adventist Board of Education, and the National Society for Hebrew Day Schools. Nonsectarian schools enroll another 800,000 pupils, most of whom pay tuition to institutions belonging to the National Association of Independent Schools (NAIS).

THE PUBLIC LIBRARY

At a bank of Internet terminals at a public library's main branch you may see a cab driver researching family genealogy on your left. On your right, a high school senior is investigating jobs with the airlines. Behind you, a stack of Mexico City newspapers wait on a reshelving cart. And in front, an acre of tables is laden with briefcases and bookbags where people sit reading.

Every metro area, no matter how small, poor, or isolated, has a network of public libraries. More than any of the different education institutions mentioned in this chapter, the library is a vital center and ultimate education resource for everyone.

Within greater New York's five boroughs and five suburban counties in New Jersey and New York State, there are 153 library systems acquiring 2 million books each year to add to the 42 million already housed in hundreds of libraries. Immense as this figure sounds, that's one book for less than four people. Other metro areas do better, but smaller ones in the inner South and in Texas do a lot worse.

Turnover

A better way to compare metro area libraries is to focus on how the library profession compares individual libraries. Turnover Rate is calculated by dividing the library's annual circulation by its number of books, i.e., its holdings. The result shows the activity of a library's collection, indicating the number of times each book would have circulated during the year if circulation had been spread evenly throughout the collection.

A library which emphasizes the circulation of best-sellers will have a higher Turnover Rate than a library which emphasizes subject depth in its collection and has an extensive reference collection... or, frankly, a library that is open fewer hours and has books no one likes to read.

America's 15 Largest Colleges

The highest degree a college—in the classic sense of the word—awarded was a Bachelor's. Baccalaureate institutions are now the smallest higher education classification. Many of the colleges listed below were community colleges ten years ago.

College	Students
Miami (FL) Dade College	94,561
Community College of Southern Nevada	53,951
St Petersburg (FL) College	35,021
Utah Valley State College	31,168
Metropolitan State College of Denver	25,829
South Texas (McAllen) College	21,927
Brigham Young University (Rexburg, ID)	16,659
Vincennes (IN) University	15,361
CUNY College of Technology	14,463
Okaloosa-Walton (FL) College	11,471
Midland (TX) College	10,570
Dixie State College of Utah	9,536
University of Arkansas, Fort Smith	8,528
Farmingdale (NY) State University	8,173
Clayton State University (GA)	7,687

America's 15 Largest Private Institutions

There are more private colleges and universities than public ones (1,461 versus 647), but they enroll fewer students. One reason is the higher expense.

College	Students
Brigham Young University	37,007
Excelsior College	29,884
Davenport University	23,235
New York University	22,901
Saint Leo University	22,781
Northeastern University	22,533
Park University	22,011
Boston University	21,587
Syracuse University	18,961
Columbia College	18,358
University of Southern California	18,065
Depaul University	17,811
Saint Johns University, New York	16,543
Embry Riddle Aeronautical University	15,482
Cornell University	14,163

Source: National Center for Education Statistics, Integrated Postsecondary Education Data System (IPEDS). All student figures are for unduplicated full- and part-time students who have enrolled throughout the year.

COLLEGE TOWNS

One in four metro areas have much higher porportions of young adults and college graduates than normal. The 20 mapped above score the highest in the "college town" factor.

COLLEGES AND UNIVERSITIES

Educators like to say that schooling leads to just three outcomes: more schooling, employment, or unemployment. When high school graduates go on to college or find jobs, the public education system is considered successful; if they do neither, the system is judged a flop.

In fact, nearly half of metro-area high school graduates eventually go to college, and seven of ten of these begin their freshman year at an institution within 50 miles of home.

More Than an Education

Everywhere from Abilene to Yuma, chamber of commerce promotional brochures tout local colleges and universities more frequently than other urban assets, and with good reason. Among the 20 million students taking college courses, 15 million are studying in metro areas. For 21 million other people, the typical location for their evening or weekend continuing education course is a local college classroom.

Colleges and universities contribute other things besides education. In smaller metro areas, a worthy theater where a touring group of professional players can stage *Playboy of the Western World* or an auditorium where an orchestra and choral group can perform Handel's *Messiah* can only be found at the local college campus.

Colleges and universities are stable white-collar employers, too. In Iowa City, IA, Lawrence, KS, and Tuscaloosa, AL, they are *the* major employers. And finally, there is the connection between research-oriented universities and healthy economies. Two historic examples are Stanford University's impetus to the growth of Silicon Valley high-tech enterprises in San Jose and the Bay Area, and MIT's faculty and alumni who started electronics firms along Route 128 outside Boston.

Half of the nearly 4,000 higher education institutions in North America are Associate of Arts colleges. Otherwise known as *community* or *junior* colleges, these institutions offer associate of arts certificates or degree programs (but no baccalaureate

degrees) to 10 million full- and part-time students. Several of the larger institutions take in more students than all but the largest state universities.

Five hundred thirty-three *Baccalaureate* institutions enroll 1,026,000 full- and part-time students. These colleges are undergraduate-level institutions exclusively; their highest offering is the bachelor's degree. They are typically private, although the largest baccalaureate college is public: Miami's Miami-Dade College with 94,000 students.

Comprehensive institutions enroll another 3.8 million full- and part-time students. Of 1,001 in America, the largest by far are branches of the California State University system. Comprehensive universities and colleges are mainly undergraduate institutions, although their highest offering is the master's degree.

Doctoral universities award the Ph.D. as their highest degree. These institutions tend to be public and large. With 699 campuses, they enroll well over 5 million full and part-time students.

SCORING: EDUCATION

In profiling metro-area education features, Places Rated details the local mix of public and private schools and public and private colleges and universities. To rate each area, five criteria are measured and get equal weight to produce the Education score:

School Support combines the metro area's average number of students per full-time equivalent classroom teacher (the lower the better) with its average instructional expense figure for student (the higher the better) indexed against local personal income. Winners here include Ocean City, New Jersey; Ithaca, New York; and Honolulu.

Private School Options is the product of the number of schools in the three main sectors of private K-12 schooling—Catholic, Other Religious, and Nonsectarian—and their enrollment, indexed against the average figure for all metro areas. Winners include Washington, DC; Houston, Atlanta, and Miami.

Library Popularity is another word for a measurement developed by the library profession: Turnover Rate. It shows relative library activity by dividing annual circulation by the number of books the library owns. The metro area average is 2.7. The winner here is Portland-Vancouver-Beaverton, with an enviable turnover rate of 8.1.

College Town is enrollment weighted by number of years of typical attendance to get the highest degree

www.placesrated.com

Education rankings, from 1 to 379, are in the *Place Profiles* section coming next. Education scores, from 100.0 to 0.0, are in *Putting It All Together* at the end of the book. Readers can view and print out these rankings and scores, from #1 Washington-Arlington, DC-VA-MD-WV (score: 100.0) to #379 Idaho Falls, ID (score: 0.0), by visiting *Places Rated's* website.

Here are the top twenty:

Rank	Score
1. Washington-Arlington, DC-VA-MD-WV	100.0
2. Madison, WI	99.7
3. Cambridge-Newton-Framingham, MA	99.4
4. Baltimore-Towson, MD	99.2
5. Akron, OH	98.9
6. Columbus, OH	98.6
7. Albany-Schenectady-Troy, NY	98.4
8. Syracuse, NY	98.1
9. St. Louis, MO-IL	97.8
10. Ann Arbor, MI	97.6
11. Minneapolis-St. Paul, MN-WI	97.3
12. Richmond, VA	97.0
13. Rochester, NY	96.8
14. Wilmington, DE-MD-NJ	96.5
15. Hartford-West Hartford, CT	96.2
16. Lexington-Fayette, KY	96.0
17. Milwaukee-Waukesha-West Allis, WI	95.7
18. San Jose-Sunnyvale-Santa Clara, CA	95.5
19. Columbia, MO	95.2
20. Durham, NC	94.9

At *www.placesrated.com* you'll also find more information on metro area colleges, universities, and public school districts.

Education

offered (that is, associate of arts enrollment is weighted by 2, baccalaureate enrollment by 4, comprehensive enrollment by 6, and doctoral enrollment by 9). This large number is then divided by the metro area's population.

As the map shows, places like Byran-College Station, Iowa City, Lawrence, and Columbia (MO) come out very high on this criterion. But there's only one game in town in Ames (Iowa State University), in Bryan-College Station (Texas A&M), in Lawrence (University of Kansas), and in Columbia (University of Missouri). Something else is needed to reward higher education variety.

College Options, the fifth criterion, is the variety of higher education institutions that meet the needs of residents: low-cost night and weekend continuing education courses for people who work, full-time graduate courses in the professions, courses leading to occupational certification in 2-year colleges, and the traditional bachelor's degree curriculum offered in college or university. Here, the top-ranking places are New York, Chicago, and Los Angeles.

PLACE PROFILES: EDUCATION

The following pages detail seven kinds of education in metropolitan areas: (1) public schools, (2) private schools, (3) public libraries, (4) 2-year colleges, (5) baccalaureate colleges, (6) comprehensive colleges and universities, and (7) doctoral universities.

Finding a good public school district isn't easy. Metropolitan Chicago has 332, for instance, and metro Phoenix-Mesa-Scottsdale has 228. A typical metro area has 26 or more, each with varying indicators of school quality. Still, information on how much local public education is fragmented into different systems can be useful to newcomers.

The percent of *Children in Public Schools* is shown in parentheses to the right of that heading. Underneath are the number of districts, the number of schools, and the total enrollment throughout the metro area.

The percent of *Children in Private Schools* is shown to the right of that heading. Below are the number of local Catholic schools and students, the number of local schools that are controlled by other religious groups and their total enrollment, and below that is the number of nonsectarian private schools and their students.

To the right of the *Public Libraries* heading is the metro area's number of library systems. Underneath that are the factors for calculating Turnover Rate, or library popularity.

Under the *Colleges and Universities* heading are four classifications of institutions. The "Associate of Arts" entry summarizes the number of community, junior, or 2-year college campuses and their students. Under the "Baccalaureate" subheading are the names of colleges where the highest degree granted is the bachelor's. Under the "Comprehensive" subheading are institutions where the master's is the highest degree granted. Under the "Doctoral" subheading are universities where the highest degree granted is the doctorate.

Enrollment figures (in parentheses) are the sum of full and part-time students. For Comprehensive and Doctoral institutions the first enrollment figure is undergraduate students, the second is graduate students; if there is only one figure, the institution's entire enrollment is graduate students. Publicly controlled institutions are italicized.

The last element is the metro area's *Report Card* showing five grades that go into Education scoring. An *A+* is awarded for placing in the 88th to 100th percentiles. All other grades are awarded as follows: *A*, for the 76th to 87th percentile; *B+* indicates the 63rd to 75th percentile; *B*, the 50th to 62nd percentile; *C+*, the 38th to 49th percentile; *C*, the 26th to 37th percentile; *D+*, the 13th to 25th percentile; *D* goes to anything lower. No metro area gets an *F* grade.

Data on public schools come from the U.S. Department of Education's unpublished "Common Core of Data" file (see nces.ed.gov/ccd/schoolsearch). Data on private schools come from the U.S. Department of Education's unpublished "Private School Survey (see nces.ed.gov/surveys/pss/privateschoolsearch). Public Library data come from the National Center for Education Statistics annual public library survey (see nces.ed.gov/surveys/libraries/librarysearch). Higher education data are derived from the U.S. Department of Education's unpublished "Integrated Post-Secondary Education Data System" (see surveys.nces.ed.gov/ipeds). The basic classifications used for grouping higher education institutions come from the Carnegie Foundation, A Classification of Institutions of Higher Education, 1994.

A check mark (✓) preceding the metro area's name identifies it as one of *Places Rated's* top forty places for education.

Abilene, TX

Children in Public Schools (99%)
16 districts, 88 schools, 27,975 students

Children in Private Schools (1%)
Other religious: 3 schools, 253 students

Public Library Systems: 7
338,717 books; turnover: 2.3

Colleges and Universities

Baccalaureate
McMurry University (1,599)

Doctoral
Abilene Christian University (4,416/773)
Hardin-Simmons University (2,281/464)

REPORT CARD
Public School Support ....A
Private School Options.....................................D
Library Popularity ....C+
College Town...B+
College Options ....C+

Places Rated Rank: 200

✓Akron, OH

Children in Public Schools (89%)
76 districts, 227 schools, 109,390 students

Children in Private Schools (11%)
Catholic: 25 schools, 9,551 students
Other religious: 16 schools, 2,736 students
Nonsectarian: 3 schools, 976 students

Public Library Systems: 10
2,464,960 books; turnover: 3.9

Colleges and Universities

Associate of Arts
3 campuses (1,410)

Comprehensive
Hiram College (1,214)

Doctoral
Kent State University (21,969/7,676)
University of Akron (21,279/5,829)

REPORT CARD
Public School Support ....A
Private School Options.....................................A
Library Popularity ....A
College Town...A
College Options ....A

Places Rated Rank: 5

Albany, GA

Children in Public Schools (96%)
5 districts, 53 schools, 28,593 students

Children in Private Schools (4%)
Catholic: 1 school, 284 students
Other religious: 4 schools, 314 students
Nonsectarian: 1 school, 712 students

Public Library Systems: 3
427,100 books; turnover: 1.7

Colleges and Universities

Associate of Arts
2 campuses (10,219)

Comprehensive
Albany State University (3,692/704)

REPORT CARD
Public School Support ....B
Private School Options.....................................C
Library Popularity ....D+
College Town...C+
College Options C

Places Rated Rank: 297

✓Albany-Schenectady-Troy, NY

Children in Public Schools (92%)
56 districts, 225 schools, 128,228 students

Children in Private Schools (8%)
Catholic: 33 schools, 8,520 students
Other religious: 15 schools, 1,530 students
Nonsectarian: 6 schools, 1,527 students

Public Library Systems: 45
2,479,626 books; turnover: 2.6

Colleges and Universities

Associate of Arts
6 campuses (23,405)

Baccalaureate
Albany College of Pharmacy (937)
Russell Sage College (906)
Siena College (3,630)
SUNY College at Cobleskill (2,838)
Union College (2,193)

Comprehensive
Albany Law School (830)
College of Saint Rose (3,162/6,235)
Excelsior College (29,884/522)
Skidmore College (2,822/68)
SUNY Empire State College (15,449/611)

Doctoral
Albany Medical College (655)
Rensselaer (5,423/2,224)
Sage College Albany (1,355/1,258)
SUNY at Albany (13,521/6,438)

REPORT CARD
Public School Support ....A+
Private School Options.....................................A
Library Popularity ....B
College Town...A
College Options ....A+

Places Rated Rank: 7

Albuquerque, NM

Children in Public Schools (93%)
11 districts, 244 schools, 128,378 students

Children in Private Schools (7%)
Catholic: 12 schools, 4,214 students
Other religious: 28 schools, 4,265 students
Nonsectarian: 7 schools, 1,709 students

Public Library Systems: 22
1,756,830 books; turnover: 2.5

Colleges and Universities

Associate of Arts
3 campuses (37,205)

Doctoral
University of New Mexico (20,587/10,171)

REPORT CARD
Public School Support C
Private School Options.....................................A
Library Popularity ....C+
College Town...B+
College Options ....A

Places Rated Rank: 113

Alexandria, LA

Children in Public Schools (90%)
3 districts, 62 schools, 26,550 students

Children in Private Schools (10%)
Catholic: 4 schools, 1,588 students
Other religious: 3 schools, 603 students
Nonsectarian: 2 schools, 639 students

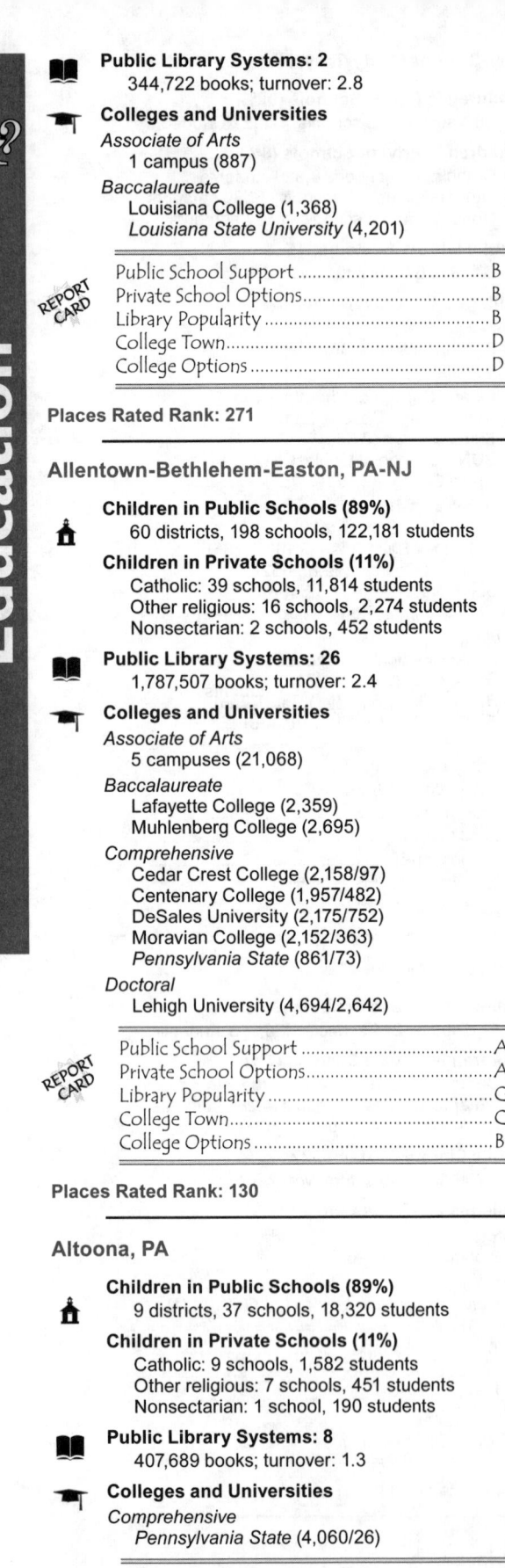

Public Library Systems: 2
344,722 books; turnover: 2.8

Colleges and Universities
Associate of Arts
1 campus (887)

Baccalaureate
Louisiana College (1,368)
Louisiana State University (4,201)

Public School Support .... B
Private School Options .... B
Library Popularity .... B
College Town .... D+
College Options .... D+

Places Rated Rank: 271

Allentown-Bethlehem-Easton, PA-NJ

Children in Public Schools (89%)
60 districts, 198 schools, 122,181 students

Children in Private Schools (11%)
Catholic: 39 schools, 11,814 students
Other religious: 16 schools, 2,274 students
Nonsectarian: 2 schools, 452 students

Public Library Systems: 26
1,787,507 books; turnover: 2.4

Colleges and Universities
Associate of Arts
5 campuses (21,068)

Baccalaureate
Lafayette College (2,359)
Muhlenberg College (2,695)

Comprehensive
Cedar Crest College (2,158/97)
Centenary College (1,957/482)
DeSales University (2,175/752)
Moravian College (2,152/363)
Pennsylvania State (861/73)

Doctoral
Lehigh University (4,694/2,642)

Public School Support .... A
Private School Options .... A
Library Popularity .... C+
College Town C
College Options .... B

Places Rated Rank: 130

Altoona, PA

Children in Public Schools (89%)
9 districts, 37 schools, 18,320 students

Children in Private Schools (11%)
Catholic: 9 schools, 1,582 students
Other religious: 7 schools, 451 students
Nonsectarian: 1 school, 190 students

Public Library Systems: 8
407,689 books; turnover: 1.3

Colleges and Universities
Comprehensive
Pennsylvania State (4,060/26)

Public School Support .... A
Private School Options .... B
Library Popularity .... D
College Town .... D+
College Options .... D

Places Rated Rank: 302

Amarillo, TX

Children in Public Schools (96%)
12 districts, 86 schools, 42,567 students

Children in Private Schools (4%)
Catholic: 4 schools, 579 students
Other religious: 5 schools, 1,416 students

Public Library Systems: 4
706,211 books; turnover: 3.2

Colleges and Universities
Associate of Arts
1 campus (13,923)

Doctoral
West Texas A&M (6,646/1,979)

Public School Support .... B
Private School Options .... D+
Library Popularity .... B+
College Town .... B+
College Options .... C+

Places Rated Rank: 175

Ames, IA

Children in Public Schools (97%)
7 districts, 30 schools, 10,400 students

Children in Private Schools (3%)
Catholic: 1 school, 182 students
Other religious: 2 schools, 133 students

Public Library Systems: 11
353,992 books; turnover: 4.6

Colleges and Universities
Doctoral
Iowa State (23,935/5,919)

Public School Support .... A
Private School Options .... D
Library Popularity .... A+
College Town .... A+
College Options .... B+

Places Rated Rank: 58

Anchorage, AK

Children in Public Schools (95%)
3 districts, 135 schools, 64,388 students

Children in Private Schools (5%)
Catholic: 3 schools, 331 students
Other religious: 15 schools, 2,892 students
Nonsectarian: 2 schools, 32 students

Public Library Systems: 8
684,149 books; turnover: 2.8

Colleges and Universities
Comprehensive
Alaska Pacific University (674/297)
University of Alaska (25,997/1,250)

Public School Support .... C+
Private School Options .... B
Library Popularity .... B
College Town .... B
College Options .... B

Places Rated Rank: 173

Anderson, IN

Children in Public Schools (93%)
5 districts, 39 schools, 20,485 students

Children in Private Schools (7%)
Catholic: 3 schools, 476 students
Other religious: 3 schools, 982 students

Public Library Systems: 4
535,263 books; turnover: 3.2

Colleges and Universities
Doctoral
Anderson University (2,389/631)

REPORT CARD
Public School Support .... B
Private School Options .... D+
Library Popularity .... B+
College Town C
College Options .... D+

Places Rated Rank: 285

Anderson, SC

Children in Public Schools (97%)
6 districts, 48 schools, 30,789 students

Children in Private Schools (3%)
Catholic: 1 school, 101 students
Other religious: 5 schools, 708 students

Public Library Systems: 1
356,688 books; turnover: 1.6

Colleges and Universities
Associate of Arts
1 campus (6,543)
Comprehensive
Anderson University (1,863)

REPORT CARD
Public School Support .... D+
Private School Options .... D
Library Popularity .... D
College Town .... D
College Options .... D+

Places Rated Rank: 374

✓Ann Arbor, MI

Children in Public Schools (94%)
19 districts, 99 schools, 48,253 students

Children in Private Schools (6%)
Catholic: 6 schools, 1,234 students
Other religious: 9 schools, 1,094 students
Nonsectarian: 3 schools, 726 students

Public Library Systems: 9
804,924 books; turnover: 4.9

Colleges and Universities
Associate of Arts
1 campus (20,409)
Baccalaureate
Ave Maria College (121)
Comprehensive
Cleary University (790/96)
Concordia University (534/45)
Doctoral
Eastern Michigan University (22,838/7,341)
University of Michigan (25,413/15,846)

REPORT CARD
Public School Support .... B
Private School Options .... B
Library Popularity .... A+
College Town .... A+
College Options .... A+

Places Rated Rank: 10

Anniston-Oxford, AL

Children in Public Schools (93%)
5 districts, 39 schools, 18,090 students

Children in Private Schools (7%)
Catholic: 1 school, 191 students
Other religious: 5 schools, 880 students
Nonsectarian: 1 school, 364 students

Public Library Systems: 4
228,216 books; turnover: 1.9

Colleges and Universities
Comprehensive
Jacksonville State University (8,416/2,500)

REPORT CARD
Public School Support .... C+
Private School Options C
Library Popularity .... D+
College Town .... B+
College Options C

Places Rated Rank: 243

Appleton, WI

Children in Public Schools (85%)
14 districts, 82 schools, 36,487 students

Children in Private Schools (15%)
Catholic: 22 schools, 4,453 students
Other religious: 16 schools, 1,789 students

Public Library Systems: 10
652,445 books; turnover: 3.1

Colleges and Universities
Associate of Arts
1 campus (12,550)
Baccalaureate
Lawrence University (1,416)

REPORT CARD
Public School Support .... B+
Private School Options .... B
Library Popularity .... B+
College Town .... D+
College Options .... D+

Places Rated Rank: 218

Asheville, NC

Children in Public Schools (93%)
9 districts, 95 schools, 53,200 students

Children in Private Schools (7%)
Catholic: 3 schools, 445 students
Other religious: 22 schools, 2,425 students
Nonsectarian: 5 schools, 1,047 students

Public Library Systems: 4
926,165 books; turnover: 3.0

Colleges and Universities
Associate of Arts
3 campuses (14,682)
Baccalaureate
Mars Hill College (1,552)
Comprehensive
Montreat College (1,410/56)
UNC Asheville (4,053/54)
Warren Wilson College (853/87)

REPORT CARD
Public School Support .... B
Private School Options .... B+
Library Popularity .... B+
College Town .... D+
College Options .... C+

Places Rated Rank: 199

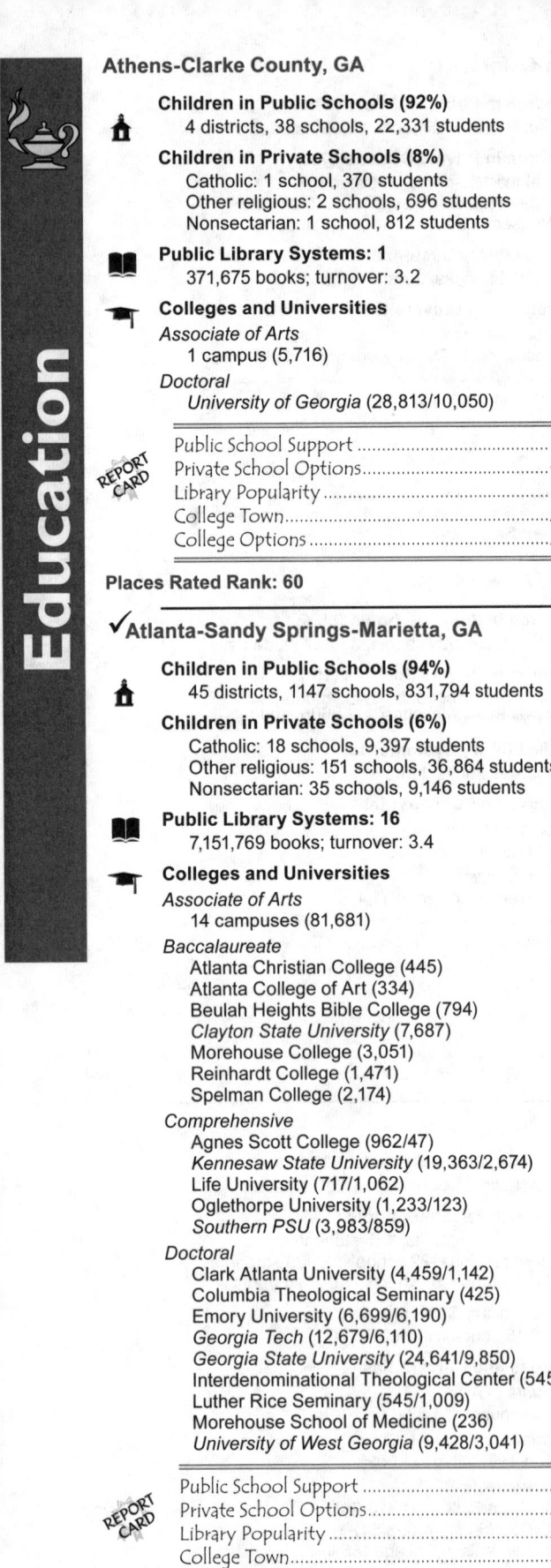

Athens-Clarke County, GA

Children in Public Schools (92%)
4 districts, 38 schools, 22,331 students

Children in Private Schools (8%)
Catholic: 1 school, 370 students
Other religious: 2 schools, 696 students
Nonsectarian: 1 school, 812 students

Public Library Systems: 1
371,675 books; turnover: 3.2

Colleges and Universities
Associate of Arts
1 campus (5,716)
Doctoral
University of Georgia (28,813/10,050)

Public School Support	B+
Private School Options	C
Library Popularity	B+
College Town	A+
College Options	A

Places Rated Rank: 60

✓Atlanta-Sandy Springs-Marietta, GA

Children in Public Schools (94%)
45 districts, 1147 schools, 831,794 students

Children in Private Schools (6%)
Catholic: 18 schools, 9,397 students
Other religious: 151 schools, 36,864 students
Nonsectarian: 35 schools, 9,146 students

Public Library Systems: 16
7,151,769 books; turnover: 3.4

Colleges and Universities
Associate of Arts
14 campuses (81,681)
Baccalaureate
Atlanta Christian College (445)
Atlanta College of Art (334)
Beulah Heights Bible College (794)
Clayton State University (7,687)
Morehouse College (3,051)
Reinhardt College (1,471)
Spelman College (2,174)
Comprehensive
Agnes Scott College (962/47)
Kennesaw State University (19,363/2,674)
Life University (717/1,062)
Oglethorpe University (1,233/123)
Southern PSU (3,983/859)
Doctoral
Clark Atlanta University (4,459/1,142)
Columbia Theological Seminary (425)
Emory University (6,699/6,190)
Georgia Tech (12,679/6,110)
Georgia State University (24,641/9,850)
Interdenominational Theological Center (545)
Luther Rice Seminary (545/1,009)
Morehouse School of Medicine (236)
University of West Georgia (9,428/3,041)

Public School Support	B+
Private School Options	A+
Library Popularity	A
College Town	C
College Options	A+

Places Rated Rank: 24

Atlantic City, NJ

Children in Public Schools (92%)
34 districts, 102 schools, 47,553 students

Children in Private Schools (8%)
Catholic: 11 schools, 3,578 students
Other religious: 4 schools, 546 students
Nonsectarian: 1 school, 71 students

Public Library Systems: 6
888,934 books; turnover: 1.3

Colleges and Universities
Associate of Arts
1 campus (8,958)
Comprehensive
Stockton SCNJ (7,655/484)

Public School Support	A+
Private School Options	B
Library Popularity	D
College Town	C
College Options	C

Places Rated Rank: 231

Auburn-Opelika, AL

Children in Public Schools (96%)
3 districts, 31 schools, 18,759 students

Children in Private Schools (4%)
Other religious: 1 school, 197 students
Nonsectarian: 2 schools, 657 students

Public Library Systems: 2
118,066 books; turnover: 2.0

Colleges and Universities
Doctoral
Auburn University (20,404/4,505)

Public School Support	B
Private School Options	D+
Library Popularity	C
College Town	A+
College Options	B+

Places Rated Rank: 178

Augusta-Richmond County, GA-SC

Children in Public Schools (93%)
7 districts, 151 schools, 93,085 students

Children in Private Schools (7%)
Catholic: 5 schools, 1,400 students
Other religious: 24 schools, 4,347 students
Nonsectarian: 4 schools, 895 students

Public Library Systems: 2
761,689 books; turnover: 2.2

Colleges and Universities
Associate of Arts
3 campuses (12,170)
Baccalaureate
Paine College (1,158)
Comprehensive
Augusta State University (6,749/1,217)
University of South Carolina (3,760/258)
Doctoral
Medical College Georgia (888/1,384)

Public School Support	B
Private School Options	B+
Library Popularity	C
College Town	C
College Options	C+

Places Rated Rank: 210

Austin-Round Rock, TX

Children in Public Schools (96%)
49 districts, 449 schools, 243,823 students

Children in Private Schools (4%)
Catholic: 12 schools, 3,074 students
Other religious: 34 schools, 6,537 students
Nonsectarian: 2 schools, 465 students

Public Library Systems: 25
2,380,069 books; turnover: 2.7

Colleges and Universities
Associate of Arts
1 campus (52,693)
Baccalaureate
Southwestern University (1,315)
Comprehensive
Concordia University (1,269/148)
Huston-Tillotson University (752)
St. Edward's University (4,094/1,211)
Doctoral
Texas State University (24,520/6,185)
University of Texas (41,646/14,173)

REPORT CARD

Public School Support ....C+
Private School Options............................A
Library Popularity ....B
College Town...A
College Options ....A+

Places Rated Rank: 47

Bakersfield, CA

Children in Public Schools (96%)
53 districts, 254 schools, 164,805 students

Children in Private Schools (4%)
Catholic: 7 schools, 1,922 students
Other religious: 34 schools, 4,000 students
Nonsectarian: 3 schools, 231 students

Public Library Systems: 1
1,048,526 books; turnover: 1.6

Colleges and Universities
Associate of Arts
3 campuses (47,414)
Comprehensive
California State University (6,624/2,907)

REPORT CARD

Public School Support ....D+
Private School Options............................B+
Library Popularity ....D
College Town...D+
College Options ....B

Places Rated Rank: 296

✓ Baltimore-Towson, MD

Children in Public Schools (86%)
9 districts, 658 schools, 397,583 students

Children in Private Schools (14%)
Catholic: 81 schools, 32,957 students
Other religious: 104 schools, 20,739 students
Nonsectarian: 28 schools, 9,732 students

Public Library Systems: 7
7,655,644 books; turnover: 3.6

Colleges and Universities
Associate of Arts
7 campuses (81,379)
Baccalaureate
Baltimore International College (767)
U. S. Naval Academy (5,587)

Comprehensive
Coppin State University (3,694/992)
Goucher College (1,382/1,696)
Maryland College of Art (2,384/280)
McDaniel College (1,829/2,784)
Sojourner-Douglass College (1,628/116)
St. John's College (493/136)
Villa Julie College (2,880/60)
Doctoral
College Notre Dame MD (2,025/2,436)
Johns Hopkins University (6,600/16,976)
Loyola College (3,565/3,455)
Morgan State University (6,938/796)
Towson University (16,571/4,754)
University of Baltimore (2,496/3,312)
UM Baltimore County (10,472/2,656)
UM Baltimore Professional (1,094/4,982)

REPORT CARD

Public School Support ....B+
Private School Options...............................A+
Library Popularity ....A
College Town...B+
College Options ....A+

Places Rated Rank: 4

Bangor, ME

Children in Public Schools (93%)
38 districts, 89 schools, 22,606 students

Children in Private Schools (7%)
Catholic: 1 school, 283 students
Other religious: 7 schools, 684 students
Nonsectarian: 2 schools, 726 students

Public Library Systems: 24
875,066 books; turnover: 1.1

Colleges and Universities
Associate of Arts
1 campus (2,592)
Comprehensive
Husson College (2,059/360)
Doctoral
Bangor Theological Seminary (53/221)
University of Maine (10,990/3,108)

REPORT CARD

Public School Support ....A+
Private School Options...............................C+
Library Popularity ....D
College Town...A+
College Options ....B

Places Rated Rank: 157

Barnstable Town, MA

Children in Public Schools (97%)
23 districts, 60 schools, 30,728 students

Children in Private Schools (3%)
Catholic: 1 school, 219 students
Other religious: 3 schools, 169 students
Nonsectarian: 2 schools, 515 students

Public Library Systems: 30
1,048,570 books; turnover: 2.4

Colleges and Universities
Associate of Arts
1 campus (5,459)
Comprehensive
Massachusetts Maritime Academy (938/21)

REPORT CARD

Public School Support ....A+
Private School Options...............................C
Library Popularity ....C+

College Town...D
College Options ....D

Places Rated Rank: 293

Education

Baton Rouge, LA

Children in Public Schools (80%)
20 districts, 247 schools, 108,761 students

Children in Private Schools (20%)
Catholic: 25 schools, 15,452 students
Other religious: 31 schools, 8,725 students
Nonsectarian: 7 schools, 2,777 students

Public Library Systems: 8
2,566,747 books; turnover: 1.4

Colleges and Universities
Associate of Arts
9 campuses (12,944)
Comprehensive
Our Lady the Lake College (2,066)
Doctoral
Louisiana State University (28,489/6,730)
Southern University (8,766/1,852)

REPORT CARD
Public School Support ....B
Private School Options..A
Library Popularity ....D
College Town...A
College Options ....A

Places Rated Rank: 114

Battle Creek, MI

Children in Public Schools (94%)
16 districts, 78 schools, 24,891 students

Children in Private Schools (6%)
Catholic: 4 schools, 1,123 students
Other religious: 4 schools, 418 students

Public Library Systems: 7
376,960 books; turnover: 2.7

Colleges and Universities
Associate of Arts
1 campus (10,285)
Baccalaureate
Albion College (1,753)

REPORT CARD
Public School Support ....A
Private School Options..D+
Library Popularity ....B
College Town...C
College Options ....D+

Places Rated Rank: 262

Bay City, MI

Children in Public Schools (87%)
7 districts, 41 schools, 16,691 students

Children in Private Schools (13%)
Catholic: 8 schools, 1,003 students
Other religious: 12 schools, 1,456 students

Public Library Systems: 1
249,138 books; turnover: 3.2

Colleges and Universities
Associate of Arts
1 campus (15,042)

REPORT CARD
Public School Support ....C+
Private School Options..C+
Library Popularity ....B+

College Town...C+
College Options ....D+

Places Rated Rank: 225

Beaumont-Port Arthur, TX

Children in Public Schools (96%)
23 districts, 143 schools, 70,916 students

Children in Private Schools (4%)
Catholic: 7 schools, 1,823 students
Other religious: 7 schools, 1,372 students
Nonsectarian: 1 school, 48 students

Public Library Systems: 14
968,295 books; turnover: 1.2

Colleges and Universities
Associate of Arts
3 campuses (9,532)
Doctoral
Lamar University (11,279/1,579)

REPORT CARD
Public School Support ....C+
Private School Options..B
Library Popularity ....D
College Town...B
College Options ....B

Places Rated Rank: 236

Bellingham, WA

Children in Public Schools (93%)
7 districts, 70 schools, 26,529 students

Children in Private Schools (7%)
Catholic: 1 school, 404 students
Other religious: 7 schools, 1,636 students
Nonsectarian: 2 schools, 77 students

Public Library Systems: 2
523,488 books; turnover: 4.7

Colleges and Universities
Associate of Arts
3 campuses (13,200)
Comprehensive
Western Washington University (14,388/2,001)

REPORT CARD
Public School Support ....D+
Private School Options..C+
Library Popularity ....A+
College Town...A
College Options ....C+

Places Rated Rank: 165

Bend, OR

Children in Public Schools (96%)
5 districts, 40 schools, 21,798 students

Children in Private Schools (4%)
Catholic: 1 school, 350 students
Other religious: 4 schools, 641 students

Public Library Systems: 1
333,602 books; turnover: 4.8

Colleges and Universities
Associate of Arts
1 campus (6,596)
Comprehensive
Oregon State University (461/149)

REPORT CARD
Public School Support ....D
Private School Options..D
Library Popularity ....A+

College Town..D
College Options ....D

Places Rated Rank: 339

Bethesda-Gaithersburg-Frederick, MD

Children in Public Schools (87%)
2 districts, 258 schools, 178,882 students

Children in Private Schools (13%)
Catholic: 34 schools, 13,421 students
Other religious: 37 schools, 9,553 students
Nonsectarian: 16 schools, 4,330 students

Public Library Systems: 2
2,762,186 books; turnover: 4.7

Colleges and Universities
Associate of Arts
2 campuses (40,982)

Baccalaureate
National Labor College (1,286)

Comprehensive
Columbia Union College (1,767/50)
Hood College (997/1,205)
Mount St. Mary's University (1,721/719)

Public School Support ....A
Private School Options.....................................A+
Library Popularity ....A+
College Town...D
College Options ....C+

Places Rated Rank: 89

Billings, MT

Children in Public Schools (95%)
36 districts, 83 schools, 23,424 students

Children in Private Schools (5%)
Catholic: 4 schools, 918 students
Other religious: 5 schools, 417 students

Public Library Systems: 5
294,798 books; turnover: 3.2

Colleges and Universities
Baccalaureate
Yellowstone Baptist College (59)

Comprehensive
Montana State University (4,419/857)
Rocky Mountain College (1,101/42)

Public School Support ....B
Private School Options.....................................D+
Library Popularity ....B+
College Town...C
College Options ....D+

Places Rated Rank: 276

Binghamton, NY

Children in Public Schools (95%)
18 districts, 79 schools, 39,058 students

Children in Private Schools (5%)
Catholic: 7 schools, 1,526 students
Other religious: 5 schools, 498 students
Nonsectarian: 1 school, 56 students

Public Library Systems: 16
652,495 books; turnover: 1.8

Colleges and Universities
Associate of Arts
1 campus (8,855)

Baccalaureate
Davis College (364)
Doctoral
SUNY Binghamton (11,546/3,279)

Public School Support ....A+
Private School Options.....................................C+
Library Popularity ....D+
College Town...A
College Options ....B

Places Rated Rank: 128

Birmingham-Hoover, AL

Children in Public Schools (92%)
22 districts, 334 schools, 172,609 students

Children in Private Schools (8%)
Catholic: 11 schools, 3,350 students
Other religious: 55 schools, 9,801 students
Nonsectarian: 5 schools, 969 students

Public Library Systems: 48
2,412,190 books; turnover: 2.4

Colleges and Universities
Associate of Arts
4 campuses (23,048)

Baccalaureate
Miles College (2,027)
SE Bible College (228)

Comprehensive
Birmingham Southern College (1,303/85)
University of Montevallo (2,964/701)

Doctoral
Samford University (3,167/1,789)
University of Alabama (13,659/6,660)

Public School Support ....B
Private School Options.....................................A
Library Popularity ....C+
College Town...C+
College Options ....B+

Places Rated Rank: 137

Bismarck, ND

Children in Public Schools (92%)
21 districts, 54 schools, 15,168 students

Children in Private Schools (8%)
Catholic: 4 schools, 959 students
Other religious: 3 schools, 340 students

Public Library Systems: 5
254,699 books; turnover: 2.3

Colleges and Universities
Associate of Arts
2 campuses (4,678)

Doctoral
University of Mary (2,369/855)

Public School Support ....B
Private School Options.....................................D+
Library Popularity ....C+
College Town...B
College Options C

Places Rated Rank: 254

Blacksburg-Christiansburg-Radford, VA

Children in Public Schools (97%)
6 districts, 42 schools, 18,517 students

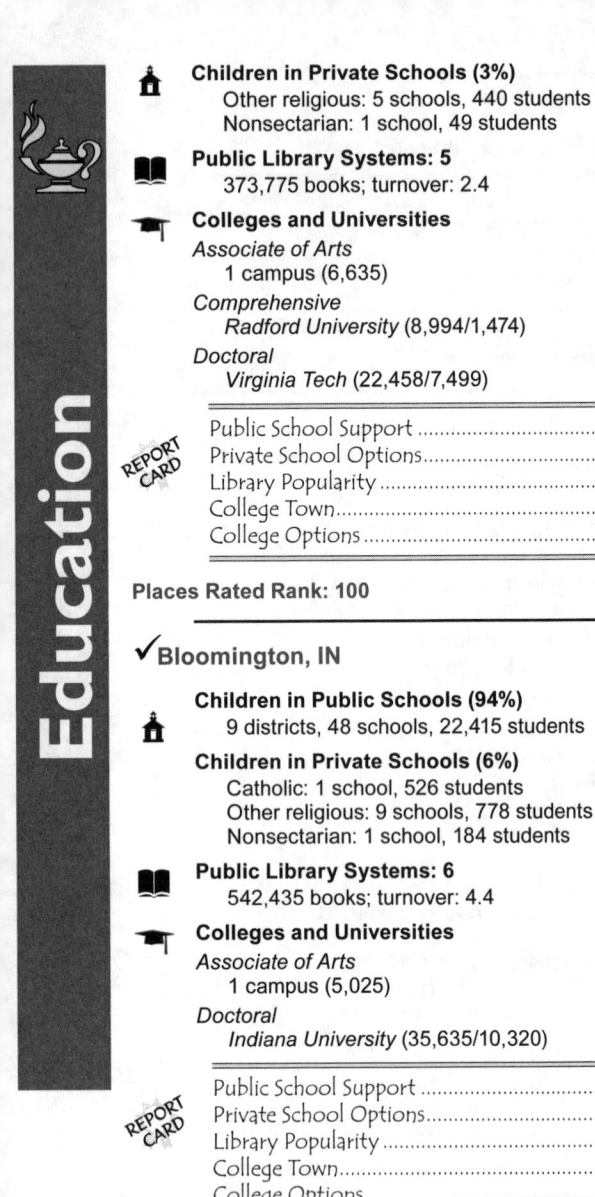

Children in Private Schools (3%)
Other religious: 5 schools, 440 students
Nonsectarian: 1 school, 49 students

Public Library Systems: 5
373,775 books; turnover: 2.4

Colleges and Universities
Associate of Arts
1 campus (6,635)
Comprehensive
Radford University (8,994/1,474)
Doctoral
Virginia Tech (22,458/7,499)

REPORT CARD
Public School Support .... A
Private School Options.....................................D+
Library Popularity ....C+
College Town...A+
College Options .... A

Places Rated Rank: 100

✓**Bloomington, IN**

Children in Public Schools (94%)
9 districts, 48 schools, 22,415 students

Children in Private Schools (6%)
Catholic: 1 school, 526 students
Other religious: 9 schools, 778 students
Nonsectarian: 1 school, 184 students

Public Library Systems: 6
542,435 books; turnover: 4.4

Colleges and Universities
Associate of Arts
1 campus (5,025)
Doctoral
Indiana University (35,635/10,320)

REPORT CARD
Public School Support .... C+
Private School Options.....................................C+
Library Popularity ....A+
College Town...A+
College Options .... A

Places Rated Rank: 38

Bloomington-Normal, IL

Children in Public Schools (90%)
17 districts, 54 schools, 24,038 students

Children in Private Schools (10%)
Catholic: 4 schools, 1,509 students
Other religious: 3 schools, 1,083 students
Nonsectarian: 2 schools, 208 students

Public Library Systems: 13
520,150 books; turnover: 2.5

Colleges and Universities
Associate of Arts
1 campus (7,530)
Baccalaureate
Illinois Wesleyan University (2,118)
Doctoral
Illinois State University (19,724/5,469)

REPORT CARD
Public School Support .... B
Private School Options.....................................C+
Library Popularity ....C+
College Town...A+
College Options .... B+

Places Rated Rank: 87

Boise City-Nampa, ID

Children in Public Schools (95%)
26 districts, 200 schools, 95,273 students

Children in Private Schools (5%)
Catholic: 6 schools, 1,924 students
Other religious: 14 schools, 2,536 students
Nonsectarian: 1 school, 224 students

Public Library Systems: 21
1,053,143 books; turnover: 3.7

Colleges and Universities
Baccalaureate
Boise Bible College (125)
Comprehensive
Albertson College (887/16)
Northwest Nazarene University (1,265/442)
Doctoral
Boise State University (21,179/4,394)

REPORT CARD
Public School Support .... D
Private School Options.....................................B
Library Popularity ....A
College Town...B+
College Options .... B+

Places Rated Rank: 150

✓**Boston-Quincy, MA**

Children in Public Schools (89%)
93 districts, 505 schools, 261,490 students

Children in Private Schools (11%)
Catholic: 67 schools, 22,648 students
Other religious: 26 schools, 4,029 students
Nonsectarian: 26 schools, 6,652 students

Public Library Systems: 59
13,182,212 books; turnover: 0.9

Colleges and Universities
Associate of Arts
9 campuses (42,145)
Baccalaureate
Benjamin Franklin Institute of Technology (323)
Berklee College of Music (4,453)
Boston Baptist College (117)
Dean College (1,389)
Fisher College (2,038)
Newbury College Brookline (1,295)
Pine Manor College (519)
Wellesley College (2,431)
Wentworth Institute of Technology (3,602)
Comprehensive
Babson College (1,748/1,902)
Boston Architectural Center (797/397)
Boston Conservatory (431/138)
Bridgewater State College (9,019/3,501)
Curry College (3,202/232)
Eastern Nazarene College (1,271/270)
Emmanuel College (1,937/340)
Massachusetts College of Art (2,782/295)
New England College of Optometry (14/427)
School Museum of Fine Arts (1,760/152)
Wheelock College (636/476)
Doctoral
Boston University (21,587/13,797)
Emerson College (3,746/1,160)
Massachusetts College Pharmacy (478/2,100)
New England Conservatory of Music (411/396)
Northeastern University (22,533/5,244)
Simmons College (1,589/2,731)
Suffolk University (4,683/4,357)
University of Massachusetts (13,875/4,244)

REPORT CARD
Public School Support .... A+
Private School Options.....................................A+

Library Popularity ....D
College Town...A
College Options ....A+

Places Rated Rank: 31

Boulder, CO

Children in Public Schools (91%)
2 districts, 54 schools, 41,425 students

Children in Private Schools (9%)
Catholic: 4 schools, 1,632 students
Other religious: 9 schools, 1,586 students
Nonsectarian: 7 schools, 1,043 students

Public Library Systems: 6
845,059 books; turnover: 3.4

Colleges and Universities
Associate of Arts
1 campus (187)
Comprehensive
Naropa University (943/851)
Doctoral
University of Colorado (29,592/7,674)

Public School Support C
Private School Options.....................................B+
Library Popularity ....A
College Town..A+
College Options ....A

Places Rated Rank: 59

Bowling Green, KY

Children in Public Schools (95%)
5 districts, 40 schools, 17,028 students

Children in Private Schools (5%)
Catholic: 1 school, 317 students
Other religious: 4 schools, 563 students

Public Library Systems: 2
167,580 books; turnover: 5.1

Colleges and Universities
Associate of Arts
1 campus (3,601)
Doctoral
Western Kentucky University (18,218/3,976)

Public School Support ....D+
Private School Options.....................................D
Library Popularity ....A+
College Town..A+
College Options ....B+

Places Rated Rank: 146

Bremerton-Silverdale, WA

Children in Public Schools (96%)
6 districts, 80 schools, 40,689 students

Children in Private Schools (4%)
Catholic: 2 schools, 234 students
Other religious: 12 schools, 999 students
Nonsectarian: 8 schools, 460 students

Public Library Systems: 1
499,912 books; turnover: 5.0

Colleges and Universities
Associate of Arts
1 campus (9,843)

Public School Support ....D+
Private School Options.....................................B

Library Popularity ....A+
College Town...D
College Options ....D

Places Rated Rank: 284

Bridgeport-Stamford-Norwalk, CT

Children in Public Schools (87%)
31 districts, 234 schools, 149,007 students

Children in Private Schools (13%)
Catholic: 39 schools, 12,637 students
Other religious: 15 schools, 2,693 students
Nonsectarian: 16 schools, 6,413 students

Public Library Systems: 28
4,287,398 books; turnover: 2.4

Colleges and Universities
Associate of Arts
4 campuses (15,695)
Baccalaureate
University of Connecticut (1,684)
Comprehensive
Fairfield University (4,944/1,463)
Doctoral
Sacred Heart University (4,739/2,540)
University of Bridgeport (1,560/2,720)
Western Connecticut State (6,412/1,206)

Public School Support ....A
Private School Options.....................................A
Library Popularity ....C+
College Town..C+
College Options ....B+

Places Rated Rank: 93

Brownsville-Harlingen, TX

Children in Public Schools (96%)
11 districts, 142 schools, 92,580 students

Children in Private Schools (4%)
Catholic: 5 schools, 1,494 students
Other religious: 11 schools, 2,226 students
Nonsectarian: 1 school, 400 students

Public Library Systems: 8
512,389 books; turnover: 0.9

Colleges and Universities
Associate of Arts
1 campus (5,997)
Comprehensive
University of Texas (13,057/1,308)

Public School Support C
Private School Options.....................................B
Library Popularity ....D
College Town..C
College Options ....C+

Places Rated Rank: 310

Brunswick, GA

Children in Public Schools (93%)
3 districts, 29 schools, 17,319 students

Children in Private Schools (7%)
Catholic: 1 school, 242 students
Other religious: 8 schools, 747 students
Nonsectarian: 1 school, 320 students

Public Library Systems: 1
268,373 books; turnover: 2.7

Education

Colleges and Universities
Associate of Arts
1 campus (4,030)

Places Rated Rank: 294

✓Buffalo-Niagara Falls, NY

Children in Public Schools (87%)
57 districts, 304 schools, 175,630 students

Children in Private Schools (13%)
Catholic: 83 schools, 22,246 students
Other religious: 33 schools, 2,900 students
Nonsectarian: 4 schools, 1,405 students

Public Library Systems: 34
4,566,518 books; turnover: 2.2

Colleges and Universities
Associate of Arts
3 campuses (26,719)

Baccalaureate
Hilbert College (1,384)
Villa Maria College (572)

Comprehensive
Canisius College (3,821/2,359)
Daemen College (1,904/571)
Medaille College (2,323/829)
Niagara University (3,009/1,177)
SUNY Buffalo (10,664/3,078)

Doctoral
D'Youville College (1,126/1,993)
SUNY Buffalo (19,761/10,555)

Places Rated Rank: 30

Burlington, NC

Children in Public Schools (96%)
5 districts, 37 schools, 22,798 students

Children in Private Schools (4%)
Catholic: 1 school, 281 students
Other religious: 3 schools, 599 students
Nonsectarian: 1 school, 179 students

Public Library Systems: 1
265,629 books; turnover: 3.0

Colleges and Universities
Associate of Arts
1 campus (6,284)

Doctoral
Elon University (5,124/315)

Places Rated Rank: 207

Burlington-South Burlington, VT

Children in Public Schools (91%)
60 districts, 91 schools, 32,829 students

Children in Private Schools (9%)
Catholic: 5 schools, 1,352 students
Other religious: 4 schools, 332 students
Nonsectarian: 7 schools, 1,441 students

Public Library Systems: 34
677,015 books; turnover: 2.2

Colleges and Universities
Baccalaureate
Burlington College (260)

Comprehensive
Champlain College (2,917/64)
Saint Michaels College (2,210/1,025)

Doctoral
University of Vermont (10,796/1,860)

Places Rated Rank: 91

✓Cambridge-Newton-Framingham, MA

Children in Public Schools (90%)
75 districts, 378 schools, 215,307 students

Children in Private Schools (10%)
Catholic: 51 schools, 15,560 students
Other religious: 16 schools, 2,715 students
Nonsectarian: 20 schools, 5,976 students

Public Library Systems: 56
5,881,176 books; turnover: 2.7

Colleges and Universities
Associate of Arts
2 campuses (11,866)

Baccalaureate
Mount Ida College (1,333)

Comprehensive
Bentley College (4,430/1,452)
Cambridge College (1,076/4,630)
Framingham State College (5,083/5,849)
Lasell College (1,126/26)
Longy School of Music (52/145)
Regis College (1,010/459)

Doctoral
Andover Newton Theological School (441)
Boston College (10,448/6,266)
Brandeis University (3,421/2,036)
Harvard University (13,306/16,855)
Lesley University (1,799/8,789)
MIT (4,307/6,697)
Tufts University (5,379/5,052)
University of Massachusetts Lowell (11,721/3,412)

Places Rated Rank: 3

Camden, NJ

Children in Public Schools (90%)
119 districts, 391 schools, 213,975 students

Children in Private Schools (10%)
Catholic: 53 schools, 17,034 students
Other religious: 33 schools, 5,745 students
Nonsectarian: 3 schools, 554 students

Public Library Systems: 43
3,656,230 books; turnover: 1.7

Colleges and Universities
Associate of Arts
3 campuses (39,130)
Comprehensive
Rutgers University (4,571/1,740)
Doctoral
Rowan University (9,653/2,017)

REPORT CARD
Public School Support ....A+
Private School Options.......................................A
Library Popularity ....D+
College Town...D+
College Options ....B+

Places Rated Rank: 151

Canton-Massillon, OH

Children in Public Schools (92%)
51 districts, 151 schools, 67,044 students

Children in Private Schools (8%)
Catholic: 16 schools, 4,280 students
Other religious: 9 schools, 1,559 students
Nonsectarian: 2 schools, 348 students

Public Library Systems: 8
1,634,100 books; turnover: 4.0

Colleges and Universities
Associate of Arts
3 campuses (13,310)
Baccalaureate
Mount Union College (2,578)
Comprehensive
Malone College (2,219/678)
Walsh University (1,823/416)

REPORT CARD
Public School Support ....B+
Private School Options.......................................B+
Library Popularity ....A+
College Town...D+
College Options ....C+

Places Rated Rank: 171

Cape Coral-Fort Myers, FL

Children in Public Schools (91%)
1 districts, 98 schools, 70,871 students

Children in Private Schools (9%)
Catholic: 3 schools, 1,987 students
Other religious: 22 schools, 3,753 students
Nonsectarian: 5 schools, 914 students

Public Library Systems: 3
1,163,772 books; turnover: 3.3

Colleges and Universities
Associate of Arts
4 campuses (19,729)
Comprehensive
Florida Gulf Coast University (5,916/1,644)

REPORT CARD
Public School Support ....D
Private School Options.......................................B+
Library Popularity ....B+
College Town...D+
College Options ....C+

Places Rated Rank: 251

Carson City, NV

Children in Public Schools (94%)
1 districts, 13 schools, 8,730 students

Children in Private Schools (6%)
Catholic: 1 school, 161 students
Other religious: 3 schools, 406 students

Public Library Systems: 1
113,384 books; turnover: 3.5

Colleges and Universities
Associate of Arts
1 campus (7,192)

REPORT CARD
Public School Support ....D+
Private School Options.......................................D
Library Popularity ....A
College Town...C
College Options ....D

Places Rated Rank: 329

Casper, WY

Children in Public Schools (97%)
2 districts, 35 schools, 11,809 students

Children in Private Schools (3%)
Catholic: 1 school, 168 students
Other religious: 3 schools, 170 students

Public Library Systems: 1
185,729 books; turnover: 2.4

Colleges and Universities
Associate of Arts
1 campus (5,227)

REPORT CARD
Public School Support ....A
Private School Options.......................................D
Library Popularity ....C+
College Town...D+
College Options ....D

Places Rated Rank: 332

Cedar Rapids, IA

Children in Public Schools (90%)
19 districts, 102 schools, 40,492 students

Children in Private Schools (10%)
Catholic: 11 schools, 3,438 students
Other religious: 8 schools, 1,028 students
Nonsectarian: 1 school, 150 students

Public Library Systems: 28
711,422 books; turnover: 3.2

Colleges and Universities
Associate of Arts
2 campuses (20,881)
Baccalaureate
Cornell College (1,140)
Mount Mercy College (1,756)
Comprehensive
Coe College (1,337/41)

REPORT CARD
Public School Support ....B+
Private School Options.......................................B
Library Popularity ....B+
College Town...C
College Options C

Places Rated Rank: 174

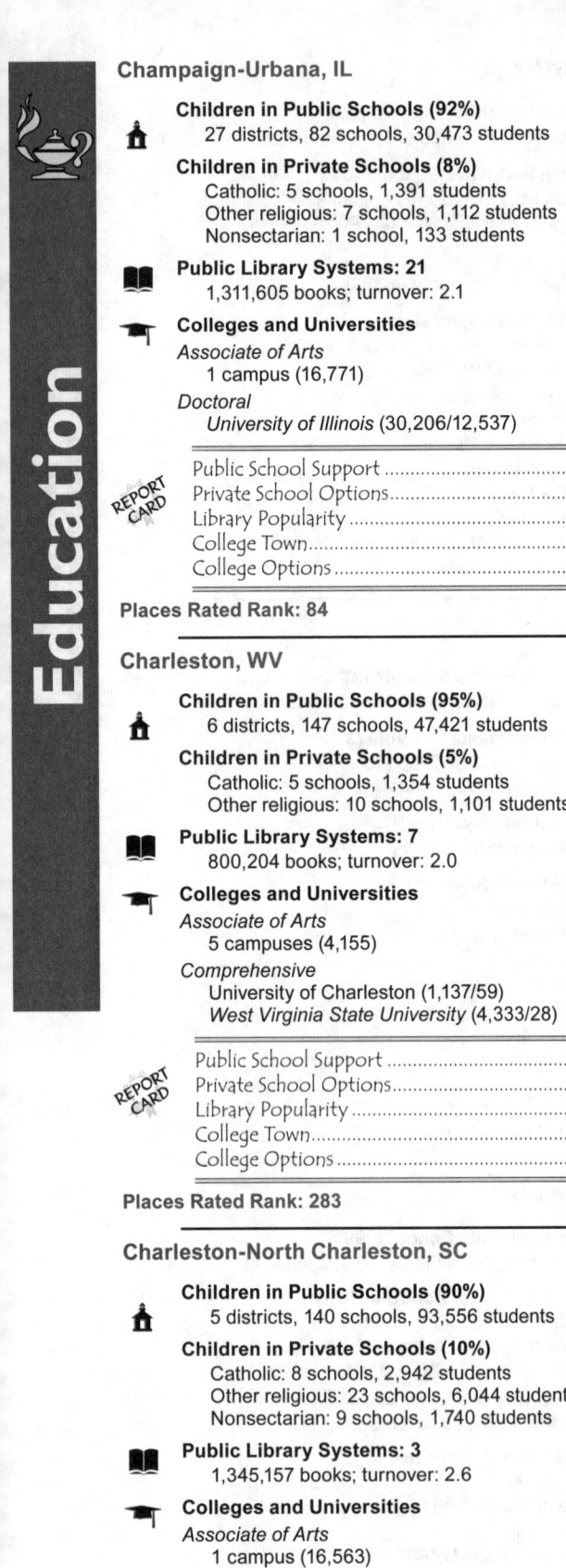

Champaign-Urbana, IL

Children in Public Schools (92%)
27 districts, 82 schools, 30,473 students

Children in Private Schools (8%)
Catholic: 5 schools, 1,391 students
Other religious: 7 schools, 1,112 students
Nonsectarian: 1 school, 133 students

Public Library Systems: 21
1,311,605 books; turnover: 2.1

Colleges and Universities
Associate of Arts
1 campus (16,771)

Doctoral
University of Illinois (30,206/12,537)

Public School Support	B+
Private School Options	B
Library Popularity	C
College Town	A+
College Options	A

Places Rated Rank: 84

Charleston, WV

Children in Public Schools (95%)
6 districts, 147 schools, 47,421 students

Children in Private Schools (5%)
Catholic: 5 schools, 1,354 students
Other religious: 10 schools, 1,101 students

Public Library Systems: 7
800,204 books; turnover: 2.0

Colleges and Universities
Associate of Arts
5 campuses (4,155)

Comprehensive
University of Charleston (1,137/59)
West Virginia State University (4,333/28)

Public School Support	A
Private School Options	C
Library Popularity	C
College Town	D
College Options	D+

Places Rated Rank: 283

Charleston-North Charleston, SC

Children in Public Schools (90%)
5 districts, 140 schools, 93,556 students

Children in Private Schools (10%)
Catholic: 8 schools, 2,942 students
Other religious: 23 schools, 6,044 students
Nonsectarian: 9 schools, 1,740 students

Public Library Systems: 3
1,345,157 books; turnover: 2.6

Colleges and Universities
Associate of Arts
1 campus (16,563)

Baccalaureate
Johnson & Wales University (1,508)

Comprehensive
Charleston Southern University (3,223/916)
Citadel Military College (2,528/2,637)
College of Charleston (11,086/3,110)

Doctoral
Medical USC (377/2,385)

Public School Support	C+
Private School Options	A

Library Popularity	B
College Town	C+
College Options	B

Places Rated Rank: 144

Charlotte-Gastonia-Concord, NC-SC

Children in Public Schools (91%)
21 districts, 325 schools, 248,412 students

Children in Private Schools (9%)
Catholic: 10 schools, 4,427 students
Other religious: 54 schools, 13,429 students
Nonsectarian: 9 schools, 5,848 students

Public Library Systems: 6
2,972,967 books; turnover: 3.6

Colleges and Universities
Associate of Arts
8 campuses (41,757)

Baccalaureate
Belmont Abbey College (945)
Cabarrus College (322)
Davidson College (1,848)
Johnson C. Smith University (1,498)

Comprehensive
Queens University (1,687/747)
Wingate University (1,391/221)
Winthrop University (5,749/2,260)

Doctoral
UNC Charlotte (18,642/5,056)

Public School Support	C
Private School Options	A
Library Popularity	A
College Town	C
College Options	A

Places Rated Rank: 117

✓Charlottesville, VA

Children in Public Schools (89%)
11 districts, 57 schools, 24,960 students

Children in Private Schools (11%)
Catholic: 1 school, 276 students
Other religious: 7 schools, 2,668 students
Nonsectarian: 4 schools, 271 students

Public Library Systems: 2
504,120 books; turnover: 3.1

Colleges and Universities
Associate of Arts
1 campus (6,497)

Doctoral
UVA (15,411/14,896)

Public School Support	A+
Private School Options	B
Library Popularity	B+
College Town	A+
College Options	B+

Places Rated Rank: 22

Chattanooga, TN-GA

Children in Public Schools (88%)
8 districts, 135 schools, 70,549 students

Children in Private Schools (12%)
Catholic: 2 schools, 784 students
Other religious: 27 schools, 6,111 students
Nonsectarian: 5 schools, 3,158 students

Public Library Systems: 8
1,387,603 books; turnover: 0.9

Colleges and Universities

Associate of Arts
2 campuses (16,496)

Comprehensive
Covenant College (1,196/78)
Southern Adventist University (2,747/395)
Tennessee Temple University (527/33)

Doctoral
University of Tennessee (8,424/1,844)

Public School Support ....C+
Private School Options..B+
Library Popularity ....D
College Town...C+
College Options ....B

Places Rated Rank: 227

Cheyenne, WY

Children in Public Schools (96%)
4 districts, 40 schools, 13,792 students

Children in Private Schools (4%)
Catholic: 1 school, 305 students
Other religious: 5 schools, 269 students

Public Library Systems: 1
256,133 books; turnover: 2.5

Colleges and Universities

Associate of Arts
1 campus (6,903)

Public School Support ....A
Private School Options..D
Library Popularity ....C+
College Town...D+
College Options ....D

Places Rated Rank: 309

Chicago-Naperville-Joliet, IL

Children in Public Schools (88%)
332 districts, 2083 schools, 1,293,426 students

Children in Private Schools (12%)
Catholic: 339 schools, 124,503 students
Other religious: 205 schools, 39,771 students
Nonsectarian: 43 schools, 9,608 students

Public Library Systems: 174
25,049,984 books; turnover: 2.4

Colleges and Universities

Associate of Arts
23 campuses (398,391)

Baccalaureate
East-West University (1,254)
Hebrew Theological College (384)
Illinois College Optometry (612)
Kendall College (836)
Robert Morris College (6,931)
St. Augustine College (2,186)
Trinity Christian College (1,408)

Comprehensive
Columbia College (10,609/697)
Dominican University (1,376/2,361)
Elmhurst College (2,729/287)
Erikson Institute (283)
Governors State University (3,854/4,338)
John Marshall Law School (1,769)
Judson College (1,580/45)
National UHS (191/431)
North Central College (2,394/552)

Northeastern IU (11,143/4,602)
Saint Xavier University (3,550/3,112)
School Art Institute (2,419/624)
University of St. Francis (2,990/2,253)
Vandercook College Music (136/1,071)

Doctoral
Aurora University (1,859/7,640)
Benedictine University (2,564/1,916)
Catholic Theological Union (522)
Chicago School Psychology (683)
Chicago State University (6,005/3,179)
Chicago Theological Seminary (236)
Concordia University (1,327/1,029)
DePaul University (17,811/12,178)
Garrett Evangelical Seminary (405)
Illinois IT (2,089/4,956)
Lewis University (3,890/1,698)
Loyola University (8,967/6,478)
Midwestern University (64/1,731)
National-Louis University (5,008/9,730)
North Park University (1,979/1,105)
Northern Illinois University (20,015/9,649)
Northwestern University (10,241/9,436)
Roosevelt University (5,501/4,431)
Rush University (270/1,296)
University of Chicago (4,475/11,192)
University of Illinois (18,512/11,590)
Wheaton College (2,553/804)

Public School Support ....D
Private School Options..A+
Library Popularity ....C+
College Town...B
College Options ....A+

Places Rated Rank: 115

Chico, CA

Children in Public Schools (95%)
16 districts, 98 schools, 33,385 students

Children in Private Schools (5%)
Catholic: 3 schools, 403 students
Other religious: 12 schools, 1,310 students
Nonsectarian: 1 school, 6 students

Public Library Systems: 1
284,355 books; turnover: 2.3

Colleges and Universities

Associate of Arts
1 campus (18,399)

Comprehensive
California State Universitt (15,353/2,045)

Public School Support C
Private School Options..C+
Library Popularity ....C+
College Town...A
College Options ....C+

Places Rated Rank: 196

✓Cincinnati-Middletown, OH-KY-IN

Children in Public Schools (85%)
124 districts, 580 schools, 319,229 students

Children in Private Schools (15%)
Catholic: 119 schools, 47,210 students
Other religious: 46 schools, 8,903 students
Nonsectarian: 6 schools, 1,334 students

Public Library Systems: 22
7,616,844 books; turnover: 3.5

Colleges and Universities

Associate of Arts
7 campuses (24,217)

Baccalaureate
God's Bible School and College (268)
Miami University Hamilton (2,974)
Miami University Middletown (2,513)
UC Walters College (5,941)

Comprehensive
Art Academy Cincinnati (212/13)
Athenaeum Ohio (144/183)
Cincinnati Christian University (638/271)
Northern Kentucky University (17,229/2,507)
Thomas More College (1,653/174)

Doctoral
College Mt St. Joseph (2,267/621)
Miami University Oxford (15,583/2,668)
Union Institute (1,563/1,984)
University of Cincinnati (22,420/10,750)
Xavier University (4,910/4,293)

Public School Support .... B
Private School Options.....................................A+
Library Popularity .... A
College Town.. B
College Options ....A+

Places Rated Rank: 21

Clarksville, TN-KY

Children in Public Schools (97%)
4 districts, 59 schools, 43,283 students

Children in Private Schools (3%)
Catholic: 2 schools, 401 students
Other religious: 5 schools, 517 students
Nonsectarian: 2 schools, 362 students

Public Library Systems: 4
331,191 books; turnover: 3.1

Colleges and Universities
Associate of Arts
1 campus (4,024)

Comprehensive
Austin Peay State University (10,259/763)

Public School Support .... D
Private School Options.....................................C+
Library Popularity ....B+
College Town.. C
College Options ....C+

Places Rated Rank: 282

Cleveland, TN

Children in Public Schools (97%)
3 districts, 33 schools, 16,565 students

Children in Private Schools (3%)
Other religious: 7 schools, 519 students

Public Library Systems: 4
121,477 books; turnover: 2.5

Colleges and Universities
Associate of Arts
1 campus (4,194)

Comprehensive
Lee University (3,900/421)

Doctoral
Church of God Theological Seminary (457)

Public School Support ....D+
Private School Options..................................... D
Library Popularity ....C+
College Town..C+
College Options ....D+

Places Rated Rank: 330

✓**Cleveland-Elyria-Mentor, OH**

Children in Public Schools (85%)

146 districts, 612 schools, 323,015 students

Children in Private Schools (15%)
Catholic: 114 schools, 44,119 students
Other religious: 46 schools, 8,558 students
Nonsectarian: 13 schools, 4,056 students

Public Library Systems: 28
11,447,518 books; turnover: 3.6

Colleges and Universities
Associate of Arts
7 campuses (65,562)

Comprehensive
Baldwin-Wallace College (4,209/1,128)
Cleveland Institute Art (648/6)
David Myers University (1,254/103)
John Carroll University (3,591/1,442)
Lake Erie College (779/849)
Notre Dame College (1,368/1,596)
Oberlin College (2,998/25)
Siegal College (17/143)
Ursuline College (1,306/467)

Doctoral
Case Western Reserve University (3,781/6,441)
Cleveland Institute Music (252/170)
Cleveland State University (14,428/9,194)
St. Mary Seminary (114)

Public School Support ....B+
Private School Options.....................................A+
Library Popularity ....A
College Town.. C
College Options ....A+

Places Rated Rank: 28

Coeur d'Alene, ID

Children in Public Schools (96%)

4 districts, 42 schools, 20,083 students

Children in Private Schools (4%)
Catholic: 1 school, 194 students
Other religious: 4 schools, 733 students

Public Library Systems: 3
251,962 books; turnover: 3.6

Colleges and Universities
Associate of Arts
1 campus (5,661)

Public School Support ....D
Private School Options..................................... D
Library Popularity ....A
College Town.. D
College Options .... D

Places Rated Rank: 355

College Station-Bryan, TX

Children in Public Schools (97%)
12 districts, 71 schools, 29,264 students

Children in Private Schools (3%)
Other religious: 3 schools, 563 students
Nonsectarian: 1 school, 346 students

Public Library Systems: 5
292,238 books; turnover: 2.6

Colleges and Universities
Doctoral
Texas A&M University (37,503/9,863)

REPORT CARD

Public School Support	B
Private School Options	D+
Library Popularity	B
College Town	A+
College Options	A

Places Rated Rank: 108

Colorado Springs, CO

Children in Public Schools (96%)
19 districts, 205 schools, 104,757 students

Children in Private Schools (4%)
Catholic: 5 schools, 1,456 students
Other religious: 18 schools, 3,053 students
Nonsectarian: 3 schools, 327 students

Public Library Systems: 5
996,038 books; turnover: 6.5

Colleges and Universities
Associate of Arts
1 campus (16,336)
Baccalaureate
Nazarene Bible College (733)
U.S. Air Force Academy (4,252)
Comprehensive
Colorado College (2,480/360)
Doctoral
University of Colorado (7,466/4,841)

REPORT CARD

Public School Support	D+
Private School Options	B+
Library Popularity	A+
College Town	C+
College Options	B

Places Rated Rank: 139

✓Columbia, MO

Children in Public Schools (93%)
9 districts, 53 schools, 22,777 students

Children in Private Schools (7%)
Catholic: 2 schools, 657 students
Other religious: 7 schools, 824 students
Nonsectarian: 1 school, 184 students

Public Library Systems: 4
463,895 books; turnover: 4.0

Colleges and Universities
Baccalaureate
Central Methodist College (919)
Comprehensive
Central Methodist University (1,918/161)
Columbia College (18,358/474)
Stephens College (678/133)
Doctoral
University of Missouri (22,493/7,893)

REPORT CARD

Public School Support	B+
Private School Options	C+
Library Popularity	A+
College Town	A+
College Options	A

Places Rated Rank: 19

Columbia, SC

Children in Public Schools (94%)
14 districts, 204 schools, 119,600 students

Children in Private Schools (6%)
Catholic: 5 schools, 1,407 students

Other religious: 24 schools, 3,515 students
Nonsectarian: 6 schools, 2,461 students

Public Library Systems: 6
1,910,232 books; turnover: 2.6

Colleges and Universities
Associate of Arts
1 campus (15,406)
Baccalaureate
Allen University (692)
Benedict College (3,223)
Comprehensive
Columbia College (1,321/598)
Lutheran Theological Seminary (210)
Doctoral
Columbia IU (755/821)
University of Southern California (18,630/10,186)

REPORT CARD

Public School Support	B+
Private School Options	A
Library Popularity	B
College Town	B+
College Options	A

Places Rated Rank: 52

Columbus, GA-AL

Children in Public Schools (92%)
7 districts, 104 schools, 51,269 students

Children in Private Schools (8%)
Catholic: 5 schools, 1,011 students
Other religious: 16 schools, 2,922 students
Nonsectarian: 1 school, 827 students

Public Library Systems: 2
331,981 books; turnover: 2.8

Colleges and Universities
Associate of Arts
3 campuses (10,102)
Comprehensive
Columbus State University (7,522/1,288)
Doctoral
Beacon University (140/82)

REPORT CARD

Public School Support	B
Private School Options	B+
Library Popularity	B
College Town	C
College Options	C+

Places Rated Rank: 184

Columbus, IN

Children in Public Schools (92%)
2 districts, 19 schools, 11,801 students

Children in Private Schools (8%)
Catholic: 1 school, 387 students
Other religious: 5 schools, 601 students

Public Library Systems: 1
180,620 books; turnover: 4.0

Colleges and Universities
Associate of Arts
1 campus (3,216)

REPORT CARD

Public School Support	C+
Private School Options	D
Library Popularity	A
College Town	D
College Options	D

Places Rated Rank: 323

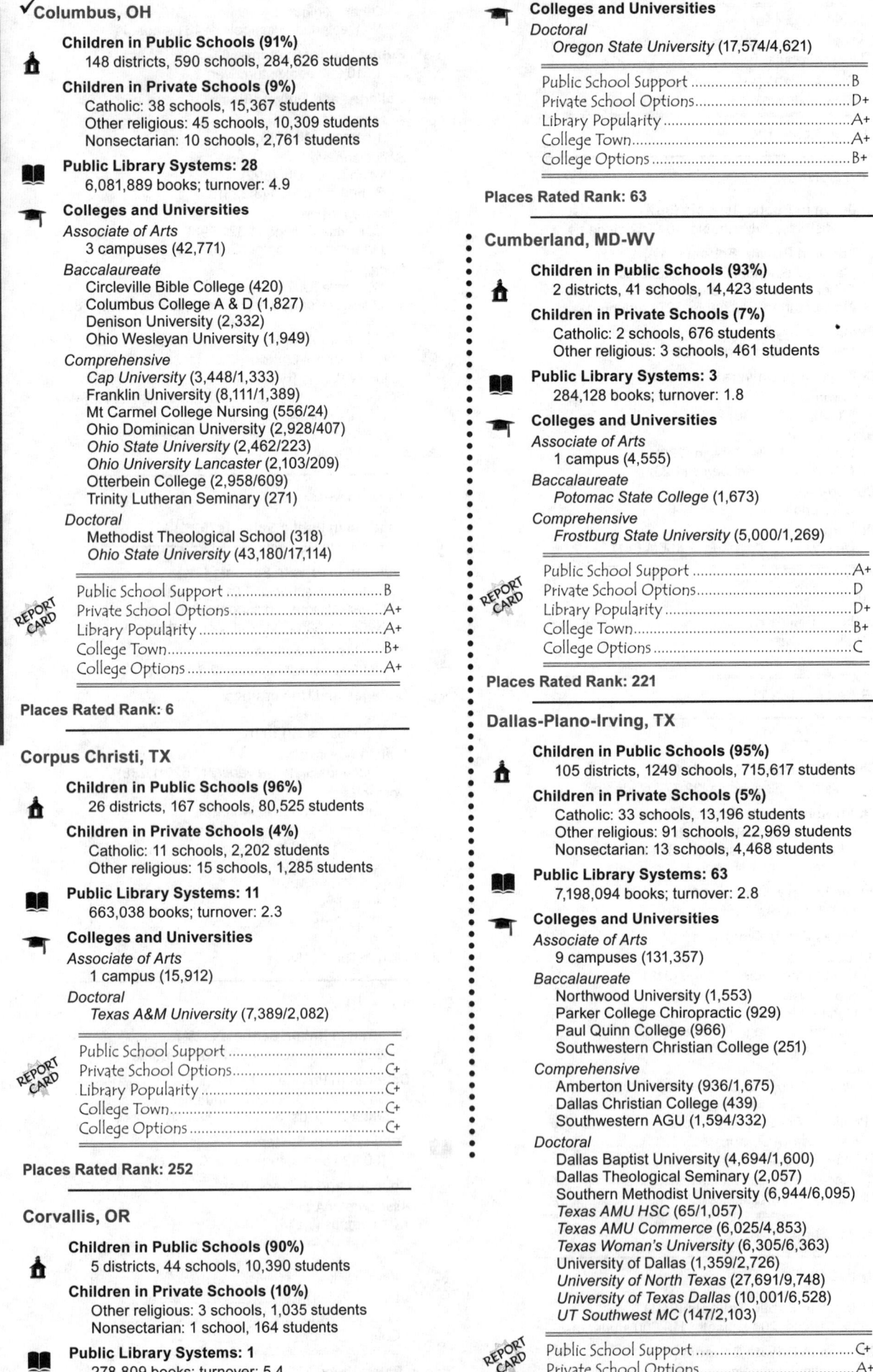

✓Columbus, OH

Children in Public Schools (91%)
148 districts, 590 schools, 284,626 students

Children in Private Schools (9%)
Catholic: 38 schools, 15,367 students
Other religious: 45 schools, 10,309 students
Nonsectarian: 10 schools, 2,761 students

Public Library Systems: 28
6,081,889 books; turnover: 4.9

Colleges and Universities
Associate of Arts
3 campuses (42,771)

Baccalaureate
Circleville Bible College (420)
Columbus College A & D (1,827)
Denison University (2,332)
Ohio Wesleyan University (1,949)

Comprehensive
Cap University (3,448/1,333)
Franklin University (8,111/1,389)
Mt Carmel College Nursing (556/24)
Ohio Dominican University (2,928/407)
Ohio State University (2,462/223)
Ohio University Lancaster (2,103/209)
Otterbein College (2,958/609)
Trinity Lutheran Seminary (271)

Doctoral
Methodist Theological School (318)
Ohio State University (43,180/17,114)

Public School Support .... B
Private School Options.................................... A+
Library Popularity .... A+
College Town.. B+
College Options .... A+

Places Rated Rank: 6

Corpus Christi, TX

Children in Public Schools (96%)
26 districts, 167 schools, 80,525 students

Children in Private Schools (4%)
Catholic: 11 schools, 2,202 students
Other religious: 15 schools, 1,285 students

Public Library Systems: 11
663,038 books; turnover: 2.3

Colleges and Universities
Associate of Arts
1 campus (15,912)

Doctoral
Texas A&M University (7,389/2,082)

Public School Support C
Private School Options.................................... C+
Library Popularity .... C+
College Town.. C+
College Options .... C+

Places Rated Rank: 252

Corvallis, OR

Children in Public Schools (90%)
5 districts, 44 schools, 10,390 students

Children in Private Schools (10%)
Other religious: 3 schools, 1,035 students
Nonsectarian: 1 school, 164 students

Public Library Systems: 1
278,809 books; turnover: 5.4

Colleges and Universities
Doctoral
Oregon State University (17,574/4,621)

Public School Support .... B
Private School Options.................................... D+
Library Popularity .... A+
College Town.. A+
College Options .... B+

Places Rated Rank: 63

Cumberland, MD-WV

Children in Public Schools (93%)
2 districts, 41 schools, 14,423 students

Children in Private Schools (7%)
Catholic: 2 schools, 676 students
Other religious: 3 schools, 461 students

Public Library Systems: 3
284,128 books; turnover: 1.8

Colleges and Universities
Associate of Arts
1 campus (4,555)

Baccalaureate
Potomac State College (1,673)

Comprehensive
Frostburg State University (5,000/1,269)

Public School Support .... A+
Private School Options.................................... D
Library Popularity .... D+
College Town.. B+
College Options C

Places Rated Rank: 221

Dallas-Plano-Irving, TX

Children in Public Schools (95%)
105 districts, 1249 schools, 715,617 students

Children in Private Schools (5%)
Catholic: 33 schools, 13,196 students
Other religious: 91 schools, 22,969 students
Nonsectarian: 13 schools, 4,468 students

Public Library Systems: 63
7,198,094 books; turnover: 2.8

Colleges and Universities
Associate of Arts
9 campuses (131,357)

Baccalaureate
Northwood University (1,553)
Parker College Chiropractic (929)
Paul Quinn College (966)
Southwestern Christian College (251)

Comprehensive
Amberton University (936/1,675)
Dallas Christian College (439)
Southwestern AGU (1,594/332)

Doctoral
Dallas Baptist University (4,694/1,600)
Dallas Theological Seminary (2,057)
Southern Methodist University (6,944/6,095)
Texas AMU HSC (65/1,057)
Texas AMU Commerce (6,025/4,853)
Texas Woman's University (6,305/6,363)
University of Dallas (1,359/2,726)
University of North Texas (27,691/9,748)
University of Texas Dallas (10,001/6,528)
UT Southwest MC (147/2,103)

Public School Support .... C+
Private School Options.................................... A+

Education

Library Popularity .... B
College Town .... C+
College Options .... A+

Places Rated Rank: 50

Dalton, GA

Children in Public Schools (98%)
3 districts, 43 schools, 26,248 students

Children in Private Schools (2%)
Other religious: 4 schools, 603 students

Public Library Systems: 1
289,435 books; turnover: 1.7

Colleges and Universities
Baccalaureate
Dalton State College (5,659)

Public School Support .... B
Private School Options .... D
Library Popularity .... D+
College Town .... D+
College Options .... D+

Places Rated Rank: 350

Danville, IL

Children in Public Schools (91%)
16 districts, 44 schools, 14,275 students

Children in Private Schools (9%)
Catholic: 4 schools, 931 students
Other religious: 4 schools, 398 students

Public Library Systems: 10
317,095 books; turnover: 1.3

Colleges and Universities
Associate of Arts
1 campus (7,605)

Baccalaureate
Lakeview College Nursing (103)

Public School Support .... B+
Private School Options .... D+
Library Popularity .... D
College Town .... D+
College Options .... D

Places Rated Rank: 347

Danville, VA

Children in Public Schools (90%)
3 districts, 38 schools, 16,612 students

Children in Private Schools (10%)
Catholic: 1 school, 368 students
Other religious: 7 schools, 1,448 students
Nonsectarian: 1 school, 18 students

Public Library Systems: 2
238,621 books; turnover: 1.9

Colleges and Universities
Associate of Arts
1 campus (6,417)

Comprehensive
Averett University (2,692/1,003)

Public School Support .... A
Private School Options C
Library Popularity .... D+
College Town .... C+
College Options .... D+

Places Rated Rank: 257

Davenport-Moline-Rock Island, IA-IL

Children in Public Schools (92%)
34 districts, 159 schools, 61,396 students

Children in Private Schools (8%)
Catholic: 13 schools, 3,687 students
Other religious: 10 schools, 1,172 students
Nonsectarian: 2 schools, 305 students

Public Library Systems: 25
1,321,263 books; turnover: 2.0

Colleges and Universities
Associate of Arts
2 campuses (23,598)

Baccalaureate
Augustana College (2,365)
Trinity College Nursing/Health (234)

Comprehensive
Palmer College Chiropractic (164/2,019)

Doctoral
St. Ambrose University (2,697/1,107)

Public School Support .... B+
Private School Options .... B+
Library Popularity C
College Town .... C+
College Options .... C+

Places Rated Rank: 194

✓Dayton, OH

Children in Public Schools (88%)
85 districts, 266 schools, 130,098 students

Children in Private Schools (12%)
Catholic: 28 schools, 11,337 students
Other religious: 21 schools, 6,003 students
Nonsectarian: 2 schools, 557 students

Public Library Systems: 14
4,066,508 books; turnover: 3.2

Colleges and Universities
Associate of Arts
1 campus (31,284)

Baccalaureate
Antioch College (638)

Comprehensive
Antioch University McGregor (215/675)
Cedarville University (3,241/75)
Central State University (1,923/15)
Kettering College Medical Arts (775)
Wilberforce University (1,330)

Doctoral
University of Dayton (7,536/4,907)
Wright State University (12,128/3,857)

Public School Support .... B+
Private School Options .... A
Library Popularity .... B+
College Town .... B+
College Options .... A

Places Rated Rank: 27

Decatur, AL

Children in Public Schools (97%)
4 districts, 60 schools, 25,234 students

Children in Private Schools (3%)
Catholic: 1 school, 223 students
Other religious: 4 schools, 573 students
Nonsectarian: 1 school, 32 students

Public Library Systems: 7
195,383 books; turnover: 1.9

Education

Colleges and Universities
Associate of Arts
1 campus (15,197)

Public School Support ....B+
Private School Options............................D+
Library Popularity ....D+
College Town..C
College Options ....D+

Places Rated Rank: 315

Decatur, IL

Children in Public Schools (89%)
12 districts, 52 schools, 17,272 students

Children in Private Schools (11%)
Catholic: 5 schools, 1,179 students
Other religious: 5 schools, 1,056 students

Public Library Systems: 8
456,809 books; turnover: 2.2

Colleges and Universities
Associate of Arts
1 campus (7,060)
Comprehensive
Millikin University (2,810/60)

Public School Support C
Private School Options.............................C
Library Popularity C
College Town...C+
College Options ....D+

Places Rated Rank: 318

Deltona-Daytona Beach-Ormond Beach, FL

Children in Public Schools (92%)
1 districts, 90 schools, 65,065 students

Children in Private Schools (8%)
Catholic: 6 schools, 1,536 students
Other religious: 24 schools, 3,735 students
Nonsectarian: 1 school, 48 students

Public Library Systems: 1
811,837 books; turnover: 5.7

Colleges and Universities
Associate of Arts
1 campus (17,736)
Baccalaureate
Bethune Cookman College (2,955)
Comprehensive
Embry Riddle Aero University (15,482/5,942)
Stetson University (2,256/1,508)

Public School Support ....D+
Private School Options.............................B
Library Popularity ....A+
College Town...B+
College Options ....B+

Places Rated Rank: 119

Denver-Aurora, CO

Children in Public Schools (94%)
30 districts, 678 schools, 389,370 students

Children in Private Schools (6%)
Catholic: 32 schools, 10,814 students
Other religious: 62 schools, 11,573 students
Nonsectarian: 12 schools, 3,257 students

Public Library Systems: 14
5,479,760 books; turnover: 4.8

Colleges and Universities
Associate of Arts
6 campuses (81,926)
Baccalaureate
Johnson & Wales University (1,558)
Metro State Colleg (25,829)
Comprehensive
Colorado Christian University (2,262/269)
Doctoral
Colorado School Mines (2,808/3,118)
Denver Seminary (927)
Iliff School Theology (386)
Regis University (6,123/5,678)
University of Colorado Denver (13,191/10,531)
University of Denver (4,907/7,297)

Public School Support ....D+
Private School Options............................A+
Library Popularity ....A+
College Town..B
College Options ....A+

Places Rated Rank: 62

Des Moines-West Des Moines, IA

Children in Public Schools (93%)
27 districts, 197 schools, 86,859 students

Children in Private Schools (7%)
Catholic: 13 schools, 4,298 students
Other religious: 9 schools, 1,886 students

Public Library Systems: 42
1,562,531 books; turnover: 2.8

Colleges and Universities
Associate of Arts
3 campuses (24,745)
Baccalaureate
Mercy College Health Sciences (740)
Comprehensive
Des Moines Osteopathic Medical College (1,244)
Faith Baptist Bible College & Seminary (409/177)
Grand View College (2,044/2)
Simpson College (2,382/25)
Doctoral
Drake University (2,909/9,383)

Public School Support ....B+
Private School Options............................B
Library Popularity ....B
College Town..B
College Options ....B+

Places Rated Rank: 126

Detroit-Livonia-Dearborn, MI

Children in Public Schools (93%)
107 districts, 692 schools, 359,259 students

Children in Private Schools (7%)
Catholic: 68 schools, 18,019 students
Other religious: 45 schools, 7,286 students
Nonsectarian: 3 schools, 96 students

Public Library Systems: 17
9,818,756 books; turnover: 0.9

Colleges and Universities
Associate of Arts
5 campuses (50,189)
Baccalaureate
Baker College (727)
College Creative Studies (1,305)
Comprehensive
Madonna University (4,314/2,435)

Marygrove College (952/6,100)
Michigan State College of Law (1,022)
Sacred Heart Major Sem (352/152)
University of Michigan (7,737/3,083)

Doctoral
Michigan Theological Seminary (14/241)
University of Detroit Mercy (4,140/2,612)
Wayne State University (24,015/14,930)

Public School Support ....B
Private School Options.......................................A
Library Popularity ....D
College Town..B
College Options ....A+

Places Rated Rank: 164

Dothan, AL

Children in Public Schools (90%)
5 districts, 50 schools, 21,544 students

Children in Private Schools (10%)
Other religious: 7 schools, 2,028 students
Nonsectarian: 1 school, 319 students

Public Library Systems: 7
340,560 books; turnover: 1.1

Colleges and Universities
Comprehensive
Troy State University (2,262/523)

Public School Support C
Private School Options.......................................C
Library Popularity ....D
College Town..D
College Options ....D

Places Rated Rank: 371

Dover, DE

Children in Public Schools (93%)
10 districts, 48 schools, 24,283 students

Children in Private Schools (7%)
Catholic: 2 schools, 837 students
Other religious: 15 schools, 1,033 students
Nonsectarian: 1 school, 33 students

Public Library Systems: 4
160,774 books; turnover: 2.8

Colleges and Universities
Associate of Arts
1 campus (8,783)

Comprehensive
Wesley College (2,424/171)

Doctoral
Delaware State University (3,377/255)

Public School Support ....B+
Private School Options.......................................C+
Library Popularity ....B
College Town..B+
College Options ....C+

Places Rated Rank: 142

Dubuque, IA

Children in Public Schools (76%)
2 districts, 27 schools, 13,018 students

Children in Private Schools (24%)
Catholic: 15 schools, 4,187 students

Public Library Systems: 4
313,116 books; turnover: 2.4

Colleges and Universities
Baccalaureate
Divine Word College (120)
Emmaus Bible College (268)

Comprehensive
Loras College (1,672/167)
Wartburg Theological Seminary (211)

Doctoral
Clarke College (1,082/183)
University of Dubuque (1,035/375)

Public School Support ....B+
Private School Options.......................................D+
Library Popularity ....C+
College Town..B
College Options ....D+

Places Rated Rank: 220

Duluth, MN-WI

Children in Public Schools (95%)
32 districts, 139 schools, 40,077 students

Children in Private Schools (5%)
Catholic: 8 schools, 1,367 students
Other religious: 7 schools, 610 students
Nonsectarian: 1 school, 81 students

Public Library Systems: 20
1,110,536 books; turnover: 2.2

Colleges and Universities
Associate of Arts
4 campuses (16,012)

Comprehensive
College St. Scholastica (2,650/669)
University of Minnesota (10,248/1,097)
University of Wisconsin (3,050/575)

Public School Support ....B+
Private School Options.......................................C+
Library Popularity C
College Town..B+
College Options ....B

Places Rated Rank: 166

✓Durham, NC

Children in Public Schools (90%)
20 districts, 111 schools, 65,181 students

Children in Private Schools (10%)
Catholic: 3 schools, 951 students
Other religious: 17 schools, 2,634 students
Nonsectarian: 7 schools, 3,383 students

Public Library Systems: 2
619,398 books; turnover: 3.6

Colleges and Universities
Associate of Arts
3 campuses (11,891)

Comprehensive
NC Central University (6,316/2,313)

Doctoral
Duke University (7,380/7,654)
UNC Chapel Hill (17,652/12,098)

Public School Support ....B
Private School Options.......................................B+
Library Popularity ....A
College Town..A+
College Options ....A

Places Rated Rank: 20

Eau Claire, WI

Children in Public Schools (89%)
13 districts, 59 schools, 22,168 students

Children in Private Schools (11%)
Catholic: 14 schools, 1,819 students
Other religious: 17 schools, 886 students
Nonsectarian: 1 school, 172 students

Public Library Systems: 10
474,905 books; turnover: 4.0

Colleges and Universities
Associate of Arts
1 campus (4,695)

Comprehensive
University of Wisconsin (11,283/948)

Public School Support ....A+
Private School Options.....................................B
Library Popularity ....A
College Town..B+
College Options ....C+

Places Rated Rank: 53

Edison, NJ

Children in Public Schools (89%)
139 districts, 556 schools, 361,859 students

Children in Private Schools (11%)
Catholic: 71 schools, 27,620 students
Other religious: 60 schools, 12,724 students
Nonsectarian: 15 schools, 5,205 students

Public Library Systems: 61
7,623,114 books; turnover: 2.3

Colleges and Universities
Associate of Arts
7 campuses (58,975)

Comprehensive
Beth Medrash Govoha (2,229/2,277)
Georgian Court University (2,367/1,313)
Monmouth University (4,869/2,289)

Doctoral
New Brunswick Theological Seminary (258)
Rutgers University New Brunswick (29,556/9,264)

Public School Support ....A+
Private School Options.....................................A+
Library Popularity ....C+
College Town..C
College Options ....A

Places Rated Rank: 46

El Centro, CA

Children in Public Schools (96%)
18 districts, 62 schools, 36,196 students

Children in Private Schools (4%)
Catholic: 3 schools, 953 students
Other religious: 5 schools, 694 students

Public Library Systems: 5
323,977 books; turnover: 1.1

Colleges and Universities
Associate of Arts
1 campus (10,381)

Comprehensive
San Diego State Imperial Valley (688/376)

Public School Support C
Private School Options.....................................D+
Library Popularity ....D

College Town..D+
College Options ....D+

Places Rated Rank: 370

Elizabethtown, KY

Children in Public Schools (95%)
5 districts, 52 schools, 19,705 students

Children in Private Schools (5%)
Catholic: 3 schools, 678 students
Other religious: 5 schools, 327 students

Public Library Systems: 2
135,954 books; turnover: 2.3

Colleges and Universities
Associate of Arts
2 campuses (7,279)

Public School Support ....B
Private School Options.....................................D+
Library Popularity C
College Town..D+
College Options ....D

Places Rated Rank: 340

Elkhart-Goshen, IN

Children in Public Schools (92%)
7 districts, 55 schools, 34,655 students

Children in Private Schools (8%)
Catholic: 3 schools, 687 students
Other religious: 29 schools, 2,507 students
Nonsectarian: 1 school, 14 students

Public Library Systems: 6
709,324 books; turnover: 3.0

Colleges and Universities
Baccalaureate
Goshen College (1,061)

Comprehensive
Mennonite Biblical Sem (239)

Public School Support ....C+
Private School Options.....................................B
Library Popularity ....B+
College Town..D
College Options ....D

Places Rated Rank: 304

Elmira, NY

Children in Public Schools (91%)
4 districts, 27 schools, 13,266 students

Children in Private Schools (9%)
Catholic: 5 schools, 1,108 students
Other religious: 2 schools, 190 students

Public Library Systems: 2
309,993 books; turnover: 1.6

Colleges and Universities
Associate of Arts
1 campus (56)

Comprehensive
Elmira College (1,694/502)

Public School Support ....A+
Private School Options.....................................D+
Library Popularity ....D
College Town..D
College Options ....D

Places Rated Rank: 338

El Paso, TX

Children in Public Schools (96%)
14 districts, 264 schools, 167,885 students

Children in Private Schools (4%)
Catholic: 13 schools, 4,368 students
Other religious: 15 schools, 3,045 students
Nonsectarian: 3 schools, 271 students

Public Library Systems: 4
947,566 books; turnover: 1.6

Colleges and Universities
Associate of Arts
1 campus (33,443)
Doctoral
University of Texas (17,479/4,750)

REPORT CARD
Public School Support ....C+
Private School Options....................................B+
Library Popularity ....D+
College Town..B
College Options ....B+

Places Rated Rank: 183

Erie, PA

Children in Public Schools (84%)
20 districts, 83 schools, 41,710 students

Children in Private Schools (16%)
Catholic: 20 schools, 6,671 students
Other religious: 9 schools, 923 students
Nonsectarian: 2 schools, 244 students

Public Library Systems: 7
648,452 books; turnover: 2.7

Colleges and Universities
Comprehensive
Edinboro University (7,840/1,396)
Lake Erie College Osteopathic (1,038)
Mercyhurst College (3,941/270)
Pennsylvania State University (3,813/176)

Doctoral
Gannon University (2,616/1,380)

REPORT CARD
Public School Support ....A
Private School Options....................................B+
Library Popularity ....B
College Town..B+
College Options ....C+

Places Rated Rank: 81

Essex County, MA

Children in Public Schools (89%)
49 districts, 212 schools, 116,398 students

Children in Private Schools (11%)
Catholic: 27 schools, 9,950 students
Other religious: 10 schools, 1,252 students
Nonsectarian: 10 schools, 3,708 students

Public Library Systems: 33
2,849,700 books; turnover: 1.8

Colleges and Universities
Associate of Arts
3 campuses (18,045)
Baccalaureate
Montserrat College Art (428)
Comprehensive
Endicott College (1,815/3,876)
Gordon College (1,780/127)
Merrimack College (3,020/24)
Salem State College (8,678/7,092)

Doctoral
Gordon-Conwell Theological Seminary (2,922)

REPORT CARD
Public School Support ....A+
Private School Options....................................A
Library Popularity ....D+
College Town..C+
College Options ....B+

Places Rated Rank: 134

Eugene-Springfield, OR

Children in Public Schools (95%)
17 districts, 129 schools, 47,026 students

Children in Private Schools (5%)
Catholic: 3 schools, 1,190 students
Other religious: 9 schools, 954 students
Nonsectarian: 1 school, 100 students

Public Library Systems: 7
638,275 books; turnover: 3.9

Colleges and Universities
Associate of Arts
1 campus (14,923)
Baccalaureate
Eugene Bible College (184)
Comprehensive
Northwest Christian College (435/100)
Doctoral
University of Oregon (18,258/5,608)

REPORT CARD
Public School Support ....D+
Private School Options....................................C+
Library Popularity ....A
College Town..A
College Options ....B+

Places Rated Rank: 116

Evansville, IN-KY

Children in Public Schools (86%)
14 districts, 105 schools, 50,342 students

Children in Private Schools (14%)
Catholic: 21 schools, 6,614 students
Other religious: 8 schools, 1,177 students
Nonsectarian: 2 schools, 482 students

Public Library Systems: 13
1,363,547 books; turnover: 2.9

Colleges and Universities
Associate of Arts
2 campuses (9,997)
Comprehensive
University of Evansville (2,799/105)
University of Southern Indiana (10,481/1,100)
Doctoral
Oakland City College (1,967/518)

REPORT CARD
Public School Support ....B
Private School Options....................................B+
Library Popularity ....B
College Town..A
College Options ....B

Places Rated Rank: 75

Fairbanks, AK

Children in Public Schools (97%)
2 districts, 47 schools, 19,409 students

Children in Private Schools (3%)
Catholic: 1 school, 235 students

Other religious: 5 schools, 359 students
Nonsectarian: 1 school, 12 students

Public Library Systems: 1
284,474 books; turnover: 2.2

Colleges and Universities
Doctoral
University of Alaska (14,738/1,380)

Public School Support ....D+
Private School Options...D+
Library Popularity C
College Town..A+
College Options ....B

Places Rated Rank: 228

Fargo, ND-MN

Children in Public Schools (94%)
17 districts, 76 schools, 27,957 students

Children in Private Schools (6%)
Catholic: 4 schools, 1,106 students
Other religious: 3 schools, 689 students

Public Library Systems: 7
610,924 books; turnover: 2.8

Colleges and Universities
Comprehensive
Concordia College (2,960)
Moorhead State University (8,346/831)
Doctoral
North Dakota State (11,233/1,792)

Public School Support ....B
Private School Options...D+
Library Popularity ....B
College Town..A
College Options ....B

Places Rated Rank: 155

Farmington, NM

Children in Public Schools (98%)
5 districts, 66 schools, 23,569 students

Children in Private Schools (2%)
Catholic: 1 school, 139 students
Other religious: 7 schools, 364 students

Public Library Systems: 3
183,247 books; turnover: 2.4

Colleges and Universities
Associate of Arts
1 campus (13,915)

Public School Support ....C+
Private School Options...D
Library Popularity ....C+
College Town..C
College Options ....D+

Places Rated Rank: 336

Fayetteville, NC

Children in Public Schools (95%)
4 districts, 115 schools, 64,977 students

Children in Private Schools (5%)
Catholic: 2 schools, 419 students
Other religious: 15 schools, 2,677 students
Nonsectarian: 2 schools, 257 students

Public Library Systems: 1
609,627 books; turnover: 2.8

Colleges and Universities
Associate of Arts
1 campus (14,818)
Comprehensive
Methodist College (3,010/45)
Doctoral
Fayetteville State University (5,177/1,569)

Public School Support ....D+
Private School Options...B
Library Popularity ....B
College Town..C+
College Options ....C+

Places Rated Rank: 215

Fayetteville-Springdale-Rogers, AR-MO

Children in Public Schools (97%)
23 districts, 119 schools, 67,853 students

Children in Private Schools (3%)
Catholic: 1 school, 320 students
Other religious: 12 schools, 1,642 students
Nonsectarian: 1 school, 367 students

Public Library Systems: 6
641,422 books; turnover: 3.6

Colleges and Universities
Associate of Arts
2 campuses (7,265)
Comprehensive
John Brown University (1,851/235)
Doctoral
University of Arkansas (14,460/4,043)

Public School Support ....D+
Private School Options...C+
Library Popularity ....A
College Town..B+
College Options ....B+

Places Rated Rank: 168

Flagstaff, AZ

Children in Public Schools (99%)
25 districts, 81 schools, 21,009 students

Children in Private Schools (1%)
Catholic: 1 school, 284 students
Other religious: 2 schools, 13 students
Nonsectarian: 1 school, 5 students

Public Library Systems: 5
304,613 books; turnover: 3.1

Colleges and Universities
Associate of Arts
1 campus (6,084)
Doctoral
Northern Arizona University (15,110/8,782)

Public School Support ....D
Private School Options...D+
Library Popularity ....B+
College Town..A+
College Options ....B+

Places Rated Rank: 188

Flint, MI

Children in Public Schools (94%)
33 districts, 177 schools, 85,552 students

Children in Private Schools (6%)
Catholic: 12 schools, 3,513 students
Other religious: 11 schools, 1,655 students

Nonsectarian: 1 school, 114 students

📖 **Public Library Systems: 2**
1,098,622 books; turnover: 1.5

🎓 **Colleges and Universities**
Associate of Arts
1 campus (18,874)
Baccalaureate
Baker College (730)
Comprehensive
Baker College GS (3,489/1,688)
Baker College (6,023/11)
Kettering University (2,787/972)
University of Michigan (6,706/809)

REPORT CARD
Public School Support .... C+
Private School Options .... B
Library Popularity .... D
College Town .... B
College Options .... B

Places Rated Rank: 219

Florence, SC

🏫 **Children in Public Schools (91%)**
6 districts, 59 schools, 34,693 students

Children in Private Schools (9%)
Catholic: 1 school, 204 students
Other religious: 13 schools, 2,333 students
Nonsectarian: 3 schools, 780 students

📖 **Public Library Systems: 2**
424,758 books; turnover: 1.5

🎓 **Colleges and Universities**
Associate of Arts
1 campus (5,748)
Baccalaureate
Coker College (1,400)
Comprehensive
Francis Marion University (3,461/968)

REPORT CARD
Public School Support .... C+
Private School Options .... B
Library Popularity .... D
College Town .... D+
College Options C

Places Rated Rank: 314

Florence-Muscle Shoals, AL

🏫 **Children in Public Schools (93%)**
6 districts, 49 schools, 21,521 students

Children in Private Schools (7%)
Catholic: 1 school, 201 students
Other religious: 4 schools, 1,019 students
Nonsectarian: 2 schools, 470 students

📖 **Public Library Systems: 9**
291,626 books; turnover: 2.5

🎓 **Colleges and Universities**
Associate of Arts
1 campus (7,123)
Comprehensive
Heritage Christian University (142/21)
University of North Alabama (6,087/1,075)

REPORT CARD
Public School Support .... B+
Private School Options C
Library Popularity .... C+
College Town .... B
College Options C

Places Rated Rank: 201

Fond du Lac, WI

🏫 **Children in Public Schools (84%)**
6 districts, 33 schools, 13,440 students

Children in Private Schools (16%)
Catholic: 9 schools, 1,383 students
Other religious: 11 schools, 1,270 students

📖 **Public Library Systems: 6**
293,815 books; turnover: 3.0

🎓 **Colleges and Universities**
Associate of Arts
1 campus (12,648)
Baccalaureate
Ripon College (1,018)
Doctoral
Marian College (2,376/2,417)

REPORT CARD
Public School Support .... A
Private School Options .... C+
Library Popularity .... B+
College Town .... A
College Options .... C+

Places Rated Rank: 98

Fort Collins-Loveland, CO

🏫 **Children in Public Schools (94%)**
4 districts, 85 schools, 41,221 students

Children in Private Schools (6%)
Catholic: 2 schools, 620 students
Other religious: 11 schools, 1,539 students
Nonsectarian: 3 schools, 407 students

📖 **Public Library Systems: 6**
574,740 books; turnover: 5.1

🎓 **Colleges and Universities**
Doctoral
Colorado State University (24,446/9,603)

REPORT CARD
Public School Support .... D+
Private School Options .... B
Library Popularity .... A+
College Town .... A+
College Options .... B+

Places Rated Rank: 68

Fort Lauderdale-Pompano Beach-Deerfield Beach, FL

🏫 **Children in Public Schools (89%)**
1 districts, 275 schools, 274,059 students

Children in Private Schools (11%)
Catholic: 23 schools, 13,078 students
Other religious: 53 schools, 14,388 students
Nonsectarian: 20 schools, 6,970 students

📖 **Public Library Systems: 5**
2,723,964 books; turnover: 3.3

🎓 **Colleges and Universities**
Associate of Arts
4 campuses (54,590)
Baccalaureate
City College (919)
Doctoral
Nova Southeastern University (6,939/25,600)

REPORT CARD
Public School Support .... D
Private School Options .... A+
Library Popularity .... B+
College Town C
College Options .... A

Places Rated Rank: 153

Fort Smith, AR-OK

Children in Public Schools (96%)
48 districts, 135 schools, 51,389 students

Children in Private Schools (4%)
Catholic: 4 schools, 1,095 students
Other religious: 6 schools, 1,229 students

Public Library Systems: 3
477,841 books; turnover: 2.5

Colleges and Universities
Associate of Arts
4 campuses (5,102)

Baccalaureate
University of Arkansas (8,528)

REPORT CARD	
Public School Support	D+
Private School Options	C
Library Popularity	C+
College Town	D+
College Options	C

Places Rated Rank: 330

Fort Walton Beach-Crestview-Destin, FL

Children in Public Schools (94%)
1 districts, 55 schools, 31,021 students

Children in Private Schools (6%)
Catholic: 1 school, 349 students
Other religious: 5 schools, 1,688 students
Nonsectarian: 1 school, 7 students

Public Library Systems: 1
229,050 books; turnover: 2.3

Colleges and Universities
Associate of Arts
1 campus (607)

Baccalaureate
Okaloosa-Walton College (11,471)

REPORT CARD	
Public School Support	D
Private School Options	C
Library Popularity	C+
College Town	C
College Options	C

Places Rated Rank: 322

Fort Wayne, IN

Children in Public Schools (85%)
12 districts, 112 schools, 65,301 students

Children in Private Schools (15%)
Catholic: 14 schools, 5,608 students
Other religious: 34 schools, 6,063 students

Public Library Systems: 5
3,466,589 books; turnover: 1.7

Colleges and Universities
Associate of Arts
1 campus (9,662)

Baccalaureate
Tri-State University (164)

Comprehensive
Indiana IT (3,609/577)
Indiana-Purdue University (13,880/1,413)
Taylor University (775/31)
University of St. Francis (1,740/320)

Doctoral
Concordia Theological Seminary (521)

REPORT CARD	
Public School Support	B
Private School Options	B

Library Popularity .... D+
College Town .... B
College Options .... B

Places Rated Rank: 213

Fort Worth-Arlington, TX

Children in Public Schools (95%)
53 districts, 617 schools, 356,518 students

Children in Private Schools (5%)
Catholic: 13 schools, 4,189 students
Other religious: 50 schools, 10,454 students
Nonsectarian: 7 schools, 3,320 students

Public Library Systems: 40
3,139,862 books; turnover: 3.6

Colleges and Universities
Associate of Arts
2 campuses (60,679)

Baccalaureate
Arlington Baptist College (217)
College of St. Thomas More (28)

Comprehensive
Southwestern Adventist University (956/45)
Texas Wesleyan University (1,983/1,320)

Doctoral
Southwestern Baptist Theological Seminary (267/3,284)
Texas Christian University (7,451/1,614)
University of Texas (23,378/8,200)
University of North Texas Health Science (1,075)

REPORT CARD	
Public School Support	D+
Private School Options	A
Library Popularity	A
College Town	C+
College Options	A+

Places Rated Rank: 89

Fresno, CA

Children in Public Schools (97%)
37 districts, 330 schools, 192,373 students

Children in Private Schools (3%)
Catholic: 7 schools, 2,275 students
Other religious: 21 schools, 3,026 students
Nonsectarian: 4 schools, 523 students

Public Library Systems: 2
2,343,034 books; turnover: 1.2

Colleges and Universities
Associate of Arts
4 campuses (54,079)

Comprehensive
Fresno Pacific University (3,674/2,451)
Mennonite Brethren Sem (282)

Doctoral
Alliant International University (386)
Cal State University (20,024/4,359)

REPORT CARD	
Public School Support	D+
Private School Options	B+
Library Popularity	D
College Town	B+
College Options	A

Places Rated Rank: 204

Gadsden, AL

Children in Public Schools (92%)
3 districts, 45 schools, 15,971 students

Children in Private Schools (8%)
Catholic: 1 school, 170 students
Other religious: 4 schools, 1,085 students
Nonsectarian: 1 school, 77 students

Public Library Systems: 6
268,430 books; turnover: 1.2

Colleges and Universities
Associate of Arts
1 campus (8,829)

REPORT CARD	
Public School Support	C+
Private School Options	C
Library Popularity	D
College Town	D+
College Options	D

Places Rated Rank: 360

Gainesville, FL

Children in Public Schools (91%)
3 districts, 75 schools, 33,122 students

Children in Private Schools (9%)
Catholic: 2 schools, 725 students
Other religious: 12 schools, 1,102 students
Nonsectarian: 7 schools, 1,548 students

Public Library Systems: 1
747,181 books; turnover: 3.5

Colleges and Universities
Associate of Arts
1 campus (19,470)
Baccalaureate
City College (606)
Doctoral
University of Florida (38,664/17,553)

REPORT CARD	
Public School Support	D
Private School Options	B
Library Popularity	A
College Town	A+
College Options	A

Places Rated Rank: 76

Gainesville, GA

Children in Public Schools (96%)
2 districts, 41 schools, 28,858 students

Children in Private Schools (4%)
Other religious: 5 schools, 717 students
Nonsectarian: 2 schools, 578 students

Public Library Systems: 1
213,836 books; turnover: 2.9

Colleges and Universities
Associate of Arts
2 campuses (12,219)
Comprehensive
Brenau University (1,773/934)

REPORT CARD	
Public School Support	C+
Private School Options	C
Library Popularity	B+
College Town	C
College Options	C

Places Rated Rank: 253

Gary, IN

Children in Public Schools (92%)
38 districts, 230 schools, 119,370 students

Children in Private Schools (8%)
Catholic: 23 schools, 6,710 students
Other religious: 27 schools, 4,191 students
Nonsectarian: 1 school, 167 students

Public Library Systems: 15
3,202,597 books; turnover: 2.2

Colleges and Universities
Associate of Arts
1 campus (8,535)
Comprehensive
Calumet College St. Joseph (1,582/153)
Indiana University Northwest (6,304/1,168)
Purdue University (10,297/1,371)
St. Joseph's College (1,081/35)
Valparaiso University (3,183/969)

REPORT CARD	
Public School Support	C+
Private School Options	B+
Library Popularity	C
College Town	C
College Options	B

Places Rated Rank: 208

Glens Falls, NY

Children in Public Schools (98%)
21 districts, 46 schools, 21,424 students

Children in Private Schools (2%)
Catholic: 1 school, 286 students
Other religious: 4 schools, 176 students
Nonsectarian: 1 school, 40 students

Public Library Systems: 19
498,238 books; turnover: 1.9

Colleges and Universities
Associate of Arts
2 campuses (5,529)

REPORT CARD	
Public School Support	A+
Private School Options	D+
Library Popularity	D+
College Town	D
College Options	D

Places Rated Rank: 321

Goldsboro, NC

Children in Public Schools (93%)
2 districts, 32 schools, 19,555 students

Children in Private Schools (7%)
Catholic: 1 school, 244 students
Other religious: 6 schools, 1,150 students

Public Library Systems: 1
118,545 books; turnover: 3.1

Colleges and Universities
Associate of Arts
1 campus (4,444)
Baccalaureate
Mount Olive College (3,310)

REPORT CARD	
Public School Support	C
Private School Options	D+
Library Popularity	B+
College Town	D+
College Options	D+

Places Rated Rank: 324

Grand Forks, ND-MN

Children in Public Schools (94%)
19 districts, 55 schools, 14,927 students

🏫 **Children in Private Schools (6%)**
Catholic: 6 schools, 734 students
Other religious: 3 schools, 135 students

📖 **Public Library Systems: 3**
340,113 books; turnover: 2.6

🎓 **Colleges and Universities**
Baccalaureate
University of Minnesota (2,934)
Doctoral
UND (11,730/3,079)

REPORT CARD	
Public School Support	A
Private School Options	D+
Library Popularity	C+
College Town	A+
College Options	B

Places Rated Rank: 138

Grand Junction, CO

🏫 **Children in Public Schools (95%)**
4 districts, 45 schools, 20,806 students

Children in Private Schools (5%)
Catholic: 1 school, 413 students
Other religious: 10 schools, 780 students

📖 **Public Library Systems: 1**
262,703 books; turnover: 3.0

🎓 **Colleges and Universities**
Comprehensive
Mesa State College (6,864/78)

REPORT CARD	
Public School Support	D+
Private School Options	D+
Library Popularity	B+
College Town	C+
College Options	D+

Places Rated Rank: 311

Grand Rapids-Wyoming, MI

🏫 **Children in Public Schools (87%)**
61 districts, 363 schools, 135,928 students

Children in Private Schools (13%)
Catholic: 29 schools, 7,368 students
Other religious: 50 schools, 13,140 students

📖 **Public Library Systems: 23**
2,565,683 books; turnover: 2.4

🎓 **Colleges and Universities**
Associate of Arts
1 campus (19,856)
Comprehensive
Aquinas College (2,007/787)
Calvin College (4,563/153)
Cornerstone University (2,084/326)
Davenport University (23,235/1,454)
Kuyper College (338)
Doctoral
Calvin Theological Seminary (349)

REPORT CARD	
Public School Support	B
Private School Options	B+
Library Popularity	C+
College Town	C+
College Options	B+

Places Rated Rank: 169

Great Falls, MT

🏫 **Children in Public Schools (94%)**
16 districts, 43 schools, 12,493 students

Children in Private Schools (6%)
Catholic: 3 schools, 603 students
Other religious: 5 schools, 254 students

📖 **Public Library Systems: 3**
154,191 books; turnover: 2.7

🎓 **Colleges and Universities**
Associate of Arts
2 campuses (2,106)
Comprehensive
University of Great Falls (845/148)

REPORT CARD	
Public School Support	B
Private School Options	D
Library Popularity	B
College Town	D
College Options	D

Places Rated Rank: 333

Greeley, CO

🏫 **Children in Public Schools (98%)**
13 districts, 115 schools, 38,756 students

Children in Private Schools (2%)
Catholic: 1 school, 203 students
Other religious: 4 schools, 500 students
Nonsectarian: 1 school, 88 students

📖 **Public Library Systems: 3**
492,868 books; turnover: 2.7

🎓 **Colleges and Universities**
Associate of Arts
1 campus (9,136)
Doctoral
University of Northern Colorado (14,427/5,288)

REPORT CARD	
Public School Support	B
Private School Options	D+
Library Popularity	B
College Town	A
College Options	B+

Places Rated Rank: 147

Green Bay, WI

🏫 **Children in Public Schools (88%)**
19 districts, 101 schools, 48,820 students

Children in Private Schools (12%)
Catholic: 25 schools, 4,690 students
Other religious: 19 schools, 1,757 students
Nonsectarian: 1 school, 150 students

📖 **Public Library Systems: 10**
606,614 books; turnover: 4.7

🎓 **Colleges and Universities**
Associate of Arts
2 campuses (14,402)
Comprehensive
Bellin College Nursing (214)
St. Norbert College (2,184/219)
University of Wisconsin (6,039/815)

REPORT CARD	
Public School Support	A
Private School Options	B+
Library Popularity	A+
College Town	C
College Options	C+

Places Rated Rank: 80

Greensboro-High Point, NC

🏫 **Children in Public Schools (94%)**
8 districts, 171 schools, 107,970 students

Children in Private Schools (6%)
Catholic: 3 schools, 1,124 students
Other religious: 25 schools, 4,657 students
Nonsectarian: 4 schools, 1,127 students

📖 **Public Library Systems: 4**
1,364,863 books; turnover: 2.2

🎓 **Colleges and Universities**
Associate of Arts
3 campuses (18,527)

Baccalaureate
Bennett College for Women (460)
Guilford College (2,481)

Comprehensive
Greensboro College (1,333/93)
High Point University (3,242/263)

Doctoral
North Carolina A & T (10,212/1,711)
UNC (12,969/4,798)

REPORT CARD
Public School Support C
Private School Options .... B+
Library Popularity C
College Town .... A
College Options .... A

Places Rated Rank: 156

Greenville, NC

🏫 **Children in Public Schools (93%)**
2 districts, 37 schools, 25,083 students

Children in Private Schools (7%)
Catholic: 1 school, 514 students
Other religious: 7 schools, 1,199 students
Nonsectarian: 1 school, 293 students

📖 **Public Library Systems: 2**
255,414 books; turnover: 1.8

🎓 **Colleges and Universities**
Associate of Arts
1 campus (7,991)

Doctoral
East Carolina University (19,007/6,712)

REPORT CARD
Public School Support .... B
Private School Options .... C+
Library Popularity .... D+
College Town .... A+
College Options .... B+

Places Rated Rank: 157

Greenville, SC

🏫 **Children in Public Schools (91%)**
4 districts, 138 schools, 90,231 students

Children in Private Schools (9%)
Catholic: 4 schools, 995 students
Other religious: 30 schools, 7,254 students
Nonsectarian: 2 schools, 988 students

📖 **Public Library Systems: 3**
1,014,537 books; turnover: 3.5

🎓 **Colleges and Universities**
Associate of Arts
1 campus (17,814)

Baccalaureate
North Greenville University (1,769)
Presbyterian College (1,207)

Comprehensive
Furman University (2,946/1,656)
Southern Wesleyan University (2,617/1,046)

Doctoral
Bob Jones University (3,919/1,347)
Clemson University (14,771/4,293)

REPORT CARD
Public School Support .... D+
Private School Options .... B+
Library Popularity .... A
College Town .... A
College Options .... B+

Places Rated Rank: 106

Gulfport-Biloxi, MS

🏫 **Children in Public Schools (90%)**
9 districts, 70 schools, 40,238 students

Children in Private Schools (10%)
Catholic: 13 schools, 3,330 students
Other religious: 6 schools, 831 students
Nonsectarian: 1 school, 128 students

📖 **Public Library Systems: 3**
450,634 books; turnover: 2.5

🎓 **Colleges and Universities**
Associate of Arts
1 campus (14,508)

REPORT CARD
Public School Support .... D+
Private School Options .... B
Library Popularity .... C+
College Town .... D
College Options .... D+

Places Rated Rank: 319

Hagerstown-Martinsburg, MD-WV

🏫 **Children in Public Schools (93%)**
3 districts, 84 schools, 38,409 students

Children in Private Schools (7%)
Catholic: 2 schools, 540 students
Other religious: 17 schools, 2,428 students
Nonsectarian: 2 schools, 20 students

📖 **Public Library Systems: 4**
513,394 books; turnover: 2.2

🎓 **Colleges and Universities**
Associate of Arts
1 campus (5,128)

REPORT CARD
Public School Support .... B+
Private School Options .... B
Library Popularity C
College Town .... D
College Options .... D

Places Rated Rank: 306

Hanford-Corcoran, CA

🏫 **Children in Public Schools (96%)**
17 districts, 62 schools, 27,372 students

Children in Private Schools (4%)
Catholic: 2 schools, 437 students
Other religious: 6 schools, 776 students

📖 **Public Library Systems: 1**
205,197 books; turnover: 0.6

REPORT CARD
Public School Support .... D+
Private School Options .... D+
Library Popularity .... D

Places Rated Rank: 378

Harrisburg-Carlisle, PA

Children in Public Schools (90%)
31 districts, 154 schools, 94,505 students

Children in Private Schools (10%)
Catholic: 13 schools, 5,007 students
Other religious: 48 schools, 2,902 students
Nonsectarian: 4 schools, 2,135 students

Public Library Systems: 14
911,647 books; turnover: 4.1

Colleges and Universities
Associate of Arts
4 campuses (20,158)
Baccalaureate
Dickinson College (2,283)
Messiah College (3,051)
Comprehensive
Dickinson School of Law (702)
Shippensburg UPenn (7,165/1,686)
Widener University (573)
Doctoral
Penn State Harrisburg (2,197/2,451)
Penn State Hershey Medical (761)

Public School Support C
Private School Options...A
Library Popularity ....A+
College Town...C+
College Options ....B

Places Rated Rank: 112

Harrisonburg, VA

Children in Public Schools (94%)
3 districts, 27 schools, 15,394 students

Children in Private Schools (6%)
Other religious: 8 schools, 981 students

Public Library Systems: 1
221,365 books; turnover: 3.0

Colleges and Universities
Baccalaureate
Bridgewater College (1,461)
Comprehensive
Eastern Mennonite University (1,180/1,010)
Doctoral
James Madison University (16,044/1,830)

Public School Support ....A+
Private School Options...D
Library Popularity ....B+
College Town...A+
College Options ....B

Places Rated Rank: 91

✓ Hartford-West Hartford-East Hartford, CT

Children in Public Schools (92%)
68 districts, 395 schools, 195,996 students

Children in Private Schools (8%)
Catholic: 37 schools, 10,445 students
Other religious: 24 schools, 2,542 students
Nonsectarian: 9 schools, 3,024 students

Public Library Systems: 66
4,924,877 books; turnover: 2.5

Colleges and Universities
Associate of Arts
7 campuses (25,863)
Baccalaureate
Charter Oak State College (2,115)
Comprehensive
Rensselaer Hartford Graduate Center (1,027)
St. Joseph College (1,308/803)
Trinity College (2,313/303)
Doctoral
Central CT State University (11,373/4,219)
Hartford Seminary (239)
University of Conn (16,294/8,008)
University of Hartford (6,257/2,454)
Wesleyan University (2,949/725)

Public School Support ....A+
Private School Options...A
Library Popularity ....C+
College Town...B+
College Options ....A+

Places Rated Rank: 15

Hattiesburg, MS

Children in Public Schools (93%)
8 districts, 44 schools, 21,540 students

Children in Private Schools (7%)
Catholic: 1 school, 338 students
Other religious: 6 schools, 1,374 students

Public Library Systems: 3
341,901 books; turnover: 1.9

Colleges and Universities
Comprehensive
William Carey College (2,322/1,723)
Doctoral
University of Southern MS (15,266/3,956)

Public School Support ....C+
Private School Options...D+
Library Popularity ....D+
College Town...A+
College Options ....B+

Places Rated Rank: 209

Hickory-Lenoir-Morganton, NC

Children in Public Schools (97%)
8 districts, 104 schools, 58,346 students

Children in Private Schools (3%)
Other religious: 11 schools, 1,467 students
Nonsectarian: 3 schools, 193 students

Public Library Systems: 5
652,546 books; turnover: 2.5

Colleges and Universities
Associate of Arts
3 campuses (16,088)
Comprehensive
Lenoir-Rhyne College (1,510/272)

Public School Support C
Private School Options...C+
Library Popularity ....C+
College Town...D
College Options C

Places Rated Rank: 306

Hinesville-Fort Stewart, GA

Children in Public Schools (98%)
2 districts, 18 schools, 15,064 students

Children in Private Schools (2%)
Other religious: 4 schools, 240 students

Public Library Systems: 1
634,758 books; turnover: 1.9

REPORT CARD
Public School Support .... D
Private School Options............................. D
Library Popularity .... D+
College Town... D
College Options .... D

Places Rated Rank: 377

Holland-Grand Haven, MI

Children in Public Schools (87%)
14 districts, 76 schools, 43,590 students

Children in Private Schools (13%)
Catholic: 4 schools, 666 students
Other religious: 19 schools, 5,951 students

Public Library Systems: 9
708,817 books; turnover: 3.3

Colleges and Universities

Baccalaureate
Hope College (3,332)

Comprehensive
Grand Valley State University (20,289/6,901)
Doctoral
Western Theological Seminary (269)

REPORT CARD
Public School Support C
Private School Options............................. C+
Library Popularity .... B+
College Town... A
College Options .... B

Places Rated Rank: 152

✓Honolulu, HI

Children in Public Schools (85%)
1 districts, 285 schools, 127,234 students

Children in Private Schools (15%)
Catholic: 19 schools, 7,556 students
Other religious: 30 schools, 9,457 students
Nonsectarian: 9 schools, 5,650 students

Public Library Systems: 1
3,177,319 books; turnover: 2.0

Colleges and Universities

Associate of Arts
6 campuses (30,206)

Baccalaureate
Brigham Young University (3,613)
University of Hawaii West Oahu (1,045)

Comprehensive
Chaminade University (3,380/911)
Hawaii Pacific University (9,738/1,522)

Doctoral
University of Hawaii Manoa (17,069/8,140)

REPORT CARD
Public School Support .... A+
Private School Options............................. A+
Library Popularity C
College Town... B+
College Options .... A

Places Rated Rank: 39

Hot Springs, AR

Children in Public Schools (96%)
8 districts, 27 schools, 13,359 students

Children in Private Schools (4%)
Catholic: 1 school, 198 students
Other religious: 4 schools, 376 students

Public Library Systems: 1
112,895 books; turnover: 4.4

Colleges and Universities
Associate of Arts
1 campus (4,661)

REPORT CARD
Public School Support C
Private School Options............................. D
Library Popularity .... A+
College Town... D
College Options .... D

Places Rated Rank: 334

Houma-Bayou Cane-Thibodaux, LA

Children in Public Schools (86%)
2 districts, 70 schools, 33,788 students

Children in Private Schools (14%)
Catholic: 11 schools, 5,178 students
Other religious: 2 schools, 544 students

Public Library Systems: 2
463,005 books; turnover: 1.7

Colleges and Universities
Associate of Arts
2 campuses (3,051)

Comprehensive
Nicholls State (7,609/1,037)

REPORT CARD
Public School Support .... B+
Private School Options............................. C
Library Popularity .... D+
College Town... C
College Options C

Places Rated Rank: 286

Houston-Sugar Land-Baytown, TX

Children in Public Schools (95%)
119 districts, 1513 schools, 1,045,691 students

Children in Private Schools (5%)
Catholic: 56 schools, 16,498 students
Other religious: 132 schools, 27,704 students
Nonsectarian: 30 schools, 5,735 students

Public Library Systems: 27
8,184,478 books; turnover: 2.9

Colleges and Universities
Associate of Arts
8 campuses (192,271)

Baccalaureate
Brazosport College (5,574)
College Biblical Studies (3,180)
Texas Chiropractic College (689)
UT Anderson Cancer Center (75)

Comprehensive
Houston Baptist University (2,273/722)
Texas A & M University (1,785/68)
University of of Houston (13,345/5,172)

Doctoral
Baylor College of Medicine (1,296)
Prairie View A & M University (6,673/2,608)
Rice University (2,969/2,017)
Texas Southern University (19,564/4,878)

UT HSC (381/3,017)
University of St. Thomas (2,062/5,098)
University of Texas Medical (591/1,561)

Public School Support .... D
Private School Options .... A+
Library Popularity .... B
College Town .... D+
College Options .... A+

Places Rated Rank: 143

Huntington-Ashland, WV-KY-OH

Children in Public Schools (96%)
19 districts, 114 schools, 44,115 students

Children in Private Schools (4%)
Catholic: 6 schools, 784 students
Other religious: 9 schools, 1,203 students

Public Library Systems: 5
840,640 books; turnover: 2.3

Colleges and Universities
Associate of Arts
5 campuses (9,117)
Baccalaureate
Tri-State Bible College (67)
Comprehensive
Ohio University Southern (2,372/649)
Doctoral
Marshall University (11,243/6,452)

Public School Support .... B+
Private School Options C
Library Popularity .... C+
College Town .... A
College Options .... B+

Places Rated Rank: 160

Huntsville, AL

Children in Public Schools (91%)
5 districts, 106 schools, 58,003 students

Children in Private Schools (9%)
Catholic: 4 schools, 1,263 students
Other religious: 13 schools, 3,260 students
Nonsectarian: 6 schools, 1,387 students

Public Library Systems: 2
636,394 books; turnover: 3.7

Colleges and Universities
Associate of Arts
1 campus (1,189)
Baccalaureate
Athens State University (3,579)
Oakwood College (1,898)
Doctoral
Alabama A&M (5,911/1,727)
University of Alabama (6,582/1,897)

Public School Support .... B
Private School Options .... B+
Library Popularity .... A
College Town .... B+
College Options .... B

Places Rated Rank: 66

Idaho Falls, ID

Children in Public Schools (99%)
6 districts, 53 schools, 23,983 students

Children in Private Schools (1%)
Catholic: 1 school, 199 students
Other religious: 2 schools, 155 students

Public Library Systems: 6
304,564 books; turnover: 2.7

Colleges and Universities
Associate of Arts
1 campus (1,581)

Public School Support .... D
Private School Options .... D
Library Popularity .... B
College Town .... D
College Options .... D

Places Rated Rank: 372

✓Indianapolis-Carmel, IN

Children in Public Schools (91%)
75 districts, 484 schools, 274,843 students

Children in Private Schools (9%)
Catholic: 42 schools, 16,361 students
Other religious: 45 schools, 8,679 students
Nonsectarian: 5 schools, 1,926 students

Public Library Systems: 28
4,387,680 books; turnover: 4.7

Colleges and Universities
Associate of Arts
1 campus (20,340)
Baccalaureate
DePauw University (2,383)
Franklin College (1,091)
Comprehensive
Butler University (3,794/1,154)
Marian College (2,281/55)
Martin University (679/129)
Doctoral
Indiana-Purdue University (28,580/12,129)
University of Indianapolis (3,560/1,414)

Public School Support .... C+
Private School Options .... A+
Library Popularity .... A+
College Town .... C+
College Options .... A

Places Rated Rank: 34

Iowa City, IA

Children in Public Schools (92%)
7 districts, 46 schools, 16,935 students

Children in Private Schools (8%)
Catholic: 3 schools, 1,100 students
Other religious: 4 schools, 411 students

Public Library Systems: 9
429,695 books; turnover: 4.3

Colleges and Universities
Doctoral
University of of Iowa (23,113/10,111)

Public School Support .... A
Private School Options .... D+
Library Popularity .... A+
College Town .... A+
College Options .... B+

Places Rated Rank: 45

Ithaca, NY ✓

🏫 **Children in Public Schools (100%)**
8 districts, 34 schools, 12,303 students

Children in Private Schools (0%)
Other religious: 1 school, 45 students

📖 **Public Library Systems: 5**
237,393 books; turnover: 4.4

🎓 **Colleges and Universities**
Associate of Arts
1 campus (4,709)
Doctoral
Cornell University (14,163/6,210)
Ithaca College (6,598/394)

Public School Support .... A+
Private School Options .... D
Library Popularity .... A+
College Town .... A+
College Options .... B+

Places Rated Rank: 36

Jackson, MI

🏫 **Children in Public Schools (91%)**
15 districts, 62 schools, 27,338 students

Children in Private Schools (9%)
Catholic: 7 schools, 2,058 students
Other religious: 5 schools, 677 students

📖 **Public Library Systems: 1**
420,011 books; turnover: 1.7

🎓 **Colleges and Universities**
Associate of Arts
1 campus (9,958)
Comprehensive
Baker College (1,868/10)
Spring Arbor University (3,384/2,277)

Public School Support .... C+
Private School Options C
Library Popularity .... D+
College Town .... B
College Options C

Places Rated Rank: 289

Jackson, MS

🏫 **Children in Public Schools (86%)**
16 districts, 155 schools, 86,050 students

Children in Private Schools (14%)
Catholic: 5 schools, 1,247 students
Other religious: 32 schools, 8,900 students
Nonsectarian: 11 schools, 3,950 students

📖 **Public Library Systems: 4**
1,079,344 books; turnover: 1.5

🎓 **Colleges and Universities**
Associate of Arts
2 campuses (17,638)
Baccalaureate
Tougaloo College (1,042)
Wesley College (96)
Comprehensive
Belhaven College (2,512/533)
Millsaps College (1,509/119)
Mississippi College (2,698/1,493)
Doctoral
Jackson State (7,336/1,953)
UMiss MC (563/1,321)

Public School Support .... D
Private School Options .... A
Library Popularity .... D
College Town .... B
College Options .... B

Places Rated Rank: 245

Jackson, TN

🏫 **Children in Public Schools (83%)**
2 districts, 35 schools, 16,880 students

Children in Private Schools (17%)
Catholic: 1 school, 377 students
Other religious: 5 schools, 1,651 students
Nonsectarian: 1 school, 1,308 students

📖 **Public Library Systems: 2**
186,050 books; turnover: 1.3

🎓 **Colleges and Universities**
Associate of Arts
2 campuses (6,123)
Baccalaureate
Lambuth University (912)
Lane College (1,048)
Comprehensive
Freed-Hardeman University (1,587/678)
Doctoral
Union University (2,427/1,161)

Public School Support .... C+
Private School Options .... C+
Library Popularity .... D
College Town .... A
College Options .... C+

Places Rated Rank: 240

Jacksonville, FL

🏫 **Children in Public Schools (89%)**
6 districts, 290 schools, 200,298 students

Children in Private Schools (11%)
Catholic: 21 schools, 8,147 students
Other religious: 70 schools, 12,605 students
Nonsectarian: 14 schools, 4,183 students

📖 **Public Library Systems: 4**
3,473,519 books; turnover: 2.1

🎓 **Colleges and Universities**
Associate of Arts
2 campuses (44,192)
Baccalaureate
Edward Waters College (1,499)
Flagler College (2,321)
Jones College (1,103)
Comprehensive
Jacksonville University (3,465/590)
Trinity Baptist College (406/37)
Doctoral
University of North Florida (14,646/2,711)

Public School Support .... D
Private School Options .... A+
Library Popularity C
College Town C
College Options .... B+

Places Rated Rank: 206

Jacksonville, NC

🏫 **Children in Public Schools (97%)**
1 districts, 33 schools, 25,503 students

Children in Private Schools (3%)
Catholic: 1 school, 201 students
Other religious: 5 schools, 597 students

Public Library Systems: 1
154,633 books; turnover: 2.2

Colleges and Universities
Associate of Arts
1 campus (6,099)

REPORT CARD
Public School Support ....D
Private School Options ....D
Library Popularity C
College Town..D
College Options ....D

Places Rated Rank: 374

Janesville, WI

Children in Public Schools (93%)
9 districts, 65 schools, 27,803 students

Children in Private Schools (7%)
Catholic: 6 schools, 1,032 students
Other religious: 7 schools, 955 students

Public Library Systems: 7
483,733 books; turnover: 3.9

Colleges and Universities
Associate of Arts
1 campus (3,761)

Baccalaureate
Beloit College (1,407)

REPORT CARD
Public School Support ....A
Private School Options C
Library Popularity ....A
College Town..D
College Options ....D

Places Rated Rank: 241

Jefferson City, MO

Children in Public Schools (81%)
20 districts, 136 schools, 20,058 students

Children in Private Schools (19%)
Catholic: 16 schools, 4,215 students
Other religious: 7 schools, 569 students

Public Library Systems: 3
195,120 books; turnover: 3.1

Colleges and Universities
Associate of Arts
2 campuses (1,082)

Baccalaureate
Westminster College (867)

Comprehensive
Lincoln University (3,402/314)
William Woods University (1,360/2,200)

REPORT CARD
Public School Support ....B+
Private School Options ....C+
Library Popularity ....B+
College Town..C+
College Options C

Places Rated Rank: 190

Johnson City, TN

Children in Public Schools (99%)
5 districts, 53 schools, 26,746 students

Children in Private Schools (1%)
Catholic: 1 school, 193 students
Other religious: 4 schools, 81 students
Nonsectarian: 1 school, 96 students

Public Library Systems: 4
268,643 books; turnover: 2.4

Colleges and Universities
Associate of Arts
1 campus (832)

Comprehensive
Milligan College (758/115)

Doctoral
East TN State University (11,259/2,725)

REPORT CARD
Public School Support C
Private School Options ....D+
Library Popularity ....C+
College Town..A
College Options ....B

Places Rated Rank: 226

Johnstown, PA

Children in Public Schools (85%)
17 districts, 43 schools, 19,933 students

Children in Private Schools (15%)
Catholic: 15 schools, 3,201 students
Other religious: 4 schools, 240 students

Public Library Systems: 14
347,186 books; turnover: 1.4

Colleges and Universities
Associate of Arts
2 campuses (2,893)

Baccalaureate
University of of Pittsburgh (3,380)

Comprehensive
Mt Aloysius College (1,995/34)
St. Francis University (1,427/805)

REPORT CARD
Public School Support ....A+
Private School Options C
Library Popularity ....D
College Town..C+
College Options C

Places Rated Rank: 261

Jonesboro, AR

Children in Public Schools (97%)
14 districts, 50 schools, 18,975 students

Children in Private Schools (3%)
Catholic: 1 school, 131 students
Other religious: 4 schools, 425 students

Public Library Systems: 2
196,509 books; turnover: 2.1

Colleges and Universities
Doctoral
Arkansas State University (11,165/1,775)

REPORT CARD
Public School Support ....C+
Private School Options ....D
Library Popularity C
College Town..A+
College Options ....C+

Places Rated Rank: 250

Joplin, MO

Children in Public Schools (94%)
13 districts, 68 schools, 27,752 students

Children in Private Schools (6%)
Catholic: 4 schools, 652 students
Other religious: 4 schools, 794 students
Nonsectarian: 1 school, 281 students

Public Library Systems: 5
233,098 books; turnover: 3.3

Colleges and Universities
Associate of Arts
1 campus (4,079)

Baccalaureate
Messenger College (121)
Ozark Christian College (899)

Comprehensive
MO Southern State University (6,618)

REPORT CARD

Public School Support .... D+
Private School Options .... C+
Library Popularity .... B+
College Town .... C+
College Options C

Places Rated Rank: 243

Kalamazoo-Portage, MI

Children in Public Schools (92%)
26 districts, 122 schools, 53,543 students

Children in Private Schools (8%)
Catholic: 8 schools, 1,713 students
Other religious: 15 schools, 2,325 students
Nonsectarian: 2 schools, 554 students

Public Library Systems: 15
1,277,121 books; turnover: 1.6

Colleges and Universities
Associate of Arts
1 campus (16,058)

Baccalaureate
Kalamazoo College (1,282)

Doctoral
Western Michigan University (25,331/8,516)

REPORT CARD

Public School Support .... C+
Private School Options .... B+
Library Popularity .... D
College Town .... A+
College Options .... A

Places Rated Rank: 134

Kankakee-Bradley, IL

Children in Public Schools (91%)
16 districts, 47 schools, 19,161 students

Children in Private Schools (9%)
Catholic: 6 schools, 1,396 students
Other religious: 5 schools, 523 students

Public Library Systems: 8
266,211 books; turnover: 1.7

Colleges and Universities
Associate of Arts
1 campus (8,720)

Comprehensive
Olivet Nazarene University (2,796/4,313)

REPORT CARD

Public School Support .... C+
Private School Options C
Library Popularity .... D+

College Town .... A
College Options C

Places Rated Rank: 266

Kansas City, MO-KS

Children in Public Schools (91%)
90 districts, 704 schools, 326,216 students

Children in Private Schools (9%)
Catholic: 57 schools, 22,583 students
Other religious: 54 schools, 8,457 students
Nonsectarian: 8 schools, 2,526 students

Public Library Systems: 30
7,180,584 books; turnover: 2.8

Colleges and Universities
Associate of Arts
9 campuses (67,966)

Baccalaureate
Cleveland Chiropractic College (582)
Kansas City Art Institute (885)
Kansas City College (244)
Ottawa University (613)
William Jewell College (1,764)

Comprehensive
Avila University (2,658/769)
Baker University School (1,254/1,948)
Mid-America Nazarene University (1,975/3,852)
Ottawa University (686/1,544)
Park University (22,011/606)
University Health Sciences (926)
University of St. Mary (805/492)

Doctoral
Midwestern Baptist Theological Seminary (210/584)
Nazarene Theological Seminary (423)
Rockhurst University (2,041/1,168)
St. Paul School Theology (317)
University Kansas Medical College (473/1,636)
University of Missouri (12,104/6,180)

REPORT CARD

Public School Support .... B+
Private School Options .... A+
Library Popularity .... B
College Town .... C+
College Options .... A+

Places Rated Rank: 48

Kennewick-Richland-Pasco, WA

Children in Public Schools (95%)
11 districts, 83 schools, 43,169 students

Children in Private Schools (5%)
Catholic: 4 schools, 1,158 students
Other religious: 7 schools, 1,245 students

Public Library Systems: 2
603,698 books; turnover: 2.6

Colleges and Universities
Associate of Arts
1 campus (9,801)

REPORT CARD

Public School Support .... D
Private School Options C
Library Popularity .... B
College Town .... D
College Options .... D

Places Rated Rank: 354

Killeen-Temple-Fort Hood, TX

Children in Public Schools (98%)
20 districts, 148 schools, 68,535 students

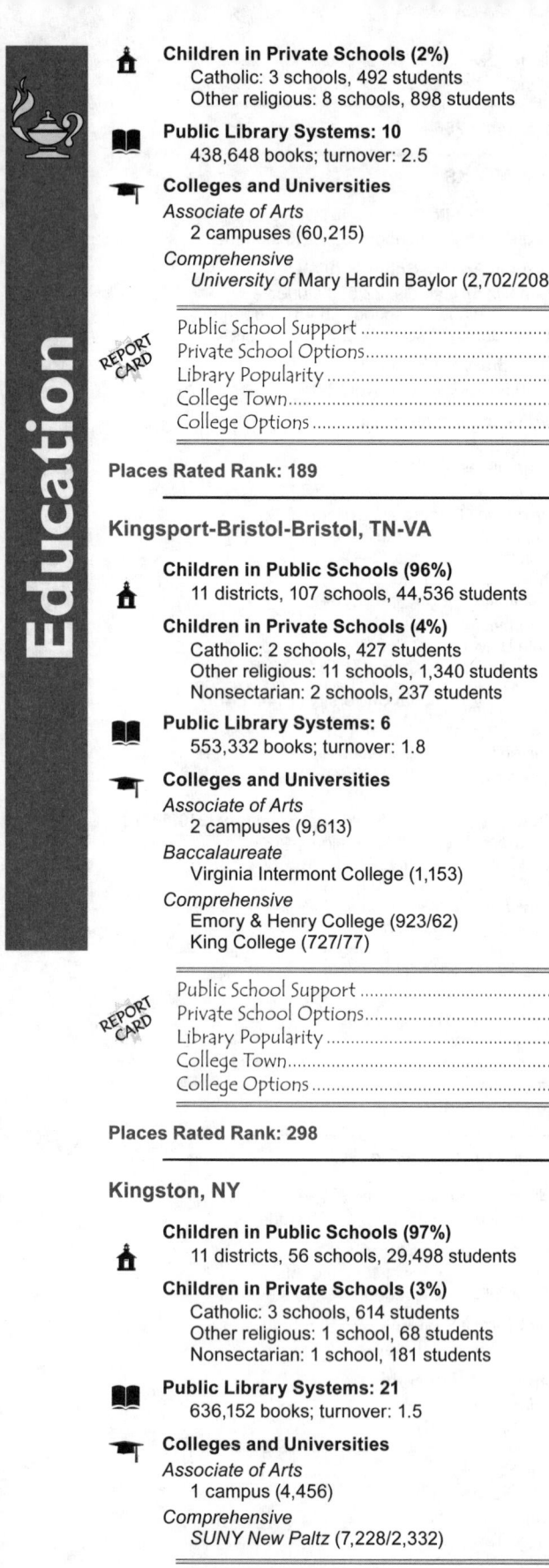

Children in Private Schools (2%)
Catholic: 3 schools, 492 students
Other religious: 8 schools, 898 students

Public Library Systems: 10
438,648 books; turnover: 2.5

Colleges and Universities
Associate of Arts
2 campuses (60,215)
Comprehensive
University of Mary Hardin Baylor (2,702/208)

REPORT CARD
Public School Support .... B+
Private School Options .... D+
Library Popularity .... C+
College Town.. B
College Options .... B

Places Rated Rank: 189

Kingsport-Bristol-Bristol, TN-VA

Children in Public Schools (96%)
11 districts, 107 schools, 44,536 students

Children in Private Schools (4%)
Catholic: 2 schools, 427 students
Other religious: 11 schools, 1,340 students
Nonsectarian: 2 schools, 237 students

Public Library Systems: 6
553,332 books; turnover: 1.8

Colleges and Universities
Associate of Arts
2 campuses (9,613)
Baccalaureate
Virginia Intermont College (1,153)
Comprehensive
Emory & Henry College (923/62)
King College (727/77)

REPORT CARD
Public School Support .... B+
Private School Options .... B
Library Popularity .... D+
College Town.. D
College Options .... D+

Places Rated Rank: 298

Kingston, NY

Children in Public Schools (97%)
11 districts, 56 schools, 29,498 students

Children in Private Schools (3%)
Catholic: 3 schools, 614 students
Other religious: 1 school, 68 students
Nonsectarian: 1 school, 181 students

Public Library Systems: 21
636,152 books; turnover: 1.5

Colleges and Universities
Associate of Arts
1 campus (4,456)
Comprehensive
SUNY New Paltz (7,228/2,332)

REPORT CARD
Public School Support .... A+
Private School Options C
Library Popularity .... D
College Town.. C+
College Options C

Places Rated Rank: 247

Knoxville, TN

Children in Public Schools (93%)
10 districts, 164 schools, 94,237 students

Children in Private Schools (7%)
Catholic: 4 schools, 1,407 students
Other religious: 19 schools, 3,641 students
Nonsectarian: 7 schools, 1,507 students

Public Library Systems: 15
1,444,897 books; turnover: 2.4

Colleges and Universities
Associate of Arts
3 campuses (13,003)
Baccalaureate
Maryville College (1,105)
Comprehensive
Johnson Bible College (792/125)
Doctoral
University of Tennessee (21,695/9,573)

REPORT CARD
Public School Support C
Private School Options .... B+
Library Popularity .... C+
College Town.. B+
College Options .... B+

Places Rated Rank: 132

Kokomo, IN

Children in Public Schools (96%)
7 districts, 36 schools, 16,853 students

Children in Private Schools (4%)
Catholic: 1 school, 88 students
Other religious: 6 schools, 644 students

Public Library Systems: 3
396,941 books; turnover: 3.2

Colleges and Universities
Associate of Arts
1 campus (4,682)
Comprehensive
Indiana University (3,837/417)

REPORT CARD
Public School Support .... B+
Private School Options .... D
Library Popularity .... B+
College Town.. C+
College Options .... D+

Places Rated Rank: 238

La Crosse, WI-MN

Children in Public Schools (87%)
12 districts, 57 schools, 19,517 students

Children in Private Schools (13%)
Catholic: 9 schools, 1,727 students
Other religious: 9 schools, 1,151 students

Public Library Systems: 7
456,777 books; turnover: 3.0

Colleges and Universities
Associate of Arts
1 campus (5,470)
Comprehensive
University of Wisconsin (8,858/2,246)
Viterbo University (2,085/8,800)

REPORT CARD
Public School Support .... A+
Private School Options .... C+
Library Popularity .... B+

College Town...A
College Options ....C+

Places Rated Rank: 72

Lafayette, IN

🏫 **Children in Public Schools (92%)**
8 districts, 47 schools, 24,599 students

Children in Private Schools (8%)
Catholic: 4 schools, 898 students
Other religious: 7 schools, 1,229 students

📖 **Public Library Systems: 11**
656,259 books; turnover: 2.9

🎓 **Colleges and Universities**
Associate of Arts
2 campuses (8,285)

Doctoral
Purdue University (34,564/9,977)

REPORT CARD
Public School Support ....C+
Private School Options.......................................C
Library Popularity ....B
College Town..A+
College Options ....A

Places Rated Rank: 105

Lafayette, LA

🏫 **Children in Public Schools (82%)**
2 districts, 62 schools, 38,351 students

Children in Private Schools (18%)
Catholic: 13 schools, 7,185 students
Other religious: 8 schools, 1,410 students

📖 **Public Library Systems: 2**
454,112 books; turnover: 3.1

🎓 **Colleges and Universities**
Associate of Arts
3 campuses (5,565)

Doctoral
University of Southwestern LA (17,209/2,076)

REPORT CARD
Public School Support ....B+
Private School Options.......................................C+
Library Popularity ....B+
College Town..A
College Options ....B

Places Rated Rank: 72

Lake Charles, LA

🏫 **Children in Public Schools (89%)**
2 districts, 66 schools, 34,246 students

Children in Private Schools (11%)
Catholic: 7 schools, 2,537 students
Other religious: 5 schools, 1,749 students

📖 **Public Library Systems: 2**
408,040 books; turnover: 2.8

🎓 **Colleges and Universities**
Associate of Arts
1 campus (2,167)

Comprehensive
McNeese State (8,544/1,527)

REPORT CARD
Public School Support ....B
Private School Options.......................................C
Library Popularity ....B

College Town...C+
College Options C

Places Rated Rank: 217

Lake County-Kenosha County, IL-WI

🏫 **Children in Public Schools (92%)**
64 districts, 247 schools, 159,539 students

Children in Private Schools (8%)
Catholic: 30 schools, 10,123 students
Other religious: 18 schools, 2,762 students
Nonsectarian: 2 schools, 740 students

📖 **Public Library Systems: 22**
3,303,791 books; turnover: 3.4

🎓 **Colleges and Universities**
Associate of Arts
2 campuses (39,025)

Baccalaureate
Shimer College (152)

Comprehensive
Carthage College (2,924/259)
Lake Forest College (1,431/18)
Lake Forest Graduate Management (1,020)
University of Wisconsin (5,818/240)

Doctoral
Rosalind Franklin University Medicine (1,679)
Trinity International University (1,144/1,471)
University of St. Mary of the Lake (236)

REPORT CARD
Public School Support ....B+
Private School Options.......................................A
Library Popularity ....A
College Town..C
College Options ....B

Places Rated Rank: 107

Lakeland, FL

🏫 **Children in Public Schools (92%)**
1 districts, 158 schools, 87,052 students

Children in Private Schools (8%)
Catholic: 5 schools, 1,641 students
Other religious: 26 schools, 5,204 students
Nonsectarian: 2 schools, 879 students

📖 **Public Library Systems: 1**
719,711 books; turnover: 2.2

🎓 **Colleges and Universities**
Associate of Arts
3 campuses (12,861)

Comprehensive
Florida Southern College (3,046/77)
Southeastern University (1,968)
Warner Southern College (1,304/55)
Webber IU (639/77)

REPORT CARD
Public School Support C
Private School Options.......................................B+
Library Popularity C
College Town..D
College Options ....C+

Places Rated Rank: 281

Lancaster, PA

🏫 **Children in Public Schools (83%)**
20 districts, 125 schools, 69,310 students

Children in Private Schools (17%)
Catholic: 8 schools, 2,475 students

Education

Other religious: 228 schools, 10,569 students
Nonsectarian: 4 schools, 793 students

Public Library Systems: 13
639,534 books; turnover: 4.2

Colleges and Universities
Associate of Arts
3 campuses (1,138)
Baccalaureate
Franklin and Marshall College (2,033)
Penn College Art & Design (419)
Comprehensive
Elizabethtown College (2,127/45)
Lancaster Bible College (833/222)
Millersville University (7,934/3,861)
Doctoral
Lancaster Theological Seminary (173)

Public School Support ....A
Private School Options.....................................A
Library Popularity ....A+
College Town...D+
College Options ....C+

Places Rated Rank: 85

Lansing-East Lansing, MI

Children in Public Schools (94%)
43 districts, 189 schools, 75,263 students

Children in Private Schools (6%)
Catholic: 13 schools, 2,858 students
Other religious: 18 schools, 1,885 students

Public Library Systems: 17
979,088 books; turnover: 2.9

Colleges and Universities
Associate of Arts
1 campus (27,615)
Baccalaureate
Great Lakes Christian College (260)
Comprehensive
Olivet College (1,110/79)
Doctoral
Michigan State University (36,773/12,322)

Public School Support ....B
Private School Options.....................................B
Library Popularity ....B+
College Town...A+
College Options ....A

Places Rated Rank: 49

Laredo, TX

Children in Public Schools (96%)
6 districts, 81 schools, 59,525 students

Children in Private Schools (4%)
Catholic: 6 schools, 1,755 students
Other religious: 1 school, 49 students
Nonsectarian: 1 school, 374 students

Public Library Systems: 1
207,097 books; turnover: 2.3

Colleges and Universities
Associate of Arts
1 campus (11,588)
Doctoral
Texas A&M IU (4,137/1,384)

Public School Support C
Private School Options.....................................C+
Library Popularity ....C+

College Town..C+
College Options ....C+

Places Rated Rank: 266

Las Cruces, NM

Children in Public Schools (99%)
3 districts, 70 schools, 39,352 students

Children in Private Schools (1%)
Catholic: 1 school, 252 students
Other religious: 1 school, 38 students

Public Library Systems: 4
165,185 books; turnover: 2.7

Colleges and Universities
Associate of Arts
1 campus (8,280)
Doctoral
New Mexico State University (14,621/4,585)

Public School Support ....D+
Private School Options.....................................D
Library Popularity ....B
College Town...A+
College Options ....B

Places Rated Rank: 211

Las Vegas-Paradise, NV

Children in Public Schools (95%)
1 districts, 308 schools, 282,984 students

Children in Private Schools (5%)
Catholic: 8 schools, 3,606 students
Other religious: 32 schools, 6,829 students
Nonsectarian: 12 schools, 3,959 students

Public Library Systems: 4
2,342,076 books; turnover: 4.9

Colleges and Universities
Associate of Arts
1 campus (41)
Baccalaureate
Community College of Southern Nevada (53,951)
NVSC Henderson (806)
Doctoral
University Nevada (25,664/7,210)

Public School Support ....D
Private School Options.....................................A
Library Popularity ....A+
College Town...C+
College Options ....A

Places Rated Rank: 102

Lawrence, KS

Children in Public Schools (96%)
3 districts, 32 schools, 13,037 students

Children in Private Schools (4%)
Catholic: 1 school, 391 students
Other religious: 1 school, 113 students

Public Library Systems: 3
262,742 books; turnover: 3.5

Colleges and Universities
Baccalaureate
Baker University College Arts & Sciences (951)
Haskell Indian Nations University (1,260)
Doctoral
University of Kansas (22,641/7,976)

Library Popularity ....D
College Town...C+
College Options ....D

Places Rated Rank: 356

Lewiston-Auburn, ME

Children in Public Schools (92%)
14 districts, 43 schools, 16,130 students

Children in Private Schools (8%)
Catholic: 4 schools, 1,089 students
Other religious: 3 schools, 273 students

Public Library Systems: 9
323,899 books; turnover: 1.5

Colleges and Universities
Associate of Arts
3 campuses (2,639)

Baccalaureate
Bates College (1,842)

REPORT CARD
Public School Support ....A+
Private School Options..................................D+
Library Popularity ....D
College Town..D
College Options ....D

Places Rated Rank: 335

✓Lexington-Fayette, KY

Children in Public Schools (89%)
9 districts, 117 schools, 59,550 students

Children in Private Schools (11%)
Catholic: 8 schools, 3,053 students
Other religious: 13 schools, 3,058 students
Nonsectarian: 4 schools, 1,220 students

Public Library Systems: 6
870,010 books; turnover: 3.9

Colleges and Universities
Associate of Arts
2 campuses (16,846)

Baccalaureate
Midway College (1,487)
Transylvania University (1,141)

Comprehensive
Asbury College (1,258/112)
Georgetown College (1,422/752)

Doctoral
Asbury Theological Seminary (2,009)
Lexington Theological Seminary (133)
University of Kentucky (19,593/8,341)

REPORT CARD
Public School Support ....B+
Private School Options..................................B+
Library Popularity ....A
College Town..A
College Options ....A

Places Rated Rank: 16

Lima, OH

Children in Public Schools (86%)
16 districts, 39 schools, 17,486 students

Children in Private Schools (14%)
Catholic: 7 schools, 2,628 students
Other religious: 3 schools, 94 students
Nonsectarian: 1 school, 45 students

Public Library Systems: 3
451,106 books; turnover: 2.7

REPORT CARD
Public School Support ....B+
Private School Options..................................D
Library Popularity ....A
College Town..A+
College Options ....B+

Places Rated Rank: 77

Lawton, OK

Children in Public Schools (99%)
11 districts, 55 schools, 21,909 students

Children in Private Schools (1%)
Catholic: 1 school, 118 students
Other religious: 2 schools, 177 students

Public Library Systems: 1
114,394 books; turnover: 1.6

Colleges and Universities
Associate of Arts
1 campus (269)

Comprehensive
Cameron University (7,108/808)

REPORT CARD
Public School Support ....D+
Private School Options..................................D
Library Popularity ....D
College Town..B
College Options C

Places Rated Rank: 348

Lebanon, PA

Children in Public Schools (91%)
7 districts, 35 schools, 18,701 students

Children in Private Schools (9%)
Catholic: 1 school, 501 students
Other religious: 19 schools, 1,259 students

Public Library Systems: 6
245,196 books; turnover: 2.7

Colleges and Universities
Associate of Arts
1 campus (94)

Comprehensive
Evangelical School of Theology (199)

Doctoral
Lebanon Valley College (1,914/380)

REPORT CARD
Public School Support ....C+
Private School Options..................................C
Library Popularity ....B
College Town..D+
College Options ....D

Places Rated Rank: 304

Lewiston, ID-WA

Children in Public Schools (95%)
5 districts, 29 schools, 9,079 students

Children in Private Schools (5%)
Catholic: 2 schools, 345 students
Other religious: 2 schools, 126 students

Public Library Systems: 3
237,935 books; turnover: 1.6

Colleges and Universities
Baccalaureate
Lewis-Clark SC (4,429)

REPORT CARD
Public School Support C
Private School Options..................................D

Colleges and Universities

Associate of Arts
 1 campus (4,015

Baccalaureate
 University of Northwestern Ohio (2,778)

Comprehensive
 Bluffton University (1,124/214)
 Ohio State University (1,547/180)

Public School Support .... C+
Private School Options.................................... C
Library Popularity .... B
College Town.. B
College Options .... D+

Places Rated Rank: 246

✓**Lincoln, NE**

Children in Public Schools (87%)
 21 districts, 99 schools, 39,229 students

Children in Private Schools (13%)
 Catholic: 11 schools, 3,561 students
 Other religious: 12 schools, 2,340 students

Public Library Systems: 4
 932,560 books; turnover: 3.4

Colleges and Universities

Associate of Arts
 1 campus (15,104)

Baccalaureate
 Bryan College Health Sciences (394)

Comprehensive
 Concordia University (1,234/248)
 Nebraska Wesleyan University (2,470/326)
 Union College (1,095)

Doctoral
 University of Nebraska (19,410/6,284)

Public School Support .... A
Private School Options.................................... B
Library Popularity .... A
College Town.. A+
College Options .... B+

Places Rated Rank: 23

Little Rock-North Little Rock, AR

Children in Public Schools (88%)
 29 districts, 204 schools, 100,957 students

Children in Private Schools (12%)
 Catholic: 12 schools, 3,842 students
 Other religious: 28 schools, 7,618 students
 Nonsectarian: 3 schools, 2,048 students

Public Library Systems: 5
 1,295,407 books; turnover: 2.0

Colleges and Universities

Associate of Arts
 2 campuses (10,944)

Baccalaureate
 Arkansas Baptist College (331)
 Central Baptist College (576)
 Philander Smith College (1,053)

Comprehensive
 Hendrix College (1,066/12)

Doctoral
 University of Arkansas (12,052/3,195)
 UAR Medical Sciences (1,022/1,503)
 University of Central Arkansas (9,615/1,502)

Public School Support C
Private School Options.................................... A

Library Popularity C
College Town.. B+
College Options .... B+

Places Rated Rank: 145

Logan, UT-ID

Children in Public Schools (100%)
 7 districts, 48 schools, 22,801 students

Public Library Systems: 9
 382,955 books; turnover: 4.2

Colleges and Universities

Doctoral
 Utah State University (16,056/3,127)

Public School Support .... D
Private School Options.................................... D
Library Popularity .... A+
College Town.. A+
College Options .... B+

Places Rated Rank: 185

Longview, TX

Children in Public Schools (97%)
 24 districts, 102 schools, 37,507 students

Children in Private Schools (3%)
 Catholic: 1 school, 183 students
 Other religious: 7 schools, 1,019 students

Public Library Systems: 6
 355,079 books; turnover: 1.9

Colleges and Universities

Associate of Arts
 1 campus (7,062)

Comprehensive
 Letourneau University (4,206/579)

Public School Support .... B+
Private School Options.................................... D
Library Popularity .... D+
College Town.. D+
College Options C

Places Rated Rank: 317

Longview, WA

Children in Public Schools (96%)
 6 districts, 41 schools, 17,911 students

Children in Private Schools (4%)
 Catholic: 1 school, 241 students
 Other religious: 4 schools, 493 students

Public Library Systems: 4
 271,409 books; turnover: 1.9

Colleges and Universities

Associate of Arts
 1 campus (4,990)

Public School Support .... D
Private School Options.................................... D
Library Popularity C
College Town.. D
College Options .... D

Places Rated Rank: 376

Los Angeles-Long Beach-Glendale, CA

Children in Public Schools (90%)
 101 districts, 1960 schools, 1,733,279 students

Children in Private Schools (10%)
Catholic: 239 schools, 83,463 students
Other religious: 308 schools, 64,138 students
Nonsectarian: 181 schools, 35,216 students

Public Library Systems: 35
22,969,913 books; turnover: 2.1

Colleges and Universities
Associate of Arts
27 campuses (533,965)

Baccalaureate
Claremont McKenna College (1,150)
Cleveland Chiropractic College (621)
Columbia College Hollywood (198)
Harvey Mudd College (719)
Life Pacific College (539)
Pitzer College (963)
Pomona College (1,529)

Comprehensive
American Film Institute (298)
Antioch University (270/669)
Art Center College (1,846/151)
California Institute Arts (809/477)
CA State Polytech University (19,342/2,753)
Cal State University (28,737/15,353)
Occidental College (1,949/38)
Otis College A & D (1,073/44)
Pacific Oaks College (248/991)
Samra University Oriental Medicine (467)
Scripps College (869/27)
Southern California Institute Architecture (174/262)
Southern California University Health Sciences (696)
Western University Health Sciences (1,736)
Whittier College (1,307/1,193)
Woodbury University (1,704/306)

Doctoral
Alliant International University (630)
Azusa Pacific University (4,819/5,303)
Biola University (3,802/2,008)
California IT (901/1,342)
Cal State University (30,686/7,966)
Cal State University (18,715/8,415)
Claremont Graduate School (2,277)
Claremont School Theology (497)
Fuller Theological Seminary (4,620)
King's College & Sem (400/367)
Loyola Marymount University (6,125/3,408)
Masters College (1,255/560)
Mt St.Mary's College (1,892/446)
Pepperdine University (3,341/5,636)
Phillips Graduate Institute (418)
University of California (27,928/11,962)
University of La Verne (4,764/5,421)
USC (18,065/16,863)

REPORT CARD	
Public School Support	D
Private School Options	A+
Library Popularity	C
College Town	B
College Options	A+

Places Rated Rank: 157

Louisville-Jefferson County, KY-IN

Children in Public Schools (84%)
29 districts, 344 schools, 176,812 students

Children in Private Schools (16%)
Catholic: 65 schools, 24,415 students
Other religious: 33 schools, 7,917 students
Nonsectarian: 5 schools, 1,782 students

Public Library Systems: 14
2,359,642 books; turnover: 2.7

Colleges and Universities
Associate of Arts
3 campuses (22,947)

Comprehensive
Indiana University Southeast (7,318/1,484)
Doctoral
Bellarmine University (2,769/744)
Louisville Presbyterian Theological Seminary (206)
Southern Baptist Theological Seminary (934/2,014)
Spalding University (1,158/1,018)
University of Louisville (17,264/7,298)

REPORT CARD	
Public School Support	C
Private School Options	A+
Library Popularity	B
College Town	C+
College Options	A

Places Rated Rank: 110

Lubbock, TX

Children in Public Schools (96%)
16 districts, 169 schools, 43,858 students

Children in Private Schools (4%)
Catholic: 2 schools, 366 students
Other religious: 5 schools, 1,355 students

Public Library Systems: 5
450,716 books; turnover: 2.1

Colleges and Universities
Associate of Arts
1 campus (291)
Comprehensive
Lubbock Christian University (2,111/265)
Doctoral
TX Tech (25,434/6,017)
TX Tech Health Science (739/1,873)

REPORT CARD	
Public School Support	A
Private School Options	D+
Library Popularity	C
College Town	A+
College Options	B+

Places Rated Rank: 136

Lynchburg, VA

Children in Public Schools (95%)
10 districts, 73 schools, 35,616 students

Children in Private Schools (5%)
Catholic: 1 school, 385 students
Other religious: 9 schools, 1,349 students
Nonsectarian: 1 school, 248 students

Public Library Systems: 5
592,078 books; turnover: 2.4

Colleges and Universities
Associate of Arts
2 campuses (6,987)

Baccalaureate
Randolph-Macon Woman's College (776)

Comprehensive
Lynchburg College (1,857/342)
Sweet Briar College (830/10)

Doctoral
Liberty University (13,014/4,570)

REPORT CARD	
Public School Support	A
Private School Options	C+
Library Popularity	C+
College Town	A
College Options	B

Places Rated Rank: 104

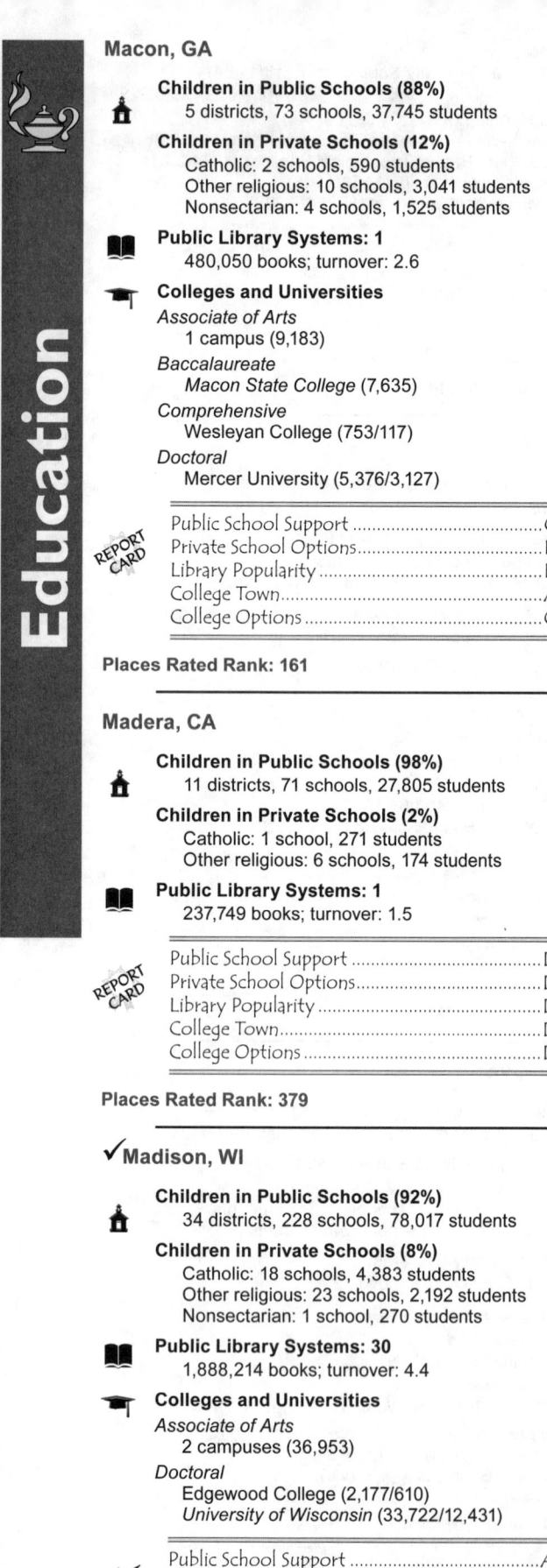

Education

Macon, GA

Children in Public Schools (88%)
5 districts, 73 schools, 37,745 students

Children in Private Schools (12%)
Catholic: 2 schools, 590 students
Other religious: 10 schools, 3,041 students
Nonsectarian: 4 schools, 1,525 students

Public Library Systems: 1
480,050 books; turnover: 2.6

Colleges and Universities
Associate of Arts
1 campus (9,183)
Baccalaureate
Macon State College (7,635)
Comprehensive
Wesleyan College (753/117)
Doctoral
Mercer University (5,376/3,127)

REPORT CARD
Public School Support ....C+
Private School Options......................................B
Library Popularity ....B
College Town..A
College Options ....C+

Places Rated Rank: 161

Madera, CA

Children in Public Schools (98%)
11 districts, 71 schools, 27,805 students

Children in Private Schools (2%)
Catholic: 1 school, 271 students
Other religious: 6 schools, 174 students

Public Library Systems: 1
237,749 books; turnover: 1.5

REPORT CARD
Public School Support ....D
Private School Options......................................D
Library Popularity ....D
College Town..D
College Options ....D

Places Rated Rank: 379

✓Madison, WI

Children in Public Schools (92%)
34 districts, 228 schools, 78,017 students

Children in Private Schools (8%)
Catholic: 18 schools, 4,383 students
Other religious: 23 schools, 2,192 students
Nonsectarian: 1 school, 270 students

Public Library Systems: 30
1,888,214 books; turnover: 4.4

Colleges and Universities
Associate of Arts
2 campuses (36,953)
Doctoral
Edgewood College (2,177/610)
University of Wisconsin (33,722/12,431)

REPORT CARD
Public School Support ....A+
Private School Options......................................B+
Library Popularity ....A+
College Town..A
College Options ....A

Places Rated Rank: 2

Manchester-Nashua, NH

Children in Public Schools (91%)
39 districts, 111 schools, 67,092 students

Children in Private Schools (9%)
Catholic: 15 schools, 5,210 students
Other religious: 7 schools, 901 students
Nonsectarian: 3 schools, 416 students

Public Library Systems: 29
1,268,161 books; turnover: 1.9

Colleges and Universities
Associate of Arts
2 campuses (9,165)
Baccalaureate
New Hampshire Institute Art (191)
St. Anselm College (2,129)
University of New Hampshire (2,253)
Comprehensive
Daniel Webster College (1,301/123)
Rivier College (1,636/1,310)
Doctoral
Southern NHU (6,572/3,204)

REPORT CARD
Public School Support ....A
Private School Options......................................B+
Library Popularity C
College Town..B
College Options ....B

Places Rated Rank: 148

Mansfield, OH

Children in Public Schools (90%)
14 districts, 49 schools, 19,701 students

Children in Private Schools (10%)
Catholic: 5 schools, 1,091 students
Other religious: 3 schools, 963 students
Nonsectarian: 1 school, 108 students

Public Library Systems: 2
572,600 books; turnover: 3.6

Colleges and Universities
Associate of Arts
1 campus (4,806)
Comprehensive
Ohio State University (1,964/115)

REPORT CARD
Public School Support ....A+
Private School Options......................................C+
Library Popularity ....A
College Town..D+
College Options ....D

Places Rated Rank: 197

McAllen-Edinburg-Mission, TX

Children in Public Schools (98%)
26 districts, 283 schools, 175,377 students

Children in Private Schools (2%)
Catholic: 3 schools, 954 students
Other religious: 15 schools, 2,097 students

Public Library Systems: 12
890,378 books; turnover: 1.7

Colleges and Universities
Baccalaureate
South Texas College (21,927)
Doctoral
UT Pan American (17,596/2,818)

REPORT CARD
Public School Support C
Private School Options......................................C

Library Popularity .... D+
College Town .... B
College Options .... B+

Places Rated Rank: 232

Medford, OR

🏫 **Children in Public Schools (95%)**
10 districts, 57 schools, 28,884 students

Children in Private Schools (5%)
Catholic: 2 schools, 287 students
Other religious: 6 schools, 1,126 students
Nonsectarian: 2 schools, 187 students

📖 **Public Library Systems: 1**
539,400 books; turnover: 2.4

🎓 **Colleges and Universities**
Comprehensive
Southern Oregon University (6,269/1,512)

REPORT CARD
Public School Support .... D
Private School Options .... C+
Library Popularity .... C+
College Town .... D+
College Options C

Places Rated Rank: 328

Memphis, TN-MS-AR

🏫 **Children in Public Schools (90%)**
16 districts, 347 schools, 229,700 students

Children in Private Schools (10%)
Catholic: 24 schools, 7,668 students
Other religious: 51 schools, 13,412 students
Nonsectarian: 8 schools, 3,540 students

📖 **Public Library Systems: 7**
2,389,205 books; turnover: 2.0

🎓 **Colleges and Universities**
Associate of Arts
7 campuses (30,829)

Baccalaureate
Baptist Memorial College Health (886)
Le Moyne-Owen College (1,240)
Rust College (1,095)

Comprehensive
Christian Brothers University (1,829/531)
Crichton College (1,643)
Memphis College Art (327/39)
Rhodes College (1,572/9)

Doctoral
Harding Graduate Sschool (255)
Memphis Theological Seminary (400)
University of Memphis (18,855/6,323)

REPORT CARD
Public School Support .... D+
Private School Options .... A+
Library Popularity C
College Town .... C+
College Options .... A

Places Rated Rank: 186

Merced, CA

🏫 **Children in Public Schools (96%)**
21 districts, 93 schools, 54,857 students

Children in Private Schools (4%)
Catholic: 4 schools, 1,016 students
Other religious: 15 schools, 1,084 students

📖 **Public Library Systems: 1**
393,967 books; turnover: 1.5

🎓 **Colleges and Universities**
Associate of Arts
1 campus (15,846)

REPORT CARD
Public School Support .... D+
Private School Options C
Library Popularity .... D
College Town .... D+
College Options .... D+

Places Rated Rank: 359

Miami-Miami Beach-Kendall, FL

🏫 **Children in Public Schools (87%)**
1 districts, 384 schools, 365,478 students

Children in Private Schools (13%)
Catholic: 43 schools, 20,716 students
Other religious: 88 schools, 21,020 students
Nonsectarian: 47 schools, 14,656 students

📖 **Public Library Systems: 5**
4,834,180 books; turnover: 1.4

🎓 **Colleges and Universities**
Associate of Arts
4 campuses (7,036)

Doctoral
University of Miami

REPORT CARD
Public School Support .... D+
Private School Options .... A+
Library Popularity .... D
College Town .... D
College Options .... D

Places Rated Rank: 337

Michigan City-La Porte, IN

🏫 **Children in Public Schools (90%)**
7 districts, 18 schools, 17,294 students

Children in Private Schools (10%)
Catholic: 6 schools, 1,409 students
Other religious: 4 schools, 446 students

📖 **Public Library Systems: 5**
441,776 books; turnover: 2.9

🎓 **Colleges and Universities**
Comprehensive
Purdue University (4,356/41)

REPORT CARD
Public School Support .... D+
Private School Options .... D+
Library Popularity .... B+
College Town C
College Options .... D+

Places Rated Rank: 324

Midland, TX

🏫 **Children in Public Schools (91%)**
6 districts, 45 schools, 23,347 students

Children in Private Schools (9%)
Catholic: 1 school, 361 students
Other religious: 5 schools, 1,625 students
Nonsectarian: 1 school, 188 students

📖 **Public Library Systems: 1**
255,046 books; turnover: 1.7

🎓 **Colleges and Universities**
Baccalaureate
Midland College (10,570)

REPORT CARD
Public School Support C
Private School Options .... C+

Education

Library Popularity .... D+
College Town .... B
College Options C

Places Rated Rank: 295

✓**Milwaukee-Waukesha-West Allis, WI**

Children in Public Schools (82%)
66 districts, 528 schools, 241,792 students

Children in Private Schools (18%)
Catholic: 99 schools, 27,133 students
Other religious: 128 schools, 20,648 students
Nonsectarian: 20 schools, 4,865 students

Public Library Systems: 41
6,062,470 books; turnover: 2.5

Colleges and Universities
Associate of Arts
3 campuses (39,779)

Baccalaureate
Milwaukee Institute Art Design (651)
Wisconsin Lutheran College (771)

Comprehensive
Alverno College (2,307/255)
Carroll College (3,087/634)
Milwaukee Engineering (2,236/467)
Mount Mary College (1,751/529)
Ottawa University (515)

Doctoral
Cardinal Stritch University (4,288/8,666)
Concordia University (3,996/1,300)
Marquette University (8,383/4,004)
Medical College Wisconsin (1,283)
University of Wisconsin (26,058/5,915)

REPORT CARD
Public School Support .... A
Private School Options .... A+
Library Popularity .... C+
College Town .... B+
College Options .... A+

Places Rated Rank: 17

✓**Minneapolis-St. Paul-Bloomington, MN-WI**

Children in Public Schools (90%)
194 districts, 1462 schools, 522,907 students

Children in Private Schools (10%)
Catholic: 103 schools, 37,065 students
Other religious: 106 schools, 18,402 students
Nonsectarian: 8 schools, 2,987 students

Public Library Systems: 30
9,512,460 books; turnover: 3.6

Colleges and Universities
Associate of Arts
11 campuses (88,300)

Baccalaureate
College Visual Arts (239)
Macalester College (2,038)
North Central University (1,310)

Comprehensive
Adler Graduate School (189)
Augsburg College (3,423/466)
Concordia College (2,562/519)
Crown College (1,925/92)
Metropolitan State University (8,392/857)
Minneapolis College A & D (658/70)
Northwestern College (2,974)
Northwestern HSU (105/870)
University of Wisconsin (6,111/1,088)

Doctoral
Bethel Seminary (904)
Bethel University (3,308/527)

College St. Catherine (4,177/1,413)
Hamline University (2,138/7,101)
Luther Seminary (798)
United Theological Seminary (234)
University of Minnesota (41,209/21,316)
University of St. Thomas (5,598/7,634)

REPORT CARD
Public School Support .... B+
Private School Options .... A+
Library Popularity .... A
College Town .... B
College Options .... A+

Places Rated Rank: 11

Missoula, MT

Children in Public Schools (93%)
16 districts, 40 schools, 13,348 students

Children in Private Schools (7%)
Catholic: 2 schools, 492 students
Other religious: 3 schools, 503 students

Public Library Systems: 1
207,210 books; turnover: 3.9

Colleges and Universities
Doctoral
University of Montana (24,745/5,209)

REPORT CARD
Public School Support .... C+
Private School Options .... D
Library Popularity .... A
College Town .... A+
College Options .... B+

Places Rated Rank: 122

Mobile, AL

Children in Public Schools (82%)
2 districts, 118 schools, 63,987 students

Children in Private Schools (18%)
Catholic: 12 schools, 4,312 students
Other religious: 32 schools, 8,270 students
Nonsectarian: 2 schools, 1,274 students

Public Library Systems: 7
666,635 books; turnover: 3.0

Colleges and Universities
Associate of Arts
1 campus (7,501)

Comprehensive
Spring Hill College (1,348/369)
University of Mobile (1,935/248)

Doctoral
University of South Alabama (12,202/3,793)

REPORT CARD
Public School Support C
Private School Options .... A
Library Popularity .... B+
College Town .... B+
College Options .... B

Places Rated Rank: 124

Modesto, CA

Children in Public Schools (95%)
30 districts, 175 schools, 105,845 students

Children in Private Schools (5%)
Catholic: 6 schools, 1,500 students
Other religious: 16 schools, 3,584 students
Nonsectarian: 1 school, 9 students

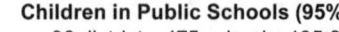

Public Library Systems: 1
721,744 books; turnover: 3.1

Colleges and Universities
Associate of Arts
1 campus (24,795)
Comprehensive
Cal State University (6,783/2,445)

Public School Support C
Private School Options...............................B
Library Popularity ....B+
College Town...D+
College Options ....C+

Places Rated Rank: 222

Monroe, LA

Children in Public Schools (92%)
4 districts, 67 schools, 31,571 students

Children in Private Schools (8%)
Catholic: 3 schools, 827 students
Other religious: 5 schools, 1,736 students
Nonsectarian: 1 school, 279 students

Public Library Systems: 2
438,130 books; turnover: 2.1

Colleges and Universities
Associate of Arts
3 campuses (2,364)
Doctoral
University of Louisiana (9,234/1,879)

Public School Support ....C+
Private School Options...............................C+
Library Popularity C
College Town...A
College Options ....C+

Places Rated Rank: 193

Monroe, MI

Children in Public Schools (92%)
13 districts, 59 schools, 26,829 students

Children in Private Schools (8%)
Catholic: 8 schools, 1,870 students
Other religious: 5 schools, 564 students

Public Library Systems: 2
539,274 books; turnover: 1.8

Colleges and Universities
Associate of Arts
1 campus (5,437)

Public School Support ....C+
Private School Options...............................C
Library Popularity ....D+
College Town...D
College Options ....D

Places Rated Rank: 361

Montgomery, AL

Children in Public Schools (86%)
6 districts, 110 schools, 56,143 students

Children in Private Schools (14%)
Catholic: 5 schools, 719 students
Other religious: 16 schools, 4,180 students
Nonsectarian: 13 schools, 4,048 students

Public Library Systems: 6
710,930 books; turnover: 1.3

Colleges and Universities
Associate of Arts
2 campuses (3,482)
Baccalaureate
Huntingdon College (685)
Comprehensive
Faulkner University (2,891/328)
Doctoral
Alabama State University (5,853/1,446)
Auburn University (6,144/1,160)
Southern Christian University (514/516)

Public School Support C
Private School Options...............................B+
Library Popularity ....D
College Town...B+
College Options ....B

Places Rated Rank: 198

Morgantown, WV

Children in Public Schools (96%)
2 districts, 39 schools, 14,662 students

Children in Private Schools (4%)
Catholic: 1 school, 380 students
Other religious: 5 schools, 285 students

Public Library Systems: 3
233,091 books; turnover: 1.9

Colleges and Universities
Doctoral
West Virginia University (19,043/10,271)

Public School Support ....A
Private School Options...............................D
Library Popularity ....D+
College Town...A+
College Options ....B+

Places Rated Rank: 163

Morristown, TN

Children in Public Schools (98%)
3 districts, 35 schools, 19,984 students

Children in Private Schools (2%)
Other religious: 5 schools, 409 students

Public Library Systems: 9
214,381 books; turnover: 2.1

Colleges and Universities
Associate of Arts
1 campus (8,278)
Comprehensive
Carson-Newman College (2,146/245)

Public School Support ....D+
Private School Options...............................D
Library Popularity C
College Town...C
College Options ....D+

Places Rated Rank: 362

Mount Vernon-Anacortes, WA

Children in Public Schools (96%)
8 districts, 52 schools, 19,171 students

Children in Private Schools (4%)
Catholic: 1 school, 266 students
Other religious: 3 schools, 455 students

Public Library Systems: 7
282,000 books; turnover: 2.8

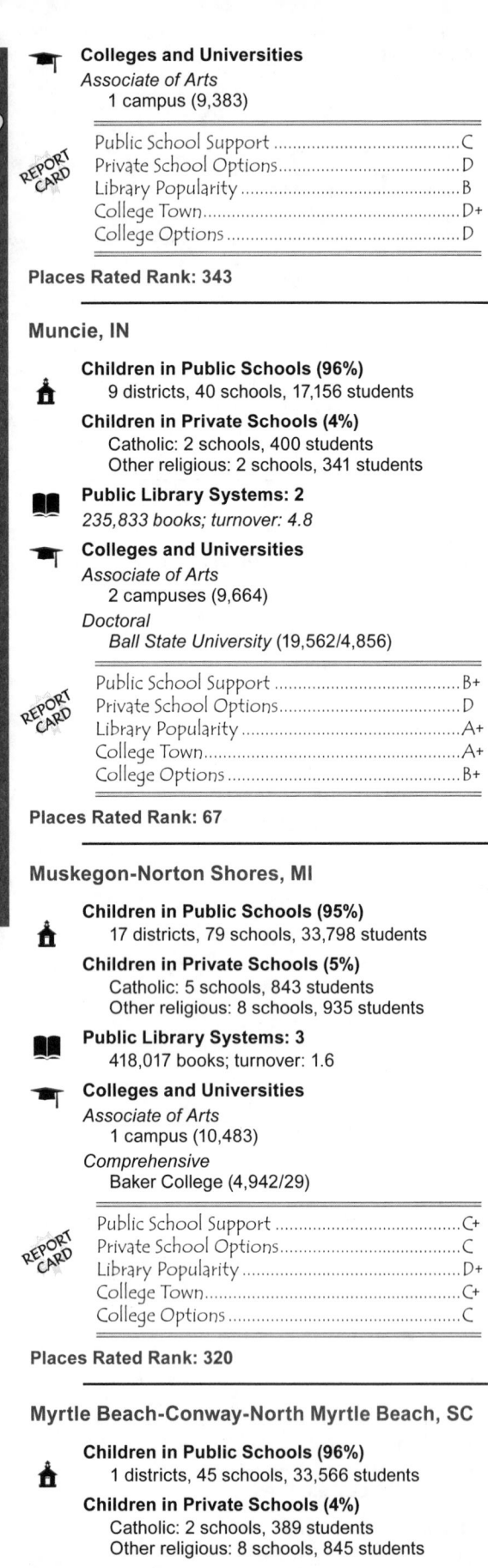

Colleges and Universities
Associate of Arts
1 campus (9,383)

Public School Support C
Private School Options.....................................D
Library Popularity ....B
College Town...D+
College Options ....D

Places Rated Rank: 343

Muncie, IN

Children in Public Schools (96%)
9 districts, 40 schools, 17,156 students

Children in Private Schools (4%)
Catholic: 2 schools, 400 students
Other religious: 2 schools, 341 students

Public Library Systems: 2
235,833 books; turnover: 4.8

Colleges and Universities
Associate of Arts
2 campuses (9,664)
Doctoral
Ball State University (19,562/4,856)

Public School Support ....B+
Private School Options.....................................D
Library Popularity ....A+
College Town...A+
College Options ....B+

Places Rated Rank: 67

Muskegon-Norton Shores, MI

Children in Public Schools (95%)
17 districts, 79 schools, 33,798 students

Children in Private Schools (5%)
Catholic: 5 schools, 843 students
Other religious: 8 schools, 935 students

Public Library Systems: 3
418,017 books; turnover: 1.6

Colleges and Universities
Associate of Arts
1 campus (10,483)
Comprehensive
Baker College (4,942/29)

Public School Support ....C+
Private School Options.....................................C
Library Popularity ....D+
College Town...C+
College Options C

Places Rated Rank: 320

Myrtle Beach-Conway-North Myrtle Beach, SC

Children in Public Schools (96%)
1 districts, 45 schools, 33,566 students

Children in Private Schools (4%)
Catholic: 2 schools, 389 students
Other religious: 8 schools, 845 students

Public Library Systems: 2
352,747 books; turnover: 2.9

Colleges and Universities
Associate of Arts
1 campus (7,020)

Comprehensive
Coastal Carolina University (6,382/2,119)
Doctoral
Cathedral Bible College (252/34)

Public School Support ....C+
Private School Options.....................................D+
Library Popularity ....B+
College Town...C
College Options C

Places Rated Rank: 265

Napa, CA

Children in Public Schools (88%)
7 districts, 52 schools, 19,841 students

Children in Private Schools (12%)
Catholic: 6 schools, 1,521 students
Other religious: 11 schools, 1,143 students

Public Library Systems: 2
267,099 books; turnover: 3.7

Colleges and Universities
Associate of Arts
1 campus (12,706)
Comprehensive
Pacific Union College (1,938/12)

Public School Support ....C+
Private School Options.....................................C
Library Popularity ....A
College Town...C
College Options ....D+

Places Rated Rank: 222

Naples-Marco Island, FL

Children in Public Schools (92%)
1 districts, 64 schools, 41,953 students

Children in Private Schools (8%)
Catholic: 4 schools, 1,114 students
Other religious: 9 schools, 1,434 students
Nonsectarian: 4 schools, 1,320 students

Public Library Systems: 1
583,694 books; turnover: 4.9

Colleges and Universities
Comprehensive
International College (1,936/284)

Public School Support C
Private School Options.....................................B
Library Popularity ....A+
College Town...D
College Options ....D

Places Rated Rank: 268

Nashville-Davidson–Murfreesboro, TN

Children in Public Schools (91%)
16 districts, 371 schools, 218,678 students

Children in Private Schools (9%)
Catholic: 11 schools, 3,452 students
Other religious: 53 schools, 13,445 students
Nonsectarian: 11 schools, 4,250 students

Public Library Systems: 22
2,679,557 books; turnover: 2.9

Colleges and Universities
Associate of Arts
7 campuses (24,531)

Baccalaureate
American Baptist College (176)
Free Will Baptist Bible College (358)
O'More College of Design (159)
Williamson Christian College (85)

Comprehensive
Aquinas College (1,136)
Cumberland University (1,034/637)
Fisk University (876/40)
Lipscomb University (2,614/331)
Watkins College Art & Design (389/40)

Doctoral
Belmont University (3,396/1,010)
Meharry Medical College (723)
Middle Tennessee State (22,265/2,699)
Tennessee State University (8,154/2,626)
Trevecca Nazarene University (1,601/1,052)
Vanderbilt University (6,412/5,328)

REPORT CARD

Public School Support C
Private School Options...A
Library Popularity ....B+
College Town...B
College Options ....A+

Places Rated Rank: 69

Nassau-Suffolk, NY

Children in Public Schools (91%)
134 districts, 667 schools, 476,515 students

Children in Private Schools (9%)
Catholic: 68 schools, 34,345 students
Other religious: 48 schools, 11,134 students
Nonsectarian: 20 schools, 4,049 students

Public Library Systems: 110
14,746,983 books; turnover: 1.8

Colleges and Universities
Associate of Arts
2 campuses (61,017)

Baccalaureate
Farmingdale State University NY (8,173)
U.S. Merchant Marine Academy (962)
Webb Institute (72)

Comprehensive
Long Island University (1,313/1,541)
Molloy College (3,052/941)
New York College Health (1,074/104)
New York IT (840/71)
Saint Josephs College (4,143/225)
SUNY Old Westbury (4,259)

Doctoral
Adelphi University (4,863/6,144)
Dowling College (4,246/4,376)
Hofstra University (10,583/4,828)
Long Island University CW Post (7,059/4,698)
New York Institute Technology (4,204/2,537)
Seminary Immaculate Conception (186)
Stony Brook University (16,949/10,329)

REPORT CARD

Public School Support ....A+
Private School Options...A+
Library Popularity ....D+
College Town...B
College Options ....A+

Places Rated Rank: 126

Newark-Union, NJ-PA

Children in Public Schools (90%)
162 districts, 646 schools, 352,082 students

Children in Private Schools (10%)
Catholic: 88 schools, 27,048 students

Other religious: 41 schools, 6,781 students
Nonsectarian: 17 schools, 3,697 students

Public Library Systems: 86
9,461,148 books; turnover: 1.3

Colleges and Universities
Associate of Arts
9 campuses (45,788)

Baccalaureate
Bloomfield College (2,479)
Rabbinical College America (246)

Comprehensive
Caldwell College (2,214/529)
College St. Elizabeth (1,479/748)
Fairleigh Dickinson University (2,926/1,431)
Kean University (11,982/3,893)

Doctoral
Drew University (1,789/1,168)
Montclair State University (13,976/5,209)
New Jersey IT (6,431/3,726)
Rutgers University Newark (7,825/4,313)
Seton Hall University (6,868/5,292)
University of Medicine & Dentistry NJ (1,167/4,598)

REPORT CARD

Public School Support ....A+
Private School Options...A+
Library Popularity ....D
College Town...B
College Options ....A+

Places Rated Rank: 54

New Haven-Milford, CT

Children in Public Schools (90%)
31 districts, 254 schools, 137,938 students

Children in Private Schools (10%)
Catholic: 37 schools, 10,368 students
Other religious: 10 schools, 1,043 students
Nonsectarian: 10 schools, 3,460 students

Public Library Systems: 29
2,990,679 books; turnover: 1.8

Colleges and Universities
Associate of Arts
2 campuses (15,577)

Baccalaureate
University of Connecticut (3,053)
Comprehensive
Albertus Magnus College (2,559/686)
University of New Haven (2,776/2,344)

Doctoral
Quinnipiac University (5,778/2,198)
Southern CT State University (9,532/5,598)
Yale University (5,430/6,199)

REPORT CARD

Public School Support ....B+
Private School Options...A
Library Popularity ....D+
College Town...B+
College Options ....A

Places Rated Rank: 79

New Orleans-Metairie-Kenner, LA

Children in Public Schools (76%)
15 districts, 325 schools, 184,166 students

Children in Private Schools (24%)
Catholic: 94 schools, 46,697 students
Other religious: 34 schools, 7,507 students
Nonsectarian: 12 schools, 5,424 students

Public Library Systems: 7
2,761,931 books; turnover: 1.6

Education

Colleges and Universities

Associate of Arts
7 campuses (29,469)

Baccalaureate
Dillard University (2,517)

Comprehensive
Loyola University (4,216/2,231)
Our Lady Holy Cross College (1,296/136)
Southern University (3,963/994)
Xavier University (3,590/919)

Doctoral
LSU MC (888/2,295)
New Orleans Baptist Theological Seminary (1,083/1,781)
Tulane University (8,711/5,567)
University of New Orleans (16,517/5,550)

Public School Support	B
Private School Options	A+
Library Popularity	D
College Town	B+
College Options	A

Places Rated Rank: 100

✓New York-White Plains-Wayne, NY-NJ

Children in Public Schools (83%)
261 districts, 2,301 schools, 1,543,196 students

Children in Private Schools (17%)
Catholic: 501 schools, 174,972 students
Other religious: 383 schools, 103,610 students
Nonsectarian: 107 schools, 33,806 students

Public Library Systems: 153
42,787,116 books; turnover: 1.6

Colleges and Universities

Associate of Arts
33 campuses (171,111)

Baccalaureate
Barnard College (2,353)
Concordia College (851)
CUNY Medgar Evers College (6,460)
CUNY NYC College Tec (14,463)
CUNY York College (7,463)
Marymount College (1,244)
Marymount Manhattan College (2,436)
Vaughn College Aero/Tech (1,691)

Comprehensive
Bank Street College Education (1,450)
Boricua College (1,552/54)
Central Yeshiva Lubavitz (556/45)
College Mount St. Vincent (1,635/916)
College New Rochelle (6,997/2,792)
Cooper Union (910/38)
CUNY Bernard Baruch College (16,524/3,341)
CUNY Brooklyn College (13,749/6,148)
CUNY City College (11,321/4,590)
CUNY Hunter College (20,123/6,251)
CUNY John Jay College Criminal Justice (13,543/1,963)
CUNY Lehman College (9,953/3,057)
CUNY Queens College (15,721/6,007)
Fashion IT (14,340/132)
Felician College (1,697/269)
Iona College (3,656/1,185)
Manhattan College (2,905/396)
Manhattanville College (1,782/1,078)
Mercy College (13,252/5,420)
Metropolitan College (1,685/459)
New Jersey City University (7,671/4,772)
New York Academy Art (142)
New York IT (2,068/872)
New York Law School (1,575)
NY School Interior Design (650/18)
Nyack College (2,626/1,016)
Pratt Institute (3,733/1,637)
Rabbinical Academy Berlin (229/135)

Rabbinical College Sofer (103/50)
Rabbinical Seminary Yereim (107/9)
Ramapo College NJ (6,358/542)
St. Joseph's College (1,332/141)
St. Joseph's Seminary & College (158)
St. Peter's College (2,929/1,058)
St. Thomas Aquinas College (2,491/327)
Sarah Lawrence College (1,372/341)
St. Francis College (2,515)
SUNY College Purchase (5,263/136)
SUNY Maritime College (1,007/232)
United Talmudical Academy (1,557/135)
Wagner College (1,955/451)
William Paterson University (10,721/2,610)
Yeshiva Nitra Rabbinical College (194/34)
Yeshiva Shaar Hatorah (89/41)

Doctoral
Columbia University (7,486/15,752)
CUNY College Staten Island (13,668/1,648)
CUNY Graduate School (4,382)
Dominican College Blauvelt (1,557/155)
Fairleigh Dickinson University (6,070/2,836)
Fordham University (8,302/9,834)
Hebrew Union College (159)
Jewish Theological Seminary (192/520)
LIU Brooklyn (5,959/3,072)
Manhattan School Music (410/500)
Mirrer Yeshiva Cent Institute (288/60)
Mount Sinai School of Medicine (650)
New York Medical College (1,514)
NYU (22,901/21,139)
Pace University (11,135/6,490)
Polytechnic University (1,745/1,560)
Rabbinical Seminary (303/187)
Rockefeller University (193)
St. John's University (16,543/5,956)
St. Vladimirs Orthodox Theological Seminary (95)
Stevens IT (1,889/3,826)
SUNY College Optometry (292)
SUNY Health Science Center (416/1,295)
Teachers College Columbia University (6,259)
The Juilliard School (742/339)
The New School (7,246/3,707)
Touro College (13,676/12,022)
Union Theological Seminary (443)
Weill Cornell Medical College (765)
Yeshiva University (2,803/3,326)
Yeshivath Viznitz (326/117)

Public School Support	A+
Private School Options	A+
Library Popularity	D
College Town	B
College Options	A+

Places Rated Rank: 33

Niles-Benton Harbor, MI

Children in Public Schools (90%)
19 districts, 73 schools, 27,950 students

Children in Private Schools (10%)
Catholic: 4 schools, 1,129 students
Other religious: 17 schools, 2,125 students

Public Library Systems: 14
775,401 books; turnover: 1.4

Colleges and Universities

Associate of Arts
1 campus (4,737)

Doctoral
Andrews University (2,019/2,120)

Public School Support	C+
Private School Options	C+
Library Popularity	D

College Town...C+
College Options C

Places Rated Rank: 301

Norwich-New London, CT

Children in Public Schools (93%)
24 districts, 100 schools, 44,439 students

Children in Private Schools (7%)
Catholic: 12 schools, 2,261 students
Other religious: 5 schools, 287 students
Nonsectarian: 2 schools, 603 students

Public Library Systems: 20
957,886 books; turnover: 2.0

Colleges and Universities
Associate of Arts
1 campus (5,139)
Baccalaureate
Mitchell College (875)
U. S. Coast Guard Academy (983)
University of Conn Avery Point (1,051)
Comprehensive
Connecticut College (2,073/15)
Lyme Academy College Fine Arts (202/4)

REPORT CARD

Public School Support ....A
Private School Options....................................B
Library Popularity C
College Town...D
College Options ....D+

Places Rated Rank: 270

Oakland-Fremont-Hayward, CA

Children in Public Schools (91%)
49 districts, 638 schools, 382,098 students

Children in Private Schools (9%)
Catholic: 59 schools, 19,330 students
Other religious: 67 schools, 12,214 students
Nonsectarian: 45 schools, 7,588 students

Public Library Systems: 10
5,176,179 books; turnover: 3.3

Colleges and Universities
Associate of Arts
12 campuses (157,369)
Comprehensive
Cifornia College Arts (1,354/189)
California State University (12,061/5,358)
Holy Names University (744/452)
Patten University (965/120)
Doctoral
Alliant International University (743)
Graduate Theological Union (271)
Jesuit School Theology Berkeley (223)
JFK University (265/1,811)
Mills College (801/511)
Northwestern Polytechnic University (166/452)
Pacific School Religion (253)
St. Mary's College (4,158/1,500)
Samuel Merritt College (348/667)
University of California (26,204/10,309)
Wright Institute (319)

REPORT CARD

Public School Support ....D+
Private School Options....................................A+
Library Popularity ....B+
College Town...B
College Options ....A+

Places Rated Rank: 57

Ocala, FL

Children in Public Schools (92%)
1 districts, 65 schools, 41,113 students

Children in Private Schools (8%)
Catholic: 1 school, 454 students
Other religious: 19 schools, 3,097 students

Public Library Systems: 1
412,107 books; turnover: 2.4

Colleges and Universities
Associate of Arts
2 campuses (9,712)

REPORT CARD

Public School Support ....D
Private School Options....................................C
Library Popularity ....C+
College Town...D
College Options ....D

Places Rated Rank: 357

Ocean City, NJ

Children in Public Schools (89%)
19 districts, 32 schools, 13,982 students

Children in Private Schools (11%)
Catholic: 6 schools, 1,577 students
Other religious: 2 schools, 212 students

Public Library Systems: 2
396,445 books; turnover: 1.6

REPORT CARD

Public School Support ....A+
Private School Options....................................D+
Library Popularity ....D
College Town...D
College Options ....D

Places Rated Rank: 342

Odessa, TX

Children in Public Schools (98%)
2 districts, 42 schools, 26,327 students

Children in Private Schools (2%)
Catholic: 1 school, 169 students
Other religious: 3 schools, 395 students

Public Library Systems: 1
125,548 books; turnover: 5.6

Colleges and Universities
Associate of Arts
1 campus (6,565)
Comprehensive
UT Permian Basin (2,775/1,142)

REPORT CARD

Public School Support ....D+
Private School Options....................................D
Library Popularity ....A+
College Town...C+
College Options ....D+

Places Rated Rank: 291

Ogden-Clearfield, UT

Children in Public Schools (98%)
10 districts, 189 schools, 103,343 students

Children in Private Schools (2%)
Catholic: 3 schools, 951 students
Other religious: 5 schools, 1,373 students
Nonsectarian: 2 schools, 184 students

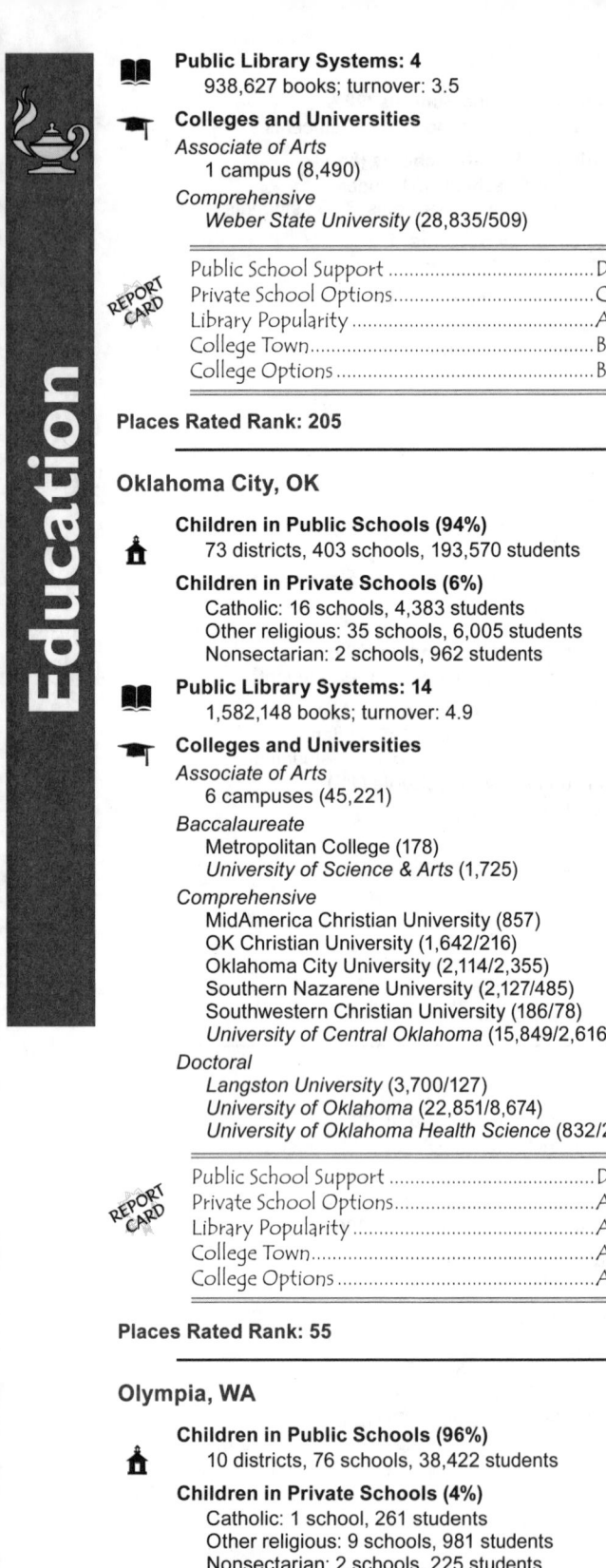

Education

📖 **Public Library Systems: 4**
938,627 books; turnover: 3.5

🎓 **Colleges and Universities**
Associate of Arts
1 campus (8,490)
Comprehensive
Weber State University (28,835/509)

REPORT CARD
Public School Support .... D
Private School Options............................. C+
Library Popularity .... A
College Town .... B
College Options .... B

Places Rated Rank: 205

Oklahoma City, OK

🏫 **Children in Public Schools (94%)**
73 districts, 403 schools, 193,570 students

Children in Private Schools (6%)
Catholic: 16 schools, 4,383 students
Other religious: 35 schools, 6,005 students
Nonsectarian: 2 schools, 962 students

📖 **Public Library Systems: 14**
1,582,148 books; turnover: 4.9

🎓 **Colleges and Universities**
Associate of Arts
6 campuses (45,221)
Baccalaureate
Metropolitan College (178)
University of Science & Arts (1,725)
Comprehensive
MidAmerica Christian University (857)
OK Christian University (1,642/216)
Oklahoma City University (2,114/2,355)
Southern Nazarene University (2,127/485)
Southwestern Christian University (186/78)
University of Central Oklahoma (15,849/2,616)
Doctoral
Langston University (3,700/127)
University of Oklahoma (22,851/8,674)
University of Oklahoma Health Science (832/2,752)

REPORT CARD
Public School Support .... D
Private School Options....................................... A
Library Popularity .... A+
College Town .... A
College Options .... A+

Places Rated Rank: 55

Olympia, WA

🏫 **Children in Public Schools (96%)**
10 districts, 76 schools, 38,422 students

Children in Private Schools (4%)
Catholic: 1 school, 261 students
Other religious: 9 schools, 981 students
Nonsectarian: 2 schools, 225 students

📖 **Public Library Systems: 1**
1,111,109 books; turnover: 4.1

🎓 **Colleges and Universities**
Associate of Arts
1 campus (9,338)
Comprehensive
Evergreen State College (5,206/315)
St. Martin's University (1,411/469)

REPORT CARD
Public School Support .... D+
Private School Options....................................... C+

Library Popularity ....A+
College Town..C
College Options C

Places Rated Rank: 233

Omaha-Council Bluffs, NE-IA

🏫 **Children in Public Schools (87%)**
64 districts, 334 schools, 134,351 students

Children in Private Schools (13%)
Catholic: 49 schools, 17,728 students
Other religious: 18 schools, 1,553 students

📖 **Public Library Systems: 40**
2,050,057 books; turnover: 2.1

🎓 **Colleges and Universities**
Associate of Arts
3 campuses (33,238)
Baccalaureate
Dana College (625)
Comprehensive
Bellevue University (6,689/2,045)
Clarkson College (562/101)
College of St. Mary (1,002/27)
Grace University (579/111)
Nebraska Methodist College Nursing (447/65)
Doctoral
Creighton University (4,343/3,262)
University of Nebraska (13,315/3,921)
University of Nebraska MC (887/2,169)

REPORT CARD
Public School Support .... B+
Private School Options....................................... B
Library Popularity C
College Town .... B+
College Options .... A

Places Rated Rank: 118

Orlando-Kissimmee, FL

🏫 **Children in Public Schools (91%)**
5 districts, 400 schools, 325,077 students

Children in Private Schools (9%)
Catholic: 14 schools, 7,247 students
Other religious: 92 schools, 20,526 students
Nonsectarian: 21 schools, 3,554 students

📖 **Public Library Systems: 9**
3,137,525 books; turnover: 3.8

🎓 **Colleges and Universities**
Associate of Arts
7 campuses (76,862)
Baccalaureate
Beacon College (88)
Florida Christian College (282)
Comprehensive
Rollins College (3,471/942)
Doctoral
University of Central Florida (39,191/10,885)

REPORT CARD
Public School Support .... D
Private School Options....................................... A+
Library Popularity .... A
College Town .... B
College Options .... A+

Places Rated Rank: 87

Oshkosh-Neenah, WI

Children in Public Schools (89%)
6 districts, 63 schools, 23,150 students

Children in Private Schools (11%)
Catholic: 9 schools, 1,446 students
Other religious: 12 schools, 1,415 students

Public Library Systems: 5
575,037 books; turnover: 3.9

Colleges and Universities
Associate of Arts
1 campus (20)
Comprehensive
University of Wisconsin (10,816/2,638)

REPORT CARD

Public School Support ....A
Private School Options......................................C+
Library Popularity ....A
College Town..B+
College Options ....C+

Places Rated Rank: 103

Owensboro, KY

Children in Public Schools (92%)
5 districts, 46 schools, 17,878 students

Children in Private Schools (8%)
Catholic: 8 schools, 1,398 students
Other religious: 3 schools, 120 students

Public Library Systems: 2
221,890 books; turnover: 2.9

Colleges and Universities
Associate of Arts
1 campus (6,836)
Baccalaureate
Kentucky Wesleyan College (672)
Comprehensive
Brescia University (787/41)

REPORT CARD

Public School Support ....C+
Private School Options......................................D+
Library Popularity ....B+
College Town..D+
College Options ....D

Places Rated Rank: 308

Oxnard-Thousand Oaks-Ventura, CA

Children in Public Schools (92%)
22 districts, 202 schools, 145,022 students

Children in Private Schools (8%)
Catholic: 15 schools, 4,344 students
Other religious: 22 schools, 5,776 students
Nonsectarian: 12 schools, 2,688 students

Public Library Systems: 4
1,620,743 books; turnover: 2.7

Colleges and Universities
Associate of Arts
4 campuses (51,989)
Baccalaureate
Thomas Aquinas College (336)
Comprehensive
California State Channel Islands (1,623/236)
St. John's Seminary (102)
Doctoral
California Lutheran University (2,082/1,358)

REPORT CARD

Public School Support ....D+
Private School Options......................................A
Library Popularity ....B
College Town..D+
College Options ....B

Places Rated Rank: 214

Palm Bay-Melbourne-Titusville, FL

Children in Public Schools (91%)
1 districts, 110 schools, 74,492 students

Children in Private Schools (9%)
Catholic: 9 schools, 2,988 students
Other religious: 27 schools, 4,250 students
Nonsectarian: 2 schools, 458 students

Public Library Systems: 1
1,219,549 books; turnover: 3.7

Colleges and Universities
Associate of Arts
1 campus (21,448)
Doctoral
Florida IT (2,419/3,049)

REPORT CARD

Public School Support ....D+
Private School Options......................................B+
Library Popularity ....A
College Town..D+
College Options ....C+

Places Rated Rank: 203

Panama City-Lynn Haven, FL

Children in Public Schools (96%)
1 districts, 45 schools, 27,004 students

Children in Private Schools (4%)
Catholic: 1 school, 229 students
Other religious: 5 schools, 929 students

Public Library Systems: 2
227,088 books; turnover: 2.3

Colleges and Universities
Associate of Arts
2 campuses (11,059)

REPORT CARD

Public School Support ....D
Private School Options......................................D
Library Popularity C
College Town..D+
College Options ....D+

Places Rated Rank: 368

Parkersburg-Marietta-Vienna, WV-OH

Children in Public Schools (95%)
11 districts, 67 schools, 26,183 students

Children in Private Schools (5%)
Catholic: 4 schools, 749 students
Other religious: 6 schools, 496 students

Public Library Systems: 5
487,702 books; turnover: 2.7

Colleges and Universities
Associate of Arts
1 campus (3,582)
Baccalaureate
Ohio Valley University (622)
WVU Parkersburg (4,867)
Comprehensive
Marietta College (1,299/153)

REPORT CARD

Public School Support ....A
Private School Options......................................D+
Library Popularity ....B
College Town..C
College Options C

Places Rated Rank: 249

Pascagoula, MS

Children in Public Schools (96%)
5 districts, 59 schools, 29,402 students

Children in Private Schools (4%)
Catholic: 4 schools, 782 students
Other religious: 4 schools, 218 students
Nonsectarian: 1 school, 200 students

Public Library Systems: 1
267,952 books; turnover: 3.4

REPORT CARD
Public School Support .... D
Private School Options C
Library Popularity .... A
College Town .... D
College Options .... D

Places Rated Rank: 346

Pensacola-Ferry Pass-Brent, FL

Children in Public Schools (91%)
2 districts, 115 schools, 68,782 students

Children in Private Schools (9%)
Catholic: 6 schools, 1,570 students
Other religious: 19 schools, 4,838 students
Nonsectarian: 2 schools, 288 students

Public Library Systems: 1
441,152 books; turnover: 2.6

Colleges and Universities
Associate of Arts
3 campuses (17,863)
Doctoral
University of West Florida (10,453/1,724)

REPORT CARD
Public School Support .... D
Private School Options .... B+
Library Popularity .... B
College Town .... C+
College Options .... B

Places Rated Rank: 216

Peoria, IL

Children in Public Schools (91%)
59 districts, 171 schools, 60,163 students

Children in Private Schools (9%)
Catholic: 12 schools, 3,353 students
Other religious: 14 schools, 2,219 students
Nonsectarian: 2 schools, 281 students

Public Library Systems: 31
1,967,390 books; turnover: 1.3

Colleges and Universities
Associate of Arts
1 campus (19,699)
Baccalaureate
Eureka College (601)
Comprehensive
St. Francis Medical Center College (236/43)
Doctoral
Bradley University (5,598/1,133)

REPORT CARD
Public School Support .... B
Private School Options .... B+
Library Popularity .... D
College Town .... C+
College Options .... C+

Places Rated Rank: 230

✓ Philadelphia, PA

Children in Public Schools (80%)
150 districts, 837 schools, 556,809 students

Children in Private Schools (20%)
Catholic: 239 schools, 98,913 students
Other religious: 149 schools, 24,991 students
Nonsectarian: 34 schools, 11,122 students

Public Library Systems: 72
10,772,432 books; turnover: 1.9

Colleges and Universities
Associate of Arts
16 campuses (81,356)
Baccalaureate
Haverford College (1,208)
Peirce College (2,296)
Swarthmore College (1,530)
Ursinus College (1,500)
Valley Forge Christian College (903)
Comprehensive
American College (839)
Cabrini College (1,888/781)
Cheyney University (1,526/447)
Delaware Valley College (2,249/106)
Gratz College (12/571)
Gwynedd Mercy College (2,607/663)
Holy Family University (2,073/1,203)
Lincoln University (1,642/477)
Moore College Art & Design (725)
Penn Academy Fine Arts (397/38)
Penn State University (3,897)
Penn State University, Delaware Campus (2,003)
Penn State University, Great Valley (2,078)
Philadelphia Biblical University (1,081/515)
Rosemont College (992/529)
St. Charles Borromeo Sem (524/349)
University Arts (2,030/191)
West Chester University Penn (12,523/3,548)
Doctoral
Arcadia University (2,004/2,154)
Bryn Mawr College (1,516/537)
Chestnut Hill College (1,152/915)
Drexel University (11,905/6,860)
Eastern University (2,512/1,448)
Immaculata University (3,077/1,425)
La Salle University (4,562/2,621)
Lutheran Theological Seminary (365)
Neumann College (2,471/720)
Pennsylvania College of Optometry (1,542)
Philadelphia College Osteopathic (1,617)
Philadelphia University (3,096/574)
St. Joseph's University (5,150/5,031)
Temple University (30,689/19,079)
Thomas Jefferson University (1,019/1,678)
University of Penn (13,390/13,203)
University of Sciences Philadelphia (1,412/1,447)
Villanova University (8,113/3,960)
Westminster Theological Seminary (833)
Widener University (3,484/1,977)

REPORT CARD
Public School Support .... B+
Private School Options .... A+
Library Popularity C
College Town .... A
College Options .... A+

Places Rated Rank: 25

Phoenix-Mesa-Scottsdale, AZ

Children in Public Schools (96%)
288 districts, 1108 schools, 688,419 students

Children in Private Schools (4%)
Catholic: 30 schools, 12,725 students
Other religious: 57 schools, 11,360 students
Nonsectarian: 7 schools, 1,940 students

Public Library Systems: 26
5,764,780 books; turnover: 4.9

Colleges and Universities

Associate of Arts
11 campuses (230,803)

Baccalaureate
IInstitute Americas (572)
Southwestern College (288)

Comprehensive
Arizona State University West (9,753/2,191)
Midwestern University (141/1,147)
Ottawa University (1,723/2,053)
Thunderbird Graduate School (1,852)

Doctoral
Arizona State University (43,920/13,218)
Arizona State East (4,403/967)
International Baptist College (85/21)

REPORT CARD
Public School Support .... D
Private School Options............................... A+
Library Popularity .... A+
College Town.. C+
College Options .... A+

Places Rated Rank: 78

Pine Bluff, AR

Children in Public Schools (96%)
14 districts, 48 schools, 17,540 students

Children in Private Schools (4%)
Catholic: 3 schools, 286 students
Other religious: 5 schools, 439 students

Public Library Systems: 1
179,303 books; turnover: 1.5

Colleges and Universities

Associate of Arts
2 campuses (3,937)

Comprehensive
University of Arkansas (3,611/180)

REPORT CARD
Public School Support .... C+
Private School Options............................... D+
Library Popularity .... D
College Town.. C
College Options .... D+

Places Rated Rank: 351

✓ Pittsburgh, PA

Children in Public Schools (89%)
139 districts, 652 schools, 340,162 students

Children in Private Schools (11%)
Catholic: 118 schools, 29,035 students
Other religious: 68 schools, 7,756 students
Nonsectarian: 13 schools, 3,200 students

Public Library Systems: 104
6,063,111 books; turnover: 2.1

Colleges and Universities

Associate of Arts
18 campuses (52,090)

Baccalaureate
University of Pittsburgh Greensburg (2,071)
Washington & Jefferson College (1,292)

Comprehensive
California University of Pennsylvania (7,427/2,524)
Carlow University (1,906/482)
Geneva College (2,249/483)
La Roche College (1,933/273)
Penn State University Beaver (825/16)
Penn State University Fayette (1,365)

Penn State University New Kensington (1,219/29)
Point Park University (3,226/611)
St. Vincent College (1,586/105)
Seton Hill University (1,571/477)

Doctoral
Carnegie Mellon University (6,435/4,594)
Chatham College (953/757)
Duquesne University (6,072/5,002)
Robert Morris University (4,180/1,445)
Slippery Rock University (7,974/1,033)
Trinity Episcopal School (474)
University of Pittsburgh (22,617/10,862)

REPORT CARD
Public School Support .... A+
Private School Options............................... A+
Library Popularity C
College Town.. B
College Options .... A+

Places Rated Rank: 29

Pittsfield, MA

Children in Public Schools (90%)
40 districts, 51 schools, 19,343 students

Children in Private Schools (10%)
Catholic: 5 schools, 1,014 students
Other religious: 3 schools, 119 students
Nonsectarian: 5 schools, 993 students

Public Library Systems: 30
716,812 books; turnover: 1.4

Colleges and Universities

Associate of Arts
1 campus (3,139)

Baccalaureate
Simons Rock College Bard (433)

Comprehensive
Massachusetts College (2,060/943)
Williams College (2,151/57)

REPORT CARD
Public School Support .... A+
Private School Options............................... C+
Library Popularity .... D
College Town.. C
College Options .... D+

Places Rated Rank: 241

Pocatello, ID

Children in Public Schools (96%)
5 districts, 44 schools, 15,098 students

Children in Private Schools (4%)
Catholic: 1 school, 170 students
Other religious: 3 schools, 531 students

Public Library Systems: 5
262,328 books; turnover: 2.4

Colleges and Universities

Doctoral
Idaho State University (14,098/3,872)

REPORT CARD
Public School Support .... D
Private School Options............................... D
Library Popularity .... C+
College Town.. A+
College Options .... B

Places Rated Rank: 256

Portland-South Portland-Biddeford, ME

Children in Public Schools (92%)
45 districts, 187 schools, 77,562 students

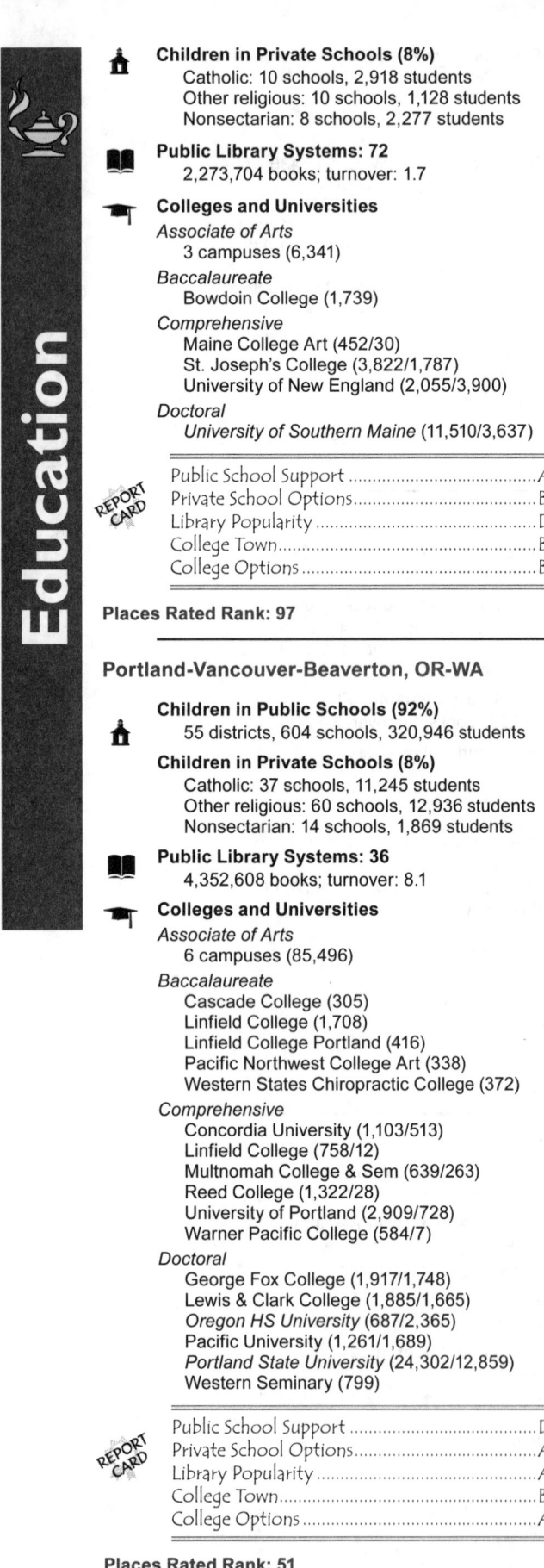

Children in Private Schools (8%)
Catholic: 10 schools, 2,918 students
Other religious: 10 schools, 1,128 students
Nonsectarian: 8 schools, 2,277 students

Public Library Systems: 72
2,273,704 books; turnover: 1.7

Colleges and Universities
Associate of Arts
3 campuses (6,341)
Baccalaureate
Bowdoin College (1,739)
Comprehensive
Maine College Art (452/30)
St. Joseph's College (3,822/1,787)
University of New England (2,055/3,900)
Doctoral
University of Southern Maine (11,510/3,637)

REPORT CARD
Public School Support ....A+
Private School Options................................B+
Library Popularity ....D+
College Town..B+
College Options ....B+

Places Rated Rank: 97

Portland-Vancouver-Beaverton, OR-WA

Children in Public Schools (92%)
55 districts, 604 schools, 320,946 students

Children in Private Schools (8%)
Catholic: 37 schools, 11,245 students
Other religious: 60 schools, 12,936 students
Nonsectarian: 14 schools, 1,869 students

Public Library Systems: 36
4,352,608 books; turnover: 8.1

Colleges and Universities
Associate of Arts
6 campuses (85,496)
Baccalaureate
Cascade College (305)
Linfield College (1,708)
Linfield College Portland (416)
Pacific Northwest College Art (338)
Western States Chiropractic College (372)
Comprehensive
Concordia University (1,103/513)
Linfield College (758/12)
Multnomah College & Sem (639/263)
Reed College (1,322/28)
University of Portland (2,909/728)
Warner Pacific College (584/7)
Doctoral
George Fox College (1,917/1,748)
Lewis & Clark College (1,885/1,665)
Oregon HS University (687/2,365)
Pacific University (1,261/1,689)
Portland State University (24,302/12,859)
Western Seminary (799)

REPORT CARD
Public School Support ....D+
Private School Options................................A+
Library Popularity ....A+
College Town..B
College Options ....A+

Places Rated Rank: 51

Port St. Lucie-Fort Pierce, FL

Children in Public Schools (91%)
2 districts, 80 schools, 52,802 students

Children in Private Schools (9%)
Catholic: 4 schools, 1,795 students
Other religious: 19 schools, 3,139 students
Nonsectarian: 1 school, 427 students

Public Library Systems: 2
581,532 books; turnover: 3.4

Colleges and Universities
Associate of Arts
1 campus (24,588)
Baccalaureate
Hobe Sound Bible College (141)

REPORT CARD
Public School Support ....D
Private School Options................................B+
Library Popularity ....A
College Town..D+
College Options C

Places Rated Rank: 279

Poughkeepsie-Newburgh-Middletown, NY

Children in Public Schools (91%)
32 districts, 176 schools, 113,755 students

Children in Private Schools (9%)
Catholic: 23 schools, 5,682 students
Other religious: 19 schools, 4,266 students
Nonsectarian: 9 schools, 1,263 students

Public Library Systems: 39
1,676,301 books; turnover: 2.2

Colleges and Universities
Associate of Arts
2 campuses (19,346)
Baccalaureate
Culinary Institute America (3,696)
U. S. Military Academy (4,209)
Comprehensive
Marist College (5,450/1,290)
Mt St. Mary College (2,459/739)
Unification Theological Seminary (232)
Vassar College (2,628)
Doctoral
Bard College (1,664/253)

REPORT CARD
Public School Support ....A
Private School Options.......................................A
Library Popularity C
College Town..C
College Options ....B

Places Rated Rank: 140

Prescott, AZ

Children in Public Schools (97%)
54 districts, 91 schools, 28,373 students

Children in Private Schools (3%)
Catholic: 1 school, 126 students
Other religious: 6 schools, 446 students
Nonsectarian: 5 schools, 426 students

Public Library Systems: 18
506,106 books; turnover: 4.1

Colleges and Universities
Associate of Arts
1 campus (15,024)
Comprehensive
Embry Riddle Aero University (1,740/39)
Doctoral
Prescott College (1,110/300)

REPORT CARD
Public School Support ....D
Private School Options................................C

Library Popularity ....A+
College Town...C
College Options C

Places Rated Rank: 277

✓ **Providence-New Bedford-Fall River, RI-MA**

🏫 **Children in Public Schools (89%)**
78 districts, 510 schools, 241,909 students

Children in Private Schools (11%)
Catholic: 81 schools, 25,514 students
Other religious: 17 schools, 2,491 students
Nonsectarian: 13 schools, 2,586 students

📖 **Public Library Systems: 68**
5,773,230 books; turnover: 1.6

🎓 **Colleges and Universities**
Associate of Arts
4 campuses (32,627)
Baccalaureate
New England IT (3,953)
Wheaton College (1,583)
Zion Bible College (347)
Comprehensive
Bryant University (3,152/601)
Providence College (4,959/1,727)
RI School Design (2,149/381)
Roger Williams University (4,647/401)
Stonehill College (2,664/16)
Doctoral
Brown University (6,479/2,012)
Johnson & Wales University (10,344/1,292)
Rhode Island College (8,084/3,623)
Salve Regina University (2,079/561)
University of Mass Dartmouth (8,399/1,257)
URI (13,350/4,673)

REPORT CARD
Public School Support ....A+
Private School Options..A
Library Popularity ....D+
College Town...B+
College Options ....A+

Places Rated Rank: 40

Provo-Orem, UT

🏫 **Children in Public Schools (99%)**
15 districts, 146 schools, 94,931 students

Children in Private Schools (1%)
Other religious: 3 schools, 229 students
Nonsectarian: 3 schools, 553 students

📖 **Public Library Systems: 13**
902,302 books; turnover: 5.0

🎓 **Colleges and Universities**
Baccalaureate
Utah Valley State College (31,168)
Doctoral
Brigham Young University (37,007/4,114)

REPORT CARD
Public School Support ....D
Private School Options..D+
Library Popularity ....A+
College Town...A+
College Options ....A

Places Rated Rank: 133

Pueblo, CO

🏫 **Children in Public Schools (96%)**
3 districts, 63 schools, 25,785 students

🏫 **Children in Private Schools (4%)**
Catholic: 2 schools, 371 students
Other religious: 6 schools, 418 students
Nonsectarian: 1 school, 184 students

📖 **Public Library Systems: 1**
424,374 books; turnover: 2.5

🎓 **Colleges and Universities**
Associate of Arts
1 campus (8,661)
Comprehensive
Colorado Southern University (7,444/1,067)

REPORT CARD
Public School Support ....D
Private School Options..C
Library Popularity ....C+
College Town...B
College Options C

Places Rated Rank: 280

Punta Gorda, FL

🏫 **Children in Public Schools (94%)**
1 districts, 23 schools, 17,409 students

Children in Private Schools (6%)
Catholic: 1 school, 319 students
Other religious: 7 schools, 738 students

📖 **Public Library Systems: 1**
217,397 books; turnover: 2.2

🎓 **Colleges and Universities**
Associate of Arts
1 campus (1,025)

REPORT CARD
Public School Support ....D
Private School Options..D+
Library Popularity C
College Town...D
College Options ....D

Places Rated Rank: 373

Racine, WI

🏫 **Children in Public Schools (85%)**
14 districts, 57 schools, 30,377 students

Children in Private Schools (15%)
Catholic: 14 schools, 2,999 students
Other religious: 10 schools, 1,797 students
Nonsectarian: 1 school, 644 students

📖 **Public Library Systems: 5**
425,558 books; turnover: 3.3

REPORT CARD
Public School Support ....B+
Private School Options..B+
Library Popularity ....B+
College Town...D
College Options ....D

Places Rated Rank: 237

Raleigh-Cary, NC

🏫 **Children in Public Schools (93%)**
19 districts, 199 schools, 153,698 students

Children in Private Schools (7%)
Catholic: 7 schools, 3,282 students
Other religious: 23 schools, 6,402 students
Nonsectarian: 6 schools, 2,504 students

📖 **Public Library Systems: 3**
1,820,587 books; turnover: 3.9

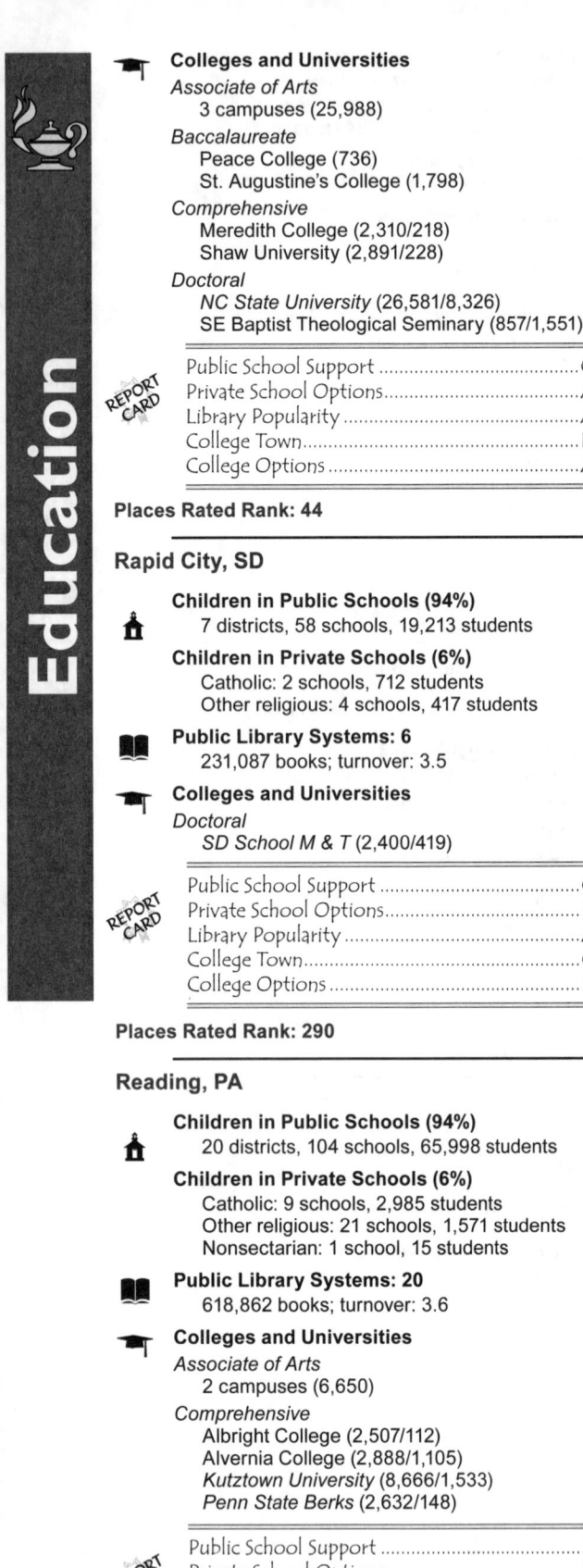

Education

Colleges and Universities
Associate of Arts
3 campuses (25,988)
Baccalaureate
Peace College (736)
St. Augustine's College (1,798)
Comprehensive
Meredith College (2,310/218)
Shaw University (2,891/228)
Doctoral
NC State University (26,581/8,326)
SE Baptist Theological Seminary (857/1,551)

Public School Support C
Private School Options.................................A
Library Popularity ....A
College Town..B+
College Options ....A

Places Rated Rank: 44

Rapid City, SD

Children in Public Schools (94%)
7 districts, 58 schools, 19,213 students

Children in Private Schools (6%)
Catholic: 2 schools, 712 students
Other religious: 4 schools, 417 students

Public Library Systems: 6
231,087 books; turnover: 3.5

Colleges and Universities
Doctoral
SD School M & T (2,400/419)

Public School Support ....C+
Private School Options.................................D
Library Popularity ....A
College Town..C
College Options ....D+

Places Rated Rank: 290

Reading, PA

Children in Public Schools (94%)
20 districts, 104 schools, 65,998 students

Children in Private Schools (6%)
Catholic: 9 schools, 2,985 students
Other religious: 21 schools, 1,571 students
Nonsectarian: 1 school, 15 students

Public Library Systems: 20
618,862 books; turnover: 3.6

Colleges and Universities
Associate of Arts
2 campuses (6,650)
Comprehensive
Albright College (2,507/112)
Alvernia College (2,888/1,105)
Kutztown University (8,666/1,533)
Penn State Berks (2,632/148)

Public School Support ....B+
Private School Options.................................B
Library Popularity ....A
College Town..C+
College Options ....C+

Places Rated Rank: 125

Redding, CA

Children in Public Schools (93%)
27 districts, 103 schools, 29,834 students

Children in Private Schools (7%)
Catholic: 4 schools, 707 students
Other religious: 11 schools, 1,637 students

Public Library Systems: 1
205,552 books; turnover: 1.7

Colleges and Universities
Associate of Arts
1 campus (11,890)
Comprehensive
Simpson University (1,083/392)

Public School Support C
Private School Options.................................C
Library Popularity ....D+
College Town..D+
College Options ....D+

Places Rated Rank: 344

Reno-Sparks, NV

Children in Public Schools (96%)
2 districts, 104 schools, 64,110 students

Children in Private Schools (4%)
Catholic: 3 schools, 1,086 students
Other religious: 9 schools, 873 students
Nonsectarian: 5 schools, 526 students

Public Library Systems: 2
796,421 books; turnover: 2.4

Colleges and Universities
Associate of Arts
1 campus (16,902)
Comprehensive
Sierra Nevada College (648/359)
Doctoral
University of Nevada (17,650/5,651)

Public School Support ....D
Private School Options.................................B
Library Popularity ....C+
College Town..A
College Options ....B+

Places Rated Rank: 178

✓Richmond, VA

Children in Public Schools (95%)
36 districts, 343 schools, 196,419 students

Children in Private Schools (5%)
Catholic: 10 schools, 2,988 students
Other religious: 40 schools, 5,712 students
Nonsectarian: 10 schools, 1,412 students

Public Library Systems: 11
2,147,019 books; turnover: 4.1

Colleges and Universities
Associate of Arts
4 campuses (27,716)
Baccalaureate
Randolph-Macon College (1,118)
Comprehensive
University of Richmond (4,370/943)
Doctoral
Baptist Theological Seminary (240)
Union Theological Seminary (460)
VA Commonwealth University (21,256/10,621)
Virginia State University (4,460/1,300)
Virginia Union University (1,581/457)

Public School Support ....A
Private School Options.................................A

Library Popularity ....A+
College Town...B
College Options ....A

Places Rated Rank: 12

Riverside-San Bernardino-Ontario, CA

Children in Public Schools (96%)
64 districts, 957 schools, 804,622 students

Children in Private Schools (4%)
Catholic: 30 schools, 8,550 students
Other religious: 132 schools, 26,787 students
Nonsectarian: 21 schools, 2,361 students

Public Library Systems: 18
4,354,623 books; turnover: 2.6

Colleges and Universities
Associate of Arts
10 campuses (148,813)

Comprehensive
California Baptist University (2,238/903)
California State University (13,927/6,265)
University of Redlands (3,650/2,002)

Doctoral
La Sierra University (1,808/851)
Loma Linda University (1,363/2,886)
University of Cal (16,431/2,215)

Public School Support ....D
Private School Options..A+
Library Popularity ....B
College Town...D+
College Options ....A+

Places Rated Rank: 177

Roanoke, VA

Children in Public Schools (97%)
10 districts, 99 schools, 44,977 students

Children in Private Schools (3%)
Catholic: 1 school, 591 students
Other religious: 6 schools, 499 students
Nonsectarian: 2 schools, 134 students

Public Library Systems: 5
978,612 books; turnover: 1.9

Colleges and Universities
Associate of Arts
2 campuses (14,552)

Baccalaureate
Ferrum College (982)
Roanoke College (2,024)

Comprehensive
Hollins University (874/466)
Jefferson College Health Sciences (874)

Public School Support ....A
Private School Options..C
Library Popularity ....D+
College Town...D+
College Options C

Places Rated Rank: 258

Rochester, MN

Children in Public Schools (89%)
17 districts, 79 schools, 29,473 students

Children in Private Schools (11%)
Catholic: 6 schools, 2,287 students
Other religious: 11 schools, 1,218 students

Public Library Systems: 9
565,028 books; turnover: 3.2

Colleges and Universities
Associate of Arts
1 campus (7,534)

Baccalaureate
Crossroads College (151)

Comprehensive
Mayo School HS (227/208)

Doctoral
Mayo Graduate School (355)

Public School Support ....B
Private School Options..C+
Library Popularity ....B+
College Town...D
College Options ....D

Places Rated Rank: 273

✓Rochester, NY

Children in Public Schools (92%)
58 districts, 300 schools, 172,241 students

Children in Private Schools (8%)
Catholic: 42 schools, 11,674 students
Other religious: 25 schools, 2,691 students
Nonsectarian: 2 schools, 524 students

Public Library Systems: 57
3,415,885 books; turnover: 2.9

Colleges and Universities
Associate of Arts
2 campuses (36,731)

Comprehensive
Hobart William SmithColleges (1,898)
Roberts Wesleyan College (1,546/830)
St. John Fisher College (2,761/843)
St. Bernard's Institute (218)
SUNY College Brockport (8,020/2,776)
SUNY College Geneseo (5,658/415)

Doctoral
Colgate Rochester Crozer Divinity School (122)
Nazareth College (2,107/1,530)
Northeastern Seminary (170)
Rochester IT (12,508/2,580)
University of Rochester (4,949/4,153)

Public School Support ....A+
Private School Options..A
Library Popularity ....B+
College Town...B+
College Options ....A

Places Rated Rank: 13

Rockford, IL

Children in Public Schools (86%)
17 districts, 112 schools, 56,879 students

Children in Private Schools (14%)
Catholic: 10 schools, 3,944 students
Other religious: 18 schools, 5,033 students
Nonsectarian: 1 school, 318 students

Public Library Systems: 51
1,785,460 books; turnover: 2.1

Colleges and Universities
Associate of Arts
1 campus (15,552)

Baccalaureate
St. Anthony College Nursing (137)

Comprehensive
Rockford College (908/2,362)

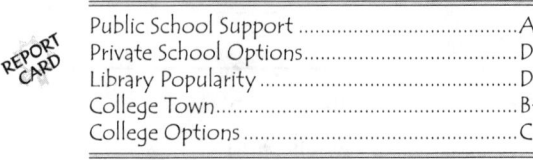

Public School Support .... C+
Private School Options .... B+
Library Popularity .... C+
College Town .... D+
College Options C

Places Rated Rank: 259

Rockingham County-Strafford County, NH

Children in Public Schools (91%)
67 districts, 121 schools, 66,095 students

Children in Private Schools (9%)
Catholic: 6 schools, 2,424 students
Other religious: 13 schools, 2,308 students
Nonsectarian: 2 schools, 1,722 students

Public Library Systems: 3
272,038 books; turnover: 2.0

Colleges and Universities
Baccalaureate
Chester College New England (201)
Comprehensive
Granite State College (2,991)
Doctoral
UNH (12,281/3,369)

Public School Support .... A+
Private School Options .... B+
Library Popularity C
College Town .... B
College Options .... B

Places Rated Rank: 120

Rocky Mount, NC

Children in Public Schools (96%)
3 districts, 45 schools, 27,280 students

Children in Private Schools (4%)
Catholic: 1 school, 80 students
Other religious: 3 schools, 487 students
Nonsectarian: 2 schools, 482 students

Public Library Systems: 1
435,089 books; turnover: 1.7

Colleges and Universities
Associate of Arts
2 campuses (7,641)
Baccalaureate
NC Wesleyan College (2,236)

Public School Support C
Private School Options C
Library Popularity C
College Town .... D+
College Options .... D+

Places Rated Rank: 353

Rome, GA

Children in Public Schools (92%)
3 districts, 34 schools, 15,871 students

Children in Private Schools (8%)
Catholic: 1 school, 371 students
Other religious: 2 schools, 1,057 students

Public Library Systems: 8
3,521,938 books; turnover: 2.6

Colleges and Universities
Associate of Arts
2 campuses (9,826)

Public School Support .... A
Private School Options .... D
Library Popularity .... D+
College Town .... B+
College Options C

Places Rated Rank: 235

Sacramento–Arden-Arcade–Roseville, CA

Children in Public Schools (94%)
63 districts, 617 schools, 358,352 students

Children in Private Schools (6%)
Catholic: 35 schools, 11,338 students
Other religious: 52 schools, 8,094 students
Nonsectarian: 24 schools, 3,755 students

Public Library Systems: 10
710,912 books; turnover: 1.3

Colleges and Universities
Associate of Arts
8 campuses (149,296)
Baccalaureate
Trinity Life Bible College (268)
Doctoral
CA State University (25,647/6,965)
University of California (25,782/6,264)

Public School Support .... D+
Private School Options .... A+
Library Popularity .... B
College Town .... B+
College Options .... A+

Places Rated Rank: 86

Saginaw-Saginaw Township North, MI

Children in Public Schools (90%)
20 districts, 95 schools, 36,882 students

Children in Private Schools (10%)
Catholic: 5 schools, 1,608 students
Other religious: 20 schools, 2,687 students

Public Library Systems: 1
843,748 books; turnover: 3.4

Colleges and Universities
Comprehensive
Saginaw Valley State University (9,633/2,573)

Public School Support .... C+
Private School Options .... C+
Library Popularity .... D
College Town .... C+
College Options C

Places Rated Rank: 288

St. Cloud, MN

Children in Public Schools (86%)
21 districts, 60 schools, 27,360 students

Children in Private Schools (14%)
Catholic: 20 schools, 4,130 students
Other religious: 5 schools, 423 students

Public Library Systems: 1
181,075 books; turnover: 5.3

Colleges and Universities
Associate of Arts
1 campus (4,808)

Baccalaureate
College St. Benedict (2,307)
Comprehensive
St. Cloud State University (17,275/2,425)
St. John's University (2,109/246)

Public School Support C
Private School Options...................................C
Library Popularity ....A
College Town...A
College Options ....C+

Places Rated Rank: 162

St. George, UT

🏫 **Children in Public Schools (100%)**
2 districts, 41 schools, 21,795 students

Children in Private Schools (0%)
Other religious: 1 school, 47 students
Nonsectarian: 1 school, 28 students

📖 **Public Library Systems: 3**
399,994 books; turnover: 1.5

🎓 **Colleges and Universities**
Baccalaureate
Dixie State College Utah (9,536)

Public School Support ....D
Private School Options...................................D
Library Popularity ....A+
College Town...C+
College Options C

Places Rated Rank: 287

St. Joseph, MO-KS

🏫 **Children in Public Schools (91%)**
15 districts, 60 schools, 18,433 students

Children in Private Schools (9%)
Catholic: 5 schools, 1,186 students
Other religious: 3 schools, 541 students

📖 **Public Library Systems: 72**
8,957,073 books; turnover: 2.6

🎓 **Colleges and Universities**
Associate of Arts
2 campuses (5,351)
Baccalaureate
MO Western State University (6,182)

Public School Support ....B+
Private School Options...................................D+
Library Popularity ....D
College Town...C+
College Options ....D+

Places Rated Rank: 299

✓ St. Louis, MO-IL

🏫 **Children in Public Schools (84%)**
158 districts, 880 schools, 423,561 students

Children in Private Schools (16%)
Catholic: 182 schools, 57,429 students
Other religious: 105 schools, 18,485 students
Nonsectarian: 15 schools, 3,862 students

📖 **Public Library Systems: 10**
890,695 books; turnover: 2.3

🎓 **Colleges and Universities**
Associate of Arts
10 campuses (111,316)

Baccalaureate
Blackburn College (639)
Harris-Stowe State University (2,213)
Logan College Chiropractic (1,284)
Principia College (572)
Ranken Tech College (1,931)
St. Louis Christian College (245)
Comprehensive
Barnes-Jewish College Nursing (867/130)
Fontbonne University (2,212/1,060)
Greenville College (1,322/248)
Lindenwood University (5,766/6,045)
McKendree College (2,590/75)
Missouri Baptist University (3,537/828)
Southern Illinois University (12,206/4,236)
St. Louis College Pharmacy (905)
Doctoral
Aquinas Institute of Theology (344)
Concordia Seminary (930)
Covenant Theological Seminary (992)
Eden Theological Seminary (232)
Maryville University St. Louis (3,208/772)
Midwest University (296)
St. Louis University (12,012/4,850)
University of Missouri (16,019/4,387)
Washington University (12,683/9,301)
Webster University (6,004/23,246)

Public School Support ....A
Private School Options...................................A+
Library Popularity ....C+
College Town...B+
College Options ....A+

Places Rated Rank: 9

Salem, OR

🏫 **Children in Public Schools (94%)**
18 districts, 149 schools, 61,021 students

Children in Private Schools (6%)
Catholic: 9 schools, 1,557 students
Other religious: 16 schools, 2,166 students

📖 **Public Library Systems: 5**
908,278 books; turnover: 2.1

🎓 **Colleges and Universities**
Associate of Arts
2 campuses (16,795)
Comprehensive
Corban College (787)
Western Oregon University (5,028/1,642)
Willamette University (1,993/652)

Public School Support C
Private School Options...................................C+
Library Popularity ....C+
College Town...C
College Options ....C+

Places Rated Rank: 272

Salinas, CA

🏫 **Children in Public Schools (95%)**
28 districts, 161 schools, 73,902 students

Children in Private Schools (5%)
Catholic: 6 schools, 2,115 students
Other religious: 8 schools, 1,277 students
Nonsectarian: 1 school, 216 students

📖 **Public Library Systems: 2**
194,049 books; turnover: 4.2

🎓 **Colleges and Universities**
Associate of Arts
4 campuses (45,565)

Comprehensive
California State University (3,721/518)
Monterey II (7/915)
Doctoral
Naval Postgraduate School (2,652)

Public School Support ....C+
Private School Options...................................B
Library Popularity C
College Town...B
College Options ....B

Places Rated Rank: 202

Salisbury, MD

Children in Public Schools (88%)
2 districts, 37 schools, 17,339 students

Children in Private Schools (12%)
Catholic: 1 school, 279 students
Other religious: 7 schools, 1,339 students
Nonsectarian: 4 schools, 748 students

Public Library Systems: 7
2,722,246 books; turnover: 6.1

Colleges and Universities
Associate of Arts
1 campus (4,265)
Comprehensive
Salisbury University (6,929/983)
Doctoral
UM Eastern Shore (3,691/540)

Public School Support ....A
Private School Options...................................C+
Library Popularity ....A+
College Town...A
College Options ....C+

Places Rated Rank: 41

Salt Lake City, UT

Children in Public Schools (96%)
21 districts, 311 schools, 194,357 students

Children in Private Schools (4%)
Catholic: 10 schools, 4,289 students
Other religious: 16 schools, 2,446 students
Nonsectarian: 7 schools, 1,283 students

Public Library Systems: 2
317,723 books; turnover: 1.8

Colleges and Universities
Associate of Arts
3 campuses (45,300)
Comprehensive
Western Governor's University (1,509/991)
Westminster College (2,189/606)
Doctoral
University of of Utah (28,981/6,821)

Public School Support ....D
Private School Options...................................A
Library Popularity ....A+
College Town...B+
College Options ....A

Places Rated Rank: 83

San Angelo, TX

Children in Public Schools (97%)
8 districts, 74 schools, 18,725 students

Children in Private Schools (3%)
Catholic: 1 school, 108 students
Other religious: 3 schools, 564 students

Public Library Systems: 25
2,374,761 books; turnover: 3.2

Colleges and Universities
Comprehensive
Angelo State University (6,360/593)

Public School Support ....C+
Private School Options...................................D
Library Popularity ....D+
College Town...B
College Options ....D+

Places Rated Rank: 327

San Antonio, TX

Children in Public Schools (94%)
67 districts, 657 schools, 356,942 students

Children in Private Schools (6%)
Catholic: 40 schools, 12,270 students
Other religious: 44 schools, 10,484 students

Public Library Systems: 8
8,190,439 books; turnover: 2.0

Colleges and Universities
Associate of Arts
4 campuses (71,900)
Baccalaureate
Texas Lutheran University (1,508)
Comprehensive
Trinity University (2,523/228)
Doctoral
Oblate School Theology (268)
Our Lady of Lake University (2,419/1,468)
St. Mary's University (2,695/1,854)
UT San Antonio (31,312/4,579)
UT Health Science (1,140/2,012)
University of Incarnate Word (4,996/1,186)

Public School Support C
Private School Options...................................B+
Library Popularity ....B+
College Town...B
College Options ....A+

Places Rated Rank: 95

San Diego-Carlsbad-San Marcos, CA

Children in Public Schools (93%)
44 districts, 710 schools, 497,959 students

Children in Private Schools (7%)
Catholic: 45 schools, 14,735 students
Other religious: 83 schools, 16,389 students
Nonsectarian: 25 schools, 5,089 students

Public Library Systems: 4
357,549 books; turnover: 3.8

Colleges and Universities
Associate of Arts
9 campuses (203,617)
Comprehensive
Bethel Seminary San Diego (255)
Cal State University (7,078/1,646)
California Western School Law (1,045)
Coleman College (1,214/54)
National University (5,820/19,864)
Point Loma Nazarene University (2,476/1,478)
San Diego Christian College (540/93)
Westminster Theological Seminary (129)

Doctoral
    Alliant IU (479/1,591)
    San Diego State University (28,731/7,409)
    Southern California Sem (81/126)
    UC (21,613/4,435)
    University of of San Diego (5,259/3,029)

Public School Support .... D
Private School Options................................... A+
Library Popularity C
College Town.. B+
College Options .... A+

Places Rated Rank: 141

Sandusky, OH

Children in Public Schools (94%)
9 districts, 32 schools, 13,373 students

Children in Private Schools (6%)
Catholic: 5 schools, 898 students

Public Library Systems: 16
8,205,695 books; turnover: 1.9

Colleges and Universities
Associate of Arts
    3 campuses (2,528)

Public School Support ....A+
Private School Options....................................D
Library Popularity ....A
College Town..D
College Options ....D

Places Rated Rank: 278

San Francisco-San Mateo-Redwood City, CA

Children in Public Schools (80%)
50 districts, 369 schools, 175,510 students

Children in Private Schools (20%)
Catholic: 74 schools, 26,117 students
Other religious: 32 schools, 6,127 students
Nonsectarian: 47 schools, 10,638 students

Public Library Systems: 9
4,486,198 books; turnover: 7.0

Colleges and Universities
Associate of Arts
    6 campuses (116,592)

Baccalaureate
    Menlo College (784)

Comprehensive
    American College Chinese Medicine (229)
    American Conservatory Theater (93/45)
    Dominican University California (1,317/742)
    New College California (893/411)
    Notre Dame de Namur University (1,114/1,034)
    SF Art Institute (518/284)
    SF Conservatory of Music (188/161)
    University Hastings College of Law (1,287)

Doctoral
    California Institute Integral Studies (56/975)
    Golden Gate University (969/4,853)
    SF State University (25,598/8,286)
    San Francisco Theological Seminary (587)
    Saybrook Institute (639)
    UCal (28/2,799)
    University of San Francisco (5,501/3,999)

Public School Support ....C+
Private School Options.....................................A+
Library Popularity C

College Town..B+
College Options ....A+

Places Rated Rank: 70

✓ San Jose-Sunnyvale-Santa Clara, CA

Children in Public Schools (89%)
46 districts, 416 schools, 264,787 students

Children in Private Schools (11%)
Catholic: 38 schools, 14,885 students
Other religious: 41 schools, 9,431 students
Nonsectarian: 30 schools, 8,163 students

Public Library Systems: 2
493,790 books; turnover: 3.5

Colleges and Universities
Associate of Arts
    8 campuses (142,201)
Baccalaureate
    Cogswell Polytechnical College (505)
Comprehensive
    National Hispanic University (391/314)
    San Jose State University (24,952/9,615)
    William Jessup University (441)
Doctoral
    Santa Clara University (5,058/4,344)
    Stanford University (6,878/14,300)

Public School Support C
Private School Options....................................A+
Library Popularity ....A+
College Town..B+
College Options ....A+

Places Rated Rank: 18

San Luis Obispo-Paso Robles, CA

Children in Public Schools (94%)
13 districts, 81 schools, 36,347 students

Children in Private Schools (6%)
Catholic: 3 schools, 995 students
Other religious: 10 schools, 1,203 students
Nonsectarian: 1 school, 180 students

Public Library Systems: 11
5,251,643 books; turnover: 3.0

Colleges and Universities
Associate of Arts
    1 campus (14,623)
Comprehensive
    California State Polytechnic (18,081/1,367)

Public School Support C
Private School Options....................................B
Library Popularity ....A
College Town..B+
College Options ....C+

Places Rated Rank: 169

Santa Ana-Anaheim-Irvine, CA

Children in Public Schools (91%)
32 districts, 602 schools, 515,222 students

Children in Private Schools (9%)
Catholic: 42 schools, 17,603 students
Other religious: 85 schools, 26,958 students
Nonsectarian: 28 schools, 6,104 students

Public Library Systems: 3
749,167 books; turnover: 3.3

Colleges and Universities

Associate of Arts
9 campuses (220,305)

Baccalaureate
Laguna College of Art & Design (342)

Comprehensive
Bethesda Christian University (138/61)
California State University (31,331/6,724)
Chapman University (4,151/7,159)
Concordia University (1,480/712)
Hope IU (1,425/345)
Vanguard USC (2,126/447)

Doctoral
Chapman University (3,748/1,938)
South Baylo University (511/367)
University of California Irvine (21,285/4,757)

Public School Support .... D
Private School Options .... A+
Library Popularity .... B+
College Town .... B
College Options .... A+

Places Rated Rank: 109

Santa Barbara-Santa Maria, CA

Children in Public Schools (92%)
25 districts, 123 schools, 67,551 students

Children in Private Schools (8%)
Catholic: 9 schools, 2,604 students
Other religious: 12 schools, 1,631 students
Nonsectarian: 12 schools, 1,847 students

Public Library Systems: 2
551,242 books; turnover: 3.9

Colleges and Universities

Associate of Arts
2 campuses (46,605)

Comprehensive
Westmont College (1,374/19)

Doctoral
Antioch University (146/269)
Fielding Institute (1,626)
University of California (19,692/3,290)

Public School Support C
Private School Options .... B+
Library Popularity .... A
College Town .... A
College Options .... B+

Places Rated Rank: 64

Santa Cruz-Watsonville, CA

Children in Public Schools (92%)
13 districts, 46 schools, 36,656 students

Children in Private Schools (8%)
Catholic: 5 schools, 1,061 students
Other religious: 6 schools, 1,469 students
Nonsectarian: 6 schools, 755 students

Public Library Systems: 5
289,173 books; turnover: 2.0

Colleges and Universities

Associate of Arts
1 campus (20,652)

Comprehensive
Bethany University (649/85)
Five Branches Institute (189)

Doctoral
UC (14,529/1,527)

Public School Support C
Private School Options .... B
Library Popularity .... A
College Town .... A
College Options .... B

Places Rated Rank: 82

Santa Fe, NM

Children in Public Schools (86%)
2 districts, 41 schools, 16,375 students

Children in Private Schools (14%)
Catholic: 4 schools, 1,317 students
Other religious: 4 schools, 335 students
Nonsectarian: 10 schools, 1,044 students

Public Library Systems: 1
689,184 books; turnover: 4.2

Colleges and Universities

Associate of Arts
1 campus (9,747)

Baccalaureate
Institute of American Indian Culture (177)

Comprehensive
College Santa Fe (1,950/632)
Southwestern College (170)
St. John's College (459/141)

Public School Support .... D+
Private School Options .... B
Library Popularity C
College Town C
College Options C

Places Rated Rank: 315

Santa Rosa-Petaluma, CA

Children in Public Schools (93%)
43 districts, 184 schools, 72,395 students

Children in Private Schools (7%)
Catholic: 9 schools, 2,951 students
Other religious: 14 schools, 1,726 students
Nonsectarian: 8 schools, 761 students

Public Library Systems: 2
1,249,558 books; turnover: 3.5

Colleges and Universities

Associate of Arts
1 campus (38,127)

Comprehensive
Sonoma State University (7,591/1,468)

Public School Support .... C+
Private School Options .... B+
Library Popularity .... A+
College Town C
College Options .... C+

Places Rated Rank: 149

Sarasota-Bradenton-Venice, FL

Children in Public Schools (92%)
2 districts, 133 schools, 82,238 students

Children in Private Schools (8%)
Catholic: 6 schools, 2,010 students
Other religious: 24 schools, 4,776 students
Nonsectarian: 7 schools, 675 students

Public Library Systems: 1
634,758 books; turnover: 1.9

Colleges and Universities

Associate of Arts
3 campuses (15,025)

Baccalaureate
New College Florida (715)
Ringling School A & D (1,004)

REPORT CARD
Public School Support C
Private School Options.....................................A
Library Popularity ....A
College Town...D
College Options C

Places Rated Rank: 239

Savannah, GA

Children in Public Schools (87%)
3 districts, 84 schools, 50,433 students

Children in Private Schools (13%)
Catholic: 8 schools, 2,362 students
Other religious: 8 schools, 3,614 students
Nonsectarian: 4 schools, 1,593 students

Public Library Systems: 21
1,185,619 books; turnover: 1.8

Colleges and Universities

Associate of Arts
1 campus (6,483)

Comprehensive
Armstrong Atlantic State University (7,484/1,361)
Savannah College A & D (5,634/1,080)
Savannah State University (3,075/187)

REPORT CARD
Public School Support ....B+
Private School Options.....................................B+
Library Popularity ....D+
College Town...B
College Options ....C+

Places Rated Rank: 181

Scranton–Wilkes-Barre, PA

Children in Public Schools (85%)
34 districts, 134 schools, 73,984 students

Children in Private Schools (15%)
Catholic: 42 schools, 11,127 students
Other religious: 19 schools, 1,859 students
Nonsectarian: 2 schools, 410 students

Public Library Systems: 6
6,754,063 books; turnover: 4.8

Colleges and Universities

Associate of Arts
3 campuses (11,584)

Comprehensive
Keystone College (1,814)
King's College (2,254/256)
Penn State University (1,634/401)
Wilkes University (2,306/4,414)

Doctoral
Baptist Bible College & Sem (775/393)
College Misericordia (2,022/257)
Marywood University (1,893/1,718)
University of Scranton (4,363/847)

REPORT CARD
Public School Support ....A
Private School Options.....................................A
Library Popularity ....D+
College Town...B
College Options ....B+

Places Rated Rank: 111

Seattle-Bellevue-Everett, WA

Children in Public Schools (92%)
34 districts, 708 schools, 361,811 students

Children in Private Schools (8%)
Catholic: 43 schools, 15,320 students
Other religious: 69 schools, 13,108 students
Nonsectarian: 33 schools, 4,972 students

Public Library Systems: 1
393,259 books; turnover: 2.6

Colleges and Universities

Associate of Arts
13 campuses (125,052)

Baccalaureate
Cornish College Arts (772)
Henry Cogswell College (285)
Puget Sound Christian College (187)

Comprehensive
City University (2,828/3,846)
Mars Hill Graduate School (294)
Northwest University (1,161/104)
Trinity Lutheran College (167/5)
University of of Washington (1,835/323)

Doctoral
Antioch University (345/926)
Bastyr University (231/960)
Seattle Pacific University (3,277/1,046)
Seattle University (4,212/3,515)
University of Washington (33,438/12,485)

REPORT CARD
Public School Support ....D+
Private School Options.....................................A+
Library Popularity ....A+
College Town...B
College Options ....A+

Places Rated Rank: 42

Sebastian-Vero Beach, FL

Children in Public Schools (90%)
1 districts, 28 schools, 16,942 students

Children in Private Schools (10%)
Catholic: 1 school, 299 students
Other religious: 8 schools, 1,399 students
Nonsectarian: 1 school, 92 students

REPORT CARD
Public School Support ....D
Private School Options.....................................C
Library Popularity ....B
College Town...D
College Options ....D

Places Rated Rank: 358

Sheboygan, WI

Children in Public Schools (88%)
9 districts, 46 schools, 19,329 students

Children in Private Schools (12%)
Catholic: 7 schools, 1,119 students
Other religious: 13 schools, 1,541 students

Public Library Systems: 8
546,552 books; turnover: 2.3

Colleges and Universities

Comprehensive
Lakeland College (4,426/841)

REPORT CARD
Public School Support ....A+
Private School Options.....................................C+
Library Popularity C

Places Rated Rank: 234

Sherman-Denison, TX

Children in Public Schools (97%)
13 districts, 67 schools, 21,031 students

Children in Private Schools (3%)
Catholic: 1 school, 119 students
Other religious: 3 schools, 505 students

Public Library Systems: 7
350,373 books; turnover: 1.9

Colleges and Universities
Associate of Arts
1 campus (5,588)
Comprehensive
Austin College (1,337/60)

Places Rated Rank: 341

Shreveport-Bossier City, LA

Children in Public Schools (95%)
3 districts, 122 schools, 67,416 students

Children in Private Schools (5%)
Catholic: 4 schools, 1,323 students
Other religious: 7 schools, 1,451 students
Nonsectarian: 3 schools, 741 students

Public Library Systems: 3
971,396 books; turnover: 1.9

Colleges and Universities
Associate of Arts
3 campuses (15,240)
Comprehensive
Centenary College (882/235)
Louisiana State University (3,655/875)
Doctoral
LSU Health Sciences (91/597)

Places Rated Rank: 269

Sioux City, IA-NE-SD

Children in Public Schools (91%)
24 districts, 82 schools, 25,334 students

Children in Private Schools (9%)
Catholic: 10 schools, 2,053 students
Other religious: 2 schools, 305 students

Public Library Systems: 16
574,841 books; turnover: 1.6

Colleges and Universities
Associate of Arts
2 campuses (8,131)
Comprehensive
Briar Cliff University (1,197/26)
Morningside College (1,055/482)

Places Rated Rank: 312

Sioux Falls, SD

Children in Public Schools (88%)
24 districts, 116 schools, 32,857 students

Children in Private Schools (12%)
Catholic: 9 schools, 2,639 students
Other religious: 9 schools, 1,780 students

Public Library Systems: 11
600,701 books; turnover: 2.6

Colleges and Universities
Associate of Arts
5 campuses (4,696)
Comprehensive
Augustana College (1,948/61)
University of Sioux Falls (1,613/349)
Doctoral
North American Baptist Seminary (152)

Places Rated Rank: 313

✓ South Bend-Mishawaka, IN-MI

Children in Public Schools (85%)
13 districts, 108 schools, 48,466 students

Children in Private Schools (15%)
Catholic: 19 schools, 6,216 students
Other religious: 16 schools, 1,683 students
Nonsectarian: 1 school, 424 students

Public Library Systems: 7
1,002,845 books; turnover: 3.8

Colleges and Universities
Associate of Arts
2 campuses (12,474)
Baccalaureate
Holy Cross College (551)
St. Mary's College (1,630)
Comprehensive
Bethel College (2,276/**143**)
Indiana University (8,415/2,155)
Doctoral
University of Notre Dame (8,583/3,747)

Places Rated Rank: 32

Spartanburg, SC

Children in Public Schools (96%)
11 districts, 78 schools, 45,242 students

Children in Private Schools (4%)
Catholic: 1 school, 140 students

Other religious: 5 schools, 1,130 students
Nonsectarian: 1 school, 461 students

Public Library Systems: 1
813,177 books; turnover: 1.8

Colleges and Universities
Associate of Arts
2 campuses (6,684)

Baccalaureate
Wofford College (1,191)

Comprehensive
Converse College (787/3,035)
USC (5,115/234)

REPORT CARD

Public School Support	B+
Private School Options	C
Library Popularity	D+
College Town	C
College Options	C+

Places Rated Rank: 273

Spokane, WA

Children in Public Schools (92%)
15 districts, 167 schools, 72,664 students

Children in Private Schools (8%)
Catholic: 14 schools, 2,979 students
Other religious: 17 schools, 2,553 students
Nonsectarian: 3 schools, 479 students

Public Library Systems: 3
942,542 books; turnover: 3.9

Colleges and Universities
Associate of Arts
2 campuses (28,352)

Comprehensive
Whitworth College (2,201/433)

Doctoral
Eastern Washington University (12,048/1,861)
Gonzaga University (4,057/2,083)

REPORT CARD

Public School Support	D+
Private School Options	B+
Library Popularity	A
College Town	A
College Options	B+

Places Rated Rank: 71

Springfield, IL

Children in Public Schools (87%)
22 districts, 127 schools, 32,010 students

Children in Private Schools (13%)
Catholic: 8 schools, 3,107 students
Other religious: 9 schools, 1,606 students

Public Library Systems: 13
640,534 books; turnover: 1.7

Colleges and Universities
Associate of Arts
2 campuses (15,723)

Doctoral
University of Illinois (3,220/2,673)

REPORT CARD

Public School Support	B
Private School Options	C+
Library Popularity	D+
College Town	B+
College Options	C+

Places Rated Rank: 212

✓ Springfield, MA

Children in Public Schools (91%)
91 districts, 241 schools, 108,963 students

Children in Private Schools (9%)
Catholic: 21 schools, 6,310 students
Other religious: 11 schools, 1,404 students
Nonsectarian: 10 schools, 2,683 students

Public Library Systems: 72
2,942,787 books; turnover: 1.7

Colleges and Universities
Associate of Arts
3 campuses (23,726)

Baccalaureate
Amherst College (2,458)
Hampshire College (1,407)

Comprehensive
Bay Path College (1,477/72)
College Our Lady the Elms (976/288)
Mount Holyoke College (2,259/230)
Western New England College (3,639/1,764)
Westfield State College (4,882/1,103)

Doctoral
American International College (1,360/591)
Smith College (2,784/510)
Springfield College (4,034/2,143)
University of Mass (22,035/7,009)

REPORT CARD

Public School Support	A+
Private School Options	A
Library Popularity	D+
College Town	A
College Options	A

Places Rated Rank: 35

Springfield, MO

Children in Public Schools (95%)
27 districts, 147 schools, 60,046 students

Children in Private Schools (5%)
Catholic: 4 schools, 1,323 students
Other religious: 11 schools, 1,338 students
Nonsectarian: 1 school, 371 students

Public Library Systems: 6
634,269 books; turnover: 5.5

Colleges and Universities
Associate of Arts
5 campuses (12,690)

Baccalaureate
Central Bible College (878)
Cox College Nursing (666)

Comprehensive
Baptist Bible College & Graduate Sschool (669/56)
Drury University (5,542/547)
Evangel University (1,887/80)

Doctoral
Assemblies of God Seminary (662)
Forest Institute Professional Psychology (265)
Missouri State University (17,724/4,463)
Southwest Baptist University (3,101/1,557)

REPORT CARD

Public School Support	D+
Private School Options	B
Library Popularity	A+
College Town	A
College Options	A

Places Rated Rank: 61

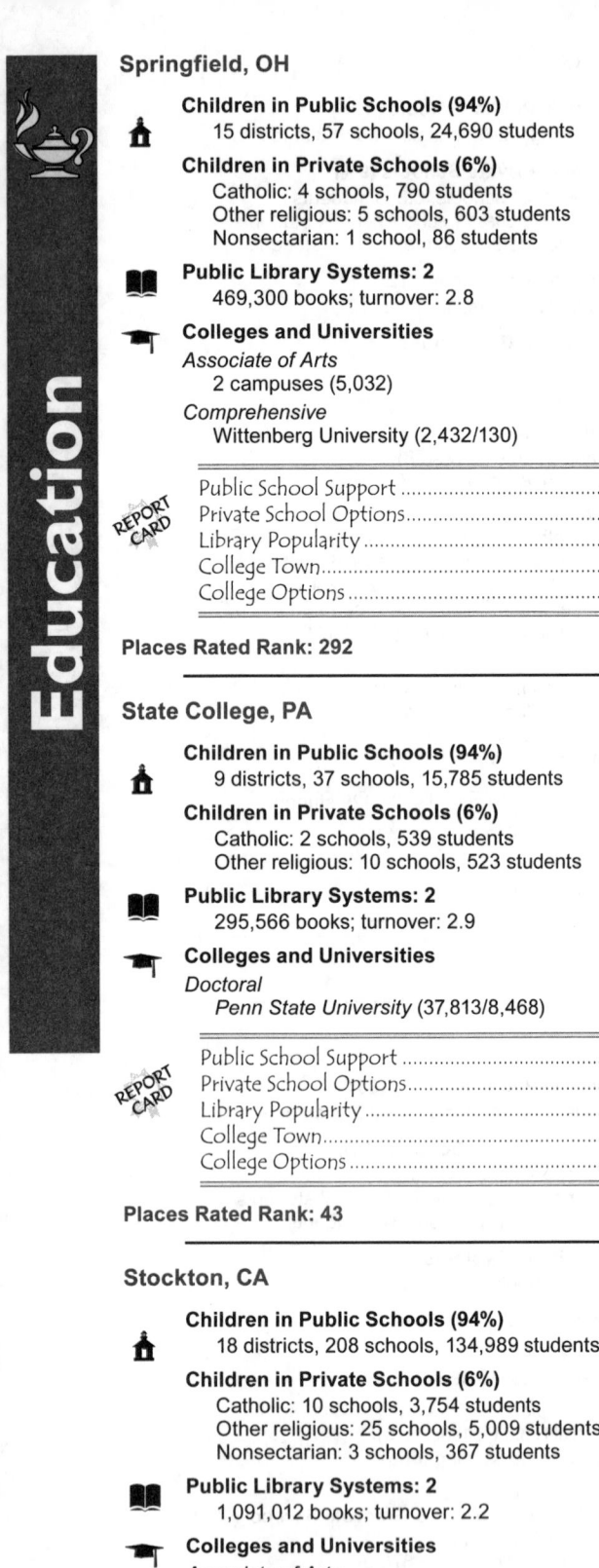

Springfield, OH

Children in Public Schools (94%)
15 districts, 57 schools, 24,690 students

Children in Private Schools (6%)
Catholic: 4 schools, 790 students
Other religious: 5 schools, 603 students
Nonsectarian: 1 school, 86 students

Public Library Systems: 2
469,300 books; turnover: 2.8

Colleges and Universities
Associate of Arts
2 campuses (5,032)
Comprehensive
Wittenberg University (2,432/130)

Public School Support	B
Private School Options	C+
Library Popularity	B
College Town	D+
College Options	D+

Places Rated Rank: 292

State College, PA

Children in Public Schools (94%)
9 districts, 37 schools, 15,785 students

Children in Private Schools (6%)
Catholic: 2 schools, 539 students
Other religious: 10 schools, 523 students

Public Library Systems: 2
295,566 books; turnover: 2.9

Colleges and Universities
Doctoral
Penn State University (37,813/8,468)

Public School Support	A+
Private School Options	D+
Library Popularity	B
College Town	A+
College Options	A

Places Rated Rank: 43

Stockton, CA

Children in Public Schools (94%)
18 districts, 208 schools, 134,989 students

Children in Private Schools (6%)
Catholic: 10 schools, 3,754 students
Other religious: 25 schools, 5,009 students
Nonsectarian: 3 schools, 367 students

Public Library Systems: 2
1,091,012 books; turnover: 2.2

Colleges and Universities
Associate of Arts
2 campuses (26,374)
Baccalaureate
Humphreys College (2,797)
Doctoral
University of Pacific (3,614/3,075)

Public School Support	D+
Private School Options	A
Library Popularity	C
College Town	D+
College Options	C+

Places Rated Rank: 263

Sumter, SC

Children in Public Schools (92%)
3 districts, 27 schools, 18,503 students

Children in Private Schools (8%)
Catholic: 2 schools, 207 students
Other religious: 2 schools, 38 students
Nonsectarian: 2 schools, 1,306 students

Public Library Systems: 1
170,905 books; turnover: 1.8

Colleges and Universities
Associate of Arts
2 campuses (6,201)
Baccalaureate
Morris College (1,134)

Public School Support	D
Private School Options	C
Library Popularity	D+
College Town	D+
College Options	D

Places Rated Rank: 366

✓Syracuse, NY

Children in Public Schools (93%)
41 districts, 189 schools, 113,147 students

Children in Private Schools (7%)
Catholic: 23 schools, 6,427 students
Other religious: 12 schools, 1,447 students
Nonsectarian: 2 schools, 622 students

Public Library Systems: 38
1,729,397 books; turnover: 3.2

Colleges and Universities
Associate of Arts
3 campuses (14,153)
Baccalaureate
Cazenovia College (1,287)
Morrisville State College (3,963)
Comprehensive
Colgate University (2,874/8)
Le Moyne College (3,279/1,106)
SUNY College Oswego (8,283/2,186)
Doctoral
SUNY College Environmental Science (1,604/583)
SUNY Health Science Center (323/923)
Syracuse University (18,961/7,625)

Public School Support	A+
Private School Options	B+
Library Popularity	B+
College Town	A
College Options	A

Places Rated Rank: 8

Tacoma, WA

Children in Public Schools (94%)
15 districts, 253 schools, 129,216 students

Children in Private Schools (6%)
Catholic: 8 schools, 3,147 students
Other religious: 21 schools, 4,851 students
Nonsectarian: 2 schools, 155 students

Public Library Systems: 4
3,183,903 books; turnover: 2.5

Colleges and Universities
Associate of Arts
5 campuses (55,595)
Comprehensive
Pacific Lutheran University (3,497/2,104)

University of Puget Sound (2,607/349)
University of Washington (2,000/502)

Doctoral
Faith Evangelical Lutheran Sem (34/222)

REPORT CARD
Public School Support ....D+
Private School Options..................................B+
Library Popularity ....C+
College Town...C
College Options ....B

Places Rated Rank: 229

Tallahassee, FL

🏫 **Children in Public Schools (91%)**
6 districts, 100 schools, 46,878 students

Children in Private Schools (9%)
Catholic: 2 schools, 560 students
Other religious: 13 schools, 2,235 students
Nonsectarian: 7 schools, 1,765 students

📖 **Public Library Systems: 3**

822,533 books; turnover: 2.9

🎓 **Colleges and Universities**
Associate of Arts
2 campuses (19,343)

Baccalaureate
Flagler College (430)

Doctoral
Florida A$M University (12,011/2,177)
Florida State University (32,938/9,346)

REPORT CARD
Public School Support ....D
Private School Options..................................B
Library Popularity ....B+
College Town...A+
College Options ....A

Places Rated Rank: 96

Tampa-St. Petersburg-Clearwater, FL

🏫 **Children in Public Schools (91%)**
5 districts, 528 schools, 382,739 students

Children in Private Schools (9%)
Catholic: 35 schools, 12,899 students
Other religious: 111 schools, 20,507 students
Nonsectarian: 26 schools, 4,931 students

📖 **Public Library Systems: 5**
4,860,184 books; turnover: 2.9

🎓 **Colleges and Universities**
Associate of Arts
6 campuses (49,553)

Baccalaureate
Clearwater Christian College (686)
Eckerd College (1,781)
Florida College (522)
St. Petersburg College (35,021)
Trinity College Florida (241)

Comprehensive
St. Leo University (22,781/782)
University of Tampa (4,651/694)

Doctoral
University of South Florida (38,168/12,651)

REPORT CARD
Public School Support ....D
Private School Options..................................A+
Library Popularity ....B+
College Town...C+
College Options ....A+

Places Rated Rank: 99

Terre Haute, IN

🏫 **Children in Public Schools (97%)**
8 districts, 58 schools, 27,423 students

Children in Private Schools (3%)
Catholic: 4 schools, 472 students
Other religious: 3 schools, 265 students

📖 **Public Library Systems: 5**
437,742 books; turnover: 2.6

🎓 **Colleges and Universities**
Associate of Arts
1 campus (6,637)

Comprehensive
Rose-Hulman IT (1,779/192)
St. Mary-of-the-Woods College (1,705/145)

Doctoral
Indiana State University (12,530/2,751)

REPORT CARD
Public School Support ....B
Private School Options..................................D
Library Popularity ....B
College Town...A+
College Options ....B

Places Rated Rank: 180

Texarkana, TX-Texarkana, AR

🏫 **Children in Public Schools (97%)**
18 districts, 60 schools, 23,429 students

Children in Private Schools (3%)
Other religious: 4 schools, 726 students

📖 **Public Library Systems: 5**
222,960 books; turnover: 1.7

🎓 **Colleges and Universities**
Associate of Arts
1 campus (6,039)

Comprehensive
Texas A&M University (1,296/896)

REPORT CARD
Public School Support ....B
Private School Options..................................D
Library Popularity ....D+
College Town...D+
College Options ....D+

Places Rated Rank: 345

✓Toledo, OH

🏫 **Children in Public Schools (87%)**
78 districts, 254 schools, 108,779 students

Children in Private Schools (13%)
Catholic: 42 schools, 13,622 students
Other religious: 14 schools, 2,351 students
Nonsectarian: 1 school, 455 students

📖 **Public Library Systems: 17**
3,493,116 books; turnover: 2.6

🎓 **Colleges and Universities**
Associate of Arts
2 campuses (26,632)

Baccalaureate
Mercy College (948)

Comprehensive
Lourdes College (1,427/96)

Doctoral
Bowling Green State University (17,081/5,089)
Medical University Ohio (1,317)
University of Toledo (20,120/4,492)

REPORT CARD
Public School Support ....B+
Private School Options..................................A

Library Popularity .... B
College Town .... A
College Options .... A

Places Rated Rank: 26

Topeka, KS

Children in Public Schools (92%)
22 districts, 109 schools, 38,017 students

Children in Private Schools (8%)
Catholic: 9 schools, 2,338 students
Other religious: 5 schools, 780 students
Nonsectarian: 2 schools, 350 students

Public Library Systems: 15
602,085 books; turnover: 4.0

Colleges and Universities
Comprehensive
Washburn University (7,357/1,344)

REPORT CARD
Public School Support .... A
Private School Options .... B
Library Popularity .... A
College Town .... D+
College Options C

Places Rated Rank: 167

Trenton-Ewing, NJ

Children in Public Schools (85%)
18 districts, 101 schools, 55,820 students

Children in Private Schools (15%)
Catholic: 15 schools, 5,948 students
Other religious: 7 schools, 1,433 students
Nonsectarian: 7 schools, 2,660 students

Public Library Systems: 6
1,579,443 books; turnover: 1.5

Colleges and Universities
Associate of Arts
3 campuses (10,200)
Comprehensive
College of NJ (6,332/1,548)
Rider University (4,812/1,533)
Thomas Edison SC (10,750/250)
Doctoral
Princeton Theological Seminary (796)
Princeton University (4,676/2,012)

REPORT CARD
Public School Support .... A+
Private School Options .... A
Library Popularity .... D
College Town .... A
College Options .... B+

Places Rated Rank: 74

Tucson, AZ

Children in Public Schools (94%)
87 districts, 343 schools, 145,806 students

Children in Private Schools (6%)
Catholic: 10 schools, 4,575 students
Other religious: 21 schools, 2,872 students
Nonsectarian: 7 schools, 1,147 students

Public Library Systems: 3
1,315,310 books; turnover: 5.1

Colleges and Universities
Associate of Arts
2 campuses (53,267)

Baccalaureate
IInstitute Americas (502)
Doctoral
University of Arizona (40,641/11,173)

REPORT CARD
Public School Support .... D
Private School Options .... A
Library Popularity .... A+
College Town .... A
College Options .... A+

Places Rated Rank: 56

Tulsa, OK

Children in Public Schools (94%)
73 districts, 323 schools, 155,413 students

Children in Private Schools (6%)
Catholic: 11 schools, 3,292 students
Other religious: 25 schools, 6,411 students
Nonsectarian: 3 schools, 492 students

Public Library Systems: 21
1,989,208 books; turnover: 2.2

Colleges and Universities
Associate of Arts
3 campuses (27,316)
Baccalaureate
Metropolitan College (157)
Oklahoma State University (4,016)
Rogers State University (4,896)
Doctoral
College Osteopathic Medicine (526)
Oral Roberts University (4,478/942)
University of Tulsa (2,924/1,658)

REPORT CARD
Public School Support .... D
Private School Options .... A
Library Popularity C
College Town C
College Options .... B

Places Rated Rank: 248

Tuscaloosa, AL

Children in Public Schools (92%)
4 districts, 66 schools, 30,780 students

Children in Private Schools (8%)
Catholic: 2 schools, 772 students
Other religious: 5 schools, 1,191 students
Nonsectarian: 4 schools, 866 students

Public Library Systems: 5
230,274 books; turnover: 2.5

Colleges and Universities
Associate of Arts
1 campus (8,256)
Baccalaureate
Stillman College (1,384)
Doctoral
University of Alabama (18,045/5,548)

REPORT CARD
Public School Support .... C+
Private School Options .... B
Library Popularity .... C+
College Town .... A+
College Options .... B+

Places Rated Rank: 129

Tyler, TX

Children in Public Schools (97%)
11 districts, 75 schools, 33,019 students

🏫 **Children in Private Schools (3%)**
Catholic: 1 school, 390 students
Other religious: 5 schools, 756 students

📖 **Public Library Systems: 6**
265,192 books; turnover: 1.2

🎓 **Colleges and Universities**
Associate of Arts
1 campus (13,153)

Comprehensive
Texas College (1,035)
UT Tyler (4,481/1,938)

REPORT CARD
Public School Support .... B
Private School Options.....................................D+
Library Popularity .... D
College Town.. B
College Options...C+

Places Rated Rank: 300

Utica-Rome, NY

🏫 **Children in Public Schools (96%)**
30 districts, 117 schools, 48,462 students

Children in Private Schools (4%)
Catholic: 7 schools, 1,883 students
Other religious: 4 schools, 158 students

📖 **Public Library Systems: 34**
952,577 books; turnover: 1.6

🎓 **Colleges and Universities**
Associate of Arts
5 campuses (13,300)

Baccalaureate
Hamilton College (1,894)

Comprehensive
SUNY IT (2,519/805)
Utica College (2,614/415)

REPORT CARD
Public School Support ....A+
Private School Options.....................................D+
Library Popularity ....D+
College Town...C
College Options...C+

Places Rated Rank: 263

Valdosta, GA

🏫 **Children in Public Schools (92%)**
5 districts, 33 schools, 21,282 students

Children in Private Schools (8%)
Catholic: 1 school, 283 students
Other religious: 9 schools, 1,212 students
Nonsectarian: 1 school, 398 students

📖 **Public Library Systems: 2**
293,336 books; turnover: 1.6

🎓 **Colleges and Universities**
Associate of Arts
2 campuses (5,313)

Doctoral
Valdosta State University (10,336/2,202)

REPORT CARD
Public School Support .... B
Private School Options.....................................C+
Library Popularity .... D
College Town...A+
College Options...C+

Places Rated Rank: 192

Vallejo-Fairfield, CA

🏫 **Children in Public Schools (92%)**
9 districts, 115 schools, 72,667 students

Children in Private Schools (8%)
Catholic: 7 schools, 2,820 students
Other religious: 17 schools, 3,192 students
Nonsectarian: 2 schools, 144 students

📖 **Public Library Systems: 3**
627,520 books; turnover: 3.8

🎓 **Colleges and Universities**
Associate of Arts
1 campus (18,596)

Baccalaureate
Cal Maritime Academy (714)

REPORT CARD
Public School Support ....D+
Private School Options.....................................B+
Library Popularity ....A
College Town..D
College Options...C

Places Rated Rank: 255

Victoria, TX

🏫 **Children in Public Schools (93%)**
7 districts, 48 schools, 21,130 students

Children in Private Schools (7%)
Catholic: 4 schools, 876 students
Other religious: 5 schools, 667 students

📖 **Public Library Systems: 3**
241,860 books; turnover: 1.9

🎓 **Colleges and Universities**
Associate of Arts
1 campus (5,885)

Comprehensive
University of Houston (1,361/1,619)

REPORT CARD
Public School Support .... B
Private School Options.....................................D+
Library Popularity ....D+
College Town..C
College Options...D+

Places Rated Rank: 326

Vineland-Millville-Bridgeton, NJ

🏫 **Children in Public Schools (93%)**
15 districts, 34 schools, 26,448 students

Children in Private Schools (7%)
Catholic: 4 schools, 1,084 students
Other religious: 2 schools, 590 students
Nonsectarian: 2 schools, 285 students

📖 **Public Library Systems: 4**
333,681 books; turnover: 1.0

🎓 **Colleges and Universities**
Associate of Arts
1 campus (3,757)

REPORT CARD
Public School Support ....B+
Private School Options.....................................C+
Library Popularity ....D
College Town..D
College Options...D

Places Rated Rank: 349

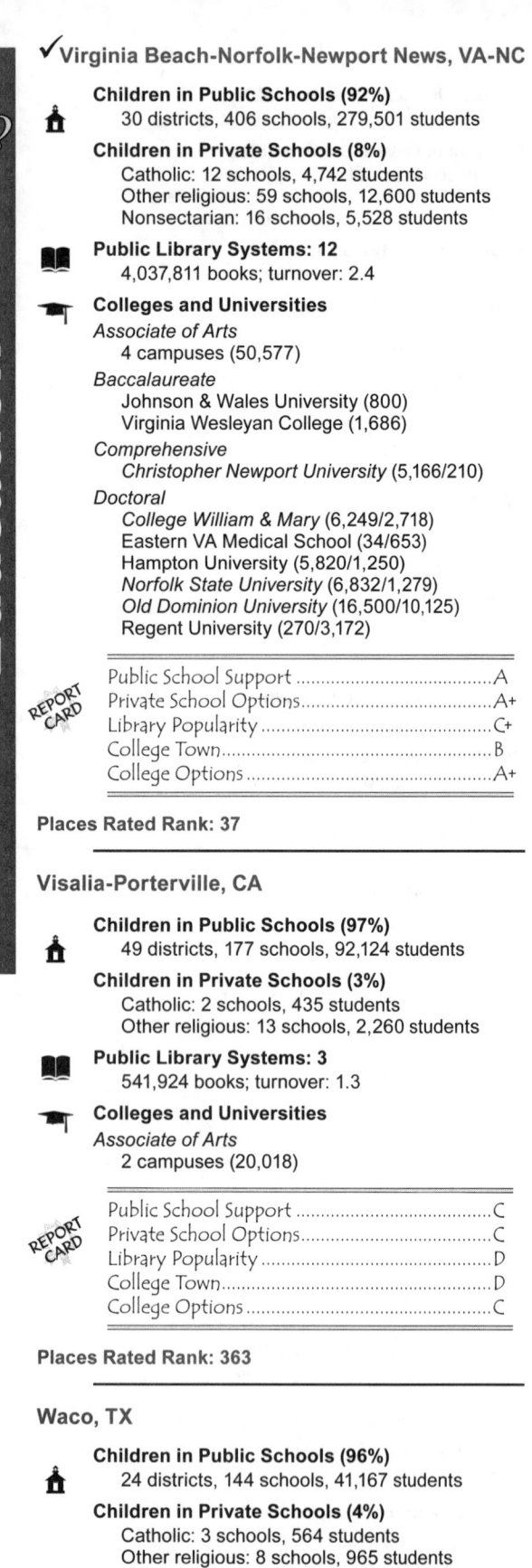

✓Virginia Beach-Norfolk-Newport News, VA-NC

Children in Public Schools (92%)
30 districts, 406 schools, 279,501 students

Children in Private Schools (8%)
Catholic: 12 schools, 4,742 students
Other religious: 59 schools, 12,600 students
Nonsectarian: 16 schools, 5,528 students

Public Library Systems: 12
4,037,811 books; turnover: 2.4

Colleges and Universities

Associate of Arts
4 campuses (50,577)

Baccalaureate
Johnson & Wales University (800)
Virginia Wesleyan College (1,686)

Comprehensive
Christopher Newport University (5,166/210)

Doctoral
College William & Mary (6,249/2,718)
Eastern VA Medical School (34/653)
Hampton University (5,820/1,250)
Norfolk State University (6,832/1,279)
Old Dominion University (16,500/10,125)
Regent University (270/3,172)

Public School Support ....A
Private School Options..................................A+
Library Popularity ....C+
College Town...B
College Options ....A+

Places Rated Rank: 37

Visalia-Porterville, CA

Children in Public Schools (97%)
49 districts, 177 schools, 92,124 students

Children in Private Schools (3%)
Catholic: 2 schools, 435 students
Other religious: 13 schools, 2,260 students

Public Library Systems: 3
541,924 books; turnover: 1.3

Colleges and Universities

Associate of Arts
2 campuses (20,018)

Public School Support C
Private School Options....................................C
Library Popularity ....D
College Town...D
College Options C

Places Rated Rank: 363

Waco, TX

Children in Public Schools (96%)
24 districts, 144 schools, 41,167 students

Children in Private Schools (4%)
Catholic: 3 schools, 564 students
Other religious: 8 schools, 965 students
Nonsectarian: 1 school, 184 students

Public Library Systems: 6
393,300 books; turnover: 1.5

Colleges and Universities

Associate of Arts
2 campuses (16,786)

Doctoral
Baylor University (12,630/2,681)

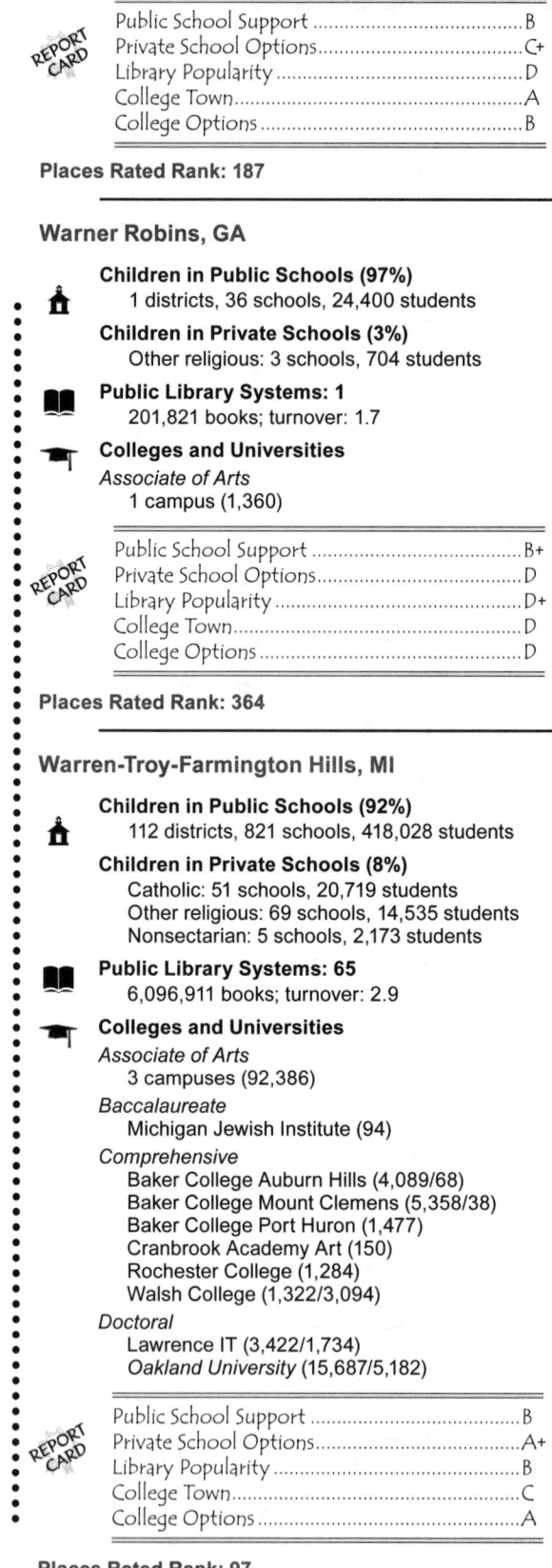

Public School Support ....B
Private School Options..................................C+
Library Popularity ....D
College Town...A
College Options ....B

Places Rated Rank: 187

Warner Robins, GA

Children in Public Schools (97%)
1 districts, 36 schools, 24,400 students

Children in Private Schools (3%)
Other religious: 3 schools, 704 students

Public Library Systems: 1
201,821 books; turnover: 1.7

Colleges and Universities

Associate of Arts
1 campus (1,360)

Public School Support ....B+
Private School Options....................................D
Library Popularity ....D+
College Town...D
College Options ....D

Places Rated Rank: 364

Warren-Troy-Farmington Hills, MI

Children in Public Schools (92%)
112 districts, 821 schools, 418,028 students

Children in Private Schools (8%)
Catholic: 51 schools, 20,719 students
Other religious: 69 schools, 14,535 students
Nonsectarian: 5 schools, 2,173 students

Public Library Systems: 65
6,096,911 books; turnover: 2.9

Colleges and Universities

Associate of Arts
3 campuses (92,386)

Baccalaureate
Michigan Jewish Institute (94)

Comprehensive
Baker College Auburn Hills (4,089/68)
Baker College Mount Clemens (5,358/38)
Baker College Port Huron (1,477)
Cranbrook Academy Art (150)
Rochester College (1,284)
Walsh College (1,322/3,094)

Doctoral
Lawrence IT (3,422/1,734)
Oakland University (15,687/5,182)

Public School Support ....B
Private School Options..................................A+
Library Popularity ....B
College Town...C
College Options ....A

Places Rated Rank: 97

✓Washington-Arlington-Alexandria, DC-VA-MD-WV

Children in Public Schools (90%)
72 districts, 1035 schools, 649,546 students

Children in Private Schools (10%)
Catholic: 87 schools, 32,815 students
Other religious: 114 schools, 26,529 students
Nonsectarian: 47 schools, 9,575 students

(Sidebar: Education)

Public Library Systems: 16
10,650,133 books; turnover: 3.2

Colleges and Universities
Associate of Arts
4 campuses (89,148)
Comprehensive
Capitol College (443/719)
Corcoran College A & D (1,028)
Dominican House Studies (73)
Shepherd University (5,794/56)
Southeastern University (870/404)
Trinity Washington University (1,153/862)
University of of Mary Washington (4,706/879)
University of District Columbia (9,504/235)
Washington Bible College (377/409)
Washington Theological Union (244)
Wesley Theological Seminary (504)
Doctoral
American University (6,013/5,682)
Bowie State University (5,243/2,380)
Catholic University (2,875/3,356)
Gallaudet University (1,334/651)
George Mason University (21,251/16,518)
George Washington University (12,425/16,291)
Georgetown University (7,904/7,524)
Howard University (7,313/3,704)
Marymount University (2,547/2,033)
UM College Park (29,248/11,431)
UM University College (26,641/10,883)

Public School Support ....A+
Private School Options..A+
Library Popularity ....B+
College Town..A
College Options ....A+

Places Rated Rank: 1

Waterloo-Cedar Falls, IA

Children in Public Schools (88%)
15 districts, 73 schools, 23,496 students

Children in Private Schools (12%)
Catholic: 8 schools, 2,284 students
Other religious: 6 schools, 896 students

Public Library Systems: 19
592,706 books; turnover: 2.1

Colleges and Universities
Associate of Arts
1 campus (7,867)
Baccalaureate
Wartburg College (1,794)
Comprehensive
Allen College (324/41)
Doctoral
University of Northern Iowa (13,786/3,293)

Public School Support ....A
Private School Options..C
Library Popularity C
College Town..A+
College Options ....B

Places Rated Rank: 131

Wausau, WI

Children in Public Schools (87%)
9 districts, 45 schools, 19,805 students

Children in Private Schools (13%)
Catholic: 13 schools, 1,940 students
Other religious: 9 schools, 953 students

Public Library Systems: 1
345,375 books; turnover: 2.2

Colleges and Universities
Associate of Arts
1 campus (5,951)

Public School Support ....A
Private School Options..C+
Library Popularity C
College Town..D
College Options ....D

Places Rated Rank: 302

Weirton-Steubenville, WV-OH

Children in Public Schools (90%)
9 districts, 55 schools, 18,878 students

Children in Private Schools (10%)
Catholic: 10 schools, 1,912 students
Other religious: 2 schools, 224 students

Public Library Systems: 5
370,785 books; turnover: 2.9

Colleges and Universities
Associate of Arts
2 campuses (2,498)
Baccalaureate
Bethany College (919)
Comprehensive
Franciscan University (2,017/881)

Public School Support ....B+
Private School Options..D+
Library Popularity ....B+
College Town..D+
College Options ....D+

Places Rated Rank: 260

Wenatchee, WA

Children in Public Schools (98%)
14 districts, 55 schools, 19,443 students

Children in Private Schools (2%)
Other religious: 4 schools, 447 students
Nonsectarian: 1 school, 28 students

Public Library Systems: 1
669,789 books; turnover: 2.2

Colleges and Universities
Associate of Arts
1 campus (5,077)

Public School Support ....D+
Private School Options..D+
Library Popularity C
College Town..D
College Options ....D

Places Rated Rank: 367

West Palm Beach-Boca Raton-Boynton Beach, FL

Children in Public Schools (88%)
2 districts, 232 schools, 174,741 students

Children in Private Schools (12%)
Catholic: 13 schools, 5,014 students
Other religious: 40 schools, 12,777 students
Nonsectarian: 22 schools, 5,072 students

Public Library Systems: 4
1,909,975 books; turnover: 4.2

Colleges and Universities
Associate of Arts
1 campus (39,326)

Baccalaureate
Northwood University (1,134)
Comprehensive
Everglades University (638/1)
Palm Beach Atlantic University (2,484/746)
Doctoral
Florida Atlantic University (28,356/5,898)
Lynn University (2,191/550)

REPORT CARD

Public School Support ....D+
Private School Options.......................................A+
Library Popularity ....A+
College Town..B
College Options ....A

Places Rated Rank: 65

Wheeling, WV-OH

Children in Public Schools (84%)
11 districts, 54 schools, 19,979 students

Children in Private Schools (16%)
Catholic: 14 schools, 2,900 students
Other religious: 7 schools, 278 students
Nonsectarian: 2 schools, 517 students

Public Library Systems: 6
578,065 books; turnover: 1.9

Colleges and Universities
Associate of Arts
2 campuses (6,810)
Baccalaureate
West Liberty State College (2,729)
Comprehensive
Ohio University Eastern (1,239/189)
Doctoral
Wheeling Jesuit University (1,459/609)

REPORT CARD

Public School Support ....A
Private School Options.......................................B
Library Popularity C
College Town..B
College Options C

Places Rated Rank: 191

Wichita, KS

Children in Public Schools (90%)
31 districts, 232 schools, 103,139 students

Children in Private Schools (10%)
Catholic: 23 schools, 7,162 students
Other religious: 14 schools, 2,246 students
Nonsectarian: 2 schools, 1,719 students

Public Library Systems: 35
1,798,687 books; turnover: 1.7

Colleges and Universities
Associate of Arts
3 campuses (17,124)
Baccalaureate
Bethel College (533)
Comprehensive
Friends University (3,452/777)
Newman University (2,627/640)
Doctoral
Wichita State University (15,161/4,768)

REPORT CARD

Public School Support C
Private School Options.......................................A
Library Popularity ....D+
College Town..B+
College Options ....B+

Places Rated Rank: 182

Wichita Falls, TX

Children in Public Schools (97%)
16 districts, 72 schools, 26,139 students

Children in Private Schools (3%)
Catholic: 1 school, 309 students
Other religious: 4 schools, 536 students

Public Library Systems: 6
289,969 books; turnover: 2.4

Colleges and Universities
Comprehensive
Midwestern State University (6,782/1,047)

REPORT CARD

Public School Support ....A
Private School Options.......................................D
Library Popularity ....C+
College Town..C+
College Options C

Places Rated Rank: 275

Williamsport, PA

Children in Public Schools (95%)
10 districts, 38 schools, 17,509 students

Children in Private Schools (5%)
Catholic: 5 schools, 684 students
Other religious: 3 schools, 284 students
Nonsectarian: 1 school, 41 students

Public Library Systems: 6
241,857 books; turnover: 4.6

Colleges and Universities
Baccalaureate
Lycoming College (1,477)
Penn College Tech (7,267)

REPORT CARD

Public School Support ....A+
Private School Options.......................................C
Library Popularity ....A+
College Town..C+
College Options ....D+

Places Rated Rank: 154

✓ Wilmington, DE-MD-NJ

Children in Public Schools (83%)
33 districts, 187 schools, 99,252 students

Children in Private Schools (17%)
Catholic: 28 schools, 10,867 students
Other religious: 24 schools, 5,485 students
Nonsectarian: 9 schools, 4,318 students

Public Library Systems: 11
1,404,636 books; turnover: 3.0

Colleges and Universities
Associate of Arts
4 campuses (14,325)
Comprehensive
Goldey-Beacom College (1,231/408)
Doctoral
University of Delaware (20,497/3,875)
Widener University (314/1,550)
Wilmington College (5,245/3,911)

REPORT CARD

Public School Support ....A
Private School Options.......................................A
Library Popularity ....B+
College Town..A
College Options ....A

Places Rated Rank: 14

Wilmington, NC

Children in Public Schools (96%)
5 districts, 67 schools, 42,372 students

Children in Private Schools (4%)
Catholic: 1 school, 164 students
Other religious: 8 schools, 759 students
Nonsectarian: 3 schools, 619 students

Public Library Systems: 3
578,185 books; turnover: 3.0

Colleges and Universities
Associate of Arts
2 campuses (11,145)
Doctoral
UNC Wilmington (11,575/1,220)

REPORT CARD
Public School Support C
Private School Options....................................C+
Library Popularity ....B+
College Town...B+
College Options ....B

Places Rated Rank: 176

Winchester, VA-WV

Children in Public Schools (97%)
5 districts, 37 schools, 19,224 students

Children in Private Schools (3%)
Catholic: 1 school, 182 students
Other religious: 4 schools, 477 students

Public Library Systems: 3
273,667 books; turnover: 2.5

Colleges and Universities
Associate of Arts
1 campus (7,015)
Doctoral
Shenandoah University (1,660/2,667)

REPORT CARD
Public School Support ....A+
Private School Options....................................D
Library Popularity ....C+
College Town...B+
College Options C

Places Rated Rank: 195

Winston-Salem, NC

Children in Public Schools (92%)
10 districts, 115 schools, 70,248 students

Children in Private Schools (8%)
Catholic: 3 schools, 1,008 students
Other religious: 18 schools, 3,637 students
Nonsectarian: 3 schools, 1,656 students

Public Library Systems: 2
697,420 books; turnover: 2.8

Colleges and Universities
Associate of Arts
1 campus (9,927)
Comprehensive
NC School of the Arts (757/84)
Piedmont Bible College (346/23)
Salem College (1,037/288)
Winston-Salem State University (4,830/230)
Doctoral
Wake Forest University (4,112/2,903)

REPORT CARD
Public School Support ....B
Private School Options....................................B+
Library Popularity ....B

College Town..C+
College Options ....C+

Places Rated Rank: 172

Worcester, MA

Children in Public Schools (90%)
82 districts, 252 schools, 132,628 students

Children in Private Schools (10%)
Catholic: 32 schools, 10,222 students
Other religious: 14 schools, 1,990 students
Nonsectarian: 7 schools, 2,563 students

Public Library Systems: 62
3,167,224 books; turnover: 1.5

Colleges and Universities
Associate of Arts
2 campuses (15,199)
Baccalaureate
Becker College (1,492)
College of Holy Cross (2,819)
Comprehensive
Anna Maria College (914/525)
Assumption College (2,767/392)
Atlantic Union College (583/31)
Fitchburg State College (4,257/7,045)
Nichols College (1,799/500)
Worcester State College (5,464/1,230)
Doctoral
Clark University (2,411/1,178)
University of Mass Medical School (940)
Worcester PI (3,088/1,328)

REPORT CARD
Public School Support ....A+
Private School Options....................................A
Library Popularity ....D
College Town...B
College Options ....B+

Places Rated Rank: 121

Yakima, WA

Children in Public Schools (96%)
16 districts, 95 schools, 48,883 students

Children in Private Schools (4%)
Catholic: 3 schools, 929 students
Other religious: 10 schools, 1,026 students

Public Library Systems: 2
435,383 books; turnover: 1.6

Colleges and Universities
Associate of Arts
2 campuses (7,781)
Comprehensive
Heritage University (948/863)

REPORT CARD
Public School Support ....D+
Private School Options....................................C
Library Popularity ....D+
College Town...D
College Options ....D+

Places Rated Rank: 365

York-Hanover, PA

Children in Public Schools (94%)
19 districts, 101 schools, 63,505 students

Children in Private Schools (6%)
Catholic: 7 schools, 2,033 students
Other religious: 18 schools, 1,557 students
Nonsectarian: 2 schools, 247 students

Public Library Systems: 9
554,722 books; turnover: 2.9

Colleges and Universities

Comprehensive
Penn State University (1,985/338)
York College (5,959/362)

Public School Support .... B
Private School Options....................................... B+
Library Popularity .... B
College Town.. D
College Options C

Places Rated Rank: 224

Youngstown-Warren-Boardman, OH-PA

Children in Public Schools (91%)
67 districts, 213 schools, 90,721 students

Children in Private Schools (9%)
Catholic: 27 schools, 6,969 students
Other religious: 17 schools, 1,838 students

Public Library Systems: 13
1,679,733 books; turnover: 2.7

Colleges and Universities

Associate of Arts
2 campuses (3,220)

Baccalaureate
Grove City College (2,346)
Thiel College (1,300)

Comprehensive
Penn State University (1,147/1)

Doctoral
Youngstown State University (13,645/2,363)

Public School Support .... A
Private School Options... B
Library Popularity .... B
College Town.. C+
College Options .... B

Places Rated Rank: 122

Yuba City, CA

Children in Public Schools (96%)
20 districts, 84 schools, 30,582 students

Children in Private Schools (4%)
Catholic: 2 schools, 308 students
Other religious: 6 schools, 892 students
Nonsectarian: 1 school, 75 students

Public Library Systems: 2
283,061 books; turnover: 1.4

Colleges and Universities

Associate of Arts
1 campus (14,413)

Public School Support C
Private School Options... C
Library Popularity .... D
College Town.. D+
College Options .... D+

Places Rated Rank: 352

Yuma, AZ

Children in Public Schools (97%)
15 districts, 54 schools, 36,081 students

Children in Private Schools (3%)
Catholic: 3 schools, 872 students
Other religious: 3 schools, 353 students

Public Library Systems: 2
256,164 books; turnover: 2.5

Colleges and Universities

Associate of Arts
1 campus (11,857)

Public School Support .... D
Private School Options... D
Library Popularity .... C+
College Town.. D
College Options .... D+

Places Rated Rank: 369

Education

Solving the SAT Puzzle

Average scores for 2006 on the SAT suffered their biggest one-year decline in thirty years: Seven points. The news is the latest in the college-entrance exam's up and down history.

After 17 years of unbroken decline, for instance, the average scores of students on the Scholastic Aptitude Tests (SAT), given by the College Entrance Examination Board, bottomed out in 1980 and started slowly upward in 1982. At the current rate of recovery, however, math scores were projected to match their 1963 high in the year 2000, and verbal scores not until well into the 21st century. Even more troubling was the slow rate of improving test scores between 1990 and 1999, when the percentage of students taking the test who had "A" averages in high school rose from 28 percent to 38 percent.

Two researchers point out that SAT scores started declining 18 years after the 1945 atomic bomb tests and began rising 18 years after the United States suspended all but underground atomic testing in 1963. The steepest drops in scores occurred in states nearest the bomb detonations, especially Nevada and Utah; smaller declines occurred in the northeastern and southeastern states far from the proving grounds. According to these researchers, those who blame the drop in SAT scores on television viewing, Internet surfing, the declining birth rate, changes in the number and mix of students taking the test, and poorer performance of schools are overlooking the effects of atomic fallout on the cognitive abilities of children.

In Texas, two other scholars of SAT trends have a different theory, however. The states that have produced the highest scores, they claim, are not those that spend the most money for education, nor those with a long tradition of quality public education, but those with the coldest winters. Average scores from cold-weather states are consistently higher than scores from warm-weather states. They offer two explanations for this link: (1) Research on thermal conditions and human behavior suggests that cool room temperatures reduce mistakes on tests, and (2) long winters force children to remain inside after school and on weekends, thereby favoring the family interaction so critical to pupil achievement.

Nonsense, other researchers contend, for if one were to rank the states by average total SATs, one would be, in effect, ranking them by the percentage of college-bound seniors who actually took the test. When the percentage is low, students taking the test are among the highest achievers; the more students in the test-taking pool, the more students of average ability are included.

The highest possible score on the SAT is 800 for the verbal and 800 for the math sections, for a total of 1600.

SAT Scores By State

	VERBAL	MATH	% TAKING TEST
UNITED STATES	508	520	49%
ALABAMA	567	559	10
ALASKA	523	519	52
ARIZONA	526	530	33
ARKANSAS	563	552	6
CALIFORNIA	504	522	50
COLORADO	560	560	26
CONNECTICUT	517	517	86
DELAWARE	503	502	74
DISTRICT OF COLUMBIA	490	478	79
FLORIDA	498	498	65
GEORGIA	497	496	75
HAWAII	490	516	61
IDAHO	544	542	21
ILLINOIS	594	606	10
INDIANA	504	508	66
IOWA	596	608	5
KANSAS	585	588	9
KENTUCKY	561	559	12
LOUISIANA	565	562	8
MAINE	509	505	75
MARYLAND	511	515	71
MASSACHUSETTS	520	527	86
MICHIGAN	568	579	10
MINNESOTA	592	597	11
MISSISSIPPI	564	554	4
MISSOURI	588	588	7
MONTANA	540	540	31
NEBRASKA	574	579	8
NEVADA	508	513	39

SAT Scores By State (Cont.)

	VERBAL	MATH	% TAKING TEST
NEW HAMPSHIRE	525	525	81
NEW JERSEY	503	517	86
NEW MEXICO	558	547	13
NEW YORK	497	511	92
NORTH CAROLINA	499	511	74
NORTH DAKOTA	590	605	4
OHIO	539	543	29
OKLAHOMA	570	563	7
OREGON	526	528	59
PENNSYLVANIA	501	503	75
RHODE ISLAND	503	505	72
SOUTH CAROLINA	494	499	64
SOUTH DAKOTA	589	589	5
TENNESSEE	572	563	16
TEXAS	493	502	54
UTAH	566	557	7
VERMONT	521	517	67
VIRGINIA	516	514	73
WASHINGTON	532	534	55
WEST VIRGINIA	523	511	20
WISCONSIN	592	599	6
WYOMING	544	543	12

Source: College Entrance Examination Board

OUTSTANDING SECONDARY SCHOOLS, 1996–2006

Every other year, the U.S. Department of Education asks each state's superintendent of instruction and the Council for American Private Education for the names of the best secondary schools in the country.

Of the thousands nominated since 2000, just 841 have received official recognition for excellence in education. The judges who do the screening are specialists in school improvement and accreditation. None of them are connected to the federal government.

The schools must survive a tough screening that includes a careful look at curricula and academic achievement. Buildings and classrooms are inspected. Judges sit in on classes and assemblies and even sample lunch in the cafeteria. They interview everyone: Students, Parents, Teachers, and Administrators.

Of these outstanding schools, 750 are located in metro areas. The schools include 315 junior high schools (JHS), middle schools (MS), and intermediate schools (IS), as well as 435 high schools (HS).

Akron, OH
Archbishop Hoban HS
Walsh Jesuit HS
Woodridge MS

Albany, GA
Cross MS

Albany-Schenectady-Troy, NY
O'Brien Academy of Science
Shaker JHS

Albuquerque, NM
Cleveland MS
Lyndon Baines Johnson MS
Mountain View MS

Allentown-Bethlehem-Easton, PA-NJ
Hackettstown MS

Amarillo, TX
James B. Bonham MS

Anchorage, AK
Stellar Secondary School

Anderson, SC
T. L. Hanna HS

Anniston-Oxford, AL
The Donoho MS

Asheville, NC
A.C. Reynolds HS
James Baxter Hunt HS

Atlanta-Sandy Springs-Marietta, GA
Carrollton JHS
Chapel Hill MS
Chattahoochee HS
Dawson County HS
Dickerson MS
Fayette County HS
Flat Rock MS
Lassiter HS
Lost Mountain MS
Roswell HS
Salem HS
Samuel Inman MS
Sequoyah HS

Atlantic City, NJ
Mainland Regional HS

Augusta-Richmond County, GA-SC
Johnson HS
Riverside MS

Austin-Round Rock, TX
C.D. Fulkes MS
Canyon Vista MS
Dripping Springs MS
Goodnight JHS

Lamar MS
Martin JHS
McNeil HS
Sidney Lanier HS

Baltimore-Towson, MD

Baltimore City College HS
Bel Air MS
Clarksville MS
Dumbarton MS
Ridgely MS
Severna Park MS

Bangor, ME

Bangor HS

Baton Rouge, LA

Baton Rouge Magnet HS
Catholic HS
St. Joseph's Academy

Bay City, MI

Herbert Henry Dow HS

Beaumont-Port Arthur, TX

George Marshall MS
Odom Academy

Bellingham, WA

Horizon MS

Bethesda-Gaithersburg-Frederick, MD

Academy of the Holy Cross
Middletown MS
Our Lady of Good Counsel HS
Paint Branch HS
Pyle MS
Thomas Spriggs Wootton HS
Windsor Knolls MS

Binghamton, NY

East MS

Birmingham-Hoover, AL

Homewood MS
Mountain Brook JHS

Bismarck, ND

Bismarck HS

Boulder, CO

Summit Middle Charter School

Bremerton-Silverdale, WA

Woodward MS

Bridgeport-Stamford-Norwalk, CT

Central MS
Newtown HS

Buffalo-Niagara Falls, NY

Clarence HS

Camden, NJ

Cherry Hill HS East
Haddonfield Memorial HS
Morrestown HS

Cape Coral-Fort Myers, FL

Cypress Lake MS
St. Michael Lutheran School

Casper, WY

Casper Classical Academy

Cedar Rapids, IA

Thomas Jefferson Senior HS
Washington HS

Champaign-Urbana, IL

Jefferson MS

Charleston, WV

George Washington HS

Charlotte-Gastonia-Concord, NC-SC

Charlotte Latin MS
Fort Mill HS

Chicago-Naperville-Joliet, IL

Alex M. Martino JHS
Buffalo Grove HS
Butler JHS
Carl Sandburg JHS
Central JHS
F.E. Peacock JHS
Field MS
Haines MS
Highland HS
Homewood-Flossmoor HS
James Hart School
Jones College Prep
Kennedy JHS
Lincoln MS
Michael Collins School
Neil Armstrong School
Oliver McCracken MS
Our Lady of the Wayside School
Palatine HS
Plum Grove Junior HS
Westbrook School

Chico, CA

Chico Senior HS

Cincinnati-Middletown, OH-KY-IN

Cincinnati Hills Christian Academy HS
Cincinnati Hills Christian Academy MS
Covington Latin School
Mariemont HS
McAuley HS
Mother of Mercy HS
Reading Central Community School
Saint Ursula Academy
Villa Madonna Academy HS
W.M. Sellman School

Cleveland-Elyria-Mentor, OH

Ballard Brady MS
Beachwood HS
Beachwood MS
Chagrin Falls HS
Chardon MS
Gesu Catholic School
Kirtland HS
Olmsted Falls HS
Rocky River HS
Rocky River MS
St. Martin of Tours School
Whitney M. Young MS

Columbia, MO

Ann Hawkins Gentry MS

Columbia, SC

Chapin MS
Dent MS
Dutch Fork HS
Hand MS
Irmo HS
Lexington HS

Columbus, GA-AL

Britt David Magnet Academy
Columbus HS

Columbus, OH

Granville HS
Granville MS
New Albany HS
New Albany MS
Olentangy HS
St. Francis DeSales HS
Worthington Kilbourne HS

Corpus Christi, TX

Gregory-Portland HS
St. Patrick School

Dallas-Plano-Irving, TX

Allen HS
Bishop Lynch HS
Clark HS
Coppell HS
Coppell MS East
Dr. Joey Pirrung School
Grapevine HS
Haggard MS
Highland Park MS
Lake Highlands HS
Lamar MS
MacArthur HS
Newman Smith HS
Northwest HS
Poteet HS
School of Science and Engineering
St. Thomas Aquinas School
Walnut Glen Academy for Excellence

Dayton, OH

Anna K. Wantz MS
Greene JROTC Academy
Miamisburg HS
Tower Heights MS
Yellow Springs HS

Deltona-Daytona Beach-Ormond Beach, FL

New Smyrna Beach HS

Denver-Aurora, CO

Campus MS
Cresthill MS
Deer Creek MS
D'Evelyn JS HS
Euclid MS
Flood MS
John Wesley Powell MS
Regis Jesuit HS
St. Mary's Academy

Des Moines-West Des Moines, IA

Adel-DeSoto-Minburn HS
Dowling Catholic HS

Detroit-Livonia-Dearborn, MI

Renaissance HS

Durham, NC

Cary HS

Edison, NJ

Bowne-Munro School
Bridgewater-Raritan Regional HS
Cambridge School
Christa McAuliffe MS
Conackamack MS
Cranbury School
Forrestdale School
High Technology HS
Hillcrest Science Magnet School
Immaculata HS
The Midland School
Montgomery MS
North Brunswick HS
Plainsboro HS North
Schoenly School

El Paso, TX

Bel Air HS
Montwood HS
Ranchland Hills MS
Silva Magnet HS
William D. Slider MS

Essex County, MA

Ipswich HS
Lynnfield HS
Steward School

Evansville, IN-KY

Reitz Memorial HS

Fort Lauderdale-Pompano Beach, FL

Cooper City HS
Forest Glen MS
Pompano Beach MS

Fort Smith, AR-OK

Southside HS

Fort Walton Beach-Crestview-Destin, FL

C.W. Ruckel MS
Okaloosa Walton Collegiate HS

Fort Wayne, IN

Bishop Dwenger HS
Shawe JS HS

Fort Worth-Arlington, TX

Colleyville Heritage HS
Decatur HS
Fort Worth Country Day
Heritage MS
Keller HS

Fresno, CA

Clovis West HS
Edison Computech 7-8
Floyd B. Buchanan HS

Gary, IN

Clifford Pierce MS

Grand Rapids-Wyoming, MI

Byron Center HS
Northview HS
Roguewood School
Troy HS

Greenville, SC

Pelham Road School
Pickens MS
R.P. Dawkins MS

Gulfport-Biloxi, MS

Pass Christian HS

Hagerstown-Martinsburg, MD-WV

Hancock Middle Senior HS

Harrisburg-Carlisle, PA

Hershey MS

Hartford-West Hartford-East Hartford, CT

Albert D. Griswold MS
Bristol Eastern HS
East Farms School
Ellen P. Hubbell School
Hartford Magnet MS
Old Saybrook MS
Sedgwick MS
Timothy Edwards MS
Vernon Center MS
West District School

Hattiesburg, MS

Oak Grove HS

Honolulu, HI

Kaimuki IS

Houston-Sugar Land-Baytown, TX

Arnold Jr. HS
Carlos Watkins MS
Cypress Falls HS
DeBakey HS
First Colony MS
Freeport IS
Grace School
Holub MS
HS for Performing Arts
James Andrew Jackson IS
Jersey Village HS
John Paul II Catholic School
Kaleidoscope MS
Katy HS
Klein Forest HS
Lawrence E. Elkins HS
Mayde Creek JHS
Memorial Parkway JHS
Rodger and Ellen Beck JHS
Spring Branch MS
Spring Woods HS
Thorton MS
V.W. Miller IS
Woodlands HS

Huntington-Ashland, WV-KY-OH

William Mason HS

Huntsville, AL

Buckhorn HS
Liberty MS
Randolph School

Indianapolis-Carmel, IN

Brownsburg JHS
Carmel HS
Carmel JHS
Cathedral HS
Clay MS
Fall Creek Valley MS
Hamilton Southeastern HS
Roncalli HS
Speedway JHS
St. Jude Catholic School
Zionsville Community HS
Zionsville MS

Jacksonville, FL

Anderson School of the Arts

Janesville, WI

Evansville HS

Jefferson City, MO

Cole Camp HS

Kansas City, MO-KS

Blue Valley MS
Brittany Hill MS
Frontier Trail JHS
Mission Valley MS
Moreland Ridge MS
Olathe East HS
Shawnee Mission Northwest HS
Shawnee Mission South HS

Kingsport-Bristol-Bristol, TN-VA

Rye Cove MS

Knoxville, TN

Farragut HS
Halls HS

Kokomo, IN

Northwestern HS

La Crosse, WI-MN

Onalaska MS

Lafayette, IN

West Lafayette JS HS

Lake County-Kenosha County, IL-WI

Adlai E. Stevenson HS
Carmel HS
Grayslake MS
Warren Township HS

Las Vegas-Paradise, NV

Academy of International Studies
Advanced Technologies Academy
Becher MS

Lawton, OK

Pioneer Park School

Lima, OH

Perry MS

Longview, TX

Pine Tree MS

Los Angeles-Long Beach-Glendale, CA

Academy of Mathematics
Arroyo Seco JHS
Beverly Hills HS
Bravo Magnet HS
Calabasas HS
Carl H Lorbeer MS
Chaminade College Preparatory
Chaparral MS
Charles Evans Hughes MS
Claremont HS
Clark Magnet HS
Crescenta Valley HS
Cubberley School
Eleanor J. Toll MS
Hill Classical MS
John A. Rowland HS

La Canada HS
Lincoln MS
Lindero Canyon MS
Lynn MS
Martin B. Tetzlaff MS
Next Century Learning Center
Pacific School
Palos Verdes Peninsula HS
Providence HS
Richard Henry Dana Jr. MS
Saint Joseph HS
Saint Matthias HS
San Marino HS
Westlake HS
Whitney HS
Will Rogers MS

Louisville-Jefferson County, KY-IN

Academy of Our Lady of Mercy
Floyd Central Junior/Senior HS
Louisville Male HS
North Oldham MS
Oldham County HS
Our Lady of Providence JSHS
Sacred Heart Academy
South Oldham HS
South Oldham MS
St. Raphael the Archangel School

Madison, WI

Middleton HS

Manchester-Nashua, NH

Clark and Wilkins Schools

Mansfield, OH

St. Peter's HS

McAllen-Edinburg-Mission, TX

Science Academy of South Texas

Memphis, TN-MS-AR

Senatobia JS HS

Miami-Miami Beach-Kendall, FL

Arvida MS
Monsignor Pace HS

Milwaukee-Waukesha-West Allis, WI

Eisenhower HS
Homestead HS
Kettle Moraine HS
Kettle Moraine MS
Pilgrim Park MS
Samuel Morse MS
Thomas Jefferson MS
Thomas More HS
Whitefish Bay MS

Minneapolis-St. Paul-Bloomington, MN-WI

Academy of Holy Angels
Benilde-St. Margaret's School
Central HS
Cretin-Derham Hall School

Delano MS
Eagan HS
Farmington MS
Highland Park Senior HS
Hillcrest Community School
Meyer MS
Rosemount MS
Shakopee Junior HS

Mobile, AL

Saint Ignatius School

Morgantown, WV

Suncrest MS

Morristown, TN

Hamblen HS East

Myrtle Beach-Conway, SC

Academy for the Arts

Nashville-Davidson–Murfreesboro, TN

Brentwood MS
Davidson Academy
Grassland MS
Holloway HS

Nassau-Suffolk, NY

Carey JSHS
Commack MS
Green Vale Upper School
Harry B. Thompson MS
Herber MS
Herricks MS
Rushmore Avenue School
South Side HS
South Woods MS
Turtle Hook MS
Wantagh HS
Westbury MS

Newark-Union, NJ-PA

Chatham HS
High Point Regional HS
Hunterdon Central Regional HS
Kittatinny Regional HS
Livingston HS
Montclair Kimberley Academy
North Hunterdon HS
Roosevelt MS
Round Valley MS
Union County Magnet HS
William F. Halloran School

New Haven-Milford, CT

Dodd MS
Harborside MS
The Peck Place School

New Orleans-Metairie-Kenner, LA

Benjamin Franklin HS
Christian Brothers School
Dwight D. Eisenhower School
Edna Karr Secondary School

Henry W. Allen Fundamental School
Mandeville HS
Saint Paul's Episcopal School
St. Benilde School
St. Scholastica Academy

New York-White Plains-Wayne, NY-NJ

Academy of the Holy Angels
Aquinas HS
Ardsley MS
Benjamin Franklin MS
Briarcliff Manor MS
Crittenden MS
Dwight D. Eisenhower MS
Fair Lawn HS
Forest Hills HS
Fox Lane HS
Hastings HS
Highland/Godwin School
Iona Preparatory School
Isaac E. Young MS
La Salle Academy
Memorial School
Mother Cabrini HS
North Salem HS
Pleasantville MS
Port Chester MS
River Dell Regional HS
Rutherford HS
Rye MS
Saunders Trades and Technical HS
Schuyler Colfax MS
St. Joan of Arc School
Tenafly HS
The Dominican Academy
The Ursuline School of New Rochelle
Urban Academy

Norwich-New London, CT

East Lyme MS
Norwich Free Academy

Oakland-Fremont-Hayward, CA

Amador Valley HS
California HS
Foothill HS
Foothill MS
Harvest Park MS
Hopkins (William) JHS
Iron Horse MS
Los Cerros MS
Middle College HS
Mission San Jose HS
Monte Vista HS
Pleasanton MS
San Ramon Valley HS
St. Joseph School
Stanley MS
William Mendenhall MS

Oklahoma City, OK

Belle Isle Enterprise MS
Central MS

Deer Creek HS
Deer Creek MS
Edmond Memorial HS

Omaha-Council Bluffs, NE-IA

George Russell MS
Millard West HS
Peter Kiewit MS
Westside MS

Orlando-Kissimmee, FL

Neptune MS
University HS

Owensboro, KY

Daviess County HS

Oxnard-Thousand Oaks-Ventura, CA

Adolfo Camarillo HS
Chaparral MS
Colina MS
Foothill Technology HS
Los Cerritos MS
Meadows School
Newbury Park HS
Redwood MS
Thousand Oaks HS
Valley View MS

Palm Bay-Melbourne-Titusville, FL

West Shore Junior/Senior HS

Parkersburg-Marietta-Vienna, WV-OH

Jackson JHS

Pascagoula, MS

Gautier HS
Ocean Springs MS
Pascagoula HS

Peoria, IL

Metamora Grade School
Tremont HS

Philadelphia, PA

Bala Cynwyd MS
Central Bucks HS - East
Garnet Valley MS
General Wayne MS
Holicong MS
Log College MS
Lower Moreland HS
Masterman Laboratory School
Neshaminy MS
Palisades MS
Strath Haven HS
Upper Merion Area HS
Upper Merion Area MS

Phoenix-Mesa-Scottsdale, AZ

Arizona School for the Arts
Highland HS
Ingleside MS
Saguaro HS

Pittsburgh, PA

Fort Couch MS
Fox Chapel Area HS
Gateway Senior HS
Ingomar MS
Marshall MS
Mt. Lebanon Senior HS
New Eagle School
Quaker Valley MS
Radnor MS
South Fayette MS
Southern Lehigh MS
Trinity HS
Upper St. Clair HS

Portland-South Portland-Biddeford, ME

Cape Elizabeth HS
Yarmouth HS

Portland-Vancouver-Beaverton, OR-WA

Jesuit HS
Saint Mary's Academy

Providence-New Bedford-Fall River, RI-MA

Barrington HS
Barrington MS
Coyle and Cassidy HS
Mercymount Country Day School
Mt. St. Charles Academy
St. Mary Academy, Bay View
Western Coventry School

Raleigh-Cary, NC

Carver Magnet School

Richmond, VA

Chickahominy MS
Harry Flood Byrd MS
James River HS
Lee-Davis HS
Pocahontas MS
Stonewall Jackson MS

Rockford, IL

Boylan Central Catholic HS

Rome, GA

Coosa MS

Sacramento–Arden-Arcade–Roseville, CA

Esparto MS
Granite Bay HS
Harriet Eddy MS
Rio Americano HS
Rolling Hills MS
Warren T. Eich IS

St. Louis, MO-IL

Brentwood HS
Carlinville HS
Forsyth School
Hoech MS
Lafayette HS

McCluer North HS
Metro Academic/Classical HS
Oak Grove MS
Robert H. Sperreng MS
Rockwood Valley MS
Rohan Woods School
Saint John Vianney HS
Shepard Accelerated School
Ste. Genevieve du Bois School
Ursuline Academy of St. Louis

Salt Lake City, UT

Judge Memorial Catholic HS

San Antonio, TX

Antonian College Prep HS
Bandera HS
Fox Academic and Technical School
Harlandale HS
Incarnate Word HS
James Madison HS
Judson HS
Kingsborough MS
Randolph MS
Sharon Christa McAuliffe JHS
Theodore Roosevelt HS
William Howard Taft HS
Winston Churchill HS

San Diego-Carlsbad-San Marcos, CA

Academy of Our Lady of Peace
Bernardo Heights MS
Black Mountain MS
Coronado HS
Diegueno JHS
Earl Warren MS
Excelsior Academy
La Costa Canyon HS
Madison MS
Meadowbrook MS
Mesa Verde MS
Mira Mesa HS
Mount Carmel HS
Rancho Bernardo HS
Rincon MS
Scripps Ranch HS
Torrey Pines HS
Twin Peaks MS
University of San Diego HS
Valley MS

San Francisco-San Mateo-Redwood City, CA

Central MS
Corte Madera School
Henry C. Hall MS
Hillview MS
Lowell HS
Nueva School
South Hillsborough School
William H. Crocker MS

San Jose-Sunnyvale-Santa Clara, CA

Abraham Lincoln Magnet School

Bret Harte MS
Castillero MS
Homestead HS
Leland HS
Millbrook School
Monta Vista HS
Sunnyvale MS
Valley Christian HS
Westmont HS

San Luis Obispo-Paso Robles, CA

Morro Bay HS
Templeton HS

Santa Ana-Anaheim-Irvine, CA

Aliso Niguel HS
Aliso Viejo MS
Bernardo Yorba MS
Corona del Mar HS
D Russell Parks Junior HS
Dana Hills HS
El Dorado HS
Hebrew Academy
HS of the Arts
Isaac Sowers MS
La Paz MS
Laguna Hills HS
Marine View MS
Mission Viejo HS
Newport Harbor HS
Northwood HS
Oak MS
Orangethorpe School
Philip J. Reilly School
Rancho San Joaquin MS
Rancho Santa Margarita IS
Santa Margarita Catholic HS
Trabuco Hills HS
Troy HS
Vista Verde School

Santa Barbara-Santa Maria, CA

Dos Pueblos HS
Goleta Valley JHS
Joe Nightingale School
Lakeview Junior HS
Orcutt Junior HS

Santa Rosa-Petaluma, CA

Meadow School

Savannah, GA

Herschel V. Jenkins HS
Savannah Arts Academy

Scranton–Wilkes-Barre, PA

Abington JHS
Abington Senior HS

Seattle-Bellevue-Everett, WA

Blanchet HS
Chief Kanim MS
Holy Names Academy

Holy Rosary School
Islander MS
Liberty HS
Mercer Island HS
Newport HS
Northshore Junior HS
Odle MS
Pine Lake MS
Shorewood HS

Sioux Falls, SD

O'Gorman HS

South Bend-Mishawaka, IN-MI

Discovery MS
Penn HS
Saint Joseph's HS
Trinity School at Greenlawn

Spartanburg, SC

D.R. Hill MS
Woodruff HS

Springfield, MA

Williams MS

Springfield, MO

Kickapoo HS

Sumter, SC

Bates MS

Syracuse, NY

Soule Road MS

Tacoma, WA

Curtis Senior HS
Sumner HS

Tallahassee, FL

Deerlake MS

Tampa-St. Petersburg-Clearwater, FL

Berkeley Preparatory School
Henry B. Plant HS
John A. Coleman MS
Seminole MS
Woodrow Wilson MS

Toledo, OH

Central Catholic HS
Notre Dame Academy
Ottawa Hills JS HS
Pettisville HS
Saint Ursula Academy
Toledo Technology Academy

Tucson, AZ

Esperero Canyon MS
Tortolita MS
University HS

Tulsa, OK

Carver MS

Saint Pius X School

Tyler, TX

Bishop Gorman MS and HS

Utica-Rome, NY

John F. Kennedy MS

Virginia Beach-Norfolk-Newport News, VA-NC

Menchville HS

Waco, TX

Bruceville-Eddy HS

Warren-Troy-Farmington Hills, MI

Adlai E. Stevenson HS
Avondale MS
Cousino HS
Donald L. Bemis JHS
Glenn W. Levey MS
Lake Orion HS
L'Anse Creuse MS North
L'Anse Creuse MS South
Novi HS
Philip A. Hart MS
Wolfe MS

Washington-Arlington, DC-VA-MD-WV

Brentsville District HS
Eleanor Roosevelt HS
George Mason MS
Phillips School
Plum Point MS
Quantico Middle/HS
Yorktown HS

Waterloo-Cedar Falls, IA

Peet JHS

Weirton-Steubenville, WV-OH

Weir HS
Weir MS

West Palm Beach-Boca Raton, FL

Boca Raton Christian School
Christa McAuliffe Community MS
Henderson University School
Suncoast Community HS

Wheeling, WV-OH

Sherrard JHS

Wichita Falls, TX

Kirby Jr High Math-Science-Technology Magnet

Wilmington, NC

Shallotte MS

Worcester, MA

Nipmuc Regional Middle/HS

Youngstown-Warren-Boardman, OH-PA

Hillview Intermediate Center
Struthers HS

HOMESCHOOLING

Call it what you will, home is the place where 1.23 million American children, most of them in grades K-9, go to school. Since the 1980s, in response to problems in the public schools, this style of education has enjoyed a small boom.

Parents have the legal right to homeschool their children in every state. Since education is governed by state law, there are as many requirements as there are states, and these are sometimes modified and interpreted by local school boards.

Forty states use the category Home Instruction by Parents in their legal language. The other states bring homeschooling under: Church School (Alabama); Private School (California, Kansas, Kentucky, Nebraska, Texas); Alternative School (Idaho); Home Education (Michigan, Pennsylvania, Wisconsin); or Home Study (Georgia).

Although twelve states require no formal notice from parents of their intent to homeschool a child, most school districts want to know when a child is being educated at home. Except in cases when the district requests an annual renewal, the notice to homeschool remains in force unless and until the parents decide to stop.

Seven states require a high school diploma or GED certificate of homeschool teachers, but the others have no specific requirements except that, in a few states, teachers should be "capable," "competent," or "qualified." Four states have "extensive requirements"; others have extensive explanations why there are no requirements.

Curricula for homeschools must match the public schools in thirty-six states. Ten states have more specific requirements in subjects ranging from reading to social studies, namely Arizona, Georgia, Hawaii, Kentucky, Missouri, Nebraska, New Mexico, South Dakota, Texas, and West Virginia. Alabama, Alaska, Arkansas, and Florida have no curriculum requirements. No standardized tests are used to evaluate the progress of homeschool students in twenty-three states.

State school attendance requirements are satisfied in most states by the submission of attendance records or by periodic reports on a child's progress. The most consistent record keeping required of homeschooling parents is the maintenance of a daily attendance register, but twenty-five states do not require any record keeping. States also vary on the amount of time a child must be in school.

REQUIREMENTS TO HOMESCHOOL

STATE	AGE	TEACHER QUALIFICATIONS'	ATTENDANCE REQUIRED	TESTING REQUIRED
ALABAMA	7 to 16	No	140 days	No
ALASKA	7 to 16	No	180 days	No
ARIZONA	6 to 16	No	No	No
ARKANSAS	5 to 17	No	No	Yes
CALIFORNIA	6 to 18	"capable"	No	No
COLORADO	7 to 16	No	172 days	Yes
CONNECTICUT	5 to 18	No	180 days	No
DELAWARE	5 to 16	No	180 days	No
DISTRICT OF COLUMBIA	5 to 18	No	No	No
FLORIDA	6 to 16	No	180 days	Yes
GEORGIA	6 to 16	HS/GED	180 days	Yes
HAWAII	6 to 18	No	No	Yes/Folio
IDAHO	7 to 16	No	"match public"	No
ILLINOIS	7 to 17	No	176 days	No
INDIANA	7 to 18	No	180 days	No
IOWA	6 to 16	No	148 days	Yes
KANSAS	7 to 18	"competent"	186 days	No
KENTUCKY	6 to 16	No	185 days	No
LOUISIANA	7 to 18	No	180 days	Yes
MAINE	7 to 17	No	175 days	Yes

Education

STATE	AGE	TEACHER QUALIFICATIONS'	ATTENDANCE REQUIRED	TESTING REQUIRED
MARYLAND	5 to 16	No	"sufficient"	Folio
MASSACHUSETTS	6 to 16	No	900/990 hours	Progress Report
MICHIGAN	6 to 16	No	No	No
MINNESOTA	7 to 16	No	No	Yes
MISSISSIPPI	6 to 16	No	"whatever"	No
MISSOURI	7 to 16	No	1000 hours	Yes/Folio
MONTANA	7 to 16	No	720/1,080 hours	No
NEBRASKA	6 to 18	No	1,032/1,080 hours	No
NEVADA	7 to 17	"extensive"	180 days	No
NEW HAMPSHIRE	6 to 16	"extensive"	No	Yes/Folio
NEW JERSEY	6 to 16	No	No	No
NEW MEXICO	5 to majority	HS/GED	"match public"	No
NEW YORK	6 to 16	No	180 days	Yes
NORTH CAROLINA	7 to 16	HS/GED	9 months	Yes
NORTH DAKOTA	7 to 16	"extensive"	175 days	Yes
OHIO	6 to 18	HS/GED	900 hours	Yes/Folio
OKLAHOMA	5 to 18	No	180 days	No
OREGON	7 to 18	No	No	Yes
PENNSYLVANIA	8 to 17	HS/GED	180 days	Yes/Folio
RHODE ISLAND	6 to 16	No	"match public"	Yes
SOUTH CAROLINA	5 to 17	HS/GED	180 days	Yes/Folio
SOUTH DAKOTA	6 to 16	No	9 months	Yes
TENNESSEE	6 to 17	B.A.	180 days	Yes
TEXAS	6 to 18	No	No	No
UTAH	6 to 18	No	"match public"	No
VERMONT	6 to 16	No	No	Yes
VIRGINIA	5 to 18	"extensive"	No	Yes
WASHINGTON	8 to 18	"extensive"	180 days	Yes
WEST VIRGINIA	6 to 16	HS/GED	180 days	Yes
WISCONSIN	6 to 18	No	875 hours	No
WYOMING	7 to 16	No	175 days	No

Source: Homeschool Legal Defense Association HS/GED: High School or general equivalency diploma. B.A.: Bachelor's degree.

Health Care

America isn't the world's healthiest nation. For all of its wealth and technological superiority, this country lags behind Canada in life expectancy and in infant mortality. For its part, Canada lags behind Sweden and Japan.

Millions of Americans are uninsured and lack access to the full range of health services. Indeed, almost one-third of all American children aren't covered by any health insurance; their school's nurse is the primary provider. In spite of an abundance of physicians packing advanced training and technical support, unfair distribution of medical care remains a central problem.

WHAT THE NUMBERS SAY

Americans continue to get healthier. Judging by two universal measures of population health, infant mortality and life expectancy, the United States is healthier now than it was a generation ago. Why are life expectancy and infant mortality such commonly accepted indicators of a nation's health? First, because these data can be found in almost every developed nation in the form of birth and death certificates.

Second, the quality of postpartum and infant care available in a nation, state, or metro area generally reflects the quality of other important health services. As for life expectancy, it remains a very broad but meaningful indicator of a nation's ability to provide sanitary food and drinking water, proper immunization and disease screening, and professional medical attention throughout life.

Infant mortality in America has dropped to its lowest level ever, with data showing 6.4 deaths per 1,000 live births. At the same time, life expectancy for girls born in 2006 is projected to exceed 80 years. For boys, life expectancy is now rising faster than girls, and will exceed 75 years.

Specialist Metro Areas

Most physicians give up general practice to specialize. Their number rises in smaller areas with medical schools and veterans' hospitals, and also where medical care is a basic industry attracting patients from outside. Below are the top ten metro areas where medical specialists are concentrated.

Metro Area	Population per Specialist
Rochester, MN	437
Durham, NC	993
Ann Arbor, MI	1,041
Iowa City, IA	1,101
Columbia, MO	1,204
Charlottesville, VA	1,246
Greenville, NC	1,372
Bethesda-Gaithersburg, MD	1,411
Gainesville, FL	1,419
Boston-Quincy, MA	1,577

Medically Generalized Metro Areas

North of the border in Canada, the proportion of physicians who are general or family practitioners is three times greater than in the United States. Below are the top ten metro areas where General/Family practitioner are concentrated.

Metro Area	People per GP/FP
Mount Vernon-Anacortes, WA	827
Duluth, MN-WI	855
Rochester, MN	883
Rome, GA	907
Eau Claire, WI	933
Iowa City, IA	954
Santa Rosa-Petaluma, CA	976
Boulder, CO	983
Santa Fe, NM	986
Grand Junction, CO	992

Osteopathic Metro Areas

Doctors of Osteopathic Medicine (D.O.s) use all accepted methods of treatment, including drugs and surgery, but they place special emphasis on the musculoskeletal system, preventive medicine, and holistic patient care. D.O.s are especially concentrated in the ten metro areas below.

Metro Area	Population per D.O.
Lansing-East Lansing, MI	1,487
Sandusky, OH	1,577
Des Moines-West Des Moines, IA	1,631
Camden, NJ	1,699
Ocean City, NJ	1,754
Joplin, MO	1,758
Tulsa, OK	1,920
Erie, PA	2,032
Warren-Troy-Farmington Hills, MI	2,042
Jefferson City, MO	2,184

Source: U.S. Department of Health and Human Services, Area Resource File.

Two Systems—Insurance, Access, and the Rest

Unfortunately, not all Americans share in these statistical gains, and the inequality contributes to the modest U.S. health ranking compared with other countries. Black/white. Rich/poor. Urban/rural. Insured/uninsured. Profit/nonprofit. Short-term/long-term care. Consumer/provider. These are the poles of a health-care system that is a business enterprise. To get at the real essence of the system, one needs to look at the providers - the hospitals and the doctors.

THE DOCTORS

Not every physician has a telephone number in the yellow pages. Some are hospital administrators, medical school professors, journalists, lawyers, or researchers for pharmaceutical companies. Others work for government public-health services or Department of Defense service branches. Still others are in residency training, or are clinical fellows at teaching hospitals, or are full-time members of hospital staffs. When it comes to the number of physicians per capita, what really counts is the number of doctors who maintain offices and see patients. It's surprising how many of them don't.

Depending on how office-based or fee-for-service physicians spend their professional hours, almost all can be classified into three groups:

Primary Care

Physicians in *General* or *Family* practice treat diseases and injuries, provide preventive care, give routine checkups, prescribe drugs and perform some surgery. Demand for General and Family Practitioners is at an all-time high in the United States for one big reason: the managed care system prefers generalists oversee a patient's total medical treatment. GPs and FPs, as they are called, use all accepted methods of medical care. They can also refer you to a specialist.

Internists diagnose and provide nonsurgical treatment for adults who have a wide range of problems associated with the internal organs, such as the stomach, kidneys, liver, and digestive tract.

Pediatricians focus on the health of infants, children, and teenagers. They specialize in the diagnosis and treatment of a variety of ailments specific to young people and track their patients' growth to adulthood.

HEALTH CARE BARGAINS

Who says quality health care is an expensive big-city amenity? These metro areas are ranked in the top 20 percent in *Places Rated's* Housing costs section and also in the top 20 percent in the Health Care section. Most are among the least expensive in "geographic practice cost indexes" which insurers use to determine physician fees.

Specialists

MDs focusing on specific medical disciplines such as cardiology, allergy, gastroenterology, and dermatology are specialists. They are the largest of the physician groups because, frankly, specializing is still where the money is. Medical specialists (and general practitioners) are likely to give attention to surgical and non-surgical approaches to treatment. If they decide that surgery is the method of treatment, they refer their patients to surgeons.

Surgeons

Physicians who treat injury, disease, and deformity through regular operations several times a week are surgeons. Of all the broadly-defined physician groups, they are the highest paid. In the United States the letters F.A.C.S. (Fellow of the American College of Surgeons) after the surgeon's name indicate that he or she has passed an evaluation of surgical training and skills as well as ethical fitness.

Where Physicians Cluster—One Measure of Health Care

Where doctors end up practicing is partly determined by sentiment, their perceptions of local quality of life, or both. But mainly it's a matter of economics. The physician has invested three to seven years in graduate medical education and frequently has to start out with an enormous loan to repay.

Some begin work on a hospital staff, develop a practice, and then open an office. Others buy practices from doctors who are preparing to retire. Still others are recruited into partnerships or group practices through advertisements such as these from the *Journal of the American Medical Association:*

INFECTIOUS DISEASE PRACTICE with two board certified ID physicians seeking third physician. Southwestern desert recreational activities abound, with proximity to Colorado, New Mexico, Utah, and California attractions. Varied, interesting patient population (winter

Hospital Services

The American Hospital Association (AHA) classifies hospital services into more than 100 categories.

Adult day-care program
Alcohol/drug abuse or dependency inpatient unit
Alcohol/drug abuse or dependency outpatient services
Alzheimer's diagnostic/assessment services
Angioplasty
Arthritis treatment center
Birthing room/LDRP room
Blood bank
Burn-care unit
Cardiac catheterization laboratory
Cardiac intensive-care unit
Cardiac rehabilitation program
Chaplaincy/Pastoral care services
Chronic obstructive pulmonary disease services
Community health promotion
Comprehensive geriatric assessment
CT scanner
Diagnostic radioisotope facility
Emergency department social work services
Emergency department
Emergency response (geriatric)
Ethics committee
Extracorporeal shock wave lithotripter
Fitness center
General inpatient care for AIDS/ARC
Genetic counseling/screening services
Geriatric acute-care unit
Geriatric clinics
Health sciences library
Hemodialysis
Histopathology laboratory
HIV/AIDS unit
Home health services
Hospice
Magnetic resonance imaging
Mammography diagnostic
Mammography screening
Medical surgical or other intensive-care unit
Megavoltage radiation therapy
Neonatal intensive-care unit
Noninvasive cardiac assessment services
Obstetrics unit

Occupational health services
Occupational therapy services
Oncology services
Open-heart surgery
Organ/tissue transplant
Organized outpatient services
Organized social work services
Orthopedic surgery
Outpatient social work services
Outpatient surgery services
Patient education
Patient representative services
Pediatric acute inpatient unit
Physical therapy services
Psychiatric child/adolescent services
Psychiatric consultation/liaison services
Psychiatric education services
Psychiatric emergency services
Psychiatric geriatric services
Psychiatric inpatient services
Psychiatric outpatient services
Psychiatric partial hospitalization program
Radioactive implants
Recreational therapy services
Rehabilitation inpatient unit
Rehabilitation outpatient services
Reproductive health services
Respiratory therapy services
Respite care
Senior membership program
Single photon emission computerized tomography (SPECT)
Skilled nursing or other long-term-care facility
Specialized outpatient program for AIDS/ARC
Speech therapy services
Sports medicine clinic/services
Therapeutic radioisotope facility
Trauma center (certified)
Ultrasound
Volunteer services department
Women's health center/services
Worksite health promotion
X-ray radiation therapy

Source: American Hospital Association, *Guide to the Health Care Field*

visitors, Native Americans, immigrants; as well as increasingly young resident Arizonans). Fax CV to 800-838-3476.

PULMONOLOGIST NEEDED immediately to join established practice. Family-oriented, peaceful community in Oklahoma. Excellent salary and benefits with progression to partnership. Send CV to Box 1205, c/o JAMA, 515 N State St, 12th Fl, Chicago, IL 60610.

By whatever means they introduce themselves professionally, new physicians who wish to specialize are mainly concerned with a place's covered (i.e., insured) census (i.e., population size).

Many physicians want to practice near a major hospital and also want to live in a city large enough to provide them with the amenities their incomes allow. In general, larger, more affluent places—Boston, New York, San Francisco, and Washington, for example—have a greater proportion of health-care facilities, medical specialists, high-tech equipment, and exotic procedures.

On the other hand, small American metro areas tend to have more general and family practitioners than specialists. The common explanation is that the smaller metro areas don't have enough patients to support a large number of specialists. There's not enough business for an allergist to open an office in one out of five smaller metro areas, for example. Doctors in these areas who want to see 30 to 40 patients a day need to be generalists.

Another pattern is for expensive, complex procedures to be available only in major metro areas or in areas with medical schools and veterans' hospitals. You can't get a bone marrow transplant in most metro areas in North America. In Utica, NY, no one performs open-heart surgery. A patient has to go to Syracuse - about 50 miles away - for that. Surgeons, too, tend to cluster in metro areas with medical schools, veterans' hospitals, and ancillary medical centers.

A counter trend in physician clustering is developing, however. Some newly graduated specialists are leaving big cities where things are so competitive that they can't find jobs and where it's simply too expensive for them to set up their own practices. They choose, instead, to go to smaller metro areas—often the towns in which they grew up—to establish a practice and to penetrate the existing referral network of doctors.

Another trend in Canada is the active and successful recruitment of physicians by American headhunters whose seminars detail the intricacies of emigration and setting up a practice in underserved areas in the United States. Some 10,000 physicians now practicing in the United States are graduates of Canadian medical schools.

Still another development is the "too many doctors, not enough jobs" prediction from as long ago as 1980. One in ten new medical school graduates have difficulty finding a suitable first post, and unemployment rates among graduates of foreign medical schools is higher than ever.

THE HOSPITAL

There is some irony in the idea that hospitals look at physicians as customers *and* providers. Hospitals market laboratories, operating rooms, beds, services, and round-the-clock monitoring not to patients but to physicians who bring in the patients. For their part, physicians care for their patients and are themselves providers.

Not all hospitals handle typical illnesses and emergencies. Many of them exclusively treat chronic diseases or alcohol and drug addiction, or they may be burn centers, psychiatric hospitals, or rehabilitation hospitals. When rating a metro area for its health care, *Places Rated* counts only general hospitals where patients stay less than 30 days.

The Bed
The number of accredited acute-care hospitals and their inpatient beds varies among places. Although the total number of hospital beds isn't as valuable an indicator as it was before advances in medicine and pharmacology shortened a hospital stay, it is still a reliable gauge of relative health-care supply. Hospitals use the bed as "the benchmark of occupancy, service, and financing," according to one textbook on hospital administration. "As it now stands, the economics of the hospital requires that the beds be filled for the hospital to stay solvent."

Hospital Services
Each year, the American Hospital Association (AHA) surveys its thousands of member hospitals, enumerating which of more than 100 AHA-defined services each institution provides. The number of services a hospital offers is one index of the level of

care you may receive there and certainly of the level of technology and specialization in that hospital.

Though most operate as nonprofits, general hospitals are actually businesses that can't afford to go deeply into the red. They offer common services such as an emergency department, postoperative recovery room, a blood bank, an intensive-care unit, and outpatient surgery. Some stake out market niches with an additional menue - a radioactive implant department, a sports medicine clinic, a histopathology laboratory, a certified trauma center, or a department with organ transplant capabilities. Of course, it really depends on one's situation; if a woman is of child-bearing years, access to genetic counseling services, an obstetrics unit, a neonatal intensive-care unit, and a pediatric inpatient unit may be extremely important.

Quality Care—What's a Consumer to Do?

Many hospitals, pressured by public and private cost-containment efforts, have had to slash services and staff. At the same time, hospitals remain critically short of qualified nurses. No wonder the quality of care is such a concern today. Since it's just about impossible to measure quality of care in any statistical way, how do we judge the skills of a doctor or hospital? Accreditation, with certain caveats, is one way.

Hospital Accreditation

The Joint Commission on Accreditation of Healthcare Organizations (JCAHO) is the private nonprofit body that investigates and certifies hospitals. The JCAHO certification determines which hospitals are eligible for federal funds or state licensure. Since JCAHO assessments have been kept confidential, consumers have no way of knowing how to interpret this discrepancy between JCAHO findings and those of federal investigators. In other words, a patient could only find out whether or not a hospital was accredited.

However, starting in 1995, you can buy a performance report from the JCAHO on local hospitals. Hospitals are scored on a scale of 0 to 100 in 28 categories, including dietary services, medication use, and staff preparation. Then each gets an overall score.

A hospital has incentives to qualify for accreditation. It makes it easier to recruit doctors and operate residency programs, and it reduces malpractice liability. Now that accreditation status is

becoming a more public matter, it may also become a useful tool for attracting patients - the consumers of health care.

Teaching Hospitals

Two of every three hospitals are *nonteaching*. That is, they are staffed almost entirely by "attending physicians" who have an outside practice, are paid by the patient, and have admitting privileges at the hospital.

Teaching hospitals grant admitting privileges to attending physicians, but they also employ full-time "house staff," taking in first-year and advanced residents and a teaching faculty. The attending physician heads a team of house staff members (including the 'hospitalist,' a newly-defined physician specialty) to make important decisions about a patient's care. The patient pays the attending physician; the hospital pays the house staff.

JUDGING: HEALTH CARE

What is being judged in this chapter is health care in each metro area, not how sick the resident population is. Moreover, *Places Rated* doesn't assess the quality of health care but its supply.

Keeping these distinctions in mind will help the reader avoid assuming that a low score in this chapter means either (1) that the people in a given place are unhealthy and don't live very long, or (2) that if one were to relocate to this place, basic health care - including even such complex emergency surgery as a coronary bypass - would be unavailable or inferior. *Both of these conclusions are incorrect.* A low score in this chapter does indicate, however, that the emphasis in that metro area is probably on basic health care and that the latest techniques and equipment, and personnel trained to implement them, are more likely to be found elsewhere.

SCORING: HEALTH CARE

To rate metro areas for relative strength in health care, *Places Rated* considers six things:

1. *General/Family Practitioners* per 100,000: physicians who generalize because of the size of the patient base or choose to specialize in family practice.

2. *Medical Specialists* per 100,000: physicians who concentrate on specific medical disciplines such as pediatrics or cardiovascular diseases.

3. *Surgical Specialists* per 100,000: physicians who operate on a regular basis several times a week.

As stated earlier, just as not all MDs see patients, not all hospitals handle typical illnesses and emergencies. In the Short-Term General Hospitals category, *Places Rated* counts only hospitals classified by the American Hospital Association as acute-care facilities whose patients stay fewer than 30 days.

4. *Accredited General Hospital Beds* set up for neonatal, pediatric, general medical-surgical, cardiac, and intensive care. In U.S. metro areas, 91 percent of short-term general hospitals are accredited by the JCAHO. While the lack of accreditation doesn't necessarily mean a facility is substandard, the presence of such accreditation means the hospital has passed rigorous and periodic reviews. While the number of hospital beds is dropping throughout North America because of cost-containment policies and the shift to outpatient services, it still is an indicator of health-care supply.

5. *Physician Residency Programs.* One-third of short-term general hospitals in the United States have approved physician training programs. Hospitals with no teaching programs aren't necessarily lagging in quality, but facilities with such programs tend to be larger urban institutions where the interaction between students and faculty encourages the development and use of the latest techniques, equipment, and therapy.

6. *Hospital Services*, a measurement that favors larger metro areas over smaller ones. All 108 American Hospital Association defined services are available in Chicago, Minneapolis, and Philadelphia, but only 33 of them are available in Bloomington, Indiana, and Morristown, Tennessee.

Affluent, big-city metro areas generally score higher in the rankings than the smaller, poorer metro areas. This doesn't mean that a person cannot receive excellent medical care in a rural clinic or, conversely, experience medical care that is bad enough to be life-threatening in even the finest of big-city hospitals. The quality of medical and nursing care most people receive depends on a number of factors, including the patient's ability to pay, blind chance, and human error.

www.placesrated.com

Health Care rankings, from 1 to 379, are in the *Place Profiles* section coming next. Health Care scores, from 100.0 to 0.0, are in *Putting It All Together* at the end of the book. Readers can view and print out these rankings and scores, from #1 Iowa City, IA (score: 100.0) to #379 Hinesville-Ft. Steward, GA (score: 0.0), by visiting *Places Rated's* website.

Here are the top twenty:

Rank	Score
1. Iowa City, IA	100.0
2. Columbia, MO	99.7
3. Sioux Falls, SD	99.4
4. Gainesville, FL	99.2
5. Durham, NC	98.9
6. Ann Arbor, MI	98.6
7. Charlottesville, VA	98.4
8. Little Rock-North Little Rock, AR	98.1
9. Rome, GA	97.8
10. Lexington-Fayette, KY	97.6
11. Morgantown, WV	97.3
12. Asheville, NC	97.0
13. Johnson City, TN	96.8
14. Eau Claire, WI	96.5
15. Shreveport-Bossier City, LA	96.2
16. Tyler, TX	96.0
17. Knoxville, TN	95.7
18. La Crosse, WI-MN	95.5
19. Madison, WI	95.2
20. Roanoke, VA	94.4
20. Billings, MT	94.4
20. Rochester, MN	94.4

At *www.placesrated.com* you'll also find more information on hospitals and medical costs as well as useful links to health and medical websites.

Health Care

The following pages show selected health-care resources for the 379 metro areas. To the right of the heading *Patient-treating Physicians* is the metro area's number of physicians who maintain offices and treat patients.

Next, under *Primary Care*, is a small table showing the number of physicians in General Practice, Family Practice, Internal Medicine, and Pediatrics. The letters AA, A, B, and C are ratings of physicians per 100,000 people. An AA means better than 80th percentile; an A, between the 60th and 80th percentiles; a B, between the 40th and 60th; and a C, below the 40th percentile.

Next, under *Specialists*, is another small table showing the number of physicians focusing on all medical specialties except internal medicine or pediatrics. Also numbered are surgeons, psychiatrists and osteopaths. The letter ratings, AA, A, B, and C indicate percentiles identical to those in primary care above.

The heading *Short-Term General Hospitals* shows the number of these institutions and their total beds. Underneath is the number accredited by the Joint Commission on Accreditation of Healthcare Organizations (JCAHO) and the number of teaching hospitals that sponsor graduate medical education in one or more clinical departments recognized by at least one residency review committee of the American Medical Association. Last is the number of defined services available within a metro area from the American Hospital Association's menu of 108.

The information is derived from these sources: American Hospital Association, *Guide to the Health Care Field, 2006; American Medical Association, Graduate Medical Education Directory, 2006, and Physician Characteristics and Distribution in the United States*, 2006; and U.S. Department of Health and Human Services, Bureau of Health-Care Professions, unpublished "Area Resource File," 2006.

A check mark (✓) in front of a metro area's name highlights it as one of the top 40 places for health care resources.

Abilene, TX

Patient-treating Physicians: 269

Primary Care			
General	Family	Internists	Pediatrics
41	34	26	15
B	C	C	C
Specialists			
Medical	Surgical	Psychiatry	Osteopathy
41	65	5	24
B	C	C	A

General Hospitals: 5 (614 beds)
  2 JCAHO, 78 of 108 services

Other Hospitals: N/A

Places Rated Rank: 221

Akron, OH

Patient-treating Physicians: 1,345

Primary Care			
General	Family	Internists	Pediatrics
148	138	147	81
C	C	B	B
Specialists			
Medical	Surgical	Psychiatry	Osteopathy
169	270	54	215
B	C	A	AA

General Hospitals: 7 (1,424 beds)
  4 JCAHO, 4 teaching, 94 of 108 services

Other Hospitals: Children, Rehab

Places Rated Rank: 276

Albany, GA

Patient-treating Physicians: 259

Primary Care			
General	Family	Internists	Pediatrics
25	19	38	17
C	C	A	B
Specialists			
Medical	Surgical	Psychiatry	Osteopathy
39	69	9	14
B	B	C	B

General Hospitals: 3 (635 beds)
  3 JCAHO, 1 teaching, 78 of 108 services

Other Hospitals: N/A

Places Rated Rank: 237

Albany-Schenectady-Troy, NY

Patient-treating Physicians: 1,866

Primary Care			
General	Family	Internists	Pediatrics
201	176	233	118
C	C	A	A
Specialists			
Medical	Surgical	Psychiatry	Osteopathy
302	463	84	87
AA	A	A	A

General Hospitals: 11 (2,543 beds)
  10 JCAHO, 5 teaching, 87 of 108 services

Other Hospitals: VA, Rehab

Places Rated Rank: 106

Albuquerque, NM

Patient-treating Physicians: 1,747

Primary Care			
General	Family	Internists	Pediatrics
246	228	224	119
A	A	A	A
Specialists			
Medical	Surgical	Psychiatry	Osteopathy
247	332	87	68
A	B	AA	B

General Hospitals: 11 (1,533 beds)
  7 JCAHO, 3 teaching, 94 of 108 services

Other Hospitals: Children, VA, Psych, Rehab

Places Rated Rank: 162

Alexandria, LA

Patient-treating Physicians: 317

Primary Care			
General	Family	Internists	Pediatrics
48	42	36	19
A	A	A	B
Specialists			
Medical	Surgical	Psychiatry	Osteopathy
40	97	17	2
B	AA	AA	C

General Hospitals: 4 (917 beds)
  4 JCAHO, 3 teaching, 79 of 108 services

Other Hospitals: VA, Psych, Rehab

Places Rated Rank: 48

Allentown-Bethlehem, PA-NJ

Patient-treating Physicians: 1,599

Primary Care			
General	Family	Internists	Pediatrics
170	155	166	84
C	C	B	B
Specialists			
Medical	Surgical	Psychiatry	Osteopathy
218	358	44	273
B	B	B	AA

General Hospitals: 10 (2,131 beds)
  9 JCAHO, 5 teaching, 97 of 108 services

Other Hospitals: Children, Rehab

Places Rated Rank: 163

Altoona, PA

Patient-treating Physicians: 264

Primary Care			
General	Family	Internists	Pediatrics
44	41	32	13
A	A	A	C
Specialists			
Medical	Surgical	Psychiatry	Osteopathy
38	53	10	26
A	C	A	AA

General Hospitals: 5 (467 beds)
  5 JCAHO, 86 of 108 services

Other Hospitals: VA, Rehab

Places Rated Rank: 109

Amarillo, TX

Patient-treating Physicians: 471

Primary Care			
General	Family	Internists	Pediatrics
58	52	51	28
B	B	B	B
Specialists			
Medical	Surgical	Psychiatry	Osteopathy
83	120	9	20
A	A	C	B

General Hospitals: 4 (1,075 beds)
  4 JCAHO, 2 teaching, 82 of 108 services

Other Hospitals: Children, VA

Places Rated Rank: 89

Ames, IA

Patient-treating Physicians: 143

Primary Care			
General	Family	Internists	Pediatrics
30	27	11	9
AA	A	C	B
Specialists			
Medical	Surgical	Psychiatry	Osteopathy
17	34	5	9
C	C	B	A

General Hospitals: 2 (292 beds)
  1 JCAHO, 75 of 108 services

Other Hospitals: N/A

Places Rated Rank: 205

Anchorage, AK

Patient-treating Physicians: 765

Primary Care			
General	Family	Internists	Pediatrics
139	125	53	54
AA	AA	C	A
Specialists			
Medical	Surgical	Psychiatry	Osteopathy
81	194	44	44
B	AA	AA	A

General Hospitals: 5 (795 beds)
  5 JCAHO, 2 teaching, 89 of 108 services

Other Hospitals: Children, Psych

Places Rated Rank: 93

Anderson, IN

Patient-treating Physicians: 150

Primary Care			
General	Family	Internists	Pediatrics
50	45	10	6
AA	AA	C	C
Specialists			
Medical	Surgical	Psychiatry	Osteopathy
16	34	8	0
C	C	B	C

General Hospitals: 2 (231 beds)
  1 JCAHO, 76 of 108 services

Other Hospitals: N/A

Places Rated Rank: 333

Anderson, SC

Patient-treating Physicians: 271

Primary Care			
General	Family	Internists	Pediatrics
65	58	27	15
AA	AA	C	C
Specialists			
Medical	Surgical	Psychiatry	Osteopathy
25	59	12	5
C	C	B	C

General Hospitals: 1 (420 beds)
  1 JCAHO, 1 teaching, 66 of 108 services
Other Hospitals: N/A

Places Rated Rank: 306

✓Ann Arbor, MI

Patient-treating Physicians: 1,723

Primary Care			
General	Family	Internists	Pediatrics
102	89	228	121
A	B	AA	AA
Specialists			
Medical	Surgical	Psychiatry	Osteopathy
321	329	118	50
AA	AA	AA	A

General Hospitals: 6 (1,658 beds)
  6 JCAHO, 3 teaching, 105 of 108 services
Other Hospitals: VA

Places Rated Rank: 6

Anniston-Oxford, AL

Patient-treating Physicians: 172

Primary Care			
General	Family	Internists	Pediatrics
29	25	23	11
B	B	B	C
Specialists			
Medical	Surgical	Psychiatry	Osteopathy
22	50	2	7
C	B	C	C

General Hospitals: 3 (447 beds)
  3 JCAHO, 61 of 108 services
Other Hospitals: N/A

Places Rated Rank: 231

Appleton, WI

Patient-treating Physicians: 318

Primary Care			
General	Family	Internists	Pediatrics
68	66	35	17
A	A	C	C
Specialists			
Medical	Surgical	Psychiatry	Osteopathy
41	74	11	8
C	C	C	C

General Hospitals: 4 (407 beds)
  2 JCAHO, 2 teaching, 85 of 108 services
Other Hospitals: N/A

Places Rated Rank: 288

✓Asheville, NC

Patient-treating Physicians: 1,052

Primary Care			
General	Family	Internists	Pediatrics
186	176	109	57
AA	AA	A	A
Specialists			
Medical	Surgical	Psychiatry	Osteopathy
157	251	47	22
AA	AA	AA	C

General Hospitals: 5 (1,363 beds)
  5 JCAHO, 2 teaching, 96 of 108 services
Other Hospitals: Children, VA, Rehab

Places Rated Rank: 12

Athens-Clarke County, GA

Patient-treating Physicians: 349

Primary Care			
General	Family	Internists	Pediatrics
38	31	38	21
C	C	B	B
Specialists			
Medical	Surgical	Psychiatry	Osteopathy
49	93	13	8
B	A	B	C

General Hospitals: 2 (617 beds)
  2 JCAHO, 75 of 108 services
Other Hospitals: N/A

Places Rated Rank: 167

Atlanta-Sandy Springs, GA

Patient-treating Physicians: 8,436

Primary Care			
General	Family	Internists	Pediatrics
799	702	1,218	799
C	C	A	AA
Specialists			
Medical	Surgical	Psychiatry	Osteopathy
1,171	2,033	395	209
B	B	A	C

General Hospitals: 41 (8,666 beds)
  34 JCAHO, 7 teaching, 104 of 108 services
Other Hospitals: Children, VA, Psych, Rehab

Places Rated Rank: 199

Atlantic City, NJ

Patient-treating Physicians: 521

Primary Care			
General	Family	Internists	Pediatrics
24	17	70	32
C	C	A	B
Specialists			
Medical	Surgical	Psychiatry	Osteopathy
55	126	18	109
C	A	B	AA

General Hospitals: 4 (726 beds)
  3 JCAHO, 1 teaching, 81 of 108 services
Other Hospitals: Rehab

Places Rated Rank: 259

Auburn-Opelika, AL

Patient-treating Physicians: 165

Primary Care			
General	Family	Internists	Pediatrics
26	19	22	17
C	C	C	A
Specialists			
Medical	Surgical	Psychiatry	Osteopathy
28	42	3	4
C	C	C	C

General Hospitals: 1 (273 beds)
  1 JCAHO, 63 of 108 services
Other Hospitals: N/A

Places Rated Rank: 332

✓Augusta, GA-SC

Patient-treating Physicians: 1,165

Primary Care			
General	Family	Internists	Pediatrics
128	112	121	83
B	B	A	A
Specialists			
Medical	Surgical	Psychiatry	Osteopathy
207	291	36	43
AA	AA	B	B

General Hospitals: 10 (2,344 beds)
  10 JCAHO, 4 teaching, 101 of 108 services
Other Hospitals: Children, VA, Psych, Rehab

Places Rated Rank: 32

Austin-Round Rock, TX

Patient-treating Physicians: 2,537

Primary Care			
General	Family	Internists	Pediatrics
396	354	271	192
B	B	B	A
Specialists			
Medical	Surgical	Psychiatry	Osteopathy
309	572	128	89
C	B	A	C

General Hospitals: 17 (2,164 beds)
  11 JCAHO, 1 teaching, 86 of 108 services
Other Hospitals: Children, Psych, Rehab

Places Rated Rank: 257

Bakersfield, CA

Patient-treating Physicians: 827

Primary Care			
General	Family	Internists	Pediatrics
124	97	144	64
C	C	B	C
Specialists			
Medical	Surgical	Psychiatry	Osteopathy
97	184	27	33
C	C	C	C

General Hospitals: 10 (1,438 beds)
  7 JCAHO, 1 teaching, 65 of 108 services
Other Hospitals: Rehab

Places Rated Rank: 362

Baltimore-Towson, MD

Patient-treating Physicians: 6,973

Primary Care			
General	Family	Internists	Pediatrics
442	375	1,212	582
C	C	AA	AA

Specialists			
Medical	Surgical	Psychiatry	Osteopathy
1,075	1,588	445	127
AA	AA	AA	C

General Hospitals: 23 (7,442 beds)
21 JCAHO, 13 teaching, 107 of 108 services
Other Hospitals: Children, VA, Psych, Rehab

Places Rated Rank: 74

Bangor, ME

Patient-treating Physicians: 373

Primary Care			
General	Family	Internists	Pediatrics
40	37	46	18
B	B	AA	B

Specialists			
Medical	Surgical	Psychiatry	Osteopathy
54	82	20	28
AA	AA	AA	AA

General Hospitals: 4 (466 beds)
2 JCAHO, 1 teaching, 75 of 108 services
Other Hospitals: Psych

Places Rated Rank: 112

Barnstable Town, MA

Patient-treating Physicians: 526

Primary Care			
General	Family	Internists	Pediatrics
50	42	107	35
C	C	AA	A

Specialists			
Medical	Surgical	Psychiatry	Osteopathy
58	123	34	21
B	A	AA	B

General Hospitals: 2 (306 beds)
2 JCAHO, 69 of 108 services
Other Hospitals: N/A

Places Rated Rank: 233

Baton Rouge, LA

Patient-treating Physicians: 1,182

Primary Care			
General	Family	Internists	Pediatrics
185	163	143	94
B	B	B	B

Specialists			
Medical	Surgical	Psychiatry	Osteopathy
169	305	35	3
C	B	C	C

General Hospitals: 16 (1,682 beds)
7 JCAHO, 2 teaching, 93 of 108 services
Other Hospitals: Children, Rehab

Places Rated Rank: 210

Battle Creek, MI

Patient-treating Physicians: 207

Primary Care			
General	Family	Internists	Pediatrics
31	31	24	8
C	B	C	C

Specialists			
Medical	Surgical	Psychiatry	Osteopathy
22	51	11	28
C	C	A	AA

General Hospitals: 3 (487 beds)
2 JCAHO, 66 of 108 services
Other Hospitals: VA, Psych, Rehab

Places Rated Rank: 318

Bay City, MI

Patient-treating Physicians: 157

Primary Care			
General	Family	Internists	Pediatrics
15	7	17	8
C	C	C	C

Specialists			
Medical	Surgical	Psychiatry	Osteopathy
16	31	5	40
C	C	C	AA

General Hospitals: 1 (309 beds)
1 JCAHO, 50 of 108 services
Other Hospitals: N/A

Places Rated Rank: 367

Beaumont-Port Arthur, TX

Patient-treating Physicians: 571

Primary Care			
General	Family	Internists	Pediatrics
88	76	62	29
C	C	C	C

Specialists			
Medical	Surgical	Psychiatry	Osteopathy
74	132	19	41
C	C	C	A

General Hospitals: 9 (1,285 beds)
6 JCAHO, 78 of 108 services
Other Hospitals: Rehab

Places Rated Rank: 303

Bellingham, WA

Patient-treating Physicians: 392

Primary Care			
General	Family	Internists	Pediatrics
90	83	36	23
AA	AA	B	B

Specialists			
Medical	Surgical	Psychiatry	Osteopathy
47	82	12	8
B	B	B	C

General Hospitals: 1 (226 beds)
1 JCAHO, 71 of 108 services
Other Hospitals: N/A

Places Rated Rank: 211

Bend, OR

Patient-treating Physicians: 324

Primary Care			
General	Family	Internists	Pediatrics
52	51	31	13
AA	AA	A	C

Specialists			
Medical	Surgical	Psychiatry	Osteopathy
35	91	5	14
B	AA	C	A

General Hospitals: 2 (220 beds)
2 JCAHO, 1 teaching, 64 of 108 services
Other Hospitals: N/A

Places Rated Rank: 165

Bethesda-Gaithersburg, MD

Patient-treating Physicians: 4,407

Primary Care			
General	Family	Internists	Pediatrics
295	250	645	419
B	B	AA	AA

Specialists			
Medical	Surgical	Psychiatry	Osteopathy
792	890	309	56
AA	AA	AA	C

General Hospitals: 7 (1,847 beds)
7 JCAHO, 3 teaching, 92 of 108 services
Other Hospitals: Psych, Rehab

Places Rated Rank: 87

✓Billings, MT

Patient-treating Physicians: 410

Primary Care			
General	Family	Internists	Pediatrics
52	47	37	19
AA	AA	A	B

Specialists			
Medical	Surgical	Psychiatry	Osteopathy
61	109	17	9
AA	AA	AA	C

General Hospitals: 3 (670 beds)
2 JCAHO, 2 teaching, 87 of 108 services
Other Hospitals: N/A

Places Rated Rank: 20

Binghamton, NY

Patient-treating Physicians: 443

Primary Care			
General	Family	Internists	Pediatrics
50	50	65	22
C	C	A	C

Specialists			
Medical	Surgical	Psychiatry	Osteopathy
62	110	26	25
B	B	A	A

General Hospitals: 2 (665 beds)
2 JCAHO, 84 of 108 services
Other Hospitals: N/A

Places Rated Rank: 241

✓ Birmingham-Hoover, AL

Patient-treating Physicians: 2,538

Primary Care			
General	Family	Internists	Pediatrics
207	181	382	183
C	C	AA	AA
Specialists			
Medical	Surgical	Psychiatry	Osteopathy
407	677	93	40
AA	AA	A	C

General Hospitals: 20 (4,531 beds)
  17 JCAHO, 10 teaching, 104 of 108 services
Other Hospitals: Children, VA, Rehab

Places Rated Rank: 36

✓ Bismarck, ND

Patient-treating Physicians: 257

Primary Care			
General	Family	Internists	Pediatrics
33	30	22	10
A	A	B	C
Specialists			
Medical	Surgical	Psychiatry	Osteopathy
39	64	8	9
AA	AA	A	B

General Hospitals: 2 (475 beds)
  2 JCAHO, 2 teaching, 86 of 108 services
Other Hospitals: N/A

Places Rated Rank: 28

Blacksburg-Christiansburg, VA

Patient-treating Physicians: 238

Primary Care			
General	Family	Internists	Pediatrics
55	51	28	11
A	AA	C	C
Specialists			
Medical	Surgical	Psychiatry	Osteopathy
15	59	7	19
C	C	C	A

General Hospitals: 4 (304 beds)
  4 JCAHO, 63 of 108 services
Other Hospitals: Psych

Places Rated Rank: 322

Bloomington, IN

Patient-treating Physicians: 295

Primary Care			
General	Family	Internists	Pediatrics
54	46	26	11
A	B	C	C
Specialists			
Medical	Surgical	Psychiatry	Osteopathy
33	66	10	8
C	C	C	C

General Hospitals: 2 (836 beds)
  2 JCAHO, 33 of 108 services
Other Hospitals: N/A

Places Rated Rank: 289

Bloomington-Normal, IL

Patient-treating Physicians: 300

Primary Care			
General	Family	Internists	Pediatrics
35	33	31	17
C	C	B	B
Specialists			
Medical	Surgical	Psychiatry	Osteopathy
38	72	10	17
B	B	B	A

General Hospitals: 2 (395 beds)
  2 JCAHO, 78 of 108 services
Other Hospitals: N/A

Places Rated Rank: 251

Boise City-Nampa, ID

Patient-treating Physicians: 965

Primary Care			
General	Family	Internists	Pediatrics
179	165	90	42
A	A	C	C
Specialists			
Medical	Surgical	Psychiatry	Osteopathy
120	268	20	39
B	A	C	B

General Hospitals: 6 (1,167 beds)
  5 JCAHO, 3 teaching, 90 of 108 services
Other Hospitals: Children, VA, Psych, Rehab

Places Rated Rank: 142

Boston-Quincy, MA

Patient-treating Physicians: 6,164

Primary Care			
General	Family	Internists	Pediatrics
234	202	1,135	495
C	C	AA	AA
Specialists			
Medical	Surgical	Psychiatry	Osteopathy
1,158	1,226	415	66
AA	AA	AA	C

General Hospitals: 23 (5,522 beds)
  17 JCAHO, 11 teaching, 105 of 108 services
Other Hospitals: Children, VA, Psych, Rehab

Places Rated Rank: 71

Boulder, CO

Patient-treating Physicians: 843

Primary Care			
General	Family	Internists	Pediatrics
156	151	87	51
AA	AA	A	AA
Specialists			
Medical	Surgical	Psychiatry	Osteopathy
95	173	57	34
A	AA	AA	A

General Hospitals: 3 (458 beds)
  3 JCAHO, 89 of 108 services
Other Hospitals: Psych

Places Rated Rank: 80

Bowling Green, KY

Patient-treating Physicians: 233

Primary Care			
General	Family	Internists	Pediatrics
30	24	27	16
B	B	A	A
Specialists			
Medical	Surgical	Psychiatry	Osteopathy
41	64	11	4
AA	AA	A	C

General Hospitals: 3 (717 beds)
  2 JCAHO, 67 of 108 services
Other Hospitals: Rehab

Places Rated Rank: 77

Bremerton-Silverdale, WA

Patient-treating Physicians: 393

Primary Care			
General	Family	Internists	Pediatrics
74	67	31	24
A	A	C	C
Specialists			
Medical	Surgical	Psychiatry	Osteopathy
47	75	17	15
C	C	B	C

General Hospitals: 2 (306 beds)
  2 JCAHO, 1 teaching, 73 of 108 services
Other Hospitals: N/A

Places Rated Rank: 339

Bridgeport-Stamford-Norwalk, CT

Patient-treating Physicians: 2,347

Primary Care			
General	Family	Internists	Pediatrics
108	91	411	207
C	C	AA	AA
Specialists			
Medical	Surgical	Psychiatry	Osteopathy
387	587	159	52
AA	AA	AA	C

General Hospitals: 6 (1,707 beds)
  6 JCAHO, 6 teaching, 101 of 108 services
Other Hospitals: Psych

Places Rated Rank: 135

Brownsville-Harlingen, TX

Patient-treating Physicians: 429

Primary Care			
General	Family	Internists	Pediatrics
66	55	50	56
C	C	C	A
Specialists			
Medical	Surgical	Psychiatry	Osteopathy
70	97	12	17
C	C	C	C

General Hospitals: 6 (1,055 beds)
  5 JCAHO, 1 teaching, 78 of 108 services
Other Hospitals: Psych

Places Rated Rank: 327

Brunswick, GA

Patient-treating Physicians: 177

Primary Care			
General	Family	Internists	Pediatrics
17	15	15	10
C	C	C	C
Specialists			
Medical	Surgical	Psychiatry	Osteopathy
24	52	14	7
B	A	AA	B

General Hospitals: 1 (278 beds)
  1 JCAHO, 61 of 108 services
Other Hospitals: Psych

Places Rated Rank: 282

Buffalo-Niagara Falls, NY

Patient-treating Physicians: 2,241

Primary Care			
General	Family	Internists	Pediatrics
212	190	361	187
C	C	AA	A
Specialists			
Medical	Surgical	Psychiatry	Osteopathy
317	554	75	90
B	A	B	B

General Hospitals: 13 (5,114 beds)
  8 JCAHO, 6 teaching, 92 of 108 services
Other Hospitals: Children, VA, Psych

Places Rated Rank: 104

Burlington, NC

Patient-treating Physicians: 169

Primary Care			
General	Family	Internists	Pediatrics
29	28	29	15
C	C	B	B
Specialists			
Medical	Surgical	Psychiatry	Osteopathy
20	42	3	0
C	C	C	C

General Hospitals: 1 (319 beds)
  1 JCAHO, 73 of 108 services
Other Hospitals: N/A

Places Rated Rank: 338

✓Burlington-South Burlington, VT

Patient-treating Physicians: 652

Primary Care			
General	Family	Internists	Pediatrics
82	75	94	53
AA	AA	AA	AA
Specialists			
Medical	Surgical	Psychiatry	Osteopathy
77	142	49	13
AA	AA	AA	C

General Hospitals: 2 (571 beds)
  2 JCAHO, 1 teaching, 86 of 108 services
Other Hospitals: Children

Places Rated Rank: 31

Cambridge-Newton, MA

Patient-treating Physicians: 4,860

Primary Care			
General	Family	Internists	Pediatrics
215	182	923	439
C	C	AA	AA
Specialists			
Medical	Surgical	Psychiatry	Osteopathy
795	891	579	32
AA	AA	AA	C

General Hospitals: 14 (2,551 beds)
  12 JCAHO, 5 teaching, 97 of 108 services
Other Hospitals: Children, VA, Psych, Rehab

Places Rated Rank: 150

Camden, NJ

Patient-treating Physicians: 2,821

Primary Care			
General	Family	Internists	Pediatrics
235	194	255	193
C	C	B	A
Specialists			
Medical	Surgical	Psychiatry	Osteopathy
385	478	92	713
A	C	B	AA

General Hospitals: 10 (2,417 beds)
  7 JCAHO, 4 teaching, 98 of 108 services
Other Hospitals: Children, Psych

Places Rated Rank: 234

Canton-Massillon, OH

Patient-treating Physicians: 762

Primary Care			
General	Family	Internists	Pediatrics
87	81	99	50
C	C	A	B
Specialists			
Medical	Surgical	Psychiatry	Osteopathy
109	143	21	114
B	C	C	AA

General Hospitals: 5 (1,445 beds)
  4 JCAHO, 2 teaching, 88 of 108 services
Other Hospitals: Children

Places Rated Rank: 212

Cape Coral-Fort Myers, FL

Patient-treating Physicians: 994

Primary Care			
General	Family	Internists	Pediatrics
84	67	101	63
C	C	B	B
Specialists			
Medical	Surgical	Psychiatry	Osteopathy
150	248	30	128
A	A	B	AA

General Hospitals: 5 (1,735 beds)
  4 JCAHO, 66 of 108 services
Other Hospitals: Children

Places Rated Rank: 209

Carson City, NV

Patient-treating Physicians: 142

Primary Care			
General	Family	Internists	Pediatrics
22	21	15	6
AA	AA	A	B
Specialists			
Medical	Surgical	Psychiatry	Osteopathy
19	31	3	15
A	AA	C	AA

General Hospitals: 1 (131 beds)
  1 JCAHO, 58 of 108 services
Other Hospitals: N/A

Places Rated Rank: 138

Casper, WY

Patient-treating Physicians: 140

Primary Care			
General	Family	Internists	Pediatrics
27	26	11	7
AA	AA	C	C
Specialists			
Medical	Surgical	Psychiatry	Osteopathy
21	35	3	2
A	A	C	C

General Hospitals: 1 (205 beds)
  1 JCAHO, 58 of 108 services
Other Hospitals: Psych

Places Rated Rank: 169

Cedar Rapids, IA

Patient-treating Physicians: 357

Primary Care			
General	Family	Internists	Pediatrics
87	81	15	19
A	AA	C	C
Specialists			
Medical	Surgical	Psychiatry	Osteopathy
48	73	13	23
C	C	C	B

General Hospitals: 4 (843 beds)
  2 JCAHO, 2 teaching, 96 of 108 services
Other Hospitals: N/A

Places Rated Rank: 206

Champaign-Urbana, IL

Patient-treating Physicians: 415

Primary Care			
General	Family	Internists	Pediatrics
67	60	51	20
A	A	A	C
Specialists			
Medical	Surgical	Psychiatry	Osteopathy
70	82	24	18
A	C	AA	B

General Hospitals: 4 (676 beds)
  3 JCAHO, 2 teaching, 81 of 108 services
Other Hospitals: Psych

Places Rated Rank: 183

Health Care

Charleston, WV

Patient-treating Physicians: 695

Primary Care			
General	Family	Internists	Pediatrics
98	82	70	44
A	A	B	A
Specialists			
Medical	Surgical	Psychiatry	Osteopathy
99	165	20	66
A	A	B	AA

General Hospitals: 7 (1,266 beds)
   5 JCAHO, 2 teaching, 96 of 108 services
Other Hospitals: Children, Psych, Rehab

Places Rated Rank: 41

Charleston-North Charleston, SC

Patient-treating Physicians: 1,503

Primary Care			
General	Family	Internists	Pediatrics
175	160	145	106
A	A	A	AA
Specialists			
Medical	Surgical	Psychiatry	Osteopathy
234	377	86	26
AA	AA	AA	C

General Hospitals: 8 (1,762 beds)
   6 JCAHO, 4 teaching, 84 of 108 services
Other Hospitals: Children, VA, Psych, Rehab

Places Rated Rank: 61

Charlotte-Gastonia, NC-SC

Patient-treating Physicians: 2,731

Primary Care			
General	Family	Internists	Pediatrics
356	341	370	215
B	B	A	A
Specialists			
Medical	Surgical	Psychiatry	Osteopathy
406	675	69	42
B	A	C	C

General Hospitals: 13 (3,206 beds)
   10 JCAHO, 1 teaching, 101 of 108 services
Other Hospitals: Children, Rehab

Places Rated Rank: 128

✓Charlottesville, VA

Patient-treating Physicians: 777

Primary Care			
General	Family	Internists	Pediatrics
78	69	88	59
AA	AA	AA	AA
Specialists			
Medical	Surgical	Psychiatry	Osteopathy
144	143	60	7
AA	AA	AA	C

General Hospitals: 2 (687 beds)
   2 JCAHO, 1 teaching, 94 of 108 services
Other Hospitals: Children

Places Rated Rank: 7

Chattanooga, TN-GA

Patient-treating Physicians: 1,036

Primary Care			
General	Family	Internists	Pediatrics
121	108	135	74
B	B	A	A
Specialists			
Medical	Surgical	Psychiatry	Osteopathy
142	254	32	47
A	A	B	A

General Hospitals: 8 (1,793 beds)
   5 JCAHO, 1 teaching, 85 of 108 services
Other Hospitals: Children, Psych, Rehab

Places Rated Rank: 96

Cheyenne, WY

Patient-treating Physicians: 170

Primary Care			
General	Family	Internists	Pediatrics
28	26	16	11
A	A	C	B
Specialists			
Medical	Surgical	Psychiatry	Osteopathy
30	44	3	4
AA	A	C	C

General Hospitals: 2 (269 beds)
   2 JCAHO, 74 of 108 services
Other Hospitals: VA

Places Rated Rank: 108

Chicago-Naperville-Joliet, IL

Patient-treating Physicians: 16,439

Primary Care			
General	Family	Internists	Pediatrics
1,688	1,430	2,725	1,287
C	C	AA	AA
Specialists			
Medical	Surgical	Psychiatry	Osteopathy
2,404	3,399	817	822
A	B	AA	A

General Hospitals: 79 (20,631 beds)
   74 JCAHO, 30 teaching, all 108 services
Other Hospitals: Children, VA, Psych, Rehab

Places Rated Rank: 115

Chico, CA

Patient-treating Physicians: 381

Primary Care			
General	Family	Internists	Pediatrics
66	56	40	20
A	A	C	C
Specialists			
Medical	Surgical	Psychiatry	Osteopathy
49	91	16	19
C	B	B	B

General Hospitals: 4 (450 beds)
   2 JCAHO, 78 of 108 services
Other Hospitals: N/A

Places Rated Rank: 253

Cincinnati-Middletown, OH-KY-IN

Patient-treating Physicians: 4,084

Primary Care			
General	Family	Internists	Pediatrics
515	465	528	375
B	B	A	AA
Specialists			
Medical	Surgical	Psychiatry	Osteopathy
575	876	168	157
B	B	A	B

General Hospitals: 23 (4,516 beds)
   17 JCAHO, 7 teaching, 103 of 108 services
Other Hospitals: Children, VA, Rehab

Places Rated Rank: 159

Clarksville, TN-KY

Patient-treating Physicians: 268

Primary Care			
General	Family	Internists	Pediatrics
44	37	32	30
C	C	C	B
Specialists			
Medical	Surgical	Psychiatry	Osteopathy
24	72	12	14
C	C	C	C

General Hospitals: 3 (472 beds)
   3 JCAHO, 66 of 108 services
Other Hospitals: Psych

Places Rated Rank: 363

Cleveland, TN

Patient-treating Physicians: 154

Primary Care			
General	Family	Internists	Pediatrics
23	19	31	12
C	C	A	B
Specialists			
Medical	Surgical	Psychiatry	Osteopathy
12	35	5	14
C	C	C	A

General Hospitals: 3 (278 beds)
   3 JCAHO, 51 of 108 services
Other Hospitals: N/A

Places Rated Rank: 345

Cleveland-Elyria-Mentor, OH

Patient-treating Physicians: 5,297

Primary Care			
General	Family	Internists	Pediatrics
390	324	819	364
C	C	AA	AA
Specialists			
Medical	Surgical	Psychiatry	Osteopathy
848	1,169	198	349
AA	A	A	AA

General Hospitals: 26 (7,670 beds)
   24 JCAHO, 6 teaching, all 108 services
Other Hospitals: Children, VA, Psych

Places Rated Rank: 53

Coeur d'Alene, ID

Patient-treating Physicians: 231

Primary Care			
General	Family	Internists	Pediatrics
54	49	18	7
AA	AA	C	C
Specialists			
Medical	Surgical	Psychiatry	Osteopathy
26	54	9	10
C	B	A	B

General Hospitals: 1 (246 beds)
1 JCAHO, 63 of 108 services
Other Hospitals: N/A

Places Rated Rank: 243

College Station-Bryan, TX

Patient-treating Physicians: 320

Primary Care			
General	Family	Internists	Pediatrics
72	68	32	19
AA	AA	C	C
Specialists			
Medical	Surgical	Psychiatry	Osteopathy
38	73	6	15
C	C	C	B

General Hospitals: 3 (423 beds)
2 JCAHO, 2 teaching, 74 of 108 services
Other Hospitals: N/A

Places Rated Rank: 269

Colorado Springs, CO

Patient-treating Physicians: 1,062

Primary Care			
General	Family	Internists	Pediatrics
120	111	84	64
C	C	C	B
Specialists			
Medical	Surgical	Psychiatry	Osteopathy
128	253	36	97
C	B	B	AA

General Hospitals: 4 (974 beds)
4 JCAHO, 91 of 108 services
Other Hospitals: Children, Psych

Places Rated Rank: 284

✓Columbia, MO

Patient-treating Physicians: 609

Primary Care			
General	Family	Internists	Pediatrics
69	61	38	30
AA	AA	A	AA
Specialists			
Medical	Surgical	Psychiatry	Osteopathy
124	141	24	38
AA	AA	AA	AA

General Hospitals: 4 (976 beds)
4 JCAHO, 4 teaching, 95 of 108 services
Other Hospitals: Children, VA, Psych, Rehab

Places Rated Rank: 2

Columbia, SC

Patient-treating Physicians: 1,313

Primary Care			
General	Family	Internists	Pediatrics
185	163	132	110
B	B	B	AA
Specialists			
Medical	Surgical	Psychiatry	Osteopathy
196	314	67	18
A	B	A	C

General Hospitals: 8 (2,028 beds)
8 JCAHO, 3 teaching, 92 of 108 services
Other Hospitals: Children, VA, Psych, Rehab

Places Rated Rank: 121

Columbus, GA-AL

Patient-treating Physicians: 456

Primary Care			
General	Family	Internists	Pediatrics
103	89	40	27
A	A	C	C
Specialists			
Medical	Surgical	Psychiatry	Osteopathy
50	118	12	20
C	C	C	B

General Hospitals: 4 (994 beds)
4 JCAHO, 2 teaching, 85 of 108 services
Other Hospitals: Psych

Places Rated Rank: 195

Columbus, IN

Patient-treating Physicians: 167

Primary Care			
General	Family	Internists	Pediatrics
30	28	17	15
AA	AA	B	AA
Specialists			
Medical	Surgical	Psychiatry	Osteopathy
18	46	3	2
B	AA	C	C

General Hospitals: 1 (256 beds)
1 JCAHO, 69 of 108 services
Other Hospitals: Psych

Places Rated Rank: 73

Columbus, OH

Patient-treating Physicians: 3,530

Primary Care			
General	Family	Internists	Pediatrics
497	454	313	225
B	A	C	A
Specialists			
Medical	Surgical	Psychiatry	Osteopathy
480	694	132	471
B	B	A	AA

General Hospitals: 15 (4,115 beds)
13 JCAHO, 4 teaching, 105 of 108 services
Other Hospitals: Children

Places Rated Rank: 141

Corpus Christi, TX

Patient-treating Physicians: 726

Primary Care			
General	Family	Internists	Pediatrics
94	84	72	65
C	C	C	A
Specialists			
Medical	Surgical	Psychiatry	Osteopathy
114	163	14	48
B	C	C	A

General Hospitals: 8 (1,500 beds)
5 JCAHO, 1 teaching, 84 of 108 services
Other Hospitals: Children, Rehab

Places Rated Rank: 189

Corvallis, OR

Patient-treating Physicians: 214

Primary Care			
General	Family	Internists	Pediatrics
30	25	33	17
AA	A	AA	AA
Specialists			
Medical	Surgical	Psychiatry	Osteopathy
24	40	12	11
A	A	AA	A

General Hospitals: 1 (134 beds)
1 JCAHO, 46 of 108 services
Other Hospitals: N/A

Places Rated Rank: 184

Cumberland, MD-WV

Patient-treating Physicians: 175

Primary Care			
General	Family	Internists	Pediatrics
24	18	21	10
C	C	B	C
Specialists			
Medical	Surgical	Psychiatry	Osteopathy
24	42	5	5
C	C	C	C

General Hospitals: 3 (450 beds)
3 JCAHO, 66 of 108 services
Other Hospitals: N/A

Places Rated Rank: 248

Dallas-Plano-Irving, TX

Patient-treating Physicians: 6,857

Primary Care			
General	Family	Internists	Pediatrics
716	639	812	497
C	C	B	A
Specialists			
Medical	Surgical	Psychiatry	Osteopathy
949	1,581	252	451
B	B	B	A

General Hospitals: 41 (8,136 beds)
33 JCAHO, 7 teaching, 104 of 108 services
Other Hospitals: Children, VA, Psych, Rehab

Places Rated Rank: 204

Dalton, GA

Patient-treating Physicians: 169

Primary Care			
General	Family	Internists	Pediatrics
22	21	26	19
C	C	B	A
Specialists			
Medical	Surgical	Psychiatry	Osteopathy
19	49	5	3
C	C	C	C

General Hospitals: 2 (290 beds)
 2 JCAHO, 68 of 108 services

Other Hospitals: N/A

Places Rated Rank: 335

Danville, IL

Patient-treating Physicians: 94

Primary Care			
General	Family	Internists	Pediatrics
22	21	12	6
B	B	C	C
Specialists			
Medical	Surgical	Psychiatry	Osteopathy
7	19	3	4
C	C	C	C

General Hospitals: 2 (659 beds)
 2 JCAHO, 1 teaching, 77 of 108 services

Other Hospitals: VA

Places Rated Rank: 280

Danville, VA

Patient-treating Physicians: 158

Primary Care			
General	Family	Internists	Pediatrics
17	17	22	10
C	C	B	C
Specialists			
Medical	Surgical	Psychiatry	Osteopathy
24	42	6	6
C	C	C	C

General Hospitals: 1 (350 beds)
 1 JCAHO, 69 of 108 services

Other Hospitals: N/A

Places Rated Rank: 320

Davenport-Moline, IA-IL

Patient-treating Physicians: 624

Primary Care			
General	Family	Internists	Pediatrics
95	92	52	29
B	B	C	C
Specialists			
Medical	Surgical	Psychiatry	Osteopathy
86	144	13	68
C	C	C	AA

General Hospitals: 7 (1,097 beds)
 5 JCAHO, 1 teaching, 94 of 108 services

Other Hospitals: N/A

Places Rated Rank: 235

Dayton, OH

Patient-treating Physicians: 1,707

Primary Care			
General	Family	Internists	Pediatrics
255	239	180	91
B	A	B	B
Specialists			
Medical	Surgical	Psychiatry	Osteopathy
248	311	54	241
A	C	B	AA

General Hospitals: 8 (2,826 beds)
 7 JCAHO, 6 teaching, 103 of 108 services

Other Hospitals: Children, VA

Places Rated Rank: 129

Decatur, AL

Patient-treating Physicians: 198

Primary Care			
General	Family	Internists	Pediatrics
39	36	28	12
B	B	C	C
Specialists			
Medical	Surgical	Psychiatry	Osteopathy
17	54	10	7
C	C	B	C

General Hospitals: 4 (558 beds)
 4 JCAHO, 56 of 108 services

Other Hospitals: N/A

Places Rated Rank: 304

Decatur, IL

Patient-treating Physicians: 202

Primary Care			
General	Family	Internists	Pediatrics
38	37	25	8
A	A	B	C
Specialists			
Medical	Surgical	Psychiatry	Osteopathy
23	46	1	5
C	C	C	C

General Hospitals: 2 (494 beds)
 2 JCAHO, 2 teaching, 78 of 108 services

Other Hospitals: N/A

Places Rated Rank: 174

Deltona-Daytona Beach, FL

Patient-treating Physicians: 763

Primary Care			
General	Family	Internists	Pediatrics
126	113	85	32
B	B	C	C
Specialists			
Medical	Surgical	Psychiatry	Osteopathy
101	162	22	65
C	C	C	A

General Hospitals: 6 (1,473 beds)
 6 JCAHO, 1 teaching, 83 of 108 services

Other Hospitals: N/A

Places Rated Rank: 262

Denver-Aurora, CO

Patient-treating Physicians: 5,148

Primary Care			
General	Family	Internists	Pediatrics
597	545	685	380
B	B	AA	AA
Specialists			
Medical	Surgical	Psychiatry	Osteopathy
742	1,087	256	258
A	A	AA	A

General Hospitals: 18 (4,249 beds)
 13 JCAHO, 8 teaching, 107 of 108 services

Other Hospitals: Children, VA

Places Rated Rank: 111

Des Moines-West Des Moines, IA

Patient-treating Physicians: 1,033

Primary Care			
General	Family	Internists	Pediatrics
100	97	63	50
C	C	C	C
Specialists			
Medical	Surgical	Psychiatry	Osteopathy
118	196	20	304
C	C	C	AA

General Hospitals: 8 (1,770 beds)
 5 JCAHO, 4 teaching, 101 of 108 services

Other Hospitals: Children, VA

Places Rated Rank: 214

Detroit-Livonia-Dearborn, MI

Patient-treating Physicians: 2,786

Primary Care			
General	Family	Internists	Pediatrics
227	190	464	167
C	C	B	C
Specialists			
Medical	Surgical	Psychiatry	Osteopathy
355	539	83	431
C	C	C	AA

General Hospitals: 16 (5,154 beds)
 14 JCAHO, 8 teaching, 104 of 108 services

Other Hospitals: Children, VA, Rehab

Places Rated Rank: 312

Dothan, AL

Patient-treating Physicians: 311

Primary Care			
General	Family	Internists	Pediatrics
35	32	33	21
B	B	A	A
Specialists			
Medical	Surgical	Psychiatry	Osteopathy
46	85	5	10
A	AA	C	B

General Hospitals: 4 (749 beds)
 3 JCAHO, 79 of 108 services

Other Hospitals: Rehab

Places Rated Rank: 60

Dover, DE

Patient-treating Physicians: 202

Primary Care			
General	Family	Internists	Pediatrics
15	15	27	16
C	C	C	B
Specialists			
Medical	Surgical	Psychiatry	Osteopathy
28	45	11	20
C	C	A	A

General Hospitals: 1 (341 beds)
1 JCAHO, 72 of 108 services
Other Hospitals: N/A

Places Rated Rank: 340

Dubuque, IA

Patient-treating Physicians: 197

Primary Care			
General	Family	Internists	Pediatrics
12	10	37	16
C	C	AA	AA
Specialists			
Medical	Surgical	Psychiatry	Osteopathy
24	55	8	7
B	AA	A	B

General Hospitals: 2 (447 beds)
2 JCAHO, 86 of 108 services
Other Hospitals: N/A

Places Rated Rank: 84

Duluth, MN-WI

Patient-treating Physicians: 601

Primary Care			
General	Family	Internists	Pediatrics
167	156	57	21
AA	AA	B	C
Specialists			
Medical	Surgical	Psychiatry	Osteopathy
74	130	13	12
B	B	C	C

General Hospitals: 11 (1,567 beds)
6 JCAHO, 2 teaching, 98 of 108 services
Other Hospitals: Children

Places Rated Rank: 35

✓ Durham, NC

Patient-treating Physicians: 2,030

Primary Care			
General	Family	Internists	Pediatrics
167	156	57	21
AA	AA	B	C
Specialists			
Medical	Surgical	Psychiatry	Osteopathy
74	130	13	12
B	B	C	C

General Hospitals: 7 (2,029 beds)
5 JCAHO, 3 teaching, 99 of 108 services
Other Hospitals: Children, VA

Places Rated Rank: 5

✓ Eau Claire, WI

Patient-treating Physicians: 411

Primary Care			
General	Family	Internists	Pediatrics
83	78	41	21
AA	AA	A	A
Specialists			
Medical	Surgical	Psychiatry	Osteopathy
58	101	13	8
AA	AA	A	C

General Hospitals: 6 (607 beds)
4 JCAHO, 2 teaching, 89 of 108 services
Other Hospitals: N/A

Places Rated Rank: 14

Edison, NJ

Patient-treating Physicians: 5,200

Primary Care			
General	Family	Internists	Pediatrics
299	253	915	494
C	C	AA	AA
Specialists			
Medical	Surgical	Psychiatry	Osteopathy
861	1,122	192	366
AA	A	A	AA

General Hospitals: 16 (4,588 beds)
14 JCAHO, 6 teaching, 105 of 108 services
Other Hospitals: Children, Psych, Rehab

Places Rated Rank: 149

El Centro, CA

Patient-treating Physicians: 101

Primary Care			
General	Family	Internists	Pediatrics
16	12	10	11
C	C	C	C
Specialists			
Medical	Surgical	Psychiatry	Osteopathy
15	28	2	1
C	C	C	C

General Hospitals: 2 (221 beds)
2 JCAHO, 44 of 108 services
Other Hospitals: N/A

Places Rated Rank: 378

Elizabethtown, KY

Patient-treating Physicians: 192

Primary Care			
General	Family	Internists	Pediatrics
22	17	24	16
C	C	B	A
Specialists			
Medical	Surgical	Psychiatry	Osteopathy
24	46	4	4
C	B	C	C

General Hospitals: 2 (344 beds)
2 JCAHO, 62 of 108 services
Other Hospitals: Psych, Rehab

Places Rated Rank: 296

Elkhart-Goshen, IN

Patient-treating Physicians: 221

Primary Care			
General	Family	Internists	Pediatrics
57	51	15	12
A	A	C	C
Specialists			
Medical	Surgical	Psychiatry	Osteopathy
14	57	5	24
C	C	C	A

General Hospitals: 2 (421 beds)
2 JCAHO, 79 of 108 services
Other Hospitals: Psych

Places Rated Rank: 326

Elmira, NY

Patient-treating Physicians: 200

Primary Care			
General	Family	Internists	Pediatrics
16	15	30	13
C	C	AA	A
Specialists			
Medical	Surgical	Psychiatry	Osteopathy
40	44	8	11
AA	A	A	A

General Hospitals: 2 (489 beds)
2 JCAHO, 88 of 108 services
Other Hospitals: N/A

Places Rated Rank: 83

El Paso, TX

Patient-treating Physicians: 839

Primary Care			
General	Family	Internists	Pediatrics
87	76	87	64
C	C	C	C
Specialists			
Medical	Surgical	Psychiatry	Osteopathy
136	227	21	37
C	C	C	C

General Hospitals: 10 (1,805 beds)
8 JCAHO, 3 teaching, 88 of 108 services
Other Hospitals: Psych, Rehab

Places Rated Rank: 336

Erie, PA

Patient-treating Physicians: 541

Primary Care			
General	Family	Internists	Pediatrics
76	73	23	18
B	B	C	C
Specialists			
Medical	Surgical	Psychiatry	Osteopathy
71	120	13	138
B	B	C	AA

General Hospitals: 6 (1,119 beds)
3 JCAHO, 1 teaching, 89 of 108 services
Other Hospitals: Children, VA, Rehab

Places Rated Rank: 188

Essex County, MA

Patient-treating Physicians: 1,342

Primary Care			
General	Family	Internists	Pediatrics
131	123	217	112
C	C	A	A
Specialists			
Medical	Surgical	Psychiatry	Osteopathy
188	307	73	44
B	C	A	C

General Hospitals: 9 (1,326 beds)
7 JCAHO, 3 teaching, 87 of 108 services
Other Hospitals: Children, Psych, Rehab

Places Rated Rank: 279

Eugene-Springfield, OR

Patient-treating Physicians: 706

Primary Care			
General	Family	Internists	Pediatrics
137	113	79	49
AA	AA	A	A
Specialists			
Medical	Surgical	Psychiatry	Osteopathy
83	151	32	18
B	B	A	C

General Hospitals: 4 (604 beds)
3 JCAHO, 66 of 108 services
Other Hospitals: N/A

Places Rated Rank: 215

Evansville, IN-KY

Patient-treating Physicians: 707

Primary Care			
General	Family	Internists	Pediatrics
141	130	54	33
AA	AA	C	C
Specialists			
Medical	Surgical	Psychiatry	Osteopathy
105	168	30	26
A	A	A	B

General Hospitals: 8 (1,385 beds)
6 JCAHO, 2 teaching, 90 of 108 services
Other Hospitals: Rehab

Places Rated Rank: 70

Fairbanks, AK

Patient-treating Physicians: 157

Primary Care			
General	Family	Internists	Pediatrics
35	30	18	12
AA	AA	B	A
Specialists			
Medical	Surgical	Psychiatry	Osteopathy
2	38	5	7
C	B	B	B

General Hospitals: 2 (260 beds)
2 JCAHO, 57 of 108 services
Other Hospitals: N/A

Places Rated Rank: 250

✓Fargo, ND-MN

Patient-treating Physicians: 422

Primary Care			
General	Family	Internists	Pediatrics
73	69	53	30
AA	AA	AA	AA
Specialists			
Medical	Surgical	Psychiatry	Osteopathy
66	87	23	7
AA	A	AA	C

General Hospitals: 3 (625 beds)
3 JCAHO, 2 teaching, 89 of 108 services
Other Hospitals: Children, VA

Places Rated Rank: 38

Farmington, NM

Patient-treating Physicians: 149

Primary Care			
General	Family	Internists	Pediatrics
32	29	13	8
B	B	C	C
Specialists			
Medical	Surgical	Psychiatry	Osteopathy
22	30	5	15
C	C	C	A

General Hospitals: 2 (215 beds)
2 JCAHO, 45 of 108 services
Other Hospitals: N/A

Places Rated Rank: 361

Fayetteville, NC

Patient-treating Physicians: 494

Primary Care			
General	Family	Internists	Pediatrics
83	77	73	32
B	B	B	C
Specialists			
Medical	Surgical	Psychiatry	Osteopathy
74	121	17	9
C	C	C	C

General Hospitals: 3 (840 beds)
3 JCAHO, 1 teaching, 89 of 108 services
Other Hospitals: VA, Psych

Places Rated Rank: 270

Fayetteville-Springdale, AR-MO

Patient-treating Physicians: 554

Primary Care			
General	Family	Internists	Pediatrics
125	113	44	36
A	A	C	C
Specialists			
Medical	Surgical	Psychiatry	Osteopathy
68	142	19	24
C	C	C	C

General Hospitals: 8 (821 beds)
5 JCAHO, 88 of 108 services
Other Hospitals: VA, Psych, Rehab

Places Rated Rank: 261

Flagstaff, AZ

Patient-treating Physicians: 267

Primary Care			
General	Family	Internists	Pediatrics
52	46	22	14
AA	AA	C	B
Specialists			
Medical	Surgical	Psychiatry	Osteopathy
26	64	14	10
C	A	AA	B

General Hospitals: 2 (336 beds)
2 JCAHO, 72 of 108 services
Other Hospitals: N/A

Places Rated Rank: 158

Flint, MI

Patient-treating Physicians: 794

Primary Care			
General	Family	Internists	Pediatrics
100	89	131	45
C	C	A	C
Specialists			
Medical	Surgical	Psychiatry	Osteopathy
79	119	15	194
C	C	C	AA

General Hospitals: 3 (1,207 beds)
3 JCAHO, 3 teaching, 86 of 108 services
Other Hospitals: Children

Places Rated Rank: 283

Florence, SC

Patient-treating Physicians: 370

Primary Care			
General	Family	Internists	Pediatrics
71	67	36	19
AA	AA	C	C
Specialists			
Medical	Surgical	Psychiatry	Osteopathy
55	94	12	5
B	A	B	C

General Hospitals: 5 (857 beds)
4 JCAHO, 1 teaching, 88 of 108 services
Other Hospitals: Rehab

Places Rated Rank: 76

Florence-Muscle Shoals, AL

Patient-treating Physicians: 230

Primary Care			
General	Family	Internists	Pediatrics
22	19	32	17
C	C	B	B
Specialists			
Medical	Surgical	Psychiatry	Osteopathy
38	64	3	10
B	B	C	B

General Hospitals: 3 (552 beds)
3 JCAHO, 54 of 108 services
Other Hospitals: N/A

Places Rated Rank: 265

Fond du Lac, WI

Patient-treating Physicians: 142

Primary Care			
General	Family	Internists	Pediatrics
29	27	17	16
B	A	C	A
Specialists			
Medical	Surgical	Psychiatry	Osteopathy
17	29	5	4
C	C	C	C

General Hospitals: 3 (149 beds)
 2 JCAHO, 82 of 108 services

Other Hospitals: Children, Psych

Places Rated Rank: 319

Fort Collins-Loveland, CO

Patient-treating Physicians: 530

Primary Care			
General	Family	Internists	Pediatrics
135	129	35	31
AA	AA	C	B
Specialists			
Medical	Surgical	Psychiatry	Osteopathy
64	121	19	23
B	B	B	B

General Hospitals: 3 (445 beds)
 2 JCAHO, 86 of 108 services

Other Hospitals: N/A

Places Rated Rank: 198

Fort Lauderdale, FL

Patient-treating Physicians: 3,650

Primary Care			
General	Family	Internists	Pediatrics
272	214	488	272
C	C	A	A
Specialists			
Medical	Surgical	Psychiatry	Osteopathy
640	778	113	377
AA	B	B	AA

General Hospitals: 18 (4,929 beds)
 16 JCAHO, 2 teaching, 95 of 108 services

Other Hospitals: Children, Psych, Rehab

Places Rated Rank: 170

Fort Smith, AR-OK

Patient-treating Physicians: 424

Primary Care			
General	Family	Internists	Pediatrics
83	73	36	20
B	B	C	C
Specialists			
Medical	Surgical	Psychiatry	Osteopathy
58	84	7	68
C	C	C	AA

General Hospitals: 8 (904 beds)
 5 JCAHO, 86 of 108 services

Other Hospitals: Psych, Rehab

Places Rated Rank: 272

Fort Walton Beach-Crestview, FL

Patient-treating Physicians: 356

Primary Care			
General	Family	Internists	Pediatrics
65	56	42	19
AA	A	A	B
Specialists			
Medical	Surgical	Psychiatry	Osteopathy
34	100	11	16
C	AA	B	B

General Hospitals: 5 (523 beds)
 5 JCAHO, 1 teaching, 72 of 108 services

Other Hospitals: N/A

Places Rated Rank: 155

Fort Wayne, IN

Patient-treating Physicians: 815

Primary Care			
General	Family	Internists	Pediatrics
126	119	43	33
A	A	C	C
Specialists			
Medical	Surgical	Psychiatry	Osteopathy
148	207	15	50
AA	A	C	A

General Hospitals: 7 (2,000 beds)
 7 JCAHO, 3 teaching, 101 of 108 services

Other Hospitals: VA, Rehab

Places Rated Rank: 47

Fort Worth-Arlington, TX

Patient-treating Physicians: 2,765

Primary Care			
General	Family	Internists	Pediatrics
344	285	234	167
C	C	C	C
Specialists			
Medical	Surgical	Psychiatry	Osteopathy
340	626	65	461
C	C	C	AA

General Hospitals: 23 (3,476 beds)
 18 JCAHO, 1 teaching, 97 of 108 services

Other Hospitals: Children, Psych, Rehab

Places Rated Rank: 323

Fresno, CA

Patient-treating Physicians: 1,274

Primary Care			
General	Family	Internists	Pediatrics
201	168	185	108
C	C	B	B
Specialists			
Medical	Surgical	Psychiatry	Osteopathy
150	282	45	34
C	C	C	C

General Hospitals: 12 (2,301 beds)
 5 JCAHO, 3 teaching, 91 of 108 services

Other Hospitals: VA, Psych, Rehab

Places Rated Rank: 264

Gadsden, AL

Patient-treating Physicians: 184

Primary Care			
General	Family	Internists	Pediatrics
30	28	21	14
B	A	B	A
Specialists			
Medical	Surgical	Psychiatry	Osteopathy
27	50	6	7
B	A	B	B

General Hospitals: 2 (415 beds)
 2 JCAHO, 57 of 108 services

Other Hospitals: Psych

Places Rated Rank: 172

✓Gainesville, FL

Patient-treating Physicians: 970

Primary Care			
General	Family	Internists	Pediatrics
112	92	112	79
AA	AA	AA	AA
Specialists			
Medical	Surgical	Psychiatry	Osteopathy
167	198	56	23
AA	AA	AA	B

General Hospitals: 4 (1,634 beds)
 4 JCAHO, 3 teaching, 90 of 108 services

Other Hospitals: Children, VA, Rehab

Places Rated Rank: 4

Gainesville, GA

Patient-treating Physicians: 289

Primary Care			
General	Family	Internists	Pediatrics
25	19	36	22
C	C	A	A
Specialists			
Medical	Surgical	Psychiatry	Osteopathy
36	88	9	9
C	AA	B	C

General Hospitals: 1 (418 beds)
 1 JCAHO, 74 of 108 services

Other Hospitals: N/A

Places Rated Rank: 226

Gary, IN

Patient-treating Physicians: 1,105

Primary Care			
General	Family	Internists	Pediatrics
159	129	118	65
C	C	C	C
Specialists			
Medical	Surgical	Psychiatry	Osteopathy
159	267	22	105
C	C	C	A

General Hospitals: 9 (2,595 beds)
 5 JCAHO, 1 teaching, 93 of 108 services

Other Hospitals: N/A

Places Rated Rank: 201

Glens Falls, NY

Patient-treating Physicians: 217

Primary Care			
General	Family	Internists	Pediatrics
34	33	19	21
B	B	C	AA

Specialists			
Medical	Surgical	Psychiatry	Osteopathy
31	55	7	6
B	B	C	C

General Hospitals: 1 (342 beds)
  1 JCAHO, 66 of 108 services
Other Hospitals: N/A

Places Rated Rank: 255

Goldsboro, NC

Patient-treating Physicians: 161

Primary Care			
General	Family	Internists	Pediatrics
31	24	16	11
B	C	C	C

Specialists			
Medical	Surgical	Psychiatry	Osteopathy
20	30	13	10
C	C	AA	B

General Hospitals: 1 (256 beds)
  1 JCAHO, 53 of 108 services
Other Hospitals: Psych

Places Rated Rank: 356

Grand Forks, ND-MN

Patient-treating Physicians: 177

Primary Care			
General	Family	Internists	Pediatrics
45	43	19	9
AA	AA	C	C

Specialists			
Medical	Surgical	Psychiatry	Osteopathy
21	37	4	4
C	C	C	C

General Hospitals: 4 (646 beds)
  2 JCAHO, 1 teaching, 91 of 108 services
Other Hospitals: N/A

Places Rated Rank: 81

Grand Junction, CO

Patient-treating Physicians: 307

Primary Care			
General	Family	Internists	Pediatrics
63	60	15	9
AA	AA	C	C

Specialists			
Medical	Surgical	Psychiatry	Osteopathy
31	64	6	53
B	A	C	AA

General Hospitals: 3 (769 beds)
  3 JCAHO, 70 of 108 services
Other Hospitals: VA

Places Rated Rank: 95

Grand Rapids-Wyoming, MI

Patient-treating Physicians: 1,476

Primary Care			
General	Family	Internists	Pediatrics
189	183	145	78
B	B	C	C

Specialists			
Medical	Surgical	Psychiatry	Osteopathy
163	324	39	247
C	B	C	AA

General Hospitals: 7 (1,599 beds)
  5 JCAHO, 1 teaching, 96 of 108 services
Other Hospitals: Children, Psych, Rehab

Places Rated Rank: 227

Great Falls, MT

Patient-treating Physicians: 199

Primary Care			
General	Family	Internists	Pediatrics
26	24	18	12
A	A	B	A

Specialists			
Medical	Surgical	Psychiatry	Osteopathy
24	48	6	17
A	AA	B	AA

General Hospitals: 1 (490 beds)
  1 JCAHO, 83 of 108 services
Other Hospitals: N/A

Places Rated Rank: 44

Greeley, CO

Patient-treating Physicians: 268

Primary Care			
General	Family	Internists	Pediatrics
65	62	16	12
A	A	C	C

Specialists			
Medical	Surgical	Psychiatry	Osteopathy
34	59	5	17
C	C	C	B

General Hospitals: 1 (276 beds)
  1 JCAHO, 78 of 108 services
Other Hospitals: N/A

Places Rated Rank: 346

Green Bay, WI

Patient-treating Physicians: 569

Primary Care			
General	Family	Internists	Pediatrics
87	76	59	30
B	B	B	C

Specialists			
Medical	Surgical	Psychiatry	Osteopathy
79	142	15	25
B	A	C	B

General Hospitals: 5 (669 beds)
  4 JCAHO, 79 of 108 services
Other Hospitals: Psych

Places Rated Rank: 193

Greensboro-High Point, NC

Patient-treating Physicians: 1,161

Primary Care			
General	Family	Internists	Pediatrics
174	160	134	82
B	B	B	B

Specialists			
Medical	Surgical	Psychiatry	Osteopathy
192	302	37	14
A	B	C	C

General Hospitals: 5 (2,117 beds)
  4 JCAHO, 1 teaching, 94 of 108 services
Other Hospitals: Psych

Places Rated Rank: 130

✓Greenville, NC

Patient-treating Physicians: 496

Primary Care			
General	Family	Internists	Pediatrics
46	40	52	35
B	B	AA	AA

Specialists			
Medical	Surgical	Psychiatry	Osteopathy
114	112	16	10
AA	AA	A	C

General Hospitals: 1 (720 beds)
  1 JCAHO, 1 teaching, 84 of 108 services
Other Hospitals: Children

Places Rated Rank: 27

Greenville, SC

Patient-treating Physicians: 1,096

Primary Care			
General	Family	Internists	Pediatrics
205	184	133	79
A	A	B	A

Specialists			
Medical	Surgical	Psychiatry	Osteopathy
136	274	30	26
C	A	C	C

General Hospitals: 8 (1,314 beds)
  5 JCAHO, 1 teaching, 91 of 108 services
Other Hospitals: Children, Psych

Places Rated Rank: 133

Gulfport-Biloxi, MS

Patient-treating Physicians: 454

Primary Care			
General	Family	Internists	Pediatrics
40	34	54	42
C	C	B	AA

Specialists			
Medical	Surgical	Psychiatry	Osteopathy
54	129	20	29
C	A	A	A

General Hospitals: 7 (1,773 beds)
  7 JCAHO, 2 teaching, 58 of 108 services
Other Hospitals: VA, Psych

Places Rated Rank: 202

Hagerstown-Martinsburg, MD-WV

Patient-treating Physicians: 338

Primary Care			
General	Family	Internists	Pediatrics
53	48	43	23
C	C	C	C
Specialists			
Medical	Surgical	Psychiatry	Osteopathy
45	90	9	17
C	C	C	B

General Hospitals: 3 (1,031 beds)
   3 JCAHO, 2 teaching, 75 of 108 services

Other Hospitals: VA, Psych

Places Rated Rank: 247

Hanford-Corcoran, CA

Patient-treating Physicians: 95

Primary Care			
General	Family	Internists	Pediatrics
30	18	9	7
C	C	C	C
Specialists			
Medical	Surgical	Psychiatry	Osteopathy
6	20	4	2
C	C	C	C

General Hospitals: 3 (157 beds)
   3 JCAHO, 53 of 108 services

Other Hospitals: N/A

Places Rated Rank: 376

Harrisburg-Carlisle, PA

Patient-treating Physicians: 1,211

Primary Care			
General	Family	Internists	Pediatrics
129	122	126	64
B	B	A	B
Specialists			
Medical	Surgical	Psychiatry	Osteopathy
179	270	40	171
A	A	A	AA

General Hospitals: 6 (1,550 beds)
   4 JCAHO, 2 teaching, 95 of 108 services

Other Hospitals: Children, Psych, Rehab

Places Rated Rank: 90

Harrisonburg, VA

Patient-treating Physicians: 191

Primary Care			
General	Family	Internists	Pediatrics
439	41	11	19
AA	AA	C	AA
Specialists			
Medical	Surgical	Psychiatry	Osteopathy
20	47	4	4
C	B	C	C

General Hospitals: 1 (244 beds)
   1 JCAHO, 66 of 108 services

Other Hospitals: N/A

Places Rated Rank: 276

Hartford-West Hartford, CT

Patient-treating Physicians: 2,705

Primary Care			
General	Family	Internists	Pediatrics
203	189	433	223
C	C	AA	AA
Specialists			
Medical	Surgical	Psychiatry	Osteopathy
432	662	185	64
AA	AA	AA	C

General Hospitals: 12 (2,087 beds)
   10 JCAHO, 5 teaching, 101 of 108 services

Other Hospitals: Children, Psych

Places Rated Rank: 143

✓Hattiesburg, MS

Patient-treating Physicians: 349

Primary Care			
General	Family	Internists	Pediatrics
53	48	30	21
AA	AA	B	AA
Specialists			
Medical	Surgical	Psychiatry	Osteopathy
60	94	13	10
AA	AA	A	B

General Hospitals: 2 (748 beds)
   2 JCAHO, 51 of 108 services

Other Hospitals: Psych

Places Rated Rank: 37

Hickory-Lenoir-Morganton, NC

Patient-treating Physicians: 547

Primary Care			
General	Family	Internists	Pediatrics
126	117	44	20
A	AA	C	C
Specialists			
Medical	Surgical	Psychiatry	Osteopathy
60	141	18	6
C	C	C	C

General Hospitals: 5 (1,136 beds)
   5 JCAHO, 87 of 108 services

Other Hospitals: N/A

Places Rated Rank: 203

Hinesville-Fort Stewart, GA

Patient-treating Physicians: 39

Primary Care			
General	Family	Internists	Pediatrics
4	3	7	7
C	C	C	C
Specialists			
Medical	Surgical	Psychiatry	Osteopathy
1	11	1	2
C	C	C	C

General Hospitals: 1 (94 beds)
   1 JCAHO, 23 of 108 services

Other Hospitals: N/A

Places Rated Rank: 379

Holland-Grand Haven, MI

Patient-treating Physicians: 322

Primary Care			
General	Family	Internists	Pediatrics
51	50	35	20
C	C	C	C
Specialists			
Medical	Surgical	Psychiatry	Osteopathy
17	66	3	67
C	C	C	AA

General Hospitals: 3 (316 beds)
   3 JCAHO, 63 of 108 services

Other Hospitals: N/A

Places Rated Rank: 370

Honolulu, HI

Patient-treating Physicians: 2,211

Primary Care			
General	Family	Internists	Pediatrics
208	162	383	195
C	C	AA	AA
Specialists			
Medical	Surgical	Psychiatry	Osteopathy
300	494	108	36
A	A	AA	C

General Hospitals: 13 (1,982 beds)
   10 JCAHO, 7 teaching, 98 of 108 services

Other Hospitals: Children, Psych, Rehab

Places Rated Rank: 99

✓Hot Springs, AR

Patient-treating Physicians: 212

Primary Care			
General	Family	Internists	Pediatrics
408	36	14	8
AA	AA	C	C
Specialists			
Medical	Surgical	Psychiatry	Osteopathy
40	55	7	9
AA	AA	A	A

General Hospitals: 4 (485 beds)
   3 JCAHO, 73 of 108 services

Other Hospitals: Psych

Places Rated Rank: 39

Houma-Bayou Cane-Thibodaux, LA

Patient-treating Physicians: 264

Primary Care			
General	Family	Internists	Pediatrics
41	33	20	22
C	C	C	B
Specialists			
Medical	Surgical	Psychiatry	Osteopathy
38	93	6	3
C	B	C	C

General Hospitals: 5 (653 beds)
   5 JCAHO, 81 of 108 services

Other Hospitals: N/A

Places Rated Rank: 267

Glens Falls, NY – Houma, LA

Houston-Sugar Land-Baytown, TX

Patient-treating Physicians: 9,000

Primary Care			
General	Family	Internists	Pediatrics
1,117	929	938	732
C	C	C	A
Specialists			
Medical	Surgical	Psychiatry	Osteopathy
1,523	2,066	314	227
A	C	B	C

General Hospitals: 56 (11,450 beds)
40 JCAHO, 6 teaching, 105 of 108 services
Other Hospitals: Children, VA, Psych, Rehab

Places Rated Rank: 187

Huntington-Ashland, WV-KY-OH

Patient-treating Physicians: 640

Primary Care			
General	Family	Internists	Pediatrics
98	86	66	35
A	A	B	B
Specialists			
Medical	Surgical	Psychiatry	Osteopathy
88	140	23	52
A	A	A	AA

General Hospitals: 5 (1,490 beds)
5 JCAHO, 3 teaching, 92 of 108 services
Other Hospitals: VA, Psych, Rehab

Places Rated Rank: 46

Huntsville, AL

Patient-treating Physicians: 676

Primary Care			
General	Family	Internists	Pediatrics
123	116	57	45
A	A	C	B
Specialists			
Medical	Surgical	Psychiatry	Osteopathy
92	174	24	18
B	A	B	C

General Hospitals: 4 (923 beds)
3 JCAHO, 1 teaching, 81 of 108 services
Other Hospitals: Rehab

Places Rated Rank: 167

Idaho Falls, ID

Patient-treating Physicians: 174

Primary Care			
General	Family	Internists	Pediatrics
24	23	12	6
C	B	C	C
Specialists			
Medical	Surgical	Psychiatry	Osteopathy
20	51	8	8
C	A	B	B

General Hospitals: 2 (299 beds)
1 JCAHO, 66 of 108 services
Other Hospitals: N/A

Places Rated Rank: 300

✓Indianapolis-Carmel, IN

Patient-treating Physicians: 3,875

Primary Care			
General	Family	Internists	Pediatrics
507	463	393	247
A	A	A	A
Specialists			
Medical	Surgical	Psychiatry	Osteopathy
655	829	119	128
AA	A	B	B

General Hospitals: 18 (4,965 beds)
10 JCAHO, 6 teaching, 103 of 108 services
Other Hospitals: Children, VA, Psych, Rehab

Places Rated Rank: 39

✓Iowa City, IA

Patient-treating Physicians: 720

Primary Care			
General	Family	Internists	Pediatrics
74	68	64	46
AA	AA	AA	AA
Specialists			
Medical	Surgical	Psychiatry	Osteopathy
123	166	35	18
AA	AA	AA	A

General Hospitals: 3 (1,043 beds)
3 JCAHO, 2 teaching, 97 of 108 services
Other Hospitals: Children, VA

Places Rated Rank: 1

Ithaca, NY

Patient-treating Physicians: 200

Primary Care			
General	Family	Internists	Pediatrics
38	35	24	11
AA	AA	A	B
Specialists			
Medical	Surgical	Psychiatry	Osteopathy
24	38	17	12
C	C	AA	A

General Hospitals: 1 (148 beds)
1 JCAHO, 57 of 108 services
Other Hospitals: N/A

Places Rated Rank: 299

Jackson, MI

Patient-treating Physicians: 186

Primary Care			
General	Family	Internists	Pediatrics
28	25	20	10
C	C	C	C
Specialists			
Medical	Surgical	Psychiatry	Osteopathy
30	37	3	38
C	C	C	AA

General Hospitals: 2 (476 beds)
1 JCAHO, 68 of 108 services
Other Hospitals: N/A

Places Rated Rank: 358

Jackson, MS

Patient-treating Physicians: 1,229

Primary Care			
General	Family	Internists	Pediatrics
149	129	111	85
B	B	B	AA
Specialists			
Medical	Surgical	Psychiatry	Osteopathy
199	321	57	21
AA	AA	AA	C

General Hospitals: 12 (3,180 beds)
7 JCAHO, 4 teaching, 76 of 108 services
Other Hospitals: Children, VA, Psych, Rehab

Places Rated Rank: 52

✓Jackson, TN

Patient-treating Physicians: 335

Primary Care			
General	Family	Internists	Pediatrics
36	35	47	19
A	A	AA	AA
Specialists			
Medical	Surgical	Psychiatry	Osteopathy
58	97	3	6
AA	AA	C	C

General Hospitals: 2 (733 beds)
2 JCAHO, 1 teaching, 66 of 108 services
Other Hospitals: Psych

Places Rated Rank: 26

Jacksonville, FL

Patient-treating Physicians: 2,574

Primary Care			
General	Family	Internists	Pediatrics
362	319	262	184
A	A	B	B
Specialists			
Medical	Surgical	Psychiatry	Osteopathy
416	538	74	132
A	B	B	A

General Hospitals: 11 (3,032 beds)
10 JCAHO, 5 teaching, 93 of 108 services
Other Hospitals: Children, Psych, Rehab

Places Rated Rank: 120

Jacksonville, NC

Patient-treating Physicians: 145

Primary Care			
General	Family	Internists	Pediatrics
29	24	13	10
C	C	C	C
Specialists			
Medical	Surgical	Psychiatry	Osteopathy
10	49	2	7
C	C	C	C

General Hospitals: 2 (250 beds)
2 JCAHO, 41 of 108 services
Other Hospitals: Psych

Places Rated Rank: 372

Janesville, WI

Patient-treating Physicians: 248

Primary Care			
General	Family	Internists	Pediatrics
33	31	41	19
C	C	A	B
Specialists			
Medical	Surgical	Psychiatry	Osteopathy
39	52	10	7
B	C	B	C

General Hospitals: 3 (394 beds)
  2 JCAHO, 86 of 108 services
Other Hospitals: N/A

Places Rated Rank: 263

Jefferson City, MO

Patient-treating Physicians: 209

Primary Care			
General	Family	Internists	Pediatrics
29	25	8	11
C	C	C	C
Specialists			
Medical	Surgical	Psychiatry	Osteopathy
22	41	8	65
C	C	C	AA

General Hospitals: 3 (332 beds)
  3 JCAHO, 75 of 108 services
Other Hospitals: N/A

Places Rated Rank: 357

✓Johnson City, TN

Patient-treating Physicians: 491

Primary Care			
General	Family	Internists	Pediatrics
72	64	71	30
AA	AA	AA	A
Specialists			
Medical	Surgical	Psychiatry	Osteopathy
61	131	22	12
A	AA	AA	C

General Hospitals: 6 (1,379 beds)
  5 JCAHO, 2 teaching, 82 of 108 services
Other Hospitals: Children, VA, Psych, Rehab

Places Rated Rank: 13

Johnstown, PA

Patient-treating Physicians: 255

Primary Care			
General	Family	Internists	Pediatrics
50	47	29	10
A	A	C	C
Specialists			
Medical	Surgical	Psychiatry	Osteopathy
33	67	5	18
C	B	C	A

General Hospitals: 3 (581 beds)
  2 JCAHO, 1 teaching, 86 of 108 services
Other Hospitals: N/A

Places Rated Rank: 145

Jonesboro, AR

Patient-treating Physicians: 243

Primary Care			
General	Family	Internists	Pediatrics
47	42	23	12
AA	AA	B	B
Specialists			
Medical	Surgical	Psychiatry	Osteopathy
33	65	10	9
A	AA	A	B

General Hospitals: 3 (409 beds)
  2 JCAHO, 65 of 108 services
Other Hospitals: Psych, Rehab

Places Rated Rank: 79

Joplin, MO

Patient-treating Physicians: 306

Primary Care			
General	Family	Internists	Pediatrics
27	24	20	15
C	C	C	C
Specialists			
Medical	Surgical	Psychiatry	Osteopathy
44	49	12	91
B	C	B	AA

General Hospitals: 4 (780 beds)
  1 JCAHO, 89 of 108 services
Other Hospitals: N/A

Places Rated Rank: 260

Kalamazoo-Portage, MI

Patient-treating Physicians: 703

Primary Care			
General	Family	Internists	Pediatrics
87	82	92	54
B	B	A	AA
Specialists			
Medical	Surgical	Psychiatry	Osteopathy
97	151	21	56
A	B	B	AA

General Hospitals: 5 (887 beds)
  4 JCAHO, 2 teaching, 91 of 108 services
Other Hospitals: Children, Rehab

Places Rated Rank: 115

Kankakee-Bradley, IL

Patient-treating Physicians: 153

Primary Care			
General	Family	Internists	Pediatrics
14	13	24	13
C	C	B	B
Specialists			
Medical	Surgical	Psychiatry	Osteopathy
20	39	6	13
C	C	C	A

General Hospitals: 2 (445 beds)
  2 JCAHO, 92 of 108 services
Other Hospitals: N/A

Places Rated Rank: 232

Kansas City, MO-KS

Patient-treating Physicians: 3,771

Primary Care			
General	Family	Internists	Pediatrics
447	417	374	259
C	B	C	A
Specialists			
Medical	Surgical	Psychiatry	Osteopathy
551	808	127	394
B	B	B	AA

General Hospitals: 38 (5,627 beds)
  28 JCAHO, 7 teaching, all 108 services
Other Hospitals: Children, VA, Psych, Rehab

Places Rated Rank: 132

Kennewick-Richland-Pasco, WA

Patient-treating Physicians: 313

Primary Care			
General	Family	Internists	Pediatrics
50	46	29	23
B	B	C	B
Specialists			
Medical	Surgical	Psychiatry	Osteopathy
42	72	4	24
C	C	C	A

General Hospitals: 4 (431 beds)
  3 JCAHO, 71 of 108 services
Other Hospitals: Psych

Places Rated Rank: 334

Killeen-Temple-Fort Hood, TX

Patient-treating Physicians: 607

Primary Care			
General	Family	Internists	Pediatrics
90	79	84	47
B	B	A	A
Specialists			
Medical	Surgical	Psychiatry	Osteopathy
89	120	14	39
B	C	C	A

General Hospitals: 6 (2,885 beds)
  6 JCAHO, 3 teaching, 89 of 108 services
Other Hospitals: VA

Places Rated Rank: 126

Kingsport-Bristol-Bristol, TN-VA

Patient-treating Physicians: 631

Primary Care			
General	Family	Internists	Pediatrics
124	114	70	24
AA	AA	B	C
Specialists			
Medical	Surgical	Psychiatry	Osteopathy
100	151	19	21
A	A	B	B

General Hospitals: 6 (1,102 beds)
  5 JCAHO, 2 teaching, 87 of 108 services
Other Hospitals: Children, Rehab

Places Rated Rank: 55

Kingston, NY

Patient-treating Physicians: 288

Primary Care			
General	Family	Internists	Pediatrics
74	67	29	18
AA	AA	C	C
Specialists			
Medical	Surgical	Psychiatry	Osteopathy
26	49	30	19
C	C	AA	A

General Hospitals: 3 (431 beds)
2 JCAHO, 44 of 108 services
Other Hospitals: N/A

Places Rated Rank: 325

Knoxville, TN

Patient-treating Physicians: 1,757

Primary Care			
General	Family	Internists	Pediatrics
229	207	207	115
AA	A	AA	AA
Specialists			
Medical	Surgical	Psychiatry	Osteopathy
307	415	61	33
AA	AA	A	C

General Hospitals: 9 (2,266 beds)
8 JCAHO, 96 of 108 services
Other Hospitals: Children, Psych

Places Rated Rank: 117

Kokomo, IN

Patient-treating Physicians: 137

Primary Care			
General	Family	Internists	Pediatrics
33	31	16	7
A	A	C	C
Specialists			
Medical	Surgical	Psychiatry	Osteopathy
17	31	7	4
C	C	B	C

General Hospitals: 4 (408 beds)
2 JCAHO, 82 of 108 services
Other Hospitals: Rehab

Places Rated Rank: 229

✓La Crosse, WI-MN

Patient-treating Physicians: 437

Primary Care			
General	Family	Internists	Pediatrics
61	59	62	20
AA	AA	AA	A
Specialists			
Medical	Surgical	Psychiatry	Osteopathy
69	93	13	9
AA	AA	A	B

General Hospitals: 2 (484 beds)
2 JCAHO, 1 teaching, 82 of 108 services
Other Hospitals: N/A

Places Rated Rank: 18

Lafayette, IN

Patient-treating Physicians: 317

Primary Care			
General	Family	Internists	Pediatrics
49	45	32	20
B	B	C	B
Specialists			
Medical	Surgical	Psychiatry	Osteopathy
45	77	8	7
B	B	C	C

General Hospitals: 1 (451 beds)
0 JCAHO, 60 of 108 services
Other Hospitals: Psych

Places Rated Rank: 297

Lafayette, LA

Patient-treating Physicians: 532

Primary Care			
General	Family	Internists	Pediatrics
66	54	66	32
B	B	A	B
Specialists			
Medical	Surgical	Psychiatry	Osteopathy
72	156	18	3
A	AA	B	C

General Hospitals: 7 (924 beds)
4 JCAHO, 1 teaching, 74 of 108 services
Other Hospitals: Psych

Places Rated Rank: 97

Lake Charles, LA

Patient-treating Physicians: 327

Primary Care			
General	Family	Internists	Pediatrics
57	51	35	16
B	B	C	C
Specialists			
Medical	Surgical	Psychiatry	Osteopathy
50	89	11	2
B	B	C	C

General Hospitals: 9 (915 beds)
5 JCAHO, 1 teaching, 80 of 108 services
Other Hospitals: N/A

Places Rated Rank: 148

Lake County-Kenosha County, IL-WI

Patient-treating Physicians: 1,890

Primary Care			
General	Family	Internists	Pediatrics
190	161	294	157
C	C	AA	AA
Specialists			
Medical	Surgical	Psychiatry	Osteopathy
238	390	84	92
B	B	A	A

General Hospitals: 9 (1,109 beds)
8 JCAHO, 1 teaching, 94 of 108 services
Other Hospitals: VA

Places Rated Rank: 191

Lakeland, FL

Patient-treating Physicians: 740

Primary Care			
General	Family	Internists	Pediatrics
79	61	117	46
C	C	B	C
Specialists			
Medical	Surgical	Psychiatry	Osteopathy
122	195	17	22
B	C	C	C

General Hospitals: 4 (1,190 beds)
4 JCAHO, 84 of 108 services
Other Hospitals: N/A

Places Rated Rank: 307

Lancaster, PA

Patient-treating Physicians: 760

Primary Care			
General	Family	Internists	Pediatrics
171	164	46	29
A	AA	C	C
Specialists			
Medical	Surgical	Psychiatry	Osteopathy
93	136	15	141
C	C	C	AA

General Hospitals: 4 (1,034 beds)
3 JCAHO, 1 teaching, 79 of 108 services
Other Hospitals: N/A

Places Rated Rank: 313

Lansing-East Lansing, MI

Patient-treating Physicians: 909

Primary Care			
General	Family	Internists	Pediatrics
97	86	75	48
C	C	C	B
Specialists			
Medical	Surgical	Psychiatry	Osteopathy
86	137	29	305
C	C	B	AA

General Hospitals: 5 (1,128 beds)
5 JCAHO, 2 teaching, 99 of 108 services
Other Hospitals: Children

Places Rated Rank: 293

Laredo, TX

Patient-treating Physicians: 192

Primary Care			
General	Family	Internists	Pediatrics
40	33	16	20
C	C	C	C
Specialists			
Medical	Surgical	Psychiatry	Osteopathy
30	45	5	6
C	C	C	C

General Hospitals: 2 (492 beds)
2 JCAHO, 57 of 108 services
Other Hospitals: N/A

Places Rated Rank: 366

Las Cruces, NM

Patient-treating Physicians: 219

Primary Care			
General	Family	Internists	Pediatrics
48	37	26	11
B	C	C	C
Specialists			
Medical	Surgical	Psychiatry	Osteopathy
27	46	9	9
C	C	C	C

General Hospitals: 2 (314 beds)
  2 JCAHO, 1 teaching, 59 of 108 services
Other Hospitals: Psych

Places Rated Rank: 360

Las Vegas-Paradise, NV

Patient-treating Physicians: 2,571

Primary Care			
General	Family	Internists	Pediatrics
283	245	415	142
B	C	A	C
Specialists			
Medical	Surgical	Psychiatry	Osteopathy
363	521	67	196
C	C	C	A

General Hospitals: 11 (2,897 beds)
  10 JCAHO, 2 teaching, 89 of 108 services
Other Hospitals: VA, Psych, Rehab

Places Rated Rank: 309

Lawrence, KS

Patient-treating Physicians: 168

Primary Care			
General	Family	Internists	Pediatrics
39	35	22	6
AA	AA	B	C
Specialists			
Medical	Surgical	Psychiatry	Osteopathy
15	35	6	11
C	C	B	A

General Hospitals: 1 (108 beds)
  1 JCAHO, 52 of 108 services
Other Hospitals: N/A

Places Rated Rank: 341

Lawton, OK

Patient-treating Physicians: 163

Primary Care			
General	Family	Internists	Pediatrics
20	18	15	9
C	C	C	C
Specialists			
Medical	Surgical	Psychiatry	Osteopathy
13	42	8	22
C	C	B	AA

General Hospitals: 4 (531 beds)
  4 JCAHO, 2 teaching, 85 of 108 services
Other Hospitals: Psych

Places Rated Rank: 285

Lebanon, PA

Patient-treating Physicians: 179

Primary Care			
General	Family	Internists	Pediatrics
40	38	10	8
A	A	C	C
Specialists			
Medical	Surgical	Psychiatry	Osteopathy
24	37	10	22
C	C	A	AA

General Hospitals: 2 (455 beds)
  2 JCAHO, 2 teaching, 74 of 108 services
Other Hospitals: VA, Psych

Places Rated Rank: 275

Lewiston, ID-WA

Patient-treating Physicians: 103

Primary Care			
General	Family	Internists	Pediatrics
21	14	12	7
AA	B	B	B
Specialists			
Medical	Surgical	Psychiatry	Osteopathy
12	25	3	6
C	B	C	A

General Hospitals: 2 (197 beds)
  2 JCAHO, 65 of 108 services
Other Hospitals: N/A

Places Rated Rank: 217

Lewiston-Auburn, ME

Patient-treating Physicians: 214

Primary Care			
General	Family	Internists	Pediatrics
31	31	28	8
B	A	A	C
Specialists			
Medical	Surgical	Psychiatry	Osteopathy
30	50	8	19
B	A	B	AA

General Hospitals: 2 (360 beds)
  2 JCAHO, 1 teaching, 83 of 108 services
Other Hospitals: N/A

Places Rated Rank: 124

✓Lexington-Fayette, KY

Patient-treating Physicians: 1,370

Primary Care			
General	Family	Internists	Pediatrics
140	132	160	78
A	A	AA	AA
Specialists			
Medical	Surgical	Psychiatry	Osteopathy
217	323	61	36
AA	AA	AA	B

General Hospitals: 10 (1,764 beds)
  9 JCAHO, 4 teaching, 95 of 108 services
Other Hospitals: N/A

Places Rated Rank: 10

Lima, OH

Patient-treating Physicians: 247

Primary Care			
General	Family	Internists	Pediatrics
37	34	18	9
A	A	C	C
Specialists			
Medical	Surgical	Psychiatry	Osteopathy
38	57	10	20
A	A	A	AA

General Hospitals: 3 (568 beds)
  2 JCAHO, 94 of 108 services
Other Hospitals: N/A

Places Rated Rank: 45

Lincoln, NE

Patient-treating Physicians: 547

Primary Care			
General	Family	Internists	Pediatrics
101	100	49	35
AA	AA	C	B
Specialists			
Medical	Surgical	Psychiatry	Osteopathy
86	131	23	12
A	A	A	C

General Hospitals: 4 (1,005 beds)
  2 JCAHO, 2 teaching, 80 of 108 services
Other Hospitals: VA, Rehab

Places Rated Rank: 88

✓Little Rock-North Little Rock, AR

Patient-treating Physicians: 1,747

Primary Care			
General	Family	Internists	Pediatrics
228	198	104	123
AA	A	C	AA
Specialists			
Medical	Surgical	Psychiatry	Osteopathy
345	401	77	17
AA	AA	AA	C

General Hospitals: 13 (3,086 beds)
  9 JCAHO, 4 teaching, 102 of 108 services
Other Hospitals: Children, VA, Psych, Rehab

Places Rated Rank: 8

Logan, UT-ID

Patient-treating Physicians: 132

Primary Care			
General	Family	Internists	Pediatrics
19	18	11	11
C	C	C	C
Specialists			
Medical	Surgical	Psychiatry	Osteopathy
12	40	3	10
C	C	C	B

General Hospitals: 2 (188 beds)
  1 JCAHO, 58 of 108 services
Other Hospitals: N/A

Places Rated Rank: 365

Longview, TX

Patient-treating Physicians: 311

Primary Care			
General	Family	Internists	Pediatrics
59	50	36	13
B	B	C	C
Specialists			
Medical	Surgical	Psychiatry	Osteopathy
44	84	5	12
C	B	C	C

General Hospitals: 4 (664 beds)
3 JCAHO, 71 of 108 services
Other Hospitals: N/A

Places Rated Rank: 246

Longview, WA

Patient-treating Physicians: 167

Primary Care			
General	Family	Internists	Pediatrics
35	32	19	14
AA	AA	B	A
Specialists			
Medical	Surgical	Psychiatry	Osteopathy
12	39	5	5
C	C	C	C

General Hospitals: 1 (202 beds)
1 JCAHO, 58 of 108 services
Other Hospitals: N/A

Places Rated Rank: 295

Los Angeles-Long Beach, CA

Patient-treating Physicians: 19,220

Primary Care			
General	Family	Internists	Pediatrics
2,208	1,587	2,847	1,475
C	C	A	A
Specialists			
Medical	Surgical	Psychiatry	Osteopathy
2,860	4,312	1,121	394
A	B	AA	C

General Hospitals: 96 (22,591 beds)
85 JCAHO, 21 teaching, all 108 services
Other Hospitals: Children, VA, Psych, Rehab

Places Rated Rank: 161

Louisville-Jefferson County, KY-IN

Patient-treating Physicians: 2,654

Primary Care			
General	Family	Internists	Pediatrics
324	279	324	185
B	B	A	A
Specialists			
Medical	Surgical	Psychiatry	Osteopathy
414	627	127	22
A	A	AA	C

General Hospitals: 18 (3,828 beds)
16 JCAHO, 4 teaching, 103 of 108 services
Other Hospitals: Children, VA, Psych, Rehab

Places Rated Rank: 57

✓Lubbock, TX

Patient-treating Physicians: 682

Primary Care			
General	Family	Internists	Pediatrics
79	69	60	40
A	A	B	A
Specialists			
Medical	Surgical	Psychiatry	Osteopathy
121	169	15	38
AA	AA	B	A

General Hospitals: 5 (1,339 beds)
3 JCAHO, 1 teaching, 87 of 108 services
Other Hospitals: Children, Psych

Places Rated Rank: 25

Lynchburg, VA

Patient-treating Physicians: 359

Primary Care			
General	Family	Internists	Pediatrics
83	80	33	20
A	AA	C	C
Specialists			
Medical	Surgical	Psychiatry	Osteopathy
50	87	8	9
C	C	C	C

General Hospitals: 2 (984 beds)
2 JCAHO, 1 teaching, 55 of 108 services
Other Hospitals: N/A

Places Rated Rank: 230

Macon, GA

Patient-treating Physicians: 527

Primary Care			
General	Family	Internists	Pediatrics
66	62	76	24
B	A	AA	B
Specialists			
Medical	Surgical	Psychiatry	Osteopathy
81	153	19	5
AA	AA	A	C

General Hospitals: 5 (872 beds)
3 JCAHO, 1 teaching, 79 of 108 services
Other Hospitals: Children, Psych, Rehab

Places Rated Rank: 56

Madera, CA

Patient-treating Physicians: 126

Primary Care			
General	Family	Internists	Pediatrics
17	10	17	29
C	C	C	AA
Specialists			
Medical	Surgical	Psychiatry	Osteopathy
16	22	6	4
C	C	C	C

General Hospitals: 2 (106 beds)
1 JCAHO, 35 of 108 services
Other Hospitals: Children

Places Rated Rank: 374

✓Madison, WI

Patient-treating Physicians: 1,515

Primary Care			
General	Family	Internists	Pediatrics
251	237	181	99
AA	AA	AA	AA
Specialists			
Medical	Surgical	Psychiatry	Osteopathy
228	301	98	26
AA	AA	AA	C

General Hospitals: 8 (1,554 beds)
8 JCAHO, 4 teaching, 100 of 108 services
Other Hospitals: Children, VA

Places Rated Rank: 19

Manchester-Nashua, NH

Patient-treating Physicians: 733

Primary Care			
General	Family	Internists	Pediatrics
87	78	107	67
C	C	A	AA
Specialists			
Medical	Surgical	Psychiatry	Osteopathy
96	169	28	24
B	B	B	C

General Hospitals: 5 (825 beds)
5 JCAHO, 91 of 108 services
Other Hospitals: VA, Rehab

Places Rated Rank: 216

Mansfield, OH

Patient-treating Physicians: 219

Primary Care			
General	Family	Internists	Pediatrics
24	21	35	10
C	C	A	C
Specialists			
Medical	Surgical	Psychiatry	Osteopathy
27	53	3	30
C	C	C	AA

General Hospitals: 1 (365 beds)
1 JCAHO, 9 of 108 services
Other Hospitals: N/A

Places Rated Rank: 317

McAllen-Edinburg-Mission, TX

Patient-treating Physicians: 625

Primary Care			
General	Family	Internists	Pediatrics
131	122	73	78
C	C	C	B
Specialists			
Medical	Surgical	Psychiatry	Osteopathy
96	133	9	14
C	C	C	C

General Hospitals: 8 (1,405 beds)
7 JCAHO, 1 teaching, 83 of 108 services
Other Hospitals: Rehab

Places Rated Rank: 344

Medford, OR

Patient-treating Physicians: 444

Primary Care			
General	Family	Internists	Pediatrics
691	63	50	22
AA	AA	A	B
Specialists			
Medical	Surgical	Psychiatry	Osteopathy
72	98	13	30
AA	A	B	A

General Hospitals: 3 (539 beds)
3 JCAHO, 70 of 108 services
Other Hospitals: N/A

Places Rated Rank: 107

Memphis, TN-MS-AR

Patient-treating Physicians: 2,323

Primary Care			
General	Family	Internists	Pediatrics
233	194	348	199
C	C	A	A
Specialists			
Medical	Surgical	Psychiatry	Osteopathy
401	571	72	21
A	B	B	C

General Hospitals: 18 (4,145 beds)
15 JCAHO, 6 teaching, 100 of 108 services
Other Hospitals: Children, VA, Psych, Rehab

Places Rated Rank: 119

Merced, CA

Patient-treating Physicians: 188

Primary Care			
General	Family	Internists	Pediatrics
55	52	24	12
B	B	C	C
Specialists			
Medical	Surgical	Psychiatry	Osteopathy
19	43	2	4
C	C	C	C

General Hospitals: 2 (289 beds)
2 JCAHO, 1 teaching, 45 of 108 services
Other Hospitals: N/A

Places Rated Rank: 371

Miami-Miami Beach-Kendall, FL

Patient-treating Physicians: 5,494

Primary Care			
General	Family	Internists	Pediatrics
679	335	696	467
B	C	AA	AA
Specialists			
Medical	Surgical	Psychiatry	Osteopathy
960	1,234	254	192
AA	A	AA	B

General Hospitals: 26 (7,416 beds)
21 JCAHO, 7 teaching, 105 of 108 services
Other Hospitals: Children, VA, Psych, Rehab

Places Rated Rank: 54

Michigan City-La Porte, IN

Patient-treating Physicians: 145

Primary Care			
General	Family	Internists	Pediatrics
29	28	19	7
B	B	C	C
Specialists			
Medical	Surgical	Psychiatry	Osteopathy
15	44	3	5
C	C	C	C

General Hospitals: 2 (444 beds)
1 JCAHO, 85 of 108 services
Other Hospitals: N/A

Places Rated Rank: 224

Midland, TX

Patient-treating Physicians: 185

Primary Care			
General	Family	Internists	Pediatrics
18	16	23	14
C	C	C	B
Specialists			
Medical	Surgical	Psychiatry	Osteopathy
27	45	9	3
C	C	B	C

General Hospitals: 3 (373 beds)
1 JCAHO, 1 teaching, 56 of 108 services
Other Hospitals: Psych, Rehab

Places Rated Rank: 329

Milwaukee-Waukesha, WI

Patient-treating Physicians: 3,833

Primary Care			
General	Family	Internists	Pediatrics
431	391	490	263
B	B	AA	AA
Specialists			
Medical	Surgical	Psychiatry	Osteopathy
556	792	156	155
AA	A	A	A

General Hospitals: 20 (4,110 beds)
17 JCAHO, 9 teaching, 102 of 108 services
Other Hospitals: Children, VA, Psych, Rehab

Places Rated Rank: 68

Minneapolis-St. Paul, MN-WI

Patient-treating Physicians: 6,288

Primary Care			
General	Family	Internists	Pediatrics
1,318	1,248	721	478
AA	AA	B	A
Specialists			
Medical	Surgical	Psychiatry	Osteopathy
861	1,271	249	95
B	C	A	C

General Hospitals: 32 (6,035 beds)
25 JCAHO, 9 teaching, all 108 services
Other Hospitals: Children, VA

Places Rated Rank: 94

Missoula, MT

Patient-treating Physicians: 300

Primary Care			
General	Family	Internists	Pediatrics
30	29	25	14
A	A	A	A
Specialists			
Medical	Surgical	Psychiatry	Osteopathy
49	83	8	5
AA	AA	A	C

General Hospitals: 2 (346 beds)
2 JCAHO, 82 of 108 services
Other Hospitals: N/A

Places Rated Rank: 42

Mobile, AL

Patient-treating Physicians: 767

Primary Care			
General	Family	Internists	Pediatrics
66	55	100	63
C	C	A	A
Specialists			
Medical	Surgical	Psychiatry	Osteopathy
125	238	18	6
A	AA	C	C

General Hospitals: 6 (1,301 beds)
5 JCAHO, 3 teaching, 77 of 108 services
Other Hospitals: Children

Places Rated Rank: 178

Modesto, CA

Patient-treating Physicians: 702

Primary Care			
General	Family	Internists	Pediatrics
143	133	99	44
B	A	B	C
Specialists			
Medical	Surgical	Psychiatry	Osteopathy
77	163	25	29
C	C	C	C

General Hospitals: 5 (1,221 beds)
4 JCAHO, 1 teaching, 71 of 108 services
Other Hospitals: N/A

Places Rated Rank: 311

Monroe, LA

Patient-treating Physicians: 328

Primary Care			
General	Family	Internists	Pediatrics
52	43	31	23
A	B	C	A
Specialists			
Medical	Surgical	Psychiatry	Osteopathy
58	71	12	6
A	C	B	C

General Hospitals: 8 (1,062 beds)
5 JCAHO, 1 teaching, 67 of 108 services
Other Hospitals: Psych

Places Rated Rank: 156

Monroe, MI

Patient-treating Physicians: 127

Primary Care			
General	Family	Internists	Pediatrics
22	16	11	9
C	C	C	C
Specialists			
Medical	Surgical	Psychiatry	Osteopathy
15	25	1	26
C	C	C	AA

General Hospitals: 1 (177 beds)
   1 JCAHO, 56 of 108 services
Other Hospitals: N/A

Places Rated Rank: 377

Montgomery, AL

Patient-treating Physicians: 573

Primary Care			
General	Family	Internists	Pediatrics
73	64	94	40
C	C	A	B
Specialists			
Medical	Surgical	Psychiatry	Osteopathy
80	144	12	32
C	C	C	B

General Hospitals: 7 (1,219 beds)
   5 JCAHO, 2 teaching, 78 of 108 services
Other Hospitals: VA, Rehab

Places Rated Rank: 238

✓Morgantown, WV

Patient-treating Physicians: 402

Primary Care			
General	Family	Internists	Pediatrics
45	42	33	20
AA	AA	A	AA
Specialists			
Medical	Surgical	Psychiatry	Osteopathy
61	106	17	14
AA	AA	AA	A

General Hospitals: 4 (632 beds)
   3 JCAHO, 1 teaching, 84 of 108 services
Other Hospitals: Rehab

Places Rated Rank: 11

Morristown, TN

Patient-treating Physicians: 155

Primary Care			
General	Family	Internists	Pediatrics
30	27	18	16
C	C	C	B
Specialists			
Medical	Surgical	Psychiatry	Osteopathy
26	28	6	11
C	C	C	B

General Hospitals: 3 (336 beds)
   3 JCAHO, 33 of 108 services
Other Hospitals: N/A

Places Rated Rank: 352

Mount Vernon-Anacortes, WA

Patient-treating Physicians: 234

Primary Care			
General	Family	Internists	Pediatrics
66	63	17	12
AA	AA	C	B
Specialists			
Medical	Surgical	Psychiatry	Osteopathy
18	48	11	7
C	B	A	C

General Hospitals: 2 (231 beds)
   1 JCAHO, 39 of 108 services
Other Hospitals: N/A

Places Rated Rank: 274

Muncie, IN

Patient-treating Physicians: 239

Primary Care			
General	Family	Internists	Pediatrics
38	30	32	11
A	B	A	C
Specialists			
Medical	Surgical	Psychiatry	Osteopathy
43	49	2	9
AA	C	C	B

General Hospitals: 1 (393 beds)
   1 JCAHO, 1 teaching, 76 of 108 services
Other Hospitals: N/A

Places Rated Rank: 171

Muskegon-Norton Shores, MI

Patient-treating Physicians: 268

Primary Care			
General	Family	Internists	Pediatrics
39	34	33	6
C	C	C	C
Specialists			
Medical	Surgical	Psychiatry	Osteopathy
27	45	4	68
C	C	C	AA

General Hospitals: 2 (382 beds)
   2 JCAHO, 72 of 108 services
Other Hospitals: N/A

Places Rated Rank: 355

Myrtle Beach-Conway, SC

Patient-treating Physicians: 382

Primary Care			
General	Family	Internists	Pediatrics
40	32	49	18
C	C	A	C
Specialists			
Medical	Surgical	Psychiatry	Osteopathy
49	91	10	32
C	B	C	A

General Hospitals: 3 (571 beds)
   3 JCAHO, 70 of 108 services
Other Hospitals: N/A

Places Rated Rank: 291

Napa, CA

Patient-treating Physicians: 344

Primary Care			
General	Family	Internists	Pediatrics
44	37	51	19
A	A	AA	A
Specialists			
Medical	Surgical	Psychiatry	Osteopathy
42	65	35	5
A	A	AA	C

General Hospitals: 2 (421 beds)
   2 JCAHO, 82 of 108 services
Other Hospitals: N/A

Places Rated Rank: 78

Naples-Marco Island, FL

Patient-treating Physicians: 642

Primary Care			
General	Family	Internists	Pediatrics
50	34	83	30
C	C	AA	B
Specialists			
Medical	Surgical	Psychiatry	Osteopathy
119	164	20	34
AA	AA	B	A

General Hospitals: 1 (539 beds)
   1 JCAHO, 59 of 108 services
Other Hospitals: Psych

Places Rated Rank: 257

Nashville-Davidson, TN

Patient-treating Physicians: 3,249

Primary Care			
General	Family	Internists	Pediatrics
296	253	442	222
C	C	AA	A
Specialists			
Medical	Surgical	Psychiatry	Osteopathy
519	833	130	42
AA	AA	A	C

General Hospitals: 24 (5,045 beds)
   20 JCAHO, 6 teaching, 102 of 108 services
Other Hospitals: Children, VA, Psych, Rehab

Places Rated Rank: 43

Nassau-Suffolk, NY

Patient-treating Physicians: 8,573

Primary Care			
General	Family	Internists	Pediatrics
425	360	1,357	781
C	C	AA	AA
Specialists			
Medical	Surgical	Psychiatry	Osteopathy
1,477	1,940	432	543
AA	AA	AA	AA

General Hospitals: 25 (8,431 beds)
   25 JCAHO, 9 teaching, 106 of 108 services
Other Hospitals: Children, VA, Psych

Places Rated Rank: 64

Newark-Union, NJ-PA

Patient-treating Physicians: 5,062

Primary Care			
General	Family	Internists	Pediatrics
302	247	793	476
C	C	AA	AA
Specialists			
Medical	Surgical	Psychiatry	Osteopathy
863	1,168	218	294
AA	A	A	A

General Hospitals: 20 (7,709 beds)
20 JCAHO, 8 teaching, 106 of 108 services
Other Hospitals: Children, VA, Psych, Rehab

Places Rated Rank: 69

New Haven-Milford, CT

Patient-treating Physicians: 2,317

Primary Care			
General	Family	Internists	Pediatrics
82	65	447	190
C	C	AA	AA
Specialists			
Medical	Surgical	Psychiatry	Osteopathy
402	524	172	29
AA	AA	AA	C

General Hospitals: 8 (2,232 beds)
8 JCAHO, 5 teaching, 97 of 108 services
Other Hospitals: Children, VA, Psych

Places Rated Rank: 102

✓New Orleans-Metairie-Kenner, LA

Patient-treating Physicians: 3,462

Primary Care			
General	Family	Internists	Pediatrics
230	187	449	260
C	C	AA	AA
Specialists			
Medical	Surgical	Psychiatry	Osteopathy
612	890	212	18
AA	AA	AA	C

General Hospitals: 28 (5,822 beds)
24 JCAHO, 7 teaching, 106 of 108 services
Other Hospitals: Children, VA, Psych, Rehab

Places Rated Rank: 29

New York-White Plains, NY-NJ

Patient-treating Physicians: 26,878

Primary Care			
General	Family	Internists	Pediatrics
1,131	862	4,877	2,424
C	C	AA	AA
Specialists			
Medical	Surgical	Psychiatry	Osteopathy
4,739	5,789	2,273	854
AA	A	AA	B

General Hospitals: 91 (36,900 beds)
83 JCAHO, 48 teaching, all 108 services
Other Hospitals: Children, VA, Psych, Rehab

Places Rated Rank: 82

Niles-Benton Harbor, MI

Patient-treating Physicians: 278

Primary Care			
General	Family	Internists	Pediatrics
55	47	35	14
A	A	B	C
Specialists			
Medical	Surgical	Psychiatry	Osteopathy
33	61	7	32
C	C	C	AA

General Hospitals: 2 (414 beds)
2 JCAHO, 64 of 108 services
Other Hospitals: N/A

Places Rated Rank: 292

Norwich-New London, CT

Patient-treating Physicians: 470

Primary Care			
General	Family	Internists	Pediatrics
48	41	78	33
C	C	A	B
Specialists			
Medical	Surgical	Psychiatry	Osteopathy
83	113	25	14
A	B	A	C

General Hospitals: 2 (417 beds)
2 JCAHO, 78 of 108 services
Other Hospitals: N/A

Places Rated Rank: 298

Oakland-Fremont-Hayward, CA

Patient-treating Physicians: 5,227

Primary Care			
General	Family	Internists	Pediatrics
550	438	940	524
C	C	AA	AA
Specialists			
Medical	Surgical	Psychiatry	Osteopathy
653	1,083	327	80
B	B	AA	C

General Hospitals: 19 (4,761 beds)
17 JCAHO, 3 teaching, 101 of 108 services
Other Hospitals: Children, Psych

Places Rated Rank: 173

Ocala, FL

Patient-treating Physicians: 442

Primary Care			
General	Family	Internists	Pediatrics
48	36	61	22
C	C	B	C
Specialists			
Medical	Surgical	Psychiatry	Osteopathy
81	103	13	27
A	C	C	A

General Hospitals: 2 (610 beds)
2 JCAHO, 57 of 108 services
Other Hospitals: N/A

Places Rated Rank: 342

Ocean City, NJ

Patient-treating Physicians: 144

Primary Care			
General	Family	Internists	Pediatrics
16	11	8	6
C	C	C	C
Specialists			
Medical	Surgical	Psychiatry	Osteopathy
13	20	2	58
C	C	C	AA

General Hospitals: 1 (208 beds)
1 JCAHO, 45 of 108 services
Other Hospitals: N/A

Places Rated Rank: 373

Odessa, TX

Patient-treating Physicians: 164

Primary Care			
General	Family	Internists	Pediatrics
16	12	27	9
C	C	B	C
Specialists			
Medical	Surgical	Psychiatry	Osteopathy
31	49	4	2
B	C	C	C

General Hospitals: 2 (438 beds)
2 JCAHO, 1 teaching, 54 of 108 services
Other Hospitals: N/A

Places Rated Rank: 321

Ogden-Clearfield, UT

Patient-treating Physicians: 576

Primary Care			
General	Family	Internists	Pediatrics
109	106	45	47
C	B	C	C
Specialists			
Medical	Surgical	Psychiatry	Osteopathy
52	151	10	22
C	C	C	C

General Hospitals: 4 (718 beds)
4 JCAHO, 85 of 108 services
Other Hospitals: N/A

Places Rated Rank: 347

Oklahoma City, OK

Patient-treating Physicians: 2,260

Primary Care			
General	Family	Internists	Pediatrics
289	245	185	115
B	B	C	C
Specialists			
Medical	Surgical	Psychiatry	Osteopathy
365	475	91	226
A	B	A	AA

General Hospitals: 23 (3,759 beds)
15 JCAHO, 4 teaching, 107 of 108 services
Other Hospitals: Children, VA, Psych, Rehab

Places Rated Rank: 125

399

Olympia, WA

Patient-treating Physicians: 464

Primary Care			
General	Family	Internists	Pediatrics
103	98	38	28
AA	AA	C	B
Specialists			
Medical	Surgical	Psychiatry	Osteopathy
53	94	17	20
B	B	A	B

General Hospitals: 2 (434 beds)
2 JCAHO, 1 teaching, 72 of 108 services

Other Hospitals: N/A

Places Rated Rank: 223

✓ Omaha-Council Bluffs, NE-IA

Patient-treating Physicians: 1,711

Primary Care			
General	Family	Internists	Pediatrics
270	260	152	125
A	AA	C	A
Specialists			
Medical	Surgical	Psychiatry	Osteopathy
266	414	58	34
A	A	B	C

General Hospitals: 14 (2,811 beds)
11 JCAHO, 7 teaching, 104 of 108 services

Other Hospitals: Children, VA, Psych

Places Rated Rank: 30

Orlando-Kissimmee, FL

Patient-treating Physicians: 3,325

Primary Care			
General	Family	Internists	Pediatrics
427	358	390	253
B	C	B	A
Specialists			
Medical	Surgical	Psychiatry	Osteopathy
501	728	85	237
B	C	C	A

General Hospitals: 12 (6,665 beds)
9 JCAHO, 2 teaching, 98 of 108 services

Other Hospitals: Children

Places Rated Rank: 122

Oshkosh-Neenah, WI

Patient-treating Physicians: 371

Primary Care			
General	Family	Internists	Pediatrics
51	48	53	24
A	A	AA	A
Specialists			
Medical	Surgical	Psychiatry	Osteopathy
38	84	26	12
C	A	AA	B

General Hospitals: 3 (338 beds)
2 JCAHO, 85 of 108 services

Other Hospitals: N/A

Places Rated Rank: 131

Owensboro, KY

Patient-treating Physicians: 195

Primary Care			
General	Family	Internists	Pediatrics
231	20	27	11
C	C	A	C
Specialists			
Medical	Surgical	Psychiatry	Osteopathy
33	54	4	6
A	A	C	C

General Hospitals: 1 (345 beds)
1 JCAHO, 69 of 108 services

Other Hospitals: N/A

Places Rated Rank: 220

Oxnard-Thousand Oaks-Ventura, CA

Patient-treating Physicians: 1,390

Primary Care			
General	Family	Internists	Pediatrics
257	227	157	95
A	A	B	B
Specialists			
Medical	Surgical	Psychiatry	Osteopathy
214	296	70	34
B	C	A	C

General Hospitals: 7 (1,353 beds)
6 JCAHO, 73 of 108 services

Other Hospitals: Psych

Places Rated Rank: 287

Palm Bay-Melbourne-Titusville, FL

Patient-treating Physicians: 984

Primary Care			
General	Family	Internists	Pediatrics
130	109	137	55
B	B	A	B
Specialists			
Medical	Surgical	Psychiatry	Osteopathy
152	217	28	51
A	B	C	A

General Hospitals: 5 (1,108 beds)
4 JCAHO, 63 of 108 services

Other Hospitals: Psych, Rehab

Places Rated Rank: 266

Panama City-Lynn Haven, FL

Patient-treating Physicians: 288

Primary Care			
General	Family	Internists	Pediatrics
36	28	33	7
C	C	B	C
Specialists			
Medical	Surgical	Psychiatry	Osteopathy
45	80	12	14
A	A	A	A

General Hospitals: 2 (547 beds)
2 JCAHO, 71 of 108 services

Other Hospitals: N/A

Places Rated Rank: 197

Parkersburg-Marietta, WV-OH

Patient-treating Physicians: 287

Primary Care			
General	Family	Internists	Pediatrics
55	50	35	6
A	A	B	C
Specialists			
Medical	Surgical	Psychiatry	Osteopathy
28	52	7	44
C	C	C	AA

General Hospitals: 5 (724 beds)
3 JCAHO, 88 of 108 services

Other Hospitals: Rehab

Places Rated Rank: 192

Pascagoula, MS

Patient-treating Physicians: 243

Primary Care			
General	Family	Internists	Pediatrics
32	26	29	14
C	C	C	C
Specialists			
Medical	Surgical	Psychiatry	Osteopathy
33	60	5	15
C	C	C	C

General Hospitals: 2 (441 beds)
1 JCAHO, 37 of 108 services

Other Hospitals: N/A

Places Rated Rank: 337

Pensacola-Ferry Pass-Brent, FL

Patient-treating Physicians: 853

Primary Care			
General	Family	Internists	Pediatrics
1382	128	71	56
A	A	C	A
Specialists			
Medical	Surgical	Psychiatry	Osteopathy
126	185	26	40
A	B	B	B

General Hospitals: 6 (1,505 beds)
5 JCAHO, 2 teaching, 93 of 108 services

Other Hospitals: N/A

Places Rated Rank: 101

Peoria, IL

Patient-treating Physicians: 707

Primary Care			
General	Family	Internists	Pediatrics
102	98	69	32
B	A	C	C
Specialists			
Medical	Surgical	Psychiatry	Osteopathy
114	148	21	38
A	C	C	A

General Hospitals: 5 (1,332 beds)
4 JCAHO, 2 teaching, 92 of 108 services

Other Hospitals: Children

Places Rated Rank: 151

Philadelphia, PA

Patient-treating Physicians: 10,732

Primary Care			
General	Family	Internists	Pediatrics
722	597	1,249	735
C	C	AA	AA

Specialists			
Medical	Surgical	Psychiatry	Osteopathy
1,774	1,955	699	1,520
AA	A	AA	AA

General Hospitals: 52 (12,872 beds)
  41 JCAHO, 22 teaching, all 108 services
Other Hospitals: Children, VA, Psych, Rehab

Places Rated Rank: 72

Phoenix-Mesa-Scottsdale, AZ

Patient-treating Physicians: 6,437

Primary Care			
General	Family	Internists	Pediatrics
739	653	755	379
C	C	B	B

Specialists			
Medical	Surgical	Psychiatry	Osteopathy
887	1,371	228	666
B	C	B	AA

General Hospitals: 30 (6,822 beds)
  26 JCAHO, 7 teaching, 104 of 108 services
Other Hospitals: Children, VA, Psych, Rehab

Places Rated Rank: 242

Pine Bluff, AR

Patient-treating Physicians: 144

Primary Care			
General	Family	Internists	Pediatrics
35	32	15	11
A	A	C	C

Specialists			
Medical	Surgical	Psychiatry	Osteopathy
18	34	3	9
C	C	C	B

General Hospitals: 1 (377 beds)
  1 JCAHO, 62 of 108 services
Other Hospitals: N/A

Places Rated Rank: 290

Pittsburgh, PA

Patient-treating Physicians: 5,429

Primary Care			
General	Family	Internists	Pediatrics
581	512	698	323
C	C	A	B

Specialists			
Medical	Surgical	Psychiatry	Osteopathy
929	1,186	219	307
AA	A	A	A

General Hospitals: 40 (8,186 beds)
  28 JCAHO, 9 teaching, all 108 services
Other Hospitals: Children, Psych, Rehab

Places Rated Rank: 66

Pittsfield, MA

Patient-treating Physicians: 341

Primary Care			
General	Family	Internists	Pediatrics
23	20	69	27
C	C	AA	AA

Specialists			
Medical	Surgical	Psychiatry	Osteopathy
45	63	33	8
A	B	AA	C

General Hospitals: 3 (435 beds)
  3 JCAHO, 1 teaching, 77 of 108 services
Other Hospitals: N/A

Places Rated Rank: 176

Pocatello, ID

Patient-treating Physicians: 138

Primary Care			
General	Family	Internists	Pediatrics
26	25	11	9
A	A	C	B

Specialists			
Medical	Surgical	Psychiatry	Osteopathy
13	35	3	8
C	B	C	B

General Hospitals: 2 (328 beds)
  1 JCAHO, 1 teaching, 66 of 108 services
Other Hospitals: N/A

Places Rated Rank: 239

Portland-South Portland, ME

Patient-treating Physicians: 1,399

Primary Care			
General	Family	Internists	Pediatrics
163	153	163	91
A	A	AA	AA

Specialists			
Medical	Surgical	Psychiatry	Osteopathy
158	266	99	219
A	A	AA	AA

General Hospitals: 9 (1,244 beds)
  7 JCAHO, 1 teaching, 99 of 108 services
Other Hospitals: Children, Psych, Rehab

Places Rated Rank: 58

Portland-Vancouver, OR-WA

Patient-treating Physicians: 4,636

Primary Care			
General	Family	Internists	Pediatrics
520	463	730	339
B	B	AA	AA

Specialists			
Medical	Surgical	Psychiatry	Osteopathy
565	1,025	193	204
B	A	A	B

General Hospitals: 16 (3,567 beds)
  16 JCAHO, 8 teaching, 101 of 108 services
Other Hospitals: Children, VA

Places Rated Rank: 123

Port St. Lucie-Fort Pierce, FL

Patient-treating Physicians: 590

Primary Care			
General	Family	Internists	Pediatrics
55	47	80	25
C	C	A	C

Specialists			
Medical	Surgical	Psychiatry	Osteopathy
84	147	20	60
B	B	B	AA

General Hospitals: 3 (847 beds)
  3 JCAHO, 73 of 108 services
Other Hospitals: Psych

Places Rated Rank: 308

Poughkeepsie-Newburgh, NY

Patient-treating Physicians: 1,215

Primary Care			
General	Family	Internists	Pediatrics
100	86	192	124
C	C	A	AA

Specialists			
Medical	Surgical	Psychiatry	Osteopathy
190	264	80	58
A	C	AA	B

General Hospitals: 8 (1,556 beds)
  8 JCAHO, 90 of 108 services
Other Hospitals: N/A

Places Rated Rank: 228

Prescott, AZ

Patient-treating Physicians: 330

Primary Care			
General	Family	Internists	Pediatrics
57	43	33	17
A	B	C	C

Specialists			
Medical	Surgical	Psychiatry	Osteopathy
38	71	18	34
C	C	A	AA

General Hospitals: 3 (463 beds)
  3 JCAHO, 72 of 108 services
Other Hospitals: VA

Places Rated Rank: 286

Providence-New Bedford, RI-MA

Patient-treating Physicians: 3,196

Primary Care			
General	Family	Internists	Pediatrics
245	210	545	274
C	C	AA	AA

Specialists			
Medical	Surgical	Psychiatry	Osteopathy
521	712	165	159
A	B	A	A

General Hospitals: 16 (3,464 beds)
  15 JCAHO, 5 teaching, 98 of 108 services
Other Hospitals: Children, VA, Psych, Rehab

Places Rated Rank: 196

Provo-Orem, UT

Patient-treating Physicians: 486

Primary Care			
General	Family	Internists	Pediatrics
93	86	31	45
C	C	C	B
Specialists			
Medical	Surgical	Psychiatry	Osteopathy
50	119	10	31
C	C	C	B

General Hospitals: 6 (675 beds)
4 JCAHO, 88 of 108 services
Other Hospitals: N/A

Places Rated Rank: 349

Pueblo, CO

Patient-treating Physicians: 315

Primary Care			
General	Family	Internists	Pediatrics
54	52	34	15
AA	AA	B	C
Specialists			
Medical	Surgical	Psychiatry	Osteopathy
34	70	17	20
C	A	AA	A

General Hospitals: 2 (543 beds)
2 JCAHO, 72 of 108 services
Other Hospitals: N/A

Places Rated Rank: 137

Punta Gorda, FL

Patient-treating Physicians: 316

Primary Care			
General	Family	Internists	Pediatrics
26	19	49	10
C	C	AA	C
Specialists			
Medical	Surgical	Psychiatry	Osteopathy
55	73	17	32
AA	A	AA	AA

General Hospitals: 3 (722 beds)
3 JCAHO, 64 of 108 services
Other Hospitals: N/A

Places Rated Rank: 182

Racine, WI

Patient-treating Physicians: 286

Primary Care			
General	Family	Internists	Pediatrics
56	51	30	16
B	B	C	C
Specialists			
Medical	Surgical	Psychiatry	Osteopathy
32	69	10	6
C	C	C	C

General Hospitals: 3 (438 beds)
2 JCAHO, 1 teaching, 83 of 108 services
Other Hospitals: N/A

Places Rated Rank: 301

Raleigh-Cary, NC

Patient-treating Physicians: 1,581

Primary Care			
General	Family	Internists	Pediatrics
205	192	214	168
C	B	A	AA
Specialists			
Medical	Surgical	Psychiatry	Osteopathy
218	366	87	22
B	B	A	C

General Hospitals: 6 (1,739 beds)
5 JCAHO, 1 teaching, 91 of 108 services
Other Hospitals: Children, Psych

Places Rated Rank: 213

✓Rapid City, SD

Patient-treating Physicians: 257

Primary Care			
General	Family	Internists	Pediatrics
41	36	22	11
A	A	C	C
Specialists			
Medical	Surgical	Psychiatry	Osteopathy
42	65	8	12
AA	AA	B	A

General Hospitals: 3 (851 beds)
3 JCAHO, 1 teaching, 88 of 108 services
Other Hospitals: VA

Places Rated Rank: 33

Reading, PA

Patient-treating Physicians: 568

Primary Care			
General	Family	Internists	Pediatrics
96	86	63	27
B	B	C	C
Specialists			
Medical	Surgical	Psychiatry	Osteopathy
80	131	18	50
C	C	C	A

General Hospitals: 3 (883 beds)
2 JCAHO, 1 teaching, 82 of 108 services
Other Hospitals: Rehab

Places Rated Rank: 314

Redding, CA

Patient-treating Physicians: 384

Primary Care			
General	Family	Internists	Pediatrics
72	65	31	11
AA	AA	C	C
Specialists			
Medical	Surgical	Psychiatry	Osteopathy
45	93	7	18
B	A	C	A

General Hospitals: 3 (492 beds)
2 JCAHO, 1 teaching, 53 of 108 services
Other Hospitals: N/A

Places Rated Rank: 186

Reno-Sparks, NV

Patient-treating Physicians: 834

Primary Care			
General	Family	Internists	Pediatrics
111	104	71	39
A	A	C	B
Specialists			
Medical	Surgical	Psychiatry	Osteopathy
113	212	27	30
A	AA	B	B

General Hospitals: 6 (1,041 beds)
4 JCAHO, 2 teaching, 85 of 108 services
Other Hospitals: VA, Psych, Rehab

Places Rated Rank: 113

Richmond, VA

Patient-treating Physicians: 2,344

Primary Care			
General	Family	Internists	Pediatrics
342	304	282	190
A	A	A	AA
Specialists			
Medical	Surgical	Psychiatry	Osteopathy
364	545	113	35
A	A	A	C

General Hospitals: 11 (3,708 beds)
10 JCAHO, 4 teaching, 105 of 108 services
Other Hospitals: Children, VA, Psych, Rehab

Places Rated Rank: 51

Riverside-San Bernardino, CA

Patient-treating Physicians: 4,187

Primary Care			
General	Family	Internists	Pediatrics
684	549	514	317
C	C	C	C
Specialists			
Medical	Surgical	Psychiatry	Osteopathy
511	962	178	195
C	C	C	C

General Hospitals: 34 (6,403 beds)
34 JCAHO, 6 teaching, 103 of 108 services
Other Hospitals: Children, VA, Psych

Places Rated Rank: 330

✓Roanoke, VA

Patient-treating Physicians: 723

Primary Care			
General	Family	Internists	Pediatrics
105	95	73	40
AA	A	A	A
Specialists			
Medical	Surgical	Psychiatry	Osteopathy
104	172	36	25
A	AA	AA	B

General Hospitals: 4 (1,553 beds)
4 JCAHO, 2 teaching, 95 of 108 services
Other Hospitals: VA

Places Rated Rank: 20

✓Rochester, MN

Patient-treating Physicians: 1,442

Primary Care			
General	Family	Internists	Pediatrics
99	93	200	49
AA	AA	AA	AA
Specialists			
Medical	Surgical	Psychiatry	Osteopathy
388	22	40	19
AA	AA	AA	A

General Hospitals: 4 (1,374 beds)
2 JCAHO, 2 teaching, 48 of 108 services
Other Hospitals: Children

Places Rated Rank: 20

Rochester, NY

Patient-treating Physicians: 2,172

Primary Care			
General	Family	Internists	Pediatrics
166	155	426	212
C	C	AA	AA
Specialists			
Medical	Surgical	Psychiatry	Osteopathy
324	475	86	40
A	B	A	C

General Hospitals: 11 (3,050 beds)
11 JCAHO, 4 teaching, 106 of 108 services
Other Hospitals: VA

Places Rated Rank: 115

Rockford, IL

Patient-treating Physicians: 637

Primary Care			
General	Family	Internists	Pediatrics
119	113	73	35
AA	AA	B	B
Specialists			
Medical	Surgical	Psychiatry	Osteopathy
97	138	16	26
A	B	C	B

General Hospitals: 5 (886 beds)
4 JCAHO, 1 teaching, 85 of 108 services
Other Hospitals: Rehab

Places Rated Rank: 154

Rockingham County, NH

Patient-treating Physicians: 687

Primary Care			
General	Family	Internists	Pediatrics
113	100	85	52
B	B	B	B
Specialists			
Medical	Surgical	Psychiatry	Osteopathy
85	153	35	39
C	C	A	B

General Hospitals: 6 (520 beds)
4 JCAHO, 88 of 108 services
Other Hospitals: Psych, Rehab

Places Rated Rank: 294

Rocky Mount, NC

Patient-treating Physicians: 185

Primary Care			
General	Family	Internists	Pediatrics
30	29	32	11
C	C	B	C
Specialists			
Medical	Surgical	Psychiatry	Osteopathy
19	50	3	6
C	C	C	C

General Hospitals: 2 (431 beds)
2 JCAHO, 68 of 108 services
Other Hospitals: N/A

Places Rated Rank: 328

✓Rome, GA

Patient-treating Physicians: 261

Primary Care			
General	Family	Internists	Pediatrics
52	50	31	11
AA	AA	AA	B
Specialists			
Medical	Surgical	Psychiatry	Osteopathy
30	75	6	8
A	AA	B	B

General Hospitals: 2 (500 beds)
2 JCAHO, 1 teaching, 89 of 108 services
Other Hospitals: N/A

Places Rated Rank: 9

Sacramento–Arden-Arcade

Patient-treating Physicians: 4,000

Primary Care			
General	Family	Internists	Pediatrics
588	499	576	304
A	B	AA	A
Specialists			
Medical	Surgical	Psychiatry	Osteopathy
463	864	189	92
B	B	A	C

General Hospitals: 15 (3,544 beds)
14 JCAHO, 5 teaching, 92 of 108 services
Other Hospitals: Children, Psych

Places Rated Rank: 177

Saginaw, MI

Patient-treating Physicians: 414

Primary Care			
General	Family	Internists	Pediatrics
71	68	49	16
A	A	B	C
Specialists			
Medical	Surgical	Psychiatry	Osteopathy
51	80	9	59
B	C	C	AA

General Hospitals: 3 (903 beds)
3 JCAHO, 1 teaching, 81 of 108 services
Other Hospitals: VA

Places Rated Rank: 164

✓St. Cloud, MN

Patient-treating Physicians: 369

Primary Care			
General	Family	Internists	Pediatrics
76	72	43	23
AA	AA	A	B
Specialists			
Medical	Surgical	Psychiatry	Osteopathy
52	81	11	7
A	B	B	C

General Hospitals: 4 (850 beds)
1 JCAHO, 1 teaching, 92 of 108 services
Other Hospitals: VA, Psych

Places Rated Rank: 34

St. George, UT

Patient-treating Physicians: 161

Primary Care			
General	Family	Internists	Pediatrics
30	25	17	4
A	B	C	C
Specialists			
Medical	Surgical	Psychiatry	Osteopathy
19	43	5	6
C	B	C	C

General Hospitals: 1 (196 beds)
1 JCAHO, 52 of 108 services
Other Hospitals: N/A

Places Rated Rank: 331

St. Joseph, MO-KS

Patient-treating Physicians: 146

Primary Care			
General	Family	Internists	Pediatrics
19	15	16	5
C	C	C	C
Specialists			
Medical	Surgical	Psychiatry	Osteopathy
20	35	2	19
C	C	C	A

General Hospitals: 1 (460 beds)
1 JCAHO, 0 of 108 services
Other Hospitals: N/A

Places Rated Rank: 353

St. Louis, MO-IL

Patient-treating Physicians: 5,578

Primary Care			
General	Family	Internists	Pediatrics
429	381	855	418
C	C	AA	A
Specialists			
Medical	Surgical	Psychiatry	Osteopathy
904	1,316	244	263
A	A	A	B

General Hospitals: 44 (9,594 beds)
35 JCAHO, 10 teaching, 107 of 108 services
Other Hospitals: Children, VA, Psych, Rehab

Places Rated Rank: 98

Salem, OR

Patient-treating Physicians: 540

Primary Care			
General	Family	Internists	Pediatrics
129	115	58	32
A	A	C	C
Specialists			
Medical	Surgical	Psychiatry	Osteopathy
47	122	21	27
C	C	B	B

General Hospitals: 4 (520 beds)
   2 JCAHO, 77 of 108 services

Other Hospitals: N/A

Places Rated Rank: 324

Salinas, CA

Patient-treating Physicians: 662

Primary Care			
General	Family	Internists	Pediatrics
118	102	69	42
B	B	C	C
Specialists			
Medical	Surgical	Psychiatry	Osteopathy
99	156	36	26
B	C	A	C

General Hospitals: 4 (637 beds)
   4 JCAHO, 1 teaching, 84 of 108 services

Other Hospitals: N/A

Places Rated Rank: 305

Salisbury, MD

Patient-treating Physicians: 280

Primary Care			
General	Family	Internists	Pediatrics
15	9	40	25
C	C	AA	AA
Specialists			
Medical	Surgical	Psychiatry	Osteopathy
52	78	9	12
AA	AA	A	A

General Hospitals: 3 (455 beds)
   2 JCAHO, 74 of 108 services

Other Hospitals: Rehab

Places Rated Rank: 110

Salt Lake City, UT

Patient-treating Physicians: 2,180

Primary Care			
General	Family	Internists	Pediatrics
234	218	223	194
C	B	B	AA
Specialists			
Medical	Surgical	Psychiatry	Osteopathy
320	492	90	38
A	A	A	C

General Hospitals: 12 (1,830 beds)
   10 JCAHO, 4 teaching, 97 of 108 services

Other Hospitals: Children, VA, Psych, Rehab

Places Rated Rank: 166

San Angelo, TX

Patient-treating Physicians: 197

Primary Care			
General	Family	Internists	Pediatrics
22	19	20	11
C	C	C	C
Specialists			
Medical	Surgical	Psychiatry	Osteopathy
27	55	9	10
B	A	A	B

General Hospitals: 2 (385 beds)
   2 JCAHO, 80 of 108 services

Other Hospitals: Psych

Places Rated Rank: 185

San Antonio, TX

Patient-treating Physicians: 3,565

Primary Care			
General	Family	Internists	Pediatrics
503	447	332	248
B	B	C	A
Specialists			
Medical	Surgical	Psychiatry	Osteopathy
551	785	153	130
A	B	A	B

General Hospitals: 24 (6,232 beds)
   17 JCAHO, 9 teaching, 97 of 108 services

Other Hospitals: Children, VA, Psych, Rehab

Places Rated Rank: 103

San Diego-Carlsbad, CA

Patient-treating Physicians: 6,337

Primary Care			
General	Family	Internists	Pediatrics
813	688	755	463
B	B	A	A
Specialists			
Medical	Surgical	Psychiatry	Osteopathy
877	1,425	355	192
A	A	AA	C

General Hospitals: 20 (6,105 beds)
   20 JCAHO, 8 teaching, 104 of 108 services

Other Hospitals: Children, VA, Psych

Places Rated Rank: 114

Sandusky, OH

Patient-treating Physicians: 158

Primary Care			
General	Family	Internists	Pediatrics
10	8	14	7
C	C	C	C
Specialists			
Medical	Surgical	Psychiatry	Osteopathy
20	25	2	50
B	C	C	AA

General Hospitals: 2 (373 beds)
   2 JCAHO, 67 of 108 services

Other Hospitals: N/A

Places Rated Rank: 315

San Francisco-San Mateo, CA

Patient-treating Physicians: 6,427

Primary Care			
General	Family	Internists	Pediatrics
413	320	1,160	490
B	C	AA	AA
Specialists			
Medical	Surgical	Psychiatry	Osteopathy
900	1,334	631	77
AA	AA	AA	C

General Hospitals: 19 (4,524 beds)
   19 JCAHO, 8 teaching, 103 of 108 services

Other Hospitals: Children, VA

Places Rated Rank: 49

San Jose-Sunnyvale, CA

Patient-treating Physicians: 4,098

Primary Care			
General	Family	Internists	Pediatrics
366	298	745	398
C	C	AA	AA
Specialists			
Medical	Surgical	Psychiatry	Osteopathy
553	931	244	50
A	A	AA	C

General Hospitals: 13 (4,078 beds)
   13 JCAHO, 5 teaching, 99 of 108 services

Other Hospitals: Children, VA

Places Rated Rank: 100

San Luis Obispo-Paso Robles, CA

Patient-treating Physicians: 606

Primary Care			
General	Family	Internists	Pediatrics
89	80	74	32
A	A	A	B
Specialists			
Medical	Surgical	Psychiatry	Osteopathy
56	122	57	17
C	A	AA	B

General Hospitals: 4 (366 beds)
   4 JCAHO, 45 of 108 services

Other Hospitals: N/A

Places Rated Rank: 256

Santa Ana-Anaheim-Irvine, CA

Patient-treating Physicians: 6,788

Primary Care			
General	Family	Internists	Pediatrics
927	729	886	536
A	B	AA	AA
Specialists			
Medical	Surgical	Psychiatry	Osteopathy
952	1,471	295	256
A	A	A	B

General Hospitals: 29 (4,962 beds)
   26 JCAHO, 3 teaching, 98 of 108 services

Other Hospitals: Children, Psych, Rehab

Places Rated Rank: 118

Santa Barbara-Santa Maria, CA

Patient-treating Physicians: 916

Primary Care			
General	Family	Internists	Pediatrics
133	109	132	53
A	A	AA	B

Specialists			
Medical	Surgical	Psychiatry	Osteopathy
117	203	49	17
B	A	AA	C

General Hospitals: 6 (874 beds)
  5 JCAHO, 1 teaching, 73 of 108 services
Other Hospitals: Rehab

Places Rated Rank: 175

Santa Cruz-Watsonville, CA

Patient-treating Physicians: 578

Primary Care			
General	Family	Internists	Pediatrics
123	105	57	36
AA	AA	B	A

Specialists			
Medical	Surgical	Psychiatry	Osteopathy
61	108	44	28
B	B	AA	A

General Hospitals: 3 (338 beds)
  2 JCAHO, 44 of 108 services
Other Hospitals: N/A

Places Rated Rank: 278

Santa Fe, NM

Patient-treating Physicians: 372

Primary Care			
General	Family	Internists	Pediatrics
70	66	45	22
AA	AA	AA	A

Specialists			
Medical	Surgical	Psychiatry	Osteopathy
45	64	28	8
A	A	AA	C

General Hospitals: 2 (285 beds)
  2 JCAHO, 1 teaching, 63 of 108 services
Other Hospitals: N/A

Places Rated Rank: 152

Santa Rosa-Petaluma, CA

Patient-treating Physicians: 1,044

Primary Care			
General	Family	Internists	Pediatrics
249	228	104	60
AA	AA	B	B

Specialists			
Medical	Surgical	Psychiatry	Osteopathy
110	224	58	33
C	A	AA	B

General Hospitals: 8 (824 beds)
  7 JCAHO, 1 teaching, 77 of 108 services
Other Hospitals: N/A

Places Rated Rank: 181

Sarasota-Bradenton-Venice, FL

Patient-treating Physicians: 1,550

Primary Care			
General	Family	Internists	Pediatrics
170	136	191	64
B	B	AA	C

Specialists			
Medical	Surgical	Psychiatry	Osteopathy
285	386	49	105
AA	AA	A	AA

General Hospitals: 7 (1,823 beds)
  6 JCAHO, 81 of 108 services
Other Hospitals: Rehab

Places Rated Rank: 92

Savannah, GA

Patient-treating Physicians: 684

Primary Care			
General	Family	Internists	Pediatrics
75	62	81	44
B	C	A	A

Specialists			
Medical	Surgical	Psychiatry	Osteopathy
106	197	18	16
A	AA	B	C

General Hospitals: 4 (1,120 beds)
  3 JCAHO, 1 teaching, 91 of 108 services
Other Hospitals: Children

Places Rated Rank: 67

Scranton–Wilkes-Barre, PA

Patient-treating Physicians: 1,046

Primary Care			
General	Family	Internists	Pediatrics
120	97	136	47
C	C	A	C

Specialists			
Medical	Surgical	Psychiatry	Osteopathy
150	231	35	159
B	C	B	AA

General Hospitals: 13 (2,057 beds)
  11 JCAHO, 3 teaching, 101 of 108 services
Other Hospitals: VA, Psych, Rehab

Places Rated Rank: 160

Seattle-Bellevue-Everett, WA

Patient-treating Physicians: 6,207

Primary Care			
General	Family	Internists	Pediatrics
1,021	925	750	379
AA	AA	AA	A

Specialists			
Medical	Surgical	Psychiatry	Osteopathy
880	1,236	344	179
AA	A	AA	B

General Hospitals: 20 (4,124 beds)
  17 JCAHO, 8 teaching, 105 of 108 services
Other Hospitals: Children, VA, Psych

Places Rated Rank: 59

Sebastian-Vero Beach, FL

Patient-treating Physicians: 321

Primary Care			
General	Family	Internists	Pediatrics
29	28	43	16
B	B	AA	A

Specialists			
Medical	Surgical	Psychiatry	Osteopathy
55	83	6	18
AA	AA	C	A

General Hospitals: 3 (676 beds)
  2 JCAHO, 68 of 108 services
Other Hospitals: Rehab

Places Rated Rank: 61

Sheboygan, WI

Patient-treating Physicians: 170

Primary Care			
General	Family	Internists	Pediatrics
37	34	14	9
A	A	C	C

Specialists			
Medical	Surgical	Psychiatry	Osteopathy
19	43	10	4
C	C	A	C

General Hospitals: 3 (392 beds)
  3 JCAHO, 78 of 108 services
Other Hospitals: N/A

Places Rated Rank: 254

Sherman-Denison, TX

Patient-treating Physicians: 196

Primary Care			
General	Family	Internists	Pediatrics
25	23	13	12
C	C	C	B

Specialists			
Medical	Surgical	Psychiatry	Osteopathy
36	52	3	6
A	B	C	C

General Hospitals: 3 (607 beds)
  3 JCAHO, 71 of 108 services
Other Hospitals: N/A

Places Rated Rank: 200

✓Shreveport-Bossier City, LA

Patient-treating Physicians: 992

Primary Care			
General	Family	Internists	Pediatrics
113	98	11	68
B	B	A	AA

Specialists			
Medical	Surgical	Psychiatry	Osteopathy
177	297	31	4
AA	AA	A	C

General Hospitals: 8 (2,136 beds)
  5 JCAHO, 4 teaching, 94 of 108 services
Other Hospitals: Children, VA, Psych

Places Rated Rank: 15

Sioux City, IA-NE-SD

Patient-treating Physicians: 224

Primary Care			
General	Family	Internists	Pediatrics
42	41	11	7
B	A	C	C

Specialists			
Medical	Surgical	Psychiatry	Osteopathy
32	57	3	24
C	C	C	AA

General Hospitals: 2 (468 beds)
2 JCAHO, 2 teaching, 83 of 108 services
Other Hospitals: N/A

Places Rated Rank: 249

✓Sioux Falls, SD

Patient-treating Physicians: 543

Primary Care			
General	Family	Internists	Pediatrics
89	84	51	20
AA	AA	A	C

Specialists			
Medical	Surgical	Psychiatry	Osteopathy
103	128	12	14
AA	AA	B	B

General Hospitals: 6 (1,321 beds)
4 JCAHO, 3 teaching, 103 of 108 services
Other Hospitals: Children, VA

Places Rated Rank: 3

South Bend-Mishawaka, IN-MI

Patient-treating Physicians: 587

Primary Care			
General	Family	Internists	Pediatrics
102	98	39	23
A	A	C	C

Specialists			
Medical	Surgical	Psychiatry	Osteopathy
78	114	12	63
B	C	C	AA

General Hospitals: 4 (786 beds)
4 JCAHO, 2 teaching, 79 of 108 services
Other Hospitals: Children

Places Rated Rank: 281

Spartanburg, SC

Patient-treating Physicians: 432

Primary Care			
General	Family	Internists	Pediatrics
81	76	40	20
A	A	C	C

Specialists			
Medical	Surgical	Psychiatry	Osteopathy
59	132	7	6
C	A	C	C

General Hospitals: 3 (626 beds)
2 JCAHO, 1 teaching, 77 of 108 services
Other Hospitals: N/A

Places Rated Rank: 218

Spokane, WA

Patient-treating Physicians: 976

Primary Care			
General	Family	Internists	Pediatrics
182	165	93	43
AA	AA	B	C

Specialists			
Medical	Surgical	Psychiatry	Osteopathy
133	230	28	35
A	A	B	B

General Hospitals: 6 (1,295 beds)
5 JCAHO, 2 teaching, 91 of 108 services
Other Hospitals: Children, VA, Rehab

Places Rated Rank: 64

✓Springfield, IL

Patient-treating Physicians: 613

Primary Care			
General	Family	Internists	Pediatrics
63	60	66	29
A	A	AA	A

Specialists			
Medical	Surgical	Psychiatry	Osteopathy
120	148	22	8
AA	AA	AA	C

General Hospitals: 2 (1,023 beds)
2 JCAHO, 2 teaching, 84 of 108 services
Other Hospitals: Children

Places Rated Rank: 23

Springfield, MA

Patient-treating Physicians: 1,403

Primary Care			
General	Family	Internists	Pediatrics
113	98	264	127
C	C	AA	AA

Specialists			
Medical	Surgical	Psychiatry	Osteopathy
199	296	102	30
B	B	AA	C

General Hospitals: 9 (1,485 beds)
8 JCAHO, 1 teaching, 94 of 108 services
Other Hospitals: Children, VA, Psych

Places Rated Rank: 208

Springfield, MO

Patient-treating Physicians: 831

Primary Care			
General	Family	Internists	Pediatrics
108	97	88	37
B	B	B	C

Specialists			
Medical	Surgical	Psychiatry	Osteopathy
110	183	24	89
B	A	B	AA

General Hospitals: 4 (1,432 beds)
3 JCAHO, 102 of 108 services
Other Hospitals: Children

Places Rated Rank: 75

Springfield, OH

Patient-treating Physicians: 188

Primary Care			
General	Family	Internists	Pediatrics
29	26	27	11
C	C	C	C

Specialists			
Medical	Surgical	Psychiatry	Osteopathy
22	40	6	13
C	C	C	B

General Hospitals: 2 (392 beds)
2 JCAHO, 70 of 108 services
Other Hospitals: N/A

Places Rated Rank: 350

State College, PA

Patient-treating Physicians: 254

Primary Care			
General	Family	Internists	Pediatrics
38	31	29	18
B	B	B	B

Specialists			
Medical	Surgical	Psychiatry	Osteopathy
34	48	14	19
B	C	A	A

General Hospitals: 2 (168 beds)
1 JCAHO, 53 of 108 services
Other Hospitals: Psych, Rehab

Places Rated Rank: 348

Stockton, CA

Patient-treating Physicians: 791

Primary Care			
General	Family	Internists	Pediatrics
136	113	115	72
C	C	C	B

Specialists			
Medical	Surgical	Psychiatry	Osteopathy
98	174	28	34
C	C	C	C

General Hospitals: 7 (1,080 beds)
7 JCAHO, 1 teaching, 77 of 108 services
Other Hospitals: Psych

Places Rated Rank: 354

Sumter, SC

Patient-treating Physicians: 134

Primary Care			
General	Family	Internists	Pediatrics
15	12	18	13
C	C	C	B

Specialists			
Medical	Surgical	Psychiatry	Osteopathy
15	33	5	7
C	C	C	C

General Hospitals: 1 (236 beds)
1 JCAHO, 47 of 108 services
Other Hospitals: N/A

Places Rated Rank: 368

Syracuse, NY

Patient-treating Physicians: 1,429

Primary Care			
General	Family	Internists	Pediatrics
207	193	149	108
A	A	B	AA
Specialists			
Medical	Surgical	Psychiatry	Osteopathy
203	356	58	34
A	A	A	C

General Hospitals: 9 (2,122 beds)
   9 JCAHO, 4 teaching, 94 of 108 services
Other Hospitals: Children, VA, Psych

Places Rated Rank: 63

Tacoma, WA

Patient-treating Physicians: 1,300

Primary Care			
General	Family	Internists	Pediatrics
223	203	131	99
A	A	C	A
Specialists			
Medical	Surgical	Psychiatry	Osteopathy
162	283	42	53
C	C	C	B

General Hospitals: 5 (1,194 beds)
   4 JCAHO, 2 teaching, 88 of 108 services
Other Hospitals: Children

Places Rated Rank: 273

Tallahassee, FL

Patient-treating Physicians: 548

Primary Care			
General	Family	Internists	Pediatrics
129	116	44	36
AA	AA	C	B
Specialists			
Medical	Surgical	Psychiatry	Osteopathy
65	118	31	25
C	C	A	B

General Hospitals: 4 (763 beds)
   2 JCAHO, 1 teaching, 76 of 108 services
Other Hospitals: Rehab

Places Rated Rank: 271

Tampa-St. Petersburg, FL

Patient-treating Physicians: 5,485

Primary Care			
General	Family	Internists	Pediatrics
529	423	724	374
C	C	A	A
Specialists			
Medical	Surgical	Psychiatry	Osteopathy
903	1,158	164	512
AA	B	B	AA

General Hospitals: 32 (8,551 beds)
   29 JCAHO, 4 teaching, 99 of 108 services
Other Hospitals: Children, VA, Psych, Rehab

Places Rated Rank: 105

Terre Haute, IN

Patient-treating Physicians: 269

Primary Care			
General	Family	Internists	Pediatrics
60	55	35	10
A	A	B	C
Specialists			
Medical	Surgical	Psychiatry	Osteopathy
34	51	9	13
C	C	C	B

General Hospitals: 5 (583 beds)
   5 JCAHO, 1 teaching, 79 of 108 services
Other Hospitals: Psych

Places Rated Rank: 240

Texarkana, TX-Texarkana, AR

Patient-treating Physicians: 254

Primary Care			
General	Family	Internists	Pediatrics
46	45	24	10
A	AA	C	C
Specialists			
Medical	Surgical	Psychiatry	Osteopathy
33	72	6	5
B	A	C	C

General Hospitals: 5 (460 beds)
   3 JCAHO, 67 of 108 services
Other Hospitals: Psych, Rehab

Places Rated Rank: 146

Toledo, OH

Patient-treating Physicians: 1,424

Primary Care			
General	Family	Internists	Pediatrics
222	197	124	108
A	A	C	A
Specialists			
Medical	Surgical	Psychiatry	Osteopathy
192	297	56	97
B	B	A	A

General Hospitals: 11 (2,736 beds)
   10 JCAHO, 3 teaching, 102 of 108 services
Other Hospitals: Children

Places Rated Rank: 50

Topeka, KS

Patient-treating Physicians: 389

Primary Care			
General	Family	Internists	Pediatrics
51	47	43	15
C	C	C	C
Specialists			
Medical	Surgical	Psychiatry	Osteopathy
66	76	20	24
A	C	A	A

General Hospitals: 6 (1,328 beds)
   4 JCAHO, 3 teaching, 89 of 108 services
Other Hospitals: VA, Rehab

Places Rated Rank: 190

Trenton-Ewing, NJ

Patient-treating Physicians: 988

Primary Care			
General	Family	Internists	Pediatrics
51	41	174	67
C	C	AA	AA
Specialists			
Medical	Surgical	Psychiatry	Osteopathy
165	218	85	50
AA	AA	AA	A

General Hospitals: 6 (1,180 beds)
   5 JCAHO, 2 teaching, 94 of 108 services
Other Hospitals: Rehab

Places Rated Rank: 86

Tucson, AZ

Patient-treating Physicians: 2,104

Primary Care			
General	Family	Internists	Pediatrics
216	193	247	132
B	B	A	A
Specialists			
Medical	Surgical	Psychiatry	Osteopathy
287	433	98	143
A	A	AA	A

General Hospitals: 9 (2,276 beds)
   9 JCAHO, 4 teaching, 94 of 108 services
Other Hospitals: VA, Rehab

Places Rated Rank: 126

Tulsa, OK

Patient-treating Physicians: 1,714

Primary Care			
General	Family	Internists	Pediatrics
184	166	167	88
C	C	C	C
Specialists			
Medical	Surgical	Psychiatry	Osteopathy
195	303	48	456
C	C	C	AA

General Hospitals: 20 (2,694 beds)
   9 JCAHO, 3 teaching, 95 of 108 services
Other Hospitals: Children, Psych, Rehab

Places Rated Rank: 252

Tuscaloosa, AL

Patient-treating Physicians: 336

Primary Care			
General	Family	Internists	Pediatrics
61	56	35	13
A	A	C	C
Specialists			
Medical	Surgical	Psychiatry	Osteopathy
48	77	17	6
B	C	A	C

General Hospitals: 4 (665 beds)
   2 JCAHO, 1 teaching, 67 of 108 services
Other Hospitals: VA

Places Rated Rank: 245

✓ Tyler, TX

Patient-treating Physicians: 562

Primary Care			
General	Family	Internists	Pediatrics
76	67	61	27
AA	AA	AA	A

Specialists			
Medical	Surgical	Psychiatry	Osteopathy
100	136	12	25
AA	AA	B	A

General Hospitals: 5 (847 beds)
   3 JCAHO, 1 teaching, 81 of 108 services
Other Hospitals: Rehab

Places Rated Rank: 16

Utica-Rome, NY

Patient-treating Physicians: 443

Primary Care			
General	Family	Internists	Pediatrics
70	66	70	28
C	B	B	C

Specialists			
Medical	Surgical	Psychiatry	Osteopathy
57	105	19	21
C	C	B	B

General Hospitals: 5 (1,138 beds)
   5 JCAHO, 81 of 108 services
Other Hospitals: N/A

Places Rated Rank: 236

Valdosta, GA

Patient-treating Physicians: 181

Primary Care			
General	Family	Internists	Pediatrics
29	24	23	9
C	C	C	C

Specialists			
Medical	Surgical	Psychiatry	Osteopathy
26	42	9	10
C	C	B	B

General Hospitals: 4 (486 beds)
   3 JCAHO, 90 of 108 services
Other Hospitals: Psych

Places Rated Rank: 222

Vallejo-Fairfield, CA

Patient-treating Physicians: 586

Primary Care			
General	Family	Internists	Pediatrics
88	71	98	57
C	C	A	A

Specialists			
Medical	Surgical	Psychiatry	Osteopathy
60	127	36	26
C	C	A	C

General Hospitals: 4 (697 beds)
   4 JCAHO, 1 teaching, 44 of 108 services
Other Hospitals: Psych

Places Rated Rank: 359

Victoria, TX

Patient-treating Physicians: 205

Primary Care			
General	Family	Internists	Pediatrics
33	30	22	16
B	B	C	A

Specialists			
Medical	Surgical	Psychiatry	Osteopathy
28	48	6	9
B	B	C	B

General Hospitals: 4 (656 beds)
   3 JCAHO, 80 of 108 services
Other Hospitals: Rehab

Places Rated Rank: 139

Vineland-Millville-Bridgeton, NJ

Patient-treating Physicians: 193

Primary Care			
General	Family	Internists	Pediatrics
21	19	25	19
C	C	C	B

Specialists			
Medical	Surgical	Psychiatry	Osteopathy
29	48	8	22
C	C	C	A

General Hospitals: 1 (457 beds)
   1 JCAHO, 55 of 108 services
Other Hospitals: N/A

Places Rated Rank: 351

Virginia Beach-Norfolk, VA-NC

Patient-treating Physicians: 3,129

Primary Care			
General	Family	Internists	Pediatrics
464	409	349	264
B	B	B	A

Specialists			
Medical	Surgical	Psychiatry	Osteopathy
419	765	119	87
B	B	B	C

General Hospitals: 16 (3,812 beds)
   16 JCAHO, 8 teaching, 98 of 108 services
Other Hospitals: Children, VA, Psych, Rehab

Places Rated Rank: 136

Visalia-Porterville, CA

Patient-treating Physicians: 400

Primary Care			
General	Family	Internists	Pediatrics
74	63	53	39
C	C	C	C

Specialists			
Medical	Surgical	Psychiatry	Osteopathy
44	91	14	15
C	C	C	C

General Hospitals: 3 (736 beds)
   2 JCAHO, 71 of 108 services
Other Hospitals: N/A

Places Rated Rank: 364

Waco, TX

Patient-treating Physicians: 341

Primary Care			
General	Family	Internists	Pediatrics
75	72	20	16
A	AA	C	C

Specialists			
Medical	Surgical	Psychiatry	Osteopathy
37	92	14	9
C	B	B	C

General Hospitals: 2 (825 beds)
   2 JCAHO, 2 teaching, 88 of 108 services
Other Hospitals: N/A

Places Rated Rank: 178

Warner Robins, GA

Patient-treating Physicians: 157

Primary Care			
General	Family	Internists	Pediatrics
21	17	30	13
C	C	A	B

Specialists			
Medical	Surgical	Psychiatry	Osteopathy
16	29	7	13
C	C	B	A

General Hospitals: 2 (231 beds)
   2 JCAHO, 44 of 108 services
Other Hospitals: N/A

Places Rated Rank: 369

Warren-Troy-Farmington Hills, MI

Patient-treating Physicians: 6,196

Primary Care			
General	Family	Internists	Pediatrics
534	462	864	414
C	C	AA	AA

Specialists			
Medical	Surgical	Psychiatry	Osteopathy
813	1,141	290	1,193
A	B	AA	AA

General Hospitals: 24 (5,196 beds)
   16 JCAHO, 5 teaching, 101 of 108 services
Other Hospitals: N/A

Places Rated Rank: 153

Washington, DC-VA-MD-WV

Patient-treating Physicians: 8,127

Primary Care			
General	Family	Internists	Pediatrics
807	707	1,317	733
C	C	AA	AA

Specialists			
Medical	Surgical	Psychiatry	Osteopathy
1,244	1,832	502	126
A	B	AA	C

General Hospitals: 33 (7,985 beds)
   33 JCAHO, 17 teaching, 107 of 108 services
Other Hospitals: Children, VA, Psych, Rehab

Places Rated Rank: 144

Waterloo-Cedar Falls, IA

Patient-treating Physicians: 278

Primary Care			
General	Family	Internists	Pediatrics
68	66	21	6
AA	AA	C	C
Specialists			
Medical	Surgical	Psychiatry	Osteopathy
28	54	10	34
C	C	B	AA

General Hospitals: 6 (709 beds)
3 JCAHO, 2 teaching, 88 of 108 services

Other Hospitals: N/A

Places Rated Rank: 180

Wausau, WI

Patient-treating Physicians: 276

Primary Care			
General	Family	Internists	Pediatrics
60	58	23	15
AA	AA	C	B
Specialists			
Medical	Surgical	Psychiatry	Osteopathy
38	58	5	15
A	B	C	A

General Hospitals: 1 (253 beds)
1 JCAHO, 1 teaching, 67 of 108 services

Other Hospitals: Children, Psych

Places Rated Rank: 207

Weirton-Steubenville, WV-OH

Patient-treating Physicians: 157

Primary Care			
General	Family	Internists	Pediatrics
23	18	27	6
C	C	B	C
Specialists			
Medical	Surgical	Psychiatry	Osteopathy
21	35	4	19
C	C	C	A

General Hospitals: 2 (576 beds)
2 JCAHO, 78 of 108 services

Other Hospitals: N/A

Places Rated Rank: 316

Wenatchee, WA

Patient-treating Physicians: 210

Primary Care			
General	Family	Internists	Pediatrics
46	44	27	7
AA	AA	A	C
Specialists			
Medical	Surgical	Psychiatry	Osteopathy
23	48	4	3
C	A	C	C

General Hospitals: 3 (193 beds)
1 JCAHO, 61 of 108 services

Other Hospitals: Rehab

Places Rated Rank: 219

West Palm Beach-Boca Raton, FL

Patient-treating Physicians: 3,001

Primary Care			
General	Family	Internists	Pediatrics
213	164	454	166
C	C	AA	A
Specialists			
Medical	Surgical	Psychiatry	Osteopathy
532	730	100	249
AA	AA	A	AA

General Hospitals: 14 (3,046 beds)
13 JCAHO, 101 of 108 services

Other Hospitals: VA, Psych, Rehab

Places Rated Rank: 91

Wheeling, WV-OH

Patient-treating Physicians: 292

Primary Care			
General	Family	Internists	Pediatrics
40	32	25	15
B	C	C	C
Specialists			
Medical	Surgical	Psychiatry	Osteopathy
32	71	9	42
C	B	B	AA

General Hospitals: 6 (1,036 beds)
6 JCAHO, 89 of 108 services

Other Hospitals: N/A

Places Rated Rank: 140

Wichita, KS

Patient-treating Physicians: 1,065

Primary Care			
General	Family	Internists	Pediatrics
216	207	88	53
AA	AA	C	C
Specialists			
Medical	Surgical	Psychiatry	Osteopathy
135	233	32	106
C	C	C	AA

General Hospitals: 11 (1,787 beds)
5 JCAHO, 3 teaching, 96 of 108 services

Other Hospitals: VA, Psych, Rehab

Places Rated Rank: 157

Wichita Falls, TX

Patient-treating Physicians: 274

Primary Care			
General	Family	Internists	Pediatrics
57	53	20	14
AA	AA	C	C
Specialists			
Medical	Surgical	Psychiatry	Osteopathy
39	65	13	13
B	B	A	B

General Hospitals: 5 (481 beds)
3 JCAHO, 1 teaching, 72 of 108 services

Other Hospitals: Psych, Rehab

Places Rated Rank: 194

Williamsport, PA

Patient-treating Physicians: 184

Primary Care			
General	Family	Internists	Pediatrics
41	39	11	4
A	A	C	C
Specialists			
Medical	Surgical	Psychiatry	Osteopathy
24	38	6	25
C	C	C	AA

General Hospitals: 2 (438 beds)
2 JCAHO, 81 of 108 services

Other Hospitals: N/A

Places Rated Rank: 244

Wilmington, DE-MD-NJ

Patient-treating Physicians: 1,237

Primary Care			
General	Family	Internists	Pediatrics
150	139	129	99
C	C	C	A
Specialists			
Medical	Surgical	Psychiatry	Osteopathy
176	266	50	128
B	C	B	AA

General Hospitals: 5 (1,467 beds)
5 JCAHO, 3 teaching, 96 of 108 services

Other Hospitals: Children, VA, Psych

Places Rated Rank: 225

Wilmington, NC

Patient-treating Physicians: 641

Primary Care			
General	Family	Internists	Pediatrics
71	65	92	29
B	B	AA	C
Specialists			
Medical	Surgical	Psychiatry	Osteopathy
98	171	30	11
A	AA	AA	C

General Hospitals: 4 (890 beds)
3 JCAHO, 1 teaching, 76 of 108 services

Other Hospitals: N/A

Places Rated Rank: 133

Winchester, VA-WV

Patient-treating Physicians: 275

Primary Care			
General	Family	Internists	Pediatrics
25	22	32	15
C	C	A	A
Specialists			
Medical	Surgical	Psychiatry	Osteopathy
43	90	7	4
AA	AA	B	C

General Hospitals: 2 (444 beds)
2 JCAHO, 69 of 108 services

Other Hospitals: N/A

Places Rated Rank: 85

Health Care

✓ Winston-Salem, NC

Patient-treating Physicians: 1,123

Primary Care			
General	Family	Internists	Pediatrics
128	114	110	74
B	B	A	AA

Specialists			
Medical	Surgical	Psychiatry	Osteopathy
217	251	56	11
AA	AA	AA	C

General Hospitals: 6 (1,901 beds)
4 JCAHO, 1 teaching, 98 of 108 services

Other Hospitals: Children

Places Rated Rank: 24

Worcester, MA

Patient-treating Physicians: 1,637

Primary Care			
General	Family	Internists	Pediatrics
184	172	328	160
C	B	AA	AA

Specialists			
Medical	Surgical	Psychiatry	Osteopathy
235	322	85	45
A	B	AA	C

General Hospitals: 10 (1,524 beds)
9 JCAHO, 2 teaching, 104 of 108 services

Other Hospitals: Children, Rehab

Places Rated Rank: 147

Yakima, WA

Patient-treating Physicians: 362

Primary Care			
General	Family	Internists	Pediatrics
83	71	36	22
AA	AA	C	C

Specialists			
Medical	Surgical	Psychiatry	Osteopathy
41	71	11	34
C	C	C	A

General Hospitals: 4 (513 beds)
3 JCAHO, 74 of 108 services

Other Hospitals: N/A

Places Rated Rank: 302

York-Hanover, PA

Patient-treating Physicians: 639

Primary Care			
General	Family	Internists	Pediatrics
113	106	60	32
B	A	C	C

Specialists			
Medical	Surgical	Psychiatry	Osteopathy
73	103	17	140
C	C	C	AA

General Hospitals: 4 (636 beds)
2 JCAHO, 1 teaching, 96 of 108 services

Other Hospitals: Rehab

Places Rated Rank: 310

Youngstown-Warren, OH-PA

Patient-treating Physicians: 1,093

Primary Care			
General	Family	Internists	Pediatrics
81	69	150	55
C	C	A	C

Specialists			
Medical	Surgical	Psychiatry	Osteopathy
123	226	22	264
C	C	C	AA

General Hospitals: 8 (1,855 beds)
6 JCAHO, 3 teaching, 94 of 108 services

Other Hospitals: Children, Psych, Rehab

Places Rated Rank: 268

Yuba City, CA

Patient-treating Physicians: 222

Primary Care			
General	Family	Internists	Pediatrics
48	42	29	21
A	A	B	A

Specialists			
Medical	Surgical	Psychiatry	Osteopathy
27	46	6	14
C	C	C	B

General Hospitals: 2 (213 beds)
1 JCAHO, 35 of 108 services

Other Hospitals: N/A

Places Rated Rank: 343

Yuma, AZ

Patient-treating Physicians: 188

Primary Care			
General	Family	Internists	Pediatrics
19	15	28	16
C	C	C	C

Specialists			
Medical	Surgical	Psychiatry	Osteopathy
30	42	7	14
C	C	C	B

General Hospitals: 1 (277 beds)
1 JCAHO, 55 of 108 services

Other Hospitals: N/A

Places Rated Rank: 375

ET CETERA: HEALTH CARE

HEALTHY LIFE/LONGER LIFE

Do you subscribe to the theory of when your time is up, you go? Then you may be surprised at current thinking. Experts now conclude that it's less likely to be a stray bullet or virus that kills you than the way you lead your life.

The most common causes of death at the turn of the century—typhoid fever, cholera, tuberculosis, smallpox, gastroenteritis, and nephritis—have been practically eliminated by scientific advances and improved sanitation. Today, more than 70 percent of the two million Americans who die each year are victims of heart disease, cancer, stroke, cirrhosis of the liver, bronchitis, asthma, and emphysema—the so-called lifestyle diseases that may be aggravated by such behavior as overeating, heavy drinking, smoking, and lack of exercise. To see how your daily habits measure up, take a look at the table "How Healthy Is Your Lifestyle?" Some risk factors are more important than others, so an entirely accurate picture of your health may not emerge from practicing self-analysis. However, changing your habits so that you qualify for the low-risk ratings will result in a longer life.

The following are some suggestions—certainly not new, but still as healthful as the first time you heard them—that can help you reduce your health risks. If you haven't yet paid heed to the wisdom of these suggestions, perhaps this will nudge you into a healthier style of living.

Stop smoking and drink only in moderation. Cigarette smokers run twice the risk that nonsmokers do of death from coronary disease. Smoking also contributes to stroke, lung cancer, emphysema, and bronchitis. Likewise, an excess of alcohol can be dangerous, increasing chances of developing cirrhosis of the liver (this condition is found six times as frequently among alcoholics as among nonalcoholics) and cardiovascular problems. Drinking, too, combined with driving multiplies the risk of dying in an automobile accident; at least half of such accidents in the United States involve drunk drivers.

Eat a balanced diet and watch your weight. Six of the ten leading causes of death have been linked to diet: heart attack, stroke, atherosclerosis, cancer, cirrhosis of the liver, and diabetes. Reducing your intake of refined flour and sugar, salt (which in excess contributes to high blood pressure), and saturated fats (which have been implicated as factors in heart disease and stroke) while choosing from a range of meat, poultry, fish, fruits, vegetables, and fiber foods (which have been shown to prevent colon cancer) is highly recommended. A balanced diet can also help you to lose extra weight, which puts added stress on the heart and organs, aggravating disease conditions.

Get regular exercise. Exercise, now seen almost as a miracle drug, can help you maintain proper weight, keep your body in good operating condition, and relieve stress (which contributes to ulcers and high blood pressure). It helps prevent premature aging and degeneration of bone (osteoporosis), muscles, and joints. The use-it-or-lose-it maxim definitely applies here.

Get regular medical care. Be sure to consult your doctor regularly and have whatever checkups or tests he or she recommends, such as a Pap smear, blood pressure, or blood cholesterol tests.

FINDING THE RIGHT DOCTOR

Not all doctors are created equal. The doctor you select and the hospital in which you're treated may be more important in determining the outcome of your illness than the disease you have. When you're selecting a surgeon, for example, you need to know how often the surgeon has done your kind of surgery (more is better) and what the outcome has been. Compare the records of several surgeons to get a sense of what a "good" track record is. Don't forget to trust your intuitions about doctors. How comfortable do you feel with the doctor? Your gut feeling could be the deciding factor.

The American Medical Association is the U.S. licensing body for physicians, but individual states vary in their licensing requirements. Highly populated states like New York and California have large staffs in their state licensing departments that can perform more thorough investigations of complaints against doctors. On the other hand, less densely populated states such as Idaho do not have the same investigative resources. But licensing boards alone cannot track down all the bad doctors. Medical schools, where students first enter the doctor track; licensing boards;

RISKY BUSINESS: HOW HEALTHY IS YOUR LIFESTYLE?

RISK CATEGORY	NO RISK	SLIGHT RISK	SUBSTANTIAL RISK	HEAVY RISK	DANGEROUS RISK
Alcohol	Non-drinker	Stopped drinking	6 drinks/week	More than 6 drinks/week	More than 2 drinks/day
Blood cholesterol	Less than 180	180-220	220-280	280-320	320 and above
Blood pressure	120/80	120/80-140/90	140/90-160/100	160/100-180/105	Above 180/105
Blood sugar	Less than 120 two hours after meal of syrup and pancakes	110-130 two hours after meal; checked every 3 months	More than 150 without diet control	More than 150 without diet control or doctor's care	Diabetes without doctor's care; <than 45 years old
Dental exams	Every 6 months	6-12 months	Infrequent orirregular visits	Only when pain or problem	Never visit dentist
Eye exam	Every 3-5 years				
Immunizations	Up-to-date	Childhood disease or immunization	Partial childhood immunizations	Partial/no childhood immunizations & compromised immune system	Compromised immune system
Nonprescription drugs	Use occasionally only for short periods; label warnings heeded				Continuing use; drinking or driving despite label warnings
Physical activity	Walk more than 2 miles/day or climb 20+ flights of stairs/day	Walk 1.5-2 miles/day or climb 15-20 flights of stairs/day	Walk only 0.5-1.5 miles/day or climb only 5-15 flights of stairs/day	Walk only 2-5 blocks/day or climb 2-4 flights of stairs/day	Walk less than 2 blocks a day or mb less than 2 flights of stairs/day
Physician visit	Have MD & see routinely every 1-2 years				Medical care on emergency room basis
Prescription drugs	With MD's consent; follow orders carefully	Take daily medication without side effects	Take medication when needed without side effects	Use sleeping/nerve pills regularly without MD supervision	Take prescribed medication with pills or alcohol w/o MD knowledge
Smoking	No smoking or stopped at least 10 years ago	Less than 10 cigarettes/day	Half a pack/day	1 pack/day	2 or more packs/day
Trimness	Lean	Slightly plump	Moderately obese	Considerably obese	Grossly obese
For Men Only					
Testicular exam	Monthly self exam & yearly by physician	Monthly self exam but not by physician	Self-exam 2-3 times/year; no physician exam	Only at physician visit	Never
For Women Only					
Breast exam	Monthly self exam & yearly by physician	Monthly self exam but not by physician	Self-exam 2-3 times/year; no physician exam	Only at physician visit	Never
Pap smear	Every year	Every 3 years	Every 4 years	Never	Never; non-menstrual bleeding

Source: Adapted from *Health Hazard Appraisal System* developed by Lewis C. Robbins, MD, Jack H. Hall, MD, and Pamela Hall.

Health Care

national, state, and local professional societies; and hospitals (where most doctors have staff privileges) must work together in order to assure that patients are treated by competent, licensed professionals.

The Health Care Financing Administration, which reimburses doctors and hospitals that treat Medicare and Medicaid patients, also has plans to help consumers in their selection of doctors. It will soon begin a longterm project of rating doctors by how well their patients do - as indicated by mortality rates and speed of recovery, for example.

In the meantime, consider the following suggestions. Chances are good that you'll have to choose a new physician at some point; even if you don't move, your doctor might. Finding a replacement for the person in whom you may have put a lot of trust isn't always easy. Give some thought to the kind of doctor you are most comfortable with. Do you want to place complete faith in your physician? Or do you have questions about your treatment? Do you like

a cooperative arrangement in which you and your doctor work as a team? It's very important to most people that they have a doctor who will listen to their complaints, worries, and concerns, rather than one who may make patients feel that they're questioning the doctor's authority.

If you're planning to move, you might ask your present doctor if he or she knows anything about doctors in your destination. Or you may get names from the nearest hospital at the new location, from friends you make, from medical societies, and from new neighbors. Given the competition for insured patients, don't be surprised to receive mail from hospitals touting their services and the quality of physicians on their referral network.

When you have decided whom you want to contact call that doctor's office, saying that you are a prospective patient, and ask to speak to the doctor briefly. You may have to agree to call back, but making connection with a professional voice is an important step. If you can't arrange this, if the doctor is "too busy," you probably ought to go to the next name on your list.

When you do make contact, tell the doctor enough about yourself so that he or she has a good idea of who you are and what your problems may be. If the doctor sounds "right" to you, you could ask about fees and emergencies. Or you may wish to save some of these questions for a personal visit. It is important to establish through the initial phone call or visit that you and the doctor will be at ease with each other.

Evaluate the doctor's attitude. If he or she doesn't want to bother with you now, you will probably get that don't-bother-me treatment sooner or later when dealing with specific problems. Make sure that:

• You can openly discuss your feelings and personal concerns about sexual and emotional problems.

• You know which hospitals he recommends and why.

• The doctor isn't vague, impatient, or unwilling to answer all your questions about the causes and treatment of your physical problems.

• The doctor takes a thorough history on you and asks about past physical and emotional problems, family medical history, medication you are taking, and other matters affecting your health.

Adult Exam Schedule

Complete Physical Examination

Every 2 years for patients under 65 years of age. Yearly for patients 65 and older

Stool Occult Blood

Every year

Vital Capacity Lung Test

Every year

Homocysteine Level

At regularly scheduled physical

Mammograms (women)

Every 2 years for women under 50. Yearly for women 50 and older. Occasionally every 6 months for previous abnormal mammograms

Cholesterol Level

Every 3-6 months for patients on cholesterol-lowering medication, or at regularly scheduled physical

Electrocardiogram

Every year

TB Skin Test

Every 2 years

Pap Smear (women)

Every year

Sigmoidoscopy/Colonoscopy

Every 3 years for patients 40 and older

PSA (men)

Every year for men 40 and older

Chest X-rays

Every 5 years. May be done if a patient has a respiratory complaint or a positive TB skin test

Paging Dr. Finder

Learning whether cardiologists, urologists, psychiatrists or other specialists practice in an area needn't mean a drudgerous session with the telephone book's yellow-pages. Call the local hospital's public relations office for a free copy of their Physician Locator or MD Directory. Hospitals in competitive markets know they will more likely have you as a customer when you're ill if they can introduce you early on to an physician that uses their facilities.

These "Dr. Finders" aren't mere telephone contact sheets. Often they are photo galleries of physicians with capsule resumés on their education from college through medical school to residency, their specialties, and their board certifications. You can also learn if they take walk-in patients and whether another doctor will cover for them on their day off. Some of these guides even detail their civic clubs and what they like to do on weekends.

The Top Killers

Below are causes of death ordered by their percent of all deaths in the United States. The first ten kill 3 of 4 of us. In fact, the top three non-accidental causes—heart disease, cancer, and stroke—account for almost 6 of every 10 deaths.

Cause	#	%
Heart diseases	652,000	27.2
Malignant neoplasms (cancer)	553,000	23.1
Cerebrovascular diseases (stroke)	150,000	6.3
Chronic lower pulmonary diseases	122,000	5.1
Accidents	112,000	4.7
Diabetes mellitus	73,000	3.1
Alzheimer's	66,000	2.8
Pneumonia and influenza	60,000	2.5
Nefritis	43,000	1.8
Septicemia	33,000	1.4
Suicide	32,000	1.4
Liver disease	27,000	1.1
Hypertension	23,000	1.0
Parkinson's Disease	18,000	0.8
Homicide and legal intervention	17,300	0.7
Pneumonitis	16,780	0.7
Perinatal Period	14,213	0.6
Aortic Aneurysm	13,753	0.6
Benign Neoplasms	13,580	0.6
HIV	13,000	0.5
All others	343,000	14.3

Source: U.S. Centers for Disease Control and Prevention

• The doctor doesn't automatically prescribe drugs rather than deal with real causes of your medical problems.

• The doctor has an associate to whom you can turn should your doctor retire or die.

Talk with the doctor about the transfer of your medical records. Some doctors like to have them, especially if there is any specific medical problem or chronic condition. Other doctors prefer to develop new records.

Even if you feel fine, arrange to have a physical or at least a quick checkup. Should an emergency occur, the doctor will have basic information about you and some knowledge of your needs, and you will avoid the stress of trying to work with a doctor who has to learn about you in an emergency.

IMMUNIZATION

The World Health Organization characterized the United States as having the third worst immunization system in the Western Hemisphere, ahead of Bolivia and Haiti. Just two of three children are immunized by age two. Reasons for the low immunization rate include the cost of vaccines, the lack of public awareness, and the attitudes of both parents and health care providers.

Some vaccines induce prolonged immunity to certain diseases, and can be given just once. But others, such as pertussis (Whooping Cough) or diphtheria, only induce temporary immunity. These vaccines require repeat booster injections to protect against such diseases.

Your immunization record should specify the types of vaccine and be dated and signed by the physician each time an immunization is given. Keep the record at home in a safe place, and take it on trips away from home.

RECOMMENDED IMMUNIZATION SCHEDULE

AGE	Diphtheria	PERTUSSIS Tetanus (DPT)	POLIO VACCINE (OPV/IPV)	VARICELLA MEASLES MUMPS RUBELLA (MMR)	HEPATITIS B (HBV)	HEMOPHILUS INFLUENZA B (Nib)	TETANUS DIPHTHERIA (Td)
Birth-2 months	•	•			•		
1-4 months	•	•			•	•	
6 months	•	•			•	•	
12-15 months			•	•	•		
18 months	•						
4-6 years	•	•	•				
14-16 years				••			Every 10 years
Adult			••				Every 10 years
Adult	Pneumococcal vaccine (one time only) Influenza vaccine (annually) Hepatitis A: a series of two shots every 6 years Hepatitis B: a series of three shots						

•• If not previously vaccinated against illness, never had illness, or tested to show not immune to illness.

Recreation

After "Where's that?" the question people ask most often about an unfamiliar place is whether there's anything to do there. Wherever they are, people want to make the most of leisure. Consider the billions spent each year on video rentals, insulated jogging clothes, season tickets at the stadium, European vacations, down-filled sleeping bags, and graphite fishing rods.

Not everyone can take advantage of all the opportunities for recreation. An Aspen ski trip or a Hilton Head golf weekend costs too much for most people. Even a backpacking trip in a national park with cheap camping fees might be out of the question for the dollars and time it takes to get there and back.

Fortunately, there are many other things to do that are inexpensive and nearby. Movies and golf are available almost anywhere; in fact, people living in smaller metro areas usually have better access to these than residents of bigger ones. On the other hand, zoos and professional sports enhance life in larger places. For more and more people, convenient outdoor recreation in a national forest or on a wild and scenic river is a lucky geographical circumstance; the protected outdoors is a part of the landscape just as developed urban land is. *Places Rated* looks at each of these kinds of recreation in determining the best places to play.

COMMON DENOMINATORS

For scuba diving, the coasts of Florida, California, and Hawaii are best bets. For skiing on powdery snow, Colorado and Utah are better than most other areas. Weather and winds turn still other areas into premier places for hang gliding. But there are certain kinds of recreation that you can find everywhere: A round of weekend golf or moviegoing at a downtown picture palace or a multiplex cinema at a suburban mall.

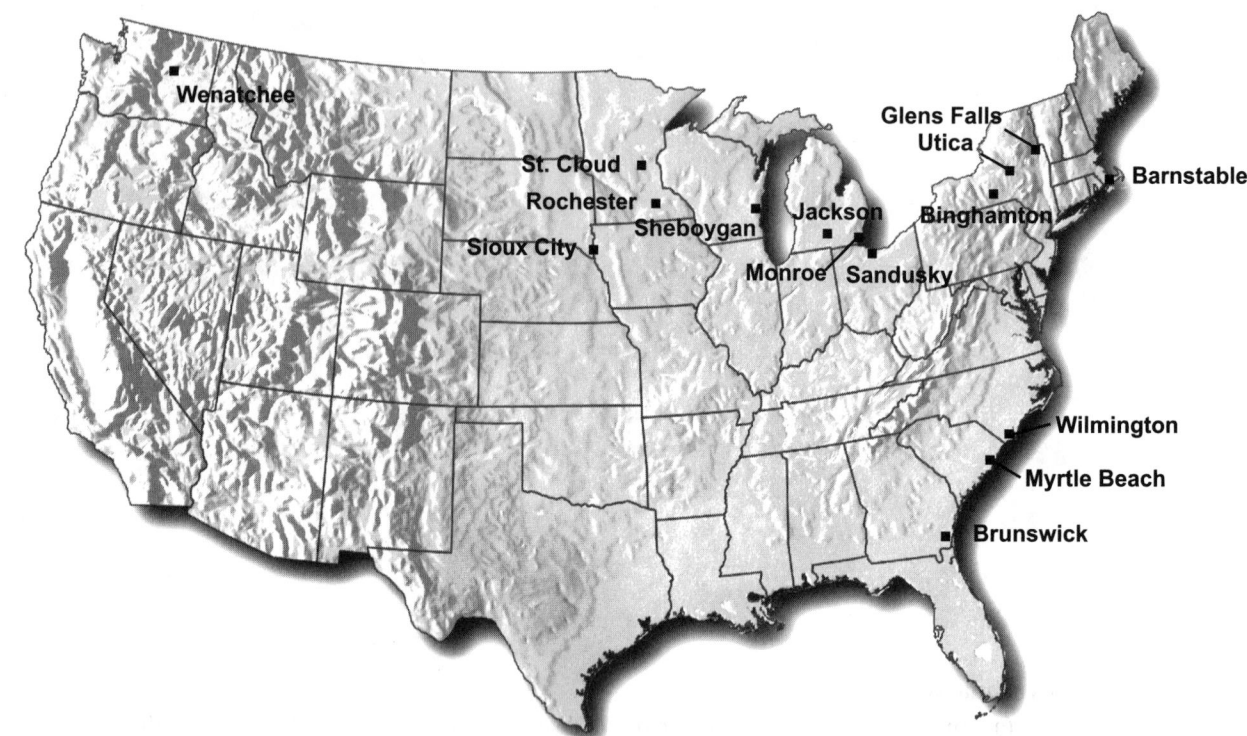

Fifteen Golf Hot Spots

Metro areas with fewer than 1,000 residents per hole of municipal or daily-fee golf are Atlantic Coast resorts like Barnstable Town, MA; Brunswick, GA; or Myrtle Beach, SC. But others are small locations in the Great Lakes states and upstate New York. According to researchers in the *Journal of Leisure Research*, by 2020 they will see a seven week longer golf season and up to one third more rounds played—thanks to global warming.

Golf: "Who Holes a Ball in Fewest Strokes Wins"

Two and a quarter centuries ago in the spring of 1779, *Rivington's Gazette* carried a small notice to New York readers:

> *To the GOLF PLAYERS: The Season for this pleasant and healthy Exercise now advancing, Gentlemen may be furnished with excellent CLUBS and the veritable Caledonian BALLS, by enquiring at the Printer's.*

The earliest reference in America to the game of golf? Perhaps, but more than a century passed before the country's first golf course would be laid out at Foxburg, Pennsylvania in 1887. The Foxburg Country Club, just north of Pittsburgh, still operates.

Certainly golf is a common denominator. It is played in every metro area—including Anchorage and Fairbanks, where games can go to midnight in the height of Alaskan summer. To find a local golf course on an idle, sunny weekend, you have three options: the *private* equity course, typically part of a country club open only to members and guests; *daily-fee* operations open to all players; and city- or county-operated *municipal* courses, again open to everyone.

If you're a golfer who can afford to join a private country club with a regulation 18-hole course or two, your dues buy one big advantage: You belong to the fortunate 14 percent of golfers who don't have to wait to tee off at a crowded municipal or daily-fee course.

On the other hand, if you're one of nearly 28 million American golfers who've played a round at a local municipal or daily-fee course, only six out of every ten of the country's 15,000 18-hole equivalent courses are open to you. Still, access to public golf is an excellent reflection of recreation opportunities in metro areas.

Movie Screens: Playing in Peoria but Bombing in Bismarck?

It's been almost 60 years since the late John Huston won his two academy awards - best director and best

screenplay - for *The Treasure of the Sierra Madre*. His father, Walter, was named best supporting actor for his portrayal of the old prospector in the same film. Jane Wyman won an Oscar for her role in *Johnny Belinda*. *Hamlet* was named best picture, and its director and star, Lawrence Olivier, best actor.

The year was 1948, when TV was just starting its expansion. In postwar America, the average American saw 28 movies a year. Popcorn was regularly swept up from the aisles between shows, the next John Wayne or Spencer Tracy film was announced on a large easel in the lobby, usherettes took you to your seat with a red-lensed flashlight, and you always got a Movietone or Warner-Pathé newsreel with the show. There were nearly 20,000 movie houses back then. Most were neighborhood establishments with a few downtown picture palaces for premieres and first-run screenings. Never again would there be so many.

Today, movie marketers count screens rather than "four wall" (as opposed to fast-disappearing drive-ins) theaters to figure access to movies. Most the country's 30,000 screens now are in multiplex cinemas run by chain exhibitors like AMC Theatres, Carmike Cinemas, National Amusements, and Regal Entertainment. Still, there are some 700 single-screen or twin Bijou, Roxy, or Strand variety of neighborhood theaters surviving in smaller metro areas and in high-density, older residential areas in larger ones.

CROWD PLEASERS

At different times of the year in Los Angeles–Long Beach, you can visit the animals at the Los Angeles Zoo; join the crowds at the Universal Studios tour; wager on the horses at Hollywood Park or Santa Anita; or take in professional baseball, basketball, and hockey, as well as NCAA Division I competition.

While few metro areas have as varied a supply of crowd pleasers as Los Angeles, some of these opportunities are common in many larger metro areas. From Six Flags Magic Mountain in suburban Los Angeles to New York's Bronx Zoo, these attractions offer Americans interesting ways to spend their leisure time.

Amusement and Theme Parks

The person who started it all was one Walter Elias Disney and his creation was Disneyland. Because he avoided the *de rigueur* waterfront location and games of chance and skill, the amusement park industry

viewed his 180-acre playland skeptically when it opened in Anaheim, California in 1955.

Disney's plan was to adapt his cartoon characters and feature films as themes to structure a family-centered park more carefully than Ocean Park in Santa Monica, Chicago's Riverview, or the Steeplechase at Coney Island - tawdry places with carny atmospheres avoided by families. Obviously, he succeeded. North America's tacky parks are largely gone, replaced by more than 200 that market themselves as family theme parks, draw millions of visitors annually, and advertise nationally and regionally as vacation attractions.

The New Ark: Zoos

The two best metro areas for seeing the animals are Chicago and San Diego. Each has not one but two of the continent's top-ranked zoological parks. Altogether, 170 metro areas have at least one zoo. Washington's National Zoo, one of the Smithsonian Institution's 17 museums, is the only one operated by the Federal Government. Almost all of the others are municipally- or state-run, and most are accredited by the American Association of Zoological Parks and Aquariums (AAZPA).

Philadelphia's Zoological Society opened the first zoo in the United States, in 1874. In 1938, it opened the country's first children's zoo. But the European idea that zoos enhance people's lives flourishes in America's Midwest. Besides Chicago's two great zoos, the Cincinnati, Cleveland, Detroit, Milwaukee, and St. Louis zoological parks are among the best in the United States. It is not coincidental that the working-class citizens of these cities can trace their roots to European countries-particularly Germany-that also have great zoos.

"Postage-stamp collecting" is the name that zookeepers give to the assembling of colorful animal specimens without regard to whether the animals fit and can thrive in a zoo's limited space. This was once a sure way of drawing more patrons and carving out a reputation as an outstanding institution. Today, professionally run zoos exhibit fewer species but more specimens of each. The standard phylogenetic exhibits (grouping African lions with Bengal tigers, timber wolves with hyenas) have been replaced with ecological displays (wildlife in desert or mountain environments) and behavioral exhibits (hibernation, burrowing, nocturnalism) that group specimens more creatively and openly.

This isn't to say that zoos no longer maintain

large, diverse collections, for the best zoos are those with the biggest animal populations. But today the benchmark of a zoo's quality isn't simply how many animals it can keep or breed; just as important is how creatively and naturally the animals are exhibited.

Aquariums

Far less common than zoos, and more often operated for profit by private firms, aquariums are found in just 34 of the 379 metro areas, most of these in areas with ocean coastlines.

These attractions are expensive. The Monterey Bay Aquarium in Monterey, CA, for instance, has a $40 million annual operating budget. Atlanta's new Georgia Aquarium, with 8 million gallons water for some 100,000 specimens, cost donor Bernie Marcus, of Home Depot, some $200 million.

They can also be disappointing. Denver's Downtown Aquarium opened to great crowds in 1999 under the name Colorado's Ocean Journey, but didn't attract its annual target 1 million visitors and filed for bankruptcy in 2002. It is now a huge seafood restaurant with a 200,000 gallon exhibit of marine and fresh water specimens.

Counting Games: Professional Sports

A frequent topic of discussion on talk shows, in bars, in magazines, and at work is where the "good" sports towns are. The question is usually argued from two perspectives: whether a town has winners or whether fans turn out to root for the teams. These two trends are often linked; over the regular seasons, the clubs with the best attendance usually have had some of the best records.

Another way to find the best sports towns is to measure the access that a metro area's fans have to regular-season games. "Game seats per capita" is an elementary measurement used most often in professional sports franchising and marketing, especially at expansion time. This figure is found by multiplying the number of home games played by all the teams in a metro area (for example, 81 baseball; 41 basketball; 8 football) by the combined seating capacity of the teams' playing arenas and then dividing that number by the metro area's population.

Counting Games: College Sports

Among the biggest crowd pleasers around are varsity teams fielded by colleges and universities. The cream of those is generally found among the teams classified Division I (split into Divisions I-A and I-AA for football only) by the National Collegiate Athletic Association (NCAA). Eligibility for this division is based on the quality of a school's typical opponent, or "schedule strength," and game attendance figures which require big stadiums and arenas. Division I men's and women's sports are on view in 282 of the 379 metro areas, from the Aces of the University of Evansville to the Zips of the University of Akron.

Nearly 35 million fans attend the 3,251 regular season games played by the 667 colleges and universities with varsity football. Although the 231 Division I-A and I-AA teams play less than one-third of these games, they draw 90 percent of the attendance.

Basketball is even more widely available. More than 28 million fans come out for the 11,000 or more regular season and tournament games played by the 897 schools that field men's varsity basketball teams. The 327 NCAA Division I men's teams play one-third of these games, yet they account for over 80 percent of total attendance. The 864 women's basketball teams draw another 5 million people to 7,305 season and tournament games, and 80 percent of the crowd watches the 291 NCAA Division I women's teams.

Auto Racing: Vrooming, Vrooming

America's love affair with fast cars started in Providence, RI, where the first automobile track race was sponsored in 1896. The affair isn't over, at least in the southeast. At the Atlanta Motor Speedway, true fanatics can live in a condominium above the bleachers and watch NASCAR Winston Cup stock cars race around the 1.522-mile highbanked asphalt oval while they do the dishes. Whether on a "short eight" crash track in rural Oregon or at the Molson Indy course in downtown Toronto, auto racing in all its variations draws million of fans.

Of the 1,405 auto racetracks in the United States and Canada, just a fraction is sanctioned by the leading racing organizations: NASCAR, CART, IRL, and SCCA. CART, or Championship Auto Racing Team, oversees the FedEx series and Indy lights; IRL, the Indy Racing League, has jurisdiction over oval-track Indy Car racing; and SCCA, the Sports Car Club of America, sanctions sports-car events.

NASCAR, the National Association for Stock Car Racing, sanctions late-model and modified stock-car racing - events restricted to American-made cars. The crowds at some NASCAR races—the Daytona 500, the Southern 500 in Darlington, SC, and the

OUTDOORS ASSETS: THE WEST RULES

These fifteen metro areas have the most of their land area in inland and offshore water, federal protected areas, and state parks. If the country had been settled from West to East, some geographers speculate, New England and much of the mid-Atlantic states might still be open, unsettled, and preserved

Talladega 500—are the largest to come together for any sporting event in North America.

The Ponies

See a horse player angrily tear up his tickets and toss the confetti into the air after a bad bet at Delaware Park, or go inside the clubhouse and watch the bored slot machine players, and you'd wonder whether gambling is recreation for anybody.

After professional baseball, however, the biggest spectator sport in North America is pari-mutuel racing at the track. Based on a system in which the players who bet on the first-, second-, and third-place finishers share the total amount of money bet, pari-mutuel racing draws more than 100 million people each year.

Thoroughbred racing dominates the American racing scene, but in Delaware, upstate New York, Michigan, and the Chicago environs, harness racing (where the jockey rides behind in a small, two-wheeled cart) attracts more bettors and more

money than their thoroughbred competition. In Canada, harness racing outdraws thoroughbred racing two to one.

OUTDOOR RECREATION ASSETS

To many people, recreation isn't something taking place entirely within four walls or in the middle of a crowded city. For them, it means turning to the open spaces for fishing, boating, swimming, hiking, running, picnicking, or just getting away from it all.

Coastlines and Inland Water

Sooners boast that Oklahoma has so many impounded lakes of every size that if you were to tip the state to the south a bit, the water would flow out and flood Texas for a good while. And Maryland crabbers point out to newcomers that the true length of estuarine shore reached by the Chesapeake Bay's tide would total more than 8,000 miles if all the bends and kinks

were straightened out.

You'll spot inland water in nine of ten metro areas. Aside from being a basic necessity for life, water can be a scenic and recreational amenity if there is enough to fish in, boat on, or swim in if the temperature is right. Where would Reno be without Lake Tahoe? Or Long Island without Long Island Sound?

Four of every five North Americans today live in metro areas within 100 miles of beaching and boating on the ocean or on any of the Great Lakes. Ocean or Great Lakes coastlines form part of the peripheries of 121 metro areas and 100 percent of another, Honolulu.

Forests, Parks, and Wildlife Refuges

Some of the most popular outdoor activities—driving for pleasure, walking, picnicking, sightseeing, bird watching, hiking, and fishing—are even more enjoyable in the country's splendid system of national forests, parks, and wildlife refuges.

One hundred fifty-five National Forests and 19 National Grasslands cover nearly 9 percent of the land area in the United States. The main purpose of the National Forest System is silviculture: growing wood, harvesting it carefully, and preserving naturally beautiful areas. More than 250,000 miles of roads lie within the forest system, built not only for loggers, but for everyone. They lead to a wide variety of recreation outlets: ski resorts, marinas, fishing lakes and streams, hiking trails, and campgrounds.

In contrast to the National Forest System, the National Park System is meant expressly for recreation. "America's best idea," began with the founding of Yellowstone National Park in 1872, the start of the oldest and now largest national park system in the world. It comprises 390 national parks, preserves, monuments, memorials, battlefields, seashores, waterways, and trails that together cover some 80 million acres.

Whereas the National Park System acts to keep irreplaceable geographical and historical treasures in the public domain, the National Wildlife Refuges protect native flora and fauna from people. There are 545 of these remarkable sanctuaries throughout the country, embracing more than 96 million acres. Most of them are open to the public for a variety of wildlife activities, particularly photography and nature observation. In certain refuges at irregular times, fishing and hunting are permitted, depending on the size of the wild populations.

Although the majority of the nation's wildlife refuges are located in open, sometimes remote country, they aren't exclusively a rural amenity. Several can be found within metropolitan areas, such as the Nisqually National Wildlife Refuge in Olympia, WA, and San Pablo Bay National Wildlife Refuge in the California metro area of Santa Rosa-Petaluma.

North of NASCAR: Skiing

Draw a line on a map of America separating regions with the best conditions for skiing from those with poor conditions or none at all and you'd have a jagged northward arc. It starts in North Carolina's Great Smoky Mountains and extends upward to Atlantic Canada, west to the foothills of the Rockies, then south along the Rocky Mountain cordillera to northern New Mexico and Arizona. Next it would reappear in the California Sierra Nevada, dropping southwest to end in the San Bernardino National Forest an hour and a half out of Los Angeles.

Although ski areas exist as far south as Alabama and Georgia, the ideal conditions are found north of this imaginary curve in the rolling, rugged terrain and predictable winter weather that everyone except skiers would consider bad.

Of the 569 ski areas in North America, half are found in nine states and provinces that border the St. Lawrence River and the Great Lakes-Michigan, Minnesota, New Hampshire, New York, Ontario, Pennsylvania, Quebec, Vermont, and Wisconsin-owing to harsh long winters and large, outdoorsy urban populations.

JUDGING: RECREATION

Is there more to do in Houston than Dallas? How do the California rivals—Los Angeles and San Francisco—compare? In recreation, let's admit it may be impossible to rank metro areas with fairness. Nevertheless, some seem shortchanged while others seem rich. To compare them, *Places Rated* considers twelve items grouped into Common Denominators, Crowd Pleasers, and Outdoor Assets.

Each factor is weighted equally within its group, i.e., public golf and movie theatres within Common Denominators, amusement parks and professional sports within Crowd Pleasers, etc. The groups are then weighted equally to produce a rank. Metro areas with an edge in recreation are frequently

large ones with a full complement of crowd pleasers and enviable outdoor assets in water and in protected recreation land.

PLACE PROFILES: RECREATION

The following profiles are a selective catalogue of recreation features in each metro area and are ordered alphabetically: Amusement/Theme Parks, Aquariums, Auto Racing, College Sports, Golf Courses, Horse Racing, Movie Theatres, Professional Sports, Recreation Areas, Ski Areas, Water Area, and Zoos.

Recreation lands include national forest, park, and wildlife refuge acres, plus state part units located within metro area counties. Units classified as 'historic' are earlier counted in *Places Rated*'s Ambiance chapter. A number of abbreviations are used in this section:

MBS .... Migratory Bird Sanctuary
NF .... National Forest
NP .... National Park
NRA .... National Recreation Area
NS .... National Seashore
NSR .... National Scenic River
NWA .... National Wildlife Area
NWR .... National Wildlife Refuge
PNA .... Provincial Natural Area
PP .... Provincial Park
SF .... State Forest
SNA .... State Natural Area
SP .... State Park
SRA .... State Recreation Area

Information comes from these sources: Association of Zoos and Aquariums, www.aza.org, 2006; American Hockey League, www.ahl.com, 2006; Baseball America, *Almanac*, 2006; Continental Basketball Association, www.cbahoopsonline.com, 2006; Central Hockey League, www.centralhockeyleague.com, 2006; East Coast Hockey League, www.echl.com, 2006; Inter-ski Associates, *White Book of Skiing*, 2006; Major League Baseball, www.mlb.com, 2006; Major League Soccer, www.mlsnet.com, 2006; National Basketball Association, www.nba.com, 2006; National Collegiate Athletic Association, National Collegiate Championships, 2006, NCAA Basketball, 2006, and NCAA Football, 2006; National Football League, www.nfl.com,

www.placesrated.com

Recreation rankings from 1 to 379 are shown at the end of each area's profile in the *Place Profiles* section coming next. Recreation scores, from 100.0 to 0.0, are in *Putting It All Together* at the end of the book. Readers can view and print out Recreation rankings and scores, from #1 Orlando-Kissimmee, FL (score: 100.0) to #379 Hanford-Corcoran, CA (score: 0.0), at *Places Rated's* website.

Here are the top twenty:

Rank	Score
1. Orlando-Kissimmee, FL	100.0
2. Seattle-Bellevue, WA	99.7
3. New York-White Plains, NY-NJ	99.4
4. Tampa-St. Petersburg, FL	99.2
5. Sacramento, CA	98.9
6. Charleston-North Charleston, SC	98.6
7. Minneapolis-St. Paul, MN-WI	98.4
8. Rochester, NY	98.1
9. Washington, DC-VA-MD-WV	97.8
10. Virginia Beach-Norfolk, VA-NC	97.6
11. San Francisco-San Mateo, CA	97.3
12. Chicago-Naperville-Joliet, IL	97.0
13. Warren-Troy-Farmington Hills, MI	96.8
14. Akron, OH	96.5
15. Houston-Sugar Land-Baytown, TX	96.2
16. Cincinnati-Middletown, OH-KY-IN	96.0
17. St. Louis, MO-IL	95.7
18. Cleveland-Elyria-Mentor, OH	95.5
19. Oakland-Fremont-Hayward, CA	95.2
20. Baltimore-Towson, MD	94.9

At *www.placesrated.com* you'll also find more information on crowd pleasers and the great outdoors as well as useful links to recreation websites.

2006; National Golf Foundation, unpublished data, 2006; National Hockey League, www.nhl.com, 2006; Quigley Publishing Company, *Motion Picture Almanac*, 2006; Southern Professional Basketball Association, www.sphl.com, 2006; United States Basketball League, www.usbl.com, 2006; U.S. Department of Agriculture, Forest Service, *Land Areas of the National Forest System*, 2006; U.S. Department of Commerce: Bureau of the Census, unpublished "Coastal Counties of the United States," and unpublished area measurements, 2006; U.S. Department of the Interior, Fish and Wildlife Service, unpublished master deed listing, 2006; and National Park Service, *Index to the National Park System and Related Areas*, 2006, and unpublished master deed listing, 2006; Women's National Basketball Association, www.wnba.com, 2006.

A check mark (✓) preceding the metro area's name highlights it as one of America's top forty areas for recreation assets.

Recreation

Abilene, TX

Golf Courses: 10
Daily fee (99 holes)
Municipal (27 holes)
Private (45 holes)

Movie Theatres: 18 screens
2 multiplexes

Recreation Areas: 1,242 acres
State
Abilene SRA

Water Area
Lakes and rivers: 8,320 acres

Zoo
Abilene Zoo

Places Rated Rank: 346

✓Akron, OH

Amusement/Theme Parks
Geauga Lake Park

Auto Racing
Nelson Ledges

College Sports: 144 games
Kent State Golden Flashes
University of Akron Zips

Golf Courses: 47
Daily fee (513 holes)
Municipal (81 holes)
Private (252 holes)

Horse Racing: 213 programs
Northfield Park (Harness)

Movie Theatres: 90 screens
8 multiplexes

Professional Sports: 61 games
Aeros (Class AA Baseball)

Recreation Areas: 25,615 acres
Federal
Cuyahoga Valley NRA
State
Eagle Creek SNA
Nelson-Kennedy Ledges SP
Portage Lakes SP
Tinkers Creek SP
West Branch SP

Ski Areas: 22,500 lift capacity/hr

Water Area
Lakes and rivers: 14,080 acres

Zoo
Akron Zoological Park

Places Rated Rank: 14

Albany, GA

Amusement/Theme Parks
The Parks At Chehaw

Golf Courses: 7
Daily fee (45 holes)
Municipal (36 holes)
Private (45 holes)

Movie Theatres: 17 screens
1 single/twin
1 multiplex

Water Area
Lakes and rivers: 15,360 acres

Places Rated Rank: 343

Albany-Schenectady, NY

College Sports: 144 games
Rensselaer Engineers
Siena College Saints
SUNY Albany Great Danes
Union College Dutchmen

Golf Courses: 42
Daily fee (405 holes)
Municipal (108 holes)
Private (243 holes)

Horse Racing: 211 programs
Saratoga (Mixed Meetings)

Movie Theatres: 69 screens
4 singles/twins
7 multiplexes

Professional Sports: 151 games
Choppers (UHL Hockey)
Patroons (CBA Basketball)
River Rats (AHL Hockey)
Valley Cats (Class A Baseball)

Recreation Areas: 7,973 acres
State
Castleton Island SP

Cherry Plain SP
Grafton Lakes SP
John B. Thatcher SP
Max V. Shaul SP
Mine Kill SP
Moreau SP
Peebles Island SP
Saratoga Lake Boat Launch SP
Saratoga Spa SP
Thompson's Lake Camp SP

Ski Areas: 108,629 lift capacity/hr

Water Area
Lakes and rivers: 39,040 acres

Places Rated Rank: 138

Albuquerque, NM

Aquarium
Albuquerque Aquarium

Auto Racing
Hollywood Hills Speedway
Sandia Motor Speedway

College Sports: 78 games
New Mexico Lobos

Golf Courses: 21
Daily fee (198 holes)
Municipal (72 holes)
Private (108 holes)

Horse Racing: 17 programs
The Downs (Thoroughbred)

Movie Theatres: 102 screens
9 multiplexes

Professional Sports: 58 games
Isotopes (Triple A Baseball)

Recreation Areas: 1,205,254 acres
Federal
Bandelier NM
Cibola NF
Cuba-Rio Puerco LUP
Petroglyph NM
Salinas Pueblo Missions NM
Santa Fe NF
Valles Caldera NP
State
Fenton Lake SP
Manzano Mountains SP
Senator Willie M. Chavez SP

Ski Areas: 36,850 lift capacity/hr

Water Area

Lakes and rivers: 6,400 acres

Zoo

Rio Grande Zoo

Places Rated Rank: 144

─────────────

Alexandria, LA

Golf Courses: 37

Daily fee (405 holes)
Municipal (36 holes)
Private (225 holes)

Movie Theatres: 21 screens

1 single/twin
2 multiplexes

Recreation Areas: 245,339 acres
Federal
Bayou Beouf PU
Kisatchie NF

Water Area

Lakes and rivers: 37,120 acres

Zoo

Alexandria Zoo

Places Rated Rank: 126

─────────────

Allentown, PA-NJ

Amusement/Theme Parks

Dorney Park/Wildwater Kingdom
Land of Make Believe

Auto Racing

Nazareth Speedway

College Sports: 208 games

Lafayette Leopards
Lehigh Mountain Hawks

Golf Courses

Daily fee (405 holes)
Municipal (36 holes)
Private (222 holes)

Movie Theatres: 79 screens

1 single/twin
7 multiplexes

Professional Sports: 15 games

Valley Dawgs (USBL Basketball)

Recreation Areas: 39,238 acres
Federal
Appalachian NT
Delaware Water Gap NRA
State
Allmuchy SP
Beltzville SP
Bursch Sugar Maple SNA
Delaware Canal SP
Finesville SP
Hickory Run SP
Jacobsburg SP
Johnsonburg SNA
Kittatinny Valley
Lehigh Gorge SP
Osmun Forest SNA

Ski Areas: 111,487 lift capacity/hr

Water Area

Lakes and rivers: 10,880 acres

Zoo

Lehigh Valley Zoo

Places Rated Rank: 83

─────────────

Altoona, PA

Amusement/Theme Parks

Delgrosso's Amusement Park
Lakemont Park

Golf Courses: 5

Daily fee (72 holes)
Private (18 holes)

Movie Theatres: 15 screens

2 multiplexes

Professional Sports: 71 games

Curve (Class AA Baseball)

Recreation Areas: 959 acres
State
Canoe Creek SP

Ski Areas: 10,000 lift capacity/hr

Water Area

Lakes and rivers: 640 acres

Places Rated Rank: 339

─────────────

Amarillo, TX

Amusement/Theme Parks

Splash Amarillo
Wonderland Park

Golf Courses: 9

Daily fee (36 holes)
Municipal (72 holes)
Private (54 holes)

Movie Theatres: 30 screens

2 multiplexes

Recreation Areas: 48,525 acres
Federal
Alibates Flint Quarries NM
Buffalo Lake NWR
Lake Meredith NRA
State
Palo Duro Canyon SP

Water Area

Lakes and rivers: 14,080 acres

Zoo

Amarillo Zoo

Places Rated Rank: 259

─────────────

Ames, IA

College Sports: 49 games

Iowa State Cyclones

Golf Courses: 6

Daily fee (54 holes)
Municipal (18 holes)
Private (36 holes)

Movie Theatres: 21 screens

3 singles/twins
2 multiplexes

Ski Areas: 4,000 lift capacity/hr

Water Area

Lakes and rivers: 640 acres

Places Rated Rank: 361

─────────────

Anchorage, AK

Auto Racing

Fur Rondy Grand Prix

College Sports: 20 games

University of Alaska Seawolves

Golf Courses: 6

Daily fee (90 holes)
Municipal (18 holes)

Movie Theatres: 50 screens

1 single/twin
6 multiplexes

Professional Sports: 36 games

Alaska Aces (ECHL Hockey)

Recreation Areas: 2,008,541 acres
Federal
Chugach NF
Denali National Preserve
Denali NP
Lake Clark NP

Ski Areas: 12,155 lift capacity/hr

Water Area

Lakes and rivers: 193,280 acres
Pacific offshore: 320,000 acres

Zoo

Alaska Zoo

Places Rated Rank: 68

─────────────

Anderson, IN

Auto Racing

Anderson Speedway

Golf Courses: 8

Daily fee (90 holes)
Municipal (18 holes)
Private (36 holes)

Horse Racing: 121 programs

Hoosier Park (Mixed Meetings)

Movie Theatres: 13 screens

3 singles/twins
1 multiplex

Water Area

Lakes and rivers: 640 acres

Places Rated Rank: 360

─────────────

Anderson, SC

Auto Racing

Anderson Motor Speedway

College Sports: 78 games

Clemson University Tigers

Golf Courses: 8
   Daily fee (135 holes)

Movie Theatres: 28 screens
   2 multiplexes

Recreation Areas: 395 acres
State
   Sadlers Creek SP

Water Area
   Lakes and rivers: 24,960 acres

Places Rated Rank: 190

Ann Arbor, MI

College Sports: 164 games
   Eastern Michigan Eagles
   Michigan Wolverines

Golf Courses: 24
   Daily fee (207 holes)
   Municipal (90 holes)
   Private (126 holes)

Movie Theatres: 33 screens
   4 singles/twins
   2 multiplexes

Recreation Areas: 13,532 acres
State
   Pinckney SRA
   W.J. Hayes SP
   Waterloo SRA

Ski Areas: 40,030 lift capacity/hr

Water Area
   Lakes and rivers: 8,320 acres

Zoo
   Michigan Zoology Museum

Places Rated Rank: 175

Anniston-Oxford, AL

College Sports: 60 games
   Jacksonville State Gamecocks

Golf Courses: 7
   Daily fee (72 holes)
   Municipal (27 holes)
   Private (18 holes)

Movie Theatres: 20 screens
   2 singles/twins
   2 multiplexes

Recreation Areas: 24,022 acres
Federal
   Talladega NF

Water Area
   Lakes and rivers: 2,560 acres

Places Rated Rank: 225

Appleton, WI

Golf Courses: 13
   Daily fee (171 holes)
   Municipal (18 holes)
   Private (45 holes)

Movie Theatres: 36 screens
   3 multiplexes

Professional Sports: 71 games
   Timber Rattlers (Class A Baseball)

Recreation Areas: 1,199 acres
State
   High Cliff SP
   Wiouwash State Trail

Ski Areas: 1,800 lift capacity/hr

Water Area
   Lakes and rivers: 51,840 acres

Places Rated Rank: 173

Asheville, NC

College Sports: 72 games
   UNC Asheville Bulldogs

Golf Courses: 25
   Daily fee (270 holes)
   Municipal (36 holes)
   Private (144 holes)

Movie Theatres: 53 screens
   6 multiplexes

Professional Sports: 71 games
   Tourists (Class A Baseball)

Recreation Areas: 242,680 acres
Federal
   Appalachian NT
   Blue Ridge Parkway
   Great Smokey Mountains NP
   Pisgah NF

Ski Areas: 14,000 lift capacity/hr

Water Area
   Lakes and rivers: 5,120 acres

Places Rated Rank: 168

Athens-Clarke County, GA

College Sports: 66 games
   Georgia Bulldogs

Golf Courses: 7
   Daily fee (72 holes)
   Private (45 holes)

Movie Theatres: 29 screens
   1 single/twin
   3 multiplexes

Recreation Areas: 4,702 acres
Federal
   Oconee NF
State
   Watson Mill Bridge SP

Water Area
   Lakes and rivers: 1,280 acres

Places Rated Rank: 337

Atlanta-Sandy Springs, GA

Amusement/Theme Parks
   American Adventures
   Six Flags Over Georgia
   White Water Atlanta

Auto Racing
   Atlanta Motor Speedway
   Road Atlanta

College Sports: 126 games
   Georgia State Panthers
   Georgia Tech Yellow Jackets

Golf Courses: 150
   Daily fee (1,278 holes)
   Municipal (225 holes)
   Private (1,197 holes)

Movie Theatres: 652 screens
   4 singles/twins
   51 multiplexes

Professional Sports: 233 games
   Braves (NL Baseball)
   Falcons (NFL Football)
   Gwinnett Gladiators (ECHL Hockey)
   Hawks (NBA Basketball)
   Krunk (CBA Basketball)
   Thrashers (NHL Hockey)

Recreation Areas: 57,132 acres
Federal
   Chattahoochee NF
   Chattahoochee River NRA
   Oconee NF
   Piedmont NWR
State
   Amicalola Falls SP
   Hard Labor Creek SP
   Indian Springs SP
   John Tanner SP
   Panola Mountain SP
   Red Top Mountain SP
   Sweetwater Creek SP

Water Area
   Lakes and rivers: 67,200 acres

Zoo
   Zoo Atlanta

Places Rated Rank: 71

Atlantic City, NJ

Golf Courses: 20
   Daily fee (234 holes)
   Municipal (18 holes)
   Private (108 holes)

Horse Racing: 4 programs
   Atlantic City (Thoroughbred)

Movie Theatres: 14 screens
   1 multiplex

Recreation Areas: 20,903 acres
Federal
   Edwin B. Forsythe NWR
   Great Egg Harbor N
State
   North Brigantine SNA

Water Area
   Lakes and rivers: 32,000 acres
   Atlantic offshore: 110,080 acres

Zoo
   Birch Grove Park Zoo

Places Rated Rank: 110

Auburn-Opelika, AL

College Sports: 66 games
Auburn Tigers

Golf Courses: 9
Daily fee (108 holes)
Municipal (18 holes)
Private (36 holes)

Movie Theatres: 16 screens
1 multiplex

Recreation Areas: 696 acres
State
Chewacla SP

Water Area
Lakes and rivers: 4,480 acres

Places Rated Rank: 305

Augusta, GA-SC

Golf Courses: 33
Daily fee (315 holes)
Municipal (18 holes)
Private (252 holes)

Movie Theatres: 63 screens
1 single/twin
5 multiplexes

Professional Sports: 107 games
Green Jackets (Class A Baseball)
Lynx (ECHL Hockey)

Recreation Areas: 34,100 acres
Federal
Sumter NF
State
Aiken SP
Mistletoe SP

Water Area
Lakes and rivers: 28,800 acres

Places Rated Rank: 231

Austin-Round Rock, TX

Amusement/Theme Parks
Aquarena Center

Auto Racing
Thunder Hill Raceway

College Sports: 126 games
Texas State Bobcats
University of Texas Longhorns

Golf Courses: 51
Daily fee (405 holes)
Municipal (135 holes)
Private (369 holes)

Movie Theatres: 159 screens
1 single/twin
15 multiplexes

Recreation Areas: 17,405 acres
Federal
Balcones Canyonlands NWR
State
Bastrop SP
Buescher SP

Lake Bastrop SRA
Lockhart SRA
McKinney Falls SP

Water Area
Lakes and rivers: 36,480 acres

Zoo
Austin Zoo

Places Rated Rank: 184

Bakersfield, CA

Auto Racing
Bakersfield Speedway
Buttonwillow Raceway Park
Willow Springs

Golf Courses: 19
Daily fee (135 holes)
Municipal (72 holes)
Private (126 holes)

Movie Theatres: 61 screens
3 singles/twins
7 multiplexes

Professional Sports: 107 games
Blaze (Class A Baseball)
Condors (ECHL Hockey)

Recreation Areas: 809,166 acres
Federal
Bitter Creek NWR
Kern NWR
Los Padres NF
Sequoia NF
State
Red Rock Canyon SP
Tule Elk SR

Ski Areas: 82,290 lift capacity/hr

Water Area
Lakes and rivers: 12,800 acres

Places Rated Rank: 243

✓Baltimore-Towson, MD

Aquarium
National Aquarium

College Sports: 516 games
Coppin State Eagles
Johns Hopkins Blue Jays
Loyola College Greyhounds
Morgan State Bears
Naval Academy Midshipmen
Towson University Tigers
UMBC Retrievers

Golf Courses: 69
Daily fee (432 holes)
Municipal (189 holes)
Private (612 holes)

Horse Racing: 75 programs
Pimlico (Thoroughbred)

Movie Theatres: 254 screens
4 singles/twins
23 multiplexes

Professional Sports: 162 games
IronBirds (Class A Baseball)
Orioles (AL Baseball)
Ravens (NFL Football)

Recreation Areas: 40,953 acres
Federal
Fort McHenry NM
National Capital Parks
Susquehanna NWR
State
Gunpowder Falls SP
Hart-Miller Island SP
Morgan Run SNA
Patapsco Valley SP
Patuxent River SP
Rocks SP
Sandy Point SP
Soldier's Delight SNA
Tuckahoe SP
Wye Island SNA

Ski Areas: 21,320 lift capacity/hr

Water Area
Lakes and rivers: 87,680 acres
Atlantic offshore: 229,120 acres

Zoo
The Maryland Zoo

Places Rated Rank: 20

Bangor, ME

College Sports: 92 games
University of Maine Black Bears

Golf Courses: 11
Daily fee (135 holes)
Municipal (36 holes)
Private (18 holes)

Horse Racing: 28 programs
Bangor Raceway (Harness)

Movie Theatres: 18 screens
2 multiplexes

Recreation Area: 200,000 acres
Baxter State Park

Ski Areas: 10,400 lift capacity/hr

Water Area
Lakes and rivers: 102,400 acres

Places Rated Rank: 228

Barnstable Town, MA

Aquarium
Aquarium of Cape Cod

Golf Courses: 33
Daily fee (180 holes)
Municipal (216 holes)
Private (198 holes)

Movie Theatres: 44 screens
2 singles/twins
6 multiplexes

Recreation Areas: 27,678 acres
Federal
Cape Cod N Seashore
State
Hawksnest SP
Nickerson SP
Scusset Beach State Reservation
South Cape Beach SP

Waquoit Bay Nat'l Estuarine
Research Reserve
Washburn Island SNA

Water Area

Lakes and rivers: 38,400 acres
Atlantic offshore: 298,240 acres

Places Rated Rank: 47

Baton Rouge, LA

Amusement/Theme Parks

Blue Bayou & Dixie Landin'

College Sports: 126 games

Louisiana State Fighting Tigers
Southern University Jaguars

Golf Courses: 22

Daily fee (207 holes)
Municipal (72 holes)
Private (108 holes)

Movie Theatres: 55 screens

5 multiplexes

Recreation Areas: 18,430 acres
Federal
Atchafalaya NWR
State
Tickfaw SP
Tunica Hills SNA

Water Area

Lakes and rivers: 117,120 acres

Zoo

Baton Rouge Zoo

Places Rated Rank: 154

Battle Creek, MI

Golf Courses: 15

Daily fee (153 holes)
Municipal (36 holes)
Private (72 holes)

Movie Theatres: 41 screens

1 single/twin
5 multiplexes

Professional Sports: 71 games

Devil Rays (Class A Baseball)

Water Area

Lakes and rivers: 6,400 acres

Zoo

Binder Park Zoo

Places Rated Rank: 291

Bay City, MI

Amusement/Theme Parks

Deer Acres Storybook Park

Golf Courses: 7

Daily fee (90 holes)
Municipal (18 holes)
Private (18 holes)

Movie Theatres: 4 screens

1 single/twin

Recreation Areas: 196 acres
State
Bay City SP

Ski Areas: 6,000 lift capacity/hr

Water Area

Lakes and rivers: 3,840 acres
Lake Huron offshore: 115,840 acres

Places Rated Rank: 156

Beaumont-Port Arthur, TX

College Sports: 48 games

Lamar University Cardinals

Golf Courses: 15

Daily fee (180 holes)
Municipal (36 holes)
Private (45 holes)

Movie Theatres: 42 screens

1 single/twin
4 multiplexes

Recreation Areas: 119,906 acres
Federal
Big Thicket N Preserve
Big Thicket NP
McFaddin NWR
Texas Point NWR
State
Sea Rim SP
Village Creek SP

Water Area

Lakes and rivers: 72,320 acres
Gulf offshore: 7,680 acres

Places Rated Rank: 127

✓Bellingham, WA

Amusement/Theme Parks

Birch Bay Water Slides

Golf Courses: 13

Daily fee (180 holes)
Municipal (18 holes)
Private (36 holes)

Movie Theatres: 15 screens

3 multiplexes

Recreation Areas: 849,632 acres
Federal
Mt. Baker NF
North Cascades NP
Ross Lake NRA
San Juan Islands NWR
State
Birch Bay SP
Larrabee SP

Ski Areas: 16,000 lift capacity/hr

Water Area

Lakes and rivers: 35,200 acres
Pacific offshore: 209,920 acres

Places Rated Rank: 37

Bend, OR

Golf Courses: 17

Daily fee (207 holes)
Private (90 holes)

Movie Theatres: 22 screens

2 multiplexes

Recreation Areas: 988,153 acres
Federal
Deschutes NF
State
Cline Falls SP
Lapine SRA
Ogden Scenic Wayside
Pilot Butte SP
Redmond-Bend Juniper Wayside
Sisters SP
Smith Rock SP
Tumalo SP

Ski Areas: 34,680 lift capacity/hr

Water Area

Lakes and rivers: 23,680 acres

Places Rated Rank: 119

Bethesda-Gaithersburg, MD

College Sports: 104 games

Mount St. Mary's Mountaineers

Golf Courses: 47

Daily fee (234 holes)
Municipal (198 holes)
Private (414 holes)

Movie Theatres: 138 screens

2 singles/twins
11 multiplexes

Professional Sports: 71 games

Keys (Class A Baseball)

Recreation Areas: 25,938 acres
Federal
Appalachian NT
Catoctin Mountain Park
George Washington Parkway
State
Cunningham Falls SP
Gambrill SP
Patuxent River SP
Seneca Creek SP
South Mountain SP

Ski Areas: 22,120 lift capacity/hr

Water Area

Lakes and rivers: 10,240 acres

Zoo

Catoctin Mountain Zoo

Places Rated Rank: 159

Billings, MT

Golf Courses: 9

Daily fee (72 holes)
Private (90 holes)

Movie Theatres: 25 screens

1 single/twin
3 multiplexes

Recreation Areas: 682,620 acres
Federal
Bighorn Canyon NRA
Custer NF
Gallatin NF

State
    Cooney Reservoir SP
    Lake Elmo SP

Ski Areas: 10,690 lift capacity/hr

Water Area
    Lakes and rivers: 17,920 acres

Zoo
    Zoo Montana

Places Rated Rank: 206

Binghamton, NY

College Sports: 104 games
    SUNY Binghamton Bearcats

Golf Courses: 22
    Daily fee (306 holes)
    Municipal (54 holes)
    Private (36 holes)

Horse Racing: 30 programs
    Tioga Downs (Harness)

Movie Theatres: 21 screens
    2 multiplexes

Professional Sports: 111 games
    Mets (Class AA Baseball)
    Senators (AHL Hockey)

Recreation Areas: 1,071 acres
State
    Chenango Valley SP

Ski Areas: 31,485 lift capacity/hr

Water Area
    Lakes and rivers: 8,320 acres

Zoo
    Ross Park Zoo

Places Rated Rank: 223

Birmingham-Hoover, AL

Amusement/Theme Parks
    Visionland
    Auto Racing
    Barber Motorsports Park

College Sports: 210 games
    Birmingham-Southern Panthers
    Samford University Bulldogs
    UAB Blazers

Golf Courses: 50
    Daily fee (441 holes)
    Municipal (108 holes)
    Private (342 holes)

Movie Theatres: 157 screens
    3 singles/twins
    13 multiplexes

Professional Sports: 71 games
    Barons (Class AA Baseball)

Recreation Areas: 94,055 acres
Federal
    Talladega NF
    Watercress Darter NWR

State
    Oak Mountain SP
    Rickwood Caverns SP

Water Area
    Lakes and rivers: 46,080 acres

Zoo
    Birmingham Zoo

Places Rated Rank: 97

Bismarck, ND

Golf Courses: 7
    Daily fee (27 holes)
    Municipal (81 holes)
    Private (18 holes)

Movie Theatres: 8 screens
    1 multiplex

Recreation Areas: 11,958 acres
Federal
    Canfield Lake NWR
    Florence Lake NWR
    Long Lake NWR
State
    Missouri River SNA

Water Area
    Lakes and rivers: 34,560 acres

Zoo
    Dakota Zoo

Places Rated Rank: 289

Blacksburg-Christiansburg, VA

College Sports: 150 games
    Radford University Highlanders
    Virginia Tech Hokies

Golf Courses: 9
    Daily fee (99 holes)
    Municipal (9 holes)
    Private (45 holes)

Movie Theatres: 11 screens
    1 multiplex

Recreation Areas: 103,916 acres
Federal
    Appalachian NT
    Jefferson NF
State
    Claytor Lake SP

Ski Areas: 13,400 lift capacity/hr

Water Area
    Lakes and rivers: 8,320 acres

Places Rated Rank: 189

Bloomington, IN

Auto Racing
    Bloomington Speedway

College Sports: 78 games
    Indiana University Hoosiers

Golf Courses: 7
    Daily fee (63 holes)
    Municipal (45 holes)
    Private (18 holes)

Movie Theatres: 25 screens
    2 singles/twins
    2 multiplexes

Recreation Areas: 20,979 acres
Federal
    Hoosier NF
    Hoosier PU
    Muscatatuck NWR
State
    McCormick's Creek SP
    Shakamak SP

Ski Areas: 5,200 lift capacity/hr

Water Area
    Lakes and rivers: 15,360 acres

Places Rated Rank: 170

Bloomington-Normal, IL

College Sports: 60 games
    Illinois State Redbirds

Golf Courses: 9
    Daily fee (45 holes)
    Municipal (72 holes)
    Private (45 holes)

Movie Theatres: 29 screens
    3 singles/twins
    3 multiplexes

Professional Sports: 20 games
    Prairie Thunder (UHL Hockey)

Recreation Areas: 1,688 acres
State
    Moraine View SP

Water Area
    Lakes and rivers: 1,920 acres

Zoo
    Miller Park Zoo

Places Rated Rank: 320

Boise City-Nampa, ID

Auto Racing
    Meridian Speedway

College Sports: 49 games
    Boise State Broncos

Golf Courses: 20
    Daily fee (189 holes)
    Municipal (90 holes)
    Private (81 holes)

Horse Racing: 46 programs
    Les Bois Park (Thoroughbred)

Movie Theatres: 66 screens
    3 singles/twins
    8 multiplexes

Professional Sports: 107 games
    Hawks (Class A Baseball)
    Idaho Steelheads (ECHL Hockey)

Recreation Areas: 938,995 acres
Federal
    Boise NF
    Deer Flat NWR

Recreation

State
Bruneau Dunes SP
Eagle Island SP
Lucky Peak SP
Veterans Memorial SP

Ski Areas: 45,250 lift capacity/hr

Water Area
Lakes and rivers: 28,800 acres

Zoo
Zoo Boise

Places Rated Rank: 139

Boston-Quincy, MA

Amusement/Theme Parks
Paragon Carousel
Star Land Sports and Fun Park
Water Wizz Water Park

Aquarium
New England Aquarium

College Sports: 167 games
Boston University Terriers
Northeastern Huskies

Golf Courses: 61
Daily fee (423 holes)
Municipal (198 holes)
Private (477 holes)

Horse Racing: 247 programs
Plainridge (Harness)
Suffolk Downs (Thoroughbred)

Movie Theatres: 205 screens
11 single/twin
18 multiplexes

Professional Sports: 190 games
Bruins (NHL Hockey)
Celtics (NBA Basketball)
New England Patriots (NFL Football)
Red Sox (AL Baseball)
Revolution (MLS Soccer)

Recreation Areas: 5,306 acres
Federal
Boston Harbor Islands
State
Bristol Blake SP
Ellisville Harbor SP
Ames Nowell SP
Boston Harbor Islands SP
Bristol Blake SP
Cushing Memorial SP
Ellisville Harbor SP
Horseneck Beach SR
Myles Standish Monument SHS
Pilgrim Memorial SHS
Roxbury Heritage SP
Webb Memorial SP
Wompatuck SP

Ski Areas: 22,705 lift capacity/hr

Water Area
Lakes and rivers: 63,360 acres
Atlantic offshore: 195,200 acres

Zoo
Franklin Park Zoo

Places Rated Rank: 69

Boulder, CO

College Sports: 49 games
University of Colorado Buffaloes

Golf Courses: 10
Daily fee (36 holes)
Municipal (81 holes)
Private (54 holes)

Movie Theatres: 34 screens
2 singles/twins
4 multiplexes

Recreation Areas: 165,806 acres
Federal
Rocky Mountain NP
Roosevelt NF
State
Eldorado Canyon SP

Ski Areas: 48,900 lift capacity/hr

Water Area
Lakes and rivers: 5,760 acres

Places Rated Rank: 188

Bowling Green, KY

Amusement/Theme Parks
Beech Bend Park

College Sports: 72 games
Western Kentucky Hilltoppers

Golf Courses: 5
Daily fee (18 holes)
Municipal (36 holes)
Private (36 holes)

Movie Theatres: 28 screens
3 multiplexes

Recreation Areas: 44,956 acres
Federal
Mammoth Cave NP

Water Area
Lakes and rivers: 4,480 acres

Places Rated Rank: 172

Bremerton-Silverdale, WA

Auto Racing
Bremerton Raceway Port

Golf Courses: 10
Daily fee (81 holes)
Municipal (54 holes)
Private (36 holes)

Movie Theatres: 32 screens
4 multiplexes

Recreation Areas: 1,083 acres
State
Blake Island SP
Camp Calvinwood
Fay-Bainbridge SP
Fort Ward SP
Harper SP
Illahee SP
Kitsap Memorial SP
Manchester SP
Scenic Beach SP

Water Area
Lakes and rivers: 40,320 acres
Pacific offshore: 68,480 acres

Places Rated Rank: 174

Bridgeport-Stamford-Norwalk, CT

College Sports: 228 games
Fairfield Stags
Sacred Heart Pioneers

Golf Courses: 42
Daily fee (36 holes)
Municipal (180 holes)
Private (540 holes)

Movie Theatres: 134 screens
8 singles/twins
15 multiplexes

Professional Sports: 36 games
Sound Tigers (AHL Hockey)

Recreation Areas: 375 acres
Federal
Appalachian NT
State
American Shakespeare Theatre SP
Collis P. Huntington SP
Indian Well SP
Mianus SP
Putnam Memorial SP
Seth Low Pierpoint SP
Sherwood Island SP
Squantz Pond SP

Ski Areas: 17,000 lift capacity/hr

Water Area
Lakes and rivers: 19,840 acres
Atlantic offshore: 115,200 acres

Zoo
Beardsley Zoo

Places Rated Rank: 164

Brownsville-Harlingen, TX

Amusement/Theme Parks
Schlitterbahn Beach Waterpark

Golf Courses: 11
Daily fee (72 holes)
Municipal (63 holes)
Private (54 holes)

Movie Theatres: 52 screens
4 multiplexes

Recreation Areas: 60,386 acres
Federal
Laguna Atascosa NWR
Lower Rio Grande Valley NWR

Water Area
Lakes and rivers: 168,320 acres

Zoo
Gladys Porter Zoo

Places Rated Rank: 64

Brunswick, GA

Amusement/Theme Parks
Summer Waves

Golf Courses: 15
Daily fee (198 holes)
Private (72 holes)

Movie Theatres: 18 screens
2 multiplexes

Recreation Areas: 19,774 acres
Federal
Blackbeard Island NWR
Fort Frederica NM
Harris Neck NWR
Wolf Island NWR
State
Sapelo Island Reserve

Water Area
Lakes and rivers: 131,200 acres
Atlantic offshore: 98,500 acres

Places Rated Rank: 66

Buffalo-Niagara Falls, NY

Aquarium
Aquarium of Niagara Falls

College Sports: 294 games
Canisius Golden Griffins
Niagara University Purple Eagles
SUNY Buffalo Bulls

Golf Courses: 49
Daily fee (288 holes)
Municipal (252 holes)
Private (342 holes)

Horse Racing: 84 programs
Buffalo Raceway (Harness)

Movie Theatres: 113 screens
1 single/twin
11 multiplexes

Professional Sports: 109 games
Bills (NFL Football)
Bisons (Triple A Baseball)
Sabres (NHL Hockey)

Recreation Areas: 5,554 acres
State
Beaver Island SP
Big Six Mile Creek Marina SP
Buckhorn Island SP
Devil's Hole SP
Earl W. Brydges Artpark
Evangola SP
Fort Niagara SP
Four Mile Creek SP
Golden Hill SP
Joseph Davis SP
Niagara Reservation SP
Reservoir SP
Whirlpool SP
Wilson-Tuscarora SP

Ski Areas: 58,010 lift capacity/hr

Water Area
Lakes and rivers: 12,800 acres
Lake Erie offshore: 498,560 acres

Zoo
Buffalo Zoological Gardens

Places Rated Rank: 53

Burlington, NC

College Sports: 72 games
Elon University Phoenix

Golf Courses: 10
Daily fee (144 holes)
Municipal (18 holes)
Private (18 holes)

Movie Theatres: 14 screens
2 multiplexes

Water Area
Lakes and rivers: 2,560 acres

Places Rated Rank: 336

Burlington-South Burlington, VT

College Sports: 124 games
University of Vermont Catamounts

Golf Courses: 14
Daily fee (207 holes)
Private (36 holes)

Movie Theatres: 20 screens
2 multiplexes

Professional Sports: 71 games
VT Lake Monsters (Class A Baseball)

Recreation Areas: 2,226 acres
State
Burton Island SP
Grand Isle SP
Knight Island SP
Lake Carmi SP
North Hero SP
Underhill SP
Woods Island SP

Ski Areas: 85,361 lift capacity/hr

Water Area
Lakes and rivers: 159,360 acres

Places Rated Rank: 171

Cambridge-Newton, MA

College Sports: 164 games
Bentley College Falcons
Boston College Eagles
Harvard Crimson
UMass-Lowell River Hawks

Golf Courses: 45
Daily fee (288 holes)
Municipal (117 holes)
Private (405 holes)

Movie Theatres: 151 screens
3 singles/twins
17 multiplexes

Professional Sports: 107 games
Devils (AHL Hockey)
Spinners (Class A Baseball)

Recreation Areas: 6,924 acres
Ashland SP
Callahan SP
Cochituate SP
Great Brook Farm SP
Hopkinton SP
Lowell Heritage SP
Pearl Hill SP
Squannacook River SNA
Walden Pond SR
Whitehall SP

Ski Areas: 35,905 lift capacity/hr

Water Area
Lakes and rivers: 15,360 acres

Zoo
Stone Zoo

Places Rated Rank: 235

Camden, NJ

Amusement/Theme Parks
Clementon Amusement Park
Mountain Creek

Aquarium
Adventure Aquarium

Golf Courses: 37
Daily fee (324 holes)
Municipal (54 holes)
Private (288 holes)

Movie Theatres: 145 screens
11 multiplexes

Recreation Areas: 4,443 acres
Federal
Edwin B. Forsythe NWR
State
Hawk Island SP
Mount Laurel SP
Rancocas SP
Warren Grove SRA

Water Area
Lakes and rivers: 20,480 acres

Places Rated Rank: 239

Canton-Massillon, OH

Golf Courses: 31
Daily fee (423 holes)
Municipal (27 holes)
Private (108 holes)

Movie Theatres: 46 screens
5 multiplexes

Recreation Areas: 704 acres
State
Jackson Bog SNA
Quail Hollow SP

Ski Areas: 16,000 lift capacity/hr

Water Area
Lakes and rivers: 5,760 acres

Places Rated Rank: 333

Cape Coral-Fort Myers, FL

Amusement/Theme Parks
Sun Splash Family Waterpark

Golf Courses: 68
Daily fee (423 holes)
Municipal (54 holes)
Private (738 holes)

Movie Theatres: 78 screens
2 singles/twins
7 multiplexes

Professional Sports: 107 games
Florida Everblades (ECHL Hockey)
Miracle (Class A Baseball)

Recreation Areas: 19,694 acres
Federal
Caloosahatchee NWR
J. N. Ding Darling NWR
Matlacha Pass NWR
Pine Island NWR
State
Cayo Cosia SP
Estero Bay Preserve SP
Gasparilla Island SP
Lovers Key SP

Water Area
Lakes and rivers: 151,040 acres
Gulf offshore: 3,840 acres

Places Rated Rank: 52

Carson City, NV

Golf Courses: 5
Daily fee (45 holes)
Municipal (36 holes)

Movie Theatres: 10 screens
1 multiplex

Recreation Areas: 17,268 acres
Federal
Toiyabe NF
Toiyabe Special Area
State
Lake Tahoe SP

Water Area
Lakes and rivers: 7,680 acres

Places Rated Rank: 57

Casper, WY

Golf Courses: 5
Daily fee (27 holes)
Municipal (27 holes)
Private (36 holes)

Movie Theatres: 19 screens
2 singles/twins
3 multiplexes

Recreation Areas: 7,452 acres
Federal
Medicine Bow NF
Pathfinder NWR
State
Wilkins SP

Ski Areas: 7,400 lift capacity/hr

Water Area
Lakes and rivers: 23,040 acres

Places Rated Rank: 332

Cedar Rapids, IA

Auto Racing
Hawkeye Downs Speedway

Golf Courses: 15
Daily fee (135 holes)
Municipal (72 holes)
Private (54 holes)

Movie Theatres: 38 screens
3 singles/twins
3 multiplexes

Professional Sports: 71 games
Kernels (Class A Baseball)

Recreation Areas: 2,935 acres
Federal
Mark Twain NWR
State
Palisades-Kepler SP
Pleasant Creek SP
Wapsipinicon SP

Ski Areas: 15,600 lift capacity/hr

Water Area
Lakes and rivers: 6,400 acres

Zoo
Beaver Park Zoo

Places Rated Rank: 278

Champaign-Urbana, IL

College Sports: 66 games
University of Illinois Fighting Illini

Golf Courses: 11
Daily fee (90 holes)
Municipal (36 holes)
Private (63 holes)

Movie Theatres: 20 screens
2 singles/twins
1 multiplex

Water Area
Lakes and rivers: 640 acres

Places Rated Rank: 378

Charleston, WV

Golf Courses: 9
Daily fee (63 holes)
Municipal (45 holes)
Private (54 holes)

Movie Theatres: 24 screens
2 multiplexes

Professional Sports: 71 games
West Virginia Power (Class A Baseball)

Water Area
Lakes and rivers: 8,960 acres

Places Rated Rank: 375

✓ Charleston-North Charleston, SC

Amusement/Theme Parks
Charles Towne Landing

Aquarium
Charleston Aquarium

College Sports: 177 games
Charleston Southern Buccaneers
College of Charleston Cougars
The Citadel Cadets

Golf Courses: 35
Daily fee (378 holes)
Municipal (45 holes)
Private (207 holes)

Movie Theatres: 102 screens
9 multiplexes

Professional Sports: 107 games
RiverDogs (Class A Baseball)
SC Stingrays (ECHL Hockey)

Recreation Areas: 300,424 acres
Federal
Ace Basin NWR
Cape Romain NWR
Fort Sumter NM
Francis Marion NF
State
Givhans Ferry SP

Water Area
Lakes and rivers: 160,640 acres
Atlantic offshore: 20,544 acres

Places Rated Rank: 6

Charlotte-Gastonia-Concord, NC-SC

Amusement/Theme Parks
Paramount's Carowinds

Auto Racing
Carolina Speedway
Concord Motorsport Park
Lowe's Motor Speedway

College Sports: 216 games
Davidson Wildcats
UNC Charlotte 49ers
Winthrop Eagles

Golf Courses: 64
Daily fee (522 holes)
Municipal (135 holes)
Private (495 holes)

Movie Theatres: 199 screens
1 single/twin
14 multiplexes

Professional Sports: 304 games
Bobcats (NBA Basketball)
Charlotte Sting (WNBA Basketball)
Checkers (ECHL Hockey)
Intimidators (Class A Baseball)
Knights (Triple A Baseball)
Panthers (NFL Football)

Recreation Areas: 12,004 acres
Federal
Kings Mountain NMP
Pee Dee NWR

State
Crowder's Mountain SP

Water Area
Lakes and rivers: 32,640 acres

Places Rated Rank: 135

Charlottesville, VA

College Sports: 110 games
University of Virginia Cavaliers

Golf Courses: 13
Daily fee (135 holes)
Municipal (18 holes)
Private (81 holes)

Movie Theatres: 16 screens
3 multiplexes

Recreation Areas: 61,251 acres
Federal
Appalachian NT
Blue Ridge Parkway
George Washington NF
Shenandoah NP

Ski Areas: 9,200 lift capacity/hr

Water Area
Lakes and rivers: 5,120 acres

Places Rated Rank: 281

Chattanooga, TN-GA

Aquarium
Tennessee Aquarium

College Sports: 43 games
UT Chattanooga Mocs

Golf Courses: 24
Daily fee (144 holes)
Municipal (72 holes)
Private (207 holes)

Movie Theatres: 77 screens
1 single/twin
8 multiplexes

Professional Sports: 71 games
Lookouts (Class AA Baseball)

Recreation Areas: 36,526 acres
Federal
Chattahoochee NF
Chick/Chatt NMP
State
Booker T. Washington SP
Cloudland Canyon SP
Harrison Bay SP
South Cumberland SRA

Ski Areas: 800 lift capacity/hr

Water Area
Lakes and rivers: 30,080 acres

Zoo
Warner Park Zoo

Places Rated Rank: 114

Cheyenne, WY

Golf Courses: 4
Daily fee (36 holes)
Municipal (27 holes)

Movie Theatres: 9 screens
2 multiplexes

Recreation Areas: 1,960 acres
State
Curt Gowdy SP

Ski Areas: 5,000 lift capacity/hr

Water Area
Lakes and rivers: 1,280 acres

Places Rated Rank: 364

✓Chicago-Naperville-Joliet, IL

Amusement/Theme Parks
Santa's Village

Aquarium
John G. Shedd Aquarium

Auto Racing
Autobahn Country Club
Chicagoland Speedway
Grundy County Speedway

College Sports: 374 games
Chicago State Cougars
DePaul Blue Demons
Loyola Ramblers
Northern Illinois Huskies
Northwestern Wildcats
University of Illinois Flames

Horse Racing: 583 programs
Arlington Park (Thoroughbred)
Balmoral Park (Harness)
Hawthorne (Mixed Meetings)
Maywood Park (Harness)
Sportsman's Park (Thoroughbred)

Movie Theatres: 775 screens
21 single/twin
69 multiplexes

Golf Courses: 216
Daily fee (1,386 holes)
Municipal (1,260 holes)
Private (1,233 holes)

Professional Sports: 509 games
Bears (NFL Football)
Blackhawks (NHL Hockey)
Bulls (NBA Basketball)
Cougars (Class A Baseball)
Cubs (NL Baseball)
Fire (MLS Soccer)
Hounds (UHL Hockey)
K.C. Cougars (Class A Baseball)
Sky (WNBA Basketball)
White Sox (AL Baseball)
Wolves (AHL Hockey)

Recreation Areas: 31,064 acres
Federal
Midewin Tallgrass Prairie OTH
State
Braidwood/Mazonia State Fish
and Wildlife Area

Des Plaines Conservation Area
Gebhard Woods SP
Goose Lake Prairie SP
Moraine Hills SP
Shabbona Lake SP
Silver Springs SP
William G. Stratton SP

Ski Areas: 34,385 lift capacity/hr

Water Area
Lakes and rivers: 31,360 acres
Lake Michigan offshore: 433,280
acres

Zoo
Brookfield Zoo
Chicago Zoological Park
Cosley Zoo
Lincoln Park Zoo
Lords Park Zoo
Phillips Park Zoo
Randall Oaks Park Zoo

Places Rated Rank: 12

Chico, CA

Golf Courses: 6
Daily fee (54 holes)
Municipal (18 holes)
Private (36 holes)

Movie Theatres: 30 screens
1 single/twin
3 multiplexes

Recreation Areas: 304,988 acres
Federal
Lassen NF
North Central Valley NWR
Plumas NF
Sacramento River NWR
State
Bidwell-Sacramento River SP
Clay Pit SVRA
Lake Oroville SRA

Ski Areas: 4,500 lift capacity/hr

Water Area
Lakes and rivers: 24,320 acres

Places Rated Rank: 155

✓Cincinnati-Middletown, OH-KY-IN

Amusement/Theme Parks
Coney Island
Paramount's King's Island
The Beach Waterpark

Aquarium
Newport Aquarium

Auto Racing
Kentucky Speedway
Lawrenceburg Speedway

College Sports: 236 games
Miami University RedHawks
University of Cincinnati Bearcats
Xavier Musketeers

Golf Courses: 110
Daily fee (792 holes)
Municipal (495 holes)
Private (684 holes)

Horse Racing: 239 programs
Lebanon Raceway (Harness)
River Downs (Thoroughbred)
Turfway Park (Thoroughbred)

Movie Theatres: 244 screens
22 multiplexes

Professional Sports: 127 games
Bengals (NFL Football)
Cyclones (AHL Hockey)
Reds (NL Baseball)

Recreation Areas: 20,250 acres
State
Big Bone Lick SP
Caesar Creek SP
East Fork SP
Hueston Woods SP
Kincaid Lake SP
Little Miami SP
Stonelick SP

Ski Areas: 14,000 lift capacity/hr
Water Area
Lakes and rivers: 42,880 acres

Zoo
Cincinnati Zoo

Places Rated Rank: 16

Clarksville, TN-KY

College Sports: 60 games
Austin Peay Governors

Golf Courses: 10
Daily fee (99 holes)
Municipal (45 holes)
Private (36 holes)

Movie Theatres: 34 screens
4 multiplexes

Recreation Areas: 135,610 acres
Federal
Cross Creeks NWR
Land Between The Lakes
State
Dunbar Cave SNA
Lake Barkley State Resort Park
Pennyrile Forest State Resort Park

Water Area
Lakes and rivers: 52,480 acres

Places Rated Rank: 122

Cleveland, TN

Golf Courses: 5
Daily fee (45 holes)
Municipal (18 holes)
Private (18 holes)

Movie Theatres: 22 screens
1 single/twin
1 multiplex

Recreation Areas: 151,503 acres
Federal
Cherokee NF
State
Hiwassee Scenic River SP

Water Area
Lakes and rivers: 6,400 acres

Places Rated Rank: 128

✓**Cleveland-Elyria-Mentor, OH**

Amusement/Theme Parks
Pioneer Waterland

Auto Racing
Burke Lakefront Airport

College Sports: 72 games
Cleveland State Vikings

Golf Courses: 112
Daily fee (1,098 holes)
Municipal (333 holes)
Private (585 holes)

Horse Racing: 187 programs
Thistledown (Thoroughbred)

Movie Theatres: 294 screens
23 multiplexes

Professional Sports: 127 games
Browns (NFL Football)
Cavaliers (NBA Basketball)
Indians (AL Baseball)
Lumberjacks (AHL Hockey)

Recreation Areas: 5,716 acres
Federal
Cuyahoga Valley NRA
State
Cleveland Lakefront SP
Findley SP
Hach-Otis SNA
Headlands Beach SP
Mentor Marsh SNA
Punderson SP

Ski Areas: 22,500 lift capacity/hr

Water Area
Lakes and rivers: 8,960 acres
Lake Erie offshore: 1,255,040 acres

Zoo
Cleveland Metroparks Zoo

Places Rated Rank: 18

✓**Coeur d'Alene, ID**

Amusement/Theme Parks
Silverwood
Wild Waters

Golf Courses: 10
Daily fee (144 holes)
Private (36 holes)

Movie Theatres: 26 screens
3 multiplexes

Recreation Areas: 497,831 acres
Federal
Coeur d' Alene NF
Kaniksu NF
State
Farragut SP
Heyburn SP

Ski Areas: 23,917 lift capacity/hr

Water Area
Lakes and rivers: 45,440 acres

Places Rated Rank: 29

College Station-Bryan, TX

Auto Racing
Texas World Speedway

College Sports: 66 games
Texas A&M Aggies

Golf Courses: 8
Daily fee (27 holes)
Municipal (27 holes)
Private (81 holes)

Movie Theatres: 18 screens
1 multiplex

Recreation Areas: 3,000 acres
State
Lake Somerville SRA

Water Area
Lakes and rivers: 17,920 acres

Places Rated Rank: 302

Colorado Springs, CO

Amusement/Theme Parks
Santa's Workshop-North Pole

Auto Racing
Pikes Peak International Raceway

College Sports: 162 games
Air Force Academy Falcons
Colorado College Tigers

Golf Courses: 22
Daily fee (162 holes)
Municipal (45 holes)
Private (189 holes)

Movie Theatres: 76 screens
4 singles/twins
6 multiplexes

Professional Sports: 58 games
Sky Sox (Triple A Baseball)

Recreation Areas: 243,569 acres
Federal
Florissant Fossil Beds NM
Pike NF
State
Mueller SP

Ski Areas: 14,400 lift capacity/hr

Water Area
Lakes and rivers: 3,200 acres

Zoo
Cheyenne Mountain Zoo

Places Rated Rank: 167

Columbia, MO

College Sports: 66 games
University of Missouri Tigers

Golf Courses: 7
> Daily fee (36 holes)
> Municipal (36 holes)
> Private (54 holes)

Movie Theatres: 16 screens
> 2 singles/twins
> 1 multiplex

Recreation Areas: 8,858 acres
Federal
> Big Muddy NFWR
> Cedar Creek PU
> Mark Twain NF

State
> Finger Lakes SP
> Rock Bridge Memorial SP

Water Area
> Lakes and rivers: 7,040 acres

Places Rated Rank: 303

Columbia, SC

Auto Racing
> Carolina Motorsports Park

College Sports: 78 games
> South Carolina Fighting Gamecocks

Golf Courses: 32
> Daily fee (297 holes)
> Municipal (18 holes)
> Private (261 holes)

Movie Theatres: 91 screens
> 8 multiplexes

Professional Sports: 36 games
> Inferno (ECHL Hockey)

Recreation Areas: 39,043 acres
Federal
> Congaree Swamp NM
> Sumter NF

State
> Lake Watereee SP
> N.R. Goodale SP
> Sesquicentennial SP

Water Area
> Lakes and rivers: 84,480 acres

Zoo
> Riverbanks Zoological Park

Places Rated Rank: 115

Columbus, GA-AL

Golf Courses: 13
> Daily fee (117 holes)
> Municipal (63 holes)
> Private (54 holes)

Movie Theatres: 43 screens
> 4 multiplexes

Professional Sports: 99 games
> Catfish (Class A Baseball)
> Cottonmouths (SPHL Hockey)

Recreation Areas: 11,547 acres
Federal
> Appalachian NT

State
> F.D. Roosevelt SP
> Sprewell Bluff SP

Water Area
> Lakes and rivers: 13,440 acres

Places Rated Rank: 207

Columbus, IN

Golf Courses: 5
> Daily fee (54 holes)
> Municipal (9 holes)
> Private (18 holes)

Movie Theatres: 27 screens
> 1 single/twin
> 2 multiplexes

Ski Areas: 5,200 lift capacity/hr

Water Area
> Lakes and rivers: 1,920 acres

Places Rated Rank: 354

Columbus, OH

Amusement/Theme Parks
> Wyandot Lake

Auto Racing
> Columbus Motor Speedway

College Sports: 130 games
> Ohio State Buckeyes

Golf Courses: 91
> Daily fee (927 holes)
> Municipal (144 holes)
> Private (567 holes)

Horse Racing: 167 programs
> Beulah Park (Thoroughbred)
> Delaware Fair (Harness)
> Scioto Downs (Harness)

Movie Theatres: 224 screens
> 14 multiplexes

Professional Sports: 75 games
> Clippers (Triple A Baseball)
> Crew (MLS Soccer)

Recreation Areas: 17,593 acres
State
> A. W. Marion SP
> Alum Creek SP
> Bigelow Cemetery Prairie SNA
> Blackhand Gorge SNA
> Buckeye Lake SP
> Deer Creek SP
> Delaware SP
> Gahanna Woods SNA
> Madison Lake SP
> Morris Woods SNA
> Mount Gilead SP
> Shallenberger SNA
> Smith Cemetery Prairie SNA
> Stage's Pond SNA
> Walther A. Tucker SNA

Ski Areas: 24,650 lift capacity/hr

Water Area
> Lakes and rivers: 18,560 acres

Zoo
> Columbus Zoo and Aquarium

Places Rated Rank: 92

Corpus Christi, TX

Aquarium
> Texas State Aquarium

Auto Racing
> Cabaniss Field NALF

College Sports: 48 games
> Texas A&M Islanders

Golf Courses: 12
> Daily fee (18 holes)
> Municipal (54 holes)
> Private (144 holes)

Movie Theatres: 39 screens
> 3 multiplexes

Recreation Areas: 57,795 acres
Federal
> Aransas NWR
State
> Copano Bay Fishing Pier SP
> Goose Island SRA
> Lake Corpus Christi SRA
> Mustang Island SP

Water Area
> Lakes and rivers: 307,200 acres
> Gulf offshore: 4,672 acres

Places Rated Rank: 101

Corvallis, OR

College Sports: 78 games
> Oregon State Beavers

Golf Courses: 4
> Daily fee (45 holes)
> Private (18 holes)

Movie Theatres: 16 screens
> 2 multiplexes

Recreation Areas: 23,698 acres
Federal
> Siuslaw NF
> William L. Finley NWR
State
> Washburn State Wayside
> Washburne Wayside
> Willamette River Greenway

Water Area
> Lakes and rivers: 1,920 acres

Places Rated Rank: 261

Cumberland, MD-WV

Golf Courses: 5
> Daily fee (72 holes)
> Private (18 holes)

Movie Theatres: 7 screens
> 1 single/twin
> 1 multiplex

Recreation Areas: 3,464 acres
State
　　Dans Mountain SP
　　Rocky Gap SP

Ski Areas: 18,100 lift capacity/hr

Water Area
　　Lakes and rivers: 3,200 acres

Places Rated Rank: 326

Dallas-Plano-Irving, TX

Amusement/Theme Parks
　　Cowtown Cattlepen Maze

Aquarium
　　Dallas World Aquarium

Auto Racing
　　Texas Motor Speedway

College Sports: 193 games
　　Dallas Baptist Patriots
　　Southern Methodist Mustangs
　　North Texas Mean Green

Golf Courses: 110
　　Daily fee (702 holes)
　　Municipal (441 holes)
　　Private (828 holes)

Horse Racing: 19 programs
　　Lone Star Park (Thoroughbred)

Movie Theatres: 426 screens
　　33 multiplexes

Professional Sports: 109 games
　　Cowboys (NFL Football)
　　FC Dallas (MLS Soccer)
　　Mavericks (NBA Basketball)
　　Stars (NHL Hockey)

Recreation Areas: 7,434 acres
State
　　Cedar Hill SRA
　　Cooper Lake SRA
　　Lake Lewisville SRA
　　Lake Tawakoni SRA
　　Ray Roberts Lake SRA

Water Area
　　Lakes and rivers: 147,840 acres

Zoo
　　Dallas Zoo
　　Fort Worth Zoo

Places Rated Rank: 44

Dalton, GA

Golf Courses: 6
　　Daily fee (45 holes)
　　Municipal (18 holes)
　　Private (36 holes)

Movie Theatres: 10 screens
　　1 single/twin
　　1 multiplex

Recreation Areas: 66,173 acres
Federal
　　Chattahoochee NF

State
　　Fort Mountain SP

Water Area
　　Lakes and rivers: 1,920 acres

Places Rated Rank: 295

Danville, IL

Golf Courses: 6
　　Daily fee (63 holes)
　　Municipal (18 holes)
　　Private (18 holes)

Movie Theatres: 8 screens
　　1 single/twin
　　1 multiplex

Recreation Areas: 2,844 acres
State
　　Kickapoo SP

Water Area
　　Lakes and rivers: 1,920 acres

Places Rated Rank: 353

Danville, VA

Golf Courses: 7
　　Daily fee (36 holes)
　　Private (81 holes)

Movie Theatres: 12 screens
　　1 multiplex

Water Area
　　Lakes and rivers: 5,120 acres

Places Rated Rank: 372

Davenport-Moline-Rock Island, IA-IL

Golf Courses: 26
　　Daily fee (162 holes)
　　Municipal (135 holes)
　　Private (162 holes)

Movie Theatres: 45 screens
　　6 singles/twins
　　3 multiplexes

Professional Sports: 91 games
　　Quad City Mallards (UHL Hockey)
　　Swing of the Quad City (Class A
　　Baseball)

Recreation Areas: 403 acres
Federal
　　Mark Twain NWR
　　Upper Mississippi NWR

Ski Areas: 6,000 lift capacity/hr

Water Area
　　Lakes and rivers: 28,160 acres

Zoo
　　Fejervary Zoo
　　Niabi Zoo

Places Rated Rank: 266

Dayton, OH

Auto Racing
　　Kil-Kare Speedway

College Sports: 144 games
　　University of Dayton Flyers
　　Wright State Raiders

Golf Courses: 37
　　Daily fee (207 holes)
　　Municipal (216 holes)
　　Private (243 holes)

Movie Theatres: 93 screens
　　3 singles/twins
　　6 multiplexes

Professional Sports: 107 games
　　Bombers (ECHL Hockey)
　　Dragons (Class A Baseball)

Recreation Areas: 6,706 acres
State
　　Hueston Woods SP
　　John Bryan SP
　　Little Miami SP
　　Sycamore SP

Water Area
　　Lakes and rivers: 5,120 acres

Places Rated Rank: 251

Decatur, AL

Amusement/Theme Parks
　　Point Mallard Park

Golf Courses: 8
　　Daily fee (54 holes)
　　Municipal (54 holes)
　　Private (36 holes)

Movie Theatres: 16 screens
　　2 multiplexes

Recreation Areas: 94,298 acres
Federal
　　Wheeler NWR
　　William B. Bankhead NF
State
　　Joe Wheeler SP

Water Area
　　Lakes and rivers: 26,880 acres

Places Rated Rank: 123

Decatur, IL

Golf Courses: 5
　　Municipal (54 holes)
　　Private (36 holes)

Movie Theatres: 23 screens
　　1 single/twin
　　2 multiplexes

Recreation Areas: 202 acres
State
　　Spitler Woods SP

Water Area
　　Lakes and rivers: 3,200 acres

Zoo

Decatur Park Zoo
Scovill Children's Zoo

Places Rated Rank: 324

Deltona-Daytona Beach, FL

Auto Racing

Daytona International Speedway
College Sports: 120 games
Bethune-Cookman Wildcats
Stetson Hatters

Golf Courses: 28

Daily fee (306 holes)
Municipal (72 holes)
Private (126 holes)

Movie Theatres: 52 screens

6 multiplexes
Professional Sports: 71 games
Cubs (Class A Baseball)

Recreation Areas: 55,238 acres

Federal
Canaveral N Seashore
Lake Woodruff NWR
Merritt Island NWR
State
Blue Spring SP
Bulow Creek SP
De Leon Springs SP
Hontoon Island SP
North Peninsula SP
Spruce Creek SRA
Tomoka SP

Water Area

Lakes and rivers: 101,760 acres
Atlantic offshore: 14,784 acres

Places Rated Rank: 41

✓ Denver-Aurora, CO

Amusement/Theme Parks

Heritage Square
Six Flags Elitch Gardens
Tiny Town and Railroad

Auto Racing

Denver Grand Prix
East Lincoln Speedway

College Sports: 107 games

University of Denver Pioneers

Golf Courses: 74

Daily fee (324 holes)
Municipal (558 holes)
Private (450 holes)

Horse Racing: 41 programs

Arapahoe Park (Thoroughbred)

Movie Theatres: 365 screens

6 singles/twins
34 multiplexes

Professional Sports: 190 games

Broncos (NFL Football)
Colorado Avalanche (NHL Hockey)
Nuggets (NBA Basketball)
Rapids (MLS Soccer)
Rockies (NL Baseball)

Recreation Areas: 2,868,843 acres

Federal
Arapaho NF
Pike NF
Roosevelt NF
San Isabel NF
State
Barr Lake SP
Castlewood Canyon SP
Chatfield SRA
Cherry Creek SRA
Eleven Mile SRA
Golden Gate SP
Roxborough SP
Spinney Mountain SRA

Ski Areas: 177,913 lift capacity/hr

Water Area

Lakes and rivers: 19,200 acres

Zoo

Denver Zoological Gardens

Places Rated Rank: 39

Des Moines-West Des Moines, IA

Amusement/Theme Parks

Adventureland Park
White Water University Fun Park

College Sports: 55 games

Drake Bulldogs

Golf Courses: 33

Daily fee (324 holes)
Municipal (90 holes)
Private (171 holes)

Horse Racing: 101 programs

Prairie Meadows (Mixed Meetings)

Movie Theatres: 116 screens

4 singles/twins
12 multiplexes

Professional Sports: 98 games

Iowa Cubs (Triple A Baseball)
Iowa Stars (AHL Hockey)

Recreation Areas: 4,715 acres

State
Badger Creek SRA
Big Creek SP
Lake Ahquabi SP
Margo Frankel Woods SP
Sheeder Prairie SHS
Springbrook SP
Walnut Woods SP

Ski Areas: 4,000 lift capacity/hr

Water Area

Lakes and rivers: 20,480 acres

Zoo

Blank Park Zoo

Places Rated Rank: 111

Detroit-Livonia-Dearborn, MI

College Sports: 75 games

Detroit Mercy Titans
Wayne State Warriors

Golf Courses: 46

Daily fee (234 holes)
Municipal (414 holes)
Private (180 holes)

Horse Racing: 77 programs

Northville Downs (Harness)

Movie Theatres: 163 screens

3 singles/twins
17 multiplexes

Professional Sports: 139 games

Red Wings (NHL Hockey)
Shock (WNBA Basketball)
Tigers (AL Baseball)

Recreation Areas: 1,248 acres

Federal
Wyandotte NWR
State
Maybury SP

Ski Areas: 22,830 lift capacity/hr

Water Area

Lakes and rivers: 12,800 acres
Lake St. Clair offshore: 24,320 acres

Zoo

Belle Isle Zoo and Aquarium

Places Rated Rank: 150

Dothan, AL

Amusement/Theme Parks

Water World

Golf Courses: 7

Daily fee (99 holes)
Private (18 holes)

Movie Theatres: 14 screens

2 multiplexes

Recreation Areas: 596 acres

State
Chattahoochee SP

Water Area

Lakes and rivers: 6,400 acres

Places Rated Rank: 348

Dover, DE

Auto Racing

Dover International Speedway

College Sports: 60 games

Delaware State Hornets

Golf Courses: 5

Daily fee (27 holes)
Private (54 holes)

Horse Racing: 238 programs

Dover Downs (Harness)
Harrington Raceway (Harness)

Movie Theatres: 16 screens

2 singles/twins
1 multiplex

Recreation Areas: 17,179 acres
Federal
Bombay Hook NWR
State
Killens Pond SP
Murderkill River Nature Preserve

Water Area
Lakes and rivers: 5,120 acres
Atlantic offshore: 128,640 acres

Places Rated Rank: 70

—————————

Dubuque, IA

Golf Courses: 7
Daily fee (45 holes)
Municipal (27 holes)
Private (45 holes)

Movie Theatres: 28 screens
3 multiplexes

Recreation Areas: 1,907 acres
Federal
Driftless Area NWR
Upper Mississippi NWR
State
Mines of Spain SP

Ski Areas: 22,400 lift capacity/hr

Water Area
Lakes and rivers: 5,120 acres

Places Rated Rank: 282

—————————

✓Duluth, MN-WI

College Sports: 20 games
University of Minnesota Bulldogs

Golf Courses: 23
Daily fee (198 holes)
Municipal (144 holes)
Private (63 holes)

Movie Theatres: 40 screens
4 singles/twins
5 multiplexes

Recreation Areas: 904,577 acres
Federal
Kabetogama PU
Saint Croix SRiver
Superior NF
Voyageurs NP
State
Amnicon Falls SP
Bear Head Lake SP
Gandy Dancer State Trail
Jay Cooke SP
McCarthy Beach SP
Moose Lake SP
Pattison SP
Saunders Grade State Trail

Ski Areas: 25,850 lift capacity/hr

Water Area
Lakes and rivers: 361,600 acres
Lake Superior offshore: 162,560 acres

Zoo
Lake Superior Zoo

Places Rated Rank: 35

Durham, NC

Amusement/Theme Parks
Pullen Park

Auto Racing
Concord Motorsport Park
Lowe's Motor Speedway

College Sports: 110 games
Duke Blue Devils

Golf Courses: 20
Daily fee (207 holes)
Private (153 holes)

Movie Theatres: 37 screens
3 multiplexes

Professional Sports: 58 games
Bulls (Triple A Baseball)

Recreation Areas: 1,965 acres
State
Eno River SP

Water Area
Lakes and rivers: 29,440 acres

Places Rated Rank: 151

—————————

Eau Claire, WI

Golf Courses: 10
Daily fee (117 holes)
Municipal (18 holes)
Private (36 holes)

Movie Theatres: 12 screens
1 multiplex

Recreation Areas: 5,788 acres
State
Brunet Island SP
Chippewa Moraine Ice Age RA
Chippewa River State Trail
Lake Wissota SP
Old Abe State Trail

Ski Areas: 5,600 lift capacity/hr

Water Area
Lakes and rivers: 24,960 acres

Places Rated Rank: 263

—————————

✓Edison, NJ

Amusement/Theme Parks
Casino Pier
Fantasy Island
Six Flags Great Adventure
Six Flags Hurricane Harbor

Auto Racing
Old Bridge Township Raceway Park
Wall Township Speedway

College Sports: 182 games
Monmouth Hawks
Rutgers Scarlet Knights

Golf Courses: 79
Daily fee (342 holes)
Municipal (306 holes)
Private (774 holes)

Horse Racing: 279 programs
Freehold Raceway (Harness)
Monmouth Park (Thoroughbred)

Movie Theatres: 189 screens
1 single/twin
17 multiplexes

Professional Sports: 71 games
BlueClaws (Class A Baseball)

Recreation Areas: 33,140 acres
Federal
Edwin B. Forsythe NWR
Gateway NRA
State
Allaire SP
Barnegat Lighthouse SP
Cheesequake SP
Cook SNA
Double Trouble SP
Hacklebarney SP
Island Beach SP
Manasquan Canal SRA
Pigeon Swamp SP
Swan Point SNA
Swimming River SNA
Washington Rock SP

Water Area
Lakes and rivers: 92,160 acres
Atlantic offshore: 35,840 acres

Places Rated Rank: 32

—————————

El Centro, CA

Auto Racing
Holtville Aerodrome International

Golf Courses: 3
Daily fee (45 holes)

Movie Theatres: 32 screens
1 single/twin
3 multiplexes

Recreation Areas: 29,642 acres
Federal
Cibola NWR
Salton Sea NWR
State
Anza-Borrego Desert SP
Ocotillo Wells SVRA
Picacho SRA
Salton Sea SRA

Water Area
Lakes and rivers: 196,480 acres

Places Rated Rank: 178

—————————

Elizabethtown, KY

Golf Courses: 5
Daily fee (72 holes)
Private (18 holes)

Movie Theatres: 16 screens
2 multiplexes

Water Area
Lakes and rivers: 1,280 acres

Places Rated Rank: 373

Elkhart-Goshen, IN

Golf Courses: 11
Daily fee (63 holes)
Municipal (36 holes)
Private (90 holes)

Movie Theatres: 27 screens
2 singles/twins
2 multiplexes

Ski Areas: 9,800 lift capacity/hr

Water Area
Lakes and rivers: 2,560 acres

Places Rated Rank: 362

Elmira, NY

Auto Racing
Chemung Speedrome

Golf Courses: 5
Daily fee (27 holes)
Municipal (36 holes)
Private (18 holes)

Movie Theatres: 12 screens
1 single/twin
1 multiplex

Professional Sports: 20 games
Jackals (UHL Hockey)

Recreation Areas: 462 acres
State
Mark Twain SP

Ski Areas: 3,200 lift capacity/hr

Water Area
Lakes and rivers: 1,920 acres

Places Rated Rank: 315

El Paso, TX

College Sports: 49 games
UTEP Miners

Golf Courses: 10
Daily fee (18 holes)
Municipal (63 holes)
Private (90 holes)

Movie Theatres: 69 screens
5 multiplexes

Professional Sports: 71 games
Diablos (Class AA Baseball)

Recreation Areas: 23,922 acres
Federal
Chamizal NMem
State
Franklin Mountains SP

Water Area
Lakes and rivers: 1,280 acres

Zoo
El Paso Zoo

Places Rated Rank: 316

Erie, PA

Amusement/Theme Parks
Waldameer Park & Water World

College Sports: 20 games
Mercyhurst Lakers

Golf Courses: 20
Daily fee (198 holes)
Municipal (72 holes)
Private (81 holes)

Movie Theatres: 23 screens
2 multiplexes

Professional Sports: 71 games
SeaWolves (Class AA Baseball)

Recreation Areas: 3,209 acres
State
Presque Isle SP

Ski Areas: 19,760 lift capacity/hr

Water Area
Lakes and rivers: 5,120 acres
Lake Erie offshore: 479,360 acres

Zoo
Erie Zoo

Places Rated Rank: 98

Essex County, MA

College Sports: 20 games
Merrimack Warriors

Golf Courses: 30
Daily fee (216 holes)
Municipal (72 holes)
Private (252 holes)

Movie Theatres: 94 screens
3 singles/twins
12 multiplexes

Recreation Areas: 3,114 acres
State
Bradley Palmer SP
Georgetown-Rowley SP
Halibut Point SP
Lawrence Heritage SP
Lynn Heritage SP
Maudslay SP
Plum Island SR
Salisbury Beach State Reservation
Sandy Point SR

Ski Areas: 24,800 lift capacity/hr

Water Area
Lakes and rivers: 24,320 acres
Atlantic offshore: 75,520 acres

Places Rated Rank: 284

Eugene-Springfield, OR

College Sports: 49 games
University of Oregon Ducks

Golf Courses: 10
Daily fee (117 holes)
Municipal (9 holes)
Private (54 holes)

Movie Theatres: 37 screens
3 multiplexes

Professional Sports: 71 games
Emeralds (Class A Baseball)

Recreation Areas: 4,284,751 acres
Federal
Oregon Islands NWR
Siuslaw NF
Umpqua NF
Willamette NF
State
Alderwood State Wayside
Armitage SP
Ben and Kay Dorris SP
Blachly Mountain Forest Wayside
Carl Washburne Memorial SP
Darlingtonia State Wayside
Devil's Elbow SP
Elijah Bristow SP
Hendricks Bridge State Wayside
Howard Morton Memorial SP
Jennie Harris State Wayside
Jessie Honeyman Memorial SP
Joaquin Miller Forest Wayside
Muriel Ponsler Memorial State
Neptune SP
Squaw Creek State Wayside
Stonefield Beach State Wayside
Willamette River Greenway

Ski Areas: 34,680 lift capacity/hr

Water Area
Lakes and rivers: 40,960 acres
Pacific offshore: 6,656 acres

Places Rated Rank: 129

Evansville, IN-KY

Auto Racing
Tri-State Speedway

College Sports: 72 games
University of Evansville Purple Aces

Golf Courses: 20
Daily fee (162 holes)
Municipal (54 holes)
Private (135 holes)

Horse Racing: 54 programs
Ellis Park (Thoroughbred)

Movie Theatres: 71 screens
2 singles/twins
6 multiplexes

Recreation Areas: 4,253 acres
Federal
Patoka NWR
State
Harmonie SP
John James Audubon SP

Water Area
Lakes and rivers: 36,480 acres

Zoo
Mesker Park Zoo

Places Rated Rank: 95

Fairbanks, AK

College Sports: 20 games
University of Alaska Nanooks

Golf Courses: 3
Daily fee (45 holes)

Movie Theatres: 17 screens
1 single/twin
1 multiplex

Recreation Area: 250,000
State
Chena River SRA

Ski Areas: 2,500 lift capacity/hr

Water Area
Lakes and rivers: 51,840 acres

Places Rated Rank: 345

Fargo, ND-MN

Amusement/Theme Parks
Driverz
Thunder Road Family Fun Park

Golf Courses: 11
Daily fee (45 holes)
Municipal (99 holes)
Private (54 holes)

Movie Theatres: 31 screens
3 multiplexes

Recreation Areas: 1,367 acres
State
Buffalo River SP

Ski Areas: 2,500 lift capacity/hr

Water Area
Lakes and rivers: 5,760 acres

Zoo
Red River Zoo

Places Rated Rank: 331

Farmington, NM

Golf Courses: 4
Daily fee (36 holes)
Municipal (18 holes)
Private (18 holes)

Horse Racing: 40 programs
SunRay Park (Thoroughbred)

Movie Theatres: 15 screens
2 singles/twins
2 multiplexes

Recreation Areas: 40 acres
Federal
Aztec Ruins NM

Ski Areas: 52,880 lift capacity/hr

Water Area
Lakes and rivers: 15,360 acres

Places Rated Rank: 338

Fayetteville, NC

Golf Courses: 13
Daily fee (162 holes)
Private (72 holes)

Movie Theatres: 34 screens
3 multiplexes

Professional Sports: 28 games
FireAntz (SPHL Hockey)

Water Area
Lakes and rivers: 3,840 acres

Places Rated Rank: 370

Fayetteville-Springdale, AR-MO

College Sports: 66 games
University of Arkansas Razorbacks

Golf Courses: 23
Daily fee (171 holes)
Private (234 holes)

Movie Theatres: 63 screens
4 singles/twins
5 multiplexes

Recreation Areas: 98,252 acres
Federal
Logan Cave NWR
Ozark NF
Pea Ridge NMP
State
Beaver Lake SP
Big Sugar Creek SP
Devil's Den SP
Withrow Springs SP

Water Area
Lakes and rivers: 25,600 acres

Places Rated Rank: 202

Flagstaff, AZ

College Sports: 43 games
Northern Arizona Lumberjacks

Golf Courses: 10
Daily fee (18 holes)
Municipal (45 holes)
Private (108 holes)

Movie Theatres: 13 screens
2 multiplexes

Recreation Areas: 13,940,795 acres
Federal
Coconino NF
Glen Canyon NRA
Grand Canyon NP
Kaibab NF
Lake Mead NRA
Navajo NM
Prescott NF
Sitgreaves NF
Sunset Crater NM
Walnut Canyon NM
Wupatki NM
State
Slide Rock SP

Ski Areas: 5,810 lift capacity/hr

Water Area
Lakes and rivers: 27,520 acres

Places Rated Rank: 209

Flint, MI

Golf Courses: 26
Daily fee (261 holes)
Municipal (45 holes)
Private (162 holes)

Horse Racing: 82 programs
Sports Creek Raceway (Harness)

Movie Theatres: 76 screens
1 single/twin
8 multiplexes

Professional Sports: 20 games
Generals (UHL Hockey)

Recreation Areas: 8 acres
Federal
Manistee NF

Ski Areas: 46,030 lift capacity/hr

Water Area
Lakes and rivers: 6,400 acres

Places Rated Rank: 272

Florence, SC

Auto Racing
Darlington Raceway

Golf Courses: 14
Daily fee (153 holes)
Private (90 holes)

Movie Theatres: 20 screens
1 single/twin
2 multiplexes

Professional Sports: 28 games
Pee Dee Cyclones (SPHL Hockey)

Recreation Areas: 931 acres
State
Long Bluff SP
Lynches River SP
Woods Bay SP

Water Area
Lakes and rivers: 5,760 acres

Places Rated Rank: 330

Florence-Muscle Shoals, AL

Golf Courses: 9
Daily fee (63 holes)
Municipal (45 holes)
Private (54 holes)

Movie Theatres: 18 screens
2 multiplexes

Recreation Areas: 6,255 acres
Federal
Natchez Trace NT
Natchez Trace Parkway
State
Joe Wheeler SP

Water Area
    Lakes and rivers: 49,920 acres
Places Rated Rank: 197

Fond du Lac, WI

Golf Courses: 4
    Daily fee (27 holes)
    Municipal (27 holes)
    Private (18 holes)

Movie Theatres: 13 screens
    1 single/twin
    1 multiplex

Recreation Areas: 1,508 acres
Federal
    Horicon NWR
State
    Campbellsport Drumlin Ice Age SP
    Wild Goose State Trail

Ski Areas: 6,900 lift capacity/hr

Water Area
    Lakes and rivers: 27,520 acres
    Lake Michigan offshore: 5,684 acres
Places Rated Rank: 237

Fort Collins-Loveland, CO

College Sports: 37 games
    Colorado State Rams

Golf Courses: 9
    Daily fee (9 holes)
    Municipal (99 holes)
    Private (54 holes)

Movie Theatres: 51 screens
    3 singles/twins
    5 multiplexes

Recreation Areas: 794,188 acres
Federal
    Rocky Mountain NP
    Roosevelt NF
State
    Boyd Lake SRA
    Lory SP
    Picnic Rock SP

Ski Areas: 53,900 lift capacity/hr

Water Area
    Lakes and rivers: 21,120 acres
Places Rated Rank: 143

Fort Lauderdale, FL

Golf Courses: 51
    Daily fee (504 holes)
    Municipal (108 holes)
    Private (306 holes)

Horse Racing: 230 programs
    Gulfstream Park (Thoroughbred)
    Pompano Park (Harness)

Movie Theatres: 283 screens
    1 single/twin
    26 multiplexes

Professional Sports: 41 games
    Florida Panthers (NHL Hockey)

Recreation Areas: 431 acres
State
    Birch SP
    Lloyd Beach SP

Water Area
    Lakes and rivers: 8,320 acres
    Atlantic offshore: 6,272 acres
Places Rated Rank: 319

Fort Smith, AR-OK

Golf Courses: 13
    Daily fee (144 holes)
    Municipal (36 holes)
    Private (45 holes)

Horse Racing: 84 programs
    Blue Ribbon Downs (Thoroughbred)

Movie Theatres: 29 screens
    3 multiplexes

Recreation Areas: 433,976 acres
Federal
    Ouachita NF
    Ozark NF
State
    Heavener-Runestone SP
    Lake Fort Smith SP
    Lake Tenkiller SP
    Lake Wister SP
    Sallisaw SP
    Talimena SP

Water Area
    Lakes and rivers: 58,880 acres
Places Rated Rank: 130

Fort Walton Beach-Crestview, FL

Golf Courses: 15
    Daily fee (153 holes)
    Municipal (36 holes)
    Private (72 holes)

Movie Theatres: 48 screens
    2 singles/twins
    5 multiplexes

Recreation Areas: 4,584 acres
Federal
    Choctawhatchee NF
    Gulf Islands N Seashore
State
    Henderson Beach SP
    Rocky Bayou SP

Water Area
    Lakes and rivers: 38,400 acres
    Gulf offshore: 15,650 acres
Places Rated Rank: 180

Fort Wayne, IN

Auto Racing
    Fort Wayne Memorial Coliseum

College Sports: 72 games
    IUPU Fort Wayne Mastodons

Golf Courses: 22
    Daily fee (288 holes)
    Municipal (18 holes)
    Private (90 holes)

Movie Theatres: 53 screens
    6 singles/twins
    4 multiplexes

Professional Sports: 107 games
    Komets (AHL Hockey)
    Wizards (Class A Baseball)

Recreation Areas: 1,065 acres
State
    Ouabache SP

Water Area
    Lakes and rivers: 3,200 acres

Zoo
    Fort Wayne Children's Zoo
Places Rated Rank: 280

Fort Worth-Arlington, TX

Amusement/Theme Parks
    Cowtown Cattlepen Maze
    Six Flags Hurricane Harbor
    Six Flags Over Texas

Auto Racing
    Motorsport Ranch
    Texas Motor Speedway

College Sports: 114 games
    Texas Christian Horned Frogs
    UT Arlington Mavericks

Golf Courses: 55
    Daily fee (405 holes)
    Municipal (279 holes)
    Private (297 holes)

Movie Theatres: 219 screens
    18 multiplexes

Professional Sports: 81 games
    Rangers (AL Baseball)

Recreation Areas: 24,587 acres
Federal
    Lyndon B. Johnson NGL
State
    Cleburne SRA
    Eagle Mountain SRA
    Lake Mineral Wells SP

Water Area
    Lakes and rivers: 40,960 acres

Zoo
    Fort Worth Zoo
Places Rated Rank: 121

Fresno, CA

Amusement/Theme Parks
    Roeding Park
    Rotary Storyland
    Wild Water Adventure Park

College Sports: 66 games
    California State Bulldogs

Golf Courses: 13
Daily fee (90 holes)
Municipal (36 holes)
Private (108 holes)

Horse Racing: 11 programs
Fresno Fair (Thoroughbred)

Movie Theatres: 76 screens
7 multiplexes

Professional Sports: 94 games
Falcons (ECHL Hockey)
Grizzlies (Triple A Baseball)

Recreation Areas: 3,319,026 acres
Federal
Inyo NF
Kings Canyon NP
Sequoia NF
Sierra NF
State
Millerton Lake SRA

Ski Areas: 96,942 lift capacity/hr

Water Area
Lakes and rivers: 35,200 acres

Zoo
Chaffee Zoological Gardens

Places Rated Rank: 89

───────────────

Gadsden, AL

Golf Courses: 9
Daily fee (108 holes)
Private (54 holes)

Movie Theatres: 18 screens
1 single/twin
1 multiplex

Ski Areas: 800 lift capacity/hr

Water Area
Lakes and rivers: 8,960 acres

Places Rated Rank: 307

───────────────

Gainesville, FL

College Sports: 66 games
University of Florida Gators

Golf Courses: 6
Daily fee (36 holes)
Municipal (18 holes)
Private (54 holes)

Movie Theatres: 36 screens
2 singles/twins
3 multiplexes

Recreation Areas: 29,586 acres
State
O'Leno SP
Paynes Prairie State Preserve
River Rise SP
San Felasco Hammock SP

Water Area
Lakes and rivers: 65,280 acres

Zoo
SFCC Teaching Zoo

Places Rated Rank: 108

Gainesville, GA

Auto Racing
Road Atlanta

Golf Courses: 3
Daily fee (45 holes)

Movie Theatres: 19 screens
2 multiplexes

Water Area
Lakes and rivers: 23,040 acres

Places Rated Rank: 304

───────────────

Gary, IN

College Sports: 72 games
Valparaiso Crusaders

Golf Courses: 32
Daily fee (288 holes)
Municipal (90 holes)
Private (189 holes)

Movie Theatres: 74 screens
8 singles/twins
6 multiplexes

Professional Sports: 24 games
Steelheads (CBA Basketball)

Recreation Areas: 11,942 acres
Federal
Indiana Dunes N Lakeshore
State
Indiana Dunes SP

Ski Areas: 3,500 lift capacity/hr

Water Area
Lakes and rivers: 6,400 acres
Lake Michigan offshore: 144,000 acres

Places Rated Rank: 141

───────────────

Glens Falls, NY

Amusement/Theme Parks
The Great Escape

Golf Courses: 14
Daily fee (225 holes)
Private (18 holes)

Movie Theatres: 9 screens
1 single/twin
1 multiplex

Recreation Areas: 5,898 acres
State
Eagle Point SRA
Hearthstone Point SRA
Lake George Beach SRA
Lake George Islands
Lake Lauderdale SP
Luzerne SRA
Prospect Mountain SRA
Rogers Rock SRA

Ski Areas: 100,897 lift capacity/hr

Water Area
Lakes and rivers: 46,080 acres

Places Rated Rank: 192

Goldsboro, NC

Golf Courses: 6
Daily fee (72 holes)
Municipal (18 holes)
Private (18 holes)

Movie Theatres: 4 screens
1 multiplex

Recreation Areas: 608 acres
State
Cliffs-Of-The-Neuse SP

Water Area
Lakes and rivers: 2,560 acres

Places Rated Rank: 356

───────────────

Grand Forks, ND-MN

College Sports: 20 games
North Dakota Fighting Sioux

Golf Courses: 9
Daily fee (108 holes)
Municipal (27 holes)
Private (18 holes)

Movie Theatres: 17 screens
2 singles/twins
2 multiplexes

Recreation Areas: 3,534 acres
Federal
Kelly's Slough NWR
Rydell NWR
State
Turtle River SP

Water Area
Lakes and rivers: 18,560 acres

Places Rated Rank: 301

───────────────

Grand Junction, CO

Auto Racing
Grand Junction Motor Speedway

Golf Courses: 5
Daily fee (45 holes)
Municipal (27 holes)
Private (18 holes)

Movie Theatres: 14 screens
2 singles/twins
2 multiplexes

Recreation Areas: 2,213,462 acres
Federal
Colorado NM
Grand Mesa NF
Manti-La Sal NF
Uncompahgre NF
White River NF
State
Highline SRA
Island Acres SRA
Vega SRA

Ski Areas: 79,763 lift capacity/hr

Water Area
Lakes and rivers: 8,320 acres

Places Rated Rank: 214

───── 442 ─────

Grand Rapids-Wyoming, MI

Auto Racing
Grattan Raceway Park
I-96 Speedway

Golf Courses: 63
Daily fee (855 holes)
Municipal (36 holes)
Private (234 holes)

Movie Theatres: 126 screens
3 singles/twins
7 multiplexes

Professional Sports: 107 games
Griffins (AHL Hockey)
Whitecaps (Class A Baseball)

Recreation Areas: 119,690 acres
Federal
Manistee NF
State
Ionia SRA
Newago SP
Yankee Springs SRA

Ski Areas: 22,100 lift capacity/hr

Water Area
Lakes and rivers: 40,320 acres
Lake Michigan offshore: 190,920 acres

Zoo
Ball Zoological Garden

Places Rated Rank: 50

Great Falls, MT

Golf Courses: 4
Daily fee (9 holes)
Municipal (36 holes)
Private (18 holes)

Movie Theatres: 10 screens
1 multiplex
Professional Sports: 24 games
Explorers (CBA Basketball)

Recreation Areas: 192,351 acres
Federal
Benton Lake NWR
Lewis & Clark NF
State
Giant Springs SP
Sluice Boxes SP

Ski Areas: 8,070 lift capacity/hr

Water Area
Lakes and rivers: 8,960 acres

Places Rated Rank: 249

Greeley, CO

Auto Racing
Continental Divide Race Park

Golf Courses: 10
Daily fee (90 holes)
Municipal (54 holes)
Private (36 holes)

Movie Theatres: 17 screens
2 multiplexes

Recreation Areas: 193,110 acres
Federal
Pawnee NGL
State
Barbour Ponds SRA

Ski Areas: 7,500 lift capacity/hr

Water Area
Lakes and rivers: 18,560 acres

Places Rated Rank: 260

✓ Green Bay, WI

Amusement/Theme Parks
Bay Beach Amusement Park

Auto Racing
College Sports: 55 games
University of Wisconsin Phoenix

Golf Courses: 22
Daily fee (342 holes)
Municipal (18 holes)
Private (36 holes)

Movie Theatres: 12 screens
2 multiplexes

Professional Sports: 5 games
Packers (NFL Football)

Recreation Areas: 141,969 acres
Federal
Nicolet NF
State
Ahnapee State Trail
Lost Dauphin SP
Mountain-Bay State Trail

Ski Areas: 1,200 lift capacity/hr

Water Area
Lakes and rivers: 17,920 acres
Lake Michigan offshore: 608,640 acres

Zoo
Northeastern Wisconsin Zoo

Places Rated Rank: 25

Greensboro-High Point, NC

College Sports: 192 games
High Point University Panthers
North Carolina A&T Aggies
UNC Greensboro Spartans

Golf Courses: 39
Daily fee (423 holes)
Municipal (90 holes)
Private (180 holes)

Movie Theatres: 84 screens
8 multiplexes

Professional Sports: 112 games
Carolina Hurricanes (NHL Hockey)
Grasshoppers (Class A Baseball)

Recreation Areas: 9,742 acres
Federal
Guilford Courthouse NMP
Uwharrie NF

Water Area
Lakes and rivers: 10,240 acres

Zoo
North Carolina Zoo

Places Rated Rank: 216

Greenville, NC

College Sports: 78 games
East Carolina Pirates

Golf Courses: 7
Daily fee (54 holes)
Municipal (18 holes)
Private (54 holes)

Movie Theatres: 12 screens
1 multiplex

Professional Sports: 71 games
Drive (Class A Baseball)

Water Area
Lakes and rivers: 1,920 acres

Places Rated Rank: 371

Greenville, SC

College Sports: 150 games
Clemson Tigers
Furman University Paladins

Golf Courses: 33
Daily fee (369 holes)
Private (216 holes)

Movie Theatres: 51 screens
5 multiplexes

Professional Sports: 107 games
Braves (Class AA Baseball)
Grrrowl (ECHL Hockey)

Recreation Areas: 37,175 acres
Federal
Sumter NF
State
Caesars Head SP
Jones Gap SP
Keowee Toxaway SP
Paris Mountain SP
Table Rock SP
Wildcat Wayside SP

Water Area
Lakes and rivers: 18,560 acres

Zoo
Greenville Zoo

Places Rated Rank: 153

✓ Gulfport-Biloxi, MS

Golf Courses: 13
Daily fee (198 holes)
Private (36 holes)

Movie Theatres: 51 screens
   6 multiplexes

Professional Sports: 36 games
   Sea Wolves (ECHL Hockey)

Recreation Areas: 127,895 acres
Federal
   De Soto NF
   Gulf Islands N Seashore
State
   Buccaneer SP

Water Area
   Lakes and rivers: 16,640 acres
   Gulf offshore: 247,680 acres

Places Rated Rank: 38

Hagerstown-Martinsburg, MD-WV

Golf Courses: 7
   Daily fee (63 holes)
   Municipal (45 holes)
   Private (18 holes)

Movie Theatres: 36 screens
   3 multiplexes

Professional Sports: 71 games
   Suns (Class A Baseball)

Recreation Areas: 14,097 acres
Federal
   Appalachian NT
   Catoctin Mountain Park
State
   Berkeley Springs SP
   Cacapon Resort SP
   Greenbrier SP
   Sideling Hill Exhibit Center
   South Mountain SP

Ski Areas: 22,120 lift capacity/hr

Water Area
   Lakes and rivers: 6,400 acres

Places Rated Rank: 218

Hanford-Corcoran, CA

Golf Courses: 3
   Daily fee (9 holes)
   Municipal (18 holes)
   Private (18 holes)

Movie Theatres: 23 screens
   1 single/twin
   4 multiplexes

Ski Areas: 10,742 lift capacity/hr

Water Area
   Lakes and rivers: 1,280 acres

Places Rated Rank: 379

Harrisburg-Carlisle, PA

Amusement/Theme Parks
   Hersheypark

Golf Courses: 23
   Daily fee (225 holes)
   Municipal (54 holes)
   Private (135 holes)

Horse Racing: 204 programs
   Penn National (Thoroughbred)

Movie Theatres: 52 screens
   1 single/twin
   5 multiplexes

Professional Sports: 111 games
   Bears (AHL Hockey)
   Senators (Class AA Baseball)

Recreation Areas: 7,351 acres
Federal
   Appalachian NT
State
   Big Spring SP
   Colonel Denning SP
   Fowlers Hollow SP
   Kings Gap SP
   Little Buffalo SP

Ski Areas: 32,520 lift capacity/hr

Water Area
   Lakes and rivers: 22,400 acres

Places Rated Rank: 176

Harrisonburg, VA

College Sports: 72 games
   James Madison Dukes

Golf Courses: 6
   Daily fee (72 holes)
   Municipal (18 holes)
   Private (18 holes)

Movie Theatres: 14 screens
   1 multiplex

Recreation Areas: 178,241 acres
Federal
   Appalachian NT
   George Washington NF
   Shenandoah NP

Ski Areas: 2,500 lift capacity/hr

Water Area
   Lakes and rivers: 1,280 acres

Places Rated Rank: 230

Hartford-West Hartford, CT

Amusement/Theme Parks
   Lake Compounce

College Sports: 274 games
   Central Connecticut Blue Devils
   Uconn Huskies
   University of Hartford Hawks

Golf Courses: 53
   Daily fee (486 holes)
   Municipal (162 holes)
   Private (306 holes)

Movie Theatres: 209 screens
   3 singles/twins
   19 multiplexes

Professional Sports: 107 games
   Rock Cats (Class AA Baseball)
   Wolf Pack (AHL Hockey)

Recreation Areas: 10,416 acres
State
   Bigelow Hollow SP
   Bolton Notch SP
   Brainard Homestead SP
   Chatfield Hollow SP
   Connecticut Valley Railroad SP
   Dart Island SP
   Devil's Hopyard SP
   Dinosaur SP
   Foster Pond SP
   Gay City SP
   George D. Seymour SP
   Gillette Castle SP
   Haddam Island SP
   Haddam Meadows SP
   Higganum Reservoir SP
   Horseguard SP
   Hurd SP
   Lamentation Mountain SP
   Mansfield Hollow SP
   Millers Pond SP
   Penwood SP
   Stratton Brook SP
   Sunset Rock SP
   Talcott Mountain SP
   Tri Mountain SP
   Wadsworth Falls SP
   Windsor Meadows SP

Ski Areas: 40,225 lift capacity/hr

Water Area
   Lakes and rivers: 25,600 acres
   Atlantic offshore: 33,280 acres

Places Rated Rank: 194

Hattiesburg, MS

College Sports: 66 games
   Southern Mississippi Golden Eagles

Golf Courses: 8
   Daily fee (99 holes)
   Private (36 holes)

Movie Theatres: 29 screens
   3 multiplexes

Recreation Areas: 214,209 acres
Federal
   De Soto NF
   De Soto PU
State
   Paul B. Johnson SP

Water Area
   Lakes and rivers: 5,760 acres

Zoo
   Hattiesburg Zoo

Places Rated Rank: 163

Hickory-Lenoir-Morganton, NC

Amusement/Theme Parks
   Tweetsie Railroad

Auto Racing
   Hickory Motor Speedway
   Tri-County Motor Speedway

Golf Courses: 19
   Daily fee (252 holes)
   Private (90 holes)

Movie Theatres: 31 screens
  1 single/twin
  4 multiplexes

Professional Sports: 71 games
  Crawdads (Class A Baseball)

Recreation Areas: 104,971 acres
Federal
  Blue Ridge Parkway
  Pisgah NF
State
  South Mountain SP

Ski Areas: 23,750 lift capacity/hr

Water Area
  Lakes and rivers: 17,920 acres

Places Rated Rank: 105

Hinesville-Fort Stewart, GA

Golf Courses: 2
  Daily fee (18 holes)
  Municipal (18 holes)

Movie Theatres: 9 screens
  1 multiplex

Water Area
  Lakes and rivers: 54,400 acres

Places Rated Rank: 306

Holland-Grand Haven, MI

Auto Racing
  Berlin Raceway

Golf Courses: 16
  Daily fee (207 holes)
  Private (72 holes)

Movie Theatres: 9 screens
  1 single/twin
  1 multiplex

Recreation Areas: 487 acres
State
  Grand Haven SP
  Holland SP
  P.J. Hoffmaster SP

Ski Areas: 17,100 lift capacity/hr

Water Area
  Lakes and rivers: 7,680 acres
  Lake Michigan offshore: 675,200
    acres

Places Rated Rank: 205

Honolulu, HI

Aquarium
  Waikiki Aquarium

Auto Racing
  Hawaii Motorsports Center
  College Sports: 66 games
  Hawaii Rainbow Warriors

College Sports: 66 games
  Hawaii Rainbow Warriors

Golf Courses: 35
  Daily fee (333 holes)
  Municipal (99 holes)
  Private (198 holes)

Movie Theatres: 140 screens
  7 singles/twins
  13 multiplexes

Recreation Areas: 10,734 acres
Federal
  Hawaiian Islands NWR
  USS Arizona Memorial
State
  Diamond Head State Monument
  Hanauma Bay Underwater Park
  Heeia SP
  Kaena Point SP
  Kahana Valley SP
  Kakaako Waterfront Park
  Keaiwa Heiau SRA
  Malaekahana SRA
  Nuuanu Pali State Wayside
  Puu Ualakaa State Wayside
  Sacred Falls SP
  Sand Island SRA
  Waahila Ridge SRA
  Wahiawa Fresh SRA

Water Area
  Lakes and rivers: 12,160 acres
  Pacific offshore: 96,512 acres

Zoo
  Honolulu Zoo

Places Rated Rank: 244

✓Hot Springs, AR

Amusement/Theme Parks
  Magic Springs & Crystal Falls

Golf Courses: 13
  Daily fee (90 holes)
  Private (144 holes)

Horse Racing: 55 programs
  Oaklawn Park (Thoroughbred)

Movie Theatres: 15 screens
  2 multiplexes

Recreation Areas: 124,962 acres
Federal
  Hot Springs NP
  Ouachita NF
State
  Lake Ouachita SP

Water Area
  Lakes and rivers: 36,480 acres

Places Rated Rank: 24

Houma-Bayou Cane-Thibodaux, LA

College Sports: 60 games
  Nicholls State Colonels

Golf Courses: 4
  Daily fee (27 holes)
  Private (45 holes)

Movie Theatres: 14 screens
  2 multiplexes

Recreation Areas: 4,416 acres
Federal
  Mandalay NWR

Water Area
  Lakes and rivers: 345,600 acres
  Gulf offshore: 203,520 acres

Places Rated Rank: 255

✓Houston-Sugar Land-Baytown, TX

Amusement/Theme Parks
  Six Flags Splashtown

Aquariums
  Houston Aquarium
  Moody Gardens Aquarium

Auto Racing
  Grand Prix of Houston
  Mercedes-Benz Sugar Land Road

College Sports: 252 games
  Prairie View A&M Panthers
  Rice University Owls
  Texas Southern Tigers
  University of Houston Cougars

Golf Courses: 155
  Daily fee (1,278 holes)
  Municipal (342 holes)
  Private (1161 holes)

Horse Racing: 87 programs
  Sam Houston (Thoroughbred)

Movie Theatres: 483 screens
  31 multiplexes

Professional Sports: 242 games
  Aeros (AHL Hockey)
  Astros (NL Baseball)
  Comets (WNBA Basketball)
  Dynamo (MLS Soccer)
  Rockets (NBA Basketball)
  Texans (NFL Football)

Recreation Areas: 225,279 acres
Federal
  Anahuac NWR
  Big Thicket N Preserve
  Brazoria NWR
  Sam Houston NF
  San Bernard NWR
  Trinity River NWR
State
  Brazos Bend SP
  Christmas Bay SRA
  Davis Hill SP
  Galveston Island SP
  Lake Houston SP

Water Area
  Lakes and rivers: 261,120 acres

Zoo
  Houston Zoo

Places Rated Rank: 15

Huntington-Ashland, WV-KY-OH

Amusement/Theme Parks
  Camden Park

College Sports: 78 games

Marshall Thundering Herd

Golf Courses: 13

Daily fee (171 holes)
Private (63 holes)

Movie Theatres: 32 screens

3 multiplexes

Recreation Areas: 76,751 acres

Federal
Wayne NF
State
Beech Fork SP
Greenbo Lake State Resort Park

Water Area

Lakes and rivers: 15,360 acres

Places Rated Rank: 152

Huntsville, AL

Amusement/Theme Parks

Point Mallard Park

College Sports: 92 games

Alabama A&M Bulldogs
UAH Chargers

Golf Courses: 17

Daily fee (189 holes)
Municipal (18 holes)
Private (90 holes)

Movie Theatres: 54 screens

1 single/twin
4 multiplexes

Professional Sports: 99 games

Havoc (SPHL Hockey)
Stars (Class AA Baseball)

Recreation Areas: 7,216 acres

Federal
Wheeler NWR
State
Joe Wheeler SP
Monte Sano SP

Water Area

Lakes and rivers: 30,080 acres

Places Rated Rank: 131

Idaho Falls, ID

Amusement/Theme Parks

Tautphaus Park

Golf Courses: 5

Daily fee (18 holes)
Municipal (54 holes)
Private (18 holes)

Movie Theatres: 21 screens

3 singles/twins
2 multiplexes

Recreation Areas: 979,392 acres

Federal
Camas NWR
Caribou NF
Grays Lake NWR
Targhee NF

Ski Areas: 19,822 lift capacity/hr

Water Area

Lakes and rivers: 26,880 acres

Zoo

Tautphaus Park Zoo

Places Rated Rank: 80

Indianapolis-Carmel, IN

Auto Racing

Indiana State Fairgrounds
Indianapolis Motor Speedway
Indianapolis Raceway Park
Putnam Park
Track Attack

College Sports: 159 games

Butler University Bulldogs
IUPU Indianapolis Jaguars

Golf Courses: 86

Daily fee (891 holes)
Municipal (243 holes)
Private (414 holes)

Horse Racing: 133 programs

Indiana Downs (Mixed Meetings)
Indiana State Fair (Harness)

Movie Theatres: 324 screens

11 single/twin
28 multiplexes

Professional Sports: 126 games

Colts (NFL Football)
Fever (WNBA Basketball)
Indians (Triple A Baseball)
Pacers (NBA Basketball)

Recreation Areas: 34,143 acres

Federal
Hoosier NF
State
Brown County SP

Ski Areas: 5,200 lift capacity/hr

Water Area

Lakes and rivers: 15,360 acres

Zoo

Indianapolis Zoo

Places Rated Rank: 72

Iowa City, IA

College Sports: 66 games

University of Iowa Hawkeyes

Golf Courses: 9

Daily fee (126 holes)
Municipal (18 holes)
Private (9 holes)

Movie Theatres: 20 screens

1 single/twin
3 multiplexes

Recreation Areas: 3,567 acres

State
Lake Darling SP
Lake Macbride SP

Water Area

Lakes and rivers: 7,040 acres

Places Rated Rank: 274

Ithaca, NY

College Sports: 124 games

Cornell University Big Red

Golf Courses: 8

Daily fee (90 holes)
Municipal (9 holes)
Private (36 holes)

Movie Theatres: 10 screens

1 multiplex

Recreation Areas: 2,633 acres

State
Allen H. Treman SP
Buttermilk Falls SP
Robert H. Treman SP
Taughannock Falls SP

Ski Areas: 14,675 lift capacity/hr

Water Area

Lakes and rivers: 10,240 acres

Places Rated Rank: 179

Jackson, MI

Auto Racing

Michigan International Speedway

Golf Courses: 22

Daily fee (306 holes)
Municipal (36 holes)
Private (45 holes)

Horse Racing: 24 programs

Jackson Raceway (Harness)

Movie Theatres: 9 screens

1 single/twin
1 multiplex

Recreation Areas: 13,104 acres

State
Lakelands Trail SP
W.J. Hayes SP
Waterloo SRA

Ski Areas: 17,200 lift capacity/hr

Water Area

Lakes and rivers: 10,880 acres

Zoo

Jackson Zoological Park

Places Rated Rank: 134

Jackson, MS

College Sports: 60 games

Jackson State Tigers

Golf Courses: 22

Daily fee (144 holes)
Municipal (72 holes)
Private (171 holes)

Movie Theatres: 54 screens

    5 multiplexes
    Professional Sports: 71 games
    Generals (Class AA Baseball)

Recreation Areas: 14,962 acres

Federal
    Homochitto NF
    Natchez Trace NT
    Natchez Trace Parkway
State
    LeFleur's Bluff SP

Water Area

    Lakes and rivers: 43,520 acres

Zoo

    Jackson Zoological Park

Places Rated Rank: 248

Jackson, TN

Golf Courses: 6

    Daily fee (36 holes)
    Municipal (36 holes)
    Private (36 holes)

Movie Theatres: 13 screens

    1 single/twin
    2 multiplexes

Professional Sports: 71 games

    Diamond Jaxx (Class AA Baseball)

Recreation Areas: 400 acres

State
    Chickasaw SP

Water Area

    Lakes and rivers: 1,280 acres

Places Rated Rank: 349

✓Jacksonville, FL

Amusement/Theme Parks

    Adventure Landing

College Sports: 72 games

    Jacksonville University Dolphins

Golf Courses: 61

    Daily fee (585 holes)
    Municipal (90 holes)
    Private (414 holes)

Movie Theatres: 140 screens

    4 singles/twins
    10 multiplexes

Professional Sports: 109 games

    Barracudas (SPHL Hockey)
    Jaguars (NFL Football)
    Suns (Class AA Baseball)

Recreation Areas: 132,405 acres

Federal
    Castillo de San Marcos NM
    Fort Caroline NMem
    Fort Matanzas NM
    Nekoosa PU
    Okefenokee NWR
    Osceola NF
    Pinhook PU
    Timucuan Ecological and Historic

State
    Amelia Island SP
    Anastasia SP
    Big Talbot Island SP
    Faver-Dykes SP
    Fort Clinch SP
    Gold Head Branch SP
    Guana River SP
    Little Talbot Island SP
    Pumpkin Hill Creek Preserve SP

Water Area

    Lakes and rivers: 131,840 acres

Zoo

    Jacksonville Zoo

Places Rated Rank: 36

Jacksonville, NC

Golf Courses: 8

    Daily fee (90 holes)
    Private (54 holes)

Movie Theatres: 16 screens

    1 multiplex

Recreation Areas: 892 acres

State
    Hammocks Beach SP

Water Area

    Lakes and rivers: 33,920 acres
    Atlantic offshore: 5,632 acres

Places Rated Rank: 279

Janesville, WI

Golf Courses: 13

    Daily fee (153 holes)
    Municipal (45 holes)
    Private (36 holes)

Movie Theatres: 29 screens

    3 multiplexes

Professional Sports: 71 games

    Snappers (Class A Baseball)

Ski Areas: 25,785 lift capacity/hr

Water Area

    Lakes and rivers: 3,840 acres

Places Rated Rank: 335

Jefferson City, MO

Golf Courses: 8

    Daily fee (81 holes)
    Municipal (18 holes)
    Private (45 holes)

Movie Theatres: 6 screens

    1 single/twin
    1 multiplex

Recreation Areas: 15,902 acres

Federal
    Big Muddy NFWR
    Mark Twain NF
State
    Katy Trail SP

Water Area

    Lakes and rivers: 16,000 acres

Places Rated Rank: 313

Johnson City, TN

College Sports: 60 games

    East Tennessee State Buccaneers

Golf Courses: 6

    Municipal (54 holes)
    Private (54 holes)

Movie Theatres: 14 screens

    1 multiplex

Recreation Areas: 160,146 acres

Federal
    Appalachian NT
    Cherokee NF
    Cherokee PU
State
    Roan Mountain SP

Ski Areas: 22,600 lift capacity/hr

Water Area

    Lakes and rivers: 6,400 acres

Places Rated Rank: 219

Johnstown, PA

College Sports: 55 games

    St. Francis Red Flash

Golf Courses: 9

    Daily fee (117 holes)
    Municipal (9 holes)
    Private (36 holes)

Movie Theatres: 11 screens

    1 single/twin
    1 multiplex

Professional Sports: 36 games

    Chiefs (ECHL Hockey)

Recreation Areas: 9,636 acres

Federal
    Johnstown Flood NMem
State
    Laurel Ridge SP
    Prince Gallitzin SP

Ski Areas: 49,700 lift capacity/hr

Water Area

    Lakes and rivers: 3,200 acres

Places Rated Rank: 245

Jonesboro, AR

College Sports: 66 games

    Arkansas State Indians

Golf Courses: 5

    Daily fee (45 holes)
    Private (45 holes)

Movie Theatres: 27 screens

    1 single/twin
    2 multiplexes

Recreation Areas: 113 acres
State
Lake Poinsett SP

Water Area
Lakes and rivers: 5,120 acres

Places Rated Rank: 352

Joplin, MO

Golf Courses: 8
Daily fee (27 holes)
Municipal (63 holes)
Private (54 holes)

Movie Theatres: 28 screens
2 singles/twins
3 multiplexes

Recreation Areas: 212 acres
Federal
George Washington Carver NM
Ozark Cavefish NWR

Water Area
Lakes and rivers: 1,280 acres

Places Rated Rank: 367

Kalamazoo-Portage, MI

Auto Racing
Gingerman

College Sports: 98 games
Western Michigan Broncos

Golf Courses: 27
Daily fee (378 holes)
Municipal (45 holes)
Private (54 holes)

Movie Theatres: 11 screens
3 singles/twins
2 multiplexes

Professional Sports: 20 games
Wings (UHL Hockey)

Recreation Areas: 3,395 acres
State
Fort Custer SRA
Kal-Haven Trail SP
Van Buren SP

Ski Areas: 21,300 lift capacity/hr

Water Area
Lakes and rivers: 19,200 acres
Lake Michigan offshore: 298,880
acres

Zoo
Kalama Zoo Nature Center

Places Rated Rank: 85

Kankakee-Bradley, IL

Golf Courses: 10
Daily fee (135 holes)
Municipal (18 holes)
Private (18 holes)

Movie Theatres: 18 screens
3 multiplexes

Recreation Areas: 3,932 acres
State
Kankakee River SP

Water Area
Lakes and rivers: 2,560 acres

Places Rated Rank: 308

Kansas City, MO-KS

Amusement/Theme Parks
Worlds of Fun

Auto Racing
Kansas Speedway

College Sports: 43 games
University of Missouri Kangaroos

Golf Courses: 80
Daily fee (558 holes)
Municipal (342 holes)
Private (540 holes)

Horse Racing: 30 programs
Woodlands (Thoroughbred)
Movie Theatres: 384 screens
8 singles/twins
34 multiplexes

Professional Sports: 144 games
Blades (AHL Hockey)
Chiefs (NFL Football)
Royals (AL Baseball)
Wizards (MLS Soccer)

Recreation Areas: 12,744 acres
Federal
Big Muddy NFWR
Marais des Cygnes NWR
Swan Lake NWR
State
Hillsdale SP
Wallace SP
Watkins Mill SP
Weston Bend SP

Ski Areas: 1,000 lift capacity/hr

Water Area
Lakes and rivers: 59,520 acres

Zoo
Fleming Park Zoo
Kansas City Zoo
Overland Park Zoo

Places Rated Rank: 88

Kennewick-Richland-Pasco, WA

Golf Courses: 7
Daily fee (54 holes)
Municipal (54 holes)
Private (18 holes)

Movie Theatres: 23 screens
3 multiplexes

Recreation Areas: 7,562 acres
Federal
Umatilla NWR
State
Crow Butte SP
Palouse Falls SP

Pasco/Fish Lake Trail
Potholes SP
Sacajawea SP

Ski Areas: 10,475 lift capacity/hr

Water Area
Lakes and rivers: 51,200 acres

Places Rated Rank: 288

Killeen-Temple-Fort Hood, TX

Golf Courses: 11
Daily fee (54 holes)
Municipal (72 holes)
Private (63 holes)

Movie Theatres: 14 screens
1 multiplex

Recreation Areas: 864 acres
State
Colorado Bend SP
Mother Neff SP

Water Area
Lakes and rivers: 22,400 acres

Places Rated Rank: 355

Kingsport-Bristol-Bristol, TN-VA

Auto Racing
Bristol Motor Speedway

Golf Courses: 16
Daily fee (117 holes)
Municipal (72 holes)
Private (90 holes)

Movie Theatres: 32 screens
3 multiplexes

Recreation Areas: 96,393 acres
Federal
Appalachian NT
Cherokee NF
Jefferson NF
State
Natural Tunnel SP
Warriors Path SP

Water Area
Lakes and rivers: 22,400 acres

Places Rated Rank: 149

Kingston, NY

Golf Courses: 11
Daily fee (153 holes)
Private (36 holes)

Movie Theatres: 12 screens
1 multiplex

Recreation Areas: 12,306 acres
State
Bristol Beach SP
Kenneth Wilson SRA
Minnewaska SP
Woodland Valley SRA

Ski Areas: 73,080 lift capacity/hr

Water Area

Lakes and rivers: 21,760 acres

Zoo

Forsyth Park Zoo

Places Rated Rank: 212

Knoxville, TN

College Sports: 66 games

University of Tennessee Volunteers

Golf Courses: 26

Daily fee (225 holes)
Municipal (72 holes)
Private (162 holes)

Movie Theatres: 104 screens

9 multiplexes

Professional Sports: 99 games

Ice Bears (SPHL Hockey)
Smokies (Class AA Baseball)

Recreation Areas: 103,996 acres

Federal
Appalachian NT
Great Smokey Mountains NP
State
Big Ridge SP
Norris Dam SP

Ski Areas: 6,000 lift capacity/hr

Water Area

Lakes and rivers: 47,360 acres

Zoo

Knoxville Zoo

Places Rated Rank: 61

Kokomo, IN

Auto Racing

Kokomo Speedway

Golf Courses: 7

Daily fee (81 holes)
Municipal (18 holes)
Private (18 holes)

Movie Theatres: 26 screens

1 single/twin
3 multiplexes

Water Area

Lakes and rivers: 640 acres

Places Rated Rank: 359

La Crosse, WI-MN

Golf Courses: 9

Daily fee (99 holes)
Municipal (27 holes)
Private (36 holes)

Movie Theatres: 17 screens

2 multiplexes

Recreation Areas: 26,080 acres

Federal
Upper Mississippi NWR

State
Beaver Creek Valley SP
Great River State Trail
La Crosse River State Trail

Ski Areas: 5,000 lift capacity/hr

Water Area

Lakes and rivers: 23,680 acres

Zoo

Myrick Park Zoo

Places Rated Rank: 137

Lafayette, IN

Amusement/Theme Parks

Columbian Park

College Sports: 66 games

Purdue University Boilermakers

Golf Courses: 11

Daily fee (162 holes)
Municipal (18 holes)
Private (9 holes)

Movie Theatres: 16 screens

1 single/twin
2 multiplexes

Water Area

Lakes and rivers: 3,840 acres

Zoo

Columbian Park Zoo

Places Rated Rank: 344

Lafayette, LA

College Sports: 66 games

University of Louisiana Ragin' Cajuns

Golf Courses: 8

Daily fee (45 holes)
Municipal (36 holes)
Private (54 holes)

Horse Racing: 87 programs

Evangeline Downs (Thoroughbred)

Movie Theatres: 60 screens

6 multiplexes

Recreation Areas: 2,128 acres

Federal
Atchafalaya NWR
State
Atchafalaya Wilderness Centre

Water Area

Lakes and rivers: 49,280 acres

Places Rated Rank: 169

Lake Charles, LA

College Sports: 60 games

McNeese State Cowboys

Golf Courses: 7

Daily fee (72 holes)
Municipal (36 holes)
Private (18 holes)

Horse Racing: 80 programs

Delta Downs (Thoroughbred)

Movie Theatres: 27 screens

3 multiplexes

Recreation Areas: 183,871 acres

Federal
Cameron Prairie NWR
Lacassine NWR
Sabine NWR
State
Sam Houston Jones SP

Water Area

Lakes and rivers: 231,680 acres

Places Rated Rank: 45

Lake County-Kenosha County, IL-WI

Amusement/Theme Parks

Six Flags Great America

Golf Courses: 63

Daily fee (333 holes)
Municipal (342 holes)
Private (459 holes)

Movie Theatres: 177 screens

3 singles/twins
14 multiplexes

Professional Sports: 71 games

Captains (Class A Baseball)

Recreation Areas: 13,556 acres

State
Bong SRA
Chain O' Lakes SP
Illinois Beach SP

Ski Areas: 31,385 lift capacity/hr

Water Area

Lakes and rivers: 17,920 acres
Lake Michigan offshore: 878,720 acres

Places Rated Rank: 43

Lakeland, FL

Amusement/Theme Parks

Cypress Gardens Adventure Park

Golf Courses: 38

Daily fee (504 holes)
Municipal (63 holes)
Private (108 holes)

Movie Theatres: 78 screens

3 singles/twins
7 multiplexes

Professional Sports: 71 games

Tigers (Class A Baseball)

Recreation Areas: 12,194 acres

Federal
Lake Wales Ridge NWR
State
Broussard Catfish Creek Preserve SP
Lake Arbuckle SP
Lake Kissimmee SP

Water Area

Lakes and rivers: 86,400 acres

Places Rated Rank: 104

_____

Lancaster, PA

Amusement/Theme Parks

Dutch Wonderland

Golf Courses: 15

Daily fee (144 holes)
Municipal (36 holes)
Private (81 holes)

Movie Theatres: 22 screens

2 multiplexes

Recreation Areas: 224 acres

State

Susquehannock SP

Ski Areas: 15,800 lift capacity/hr

Water Area

Lakes and rivers: 22,400 acres

Places Rated Rank: 317

_____

Lansing-East Lansing, MI

College Sports: 98 games

Michigan State Spartans

Golf Courses: 31

Daily fee (477 holes)
Municipal (36 holes)
Private (45 holes)

Movie Theatres: 53 screens

4 singles/twins
4 multiplexes

Professional Sports: 71 games

Lugnuts (Class A Baseball)

Recreation Areas: 2,682 acres

State

Lakelands Trail SP
Sleepy Hollow SP

Ski Areas: 17,200 lift capacity/hr

Water Area

Lakes and rivers: 5,120 acres

Zoo

Potter Park Zoo

Places Rated Rank: 285

_____

Laredo, TX

Golf Courses: 2

Municipal (18 holes)
Private (18 holes)

Movie Theatres: 22 screens

2 multiplexes

Recreation Areas: 742 acres

State

Lake Casa Blanca SRA

Water Area

Lakes and rivers: 12,160 acres

Places Rated Rank: 374

Las Cruces, NM

College Sports: 54 games

New Mexico State Aggies

Golf Courses: 8

Daily fee (63 holes)
Private (81 holes)

Horse Racing: 87 programs

Sunland Park (Thoroughbred)

Movie Theatres: 20 screens

3 multiplexes

Recreation Areas: 52,780 acres

Federal

San Andres NWR
White Sands NM

Water Area

Lakes and rivers: 4,480 acres

Places Rated Rank: 325

_____

✓Las Vegas-Paradise, NV

Amusement/Theme Parks

Adventuredome
Stratosphere Tower

Auto Racing

Las Vegas Motor Speedway
Ramada Express International

College Sports: 78 games

University of Nevada Rebels

Golf Courses: 61

Daily fee (711 holes)
Municipal (135 holes)
Private (243 holes)

Movie Theatres: 216 screens

17 multiplexes
Professional Sports: 94 games
51s (Triple A Baseball)
Wranglers (ECHL Hockey)

Recreation Areas: 1,775,392 acres

Federal

Desert NWR
Lake Mead NRA
Moapa Valley NWR
Toiyabe NF
Toiyabe Special Area

State

Floyd Lamb SP
Spring Mountain Ranch SP
Valley of Fire SP

Ski Areas: 71,890 lift capacity/hr

Water Area

Lakes and rivers: 115,200 acres

Zoo

Las Vegas Zoological Park

Places Rated Rank: 22

_____

Lawrence, KS

College Sports: 66 games

University of Kansas Jayhawks

Golf Courses: 5

Daily fee (45 holes)
Municipal (18 holes)
Private (18 holes)

Movie Theatres: 14 screens

1 single/twin
1 multiplex

Recreation Areas: 1,425 acres

State

Clinton SP

Water Area

Lakes and rivers: 11,520 acres

Places Rated Rank: 229

_____

Lawton, OK

Golf Courses: 6

Daily fee (27 holes)
Municipal (18 holes)
Private (54 holes)

Movie Theatres: 28 screens

3 multiplexes

Recreation Areas: 59,019 acres

Federal

Wichita Mountains NWR

Water Area

Lakes and rivers: 8,960 acres

Places Rated Rank: 200

_____

Lebanon, PA

Golf Courses: 9

Daily fee (126 holes)
Municipal (9 holes)
Private (18 holes)

Movie Theatres: 12 screens

1 multiplex

Recreation Areas: 2,085 acres

Federal

Appalachian NT

State

Memorial Lake SP
Swatara SP

Ski Areas: 5,400 lift capacity/hr

Water Area

Lakes and rivers: 640 acres

Places Rated Rank: 347

_____

Lewiston-Auburn, ME

Golf Courses: 5

Daily fee (27 holes)
Municipal (18 holes)
Private (36 holes)

Movie Theatres: 30 screens

3 multiplexes

Recreation Areas: 740 acres

State

Range Ponds SP

Ski Areas: 75,405 lift capacity/hr

Water Area
Lakes and rivers: 17,280 acres

Places Rated Rank: 271

Lewiston, ID-WA

Golf Courses: 9
Daily fee (135 holes)
Private (18 holes)

Movie Theatres: 15 screens
2 multiplexes

Recreation Areas: 60,516 acres
Federal
Clearwater NF
Umatilla NF
Wallowa NF
State
Chief Timothy SP
Fields Spring SP
Hells Gate SP

Ski Areas: 1,750 lift capacity/hr

Water Area
Lakes and rivers: 7,680 acres

Places Rated Rank: 227

Lexington-Fayette, KY

College Sports: 78 games
University of Kentucky Wildcats

Golf Courses: 29
Daily fee (234 holes)
Municipal (81 holes)
Private (207 holes)

Horse Racing: 58 programs
Keeneland (Thoroughbred)
The Red Mile (Harness)

Movie Theatres: 99 screens
2 singles/twins
10 multiplexes

Professional Sports: 71 games
Legends (Class A Baseball)

Water Area
Lakes and rivers: 2,560 acres

Places Rated Rank: 334

Lima, OH

Auto Racing
Limaland Motorsports Park

Golf Courses: 9
Daily fee (126 holes)
Private (36 holes)

Movie Theatres: 10 screens
2 multiplexes

Water Area
Lakes and rivers: 1,280 acres

Places Rated Rank: 363

Lincoln, NE

College Sports: 66 games
University of Nebraska Cornhuskers

Golf Courses: 14
Daily fee (99 holes)
Municipal (72 holes)
Private (81 holes)

Movie Theatres: 41 screens
5 multiplexes

Recreation Areas: 5,822 acres
State
Blue River SRA
Bluestem SRA
Branched Oak SRA
Conestoga SRA
Olive Creek SRA
Pawnee SRA
Stagecoach SRA
Wagon Train SRA

Water Area
Lakes and rivers: 5,760 acres

Zoo
Folsom Children's Zoo

Places Rated Rank: 276

Little Rock-North Little Rock, AR

Amusement/Theme Parks
Wild River Country

College Sports: 60 games
University of Arkansas Trojans

Golf Courses: 34
Daily fee (243 holes)
Municipal (99 holes)
Private (261 holes)

Movie Theatres: 103 screens
11 multiplexes

Professional Sports: 71 games
Arkansas Travelers (Class AA Baseball)

Recreation Areas: 160,323 acres
Federal
Ouachita NF
State
Pinnacle Mountain SP
Wooly Hollow SP

Water Area
Lakes and rivers: 69,120 acres

Zoo
Little Rock Zoo

Places Rated Rank: 75

Logan, UT-ID

College Sports: 49 games
Utah State University Aggies

Golf Courses: 5
Daily fee (27 holes)
Municipal (36 holes)
Private (18 holes)

Movie Theatres: 20 screens
1 single/twin
4 multiplexes

Recreation Areas: 818,876 acres
Federal
Cache NF
Caribou NF
State
Hyrum Lake SP

Ski Areas: 29,355 lift capacity/hr

Water Area
Lakes and rivers: 7,680 acres

Zoo
Willow Park Zoo

Places Rated Rank: 148

Longview, TX

Golf Courses: 10
Daily fee (108 holes)
Municipal (9 holes)
Private (54 holes)

Movie Theatres: 46 screens
6 multiplexes

Recreation Areas: 287 acres
State
Martin Creek Lake SRA

Water Area
Lakes and rivers: 14,080 acres

Places Rated Rank: 322

Longview, WA

Golf Courses: 4
Daily fee (36 holes)
Municipal (18 holes)
Private (18 holes)

Movie Theatres: 9 screens
2 multiplexes

Recreation Areas: 35,012 acres
Federal
Gifford Pinchot NF
State
Seaquest SP

Water Area
Lakes and rivers: 17,920 acres

Places Rated Rank: 221

✓Los Angeles-Long Beach, CA

Amusement/Theme Parks
Raging Waters
Six Flags Hurricane Harbor
Six Flags Magic Mountain

Aquariums
Universal Studios Hollywood
Aquarium of the Pacific
Cabrillo Marine Aquarium

Auto Racing
Barona Speedway
Irwindale Speedway
Long Beach Grand Prix

College Sports: 408 games
Cal State, Northridge Matadors

Long Beach State 49ers
Loyola Marymount Lions
Pepperdine Waves
UCLA Bruins
USC Trojans

Golf Courses: 77

Daily fee (243 holes)
Municipal (567 holes)
Private (576 holes)

Horse Racing: 162 programs

Fairplex Park (Thoroughbred)
Hollywood Park (Thoroughbred)
Santa Anita (Thoroughbred)

Movie Theatres: 998 screens

48 singles/twins
93 multiplexes

Professional Sports: 345 games

Clippers (NBA Basketball)
Dodgers (NL Baseball)
Galaxy (MLS Soccer)
Ice Dogs (AHL Hockey)
Ice Dogs (ECHL Hockey)
JetHawks (Class A Baseball)
Lakers (NBA Basketball)
Los Angeles Kings (NHL Hockey)
Sparks (WNBA Basketball)

Recreation Areas: 1,385,726 acres
Federal
Angeles NF
Angeles OTH
Los Padres NF
Santa Monica Mountains NRA
State
Antelope Valley Poppy SR
Castaic Lake SRA
Dan Blocker Beach
Dockweiler SB
Hungry Valley SVRA
Kenneth Hahn SRA
Las Tunas SB
Leo Carrillo SB
Malibu Creek SP
Malibu Lagoon SB
Manhattan SB
Placerita Canyon SP
Point Dume SB
Redondo SB
Robert H. Meyer Memorial SB
Royal Palms SB
Saddleback Butte SP
Santa Monica SB
Santa Susana Mountains
Topanga SB
Topanga SP
Will Rogers SB

Ski Areas: 82,290 lift capacity/hr

Water Area

Lakes and rivers: 28,160 acres
Pacific offshore: 42,472 acres

Zoo

Parnell Park Zoo
The Los Angeles Zoo

Places Rated Rank: 28

Louisville-Jefferson County, KY-IN

Amusement/Theme Parks

Six Flags Kentucky Kingdom

Auto Racing

Salem Speedway

College Sports: 78 games

University of Louisville Cardinals

Golf Courses: 58

Daily fee (468 holes)
Municipal (189 holes)
Private (378 holes)

Horse Racing: 27 programs

Churchill Downs (Thoroughbred)

Movie Theatres: 141 screens

4 singles/twins
12 multiplexes

Professional Sports: 58 games

Bats (Triple A Baseball)

Recreation Areas: 8,310 acres
State
Charlestown SP
Dream Lake SRA
Sawyer SP
Taylorsville Lake SP
Wyandotte Woods SRA

Ski Areas: 11,200 lift capacity/hr

Water Area

Lakes and rivers: 37,760 acres

Zoo

Louisville Zoological Gardens

Places Rated Rank: 81

Lubbock, TX

Amusement/Theme Parks

McKenzie Park/Joyland

College Sports: 66 games

Texas Tech Red Raiders

Golf Courses: 11

Daily fee (99 holes)
Municipal (45 holes)
Private (54 holes)

Movie Theatres: 33 screens

2 multiplexes

Water Area

Lakes and rivers: 1,920 acres

Places Rated Rank: 365

Lynchburg, VA

College Sports: 72 games

Liberty University Flames

Golf Courses: 14

Daily fee (171 holes)
Private (72 holes)

Movie Theatres: 22 screens

3 multiplexes

Professional Sports: 71 games

Hillcats (Class A Baseball)

Recreation Areas: 107,622 acres
Federal
Appalachian NT
Blue Ridge Parkway
George Washington NF
Jefferson NF
State
Holliday Lake SP
Smith Mountain Lake SP

Ski Areas: 9,200 lift capacity/hr

Water Area

Lakes and rivers: 14,720 acres

Places Rated Rank: 166

Macon, GA

College Sports: 72 games

Mercer University Bears

Golf Courses: 10

Daily fee (72 holes)
Municipal (36 holes)
Private (72 holes)

Movie Theatres: 41 screens

1 single/twin
3 multiplexes

Professional Sports: 71 games

Braves (Class A Baseball)

Recreation Areas: 52,199 acres
Federal
Bond Swamp NWR
Ocmulgee NM
Oconee NF
Piedmont NWR
State
High Falls SP

Water Area

Lakes and rivers: 8,320 acres

Places Rated Rank: 211

Madera, CA

Auto Racing

Madera Speedway

Golf Courses: 5

Daily fee (54 holes)
Municipal (18 holes)
Private (18 holes)

Movie Theatres: 13 screens

1 single/twin
2 multiplexes

Recreation Areas: 908,720 acres
Federal
Devils Postpile NM
Inyo NF
San Joaquin EA
Sierra NF
Yosemite NP
State
Millerton Lake SRA

Ski Areas: 98,942 lift capacity/hr

Water Area

Lakes and rivers: 9,600 acres

Places Rated Rank: 204

Madison, WI

Amusement/Theme Parks

Bay of Dreams
Family Land
Noah's Ark Waterpark
Riverview Park and Waterworld
Tommy Bartlett Exploratory

Auto Racing

Angell Park Speedway
Madison International Speedway

College Sports: 81 games

University of Wisconsin Badgers

Golf Courses: 36

Daily fee (414 holes)
Municipal (99 holes)
Private (126 holes)

Movie Theatres: 61 screens

1 single/twin
5 multiplexes

Recreation Areas: 7,810 acres
State

Blackhawk Lake SRA
Blue Mound SP
Blue Mounds SP
Cross Plains Ice Age SP
Governor Dodge SP
Governor Nelson SP
Lake Kegonsa SP
Military Ridge State Trail

Ski Areas: 40,150 lift capacity/hr

Water Area

Lakes and rivers: 40,320 acres

Zoo

Henry Vilas Zoo

Places Rated Rank: 107

Manchester-Nashua, NH

Golf Courses: 15

Daily fee (189 holes)
Municipal (18 holes)
Private (54 holes)

Movie Theatres: 28 screens

3 multiplexes

Professional Sports: 107 games

Fisher Cats (Class AA Baseball)
Monarchs (AHL Hockey)

Recreation Areas: 1,176 acres
State

Binney Pond SNA
Bradford Pines SNA
Clough SP
Curtiss Dogwood SNA
Greenfield SP
Jeremy Hill SNA
Miller SP
Silver Lake SP

Ski Areas: 61,125 lift capacity/hr

Water Area

Lakes and rivers: 10,240 acres

Places Rated Rank: 329

Mansfield, OH

Auto Racing

Mansfield Motorsports Speedway
Mid-Ohio Sports Car Course

Golf Courses: 9

Daily fee (117 holes)
Private (36 holes)

Movie Theatres: 28 screens

3 multiplexes

Recreation Areas: 133 acres
State

Fowler Woods SNA

Ski Areas: 15,050 lift capacity/hr

Water Area

Lakes and rivers: 1,920 acres

Places Rated Rank: 323

McAllen-Edinburg-Mission, TX

College Sports: 48 games

UT, Pan American Broncs

Golf Courses: 14

Daily fee (135 holes)
Municipal (72 holes)
Private (45 holes)

Movie Theatres: 78 screens

6 multiplexes

Recreation Areas: 24,855 acres
Federal

Lower Rio Grande Valley NWR
Santa Ana NWR
State

Bentsen-Rio Grande Valley SP

Water Area

Lakes and rivers: 8,960 acres

Places Rated Rank: 300

Medford, OR

Golf Courses: 6

Daily fee (72 holes)
Municipal (9 holes)
Private (27 holes)

Movie Theatres: 32 screens

4 multiplexes

Recreation Areas: 1,347,917 acres
Federal

Crater Lake NP
Klamath NF
Rogue River NF
Umpqua NF
State

Ben Hur Lampman State Wayside
Casey SP
Joseph Stewart SP

Prospect State Wayside
Tou Velle SP
Tubb Springs State Wayside
Vally of the Rogue SP

Ski Areas: 17,950 lift capacity/hr

Water Area

Lakes and rivers: 10,880 acres

Places Rated Rank: 215

Memphis, TN-MS-AR

Amusement/Theme Parks

Libertyland
Mud Island River Park

Auto Racing

Memphis Motorsports Park

College Sports: 78 games

University of Memphis Tigers

Golf Courses: 42

Daily fee (270 holes)
Municipal (126 holes)
Private (360 holes)

Movie Theatres: 182 screens

17 multiplexes

Professional Sports: 41 games

Grizzlies (NBA Basketball)

Recreation Areas: 44,614 acres
Federal

Holly Springs NF
Lower Hatchie NWR
Wapanocca NWR
State

Meeman-Shelby Forest SP
T.O. Fuller SP
Wall Doxey SP

Water Area

Lakes and rivers: 80,640 acres

Zoo

Memphis Zoo

Places Rated Rank: 63

Merced, CA

Golf Courses: 4

Daily fee (45 holes)
Private (18 holes)

Movie Theatres: 46 screens

2 singles/twins
6 multiplexes

Recreation Areas: 72,711 acres
Federal

Grasslands WMA
Kesterson NWR
Merced NWR
San Luis NWR
State

George J. Hatfield SRA
Great Valley Grasslands SP
McConnell SRA
San Luis Reservoir SRA

Ski Areas: 26,942 lift capacity/hr

Water Area

Lakes and rivers: 27,520 acres

Zoo

Applegate Park Zoo

Places Rated Rank: 185

Miami-Miami Beach-Kendall, FL

Aquarium

Miami Seaquarium

Auto Racing

Homestead Miami Speedway

College Sports: 144 games

Florida International Golden Panthers
University of Miami Hurricanes

Golf Courses: 33

Daily fee (297 holes)
Municipal (162 holes)
Private (135 holes)

Horse Racing: 126 programs

Calder Race Course (Thoroughbred)

Movie Theatres: 268 screens

4 singles/twins
19 multiplexes

Professional Sports: 156 games

Dolphins (NFL Football)
Florida Pit Bulls (CBA Basketball)
Heat (NBA Basketball)
Marlins (NL Baseball)

Recreation Areas: 1,258 acres
State
Cape Florida SRA
Oleta River SRA

Water Area

Lakes and rivers: 49,280 acres
Atlantic offshore: 128,000 acres

Zoo

Metro Zoo-Crandon Park

Places Rated Rank: 142

Michigan City-La Porte, IN

Golf Courses: 6

Daily fee (27 holes)
Municipal (36 holes)
Private (36 holes)

Movie Theatres: 4 screens

1 multiplex

Recreation Areas: 643 acres
Federal
Indiana Dunes N Lakeshore

Ski Areas: 3,500 lift capacity/hr

Water Area

Lakes and rivers: 5,760 acres
Lake Michigan offshore: 3,200 acres

Zoo

Washington Park Zoo

Places Rated Rank: 310

Midland, TX

Golf Courses: 7

Daily fee (36 holes)
Municipal (36 holes)
Private (45 holes)

Movie Theatres: 4 screens

1 multiplex

Professional Sports: 71 games

Rock Hounds (Class AA Baseball)

Water Area

Lakes and rivers: 1,280 acres

Places Rated Rank: 376

Milwaukee-Waukesha-West Allis, WI

Auto Racing

The Milwaukee Mile

College Sports: 127 games

Marquette University Golden Eagles
University of Wisconsin Panthers

Golf Courses: 66

Daily fee (612 holes)
Municipal (243 holes)
Private (324 holes)

Movie Theatres: 180 screens

2 singles/twins
16 multiplexes

Professional Sports: 203 games

Admirals (AHL Hockey)
Brewers (NL Baseball)
Bucks (NBA Basketball)
Packers (NFL Football)

Recreation Areas: 1,689 acres
State
Glacial Drumlin State Trail
Harrington Beach SP
Pike Lake SP

Ski Areas: 45,485 lift capacity/hr

Water Area

Lakes and rivers: 21,120 acres
Lake Michigan offshore: 1,170,560 acres

Zoo

Milwaukee County Zoo

Places Rated Rank: 62

✓ Minneapolis-St. Paul, MN-WI

Amusement/Theme Parks

Camp Snoopy
Mall of America
Valleyfair

College Sports: 106 games

University of Minnesota Golden Gophers

Golf Courses: 152

Daily fee (1,575 holes)
Municipal (549 holes)
Private (612 holes)

Horse Racing: 68 programs

Canterbury Park (Thoroughbred)

Movie Theatres: 533 screens

17 singles/twins
48 multiplexes

Professional Sports: 149 games

Lynx (WNBA Basketball)
Timberwolves (NBA Basketball)
Twins (AL Baseball)
Vikings (NFL Football)

Recreation Areas: 63,128 acres
Federal
Lower Saint Croix NS River
Minnesota Valley NWR
Mississippi NSRiver
Mississippi River NRA
Saint Croix NS River
Sherburne NWR
State
Afton SP
Fort Snelling SP
Interstate SP
Kinnickinnic SP
Lake Maria SP
Wild River SP
William O'Brien SP
Willow River SP

Ski Areas: 73,600 lift capacity/hr

Water Area

Lakes and rivers: 192,000 acres

Zoo

Como Zoo
Minnesota Zoo

Places Rated Rank: 7

Missoula, MT

College Sports: 43 games

University of Montana Grizzlies

Golf Courses: 6

Daily fee (63 holes)
Municipal (27 holes)
Private (18 holes)

Movie Theatres: 19 screens

3 multiplexes

Recreation Areas: 2,102,856 acres
Federal
Aerial Fire Depot OTH
Bitterroot NF
Flathead NF
Lolo NF
State
Beavertail Hill SP
Frenchtown Pond SP
Placid Lake SP
Salmon Lake SP

Ski Areas: 14,930 lift capacity/hr

Water Area

Lakes and rivers: 12,800 acres

Places Rated Rank: 136

Mobile, AL

College Sports: 60 games
University of South Alabama Jaguars

Golf Courses: 11
Daily fee (54 holes)
Municipal (99 holes)
Private (36 holes)

Movie Theatres: 59 screens
4 multiplexes

Professional Sports: 71 games
BayBears (Class AA Baseball)

Recreation Areas: 1,691 acres
Federal
Bon Secour NWR
Grand Bay NWR

Water Area
Lakes and rivers: 24,320 acres
Gulf offshore: 181,760 acres

Places Rated Rank: 183

Modesto, CA

Golf Courses: 8
Daily fee (36 holes)
Municipal (45 holes)
Private (63 holes)

Movie Theatres: 69 screens
2 singles/twins
5 multiplexes

Professional Sports: 71 games
Nuts (Class A Baseball)

Recreation Areas: 29,216 acres
Federal
San Joaquin River NWR
State
Henry W. Coe SP
Turlock Lake SRA

Ski Areas: 17,700 lift capacity/hr

Water Area
Lakes and rivers: 12,800 acres

Places Rated Rank: 258

Monroe, LA

College Sports: 66 games
University of Louisiana Indians

Golf Courses: 8
Daily fee (54 holes)
Municipal (36 holes)
Private (45 holes)

Movie Theatres: 27 screens
2 multiplexes

Recreation Areas: 39,610 acres
Federal
D'Arbonne NWR
Upper Ouachita NWR
State
Lake D'Arbonne SP

Water Area
Lakes and rivers: 32,000 acres

Zoo
Louisiana Purchase Zoo

Places Rated Rank: 133

Monroe, MI

Golf Courses: 24
Daily fee (405 holes)
Private (18 holes)

Movie Theatres: 11 screens
2 multiplexes

Recreation Areas: 1,000 acres
State
Sterling SP

Water Area
Lakes and rivers: 8,960 acres
Lake Erie offshore: 73,600 acres

Places Rated Rank: 210

Montgomery, AL

College Sports: 60 games
Alabama State Hornets

Golf Courses: 19
Daily fee (162 holes)
Municipal (36 holes)
Private (144 holes)

Movie Theatres: 47 screens
1 single/twin
4 multiplexes

Professional Sports: 71 games
Biscuits (Class AA Baseball)

Water Area
Lakes and rivers: 39,040 acres
Gulf offshore: 181,760 acres

Zoo
Montgomery Zoo

Places Rated Rank: 292

Morgantown, WV

College Sports: 78 games
West Virginia Mountaineers

Golf Courses: 9
Daily fee (126 holes)
Private (27 holes)

Movie Theatres: 24 screens
2 multiplexes

Recreation Areas: 4,029 acres
Federal
Monongahela NF
State
Cathedral SP

Ski Areas: 25,700 lift capacity/hr

Water Area
Lakes and rivers: 5,120 acres

Places Rated Rank: 277

Morristown, TN

Golf Courses: 9
Daily fee (153 holes)

Movie Theatres: 9 screens
1 multiplex

Recreation Areas: 1,440 acres
State
Panther Creek SP

Ski Areas: 6,000 lift capacity/hr

Water Area
Lakes and rivers: 49,920 acres

Places Rated Rank: 201

Mount Vernon-Anacortes, WA

Auto Racing
Skagit Speedway

Golf Courses: 5
Daily fee (72 holes)
Private (18 holes)

Movie Theatres: 14 screens
1 multiplex

Recreation Areas: 545,131 acres
Federal
Brazier PU
Golden Phoenix PU
Illabot Creek PU
Mt. Baker NF
North Cascades NP
Ross Lake NRA
San Juan Islands NWR
Skagit PU
State
Bay View SP
Burrows Island SP
Cascade Island
Cone Island SP
Deception Pass SP
Everett Property
Heart Lake SP
Huckleberry Island SP
Larrabee SP
Northwest Region
O'Brien-Riggs SP
Rasar SP
Rockport SP
Saddlebag Island SP
Skagit River SP

Ski Areas: 22,500 lift capacity/hr

Water Area
Lakes and rivers: 25,600 acres
Pacific offshore: 92,800 acres

Places Rated Rank: 42

Muncie, IN

College Sports: 66 games
Ball State Cardinals

Golf Courses: 8
Daily fee (108 holes)
Private (36 holes)

Movie Theatres: 21 screens
1 single/twin
2 multiplexes

Water Area
Lakes and rivers: 1,920 acres

Places Rated Rank: 342

────────────

✓**Muskegon-Norton Shores, MI**

Amusement/Theme Parks
Michigan's Adventure

Golf Courses: 16
Daily fee (243 holes)
Private (36 holes)

Horse Racing: 118 programs
Great Lakes Downs (Thoroughbred)

Movie Theatres: 27 screens
2 singles/twins
3 multiplexes

Professional Sports: 44 games
Fury (UHL Hockey)
Michigan Mayhem (CBA Basketball)

Recreation Areas: 15,162 acres
Federal
Manistee NF
State
Duck Lake SP
Muskegon SP
P.J. Hoffmaster SP

Ski Areas: 15,600 lift capacity/hr

Water Area
Lakes and rivers: 11,520 acres
Lake Michigan offshore: 596,480 acres

Places Rated Rank: 33

────────────

Myrtle Beach-Conway Beach, SC

Amusement/Theme Parks
Alligator Adventure
Barefoot Landing
Broadway At The Beach
Family Kingdom Amusement Park
Myrtle Waves Water Park
NASCAR Speedpark
North Myrtle Beach Grand Prix
Pavilion Amusement Park

Aquarium
Ripleys Aquarium

College Sports: 72 games
Coastal Carolina Chanticleers

Golf Courses: 72
Daily fee (1,197 holes)
Municipal (18 holes)
Private (72 holes)

Movie Theatres: 42 screens
3 multiplexes

Professional Sports: 71 games
Pelicans (Class A Baseball)

Recreation Areas: 312 acres
State
Myrtle Beach SP

Water Area
Lakes and rivers: 7,680 acres
Atlantic offshore: 6,976 acres

Places Rated Rank: 217

────────────

Napa, CA

Golf Courses: 8
Daily fee (54 holes)
Municipal (27 holes)
Private (54 holes)

Movie Theatres: 9 screens
1 single/twin
1 multiplex

Recreation Areas: 3,840 acres
State
Bothe-Napa Valley SP
Robert Louis Stevenson SP
Sugarloaf Ridge SP

Water Area
Lakes and rivers: 21,760 acres

Places Rated Rank: 265

────────────

Naples-Marco Island, FL

Golf Courses: 73
Daily fee (216 holes)
Private (1,098 holes)

Movie Theatres: 38 screens
1 single/twin
4 multiplexes

Recreation Areas: 643,499 acres
Federal
Big Cypress Addition
Big Cypress N Preserve
Everglades NP
Florida Panther NWR
State
Collier-Seminole SP
Delnor-Wiggins Pass SP
Fakahatchee Strand Preserve SP

Water Area
Lakes and rivers: 58,240 acres
Gulf offshore: 12,096 acres

Zoo
Naples Zoo

Places Rated Rank: 79

────────────

Nashville-Davidson, TN

Amusement/Theme Parks
Nashville Shores
Travellers Rest Plantation
Trinity Music City
Wave Country

Auto Racing
Nashville Superspeedway

College Sports: 319 games
Belmont Bruins
Lipscomb Bisons

Middle Tennessee State Blue Raiders
Tennessee State Tigers
Vanderbilt Commodores

Golf Courses: 51
Daily fee (342 holes)
Municipal (207 holes)
Private (369 holes)

Movie Theatres: 167 screens
1 single/twin
12 multiplexes

Professional Sports: 109 games
Predators (NHL Hockey)
Sounds (Triple A Baseball)
Titans (NFL Football)

Recreation Areas: 11,630 acres
Federal
Natchez Trace NT
Natchez Trace Parkway
State
Bledsoe Creek SP
Cedars of Lebanon SP
Long Hunter SP
Montgomery Bell SP
Radnor Lake SNA

Water Area
Lakes and rivers: 48,000 acres

Zoo
Nashville Zoo

Places Rated Rank: 120

────────────

Nassau-Suffolk, NY

College Sports: 237 games
Adelphi Panthers
Hofstra Flying Dutchmen
New York Tech Bears
Stony Brook University Seawolves

Golf Courses: 114
Daily fee (387 holes)
Municipal (459 holes)
Private (1206 holes)

Horse Racing: 38 programs
Belmont Park (Thoroughbred)

Movie Theatres: 261 screens
1 single/twin
31 multiplexes

Professional Sports: 56 games
Long Island Primetime (USBL Basketball)
New York Islanders (NHL Hockey)

Recreation Areas: 40,952 acres
Federal
Amagansett NWR
Conscience Point NWR
Elizabeth A. Morton NWR
Fire Island Seashore
Oyster Bay NWR
Seatuck NWR
Target Rock NWR
Wertheim NWR
State
Belmont Lake SP
Bethpage SP

Brookhaven SP
Caleb Smith SP
Cannetoquot River SP
Captree SP
Caumsett SP
Connetquot River SP
Heckscher SP
Hempstead Lake SP
Hither Hills SP
Jones Beach SP
Massapequa SP
Montauk Downs SP
Montauk Point SP
Orient Beach SP
Robert Moses SP
Sunken Meadow SP
Valley Stream SP
Wildwood SP

Water Area
Lakes and rivers: 185,600 acres
Atlantic offshore: 570,240 acres

Places Rated Rank: 60

Newark-Union, NJ-PA

Amusement/Theme Parks
Mountain Creek
Wild West City

Auto Racing
New Jersey Motorsports Park

College Sports: 84 games
New Jersey Tech Highlanders
Seton Hall Pirates

Golf Courses: 74
Daily fee (360 holes)
Municipal (252 holes)
Private (711 holes)

Movie Theatres: 136 screens
2 singles/twins
16 multiplexes

Recreation Areas: 95,436 acres
Federal
Appalachian NT
Delaware Water Gap NRA
Great Swamp NWR
Upper Delaware NSRiver
Wallkill River NWR
State
Allmuchy SP
Cranberry Lake SP
Farney SP
Great Piece Meadow SP
Hacklebarney SP
High Point SP
Hopatcong SP
Kittatinny Valley
Musconetong SP
Promised Land SP
Round Valley SRA
Spruce Run SRA
Swartswood SP
Troy Meadows SNA
Voorhees SP
Wawayanda SP

Ski Areas: 90,210 lift capacity/hr

Water Area
Lakes and rivers: 38,400 acres

Zoo
Birch Grove Park Zoo
Space Farms Zoo
Turtle Back Zoo

Places Rated Rank: 55

New Haven-Milford, CT

Amusement/Theme Parks
Quassy Amusement Park

College Sports: 248 games
Quinnipiac Bobcats
Yale Bulldogs

Golf Courses: 24
Daily fee (135 holes)
Municipal (90 holes)
Private (207 holes)

Movie Theatres: 115 screens
3 singles/twins
12 multiplexes

Professional Sports: 71 games
Ravens (Class AA Baseball)

Recreation Areas: 8,149 acres
State
George C. Waldo SP
Hammonasset Beach SRA
Kettletown SP
Osbornedale SP
Qunnipiac SP
Silver Sands SP
Sleeping Giant SP
Southford Falls SP
West Peak SP
West Rock Ridge SP
Wharton Brook SP
Whittemore Glen SP

Ski Areas: 27,000 lift capacity/hr

Water Area
Lakes and rivers: 12,800 acres
Atlantic offshore: 151,040 acres

Places Rated Rank: 109

✓New Orleans-Metairie-Kenner, LA

Amusement/Theme Parks
Six Flags New Orleans

Aquarium
Aquarium of the Americas

College Sports: 114 games
Tulane Green Wave
University of New Orleans
Privateers

Golf Courses: 33
Daily fee (279 holes)
Municipal (99 holes)
Private (216 holes)

Horse Racing: 85 programs
Fair Grounds (Thoroughbred)

Movie Theatres: 136 screens
4 singles/twins
12 multiplexes

Professional Sports: 109 games
Hornets (NBA Basketball)
Saints (NFL Football)
Zephyrs (Triple A Baseball)

Recreation Areas: 113,877 acres
Federal
Bayou Sauvage NWR
Big Branch Marsh NWR
Bogue Chitto NWR
Breton NWR
Delta NWR
State
Bayou Segnette SP
Fairview-Riverside SP
Fontainebleau SP
Grand Isle East SP
Grand Isle West SP
Slidell SP
St. Bernard SP

Water Area
Lakes and rivers: 1,166,080 acres
Gulf offshore: 599,680 acres

Zoo
Audubon Zoo

Places Rated Rank: 23

✓New York-White Plains, NY-NJ

Amusement/Theme Parks
Coney Island Beach and Boardwalk
Six Flags Great Adventure
Six Flags Hurricane Harbor

College Sports: 792 games
Columbia University Lions
Fairleigh Dickinson Knights
Fordham Rams
Iona College Gaels
Manhattan College Jaspers
St. Francis College Terriers
St. John's University Red Storm
St. Peter's Peacocks
Wagner College Seahawks

Golf Courses: 112
Daily fee (234 holes)
Municipal (558 holes)
Private (1,215 holes)

Horse Racing: 314 programs
Aqueduct (Thoroughbred)
The Meadowlands (Mixed Meetings)
Yonkers Raceway (Harness)

Movie Theatres: 697 screens
12 singles/twins
77 multiplexes

Professional Sports: 380 games
Giants (NFL Football)
Jets (NFL Football)
Knicks (NBA Basketball)
Liberty (WNBA Basketball)
Mets (NL Baseball)
Nets (NBA Basketball)
New Jersey Devils (NHL Hockey)
New York Red Bulls (MLS Soccer)
Rangers (NHL Hockey)
Yankees (AL Baseball)

Recreation Areas: 75,809 acres

Federal
Appalachian NT
Castle Clinton NM
Federal Hall NM
Gateway NRA
General Grant NM
Hamilton Grange NM
Statue of Liberty NM

State
Appalachian Trail SP
Bayswater Point SP
Bear Mountain/Iona SP
Blauvelt SP
Clarence Fahnestock SP
Clay Pit Pond SP
Franklin D. Roosevelt SP
Greenwood Lake SP
Harriman SP
Haverstraw Beach SP
High Tor SP
Hook Mountain SP
Hudson Highlands SP
Liberty SP
Nyack Beach SP
Old Croton Trailway SP
Palisades Parkway SP
Ringwood SP
Riverbank SP
Roberto Clemente SP
Rockefeller Preserve SP
Rockland Lake SP
Rockwood Hall SP
Tallman Mountain SP
Wawayanda SP

Ski Areas: 31,600 lift capacity/hr

Water Area
Lakes and rivers: 124,160 acres
Atlantic offshore: 48,640 acres

Zoo
Bergen County Zoo
Queens Zoo WCS

Places Rated Rank: 3

Niles-Benton Harbor, MI

Golf Courses: 16
Daily fee (162 holes)
Municipal (18 holes)
Private (108 holes)

Movie Theatres: 25 screens
2 singles/twins
3 multiplexes

Recreation Areas: 3,246 acres
State
Grand Mere SP
Warren Dunes SP
Warren Woods SP

Ski Areas: 19,800 lift capacity/hr

Water Area
Lakes and rivers: 5,760 acres
Lake Michigan offshore: 640,000 acres

Places Rated Rank: 146

Norwich-New London, CT

Aquarium
Mystic Marinelife Aquarium

Auto Racing
Waterford Speedbowl

Golf Courses: 13
Daily fee (117 holes)
Municipal (36 holes)
Private (81 holes)

Movie Theatres: 54 screens
3 singles/twins
7 multiplexes

Professional Sports: 159 games
Defenders (Class AA Baseball)
Navigators (Class AA Baseball)
Sun (WNBA Basketball)

Recreation Areas: 4,808 acres
Beckett Hill SP
Bluff Point Coastal Reserve SP
Day Pond SP
Fort Griswold SP
Fort Shantok SP
Haley Farm SP
Harkness Memorial SP
Hopemead SP
Hopeville Pond SP
Minnie Island SP
Pomeroy SP
Rocky Neck SP
Selden Neck SP
Stoddard Hill SP

Ski Areas: 14,250 lift capacity/hr

Water Area
Lakes and rivers: 23,040 acres
Atlantic offshore: 44,800 acres

Zoo
Mohegan Park Zoo

Places Rated Rank: 161

✓**Oakland-Fremont-Hayward, CA**

Amusement/Theme Parks
Children's Fairyland
Rapids Waterslide

College Sports: 150 games
St. Mary's College Gaels
University of California Golden Bears

Golf Courses: 48
Daily fee (288 holes)
Municipal (243 holes)
Private (333 holes)

Horse Racing: 120 programs
Golden Gate Fields (Thoroughbred)
Pleasanton (Thoroughbred)

Movie Theatres: 289 screens
18 singles/twins
25 multiplexes

Professional Sports: 132 games
Athletics (AL Baseball)
Golden State Warriors (NBA Basketball)
Raiders (NFL Football)

Recreation Areas: 40,916 acres
Federal
Antoich Dunes NWR
San Francisco Bay NWR
State
Bethany Reservoir SRA
Franks Tract SRA
Lake Del Valle SRA
Mount Diablo SP
Robert W. Crown Memorial SB

Water Area
Lakes and rivers: 106,240 acres

Zoo
Knowland Park Zoo
Walnut Creek Zoo

Places Rated Rank: 19

Ocala, FL

Golf Courses: 23
Daily fee (297 holes)
Municipal (45 holes)
Private (72 holes)

Movie Theatres: 25 screens
2 singles/twins
2 multiplexes

Recreation Areas: 282,883 acres
Federal
Ocala NF
State
Lake Rousseau SRA
Rainbow Springs SP
Silver River SP

Water Area
Lakes and rivers: 53,760 acres
Atlantic offshore

Places Rated Rank: 102

Ocean City, NJ

Amusement/Theme Parks
Morey's Piers
Playland
Wonderland Pier

Aquarium
Atlantic City Aquarium

Golf Courses: 8
Daily fee (108 holes)
Private (36 holes)

Movie Theatres: 8 screens
1 multiplex

Recreation Areas: 12,657 acres
Federal
Cape May NWR
State
Cape May Point SP
Cape May Wetlands SNA
Corson's Inlet SP
Great Sound SP
Strathmere SNA

Water Area
Lakes and rivers: 19,200 acres
Atlantic offshore: 110,080 acres

Places Rated Rank: 91

_____

Odessa, TX

Golf Courses: 4
Daily fee (36 holes)
Private (36 holes)

Movie Theatres: 30 screens
3 multiplexes

Water Area
Lakes and rivers: 640 acres

Places Rated Rank: 377

_____

✓Ogden-Clearfield, UT

Amusement/Theme Parks
Lagoon Amusement Park
College Sports: 43 games
Weber State Wildcats

Golf Courses: 19
Daily fee (171 holes)
Municipal (117 holes)
Private (54 holes)

Movie Theatres: 40 screens
3 multiplexes

Recreation Areas: 237,261 acres
Federal
Cache NF
Wasatch NF
State
Antelope Island SP
East Canyon SP
Lost Creek Lake SP
Saltaire Beach SP

Ski Areas: 172,950 lift capacity/hr

Water Area
Lakes and rivers: 265,600 acres

Places Rated Rank: 40

_____

Oklahoma City, OK

Amusement/Theme Parks
Frontier City
White Water Bay

Aquarium
Aquaticus Aquarium

College Sports: 66 games
University of Oklahoma Sooners

Golf Courses: 48
Daily fee (342 holes)
Municipal (243 holes)
Private (270 holes)

Horse Racing: 65 programs
Remington Park (Thoroughbred)

Movie Theatres: 142 screens
12 multiplexes

Professional Sports: 58 games
RedHawks (Triple A Baseball)

Recreation Areas: 2,055 acres
Federal
Oklahoma City NMEM
State
John Miskelley SP
Little River SP
State Capitol Park SP

Water Area
Lakes and rivers: 39,040 acres

Zoo
Oklahoma City Zoo

Places Rated Rank: 186

_____

Olympia, WA

Auto Racing
South Sound Speedway

Golf Courses: 8
Daily fee (81 holes)
Municipal (18 holes)
Private (36 holes)

Movie Theatres: 16 screens
1 multiplex

Recreation Areas: 4,636 acres
Federal
Nisqually NWR
Olympic NF
Snoqualmie NF
State
Elbow Lake SP
Millersylvania Memorial SP
Nisqually
Tolmie SP

Water Area
Lakes and rivers: 30,080 acres
Pacific offshore: 2,180 acres

Places Rated Rank: 234

_____

Omaha-Council Bluffs, NE-IA

Amusement/Theme Parks
Fun Plex Amusement Park

Aquarium
Ak-Sar-Ben Aquarium

Auto Racing
Eagle Raceway
Mid America Motorplex

College Sports: 92 games
Creighton University Bluejays
University of Nebraska Mavericks

Golf Courses: 45
Daily fee (468 holes)
Municipal (153 holes)
Private (189 holes)

Horse Racing: 4 programs
Horsemen's Park (Thoroughbred)

Movie Theatres: 139 screens
4 singles/twins
10 multiplexes

Professional Sports: 94 games
Ak-Sar-Ben Knights (AHL Hockey)
Royals (Triple A Baseball)

Recreation Areas: 11,763 acres
Federal
De Soto NWR
DeSoto NWR
State
Lake Manawa SP
Louisville SRA
Mahoney SP
Memphis SRA
Pioneer SRA
Platte River SP
Schramm Park SRA
Two Rivers SRA
Wilson Island SRA

Ski Areas: 3,100 lift capacity/hr

Water Area
Lakes and rivers: 28,160 acres

Zoo
Henry Doorly Zoo

Places Rated Rank: 78

_____

✓Orlando-Kissimmee, FL

Amusement/Theme Parks
Disney-MGM Studios
Disney's Blizzard Beach
Disney's Typhoon Lagoon
EPCOT Center
Holy Land Experience
Magic Kingdom Park
Seaworld Orlando
Universal Orlando Resort
Universal Studios
Universal's Islands of Adventure
Walt Disney World Resort
Water Mania
Wet 'N Wild

Auto Racing
Orlando Speedworld Speedway
College Sports: 78 games
UCF Golden Knights

Golf Courses: 104
Daily fee (1,449 holes)
Municipal (27 holes)
Private (387 holes)

Movie Theatres: 317 screens
4 singles/twins
25 multiplexes

Professional Sports: 140 games
Cobras (Class A Baseball)
Magic (NBA Basketball)
Seals (SPHL Hockey)

Recreation Areas: 154,049 acres
Federal
Lake Woodruff NWR
Ocala NF
State
Hontoon Island SP
Lake Griffin SP
Lake Louisa SP
Lower Wekiva River SNA
Rock Springs Run State Reserve
Tosohatchee SNA
Wekiwa Springs SP

Water Area

Lakes and rivers: 333,440 acres

Zoo

Central Florida Zoo

Places Rated Rank: 1

Oshkosh-Neenah, WI

Golf Courses: 12

Daily fee (135 holes)
Municipal (18 holes)
Private (54 holes)

Movie Theatres: 12 screens

1 multiplex

Recreation Areas: 54 acres
State
Wiouwash State Trail

Ski Areas: 6,000 lift capacity/hr

Water Area

Lakes and rivers: 89,600 acres

Places Rated Rank: 252

Owensboro, KY

Golf Courses: 7

Daily fee (45 holes)
Municipal (27 holes)
Private (45 holes)

Movie Theatres: 16 screens

1 multiplex

Recreation Areas: 297 acres
State
Hawes SP

Water Area

Lakes and rivers: 16,640 acres

Places Rated Rank: 287

Oxnard-Thousand Oaks-Ventura, CA

Auto Racing

Ventura Raceway

Golf Courses: 27

Daily fee (252 holes)
Municipal (72 holes)
Private (153 holes)

Movie Theatres: 131 screens

5 singles/twins
13 multiplexes

Recreation Areas: 1,146,206 acres
Federal
Angeles NF
Bitter Creek NWR
Channel Islands NP
Hopper Mountain NWR
Los Padres NF
Los Padres OTH
Santa Monica Mountains NRA
State
Emma Wood SB
Hungry Valley SVRA
Leo Carrillo SB
Mandalay SB

McGrath SB
Oxnard SB
Point Mugu SP
San Buenaventura SB

Ski Areas: 12,600 lift capacity/hr

Water Area

Lakes and rivers: 7,680 acres

Places Rated Rank: 191

Palm Bay-Melbourne-Titusville, FL

Golf Courses: 24

Daily fee (180 holes)
Municipal (135 holes)
Private (108 holes)

Movie Theatres: 113 screens

2 singles/twins
9 multiplexes

Professional Sports: 71 games

Brevard County Manatees
(Class A Baseball)

Recreation Areas: 36,427 acres
Federal
Archie Carr NWR
Canaveral N Seashore
St. Johns NWR
State
Indian River Lagoon Preserve SP
Sebastian Inlet SP

Water Area

Lakes and rivers: 176,640 acres
Atlantic offshore: 16,832 acres

Zoo

Brevard Zoo

Places Rated Rank: 59

Panama City-Lynn Haven, FL

Amusement/Theme Parks

Shipwreck Island Waterpark

Golf Courses: 11

Daily fee (144 holes)
Private (54 holes)

Movie Theatres: 35 screens

4 multiplexes

Recreation Areas: 1,450 acres
State
Camp Helen SP
St. Andrews SRA

Water Area

Lakes and rivers: 76,160 acres
Gulf offshore: 9,600 acres

Places Rated Rank: 158

Parkersburg-Marietta, WV-OH

Golf Courses: 11

Daily fee (153 holes)
Private (36 holes)

Movie Theatres: 19 screens

2 multiplexes

Recreation Areas: 39,694 acres
Federal
Ohio River Islands NWR
Wayne NF
Wayne PU
State
Muskingum River Parkway SP

Water Area

Lakes and rivers: 13,440 acres

Places Rated Rank: 213

Pascagoula, MS

Golf Courses: 6

Daily fee (90 holes)
Municipal (18 holes)

Movie Theatres: 21 screens

2 multiplexes

Recreation Areas: 110,369 acres
Federal
De Soto NF
Grand Bay NWR
Gulf Islands N Seashore
Mississippi Sandhill Crane NWR
State
Shepard SP

Water Area

Lakes and rivers: 19,840 acres
Gulf offshore: 130,560 acres

Places Rated Rank: 77

Pensacola-Ferry Pass-Brent, FL

Golf Courses: 16

Daily fee (225 holes)
Municipal (18 holes)
Private (45 holes)

Movie Theatres: 52 screens

6 multiplexes

Professional Sports: 36 games

Ice Pilots (ECHL Hockey)

Recreation Areas: 28,562 acres
Federal
Choctawhatchee NF
Gulf Islands N Seashore
State
Big Lagoon SP
Blackwater River SP
Navarre Beach SP
Perdido Key SRA
Yellow River Marsh Preserve SP

Water Area

Lakes and rivers: 138,880 acres
Gulf offshore: 9,088 acres

Places Rated Rank: 147

Peoria, IL

College Sports: 60 games

Bradley University Braves

Golf Courses: 22

Daily fee (153 holes)
Municipal (126 holes)
Private (108 holes)

Movie Theatres: 92 screens

    3 singles/twins
    8 multiplexes

Professional Sports: 111 games

    Chiefs (Class A Baseball)
    Rivermen (AHL Hockey)

Recreation Areas: 15,541 acres

Federal
    Chautauqua NWR
State
    Mackinaw River State Wildlife Area
    Marshall State Fish and Wildlife
    Powerton Lake State Fish and
    Rock Island Trail SP
    Spring Lake State Fish and Wildlife
    Woodford State Fish and Wildlife

Water Area

    Lakes and rivers: 30,080 acres

Zoo

    Glen Oak Zoo

Places Rated Rank: 87

Philadelphia, PA

Amusement/Theme Parks

    Sesame Place

College Sports: 561 games

    Drexel University Dragons
    La Salle University Explorers
    Philadelphia University Rams
    Saint Joseph's University Hawks
    Temple University Owls
    University of Pennsylvania Quakers
    Villanova University Wildcats

Golf Courses: 119

    Daily fee (720 holes)
    Municipal (252 holes)
    Private (1,161 holes)

Horse Racing: 227 programs

    Philadelphia Park (Thoroughbred)

Movie Theatres: 328 screens

    1 single/twin
    30 multiplexes

Professional Sports: 209 games

    76ers (NBA Basketball)
    Eagles (NFL Football)
    Flyers (NHL Hockey)
    Phantoms (AHL Hockey)
    Phillies (NL Baseball)

Recreation Areas: 19,339 acres

Federal
    John Heinz NWR
    Thaddeus Kosciuszko NM
State
    Benjamin Rush SP
    Delaware Canal SP
    Evansburg SP
    Fort Washington SP
    French Creek SP
    Marsh Creek SP
    Neshaminy SP
    Nockamixon SP
    Ralph Stover SP
    Ridley Creek SP
    Tyler SP
    White Clay Creek SP

Ski Areas: 19,400 lift capacity/hr

Water Area

    Lakes and rivers: 23,680 acres
    Atlantic offshore: 1,560 acres

Zoo

    Elmwood Park Zoo
    Philadelphia Zoo

Places Rated Rank: 73

Phoenix-Mesa-Scottsdale, AZ

Amusement/Theme Parks

    Big Surf
    Goldfield Ghost Town
    Golfland/Sunsplash
    Rawhide Western Town
    Rockin' R Ranch
    Surfside Skateland
    Waterworld Safari

Auto Racing

    Arizona Motorsports Park
    Canyon Raceway
    Firebird International Raceway
    Manzanita Speedway
    Phoenix International Raceway

College Sports: 66 games

    Arizona State Sun Devils

Golf Courses: 177

    Daily fee (1,935 holes)
    Municipal (171 holes)
    Private (1,071 holes)

Horse Racing: 170 programs

    Turf Paradise (Thoroughbred)

Movie Theatres: 341 screens

    3 singles/twins
    25 multiplexes

Professional Sports: 226 games

    Cardinals (NFL Football)
    Coyotes (NHL Hockey)
    Diamondbacks (NL Baseball)
    Mercury (WNBA Basketball)
    RoadRunners (ECHL Hockey)
    Suns (NBA Basketball)

Recreation Areas: 1,111,678 acres

Federal
    Casa Grande Ruins NM
    Coronado NF
    Hohokam Pima NM
    Tonto NF
State
    Lost Dutchman SP
    Oracle WR
    Pichaco Peak SP

Ski Areas: 3,200 lift capacity/hr

Water Area

    Lakes and rivers: 16,000 acres

Zoo

    Phoenix Zoo
    Wildlife World Zoo

Places Rated Rank: 103

Pine Bluff, AR

College Sports: 60 games

    University of Arkansas Golden Lions

Golf Courses: 4

    Daily fee (27 holes)
    Municipal (9 holes)
    Private (36 holes)

Movie Theatres: 8 screens

    1 multiplex

Recreation Areas: 2,066 acres

State
    Cane Creek SP

Water Area

    Lakes and rivers: 26,240 acres

Places Rated Rank: 312

✓Pittsburgh, PA

Amusement/Theme Parks

    Idlewild Park
    Kennywood Park
    Sandcastle

Auto Racing

    BeaveRun Motorsports Complex
    Lernerville Speedway
    Pittsburgh Vintage Grand Prix

College Sports: 257 games

    Duquesne Dukes
    Robert Morris Colonials
    University of Pittsburgh Panthers

Golf Courses: 142

    Daily fee (1,539 holes)
    Municipal (108 holes)
    Private (900 holes)

Horse Racing: 206 programs

    The Meadows (Harness)

Movie Theatres: 249 screens

    23 multiplexes
    Professional Sports: 132 games
    Penguins (NHL Hockey)
    Pirates (NL Baseball)
    Steelers (NFL Football)

Recreation Areas: 54,650 acres

Federal
    Ohio River Islands NWR
State
    Hillman SP
    Jennings SP
    Keystone SP
    Laurel Mountain SP
    Laurel Ridge SP
    Laurel Summit SP
    Linn Run SP
    Moraine SP
    Ohiopyle SP
    Point SP
    Raccoon Creek SP

Ski Areas: 55,300 lift capacity/hr

Water Area

    Lakes and rivers: 42,880 acres

Zoo

    Pittsburgh Zoo & PPG Aquarium

Places Rated Rank: 21

Pittsfield, MA

Golf Courses: 14
Daily fee (180 holes)
Private (72 holes)

Movie Theatres: 20 screens
1 single/twin
3 multiplexes

Recreation Areas: 25,110 acres
Federal
Appalachian NT
State
Bash Bish Falls SP
Clarksburg SP
East Mountain SP
Mt. Everett SR
Mt. Greylock SR
Natural Bridge SP
Taconic Trail SP
Wahconah Falls SP
Western Gateway Heritage SP

Ski Areas: 77,999 lift capacity/hr

Water Area
Lakes and rivers: 9,600 acres

Places Rated Rank: 232

Pocatello, ID

College Sports: 43 games
Idaho State Bengals

Golf Courses: 4
Daily fee (9 holes)
Municipal (45 holes)
Private (18 holes)

Movie Theatres: 13 screens
2 singles/twins
2 multiplexes

Recreation Areas: 227,496 acres
Federal
Caribou NF
Curlew NGL
Minidoka NWR
Sawtooth NF

Ski Areas: 34,135 lift capacity/hr

Water Area
Lakes and rivers: 45,440 acres

Zoo
Ross Park Zoo

Places Rated Rank: 94

Portland-South Portland, ME

Amusement/Theme Parks
Aquaboggan Water Park
Funtown/Splashtown USA

Aquarium
Maine Aquarium

Golf Courses: 37
Daily fee (477 holes)
Municipal (54 holes)
Private (126 holes)

Horse Racing: 103 programs
Scarborough Downs (Harness)

Movie Theatres: 115 screens
8 singles/twins
13 multiplexes

Professional Sports: 111 games
Pirates (AHL Hockey)
Sea Dogs (Class AA Baseball)
Recreation Areas: 4,067 acres
Bradbury Mountain SP
Crescent Beach SP
Ferry Beach SP
Peacock Beach SP
Popham Beach SP
Reid SP
Scarboro Beach SP
Sebago Lake SP
Two Lights SP
Wolfe's Neck Woods SP

Ski Areas: 76,700 lift capacity/hr

Water Area
Lakes and rivers: 172,160 acres
Atlantic offshore: 91,520 acres

Places Rated Rank: 106

✓Portland-Vancouvern, OR-WA

Amusement/Theme Parks
Oaks Park

Auto Racing
Portland International Raceway

College Sports: 115 games
Portland State Vikings
University of Portland Pilots

Golf Courses: 54
Daily fee (585 holes)
Municipal (117 holes)
Private (270 holes)

Horse Racing: 82 programs
Portland Meadows (Thoroughbred)

Movie Theatres: 243 screens
22 multiplexes

Professional Sports: 41 games
Trail Blazers (NBA Basketball)

Recreation Areas: 2,090,766 acres
Federal
Franz Lake NWR
Gifford Pinchot NF
Julia Butler Hansen NWR
Little White Salman NWR
McQuinn Strip
Mt. Hood NF
Pierce NWR
Ridgefield NWR
Siuslaw NF
Steigerwald Lake NWR
Tualatin River NWR
Willamette NF
State
Ainsworth SP
Bald Peak SP
Banks-Vernonia SP
Battle Ground Lake SP

Beacon Rock SP
Benson SP
Bonneville SP
Bonnie Lure SP
Bridal Veil Falls SP
Clackamas River Scenic Waterway
Columbia River
Crown Point SP
Dabney SP
Erratic Rock SP
George Joseph SP
Guy Talbot SP
John Yeon SP
Lewis and Clark SP
Mary S. Young SP
Maud Williamson SP
McLoughlin SP
Milo McIver SP
Molalla River SP
Paradise Point SP
Portland Women's Forum SP
Reed Island SP
Rocky Butte SP
Rooster Rock SP
Sandy River Scenic Waterway
Shepperd's Dell SP
Sunset Highway Forest Wayside
Tryon Creek SP
Willamette Mission SP
Willamette River Greenway
Willamette Stone SP
Wilson River Highway Forest
    Wayside
Wormald SP

Ski Areas: 32,855 lift capacity/hr

Water Area
Lakes and rivers: 85,760 acres

Zoo
Oregon Zoo

Places Rated Rank: 26

Port St. Lucie-Fort Pierce, FL

Golf Courses: 45
Daily fee (270 holes)
Municipal (90 holes)
Private (450 holes)

Movie Theatres: 55 screens
1 single/twin
6 multiplexes

Recreation Areas: 27,344 acres
Federal
Hobe Sound NWR
State
Atlantic Ridge Preserve SP
Avalon SP
Dickinson SP
Fort Pierce Inlet SP
Savannas Preserve SP
Seabranch Preserve SP
St. Lucie Inlet SP

Water Area
Lakes and rivers: 104,960 acres
Atlantic offshore: 9,536 acres

Places Rated Rank: 100

Poughkeepsie-Newburgh, NY

College Sports: 234 games
Marist College Red Foxes
U.S. Military Academy Cadets

Golf Courses: 33
Daily fee (279 holes)
Municipal (108 holes)
Private (198 holes)
Horse Racing: 8 programs
Goshen (Harness)

Movie Theatres: 50 screens
4 multiplexes
Professional Sports: 71 games
Renegades (Class A Baseball)

Recreation Areas: 43,691 acres
Federal
Appalachian NT
Upper Delaware NSRiver
Wallkill River NWR
State
Bear Mountain/Iona SP
Clermont SP
Goose Pond Mountain SP
Harriman SP
Highland Lakes SP
Hudson Highlands SP
James Baird SP
Margaret L. Norrie SP
Ogden Mills SP
Storm King SP
Taconic SP

Ski Areas: 73,880 lift capacity/hr

Water Area
Lakes and rivers: 29,440 acres

Zoo
Trevor Zoo

Places Rated Rank: 76

———————————

Prescott, AZ

Auto Racing
Canyon Raceway

Golf Courses: 14
Daily fee (135 holes)
Municipal (36 holes)
Private (72 holes)

Horse Racing: 56 programs
Yavapai Downs (Thoroughbred)

Movie Theatres: 32 screens
2 singles/twins
3 multiplexes

Recreation Areas: 7,877,542 acres
Federal
Coconino NF
Kaibab NF
Montezuma Castle NM
Prescott NF
Tonto NF
Tuzigoot NM
State
Dead Horse Ranch SP
Red Rock SP

Ski Areas: 5,810 lift capacity/hr

Water Area
Lakes and rivers: 3,200 acres

Places Rated Rank: 162

———————————

✓Providence-New Bedford, RI-MA

Amusement/Theme Parks
Fall River Carousel

Auto Racing
Seekonk Speedway

College Sports: 303 games
Brown University Bears
Providence College Friars
University of Rhode Island Rams

Golf Courses: 67
Daily fee (657 holes)
Municipal (45 holes)
Private (504 holes)

Movie Theatres: 246 screens
3 singles/twins
25 multiplexes

Professional Sports: 98 games
Bruins (AHL Hockey)
Red Sox (Triple A Baseball)

Recreation Areas: 15,023 acres
Federal
New Bedford Whaling NM
Roger Williams NM
State
Bay Island SP
Beavertail SP
Borderland SP
Brenton Point SP
Burlingame SP
Charlestown Beachway SB
Colt SP
Demarest Lloyd SP
Diamond Hill SP
Dighton Rock SP
East Beach SB
Fall River Heritage SP
Fishermen's Memorial SP
Fort Adams SP
Fort Phoenix SNA
Fort Wetherill SP
Goddard Memorial SP
Haines Memorial SP
Lincoln Woods SP
Massasoit SP
Misquamicut SB
Salty Brine SB
Scarborough SB
Teddy's Beach SB
Watson Pond SP
Wheeler SB

Ski Areas: 14,355 lift capacity/hr

Water Area
Lakes and rivers: 132,480 acres
Atlantic offshore: 44,800 acres

Zoo
Buttonwood Park Zoo
Capron Park Zoo
Roger Williams Park Zoo

Places Rated Rank: 31

Provo-Orem, UT

College Sports: 126 games
Brigham Young Cougars
Utah Valley State Wolverines

Golf Courses: 14
Daily fee (90 holes)
Municipal (117 holes)
Private (36 holes)

Movie Theatres: 48 screens
4 multiplexes

Recreation Areas: 1,841,425 acres
Federal
Ashley NF
Fish Springs NWR
Fishlake NF
Manti-La Sal NF
Timpanogos Cave NM
Uinta NF
Wasatch NF
State
Scofield SP
Utah Lake SP
Yuba Lake SP

Ski Areas: 55,817 lift capacity/hr

Water Area
Lakes and rivers: 101,120 acres

Places Rated Rank: 99

———————————

Pueblo, CO

Amusement/Theme Parks
Rock Canyon Water Slide

Auto Racing
Pueblo Motorsports Park

Golf Courses: 6
Municipal (81 holes)
Private (18 holes)

Movie Theatres: 17 screens
2 multiplexes

Recreation Areas: 41,806 acres
Federal
San Isabel NF
State
Pueblo SRA

Water Area
Lakes and rivers: 5,760 acres

Zoo
Pueblo Zoo

Places Rated Rank: 273

———————————

Punta Gorda, FL

Golf Courses: 12
Daily fee (135 holes)
Private (72 holes)

Movie Theatres: 16 screens
1 multiplex

Professional Sports: 71 games
Rangers (Class A Baseball)

Recreation Areas: 35,346 acres
Federal
    Island Bay NWR
State
    Charlotte Harbor Preserve SP
    Don Pedro Island SRA
    Port Charlotte Beach SRA

Water Area
    Lakes and rivers: 78,080 acres
    Gulf offshore

Places Rated Rank: 96

___

Racine, WI

Golf Courses: 11
    Daily fee (36 holes)
    Municipal (126 holes)
    Private (36 holes)

Movie Theatres: 13 screens
    2 multiplexes

Ski Areas: 51,085 lift capacity/hr

Water Area
    Lakes and rivers: 4,480 acres
    Lake Michigan offshore: 289,280 acres

Zoo
    Racine Zoo

Places Rated Rank: 254

___

Raleigh-Cary, NC

Amusement/Theme Parks
    Pullen Park
    Auto Racing
    Southern National Speedway

College Sports: 188 games
    North Carolina State Wolfpack
    UNC Chapel Hill Tar Heels

Golf Courses: 38
    Daily fee (432 holes)
    Private (243 holes)

Movie Theatres: 141 screens
    10 multiplexes

Professional Sports: 129 games
    Mudcats (Class AA Baseball)

Recreation Areas: 7,909 acres
Federal
    Blue Ridge Parkway
State
    Falls Lake SRA
    Jordan Lake SRA
    W.B. Umstead SP

Water Area
    Lakes and rivers: 19,840 acres
    Gulf offshore: 2,752 acres

Places Rated Rank: 116

___

Rapid City, SD

Golf Courses: 8
    Daily fee (99 holes)
    Municipal (18 holes)
    Private (18 holes)

Movie Theatres: 14 screens
    2 multiplexes

Recreation Areas: 1,334,909 acres
Federal
    Badlands NP
    Black Hills NF
    Buffalo Gap NGL
    Mount Rushmore NM
State
    Bear Butte SP

Ski Areas: 11,500 lift capacity/hr

Water Area
    Lakes and rivers: 12,800 acres

Places Rated Rank: 220

___

Reading, PA

Amusement/Theme Parks
    Koziar's Christmas Village

Auto Racing
    Liberty Bell Motorsports Park

Golf Courses: 20
    Daily fee (261 holes)
    Municipal (18 holes)
    Private (72 holes)

Movie Theatres: 18 screens
    2 multiplexes

Professional Sports: 107 games
    Phillies (Class AA Baseball)
    Royals (ECHL Hockey)

Recreation Areas: 8,725 acres
Federal
    Appalachian NT
State
    French Creek SP
    Nolde Forest SP

Ski Areas: 19,400 lift capacity/hr

Water Area
    Lakes and rivers: 3,840 acres

Places Rated Rank: 268

___

Redding, CA

Amusement/Theme Parks
    Waterworks Park
    Auto Racing
    Shasta Raceway Park

Golf Courses: 6
    Daily fee (63 holes)
    Private (45 holes)

Movie Theatres: 21 screens
    3 singles/twins
    2 multiplexes

Recreation Areas: 2,362,460 acres
Federal
    Lassen NF
    Lassen Volcanic NP
    Shasta NF
    Trinity NF
    Whiskeytown-Shasta-Trinity NRA

State
    Ahjumawi Lava Springs SP
    Castle Crags SP
    McArthur-Burney Falls Memorial SP

Ski Areas: 8,700 lift capacity/hr

Water Area
    Lakes and rivers: 39,680 acres

Places Rated Rank: 117

___

Reno-Sparks, NV

Amusement/Theme Parks
    Wild Island

College Sports: 66 games
    University of Nevada Wolf Pack

Golf Courses: 19
    Daily fee (144 holes)
    Municipal (81 holes)
    Private (108 holes)

Movie Theatres: 46 screens
    4 multiplexes

Recreation Areas: 309,505 acres
Federal
    Anaho Island NWR
    Sheldon NWR
    Toiyabe NF
    Toiyabe Special Area
State
    Lake Tahoe SP
    Washoe Lake SRA

Ski Areas: 165,182 lift capacity/hr

Water Area
    Lakes and rivers: 133,760 acres

Places Rated Rank: 118

___

Richmond, VA

Amusement/Theme Parks
    Paramount's Kings Dominion

Auto Racing
    Dragons Ridge Motorsports Park
    Richmond International Raceway
    Shenandoah Speedway

College Sports: 144 games
    University of Richmond Spiders
    Virginia Commonwealth Rams

Horse Racing: 68 programs
    Colonial Downs (Mixed Meetings)

Golf Courses: 46
    Daily fee (450 holes)
    Municipal (18 holes)
    Private (360 holes)

Movie Theatres: 97 screens
    1 single/twin
    8 multiplexes

Professional Sports: 86 games
    Braves (Triple A Baseball)
    Renegades (SPHL Hockey)

Recreation Areas: 13,527 acres

Federal
Fredericksburg and Spotsylvania NMP
James River NWR
Presquile NWR

State
Bear Creek Lake SP
Pocahontas SP

Water Area

Lakes and rivers: 80,640 acres

Places Rated Rank: 56

Riverside-San Bernardino, CA

Amusement/Theme Parks

Knott's Soak City
Pharaoh's Lost Kingdom

Auto Racing

California Speedway
Lucas Oil I-10 Speedway
Orange Show Speedway
Perris Auto Speedway

College Sports: 72 games

UC Riverside Highlanders

Golf Courses: 162

Daily fee (1,476 holes)
Municipal (243 holes)
Private (1,188 holes)

Movie Theatres: 473 screens

6 singles/twins
47 multiplexes

Professional Sports: 284 games

High Desert Mavericks
(Class A Baseball)
Inland Empire 66ers
(Class A Baseball)
Quakes (Class A Baseball)
Storm (Class A Baseball)

Recreation Areas: 3,826,353 acres

Federal
Angeles NF
Cleveland NF
Cleveland OTH
Coachella Valley NWR
Death Valley NP
Joshua Tree NM
Joshua Tree NP
Mojave Desert N Preserve
San Bernardino NF

State
Anza-Borrego Desert SP
Chino Hills SP
Lake Elsinore SRA
Lake Perris SRA
Mount San Jacinto SP
Providence Mountains SRA
Salton Sea SRA
Seccombe Lake SRA
Silverwood Lake SRA

Ski Areas: 84,490 lift capacity/hr

Water Area

Lakes and rivers: 90,240 acres

Zoo

Moonridge Zoo

Places Rated Rank: 86

Roanoke, VA

Golf Courses: 12

Daily fee (126 holes)
Municipal (9 holes)
Private (72 holes)

Movie Theatres: 34 screens

3 multiplexes

Recreation Areas: 295,838 acres

Federal
Appalachian NT
Blue Ridge Parkway
Booker T. Washington NM
George Washington NF
Jefferson NF

Water Area

Lakes and rivers: 14,080 acres

Zoo

Mill Mountain Zoo

Places Rated Rank: 187

Rochester, MN

Golf Courses: 17

Daily fee (225 holes)
Municipal (45 holes)
Private (36 holes)

Movie Theatres: 39 screens

1 single/twin
3 multiplexes

Recreation Areas: 3,603 acres

Federal
Upper Mississippi NWR
State
Carley SP

Ski Areas: 16,300 lift capacity/hr

Water Area

Lakes and rivers: 16,640 acres

Places Rated Rank: 257

✓ Rochester, NY

Amusement/Theme Parks

Seabreeze Park/Raging RiverS

Auto Racing

Canandaigua Speedway

College Sports: 32 games

Hobart College Statesmen

Golf Courses: 73

Daily fee (900 holes)
Municipal (81 holes)
Private (333 holes)

Horse Racing: 160 programs

Finger Lakes (Thoroughbred)

Movie Theatres: 120 screens

10 multiplexes

Professional Sports: 98 games

Americans (AHL Hockey)
Red Wings (Triple A Baseball)

Recreation Areas: 18,825 acres

Federal
Iroquois NWR
State
Canandaigua Lake Boat Launch SP
Chimney Bluffs SP
Conesus Lake Boat Launch SP
Hamlin Beach SP
Harriet Spencer SP
Honeoye Boat Launch SP
Irondequoit Bay Marine Park
Lakeside Beach SP
Letchworth SP
Oak Orchard Marine Park
Seneca Lake SP

Ski Areas: 20,600 lift capacity/hr

Water Area

Lakes and rivers: 28,160 acres
Lake Ontario offshore: 1,211,520 acres

Zoo

Seneca Park Zoo

Places Rated Rank: 8

Rockford, IL

Auto Racing

Blackhawk Farms Raceway

Golf Courses: 15

Daily fee (72 holes)
Municipal (117 holes)
Private (72 holes)

Movie Theatres: 41 screens

4 multiplexes
Professional Sports: 44 games
Ice Hogs (UHL Hockey)
Lightning (CBA Basketball)
Recreation Areas: 3,092 acres
State
Rock Cut SP

Ski Areas: 18,885 lift capacity/hr

Water Area

Lakes and rivers: 3,840 acres

Places Rated Rank: 286

Rockingham County, NH

Amusement/Theme Parks

Canobie Lake Park
Water Country

College Sports: 75 games

University of New Hampshire Wildcats

Golf Courses: 23

Daily fee (306 holes)
Private (108 holes)

Horse Racing: 100 programs

Rockingham Park (Harness)

Movie Theatres: 52 screens

8 multiplexes

Recreation Areas: 6,723 acres
State
    Hampton Beach SP
    Jenness Beach SB
    Kingston SP
    North Hampton SB
    Northwood Meadows SNA
    Odiorne Point SP
    Pawtuckaway SP
    Portsmouth Fish Pier SRA
    Rye Harbor SP
    Seabrook Fish Pier SRA
    Wallis Sands SB

Ski Areas: 78,165 lift capacity/hr

Water Area
    Lakes and rivers: 29,440 acres
    Atlantic offshore: 4,352 acres

Places Rated Rank: 222

Rocky Mount, NC

Golf Courses: 7
    Daily fee (54 holes)
    Private (63 holes)

Movie Theatres: 13 screens
    1 multiplex

Professional Sports: 71 games
    Crawdads (Class A baseball)

Water Area
    Lakes and rivers: 2,560 acres

Places Rated Rank: 368

Rome, GA

Golf Courses: 5
    Daily fee (18 holes)
    Municipal (18 holes)
    Private (45 holes)

Movie Theatres: 20 screens
    3 multiplexes

Recreation Areas: 6,621 acres
Federal
    Chattahoochee NF

Water Area
    Lakes and rivers: 3,200 acres

Places Rated Rank: 290

✓Sacramento–Arden-Arcade, CA

Amusement/Theme Parks
    Six Flags Waterworld
    Auto Racing
    Barona Speedway

College Sports: 72 games
    California State Hornets

Golf Courses: 48
    Daily fee (369 holes)
    Municipal (180 holes)
    Private (315 holes)

Horse Racing: 211 programs
    Cal Expo (Harness)
    Sacramento (Thoroughbred)

Movie Theatres: 227 screens
    4 singles/twins
    24 multiplexes

Professional Sports: 58 games
    Kings (NBA Basketball)
    Monarchs (WNBA Basketball)

Recreation Areas: 2,233,117 acres
Federal
    Eldorado NF
    Tahoe NF
    Toiyabe NF
State
    Auburn SRA
    Brannan Island SRA
    Burton Creek SP
    D. L. Bliss SP
    Delta Meadows River Park
    Emerald Bay SP
    Folsom Lake SRA
    Kings Beach SRA
    Lake Valley SRA
    Prairie City SVRA
    Sugar Pine Point SP
    Tahoe SRA
    Washoe Meadows SP

Ski Areas: 231,007 lift capacity/hr

Water Area
    Lakes and rivers: 138,240 acres

Zoo
    Folsom Zoo
    Roseville City Zoo
    Sacramento Zoo

Places Rated Rank: 5

Saginaw, MI

Auto Racing
    Dixie Motor Speedway

Golf Courses: 17
    Daily fee (252 holes)
    Private (54 holes)

Horse Racing: 34 programs
    Saginaw Raceway (Harness)

Movie Theatres: 22 screens
    2 singles/twins
    2 multiplexes

Recreation Areas: 2,053 acres
Federal
    Shiawassee NWR

Ski Areas: 6,000 lift capacity/hr

Water Area
    Lakes and rivers: 4,480 acres
    Lake Huron offshore: 11,540 acres

Zoo
    Saginaw Children's Zoo

Places Rated Rank: 256

St. Cloud, MN

College Sports: 20 games
    St. Cloud State Huskies

Golf Courses: 16
    Daily fee (252 holes)
    Municipal (18 holes)
    Private (18 holes)

Movie Theatres: 36 screens
    1 single/twin
    4 multiplexes

Ski Areas: 10,000 lift capacity/hr

Water Area
    Lakes and rivers: 32,000 acres

Places Rated Rank: 283

St. George, UT

Golf Courses: 10
    Daily fee (54 holes)
    Municipal (108 holes)
    Private (18 holes)

Movie Theatres: 25 screens
    5 multiplexes

Recreation Areas: 535,360 acres
Federal
    Dixie NF
    Zion NP
State
    Gunlock Lake SP
    Quail Creek SP
    Snow Canyon SP

Ski Areas: 10,500 lift capacity/hr

Water Area
    Lakes and rivers: 1,920 acres

Places Rated Rank: 224

St. Joseph, MO-KS

Golf Courses: 5
    Municipal (36 holes)
    Private (45 holes)

Movie Theatres: 20 screens
    2 singles/twins
    2 multiplexes

Recreation Areas: 121 acres
State
    Lewis & Clark SP

Ski Areas: 1,000 lift capacity/hr

Water Area
    Lakes and rivers: 8,320 acres

Places Rated Rank: 358

✓St. Louis, MO-IL

Amusement/Theme Parks
    Six Flags St. Louis

Auto Racing
    Gateway International Raceway
    Tri-City Speedway

College Sports: 72 games
    Saint Louis University Billikens

Golf Courses: 120
    Daily fee (1,305 holes)
    Municipal (144 holes)
    Private (702 holes)

Horse Racing: 102 programs
    Fairmount Park (Thoroughbred)

Movie Theatres: 345 screens
    11 single/twin
    35 multiplexes

Professional Sports: 172 games
    Blues (NHL Hockey)
    Cardinals (NL Baseball)
    Chicago Wolves (AHL Hockey)
    Rams (NFL Football)

Recreation Areas: 144,698 acres
Federal
    Jefferson National Expansion NM
    Mark Twain NF
    Mark Twain NWR
State
    Beaver Dam SP
    Castlewood SP
    Cuivre River SP
    Edmund Babler Memorial SP
    Eldon Hazlett SP
    Frank Holton SP
    Horsehoe Lake SP
    Meramec SP
    Mississippi River State Fish and
    Pere Marquette SP
    Robertsville SP
    South Shore SP
    Washington SP

Ski Areas: 6,000 lift capacity/hr

Water Area
    Lakes and rivers: 123,520 acres

Zoo
    St. Louis Zoo

Places Rated Rank: 17

Salem, OR

Golf Courses: 12
    Daily fee (153 holes)
    Private (54 holes)

Movie Theatres: 11 screens
    1 multiplex

Professional Sports: 71 games
    Volcanoes (Class A Baseball)

Recreation Areas: 431,056 acres
Federal
    Ankeny NWR
    Baskett Slough NWR
    McQuinn Strip
    Mt. Hood NF
    Siuslaw NF
    Willamette NF
State
    Champoeg SP
    Detroit Lake SP
    Holman State Wayside
    North Santiam SP
    Sarah Helmich SP
    Silver Falls SP

Van Duzer Forest Corridor Wayside
    Willamette Mission SP
    Willamette River Greenway

Ski Areas: 10,185 lift capacity/hr

Water Area
    Lakes and rivers: 8,320 acres

Places Rated Rank: 247

Salinas, CA

Aquarium
    Monterey Bay Aquarium

Auto Racing
    Mazda Raceway Laguna Seca

Golf Courses: 24
    Daily fee (180 holes)
    Municipal (81 holes)
    Private (162 holes)

Movie Theatres: 70 screens
    1 single/twin
    9 multiplexes

Recreation Areas: 326,304 acres
Federal
    Los Padres NF
    Pinnacles NM
    Salinas River NWR
    Sur Sur PU
State
    Andrew Molera SP
    Asilomar Conference and SB
    Carmel River SB
    Fremont Peak SP
    Garrapata SP
    John Little SR
    Julia Pfeiffer Burns SP
    Marina SB
    Monterey SB
    Moss Landing SB
    Pfeiffer Big Sur SP
    Point Lobos SR
    Salinas River SB
    Zmudowski SB

Ski Areas: 10,742 lift capacity/hr

Water Area
    Lakes and rivers: 8,320 acres
    Pacific offshore: 84,480 acres

Places Rated Rank: 65

Salisbury, MD

College Sports: 48 games
    UM Eastern Shore Fighting Hawks

Golf Courses: 4
    Daily fee (18 holes)
    Municipal (18 holes)
    Private (27 holes)

Movie Theatres: 10 screens
    1 multiplex

Professional Sports: 71 games
    Shorebirds (Class A Baseball)

Recreation Areas: 7,570 acres
Federal
    Martin NWR

State
    Janes Island SP

Water Area
    Lakes and rivers: 38,400 acres
    Atlantic offshore: 156,800 acres

Zoo
    Salisbury Zoo

Places Rated Rank: 125

✓Salt Lake City, UT

Auto Racing
    Miller Motorsports Park
    Rocky Mountain Raceways

College Sports: 66 games
    University of Utah Utes

Golf Courses: 32
    Daily fee (81 holes)
    Municipal (333 holes)
    Private (162 holes)

Movie Theatres: 119 screens
    11 multiplexes

Professional Sports: 188 games
    Bees (Triple A Baseball)
    Grizzlies (AHL Hockey)
    Jazz (NBA Basketball)
    Real (MLS Soccer)
    Utah Grizzlies (ECHL Hockey)

Recreation Areas: 1,298,307 acres
Federal
    Ashley NF
    Wasatch NF
State
    Bonneville Salt Flats SP
    Jordan River Parkway SP
    Rail Trail SP
    Rockport Lake SP
    Saltaire Beach SP

Ski Areas: 175,417 lift capacity/hr

Water Area
    Lakes and rivers: 270,720 acres

Zoo
    Utah's Hogle Zoo

Places Rated Rank: 34

San Angelo, TX

Golf Courses: 5
    Daily fee (36 holes)
    Municipal (9 holes)
    Private (36 holes)

Movie Theatres: 14 screens
    1 multiplex

Water Area
    Lakes and rivers: 11,520 acres

Places Rated Rank: 369

San Antonio, TX

Amusement/Theme Parks
    Aquarena Center

Natural Bridge Wildlife Ranch
Schlitterbahn Waterpark
Seaworld San Antonio
Seguin Wave Pool
Six Flags Fiesta Texas
Splashtown

College Sports: 108 games
Texas State University Bobcats
University of Texas Roadrunners

Golf Courses: 49
Daily fee (495 holes)
Municipal (171 holes)
Private (207 holes)

Horse Racing: 4 programs
Retama Park (Thoroughbred)

Movie Theatres: 228 screens
17 multiplexes
Professional Sports: 98 games
Rampage (AHL Hockey)
Silver Stars (WNBA Basketball)
Spurs (NBA Basketball)

Recreation Areas: 9,142 acres
State
Guadalupe River SP
Hill Country SNA
Lost Maples SNA

Water Area
Lakes and rivers: 28,800 acres

Zoo
San Antonio Zoo & Aquarium

Places Rated Rank: 182

✓**San Diego-Carlsbad, CA**

Amusement/Theme Parks
Belmont Park
Legoland California
Seaworld

Aquarium
Birch Aquarium

Auto Racing
Barona Speedway

College Sports: 150 games
San Diego State Aztecs
University of San Diego Toreros

Golf Courses: 71
Daily fee (621 holes)
Municipal (126 holes)
Private (531 holes)

Horse Racing: 43 programs
Del Mar (Thoroughbred)

Movie Theatres: 383 screens
5 singles/twins
33 multiplexes

Professional Sports: 127 games
Chargers (NFL Football)
Gulls (ECHL Hockey)
Padres (NL Baseball)

Recreation Areas: 898,711 acres
Federal
Cabrillo NM

Cleveland NF
Guatay Mtn PU
Sweetwater Marsh NWR
Tijuana Slough NWR
State
Anza-Borrego Desert SP
Border Field SP
Cardiff SB
Carlsbad SB
Cuyamaca Rancho SP
Leucadia SB
Moonlight SB
Ocotillo Wells SVRA
Palomar Mountain SP
San Elijo SB
San Onofre SB
Silver Strand SB
South Carlsbad SB
Torrey Pines SB
Torrey Pines SR

Water Area
Lakes and rivers: 34,560 acres
Pacific offshore: 17,152 acres

Zoo
National City Zoo
Roseville City Zoo
San Diego Zoo

Places Rated Rank: 27

Sandusky, OH

Amusement/Theme Parks
Cedar Point

Golf Courses: 8
Daily fee (108 holes)
Municipal (9 holes)
Private (18 holes)

Movie Theatres: 18 screens
2 multiplexes

Recreation Areas: 1,048 acres
State
Kelleys Island SP
Sheldon Marsh SNA

Water Area
Lakes and rivers: 19,200 acres
Lake Erie offshore: 218,240 acres

Zoo
Cedar Point Zoo

Places Rated Rank: 93

✓**San Francisco-San Mateo, CA**

Aquariums
Aquarium of the Bay
Steinhart Aquarium

Auto Racing
3Com Park

College Sports: 72 games
University of San Francisco Dons

Golf Courses: 25
Daily fee (153 holes)
Municipal (72 holes)
Private (216 holes)

Horse Racing: 50 programs
Bay Meadows (Thoroughbred)

Movie Theatres: 198 screens
22 singles/twins
25 multiplexes

Professional Sports: 132 games
49ers (NFL Football)
Giants (NL Baseball)
San Jose Sharks (NHL Hockey)

Recreation Areas: 126,239 acres
Federal
Farallon NWR
Golden Gate NRA
Marin Islands NWR
Muir Woods NM
Point Reyes N Seashore
San Francisco Bay NWR
State
Angel Island SP
Ano Nuevo SR
Bean Hollow SB
Big Basin Redwoods SP
Burleigh Murray Ranch
Butano SP
Candlestick Point SRA
China Camp SP
Gray Whale Cove SB
Half Moon Bay SB
Montara SB
Mount Tamalpais SP
Pacifica SB
Pescadero SB
Pomponio SB
Portola SP
Samuel P. Taylor SP
San Bruno Mountain SP
San Gregorio SB
Thornton SB
Tomales Bay SP

Water Area
Lakes and rivers: 158,080 acres
Pacific offshore: 3,840 acres

Zoo
San Francisco Zoo

Places Rated Rank: 11

San Jose-Sunnyvale, CA

Amusement/Theme Parks
Bonfante Gardens
Paramount's Great America

College Sports: 228 games
San Jose State Spartans
Santa Clara Broncos
Stanford Cardinal

Golf Courses: 31
Daily fee (180 holes)
Municipal (153 holes)
Private (225 holes)

Movie Theatres: 284 screens
6 singles/twins
24 multiplexes

Professional Sports: 71 games
Giants (Class A Baseball)

Recreation Areas: 66,515 acres

Federal
    Pinnacles NM
    San Francisco Bay NWR
State
    Castle Rock SP
    Fremont Peak SP
    Henry W. Coe SP
    Hollister Hills SVRA

Ski Areas: 24,942 lift capacity/hr

Water Area
    Lakes and rivers: 9,600 acres

Zoo
    Happy Hollow Zoo
    San Jose Baby Zoo

Places Rated Rank: 157

San Luis Obispo-Paso Robles, CA

College Sports: 72 games
    Cal Poly Mustangs

Golf Courses: 12
    Daily fee (144 holes)
    Municipal (54 holes)
    Private (18 holes)

Movie Theatres: 42 screens
    3 singles/twins
    6 multiplexes

Recreation Areas: 207,006 acres
Federal
    Los Padres NF
    Sur Sur PU
State
    Cayuccos SB
    Los Osos Oaks SR
    Montana De Oro SP
    Morro Bay SP
    Morro Strand SB
    Pismo Dunes SVRA
    Pismo SB
    San Simeon SP
    William Randolph Hearst SB

Ski Areas: 1,500 lift capacity/hr

Water Area
    Lakes and rivers: 12,160 acres
    Pacific offshore: 34,840 acres

Zoo
    Charles Paddock Zoo

Places Rated Rank: 198

Santa Ana-Anaheim-Irvine, CA

Amusement/Theme Parks
    Balboa Fun Zone
    Disneyland
    Disney's California Adventure
    Knott's Berry Farm
    Wild Rivers Waterpark

Aquarium
    Birch Aquarium

College Sports: 144 games
    California State Titans
    UC Irvine Anteaters

Golf Courses: 48
    Daily fee (288 holes)
    Municipal (198 holes)
    Private (369 holes)

Horse Racing: 205 programs
    Los Alamitos (Thoroughbred)

Movie Theatres: 433 screens
    6 singles/twins
    38 multiplexes

Professional Sports: 122 games
    Anaheim Ducks (NHL Hockey)
    Angels (AL Baseball)

Recreation Areas: 65,074 acres
Federal
    Cleveland NF
State
    Bolsa Chica SB
    Chino Hills SP
    Corona Del Mar SB
    Crystal Cove SP
    Doheny SB
    Huntington SB
    San Clemente SB

Ski Areas: 80,790 lift capacity/hr

Water Area
    Lakes and rivers: 6,400 acres
    Pacific offshore: 9,472 acres

Zoo
    Orange County Zoo
    Santa Ana Zoo

Places Rated Rank: 54

Santa Barbara-Santa Maria, CA

Auto Racing
    Santa Maria Speedway
    College Sports: 72 games
    UC Santa Barbara Gauchos

Golf Courses: 16
    Daily fee (117 holes)
    Municipal (36 holes)
    Private (126 holes)

Movie Theatres: 50 screens
    8 singles/twins
    7 multiplexes

Recreation Areas: 702,346 acres
Federal
    Channel Islands NP
    Los Padres NF
    Los Padres OTH
State
    Carpinteria SB
    El Capitan SB
    Gaviota SP
    Point Sal SB
    Refugio SB

Ski Areas: 1,500 lift capacity/hr

Water Area
    Lakes and rivers: 8,320 acres
    Pacific offshore: 66,496 acres

Zoo
    Santa Barbara Zoo

Places Rated Rank: 195

Santa Cruz-Watsonville, CA

Amusement/Theme Parks
    Santa Cruz Beach Boardwalk
    Auto Racing
    Watsonville Speedway

Golf Courses: 5
    Daily fee (72 holes)
    Municipal (18 holes)

Movie Theatres: 40 screens
    3 singles/twins
    7 multiplexes

Recreation Areas: 40,600 acres
Federal
    Ellicott Slough NWR
State
    Big Basin Redwoods SP
    Castle Rock SP
    Forest of Nisene Marks SP
    Henry Cowell Redwoods SP
    Lighthouse Field SB
    Manresa SB
    Natural Bridges SB
    New Brighton SB
    Seacliff SB
    Sunset SB
    Twin Lakes SB
    Wilder Ranch SP

Water Area
    Lakes and rivers: 640 acres
    Pacific offshore: 53,120 acres

Places Rated Rank: 49

Santa Fe, NM

Golf Courses: 6
    Daily fee (45 holes)
    Municipal (18 holes)
    Private (45 holes)

Movie Theatres: 19 screens
    1 single/twin
    3 multiplexes

Recreation Areas: 247,826 acres
Federal
    Bandelier NM
    Bruns Hospital Area OTH
    Santa Fe NF
State
    Hyde Memorial SP
    Santa Fe River SP

Ski Areas: 20,350 lift capacity/hr

Water Area
    Lakes and rivers: 1,280 acres

Places Rated Rank: 297

Santa Rosa-Petaluma, CA

Amusement/Theme Parks
    Windsor Waterworks and Slides

Auto Racing
    Infineon Raceway
    Petaluma Speedway

Golf Courses: 14
    Daily fee (108 holes)
    Municipal (63 holes)
    Private (81 holes)

Horse Racing: 12 programs
  Santa Rosa (Thoroughbred)

Movie Theatres: 108 screens
  2 singles/twins
  13 multiplexes

Recreation Areas: 25,779 acres
Federal
  San Pablo Bay NWR
State
  Annadel SP
  Armstrong Redwoods SR
  Austin Creek SRA
  Bothe-Napa Valley SP
  Kruse Rhododendron SR
  Robert Louis Stevenson SP
  Salt Point SP
  Sonoma Coast SB
  Sugarloaf Ridge SP

Water Area
  Lakes and rivers: 18,560 acres
  Pacific offshore: 10,432 acres

Places Rated Rank: 140

Sarasota-Bradenton-Venice, FL

Aquarium
  Mote Marine Aquarium

Auto Racing
  DeSoto Super Speedway

Golf Courses: 70
  Daily fee (594 holes)
  Municipal (90 holes)
  Private (567 holes)

Movie Theatres: 79 screens
  7 multiplexes

Professional Sports: 71 games
  Reds (Class A Baseball)

Recreation Areas: 30,869 acres
Federal
  De Soto NMem
  Passage Key NWR
State
  Lake Manatee SP
  Myakka River SP
  Oscar Scherer SP

Water Area
  Lakes and rivers: 56,960 acres
  Gulf offshore: 30,080 acres

Places Rated Rank: 46

Savannah, GA

Auto Racing
  Roebling Road

College Sports: 48 games
  Savannah State Tigers

Golf Courses: 20
  Daily fee (153 holes)
  Municipal (45 holes)
  Private (153 holes)

Movie Theatres: 40 screens
  2 singles/twins
  4 multiplexes

Professional Sports: 71 games
  Sand Gnats (Class A Baseball)

Recreation Areas: 27,959 acres
Federal
  Fort Pulaski NM
  Savannah Coastal NWR
  Wassaw NWR
State
  Skidaway Island SP

Water Area
  Lakes and rivers: 44,800 acres
  Atlantic offshore: 13,440 acres

Places Rated Rank: 74

Scranton–Wilkes-Barre, PA

Golf Courses: 31
  Daily fee (342 holes)
  Municipal (27 holes)
  Private (189 holes)

Horse Racing: 143 programs
  Pocono Downs (Harness)

Movie Theatres: 48 screens
  5 multiplexes

Professional Sports: 94 games
  Penguins (AHL Hockey)
  Red Barons (Triple A Baseball)

Recreation Areas: 17,035 acres
State
  Archbald Pothole SP
  Frances Slocum SP
  Lackawanna SP
  Lehigh Gorge SP
  Nescopeck SP
  Ricketts Glen SP

Ski Areas: 93,297 lift capacity/hr

Water Area
  Lakes and rivers: 19,200 acres

Places Rated Rank: 165

✓Seattle-Bellevue-Everett, WA

Amusement/Theme Parks
  Fun Forest Amusement Park
  Wild Waves Enchanted Village

Aquarium
  Seattle Aquarium

Auto Racing
  Evergreen Speedway
  Pacific Raceways
  Seattle International Raceway

College Sports: 78 games
  University of Washington Huskies

Golf Courses: 56
  Daily fee (432 holes)
  Municipal (216 holes)
  Private (351 holes)

Horse Racing: 92 programs
  Emerald Downs (Thoroughbred)

Movie Theatres: 264 screens
  6 singles/twins
  27 multiplexes

Professional Sports: 258 games
  AquaSox (Class A Baseball)
  Dust Devils (Class A Baseball)
  Mariners (AL Baseball)
  Seahawks (NFL Football)
  Storm (WNBA Basketball)
  Supersonics (NBA Basketball)

Recreation Areas: 1,651,521 acres
Federal
  Gold Basin PU
  Mt. Baker NF
  Snoqualmie NF
State
  Black Diamond SP
  Bridle Trails SP
  Dash Point SP
  Everett Jetty SP
  Federation Forest SP
  Flaming Geyser SP
  Hanging Gardens SP
  Iron Horse West SP
  Jellum SP
  Kanaskat-Palmer SP
  Lake Sammamish SP
  Lord Hill
  Lower Green River SP
  Mahler SP
  Mercer Slough SP
  Mount Pilchuck SP
  Mukilteo SP
  Nolte SP
  Olallie SP
  Saltwater SP
  Skykomish River SP
  Squak Mountain SP
  Wallace Falls SP
  Wenberg SP
  West Hylebos SP

Ski Areas: 78,075 lift capacity/hr

Water Area
  Lakes and rivers: 62,720 acres
  Pacific offshore: 120,320 acres

Zoo
  Washington Zoological Park
  Woodland Park Zoo

Places Rated Rank: 2

Sebastian-Vero Beach, FL

Golf Courses: 20
  Daily fee (45 holes)
  Municipal (54 holes)
  Private (261 holes)

Movie Theatres: 14 screens
  1 single/twin
  1 multiplex

Professional Sports: 71 games
  Dodgers (Class A Baseball)

Recreation Areas: 684 acres
Federal
  Archie Carr NWR
  Pelican Island NWR

State
Sebastian Inlet SP

Water Area
Lakes and rivers: 23,680 acres
Atlantic offshore: 12,500 acres

Places Rated Rank: 241

Sheboygan, WI

Auto Racing
Road America

Golf Courses: 11
Daily fee (171 holes)
Private (18 holes)

Movie Theatres: 13 screens
1 multiplex

Recreation Areas: 962 acres
State
Kohler-Andrae SP

Ski Areas: 8,100 lift capacity/hr

Water Area
Lakes and rivers: 2,560 acres
Lake Michigan offshore: 481,920 acres

Places Rated Rank: 160

Sherman-Denison, TX

Golf Courses: 5
Daily fee (72 holes)
Private (18 holes)

Movie Theatres: 19 screens
2 multiplexes

Recreation Areas: 457 acres
State
Eisenhower SRA

Water Area
Lakes and rivers: 29,440 acres

Places Rated Rank: 270

Shreveport-Bossier City, LA

Amusement/Theme Parks
Watertown Usa

College Sports: 72 games
Centenary College Gentlemen

Golf Courses: 15
Daily fee (108 holes)
Municipal (45 holes)
Private (117 holes)

Horse Racing: 102 programs
Louisiana Downs (Thoroughbred)

Movie Theatres: 40 screens
3 multiplexes

Recreation Areas: 585 acres
State
C. Bickham Dickson SP

Water Area
Lakes and rivers: 64,640 acres

Places Rated Rank: 226

Sioux City, IA-NE-SD

Golf Courses: 15
Daily fee (180 holes)
Municipal (36 holes)
Private (45 holes)

Movie Theatres: 28 screens
1 single/twin
2 multiplexes

Recreation Areas: 859 acres
Federal
Missouri NS River
Missouri NSRiver
State
Ponca SP

Water Area
Lakes and rivers: 13,440 acres

Places Rated Rank: 299

Sioux Falls, SD

Amusement/Theme Parks
Wild Water West Waterpark

Golf Courses: 14
Daily fee (135 holes)
Municipal (63 holes)
Private (45 holes)

Movie Theatres: 22 screens
1 single/twin
2 multiplexes

Recreation Areas: 1,962 acres
State
Beaver Creek SNA
Big Sioux SRA
Lake Vermillion SRA
Newton Hills SP
Palisades SP

Water Area
Lakes and rivers: 5,760 acres

Zoo
Great Plains Zoo

Places Rated Rank: 328

South Bend-Mishawaka, IN-MI

Auto Racing
South Bend Motor Speedway
College Sports: 130 games
Notre Dame Fighting Irish

Golf Courses: 20
Daily fee (207 holes)
Municipal (72 holes)
Private (72 holes)

Movie Theatres: 38 screens
2 singles/twins
3 multiplexes

Professional Sports: 71 games
Silver Hawks (Class A Baseball)

Recreation Areas: 3,815 acres
State
Potato Creek SP

Ski Areas: 19,800 lift capacity/hr

Water Area
Lakes and rivers: 12,800 acres

Zoo
Potawatomi Zoo

Places Rated Rank: 132

Spartanburg, SC

Amusement/Theme Parks
Hollywild Animal Park

College Sports: 72 games
Wofford College Terriers

Golf Courses: 11
Daily fee (108 holes)
Private (81 holes)

Movie Theatres: 44 screens
5 multiplexes

Recreation Areas: 7,054 acres
State
Croft SP

Water Area
Lakes and rivers: 5,120 acres

Places Rated Rank: 250

Spokane, WA

Amusement/Theme Parks
Carrousel
Splashdown Family Waterpark

Auto Racing
Spokane Raceway Park
College Sports: 115 games
Eastern Washington Eagles
Gonzaga University Zags

Golf Courses: 14
Daily fee (81 holes)
Municipal (126 holes)
Private (36 holes)

Horse Racing: 75 programs
Playfair (Thoroughbred)

Movie Theatres: 44 screens
3 multiplexes

Professional Sports: 71 games
Indians (Class A Baseball)

Recreation Areas: 37,482 acres
Federal
Turnbull NWR
State
Centennial Trail SP
Mount Spokane SP
Pasco/Fish Lake Trail
Riverside SP
Spokane River Cent Trail

Ski Areas: 19,027 lift capacity/hr

Water Area
Lakes and rivers: 10,880 acres

Zoo

Inland Northwest Zoo

Places Rated Rank: 124

Springfield, IL

Auto Racing

Illinois State Fairgrounds
Golf Courses: 12
Daily fee (117 holes)
Municipal (54 holes)
Private (36 holes)

Horse Racing: 6 programs

Illinois State Fair (Harness)

Movie Theatres: 35 screens

1 single/twin
4 multiplexes

Water Area

Lakes and rivers: 6,400 acres

Zoo

Henson Robinson Zoo

Places Rated Rank: 311

Springfield, MA

Amusement/Theme Parks

Six Flags New England

Auto Racing

Palmer Motorsports Park

College Sports: 144 games

American International Yellow Jackets
UMass-Amherst Minutemen

Golf Courses: 37

Daily fee (342 holes)
Municipal (117 holes)
Private (207 holes)

Movie Theatres: 57 screens

4 singles/twins
4 multiplexes

Professional Sports: 40 games

Falcons (AHL Hockey)

Recreation Areas: 7,540 acres

C.M. Gardner SP
Chicopee Memorial SP
Deer Hill SP
Elwell SP
Hampton Ponds SP
Holland Pond SRA
Holyoke Heritage SP
Holyoke Range SP
Krug Sugarbush SNA
Lake Lorraine SP
Mt. Tom SR
Red Bridge SP
Robinson SP
Skinner SP
Springfield Heritage SP

Ski Areas: 162,806 lift capacity/hr

Water Area

Lakes and rivers: 35,200 acres

Zoo

Forest Park Children's Zoo
Museum of Zoology

Places Rated Rank: 203

Springfield, MO

College Sports: 96 games

Drury University Panthers
Southwest Missouri State Bears

Golf Courses: 18

Daily fee (153 holes)
Municipal (54 holes)
Private (108 holes)

Movie Theatres: 31 screens

3 singles/twins
3 multiplexes

Professional Sports: 71 games

Cardinals (Class AA Baseball)

Recreation Areas: 52,527 acres

Federal
Mark Twain NF
State
Bennett Spring SP

Water Area

Lakes and rivers: 6,400 acres

Zoo

Dickerson Park Zoo

Places Rated Rank: 293

Springfield, OH

Golf Courses: 12

Daily fee (108 holes)
Municipal (54 holes)
Private (45 holes)

Movie Theatres: 18 screens

2 singles/twins
2 multiplexes

Recreation Areas: 1,910 acres

State
Buck Creek SP

Water Area

Lakes and rivers: 2,560 acres

Places Rated Rank: 296

State College, PA

College Sports: 110 games

Penn State Nittany Lions

Golf Courses: 7

Daily fee (63 holes)
Private (54 holes)

Movie Theatres: 11 screens

2 multiplexes

Professional Sports: 71 games

Spikes (Class A Baseball)

Recreation Areas: 9,986 acres

State
Bald Eagle SP

Black Moshannon SP
McCall Dam SP
Penn Roosevelt SP
Poe Paddy SP
Poe Valley SP

Ski Areas: 10,000 lift capacity/hr

Water Area

Lakes and rivers: 2,560 acres

Places Rated Rank: 327

Stockton, CA

Amusement/Theme Parks

Pixie Woods Wonderland

Auto Racing

Altamont Motorsports Park
Stockton '99' Speedway

College Sports: 60 games

University of the Pacific Tigers

Golf Courses: 15

Daily fee (63 holes)
Municipal (72 holes)
Private (126 holes)

Horse Racing: 10 programs

Stockton Fair (Thoroughbred)

Movie Theatres: 61 screens

1 single/twin
5 multiplexes

Professional Sports: 107 games

Ports (Class A Baseball)
Thunder (ECHL Hockey)

Recreation Areas: 441 acres

State
Caswell Memorial SP
Durham Ferry SRA

Water Area

Lakes and rivers: 17,280 acres

Zoo

Micke Grove Zoo

Places Rated Rank: 199

Sumter, SC

Golf Courses: 6

Daily fee (72 holes)
Municipal (18 holes)
Private (18 holes)

Movie Theatres: 13 screens

2 multiplexes

Recreation Areas: 1,924 acres

State
Poinsett SP
Woods Bay SP

Water Area

Lakes and rivers: 10,880 acres

Places Rated Rank: 267

Syracuse, NY

Auto Racing

Oswego Speedway

College Sports: 217 games
Colgate University Raiders
Le Moyne College Dolphins
Syracuse University Orange

Golf Courses: 57
Daily fee (702 holes)
Municipal (36 holes)
Private (279 holes)

Movie Theatres: 56 screens
1 single/twin
5 multiplexes

Professional Sports: 98 games
Crunch (AHL Hockey)
SkyChiefs (Triple A Baseball)

Recreation Areas: 3,170 acres
State
Battle Island SP
Chittenango Falls SP
Clark Reservation
Green Lakes SP
Mexico Point Boat Launch SP
Otisco Lake Boat Launch SP
Selkirk Shores SP
South Shore Boat Launch SP

Ski Areas: 40,775 lift capacity/hr

Water Area
Lakes and rivers: 62,080 acres

Zoo
Burnet Park Zoo
Gifford Zoo at Burnet Park

Places Rated Rank: 67

Tacoma, WA

Golf Courses: 20
Daily fee (189 holes)
Municipal (63 holes)
Private (108 holes)

Movie Theatres: 74 screens
8 multiplexes

Professional Sports: 58 games
Rainiers (Triple A Baseball)

Recreation Areas: 339,880 acres
Federal
Mount Ranier NP
Nisqually NWR
Snoqualmie NF
State
Dash Point SP
Eagle Island SP
Haley Property
Joemma Beach
Kopachuck SP
Nisqually
Pensrose Point SP
Puyallup 40 SP
Steilacom Lake Tidelands SP

Ski Areas: 71,575 lift capacity/hr

Water Area
Lakes and rivers: 73,600 acres
Pacific offshore: 10,240 acres

Zoo
Port Defiance Zoo and Aquarium

Places Rated Rank: 84

Tallahassee, FL

College Sports: 114 games
Florida A&M Rattlers
Florida State Seminoles

Golf Courses: 11
Daily fee (99 holes)
Municipal (27 holes)
Private (72 holes)

Movie Theatres: 45 screens
4 multiplexes

Recreation Areas: 348,893 acres
Federal
Apalachicola NF
St. Marks NWR
State
Lake Talquin SP
Ochlockonee River SP
Wakulla Springs SP

Water Area
Lakes and rivers: 60,800 acres

Places Rated Rank: 82

✓Tampa-St. Petersburg, FL

Amusement/Theme Parks
Adventure Island
Weeki Wachee Springs

Aquariums
C.M.S.C. Aquarium
The Florida Aquarium

Auto Racing
East Bay Raceway Park
St. Pete Grand Prix

College Sports: 78 games
University of South Florida Bulls

Golf Courses: 116
Daily fee (1,125 holes)
Municipal (144 holes)
Private (819 holes)

Horse Racing: 94 programs
Tampa Bay Downs (Thoroughbred)

Movie Theatres: 322 screens
6 singles/twins
25 multiplexes

Professional Sports: 345 games
Blue Jays (Class A Baseball)
Tampa Bay Buccaneers
(NFL Football)
Tampa Bay Devil Rays
(AL Baseball)
Tampa Bay Lightning (NHL Hockey)
Threshers (Class A Baseball)
Yankees (Class A Baseball)

Recreation Areas: 25,165 acres
Federal
Chassahowitzka NWR
Egmont Key NWR

Pinellas NWR
State
Alafia River SP
Anclote Key Preserve SP
Caladesi Island SP
Cockroach Bay Preserve SP
Egmont Key SP
Hillsborough River SP
Honeymoon Island SP
Little Manatee River SP
Salt Springs SP

Water Area
Lakes and rivers: 97,280 acres
Gulf offshore: 160,640 acres

Zoo
Lowry ParkZoo

Places Rated Rank: 4

Terre Haute, IN

Auto Racing
Terre Haute Action Track

College Sports: 60 games
Indiana State Sycamores

Golf Courses: 9
Daily fee (63 holes)
Municipal (63 holes)
Private (36 holes)

Movie Theatres: 22 screens
2 singles/twins
2 multiplexes

Recreation Areas: 1,693 acres
State
Shakamak SP

Water Area
Lakes and rivers: 12,800 acres

Places Rated Rank: 246

Texarkana, TX-Texarkana, AR

Golf Courses: 5
Daily fee (54 holes)
Private (36 holes)

Movie Theatres: 14 screens
1 multiplex

Water Area
Lakes and rivers: 30,720 acres

Places Rated Rank: 340

✓Toledo, OH

Auto Racing
Toledo Speedway

College Sports: 164 games
Bowling Green Falcons
University of Toledo Rockets

Golf Courses: 32
Daily fee (360 holes)
Municipal (72 holes)
Private (135 holes)

Horse Racing: 116 programs
Raceway Park (Harness)

Movie Theatres: 61 screens

  5 multiplexes
  Professional Sports: 94 games
  Mud Hens (Triple A Baseball)
  Storm (ECHL Hockey)

Recreation Areas: 12,298 acres

Federal
  Cedar Point NWR
  Ottawa NWR
  Perry's Victory Peace NM
  West Sister Island NWR
State
  Catawba Island SP
  Crane Creek SP
  East Harbor SP
  Goll Woods SNA
  Harrison Lake SP
  Irwin Prairie SNA
  Mary Jane Thurston SP
  Maumee Bay SP
  South Bass Island SP

Water Area

  Lakes and rivers: 32,640 acres
  Lake Erie offshore: 344,320 acres

Zoo

  Toledo Zoological Gardens

Places Rated Rank: 29

Topeka, KS

Auto Racing

  Heartland Park

Golf Courses: 12

  Daily fee (72 holes)
  Municipal (45 holes)
  Private (90 holes)

Movie Theatres: 22 screens

  2 multiplexes

Recreation Areas: 3,872 acres

State
  Melvern SP
  Perry SP
  Pomona SP

Water Area

  Lakes and rivers: 29,440 acres

Zoo

  Gage Park Zoo
  Topeka Zoological Park

Places Rated Rank: 253

Trenton-Ewing, NJ

College Sports: 196 games

  Princeton University Tigers
  Rider University Broncs

Golf Courses: 14

  Daily fee (54 holes)
  Municipal (72 holes)
  Private (117 holes)

Movie Theatres: 61 screens

  4 multiplexes

Professional Sports: 107 games

  Thunder (Class AA Baseball)
  Titans (ECHL Hockey)

Water Area

  Lakes and rivers: 1,920 acres

Places Rated Rank: 321

Tucson, AZ

Amusement/Theme Parks

  Old Tucson Studios
  Auto Racing
  USA Race Park

College Sports: 66 games

  University of Arizona Wildcats

Golf Courses: 42

  Daily fee (405 holes)
  Municipal (108 holes)
  Private (234 holes)

Horse Racing: 30 programs

  Rillito Park (Thoroughbred)

Movie Theatres: 127 screens

  1 single/twin
  13 multiplexes

Professional Sports: 58 games

  Sidewinders (Triple A Baseball)

Recreation Areas: 1,341,692 acres

Federal
  Buenos Aires NWR
  Cabeza Prieta NWR
  Coronado NF
  Grand Canyon NP
  Organ Pipe Cactus NM
  Saguaro NM
State
  Catalina SP

Ski Areas: 3,200 lift capacity/hr

Water Area

  Lakes and rivers: 1,280 acres

Zoo

  Reid Park Zoo

Places Rated Rank: 113

Tulsa, OK

Amusement/Theme Parks

  Bell's Amusement Park

Auto Racing

  Creek County Speedway
  Hallett Motor Racing Circuit

College Sports: 133 games

  Oral Roberts University Golden
    Eagles
  University of Tulsa Golden
    Hurricane

Golf Courses: 34

  Daily fee (216 holes)
  Municipal (189 holes)
  Private (198 holes)

Horse Racing: 30 programs

  Fair Meadows (Thoroughbred)

Movie Theatres: 149 screens

  12 multiplexes

Professional Sports: 71 games

  Drillers (Class AA Baseball)

Recreation Areas: 12,732 acres

Federal
  Deep Fork NWR
State
  Dripping Springs SP
  Feyodi Creek SP
  Heyburn SP
  Lake Keystone SP
  Okmulgee SP
  Osage Hills SP
  Sequoyah Bay SP
  Wah-Sha-She SP
  Walnut Creek SP

Water Area

  Lakes and rivers: 113,920 acres

Zoo

  Tulsa Zoological Park

Places Rated Rank: 51

Tuscaloosa, AL

College Sports: 66 games

  University of Alabama Crimson Tide

Golf Courses: 9

  Daily fee (45 holes)
  Municipal (27 holes)
  Private (90 holes)

Movie Theatres: 24 screens

  2 singles/twins
  2 multiplexes

Recreation Areas: 40,665 acres

Federal
  Talladega NF
State
  Lake Lurleen SP

Water Area

  Lakes and rivers: 34,560 acres

Places Rated Rank: 238

Tyler, TX

Golf Courses: 13

  Daily fee (126 holes)
  Private (99 holes)

Movie Theatres: 28 screens

  2 multiplexes

Recreation Areas: 986 acres

State
  Tyler SP

Water Area

  Lakes and rivers: 13,440 acres

Zoo

  Caldwell Zoo

Places Rated Rank: 275

Utica-Rome, NY

Amusement/Theme Parks

  Enchanted Forest/Water Safari

Golf Courses: 33

Daily fee (459 holes)
Municipal (27 holes)
Private (99 holes)

Horse Racing: 36 programs

The Syracuse Mile (Harness)
Vernon Downs (Harness)

Movie Theatres: 31 screens

3 singles/twins
3 multiplexes

Recreation Areas: 5,684 acres
Federal
Fort Stanwix NM
State
Alger Island SRA
Delta Lake SP
Fourth Lake SRA
Hinckley Reservoir SRA
Nicks Lake SRA
Pixley Falls SP
Verona Beach SP

Ski Areas: 16,300 lift capacity/hr

Water Area

Lakes and rivers: 58,240 acres

Zoo

Utica Zoo

Places Rated Rank: 145

Valdosta, GA

Amusement/Theme Parks
Wild Adventures

Golf Courses: 7

Daily fee (81 holes)
Private (36 holes)

Movie Theatres: 24 screens

2 multiplexes

Recreation Areas: 3,559 acres
Federal
Banks Lake NWR

Water Area

Lakes and rivers: 25,600 acres

Places Rated Rank: 236

Vallejo-Fairfield, CA

Amusement/Theme Parks
Scandia Family Center
Six Flags Marine World

Golf Courses: 10

Daily fee (72 holes)
Municipal (72 holes)
Private (36 holes)

Movie Theatres: 50 screens

4 multiplexes

Recreation Areas: 2,180 acres
Federal
San Pablo Bay NWR
State
Benicia SRA

Water Area

Lakes and rivers: 50,560 acres

Places Rated Rank: 196

Victoria, TX

Amusement/Theme Parks
Riverside Park

Golf Courses: 5

Daily fee (36 holes)
Municipal (27 holes)
Private (18 holes)

Movie Theatres: 12 screens

1 multiplex

Recreation Areas: 42,972 acres
Federal
Aransas NWR
State
Matagorda Island SP
Port Lavaca Fishing Pier SP

Water Area

Lakes and rivers: 264,960 acres

Zoo

The Texas Zoo

Places Rated Rank: 112

Vineland-Millville-Bridgeton, NJ

Auto Racing
New Jersey Motorsports Park

Golf Courses: 1

Daily fee (18 holes)

Movie Theatres: 15 screens

1 single/twin
1 multiplex

Recreation Areas: 1,415 acres
State
Bear Swamp East SNA

Water Area

Lakes and rivers: 9,600 acres
Atlantic offshore: 110,080 acres

Zoo

Cohanzick Zoo

Places Rated Rank: 193

✓ Virginia Beach-Norfolk, VA-NC

Amusement/Theme Parks
Busch Gardens Williamsburg
Ocean Breeze Waterpark
Water Country USA

Aquarium
Virginia Aquarium

College Sports: 223 games
Hampton University Pirates
Norfolk State Spartans
Old Dominion Monarchs
William and Mary Tribe

Golf Courses: 60

Daily fee (531 holes)
Municipal (234 holes)
Private (306 holes)

Movie Theatres: 193 screens

14 multiplexes

Professional Sports: 129 games
Avalanche (Class A Baseball)
Tides (Triple A Baseball)

Recreation Areas: 110,003 acres
Federal
Back Bay NWR
Cape Hatteras N Seashore
Currituck NWR
Great Dismal Swamp NWR
Mackay Island NWR
Nansemond NWR
Plum Tree Island NWR
State
False Cape SP
Seashore SP

Water Area

Lakes and rivers: 273,280 acres
Atlantic offshore: 408,320 acres

Zoo

Newport News Zoo
Virginia Zoological Park

Places Rated Rank: 10

Visalia-Porterville, CA

Auto Racing
Plaza Park Raceway

Golf Courses: 8

Daily fee (63 holes)
Municipal (36 holes)
Private (36 holes)

Movie Theatres: 55 screens

3 singles/twins
5 multiplexes

Professional Sports: 71 games
Oaks (Class A Baseball)

Recreation Areas: 2,297,374 acres
Federal
Blue Ridge NWR
Inyo NF
Kings Canyon NP
Pixley NWR
Sequoia NF
Sequoia NP

Ski Areas: 10,742 lift capacity/hr

Water Area

Lakes and rivers: 9,600 acres

Places Rated Rank: 208

Waco, TX

College Sports: 66 games
Baylor University Bears

Golf Courses: 7

Daily fee (72 holes)
Municipal (36 holes)
Private (18 holes)

Movie Theatres: 38 screens

3 multiplexes

Water Area

Lakes and rivers: 11,520 acres

Zoo

Cameron Park Zoo

Places Rated Rank: 318

Warner Robins, GA

Golf Courses: 7

Daily fee (90 holes)
Municipal (18 holes)
Private (18 holes)

Movie Theatres: 6 screens

1 multiplex

Water Area

Lakes and rivers: 1,920 acres

Places Rated Rank: 366

✓Warren-Troy-Farmington Hills, MI

Auto Racing

Waterford Hills

College Sports: 72 games

Oakland University Golden Grizzlies

Golf Courses: 155

Daily fee (1,728 holes)
Municipal (342 holes)
Private (711 holes)

Horse Racing: 140 programs

Hazel Park (Harness)

Movie Theatres: 335 screens

9 singles/twins
24 multiplexes

Professional Sports: 51 games

Lions (NFL Football)
Pistons (NBA Basketball)

Recreation Areas: 44,779 acres

State

Bald Mountain SRA
Brighton SRA
Highland SRA
Holly SRA
Island Lake SRA
Lakelands Trail SP
Metamora-Hadley SRA
Ortonville SRA
Pinckney SRA
Pontiac Lake SRA
Proud Lake SRA
Seven Lakes SP
W.C. Wetzel SP

Ski Areas: 40,030 lift capacity/hr

Water Area

Lakes and rivers: 56,960 acres
Lake St. Clair offshore: 108,160 acres

Zoo

Detroit Zoological Park

Places Rated Rank: 13

✓Washington, DC-VA-MD-WV

Amusement/Theme Parks

Six Flags America

Aquarium

National Aquarium

Auto Racing

Summit Point Raceway

College Sports: 468 games

American University Eagles
George Mason Patriots
George Washington Colonials
Georgetown University Hoyas
Howard University Bison
University of Maryland Terrapins

Golf Courses: 101

Daily fee (774 holes)
Municipal (297 holes)
Private (738 holes)

Horse Racing: 467 programs

Charles Town (Thoroughbred)
Laurel Park (Thoroughbred)
Rosecroft Raceway (Harness)

Movie Theatres: 437 screens

6 singles/twins
39 multiplexes

Professional Sports: 349 games

BaySox (Class AA Baseball)
D.C. United (MLS Soccer)
Mystics (WNBA Basketball)
Nationals (Class A Baseball)
Nationals (NL Baseball)
Redskins (NFL Football)
Washington Capitals (NHL Hockey)
Wizards (NBA Basketball)

Recreation Areas: 81,951 acres

Federal

Appalachian NT
Arlington House-Robert E. Lee NM
Blue Ridge Parkway
Constitution Gardens
FDR Memorial
Featherstone NWR
Fort Washington Park
Fredericksburg/Spotsylvania NMP
George Washington NF
George Washington Parkway
Greenbelt Park
Korean War Veterans NM
Lincoln NMem
Lyndon B. Johnson NM Grove
Marumsco NWR
Mason Neck NWR
National Capital Parks
National Mall
Piscataway Park
Potomac Heritage NT
Prince William Forest Park
Rock Creek Park
Shenandoah NP
Theodore Roosevelt Island
Thomas Jefferson NM
Vietnam Veterans NM
Washington Monument
White House
Wolf Trap Farm Park

State

Calvert Cliffs SP
Lake Anna SP
Leesylvania SP
Mason Neck SP
Merkle Wildlife Sanctuary
Sky Meadows SP

Ski Areas: 2,500 lift capacity/hr

Water Area

Lakes and rivers: 80,000 acres
Atlantic offshore: 167,040 acres

Zoo

National Zoo

Places Rated Rank: 9

Waterloo-Cedar Falls, IA

College Sports: 60 games

University of Northern Iowa Panthers

Golf Courses: 14

Daily fee (108 holes)
Municipal (90 holes)
Private (54 holes)

Movie Theatres: 25 screens

2 singles/twins
3 multiplexes

Water Area

Lakes and rivers: 4,480 acres

Places Rated Rank: 357

Wausau, WI

Golf Courses: 6

Daily fee (72 holes)
Private (36 holes)

Movie Theatres: 14 screens

2 multiplexes

Recreation Areas: 1,283 acres

State

Mountain-Bay State Trail
Rib Mountain SP

Ski Areas: 17,225 lift capacity/hr

Water Area

Lakes and rivers: 19,840 acres

Zoo

Wildwood Park Zoo

Places Rated Rank: 309

Weirton-Steubenville, WV-OH

Golf Courses: 10

Daily fee (117 holes)
Private (63 holes)

Horse Racing: 226 programs

Mountaineer Park (Thoroughbred)

Movie Theatres: 6 screens

1 multiplex

Recreation Areas: 2,304 acres
State
    Jefferson Lake SP
    Tomlinson Run SP

Water Area
    Lakes and rivers: 5,760 acres

Places Rated Rank: 242

Wenatchee, WA

Auto Racing
    Wenatchee Valley's Super Oval

Golf Courses: 10
    Daily fee (108 holes)
    Municipal (45 holes)
    Private (18 holes)

Movie Theatres: 12 screens
    2 multiplexes

Recreation Areas: 1,456,258 acres
Federal
    Lake Chelan NRA
    North Cascades NP
    Wenatchee NF
State
    Chief Joseph SP
    Daroga
    Ice Caves SP
    Lake Chelan SP
    Lake Wenatchee SP
    Lincoln Rock SP
    Peshastin Pinnacles
    Rock Island SP
    Squilchuck SP
    Twenty-Five Mile Creek SP
    Wenatchee Confluence

Ski Areas: 77,350 lift capacity/hr

Water Area
    Lakes and rivers: 64,000 acres

Places Rated Rank: 58

West Palm Beach-Boca Raton, FL

Amusement/Theme Parks
    Lion Country Safari

Aquarium
    South Florida Aquarium

Auto Racing
    Moroso Motorsports Park

College Sports: 78 games
    Florida Atlantic Owls

Golf Courses: 133
    Daily fee (297 holes)
    Municipal (189 holes)
    Private (1,908 holes)

Movie Theatres: 228 screens
    3 singles/twins
    19 multiplexes

Professional Sports: 71 games
    Hammerheads (Class A Baseball)

Recreation Areas: 2,775 acres
Federal
    Loxahatchee NWR

State
    MacArthur Beach SP

Water Area
    Lakes and rivers: 163,840 acres
    Atlantic offshore: 6,208 acres

Zoo
    Dreher Park Zoo

Places Rated Rank: 90

Wheeling, WV-OH

Golf Courses: 9
    Daily fee (45 holes)
    Municipal (63 holes)
    Private (54 holes)

Movie Theatres: 9 screens
    1 multiplex

Professional Sports: 36 games
    Nailers (ECHL Hockey)

Recreation Areas: 1,133 acres
Federal
    Ohio River Islands NWR
State
    Barkcamp SP

Water Area
    Lakes and rivers: 7,680 acres

Zoo
    Oglebay Good Zoo

Places Rated Rank: 294

Wichita, KS

College Sports: 48 games
    Wichita State Shockers

Golf Courses: 27
    Daily fee (153 holes)
    Municipal (153 holes)
    Private (180 holes)

Movie Theatres: 101 screens
    3 singles/twins
    11 multiplexes

Professional Sports: 71 games
    Wranglers (Class AA Baseball)

Recreation Areas: 4,003 acres
State
    Cheney SP
    El Dorado SP

Water Area
    Lakes and rivers: 19,840 acres

Zoo
    Clay Center Zoo
    Sedgwick County Zoo

Places Rated Rank: 269

Wichita Falls, TX

Golf Courses: 7
    Daily fee (36 holes)
    Municipal (54 holes)
    Private (27 holes)

Movie Theatres: 30 screens
    3 multiplexes

Recreation Areas: 524 acres
State
    Lake Arrowhead SRA

Water Area
    Lakes and rivers: 24,960 acres

Places Rated Rank: 314

Williamsport, PA

Golf Courses: 3
    Municipal (36 holes)
    Private (18 holes)

Movie Theatres: 12 screens
    1 multiplex

Professional Sports: 71 games
    Crosscutters (Class A Baseball)

Recreation Areas: 2,183 acres
State
    Little Pine SP
    Susquehanna SP
    Upper Pine Bottom SP

Ski Areas: 7,900 lift capacity/hr

Water Area
    Lakes and rivers: 5,760 acres

Places Rated Rank: 351

Wilmington, DE-MD-NJ

College Sports: 104 games
    Delaware Fightin' Blue Hens

Golf Courses: 28
    Daily fee (261 holes)
    Municipal (18 holes)
    Private (216 holes)

Horse Racing: 141 programs
    Delaware Park (Thoroughbred)

Movie Theatres: 49 screens
    3 singles/twins
    4 multiplexes

Professional Sports: 71 games
    Blue Rocks (Class A Baseball)

Recreation Areas: 17,839 acres
Federal
    Supawna Meadows NWR
State
    Brandywine Creek SP
    Carpenter SP
    Elk Neck SP
    Fail Hill SNA
    Flint Woods Nature Preserve
    Fort DuPont SP
    Fox Point SP
    Lums Pond SP
    Parvin SP
    White Clay Creek Preserve
    White Clay Creek SP

Ski Areas: 10,400 lift capacity/hr

Water Area
    Lakes and rivers: 41,600 acres
    Atlantic offshore: 68,480 acres

Zoo
Brandywine Zoo

Places Rated Rank: 48

Wilmington, NC

Aquarium
North Carolina Aquarium

College Sports: 72 games
UNC Wilmington Seahawks

Golf Courses: 48
Daily fee (747 holes)
Municipal (18 holes)
Private (99 holes)

Movie Theatres: 42 screens
4 multiplexes

Recreation Areas: 1,773 acres
State
Carolina Beach SP

Water Area
Lakes and rivers: 44,160 acres
Atlantic offshore: 16,960 acres

Places Rated Rank: 181

Winchester, VA-WV

Golf Courses: 5
Daily fee (54 holes)
Private (27 holes)

Movie Theatres: 12 screens
2 multiplexes

Recreation Areas: 8,403 acres
Federal
George Washington NF

Ski Areas: 2,500 lift capacity/hr

Water Area
Lakes and rivers: 2,560 acres

Places Rated Rank: 350

Winston-Salem, NC

College Sports: 78 games
Wake Forest Demon Deacons

Golf Courses: 28
Daily fee (315 holes)
Municipal (72 holes)
Private (108 holes)

Movie Theatres: 22 screens
2 multiplexes

Professional Sports: 71 games
Warthogs (Class A Baseball)

Recreation Areas: 6,160 acres
State
Hanging Rock SP
Pilot Mountain SP

Water Area
Lakes and rivers: 7,040 acres

Places Rated Rank: 264

Worcester, MA

College Sports: 124 games
Holy Cross Crusaders

Golf Courses: 40
Daily fee (486 holes)
Municipal (63 holes)
Private (162 holes)

Movie Theatres: 78 screens
5 singles/twins
7 multiplexes

Professional Sports: 36 games
Sharks (AHL Hockey)

Recreation Areas: 11,785 acres
State
Buffumville SRA
Campbell's Falls SP
Dunn Pond SP
Gardner Heritage SP
Lake Dennison SRA
Moore SP
Purgatory Chasm SP
Quinsigamond SP
Rutland SP
Streeter Point SRA
Tully Lake SRA
Wachusett Mountain SR
Wells SP

Ski Areas: 51,025 lift capacity/hr

Water Area
Lakes and rivers: 42,240 acres

Places Rated Rank: 233

Yakima, WA

Golf Courses: 6
Daily fee (72 holes)
Private (36 holes)

Movie Theatres: 24 screens
3 multiplexes

Professional Sports: 95 games
Bears (Class A Baseball)
Sun Kings (CBA Basketball)

Recreation Areas: 996,905 acres
Federal
Gifford Pinchot NF
Snoqualmie NF
Toppenish NWR
State
Yakima Sportsmans SP

Ski Areas: 71,575 lift capacity/hr

Water Area
Lakes and rivers: 10,240 acres

Places Rated Rank: 262

York-Hanover, PA

Golf Courses: 18
Daily fee (252 holes)
Private (72 holes)

Movie Theatres: 22 screens
2 multiplexes

Recreation Areas: 5,699 acres
State
Codorus SP
Gifford Pinchot SP
Samuel Lewis SP

Ski Areas: 21,320 lift capacity/hr

Water Area
Lakes and rivers: 3,840 acres

Places Rated Rank: 341

Youngstown-Warren, OH-PA

College Sports: 60 games
Youngstown State Penguins

Golf Courses: 45
Daily fee (621 holes)
Municipal (63 holes)
Private (126 holes)

Movie Theatres: 60 screens
7 multiplexes

Professional Sports: 71 games
Scrappers (Class A Baseball)

Recreation Areas: 6,900 acres
State
Kyle Woods SNA
M.K. Goddard SP
Mosquito Creek SP

Ski Areas: 6,500 lift capacity/hr

Water Area
Lakes and rivers: 23,680 acres

Places Rated Rank: 177

Yuba City, CA

Golf Courses: 6
Daily fee (63 holes)
Private (36 holes)

Movie Theatres: 12 screens
1 single/twin
2 multiplexes

Recreation Areas: 88,971 acres
Federal
Butte Sink WMA
Plumas NF
Sutter NWR
Tahoe NF

Ski Areas: 150,824 lift capacity/hr

Water Area
Lakes and rivers: 12,160 acres

Places Rated Rank: 240

Yuma, AZ

Golf Courses: 7
Daily fee (81 holes)
Municipal (18 holes)
Private (18 holes)

Movie Theatres: 22 screens
2 multiplexes

Recreation Areas: 972,281 acres
Federal
Cabeza Prieta NWR
Kofa NWR

Ski Areas: 3,200 lift capacity/hr

Water Area
Lakes and rivers: 3,200 acres

Places Rated Rank: 298

GAMBLING

Twenty-five years ago, gambling was legal in only three locations: Nevada, New Jersey, and Puerto Rico. Now, Utah and Hawaii are the last holdouts. Besides the lottery and pari-mutuel racing, you can place a legal bet in nearly 900 casinos—455 of them privately run, 406 others on Native American reservations—according to *stateline.org*, the online news source covering state governments.

The change represents a rapid shift in voter attitudes from first viewing gambling as sinful and ruinous, to then considering it a vice and a human weakness, to finally seeing it as harmless and entertaining activity.

Periodic economic slumps, too, have forced states to find other revenue sources. Last year, to avoid raising taxes, states collected more than $20 billion in revenue from gambling operations for health care, education, transportation and infrastructure. Gambling now pulls in more dollars than Americans spend on movie tickets, CDs, sporting events and concerts.

A hot craze in is installing casino gambling in dog and horse track clubhouses. Currently there are 29 *racinos* in 11 states: Delaware, Florida, Iowa, Louisiana, Maine, New Mexico, New York, Oklahoma, Pennsylvania, Rhode Island and West Virginia.

Arkansas, Alabama and Wyoming are considering joining the 42 states that operate lotteries, including North Carolina, which just started playing in the spring of 2005, Oklahoma in the fall of 2005, and Tennessee in 2004.

One concern is the rapid expansion of unregulated offshore Internet gambling Web sites. Internet gambling - with an estimated $13 billion wagered online in 2005 on Texas Hold'em poker, blackjack and other games - is the fastest-growing form of gambling. Another growing form of Internet gambling are Internet sites where players make wagers with one another – say, which college basketball teams will be in the NCAA Final Four tournament - with the Web site taking a small cut of each wager in exchange for organizing and handling the transaction.

LEGALIZED GAMBLING BY STATE

State	Lotteries	Horses	Greyhounds	Casinos
ALABAMA			•	T
ALASKA				T
ARIZONA	•	•	•	T
ARKANSAS		•	•	
CALIFORNIA	•	•		T
COLORADO	•	•	•	C,T
CONNECTICUT	•		•	T
DELAWARE	•	•		RC
D.C.	•			
FLORIDA	•	•	•	C,RC,S
GEORGIA	•			S
HAWAII				
IDAHO	•	•		T
ILLINOIS	•	•		R
INDIANA	•	•		R
IOWA	•	•	•	R,RC,T
KANSAS	•	•	•	T
KENTUCKY		•		C
LOUISIANA	•	•		R,RC,T
MAINE		•		RC
MARYLAND	•	•		
MASSACHUSETTS	•	•	•	S
MICHIGAN	•	•		T
MINNESOTA	•	•		T
MISSISSIPPI				R,T
MISSOURI	•			R
MONTANA	•			T
NEBRASKA	•	•		T
NEVADA				C,T
NEW HAMPSHIRE	•	•	•	
NEW JERSEY	•	•		C
NEW MEXICO	•	•		RC
NEW YORK	•	•		RC,T
NORTH CAROLINA	•			T
NORTH DAKOTA				T
OHIO	•	•		
OKLAHOMA	•	•		RC,T
OREGON	•	•	•	T
PENNSYLVANIA	•	•		RC
RHODE ISLAND	•		•	RC
SOUTH CAROLINA	•			S
SOUTH DAKOTA	•			C,T
TENNESSEE	•			
TEXAS	•	•	•	
UTAH				
VERMONT	•			
VIRGINIA	•	•		
WASHINGTON	•	•		T
WEST VIRGINIA	•	•	•	RC
WISCONSIN	•		•	T
WYOMING		•		

Source: Stateline.org

Key: T = Tribal casinos, RC = Racinos, C = Privately-run casinos, R = Riverboat casinos, S = offshore ship casinos

Gambling

Where Is The Best Skiing?

A ski area is more than a snow-covered hill or mountain. It also has developed trails and lift machinery. Usually, too, there is a lodge for meals and overnight stays. If the area is large and popular, it also has apres-ski—nighttime entertainment from music to movies to disco - that is as critical as fresh snow and challenging runs to many skiers.

But if you're a skier with time and money, skiing Hanley's Happy Hill in Pennsylvania, Little Switzerland in Wisconsin, or even Vermont's Killington or Stowe isn't quite the same as skiing destination areas in the West such as Aspen, Park City, Jackson Hole, or Whistler/Blackcomb. Ski areas are where you find them, but the best *skiing* is in the highest part of the continent: the Rocky Mountain West and the Sierra Nevada near Lake Tahoe.

This statement isn't purely a matter of opinion. According to ski-industry surveys, most of North America's ten to twelve million skiers are of intermediate ability, tending toward advanced. If they could ski anywhere, they would choose areas that enhance their ability; that is, places with high mountains, great vertical rises, long runs, and heavy powder snowfalls that begin early in winter and last into spring. You'll find more of these qualities within short drives of Calgary, Denver, Boulder, Reno, Salt Lake City, Seattle, Tacoma, Spokane, and Vancouver than anywhere else.

Vertical Rise...

The perpendicular distance from the base to the highest ski able point on a hill or mountain is a ski area's *vertical*. Although vertical rise has little to do with the quality of trails, it is a good indication of length of the runs and the mountain's challenge.

Area	Vertical
Blackcomb Mountain, BC	5,280 feet
Whistler Mountain, BC	5,000
Panorama Resort, BC	4,300
Jackson Hole, WY	4,139
Snowmass, CO	3,721
Aspen Highlands, CO	3,635
Steamboat, CO	3,600
Heavenly Valley, CA	3,600
Telluride, CO	3,522
Sunshine Village, AB	3,514

...and Longest Runs

The longest run is the longest continuous trail on the mountain, from the top to the runout at the base lodge's parking lot. The average is 7,000 feet. At ten resorts, it's more than three times that length.

Area	Longest Run
Killington, VT	6.6 miles
Big Sky Resort, MT	6.00
Heavenly Valley, CA	5.50
Taos Ski Valley, NM	5.25
Solvista Ski Ranch, CO	5.10
Snowmass, CO	5.05
Telluride Ski, CO	4.60
Okemo Mountain, VT	4.50
Jackson Hole, WY	4.50
Vail, CO	4.00

...and Lift Capacities

A ski area's lift capacity is the number of people its lifts can move up the mountain in one hour. The total lift capacity is a good indication of how developed the ski area is and often how fast the lift lines move. Ten North American ski areas have lift capacities of at least 30,000 skiers per hour.

Area	Lift Capacity
Mammoth Mountain, CA	60,000 skiers/hour
Vail, CO	53,381
Killington/Pico Ski, VT	52,973
Squaw Valley, CA	49,000
Deer Valley Resort, UT	43,500
Breckenridge, CO	37,280
Mount Snow/Haystack, VT	36,252
Steamboat, CO	36,195
Winter Park, CO	33,700
Heavenly Valley, CA	33,000

Source: Inter-Ski Services, *The White Book of Ski Areas*

Major League Title Towns

For a baseball fan in the mid-1970s, the place to be was Oakland as the A's hauled in three straight World Series championships. Or fast forward to the 1990s, when the New York Yankees won four World Series in the last years of the millennium.

In the 1960s, football fans found a warm welcome in frosty Green Bay, the only city to actually own a

Baseball's Odyssey

No sport inspires patriotic nostalgia nor has as many heroes and memorable moments as baseball. The logos and names of many of today's major-league teams are as well-traveled as the southward and westward history of this country. Still others stick to one single, loyal lineage. The Atlanta Braves, for example, is one of the nation's oldest clubs, but the team started neither in Atlanta nor as the Braves. The year was 1876 and the ancestral team was the Boston Red Caps. A series of name changes and relocations followed, and the team wouldn't settle in Atlanta until 1966. Other teams have similar stories.

Los Angeles Angels of Anaheim (AL) - *1961*, began as Los Angeles Angels; 1965, moved to Orange County and renamed California Angels; 1997, renamed Anaheim Angels; 2005, renamed Los Angeles Angels of Anaheim.

Atlanta Braves (NL) - *1876*, began as Boston Red Caps; 1883, renamed Beaneaters; 1907, renamed Doves; 1909, renamed Pilgrims; 1936, renamed Bees; 1941, renamed Braves; 1953, moved to Milwaukee and renamed Milwaukee Braves; 1966, moved to Atlanta and renamed Atlanta Braves.

Baltimore Orioles (AL) - *1901*, began as Milwaukee Brewers; 1902, moved to St. Louis and renamed St. Louis Browns; 1954, moved to Baltimore and renamed Orioles.

Boston Red Sox (AL) - *1901*, began as Somersets; 1905, renamed Puritans; 1907, renamed Red Sox.

Chicago Cubs (NL) - *1876*, began as White Stockings; 1894, renamed Colts; 1898, renamed Orphans; 1903, renamed Cubs.

Cincinnati Reds (NL) - *1876*, began as Red Stockings; 1880, renamed Reds; 1953, renamed Red Legs; 1959, renamed Reds.

Cleveland Indians (AL) - *1901*, began as Blues; 1902, renamed Bronchos [sic]; 1903, renamed Naps; 1914, renamed Indians.

Houston Astros (NL) - *1962*, began as Houston Colt .45's; 1964, renamed Astros.

Los Angeles Dodgers (NL) - *1890*, began as Brooklyn Bridegrooms; 1898, renamed Superbas; 1914, renamed Robins; 1931, renamed Dodgers; 1958, moved to Los Angeles and renamed Los Angeles Dodgers. Milwaukee Brewers (AL)-1969, began as Seattle Pilots; 1970, moved to Milwaukee and renamed Milwaukee Brewers.

Minnesota Twins (AL) - *1901*, began as Washington Senators; 1960, moved to Minneapolis-St. Paul and renamed Minnesota Twins.

New York Yankees (AL) - *1901*, began as Baltimore Orioles; 1903, moved to New York and renamed New York Highlanders; 1912, renamed Yankees.

Oakland As (AL) - *1901*, began as Philadelphia Athletics; 1955, moved to Kansas City and renamed Kansas City Athletics; 1968, moved to Oakland and renamed Oakland Athletics; 1974, renamed A's.

Philadelphia Phillies (NL) - *1883*, began as Phillies; 1944, renamed Blue Jays; 1946, renamed Phillies.

Pittsburgh Pirates (NL) - *1887*, began as Alleghenys; 1890, renamed Innocents; 1891, renamed Pirates.

San Francisco Giants (NL) - *1879*, began as Troy (NY) Trojans; 1883, moved to New York City and renamed New York Gothams; 1886, renamed Giants; 1958, moved to San Francisco and renamed San Francisco Giants.

St. Louis Cardinals (NL) - *1892*, began as Perfectos; 1899, renamed Cardinals.

Texas Rangers (AL) - *1961*, began as Washington Senators; 1971, moved to Arlington and renamed Texas Rangers.

Washington Nationals (NL) – *1969*, began as Montreal Expos; 2005 moved to Washington, DC, and renamed Washington Nationals.

The *Chicago White Sox* (AL, 1901), *Detroit Tigers* (AL, 1901), *New York Mets* (NL, 1962), *Kansas City Royals* (AL, 1969), *San Diego Padres* (NL, 1969), *Seattle Mariners* (AL, 1977), *Toronto Blue Jays* (AL, 1977), *Colorado Rockies* (NL, 1993), *Florida Marlins* (NL, 1993), *Arizona Diamondbacks* (NL, 1997), and *Tampa Bay Devil Rays* (AL, 1997) have neither changed their name nor moved.

Hockey's Odyssey

No one really knows when or where hockey originated. But, as the *New York Times* headline said when Canada's men's and women's teams came out on top in the 2002 Winter Olympics: "Their Game, Their Medals". At Montreal's Windsor Hotel nearly 80 years ago, five men who wanted to bankroll teams met to form the National Hockey League (NHL).

Since 1998, four new teams have skated into the NHL. And an icy cold winter isn't any longer the common metaphor for team locations. Zamboni ice resurfacers now operate in southern California, Florida, North Carolina, and Georgia. The following list marks the changes and relocations of NHL teams from their entrance into the league.

Calgary Flames - *1972*, began as Atlanta Flames; 1980, moved to Calgary and renamed Calgary Flames.

Carolina Hurricanes - *1992*, began as New England Whalers (Boston) of the World Hockey Association; 1977, moved to Hartford; 1979, joined NHL; 1997, moved to Greensboro, renamed Carolina Hurricanes; 1999, moved to Raleigh.

Colorado Avalanche - **1972**, began as Quebec Nordiques of the World Hockey Association; 1979, joined NHL; 1995, moved to Denver and renamed Colorado Avalanche.

Dallas Stars - **1967**, began as Minnesota North Stars; 1993, moved to Dallas and renamed Dallas Stars.

Detroit Red Wings - **1926**, began as Cougars; 1929, renamed Falcons; 1932, renamed Red Wings.

Edmonton Oilers - **1972**, began as Alberta Oilers of the World Hockey Association; 1973, renamed Edmonton Oilers; 1979, joined NHL.

New Jersey Devils - **1974**, began as Kansas City Scouts; 1976, moved to Denver and renamed Colorado Rockies; 1982, moved to East Rutherford and renamed New Jersey Devils.

Phoenix Coyotes - **1979**, began as Winnipeg Jets; 1996 moved to Phoenix and renamed Phoenix Coyotes.

Toronto Maple Leafs - **1917**, began as Arenas; 1919, changed name to St. Patricks; 1926, changed name to Maple Leafs.

The *Anaheim Mighty Ducks* (1993), *Atlanta Thrashers* (1999), *Boston Bruins* (1924), *Buffalo Sabres* (1970), *Chicago Black Hawks* (1926), *Columbus Blue Jackets* (2000), *Florida Panthers* (1993), *Los Angeles Kings* (1967), *Minnesota Wild* (2000), *Montreal Canadiens* (1917), *Nashville Predators* (1998), *New York Islanders* (1972), *New York Rangers* (1926), *Ottawa Senators* (1992), *Philadelphia Flyers* (1967), *Pittsburgh Penguins* (1967), *St. Louis Blues* (1967), *San Jose Sharks* (1991), *Tampa Bay Lightning* (1992), *Vancouver Canucks* (1970), and *Washington Capitals* (1974) have neither changed their name nor moved.

big-time sports franchise. There the Packers took five NFL Championships over a seven-year span. No baseball team can really be called a dominant World Series champ for the 1980s. Neither has any football team topped the Packers' record for the 1960s. But the Pittsburgh Steelers, with four Super Bowl wins, the San Francisco 49ers, with three, and the Washington Redskins, with two, have inspired devotion among fans in the late 1970s and throughout the 1980s. The Dallas Cowboys dominated the early 1990s, while the late 1990s belonged to the Denver Broncos.

For basketball fans, Boston was the place to be in the 1960s and through the 1980s. For nearly three decades, the Celtics dominated the sport, winning more titles than any other team in NBA history. With all their tradition and mystique - and the renowned parquet floor of the Boston Garden where they played - they have left many opponents bewitched, bothered, and bewildered. Still, in the 1980s the Los Angeles Lakers didn't do too badly either, with more championships in that decade than any other team. In the 1990s, the Chicago Bulls and the Houston Rockets were the teams to watch. And as we make our way into the 21st century, the Lakers are once again dominating, taking the first three championships of this decade.

Enter Soccer, Women's Basketball

Women weren't far behind men when basketball bounded into the sports scene. Senda Berenson brought the game to women at Smith College and its popularity spread around the country. But while more and more women were participating, they were hindered for years by long hemlines and rules that restricted them from 'unfeminine' play, such as ball snatching and body blocking. The restrictions would fall away with the years, and so would the air balls. In 1996, women's basketball finally gained recognition with Olympic gold. A year later, the inaugural season for the Women's National Basketball Association (WNBA) began.

But women's basketball isn't the only new professional sport. For years, while Americans cheered their professional baseball, football, basketball, and ice hockey teams, fans in Europe and South America packed stadiums for another kind of football commonly known among Americans as soccer. The sport has been hot among American youth for years, but not until the mid-1990s did the sport turn pro.

Basketball's Odyssey

On November 1, 1946, the Toronto Huskies tipped off against the New York Knickerbockers in the historic first game of the Basketball Association of America (BAA). Sadly, 12 games later the Huskies traded their player-coach to Cleveland and by the end of the season the team folded - another rough episode that often marks the start of professional sports associations.

After the 1948-49 season, the BAA changed its name to the National Basketball Association. Today, the Knicks, the Boston Celtics, and the Golden State Warriors (the old Philadelphia Warriors) are the only former BAA franchises remaining. As for the NBA, the list below shows which teams have later moved to another city and changed their name since their founding date.*

Atlanta Hawks – 1946, began as Tri-Cities Blackhawks; 1951, moved to Milwaukee and renamed Milwaukee Hawks; 1955, moved to St. Louis and renamed St. Louis Hawks; 1968, moved to Atlanta and renamed Atlanta Hawks.

Detroit Pistons – 1948, began as Fort Wayne Pistons; 1957, moved to Detroit and renamed Detroit Pistons.

Golden State Warriors – 1946, began as Philadelphia Warriors; 1962, moved to San Francisco and renamed San Francisco Warriors; 1971, moved to Oakland and renamed Golden State Warriors.

Houston Rockets – 1967, began as San Diego Rockets; 1971, moved to Houston and renamed Houston Rockets.

Los Angeles Clippers – 1970, began as Buffalo Braves; 1978, moved to San Diego and renamed San Diego Clippers; 1984, moved to Los Angeles and renamed Los Angeles Clippers.

Los Angeles Lakers – 1948, began as Minneapolis Lakers; 1960, moved to Los Angeles and renamed Los Angeles Lakers.

Memphis Grizzlies – 1995, began as Vancouver Grizzlies; 2001, moved to Memphis and renamed Memphis Grizzlies.

New Jersey Nets – 1967, began as New York Nets of the American Basketball Association; 1976, joined the NBA; 1977, moved to New Jersey and renamed New Jersey Nets.

New Orleans (Oklahoma City) Hornets – 1988, began as Charlotte Hornets; 2002, moved to New Orleans; 2005, Hurricane Katrina forces temporary move to Oklahoma City.

Philadelphia 76ers – 1949, began as Syracuse Nationals; 1963, moved to Philadelphia and renamed Philadelphia 76ers.

Sacramento Kings – 1945, began as Rochester (NY) Royals; 1958, moved to Cincinnati and renamed Cincinnati Royals; 1972, moved to split home courts in Kansas City and Omaha and renamed Kansas City-Omaha Kings; 1975, quit Omaha for Kansas City and renamed Kansas City Kings; 1985, moved to Sacramento and renamed Sacramento Kings.

San Antonio Spurs – 1967, began as Dallas Spurs of the American Basketball Association; 1973, moved to San Antonio and renamed San Antonio Spurs; 1976, joined the NBA.

Utah Jazz – 1974, began as New Orleans Jazz; 1979, moved to Salt Lake City and renamed Utah Jazz.

Washington Wizards – 1961, began as Chicago Packers; 1962, renamed Chicago Zephyrs; 1963, moved to Baltimore and renamed Baltimore Bullets; 1973, moved to Landover, MD, and renamed Capital Bullets; 1974, renamed Washington Bullets; 1997, moved to Washington, DC, and renamed Washington Wizards.

*The *Boston Celtics* (1946), *New York Knickerbockers* (1946), *Chicago Bulls* (1966), *Seattle Supersonics* (1967), *Milwaukee Bucks* (1968), *Phoenix Suns* (1968), *Cleveland Cavaliers* (1970), *Portland Trail Blazers* (1970), *Dallas Mavericks* (1980), *Miami Heat* (1988), *Minnesota Timberwolves* (1989), *Orlando Magic* (1989), *Toronto Raptors* (1995), and Charlotte Bobcats (2004) began as NBA teams and have neither moved nor changed their team name.

The *Denver Nuggets* (1967) and *Indiana Pacers* (1967) are former American Basketball League franchises that joined the NBA in 1976.

Professional Champs: A Metro Retrospective

Our survey of metro areas in the list just below looks at the winners in five professional team sports: baseball, football, basketball, ice hockey, and soccer. In the cases of baseball and ice hockey, we include the winners of the World Series (since 1903) and the Stanley Cup (since 1894). For football and men's basketball, we include the NFL Super Bowl, and NBA Championship winners. New to this year's edition are championship listings for major league soccer (MLS) starting in 1996, and women's professional basketball (WNBA), which began play in 1997.

Going back a little more toward the roots, we also list the championship winners from the leagues that preceded the modern NFL (the National Football League, 1933-1969, and the American Football League, 1960-1969) and the NBA (the Basketball Association of America, 1947-1949). The NFL and AFL champions of 1966, 1967, and 1968 met in the Super Bowls of 1967, 1968, and 1969, before the formation of the modern NFL; for those years, we name the winners of both the individual league championships and the Super Bowl.

If a team has changed names or towns, we list it with the name it used and in the town it played at the time it won the championship.

PROFESSIONAL CHAMPIONSHIPS IN THE METRO AREAS

Anaheim-Santa Ana-Irvine, CA
NFL Championship: Los Angeles Rams, 1951

Atlanta-Sandy Springs-Marietta, GA
World Series: Braves, 1995

Baltimore-Towson, MD
World Series: Orioles, 1966, 1970, 1983
Super Bowl: Colts, 1971; Ravens, 2001;
NFL Championship: Colts 1958, 1959, 1968
NBA Championship: Bullets, 1948

Boston-Quincy, MA
World Series: Somersets, 1903; Red Sox, 1912, 1914, 1915, 1916, 1918, 2004
Super Bowl: Patriots, 2002, 2004, 2005
NBA Championship: Celtics, 1957, 1959, 1960, 1961, 1962, 1963, 1964, 1965, 1966, 1968, 1969, 1974, 1976, 1981, 1984, 1986
NHL Stanley Cup: Bruins, 1929, 1939, 1941, 1970, 1972

Buffalo-Niagara Falls, NY
AFL Championship: Bills, 1964, 1965

Chicago-Naperville-Joliet, IL
World Series: White Sox, 1906, 1917, 2005; Cubs, 1907, 1908
Super Bowl: Bears, 1986
NFL Championship: Bears, 1933, 1940, 1941, 1943, 1946; Cardinals, 1947; Bears, 1963
NBA Championship: Bulls, 1991, 1992, 1993, 1996, 1997, 1998
NHL Stanley Cup: Black Hawks, 1934, 1938, 1961
MLS Championship: Fire, 1998

Cincinnati-Middletown, OH-KY-IN
World Series: Reds, 1919, 1940, 1975, 1976, 1990

Cleveland, OH
World Series: Indians, 1920, 1948
NFL Championship: Rams, 1945; Browns, 1950, 1954, 1955, 1964

Dallas-Plano-Irving, TX
Super Bowl: Cowboys, 1972, 1978, 1993, 1994, 1996
AFL Championship: Texans, 1962
NHL Stanley Cup: Stars, 1999

Denver-Aurora, CO
Super Bowl: Broncos, 1998, 1999
NHL Stanley Cup: Colorado Avalanche, 1996, 2001

Detroit-Livonia-Dearborn, MI
World Series: Tigers, 1935, 1945, 1968, 1984
NFL Championship: Lions, 1935, 1952, 1953, 1957
NBA Championship: Pistons, 1989, 1990, 2004
NHL Stanley Cup: Red Wings, 1936, 1937, 1943, 1950, 1952, 1954, 1955, 1997, 1998, 2002
WNBA Championship: Shock, 2003

Green Bay, WI
Super Bowl: Packers, 1967, 1968, 1997
NFL Championship: Packers, 1936, 1937, 1939, 1944, 1961, 1962, 1965, 1966, 1967

Houston-Sugarland-Baytown, TX
AFL Championship: Oilers, 1960, 1961
NBA Championship: Rockets, 1994, 1995
WNBA Championship: Comets, *1997 inaugural season, 1998, 1999, 2000

Kansas City, MO-KS
World Series: Royals, 1985

Football's Odyssey

The first NFL franchise in Cleveland belonged not to the Browns but to the Rams, who played such opponents as the Brooklyn Dodgers, Chicago Cardinals, and Pittsburgh Pirates back in the 1930s. Today these early teams seem ragtag compared to the juggernauts that now come together in a Super Bowl.

Some of the greatest moments in the history of professional football are just that: moments. Never again will a play fall into place in quite the same way, or a mix of players click to form an unstoppable team. Since professional football began to take shape in 1922 with the establishment of the National Football League, team names, locations, leagues and loyalties have been in flux. The list below recaps the moves and name changes of today's NFL teams since their founding date.

Arizona Cardinals - *1913*, began as Racine Avenue (Chicago) Cardinals; 1922, renamed Chicago Cardinals; 1960, moved to St. Louis and renamed St. Louis Cardinals; 1988, moved to Phoenix and renamed Phoenix Cardinals; 1994, renamed Arizona Cardinals.

Baltimore Ravens - *1946*, began as Cleveland Browns of the All-America Football Conference; 1950, joined NFL; 1996, moved to Baltimore, renamed Ravens.

Detroit Lions - *1930*, began as Portsmouth (OH) Spartans; 1934, moved to Detroit and renamed Detroit Lions.

Indianapolis Colts - *1952*, defunct Dallas Texans of the All-America Football Conference moved to Baltimore, renamed Baltimore Colts, and joined the NFL; 1983, moved to Indianapolis and renamed Indianapolis Colts.

Kansas City Chiefs - *1959*, began as Dallas Texans of the American Football League; 1963, moved to Kansas City and renamed Kansas City Chiefs; 1970, joined NFL.

New England Patriots - *1959*, began as Boston Patriots of the American Football League; 1970, joined NFL; 1971, renamed New England Patriots.

New York Jets - *1959*, began as New York Titans of the American Football League; 1963, renamed New York Jets; 1970, joined NFL.

Oakland Raiders - *1959*, began as Oakland Raiders of the American Football League; 1970, joined NFL; 1982, moved to Los Angeles and renamed Los Angeles Raiders; 1995, moved to Oakland and renamed Oakland Raiders.

St. Louis Rams - *1937*, began as Cleveland Rams; 1946, moved to Los Angeles and renamed Los Angeles Rams; 1995, moved to St. Louis and renamed St. Louis Rams.

San Diego Chargers - *1959*, franchised as Los Angeles Chargers of the American Football League; 1961, moved to San Diego and renamed San Diego Chargers; 1970, joined NFL.

Tennessee Titans - *1959*, franchised as Houston Oilers of the American Football League; 1997, moved to Memphis as Tennessee Oilers; 1998, moved to Nashville; 1999, renamed Tennessee Titans.

Washington Redskins - *1932*, began as Boston Braves; 1933, renamed Boston Redskins; 1937, moved to Washington and renamed Washington Redskins.

The *Chicago Bears* (1922), *Green Bay Packers* (1922), *New York Giants* (1925), *Philadelphia Eagles* (1933), *Pittsburgh Steelers* (1933), *Dallas Cowboys* (1960), *Minnesota Vikings* (1960), *Atlanta Falcons* (1965), *New Orleans Saints* (1966), *Seattle Seahawks* (1974), *Tampa Bay Buccaneers* (1974), *Carolina Panthers* (1994), and *Jacksonville Jaguars* (1994) began as NFL teams and have neither moved nor changed their team name. The *Cleveland Browns* (1999), a new NFL team, revived the name of the 1946-1996 home team that moved to Baltimore and was renamed the Ravens. The *Houston Texans* (2002), is the newest NFL team in the league. To accommodate them, the NFL was realigned into eight four-team divisions in 2001.

The *San Francisco 49ers* (1946) are a former All-American Football Conference team that joined the NFL in 1949. The *Buffalo Bills* (1959), *Denver Broncos* (1959), *Miami Dolphins* (1965), and *Cincinnati Bengals* (1967) are former American Football League franchises that merged with the NFL in 1970.

Super Bowl: Chiefs, 1970
AFL Championship: Chiefs, 1966, 1969
MLS Championship: Wizards, 2000

Los Angeles-Long Beach-Glendale, CA

World Series: Anaheim Angels, 2002; Dodgers, 1959, 1963, 1965, 1981, 1988
Super Bowl: Raiders, 1984
MLS Championship: Galaxy, 2002
NFL Championship: Rams, 1951
NBA Championship: Lakers, 1972, 1980, 1982, 1985, 1987, 1988, 2000, 2001, 2002
WNBA Championship: Sparks, 2001, 2002

Miami-Miami Beach-Kendall, FL

World Series: Florida Marlins, 1997, 2003
Super Bowl: Dolphins, 1973, 1974
NBA Championship: Heat, 2006

Milwaukee-Waukesha-West Alles, WI

World Series: Braves, 1957
NBA Championship: Bucks, 1971

Minneapolis-St. Paul-Bloomington, MN

World Series: Twins, 1987, 1991
NFL Championship: Minnesota Vikings, 1969
NBA Championship: Minneapolis Lakers, 1949, 1950, 1952, 1953, 1954

Nashville

Super Bowl: Tennessee Titals,

Nassau-Suffolk, NY

NHL Stanley Cup: New York Islanders, 1980, 1981, 1982, 1983

New York-White Plains-Wayne, NY-NJ

World Series: Yankees, 1923, 1927, 1928, 1932, 1936, 1937, 1938, 1939, 1941, 1943, 1947, 1949, 1950, 1951, 1952, 1953, 1956, 1958, 1961, 1962, 1977, 1978; Brooklyn Dodgers, 1955; Mets, 1969, 1986; Yankees, 1996, 1998, 1999, 2000
Super Bowl: Jets, 1969; Giants, 1987, 1991
AFL Championship: Jets, 1968
NFL Championship: Giants, 1934, 1938, 1944, 1956
NBA Championship: Knickerbockers, 1970, 1973
NHL Stanley Cup: New Jersey Devils, 1995, 2000, 2003; Rangers, 1928, 1933, 1940, 1994

Oakland-Fremont-Hayward, CA

World Series: Athletics, 1972, 1973, 1974, 1989
Super Bowl: Raiders, 1977, 1981, 2002
AFL Championship: Raiders, 1967
NBA Championship: Golden State Warriors, 1975

Philadelphia, PA

World Series: Athletics, 1910, 1911, 1913, 1929, 1930; Phillies, 1980
NFL Championship: Eagles, 1948, 1949, 1960
NBA Championship: Warriors, 1947, 1956; 76ers, 1967, 1983
NHL Stanley Cup: Flyers, 1974, 1975

Phoenix-Mesa-Scottsdale, AZ

World Series: Arizona Diamondbacks, 2001

Pittsburgh, PA

World Series: Pirates, 1909, 1925, 1960, 1971, 1979
Super Bowl: Steelers, 1975, 1976, 1979, 1980, 2005
NHL Stanley Cup: Penguins, 1991, 1992

Portland-Vancouver-Beaverton, OR

NBA Championship: Trail Blazers, 1977

Raleigh-Cary, NC

NHL Stanley Cup: Carolina Hurricanes, 2006

Rochester, NY

NBA Championship: Royals, 1951

Sacramento–Arden-Arcade–Roseville, CA

WNBA Championship: Monarchs, 2005

St. Louis, MO-IL

World Series: Cardinals, 1926, 1931, 1934, 1942, 1944, 1946, 1964, 1967, 1982, 2006
Super Bowl: Rams, 2000
NBA Championship: Hawks, 1958

San Antonio, TX

NBA Championship: Spurs, 1999, 2003, 2005

San Diego-Carlsbad-San Marcos, CA

AFL Championship: Chargers, 1963

San Francisco-San Mateo-Redwood, CA

World Series: Giants, 1905, 1921, 1922, 1933, 1954;
Super Bowl: 49ers, 1982, 1985, 1989, 1990, 1995

San Jose-Sunnyvale-Santa Clara, CA

MLS Championship: Earthquakes, 2001, 2003

Seattle-Bellvue-Everett, WA

NBA Championship: Supersonics, 1979
NHL Stanley Cup: Metropolitans, 1917

WNBA Championship: Storm, 2004

Syracuse, NY
NBA Championship: Nationals, 1955

Tampa-St. Petersburg-Clearwater, FL
Super Bowl: Bucs, 2003
NHL Stanley Cup: Lightning, 2004

Washington-Arlington, DC-MD-VA
World Series: Senators, 1924
Super Bowl: Redskins, 1983, 1988, 1992
NFL Championship: Redskins, 1937, 1942
NBA Championship: Bullets, 1978
MLS Championship: DC United, 1996, 1997, 1999, 2004

COLLEGIATE TITLE TOWNS

For many, collegiate play is more entertaining than professional competition. The passion of amateur athletes along with pride in the alma mater's teams are enough to turn dignified and learned alumni into rabid fans.

The 2006-2007 academic year marks the 123rd season of American college athletic championships, beginning when Harvard University's J. S. Clark captured the first singles title in college tennis in 1883. Founded in 1906, the National Collegiate Athletic Association (NCAA) began sponsoring college athletic championships in 1921 with its first outdoor track meet. The University of Illinois took the championship title that year, but the University of Southern California would dominate the sport until the 1990s, when the University of Arkansas took over the lead.

It was not until 1981 that the association initiated women's championships. Two sports and two schools made their mark in collegiate history that year. The University of Virginia won the women's cross country title and the University of Southern California won the volleyball title. Most other women's sports held inaugural championships in 1982. Women's water polo is the latest sport to be sanctioned, with UCLA taking the 2001 title.

Over the years, some 600 colleges and universities have been named national champions in each of the NCAA's three divisions. What follows is a list of every NCAA Division I championship won by schools within metropolitan areas. Many NCAA sports, such as basketball and soccer, have both men's and women's championships. An M or W after the sport in the list below indicates whether the title was in men's or women's competition. Sports such as baseball, football, ice hockey, and wrestling are played at the championship level by men only, whereas field hockey, softball, and rowing championships are for women only; accordingly, no M or W designation is given for those sports. Ski and fencing teams are coed.

Ever since Yale first won the title in 1893, there has been an unofficial national champion football team selected by various polls of coaches, sportswriters, and statisticians at the end of each season. In some years, two teams were proclaimed champions by different polls. Division I-AA champions are identified by (I-AA).

NCAA DIVISION I CHAMPIONS BY METRO AREA

Albany-Schenectady-Troy, NY
Rensselaer Polytechnic Institute: Ice Hockey, 1954, 1985

Ames, IA
Iowa State University: Wrestling, 1933, 1965, 1969, 1970, 1972, 1973, 1977, 1987; Cross Country (M), 1989, 1994; Gymnastics (M), 1971, 1973, 1974;

Ann Arbor, MI
University of Michigan: Baseball, 1953, 1962; Basketball (M), 1989; Field Hockey, 2001; Football, 1901, 1902, 1932, 1933, 1947, 1948, 1952, 1948, 1997; Gymnastics (M), 1963, 1969, 1970, 1999; Ice Hockey, 1948, 1951, 1952, 1953, 1955, 1956, 1964, 1996, 1998; Outdoor Track (M), 1923; Swimming and Diving (M), 1937, 1938, 1939, 1940, 1941, 1948, 1957, 1958, 1959, 1961, 1995; Tennis (M), 1957

Athens-Clarke County, GA
University of Georgia: Baseball, 1990; Football, 1980; Golf (M), 1999; Golf (W), 2001; Gymnastics (W), 1987, 1989, 1993, 1998, 1999, 2005, 2006; Swimming and Diving (W), 1999, 2000, 2001, 2005; Tennis (M), 1985, 1987, 1999, 2001; Tennis (W), 1994, 2000

Atlanta-Sandy Springs-Marietta, GA
Georgia Institute of Technology: Football, 1917, 1928, 1990

Timeline: NCAA First Championships

June 1921 – Outdoor Track & Field, at the University of Chicago

April 1924 – Swimming & Diving, at the U.S. Naval Academy

March 1928 – Wrestling, at Iowa State University

April 1937 – Boxing, at the University of California, Davis

April 1938 – Gymnastics, at the University of Chicago

November 1938 – Cross Country, at Michigan State University

March 1939 – Basketball, at Northwestern University

March 1941 - Fencing, at Ohio State University

May 1946 - Team Tennis, at Northwestern University

June 1947 – Baseball, at Western Michigan University

March 1948 - Ice Hockey, at Colorado College

March 1954 – Skiing, at the University of Nevada

December 1959 – Men's Soccer, at the University of Connecticut

March 1965 - Indoor Track, in Detroit

April 1969 – Trampoline, at the University of Michigan

November 1969 - Water Polo, at California State, Long Beach

April 1970 – Volleyball, at UCLA

June 1971 – Lacrosse, at Hofstra University

April 1980 – Rifle, in Johnson City, Tennessee

November 1981 - Field Hockey at University of Connecticut

November 1981 - Women's Cross Country, at Wichita State University

November 1981 – Women's Soccer, at University of Central Florida

December 1981 - Women's Volleyball, at UCLA

March 1982 - Women's Swimming & Diving, at the University of Florida

March 1982 - Women's Basketball, in Norfolk, Virginia

April 1982 - Women's Gymnastics, at the University of Utah

May 1982 - Women's Golf, at Stanford University

May 1982 - Women's Lacrosse, at College of New Jersey

May 1982 - Women's Softball, in Omaha, Nebraska

May 1982 - Women's Tennis, in Salt Lake City, Utah

May 1982 - Women's Outdoor Track & Field, at Brigham Young University

March 1983 - Women's Indoor Track & Field, in Pontiac, Michigan

Source: NCAA, Collegiate Championships

Auburn-Opelika, AL

Auburn University: Football, 1957; Swimming and Diving (M), 1997, 1999, 2003, 2004, 2005, 2006; Swimming and Diving (W), 2002, 2003, 2004, 2006

Austin-Round Rock, TX

University of Texas: Baseball, 1949, 1950, 1975, 1983, 2002, 2005; Basketball (W), 1986; Cross Country (W), 1986; Football, 1963, 1969, 1970, 2005; Golf (M), 1971, 1972; Gymnastics (W), 1987; Indoor Track (W), 1986, 1988, 1990, 1998, 1999; Outdoor Track (W), 1986, 1998, 1999; Swimming and Diving (M), 1981, 1988, 1989, 1990, 1991, 1996, 2000, 2001, 2002; Swimming and Diving (W), 1984, 1985, 1986, 1987, 1988, 1990, 1991; Tennis (W), 1993, 1995; Volleyball (W), 1988

Baltimore-Towson, MD

Johns Hopkins University: Lacrosse (M), 1974, 1978, 1979, 1980, 1984, 1985, 1987

Bangor, ME

University of Maine, Orono: Ice Hockey, 1993, 1999

Baton Rouge, LA

Louisiana State University: Baseball, 1991, 1993, 1996, 1997, 2000; Football, 1958, 2003; Golf (M), 1940, 1942, 1947, 1955; Indoor Track (M), 2001, 2005; Indoor Track (W), 1987, 1989, 1991, 1993, 1994, 1995, 1996, 1997, 2002, 2003, 2004; Outdoor Track (M), 1933, 1989, 1990, 2002; Outdoor Track (W), 1987, 1988, 1989, 1990, 1991, 1992, 1993, 1994, 1995, 1996, 1997, 2000

Bloomington, IN

Indiana University: Basketball (M), 1940, 1953, 1976, 1981, 1987; Cross Country (M), 1938, 1940, 1942; Outdoor Track (M), 1932; Soccer (M), 1982, 1983, 1988, 1998, 1999, 2003, 2004; Swimming and Diving (M), 1968, 1969, 1970, 1971, 1972, 1973; Wrestling, 1932

Boise City-Nampa, ID

Boise State University: Football (I-AA), 1980

Boston-Quincy, MA

Boston College: Ice Hockey, 1949, 2001
Boston University: Ice Hockey, 1971, 1972, 1978, 1995
Harvard University: Football, 1890, 1898, 1899, 1910, 1912, 1913, 1919; Ice Hockey, 1989; Lacrosse (W), 1990

Boulder, CO

University of Colorado: Cross Country (M), 2001; Cross Country (W), 2000; Football, 1990; Skiing, 1959, 1960, 1972, 1973, 1974, 1975, 1976, 1977, 1978, 1979, 1982, 1991, 1995, 1998, 1999

Burlington-South Burlington, VT

University of Vermont: Skiing, 1980, 1989, 1990, 1992, 1994

Cedar Rapids, IA

Cornell College, Wrestling, 1947

Champaign-Urbana, IL

University of Illinois: Football, 1923, 1927, Gymnastics (M), 1939, 1940, 1941, 1942, 1950, 1955, 1956, 1958, 1989; Outdoor Track (M), 1921, 1927, 1944, 1946, 1947

Charlottesville, VA

University of Virginia: Cross Country (W) 1981, 1982; Lacrosse (M), 1972, 1999; Lacrosse (W), 1991, 1993; Soccer (M), 1989, 1991, 1992, 1993, 1994

Chicago-Naperville-Joliet, IL

Loyola University: Basketball (M), 1963
University of Chicago: Football, 1905; Gymnastics (M), 1938

Cincinnati-Middletown, OH-KY-IN

University of Cincinnati: Basketball (M), 1961, 1962

College Station-Bryan, TX

Texas A & M University: Football, 1939; Softball, 1983, 1987

Colorado Springs, CO

Colorado College: Ice Hockey, 1950, 1957

Columbia, MO

University of Missouri: Baseball, 1954; Indoor Track (M), 1965

Columbia, SC

University of South Carolina: Outdoor Track (W), 2002

Columbus, OH

Ohio State University: Baseball, 1966; Basketball (M), 1960; Football, 1942, 1954, 1957, 1968, 2002; Golf (M), 1945, 1979; Gymnastics (M), 1985, 1996, 2001; Outdoor Track (M), 1929; Swimming and Diving (M), 1943, 1945, 1946, 1947, 1949,

1950, 1952, 1954, 1955, 1956, 1962

Dallas-Plano-Irving, TX

Southern Methodist University: Golf (M), 1954; Indoor Track (M), 1983; Outdoor Track (M), 1983, 1986

Denver-Aurora, CO

University of Denver: Gymnastics (W), 1983; Ice Hockey, 1958, 1960, 1961, 1968, 1969, 2004, 2005; Skiing, 1954, 1955, 1956, 1957, 1961, 1962, 1963, 1964, 1965, 1966, 1967, 1969, 1970, 1971, 2000, 2001, 2002

Des Moines, IA

Drake University: Cross Country (M), 1944, 1945, 1946

Duluth, MN-WI

University of Minnesota: Ice Hockey (W), 2001, 2002

Durham, NC

Duke University: Basketball (M), 1991, 1992, 2001; Golf (W), 1999, 2002, 2004, 2005, 2006; Soccer (M), 1986

El Paso, TX

University of Texas, El Paso: Basketball (M), 1966; Cross Country (M), 1969, 1975, 1976, 1978, 1979, 1980, 1981, 1983; Indoor Track (M), 1974, 1975, 1976, 1978, 1980, 1981, 1982; Outdoor Track (M), 1975, 1978, 1979, 1980, 1981, 1982

Eugene-Springfield, OR

University of Oregon: Basketball (M), 1939; Cross Country (M), 1971, 1973, 1974, 1977; Cross Country (W), 1983, 1987; Outdoor Track (M), 1962, 1964, 1965, 1970, 1984; Outdoor Track (W), 1985

Fairbanks, AK

University of Alaska: Rifle, 1994, 1999, 2000, 2001, 2002, 2003, 2004, 2006

Fayetteville-Springdale-Rogers, AR

University of Arkansas: Basketball (M), 1994; Cross Country (M), 1984, 1986, 1987, 1990, 1991, 1992, 1993, 1995, 1998, 1999, 2000; Indoor Track (M), 1984, 1985, 1986, 1987, 1988, 1989, 1990, 1991, 1992, 1993, 1994, 1995, 1997, 1998, 1999, 2000, 2003; Outdoor Track (M), 1985, 1992, 1993, 1994, 1995, 1996, 1997, 1998, 1999

Fort Worth-Arlington, TX

Texas Christian University: Football, 1938; Golf (W), 1983

Fresno, CA

California State University: Softball, 1998

Gainesville, FL

University of Florida: Basketball, 2006 (M); Football, 1996, 2006; Golf (M), 1968, 1973, 1993, 2001; Golf (W), 1985, 1986; Indoor Track (W), 1992; Soccer (W), 1998; Swimming and Diving (M), 1983, 1984; Swimming and Diving (W), 1982; Tennis (W), 1992, 1996, 1998

Grand Forks, ND-MN

University of North Dakota: Ice Hockey, 1959, 1963, 1980, 1982, 1987, 1997, 2000

Greensboro-High Point, NC

Wake Forest University: Baseball, 1955; Golf (M), 1974, 1975, 1986

Greenville, SC

Clemson University: Football, 1981; Soccer (M), 1984, 1987
Furman University: Football (I-AA), 1988

Hartford-West Hartford, CT

University of Connecticut: Basketball (M), 1999, 2004; Basketball (W), 1995, 2000, 2002, 2003, 2004

Honolulu, HI

University of Hawaii: Volleyball (M), 2002; Volleyball (W), 1982, 1983, 1987

Houston-Sugarland-Baytown, TX

Rice University: Baseball, 2003
University of Houston: Cross Country (M), 1960; Golf (M), 1956, 1957, 1958, 1959, 1960, 1962, 1964, 1965, 1966, 1967, 1969, 1970, 1977, 1982, 1984, 1985

Huntington-Ashland, WV-KY-OH

Marshall University: Football (I-AA), 1992, 1996

Iowa City, IA

University of Iowa: Field Hockey, 1986; Gymnastics (M), 1969; Wrestling, 1975, 1976, 1978, 1979, 1980, 1981, 1982, 1983, 1984, 1985, 1986, 1991, 1992, 1993, 1995, 1996, 1997, 1998, 1999, 2000

Ithaca, NY

Cornell University: Football, 1915, 1921, 1922

Kalamazoo-Portage, MI

Western Michigan University: Cross Country (M), 1964, 1965

Knoxville, TN

University of Tennessee: Basketball (W), 1987, 1989, 1991, 1996, 1997, 1998; Cross Country (M), 1972; Football, 1951, 1998; Indoor Track (M), 2002; Outdoor Track (M), 1974, 1991, 2001; Swimming and Diving (M), 1978

Lafayette, IN

Purdue University: Basketball (W), 1999; Golf (M), 1961

Lansing-East Lansing, MI

Michigan State University: Basketball (M), 1979, 2000; Cross Country (M), 1939, 1948, 1949, 1952, 1955, 1956, 1958, 1959; Football, 1952, 1965; Gymnastics (M), 1958; Ice Hockey, 1966, 1986; Soccer (M), 1967, 1968; Wrestling, 1967

Las Vegas-Paradise, NV

University of Nevada: Basketball (M), 1990; Golf (M), 1998

Lawrence, KS

Kansas University: Basketball (M), 1952, 1988; Cross Country (M), 1953; Indoor Track (M), 1966, 1969, 1970; Outdoor Track (M), 1959, 1960, 1970

Lexington-Fayette, KY

Eastern Kentucky University: Football (I-AA), 1979, 1982
University of Kentucky: Basketball (M), 1948, 1949, 1951, 1958, 1978, 1996, 1998; Cross Country (W), 1988

Lincoln, NE

University of Nebraska: Football, 1970, 1971, 1994, 1995, 1997; Gymnastics (M), 1979, 1980, 1981, 1982, 1983, 1988, 1990, 1994; Indoor Track (W), 1983, 1984; Volleyball (W), 1995, 2000

Los Angeles-Long Beach-Glendale, CA

California State University, Fullerton: Baseball, 1979, 1984, 1995, 2004; Softball, 1986
California State University, Long Beach: Volleyball (M), 1991; Volleyball (W), 1989, 1993, 1998
California State University, Northridge: Gymnastics (W), 1982
Pepperdine University: Baseball, 1992; Golf (M),

1997; Volleyball (M), 1978, 1985, 1986, 1992, 2005; Water Polo (M), 1997

University of California, Irvine: Water Polo (M), 1970, 1982, 1989

University of California, Los Angeles: Basketball (M), 1964, 1965, 1967, 1968, 1969, 1970, 1971, 1972, 1973, 1975, 1995; Football, 1954; Golf (M), 1988; Golf (W), 1991; Gymnastics (M), 1984, 1987; Gymnastics (W), 1997, 2000, 2001, 2003, 2004; Indoor Track (W), 2000, 2001; Outdoor Track (M), 1956, 1966, 1971, 1972, 1973, 1978, 1987, 1988; Outdoor Track (W), 1982, 1983; Soccer (M), 1985, 1990, 1997, 2002; Softball, 1982, 1984, 1985, 1988, 1989 1990, 1992, 1995, 1999, 2003, 2004; Swimming and Diving (M), 1982; Tennis (M), 1950, 1952, 1953, 1954, 1956, 1960, 1961, 1965, 1970, 1971, 1975, 1976, 1979, 1982, 1984; Volleyball (M), 1970, 1971, 1972, 1974, 1975, 1976, 1979, 1981, 1982, 1983, 1984, 1987, 1989, 1993, 1995, 1996, 1998, 2000; Volleyball (W), 1984, 1990, 1991; Water Polo (M), 1969, 1971, 1972, 1995, 1996, 1999, 2000; Water Polo (W), 2001

University of Southern California: Baseball, 1948, 1958, 1961, 1963, 1968, 1970, 1971, 1972, 1973, 1974, 1978, 1998; Basketball (W), 1983, 1984; Football, 1928, 1931, 1932, 1939, 1962, 1967, 1972, 1974, 1978, 2003, 2004; Gymnastics (M), 1962; Indoor Track (M), 1967, 1972; Outdoor Track (M), 1926, 1930, 1931, 1935, 1936, 1937, 1938, 1939, 1940, 1941, 1942, 1943, 1949, 1950, 1951, 1952, 1953, 1954, 1955, 1958, 1961, 1963, 1965, 1967, 1968, 1976; Outdoor Track (W), 2001; Swimming and Diving (M), 1960, 1963, 1964, 1965, 1966, 1974, 1975, 1976, 1977; Swimming and Diving (W), 1997; Tennis (M), 1946, 1951, 1955, 1958, 1962, 1963, 1964, 1966, 1967, 1968, 1969, 1976, 1991, 1993, 1994, 2002; Tennis (W), 1983, 1985; Volleyball (M), 1977, 1980, 1988, 1990; Volleyball (W), 1981, 2002, 2003; Water Polo (M), 1998

Louisville, KY-IN

University of Louisville: Basketball (M), 1980, 1986

Lubbock, TX

Texas Tech University: Basketball (W), 1993

Madison, WI

University of Wisconsin: Basketball (M), 1941; Cross Country (M), 1982, 1985, 1988; Cross Country (W), 1984, 1985; Ice Hockey, 1973, 1977, 1981, 1983, 1990, 2006; Soccer (M), 1995

Miami-Miami Beach-Kendall, FL

University of Miami: Baseball, 1982, 1985, 1999, 2001; Football, 1983, 1987, 1989, 1991, 2001; Golf (W), 1984

Milwaukee-Waukesha-West Allis, WI

Marquette University: Basketball (M), 1977

Minneapolis-St. Paul-Bloomington, MN-WI

University of Minnesota: Baseball, 1956, 1960, 1964; Football, 1934, 1935, 1936, 1940, 1941, 1960; Golf (M), 2002; Ice Hockey, 1974, 1976, 1979, 2002, 2003; Outdoor Track (M), 1948; Wrestling, 2001, 2002

Missoula, MT

University of Montana: Football (I-AA), 1995, 2001

Monroe, LA

Northeast Louisiana University: Football (I-AA), 1987

Morgantown, WV

West Virginia University: Rifle, 1983, 1984, 1986, 1988, 1989, 1990, 1991, 1992, 1993, 1995, 1996, 1997, 1998

New Haven-Milford, CT

Yale University: Football, 1883, 1884, 1886, 1887, 1888, 1891, 1892, 1894, 1900, 1907, 1909; Golf (M), 1924, 1925, 1926, 1931, 1932, 1933, 1936, 1943; Swimming and Diving (M), 1942, 1944, 1951, 1953

New Orleans-Metairie-Kenner, LA

Tulane University: Tennis (M), 1959

New York-White Plains-Wayne, NY-NJ

Columbia University: Fencing, 1992, 1993
City College of New York: Basketball (M), 1950
Manhattan College, Indoor Track (M), 1973
St. John's University: Fencing, 2001; Soccer (M), 1996

Oakland-Fremont-Hayward, CA

University of California, Berkeley: Baseball, 1947, 1957; Basketball (M), 1959; Football, 1920; Gymnastics (M), 1968, 1975, 1997, 1998; Outdoor Track (M), 1922; Softball, 2002; Swimming and Diving (M), 1979, 1980; Water Polo (M), 1973, 1974, 1975, 1977, 1983, 1984, 1987, 1988, 1990, 1991, 1992

Oklahoma City, OK

University of Oklahoma: Baseball, 1951, 1994; Football, 1950, 1955, 1956, 1974, 1975, 1985, 2000; Golf (M), 1989; Gymnastics

(M), 1977, 1978, 1991, 2002, 2003, 2005, 2006; Softball, 2000; Wrestling, 1936, 1951, 1952, 1957, 1960, 1963, 1974

Philadelphia, PA

La Salle University: Basketball (M), 1954
Temple University: Gymnastics (M), 1949; Lacrosse (W), 1984, 1988
University of Pennsylvania: Football, 1895, 1897, 1904, 1908
Villanova University: Basketball (M), 1985; Cross Country (M), 1966, 1967, 1968, 1970; Cross Country (W), 1989, 1990, 1991, 1992, 1993, 1994, 1998; Indoor Track (M), 1968, 1971, 1979; Outdoor Track (M), 1957

Phoenix-Mesa Scottsdale, AZ

Arizona State University: Baseball, 1965, 1967, 1969, 1977, 1981; Golf (M), 1990, 1996; Golf (W), 1990, 1993, 1994, 1995, 1997, 1998; Gymnastics (M), 1986; Outdoor Track (M), 1977; Wrestling, 1988

Pittsburgh, PA

University of Pittsburgh: Football, 1916, 1918, 1937, 1976

Pocatello, ID

Idaho State University: Football (I-AA), 1981

Portland-Vancouver-Beaverton, OR

University of Portland: Soccer (W), 2002, 2005

Poughkeepsie-Newburgh, NY-PA

United States Military Academy: Football, 1914, 1944, 1945

Providence-New Bedford-Fall River, RI-MA

Brown University: Rowing, 1999, 2000, 2002, 2004, 2006
Providence College: Cross Country (W), 1995

Provo-Orem, UT

Brigham Young University: Cross Country (W), 1997, 1999, 2001, 2002; Football, 1984; Golf (M), 1981; Outdoor Track (M), 1970; Volleyball (M), 1999, 2001, 2004

Raleigh-Cary, NC

North Carolina State University: Basketball (M), 1974, 1983
University of North Carolina: Basketball (M), 1957, 1982, 1993, 2005; Basketball (W), 1994; Field Hockey, 1989, 1995, 1996, 1997; Lacrosse (M), 1981, 1982, 1986, 1991; Soccer (M), 2001; Soccer (W), 1982, 1983,

1984, 1986, 1987, 1988, 1989, 1990, 1991, 1992, 1993, 1994, 1996, 1997, 1999, 2000, 2003

Richmond, VA

University of Richmond: Soccer (M), 1998

Rockingham County-Strafford County, NH

University of New Hampshire: Lacrosse (W), 1985

St. Louis, MO-IL

St. Louis University: Soccer (M), 1959, 1960, 1962, 1963, 1965, 1967, 1969, 1970, 1972, 1973

Salt Lake City, UT

University of Utah: Basketball (M), 1944; Gymnastics (W), 1982, 1983, 1984, 1985, 1986, 1990, 1992, 1994, 1995; Skiing, 1981, 1983, 1984, 1986, 1987, 1988, 1993, 1996, 1997

San Antonio, TX

Trinity University: Tennis (M), 1972

San Diego-Carlsbad-San Marcos, CA

San Diego State University: Volleyball (M), 1973

San Francisco-San Mateoy, CA

University of San Francisco: Basketball (M), 1955, 1956; Soccer (M), 1966, 1975, 1976, 1978, 1980; Tennis (M), 1949

San Jose-Sunnyvale-Santa Clara, CA

San Jose State University: Cross Country (M), 1962, 1963; Golf (M), 1948; Golf (W), 1987, 1989, 1992; Outdoor Track (M), 1969
Stanford University: Baseball, 1987, 1988; Basketball (M), 1942; Basketball (W), 1990, 1992; Cross Country (M), 1996, 1997, **2002**, 2003; Cross Country (W), 1996, 2003, **2005**; Golf (M), 1939, 1941, 1942, 1946, 1953, 1994; Football, 1926; Gymnastics (M), 1992, 1993, 1995; Outdoor Track (M), 1925, 1928, 1934, 2000; Swimming and Diving (M), 1967, 1985, 1986, 1987, 1992, 1993, 1994, 1998; Swimming and Diving (W), 1983, 1989, 1992, 1993, 1994, 1995, 1996, 1998; Tennis (M), 1973, 1974, 1977, 1978, 1980, 1981, 1983, 1986, 1988, 1989, 1990, 1992, 1995, 1996, 1997, 1998, 2000; Tennis (W), 1982, 1984, 1986, 1987, 1988, 1989, 1990, 1991, 1997, 1999, 2001, 2002; Volleyball (M), 1997; Volleyball (W), 1992, 1994, 1996, 1997, 2001, 2002; Water Polo (M), 1976, 1978, 1980, 1981, 1985, 1986, 1993, 1994, 2001, 2002
University of Santa Clara: Soccer (M), 1989; Soccer (W), 2001

Santa Barbara-Santa Maria, CA

University of California, Santa Barbara: Water Polo (M), 1979

Seattle-Bellevue-Everett, WA

University of Washington: Football, 1992; Rowing, 1997, 1998

South Bend-Mishawaka, IN-MI

University of Notre Dame: Basketball (W), 2001; Cross Country (M), 1957; Fencing, 1994, 2003, 2005; Football, 1924, 1929, 1943, 1946, 1947, 1949, 1966, 1973, 1977, 1988; Golf (M), 1944; Soccer (W), 1995, 2004; Tennis (M), 1959

Springfield, MA

University of Massachusetts: Football (I-AA), 1998; Lacrosse (W), 1982

State College, PA

Pennsylvania State University: Cross Country (M), 1942, 1947, 1950; Fencing, 1990, 1991, 1995, 1996, 1997, 1998, 1999, 2000, 2002; Football, 1982, 1986; Gymnastics (M), 1948, 1953, 1954, 1957, 1959, 1960, 1961, 1965, 1976, 2000, 2004; Lacrosse (W), 1987, 1989; Volleyball (M), 1994; Volleyball (W), 1999; Wrestling, 1953

Stockton, CA

University of the Pacific: Volleyball (W), 1985, 1986

Syracuse, NY

Syracuse University: Basketball (M), 2003; Cross Country (M), 1951; Football, 1959; Lacrosse (M), 1983, 1988, 1989, 1990, 1993, 1995, 2000, 2002

Tallahassee, FL

Florida State University: Football, 1993, 1999; Gymnastics (M), 1951, 1952; Indoor Track (W), 1985; Outdoor Track (W), 1984
Florida A & M University: Football (I-AA), 1978

Terre Haute, IN

Indiana State University: Gymnastics (M), 1977

Toledo, OH

Bowling Green University: Ice Hockey, 1984

Trenton-Ewing, NJ

Princeton University: Football, 1889, 1893, 1896, 1903, 1906, 1911; Golf (M), 1922, 1923, 1927, 1928, 1929, 1930, 1937, 1940; Lacrosse (M), 1992, 1994, 1996, 1997, 1998, 2001; Lacrosse (W), 1994, 2002

Tucson, AZ

University of Arizona: Baseball, 1976, 1980, 1986; Basketball (M), 1997; Golf (M), 1992; Golf (W), 1996, 2000; Softball, 1991, 1993, 1994, 1996, 1997, 2001, 2006

Tulsa, OK

University of Tulsa: Golf (W), 1982, 1988

Tuscaloosa, AL

University of Alabama: Football, 1925, 1926, 1961, 1964, 1965, 1973, 1978, 1979, 1992; Gymnastics (W), 1988, 1991, 1996, 2002

Virginia Beach-Norfolk, VA-NC

Old Dominion University: Basketball (W), 1985; Field Hockey, 1982, 1983, 1984, 1988, 1990, 1991, 1992, 1998, 2000

Waco, TX

Baylor University: Basketball (W), 2005

Washington-Arlington, DC-MD-VA-WV

George Mason University: Indoor Track (M), 1996; Soccer (W), 1985
Georgetown University: Basketball (M), 1984
Howard University: Soccer (M), 1971, 1974
University of Maryland: Basketball (M), 2002; Basketball (W), 2006; Field Hockey, 1987, 1993, 1999, 2005; Football, 1953; Lacrosse (M), 1973, 1975; Lacrosse (W), 1986, 1992, 1995, 1996, 1997, 1998, 1999, 2000, 2001; Soccer (M), 1968

Waterloo-Cedar Falls, IA

University of Northern Iowa: Wrestling, 1950

Wichita, KS

Wichita State University: Baseball, 1989

Wilmington, DE-NJ-MD

University of Delaware: Lacrosse (W), 1983

Worcester, MA

Holy Cross College: Baseball, 1952; Basketball (M), 1947

Youngstown-Warren-Boardman, OH

Youngstown State University: Football (I-AA), 1991, 1993, 1994, 1997

Source: National Collegiate Athletic Association, College Champions, Official NCAA Championships Record Book; www.ncaachampionships.com and www.finalfour.net.

Climate

T he fortunate people of the planet," John Kenneth Galbraith wrote years ago in *Harper's*, "are those who live by the seasons. There is far more difference between a Vermont farm in the summer and that farm in the winter than there is between San Diego and Sao Paulo. This means that people who live where the seasons are good and strong have no need to travel; they can stay at home and let change come to them. This simple truth will one day be recognized and then we will see a great reverse migration from Florida to Maine and on into Quebec."

Galbraith's forecast may be a tad optimistic. Pathways to seasonal sun are too well worn. Check out the number of Maine and Minnesota license plates in Florida and Texas Gulf parking lots in February. Americans say they prefer mild, sunny climates, and when asked where these climates are, they point to the fast-growing lower half of the Pacific Coast, Florida, and anywhere along the South Atlantic and Gulf Coast shore. Certainly this area, between 25 degrees and 35 degrees latitude, has been drawing migrants for decades.

But other places north of the Mason-Dixon line and hundreds of miles from ocean beaches benefit from population growth, and many of these enjoy mild climates, too. The names of some might surprise you.

What has always been surprising is the enormous variety of global climates found right here at home. Northern maritime, mild Mediterranean, southerly mountain, lowland desert, tropical "paradise," desert highland, rugged northern continental, windward slope, leeward slope, humid subtropical - you name it, and you'll meet up with it somewhere in America.

Climate is a part of your circumstances that can't be bought, built, remodeled, or relocated. A place's climate is there for keeps, and the weather events that make up a place's climate - rain, snow, heat, cold, drought, wind - will have a profound effect on your life.

THE DIFFERENCE IS GEOPHYSICAL

If you can live anywhere you wish and are open to all the variety America offers, know that a combination of water, latitude and longitude, elevation, prevailing winds, mountain ranges, and urban development lies behind any metro area's climate.

Water

Oceans and other large bodies of water take the edge off temperature. Water warms up slowly, holds much more heat than land, and cools more slowly. Places near or surrounded by water tend to be cooler in summer and warmer in winter than others far from water.

The hottest it gets in July on the Santa Monica Pier in Los Angeles is 75°F; meanwhile, 15 miles north in the San Fernando Valley, away from the Pacific Ocean, it's 95°F. If Buffalo were to be gathered up and then set down hundreds of miles directly west of its location near Lakes Erie and Ontario, winter would arrive a month sooner and spring a month later.

While bodies of water soften hot and cold temperatures, they also influence a place's microclimate. Utah's ancient Great Salt Lake is the big reason there is much more snow in Salt Lake City than in other nearby areas. Face Lake Michigan in a blustery Chicago winter and you may have to grab a rail, so strong is the easterly wind that comes in unobstructed from miles offshore.

Latitude

Places located in the continent's heartland away from the moderating effects of water experience wide swings of temperature. These continental climates tend to be even more rigorous in the higher latitudes. The closer to the poles you get, the more exaggerated the seasonal shifts because extreme northerly or southerly locations see the greatest seasonal variation in the amount and intensity of sunlight.

In late December in Anchorage, AK, (61.10 N), 275,000 residents see 10:15am sunrises and 3:50pm sunsets with daylight saving time, a six-hour day for last-minute Christmas shopping. In late July, building contractors there schedule double shifts as the day lengthens to 18 hours and the city becomes an intensely sunlit spot.

Far to the southwest, the solar energy pouring over Honolulu (21.20 N) varies by just 50 percent from time of maximum in June to time of minimum in December, but in Anchorage it is twenty times

as great. Places in the far north experience not only Siberian winters but short, sun-baked summers.

Elevation

Greater height above sea level has the same effect as higher latitude. Each 1,000 feet of elevation lowers the average temperature by 3.3°F. In New Mexico, for example, there are just 3° of difference in annual average temperature between Clayton and Lordsburg, two locations with similar elevations. But Clayton sits up near the Oklahoma panhandle while Lordsburg is 440 miles southwest near the Sonoran Desert in Mexico. At Albuquerque's airport and at the top of Sandia Peak, two weather stations just 15 miles apart but differing in elevation by 4,700 feet, the average annual temperatures differ by 16°F.

In the United States, places that combine high altitudes with southerly latitudes get the mild, short winters of the south and the cooler nights and crisp falls of the north. Asheville, NC, in the southern Appalachians, and Santa Fe, NM, in the southern Rockies have long been known for their mild, four-season climates.

Wind

Consider a pair of metro areas 3,200 miles apart: Bellingham, WA, and Portland, ME. Both sit high in northern latitudes on their respective coasts. Both peek through some of the foggiest mornings on the continent. You'd naturally suppose the two have similar climates.

But Bellingham is much milder because of the winds that blow from west to east across the continent. The west coast is a landfall for air that has moved thousands of miles over water. Cities hundreds of miles inland still feel the beneficial effects of the Pacific winds. Interior cities in the east feel few consequences of the Atlantic except on those rare occasions when the prevailing wind direction doesn't prevail. This reversal of wind direction often means a storm.

Mountain Ranges

The only barriers big enough to deflect and channel winds, rain, and snow are mountains. Mountain people aren't telling tall tales when they tell visitors that the weather on one side of a mountain range is often radically different from that on the other.

The windward side of British Columbia's Coast Mountains is a lush coastal rain forest; the leeward side, a dry grass and sagebrush steppe. In winter, the Great

Divide shields Colorado Springs from much of the Arctic air that moves down the continent. In summer, the hidden, windward side of the city's mountain vista is a lush, evergreen parkland at lower elevations; the leeward side where the city sits is a semi-arid steppe descending to dry, short-grass prairie.

Urban Development

Finally, urban development makes heat islands within the surrounding countryside. Office buildings, factories, and cars produce enormous amounts of waste heat. Brick, concrete, and asphalt surfaces absorb and store heat during the day; at night the stored heat drifts up into the air, keeping the city from cooling off. At night in winter, a large northern metropolis's core can be 30° warmer than its suburbs. In general, wind speed, visibility, sunshine, and heating needs are less in the center of the city than in nearby country, but temperature, cloudiness, thunderstorm frequency, and air pollution levels are higher.

JUDGING: CLIMATE

You might have trouble naming many important aspects in life that aren't influenced in some way by climate. It decides what we'll wear, when we vacation, whether we'll work outside, how much we pay to keep the indoors comfortable. It affects travel safety and mobility. Certainly, it affects how we feel and behave.

Places Rated's judging climates isn't new. Canada has a "severity index" for hundreds of locations. There's one for New Zealand's cities rating human comfort using rainfall, sunshine, temperature, humidity, and wind. In the United States, the "weather stress index" from the National Oceanic and Atmospheric Administration (NOAA) uses temperature, humidity, and wind speed to calculate discomfort in certain cities based on deviation of those three elements from the normal.

To rate the climates in 379 metro areas, *Places Rated* considers multiple data elements, including monthly high and low temperatures, wind speeds, humidity, darkness, clear days, partly cloudy days, cloudy days, thunderstorms, fog, and precipitation in the form of rain and snow.

Mild Winters

To measure how mild the winters are, windchill (air temperatures reduced by wind, derived according to

The Difference Is Geophysical

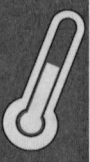

Climate

Not for Depressives

Over 150 years ago, physicians first noted persons suffering from symptoms of depression in winter experienced relief during the spring and summer. Seasonal Affective Disorder (SAD) was officially named in 1984. SAD is a mood disorder related to seasonal variations of light. Based on northerly latitudes and a high number of foggy, wet, and cloudy days, below in alphabetical order are the lowest-rated metro areas for seasonal brightness.

Bellingham, WA	Mount Vernon, WA
Binghamton, NY	Olympia, WA
Bremerton, WA	Parkersburg, WV
Charleston, WV	Salem, OR
Corvallis, OR	Seattle, WA
Eugene, OR	Tacoma, WA
Fairbanks, AK	Utica-Rome, NY
Huntington, WV	Weirton, WV-OH
Johnstown, PA	Williamsport, PA
Morgantown, WV	Youngstown, OH

Most Hazardous

Are there perilous climates? Sure there are. How about January blizzards for Fargo, Grand Forks, and Rapid City? How about funnel clouds and thunderheads for Wichita Falls or Oklahoma City in July? Ironically, metros with the least hazardous weather also have the mildest winters. Life is unfair. Listed in alphabetical order are metro areas in the bottom five percent of hazard-free climates.

Ames, IA	Great Falls, MT
Billings, MT	Lake County, IL-WI
Casper, WY	Milwaukee, WI
Cedar Rapids, IA	Minneapolis, MN-WI
Cheyenne, WY	Racine, WI
Dubuque, IA	Rapid City, SD
Duluth, MN-WI	Rochester, MN
Eau Claire, WI	Sioux City, IA-NE-SD
Fargo, ND-MN	Sioux Falls, SD
Grand Forks, ND-MN	Waterloo, IA

newly revised National Oceanic and Atmospheric Administration standards. See "Windchill" in this chapter's Et Cetera section.), the number of days the temperature falls to 32°F or less, and the average 24-hour temperature for the coldest month are taken into account. San Diego has the highest figure for these months, resulting in a winter mildness score of 100. New York hits the middle with a 50 score, meaning it sees a milder winter than 50 percent of metro areas in the United States. Alas, locations in the frozen and snowy northern prairie – Grand Forks, ND-MN, Fargo, ND-MN, and Duluth, MN-WI – score at the bottom.

Mild Summers

To measure how mild the summers are, humidity, the average 24-hour temperature of the hottest month, and the number of months the thermometer tops 90°F are taken into account. Flagstaff, high and dry in Arizona's Coconino National Forest, has the lowest figure; its summer mildness score is 100. Lynchburg - in Virginia's Piedmont - gets the middle 50, meaning it sees a milder summer than half of America's other metro areas. Corpus Christi, on the hot and humid southern Gulf coast in Texas, gets a 0. These metro areas are respectively the best, average, and worst for summer mildness.

Hazard Free

Bad weather isn't just inconvenient - it is downright dangerous. Aside from delaying and canceling social and business events, it contributes to injury and even death. The general hazardousness of an area is measured by normal winter snowfall and the frequencies of two other elements: strong winds and thunderstorms.

To score for relative freedom from these hazards, *Places Rated* counts snow three times as heavily as thunderstorms, and thunderstorms three times as heavily as strong winds. The higher the score, the freer the metro area is from these weather hazards. San Diego, Santa Barbara, Los Angeles and three other nearby areas on the southern California coast, each with 99 scores, do best here. Again New York, at 50, is average, and Cheyenne on the wind-bullied Great Plains earns a hazard-ridden score of 0.

Seasonal Affect

If you need a single guilty party to blame for tiredness, depression, irritability, lack of sleep, lack of focus, lack of ambition, lack of interest in sex or food, headache, chest and joint pains, hallucinations,

and any other ailments, stick it to the weather.

To measure the local weather's seasonal affect, or psychological impact, the number of cloudy days (more than 80 percent cloud cover) and wet days (precipitation greater than 0.1 inch) is weighted twice as heavily as the number of fog (visibility less than one-half mile) days, and fog days are weighted as heavily as latitude, and indicator of potential sunlight. Phoenix earns a perfect 100 score. Memphis gets 50. Seattle, Olympia, and Bremerton, up north on Washington's dripping Puget Sound shore, score at the bottom. These metro areas are respectively the best, average, and worst for bright seasons.

SCORING EXAMPLES: CLIMATE

Each metro area's *Places Rated* score for climate comes from adding four broad factors: winter mildness, summer mildness, seasonal affect, and hazardousness. A metro area's final score is its percentile on a scale of 0 to 100 corresponding to its rank.

A location near the center of California's Pacific coast, another in Southside Virginia, and still another in Western Michigan illustrate the best, average, and worst metro areas by *Places Rated*'s scoring method for climate.

The Best: San Francisco, CA

Mark Twain once said in an after dinner speech that the coldest winter he had ever spent was the summer in San Francisco. San Francisco's average temperature is 57°F. So is St. Louis's. But San Francisco enjoys both a diurnal (24-hour) temperature range of 12° and an annual range (the difference between January's and July's average temperatures) of 12°. St. Louis has a diurnal range of 17° and an annual range of 47°.

The temperature swings in these two cities highlight the difference between a marine climate and a hot continental climate. San Francisco's somewhat cool climate is remarkably stable year-round; St. Louis's is neither.

In spite of sea fogs and the low stratus associated with them, this metro area's percent of possible sunshine is greater than that of New York, Boston, and Washington, DC. Thunderstorms here are rare. On none of the year's 365 days do temperatures hit zero. There is no snow. Just a handful of days record a fall to freezing or a heat wave exceeding 90°F. More than any other factor, it is San Francisco's infrequent extremes of heat and cold, coupled with a temperature

Great Summer Homes?

Perhaps it's a stretch for Altoona, Buffalo, or Pittsburgh to be summer escapes. But Flagstaff, Bend, and Prescott certainly are. So also are Pittsfield and Rockingham-Strafford counties, and a few more besides. Mild summers are found in all parts of the country. Listed below in alphabetical order are metro areas in the top five percent for mild summers.

Altoona, PA	Missoula, MT
Anchorage, AK	Pittsburgh, PA
Bangor, ME	Pittsfield, MA
Bend, OR	Portland, ME
Buffalo, NY	Portland, OR-WA
Burlington, VT	Prescott, AZ
Cheyenne, WY	Providence, RI-MA
Corvallis, OR	Rockingham, NH
Flagstaff, AZ	Salem, OR
Great Falls, MT	Santa Fe, NM
Longview, WA	Springfield, MA
Manchester, NH	

Great Winter Homes

It's a fact that many of the great metro areas in California and in the southwest got their start as winter health resorts. And Florida? Metro areas in the Sunshine State are winter resorts, too, but they slightly lag spots in the Pacific and Mountains time zones for winter mildness. Listed below in alphabetical order are metro areas in the top five percent in mild winters.

Bakersfield, CA	San Diego, CA
El Centro, CA	San Francisco, CA
Los Angeles, CA	San Luis Obispo, CA
Merced, CA	Santa Ana, CA
Napa, CA	Santa Barbara, CA
Oakland, CA	Stockton, CA
Oxnard, CA	Tucson, AZ
Phoenix, AZ	Vallejo, CA
Riverside, CA	Visalia, CA
Sacramento, CA	Yuma, AZ

Source: National Climatic Data Center. Not shown: Alaska's 9 divisions and Hawaii's 6 divisions.

range ideal for human activity and comfort that produces a top *Places Rated* climate rating.

The Average: Richmond, VA

This old city, historic capital of the Commonwealth of Virginia, sits on the James River at its highest navigable point. The climate here is *Subtropical*, defined as having at least 8 months where the average temperature is over 50°F and no dry season in any month.

For mildness, RVA (the local moniker) earns a respectable 54 for mild winters and 41 for hot and humid summers. Its seasonal affect is 43, due to a cloudy or partly cloudy year. The city earns a hazard-free score of 63, thanks to minor amounts of snow and number of thunderstorms. When all the factors are weighted by their importance in *Places Rated*'s scoring method, they produce a ranking in the exact middle of America's metro areas.

The Worst: Kalamazoo, MI

The climate for this metro area is *Hot Continental*, defined as 4 to 7 months where the average temperature is over 50°F, at least one month where it is under 32°F, and at least one month where it is over 72°F. *Hot Continental* is America's defining climate type. It's a category for most of the country. It is what people mean when they say: "Don't like the weather? Wait a few days."

Kalamazoo's best period is a summer that is milder than almost half of all metro areas in the country. Winters, made worse by weather hazards and a big dose of cloudiness, are quite another matter. The Pacific is 2,000 miles west and the Atlantic 1,000 miles east; any moderating effect from either ocean has dissipated long before getting here. Moreover, cold arctic air moves unobstructed over the prairie and isn't altered in the slightest when it hits.

379 PLACE THUMBNAILS: CLIMATE

The following pages are capsule climate summaries for 379 metro areas. Next to the metro area's name are its elevation and its latitude north of the equator and longitude west of Greenwich, England. With these coordinates, you can roughly determine whether the place you may be coming from is farther north, south, east, or west from the place you may be headed. Big

differences in geographical coordinates can produce big differences in the climate.

Underneath the metro area name is the Climate Division, in *italics*, where the metro area is located. There are 344 Climate Divisions in America, defined by state climatologists into homogeneous geographical and climatological groupings of weather stations using 100-year records for temperature and precipitation.

Places Rated groups 379 metro areas into 132 of these divisions, renaming most of them. Abilene, for instance, is one of 5 metro areas on the *Texas High Plains*; Atlantic City is one of 3 on the *New Jersey Shore*; and Boston is one of 4 on *Massachusetts Bay*.

Rounding out each metro area's capsule summary are its percentiles (a scale of 0 to 100, the higher the better) versus other metro areas in mildness of its **Winters**, mildness of its **Summers**, how bright the **Seasonal Affect** is, and how **Hazard-free** the area's climate is (see the section, **JUDGING: CLIMATE**, a few pages back for an explanation of these terms).

Places Rated rankings are determined by adding the four percentiles; the higher the total, the better. A check mark (✓) preceding a metro area's name highlights it as one of the top forty metro areas in the country for a combination of mild summers, mild winters, seasonal brightness, and relative lack of hazards.

Abilene, TX
(32.25N, 99.41W at 1,780')

see *Texas High Plains*

Winters 54
Summers 24
Seasonal Affect................88
Hazard-free 49

Places Rated Rank: 223

Akron, OH
(40.55N, 81.26W at 1,210')

see *Northeast Ohio Hills*

Winters 10
Summers 88
Seasonal Affect..................7
Hazard-free 28

Places Rated Rank: 257

Albany, GA
(31.32N, 84.08W at 180')

see *Southern Georgia*

Winters 86
Summers 17
Seasonal Affect................57
Hazard-free 85

Places Rated Rank: 93

Albany-Schenectady, NY
(42.45N, 73.48W at 270')

see *Upper Hudson*

Winters 22
Summers 79
Seasonal Affect................17
Hazard-free 19

Places Rated Rank: 237

Albuquerque, NM
(35.03N, 106.37W at 5,310')

see *New Mexico Northern Mountain*

Winters 61
Summers 49
Seasonal Affect................97
Hazard-free 51

Places Rated Rank: 69

Alexandria, LA
(31.19N, 92.28W at 90')

see *Central Louisiana*

Winters 65
Summers 6
Seasonal Affect................70
Hazard-free 76

Places Rated Rank: 252

Allentown-Bethlehem, PA-NJ
(40.39N, 75.26W at 390')

see *Pennsylvania Poconos*

Winters 42
Summers 61
Seasonal Affect................33
Hazard-free 36

Places Rated Rank: 192

Altoona, PA
(40.18N, 78.19W at 1,480')

see *Pennsylvania Central Mountains*

Winters 23
Summers 94
Seasonal Affect................12
Hazard-free 35

Places Rated Rank: 143

Amarillo, TX
(35.14N, 101.42W at 3,600')

see *Texas High Plains*

Winters 33
Summers 42
Seasonal Affect................91
Hazard-free 27

Places Rated Rank: 269

Ames, IA
(42.02N, 93.37W at 922')

see *Central Iowa*

Winters 9
Summers 59
Seasonal Affect................54
Hazard-free 5

Places Rated Rank: 357

Anchorage, AK
(61.1N, *150.01W at 110'*)

see *Alaska Cook Inlet*

Winters 38
Summers 99
Seasonal Affect................19
Hazard-free 34

Places Rated Rank: 64

Anderson, IN
(40.06N, 85.4W at 874')

see *Central Indiana*

Winters 39
Summers 49
Seasonal Affect................20
Hazard-free 33

Places Rated Rank: 295

Anderson, SC
(34.3N, 82.39W at 771')

see *Upcountry South Carolina*

Winters 77
Summers 35
Seasonal Affect................57
Hazard-free 76

Places Rated Rank: 77

Ann Arbor, MI
(42.18N, 83.43W at 900')

see *Southeast Michigan*

Winters 29
Summers 85
Seasonal Affect..........................24
Hazard-free 15

Places Rated Rank: 170

Anniston-Oxford, AL
(33.35N, 85.51W at 610')

see *Alabama Appalachians*

Winters 75
Summers 15
Seasonal Affect................36
Hazard-free 75

Places Rated Rank: 208

Appleton, WI
(44.14N, 88.24W at 709')

see *East Central Wisconsin*

Winters 17
Summers 66
Seasonal Affect...........................31
Hazard-free 7

Places Rated Rank: 327

Asheville, NC
(35.26N, 82.33W at 2,140')

see *North Carolina Southern Mountains*

Winters 50
Summers 47
Seasonal Affect...........................43
Hazard-free 54

Places Rated Rank: 187

Athens-Clarke County, GA
(33.57N, 83.19W at 800')

see *North Central Georgia*

Winters 70
Summers 20
Seasonal Affect...........................53
Hazard-free 77

Places Rated Rank: 178

Atlanta-Sandy Springs, GA
(33.39N, 84.26W at 1,010')

see *North Central Georgia*

Winters 66
Summers 33
Seasonal Affect...........................59
Hazard-free 63

Places Rated Rank: 138

Atlantic City, NJ
(39.27N, 74.34W at 60')

see *New Jersey Shore*

Winters 64
Summers 57
Seasonal Affect...........................48
Hazard-free 36

Places Rated Rank: 80

Auburn-Opelika, AL
(32.36N, 85.28W at 709')

see *Lower Chatahoochee Watershed*

Winters 80
Summers 23
Seasonal Affect...........................58
Hazard-free 84

Places Rated Rank: 92

Augusta, GA-SC
(33.22N, 81.58W at 150')

see *South Carolina Midlands*

Winters 76
Summers 22
Seasonal Affect...........................60
Hazard-free 81

Places Rated Rank: 120

Austin-Round Rock, TX
(30.17N, 97.42W at 590')

see *South Central Texas*

Winters 81
Summers 20
Seasonal Affect...........................81
Hazard-free 78

Places Rated Rank: 84

√ **Bakersfield, CA**
(35.25N, 119.03W at 490')

see *San Joaquin Basin*

Winters 98
Summers 29
Seasonal Affect...........................97
Hazard-free 98

Places Rated Rank: 40

Baltimore-Towson, MD
(39.17N, 76.37W at 10')

see *Baltimore-Washington Corridor*

Winters 62
Summers 46
Seasonal Affect...........................60
Hazard-free 53

Places Rated Rank: 104

Bangor, ME
(44.48N, 68.49W at 190')

see *Maine Southern Interior*

Winters 17
Summers 96
Seasonal Affect...........................14
Hazard-free 15

Places Rated Rank: 191

Barnstable Town,MA
(41.4N, 69.58W at 50')

see *Massachusetts Bay*

Winters 43
Summers 65
Seasonal Affect...........................40
Hazard-free 29

Places Rated Rank: 161

Baton Rouge, LA
(30.32N, 91.08W at 60')

see *Central Louisiana*

Winters 78
Summers 3
Seasonal Affect...........................62
Hazard-free 86

Places Rated Rank: 202

Battle Creek, MI
(42.19N, 85.1W at 819')

see *Central Michigan*

Winters 16
Summers 54
Seasonal Affect...........................13
Hazard-free 17

Places Rated Rank: 373

Bay City, MI
(43.35N, 83.53W at 594')

see *Saginaw Bay*

Winters 28
Summers 84
Seasonal Affect...........................21
Hazard-free 9

Places Rated Rank: 200

Beaumont-Port Arthur, TX
(29.57N, 94.01W at 20')

see *Upper Texas Gulf*

Winters 63
Summers 2
Seasonal Affect...........................62
Hazard-free 70

Places Rated Rank: 308

Bellingham, WA
(48.48N, 122.32W at 150')

see *Puget Sound Shore*

Winters 86
Summers 70
Seasonal Affect.............................1
Hazard-free 74

Places Rated Rank: 41

√ **Bend, OR**
(44.03N, 121.18W at 3,629')

see *South Central Oregon*

Winters 49
Summers 99
Seasonal Affect...........................79
Hazard-free 49

Places Rated Rank: 35

Bethesda-Gaithersburg, MD
(38.58N, 77.06W at 303')

see *Baltimore-Washington Corridor*

Winters 55
Summers 60
Seasonal Affect...........................24
Hazard-free 51

Places Rated Rank: 112

Billings, MT
(45.48N, 108.32W at 3,570')

see *South Central Montana*

Winters 11
Summers 80
Seasonal Affect...........................63
Hazard-free 4

Places Rated Rank: 246

Binghamton, NY
(42.13N, 75.59W at 1,600')

see *New York's Southern Tier*

Winters 4
Summers 82
Seasonal Affect.............................2
Hazard-free 11

Places Rated Rank: 341

Birmingham-Hoover, AL
(33.34N, 86.45W at 620')

see *Alabama Appalachians*

Winters 66
Summers 22
Seasonal Affect 45
Hazard-free 76

Places Rated Rank: 210

Bismarck, ND
(46.46N, 100.45W at 1,650')

see *Central North Dakota*

Winters 24
Summers 87
Seasonal Affect 61
Hazard-free 8

Places Rated Rank: 150

Blacksburg-Christiansburg, VA
(37.13N, 80.24W at 2,080')

see *Virginia Mountains*

Winters 54
Summers 71
Seasonal Affect 64
Hazard-free 48

Places Rated Rank: 60

Bloomington, IN
(39.1N, 86.31W at 820')

see *South Central Indiana*

Winters 37
Summers 42
Seasonal Affect 16
Hazard-free 34

Places Rated Rank: 335

Bloomington-Normal, IL
(40.31N, 89W at 790')

see *Illinois Prairie*

Winters 21
Summers 45
Seasonal Affect 41
Hazard-free 25

Places Rated Rank: 358

Boise City-Nampa, ID
(43.34N, 116.13W at 2,840')

see *Treasure Valley*

Winters 71
Summers 66
Seasonal Affect 72
Hazard-free 49

Places Rated Rank: 46

Boston-Quincy, MA
(42.22N, 71.02W at 20')

see *Massachusetts Bay*

Winters 33
Summers 85
Seasonal Affect 44
Hazard-free 30

Places Rated Rank: 102

Boulder, CO
(40N, 105.16W at 5,480')

see *Colorado Northern Front Range*

Winters 2
Summers 74
Seasonal Affect 84
Hazard-free 43

Places Rated Rank: 245

Bowling Green, KY
(36.59N, 86.26W at 529')

see *West Central Kentucky*

Winters 44
Summers 29
Seasonal Affect 29
Hazard-free 58

Places Rated Rank: 321

✓ Bremerton, WA
(47.34N, 122.4W at 160')

see *Puget Sound Shore*

Winters 84
Summers 75
Seasonal Affect 0
Hazard-free 77

Places Rated Rank: 39

Bridgeport-Stamford, CT
(41.1N, 73.08W at 10')

see *Long Island Sound*

Winters 49
Summers 79
Seasonal Affect 39
Hazard-free 31

Places Rated Rank: 74

Brownsville-Harlingen, TX
(25.54N, 97.26W at 20')

see *Lower Rio Grande Valley*

Winters 92
Summers 0
Seasonal Affect 81
Hazard-free 67

Places Rated Rank: 137

Brunswick, GA
(31.08N, 81.29W at 10')

see *Colonial Coast*

Winters 74
Summers 11
Seasonal Affect 62
Hazard-free 88

Places Rated Rank: 176

Buffalo-Niagara Falls, NY
(42.56N, 78.44W at 710')

see *Western New York*

Winters 3
Summers 97
Seasonal Affect 12
Hazard-free 13

Places Rated Rank: 255

Burlington, NC
(36.05N, 79.26W at 663')

see *North Carolina Piedmont*

Winters 67
Summers 37
Seasonal Affect 47
Hazard-free 69

Places Rated Rank: 117

Burlington, VT
(44.28N, 73.09W at 330')

see *Northwestern Vermont*

Winters 14
Summers 98
Seasonal Affect 10
Hazard-free 15

Places Rated Rank: 208

Cambridge-Newton, MA
(42.21N, 71.06W at 40')

see *Massachusetts Bay*

Winters 33
Summers 81
Seasonal Affect 44
Hazard-free 30

Places Rated Rank: 121

Camden, NJ
(39.55N, 75.07W at 33')

see *Delaware Valley*

Winters 59
Summers 60
Seasonal Affect 37
Hazard-free 46

Places Rated Rank: 89

Canton-Massillon, OH
(40.55N, 81.26W at 1,210')

see *Northeast Ohio Hills*

Winters 10
Summers 88
Seasonal Affect 7
Hazard-free 28

Places Rated Rank: 257

Cape Coral-Fort Myers, FL
(26.35N, 81.52W at 20')

see *Florida Southwest Coast*

Winters 84
Summers 2
Seasonal Affect 83
Hazard-free 97

Places Rated Rank: 127

✓ Carson City, NV
(39.09N, 119.45W at 4,665')

see *Tahoe Basin*

Winters 68
Summers 82
Seasonal Affect 92
Hazard-free 46

Places Rated Rank: 25

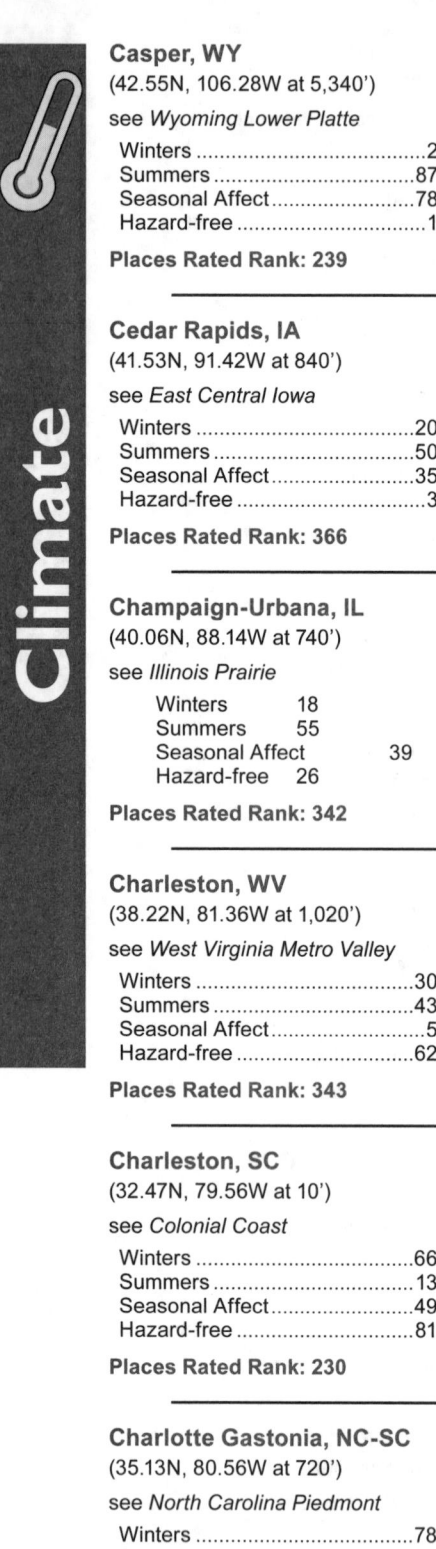

Casper, WY
(42.55N, 106.28W at 5,340')

see *Wyoming Lower Platte*

Winters 2
Summers 87
Seasonal Affect....................78
Hazard-free 1

Places Rated Rank: 239

Cedar Rapids, IA
(41.53N, 91.42W at 840')

see *East Central Iowa*

Winters 20
Summers 50
Seasonal Affect....................35
Hazard-free 3

Places Rated Rank: 366

Champaign-Urbana, IL
(40.06N, 88.14W at 740')

see *Illinois Prairie*

Winters   18
Summers   55
Seasonal Affect   39
Hazard-free   26

Places Rated Rank: 342

Charleston, WV
(38.22N, 81.36W at 1,020')

see *West Virginia Metro Valley*

Winters 30
Summers 43
Seasonal Affect......................5
Hazard-free 62

Places Rated Rank: 343

Charleston, SC
(32.47N, 79.56W at 10')

see *Colonial Coast*

Winters 66
Summers 13
Seasonal Affect....................49
Hazard-free 81

Places Rated Rank: 230

Charlotte Gastonia, NC-SC
(35.13N, 80.56W at 720')

see *North Carolina Piedmont*

Winters 78
Summers 34
Seasonal Affect....................48
Hazard-free 72

Places Rated Rank: 81

Charlottesville, VA
(38.02N, 78.31W at 870')

see *Virginia's Western Piedmont*

Winters 45
Summers 47
Seasonal Affect....................69
Hazard-free 62

Places Rated Rank: 164

Chattanooga, TN-GA
(35.02N, 85.12W at 690')

see *Upper Tennessee Watershed*

Winters 60
Summers 28
Seasonal Affect....................29
Hazard-free 72

Places Rated Rank: 222

Cheyenne, WY
(41.09N, 104.49W at 6,120')

see *Wyoming Lower Platte*

Winters 0
Summers 100
Seasonal Affect....................84
Hazard-free 2

Places Rated Rank: 186

Chicago-Naperville-Joliet, IL
(41.44N, 87.46W at 620')

see *Chicagoland*

Winters 18
Summers 63
Seasonal Affect....................28
Hazard-free 14

Places Rated Rank: 332

✓ **Chico, CA**
(39.42N, 121.49W at 190')

see *Sacramento Valley*

Winters 93
Summers 45
Seasonal Affect....................85
Hazard-free 89

Places Rated Rank: 32

Cincinnati, OH-KY-IN
(39.06N, 84.31W at 683')

see *Southwest Ohio*

Winters 41
Summers 55
Seasonal Affect....................16
Hazard-free 41

Places Rated Rank: 234

Clarksville, TN
(36.33N, 87.22W at 380')

see *Middle Tennessee*

Winters 47
Summers 25
Seasonal Affect....................34
Hazard-free 54

Places Rated Rank: 325

Cleveland, TN
(35.09N, 84.52W at 864')

see *Upper Tennessee Watershed*

Winters 60
Summers 33
Seasonal Affect....................29
Hazard-free 71

Places Rated Rank: 204

Cleveland-Elyria-Mentor, OH
(41.25N, 81.52W at 770')

see *Ohio's Lake Erie Shore*

Winters 7
Summers 83
Seasonal Affect......................7
Hazard-free 24

Places Rated Rank: 309

Coeur d'Alene, ID
(47.4N, 116.46W at 2,152')

see *Northwest Inland Empire*

Winters 27
Summers 93
Seasonal Affect....................26
Hazard-free 44

Places Rated Rank: 96

College Station, TX
(30.35N, 96.22W at 320')

see *North Central Texas*

Winters 80
Summers 18
Seasonal Affect....................81
Hazard-free 60

Places Rated Rank: 119

Colorado Springs, CO
(38.49N, 104.43W at 6,090')

see *Colorado Southern Front Range*

Winters 4
Summers 92
Seasonal Affect....................89
Hazard-free 23

Places Rated Rank: 166

Columbia, MO
(38.49N, 92.13W at 890')

see *Northeast Missouri Prairie*

Winters 24
Summers 30
Seasonal Affect....................46
Hazard-free 34

Places Rated Rank: 377

Columbia, SC
(33.57N, 81.07W at 210')

see *South Carolina Midlands*

Winters 74
Summers 20
Seasonal Affect....................62
Hazard-free 79

Places Rated Rank: 141

Columbus, GA
(32.31N, 84.57W at 450')

see *Lower Chatahoochee Watershed*

Winters 80
Summers 17
Seasonal Affect....................59
Hazard-free 87

Places Rated Rank: 116

Columbus, IN

(39.12N, 85.55W at 629')

see *South Central Indiana*

Winters	34
Summers	48
Seasonal Affect	45
Hazard-free	29

Places Rated Rank: 298

Columbus, OH

(40N, 82.53W at 810')

see *Central Ohio*

Winters	37
Summers	66
Seasonal Affect	8
Hazard-free	42

Places Rated Rank: 218

Corpus Christi, TX

(27.46N, 97.3W at 40')

see *Texas Coastal Bend*

Winters	91
Summers	0
Seasonal Affect	80
Hazard-free	64

Places Rated Rank: 150

✓ Corvallis, OR

(44.33N, 123.15W at 225')

see *Willamette Valley-Lower Columbia*

Winters	90
Summers	96
Seasonal Affect	4
Hazard-free	79

Places Rated Rank: 11

Cumberland, MD-WV

(39.38N, 78.45W at 730')

see *National Freeway*

Winters	34
Summers	57
Seasonal Affect	11
Hazard-free	40

Places Rated Rank: 275

Dallas-Plano-Irving, TX

(32.51N, 96.51W at 440')

see *North Central Texas*

Winters	56
Summers	19
Seasonal Affect	83
Hazard-free	57

Places Rated Rank: 235

Dalton, GA

(34.46N, 84.58W at 759')

see *Upper Tennessee Watershed*

Winters	66
Summers	30
Seasonal Affect	30
Hazard-free	72

Places Rated Rank: 184

Danville, IL

(40.07N, 87.37W at 597')

see *Middle Wabash Valley*

Winters	38
Summers	46
Seasonal Affect	25
Hazard-free	24

Places Rated Rank: 310

Danville, VA

(36.35N, 79.23W at 410')

see *Virginia's Western Piedmont*

Winters	71
Summers	40
Seasonal Affect	54
Hazard-free	55

Places Rated Rank: 94

Davenport-Moline, IA-IL

(41.35N, 90.25W at 580')

see *East Central Iowa*

Winters	19
Summers	62
Seasonal Affect	50
Hazard-free	16

Places Rated Rank: 307

Dayton, OH

(39.53N, 84.53W at 1,020')

see *West Central Ohio*

Winters	35
Summers	79
Seasonal Affect	11
Hazard-free	19

Places Rated Rank: 185

Decatur, AL

(34.45N, 87.37W at 540')

see *Northern Alabama*

Winters	57
Summers	16
Seasonal Affect	33
Hazard-free	60

Places Rated Rank: 317

Decatur, IL

(39.5N, 89.01W at 620')

see *Illinois Prairie*

Winters	25
Summers	44
Seasonal Affect	36
Hazard-free	26

Places Rated Rank: 354

Deltona-Daytona Beach, FL

(29.11N, 81.03W at 30')

see *North Central Florida*

Winters	86
Summers	10
Seasonal Affect	68
Hazard-free	90

Places Rated Rank: 103

Denver-Aurora, CO

(39.46N, 104.52W at 5,290')

see *Colorado Northern Front Range*

Winters	6
Summers	72
Seasonal Affect	85
Hazard-free	33

Places Rated Rank: 252

Des Moines, IA

(41.32N, 93.39W at 940')

see *Central Iowa*

Winters	9
Summers	54
Seasonal Affect	55
Hazard-free	6

Places Rated Rank: 368

Detroit-Livonia-Dearborn, MI

(42.14N, 83.2W at 630')

see *Southeast Michigan*

Winters	26
Summers	84
Seasonal Affect	24
Hazard-free	12

Places Rated Rank: 198

Dothan, AL

(31.53N, 85.28W at 600')

see *Lower Chatahoochee Watershed*

Winters	89
Summers	9
Seasonal Affect	71
Hazard-free	88

Places Rated Rank: 97

Dover, DE

(39.09N, 75.31W at 30')

see *PA's Southeastern Piedmont*

Winters	63
Summers	53
Seasonal Affect	33
Hazard-free	51

Places Rated Rank: 99

Dubuque, IA

(42.24N, 90.42W at 1,060')

see *Coulee Region*

Winters	3
Summers	71
Seasonal Affect	31
Hazard-free	3

Places Rated Rank: 361

Duluth, MN-WI

(46.5N, 92.11W at 1,430')

see *Northeast Minnesota*

Winters	3
Summers	86
Seasonal Affect	25
Hazard-free	1

Places Rated Rank: 320

Climate

Durham, NC
(35.59N, 78.53W at 394')

see *NC Central Coastal Plain*

Winters 64
Summers 28
Seasonal Affect 52
Hazard-free 60

Places Rated Rank: 193

Eau Claire, WI
(44.52N, 91.29W at 890')

see *East Central Minnesota*

Winters 5
Summers 93
Seasonal Affect 48
Hazard-free 3

Places Rated Rank: 231

Edison, NJ
(40.19N, 73.58W at 10')

see *New Jersey Shore*

Winters 51
Summers 78
Seasonal Affect 55
Hazard-free 42

Places Rated Rank: 62

El Centro, CA
(32.47N, 115.33W at 41')

see *Lower Colorado Valley*

Winters 97
Summers 26
Seasonal Affect 98
Hazard-free 72

Places Rated Rank: 48

Elizabethtown, KY
(37.41N, 85.51W at 731')

see *West Central Kentucky*

Winters 51
Summers 39
Seasonal Affect 23
Hazard-free 53

Places Rated Rank: 243

Elkhart-Goshen, IN
(41.14N, 85.52W at 810')

see *Michiana*

Winters 1
Summers 73
Seasonal Affect 9
Hazard-free 13

Places Rated Rank: 365

Elmira, NY
(42.06N, 76.48W at 840')

see *New York's Southern Tier*

Winters 29
Summers 83
Seasonal Affect 15
Hazard-free 12

Places Rated Rank: 207

El Paso, TX
(31.48N, 106.24W at 3,920')

see *Trans Pecos*

Winters 80
Summers 33
Seasonal Affect 99
Hazard-free 63

Places Rated Rank: 59

Erie, PA
(42.05N, 80.11W at 730')

see *Western New York*

Winters 2
Summers 84
Seasonal Affect 6
Hazard-free 20

Places Rated Rank: 333

Essex County, MA
(42.31N, 70.55W at 17')

see *Massachusetts Bay*

Winters 19
Summers 85
Seasonal Affect 43
Hazard-free 30

Places Rated Rank: 180

✓ **Eugene-Springfield, OR**
(44.07N, 123.13W at 360')

see *Willamette Valley-Lower Columbia*

Winters 90
Summers 93
Seasonal Affect 2
Hazard-free 83

Places Rated Rank: 13

Evansville, IN
(38.03N, 87.32W at 380')

see *Lower Ohio Valley*

Winters 53
Summers 51
Seasonal Affect 35
Hazard-free 45

Places Rated Rank: 171

Fairbanks, AK
(64.5N, 147.43W at 440')

see *Alaska Interior Basin*

Winters 40
Summers 81
Seasonal Affect 4
Hazard-free 33

Places Rated Rank: 129

Fargo, ND-MN
(46.54N, 96.48W at 900')

see *North Dakota Red River Valley*

Winters 27
Summers 86
Seasonal Affect 53
Hazard-free 1

Places Rated Rank: 155

Farmington, NM
(36.44N, 108.12W at 5,311')

see *Four Corners*

Winters 56
Summers 56
Seasonal Affect 96
Hazard-free 45

Places Rated Rank: 71

Fayetteville, NC
(35.04N, 78.52W at 100')

see *N. Carolina's Central Coastal Plain*

Winters 79
Summers 17
Seasonal Affect 55
Hazard-free 65

Places Rated Rank: 162

Fayetteville-Rogers, AR-MO
(36.06N, 94.1W at 1,270')

see *Ozark Plateau*

Winters 40
Summers 35
Seasonal Affect 78
Hazard-free 41

Places Rated Rank: 267

Flagstaff, AZ
(35.08N, 111.4W at 7,000')

see *North Central Arizona*

Winters 5
Summers 100
Seasonal Affect 93
Hazard-free 36

Places Rated Rank: 98

Flint, MI
(42.58N, 83.45W at 770')

see *Saginaw Bay*

Winters 18
Summers 90
Seasonal Affect 19
Hazard-free 10

Places Rated Rank: 219

Florence, SC
(34.11N, 79.43W at 150')

see *South Carolina Midlands*

Winters 70
Summers 23
Seasonal Affect 68
Hazard-free 83

Places Rated Rank: 128

Florence-Muscle Shoals, AL
(34.45N, 87.37W at 540')

see *Northern Alabama*

Winters 57
Summers 16
Seasonal Affect 33
Hazard-free 60

Places Rated Rank: 317

Fond du Lac, WI
(43.46N, 88.26W at 760')

see *East Central Wisconsin*

Winters 31
Summers 67
Seasonal Affect.......................32
Hazard-free 7

Places Rated Rank: 249

Fort Collins-Loveland, CO
(40.35N, 105.05W at 5,000')

see *Colorado Northern Front Range*

Winters 0
Summers 89
Seasonal Affect.......................85
Hazard-free 15

Places Rated Rank: 221

Fort Lauderdale, FL
(26.06N, 80.12W at 20')

see *Florida Lower East Coast*

Winters 82
Summers 5
Seasonal Affect.......................75
Hazard-free 89

Places Rated Rank: 145

Fort Smith, AR-OK
(35.2N, 94.22W at 450')

see *Ozark Plateau*

Winters 51
Summers 15
Seasonal Affect.......................76
Hazard-free 63

Places Rated Rank: 290

Ft. Walton Beach, FL
(30.31N, 86.3W at 60')

see *Central Gulf Coast*

Winters 72
Summers 10
Seasonal Affect.......................72
Hazard-free 79

Places Rated Rank: 194

Fort Wayne, IN
(41N, 85.12W at 790')

see *Northeast Indiana*

Winters 25
Summers 64
Seasonal Affect.......................18
Hazard-free 20

Places Rated Rank: 302

Fort Worth-Arlington, TX
(32.51N, 96.51W at 440')

see *North Central Texas*

Winters 56
Summers 19
Seasonal Affect.......................83
Hazard-free 57

Places Rated Rank: 235

Fresno, CA
(36.47N, 119.43W at 340')

see *San Joaquin Basin*

Winters 94
Summers 32
Seasonal Affect.......................94
Hazard-free 96

Places Rated Rank: 43

Gadsden, AL
(34.02N, 86W at 560')

see *Alabama Appalachians*

Winters 73
Summers 18
Seasonal Affect.......................40
Hazard-free 69

Places Rated Rank: 206

Gainesville, FL
(29.41N, 82.16W at 140')

see *North Central Florida*

Winters 88
Summers 7
Seasonal Affect.......................60
Hazard-free 97

Places Rated Rank: 118

Gainesville, GA
(34.17N, 83.49W at 1,249')

see *North Central Georgia*

Winters 60
Summers 38
Seasonal Affect.......................58
Hazard-free 61

Places Rated Rank: 152

Gary, IN
(41.33N, 87.17W at 60')

see *Chicagoland*

Winters 21
Summers 52
Seasonal Affect.......................15
Hazard-free 16

Places Rated Rank: 363

Glens Falls, NY
(43.21N, 73.37W at 320')

see *Upper Hudson*

Winters 14
Summers 88
Seasonal Affect.......................13
Hazard-free 8

Places Rated Rank: 257

Goldsboro, NC
(35.2N, 77.58W at 110')

see *NC Central Coastal Plain*

Winters 74
Summers 16
Seasonal Affect.......................43
Hazard-free 68

Places Rated Rank: 211

Grand Forks, ND-MN
(47.57N, 97.1W at 850')

see *North Dakota Red River Valley*

Winters 28
Summers 93
Seasonal Affect.......................56
Hazard-free 0

Places Rated Rank: 105

Grand Junction, CO
(39.06N, 108.33W at 4,840')

see *Western Slope of Colorado*

Winters 45
Summers 49
Seasonal Affect.......................87
Hazard-free 45

Places Rated Rank: 149

Grand Rapids-Wyoming, MI
(42.53N, 85.31W at 780')

see *Western Michigan*

Winters 6
Summers 77
Seasonal Affect.........................8
Hazard-free 16

Places Rated Rank: 345

Great Falls, MT
(47.29N, 111.22W at 3,660')

see *Central Montana*

Winters 10
Summers 97
Seasonal Affect.......................49
Hazard-free 2

Places Rated Rank: 197

Greeley, CO
(40.25N, 104.42W at 4,720')

see *Colorado Northern Front Range*

Winters 6
Summers 66
Seasonal Affect.......................87
Hazard-free 12

Places Rated Rank: 312

Green Bay, WI
(44.29N, 88.08W at 700')

see *East Central Wisconsin*

Winters 20
Summers 77
Seasonal Affect.......................31
Hazard-free 6

Places Rated Rank: 264

Greensboro-High Point, NC
(36.05N, 79.57W at 900')

see *North Carolina Piedmont*

Winters 62
Summers 33
Seasonal Affect.......................70
Hazard-free 64

Places Rated Rank: 139

Greenville, NC
(35.37N, 77.23W at 30')

see *NC Central Coastal Plain*

Winters 67
Summers 24
Seasonal Affect.........................42
Hazard-free 66

Places Rated Rank: 214

Greenville, SC
(34.51N, 82.23W at 970')

see *Upcountry South Carolina*

Winters 77
Summers 38
Seasonal Affect.........................57
Hazard-free 73

Places Rated Rank: 70

Gulfport-Biloxi, MS
(30.23N, 88.59W at 10')

see *Central Gulf Coast*

Winters 65
Summers 8
Seasonal Affect.........................63
Hazard-free 84

Places Rated Rank: 238

Hagerstown, MD-WV
(39.39N, 77.44W at 660')

see *National Freeway*

Winters 42
Summers 61
Seasonal Affect.........................10
Hazard-free 42

Places Rated Rank: 215

✓ **Hanford-Corcoran, CA**
(36.19N, 119.38W at 248')

see *San Joaquin Basin*

Winters 94
Summers 39
Seasonal Affect.........................94
Hazard-free 93

Places Rated Rank: 36

Harrisburg-Carlisle, PA
(40.13N, 76.51W at 340')

see *PA's Southeastern Piedmont*

Winters 44
Summers 64
Seasonal Affect.........................20
Hazard-free 53

Places Rated Rank: 163

Harrisonburg, VA
(38.26N, 78.52W at 1,352')

see *Virginia Mountains*

Winters 48
Summers 58
Seasonal Affect.........................67
Hazard-free 49

Places Rated Rank: 106

Hartford, CT
(41.56N, 72.41W at 160')

see *Windsor Locks*

Winters 35
Summers 78
Seasonal Affect.........................15
Hazard-free 34

Places Rated Rank: 159

Hattiesburg, MS
(31.19N, 89.18W at 160')

see *Central Mississippi*

Winters 70
Summers 4
Seasonal Affect.........................49
Hazard-free 80

Places Rated Rank: 262

Hickory-Lenoir-Morganton, NC
(35.44N, 81.23W at 1,140')

see *North Carolina Piedmont*

Winters 59
Summers 34
Seasonal Affect.........................50
Hazard-free 65

Places Rated Rank: 181

Hinesville-Fort Stewart, GA
(31.5N, 81.35W at 48')

see *Colonial Coast*

Winters 85
Summers 22
Seasonal Affect.........................61
Hazard-free 88

Places Rated Rank: 76

Holland-Grand Haven, MI
(42.47N, 86.06W at 612')

see *Western Michigan*

Winters 4
Summers 81
Seasonal Affect...........................8
Hazard-free 22

Places Rated Rank: 331

✓ **Honolulu, HI**
(21.2N, 157.55W at 10')

see *Island of Oahu*

Winters 93
Summers 54
Seasonal Affect.........................96
Hazard-free 84

Places Rated Rank: 16

Hot Springs, AR
(34.3N, 93.03W at 579')

see *Central Arkansas*

Winters 53
Summers 14
Seasonal Affect.........................69
Hazard-free 67

Places Rated Rank: 285

Houma-Bayou Cane, LA
(29.35N, 90.44W at 20')

see *Central Gulf Coast*

Winters 79
Summers 4
Seasonal Affect.........................56
Hazard-free 84

Places Rated Rank: 203

Houston-Sugar Land, TX
(29.39N, 95.17W at 50')

see *Upper Texas Gulf*

Winters 74
Summers 1
Seasonal Affect.........................51
Hazard-free 89

Places Rated Rank: 233

Huntington, WV-KY-OH
(38.22N, 82.33W at 830')

see *West Virginia Metro Valley*

Winters 42
Summers 40
Seasonal Affect...........................5
Hazard-free 62

Places Rated Rank: 304

Huntsville, AL
(34.39N, 86.46W at 620')

see *Northern Alabama*

Winters 61
Summers 19
Seasonal Affect.........................26
Hazard-free 60

Places Rated Rank: 281

Idaho Falls, ID
(43.28N, 112.02W at 4,699')

see *Eastern Idaho*

Winters 32
Summers 80
Seasonal Affect.........................64
Hazard-free 8

Places Rated Rank: 133

Indianapolis, IN
(39.44N, 86.16W at 790')

see *Central Indiana*

Winters 37
Summers 43
Seasonal Affect.........................21
Hazard-free 32

Places Rated Rank: 328

Iowa City, IA
(41.39N, 91.32W at 640')

see *East Central Iowa*

Winters 25
Summers 42
Seasonal Affect.........................38
Hazard-free 6

Places Rated Rank: 370

Ithaca, NY

(42.26N, 76.29W at 814')

see *New York's Southern Tier*

Winters 12
Summers 91
Seasonal Affect..........................10
Hazard-free 21

Places Rated Rank: 229

Jackson, MI

(42.16N, 84.28W at 1,000')

see *Central Michigan*

Winters 31
Summers 56
Seasonal Affect..........................21
Hazard-free 11

Places Rated Rank: 322

Jackson, MS

(32.19N, 90.05W at 310')

see *Central Mississippi*

Winters 69
Summers 6
Seasonal Affect..........................52
Hazard-free 78

Places Rated Rank: 254

Jackson, TN

(35.36N, 88.55W at 430')

see *Lower Mississippi Watershed*

Winters 46
Summers 32
Seasonal Affect..........................40
Hazard-free 56

Places Rated Rank: 282

Jacksonville, FL

(30.3N, 81.42W at 30')

see *Northern Florida*

Winters 88
Summers 8
Seasonal Affect..........................69
Hazard-free 91

Places Rated Rank: 100

Jacksonville, NC

(34.5N, 77.18W at 40')

see *Carolina Coastal Plain*

Winters 71
Summers 19
Seasonal Affect..........................53
Hazard-free 67

Places Rated Rank: 195

Janesville, WI

(42.3N, 89.02W at 780')

see *Rock River Run*

Winters 17
Summers 61
Seasonal Affect..........................38
Hazard-free 10

Places Rated Rank: 340

Jefferson City, MO

(38.34N, 92.1W at 555')

see *Northeast Missouri Prairie*

Winters 32
Summers 30
Seasonal Affect..........................46
Hazard-free 29

Places Rated Rank: 362

Johnson City, TN

(36.31N, 82.32W at 1,280')

see *Upper Tennessee Watershed*

Winters 55
Summers 31
Seasonal Affect..........................16
Hazard-free 70

Places Rated Rank: 247

Johnstown, PA

(40.2N, 78.55W at 1,210')

see *Pennsylvania Central Mountains*

Winters 12
Summers 69
Seasonal Affect............................2
Hazard-free 37

Places Rated Rank: 338

Jonesboro, AR

(35.5N, 90.42W at 302')

see *Lower Mississippi Watershed*

Winters 41
Summers 30
Seasonal Affect..........................35
Hazard-free 57

Places Rated Rank: 324

Joplin, MO

(37.09N, 94.3W at 980')

see *Ozark Plateau*

Winters 34
Summers 27
Seasonal Affect..........................65
Hazard-free 38

Places Rated Rank: 347

Kalamazoo-Portage, MI

(42.17N, 85.36W at 950')

see *Western Michigan*

Winters 6
Summers 47
Seasonal Affect..........................13
Hazard-free 21

Places Rated Rank: 379

Kankakee-Bradley, IL

(41.3N, 87.41W at 710')

see *Illinois Prairie*

Winters 24
Summers 69
Seasonal Affect..........................35
Hazard-free 9

Places Rated Rank: 271

Kansas City, MO-KS

(39.19N, 94.43W at 970')

see *Missouri River Prairie*

Winters 26
Summers 35
Seasonal Affect..........................72
Hazard-free 28

Places Rated Rank: 350

✓ Kennewick, WA

(46.19N, 119.16W at 370')

see *Eastern Slope of the Cascades*

Winters 89
Summers 60
Seasonal Affect..........................65
Hazard-free 69

Places Rated Rank: 31

Killeen-Temple-Fort Hood, TX

(31.05N, 97.19W at 630')

see *North Central Texas*

Winters 71
Summers 16
Seasonal Affect..........................82
Hazard-free 56

Places Rated Rank: 179

Kingsport-Bristol, TN-VA

(36.31N, 82.32W at 1,280')

see *Upper Tennessee Watershed*

Winters 55
Summers 31
Seasonal Affect..........................16
Hazard-free 70

Places Rated Rank: 247

Kingston, NY

(41.55N, 73.59W at 223')

see *Lower Hudson Valley*

Winters 38
Summers 75
Seasonal Affect..........................18
Hazard-free 24

Places Rated Rank: 174

Knoxville, TN

(35.49N, 83.59W at 880')

see *Upper Tennessee Watershed*

Winters 52
Summers 27
Seasonal Affect..........................22
Hazard-free 67

Places Rated Rank: 288

Kokomo, IN

(40.19N, 86.3W at 840')

see *Central Indiana*

Winters 31
Summers 45
Seasonal Affect..........................23
Hazard-free 25

Places Rated Rank: 344

La Crosse, WI-MN
(43.52N, 91.15W at 650')
see *Coulee Region*
Winters 25
Summers 59
Seasonal Affect 47
Hazard-free 21
Places Rated Rank: 293

Lafayette, IN
(40.28N, 87W at 710')
see *Middle Wabash Valley*
Winters 36
Summers 53
Seasonal Affect 25
Hazard-free 18
Places Rated Rank: 300

Lafayette, LA
(30.12N, 91.59W at 40')
see *Central Louisiana*
Winters 65
Summers 3
Seasonal Affect 45
Hazard-free 80
Places Rated Rank: 303

Lake Charles, LA
(30.07N, 93.13W at 10')
see *Upper Texas Gulf*
Winters 68
Summers 4
Seasonal Affect 46
Hazard-free 80
Places Rated Rank: 274

Lake-Kenosha, IL-WI
(42.33N, 87.48W at 600')
see *Chicagoland*
Winters 16
Summers 78
Seasonal Affect 34
Hazard-free 4
Places Rated Rank: 276

Lakeland, FL
(28.01N, 81.55W at 150')
see *South Central Florida*
Winters 83
Summers 2
Seasonal Affect 74
Hazard-free 95
Places Rated Rank: 153

Lancaster, PA
(40.03N, 76.17W at 270')
see *PA's Southeastern Piedmont*
Winters 59
Summers 74
Seasonal Affect 37
Hazard-free 38
Places Rated Rank: 63

Lansing-East Lansing, MI
(42.46N, 84.36W at 840')
see *Central Michigan*
Winters 15
Summers 63
Seasonal Affect 20
Hazard-free 10
Places Rated Rank: 351

Laredo, TX
(27.34N, 99.3W at 430')
see *Lower Rio Grande Valley*
Winters 91
Summers 25
Seasonal Affect 98
Hazard-free 88
Places Rated Rank: 51

Las Cruces, NM
(32.37N, 106.44W at 4,270')
see *Trans Pecos*
Winters 80
Summers 43
Seasonal Affect 99
Hazard-free 58
Places Rated Rank: 49

Las Vegas-Paradise, NV
(36.05N, 115.1W at 2,160')
see *Southern Nevada*
Winters 91
Summers 27
Seasonal Affect 99
Hazard-free 79
Places Rated Rank: 50

Lawrence, KS
(38.58N, 95.16W at 980')
see *Missouri River Prairie*
Winters 29
Summers 22
Seasonal Affect 67
Hazard-free 39
Places Rated Rank: 372

Lawton, OK
(34.37N, 98.27W at 1,150')
see *Oklahoma-Texas Red River Valley*
Winters 46
Summers 24
Seasonal Affect 86
Hazard-free 39
Places Rated Rank: 296

Lebanon, PA
(40.2N, 76.24W at 464')
see *PA's Southeastern Piedmont*
Winters 44
Summers 73
Seasonal Affect 19
Hazard-free 51
Places Rated Rank: 110

Lewiston, ID-WA
(46.22N, 116.58W at 1,360')
see *The Palouse*
Winters 35
Summers 83
Seasonal Affect 26
Hazard-free 61
Places Rated Rank: 85

Lewiston-Auburn, ME
(44.06N, 70.13W at 180')
see *Maine Southern Interior*
Winters 18
Summers 92
Seasonal Affect 12
Hazard-free 23
Places Rated Rank: 196

Lexington-Fayette, KY
(38.02N, 84.36W at 970')
see *Kentucky Blue Grass*
Winters 44
Summers 46
Seasonal Affect 18
Hazard-free 44
Places Rated Rank: 265

Lima, OH
(40.43N, 84.08W at 850')
see *West Central Ohio*
Winters 38
Summers 69
Seasonal Affect 15
Hazard-free 20
Places Rated Rank: 217

Lincoln, NE
(40.51N, 96.45W at 1,190')
see *Mid-Missouri Watershed*
Winters 19
Summers 41
Seasonal Affect 75
Hazard-free 12
Places Rated Rank: 359

Little Rock, AR
(34.44N, 92.14W at 260')
see *Central Arkansas*
Winters 53
Summers 13
Seasonal Affect 69
Hazard-free 68
Places Rated Rank: 297

Logan, UT-ID
(41.44N, 111.5W at 4,499')
see *Wasatch Front*
Winters 5
Summers 67
Seasonal Affect 79
Hazard-free 43
Places Rated Rank: 280

Longview, TX
(32.32N, 94.21W at 350')

see *Ark-La-Tex*

Winters 63
Summers 6
Seasonal Affect 71
Hazard-free 66

Places Rated Rank: 272

Longview, WA
(46.08N, 122.56W at 21')

see *Willamette Valley-Lower Columbia*

Winters 41
Summers 98
Seasonal Affect 5
Hazard-free 74

Places Rated Rank: 54

✓ **Los Angeles, CA**
(33.56N, 118.24W at 100')

see *California South Coast*

Winters 99
Summers 65
Seasonal Affect 91
Hazard-free 100

Places Rated Rank: 8

Louisville, KY-IN
(38.11N, 85.44W at 480')

see *Kentucky Blue Grass*

Winters 46
Summers 39
Seasonal Affect 23
Hazard-free 52

Places Rated Rank: 270

Lubbock, TX
(33.39N, 101.49W at 3,250')

see *Texas High Plains*

Winters 40
Summers 37
Seasonal Affect 93
Hazard-free 35

Places Rated Rank: 242

Lynchburg, VA
(37.2N, 79.12W at 920')

see *Virginia's Western Piedmont*

Winters 60
Summers 50
Seasonal Affect 68
Hazard-free 59

Places Rated Rank: 82

Macon, GA
(32.42N, 83.39W at 350')

see *Central Georgia*

Winters 78
Summers 14
Seasonal Affect 47
Hazard-free 82

Places Rated Rank: 169

✓ **Madera, CA**
(36.57N, 120.03W at 272')

see *San Joaquin Basin*

Winters 94
Summers 37
Seasonal Affect 94
Hazard-free 96

Places Rated Rank: 38

Madison, WI
(43.08N, 89.2W at 860')

see *Rock River Run*

Winters 11
Summers 65
Seasonal Affect 27
Hazard-free 7

Places Rated Rank: 353

Manchester-Nashua, NH
(42.59N, 71.27W at 173')

see *Central New England*

Winters 12
Summers 96
Seasonal Affect 42
Hazard-free 11

Places Rated Rank: 188

Mansfield, OH
(40.49N, 82.31W at 1,300')

see *Central Ohio*

Winters 13
Summers 81
Seasonal Affect 7
Hazard-free 14

Places Rated Rank: 301

McAllen, TX
(26.11N, 98.14W at 100')

see *Lower Rio Grande Valley*

Winters 92
Summers 1
Seasonal Affect 82
Hazard-free 65

Places Rated Rank: 134

✓ **Medford, OR**
(42.23N, 122.53W at 1,300')

see *Oregon's Rogue River Valley*

Winters 90
Summers 63
Seasonal Affect 51
Hazard-free 78

Places Rated Rank: 26

Memphis, TN-MS-AR
(35.03N, 90W at 270')

see *Lower Mississippi Watershed*

Winters 48
Summers 20
Seasonal Affect 50
Hazard-free 61

Places Rated Rank: 315

✓ **Merced, CA**
(37.17N, 120.31W at 150')

see *San Joaquin Basin*

Winters 98
Summers 40
Seasonal Affect 93
Hazard-free 94

Places Rated Rank: 28

Miami-Miami Beach, FL
(25.48N, 80.18W at 10')

see *Florida Lower East Coast*

Winters 82
Summers 9
Seasonal Affect 76
Hazard-free 89

Places Rated Rank: 124

Michigan City, MI
(41.42N, 86.53W at 597')

see *Michiana*

Winters 1
Summers 57
Seasonal Affect 14
Hazard-free 13

Places Rated Rank: 378

Midland, TX
(43.36N, 84.14W at 611')

see *Texas High Plains*

Winters 69
Summers 29
Seasonal Affect 90
Hazard-free 50

Places Rated Rank: 122

Milwaukee, WI
(42.57N, 87.54W at 670')

see *Chicagoland*

Winters 11
Summers 74
Seasonal Affect 29
Hazard-free 4

Places Rated Rank: 330

Minneapolis-St. Paul, MN
(44.53N, 93.13W at 830')

see *East Central Minnesota*

Winters 7
Summers 76
Seasonal Affect 51
Hazard-free 5

Places Rated Rank: 313

Missoula, MT
(46.52N, 113.59W at 3,220')

see *Western Montana*

Winters 39
Summers 95
Seasonal Affect 34
Hazard-free 43

Places Rated Rank: 61

Mobile, AL

(30.41N, 88.15W at 210')

see *Central Gulf Coast*

Winters 58
Summers 9
Seasonal Affect............................58
Hazard-free 75

Places Rated Rank: 291

✓ **Modesto, CA**

(37.39N, 121W at 90')

see *San Joaquin Basin*

Winters 94
Summers 46
Seasonal Affect............................92
Hazard-free 95

Places Rated Rank: 23

Monroe, LA

(32.31N, 92.03W at 80')

see *North Central Louisiana*

Winters 55
Summers 2
Seasonal Affect............................54
Hazard-free 68

Places Rated Rank: 346

Monroe, MI

(41.54N, 83.23W at 593')

see *Southeast Michigan*

Winters 30
Summers 62
Seasonal Affect............................22
Hazard-free 22

Places Rated Rank: 277

Montgomery, AL

(32.18N, 86.24W at 220')

see *Lower Chatahoochee Watershed*

Winters 79
Summers 10
Seasonal Affect............................52
Hazard-free 87

Places Rated Rank: 166

Morgantown, WV

(39.37N, 79.57W at 823')

see *National Freeway*

Winters 31
Summers 51
Seasonal Affect..............................4
Hazard-free 58

Places Rated Rank: 306

Morristown, TN

(36.12N, 83.17W at 1,283')

see *Upper Tennessee Watershed*

Winters 52
Summers 31
Seasonal Affect............................21
Hazard-free 65

Places Rated Rank: 273

✓ **Mount Vernon, WA**

(48.25N, 122.19W at 23')

see *Puget Sound Shore*

Winters 88
Summers 92
Seasonal Affect..............................1
Hazard-free 70

Places Rated Rank: 15

Muncie, IN

(40.06N, 85.43W at 840')

see *Central Indiana*

Winters 39
Summers 51
Seasonal Affect............................17
Hazard-free 30

Places Rated Rank: 284

Muskegon-Norton Shores, MI

(43.14N, 86.14W at 592')

see *Western Michigan*

Winters 4
Summers 82
Seasonal Affect..............................8
Hazard-free 25

Places Rated Rank: 323

Myrtle Beach, SC

(34.03N, 78.53W at 90')

see *Carolina Coastal Plain*

Winters 58
Summers 15
Seasonal Affect............................56
Hazard-free 65

Places Rated Rank: 278

✓ **Napa, CA**

(38.17N, 122.17W at 17')

see *California North Coast*

Winters 95
Summers 47
Seasonal Affect............................88
Hazard-free 84

Places Rated Rank: 27

Naples-Marco Island, FL

(26.1N, 81.47W at 0')

see *Florida Southwest Coast*

Winters 84
Summers 5
Seasonal Affect............................81
Hazard-free 97

Places Rated Rank: 114

Nashville-Davidson, TN

(36.07N, 86.41W at 590')

see *Middle Tennessee*

Winters 47
Summers 24
Seasonal Affect............................30
Hazard-free 59

Places Rated Rank: 326

Nassau-Suffolk, NY

(40.44N, 73.37W at 100')

see *Long Island Sound*

Winters 53
Summers 70
Seasonal Affect............................74
Hazard-free 54

Places Rated Rank: 57

Newark-Union, NJ-PA

(40.42N, 74.1W at 10')

see *New York-Newark*

Winters 49
Summers 67
Seasonal Affect............................54
Hazard-free 44

Places Rated Rank: 83

New Haven-Milford, CT

(41.1N, 73.08W at 10')

see *Long Island Sound*

Winters 49
Summers 79
Seasonal Affect............................39
Hazard-free 31

Places Rated Rank: 74

New Orleans-Metairie, LA

(29.59N, 90.15W at 0')

see *Central Gulf Coast*

Winters 76
Summers 7
Seasonal Affect............................56
Hazard-free 84

Places Rated Rank: 211

New York, NY-NJ

(40.47N, 73.58W at 130')

see *New York-Newark*

Winters 50
Summers 69
Seasonal Affect............................66
Hazard-free 50

Places Rated Rank: 67

Niles-Benton Harbor, MI

(42.08N, 86.26W at 630')

see *Michiana*

Winters 1
Summers 75
Seasonal Affect..............................9
Hazard-free 22

Places Rated Rank: 356

Norwich-New London, CT

(41.32N, 72.04W at 20')

see *Long Island Sound*

Winters 45
Summers 87
Seasonal Affect............................28
Hazard-free 23

Places Rated Rank: 78

✓ Oakland, CA
(37.56N, 122.21W at 60')

see *California North Coast*

Winters 95
Summers 90
Seasonal Affect.....................88
Hazard-free 91

Places Rated Rank: 3

Ocala, FL
(29.12N, 82.05W at 80')

see *North Central Florida*

Winters 87
Summers 1
Seasonal Affect.....................60
Hazard-free 98

Places Rated Rank: 147

Ocean City, NJ
(39.16N, 74.13W at 6')

see *New Jersey Shore*

Winters 67
Summers 57
Seasonal Affect.....................49
Hazard-free 36

Places Rated Rank: 73

Odessa, TX
(31.5N, 102.22W at 2,890')

see *Texas High Plains*

Winters 69
Summers 29
Seasonal Affect.....................96
Hazard-free 50

Places Rated Rank: 115

Ogden-Clearfield, UT
(41.13N, 111.58W at 4,296')

see *Wasatch Front*

Winters 17
Summers 52
Seasonal Affect.....................80
Hazard-free 48

Places Rated Rank: 294

Oklahoma City, OK
(35.24N, 97.36W at 1,280')

see *Central Oklahoma*

Winters 40
Summers 31
Seasonal Affect.....................84
Hazard-free 38

Places Rated Rank: 292

Olympia, WA
(46.58N, 122.54W at 190')

see *Puget Sound Shore*

Winters 84
Summers 73
Seasonal Affect.......................0
Hazard-free 74

Places Rated Rank: 42

Omaha-Council Bluffs, NE-IA
(41.18N, 95.54W at 1,000')

see *Mid-Missouri Watershed*

Winters 15
Summers 44
Seasonal Affect.....................73
Hazard-free 8

Places Rated Rank: 369

Orlando-Kissimmee, FL
(28.27N, 81.19W at 100')

see *South Central Florida*

Winters 85
Summers 5
Seasonal Affect.....................77
Hazard-free 90

Places Rated Rank: 125

Oshkosh-Neenah, WI
(44.01N, 88.32W at 743')

see *East Central Wisconsin*

Winters 13
Summers 70
Seasonal Affect.....................31
Hazard-free 6

Places Rated Rank: 329

Owensboro, KY
(37.46N, 87.09W at 400')

see *Lower Ohio Valley*

Winters 52
Summers 34
Seasonal Affect.....................34
Hazard-free 53

Places Rated Rank: 251

✓ Oxnard-Thousand Oaks, CA
(34.19N, 119.09W at 240')

see *California South Coast*

Winters 100
Summers 59
Seasonal Affect.....................97
Hazard-free 99

Places Rated Rank: 10

Palm Bay-Melbourne, FL
(28.07N, 80.39W at 40')

see *South Central Florida*

Winters 87
Summers 10
Seasonal Affect.....................78
Hazard-free 92

Places Rated Rank: 91

Panama City-Lynn Haven, FL
(30.13N, 85.36W at 30')

see *Central Gulf Coast*

Winters 72
Summers 17
Seasonal Affect.....................73
Hazard-free 86

Places Rated Rank: 140

Parkersburg, WV-OH
(39.21N, 81.26W at 830')

see *Allegheny Plateau*

Winters 48
Summers 43
Seasonal Affect.......................2
Hazard-free 57

Places Rated Rank: 261

Pascagoula, MS
(30.21N, 88.33W at 16')

see *Central Gulf Coast*

Winters 65
Summers 8
Seasonal Affect.....................63
Hazard-free 82

Places Rated Rank: 240

Pensacola, FL
(30.28N, 87.12W at 110')

see *Central Gulf Coast*

Winters 72
Summers 11
Seasonal Affect.....................72
Hazard-free 85

Places Rated Rank: 175

Peoria, IL
(40.4N, 89.41W at 650')

see *Illinois Prairie*

Winters 21
Summers 41
Seasonal Affect.....................41
Hazard-free 17

Places Rated Rank: 374

Philadelphia, PA
(39.53N, 75.15W at 0')

see *Delaware Valley*

Winters 59
Summers 60
Seasonal Affect.....................37
Hazard-free 46

Places Rated Rank: 87

Phoenix-Mesa-Scottsdale, AZ
(33.26N, 112.01W at 1,110')

see *South Central Arizona*

Winters 96
Summers 26
Seasonal Affect...................100
Hazard-free 98

Places Rated Rank: 45

Pine Bluff, AR
(34.13N, 92.01W at 210')

see *Central Arkansas*

Winters 57
Summers 12
Seasonal Affect.....................71
Hazard-free 71

Places Rated Rank: 268

Pittsburgh, PA
(40.3N, 80.13W at 1,140')

see *Allegheny Plateau*

Winters 23
Summers 95
Seasonal Affect.......................11
Hazard-free 36

Places Rated Rank: 135

Pittsfield, MA
(42.11N, 73.24W at 730')

see *Upper Hudson*

Winters 22
Summers 98
Seasonal Affect.......................12
Hazard-free 14

Places Rated Rank: 154

Pocatello, ID
(42.52N, 112.26W at 4,462')

see *Eastern Idaho*

Winters 32
Summers 75
Seasonal Affect.......................65
Hazard-free 13

Places Rated Rank: 158

Portland, ME
(43.39N, 70.19W at 40')

see *New England Mid-Coast*

Winters 24
Summers 97
Seasonal Affect.......................13
Hazard-free 20

Places Rated Rank: 144

Portland-Vancouver, OR-WA
(45.36N, 122.36W at 20')

see *Willamette Valley-Lower Columbia*

Winters 43
Summers 98
Seasonal Affect...........................6
Hazard-free 75

Places Rated Rank: 52

Port St. Lucie, FL
(27.28N, 80.21W at 20')

see *South Central Florida*

Winters 87
Summers 11
Seasonal Affect.......................75
Hazard-free 93

Places Rated Rank: 90

Poughkeepsie, NY
(41.07N, 74.09W at 270')

see *Lower Hudson Valley*

Winters 36
Summers 84
Seasonal Affect.......................74
Hazard-free 40

Places Rated Rank: 65

✓**Prescott, AZ**
(34.32N, 112.28W at 5,368')

see *North Central Arizona*

Winters 50
Summers 99
Seasonal Affect.......................93
Hazard-free 46

Places Rated Rank: 29

Providence, RI
(41.44N, 71.26W at 50')

see *Long Island Sound*

Winters 39
Summers 94
Seasonal Affect.......................27
Hazard-free 31

Places Rated Rank: 66

Provo-Orem, UT
(40.05N, 111.36W at 4,720')

see *Wasatch Front*

Winters 9
Summers 56
Seasonal Affect.......................79
Hazard-free 47

Places Rated Rank: 311

Pueblo, CO
(38.17N, 104.31W at 4,680')

see *Colorado Southern Front Range*

Winters 15
Summers 50
Seasonal Affect.......................89
Hazard-free 32

Places Rated Rank: 319

Punta Gorda, FL
(26.55N, 82W at 20')

see *South Central Florida*

Winters 84
Summers 3
Seasonal Affect.......................83
Hazard-free 96

Places Rated Rank: 126

Racine, WI
(42.42N, 87.46W at 600')

see *Chicagoland*

Winters 8
Summers 70
Seasonal Affect.......................30
Hazard-free 4

Places Rated Rank: 348

Raleigh-Cary, NC
(35.52N, 78.47W at 420')

see *NC Central Coastal Plain*

Winters 67
Summers 26
Seasonal Affect.......................52
Hazard-free 64

Places Rated Rank: 189

Rapid City, SD
(44.03N, 103.04W at 3,160')

see *South Dakota Black Hills*

Winters 7
Summers 76
Seasonal Affect.......................76
Hazard-free 2

Places Rated Rank: 279

Reading, PA
(40.25N, 75.56W at 360')

see *PA's Southeastern Piedmont*

Winters 42
Summers 74
Seasonal Affect.......................17
Hazard-free 35

Places Rated Rank: 146

Redding, CA
(40.3N, 122.18W at 500')

see *Sacramento Valley*

Winters 92
Summers 35
Seasonal Affect.......................86
Hazard-free 93

Places Rated Rank: 44

✓**Reno-Sparks, NV**
(39.3N, 119.47W at 4,400')

see *Tahoe Basin*

Winters 72
Summers 76
Seasonal Affect.......................92
Hazard-free 46

Places Rated Rank: 30

Richmond, VA
(37.3N, 77.2W at 160')

see *Southside Virginia*

Winters 54
Summers 41
Seasonal Affect.......................43
Hazard-free 63

Places Rated Rank: 183

✓**Riverside-San Bernardino, CA**
(33.57N, 117.23W at 840')

see *California South Coast*

Winters 98
Summers 42
Seasonal Affect.......................98
Hazard-free 98

Places Rated Rank: 22

Roanoke, VA
(37.19N, 79.58W at 1,150')

see *Virginia's Western Piedmont*

Winters 52
Summers 53
Seasonal Affect.......................63
Hazard-free 54

Places Rated Rank: 111

Rochester, MN
(43.55N, 92.3W at 1,300')

see *Coulee Region*

Winters 3
Summers 67
Seasonal Affect 28
Hazard-free 0

Places Rated Rank: 371

Rochester, NY
(43.08N, 77.4W at 600')

see *Western New York*

Winters 8
Summers 88
Seasonal Affect 14
Hazard-free 26

Places Rated Rank: 260

Rockford, IL
(42.12N, 89.06W at 720')

see *Rock River Run*

Winters 13
Summers 65
Seasonal Affect 38
Hazard-free 10

Places Rated Rank: 339

Rockingham-Strafford, NH
(43.01N, 70.5W at 80')

see *New England Mid-Coast*

Winters 16
Summers 99
Seasonal Affect 39
Hazard-free 7

Places Rated Rank: 156

Rocky Mount, NC
(35.54N, 77.43W at 110')

see *NC Central Coastal Plain*

Winters 67
Summers 18
Seasonal Affect 42
Hazard-free 69

Places Rated Rank: 226

Rome, GA
(34.15N, 85.09W at 605')

see *North Central Georgia*

Winters 69
Summers 36
Seasonal Affect 58
Hazard-free 59

Places Rated Rank: 113

✓ Sacramento, CA
(38.31N, 121.3W at 20')

see *Sacramento Valley*

Winters 96
Summers 49
Seasonal Affect 91
Hazard-free 91

Places Rated Rank: 19

Saginaw, MI
(43.37N, 84.13W at 640')

see *Saginaw Bay*

Winters 28
Summers 80
Seasonal Affect 20
Hazard-free 11

Places Rated Rank: 216

St. Cloud, MN
(45.33N, 94.04W at 1,030')

see *East Central Minnesota*

Winters 22
Summers 72
Seasonal Affect 51
Hazard-free 28

Places Rated Rank: 220

St. George, UT
(37.06N, 113.34W at 2,880')

see *Utah's Dixie*

Winters 89
Summers 28
Seasonal Affect 99
Hazard-free 71

Places Rated Rank: 55

St. Joseph, MO-KS
(39.3N, 94.37W at 840')

see *Missouri River Prairie*

Winters 21
Summers 37
Seasonal Affect 73
Hazard-free 21

Places Rated Rank: 364

St. Louis, MO-IL
(38.45N, 90.22W at 570')

see *Northeast Missouri Prairie*

Winters 37
Summers 39
Seasonal Affect 42
Hazard-free 40

Places Rated Rank: 314

✓ Salem, OR
(44.55N, 123W at 200')

see *Willamette Valley-Lower Columbia*

Winters 90
Summers 95
Seasonal Affect 3
Hazard-free 77

Places Rated Rank: 12

✓ Salinas, CA
(36.36N, 121.54W at 380')

see *California Central Coast*

Winters 93
Summers 91
Seasonal Affect 89
Hazard-free 93

Places Rated Rank: 2

Salisbury, MD
(38.21N, 75.35W at 23')

see *Maryland Eastern Shore*

Winters 72
Summers 55
Seasonal Affect 61
Hazard-free 52

Places Rated Rank: 58

Salt Lake City, UT
(40.47N, 111.57W at 4,220')

see *Wasatch Front*

Winters 8
Summers 52
Seasonal Affect 80
Hazard-free 48

Places Rated Rank: 334

San Angelo, TX
(31.22N, 100.3W at 1,900')

see *Edwards Plateau of Texas*

Winters 75
Summers 23
Seasonal Affect 92
Hazard-free 56

Places Rated Rank: 107

San Antonio, TX
(29.32N, 98.28W at 790')

see *South Central Texas*

Winters 88
Summers 12
Seasonal Affect 79
Hazard-free 80

Places Rated Rank: 88

✓ San Diego-Carlsbad, CA
(32.44N, 117.1W at 10')

see *California South Coast*

Winters 99
Summers 72
Seasonal Affect 95
Hazard-free 100

Places Rated Rank: 6

Sandusky, OH
(41.26N, 82.42W at 597')

see *Ohio's Lake Erie Shore*

Winters 36
Summers 62
Seasonal Affect 22
Hazard-free 27

Places Rated Rank: 232

✓ San Francisco, CA
(37.46N, 122.26W at 80')

see *California North Coast*

Winters 95
Summers 90
Seasonal Affect 87
Hazard-free 92

Places Rated Rank: 1

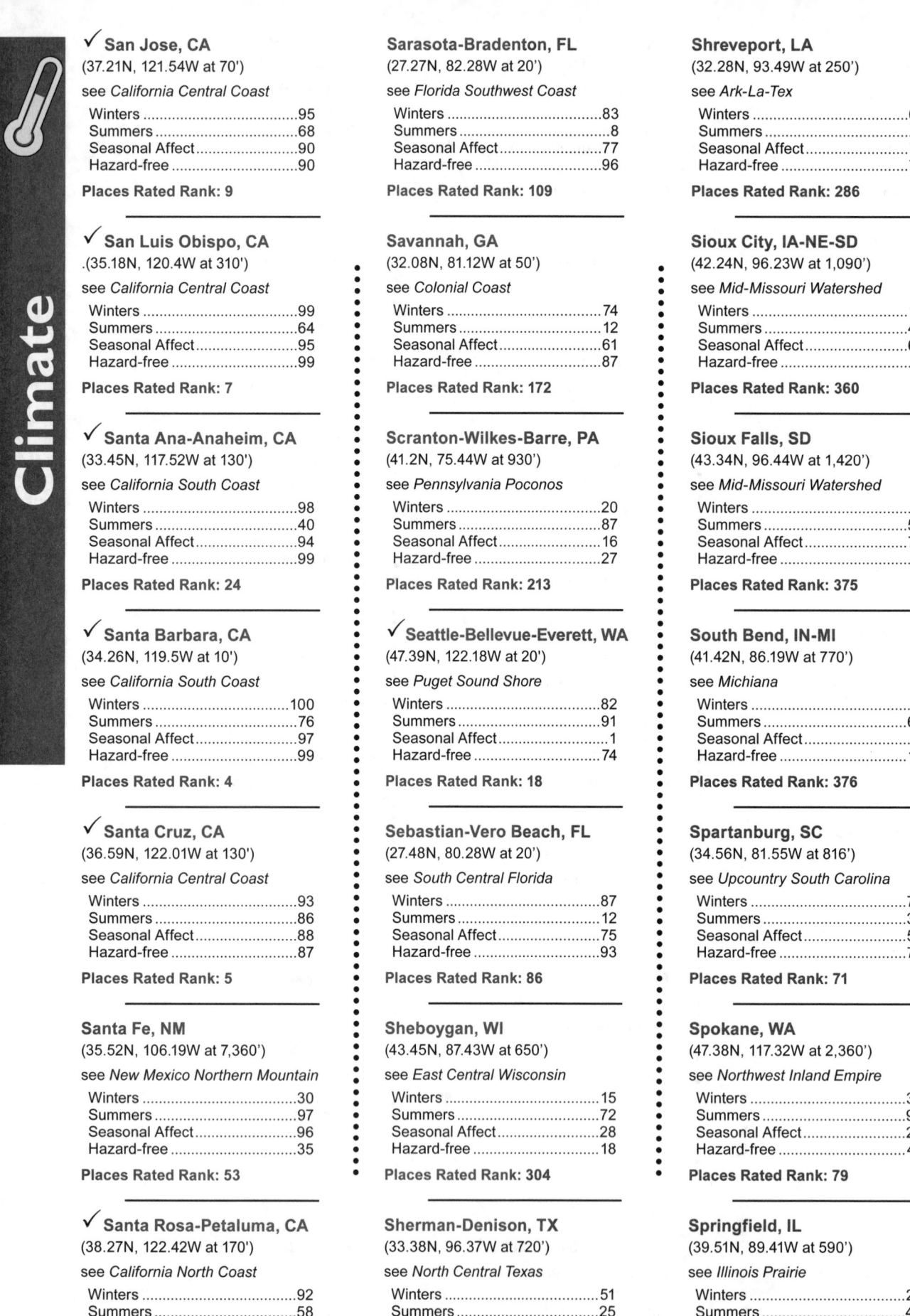

✓ **San Jose, CA**

(37.21N, 121.54W at 70')

see *California Central Coast*

Winters 95
Summers 68
Seasonal Affect.........................90
Hazard-free 90

Places Rated Rank: 9

✓ **San Luis Obispo, CA**

.(35.18N, 120.4W at 310')

see *California Central Coast*

Winters 99
Summers 64
Seasonal Affect.........................95
Hazard-free 99

Places Rated Rank: 7

✓ **Santa Ana-Anaheim, CA**

(33.45N, 117.52W at 130')

see *California South Coast*

Winters 98
Summers 40
Seasonal Affect.........................94
Hazard-free 99

Places Rated Rank: 24

✓ **Santa Barbara, CA**

(34.26N, 119.5W at 10')

see *California South Coast*

Winters 100
Summers 76
Seasonal Affect.........................97
Hazard-free 99

Places Rated Rank: 4

✓ **Santa Cruz, CA**

(36.59N, 122.01W at 130')

see *California Central Coast*

Winters 93
Summers 86
Seasonal Affect.........................88
Hazard-free 87

Places Rated Rank: 5

Santa Fe, NM

(35.52N, 106.19W at 7,360')

see *New Mexico Northern Mountain*

Winters 30
Summers 97
Seasonal Affect.........................96
Hazard-free 35

Places Rated Rank: 53

✓ **Santa Rosa-Petaluma, CA**

(38.27N, 122.42W at 170')

see *California North Coast*

Winters 92
Summers 58
Seasonal Affect.........................86
Hazard-free 81

Places Rated Rank: 17

Sarasota-Bradenton, FL

(27.27N, 82.28W at 20')

see *Florida Southwest Coast*

Winters 83
Summers 8
Seasonal Affect.........................77
Hazard-free 96

Places Rated Rank: 109

Savannah, GA

(32.08N, 81.12W at 50')

see *Colonial Coast*

Winters 74
Summers 12
Seasonal Affect.........................61
Hazard-free 87

Places Rated Rank: 172

Scranton-Wilkes-Barre, PA

(41.2N, 75.44W at 930')

see *Pennsylvania Poconos*

Winters 20
Summers 87
Seasonal Affect.........................16
Hazard-free 27

Places Rated Rank: 213

✓ **Seattle-Bellevue-Everett, WA**

(47.39N, 122.18W at 20')

see *Puget Sound Shore*

Winters 82
Summers 91
Seasonal Affect...........................1
Hazard-free 74

Places Rated Rank: 18

Sebastian-Vero Beach, FL

(27.48N, 80.28W at 20')

see *South Central Florida*

Winters 87
Summers 12
Seasonal Affect.........................75
Hazard-free 93

Places Rated Rank: 86

Sheboygan, WI

(43.45N, 87.43W at 650')

see *East Central Wisconsin*

Winters 15
Summers 72
Seasonal Affect.........................28
Hazard-free 18

Places Rated Rank: 304

Sherman-Denison, TX

(33.38N, 96.37W at 720')

see *North Central Texas*

Winters 51
Summers 25
Seasonal Affect.........................85
Hazard-free 48

Places Rated Rank: 241

Shreveport, LA

(32.28N, 93.49W at 250')

see *Ark-La-Tex*

Winters 62
Summers 3
Seasonal Affect.........................71
Hazard-free 73

Places Rated Rank: 286

Sioux City, IA-NE-SD

(42.24N, 96.23W at 1,090')

see *Mid-Missouri Watershed*

Winters 16
Summers 48
Seasonal Affect.........................66
Hazard-free 3

Places Rated Rank: 360

Sioux Falls, SD

(43.34N, 96.44W at 1,420')

see *Mid-Missouri Watershed*

Winters 1
Summers 58
Seasonal Affect.........................70
Hazard-free 1

Places Rated Rank: 375

South Bend, IN-MI

(41.42N, 86.19W at 770')

see *Michiana*

Winters 1
Summers 67
Seasonal Affect...........................9
Hazard-free 19

Places Rated Rank: 376

Spartanburg, SC

(34.56N, 81.55W at 816')

see *Upcountry South Carolina*

Winters 77
Summers 38
Seasonal Affect.........................57
Hazard-free 73

Places Rated Rank: 71

Spokane, WA

(47.38N, 117.32W at 2,360')

see *Northwest Inland Empire*

Winters 33
Summers 94
Seasonal Affect.........................26
Hazard-free 41

Places Rated Rank: 79

Springfield, IL

(39.51N, 89.41W at 590')

see *Illinois Prairie*

Winters 21
Summers 48
Seasonal Affect.........................44
Hazard-free 17

Places Rated Rank: 355

Springfield, MA

(42.23N, 72.32W at 180')

see *Windsor Locks*

Winters 30
Summers 96
Seasonal Affect.......................19
Hazard-free 9

Places Rated Rank: 122

Springfield, MO

(37.14N, 93.23W at 1,270')

see *Ozark Plateau*

Winters 28
Summers 34
Seasonal Affect.......................65
Hazard-free 31

Places Rated Rank: 352

Springfield, OH

(39.55N, 83.48W at 980')

see *West Central Ohio*

Winters 35
Summers 83
Seasonal Affect.......................11
Hazard-free 18

Places Rated Rank: 165

State College, PA

(40.48N, 77.52W at 1,170')

see *Pennsylvania Central Mountains*

Winters 13
Summers 63
Seasonal Affect.........................6
Hazard-free 33

Places Rated Rank: 349

✓ **Stockton, CA**

(38.07N, 121.17W at 40')

see *San Joaquin Basin*

Winters 97
Summers 58
Seasonal Affect.......................90
Hazard-free 91

Places Rated Rank: 14

Sumter, SC

(33.56N, 80.21W at 180')

see *South Carolina Midlands*

Winters 82
Summers 13
Seasonal Affect.......................59
Hazard-free 81

Places Rated Rank: 130

Syracuse, NY

(43.07N, 76.07W at 410')

see *Western New York*

Winters 7
Summers 89
Seasonal Affect.......................10
Hazard-free 25

Places Rated Rank: 266

✓ **Tacoma, WA**

(47.12N, 122.2W at 50')

see *Puget Sound Shore*

Winters 85
Summers 90
Seasonal Affect.........................1
Hazard-free 62

Places Rated Rank: 19

Tallahassee, FL

(30.23N, 84.22W at 60')

see *Northern Florida*

Winters 89
Summers 6
Seasonal Affect.......................67
Hazard-free 94

Places Rated Rank: 108

Tampa-St. Petersburg, FL

(27.58N, 82.32W at 20')

see *South Central Florida*

Winters 83
Summers 4
Seasonal Affect.......................77
Hazard-free 94

Places Rated Rank: 132

Terre Haute, IN

(39.21N, 87.25W at 560')

see *Middle Wabash Valley*

Winters 47
Summers 54
Seasonal Affect.......................39
Hazard-free 39

Places Rated Rank: 190

Texarkana, TX-AR

(33.27N, 94W at 360')

see *Ark-La-Tex*

Winters 63
Summers 21
Seasonal Affect.......................76
Hazard-free 82

Places Rated Rank: 173

Toledo, OH

(41.36N, 83.48W at 670')

see *Ohio's Lake Erie Shore*

Winters 27
Summers 71
Seasonal Affect.......................22
Hazard-free 19

Places Rated Rank: 244

Topeka, KS

(39.04N, 95.38W at 880')

see *Missouri River Prairie*

Winters 26
Summers 28
Seasonal Affect.......................67
Hazard-free 32

Places Rated Rank: 367

Trenton, NJ

(40.16N, 74.34W at 100')

see *Delaware Valley*

Winters 48
Summers 71
Seasonal Affect.......................36
Hazard-free 40

Places Rated Rank: 95

Tucson, AZ

(32.08N, 110.56W at 2,580')

see *Southeast Arizona*

Winters 81
Summers 26
Seasonal Affect.....................100
Hazard-free 90

Places Rated Rank: 56

Tulsa, OK

(36.12N, 95.54W at 650')

see *Green Country Oklahoma*

Winters 43
Summers 21
Seasonal Affect.......................80
Hazard-free 47

Places Rated Rank: 316

Tuscaloosa, AL

(33.14N, 87.37W at 170')

see *Alabama Appalachians*

Winters 76
Summers 11
Seasonal Affect.......................48
Hazard-free 78

Places Rated Rank: 201

Tyler, TX

(32.1N, 95.5W at 460')

see *Ark-La-Tex*

Winters 56
Summers 21
Seasonal Affect.......................84
Hazard-free 58

Places Rated Rank: 227

Utica-Rome, NY

(43.09N, 75.23W at 710')

see *Western New York*

Winters 8
Summers 93
Seasonal Affect.........................3
Hazard-free 17

Places Rated Rank: 256

Valdosta, GA

(30.49N, 83.16W at 229')

see *Southern Georgia*

Winters 74
Summers 7
Seasonal Affect.......................66
Hazard-free 95

Places Rated Rank: 182

✓ **Vallejo, CA**

(38.17N, 122.04W at 40')

see *California North Coast*

Winters 95
Summers 44
Seasonal Affect.....................88
Hazard-free 83

Places Rated Rank: 33

Victoria, TX

(28.51N, 96.55W at 100')

see *Texas Coastal Bend*

Winters 79
Summers 1
Seasonal Affect.....................53
Hazard-free 75

Places Rated Rank: 228

Vineland, NJ

(39.22N, 75.04W at 70')

see *Delaware Valley*

Winters 64
Summers 52
Seasonal Affect.....................44
Hazard-free 39

Places Rated Rank: 101

Virginia Beach, VA

(36.54N, 76.12W at 20')

see *Southside Virginia*

Winters 58
Summers 44
Seasonal Affect.....................46
Hazard-free 52

Places Rated Rank: 157

✓ **Visalia, CA**

(36.2N, 119.18W at 330')

see *San Joaquin Basin*

Winters 98
Summers 36
Seasonal Affect.....................95
Hazard-free 97

Places Rated Rank: 34

Waco, TX

(31.37N, 97.13W at 500')

see *North Central Texas*

Winters 70
Summers 15
Seasonal Affect.....................82
Hazard-free 55

Places Rated Rank: 205

Warner Robins, GA

(32.37N, 83.36W at 381')

see *Central Georgia*

Winters 78
Summers 14
Seasonal Affect.....................47
Hazard-free 82

Places Rated Rank: 168

Warren, MI

(42.28N, 83.01W at 619')

see *Southeast Michigan*

Winters 9
Summers 89
Seasonal Affect.....................24
Hazard-free 16

Places Rated Rank: 250

Washington, DC-MD-VA

(38.51N, 77.02W at 10')

see *Baltimore-Washington Corridor*

Winters 62
Summers 47
Seasonal Affect.....................25
Hazard-free 55

Places Rated Rank: 135

Waterloo, IA

(42.33N, 92.24W at 870')

see *East Central Iowa*

Winters 20
Summers 61
Seasonal Affect.....................38
Hazard-free 2

Places Rated Rank: 336

Wausau, WI

(44.55N, 89.37W at 1,200')

see *North Central Wisconsin*

Winters 12
Summers 78
Seasonal Affect.....................32
Hazard-free 5

Places Rated Rank: 299

Weirton-Steubenville, WV-OH

(40.23N, 80.38W at 990')

see *Allegheny Plateau*

Winters 26
Summers 67
Seasonal Affect.......................3
Hazard-free 29

Places Rated Rank: 283

Wenatchee, WA

(47.25N, 120.18W at 645')

see *Eastern Slope of the Cascades*

Winters 53
Summers 77
Seasonal Affect.....................27
Hazard-free 43

Places Rated Rank: 68

West Palm Beach, FL

(26.41N, 80.07W at 20')

see *Florida Lower East Coast*

Winters 81
Summers 7
Seasonal Affect.....................74
Hazard-free 85

Places Rated Rank: 148

Wheeling, WV

(39.54N, 80.45W at 620')

see *Allegheny Plateau*

Winters 23
Summers 79
Seasonal Affect.......................6
Hazard-free 38

Places Rated Rank: 223

Wichita, KS

(37.39N, 97.26W at 1,320')

see *South Central Kansas*

Winters 29
Summers 36
Seasonal Affect.....................78
Hazard-free 26

Places Rated Rank: 337

Wichita Falls, TX

(33.58N, 98.29W at 990')

see *Oklahoma-Texas Red River Valley*

Winters 47
Summers 21
Seasonal Affect.....................87
Hazard-free 44

Places Rated Rank: 289

Williamsport, PA

(41.15N, 76.55W at 520')

see *Pennsylvania Central Mountains*

Winters 34
Summers 56
Seasonal Affect.......................4
Hazard-free 42

Places Rated Rank: 287

Wilmington, DE

(39.4N, 75.36W at 80')

see *Delaware Valley*

Winters 58
Summers 51
Seasonal Affect.....................32
Hazard-free 47

Places Rated Rank: 141

Wilmington, NC

(34.16N, 77.54W at 30')

see *Carolina Coastal Plain*

Winters 72
Summers 13
Seasonal Affect.....................41
Hazard-free 71

Places Rated Rank: 225

Winchester, VA

(39.11N, 78.09W at 720')

see *Virginia Mountains*

Winters 46
Summers 53
Seasonal Affect.....................66
Hazard-free 56

Places Rated Rank: 131

Winston-Salem, NC

(36.05N, 80.14W at 912')

see *North Carolina Piedmont*

Winters 61
Summers 31
Seasonal Affect.......................70
Hazard-free 66

Places Rated Rank: 160

Worcester, MA

(42.16N, 71.52W at 990')

see *Central New England*

Winters 14
Summers 92
Seasonal Affect.......................30
Hazard-free 22

Places Rated Rank: 199

✓ **Yakima, WA**

(46.34N, 120.32W at 1,060')

see *Eastern Slope of the Cascades*

Winters 76
Summers 85
Seasonal Affect.......................64
Hazard-free 52

Places Rated Rank: 21

York-Hanover, PA

(39.55N, 76.45W at 390')

see *PA's Southeastern Piedmont*

Winters 43
Summers 62
Seasonal Affect.......................37
Hazard-free 36

Places Rated Rank: 177

Youngstown, OH

(41.15N, 80.4W at 1,180')

see *Northeast Ohio Hills*

Winters 11
Summers 89
Seasonal Affect.........................3
Hazard-free 24

Places Rated Rank: 263

✓ **Yuba City, CA**

(39.09N, 121.36W at 60')

see *Sacramento Valley*

Winters 96
Summers 38
Seasonal Affect.......................90
Hazard-free 91

Places Rated Rank: 37

Yuma, AZ

(32.4N, 114.36W at 210')

see *Lower Colorado Valley*

Winters 97
Summers 25
Seasonal Affect.......................98
Hazard-free 76

Places Rated Rank: 47

CLIMATE DIVISIONS

The following pages are brief profiles of 132 Climate Divisions where America's 379 metro areas are found. Climate Divisions go back to 1908 when the Agriculture Department was responsible for collecting the country's climate data. The 12 'drainage basins' identified for crop and water reporting purposes that year has grown to 344 climate divisions defined to monitor everything from crops to energy consumption to health – all of it now collected by the Commerce Department.

Places Rated averages the climate data for metro areas in each division. Temperature and precipitation data come from the National Oceanic and Atmospheric Administration (NOAA) *Series 20* publications. Data on humidity, wind, fog, thunderstorms, as well as clear, partly cloudy, and cloudy days are derived from the closest station reporting in NOAA's *Local Climatological Data.*

The descriptions for climate are capsule summaries of each division's location, landscape, and climate features. The tables to the right of each description include monthly high and low temperatures, relative humidity observed nearest to noon, wind speed, precipitation, and snowfall. Each profile also includes a visual legend for the average number of days per year that a region sees such conditions as a partly cloudy sky, temperatures below zero, and thunderstorms (see sample legend below).

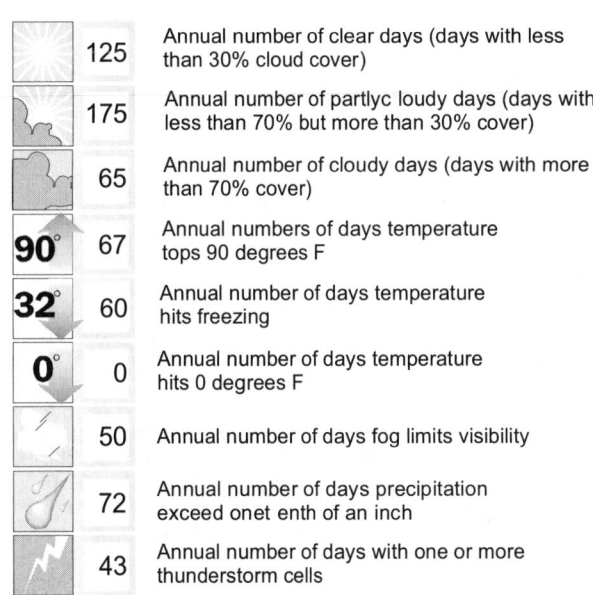

125	Annual number of clear days (days with less than 30% cloud cover)
175	Annual number of partlyc loudy days (days with less than 70% but more than 30% cover)
65	Annual number of cloudy days (days with more than 70% cover)
90° 67	Annual numbers of days temperature tops 90 degrees F
32° 60	Annual number of days temperature hits freezing
0° 0	Annual number of days temperature hits 0 degrees F
50	Annual number of days fog limits visibility
72	Annual number of days precipitation exceed onet enth of an inch
43	Annual number of days with one or more thunderstorm cells

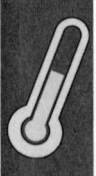

Climate

Alabama Appalachians

Location: In northeast Alabama, where the great Appalachians, possibly the oldest mountains in the United States, soften into foothills and then disappear. Sometimes called the Coosa Valley.

Landscape: Irregular plains and open high hills. At least 50 percent of the trees are loblolly pine, shortleaf pine, and other southern yellow pine.

Climate: Subtropical. The climate is uniform throughout the region. Mild winters and hot, humid summers are the rule. The growing season is long, but frost occurs nearly every winter. Precipitation is evenly distributed throughout the year, but peaks slightly in midsummer or early spring when it falls during thunderstorms. Snow falls rarely and melts almost immediately.

	99
	111
	155
90°	62
32°	62
0°	0
	159
	76
	57

	High °F	Low °F	Hum %	Wind mph	Precip inches	Snow inches
JAN	52	31	71	8.1	5.2	0.5
FEB	57	34	67	8.7	5.0	0.4
MAR	66	42	66	9.1	6.3	0.1
APR	75	49	67	8.3	5.3	0.0
MAY	81	58	71	6.8	4.5	0.0
JUN	88	65	71	6.1	3.8	0.0
JUL	90	69	75	5.7	5.0	0.0
AUG	90	69	75	5.4	3.7	0.0
SEP	84	63	74	6.3	3.6	0.0
OCT	75	50	71	6.2	2.9	0.0
NOV	65	41	71	7.3	4.1	0.0
DEC	56	34	71	7.8	5.1	0.2

Alaska Cook Inlet

Location: State climatologists define this area as the watershed of the Matunuska and Susitna (the Mat-Su) Rivers down to greater Anchorage and the Kenai Peninsula. Four of five Alaskans live here. Cook Inlet is the 200-mile long inlet that leads from Anchorage's waterfront to the Pacific Ocean.

Landscape: Irregular plains, open hills, and low mountains. Lowland spruce-hardwood forests are abundant.

Climate: Subarctic. The four seasons are well marked but their length is a lot different from seasons in the lower 48. Though rivers and lakes begin to thaw in late April, the last freeze is May 29. Ninety days later, the first freeze arrives with snow following in early October. Mountains block warm air and moisture from the Gulf of Alaska and they also block the deep cold air from the interior.

	61
	64
	240
90°	12
32°	194
0°	34
	73
	57
	0

	High °F	Low °F	Hum %	Wind mph	Precip inches	Snow inches
JAN	21	8	73	6.4	0.8	10.7
FEB	26	12	70	6.8	0.8	11.5
MAR	33	18	64	6.9	0.7	9.0
APR	43	29	60	7.2	0.7	4.8
MAY	54	39	56	8.4	0.7	0.4
JUN	62	47	62	8.3	1.1	0.0
JUL	65	52	68	7.3	1.7	0.0
AUG	63	50	71	6.9	2.4	0.0
SEP	55	42	71	6.7	2.7	0.3
OCT	41	29	72	6.7	2.0	7.3
NOV	27	15	75	6.5	1.1	10.7
DEC	23	10	77	6.2	1.1	14.8

Alaska Interior Basin

Location: State climatologists place this huge area between the Arctic and the maritime Cook Inlet to the south. Here, Fairbanks North Star borough, some 45 minutes north of Anchorage on a Boeing 737, is America's northernmost metro area.

Landscape: Tablelands, open hills, and low mountains with dense stands of white spruce and black spruce.

Climate: Subarctic. From June through July, the sun is up 18 to 21 hours a day, daily temperatures reach 70 degrees or more, and vegetables and grains grow luxuriantly. Ice will support a person's weight by October 27. From November to early March, when the period of daylight drops to less than 4 hours, the thermometer drops below zero, and temperatures of -40 degrees or colder occur. Snowfalls of 4 inches or more in a day hit only three times during winter. Blizzards are almost never seen, as winds rarely reach more than 20 miles an hour. Breakup of the river ice usually occurs in the first week of May.

	70
	86
	210
90°	55
32°	225
0°	116
	73
	106
	0

	High °F	Low °F	Hum %	Wind mph	Precip inches	Snow inches
JAN	-2	-19	70	3.0	0.5	10.9
FEB	7	-14	65	4.0	0.4	8.5
MAR	24	-2	60	5.0	0.4	6.1
APR	41	20	53	6.0	0.3	3.0
MAY	59	38	44	8.0	0.6	0.8
JUN	70	50	52	7.0	1.4	0.0
JUL	72	53	60	7.0	1.9	0.0
AUG	66	47	65	6.0	2.0	0.0
SEP	55	36	65	6.0	0.9	1.4
OCT	32	18	72	5.0	0.9	10.7
NOV	11	-6	75	4.0	0.8	13.2
DEC	2	-15	72	3.0	0.9	12.6

Allegheny Plateau

Location: This is a large, dissected plateau area in western Pennsylvania and northern West Virginia. It includes metro Pittsburgh and three metro areas in West Virginia's northern panhandle and Ohio Valley: Parkersburg, Weirton and Wheeling.

Landscape: Open high hills and low mountains. The trees are Appalachian oak, tall broadleaf trees that provide a dense, continuous canopy in summer and shed their leaves completely in winter.

Climate: Hot Continental, modified slightly by nearness to the Atlantic and Great Lakes. The predominant air comes from Canada and moves in by way of storm tracks, which vary in origin from the Hudson Bay to the Rockies. There are frequent inversions of air from the Gulf of Mexico during the summer, resulting in spells of warm, humid weather. Rain is evenly distributed and there is a 50 percent chance of measurable precipitation on any given day. During winter, one fourth of it is in the form of snow.

	61
	101
	204
90°	13
32°	118
0°	3
	183
	78
	36

	High °F	Low °F	Hum %	Wind mph	Precip inches	Snow inches
JAN	36	19	72	10.1	2.5	10.8
FEB	40	21	70	9.9	2.5	8.4
MAR	52	30	67	10.2	3.6	6.9
APR	63	39	65	9.8	3.4	1.3
MAY	73	49	70	8.3	3.9	0.1
JUN	81	58	71	7.5	3.9	0.0
JUL	84	62	69	6.9	4.1	0.0
AUG	82	61	70	6.6	3.7	0.0
SEP	76	55	73	7.1	3.1	0.0
OCT	65	43	69	8.0	2.7	0.2
NOV	53	34	70	9.4	3.2	2.9
DEC	41	25	72	9.9	3.0	7.1

Ark-La-Tex

Location: The name for this region, centered on metro Shreveport in northwest Louisiana, is a local colloquialism for where Arkansas, Oklahoma, Texas and Louisiana come together.

Landscape: Smooth and irregular plains. This area once was covered by a bottom-land deciduous forest with Carolina ash, elm, cottonwood, sugarberry, sweetgum, and water tupelo, as well as oak and bald cypress.

Climate: Subtropical. Winters are mild with cold spells that generally don't last long. The typical pattern is a drop in temperature the first day, minimum temperatures the second day, and gradual warming on the third. Summers are hot and humid, relieved by thunderstorms that come about eight times per month. April and May are pleasant. Fall lasts from late September to December and is delightful. The freeze-free growing season is long, from mid-May to mid-November.

	122
	98
	146
90°	90
32°	41
0°	0
	97
	60
	55

	High °F	Low °F	Hum %	Wind mph	Precip inches	Snow inches
JAN	55	34	73	9.3	3.3	0.9
FEB	61	38	71	9.9	3.6	0.6
MAR	69	46	69	10.6	3.8	0.2
APR	77	54	70	10.2	4.1	0.0
MAY	83	61	71	8.8	4.9	0.0
JUN	90	68	73	8.0	4.2	0.0
JUL	93	72	72	7.5	3.0	0.0
AUG	94	71	71	7.2	2.4	0.0
SEP	87	65	73	7.5	3.5	0.0
OCT	79	54	71	7.9	3.8	0.0
NOV	68	45	72	8.9	4.3	0.1
DEC	58	37	72	9.2	4.2	0.2

Baltimore-Washington

Location: Some 50 miles east of the Blue Ridge Mountains, this region lies along the western shore of Chesapeake Bay. Its twin metro areas 40 miles from each other, make up a huge urban and suburban area.

Landscape: Flat plains and tablelands with moderate relief. Common trees include evergreen oaks and members of the laurel and magnolia families.

Climate: Hot Continental. The Appalachians to the west and the Atlantic Ocean to the east produce a milder climate compared with other locations. Summers are hot and humid. The first freeze arrives at the end of October, followed by a chilly and rainy winter. Snow is minimal and doesn't last long. Rain falls throughout the year, but is greatest in late summer and early fall.

	100
	106
	159
90°	33
32°	80
0°	0
	133
	81
	29

	High °F	Low °F	Hum %	Wind mph	Precip inches	Snow inches
JAN	41	25	64	9.9	2.9	5.6
FEB	45	27	62	10.4	2.9	6.1
MAR	55	36	61	10.9	3.4	3.2
APR	65	45	60	10.5	3.0	0.1
MAY	75	55	64	9.2	4.0	0.0
JUN	84	64	65	8.8	3.5	0.0
JUL	88	69	66	8.2	3.7	0.0
AUG	86	68	69	8.0	4.1	0.0
SEP	79	60	69	8.3	3.4	0.0
OCT	68	48	68	8.7	3.1	0.0
NOV	57	39	66	9.3	3.3	1.0
DEC	46	30	65	9.5	3.3	3.5

Climate

California Central Coast

Location: The Central Coast Drainage region extends 250 miles south from San Jose and centers on Monterey and San Luis Obispo counties.

Landscape: Open low mountains and high mountains. Trees include the Monterey cypress, Torrey pine, Monterey pine, and white oak. On steep hill and mountain slopes much of the vegetation is scrub or chaparral.

Climate: Mediterranean. Year-round mild temperatures move through gradual transitions. Under the influence of the Pacific High, cooling produces nightly low-stratus clouds, known as California stratus, and early morning fog. Both dissipate before noon leaving most afternoons clear and sunny. Most rain falls from December through March. Winter fog is also common. Summers are dry and thunderstorms are rare.

	163
	103
	99
90°	10
32°	7
0°	0
	100
	33
	0

	High °F	Low °F	Hum %	Wind mph	Precip inches	Snow inches
JAN	61	41	74	6.6	4.2	0.1
FEB	63	43	73	8.1	3.6	0.0
MAR	64	44	72	9.5	3.6	0.0
APR	67	45	70	11.0	1.7	0.0
MAY	70	48	71	11.8	0.3	0.0
JUN	74	51	72	12.1	0.1	0.0
JUL	76	53	74	11.8	0.1	0.0
AUG	77	54	75	11.1	0.1	0.0
SEP	77	53	73	9.8	0.3	0.0
OCT	74	50	71	8.4	1.1	0.0
NOV	66	45	71	6.9	3.0	0.0
DEC	60	41	74	6.5	3.3	0.0

California North Coast

Location: State climatologists define the North Coast Drainage area as a group of counties surrounding all sides of San Francisco Bay.

Landscape: Low mountains. Trees include the Monterey cypress, Torrey pine, Monterey pine, Bishop Pine, and white oak. On steep slopes much of the vegetation is scrub or chaparral.

Climate: Mediterranean. This climate is confined to coasts washed by cool currents. The annual temperature cycle is very weak, reflecting the powerful influence of the cold California sea current with its cool marine air layer. Cool summers are typical, and winter temperatures are much milder than those of inland locations at similar latitudes. All months are above freezing. Rainfall drops to nearly zero for 2 consecutive summer months, but rises to substantial amounts in the rainy winter season. Annual rainfall ranges from 40" to 100". Dense fogs are common along the coast in summer.

	160
	101
	104
90°	28
32°	18
0°	0
	100
	40
	0

	High °F	Low °F	Hum %	Wind mph	Precip inches	Snow inches
JAN	56	40	76	7.2	5.1	0.0
FEB	62	43	75	8.7	3.7	0.0
MAR	64	44	73	10.5	3.5	0.0
APR	68	46	71	12.2	1.5	0.0
MAY	73	49	71	13.4	0.3	0.0
JUN	77	53	71	13.9	0.1	0.0
JUL	79	54	73	13.6	0.0	0.0
AUG	79	54	74	12.8	0.1	0.0
SEP	80	54	72	11.1	0.4	0.0
OCT	75	51	71	9.4	1.5	0.0
NOV	64	45	73	7.5	3.7	0.0
DEC	56	40	76	7.1	3.8	0.0

California South Coast

Location: California climatologists define the South Coast Drainage region as the area from San Diego north on Interstate 5 to Los Angeles, including suburban Orange, Riverside, and San Bernardino counties.

Landscape: Plains with open low mountains and high mountains. Trees include the Monterey cypress, Torrey pine, Monterey pine, and white oak. On steep slopes much of the vegetation is chaparral; east in the desert, the vegetation is thorny bush and Joshua trees.

Climate: Mediterranean. There are few freezing or 90-degree days. Dry easterly winds sometimes blow for several days at a time, bringing temperatures in the 90s and higher. Summers tend to be dry and mild. Springs are cooler, and there is rain from November through March. Storms are practically unknown. Sunshine is abundant though there is considerable fog along the coast and many low clouds in early morning and evening during the summer.

	164
	109
	94
90°	23
32°	5
0°	0
	93
	19
	1

	High °F	Low °F	Hum %	Wind mph	Precip inches	Snow inches
JAN	67	44	68	5.7	2.6	0.0
FEB	68	46	69	6.6	2.6	0.0
MAR	68	47	70	7.1	2.2	0.0
APR	71	50	67	7.5	0.9	0.0
MAY	73	54	68	7.4	0.2	0.0
JUN	76	57	70	7.2	0.0	0.0
JUL	81	61	71	6.8	0.0	0.0
AUG	82	62	72	6.6	0.1	0.0
SEP	80	60	70	6.2	0.4	0.0
OCT	77	55	69	5.9	0.4	0.0
NOV	71	48	67	5.7	1.8	0.0
DEC	67	44	68	5.5	1.8	0.0

Carolina Coastal Plain

Location: This is an area in North and South Carolina (where it is called Lowcountry) that extends from Atlantic beaches inland to an area called the Fall Line, where waterfalls first appear in rivers and streams.

Landscape: Flat plains. Common trees include evergreen oaks and members of the laurel and magnolia families. Sandy uplands have forests of loblolly and slash pine. Bald Cypress is a dominant tree in swamps.

Climate: Subtropical. A strong influence from the Atlantic moderates all four seasons. Summers are iced-tea warm and humid, but excessive heat is rare. During winter, polar air occasionally sails in, but the bite is gone by the time it reaches this area. Snowfall is slight. Rainfall is ample and well distributed, with most occurring in summer thundershowers. In winter, rain may fall steadily for several days.

	108
	106
	151
90°	49
32°	50
0°	0
	169
	73
	51

	High °F	Low °F	Hum %	Wind mph	Precip inches	Snow inches
JAN	56	32	69	9.0	4.0	0.4
FEB	59	34	66	9.7	3.8	0.7
MAR	67	41	68	10.1	4.1	0.4
APR	75	48	65	10.0	3.0	0.0
MAY	81	57	72	8.9	4.6	0.0
JUN	86	65	73	8.4	5.6	0.0
JUL	89	69	76	7.9	7.0	0.0
AUG	88	69	79	7.4	6.7	0.0
SEP	85	63	77	7.8	4.8	0.0
OCT	76	51	74	8.0	2.9	0.0
NOV	69	43	71	8.1	3.0	0.0
DEC	60	35	70	8.4	3.6	0.5

Central Arkansas

Location: The region embraces a clutch of rural and urban counties surrounding the capital city of Little Rock, and includes Pine Bluff and Hot Springs, the spa-resort-retirement city just southwest on I-30.

Landscape: Plains with hills and open low mountains. Half the trees are typical southern yellow pine. The rest are oak, hickory, sweetgum, blackgum, red maple, and winged elm. Dogwood and numerous woody vines are common.

Climate: Subtropical. Mild winters and hot, humid summers are the rule. The growing season is long, but frost occurs nearly every winter. Precipitation is even throughout the year, but peaks slightly in early spring when it falls mostly during thunderstorms. Snow falls rarely and melts almost immediately.

	119
	100
	147
90°	76
32°	54
0°	0
	142
	71
	57

	High °F	Low °F	Hum %	Wind mph	Precip inches	Snow inches
JAN	50	29	71	8.5	3.5	2.0
FEB	55	33	70	8.9	4.0	1.3
MAR	65	42	68	9.6	5.1	0.4
APR	74	51	70	9.0	5.3	0.0
MAY	81	59	73	7.7	5.6	0.0
JUN	89	67	71	7.2	3.8	0.0
JUL	93	71	72	6.7	4.2	0.0
AUG	92	69	73	6.3	3.5	0.0
SEP	85	63	74	6.7	3.9	0.0
OCT	76	51	70	6.8	4.0	0.0
NOV	63	41	71	8.0	5.1	0.1
DEC	53	33	71	8.2	5.1	0.6

Central Georgia

Location: This region includes metro Macon and metro Warner Robins in the Old South's cotton belt, near the exact center of the state.

Landscape: Irregular plains and open low hills. Half the trees are typical southern yellow pine. The rest are oak, hickory, sweetgum, blackgum, red maple, and winged elm. Dogwood and numerous woody vines are common.

Climate: Subtropical. The first frost comes rather late in the year, in the first week of November. The Appalachian Mountains north of here block cold air in the winter. Each year, there are traces of snow. By mid-March, there are no more frosts. Summers are hot and humid, but relieved by showers and thunderstorms.

	112
	107
	147
90°	87
32°	42
0°	0
	180
	83
	54

	High °F	Low °F	Hum %	Wind mph	Precip inches	Snow inches
JAN	57	34	71	8.0	4.6	0.3
FEB	61	37	69	8.6	4.7	0.6
MAR	70	44	69	9.0	4.8	0.1
APR	78	51	68	8.5	3.5	0.0
MAY	85	59	69	7.5	3.6	0.0
JUN	90	67	70	7.1	3.6	0.0
JUL	92	71	73	6.8	4.3	0.0
AUG	91	70	75	6.3	3.6	0.0
SEP	86	64	75	6.8	2.8	0.0
OCT	78	52	70	6.7	2.2	0.0
NOV	69	43	70	7.0	2.7	0.0
DEC	60	37	70	7.5	4.3	0.0

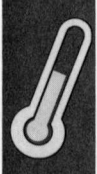

Climate

Central Gulf Coast

Location: This region is a chain of metro areas from the Florida panhandle to New Orleans, all fronting the Gulf or within a few miles of it. Because of the water's warm temperatures, the region sees tropical hurricanes.

Landscape: Flat and irregular plains. Common trees include evergreen oaks and members of the laurel and magnolia families. Sandy uplands have forests of loblolly and slash pine. Bald Cypress is a dominant tree in swamps. Sometimes the trees are festooned with Spanish moss.

Climate: Subtropical. Precipitation amounts are among the highest in the United States and fall evenly throughout the year. The Gulf moderates the weather, tempering the cold winter northers and causing cool and refreshing sea breezes during summer. Summer days typically start in the low seventies. Then the temperature rises rapidly before noon to the high 80s or low 90s where it is checked by the sea breeze. Winters see predictable freezes - the first occurring November 14 and the latest around March 9.

	103
	120
	142
90°	62
32°	18
0°	0
	173
	72
	70

	High °F	Low °F	Hum %	Wind mph	Precip inches	Snow inches
JAN	60	40	74	9.3	5.0	0.1
FEB	64	43	72	9.8	5.6	0.1
MAR	70	50	72	9.9	5.4	0.1
APR	78	57	72	9.5	4.2	0.0
MAY	84	65	74	8.4	4.7	0.0
JUN	89	71	75	7.3	5.8	0.0
JUL	90	73	77	6.5	7.3	0.0
AUG	90	73	78	6.4	7.0	0.0
SEP	87	69	76	7.5	5.8	0.0
OCT	80	58	72	7.8	3.5	0.0
NOV	71	50	73	8.7	4.0	0.0
DEC	64	43	75	9.1	5.0	0.1

Central Indiana

Location: This region is Indiana's exact center. It takes in the nine counties of greater Indianapolis plus three other, nearby metro areas within the Indianapolis media market.

Landscape: Smooth and irregular plains, open hills. Vegetation is intermingled prairie, groves, and strips of deciduous trees commonly found near streams and on north facing slopes.

Climate: Hot Continental, with warm summers, moderately cold winters, and occasional wide variations in temperatures during the cold season. Snowfalls of 3 inches or more occur about three times annually. Air from the Gulf of Mexico bring periods of muggy weather in summer but are usually replaced by cooler air from the northern Plains and Great Lakes. The last freeze is April 21. The first freeze is five months later around October 18. Precipitation is well distributed throughout the year.

	88
	99
	179
90°	19
32°	126
0°	8
	163
	71
	43

	High °F	Low °F	Hum %	Wind mph	Precip inches	Snow inches
JAN	33	17	76	10.9	2.1	6.1
FEB	37	21	74	10.8	2.2	5.6
MAR	49	31	71	11.7	3.5	3.7
APR	62	41	68	11.2	3.9	0.4
MAY	73	50	69	9.5	3.9	0.0
JUN	82	60	69	8.5	3.7	0.0
JUL	85	64	74	7.5	4.1	0.0
AUG	83	61	76	7.2	3.6	0.0
SEP	77	55	74	8.0	3.0	0.0
OCT	65	43	72	8.8	2.7	0.1
NOV	51	34	76	10.4	3.2	1.9
DEC	38	23	78	10.5	3.2	5.3

Central Iowa

Location: Two of America's great Interstates, I-35 and I-80, meet in Des Moines, Iowa's capital city. Ames, the university metro area, is a short distance north of here.

Landscape: Irregular plains and open low hills. Vegetation is mixed prairie, groves, and strips of deciduous trees commonly found near streams and on north facing slopes.

Climate: Prairie, with long, cold winters, hot summers, and short springs and falls. The first freeze arrives before mid-October. The last freeze occurs in the beginning of May. The winter is a season of dry cold, occasionally broken by snowstorms of short duration. Winter winds are from the northwest and often intensify the cold as they sweep over the flat land, though bitterly cold days are rare. Summer winds are southerly and precipitation falls in showers or thunderstorms from late April through October. Autumn is sunny with diminishing precipitation.

	105
	97
	164
90°	26
32°	137
0°	16
	109
	54
	46

	High °F	Low °F	Hum %	Wind mph	Precip inches	Snow inches
JAN	28	10	72	11.5	0.8	8.1
FEB	33	15	72	11.4	1.0	7.2
MAR	46	27	70	12.7	2.2	6.2
APR	62	39	67	12.7	3.4	1.9
MAY	73	51	67	11.1	4.0	0.0
JUN	82	60	68	10.2	4.8	0.0
JUL	86	65	70	8.9	3.8	0.0
AUG	84	62	72	8.6	4.1	0.0
SEP	76	53	72	9.4	3.5	0.0
OCT	64	42	67	10.3	2.6	0.2
NOV	47	29	72	11.3	1.7	3.0
DEC	32	15	75	11.2	1.2	6.6

Central Louisiana

Location: This region, centered in greater Alexandria, lies just outside of the group of 22 parishes that are officially defined by Louisiana as Acadiana.

Landscape: Flat and irregular plains. Common trees include evergreen oaks and members of the laurel and magnolia families. Sandy uplands have forests of loblolly and slash pine. Bald Cypress is a dominant tree in swamps.

Climate: Subtropical, reflecting the nearness of the Gulf of Mexico. Rain is evenly distributed through the year. Early summer mornings may be as much as twenty degrees cooler than the afternoons. There are tropical storms in summer and hurricanes in summer and fall, sometimes sprouting tornadoes.

	104
	111
	150
90°	88
32°	24
0°	0
	167
	71
	68

	High °F	Low °F	Hum %	Wind mph	Precip inches	Snow inches
JAN	59	39	77	9.3	5.0	0.2
FEB	63	42	76	9.7	4.9	0.3
MAR	71	50	75	10.0	4.8	0.0
APR	79	58	73	9.5	4.5	0.0
MAY	85	64	73	8.3	5.1	0.0
JUN	90	70	75	7.3	4.7	0.0
JUL	92	73	77	6.5	6.1	0.0
AUG	91	72	77	6.2	5.3	0.0
SEP	87	68	76	7.1	4.8	0.0
OCT	80	57	74	7.3	3.8	0.0
NOV	71	49	75	8.5	4.5	0.0
DEC	63	42	78	8.9	5.9	0.0

Central Michigan

Location: This includes a triangle of cities, Lansing (the state's capital), Battle Creek and Jackson. Each is about 40 miles from one another.

Landscape: Smooth and irregular plains. Stands of white oak, red oak, black oak, bitternut hickory, and shagbark hickory trees form a mosaic pattern with prairie. The understory is flowering dogwood.

Climate: Hot Continental. The Great Lakes influences temperature, the number of frost-free days, and the ratio of sunshine to cloudy days. Frost-free periods average 170 to 180 days, from the beginning of May to mid-October. Precipitation averages 31 inches annually, a lot of it as snow. Sleet, hail, and ice storms are common, and tornadoes and blizzards sometimes occur. Heavy cloud cover in the fall and early winter is common.

	71
	104
	190
90°	14
32°	143
0°	10
	153
	67
	32

	High °F	Low °F	Hum %	Wind mph	Precip inches	Snow inches
JAN	29	14	79	11.8	1.5	11.7
FEB	32	15	76	11.0	1.4	8.6
MAR	44	26	74	11.3	2.4	7.6
APR	58	36	69	11.2	3.0	2.3
MAY	70	46	68	9.9	3.1	0.1
JUN	79	56	69	9.0	3.5	0.0
JUL	83	60	72	8.0	3.1	0.0
AUG	81	58	75	7.5	3.3	0.0
SEP	73	51	77	8.2	3.5	0.0
OCT	60	40	75	9.3	2.3	0.2
NOV	47	31	78	10.8	2.7	4.8
DEC	34	20	81	11.2	2.4	10.2

Central Mississippi

Location: This area includes metro Jackson and metro Hattiesburg and the 90 miles of farmland between them along old U.S. 49.

Landscape: Irregular plains. Half the trees are typical southern yellow pine. The rest are oak, hickory, sweetgum, blackgum, red maple, and winged elm. Dogwood and numerous woody vines are common.

Climate: Subtropical. Quite humid during most of the year, with one short cold season and one long warm one. In summer, the southerly winds and warm Gulf air masses predominate, resulting in a warm, humid Maritime climate. Summer days are sultry, and so are the nights. In winter, northern air sometimes invades the area, causing rapid and dramatic temperature drops.

	111
	104
	150
90°	90
32°	47
0°	0
	195
	74
	68

	High °F	Low °F	Hum %	Wind mph	Precip inches	Snow inches
JAN	57	34	76	8.4	5.5	0.5
FEB	61	36	74	8.6	5.2	0.3
MAR	70	45	72	9.1	6.0	0.1
APR	78	53	73	8.5	5.2	0.0
MAY	84	60	74	7.3	5.1	0.0
JUN	90	67	74	6.4	3.7	0.0
JUL	92	71	77	5.9	5.0	0.0
AUG	92	70	77	5.6	4.5	0.0
SEP	88	64	76	6.4	3.6	0.0
OCT	79	51	73	6.5	3.2	0.0
NOV	70	43	74	7.6	4.8	0.0
DEC	61	37	76	8.3	6.1	0.0

Climate Divisions (Ce)

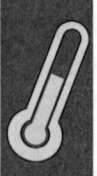

Central Montana

Location: This region, centered on Great Falls, is east of the Continental Divide. Here the land turns into a prairie province and extends a thousand miles to the Great Lakes.

Landscape: Open high mountains declining to tablelands. The lower ground is a shortgrass prairie with scattered trees and sagebrush and rabbitbrush.

Climate: Temperate Steppe. Summers are cool, sunny, and pleasant. Seventy percent of the annual rainfall occurs between April and September, the freeze-free growing season. The first frost arrives in mid-September. Winters are quite cold but continually modified by Chinook winds bringing warm air from the Pacific, causing rapid warming and preventing accumulation of snow. By mid-May, the last frost has departed, though there are snow traces throughout spring and sometimes into summer.

	79
	106
	180
90°	18
32°	155
0°	28
	45
	32
	25

	High °F	Low °F	Hum %	Wind mph	Precip inches	Snow inches
JAN	31	12	63	15.2	0.9	9.9
FEB	38	17	61	14.2	0.6	8.3
MAR	44	23	59	12.9	1.1	10.4
APR	55	32	55	12.8	1.4	7.2
MAY	65	41	56	11.3	2.5	1.8
JUN	75	49	56	11.1	2.4	0.3
JUL	83	53	49	10.0	1.2	0.0
AUG	82	52	48	10.2	1.5	0.1
SEP	70	44	53	11.2	1.2	1.5
OCT	59	36	54	13.1	0.8	3.4
NOV	44	24	60	14.6	0.7	7.5
DEC	33	15	63	15.6	0.9	8.7

Central New England

Location: This is a joining of Southern New Hampshire with Central Massachusetts climate areas officially defined by the respective states' climatologists.

Landscape: Open hills and low mountains. The forests are mixed stands of pine and deciduous species - yellow birch, sugar maple, and American beech.

Climate: Hot Continental. Typical New England four-season climate with air that is cold and dry in winter, cool and dry in summer. Hot summer weather is infrequent. The winter wind-chill factor is low as the area is protected from strong winds by the hilly terrain. The annual precipitation is 37 inches with annual snowfall averaging 60 inches.

	94
	106
	166
90°	11
32°	115
0°	3
	54
	75
	21

	High °F	Low °F	Hum %	Wind mph	Precip inches	Snow inches
JAN	31	13	65	12.8	3.5	16.6
FEB	34	14	64	12.7	3.4	15.9
MAR	43	24	64	12.5	3.8	13.5
APR	55	34	62	12.1	3.8	3.0
MAY	67	44	65	11.1	3.9	0.2
JUN	76	53	67	10.2	3.8	0.0
JUL	80	59	68	9.7	3.6	0.0
AUG	79	57	70	9.6	3.6	0.0
SEP	71	49	72	10.0	3.6	0.0
OCT	61	38	69	10.7	4.0	0.3
NOV	48	30	69	11.5	4.4	3.5
DEC	35	18	68	12.3	4.0	14.1

Central North Dakota

Location: Bismarck, the state capital, anchors this area at the headwaters of the Missouri River about midway between the Great Lakes and the Rocky Mountains.

Landscape: Tablelands with hills, in a shortgrass prairie. There are scattered trees and sagebrush and rabbitbrush. Because ground cover is scarce, much soil is exposed to wind erosion.

Climate: Steppe. The temperature range from summer's hottest to winter's coldest is 135 degrees, typical of the northern Great Plains. In summer, readings of 100°F or more may be expected 6 years out of 10. Readings of -30°F in winter are seen 7 years out of 10. January averages just 8°F, while July averages 71°F. The first freeze hits September 23, the last around May 13. Wind is often steady and clothes dry quickly on the line.

	93
	107
	165
90°	23
32°	186
0°	51
	59
	34
	34

	High °F	Low °F	Hum %	Wind mph	Precip inches	Snow inches
JAN	20	-2	72	10.0	0.4	7.2
FEB	26	5	73	9.8	0.4	6.7
MAR	39	18	72	10.9	0.8	8.1
APR	55	31	65	11.9	1.7	3.8
MAY	68	42	63	11.6	2.2	0.9
JUN	77	52	68	10.4	2.7	0.0
JUL	84	56	66	9.2	2.1	0.0
AUG	83	54	65	9.4	1.7	0.0
SEP	71	43	67	9.9	1.5	0.3
OCT	59	33	65	10.0	0.9	1.7
NOV	39	18	73	9.9	0.5	6.3
DEC	25	3	75	9.5	0.5	6.9

Central Ohio

Location: The area is centered on Columbus, the state capital, and includes the rural expanse up to Mansfield, some 60 miles north on Interstate Highway 71.

Landscape: Irregular plains and tablelands with moderate relief. Vegetation is intermingled prairie, groves, and strips of deciduous trees commonly found near streams and on north facing slopes.

Climate: Hot Continental. The first freeze is October 6. Cold air masses from Canada frequently invade the region. Winters are typical of the latitude with cold temperatures and snow. The last frost departs May 3. Tropical Gulf air masses often reach here during the summer but to a much lesser extent in fall and winter. Summers are warm and humid. The area's rivers contribute to the formation of shallow ground fog at daybreak in the summer and fall.

	73
	102
	191
90°	13
32°	125
0°	5
	162
	81
	39

	High °F	Low °F	Hum %	Wind mph	Precip inches	Snow inches
JAN	33	18	75	11.6	2.1	9.6
FEB	37	20	73	11.2	2.1	8.2
MAR	49	30	69	11.3	3.3	5.8
APR	60	39	66	11.0	3.4	1.4
MAY	71	49	68	9.2	4.1	0.1
JUN	79	58	69	8.6	4.0	0.0
JUL	83	62	71	7.5	4.2	0.0
AUG	81	61	74	7.3	3.9	0.0
SEP	75	54	73	7.8	3.2	0.0
OCT	63	43	70	9.0	2.2	0.3
NOV	50	34	73	10.5	3.4	2.4
DEC	38	24	76	11.2	3.0	7.1

Central Oklahoma

Location: This region is anchored by greater Oklahoma City and lies in the southern Great Plains.

Landscape: Irregular plains, hills. A bluestem-grama grassland prairie.

Climate: Prairie. The climate is typical of the Great Plains with some influence exerted by warm, moist air from the Gulf of Mexico. There is pronounced daily and seasonal temperature changes and considerable variation in seasonal and annual precipitation. The first freeze is early November and the last is early May. Summers are long and hot, broken by rain falling both as showers and thunderstorms. Occasionally there will be hail and destructive winds. Winters are comparatively mild and short, with moisture in the form of sleet arriving on frontal passages from the north.

	139
	96
	130
90°	70
32°	79
0°	0
	89
	48
	50

	High °F	Low °F	Hum %	Wind mph	Precip inches	Snow inches
JAN	47	25	69	12.6	1.1	3.0
FEB	52	30	68	13.1	1.6	2.4
MAR	62	39	65	14.5	2.7	1.4
APR	72	49	65	14.2	2.8	0.0
MAY	79	58	71	12.6	5.2	0.0
JUN	87	66	70	11.9	4.3	0.0
JUL	93	71	65	10.9	2.6	0.0
AUG	93	70	65	10.4	2.6	0.0
SEP	84	62	70	11.0	3.8	0.0
OCT	74	50	66	11.8	3.2	0.0
NOV	60	39	68	12.4	2.0	0.5
DEC	50	29	68	12.4	1.4	1.8

Chicagoland

Location: This region's name first appeared in the *Chicago Tribune* a century ago. It describes the Windy City and a clutch of surrounding counties in Illinois, Indiana, and Wisconsin.

Landscape: Flat, smooth, and irregular plains. . Vegetation is intermingled prairie, groves, and strips of deciduous trees commonly found near streams and on north facing slopes.

Climate: Hot Continental. The first freeze occurs in mid-October, the last in the beginning of May. Lake Michigan exerts a strong influence on the climate. Summer temperatures near the shore are often 10 degrees cooler than inland. Hot spells bring high temperature and high humidity, which may last for several days, then end abruptly with a shift of winds to the north or northwest. They are often accompanied by thunderstorms. Winters can be severely cold and snowy owing to the Lake's precipitation effect and wind chill.

	85
	101
	179
90°	15
32°	137
0°	12
	140
	65
	36

	High °F	Low °F	Hum %	Wind mph	Precip inches	Snow inches
JAN	29	13	73	12.3	1.6	12.0
FEB	33	17	73	12.0	1.4	8.8
MAR	44	27	71	12.5	2.6	7.7
APR	55	37	69	12.4	3.6	1.4
MAY	67	47	68	11.1	3.2	0.1
JUN	77	56	69	9.9	3.6	0.0
JUL	82	63	71	9.1	3.8	0.0
AUG	80	61	74	8.9	3.7	0.0
SEP	73	54	74	9.7	3.8	0.0
OCT	62	43	71	10.8	2.5	0.2
NOV	47	32	74	11.9	2.8	2.5
DEC	34	19	77	11.8	2.4	9.3

Climate

Colonial Coast

Location: This region's name is an invention of Georgia's travel and tourism agencies and defines the state's Atlantic coast from Brunswick to Savannah. Charleston, SC, is included here.

Landscape: Flat and smooth plains. Common trees include evergreen oaks and members of the laurel and magnolia families. Sandy uplands have forests of loblolly and slash pine. Bald Cypress is a dominant tree in swamps. Sometimes the trees are festooned with Spanish moss.

Climate: Subtropical. Summer temperatures are moderated by the Atlantic and by thundershowers that occur almost every afternoon. Sunshine is adequate in all seasons; seldom are there more than two or three days in succession without it. The long growing season - from the end of February to the beginning of December - is accompanied by abundant rain that peaks in late summer.

	106
	109
	151
90°	67
32°	38
0°	0
	173
	70
	60

	High °F	Low °F	Hum %	Wind mph	Precip inches	Snow inches
JAN	59	39	69	8.3	3.6	0.1
FEB	62	42	66	8.9	3.4	0.2
MAR	70	49	66	9.1	4.0	0.0
APR	77	56	66	8.6	2.7	0.0
MAY	83	63	68	7.6	3.9	0.0
JUN	88	70	71	7.4	5.4	0.0
JUL	90	73	73	7.0	6.2	0.0
AUG	89	73	76	6.5	7.0	0.0
SEP	85	69	76	6.9	4.9	0.0
OCT	78	59	71	7.2	2.5	0.0
NOV	70	50	69	7.3	2.3	0.0
DEC	62	43	69	7.7	3.0	0.1

Colorado Northern Front Range

Location: This region is an area just east of Rocky Mountain foothills on the western edge of the Great Plains. It starts at the Wyoming border and runs south along I-25 to Denver, taking in a number of fast-growing cities.

Landscape: Irregular plains, tablelands, and high mountains. Ponderosa pine dominates on lower, drier, more exposed slopes. After fires the original forest trees are usually succeeded by aspen or lodgepole pine. East, the land is a shortgrass prairie.

Climate: Temperate Steppe. Mild, sunny, semiarid, and lacking the cold winter mornings of higher elevations or the hot summer afternoons of lower altitudes. There is little humidity or precipitation and lots of sunshine. During winter, cold air invasion from the north can be abrupt and severe, yet many of the polar masses that spread southward out of Canada over the plains are too shallow to reach Denver's altitude. The last freeze is May 11; the first freeze arrives around September 30. Spring is wet, cloudy, and windy. Summers are cool. Fall is most pleasant.

	121
	125
	119
90°	33
32°	158
0°	10
	54
	34
	45

	High °F	Low °F	Hum %	Wind mph	Precip inches	Snow inches
JAN	42	16	55	9.1	0.5	7.7
FEB	47	20	53	9.4	0.5	7.2
MAR	53	26	52	10.4	1.3	12.8
APR	62	34	50	10.8	1.8	8.0
MAY	71	44	54	10.3	2.7	1.4
JUN	81	52	52	9.6	2.0	0.0
JUL	88	58	53	8.8	1.8	0.0
AUG	85	56	55	8.5	1.3	0.0
SEP	76	47	52	8.6	1.4	1.0
OCT	66	36	49	8.7	1.0	3.6
NOV	52	26	56	8.8	0.8	8.1
DEC	43	17	56	8.9	0.6	7.3

Colorado Southern Front Range

Location: This region is the southern part of Colorado's Front Range, an area along I-25 immediately east of Rocky Mountain foothills on the western edge of the Great Plains. Colorado Springs and Pueblo, 40 miles apart, are here.

Landscape: Tablelands and high mountains. Ponderosa pine dominates on lower, drier, more exposed slopes. After fires the original forest trees are usually succeeded by aspen or lodgepole pine. East, the land is a shortgrass prairie.

Climate: Temperate Steppe. The area's climate is moderated by outlying elevations that give it the pleasant plains-and-mountain mixture. Precipitation is generally light, with 80 percent falling as rain from April to October. The last freeze is around May 3; the first is October 12. Temperatures are on the mild side for this latitude and at this elevation.

	133
	120
	113
90°	40
32°	157
0°	9
	55
	29
	50

	High °F	Low °F	Hum %	Wind mph	Precip inches	Snow inches
JAN	43	15	56	8.8	0.3	5.5
FEB	48	19	51	9.3	0.4	4.7
MAR	54	25	50	10.4	0.9	8.1
APR	64	34	48	11.0	1.0	4.8
MAY	73	44	51	10.4	1.7	1.1
JUN	83	53	50	9.9	1.8	0.0
JUL	89	59	54	9.1	2.5	0.0
AUG	86	57	56	8.5	2.5	0.0
SEP	77	49	52	8.7	1.1	0.8
OCT	67	36	49	8.6	0.7	2.3
NOV	54	25	57	8.5	0.5	5.1
DEC	44	16	57	8.6	0.4	5.5

Coulee Region

Location: This is a colloquial name for an area in western Wisconsin, northeastern Iowa, and southeastern Minnesota bypassed by the last continental glaciers. Consequently, the topography is more rugged that the flat prairie nearby.

Landscape: Irregular plains and open hills. Vegetation is intermingled prairie, groves, and strips of deciduous trees commonly found near streams and on north facing slopes.

Climate: Hot Continental, with four well-defined seasons. Winters are cold and snowy, but summers are extremely pleasant with temperatures reaching as high as 90°F on only seven days in a typical season. On the average, heavy fog occurs 35 times a year, and thunderstorms occur about once every three days during the growing season. These storms are often heavy downpours with high winds bringing occasional flash flooding. Hail falls about four times each year. Tornadoes are rare. The first freeze comes at the beginning of October; the last occurs at the beginning of May.

	91
	98
	176
90°	10
32°	158
0°	26
	115
	61
	41

	High °F	Low °F	Hum %	Wind mph	Precip inches	Snow inches
JAN	23	5	74	11.6	1.0	9.7
FEB	28	10	74	11.3	1.0	7.9
MAR	41	23	73	12.0	2.2	9.5
APR	57	36	68	12.5	3.1	2.7
MAY	69	47	68	11.3	3.6	0.0
JUN	79	56	70	10.3	3.9	0.0
JUL	83	61	73	9.1	4.0	0.0
AUG	80	59	75	8.9	4.2	0.0
SEP	71	50	76	9.8	4.0	0.0
OCT	60	39	71	10.8	2.4	0.3
NOV	43	27	76	11.5	2.0	4.6
DEC	27	12	78	11.3	1.4	10.1

Delaware Valley

Location: This region is Philadelphia's suburban counties in New Jersey. The area includes Trenton, New Jersey's capital, and two other metros - Camden and Vineland - along the Delaware River and Bay.

Landscape: Tablelands with moderate relief. The valleys support a mixed oak-pine forest. Chestnut was once abundant, but blight eliminated it as a canopy tree.

Climate: Hot Continental. Sustained periods of extreme highs or lows seldom last for more than three or four days. During the summer, high humidity adds to the discomfort of warm temperatures. Precipitation is evenly distributed throughout the year. Snowfall often is considerably higher in the northern part of the region, where rain sometimes falls instead. Winters often bring high winds and cold air.

	94
	110
	161
90°	21
32°	101
0°	1
	166
	72
	27

	High °F	Low °F	Hum %	Wind mph	Precip inches	Snow inches
JAN	38	22	67	10.3	3.2	6.5
FEB	41	24	64	10.9	3.0	6.4
MAR	51	32	63	11.4	3.6	3.8
APR	62	41	62	11.0	3.7	0.3
MAY	73	52	66	9.5	3.9	0.0
JUN	81	61	67	8.8	3.6	0.0
JUL	86	66	68	8.2	4.3	0.0
AUG	84	65	70	7.8	3.9	0.0
SEP	77	57	71	8.2	3.5	0.0
OCT	66	45	70	8.8	2.9	0.0
NOV	55	37	68	9.7	3.4	0.7
DEC	44	28	68	10.0	3.5	3.4

East Central Iowa

Location: On the eastern side of the Corn State are a group of metro areas connected by I-80 and its spur, I-380: Davenport, Cedar Rapids, Iowa City, and Waterloo.

Landscape: Irregular plains. Vegetation is intermingled prairie, groves, and strips of deciduous trees commonly found near streams and on north facing slopes.

Climate: Prairie, with extremes in temperature, precipitation, and potential for violent storms. Summer highs can reach 100°F accompanied by high humidity. Winter low temperatures range from 15°F to 25°F, but can get much colder. The typical frost-free season is 150 days, from April 22 to October 11. Precipitation can be highly variable, with large amounts falling all at once and then none at all for long periods. The area is typical of the entire state: Susceptible to droughts, floods, blizzards, and tornadoes.

	93
	100
	172
90°	20
32°	145
0°	20
	134
	60
	42

	High °F	Low °F	Hum %	Wind mph	Precip inches	Snow inches
JAN	27	9	73	11.3	1.0	7.2
FEB	32	14	73	11.2	1.0	6.2
MAR	45	27	73	12.3	2.3	5.8
APR	61	39	69	12.5	3.4	1.5
MAY	72	50	68	10.9	3.9	0.0
JUN	82	60	69	9.8	4.5	0.0
JUL	85	64	73	8.4	4.4	0.0
AUG	83	61	75	8.1	4.1	0.0
SEP	75	53	74	8.9	3.7	0.0
OCT	64	42	70	9.9	2.6	0.2
NOV	47	29	74	11.1	2.0	2.6
DEC	32	16	76	11.0	1.6	6.9

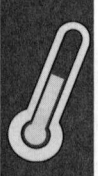

East Central Minnesota

Location: State climatologists define this as a 12-county area centered around the Twin Cities - Minneapolis and St. Paul. Included here is a pair of smaller metros some 60 miles east and west of the Twin Cities via Interstate Highway 94: St. Cloud and Eau Claire.

Landscape: Irregular plains and open hills. Stands of white oak, red oak, black oak, bitternut hickory, and shagbark hickory trees form a mosaic pattern with prairie. Spring reveals a flowering dogwood understory.

Climate: Hot Continental. Since the region isn't far from North America's geographic center, there are wide variations in temperature, ample summer rainfall, and scanty winter precipitation. In general, there also exists a tendency toward extremes in almost all climate features. Severe storms of all types -- blizzards, freezing rain, tornadoes, wind, and hail -- occur. The first freeze is an early October 1; the last is in mid-May.

			96
			101
			168
90°			12
32°			165
0°			38
			96
			57
			37

	High °F	Low °F	Hum %	Wind mph	Precip inches	Snow inches
JAN	21	0	72	9.9	0.9	10.6
FEB	27	6	72	9.7	0.7	9.3
MAR	39	20	70	10.7	1.7	10.4
APR	57	34	65	11.6	2.6	2.7
MAY	70	45	65	10.6	3.5	0.1
JUN	78	55	68	9.9	4.3	0.0
JUL	83	60	69	8.8	3.6	0.0
AUG	80	57	72	8.6	4.1	0.0
SEP	70	48	73	9.3	3.4	0.0
OCT	58	37	70	9.8	2.3	0.5
NOV	41	23	74	10.2	1.5	7.8
DEC	25	8	75	9.7	1.0	9.0

East Central Wisconsin

Location: Wisconsin climatologists locate this region at Green Bay at the mouth of the Fox River and stretch it south to take in Appleton, Oshkosh, and Sheboygan. This is Ground Zero in Packer Country.

Landscape: Irregular plains. Stands of white oak, red oak, black oak, bitternut hickory, and shagbark hickory trees form a mosaic pattern with prairie. Spring reveals a flowering dogwood understory.

Climate: Hot Continental, modified by Lake Superior to the northwest and Lake Michigan and Green Bay to the east. The first freeze is early October, the last is mid-May. Summers are pleasant with cool evenings and nights. Thunderstorms and heavy rains can be expected in late summer and fall. Winters arrive early and tend to be long and cold. The area experiences a moderate amount of snow for this latitude.

			86
			102
			177
90°			7
32°			158
0°			26
			124
			63
			33

	High °F	Low °F	Hum %	Wind mph	Precip inches	Snow inches
JAN	25	8	74	10.9	1.2	11.1
FEB	29	12	74	10.5	1.1	9.0
MAR	40	23	73	10.8	2.1	9.2
APR	54	35	69	11.2	2.7	1.7
MAY	67	46	67	10.1	3.0	0.1
JUN	76	55	69	9.2	3.4	0.0
JUL	82	61	72	8.2	3.2	0.0
AUG	79	59	76	7.9	3.7	0.0
SEP	71	51	76	8.9	3.7	0.0
OCT	59	41	74	9.9	2.4	0.2
NOV	44	29	76	10.9	2.2	3.7
DEC	29	14	77	10.5	1.6	10.6

Eastern Idaho

Location: State climatologists call this area the Eastern Highlands. It takes in Pocatello and Idaho Falls, two cities 50 miles apart, that periodically trade places as the state's 3rd largest.

Landscape: Plains with hills and high mountains. Ponderosa pine and Douglas-fir predominate on the mountains slopes.

Climate: Temperate Steppe. The climate is variable and invigorating. Cloudy and unsettled weather is the rule through the winter with precipitation one of every three days, with occasional heavy snow. Late May sees the end of frost. Spring is the wettest and windiest season. Summers are somewhat hot and dry, with occasional thunderstorms and generally cool evenings. Fall, as elsewhere, is the finest season. At the end of September, the first frost appears.

			106
			98
			126
90°			61
32°			157
0°			4
			49
			95
			24

	High °F	Low °F	Hum %	Wind mph	Precip inches	Snow inches
JAN	29	12	76	10.6	0.9	9.8
FEB	36	17	73	10.6	0.8	6.3
MAR	45	25	65	11.2	1.0	5.7
APR	57	32	54	11.6	1.1	4.2
MAY	67	39	52	10.5	1.4	0.6
JUN	77	47	48	10.1	1.1	0.0
JUL	87	52	40	9.1	0.6	0.0
AUG	85	50	39	8.9	0.7	0.0
SEP	74	42	45	9.0	0.9	0.1
OCT	61	32	54	9.4	0.9	1.8
NOV	44	25	69	10.4	1.1	5.3
DEC	31	14	76	10.5	1.0	8.9

Eastern Slope of the Cascades

Location: Otherwise called South Central Washington, this region lies east of the Cascade Mountains in a broad valley. Yakima and the Tri-Cities (Kennewick, Pasco and Richland) are here.

Landscape: Tablelands, open hills, and high mountains. Principal trees are western red cedar, western hemlock, and Douglas-fir. In interior valleys there are big-leaf maple, Oregon ash, and black cottonwood.

Climate: Temperate Desert. Relatively mild and dry, with Maritime and Continental climate features, modified by the Cascade and Rocky Mountain ranges. Precipitation is generally light here in the rain shadow of the Cascades. The first freeze is October 13, the last is May 1. Summers are dry and hot, with rapid temperature drops after sunset, making the nights pleasantly cool. Shielded from most of the cold air masses from Canada, winters are cool with only light snowfall of 20 inches to 25 inches per year.

	101
	90
	173
90°	35
32°	126
0°	3
	71
	33
	8

	High °F	Low °F	Hum %	Wind mph	Precip inches	Snow inches
JAN	38	23	79	6.7	1.1	8.2
FEB	46	28	73	7.3	0.8	2.9
MAR	56	33	62	8.5	0.6	1.2
APR	64	39	56	9.1	0.5	0.0
MAY	73	46	54	8.8	0.5	0.0
JUN	81	53	52	8.5	0.5	0.0
JUL	88	57	47	8.1	0.2	0.0
AUG	87	57	49	7.7	0.4	0.0
SEP	78	48	54	7.6	0.4	0.0
OCT	65	38	63	7.1	0.5	0.0
NOV	49	32	77	6.7	1.1	2.0
DEC	38	25	82	6.3	1.3	7.2

Edwards Plateau of Texas

Location: This limestone belt in west-central Texas is more suitable for grazing that for raising row crops. Greater San Angelo is here.

Landscape: Tablelands with moderate relief. Vegetation is oak and juniper mixed with grasses and mesquite.

Climate: Steppe. Between the humid climate of east Texas and the dry High Plains of west Texas, desert characteristics prevail. Summers are long and hot, and welcome temperature drops occur rapidly after sunset. Precipitation is typical of the Great Plains, most often coming from thunderstorms. Tropical disturbances moving in from the Gulf bring late summer rains. The prevailing south to southwest winds are brisk and modify summer heat, though occasional uncomfortable hot spells with humid air permeate the area. Winters are short and mild.

	154
	97
	114
90°	109
32°	52
0°	0
	43
	33
	38

	High °F	Low °F	Hum %	Wind mph	Precip inches	Snow inches
JAN	57	31	65	10.2	0.8	1.5
FEB	62	35	63	10.8	1.1	0.7
MAR	73	44	58	12.3	0.9	0.2
APR	81	53	59	12.0	1.7	0.0
MAY	87	61	65	11.2	3.0	0.0
JUN	93	66	66	11.0	2.3	0.0
JUL	96	69	61	9.8	1.1	0.0
AUG	95	68	62	9.1	1.9	0.0
SEP	87	64	69	9.0	3.4	0.0
OCT	79	54	68	9.3	2.4	0.0
NOV	68	43	66	10.0	1.1	0.5
DEC	59	33	65	10.0	0.8	0.2

Florida Lower East Coast

Location: This region is locally referred to as South Florida, the Tri-County Area, or The Gold Coast. It takes in Miami-Dade, Broward, and Brevard counties at the southern end of I-95 and is the largest urbanized area in the South.

Landscape: Flat plains. Common trees include evergreen oaks and members of the laurel and magnolia families. Sandy uplands have forests of loblolly and slash pine. Bald Cypress is a dominant tree in swamps.

Climate: Savannah, with a long, warm summer, abundant rainfall, and a mild, dry winter. The Atlantic Ocean is responsible for the small range of daily temperatures, and it aids the rapid warming of colder air masses passing east of the state. Freezing temperatures occur occasionally in surrounding farming districts, but almost never near the ocean. Hurricanes affect the area and are most frequent in early fall.

	75
	170
	120
90°	69
32°	0
0°	0
	40
	80
	76

	High °F	Low °F	Hum %	Wind mph	Precip inches	Snow inches
JAN	75	58	72	9.7	2.3	0.0
FEB	77	58	70	10.3	2.5	0.0
MAR	79	63	69	10.7	2.9	0.0
APR	83	66	67	10.6	3.0	0.0
MAY	86	71	70	9.8	6.3	0.0
JUN	88	74	75	8.4	9.0	0.0
JUL	90	75	74	7.9	6.2	0.0
AUG	90	76	75	7.9	6.8	0.0
SEP	88	75	77	8.4	7.9	0.0
OCT	85	71	74	9.6	6.2	0.0
NOV	81	66	73	9.9	3.8	0.0
DEC	77	60	71	9.5	2.1	0.0

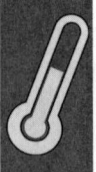

Florida Southwest Coast

Location: Florida state climatologists define this region as the state's southern tip - minus the densely settled Lower East Coast along I-95. Here are the Everglades and rapidly-growing Naples, Fort Myers, and Sarasota-Bradenton.

Landscape: Flat plains. Common trees include evergreen oaks and members of the laurel and magnolia families. Sandy uplands have forests of loblolly and slash pine. Bald Cypress is a dominant tree in swamps. Sometimes the trees are festooned with Spanish moss.

Climate: Savannah. Summer and winter temperature extremes are effectively checked by the influence of the Gulf. Winters are mild have many bright, warm days. Traces of snow have occurred only a few times this century. Nights are moderately cool. Rainfall averages more than 50 inches annually, with two-thirds of it falling daily between June and September in the form of late afternoon or early evening summer thunderstorms.

	100
	160
	106
90°	98
32°	0
0°	0
	111
	71
	88

	High °F	Low °F	Hum %	Wind mph	Precip inches	Snow inches
JAN	74	52	73	8.5	2.0	0.0
FEB	75	53	72	9.1	2.5	0.0
MAR	79	57	71	9.3	2.9	0.0
APR	84	61	68	8.9	1.3	0.0
MAY	88	66	69	8.3	3.6	0.0
JUN	90	71	74	7.4	8.6	0.0
JUL	91	73	74	6.8	8.3	0.0
AUG	91	73	76	6.8	9.1	0.0
SEP	90	73	76	7.6	8.1	0.0
OCT	86	67	73	8.4	2.9	0.0
NOV	81	60	73	8.3	1.8	0.0
DEC	76	54	73	8.1	1.7	0.0

Four Corners

Location: A marker in the middle of a Navajo reservation locates the only spot where four states come together at one point: Utah, Colorado, New Mexico and Arizona. Farmington, New Mexico, is the only metro area here.

Landscape: Plains with low mountains. At low elevations, several kinds of cactus and yucca are common. The woodland zone is dominated by open stands of two-needle pinyon pine and several species of juniper. Sagebrush dominates the outlying plains.

Climate: Steppe. Low humidity and warm daytime temperatures are the rule. Winters are mild, summers are hot. In the evening, temperatures drop and jackets and sweaters show up in downtown streets. This is an extremely arid location, with typical precipitation seldom exceeding 10 inches per year.

	168
	110
	87
90°	66
32°	114
0°	1
	14
	33
	38

	High °F	Low °F	Hum %	Wind mph	Precip inches	Snow inches
JAN	41	17	56	8.0	0.6	4.3
FEB	48	23	49	8.8	0.6	2.1
MAR	57	29	41	10.0	0.9	1.7
APR	67	35	34	10.8	0.6	0.5
MAY	77	44	34	10.5	0.5	0.0
JUN	88	53	32	9.9	0.4	0.0
JUL	92	60	44	9.0	1.1	0.0
AUG	89	59	49	8.2	1.3	0.0
SEP	81	51	46	8.5	1.0	0.0
OCT	69	39	45	8.2	1.1	0.0
NOV	54	29	51	7.9	0.8	1.0
DEC	43	20	57	7.7	0.6	4.6

Green Country Oklahoma

Location: The region's name is a 40-year old invention of Oklahoma tourism boosters and describes the state's extreme northeast section of forests, lakes, and Ozark foothills. Tulsa is here.

Landscape: Irregular plains and open hills. . Vegetation is intermingled prairie, groves, and strips of deciduous trees commonly found near streams and on north facing slopes.

Climate: Prairie. Far enough north to escape the sweltering heat of the Deep South, yet far enough south to miss the extreme cold of winter. Warm moist air from the Gulf of Mexico contributes to the high humidity. Winter months are generally mild. Temperatures of 100°F or higher are experienced from late July to early September but are accompanied by low humidity and a good southerly breeze. Fall is the finest season with long, sunny days and cool, bracing nights.

	127
	103
	136
90°	74
32°	78
0°	1
	92
	54
	50

	High °F	Low °F	Hum %	Wind mph	Precip inches	Snow inches
JAN	45	25	69	10.3	1.5	3.3
FEB	51	30	67	10.8	2.0	2.4
MAR	62	39	65	12.1	3.5	1.4
APR	73	50	65	11.9	3.7	0.0
MAY	80	59	72	10.6	5.6	0.0
JUN	88	68	73	10.0	4.4	0.0
JUL	94	73	68	9.4	3.1	0.0
AUG	93	71	69	8.9	3.1	0.0
SEP	84	63	73	9.1	4.7	0.0
OCT	74	51	68	9.7	3.7	0.0
NOV	60	40	69	10.3	3.1	0.4
DEC	49	29	70	10.2	2.2	1.6

Illinois Prairie

Location: This region embraces a huge area of level land radiating southwest out of Chicago that includes the college metros of Champaign-Urbana and Bloomington-Normal, plus other metros including the state capital at Springfield.

Landscape: Flat, smooth, and irregular plains. . Vegetation is intermingled prairie, groves, and strips of deciduous trees commonly found near streams and on north facing slopes.

Climate: Prairie, marked with changeable weather and a wide range of temperatures. An extreme example was the year 1936: 17 days with temperatures of 100°F or higher in July, and 26 days within a 31-day winter period when the temperature was zero. June and September are usually the most pleasant months of the year. During October and early November, residents enjoy Indian summer, with its extended period of warm, dry weather. The average first freeze is late October; the average last freeze is late April.

	95
	99
	173
90°	28
32°	124
0°	9
	112
	65
	48

	High °F	Low °F	Hum %	Wind mph	Precip inches	Snow inches
JAN	32	15	74	11.4	1.6	7.2
FEB	36	19	74	11.4	1.7	5.9
MAR	49	30	72	12.3	3.1	4.5
APR	63	41	68	12.1	3.8	0.8
MAY	74	51	67	10.3	3.9	0.0
JUN	83	61	68	9.1	3.9	0.0
JUL	86	65	72	8.0	4.1	0.0
AUG	84	63	75	7.7	3.6	0.0
SEP	78	55	73	8.6	3.6	0.0
OCT	66	44	69	9.7	2.7	0.1
NOV	51	33	74	11.3	2.9	2.2
DEC	36	21	78	11.1	2.7	5.8

Island of Oahu

Location: This is the third largest of the Hawaiian Islands and most populous island in the State of Hawaii. Oahu is also coextensive with greater Honolulu, America's westernmost and southernmost metro area.

Landscape: Smooth plains, tablelands, and low mountains. Many species were endemic before human settlement. Native plants form a variety of community types, including shrub land, forest, and areas of bog and moss-lichen.

Climate: Tropical and Rainforest, showing the least seasonal temperature change of any American metro area. The difference between January minimum and August maximum is only about 22°. There is no snow, fog, or freezing weather, an average of twenty-three 90° days and fourteen thunderstorms a year. Although it is sometimes uncomfortably warm, persistent trade winds provide relief.

	90
	180
	95
90°	23
32°	0
0°	0
	0
	47
	14

	High °F	Low °F	Hum %	Wind mph	Precip inches	Snow inches
JAN	80	66	71	9.5	3.5	0.0
FEB	81	65	69	10.1	2.2	0.0
MAR	82	67	65	11.4	2.2	0.0
APR	83	69	62	11.8	1.5	0.0
MAY	85	70	60	11.8	1.1	0.0
JUN	87	72	59	12.7	0.5	0.0
JUL	88	74	59	13.2	0.6	0.0
AUG	89	74	60	12.8	0.4	0.0
SEP	89	74	60	11.2	0.8	0.0
OCT	87	72	63	10.5	2.3	0.0
NOV	84	70	67	10.7	3.0	0.0
DEC	81	67	70	10.4	3.8	0.0

Kentucky Blue Grass

Location: Kentucky climatologists named the area that embraces the state's two largest metro areas - Lexington and Louisville - after the lawn and pasture grass that dominates the eastern United States.

Landscape: Irregular plains and open hills. Vegetation is mixed prairie, groves, and strips of deciduous trees commonly found near streams and on north facing slopes.

Climate: Hot Continental. Precipitation is evenly distributed throughout the winter, spring, and summer, with an average of 12 inches falling in each of these seasons. Snowfall is variable, but the ground does not retain snow for more than a few days at a time. The months of September and October are the most pleasant of the year as they have the least precipitation, the most clear days, and generally comfortable temperatures.

	92
	102
	173
90°	29
32°	94
0°	2
	147
	76
	45

	High °F	Low °F	Hum %	Wind mph	Precip inches	Snow inches
JAN	40	23	72	10.3	2.9	5.3
FEB	44	26	71	10.2	3.3	4.7
MAR	56	36	68	10.7	4.5	3.0
APR	66	45	65	10.2	4.1	0.2
MAY	75	54	69	8.3	4.5	0.0
JUN	83	62	70	7.7	3.6	0.0
JUL	86	67	72	7.1	4.8	0.0
AUG	85	65	74	6.7	3.7	0.0
SEP	79	58	74	7.2	3.2	0.0
OCT	68	46	70	7.7	2.6	0.1
NOV	56	37	71	9.4	3.5	0.8
DEC	45	28	74	9.9	3.8	2.1

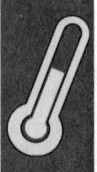

Long Island Sound

Location: Includes all the metro areas along I-95 from Rhode Island southbound to New York City's Connecticut suburbs. Long Island Sound is an estuary, a place where salt water from the ocean mixes with fresh water from rivers.

Landscape: Urban, on irregular plains with open hills. Uncleared land has stands of tall oak and maple trees that provide a dense, continuous canopy in summer and shed their leaves completely in winter.

Climate: Hot Continental, with four well-defined seasons and considerable diversity of weather over short time periods. Nearness to the Sound moderates the temperatures, often by cloud cover. Precipitation usually falls as snow in winter and as thunderstorms in summer. Hurricanes occasionally strike along the shore during August or September.

Icon readings: 101 · 110 · 155 · 90° 8 · 32° 104 · 0° 1 · 131 · 74 · 23

	High °F	Low °F	Hum %	Wind mph	Precip inches	Snow inches
JAN	37	21	67	12.0	3.6	7.9
FEB	38	23	65	12.5	3.4	8.2
MAR	47	30	64	12.6	4.0	5.5
APR	57	39	64	12.2	4.1	0.6
MAY	68	49	67	10.8	4.0	0.0
JUN	77	58	69	10.0	3.4	0.0
JUL	82	64	70	9.4	3.6	0.0
AUG	81	64	71	9.4	3.5	0.0
SEP	74	56	72	10.1	3.4	0.0
OCT	64	45	69	10.7	3.5	0.0
NOV	53	37	69	11.6	4.2	0.7
DEC	41	26	67	11.9	4.0	5.2

Lower Chatahoochee Watershed

Location: Named after the river that forms the southern boundary between Georgia and Alabama. Along its low-lying and winding valley are several small to mid-size metro areas.

Landscape: Irregular plains and open hills. Common trees include evergreen oaks and members of the laurel and magnolia families. Sandy uplands have forests of loblolly and slash pine. Bald Cypress is a dominant tree in swamps.

Climate: Subtropical. Summers are long, hot, and humid and are relieved somewhat by afternoon thunderstorms. While there are occasional freezes, winter is relatively mild, but overcast and wet.

Icon readings: 108 · 111 · 147 · 90° 81 · 32° 44 · 0° 0 · 181 · 72 · 63

	High °F	Low °F	Hum %	Wind mph	Precip inches	Snow inches
JAN	55	35	72	7.3	4.8	0.1
FEB	60	37	69	7.8	5.2	0.2
MAR	68	45	69	8.0	6.3	0.1
APR	76	52	68	7.2	4.4	0.0
MAY	82	60	69	6.4	4.0	0.0
JUN	89	67	71	5.9	4.1	0.0
JUL	90	70	75	5.6	5.5	0.0
AUG	90	70	76	5.3	3.9	0.0
SEP	86	65	74	6.2	3.6	0.0
OCT	77	54	71	6.2	2.5	0.0
NOV	68	45	71	6.5	3.9	0.0
DEC	59	38	72	6.8	5.1	0.0

Lower Colorado Valley

Location: El Centro, CA, and Yuma, AZ, 55 miles apart, lie in a broad valley in the Sonoran Desert in the southwestern United States. Just below here the Colorado River, which began 1,500 away in the Rocky Mountains, crosses into Mexico.

Landscape: Plains with low mountains. Desert vegetation is usually very sparse. Cacti and thorny shrubs are conspicuous. Mesquite is less widespread and grows only along washes and watercourses.

Climate: Desert. Summers are long and hot. Home heating is necessary from late October to mid-April, when evenings and nights cool dramatically. In winter the rains are widespread and usually gentle, but in summer they are usually thunderstorms. There are virtually no summer rains. The area is so dry, many places in the world get more rain in a year than has fallen here in the past century. Yuma is officially the sunniest place in America.

Icon readings: 242 · 71 · 52 · 90° 92 · 32° 60 · 0° 0 · 97 · 8 · 1

	High °F	Low °F	Hum %	Wind mph	Precip inches	Snow inches
JAN	69	42	43	7.3	0.4	0.0
FEB	75	45	38	7.4	0.2	0.0
MAR	79	49	34	7.9	0.2	0.0
APR	86	54	30	8.3	0.1	0.0
MAY	94	61	27	8.3	0.0	0.0
JUN	103	69	25	8.5	0.0	0.0
JUL	107	78	35	9.5	0.2	0.0
AUG	106	78	39	8.9	0.5	0.0
SEP	101	71	39	7.3	0.3	0.0
OCT	91	60	37	6.6	0.3	0.0
NOV	78	49	38	6.9	0.3	0.0
DEC	69	42	42	7.2	0.4	0.0

Lower Hudson Valley

Location: The land of the two-hour commute, some locals call this region on the Hudson River some 50 miles above New York City. The main-traveled route from Kingston, Poughkeepsie, and Newburgh is Interstate Highway 87.

Landscape: Open low mountains. The valleys support a mixed oak-pine forest. Higher up is an Appalachian oak forest, dominated by white oak and black oak. Chestnut was once abundant, but blight eliminated it as a canopy tree.

Climate: Hot Continental. Summers are warm and frequently humid, with evenings cooled by breezes from all directions. Summer thunderstorms and showers are common in the Hudson Valley. The first freeze comes in early October. Winters are cold, overcast, wet and snowy.

	88
	119
	159
90°	13
32°	118
0°	9
	129
	71
	24

	High °F	Low °F	Hum %	Wind mph	Precip inches	Snow inches
JAN	35	15	68	10.3	3.0	10.9
FEB	37	17	66	10.5	2.9	10.8
MAR	48	27	64	10.8	3.5	8.3
APR	59	37	61	10.4	4.1	1.5
MAY	71	47	64	8.9	4.6	0.1
JUN	79	56	67	8.2	3.9	0.0
JUL	84	61	68	7.5	4.2	0.0
AUG	82	59	71	7.3	4.1	0.0
SEP	75	51	72	7.8	3.9	0.0
OCT	64	39	70	8.5	3.5	0.0
NOV	52	32	70	9.5	4.1	1.7
DEC	39	21	70	9.8	3.4	9.3

Lower Mississippi Watershed

Location: Anchored by greater Memphis on the Mississippi River; includes Jackson, TN, inland on the east and Jonesboro, AR, inland on the west.

Landscape: Flat and irregular plains. Stands of white oak, red oak, black oak, bitternut hickory, and shagbark hickory trees form a mosaic pattern with prairie. The understory is flowering dogwood.

Climate: Hot Continental. Though not in the normal paths of storms coming from the Gulf of Mexico or from Canada, the area is affected by both and has frequent changes in weather. Freezing days are common during winter. Hot, steamy weather can be expected during summer. But extremes in highs and lows are rare. The typical growing season is 230 days with annual rainfall of more than 40 inches.

	118
	96
	151
90°	74
32°	66
0°	0
	182
	76
	59

	High °F	Low °F	Hum %	Wind mph	Precip inches	Snow inches
JAN	47	29	72	10.0	3.7	2.6
FEB	52	33	70	10.1	4.2	2.1
MAR	62	42	67	10.8	5.1	1.1
APR	73	51	66	10.3	5.3	0.0
MAY	81	59	68	8.8	5.2	0.0
JUN	89	67	69	7.9	3.6	0.0
JUL	92	71	70	7.5	3.6	0.0
AUG	90	69	72	6.9	3.2	0.0
SEP	84	63	71	7.4	3.7	0.0
OCT	74	50	67	7.7	3.2	0.0
NOV	61	42	68	9.1	4.8	0.3
DEC	51	33	71	9.7	5.2	0.5

Lower Ohio Valley

Location: Takes in a pair of metro areas - Evansville, Indiana, and Owensboro, Kentucky - 40 miles apart on opposite banks of the Ohio River, just above where it flows into the Mississippi.

Landscape: Irregular plains and open hills. Vegetation is mixed prairie, groves, and strips of deciduous trees commonly found near streams and on north facing slopes.

Climate: Hot Continental. Prevailing wind here is from the south, and, although the area is 550 miles from the Gulf of Mexico, the weather resembles that of its neighbors to the south. Strong cold winds sometimes blow from the north following cold fronts. As soon as the high-pressure ridge moves by, the wind backs around again from the south. Snowfall varies a great deal from year to year but accumulation is rare. Average growing season: 199 days.

	102
	100
	163
90°	36
32°	105
0°	3
	163
	74
	43

	High °F	Low °F	Hum %	Wind mph	Precip inches	Snow inches
JAN	40	22	71	9.2	2.9	4.8
FEB	45	26	71	9.4	3.4	3.5
MAR	57	36	69	10.1	4.8	2.8
APR	68	45	66	9.7	4.4	0.2
MAY	78	54	69	8.0	4.6	0.0
JUN	86	63	69	7.2	3.6	0.0
JUL	89	67	72	6.2	3.9	0.0
AUG	88	65	73	5.8	3.3	0.0
SEP	82	58	74	6.4	3.2	0.0
OCT	71	45	70	6.9	2.9	0.1
NOV	57	37	71	8.7	4.0	0.7
DEC	45	27	73	8.9	3.8	1.9

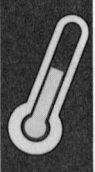

Lower Rio Grande Valley

Location: After Florida's Lower East Coast, this is the southernmost climate region on the United States Mainland. It takes in Brownsville, McAllen, and Laredo along the Rio Grande opposite the State of Tamaulipas, Mexico.

Landscape: Flat, smooth, and irregular plains. Arid grasslands are mixed with oak, juniper and mesquite.

Climate: Subtropical, influenced by the Gulf of Mexico. Winters are mild. Summers are hot, humid, and frequently stormy. There are more than 100 days over 90°F. High humidity is constant throughout the year; during the months of May through August it feels oppressive. While the Sierra Madre Oriental Mountains in Mexico block dry air from the Chihuahuan Desert, both affect the climate of this river plain.

	128
	121
	116
90°	129
32°	6
0°	0
	78
	34
	29

	High °F	Low °F	Hum %	Wind mph	Precip inches	Snow inches
JAN	68	47	69	10.2	1.2	0.0
FEB	72	50	65	11.0	1.1	0.0
MAR	80	58	61	12.5	0.5	0.0
APR	86	65	59	12.8	1.4	0.0
MAY	90	71	61	12.1	2.9	0.0
JUN	94	74	61	11.0	2.8	0.0
JUL	96	75	64	10.3	1.6	0.0
AUG	96	75	65	9.4	2.6	0.0
SEP	92	72	67	8.8	4.5	0.0
OCT	86	65	65	8.8	2.5	0.0
NOV	78	57	65	9.7	1.2	0.0
DEC	70	50	68	9.8	1.1	0.0

Maine Southern Interior

Location: Anchored by Bangor on the north and Lewiston-Auburn on the south. The two metro areas are connected by an 85-mile stretch of I-95 in Maine's southern interior.

Landscape: Plains with high hills. The forests are mixed stands of pine and deciduous species - yellow birch, sugar maple, and American beech.

Climate: Warm Continental. Alternating air masses create strong seasonal contrasts in temperature. Winters are moderately long and somewhat severe. Snow tends to cover the ground all winter. Though daily highs top 50°F one-third of the year, typical springs and falls are short and aren't warm. Spring is often referred to as mud season. Summer is mild. The frost-free growing season here is just 140 days, from around May 27 to September 18.

	101
	99
	165
90°	7
32°	159
0°	16
	170
	81
	16

	High °F	Low °F	Hum %	Wind mph	Precip inches	Snow inches
JAN	28	10	68	9.2	3.2	20.8
FEB	31	12	67	9.4	3.1	20.6
MAR	40	23	66	10.0	3.6	13.8
APR	52	34	64	10.0	3.7	4.0
MAY	65	44	67	9.2	3.6	0.6
JUN	74	54	69	8.3	3.5	0.0
JUL	79	60	70	7.6	3.4	0.0
AUG	77	58	71	7.5	3.3	0.0
SEP	69	50	73	7.9	3.2	0.0
OCT	58	40	72	8.4	3.6	0.7
NOV	45	30	72	8.8	4.8	4.2
DEC	32	16	70	9.0	4.2	18.4

Maryland's Eastern Shore

Location: This area lies on the east side of Chesapeake Bay accessible from the rest of Maryland by the two William Preston Lane Memorial Bridges over the Bay. The only metro area here is Salisbury, MD.

Landscape: Flat plains. Common trees include evergreen oaks and members of the laurel and magnolia families. Sandy uplands have forests of loblolly and slash pine.

Climate: Subtropical, with a definite marine influence. Summers are hot and humid though frequently lifted by a Bay breeze. Some winters can be freezing and snowy, but are normally overcast, chilly and rainy. The first frost arrives October 29 and the last frost is out by April 9. Snow falls every year, but is minimal and the cover is quickly gone.

	105
	109
	151
90°	31
32°	97
0°	0
	146
	70
	27

	High °F	Low °F	Hum %	Wind mph	Precip inches	Snow inches
JAN	45	26	65	9.7	3.6	4.5
FEB	48	28	63	10.3	3.5	5.3
MAR	57	35	62	10.8	4.2	2.6
APR	67	43	61	10.5	3.2	0.2
MAY	76	53	65	9.1	3.6	0.0
JUN	83	62	66	8.5	3.6	0.0
JUL	87	67	67	8.0	4.3	0.0
AUG	86	66	70	7.8	5.3	0.0
SEP	80	58	70	8.0	3.7	0.0
OCT	70	47	69	8.6	3.4	0.0
NOV	60	38	67	9.2	3.2	0.8
DEC	50	30	66	9.3	3.7	2.0

Massachusetts Bay

Location: The entire Atlantic shoreline between Cape Ann and Cape Cod in Massachusetts. It includes greater Boston and three suburban metro areas.

Landscape: Irregular plains with hills. The valleys support a mixed oak-pine forest. Chestnut was once abundant, but blight eliminated it as a canopy tree.

Climate: Hot Continental. The Atlantic greatly influences the climate, roughly described as damp, changeable, and relatively mild considering its northern location. Sea breezes moderate summer and winter temperatures. The first freeze is around mid-October; the last is in early May. Rain is plentiful and distributed evenly. Greater Boston receives lots of snow, though in the city and south it often becomes sleet with little accumulation.

	98
	104
	163
90°	10
32°	104
0°	1
	24
	75
	21

	High °F	Low °F	Hum %	Wind mph	Precip inches	Snow inches
JAN	36	22	65	13.8	3.6	11.4
FEB	37	23	65	13.8	3.7	11.5
MAR	45	31	66	13.7	3.7	8.2
APR	55	40	65	13.2	3.6	0.8
MAY	65	49	69	12.2	3.4	0.1
JUN	75	58	69	11.5	3.1	0.0
JUL	80	64	68	11.0	2.9	0.0
AUG	79	63	71	10.8	3.2	0.0
SEP	72	57	73	11.3	3.2	0.0
OCT	62	47	71	12.0	3.5	0.0
NOV	52	38	70	12.9	4.2	1.1
DEC	40	27	68	13.6	4.1	7.5

Michiana

Location: This area in northern Indiana and southwest Michigan has more than 1 million people and is centered on South Bend. The name contracts "Michigan" with "Indiana", and was coined by the *South Bend Tribune* a hundred years ago.

Landscape: Flat, smooth, and irregular plains. Vegetation is mixed prairie, groves, and strips of deciduous trees commonly found near streams and on north facing slopes.

Climate: Hot Continental. Lake Michigan's moderating effect on temperature is apparent. Readings of 100° are rare, and cold waves aren't severe latitude. The typical first freeze is October 5 and the last one is May 6. Precipitation is even throughout the year with higher amounts during the growing season. Winter is marked by cloudiness and high humidity along with frequent periods of snow from November to March. Heavy snowfalls, from a cold northwest wind passing over Lake Michigan aren't uncommon.

	76
	101
	189
90°	16
32°	131
0°	9
	168
	73
	39

	High °F	Low °F	Hum %	Wind mph	Precip inches	Snow inches
JAN	31	15	77	11.7	2.0	14.0
FEB	34	18	75	11.2	1.8	11.2
MAR	46	28	72	11.9	2.8	7.2
APR	59	38	68	11.6	3.5	1.7
MAY	70	49	67	10.1	3.4	0.0
JUN	80	58	68	9.1	3.7	0.0
JUL	83	63	70	8.1	3.5	0.0
AUG	81	60	74	7.5	3.5	0.0
SEP	75	53	74	8.4	3.3	0.0
OCT	63	42	72	9.4	2.8	0.4
NOV	49	33	76	11.0	3.0	5.4
DEC	35	21	79	11.2	3.0	12.5

Mid-Missouri Watershed

Location: This area encompasses a large section of prairie around where South Dakota, Iowa, and Nebraska meet. The common element is the Missouri River.

Landscape: Smooth and irregular plains, open low hills. Vegetation is intermingled prairie, groves, and strips of deciduous trees commonly found near streams and on north facing slopes.

Climate: Prairie. Winters are cold and summers are warm with most rain failing between April and September. Except for an occasional dry year, rain is plentiful. As elsewhere in the Northern Plains, there is considerable fluctuation in temperature and precipitation from season to season and year to year. The typical growing season extends 160 days. The first frost is in early October, the last is out in late April.

	110
	103
	153
90°	33
32°	151
0°	21
	84
	47
	48

	High °F	Low °F	Hum %	Wind mph	Precip inches	Snow inches
JAN	29	8	72	10.8	0.6	6.5
FEB	34	14	73	10.8	0.7	6.5
MAR	47	26	71	12.3	1.9	7.3
APR	62	38	66	12.8	2.6	1.5
MAY	73	49	68	11.3	3.8	0.1
JUN	83	59	69	10.4	3.7	0.0
JUL	88	65	71	9.4	3.2	0.0
AUG	85	62	73	9.3	3.1	0.0
SEP	75	52	72	9.8	3.3	0.0
OCT	64	39	68	10.2	2.0	0.5
NOV	47	26	73	11.0	1.2	3.7
DEC	32	13	75	10.6	0.8	6.0

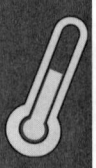

Climate

Middle Tennessee

Location: By local usage, this region contains Tennessee counties in the central time zone and east of the Tennessee River's western crossing. Clarkesville and Nashville are here.

Landscape: Tablelands and open hills. Stands of white oak, red oak, black oak, bitternut hickory, and shagbark hickory trees form a mosaic pattern with prairie. The understory is flowering dogwood.

Climate: Hot Continental, but with rare extremes of heat or cold. Humidity is moderate when compared with other locations east of the Mississippi and south of the Ohio River. The area is not in highly traveled paths of general storm systems. However, it is in a zone that gets thunderstorms often and snow falls each winter. The growing season is some 211 days with rainfall averaging 47 inches each year.

	103
	106
	156
90°	54
32°	85
0°	2
	150
	80
	54

	High °F	Low °F	Hum %	Wind mph	Precip inches	Snow inches
JAN	45	25	72	9.1	3.6	3.8
FEB	50	29	70	9.3	4.0	3.3
MAR	61	38	66	9.9	5.3	1.6
APR	71	46	66	9.3	4.4	0.0
MAY	79	55	71	7.7	4.6	0.0
JUN	86	63	71	7.1	3.7	0.0
JUL	90	68	73	6.6	4.1	0.0
AUG	89	66	74	6.2	3.6	0.0
SEP	83	59	74	6.5	3.5	0.0
OCT	72	46	70	6.8	2.9	0.0
NOV	60	38	71	8.4	4.3	0.4
DEC	50	29	72	8.9	4.9	1.4

Middle Wabash Valley

Location: The Wabash glides past Lafayette (IN), Danville (IL), and Terre Haute (IN) on its way to the Ohio. It is the longest free-flowing river east of the Mississippi.

Landscape: Smooth and irregular plains. Vegetation is mixed prairie, groves, and strips of deciduous trees commonly found near streams and on north facing slopes.

Climate: Hot Continental, with by changeable weather and a wide range of temperatures. June and September are usually the most pleasant months of the year. After the last freeze in late October, residents enjoy Indian summer for several weeks with its extended period of warm, dry weather. The last freeze is late April.

	93
	99
	174
90°	19
32°	132
0°	10
	163
	67
	43

	High °F	Low °F	Hum %	Wind mph	Precip inches	Snow inches
JAN	33	15	75	10.3	1.9	5.9
FEB	38	19	73	10.3	1.9	4.9
MAR	50	30	71	11.2	3.2	3.6
APR	63	41	68	10.7	3.9	0.4
MAY	74	50	69	9.0	4.2	0.0
JUN	83	60	69	8.1	3.8	0.0
JUL	86	64	73	7.1	4.4	0.0
AUG	84	61	75	6.7	3.8	0.0
SEP	78	54	74	7.5	3.2	0.0
OCT	66	42	71	8.2	2.8	0.0
NOV	52	33	74	9.8	3.2	1.9
DEC	38	22	77	10.0	2.9	4.5

Missouri River Prairie

Location: Where the Missouri and Kansas Rivers meet, this region is centered on metro "KC" (Kansas City) and several smaller metro areas within commuting distance of it.

Landscape: Irregular plains and open low hills. Vegetation is mixed prairie, groves, and strips of deciduous trees commonly found near streams and on north facing slopes.

Climate: Prairie. Early spring brings rapid weather changes. Summer days are warm, sometimes hot, but nights are mild with moderate humidity. As in so many locations in the heartland, fall is the most pleasant season, marked by many mild sunny days and cool nights. The typical date of winter's last freeze is April 7. Winters can be quite cold. The first freeze occurs at the end of October.

	118
	97
	152
90°	45
32°	110
0°	5
	116
	58
	53

	High °F	Low °F	Hum %	Wind mph	Precip inches	Snow inches
JAN	37	17	71	10.6	1.1	6.3
FEB	43	22	71	10.8	1.1	4.9
MAR	55	32	69	12.3	2.6	3.6
APR	67	43	68	12.1	3.2	0.7
MAY	76	53	71	10.4	4.9	0.0
JUN	85	63	73	9.8	5.2	0.0
JUL	90	67	72	9.1	4.3	0.0
AUG	88	65	73	8.7	4.1	0.0
SEP	80	56	73	9.2	4.4	0.0
OCT	69	45	69	9.8	3.2	0.0
NOV	54	33	71	10.8	2.0	1.1
DEC	41	22	73	10.5	1.6	4.5

National Freeway

Location: Interstate Highway 68 runs 110 miles east-west between Morgantown, WV, and Hancock, MD, in the Appalachian Highlands.

Landscape: High hills and open low mountains. The valleys support a mixed oak-pine forest. Higher up is an Appalachian oak forest, dominated by white oak and black oak. Chestnut was once abundant, but blight eliminated it as a canopy tree.

Climate: Hot Continental. Thanks to the elevation, summers, though warm and somewhat humid with occasional thundershowers, are more pleasant than southern locations. The mountains interfere with winter storm tracks, but periods of cold and snow with freezing rain occur annually. Frost appears in late October, and is out by early April.

	60
	106
	199
90°	27
32°	109
0°	2
	197
	79
	38

	High °F	Low °F	Hum %	Wind mph	Precip inches	Snow inches
JAN	38	20	71	9.5	2.5	9.0
FEB	42	22	69	9.5	2.4	7.8
MAR	54	32	65	9.8	3.3	6.1
APR	64	41	62	9.4	3.3	0.5
MAY	74	50	65	7.9	3.9	0.0
JUN	82	58	68	7.1	3.7	0.0
JUL	86	63	70	6.5	3.7	0.0
AUG	84	62	72	6.1	3.6	0.0
SEP	78	55	73	6.5	3.2	0.0
OCT	66	43	69	7.3	2.9	0.0
NOV	54	35	70	8.7	3.1	1.8
DEC	43	26	71	9.3	2.9	5.8

New England Mid-Coast

Location: This area takes in New Hampshire's entire 25-mile seacoast plus a short stretch of Maine's coastal towns up I-95 to greater Portland. The area lies south of what Mainers call 'downeast'.

Landscape: Plains with high hills. The forests are mixed stands of pine and deciduous species - yellow birch, sugar maple, and American beech.

Climate: Hot Continental. As a rule, the region gets pleasant summers and falls, cold winters with frequent thaws, and disagreeable muddy springs. Autumn has the greatest number of sunny days. Winters are severe; they begin late but extend deep into springtime and temperatures well below zero are recorded frequently. Precipitation falls evenly throughout the year, but heavy snowfalls, sometimes totaling more than 100 inches per year, do occur.

	100
	102
	164
90°	6
32°	143
0°	10
	97
	79
	19

	High °F	Low °F	Hum %	Wind mph	Precip inches	Snow inches
JAN	32	12	65	11.5	3.7	16.5
FEB	35	14	65	11.6	3.5	15.2
MAR	43	25	65	11.8	3.8	11.0
APR	54	34	63	11.6	4.1	2.5
MAY	65	43	67	10.7	3.6	0.1
JUN	74	52	68	9.9	3.4	0.0
JUL	80	58	68	9.3	3.2	0.0
AUG	79	56	70	9.2	3.0	0.0
SEP	70	48	72	9.6	3.3	0.0
OCT	60	38	70	10.2	4.0	1.1
NOV	48	30	70	10.8	5.1	3.5
DEC	36	18	68	11.3	4.6	11.8

New Jersey Shore

Location: This is a New Jersey and Philadelphia term used for the Atlantic Ocean coast of New Jersey from Cape May on the south all the way up 160 miles to Sandy Hook at New York Harbor.

Landscape: Smooth plains with hills. Vegetation is a mixed oak-pine forest. Chestnut was once abundant, but blight eliminated it as a canopy tree.

Climate: Hot Continental. Summers are relatively cooler, winters warmer than those of other places at the same latitude. Summer sea breezes in the late morning and the afternoon prevent excessive heat. Fall is long, lasting until the first freeze around November 10. Spring warming is somewhat delayed; the last freeze occurs around March 30. Average ocean temperatures range from near 37°F in winter to 72°F in August. Precipitation is moderate and well distributed throughout the year.

	94
	111
	160
90°	17
32°	99
0°	2
	152
	65
	25

	High °F	Low °F	Hum %	Wind mph	Precip inches	Snow inches
JAN	39	21	67	11.0	3.5	5.8
FEB	42	23	66	11.4	3.0	6.1
MAR	51	31	64	11.9	3.7	3.3
APR	61	39	62	11.5	3.7	0.2
MAY	71	50	66	10.1	3.7	0.0
JUN	80	59	66	9.2	2.9	0.0
JUL	85	65	67	8.6	4.2	0.0
AUG	83	63	70	8.2	4.2	0.0
SEP	77	55	71	8.5	3.4	0.0
OCT	66	44	70	9.1	2.9	0.0
NOV	55	36	70	10.3	3.8	0.4
DEC	44	26	68	10.7	3.5	3.0

Climate

New Mexico Northern Mountain

Location: Fifty-five miles of Interstate Highway separate Santa Fe, New Mexico's capital, and Albuquerque, its largest city. The areas may never meet, since protected federal land and rough topography discourages developers.

Landscape: Plains with high mountains. The foothills have mixed grasses, chaparral brush, oak-juniper woodland, and pinyon-juniper woodland. At about 7,000 ft (2,100 m), open forests of ponderosa pine are found.

Climate: Temperate Steppe. There are no muggy days and nights are cool. Half the annual precipitation falls as brief but severe thunderstorms between July and September. These storms have a moderating effect on the heat and do not interfere much with outdoor activities. Long drizzles are unknown. The low rainfall and mild temperatures--91°F in July, 46° in January--make the area a health resort.

	168
	110
	87
90°	45
32°	136
0°	2
	14
	33
	38

	High °F	Low °F	Hum %	Wind mph	Precip inches	Snow inches
JAN	43	20	56	8.0	0.7	4.0
FEB	49	24	49	8.8	0.6	3.8
MAR	56	29	41	10.0	0.9	4.4
APR	65	36	34	10.8	0.8	2.3
MAY	74	45	34	10.5	0.8	0.0
JUN	84	55	32	9.9	1.0	0.0
JUL	87	60	44	9.0	2.3	0.0
AUG	83	58	49	8.2	2.6	0.0
SEP	77	51	46	8.5	1.6	0.0
OCT	66	40	45	8.2	1.1	0.6
NOV	53	29	51	7.9	0.7	2.6
DEC	44	21	57	7.7	0.8	4.8

New York's Southern Tier

Location: Refers to New York's counties west of the Catskill Mountains along the northern border of Pennsylvania. Binghamton and Elmira are here. Ithaca, though just outside the Southern Tier, is included here.

Landscape: Open high hills. The forests are mixed stands of pine and deciduous species - yellow birch, sugar maple, and American beech.

Climate: Warm Continental. Since the area is next to the St. Lawrence Valley storm track and subject to intruding arctic air masses that approach from the west and north, the local weather undergoes frequent and rapid changes. Winters are cold, but usually not severe, but moisture-laden winds from the Great Lakes bring much snow. Summers are pleasantly cool and invigorating.

	59
	99
	207
90°	9
32°	147
0°	9
	142
	77
	28

	High °F	Low °F	Hum %	Wind mph	Precip inches	Snow inches
JAN	30	14	74	11.0	2.0	15.9
FEB	32	14	72	11.0	2.1	14.5
MAR	42	24	70	11.1	2.5	11.5
APR	55	34	65	10.8	2.9	3.6
MAY	67	44	66	9.3	3.3	0.3
JUN	76	53	69	8.6	3.7	0.0
JUL	80	58	70	8.1	3.4	0.0
AUG	78	56	74	7.9	3.3	0.0
SEP	71	49	76	8.4	3.3	0.0
OCT	59	39	73	9.1	3.0	0.4
NOV	47	31	75	10.4	3.1	5.7
DEC	35	20	53	10.7	2.6	14.5

New York-Newark

Location: This region merges New York's five boroughs with greater Newark immediately across the Hudson River in New Jersey. New York is the point where New England meets the Atlantic coastal plain. After Tokyo and Mexico City, New York-Newark is the world's third largest metro area.

Landscape: Smooth plains and open high hills. Vegetation is a mixed oak-pine forest. Chestnut was once abundant, but blight eliminated it as a canopy tree.

Climate: Hot Continental. Close to the path of most storm and frontal systems that move across the continent. Weather changes approach from the west. The area can thus expect higher temperatures in summer and lower ones in winter than usual for a coastal area. Sea breezes moderate summer afternoon heat and delay winter snows. The Atlantic's influence is also measured in the 200-day frost-free season, from mid-April to mid-November.

	100
	120
	146
90°	16
32°	81
0°	0
	107
	74
	24

	High °F	Low °F	Hum %	Wind mph	Precip inches	Snow inches
JAN	38	24	65	10.9	3.4	7.5
FEB	40	26	63	11.2	3.2	8.1
MAR	50	34	61	11.4	4.0	5.0
APR	62	43	58	10.8	4.0	0.8
MAY	72	53	62	9.4	4.3	0.0
JUN	81	63	63	8.8	3.4	0.0
JUL	86	69	64	8.2	4.4	0.0
AUG	85	67	66	8.1	4.0	0.0
SEP	77	60	68	8.6	3.8	0.0
OCT	66	49	66	9.1	3.3	0.0
NOV	55	40	67	10.0	4.2	0.7
DEC	43	30	66	10.6	3.7	5.5

North Carolina Piedmont

Location: Piedmont or "foothill" is a common region in the Carolinas and Virginia, lying between the coastal plain and the highlands. In North Carolina, it is at its widest (300 miles) and embraces most of the state's population.

Landscape: Plains with high hills. Most of the land is cultivated, but there are stands of tall broadleaf trees that provide a dense, continuous canopy in summer and shed their leaves completely in winter.

Climate: Hot Continental. Winter temperatures and rainfall are modified by the mountain barrier. Freezing temperatures occur on more than half the winter days, but zero weather is almost unknown. Light snow may fall, perhaps two snows of an inch or more per year; ice glazing is more common here than in most of North Carolina - an average of four times a year - but it is seldom severe or long lasting.

	110
	105
	150
90°	37
32°	76
0°	0
	166
	69
	42

	High °F	Low °F	Hum %	Wind mph	Precip inches	Snow inches
JAN	48	28	68	8.0	3.5	3.0
FEB	52	30	64	8.4	3.7	2.5
MAR	61	38	64	9.0	4.2	1.8
APR	71	47	63	8.8	3.0	0.0
MAY	78	55	69	7.6	4.2	0.0
JUN	85	64	71	6.9	4.0	0.0
JUL	88	68	73	6.5	4.3	0.0
AUG	87	67	75	6.3	4.1	0.0
SEP	81	60	74	6.6	3.6	0.0
OCT	71	48	70	6.9	3.5	0.0
NOV	62	40	68	7.3	3.2	0.1
DEC	52	32	68	7.5	3.6	0.9

North Carolina Southern Mountains

Location: State climatologists locate this area in the extreme southwestern part of the Blue Ridge Mountains near Tennessee and Georgia. Asheville is the only metro area here.

Landscape: Low mountains, including Mt. Mitchell (6,684') highest point east of the Mississippi. The valleys support a mixed oak-pine forest. Higher up is an Appalachian oak forest, dominated by white oak and black oak. Chestnut was once abundant, but blight eliminated it as a canopy tree.

Climate: Hot Continental. Temperate but invigorating, with sharp daily temperature variation occurring throughout the year. Spring arrives early - around April 10 - and summers are long, with warm, clear days. Destructive weather events are rare. However, the valleys are subject to flooding, with high water occurring in 12-year cycles. The first freeze is October 24. Winter is short, dreary, and wet.

	101
	113
	151
90°	11
32°	99
0°	1
	209
	75
	45

	High °F	Low °F	Hum %	Wind mph	Precip inches	Snow inches
JAN	47	25	72	9.5	3.3	4.6
FEB	50	27	69	9.5	3.9	4.6
MAR	59	35	69	9.4	4.6	3.0
APR	68	43	68	8.8	3.4	0.7
MAY	75	51	75	7.1	4.4	0.0
JUN	80	58	77	6.1	4.2	0.0
JUL	83	63	79	5.9	4.5	0.0
AUG	82	62	80	5.4	4.7	0.0
SEP	77	56	80	5.7	3.9	0.0
OCT	68	44	75	6.7	3.6	0.0
NOV	59	36	73	8.2	3.6	0.7
DEC	50	29	72	8.9	3.5	2.0

North Carolina's Central Coastal Plain

Location: This state climate zone extends from Atlantic beaches inland over mostly flat and low terrain to where waterfalls are first spied in the rivers streams. Here is the state capital at Raleigh and an assortment of military and tobacco metro areas.

Landscape: Flat, smooth, and irregular plains. Common trees include evergreen oaks and members of the laurel and magnolia families. Sandy uplands have forests of loblolly and slash pine. Bald Cypress is a dominant tree in swamps.

Climate: Subtropical. The western mountains form a partial barrier to cold air masses moving east from the nation's interior. There are few days in the dead of the winter when the temperature falls below 20°F. Tropical air is present during much of the warm and humid summer. In midsummer, afternoon temperatures reach 90°F or higher every fourth day. Rainfall is well distributed throughout the year. The frost-free season extends from mid-April to mid-October.

	111
	106
	149
90°	49
32°	75
0°	0
	181
	75
	42

	High °F	Low °F	Hum %	Wind mph	Precip inches	Snow inches
JAN	50	29	67	8.5	3.9	2.1
FEB	54	31	65	8.9	3.8	2.2
MAR	63	39	65	9.3	4.1	1.3
APR	72	47	63	9.0	3.1	0.0
MAY	80	56	70	7.7	4.1	0.0
JUN	86	64	72	7.0	4.2	0.0
JUL	89	68	74	6.7	5.0	0.0
AUG	88	67	76	6.4	5.2	0.0
SEP	83	60	75	6.8	3.9	0.0
OCT	73	48	71	7.1	3.0	0.0
NOV	64	39	68	7.6	3.0	0.1
DEC	54	32	68	8.0	3.4	0.8

Climate Divisions (Ne-No)

North Central Arizona

Location: Flagstaff and Prescott, 63 miles apart and at different elevations, sit in a mountainous region oriented southeast to northwest with maximum elevations between 9,000 and 12,000 feet.

Landscape: Tablelands and open high mountains. At low elevations, several kinds of cactus and yucca are common. The woodland zone is dominated by open stands of two-needle pinyon pine and several species of juniper. East of here is the largest stand of Ponderosa Pine in the world.

Climate: Steppe. Varies considerably with altitude. Average annual temperature is about 55F in the lower foothills and 40F on the upper mountain slopes. During late spring, there is a moisture deficit until the arrival of summer rains, which appear as thunderstorms. Rains also come in early autumn and winter. In the mountains, most precipitation is snow. Accumulations vary from year to year, but five feet on the upper slopes isn't unusual.

	162
	102
	101
90°	2
32°	210
0°	8
	12
	39
	38

	High °F	Low °F	Hum %	Wind mph	Precip inches	Snow inches
JAN	46	19	63	6.8	1.8	12.6
FEB	50	21	60	6.7	1.8	10.9
MAR	53	25	57	7.2	2.2	14.5
APR	61	30	49	7.6	1.1	5.8
MAY	71	37	46	7.3	0.6	0.9
JUN	81	46	38	6.9	0.4	0.0
JUL	85	54	53	5.5	3.0	0.0
AUG	82	52	60	5.1	3.1	0.0
SEP	77	45	55	5.7	2.0	0.1
OCT	67	35	54	5.8	1.4	1.1
NOV	55	25	57	6.8	1.7	6.0
DEC	47	19	62	6.7	2.0	10.5

North Central Florida

Location: State climatologists define this region as a 60-mile wide band from the Atlantic Ocean across the state to the Gulf of Mexico, taking in Daytona Beach, Gainesville, and Ocala.

Landscape: Flat plains. Common trees include evergreen oaks and members of the laurel and magnolia families. Sandy uplands have forests of loblolly and slash pine. Bald Cypress is a dominant tree in swamps.

Climate: Subtropical, with summers that are hotter and more humid than coastal locations, but that are cooled by afternoon thunderstorms. Winters are mild and snowless. The annual range of temperature changes is small, but there is a subtle though definite four-season climate. Freezes do occur from December 9 until mid-February.

	101
	130
	134
90°	84
32°	10
0°	0
	176
	78
	80

	High °F	Low °F	Hum %	Wind mph	Precip inches	Snow inches
JAN	68	45	74	7.8	3.1	0.0
FEB	70	46	73	8.3	3.7	0.0
MAR	76	52	71	8.6	3.4	0.0
APR	82	57	70	8.1	2.6	0.0
MAY	87	64	72	7.6	3.8	0.0
JUN	90	69	76	6.8	6.7	0.0
JUL	91	71	78	6.4	6.7	0.0
AUG	90	72	80	6.1	6.9	0.0
SEP	88	70	81	6.7	5.7	0.0
OCT	82	62	77	7.5	2.7	0.0
NOV	76	53	76	7.3	2.5	0.0
DEC	70	47	75	7.0	2.8	0.0

North Central Georgia

Location: Sometimes called Georgia's Inland Empire, this region takes in areas within sight of the state's Appalachian foothills, including greater Atlanta, Athens, and Gainesville.

Landscape: Tablelands, open high hills and low mountains. Here the soil is classic 'red land', and is dominated by tall broadleaf trees that provide a dense, continuous canopy in summer and shed their leaves completely in winter.

Climate: Hot Continental, moderated by the Atlantic Ocean 200 miles southeast, the Gulf of Mexico 275 miles south, and the Appalachians to the north. Summers are sweltering, but without long stretches of extreme heat. Precipitation falls evenly throughout the year, usually as rain, but snow is possible. The first freeze arrives around November 6. Winters aren't severe. Cold spells are short-lived and broken up by periods of warm southerly airflow.

	111
	106
	148
90°	41
32°	50
0°	0
	157
	76
	49

	High °F	Low °F	Hum %	Wind mph	Precip inches	Snow inches
JAN	50	30	69	9.9	5.1	0.9
FEB	55	33	66	10.3	4.8	0.7
MAR	64	40	66	10.3	6.1	0.5
APR	73	48	65	9.7	4.6	0.0
MAY	79	57	69	8.3	4.4	0.0
JUN	85	64	70	7.7	4.0	0.0
JUL	88	68	74	7.3	4.8	0.0
AUG	87	68	75	6.8	3.8	0.0
SEP	81	62	74	7.6	3.7	0.0
OCT	72	49	70	8.1	3.3	0.0
NOV	63	41	69	8.7	4.0	0.1
DEC	54	33	69	9.4	4.6	0.2

North Central Louisiana

Location: The region takes in a group of Louisiana's parishes, centered on Monroe, that border Arkansas and the Mississippi River.

Landscape: Irregular plains. In the midst of hardwood stands and Louisiana Longleaf Pine forests.

Climate: Subtropical. Summers are extremely hot and humid but are relieved by frequent thunderstorms. Winters are usually mild and rainy, thanks to the Gulf of Mexico, though northern weather sweeps in with occasional below- freezing temperatures and ice storms. Early November sees the first freeze, and the last happens in late March.

	98
	115
	152
90°	90
32°	41
0°	0
	197
	66
	76

	High °F	Low °F	Hum %	Wind mph	Precip inches	Snow inches
JAN	54	35	79	10.0	4.7	0.6
FEB	59	39	76	10.3	4.7	0.5
MAR	68	46	76	10.5	5.3	0.1
APR	77	55	76	10.1	4.3	0.0
MAY	84	63	78	8.9	5.5	0.0
JUN	91	70	78	7.7	3.8	0.0
JUL	92	72	79	6.5	3.7	0.0
AUG	92	70	79	6.2	2.7	0.0
SEP	87	65	78	7.3	3.5	0.0
OCT	78	52	74	7.7	3.2	0.0
NOV	67	44	75	9.1	4.7	0.0
DEC	58	37	77	9.5	5.5	0.2

North Central Texas

Location: This region is the most populous in Texas, and takes in the famous 'metroplex' (Dallas and Fort Worth) plus Waco, Killeen, and others.

Landscape: Plains and tablelands with hills. Arid grasslands are mixed with oak, juniper and mesquite.

Climate: Prairie and Subtropical, with hot summers and rain at night and marked by a wide range in annual temperature. The first freeze occurs around November 12, the last around March 25. Winters tend to be mild, but northers bring cold air masses down from the Great Plains and the Rocky Mountains. These cold snaps are not prolonged, however. Heavy downpours may accompany thunderstorms during April and May. July and August are relatively dry. Snowfall is slight and doesn't accumulate.

	136
	97
	132
90°	102
32°	37
0°	0
	88
	50
	45

	High °F	Low °F	Hum %	Wind mph	Precip inches	Snow inches
JAN	55	34	72	11.2	1.9	0.9
FEB	60	38	70	11.9	2.5	0.9
MAR	69	47	69	12.9	2.9	0.1
APR	77	56	70	12.7	3.5	0.0
MAY	84	63	74	11.5	5.0	0.0
JUN	91	70	71	11.2	3.6	0.0
JUL	95	74	64	10.5	2.2	0.0
AUG	96	74	65	9.7	2.2	0.0
SEP	88	67	70	9.6	4.1	0.0
OCT	79	56	69	10.1	3.7	0.0
NOV	68	46	71	10.9	2.7	0.1
DEC	58	37	71	11.0	2.1	0.1

North Central Wisconsin

Location: This region, centered on Wausau, is 20 miles from a point in North America exactly halfway between the Equator and the North Pole and a quarter of the way around the world from Greenwich, England.

Landscape: Irregular plains. The forests are mixed stands of pine and deciduous species - yellow birch, sugar maple, and American beech.

Climate: Warm Continental. Summers are pleasant, with less than a week's worth of 90°F days. Springs and falls are transitional. By the first week in October, frost appears. Winters are severely cold, with lingering moisture from Lake Superior delivering heavy snowfalls. Snow cover persists through the winter. Mid-May sees the last frost.

	86
	102
	177
90°	5
32°	171
0°	37
	124
	62
	33

	High °F	Low °F	Hum %	Wind mph	Precip inches	Snow inches
JAN	21	3	74	10.9	0.9	10.9
FEB	27	7	74	10.5	0.9	9.7
MAR	38	19	73	10.8	2.0	11.3
APR	54	33	69	11.2	2.8	2.7
MAY	67	44	67	10.1	3.6	0.2
JUN	76	54	69	9.2	4.0	0.0
JUL	81	59	72	8.2	3.9	0.0
AUG	78	57	76	7.9	4.4	0.0
SEP	68	48	76	8.9	4.3	0.0
OCT	56	38	74	9.9	2.6	0.2
NOV	40	25	76	10.9	2.0	5.0
DEC	26	10	77	10.5	1.4	10.8

Climate

North Dakota Red River Valley

Location: This region in the center of North America is drained by the Red River of the North and includes Fargo and Grand Forks, some 75 miles apart.

Landscape: Smooth and irregular plains. Vegetation is mixed prairie, groves, and strips of deciduous trees commonly found near streams and on north facing slopes.

Climate: Prairie. Summers are generally comfortable, with a few days of hot and humid weather. Nights are cool. Winters are cold and dry, with maximum temperatures rising above freezing only six times a month. At night, the temperature drops below zero half the time. The first freeze is mid-September and the last, mid-May. With the flat terrain, surface friction has little slowing effect on the wind, contributing to the legendary Dakota blizzards. Strong winds with even a light snowfall will cause heavy snowdrifts.

	88
	109
	168
90°	14
32°	184
0°	60
	77
	44
	31

	High °F	Low °F	Hum %	Wind mph	Precip inches	Snow inches
JAN	15	-4	74	12.7	0.7	8.4
FEB	20	2	75	12.4	0.5	5.5
MAR	34	16	76	13.1	1.0	6.8
APR	53	32	68	13.9	1.6	2.8
MAY	68	43	64	12.9	2.3	0.2
JUN	77	53	69	11.6	2.8	0.0
JUL	83	58	70	10.5	2.7	0.0
AUG	81	55	70	11.0	2.4	0.0
SEP	69	45	72	11.9	2.1	0.0
OCT	56	34	69	12.6	1.5	0.7
NOV	36	19	76	12.8	0.7	5.7
DEC	20	2	76	12.3	0.6	6.7

Northeast Indiana

Location: This industrial region is roughly equidistant from Chicago, Detroit, and Cincinnati. The city of Fort Wayne predominates here and sits at the high point between two Indiana watersheds; hence its nickname, "Summit City."

Landscape: Flat, smooth, or irregular plains. Stands of white oak, red oak, black oak, bitternut hickory, and shagbark hickory trees form a mosaic pattern with prairie. The understory is flowering dogwood.

Climate: Hot Continental. Lake Michigan moderates temperatures slightly throughout the region, but also contributes to frequent snowfalls. The last freeze is late April. Summers are moderately warm and humid, with occasional afternoon and evening thunderstorms. The year's first frost occurs by mid-October. Winters are somewhat cold and cloudy.

	76
	101
	189
90°	16
32°	131
0°	9
	168
	73
	39

	High °F	Low °F	Hum %	Wind mph	Precip inches	Snow inches
JAN	30	15	77	11.7	2.0	14.0
FEB	34	18	75	11.2	1.8	11.2
MAR	46	28	72	11.9	2.8	7.2
APR	60	38	68	11.6	3.5	1.7
MAY	71	49	67	10.1	3.4	0.0
JUN	81	58	68	9.1	3.7	0.0
JUL	85	63	70	8.1	3.5	0.0
AUG	82	60	74	7.5	3.5	0.0
SEP	76	53	74	8.4	3.3	0.0
OCT	63	42	72	9.4	2.8	0.4
NOV	49	33	76	11.0	3.0	5.4
DEC	36	21	79	11.2	3.0	12.5

Northeast Minnesota

Location: An area where Minnesota and Wisconsin and Lake Superior come together. Duluth, the northern terminus of I-35, is the only metro area here.

Landscape: Tablelands and plains with hills. The forests are mixed stands of pine and deciduous species - yellow birch, sugar maple, and American beech.

Climate: Warm Continental. Winters are long and severely cold. Snow comes early and remains on the ground until springtime. The first freeze is normally recorded on September 22, the last on May 26. All months are windy. Summers are bright, dry, and seldom hot due to the northerly latitude and proximity of Lake Superior.

	77
	102
	186
90°	7
32°	186
0°	51
	134
	60
	34

	High °F	Low °F	Hum %	Wind mph	Precip inches	Snow inches
JAN	16	-2	74	11.6	1.2	16.8
FEB	22	3	71	11.2	0.8	11.2
MAR	33	16	71	11.8	1.9	13.3
APR	48	29	66	12.4	2.3	6.5
MAY	62	40	65	11.6	3.0	0.8
JUN	71	49	71	10.5	3.8	0.0
JUL	77	55	72	9.4	3.6	0.0
AUG	74	53	76	9.4	4.0	0.0
SEP	64	45	76	10.5	3.8	0.1
OCT	52	35	72	11.1	2.5	1.4
NOV	35	22	76	11.6	1.8	12.5
DEC	21	5	77	11.2	1.2	15.4

Northeast Missouri Prairie

Location: Here, the Missouri River flows past Columbia (the state's university town) and Jefferson City (the capital) on its way to joining the Mississippi River just south of St. Louis.

Landscape: Irregular plains and open hills. Vegetation is mixed prairie, groves, and strips of deciduous trees commonly found near streams and on north facing slopes.

Climate: Prairie. The first freeze is around October 16, followed by a moderately cold winter. The latest frost occurs at the beginning of May, followed by a warm and often humid summer. Each summer sees a few days over 100°F, and winter lows reach zero two or three times annually. Summer hot spells are often relieved by thunderstorms, and winter cold snaps are often interrupted by days that are almost balmy. The late spring and early summer months are the rainiest, but the rain diminishes by late summer.

	103
	94
	168
90°	37
32°	108
0°	2
	129
	64
	50

	High °F	Low °F	Hum %	Wind mph	Precip inches	Snow inches
JAN	38	18	73	10.7	1.5	5.2
FEB	43	22	72	10.9	1.9	5.1
MAR	55	33	69	11.9	3.3	4.0
APR	67	44	67	11.4	3.6	0.5
MAY	75	53	72	9.2	4.6	0.0
JUN	84	62	72	8.7	4.2	0.0
JUL	89	67	71	8.2	3.5	0.0
AUG	87	65	73	7.8	3.1	0.0
SEP	80	57	73	8.4	3.6	0.0
OCT	69	45	71	9.3	3.1	0.0
NOV	55	35	73	10.4	3.0	1.6
DEC	42	23	75	10.7	2.7	3.8

Northeast Ohio Hills

Location: State climatologists have collected 13 counties here into a coherent climate region. Some Ohioans consider this region one vast industrial megalopolis, combining greater Cleveland, Akron, Canton, and Youngstown.

Landscape: Irregular plains, tablelands, and hills. The valleys support a mixed oak-pine forest. Chestnut was once abundant, but blight eliminated it as a canopy tree.

Climate: Hot Continental, in the path of cold winter air masses advancing south and east out of Canada. Extreme low temperatures are modified as the air passes over the comparatively warm water of Lake Erie. But this also means considerable winter cloudiness and frequent snows. Throughout the year, one of three days is foggy. Spring is a brief transition period with the last freeze out by around May 4. Summer heat is also moderated by the lake. Fall is the most pleasant season, with mild, sunny weather often extending into November or even early December.

	66
	98
	200
90°	8
32°	130
0°	5
	174
	77
	36

	High °F	Low °F	Hum %	Wind mph	Precip inches	Snow inches
JAN	32	17	75	11.6	2.2	11.8
FEB	35	19	73	11.1	2.2	10.0
MAR	47	28	70	11.4	3.3	9.6
APR	59	38	66	10.8	3.1	2.6
MAY	69	48	66	9.3	3.7	0.1
JUN	78	56	68	8.4	3.4	0.0
JUL	82	61	70	7.6	4.1	0.0
AUG	80	59	73	7.4	3.3	0.0
SEP	73	53	74	8.1	3.4	0.0
OCT	62	42	71	9.1	2.4	0.6
NOV	49	34	73	10.9	3.0	4.9
DEC	37	23	76	11.3	2.9	10.9

Northern Alabama

Location: This region consists of a long string of cities, dominated by Huntsville, along the broad and winding Tennessee River in the northern quarter of the state. Alabamians call it the Tennessee Valley.

Landscape: Irregular plains, tablelands, and open hills. Stands of white oak, red oak, black oak, bitternut hickory, and shagbark hickory trees form a mosaic pattern with prairie. The understory is flowering dogwood.

Climate: Hot Continental. Cold air from the north predominates during the winter, but occasional mild air from the Gulf of Mexico comes up for several days. Severe cold is brief. Springs are variable and stormy as cold polar air and warm Gulf air meet. Summers are hot and humid, relieved by showers that come about every three days. Falls are dry, cool, and pleasant.

	100
	101
	164
90°	55
32°	66
0°	0
	148
	76
	54

	High °F	Low °F	Hum %	Wind mph	Precip inches	Snow inches
JAN	48	29	73	9.3	4.7	1.7
FEB	54	33	70	9.7	4.6	0.9
MAR	63	41	69	10.1	6.1	0.4
APR	73	49	67	9.3	4.6	0.0
MAY	80	57	72	8.1	5.1	0.0
JUN	87	65	72	7.0	4.1	0.0
JUL	90	69	75	6.3	4.7	0.0
AUG	89	68	75	6.0	3.3	0.0
SEP	83	62	75	6.9	4.1	0.0
OCT	73	49	71	7.5	3.2	0.0
NOV	62	41	71	8.6	4.6	0.0
DEC	52	33	72	9.4	5.8	0.5

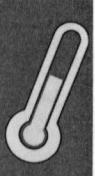

Northern Florida

Location: This region, along I-10 just below Florida's border with Georgia, takes in the state's largest city (Jacksonville) and its capital (Tallahassee).

Landscape: Flat and irregular plains. The landscape of North Central Florida is dominated by forests of loblolly and slash pine. Bald Cypress is a dominant tree in swamps. Sometimes the trees are festooned with Spanish moss.

Climate: Subtropical. Average temperatures compare with those of southern portions of California, Brazil, China, and Australia. In contrast to south Florida, there is a more definite march of the four seasons here, with considerable winter rainfall and much less winter sunshine. The freeze-free growing season is from March 9 to November 16. Summer is the least pleasant time of the year, with humidity and high temperature bringing discomfort. Thunderstorms occur every other day during those months.

	99
	128
	139
90°	85
32°	22
0°	0
	189
	72
	74

	High °F	Low °F	Hum %	Wind mph	Precip inches	Snow inches
JAN	64	39	73	7.5	4.0	0.0
FEB	67	42	71	8.2	4.7	0.0
MAR	73	48	69	8.3	4.9	0.0
APR	80	54	68	7.8	3.3	0.0
MAY	86	61	69	7.2	4.1	0.0
JUN	90	69	73	6.7	6.3	0.0
JUL	91	72	76	6.1	7.2	0.0
AUG	91	72	78	5.8	7.7	0.0
SEP	88	69	77	6.7	6.3	0.0
OCT	81	58	74	7.1	2.9	0.0
NOV	73	48	73	7.0	3.0	0.0
DEC	66	42	73	7.1	3.9	0.0

Northwest Inland Empire

Location: This region in the Pacific Northwest centers on Spokane, Washington, and includes much of the surrounding Columbia River basin. It extends into northern Idaho.

Landscape: Open low and high mountains. Mixed evergreen-deciduous forest predominates; Douglas-fir forest and cedar-hemlock-Douglas-fir forest are the two major types.

Climate: Temperate Steppe, with a mingle of damp coastal climate and an arid interior climate. Air masses come from the west or southwest and lose most of their moisture passing over the mountains. Sometimes dry, Continental air masses from the east invade the area, bringing high temperatures with low humidity in the summer and subzero temperatures in the winter. Generally, the region has a mild climate during summer and a cold climate during winter with heavy snowfalls in December and January.

	86
	87
	192
90°	21
32°	141
0°	5
	101
	57
	11

	High °F	Low °F	Hum %	Wind mph	Precip inches	Snow inches
JAN	35	22	82	8.8	2.7	20.1
FEB	42	26	77	9.2	2.0	8.8
MAR	49	30	68	9.6	1.9	4.6
APR	58	35	61	10.0	1.4	0.5
MAY	67	42	59	9.3	1.7	0.1
JUN	76	49	55	9.2	1.6	0.0
JUL	84	54	47	8.6	0.8	0.0
AUG	84	54	46	8.2	1.0	0.0
SEP	74	46	53	8.3	1.0	0.0
OCT	60	37	64	8.1	1.3	0.4
NOV	44	30	82	8.6	2.7	6.0
DEC	35	24	86	8.6	3.0	15.5

Northwest Vermont

Location: Vermont's only metro area, Burlington, is just above the center of a great valley created by Lake Champlain. Quebec is north of here, and New York State is on the lake's western shore.

Landscape: Plains with open low mountains. The forests are mixed stands of pine and deciduous species - yellow birch, sugar maple, and American beech.

Climate: Warm Continental. The northerly latitude assures the variety and vigor of a true New England climate. The summer, while not long, is pleasant. Fall is cool; the first freeze occurs in late September. Winters are cold, with brief, intense cold snaps formed by high-pressure systems moving down from central Canada and Hudson Bay. Lake Champlain's tempering effect produces temperatures along the lakeshore from 5 to 10°F warmer than those at the airport, 3.5 miles inland. This is one of the cloudiest areas in the United States.

	58
	101
	206
90°	6
32°	157
0°	28
	120
	75
	22

	High °F	Low °F	Hum %	Wind mph	Precip inches	Snow inches
JAN	25	8	68	9.7	1.8	18.8
FEB	28	9	68	9.4	1.6	16.8
MAR	39	22	67	9.5	2.2	12.4
APR	54	34	64	9.5	2.8	3.8
MAY	67	45	63	9.0	3.1	0.2
JUN	76	55	66	8.5	3.5	0.0
JUL	81	60	66	8.0	3.7	0.0
AUG	78	58	70	7.6	4.1	0.0
SEP	69	49	74	8.3	3.3	0.0
OCT	57	39	71	8.8	2.9	0.2
NOV	44	30	72	9.7	3.1	6.6
DEC	30	16	72	9.9	2.4	18.1

Ohio's Lake Erie Shore

Location: This region is located on the southern shore of Lake Erie along 100 miles of Interstate Highway 90 between Cleveland to Toledo.

Landscape: Flat, smooth, and irregular plains. Vegetation is mixed prairie, groves, and strips of deciduous trees commonly found near streams and on north facing slopes.

Climate: Hot Continental. Lake Erie moderates temperature, and extremes are seldom recorded. The typical first freeze comes at the end of October; the latest is mid-April. Summers are moderate, though humidity is high. There is an excessive amount of cloudiness; in winter, the sun shines during only 30 percent of the daylight hours; December and January, the cloudiest months, sometimes receive as little as 16 percent of the possible amount of sunshine. Snowfall is light and distributed evenly from November to March.

	71
	104
	191
90°	13
32°	138
0°	7
	153
	72
	36

	High °F	Low °F	Hum %	Wind mph	Precip inches	Snow inches
JAN	31	17	75	11.3	1.8	10.1
FEB	34	19	73	11.0	1.9	9.1
MAR	45	28	71	11.4	2.7	7.3
APR	58	38	68	11.1	3.0	1.6
MAY	69	48	67	9.7	3.3	0.0
JUN	79	58	68	8.7	3.8	0.0
JUL	83	62	70	7.8	3.5	0.0
AUG	81	61	74	7.5	3.4	0.0
SEP	74	54	74	8.1	3.1	0.0
OCT	62	43	71	9.2	2.3	0.2
NOV	49	34	74	10.7	2.9	3.2
DEC	37	23	77	11.0	2.9	9.1

Oklahoma-Texas Red River Valley

Location: Lawton and Wichita Falls are 50 miles from each other on Interstate Highway 44. The Red River, the Texas-Oklahoma boundary, runs between the metro areas.

Landscape: Irregular plains with low mountains. Post oak and blackjack oak dominate the cross timbers region of Oklahoma and Texas. Arid grasslands are mixed with oak, juniper and mesquite.

Climate: Prairie, with large daily and annual temperature extremes and erratic rainfall. While Blue Northers may drop the temperature 20° to 30° within an hour, winters are relatively mild. Snow over an inch occurs only two days a year. Summer temperatures average in the mid-80s, but 100° days are frequent in periods of hot weather. Prolonged dry periods are common. Winds are southerly and are strong in all months. Dust storms are rare.

	151
	93
	120
90°	103
32°	73
0°	0
	70
	40
	47

	High °F	Low °F	Hum %	Wind mph	Precip inches	Snow inches
JAN	51	26	69	11.2	1.0	2.0
FEB	56	30	68	11.9	1.4	2.1
MAR	65	39	65	13.2	2.2	0.7
APR	75	50	65	13.1	2.7	0.0
MAY	83	59	70	12.2	4.5	0.0
JUN	91	67	68	12.0	3.6	0.0
JUL	97	72	61	11.1	1.8	0.0
AUG	95	71	63	10.3	2.3	0.0
SEP	86	63	70	10.4	3.7	0.0
OCT	76	51	68	10.7	2.9	0.0
NOV	64	39	69	11.4	1.7	0.3
DEC	54	29	69	11.2	1.3	1.2

Oregon's Rogue River Valley

Location: This area in southwestern Oregon near the California border is a fruit, wine, and timber-producing river valley. The valley forms a relatively isolated enclave west of the Cascades.

Landscape: High mountains. Trees include the Torrey pine, Monterey pine, and Bishop Pine, and white oak.

Climate: Mediterranean, with marked seasonal characteristics. Late fall, winter, and early spring are cloudy, damp, and cool. The rest of the year is sunny, warm, and dry. The rain shadow afforded by the Siskiyous and the Coastal Range results in relatively light rainfall, most of it falling in the wintertime. Snowfalls are light. Winters are mild, with the temperatures just dipping below freezing during December and January. Summer days can reach 90°F, but nights are cool.

	118
	79
	169
90°	54
32°	86
0°	0
	100
	49
	7

	High °F	Low °F	Hum %	Wind mph	Precip inches	Snow inches
JAN	46	30	81	4.1	2.7	3.3
FEB	53	32	73	4.5	1.9	1.2
MAR	59	35	68	5.2	1.8	0.7
APR	65	38	64	5.7	1.2	0.2
MAY	73	43	61	5.7	1.0	0.0
JUN	82	51	56	5.9	0.6	0.0
JUL	91	55	50	5.8	0.3	0.0
AUG	90	55	51	5.3	0.5	0.0
SEP	83	48	54	4.5	0.9	0.0
OCT	69	40	65	3.7	1.5	0.0
NOV	53	36	80	3.6	3.2	0.5
DEC	44	31	84	3.7	3.3	1.4

Ozark Plateau

Location: This region is where Missouri, Arkansas, Kansas, and Oklahoma come closest together.

Landscape: Tablelands, high hills, and low mountains. Stands of white oak, red oak, black oak, bitternut hickory, and shagbark hickory trees form a mosaic pattern with prairie. The understory is flowering dogwood.

Climate: Hot Continental, with hot, humid summers and briefer winters than other locations at this latitude. Winters vary from warm and humid Maritime to cold and dry Continental, but each winter is relatively free from extremes. Snowfalls are minimal; precipitation in January and February falls as icy rain. Temperatures start freezing late November through February, but seldom fall to zero or below. Spring is likely to be a wet transition period from late February through April. Freezes arrive by mid-October and depart by late April.

	120
	98
	148
90°	56
32°	94
0°	1
	106
	62
	54

	High °F	Low °F	Hum %	Wind mph	Precip inches	Snow inches
JAN	44	23	70	10.4	1.8	3.4
FEB	49	27	69	10.8	2.3	3.3
MAR	60	37	66	11.8	3.8	2.3
APR	70	47	67	11.3	4.1	0.2
MAY	77	56	72	9.7	4.8	0.0
JUN	85	64	73	9.0	4.7	0.0
JUL	91	69	71	8.2	2.9	0.0
AUG	89	67	71	8.1	3.6	0.0
SEP	82	60	74	8.6	4.5	0.0
OCT	72	48	68	9.2	3.7	0.0
NOV	59	37	70	10.1	3.7	1.0
DEC	48	27	71	10.3	2.9	1.7

The Palouse

Location: An area in northwestern Idaho and southeastern Washington, The Palouse takes in the rolling, fertile hills of the Palouse prairie and the forested hills and canyon lands.

Landscape: Tablelands and open low mountains. Large areas of level land are rare. There are scattered trees and sagebrush and rabbitbrush. Because ground cover is scarce, much soil is exposed to wind erosion.

Climate: Temperate Steppe, lying in the rain shadow east of the Cascade Range. The climate closely resembles that of the Great Plains. Winters are cold and dry, except for two extremely snowy months. Summers are warm to hot. The average annual temperature is 45°F throughout most of the region.

	106
	98
	162
90°	18
32°	133
0°	3
	49
	95
	24

	High °F	Low °F	Hum %	Wind mph	Precip inches	Snow inches
JAN	40	28	76	6.0	1.3	20.0
FEB	47	32	73	7.0	0.9	9.0
MAR	54	35	65	6.0	1.1	4.0
APR	62	40	54	7.0	1.1	1.0
MAY	70	47	52	6.0	1.3	0.1
JUN	80	54	48	6.0	1.3	0.0
JUL	89	59	40	6.0	0.7	0.0
AUG	88	59	39	5.0	0.8	0.0
SEP	77	51	45	5.0	0.8	0.0
OCT	63	41	54	5.0	0.9	0.3
NOV	48	34	69	6.0	1.1	5.0
DEC	40	29	76	6.0	1.2	15.0

Pennsylvania Central Mountains

Location: The region includes Altoona, Johnstown, and State College in Pennsylvania's Allegheny Mountains near the center of the state.

Landscape: Open low mountains. The valleys support a mixed oak-pine forest. Higher up is an Appalachian oak forest, dominated by white oak and black oak. Chestnut was once abundant, but blight eliminated it as a canopy tree.

Climate: Hot Continental. The area is one of America's cloudiest, with precipitation distributed evenly throughout the year. Frost arrives in late October, followed by winter months that aren't as severe and snowy as upstate New York. Springs are transitional, overcast, and wet. Thanks to clear weather and elevation, summer and fall are the most pleasant seasons of the year.

	58
	103
	204
90°	14
32°	130
0°	3
	178
	77
	35

	High °F	Low °F	Hum %	Wind mph	Precip inches	Snow inches
JAN	34	18	69	10.6	2.8	12.8
FEB	37	20	68	10.5	2.8	11.5
MAR	48	29	65	10.7	3.5	9.7
APR	60	38	64	10.3	3.3	1.4
MAY	71	48	69	8.9	3.9	0.0
JUN	79	56	70	8.0	4.2	0.0
JUL	83	61	68	7.3	4.1	0.0
AUG	81	59	68	6.9	3.4	0.0
SEP	74	52	73	7.4	3.4	0.0
OCT	63	41	69	8.4	2.9	0.2
NOV	51	34	70	9.8	3.4	3.4
DEC	38	24	69	10.4	3.0	9.1

Pennsylvania Poconos

Location: Describes a mountainous area in northeast Pennsylvania just above Allentown and extending north to Wilkes-Barre, Scranton, and Hazleton.

Landscape: Open low mountains, woodlands and lakes. The valleys support a mixed oak-pine forest. Higher up is an Appalachian oak forest, dominated by white oak and black oak. Chestnut was once abundant, but blight eliminated it as a canopy tree.

Climate: Hot Continental; cool in summer with frequent, brief showers. The first freeze is mid-October. Winter temperatures in the valley are not severe. Though the annual snowfall is 47 inches, severe snowstorms are infrequent. Annual precipitation is 36 inches. Some tropical storm effect can be felt.

	82
	108
	176
90°	12
32°	125
0°	4
	165
	71
	30

	High °F	Low °F	Hum %	Wind mph	Precip inches	Snow inches
JAN	33	18	70	11.0	2.6	9.8
FEB	36	20	68	11.3	2.6	9.8
MAR	47	29	65	11.5	2.9	7.6
APR	59	38	63	11.1	3.2	1.9
MAY	70	49	65	9.5	3.9	0.1
JUN	79	58	69	8.8	3.9	0.0
JUL	83	63	70	7.8	4.0	0.0
AUG	81	61	73	7.5	3.8	0.0
SEP	74	54	75	8.0	3.6	0.0
OCT	62	42	73	9.0	2.9	0.2
NOV	50	34	72	10.3	3.5	2.3
DEC	38	24	72	10.6	3.0	7.5

Pennsylvania's Southeastern Piedmont

Location: Lies between greater Philadelphia and the Appalachians to the west. It is a broad plateau and contains the state capital at Harrisburg and a group of metro areas in the heart of Pennsylvania Dutch Country.

Landscape: Flat plains with high hills. The valleys support a mixed oak-pine forest. Higher up is an Appalachian oak forest, dominated by white oak and black oak. Chestnut was once abundant, but blight eliminated it as a canopy tree.

Climate: Hot Continental. Topographic differences result in local eccentricities. In general, this region has long, hot summers and comparatively mild winters. The growing season is 170 to 200 days, starting usually the first week in May and ending mid-October. Precipitation is more than adequate, averaging 35 to 50 inches. Average annual snowfall is 30 inches. The seasons are distinct but not harsh.

	92
	110
	164
90°	22
32°	112
0°	2
	164
	75
	29

	High °F	Low °F	Hum %	Wind mph	Precip inches	Snow inches
JAN	38	20	67	9.6	3.1	8.0
FEB	41	22	64	10.2	2.8	8.2
MAR	52	31	63	10.7	3.3	5.2
APR	63	40	61	10.2	3.5	0.4
MAY	73	50	64	8.7	4.1	0.0
JUN	82	59	65	8.0	4.1	0.0
JUL	86	64	67	7.3	4.1	0.0
AUG	84	62	69	7.0	3.7	0.0
SEP	77	55	71	7.3	3.7	0.0
OCT	66	43	69	7.9	3.1	0.0
NOV	54	35	68	8.9	3.5	1.4
DEC	42	26	68	9.3	3.3	5.3

Puget Sound Shore

Location: Washington State climatologists call this region the Puget Sound Lowlands. Puget Sound is the saltwater extension of the Pacific Ocean. The lowlands, or shore, includes almost all of Washington's largest cities and is home to about 5 million people.

Landscape: Tablelands, open hills, and high mountains. Principal trees are western red cedar, western hemlock, and Douglas-fir.

Climate: Marine, with moderate temperatures, a pronounced rainy season, and considerable cloudiness, particularly during winter. Sometimes severe winter storms come in from the north. Summers are pleasant and winters are relatively mild, with prevailing temperatures in the 40s. Summer heat and winter cold are modified by the nearness of the ocean. There is measurable rainfall on an average of 150 days a year. The first freeze is November 15th, the last in later March.

	57
	83
	225
90°	4
32°	62
0°	0
	182
	100
	6

	High °F	Low °F	Hum %	Wind mph	Precip inches	Snow inches
JAN	45	33	81	8.5	6.0	5.2
FEB	50	35	79	8.4	4.5	1.9
MAR	53	36	76	8.7	4.0	1.6
APR	58	40	73	8.6	2.8	0.1
MAY	64	44	72	8.0	2.1	0.0
JUN	70	49	71	7.8	1.7	0.0
JUL	75	52	70	7.4	1.0	0.0
AUG	75	53	72	7.1	1.3	0.0
SEP	70	48	75	7.1	2.0	0.0
OCT	60	42	82	7.4	3.6	0.0
NOV	51	38	83	8.2	6.2	0.9
DEC	45	34	84	8.5	6.4	3.0

Rock River Run

Location: The Rock River starts in southeast Wisconsin and winds 300 miles south through Beloit, Janesville, and Rockford (IL) to the Mississippi. Wisconsin's capital at Madison isn't on the river but is included in this region.

Landscape: Irregular plains and open hills. Vegetation is intermingled prairie, groves, and strips of deciduous trees commonly found near streams and on north facing slopes.

Climate: Prairie, typical of interior North America with its wide annual temperature range and frequent short periods of temperature changes. Summer temperatures average 68°F, winter ones 20°F, with occasional outbreaks of arctic air. Much of the precipitation falls between May and September. Lighter winter precipitation falls over a longer period of time. The average growing season is 175 days, from the end of April to mid-October.

			92
			97
			176
90°			15
32°			148
0°			18
			141
			59
			42

	High °F	Low °F	Hum %	Wind mph	Precip inches	Snow inches
JAN	26	9	75	10.6	1.2	9.1
FEB	31	13	73	10.5	1.1	6.7
MAR	43	24	72	11.5	2.3	7.4
APR	58	36	68	11.7	3.2	1.6
MAY	70	46	67	10.3	3.3	0.0
JUN	80	56	68	9.3	4.0	0.0
JUL	83	61	72	8.1	3.8	0.0
AUG	81	59	75	7.9	4.1	0.0
SEP	73	50	75	8.6	3.7	0.0
OCT	62	39	72	9.5	2.5	0.1
NOV	45	28	76	10.7	2.4	2.9
DEC	31	15	78	10.4	1.9	9.3

Sacramento Valley

Location: Lies to the north of the San Joaquin-Sacramento River Delta in central California. It encompasses greater Sacramento, the capital, and three other metro areas.

Landscape: Flat or irregular plains and low mountains. Native trees include white oak and Bishop Pine. Steep slopes are covered with chaparral. Native grasses have disappeared.

Climate: Mediterranean. Mountains shelter the area from storms and violent weather. Northerly winds sometimes reach the valley over the Siskiyou Mountains, bringing bring heavy rains in winter or increased heat in summer. Summers are sunny and hot, but with low humidity. Winters are short and mild. Snow is rare, though the Sierra Nevada snowfields east of here provide the region's water. The first frost comes soon after Thanksgiving; the latest is around March 1.

			182
			77
			107
90°			88
32°			24
0°			0
			95
			35
			4

	High °F	Low °F	Hum %	Wind mph	Precip inches	Snow inches
JAN	54	36	75	6.7	4.8	0.2
FEB	61	40	69	7.3	3.6	0.1
MAR	64	42	68	8.2	3.5	0.1
APR	72	46	61	8.0	1.6	0.0
MAY	81	52	55	8.6	0.6	0.1
JUN	89	58	50	8.9	0.3	0.0
JUL	95	61	46	8.3	0.1	0.0
AUG	94	60	48	7.7	0.2	0.0
SEP	88	56	49	7.0	0.6	0.0
OCT	78	49	56	6.4	1.6	0.0
NOV	63	42	68	6.2	3.9	0.0
DEC	54	36	75	6.8	3.8	0.6

Saginaw Bay

Location: On Lake Huron, this bay is the crook between "The Thumb" and the rest of Michigan's Lower Peninsula.

Landscape: Flat and irregular plains. Stands of white oak, red oak, black oak, bitternut hickory, and shagbark hickory trees form a mosaic pattern with prairie. The understory is flowering dogwood.

Climate: Hot Continental. In spring, the cooling effect of Lake Huron retards the growth of vegetation until the danger of frost is past. In the fall, the warming effect holds off frost until the crops have matured. Summer days are warm and pleasant, with cooler nights. Winters are snowy and cold, but extremely cold temperatures or prolonged cold spells are rare because of the warm lake breeze.

			66
			105
			195
90°			10
32°			144
0°			10
			143
			61
			33

	High °F	Low °F	Hum %	Wind mph	Precip inches	Snow inches
JAN	28	14	75	11.8	1.4	11.1
FEB	31	16	73	11.2	1.2	8.3
MAR	42	25	70	11.9	2.2	7.2
APR	56	36	67	11.5	2.9	1.8
MAY	69	46	66	10.1	2.7	0.0
JUN	78	55	68	9.1	3.0	0.0
JUL	82	60	70	8.2	2.4	0.0
AUG	80	58	73	7.8	3.4	0.0
SEP	72	51	75	8.8	3.8	0.0
OCT	60	41	72	9.8	2.4	0.3
NOV	46	32	75	11.2	2.5	3.3
DEC	33	21	77	11.3	2.2	9.0

San Joaquin Basin

Location: This region is the southern section of California's Central Valley from Stockton (San Joaquin County) south some 250 miles to Bakersfield (Kern County).

Landscape: Plains with hills and low mountains. The Central Valley was once dominated by natural grasses that farming and fire have eliminated except in a few remaining stands. These stands suggest that the dominants were bunch grasses on lands similar in appearance to mixed prairie.

Climate: Mediterranean, warm and semiarid. Almost all of the precipitation falls between October and April, which is typical of southern California. Thunderstorms and snow are rare in the valley. Summers are hot, cloudless, dry, and occasionally relieved by ocean breezes from the west. Winters are mild. The first freeze comes around Thanksgiving; the last is an early February 18.

	193
	75
	98
90°	98
32°	25
0°	0
	92
	26
	5

	High °F	Low °F	Hum %	Wind mph	Precip inches	Snow inches
JAN	54	37	79	5.6	1.9	0.1
FEB	62	40	72	6.0	1.8	0.0
MAR	67	43	66	6.9	1.8	0.0
APR	74	47	57	7.6	1.0	0.0
MAY	83	52	49	8.4	0.3	0.0
JUN	91	58	44	8.5	0.1	0.0
JUL	96	62	42	7.6	0.0	0.0
AUG	94	61	45	7.0	0.0	0.0
SEP	89	57	49	6.4	0.2	0.0
OCT	80	50	56	5.5	0.6	0.0
NOV	65	42	69	5.0	1.6	0.0
DEC	54	36	79	5.2	1.5	0.0

South Carolina Midlands

Location: This region's name was created by television outlets in Columbia, the state capital, to attract viewers outside greater Columbia. It contains the center band of South Carolina counties from the Atlantic Ocean west to Georgia.

Landscape: Smooth and irregular plains with open low hills. Common trees include evergreen oaks and members of the laurel and magnolia families. Sandy uplands have forests of loblolly and slash pine. Bald Cypress is a dominant tree in swamps.

Climate: Subtropical. Although the Appalachians shield the area from northern cold fronts in winter, they offer little moderating effect on summer heat. Summers are long and hot, with high temperatures from May to September. Temperatures will surpass 100°F an average of six times a year. Winters are mild, only about a third of the days have freezing temperatures. Snow accumulation is rare. Spring is changeable and may bring some violent weather. Fall is cool, pleasant, and sunny.

	114
	105
	148
90°	71
32°	54
0°	0
	176
	71
	51

	High °F	Low °F	Hum %	Wind mph	Precip inches	Snow inches
JAN	55	32	69	7.1	4.0	0.4
FEB	59	35	65	7.7	3.8	1.0
MAR	68	43	66	8.2	4.5	0.3
APR	76	50	64	8.1	3.1	0.0
MAY	83	58	69	6.9	3.7	0.0
JUN	89	66	70	6.5	4.8	0.0
JUL	91	70	72	6.2	5.2	0.0
AUG	90	69	75	5.7	5.2	0.0
SEP	85	63	74	5.9	3.4	0.0
OCT	76	51	71	6.0	2.8	0.0
NOV	68	42	69	6.3	2.7	0.0
DEC	59	35	69	6.7	3.4	0.2

South Central Arizona

Location: Maricopa and Pinal counties (greater Phoenix) make this official Arizona climate region the most populous in the state. Boosters call it the Valley of the Sun. Sprawl extends deep into the dry mountains and south along I-10 toward Tucson.

Landscape: Plains with low and open high mountains. Desert vegetation is usually very sparse. Cacti and thorny shrubs are conspicuous. Mesquite is less widespread and grows only along washes and watercourses.

Climate: Desert, with low annual rainfall and humidity. Daytime temperatures are high throughout the summer. Many days exceed 100°F in the afternoon and remain above 85°F all night. Winters are mild, but nighttime temperatures frequently drop below freezing from the beginning of December through mid-February. Most days are clear and sunny, and the valley floor is generally free of wind except during the thunderstorm season in July and August.

	211
	85
	70
90°	167
32°	10
0°	0
	6
	14
	23

	High °F	Low °F	Hum %	Wind mph	Precip inches	Snow inches
JAN	66	41	50	5.3	0.7	0.0
FEB	71	45	44	5.9	0.7	0.0
MAR	76	49	41	6.7	0.9	0.0
APR	85	55	30	6.9	0.2	0.0
MAY	94	64	24	7.0	0.1	0.0
JUN	104	73	22	6.8	0.1	0.0
JUL	106	81	32	7.1	0.8	0.0
AUG	104	79	37	6.6	1.0	0.0
SEP	98	73	36	6.3	0.9	0.0
OCT	88	61	36	5.8	0.6	0.0
NOV	75	49	42	5.3	0.7	0.0
DEC	66	42	51	5.1	1.0	0.0

Climate Divisions (R-So)

South Central Florida

Location: Florida state climatologists define this region as a 70-mile wide band from the Atlantic across the state to the Gulf, just above the Gold Coast and the Everglades, taking in Orlando and Tampa and several smaller metro areas along the way.

Landscape: Flat plains. Common trees include evergreen oaks and members of the laurel and magnolia families. Sandy uplands have forests of loblolly and slash pine. Bald Cypress is a dominant tree in swamps. Sometimes the trees are festooned with Spanish moss.

Climate: Subtropical, with high year-round relative humidity near 90 percent at night and dipping to 50 percent in the afternoon. The rainy season extends from June through September; afternoon thundershowers occur daily. Rain is light during the winter, and snow and sleet are rare. Winter temperatures may drop to freezing at night, but days are clear and dry, with brilliant sunshine.

		95
		147
		124
90°		81
32°		2
0°		0
		100
		71
		81

	High °F	Low °F	Hum %	Wind mph	Precip inches	Snow inches
JAN	72	50	73	8.6	2.1	0.0
FEB	73	52	71	9.2	2.9	0.0
MAR	78	57	71	9.6	3.0	0.0
APR	82	61	68	9.3	1.6	0.0
MAY	87	67	69	8.8	3.9	0.0
JUN	90	71	74	7.8	6.6	0.0
JUL	91	73	75	7.0	6.4	0.0
AUG	91	73	77	6.7	6.7	0.0
SEP	89	72	76	7.6	6.5	0.0
OCT	84	66	74	8.6	3.5	0.0
NOV	79	59	74	8.8	2.4	0.0
DEC	74	53	73	8.2	2.1	0.0

South Central Indiana

Location: This region takes in two metro areas - Bloomington and Columbus - on opposite sides of the Hoosier National Forest about midway between Indianapolis and Louisville.

Landscape: Irregular plains and open hills. Vegetation is intermingled prairie, groves, and strips of deciduous trees.

Climate: Hot Continental. Summers are warm and humid with frequent thundershowers. This region is on the border between cold air from the Great Lakes and warm moist air from the Gulf of Mexico, creating periods of wet, unstable weather. The first freeze arrives in mid-October and the last freeze departs in late April.

		92
		99
		176
90°		28
32°		121
0°		8
		133
		70
		47

	High °F	Low °F	Hum %	Wind mph	Precip inches	Snow inches
JAN	36	18	75	11.0	2.4	5.8
FEB	41	21	75	11.0	2.6	5.3
MAR	52	31	72	11.9	4.1	3.4
APR	64	42	68	11.5	4.0	0.3
MAY	74	51	68	9.8	4.7	0.0
JUN	82	61	69	8.7	3.1	0.0
JUL	86	65	73	7.7	4.7	0.0
AUG	84	62	76	7.4	3.8	0.0
SEP	78	55	74	8.2	2.9	0.0
OCT	67	43	71	9.1	2.8	0.1
NOV	54	34	75	10.7	3.5	1.6
DEC	41	24	78	10.7	3.4	3.8

South Central Kansas

Location: This region above the Oklahoma line lies across Interstate Highway 35, the middle route running between Canada and Mexico. The region's enter is Wichita, the largest city in Kansas.

Landscape: Smooth and irregular plains, open hills. Vegetation is intermingled prairie, groves, and strips of deciduous trees commonly found near streams and on north facing slopes.

Climate: Prairie, lying in the path of warm, moist air from the Gulf of Mexico and cold, dry air from the Polar Regions. The average freeze-free growing season is from April 15 to October 24. Winds are generally from the south. Summers can be hot, with more than 60 days over 90°F normally recorded during that time. Winters are mild, and snowfalls are light, averaging 16 inches a year. Thunderstorms occur mainly during the spring and early summer. They can be severe and cause damage from heavy rain, large hail, strong winds, and tornadoes.

		128
		97
		140
90°		62
32°		114
0°		2
		90
		48
		54

	High °F	Low °F	Hum %	Wind mph	Precip inches	Snow inches
JAN	40	19	71	12.1	0.8	4.6
FEB	46	24	70	12.6	1.0	4.2
MAR	57	34	66	14.1	2.4	2.4
APR	68	45	66	14.0	2.4	0.3
MAY	77	54	70	12.4	3.8	0.0
JUN	87	65	68	12.1	4.3	0.0
JUL	93	70	64	11.4	3.1	0.0
AUG	91	68	65	11.1	3.0	0.0
SEP	81	59	68	11.6	3.5	0.0
OCT	71	47	67	11.9	2.2	0.0
NOV	55	34	69	12.2	1.6	1.3
DEC	43	23	71	12.0	1.2	3.3

South Central Montana

Location: Centered on metropolitan Billings at the mid-point of Montana's 550-mile long stretch of Interstate Highway 90. Just south is the Crow Indian Reservation, the Bighorn Mountains and Wyoming.

Landscape: Open high hills and high mountains with evergreen slopes are visible to the west. The setting east is a shortgrass prairie. There are scattered trees and sagebrush and rabbitbrush. Because ground cover is scarce, much soil is exposed.

Climate: Temperate Steppe. Winters are usually dry and cold, but heavy snows occur anytime, especially in spring or fall when the temperatures drop unexpectedly and sometimes lead to Blizzards. Severe cold spells are sometimes relieved by the Chinook winds moving down the Yellowstone Valley bringing warm Pacific air. Springs are changeable, cloudy, and cool. Summers are mild, dry, and sunny, with cool to cold nights.

	89
	112
	164
90°	29
32°	150
0°	18
	48
	29
	27

	High °F	Low °F	Hum %	Wind mph	Precip inches	Snow inches
JAN	32	14	60	13.0	0.9	9.1
FEB	39	19	59	12.2	0.6	7.8
MAR	46	25	57	11.4	1.2	10.1
APR	57	34	55	11.5	1.7	7.9
MAY	67	43	56	10.7	2.6	1.5
JUN	78	52	55	10.1	2.0	0.0
JUL	87	58	48	9.5	0.9	0.0
AUG	85	57	46	9.5	1.0	0.0
SEP	72	47	51	10.2	1.4	1.1
OCT	61	38	52	11.0	1.1	3.7
NOV	45	26	59	12.1	0.8	6.8
DEC	34	17	60	13.1	0.8	8.5

South Central Oregon

Location: This region is centered on Bend, one of the fastest-growing metro areas in the country. West of here are the Cascades and Ponderosa Pine and Douglas-fir logging country, and east of here is the high desert plateau.

Landscape: Open high mountains. Principal trees are western red cedar, western hemlock, and Douglas-fir. In interior valleys are deciduous trees.

Climate: Temperate Desert. The Cascades restrain summer temperatures and also block moisture-laden Pacific winds. Rains are light, with only a rare rainfall of an inch or more. The average growing season is only 82 days, with frost coming as early as late August and departing as late as the following July. Moderate days and cool nights characterize temperatures here. The area is famous for its Indian Summer.

	130
	90
	145
90°	13
32°	196
0°	4
	49
	27
	24

	High °F	Low °F	Hum %	Wind mph	Precip inches	Snow inches
JAN	42	22	77	4.1	1.8	12.3
FEB	46	25	71	4.5	1.0	4.7
MAR	51	26	59	5.3	0.9	5.6
APR	58	29	53	5.7	0.6	2.3
MAY	65	35	51	5.7	0.8	0.4
JUN	74	41	51	5.9	0.9	0.0
JUL	81	45	47	5.8	0.5	0.0
AUG	81	45	50	5.3	0.6	0.0
SEP	73	38	55	4.5	0.5	0.0
OCT	63	32	62	3.7	0.6	0.2
NOV	48	27	74	3.6	1.6	5.3
DEC	42	22	80	3.6	2.0	9.4

South Central Texas

Location: This 75-mile long region along I-35 is anchored by San Antonio on the south and Austin on the north and includes part of the famous Texas Hill Country.

Landscape: Tablelands with open high hills. In much of this area, mesquite and juniper grow in open stands among the grasses.

Climate: Steppe. Summers are hot although night temperatures usually drop to the 70's. Winters are mild, with few days below-freezing. Prevailing winds are southerly, but strong northers bring cold snaps rarely lasting more than a few days. Precipitation is well distributed, though heaviest in late spring with a secondary peak in September. Summer produces thunderstorms while rains in winter are slow and steady. Snowfall is inconsequential and destructive weather is infrequent.

	111
	116
	138
90°	109
32°	22
0°	0
	115
	47
	39

	High °F	Low °F	Hum %	Wind mph	Precip inches	Snow inches
JAN	60	38	70	9.3	1.7	0.5
FEB	65	42	68	9.8	2.0	0.3
MAR	73	50	65	10.5	1.7	0.0
APR	80	59	69	10.3	2.5	0.0
MAY	85	66	73	9.7	4.5	0.0
JUN	91	72	71	9.5	3.8	0.0
JUL	95	74	68	8.7	2.1	0.0
AUG	95	74	67	8.1	2.3	0.0
SEP	90	70	69	8.1	3.4	0.0
OCT	82	59	68	8.2	3.3	0.0
NOV	72	49	68	8.8	2.5	0.1
DEC	63	41	69	8.8	1.7	0.0

South Dakota Black Hills

Location: The Black Hills are a small, isolated range of mountains in western South Dakota. Rapid City dominates this sparsely-settled region.

Landscape: Tablelands with low mountains with evergreen slopes. The setting east is a typical a shortgrass prairie. There are scattered trees and sagebrush and rabbitbrush. Because ground cover is scarce, much soil is exposed to wind erosion.

Climate: Temperate Steppe. Greatly affected by mountains, there are large daily and seasonal temperature ranges. In the lee of the Black Hills, storms are deflected from Rapid City making winters here among the warmest in South Dakota. Snowfall is light, averaging 40 inches annually. Spring temperatures vary widely. Summer days are warm; nights are cool.

	111
	115
	139
90°	32
32°	169
0°	25
	40
	60
	40

	High °F	Low °F	Hum %	Wind mph	Precip inches	Snow inches
JAN	34	11	66	10.8	0.4	8.0
FEB	38	15	67	11.1	0.5	8.0
MAR	46	22	64	12.7	1.0	7.8
APR	58	32	60	13.3	1.9	6.1
MAY	68	42	61	12.4	2.7	0.8
JUN	78	52	63	10.9	3.1	0.1
JUL	86	58	57	10.2	2.0	0.0
AUG	85	56	54	10.3	1.7	0.0
SEP	74	46	53	11.0	1.2	0.1
OCT	63	35	56	11.2	1.1	1.6
NOV	47	23	64	10.9	0.6	5.1
DEC	36	13	67	10.6	0.5	5.1

Southeast Arizona

Location: This official Arizona climate region takes in Graham, Pima (metro Tucson), and Santa Cruz counties in the Sonora Desert just above the Mexican border. New Mexico is immediately east.

Landscape: Plains with high mountains. Vegetation is usually very sparse; cacti and thorny shrubs are conspicuous. Mesquite is less widespread and grows only along washes and watercourses.

Climate: Desert. A long, hot season starts in April and lasts until October. High temperatures are modified by low humidity. July and August can be unpleasant. Clear skies or thin, high clouds permit intense surface heating during the day and active radiational cooling at night. Temperatures below freezing are rare, as is snowfall. The freeze-free growing season lasts from mid-February to the beginning of December. Summer is the rainy season with active thunderstorms, filling the normally dry Cruz River.

	194
	90
	81
90°	140
32°	18
0°	0
	3
	12
	42

	High °F	Low °F	Hum %	Wind mph	Precip inches	Snow inches
JAN	64	39	48	7.9	0.9	0.3
FEB	68	41	43	8.1	0.7	0.2
MAR	73	45	39	8.5	0.7	0.3
APR	81	50	29	8.9	0.3	0.1
MAY	90	58	24	8.8	0.2	0.0
JUN	100	68	23	8.7	0.2	0.0
JUL	99	74	43	8.4	2.4	0.0
AUG	97	72	49	7.9	2.2	0.0
SEP	93	68	41	8.3	1.7	0.0
OCT	84	57	39	8.2	1.1	0.0
NOV	73	46	41	8.1	0.7	0.1
DEC	64	40	49	7.8	1.1	0.3

Southeast Michigan

Location: Centered on Metro Detroit, this ten-county area is where most of the state's residents, businesses, and industries are found.

Landscape: Flat, smooth, and irregular plains. Vegetation is intermingled prairie, groves, and strips of deciduous trees commonly found near streams and on north facing slopes.

Climate: Hot Continental. Winter cold is modified by the Great Lakes, warming and moistening the arctic air that passes over the northern Plains. As a result the area is quite cloudy, especially from December through March. Summers in the city are warm and sunny. Brief showers can occur every few days but often fall on only part of the city. Winter storms may bring rain, snow, or both. Freezing rain and sleet are common. The first freeze is around October 22, and the last is late April.

	75
	106
	185
90°	12
32°	138
0°	7
	157
	66
	33

	High °F	Low °F	Hum %	Wind mph	Precip inches	Snow inches
JAN	30	16	75	11.6	1.7	11.5
FEB	33	18	72	11.3	1.7	8.4
MAR	44	27	70	11.6	2.5	6.8
APR	57	37	67	11.4	3.0	1.6
MAY	69	48	66	10.0	2.9	0.0
JUN	79	57	67	9.1	3.5	0.0
JUL	83	62	69	8.2	3.1	0.0
AUG	81	60	72	8.0	3.3	0.0
SEP	74	53	73	8.5	3.0	0.0
OCT	61	42	71	9.6	2.1	0.2
NOV	48	33	74	11.0	2.7	3.6
DEC	35	22	77	11.3	2.8	10.8

Southern Georgia

Location: This region surrounding Valdosta and Albany lies just above the Florida border. The area's rivers are prone to flooding after extended periods of rain.

Landscape: Flat, smooth and irregular plains. Common trees include evergreen oaks and members of the laurel and magnolia families. Sandy uplands have forests of loblolly and slash pine. Bald Cypress is a dominant tree in swamps.

Climate: Subtropical. Summers are very warm and humid. Like Florida, afternoon thunderstorms here are predictable and welcome. The first freeze is late in the year - early December. Winters are short, cloudy, and somewhat rainy. The last frosts depart six weeks after they first occur.

	106
	117
	143
90°	91
32°	37
0°	0
	190
	73
	69

	High °F	Low °F	Hum %	Wind mph	Precip inches	Snow inches
JAN	61	36	73	7.1	5.0	0.1
FEB	65	39	70	7.6	4.9	0.2
MAR	72	46	70	7.8	5.2	0.0
APR	80	52	68	7.1	3.7	0.0
MAY	86	60	69	6.5	4.1	0.0
JUN	91	67	71	5.9	5.3	0.0
JUL	92	70	76	5.5	6.0	0.0
AUG	91	70	77	5.3	4.7	0.0
SEP	88	65	75	6.2	3.5	0.0
OCT	81	54	72	6.3	2.1	0.0
NOV	72	45	72	6.4	3.1	0.0
DEC	64	39	73	6.6	4.1	0.0

Southern Nevada

Location: Nevada state climatologists may eventually call this region what locals call it: The Las Vegas Valley. It refers to the southernmost part of the state where California, Arizona, and Nevada meet.

Landscape: Plains with high mountains. Desert vegetation is usually very sparse. Cacti and thorny shrubs are conspicuous. Mesquite is less widespread and grows only along washes and watercourses.

Climate: Desert. Summer humidity is low with maximum temperatures in the 100 degree levels. Nearby mountains contribute to relatively cool nights. Spring and fall are ideal, rarely interrupted by adverse weather conditions. Winters are also mild, with daytime averages of 60°F, clear skies, and warm sunshine. There are few overcast or rainy days.

	211
	82
	72
90°	134
32°	37
0°	0
	4
	13
	13

	High °F	Low °F	Hum %	Wind mph	Precip inches	Snow inches
JAN	57	34	44	7.4	0.5	1.0
FEB	63	39	39	8.6	0.5	0.1
MAR	69	44	34	10.2	0.4	0.0
APR	78	51	26	11.0	0.2	0.0
MAY	88	60	23	11.1	0.3	0.0
JUN	100	69	18	11.1	0.1	0.0
JUL	106	76	22	10.3	0.3	0.0
AUG	103	74	26	9.6	0.5	0.0
SEP	95	66	25	9.0	0.3	0.0
OCT	82	54	28	8.1	0.2	0.0
NOV	67	43	36	7.8	0.4	0.1
DEC	58	34	44	7.3	0.4	0.1

Southside Virginia

Location: To Virginians, this region's name means a broad swath of counties in the southeast and south central part of the Commonwealth, including greater Norfolk-Virginia Beach and Richmond.

Landscape: Flat and irregular plains. Half the trees are typical southern yellow pine. The rest are oak, hickory, sweetgum, blackgum, red maple, and winged elm. Dogwood and numerous woody vines are common.

Climate: Subtropical, with warm, humid summers and generally mild winters. The mountains to the west act as a barrier to cold air in winter; the open waters of the Chesapeake Bay and the Atlantic contribute to mild winters and to humid summers. Coldest weather occurs in late December and in January, with a normal temperature range from 20°F to 50°F. Precipitation is evenly distributed throughout the year, though dry periods do occur in the autumn, when long periods of pleasant, mild weather are most common.

	103
	107
	157
90°	36
32°	70
0°	0
	148
	75
	40

	High °F	Low °F	Hum %	Wind mph	Precip inches	Snow inches
JAN	47	28	68	9.8	3.5	3.8
FEB	49	30	66	10.3	3.3	3.5
MAR	59	38	64	10.8	3.7	1.7
APR	68	46	62	10.4	3.0	0.1
MAY	77	56	67	9.2	3.8	0.0
JUN	84	64	68	8.6	3.7	0.0
JUL	87	69	71	8.0	5.0	0.0
AUG	86	68	73	7.6	4.6	0.0
SEP	80	62	73	8.2	3.6	0.0
OCT	70	50	71	8.7	3.3	0.0
NOV	61	41	68	9.1	3.0	0.2
DEC	51	33	68	9.5	3.2	1.4

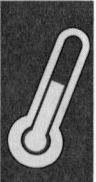

Southwest Ohio

Location: This region is anchored by Cincinnati, the Queen City. The Ohio River flows southwest past the city and on the opposite bank is Kentucky. Just west of the city is the Indiana border.

Landscape: Irregular plains and tablelands with moderate relief. Stands of white oak, red oak, black oak, bitternut hickory, and shagbark hickory trees form a mosaic pattern with prairie. The understory is flowering dogwood.

Climate: Hot Continental, with a twenty degree range in daily temperatures. Winters on the lower Ohio aren't severe, but they are overcast. Heavy snowfalls are uncommon. Summers are warm and humid. Changes in regional weather are frequent due to the passage of numerous cyclonic storms in winter and spring, and thunderstorms during the summer. Fall is the most pleasant season, with the least rainfall of any period, a lot of sunshine, and comfortable temperatures.

	82
	98
	186
90°	23
32°	107
0°	2
	160
	73
	39

	High °F	Low °F	Hum %	Wind mph	Precip inches	Snow inches
JAN	37	20	74	10.7	2.6	6.7
FEB	41	23	71	10.4	2.7	5.5
MAR	53	33	69	11.1	4.2	4.2
APR	64	42	65	10.7	3.8	0.5
MAY	74	52	68	8.7	4.3	0.0
JUN	82	60	69	8.0	3.8	0.0
JUL	86	65	71	7.2	4.2	0.0
AUG	84	63	73	6.8	3.3	0.0
SEP	78	57	73	7.4	2.9	0.0
OCT	66	44	70	8.2	2.9	0.3
NOV	53	35	72	9.7	3.5	2.1
DEC	42	25	75	10.2	3.2	3.9

Tahoe Basin

Location: Climatologists define this as the area surrounding Lake Tahoe, a huge freshwater lake in the Sierra Nevada. Carson City, Nevada's capital, and Reno, its second largest city, are here.

Landscape: Plains with high mountains. Douglas-fir, Ponderosa Pine and grasses grow principally in the basins and ranges.

Climate: Temperate Desert. Sunshine is abundant year round. Temperatures are mild, but the daily range may exceed 45°F. Even when afternoons reach the upper 90s, a light jacket is needed shortly after sunset. Nights with a minimum temperature over 60°F are rare. Afternoon temperatures are moderate, and only about ten days a year fail to reach a level above freezing. The first noted freeze is September 22, the last around Memorial Day. Humidity is low during the summer months and moderately low during winter.

	159
	93
	113
90°	52
32°	189
0°	3
	15
	23
	14

	High °F	Low °F	Hum %	Wind mph	Precip inches	Snow inches
JAN	46	21	65	5.6	1.5	6.4
FEB	52	24	58	6.2	1.3	4.8
MAR	56	29	51	7.8	0.9	4.5
APR	64	33	46	8.3	0.4	1.4
MAY	73	39	46	8.0	0.6	0.9
JUN	82	46	43	7.7	0.4	0.0
JUL	91	51	41	7.1	0.3	0.0
AUG	89	49	42	6.6	0.3	0.0
SEP	80	41	45	5.8	0.4	0.1
OCT	69	33	50	5.4	0.5	0.3
NOV	55	26	58	5.5	1.1	1.9
DEC	46	20	64	5.2	1.3	5.2

Texas Coastal Bend

Location: This Gulf coast region in Texas is centered on greater Corpus Christi. It describes the area where the coast bends directly south and heads for Mexico.

Landscape: Flat and irregular plains. In much of this area, mesquite and juniper grow in open stands among the grasses.

Climate: Subtropical. Tropical storms, usual from June through November, add to the total rainfall. Peak rainfall months are May and September. There is little daily variation in the summer temperature, averaging in the high 80s or low 90s. Sea breezes bring cooler nights, with temperatures dropping into the low 70s.

	95
	120
	152
90°	106
32°	9
0°	0
	146
	47
	39

	High °F	Low °F	Hum %	Wind mph	Precip inches	Snow inches
JAN	64	44	77	11.2	1.9	0.1
FEB	68	47	76	11.9	2.0	0.0
MAR	75	54	73	12.8	1.2	0.0
APR	81	62	76	12.9	2.1	0.0
MAY	86	69	78	11.8	3.9	0.0
JUN	91	73	77	10.7	4.1	0.0
JUL	93	75	75	10.3	2.9	0.0
AUG	94	75	75	9.7	3.2	0.0
SEP	89	71	76	9.5	5.6	0.0
OCT	83	62	74	9.6	3.2	0.0
NOV	75	54	74	10.8	2.0	0.0
DEC	67	47	75	10.9	1.6	0.0

Texas High Plains

Location: This is the southern part of the Great Plains that run from Manitoba all the way south to the beginnings of desert in West Texas. It takes in metro areas on the *Llano Estacado* and the Permian Basin.

Landscape: Smooth and irregular plains with hills. In much of this area, mesquite and juniper grow in open stands among the grasses.

Climate: Steppe. Droughts occur with monotonous frequency. Severe windstorms leave dust in the air several days after the storm has passed. Though summer afternoon temperatures are frequently above 90°F, low humidity and rapid evaporation have a cooling effect. The climate is generally pleasant, with the most disagreeable weather concentrated in late winter and spring. Violent thunderstorms in spring and early summer bring the major precipitation.

	159
	98
	107
90°	91
32°	76
0°	1
	54
	30
	43

	High °F	Low °F	Hum %	Wind mph	Precip inches	Snow inches
JAN	54	27	61	11.4	0.5	2.1
FEB	59	31	60	12.4	0.7	2.0
MAR	68	39	53	13.9	0.9	1.1
APR	77	48	53	13.9	1.1	0.2
MAY	84	57	59	13.3	2.4	0.0
JUN	91	65	61	13.0	2.5	0.0
JUL	94	69	58	11.3	2.1	0.0
AUG	92	67	60	10.4	2.4	0.0
SEP	84	61	65	10.8	2.6	0.0
OCT	76	50	61	11.1	1.8	0.1
NOV	64	38	60	11.4	0.9	1.0
DEC	56	29	60	11.3	0.6	1.3

Trans Pecos

Location: This region, considered synonymous among natives with "West Texas," lies west of the Pecos River and all the way to New Mexico and the Mountain Time Zone. El Paso and nearby Las Cruces, NM, are here.

Landscape: Plains with high mountains. All mountains over 5,000' in Texas are in the Trans Pecos.

Climate: Desert. Dry and sunny, with summer temperatures that are high but not extreme. The low relative humidity lessens the felt heat. The winter is mild, typical of arid areas at low altitudes. The first freeze comes by November 1, and the last by April 11. Rainfall is scarce year-round and fosters only scrub-like desert vegetation. Winter nights can be cold, but the days are warm, averaging in the 50's. Days can be windy, with annoying dust and sandstorms.

	193
	100
	73
90°	96
32°	50
0°	0
	9
	22
	34

	High °F	Low °F	Hum %	Wind mph	Precip inches	Snow inches
JAN	56	24	51	8.3	0.5	1.4
FEB	62	29	42	9.1	0.4	0.8
MAR	69	35	34	11.0	0.3	0.4
APR	78	42	28	11.0	0.2	0.3
MAY	86	51	30	10.3	0.3	0.0
JUN	95	60	32	9.3	0.7	0.0
JUL	96	65	47	8.3	1.7	0.0
AUG	93	63	50	7.7	2.0	0.0
SEP	87	57	51	7.6	1.6	0.0
OCT	78	45	47	7.5	0.8	0.0
NOV	66	33	47	8.0	0.5	0.9
DEC	57	26	52	7.9	0.7	1.7

Treasure Valley

Location: This is a region in extreme southwestern Idaho which includes the five-county Boise Metropolitan Area and Malheur County over the border in Oregon.

Landscape: Tablelands and high mountains. Douglas-fir, Ponderosa Pine and grasses grow principally in the basins and ranges. On the lower slopes is a semi desert.

Climate: Temperate Steppe, with periods of cloudy, stormy, and mild weather almost every winter. The cause is the flow of warm Chinook winds. Summer hot spells rarely last longer than a few days, but temperatures may reach 100°F. Due to the low humidity, the average July evening temperature of 62°F is comfortable. The last freeze arrives around Memorial Day, the first in mid-September. In general, the climate is dry and temperate, with enough variation to be stimulating.

	120
	90
	155
90°	44
32°	124
0°	2
	51
	34
	15

	High °F	Low °F	Hum %	Wind mph	Precip inches	Snow inches
JAN	36	22	76	8.0	1.5	6.8
FEB	44	28	70	8.9	1.1	3.6
MAR	53	32	60	9.9	1.3	1.7
APR	61	37	53	9.9	1.2	0.6
MAY	71	44	52	9.5	1.1	0.1
JUN	81	52	49	9.0	0.8	0.0
JUL	90	58	38	8.4	0.3	0.0
AUG	88	57	38	8.2	0.4	0.0
SEP	77	48	44	8.2	0.8	0.0
OCT	65	39	53	8.3	0.8	0.1
NOV	49	31	69	8.4	1.5	2.2
DEC	38	23	76	8.1	1.4	5.8

Upcountry South Carolina

Location: This is the smallest of three basic South Carolina regions (the others: Lowcountry and Piedmont), and is located in low-rise mountains in the extreme northwestern part of the state. The six counties that make up Greenville, Spartanburg, and Anderson are the heart of Upcountry.

Landscape: Irregular plains, high hills, and low mountains. Half the trees are typical southern yellow pine. The rest are oak, hickory, sweetgum, blackgum, red maple, and winged elm. Dogwood and numerous woody vines are common.

Climate: Hot Continental, with humid hot summers and winters that are generally mild. There are no zero degree days. Nearby mountains protect the area from cold fronts. Rain falls throughout the year with thunderstorms peaking in July and August. Occasional tropical storms and hurricanes from the Atlantic Ocean, beyond the Outer Banks some 100 miles east, may strike this location.

	121
	100
	144
90°	29
32°	68
0°	0
	151
	81
	44

	High °F	Low °F	Hum %	Wind mph	Precip inches	Snow inches
JAN	51	31	66	7.5	4.1	1.0
FEB	56	33	63	8.0	4.4	1.2
MAR	65	41	64	8.2	5.4	0.9
APR	73	48	63	8.0	3.9	0.0
MAY	80	57	69	6.9	4.4	0.0
JUN	86	65	70	6.5	4.8	0.0
JUL	89	69	72	6.0	4.6	0.0
AUG	88	68	75	5.8	4.0	0.0
SEP	82	62	74	6.1	4.0	0.0
OCT	73	50	69	6.6	4.0	0.0
NOV	64	41	68	6.8	3.7	0.0
DEC	54	34	67	7.4	4.1	0.4

Upper Hudson

Location: New York's upper Hudson Valley includes Albany, the capital city, and Glens Falls. It also takes in Pittsfield, 30 miles east over the Massachusetts border.

Landscape: Tablelands and open low mountains. The forests are mixed stands of pine and deciduous species - yellow birch, sugar maple, and American beech.

Climate: Hot Continental. The area sees some moderating influences from the Atlantic Ocean to the south. The first frost arrives at the end of September. Winters are cold and occasionally severe with maximum temperatures not rising above 32°F over long stretches. The last frost occurs mid-May, and during the warmer months, temperatures rise quickly to moderate levels during the day, then plunge to cool at night. Occasional hot spells of a week or more occur during the summer.

	67
	107
	192
90°	6
32°	159
0°	17
	144
	72
	25

	High °F	Low °F	Hum %	Wind mph	Precip inches	Snow inches
JAN	29	9	71	10.1	2.7	16.1
FEB	32	12	68	10.4	2.5	14.6
MAR	43	23	65	10.7	3.0	11.3
APR	56	34	62	10.4	3.3	2.3
MAY	68	44	65	9.0	3.8	0.1
JUN	77	53	69	8.3	3.6	0.0
JUL	82	58	69	7.7	3.4	0.0
AUG	79	56	73	7.2	3.9	0.0
SEP	71	48	75	7.7	3.2	0.0
OCT	60	37	73	8.3	3.1	0.2
NOV	47	29	73	9.5	3.4	3.9
DEC	34	17	73	9.7	3.2	15.3

Upper Tennessee Watershed

Location: This is an area in eastern Tennessee that runs southwest by northeast along the Tennessee River. Visible to the east are the Blue Ridge Mountains.

Landscape: Open hills and low mountains. The valleys support a mixed oak-pine forest. Higher up is an Appalachian oak forest, dominated by white oak and black oak. Chestnut was once abundant, but blight eliminated it as a canopy tree.

Climate: Hot Continental. Though summers are long and hot, the nights are almost always cool, with the average diurnal variation being about 20 degrees. The earliest frost arrives by the end of October. Freezing temperatures are common from December to March but seldom fall to zero or below.

	98
	108
	160
90°	38
32°	77
0°	0
	166
	83
	49

	High °F	Low °F	Hum %	Wind mph	Precip inches	Snow inches
JAN	46	26	72	7.0	4.3	3.6
FEB	52	29	69	7.4	4.2	2.9
MAR	62	37	67	7.9	5.1	1.5
APR	71	45	66	7.6	4.0	0.1
MAY	78	53	71	6.0	4.3	0.0
JUN	85	61	73	5.5	3.8	0.0
JUL	88	65	75	5.1	4.8	0.0
AUG	87	65	76	4.7	3.6	0.0
SEP	82	59	75	5.0	3.7	0.0
OCT	71	46	72	5.1	3.1	0.0
NOV	61	38	71	6.1	3.9	0.5
DEC	50	30	73	6.5	4.5	1.4

Upper Texas Gulf

Location: This region runs from Houston and Galveston Bay some 60 miles east along the Gulf of Mexico to Sabine Pass and the Louisiana border. Lake Charles, LA, is included here.

Landscape: Flat and irregular plains. Common trees include evergreen oaks and members of the laurel and magnolia families. Sandy uplands have forests of loblolly and slash pine. Bald cypress is found in the swamps.

Climate: Subtropical. Temperatures are modified by winds from the Gulf, but the breezes also assure high humidity and mosquito-swatting weather year-round. Summer days are hot and humid, though the evenings are relatively cool. The first freeze is December 6. Winters are mild. Polar air penetrates the area frequently enough to provide some stimulating variety and temperatures occasionally dip below freezing. The last frost is February 16. Destructive storms are infrequent, but heavy thunderstorms and hurricanes do occur.

	95
	115
	155
90°	84
32°	18
0°	0
	186
	67
	69

	High °F	Low °F	Hum %	Wind mph	Precip inches	Snow inches
JAN	61	42	77	9.6	4.3	0.2
FEB	64	45	75	10.1	3.4	0.2
MAR	72	52	75	10.5	3.1	0.0
APR	78	60	75	10.3	3.3	0.0
MAY	84	66	77	9.1	5.5	0.0
JUN	89	72	78	8.1	5.7	0.0
JUL	92	74	78	7.0	5.1	0.0
AUG	92	74	78	6.6	5.1	0.0
SEP	87	70	78	7.5	5.8	0.0
OCT	81	59	74	7.8	4.1	0.0
NOV	72	51	75	9.1	4.4	0.0
DEC	64	44	77	9.3	4.4	0.0

Utah's Dixie

Location: The name of this region, in the extreme southwestern corner of Utah, comes from a failed attempt to grow cotton nearly 150 years ago during the Civil War.

Landscape: Plains with high mountains. At low elevations, several kinds of cactus and yucca are common. The woodland zone is dominated by open stands of two-needle pinyon pine and several species of juniper.

Climate: Steppe. The most striking features are bright sunshine, small annual precipitation, dryness, purity of air, and large daily variations in temperature. Summers are hot and dry. Winters are short and mild, with the Rocky Mountains blocking cold air masses from the north and east. The first frost comes in early November, and the last frost leaves by April 1.

	211
	82
	72
90°	134
32°	37
0°	0
	4
	13
	13

	High °F	Low °F	Hum %	Wind mph	Precip inches	Snow inches
JAN	54	27	44	7.4	1.0	1.6
FEB	61	32	39	8.6	0.9	0.7
MAR	68	38	34	10.2	1.1	0.0
APR	77	44	26	11.0	0.5	0.0
MAY	86	53	23	11.1	0.4	0.0
JUN	97	62	18	11.1	0.2	0.0
JUL	102	69	22	10.3	0.6	0.0
AUG	100	67	26	9.6	0.8	0.0
SEP	93	58	25	9.0	0.5	0.0
OCT	81	46	28	8.1	0.5	0.0
NOV	65	35	36	7.8	0.9	0.0
DEC	54	28	44	7.3	0.7	0.7

Virginia Mountains

Location: This region of western Virginia, from Winchester south along Interstate Highway 81, is bounded by the Blue Ridge mountains to the East and the Allegheny mountains to the West.

Landscape: Low mountains. The mountains contain a typical Appalachian oak forest, dominated by a dozen species each in the white oak and black oak groups. Chestnut was once abundant, but blight eliminated it as a canopy tree.

Climate: Hot Continental. Mountains moderate cold air from the north. The elevation produces cool summer nights. Rain falls throughout the year, with an average of 23 inches in the warm season. Snow falls each winter, with extremes ranging from a trace to 60 inches. The first freeze is October 13; the last is April 26.

	109
	109
	148
90°	31
32°	92
0°	0
	122
	72
	35

	High °F	Low °F	Hum %	Wind mph	Precip inches	Snow inches
JAN	40	20	62	9.1	2.5	6.9
FEB	44	21	61	9.3	2.6	6.5
MAR	54	30	61	9.7	3.2	5.3
APR	64	39	59	9.4	3.2	0.5
MAY	73	48	67	7.7	3.8	0.0
JUN	81	56	69	6.9	3.3	0.0
JUL	84	61	71	6.5	3.8	0.0
AUG	83	59	73	6.2	3.6	0.0
SEP	77	52	73	6.4	3.4	0.0
OCT	66	40	69	7.0	3.5	0.1
NOV	55	32	65	8.1	3.0	1.4
DEC	45	24	64	8.4	2.6	4.4

Virginia's Western Piedmont

Location: Commonwealth climatologists break Virginia's Piedmont in two, and locate this one immediately east of the mountains. Charlottesville, Danville, Lynchburg, and Roanoke are here.

Landscape: Plains with open low mountains. The valleys support a mixed oak-pine forest. Higher up is an Appalachian oak forest, dominated by white oak and black oak. Chestnut was once abundant, but blight eliminated it as a canopy tree.

Climate: Hot Continental, with mild winters and warm, humid summers. The mountains produce various steering and blocking effects on storms and air masses. Chesapeake Bay further modifies the climate, making it warmer in winter, cooler in summer. Precipitation is well distributed throughout the year, with the maximum in July, the minimum in January. First freeze is around November 4, the last around April 7. Tornadoes and violent storms are rare, but severe thunderstorms occur each year.

	107
	110
	149
90°	37
32°	91
0°	0
	122
	73
	36

	High °F	Low °F	Hum %	Wind mph	Precip inches	Snow inches
JAN	44	25	62	9.0	3.0	5.9
FEB	48	27	61	9.2	3.2	5.6
MAR	58	36	61	9.6	3.6	3.6
APR	68	44	59	9.3	3.2	0.3
MAY	77	53	67	7.7	4.2	0.0
JUN	84	61	69	6.9	3.5	0.0
JUL	87	66	71	6.5	4.3	0.0
AUG	86	65	73	6.2	4.1	0.0
SEP	80	58	73	6.5	3.6	0.0
OCT	69	46	69	7.1	3.9	0.0
NOV	59	38	65	8.0	3.3	0.9
DEC	48	29	64	8.3	3.2	2.9

Wasatch Front

Location: This is a north-south chain of urban areas in Utah that embraces more than two-thirds of the state's population and includes the state capital, Salt Lake City. Visible from each area to the east is the Wasatch mountain range.

Landscape: Plains with high mountains. Ponderosa pine dominates on lower, drier, more exposed slopes. After fires the original forest trees are usually succeeded by aspen or lodgepole pine. West, the land is a sagebrush prairie.

Climate: Temperate Steppe. Though not mild, the climate here is modified by the surrounding mountains that deflect stormy weather elsewhere. There are four well-defined seasons, including a long winter. Summers are hot, but the dry air lessens felt heat, and nights are cool. Winters are cold but not severe. Most of the precipitation is snow, with accumulations staying on the ground for most of the winter. Fall is short; spring is longer and sometimes stormy.

	125
	101
	139
90°	58
32°	134
0°	3
	42
	43
	38

	High °F	Low °F	Hum %	Wind mph	Precip inches	Snow inches
JAN	35	18	75	7.5	1.3	13.5
FEB	42	23	69	8.1	1.5	9.9
MAR	51	30	59	9.3	2.0	9.1
APR	61	37	53	9.6	2.1	3.6
MAY	71	45	49	9.5	1.9	0.5
JUN	82	54	43	9.4	1.2	0.0
JUL	91	62	37	9.5	0.8	0.0
AUG	88	60	39	9.7	1.0	0.0
SEP	78	50	45	9.1	1.4	0.1
OCT	65	40	55	8.5	1.7	1.2
NOV	49	30	67	7.9	1.6	5.7
DEC	37	21	75	7.5	1.6	11.9

West Central Kentucky

Location: Mammoth Cave National Park sits between two small metro areas - Bowling Green and Elizabethtown - some 60 miles apart on I-65 just west of Kentucky's center.

Landscape: Open hills. Stands of white oak, red oak, black oak, bitternut hickory, and shagbark hickory trees form a mosaic pattern with prairie. The understory is flowering dogwood.

Climate: Hot Continental, but with features like the subtropical climate to the south. Summers are hot, with frequent tornadoes. Most precipitation takes place during the growing season. Winters can be cold with occasional snow, but the mid-latitude location insures against prolonged severe cold snaps.

	98
	104
	164
90°	43
32°	83
0°	2
	146
	79
	50

	High °F	Low °F	Hum %	Wind mph	Precip inches	Snow inches
JAN	43	23	71	9.4	3.5	4.5
FEB	48	27	70	9.5	4.1	3.2
MAR	59	37	67	10.0	4.8	2.4
APR	70	45	65	9.5	4.3	0.1
MAY	78	54	70	7.8	4.9	0.0
JUN	86	63	71	7.3	3.8	0.0
JUL	89	67	73	6.7	4.6	0.0
AUG	87	65	74	6.3	3.4	0.0
SEP	81	58	74	6.7	3.8	0.0
OCT	71	45	70	7.0	3.0	0.0
NOV	58	37	71	8.6	4.3	0.6
DEC	47	28	72	9.0	4.7	1.4

West Central Ohio

Location: State climatologists place this region against the Indiana border along I-75 from Dayton 65 miles north to Lima.

Landscape: Smooth and irregular plains. Stands of white oak, red oak, black oak, bitternut hickory, and shagbark hickory trees form a mosaic pattern with prairie. The understory is flowering dogwood.

Climate: Hot Continental. Cold, polar air flowing across the Great Lakes causes cloudiness during the winter, accompanied by frequent snow flurries that add little to the total snowfall. Extreme temperatures are usually of short duration in summer or winter. High relative humidity during much of the year causes some discomfort. The first freeze is usually October 8, the last at the beginning of May.

	76
	100
	189
90°	15
32°	132
0°	8
	166
	74
	38

	High °F	Low °F	Hum %	Wind mph	Precip inches	Snow inches
JAN	33	15	74	11.4	2.1	7.4
FEB	37	18	72	11.3	2.0	6.1
MAR	49	28	70	11.8	3.3	5.0
APR	61	38	66	11.3	3.6	0.6
MAY	72	48	66	9.5	4.2	0.0
JUN	81	57	67	8.8	3.8	0.0
JUL	84	62	69	7.9	4.0	0.0
AUG	82	59	72	7.3	3.5	0.0
SEP	76	52	72	8.1	3.0	0.0
OCT	64	40	70	8.9	2.6	0.2
NOV	51	32	74	10.9	3.2	2.0
DEC	38	22	76	11.2	2.9	5.8

West Virginia Metro Valley

Location: This mountainous region lies along I-64 from Huntington, on the Ohio River, inland 45 miles to Charleston, West Virginia's capital.

Landscape: High hills and low mountains. The valleys support a mixed oak-pine forest. Higher up is an Appalachian oak forest, dominated by white oak and black oak. Chestnut was once abundant, but blight eliminated it as a canopy tree.

Climate: Hot Continental, with sharp temperature swings, both seasonal and day-to-day. May through September is generally warm; November through March moderately cold. The last freeze is at the beginning of May, the first at the beginning of October. Cold spells in winter don't last long. Precipitation is evenly distributed throughout the year, with a maximum in July and a minimum in October. Fogs are more frequent in this region than any other in the United States.

	64
	106
	196
90°	21
32°	99
0°	6
	217
	86
	44

	High °F	Low °F	Hum %	Wind mph	Precip inches	Snow inches
JAN	41	23	71	7.5	2.9	9.2
FEB	45	26	69	7.5	3.0	8.0
MAR	57	35	65	8.1	3.7	4.7
APR	67	43	62	7.7	3.4	0.8
MAY	75	52	69	6.1	4.1	0.0
JUN	82	60	72	5.5	3.5	0.0
JUL	85	65	75	5.2	4.8	0.0
AUG	84	64	76	4.8	3.9	0.0
SEP	78	57	75	5.0	3.1	0.0
OCT	68	45	71	5.5	2.9	0.2
NOV	57	37	69	6.8	3.4	1.7
DEC	46	28	71	7.3	3.4	4.5

Western Michigan

Location: Also locally known as West Michigan, this region includes a group of metro areas near the eastern shore of Lake Michigan. The largest city is Grand Rapids.

Landscape: Smooth and irregular plains with hills. Stands of white oak, red oak, black oak, bitternut hickory, and shagbark hickory trees form a mosaic pattern with prairie. The understory is flowering dogwood.

Climate: Hot Continental. Summer days are warm and pleasant, with cooler nights. Winters are snowy and cold, but extremely cold temperatures or prolonged cold spells are rare because of the warm Lake Michigan breeze. The growing season averages 170 days. The date of the last freeze is usually May 10. The first freeze comes on October 17.

	66
	97
	202
90°	13
32°	144
0°	8
	141
	75
	34

	High °F	Low °F	Hum %	Wind mph	Precip inches	Snow inches
JAN	30	16	78	11.6	2.1	24.6
FEB	32	17	75	10.8	1.5	14.0
MAR	43	26	73	11.2	2.5	9.7
APR	57	36	68	11.0	3.3	2.4
MAY	69	46	67	9.7	3.0	0.0
JUN	78	56	68	8.9	3.3	0.0
JUL	82	61	71	8.1	3.1	0.0
AUG	80	59	74	7.8	3.5	0.0
SEP	73	52	76	8.3	4.1	0.0
OCT	61	41	74	9.4	2.9	0.7
NOV	47	32	77	10.6	3.2	7.9
DEC	34	22	80	10.8	3.0	19.5

Climate

Western Montana

Location: The western third of the state's land area. Missoula, in a deep valley surrounded by mountains, predominates. Three major rivers cut through here - the Clark Fork, the Bitterroot, and the Blackfoot.

Landscape: High mountains. In the Bitterroot Range, mountain hemlock is found in high elevations and red cedar and western hemlock are found lower down. Tall Douglas-fir is ubiquitous, along with western white pine, western larch, grand fir, and western ponderosa pine.

Climate: Temperate Steppe. Mountain ranges have a marked effect on the climate. There are about 137 growing days each year, from May 10 to September 20. The summer months are dry with moderate temperatures and cool nights. In winter, the Continental Divide shields the area from severely cold air. On occasion, however, there can be severe blizzard conditions, referred to locally as Hell Gate Blizzards.

	115
	92
	153
90°	21
32°	137
0°	15
	67
	123
	23

	High °F	Low °F	Hum %	Wind mph	Precip inches	Snow inches
JAN	30	14	81	8.0	1.2	12.5
FEB	37	20	77	6.0	0.8	7.7
MAR	46	25	69	7.0	0.9	5.9
APR	57	32	61	8.0	1.0	2.1
MAY	66	39	61	8.0	1.8	0.8
JUN	74	46	61	8.0	1.9	0.0
JUL	84	50	52	8.0	1.0	0.0
AUG	83	49	51	8.0	1.0	0.0
SEP	71	40	60	7.0	1.1	0.0
OCT	57	31	70	7.0	0.8	0.9
NOV	40	24	80	6.0	0.9	5.8
DEC	31	17	83	7.0	1.1	10.6

Western New York

Location: This area takes in the western counties near Lakes Erie and Ontario. It is a both a geographical and colloquial region not to be confused with "upstate New York," any area north of New York City.

Landscape: Tablelands with high hills. The forests are mixed stands of pine and deciduous species - yellow birch, sugar maple, and American beech.

Climate: Hot Continental. Cyclonic systems moving from the interior of the country and passing through the St. Lawrence Valley affect this area. Seasonal and daily changes are marked and invigorating. Winters can be cold and severe with daytime temperatures averaging 35°F, and 18°F overnight. Summer nights generally are cool, but days can be warm and humid. The first freeze is an early October 5, and the last, mid-May. The area is overcast, and the cloudiest months are December, January, and February.

	61
	100
	204
90°	6
32°	135
0°	9
	135
	78
	29

	High °F	Low °F	Hum %	Wind mph	Precip inches	Snow inches
JAN	30	16	74	12.1	2.6	24.0
FEB	32	16	73	11.7	2.4	20.4
MAR	42	26	71	11.6	2.8	14.0
APR	55	36	66	11.2	3.1	3.3
MAY	67	47	66	9.7	3.3	0.2
JUN	76	55	68	9.1	3.7	0.0
JUL	81	61	69	8.7	3.4	0.0
AUG	78	59	73	8.4	3.8	0.0
SEP	71	53	74	8.9	3.8	0.0
OCT	60	42	72	9.8	3.2	0.3
NOV	47	34	74	11.3	3.8	9.3
DEC	35	22	76	11.7	3.5	22.7

Western Slope of Colorado

Location: Coloradoans use this name to describe that part of the state beyond the Rocky Mountains to the western border. The area is drained by the Colorado River and its unofficial capital is Grand Junction.

Landscape: Open high mountains. Ponderosa pine dominates on lower, drier, more exposed slopes, and Douglas-fir is predominant in higher, moister, more sheltered areas. After fires, they are succeeded by aspen or lodgepole pine.

Climate: Temperate Steppe. The interior location plus the ring of high mountains mean low rainfall. Winter snows are frequent but light and do not remain long. Summer humidity is low, making the region as dry as parts of Arizona. Sunny days predominate in all seasons. The area's climate is marked by wide seasonal temperature changes. The first freeze arrives at the end of September; the last comes at the end of May.

	137
	107
	122
90°	62
32°	134
0°	5
	26
	27
	36

	High °F	Low °F	Hum %	Wind mph	Precip inches	Snow inches
JAN	36	15	71	5.7	0.6	7.3
FEB	45	24	61	6.7	0.5	4.2
MAR	56	31	50	8.3	0.9	3.8
APR	66	39	43	9.4	0.8	1.1
MAY	76	48	40	9.6	0.9	0.1
JUN	88	57	32	9.7	0.5	0.0
JUL	94	64	35	9.3	0.6	0.0
AUG	91	62	38	9.1	0.8	0.0
SEP	81	53	39	9.0	0.8	0.1
OCT	68	42	46	7.9	1.0	0.5
NOV	51	29	59	6.8	0.7	2.7
DEC	39	19	69	5.9	0.6	5.3

Willamette Valley-Lower Columbia

Location: This region takes in metro areas in northwest Oregon on the Willamette River as it flows northward from mountains near Eugene to the Columbia River at Portland. Included here is Longview, Washington, upriver on the Columbia some 50 miles from Portland.

Landscape: Low and high mountains. Principal trees are western red cedar, western hemlock, and Douglas-fir. The valley often contains deciduous trees, such as big-leaf maple, Oregon ash, and black cottonwood.

Climate: Marine. A continual windshield-wiper kind of climate in winter, marked by relatively mild temperatures and cloudy skies. Summers are pleasantly mild with northwesterly winds and little precipitation. Fall and spring are transitional. Fog occurs frequently in fall and winter. At all times, incursions of Marine air are a moderating influence. Extremes in winter and summer come from the continental interior.

	73
	78
	214
90°	13
32°	55
0°	0
	90
	94
	37

	High °F	Low °F	Hum %	Wind mph	Precip inches	Snow inches
JAN	46	33	82	8.8	6.5	3.3
FEB	51	35	78	8.3	4.8	0.9
MAR	56	37	74	8.1	4.5	0.7
APR	60	39	72	7.4	2.8	0.0
MAY	67	44	70	7.0	2.1	0.0
JUN	73	50	68	7.0	1.5	0.0
JUL	80	52	64	7.3	0.6	0.0
AUG	81	53	64	6.9	1.1	0.0
SEP	75	49	67	6.5	1.8	0.0
OCT	64	43	76	6.3	3.2	0.0
NOV	52	39	83	7.9	6.7	0.4
DEC	46	34	85	8.5	7.3	1.3

Windsor Locks

Location: Hartford, CT, and Springfield, MA, are some 30 miles apart on the Connecticut River that flows past them to Long Island Sound. Windsor Locks is the location for Bradley International Airport, shared by both cities.

Landscape: Open hills and low mountains. The forests are mixed stands of pine and deciduous species - yellow birch, sugar maple, and American beech.

Climate: Hot Continental. Summers are hot and humid with afternoon showers. There are 10 to 15 days between June and September when afternoon temperatures exceed 90°F. Winters can be cold with icy rain. Snowfall is light, falling a few inches per storm. Occasionally tropical weather systems produce strong winds and heavy rain in the late summer or fall, and coastal low pressure systems will bring a heavy snowfall in winter.

	86
	108
	172
90°	14
32°	143
0°	9
	165
	76
	20

	High °F	Low °F	Hum %	Wind mph	Precip inches	Snow inches
JAN	34	14	65	10.4	3.3	11.8
FEB	37	17	64	10.6	3.1	11.4
MAR	47	27	62	10.7	3.4	9.3
APR	60	36	59	10.5	3.7	1.6
MAY	72	46	60	9.4	4.0	0.1
JUN	80	55	65	8.5	3.8	0.0
JUL	85	61	66	7.9	3.5	0.0
AUG	83	59	69	7.8	3.7	0.0
SEP	75	50	71	8.0	3.6	0.0
OCT	64	40	68	8.6	3.5	0.1
NOV	52	32	69	9.3	3.9	2.0
DEC	38	20	69	9.8	3.8	10.2

Wyoming Lower Platte

Location: Climatologists divide this least populous state into ten climate divisions. The only one with metro areas - Cheyenne and Casper - lies along Interstate Highway 25 in the southeast.

Landscape: Plains with low mountains. Most of the area is a shortgrass prairie. There are scattered trees and sagebrush and rabbitbrush. Because ground cover is scarce, much soil is exposed to wind erosion.

Climate: Temperate Steppe. Dry, thanks to the effective moisture barrier of the Rocky Mountains to the west. Summertime precipitation descends from thunderstorms, which generally provide ample moisture for grasslands. Annual snowfall averages 80 inches, and the winter season can be severe. The dryness of the air prevents discomfort during both the warm summer months and winter cold snaps. This is one of America's windiest climate regions.

	107
	119
	140
90°	19
32°	177
0°	17
	48
	33
	42

	High °F	Low °F	Hum %	Wind mph	Precip inches	Snow inches
JAN	35	14	60	15.9	0.5	8.2
FEB	39	17	59	14.9	0.5	8.1
MAR	45	22	59	14.2	1.0	13.1
APR	55	30	57	13.4	1.5	10.8
MAY	66	39	59	12.1	2.3	3.6
JUN	77	48	56	11.2	1.8	0.3
JUL	85	54	52	10.3	1.7	0.0
AUG	83	52	50	10.4	1.2	0.0
SEP	72	43	51	11.1	1.1	1.0
OCT	60	33	53	12.2	0.9	4.4
NOV	46	23	60	13.9	0.6	9.0
DEC	36	15	61	15.3	0.5	8.5

A CENTURY FORECAST

Hotter, Wetter...then a lot Hotter, Drier

Ice Station Zebra or Hothouse Earth? For most of the 20th century, climate speculation focused on those two long-range scenarios. Today there is general agreement that a frozen future is out of the running, assuming the world stays out of nuclear war. Near term, the likeliest forecast is a 5-9°F warming over the next century according to the U.S. Global Change Research Program. A similar, previous, temperature rise took 10,000 years to achieve, according to researchers. Here are several of the Research Program's big findings.

Increased warming

Thanks to increased use of fossil fuels tripling CO_2 and sulfur dioxide emissions (greenhouse gas), average annual temperatures in the United States will rise 5-9°F over the next 100 years, more than the expected *global* increase. This rise will go hand in hand with more precipitation and faster evaporation of water, leading to more very wet and very dry conditions.

Wintertime warming will be greater than summertime warming, and nighttime warming greater than daytime warming. The eastern half of the country, especially the southeastern part, will be doubly impacted because of the effects of heat combined with humidity. New York's summer days will be like those now seen in Atlanta, those in Atlanta like those in Houston, and those in Houston like those in Panama City.

Uncertainties remain and surprises are expected

Some features of climate change will be completely unexpected as complex systems respond. Animal species dislocations and insect and rodent pest outbreaks are examples. To offer three more conjectures: Dramatic changes in ocean circulation patterns, clearer heat-intense days for Indianapolis, and increased thunderstorms in Washington, DC.

In addition, Canada could become one of the world's richest countries for its surplus of fresh water, energy technology may regain its importance, the southeastern and southwestern United States may share common water and power issues in opposition

to the rest of the country. And there will be no more maple syrup produced; stands of sugar maples will gradually move north of the New England.

Differing regional impacts

Climate change will vary widely across the country. Temperature increases will vary somewhat from one region to the next. Heavy and extreme precipitation events are likely to become more frequent, yet some regions will get drier. The potential impacts of climate change will also vary widely across the nation.

Vulnerable ecosystems

Many ecosystems are highly vulnerable to the projected rate and magnitude of climate change. A few, such as alpine meadows in some areas of the Rocky Mountains and some barrier islands, are likely to disappear entirely. Others, such as forests of the Southeast, are likely to experience major species shifts or break up into a mosaic of grasslands, woodlands, and forests. The goods and services lost through the disappearance or fragmentation of certain ecosystems are likely to be costly or impossible to replace.

Widespread Drought

Lack of water will be an ominous issue in every region. Especially vulnerable: the West, Pacific Northwest, and Alaska because of reduced summer runoff, increased winter runoff, and increased demands. Other issues: floods and water quality.

No Danger to Food Supply

Farming will adapt to climate change. Crop productivity will increase over the next few decades, but gains won't be shared in every region. Falling prices and competitive pressures, while benefiting consumers, are very likely to stress some farmers. Expect farm abandonment in extremely dry areas.

Near-term increase in forest growth

Timber inventories will shift from softwoods to hardwoods and will increase over the next several decades in some areas as trees respond to higher carbon dioxide levels. Over the longer term, changes in larger-scale processes such as fire, insects, droughts, and disease will possibly decrease forest productivity. In addition, climate change is likely to cause permanent shifts in forest species.

Damage to coastal and permafrost areas

Sea level, which has risen from 4 to 8 inches in the last century, will rise another 5 to 37 inches depending on which of the differing forecast models is used. The range is so broad because of uncertainties related to the Antarctic and Greenland ice caps.

Climate change and the resulting rise in sea level are likely to exacerbate threats to buildings, roads, power lines, and other infrastructure in sensitive places. For example, infrastructure damage is related to permafrost melting in Alaska, and to sea-level rise and storm surge in low-lying coastal areas.

Adaptation determines health outcomes

A range of negative health impacts is possible from climate change, but adaptation is likely to help protect much of the U.S. population. Maintaining our nation's public health and community infrastructure, from water treatment systems to emergency shelters, will be important for minimizing the impacts of water-borne diseases, heat stress, air pollution, extreme weather events, and diseases transmitted by insects, ticks, and rodents.

Other stresses magnified by climate change

Climate change will magnify other stresses, such as air and water pollution and habitat destruction due to human development patterns. For some systems, such as coral reefs, the combined effects of climate change and other stresses will bring large, possibly irreversible impacts.

Source: U.S. Global Change Research Program, *Climate Change Impacts on the United States*

THOSE DIGITAL BANK CLOCKS ARE WRONG

Air temperature is one thing, but how temperature really feels is quite another. Most digital readouts seen on the corners of small town Main Streets showing the time and temperature may be low in summer and high in winter, since their internal instruments aren't sophisticated enough to sense wet air or wind speed.

It's not the heat, it's the humidity

Because it intensifies heat, the amount of moisture in the air is a big factor in climatic comfort. Hot days that are also humid aren't comfortable when the body's natural evaporative cooling becomes overloaded.

Moreover, just as warm air is able to hold more moisture, so damp air is able to hold heat better and longer. In hot, humid climates, heat is retained in the damp air even after sundown, producing nights almost as hot as the days. In contrast, drier climates offer greater comfort not only during hot summer days but also at night, which can be cool and sometimes even chilly.

Excessive humidity can aggravate certain types of arthritis and rheumatism and, combined with low temperatures, can have a harmful effect on those suffering from pulmonary diseases. Very moist air also encourages the growth of a wide variety of bacteria and molds, increasing the chances of infection.

Humidity affects hair, too. The range between dry and saturated air produces a 3 percent difference in hair length. In moist air, people with naturally curly hair have the frizzies as hair length increases, while others with long straight hair find it going limp. Hair is such a reliable indicator of humidity that it is the primary element of the hair hygrometer, a meteorological instrument in use from the late 1700s

Heat Index — Apparent Temperature (°F)

Air Temperature (°F)	0%	5%	10%	15%	20%	25%	30%	35%	40%	45%	50%	55%	60%	65%	70%	75%	80%	85%	90%
110	99	102	105	108	112	117	123	130	137	143	150								
105	95	97	100	102	105	109	113	118	123	129	135	142	149						
100	91	93	95	97	99	101	104	107	110	115	120	126	132	138	144				
95	87	88	90	91	93	94	96	98	101	104	107	110	114	119	124	130	136		
90	83	84	85	86	87	88	90	91	93	95	96	98	100	102	106	109	113	117	122
85	78	79	80	81	82	83	84	85	86	87	88	89	90	91	93	95	97	99	102
80	73	74	75	76	77	77	78	79	79	80	81	81	82	83	85	86	86	87	88
75	69	69	70	71	72	72	73	73	74	74	75	75	76	76	77	77	78	78	79
70	64	64	65	65	66	66	67	67	68	68	69	69	70	70	70	70	71	71	71

Relative Humidity (%)

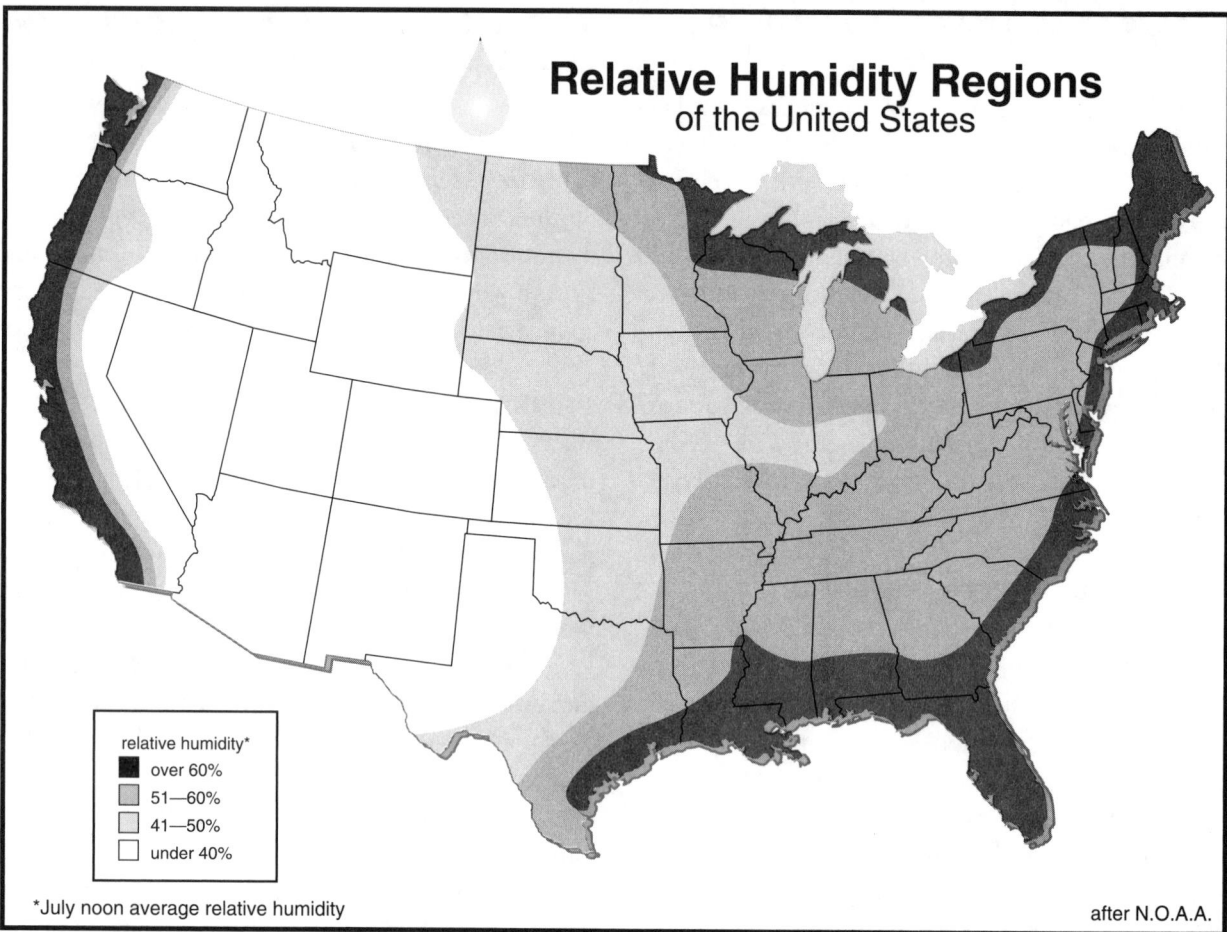

Relative Humidity Regions
of the United States

relative humidity*

- over 60%
- 51—60%
- 41—50%
- under 40%

*July noon average relative humidity

after N.O.A.A.

through the 1960s.

Low humidity brings different consequences. When it drops below 50 percent, most people experience dry nasal passages and perhaps a dry, tickling throat. In the Southwest, many people suffer from nosebleeds, flaking skin, and a chronic sore throat when relative humidity drops to 20 percent.

The table "Heat Index" shows the relationship between relative humidity and temperature. To find the apparent temperature, locate air temperature at the left and relative humidity along the bottom. The intersection of the temperature figure with the humidity figure produces the apparent temperature. For example, air temperature of 85°F feels like 88° at 50 percent humidity and 102° when the humidity is 90 percent.

When the wind kicks up

As long as air temperature is lower than skin temperature, when the wind blows your body loses heat more quickly than if the wind is calm. Each molecule of air that touches exposed skin carries off some body heat. The faster the wind, the more molecules of air come in contact with skin, which in turn gives up heat to each molecule by conduction.

Windchill is a centuries-old concept, but it was first experimentally measured in Antarctica during World War II when two explorers, Charles Passel and Paul Siple, exposed a plastic container of water 33 feet above the ground to varying combinations of wind speed and air temperature and timed how long the water turned to ice. Windchill soon became a popular index heard on local weather reports.

The idea remains controversial. After all, sunshine and exercise warm the body even as it gives up heat from windchill. Also, human bodies shiver while plastic cups of water don't. Moreover, the index assumes the skin is bare, which is unlikely if people dress properly.

In the winter of 2001-02, the United States and Canada introduced a new index based on heat lost from the exposed faces of 12 volunteer soldiers walking on treadmills in a chilled wind tunnel. The new, 'warmer' index is now in use by both the United States and Canadian weather offices and is employed in local weather reports. It is expressed, in temperaturelike units, as to the how the skin feels on a calm day.

566

Windchill

Air Temperature (°F)

Wind Speed (MPH)	40°	35°	30°	25°	20°	15°	10°	5°	0°	-5°	-10°	-15°	-20°	-25°	-30°	-35°	-40°
5	36	31	25	19	13	7	1	-5	-11	-16	-22	-28	-34	-40	-46	-52	-57
10	34	27	21	15	9	3	-4	-10	-16	-22	-28	-35	-41	-47	-53	-59	-66
15	32	25	19	13	6	0	-7	-13	-19	-26	-32	-39	-45	-51	-58	-64	-71
20	30	24	17	11	4	-2	-9	-15	-22	-29	-35	-42	-48	-55	-61	-68	-74
25	29	23	16	9	3	-4	-11	-17	-24	-31	-37	-44	-51	-58	-64	-71	-78
30	28	22	15	8	1	-5	-12	-19	-26	-33	-39	-46	-53	-60	-67	-73	-80
35	28	21	14	7	0	-7	-14	-21	-27	-34	-41	-48	-55	-62	-69	-76	-82
40	27	20	13	6	-1	-8	-15	-22	-29	-36	-43	-50	-57	-64	-71	-78	-84
45	26	19	12	5	-2	-9	-16	-23	-30	-37	-44	-51	-58	-65	-72	-79	-86
50	26	19	12	4	-3	-10	-17	-24	-31	-38	-45	-52	-60	-67	-74	-81	-88
55	25	18	11	4	-3	-11	-18	-25	-32	-39	-46	-54	-61	-68	-75	-82	-89
60	25	17	10	3	-4	-11	-19	-26	-33	-40	-48	-55	-62	-69	-76	-84	-91

Apparent Temperature

The table "Windchill" gives the windchill temperature as a relationship between air temperature and the wind's speed. First locate the air temperature across the top, then the wind speed in the left column. At 0°F, for example, the windchill index in a wind of 20 miles per hour would mean your face would feel as cold as it would on a calm day when the temperature is minus 22°F. When it's 40°F outside and the wind gusts to 35 miles per hour the temperature feels more like 28°F to the face on a calm day.

NATURAL HAZARDS

Perhaps no natural sight was more dramatic on live TV than the eruption of Mount St. Helens in 1980. An internal blast equal to 10 million tons of TNT blew off the topmost 1,300 feet of the mountain. Fortunately, volcanoes usually give warning. Even more fortunately, the places where volcanic activity is a potential hazard are very few.

Other violent natural events are more common and, although less cataclysmic than a volcanic eruption, can cause great damage and threaten lives. Many of these natural hazards follow definite geographic patterns in North America, and some metro areas are at much greater risk than others.

The Sun Belt Is Also a Storm Belt

Most severe storms occur in the southern half of the United States. For this reason, you might say that the Sun Belt is also a storm belt.

• *Thunderstorms and Lightning*. Thunderstorms are common and don't usually cause death. But lightning kills 250 North Americans a year. It remains the most common and frequent natural danger. At any given moment there are about 2,000 thunderstorms in progress around the globe. In the time it takes to read this paragraph, lightning will have struck the earth 700 times.

Florida, the Sunshine State, is actually the country's stormiest state, with three times as much thunder and lightning as any other. California, along with Oregon and Washington, is one of the most storm-free states. In a typical year, coastal California towns will average between two and five thunderstorm episodes. Most American places average between 35 and 50. Fort Myers-Cape Coral, Florida, averages 128. (A thunderstorm episode represents the presence of a single storm cell; a metro area like Fort Myers-Cape Coral can register four or five episodes in a single day.)

The *Place Profiles* earlier in this chapter tell how many thunderstorm days each of America's metro climate regions can expect in an average year. The southeastern quadrant of the country generally receives more rain and thunderstorms than the rest, although the thunderstorms of the Great Plains are awesome spectacles.

• *Tornadoes.* While they are not nearly as large or long-lived as hurricanes and they release far less total force, tornadoes have more destructive and killing power concentrated in a small area than any other storm known. For absolute ferocity and wind speed, a tornado has no rival.

The hallmark of this vicious inland storm is the violently rotating air column that sweeps and bounces along the ground. Inside, pressure drops to less than 90 per cent of normal atmosphere. This vacuum wrecks buildings and sweeps up cars, trains,

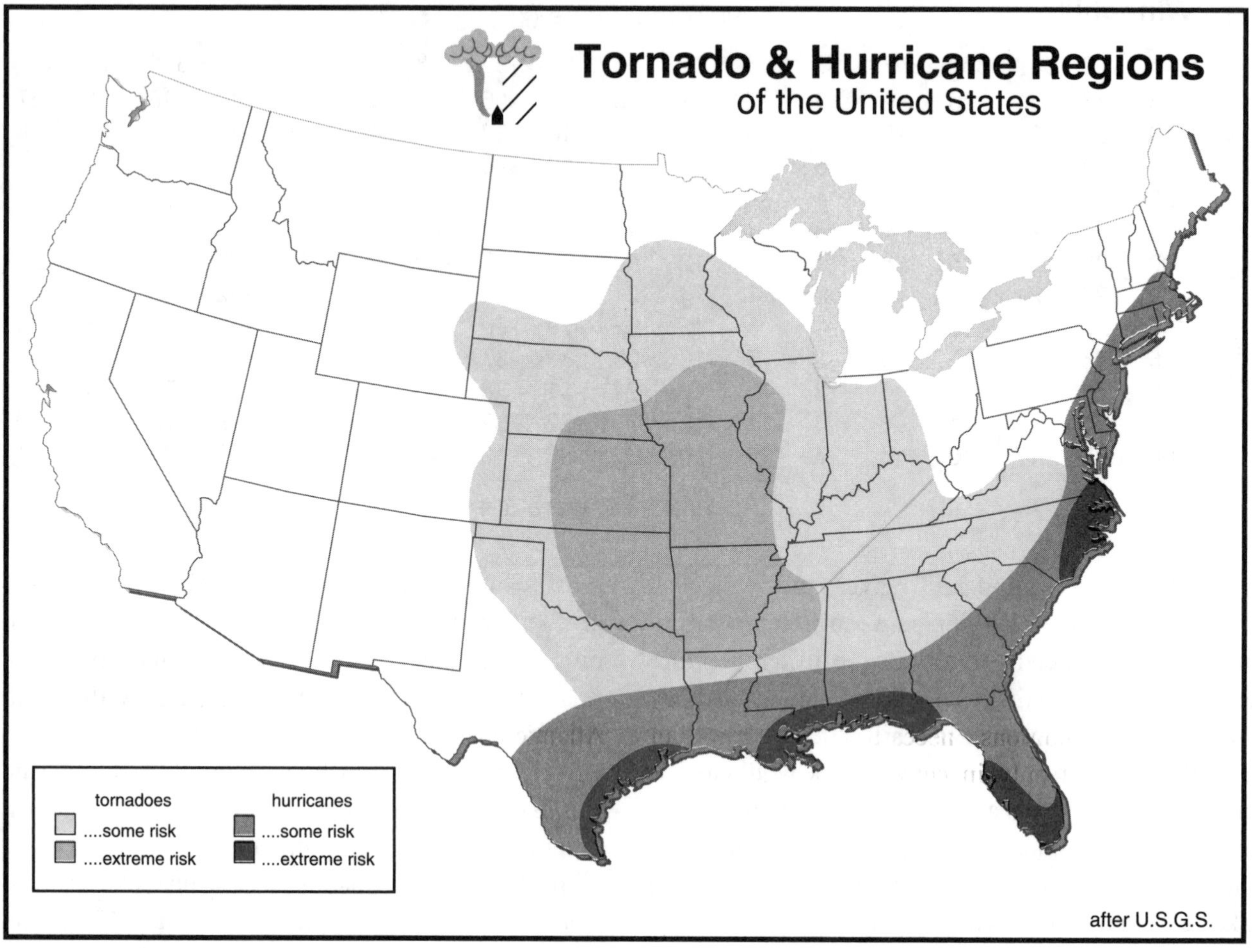

Tornado & Hurricane Regions
of the United States

tornadoes
☐ ....some risk
☐ ....extreme risk

hurricanes
☐ ....some risk
■ ....extreme risk

after U.S.G.S.

livestock, and trees, sucking them up hundreds of feet into a whirling vortex. Wind speeds close to 300 miles per hour have been recorded.

Although no one can tell for certain just where tornadoes might touch down, their season, origin, and direction of travel are predictable. Tornadoes peak in late spring and early summer, and most originate in the central and southern American Great Plains, in Oklahoma, Texas, Arkansas, Kansas, and Missouri.

After forming in intense heat and rising air, the storms proceed northeastward at 25 to 40 miles per hour. Most do not last very long or travel very far. Half travel less than 5 miles, although several have been tracked over 200 miles.

In season, one tornado every 5 days is reported in Canada, compared to five tornadoes every day in the United States. One-third of all tornadoes reported in North America occur in Kansas, Oklahoma, and Texas. Metro areas in Oklahoma, eastern Texas, Arkansas, northern Louisiana and Mississippi, eastern Tennessee, Kansas, Missouri, and parts of Nebraska, Iowa, and Illinois have a high potential for tornado danger. About 70 or 80 hit Canada's populated places

in a typical year, mainly in Ontario. Most are too weak to cause serious damage.

•   *Hurricanes.* Giant tropical cyclonic storms starting up at sea, hurricanes are unmatched for sheer power over a very large area. They last for days, measure hundreds of miles across, and release tremendous energy in the form of high winds, torrential rains, lightning, and tidal surges. They usually occur from June through November and strike the Gulf and southern Atlantic Coast, though they will also strike locations farther north. Like thunderstorms, hurricanes are much less frequent and less severe on the Pacific Coast.

Hurricanes usually originate in the tropical waters of the Atlantic Ocean. Most occur toward summer's end because it takes that long for the water temperature and evaporation rate to rise sufficiently to begin the spiraling, counterclockwise rotation of wind around a low pressure system. When the winds are less than 39 miles per hour, the cyclone is a tropical depression; when winds speed up to between 39 and 74 miles per hour, the cyclone becomes a tropical storm. And when the winds reach 75 miles per hour,

the storm becomes a hurricane.

Often the greatest danger and destruction from hurricanes aren't winds but tidal surges that sweep ashore with seas 15 or more feet higher than normal high tides. Although Florida and the southern coasts are most vulnerable to hurricanes, locations as far north as Cape Cod and Maine are not immune.

Earthquake Risks

The cause of an earthquake is the pressure building between two contiguous masses of rock - called tectonic plates - that move slowly but inexorably toward each other in slightly different directions. When the pressure becomes too great for the rock substance to hold, it shears suddenly. This shearing, along with the consequent shuddering, swaying, and even shifting of immense masses of underground rock, is experienced on the earth's surface as an earthquake.

Those conditions necessary to cause an earthquake exist only in certain areas. The entire area ringing the Pacific Ocean is earthquake prone- from western South America to Central America, to North America's Pacific states and provinces, through Alaska's Aleutian Island chain across to Japan, down through China, and ending in New Zealand. This last area has more earthquakes than any other place in the world.

According to the map "Earthquake Regions of the United States," although much of North America is free from the threat of earthquakes, some areas appear to be resting on powder kegs. (U.S. Geological Survey seismologists warn that the map is experimental and that its predictions cannot be guaranteed.)

• *Northeast.* There is much disagreement among geologists concerning earthquake risk in the northeast. A number of theories about seismic trends have been advanced, and attempts have been made to relate these trends to various fault systems. The best known of these systems is the Boston-Ottawa trend, shown on the map as a continuous area from the Atlantic coast of Massachusetts to the St. Lawrence River valley, encompassing the two cities for which it is named. Most people are unaware that Boston suffered a severe earthquake in the 1700s and that it

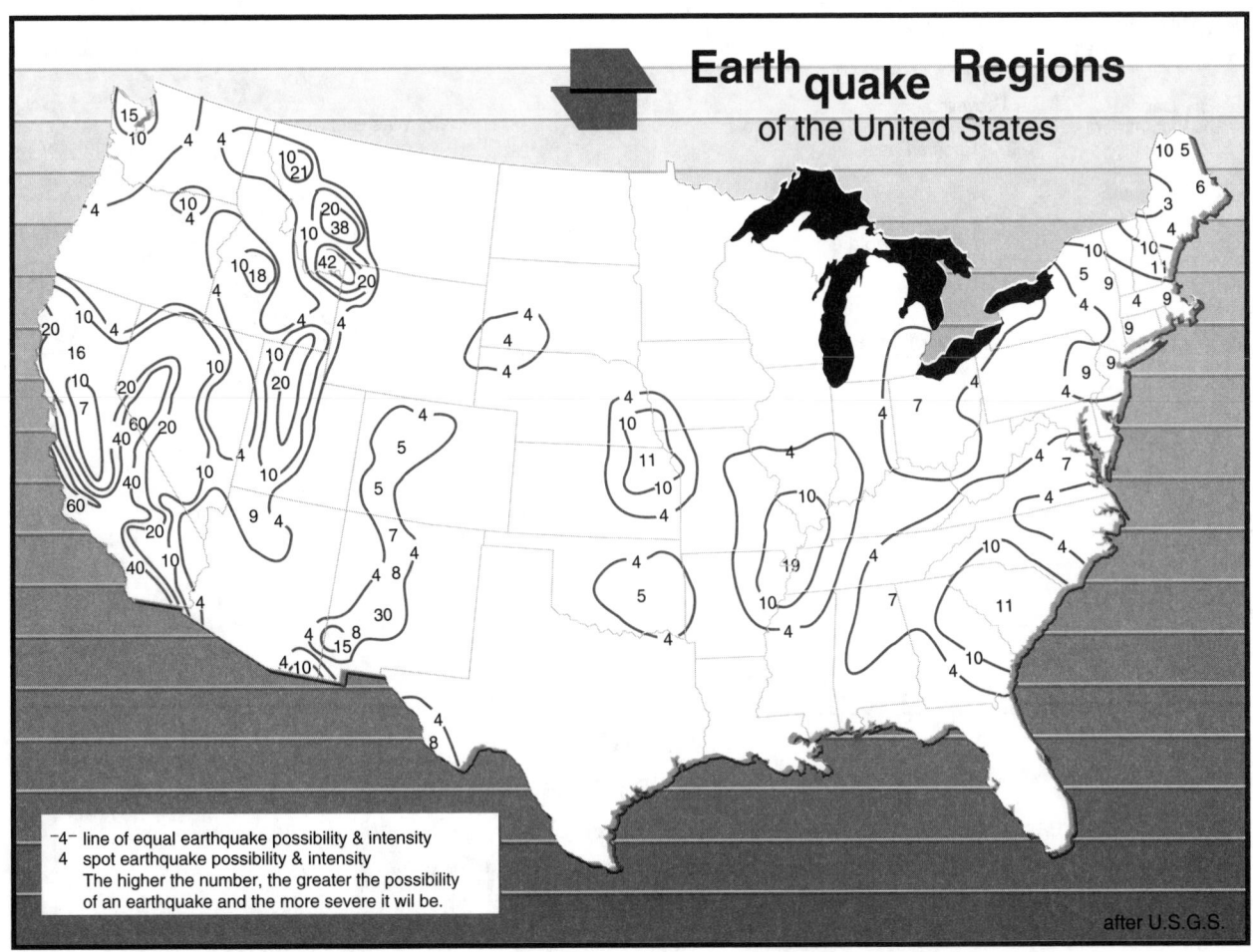

Earthquake Regions
of the United States

-4- line of equal earthquake possibility & intensity
4 spot earthquake possibility & intensity
The higher the number, the greater the possibility of an earthquake and the more severe it wil be.

after U.S.G.S.

remains earthquake-prone today.

• *Southeast.* One theory about earthquake risk is that possible earthquake epicenters - the points of origin of ground tremors - are not randomly distributed but occur in zones. In the southeast, these zones run both parallel to and across the Appalachians. Historically, the greatest shock recorded east of the Mississippi occurred in Charleston, South Carolina, in 1886. The present hazard in South Carolina and eastern Georgia is as high as in the Boston Ottawa trend.

• *Midwest and Rocky Mountains.* The zone of greatest hazard in the Mississippi Valley lies around the side of the cataclysmic series of quakes that occurred near New Madrid, Missouri. The biggest city in this zone is Memphis. The risk of seismic activity is greater in the Rocky Mountains region. The three biggest mountain citiesDenver, Albuquerque, and Salt Lake City-all lie within risk zones.

• *Pacific Northwest.* The Puget Sound area near Seattle has experienced three major shocks within the past 40 years, causing considerable damage. In 1964, an earthquake in Anchorage registered 8.4 on

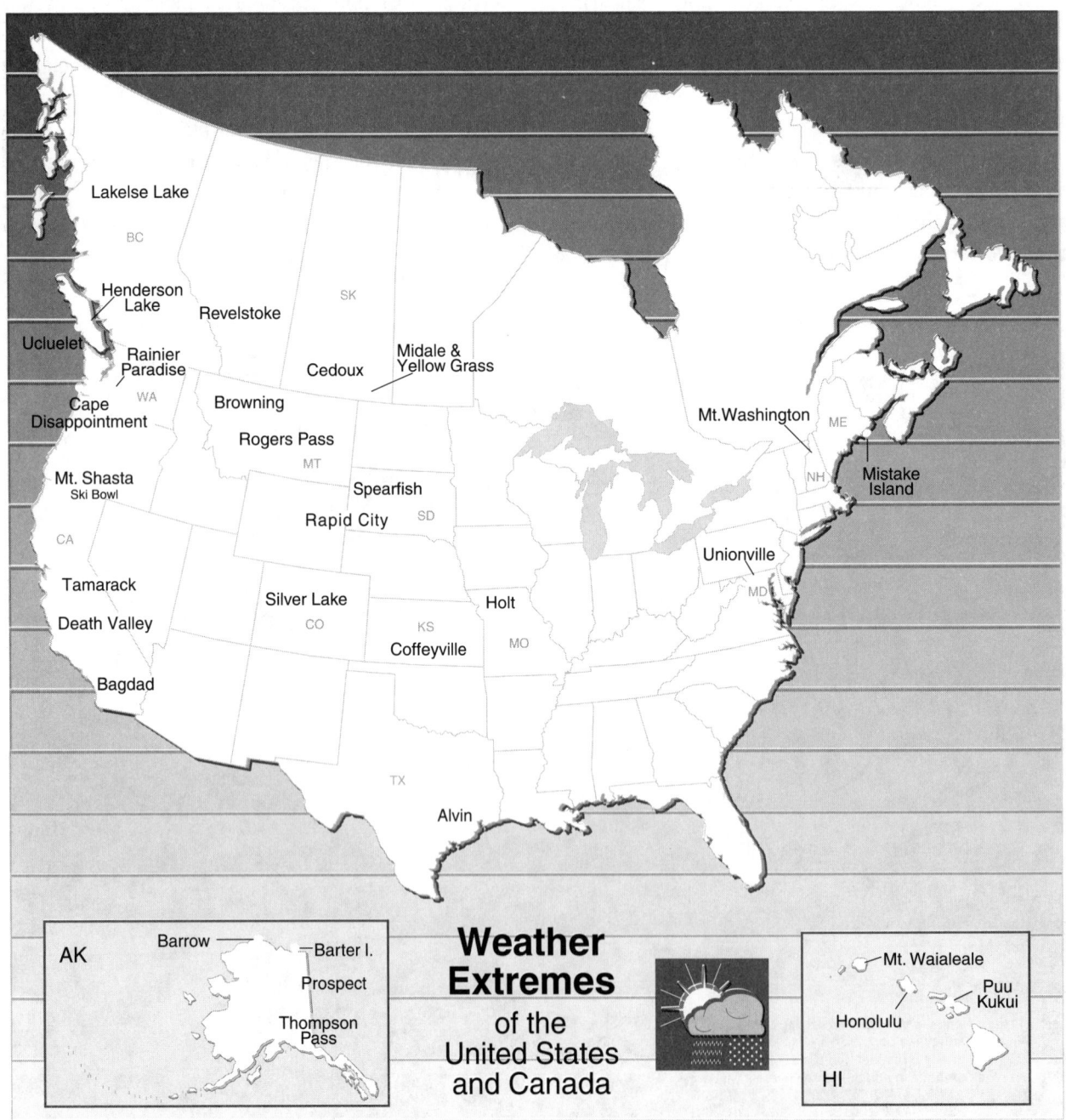

Weather Extremes of the United States and Canada

Going to Extremes

Among the 50 states, Honolulu is both the southernmost and westernmost metro area. The longest distance is 5,859 miles between Log Point, Elliot Key, Florida and Kure Island, Hawaii.

Coterminous United States

Geographic center: ....near Lebanon, Smith County, Kansas
Most Central metro area: ....Lincoln, Nebraska
Northernmost point: ....Lake of the Woods Projection, Minnesota
Northernmost metro area: ....Bellingham, Washington
Southernmost point: ....Cape Sable, Florida
Southernmost metro area: ....Miami, Florida
Easternmost point: .... West Quoddy Head, Maine
Easternmost metro area: .... Bangor, Maine
Westernmost point: .... Cape Alava, Washington
Westernmost metro area: ....Eugene-Springfield, Oregon

Elevations

Air temperature decreases with increasing elevation. The usual rate of increase – called the *lapse rate* – is 3.3°F lower per 1,000 feet of elevation than that of nearby lower-altitude stations.

	Highest Place (Elevation ft.)	Lowest Place (Elevation ft.)
United States	**Mount McKinley, AK (20,320)**	**Death Valley, CA (-282)**
Alabama	Cheaha Mountain (2,407)	Gulf of Mexico (sea level)
Alaska	Mount McKinley (20,320)	Pacific Ocean (sea level)
Arizona	Humphreys Peak (12,633)	Colorado River (70)
Arkansas	Magazine Mountain (2,753)	Ouachita River (55)
California	Mount Whitney (14,494)	Death Valley (-282)
Colorado	Mount Elbert (14,433)	Arkansas River (3,350)
Connecticut	Mount Frissell (2,380)	Long Island Sound (sea level)
Delaware	On Ebright Road (442)	Atlantic Ocean (sea level)
Florida	Sec. 30, T. 6N., R. 20W (345)	Atlantic Ocean (sea level)
Georgia	Brasstown Bald (4,784)	Atlantic Ocean (sea level)
Hawaii	Mauna Kea (13,796)	Pacific Ocean (sea level)
Idaho	Borah Peak (12,662)	Snake River (710)
Illinois	Charles Mound (1,235)	Ohio River (320)

the Richter scale (a 9-point span on a seismograph used to express the relative magnitude of an earthquake).

• *California and Nevada.* Much more seismic activity (and, therefore, more research and data) is present in California and Nevada than anywhere else in North America. The greatest hazards are found in the San Andreas, Owens Valley, and Garlock fault systems, shown on the map as zones numbered as high as 60. All the metro areas in California are affected by these faults, particularly Bakersfield, Los Angeles-Long Beach, Oakland, San Francisco, San Jose, and Santa-Cruz-Watsonville. These places, most of which have mild climates and pleasant terrain, are in real danger.

NORTH AMERICAN WEATHER EXTREMES

No organization validates world records for climate. Data from Environment Canada and from the U.S. Environmental Data Service are current and reliable for North America. These agencies also recognize several world records for temperature, differing forms of precipitation, and other phenomena.

• *Temperature* records are reported by more than 10,000 stations around the world. Theoretically, the hottest it can ever get is just under 140°F, because hot air is lighter and quickly rises above overlying, cooler layers. More than 80 years ago, the highest point a thermometer ever reached in ambient air

Going to Extremes (Cont.)

State	Highest Point	Lowest Point
Illinois	Charles Mound (1,235)	Ohio River (320)
Indiana	Franklin Township (1,257)	Ohio River (320)
Iowa	Sec. 29, T. 100N, R. 41W (1,670)	Mississippi River (480)
Kansas	Mount Sunflower (4,039)	Verdigris River (680)
Kentucky	Black Mountain (4,145)	Mississippi River (257)
Louisiana	Driskill Mountain (535)	New Orleans (-5)
Maine	Mount Katahdin (5,268)	Atlantic Ocean (sea level)
Maryland	Backbone Mountain (3,360)	Atlantic Ocean (sea level)
Massachusetts	Mount Greylock (3,491)	Atlantic Ocean (sea level)
Michigan	Mount Curwood (1,980)	Gulf of Mexico (sea level)
Missouri	Taum Sauk Mountain (1,772)	St. Francis River (230)
Montana	Granite Peak (12,799)	Kootenai River (1,800)
Nebraska	Johnson Township (5,426)	SE corner of State (840)
Nevada	Boundary Peak (13,145)	Colorado River (470)
New Hampshire	Mount Washington (6,288)	Atlantic Ocean (sea level)
New Jersey	High Point (1,803)	Atlantic Ocean (sea level)
New Mexico	Wheeler Peak (13,161)	Red Bluff Reservoir (2,817)
New York	Mount Marcy (5,344)	Atlantic Ocean (sea level)
North Carolina	Mount Mitchell (6,684)	Atlantic Ocean (sea level)
North Dakota	White Butte (3,506)	Red River (750)
Ohio	Campbell Hill (1,550)	Ohio River (433)
Oklahoma	Black Mesa (4,978)	Little River (287)
Oregon	Mount Hood (11,239)	Pacific Ocean (sea level)
Pennsylvania	Mount Davis (3,213)	Delaware River (sea level)
Rhode Island	Jerimoth Hill (812)	Atlantic Ocean (sea level)
South Carolina	Sassafras Mountain (3,560)	Atlantic Ocean (sea level)
South Dakota	Harney Peak (7,242)	Big Stone Lake (962)
Tennessee	Clingmans Dome (6,643)	Mississippi River (182)
Texas	Guadalupe Peak (8,749)	Gulf of Mexico (sea level)
Utah	Kings Peak (13,528)	Beaverdam Creek (2,000)
Vermont	Mount Mansfield (4,393)	Lake Champlain (95)
Virginia	Mount Rogers (5,729)	Atlantic Ocean (sea level)
Washington	Mount Rainier (14,410)	Pacific Ocean (sea level)
West Virginia	Spruce Knob (4,862)	Potomac River (240)
Wisconsin	Timms Hill (1,951)	Lake Michigan (581)
Wyoming	Gannett Peak (13,804)	Belle Fourche River (3,100)

Source: U.S. Geological Survey, *Elevations and Distances*

in the shade was 136°F at El Azizia, Libya, in the northern Sahara.

The current North American heat record, 134°F, was set more than nine decades ago at Greenland Ranch [now called Furnace Creek] station in California's Death Valley. Canada's record high temperature, a milder 113°F, hit Midale and Yellow Grass, Saskatchewan, in 1937.

In theory, the coldest it can get on the earth's surface is around minus 130°F, in still air, at 14,000 feet in the middle of polar night. The new world record is minus 129°F, measured at 11,000 feet at Vostok, Antarctica, in 1983. The North American record is minus 81 °F, measured at 2,000 feet at Snag, in Canada's Yukon Territory. An imperceptibly milder reading, minus 80°F, resulted in the United States record, at Prospect Creek Camp, Alaska, in 1971.

• World *snowfall* records are entirely North American for two reasons: 1. Snow falls on just 23 percent of the earth's landmass, meaning few countries ever record it, and 2. Among countries that experience snow, Canada and the United States record snow depth while others measure snow in terms of water content.

Thus, the world's greatest recorded 24-hour snowfall, 76 inches, occurred at Silver Lake, Colorado, in mid-April of 1921. Over the 1997-98 season, Mount Baker, Oregon, received almost 98 feet of snow, surpassing the 95 feet total that fell on

Rainier Paradise Ranger Station, Washington, during the 1971-72 season. The greatest depth of snow on the ground, nearly 38 feet, was measured at Tamarack, California, on March, 11, 1911. Canadian snowfall records, all set in British Columbia, are nowhere near these amounts.

The world's heaviest annual average rainfall has been recorded by gauges set 5,000 feet up on Mt. Waialeale, Kauai Island, Hawaii: 460 inches. The North American record outside of Hawaii, 256 inches, was established at Henderson Lake on Vancouver Island, British Columbia.

The world's heaviest 1-hour rainfall, 12 inches, hit Holt, Missouri, on June 22, 1947. Nine years later, in 1956, an identical amount fell on Kilauea Sugar Plantation, Kauai Island, Hawaii. Reunion Island, in the path of Indian Ocean tropical storms, regularly gets the world's heaviest short-term rains: 12-hour rain, 53 inches; 24hour rain, 74 inches; 5-day rain, 152 inches.

Two locations are noteworthy for lack of rain. Nearly 9 decades ago, at Bagdad, California, weather instruments recorded not a trace of moisture for over 2 years, the North American record. At Arica, Chile, the annual readings were 0.00 mm for 14 consecutive years.

• *Wind* is climate's most variable element. The values include peak wind, or the greatest 5-second average wind speed during the previous hour, and fastest mile, the fastest speed in miles per hour of any wind over a 24-hour observation day. Canada's highest average annual wind, 22 miles per hour, is measured at Cape Warwick, on Resolution Island, Northwest Territories. The North American record is 35 miles per hour, measured on top of New Hampshire's Mt. Washington, where the world's fastest peak wind (231 m.p.h.) and fastest mile (188 m.p.h.) were also recorded in the spring of 1934.

• *Fog*, simply put, is a cloud that touches the ground. As a cloud, it is composed of uncountable millions of visible water droplets formed when air is cooled to the saturation point. Cooling occurs when strong nighttime surface radiation cools the air near the ground; when humid and warm air moves across colder land; and when moist air moves up and over higher terrain. Thick fog is reported when visibility is less than half a mile; a day of fog is defined as one on which thick fog occurred once during the day.

The foggiest area in Canada (indeed one of the world's foggiest) is Newfoundland's Avalon Peninsula, socked in more than half the year. The two foggiest points in the United States, at opposite ends of the country, are Cape Disappointment, at the mouth of the Columbia River in Washington, and Moose Peak Lighthouse, off Maine's northern coast.

• *Hail* is rain collecting into ice lumps as it falls to earth from a convective cloud during a thunderstorm. In North America, the area along the eastern slope of the Rocky Mountains from New Mexico on up to Alberta gets more hail days, more hailstorms, and more and bigger hailstones than any other area on the continent. The heaviest authenticated hailstone (1.67 pounds) fell east of here at Coffeyville, Kansas in 1970. Canada's heaviest hailstone (10.23 ounces) fell near Cedoux, Saskatchewan in 1973.

Putting It All Together

Questions: Where will you find rock-bottom living costs and weather that's bright and shirt-sleeve mild all year? Where are the great hospitals? In which metropolitan areas is the crime rate so low that no one remembers how a police siren sounds? How about a short commute, easy parking, excellent schools, top universities, a nearby beach *and* nearby alpine skiing, a generous helping of the arts, some historic neighborhoods, and a rosy job outlook? Where will you find men and women who are good-looking and children who are above-average?

Answer: The best place to live. But if you think about the odds of finding these qualities in one place, it all sounds too good to be true. Does such a place exist?

To meet all the requirements, this ideal place would resemble San Francisco or Oakland, where the weather is moderated by the warm Pacific Ocean and the temperature seldom varies much from a mild 65°F. The place's overall costs of living might resemble that of Texarkana, a small metro area astride the Arkansas and Texas border.

This ideal place must be large enough to match Boston's variety of higher education options, New York's array of arts attractions, Atlanta's public transit system, Chicago's ease of travel to other parts of the continent, and Philadelphia's supply of physicians and hospitals.

Yet this place would also need to be small if it were to have a crime rate as low as Appleton, WI. For quality and variety of man-made and natural recreation amenities, the standard set by Miami would have to be met. Finally, our ideal location would have to present individuals with employment prospects as bright as those of Austin, the capital of Texas.

Obviously, this ideal spot is fictional. You can explore the geography long and hard, but you will never find the one metro area that combines all of the "bests" in each of *Places Rated*'s nine categories. Moreover, because one person's long-sought heaven can be another's purgatory, one can argue that there really is no such thing as the ideal metro area.

If you could move anywhere you wish, choosing your destination would still not be easy. The best strategy is to focus on your own preferences and needs. (The section "Decisions, Decisions" at the beginning of the book can help you identify what these preferences and needs might be.) Having said as much, we can still try to discover which of America's 379 officially-defined metro areas come closest to the ideal.

THE MOST NORMAL METRO AREAS IN AMERICA

Here are fifteen areas (average population: 325,000) whose scores across all nine of *Places Rated*'s categories differ the least from the average. In other words, these are the most normal metro areas among all 379 in the United States.

FINDING THE BEST PLACES IN AMERICA

Thirty-five years ago, the Environmental Protection Agency rated 243 American metro areas for livability by such diverse factors as unemployment rates, crime rates, and per capita contributions to charity. Their method for determining the best all-around city (it was Minneapolis, by the way) was very simple: For a final ranking, the scores for each place in each of the factors were averaged—the higher this mean score, the better.

Places Rated's method is no different. Atlanta, for example, has a score of 99 in ambiance, 34 in housing costs, 97 in job outlook, 33 in personal safety, 98 in transportation, 94 in education, 48 in health care, 81 in recreation, and 64 in climate. If you think of these scores as percentages (which they actually are), Atlanta's job outlook elevates it above 97 out of 100 metro areas in America, its recreation beats 8 out of 10 areas, but some two-thirds of America's metro areas are better than the Georgia capital when it comes to crime and housing costs.

Because the system is based on scores, the higher the average (or overall) score, the better the metro area is judged to be all-around. (Atlanta places 21st overall among metro areas.)

The leading metro areas closely resemble those in *Places Rated*'s previous (1999) edition. Although their rankings have changed somewhat, twenty-four were in the top forty before. Of the sixteen newcomers to the list, four were among the previous top fifty.

By no means are these top-rated places untarnished. Most score near the bottom in costs of living, eleven are among the worst in crime, and four have low scores in climate. More importantly, just one metro area—Pittsburgh—of all 379 metro areas in America ranks in the upper half in each of *Places Rated*'s nine categories.

Back to the point: There isn't an ideal haven in America. In spite of a blot or two, many come close through a combination of strengths. Whether their strengths are vital or unimportant, or whether their blots are knockout factors or trivial, is for you to decide.

If You Read This Chapter First

Readers who've skipped ahead to see how it all comes out may be surprised by many of the results shown in the table on the following pages. If you are curious about how a metro area is scored in a particular category, see the explanation in the SCORING section in the appropriate chapter.

Places Rated's categories include five relating mainly to facilities (health care, education, recreation, transportation, and ambience) and four relating to indicators (climate, crime, housing costs, and jobs). Smaller metro areas do better on the indicators (these places typically have lower crime rates, lower costs of living, and frequently faster rates of job growth), while larger places score higher on facilities. Climate favors neither large places nor small ones. Because of *Places Rated*'s emphasis on facilities, larger metro areas have an edge.

When you review the rankings in each of the chapters, be aware that the percentile scores shown on the following pages area closely grouped. With such close results, ranking metro areas from 1 to 379 may give the impression of greater differences among them than actually exist. Remember, too, that throughout this almanac the unit of comparison is not the incorporated city but the officially defined metropolitan area, typically made up of cities, towns, and other minor political divisions in New England, and one or more counties in the rest of the United States.

FINDING *YOUR* BEST PLACE TO LIVE

Using *Places Rated*, you can put together a custom-made list of possibilities. Just add up the scores in the categories you think are important and eliminate the others, thereby separating out the ones best suited to your own preferences. The "Decisions, Decisions" chapter at the beginning of the book may help.

One way to start is to note the scores of each metro area in the chapters most important to you and consider only the places that rank in the first 50 or 100. You may want to add a certain category's score twice if it is a critical need for you.

If you're a recent graduate, unmarried and just entering the job market, you might be interested mainly in the prospects for employment and having a good time. For you, the best areas could be those that have the best scores for recreation and job outlook. Here are the six that score higher than the 95th percentile in both those categories.

METRO AREA	JOBS	RECREATION
Houston-Sugar Land, TX	98.9	96.2
Orlando-Kissimmee, FL	95.2	100.0
Sacramento–Arden-Arcade, CA	98.1	98.9
Seattle-Bellevue, WA	95.5	99.7
Warren-Troy, MI	96.0	96.8
Washington, DC-VA-MD-WV	96.5	97.8

Finding the ideal spot is a matter of personal choice. *Places Rated* doesn't pretend to be the final arbiter of the best and worst metro areas; rather, it is designed as an instrument you can fine-tune and adjust to help you find the kind of place where you want to live.

A BIG POND OR A SMALL ONE?

Places Rated's top forty metro areas include just three with populations under one million. Yet there are many persons who would prefer not to live in a large city or even a medium-sized one if they could help it.

In 1974, the National Science Foundation (NSF) published *City Size and Quality of Life*. The study pointed out that large metro areas offer desirable social opportunities for many people: economic diversity, cultural events, anonymity, free expression of diverse life-styles, and the chance for personal achievement.

On the other hand, rates of violent crime increase as places get larger; air and water pollution increases; there is less discretionary time; larger places tend to diminish an individual's sense of relative significance; and access to the natural environment shrinks. Ominously, the NSF predicted larger cities would grow "to a point where they yield diminishing returns to scale."

Most important, perhaps, the study found that although the trend was toward growth of big metro areas, most people didn't want to live in big cities. They preferred small towns or suburbs but were

America's Best 25 Small Metro Areas

Almost half (185) of the metro areas have fewer than 250,000 people. These 25 rank the highest overall in *Places Rated*. Interestingly, most of them are within a few hundred miles of each other.

Bangor, ME	149,782
Bellingham, WA	188,175
Billings, MT	147,880
Bismarck, ND	100,445
Bloomington, IN	186,617
Burlington-South Burlington, VT	210,872
Charlottesville, VA	190,968
Columbia, MO	160,037
Eau Claire, WI	155,616
Fargo, ND-MN	186,442
Gainesville, FL	249,757
Grand Forks, ND-MN	96,712
Iowa City, IA	144,893
Ithaca, NY	102,303
Johnson City, TN	192,241
La Crosse, WI-MN	132,266
Lynchburg, VA	238,314
Medford, OR	207,528
Missoula, MT	106,325
Morgantown, WV	116,366
Napa, CA	138,654
Oshkosh-Neenah, WI	164,027
Pocatello, ID	86,738
Rochester, MN	182,098
St. Cloud, MN	182,768

being forced by economics to leave the smaller places for the bigger ones. By the year 2000, the study predicted, 63 percent of Americans—as compared with 38 percent in 1960—would live in the forty-four largest metropolitan areas, each of which would have a population greater than one million.

The NSF's forecast, it turns out 33 years later, was wrong. Just half of us live in metro areas with more than 1 million people; yet there are now sixty-one such areas in America, not forty-four.

During this century, a general worldwide trend has been "smaller pieces into bigger ones." Large corporations buy up smaller ones and grow even larger; people flock from the countryside or small towns into ever-swelling cities and their surrounding suburbs.

However, we may have reached a population watershed during the last 2 decades. The latest mobility data indicate that people are moving out of large cities and into the less populous places.

Could the early years of the 21st century usher in the era of "bigger pieces into smaller ones"? Certainly, the advent of the Internet has robbed the biggest metro areas of the advantage in one of the most significant factors in their development: Swift and effective communication between all branches of business, industry, and commerce.

For those readers who have already decided that they would prefer a smaller metro area, a careful consideration of population size may be the fairest way to compare Places Rated rankings.

SCORES: PUTTING IT ALL TOGETHER

The following table shows each metro area's score in *Places Rated*'s nine categories. Scores are expressed as percentiles and range from 0 (the Worst) to 100 (the Best) and are normalized such that the 50th percentile is the average for all metro areas. Scores that are among the top 40 in each category are **bolded**.

Abilene, for example, has a score of 24 in ambiance, 98 in housing costs, 6 in job outlook, 51 in crime, 58 in transportation, 47 in education, 42 in health care, 9 in recreation, and 41 in climate mildness. If you think of these scores as percentages (which they actually are), Abilene's housing affordability elevates it above 98 out of 100 metro areas in America, but 94 of 100 metro areas are better than Abilene when it comes to job outlook. Abilene's mean score is 42, producing a rank of 267 among 379 metro areas.

Metro Area	🎭	🏠	🔭	🔍	📷	💡	⚕	🏛	🎿	Mean Score	Rank
Metro Area Average	*50*	*50*	*50*	*50*	*50*	*50*	*50*	*50*	*50*	*50*	*–*
Abilene, TX	24	**98**	6	51	58	47	42	9	41	42	267
Akron, OH	69	51	72	68	71	**99**	27	**97**	32	65	59
Albany, GA	28	**95**	24	28	46	22	38	10	76	41	282
Albany-Schenectady, NY	**97**	32	71	73	86	**98**	72	64	38	70	28
Albuquerque, NM	**93**	45	87	3	80	71	57	62	82	64	64
Alexandria, LA	18	**95**	34	1	43	29	88	67	33	45	237
Allentown-Bethlehem, PA-NJ	79	27	68	85	49	66	57	78	49	62	85
Altoona, PA	22	87	17	79	38	20	71	11	62	45	238
Amarillo, TX	61	70	21	16	74	54	77	32	29	48	200
Ames, IA	50	38	11	**91**	60	85	46	5	6	44	253
Anchorage, AK	58	20	81	46	82	55	76	82	83	65	60
Anderson, IN	31	87	7	88	17	25	12	5	22	33	341
Anderson, SC	22	81	20	22	3	1	19	50	80	33	339
Ann Arbor, MI	**94**	27	73	66	45	**98**	**99**	54	55	68	44
Anniston-Oxford, AL	10	**94**	4	5	5	36	39	41	45	31	353
Appleton, WI	55	46	55	**100**	75	43	24	54	14	52	168
Asheville, NC	**92**	39	47	64	61	48	**97**	56	51	62	91
Athens-Clarke County, GA	44	56	43	41	35	85	56	11	53	47	209
Atlanta-Sandy Springs, GA	**99**	34	**97**	33	**98**	**94**	48	81	64	72	21
Atlantic City, NJ	63	15	60	39	40	39	32	71	79	49	191
Auburn-Opelika, AL	36	78	23	19	25	53	12	20	76	38	303
Augusta, GA-SC	47	81	61	44	39	45	**92**	39	69	57	114
Austin-Round Rock, TX	**98**	30	**100**	48	**95**	88	32	52	78	69	35
Bakersfield, CA	10	21	79	38	49	22	4	36	90	39	294
Baltimore-Towson, MD	**94**	14	**92**	23	90	**99**	81	**95**	73	73	12
Bangor, ME	62	52	14	**91**	63	58	71	40	50	56	128
Barnstable Town, MA	82	7	42	64	31	23	39	88	58	48	200
Baton Rouge, LA	48	65	75	8	59	70	45	60	47	53	153
Battle Creek, MI	34	74	23	9	39	31	16	23	2	28	366
Bay City, MI	35	80	8	77	28	41	3	59	47	42	265
Beaumont-Port Arthur, TX	6	**92**	54	26	45	38	20	67	19	41	280
Bellingham, WA	52	15	44	44	54	57	44	90	89	55	136
Bend, OR	18	10	58	65	45	11	57	69	**91**	47	212
Bethesda-Gaithersburg, MD	75	5	87	86	10	77	77	58	71	61	95
Billings, MT	57	47	19	76	71	27	**94**	46	35	52	158
Binghamton, NY	53	82	16	**95**	60	67	37	41	10	51	172
Birmingham-Hoover, AL	70	69	86	34	63	64	**91**	75	45	66	53
Bismarck, ND	28	56	23	**98**	56	33	**93**	24	60	52	160
Blacksburg, VA	71	67	14	**94**	17	74	15	50	84	54	143
Bloomington, IN	82	68	35	78	43	**90**	24	55	12	54	139
Bloomington-Normal, IL	45	52	87	56	81	77	34	16	6	50	177
Boise City-Nampa, ID	74	29	**90**	67	78	61	63	63	88	68	38
Boston-Quincy, MA	**100**	8	82	59	89	**92**	81	82	73	74	9
Boulder, CO	88	12	**95**	87	42	85	79	51	35	64	70
Bowling Green, KY	43	67	25	10	16	62	80	55	15	41	272
Bremerton-Silverdale, WA	11	17	70	52	13	25	11	54	90	38	300
Bridgeport-Stamford, CT	**93**	3	82	81	21	76	65	57	80	62	87
Brownsville-Harlingen, TX	0	**100**	46	28	87	18	14	83	64	49	190
Brunswick, GA	22	54	31	12	14	22	26	83	54	35	322
Buffalo-Niagara Falls, NY	89	76	46	61	**92**	**92**	73	86	33	72	23
Burlington, NC	11	61	20	36	11	46	11	11	69	31	354
Burlington-South Burlington, VT	86	20	54	79	82	76	**92**	55	45	65	55
Cambridge-Newton, MA	**92**	7	80	**95**	8	**99**	61	38	68	61	94
Camden, NJ	52	23	78	72	0	61	38	37	77	49	192
Canton-Massillon, OH	46	59	34	66	70	55	44	12	32	46	221
Cape Coral-Fort Myers, FL	43	11	84	28	68	34	45	87	67	52	167

Metro Area	🎭	🏠	⛱	〰	📻	⚗	⚕	🏛	⛳	Mean Score	Rank
Metro Area Average	50	50	50	50	50	50	50	50	50	50	–
Carson City, NV	36	8	57	57	20	13	64	85	94	48	197
Casper, WY	15	37	13	47	42	12	56	12	37	30	356
Cedar Rapids, IA	33	55	66	73	87	54	46	27	3	49	187
Champaign-Urbana, IL	51	59	21	37	83	78	52	0	10	43	255
Charleston, SC	88	28	83	17	69	62	84	99	39	63	76
Charleston, WV	30	91	63	54	65	25	89	1	10	48	207
Charlotte-Gastonia, NC-SC	86	42	96	4	92	70	66	65	79	67	52
Charlottesville, VA	85	19	61	85	55	94	98	26	57	65	61
Chattanooga, TN-GA	88	70	56	17	52	40	75	70	42	57	122
Cheyenne, WY	30	36	12	88	42	19	72	4	51	39	291
Chicago-Naperville-Joliet, IL	99	17	88	2	100	70	69	97	12	62	90
Chico, CA	59	16	30	49	35	48	33	59	92	47	215
Cincinnati, OH-KY-IN	87	51	84	52	98	95	58	96	38	73	16
Clarksville, TN-KY	9	91	70	44	22	26	4	68	14	39	295
Cleveland, TN	7	78	25	55	11	13	9	66	46	35	330
Cleveland-Elyria-Mentor, OH	87	48	80	54	97	93	86	96	19	73	14
Coeur d'Alene, ID	17	26	51	62	8	6	36	92	75	42	269
College Station-Bryan, TX	44	66	51	43	56	72	29	20	69	50	179
Colorado Springs, CO	83	32	92	56	74	64	25	56	56	60	100
Columbia, MO	35	58	44	75	56	95	100	20	1	54	147
Columbia, SC	78	63	73	21	66	87	68	70	63	65	54
Columbus, GA-AL	37	73	50	40	40	52	49	46	70	51	176
Columbus, IN	49	66	55	93	26	15	81	7	21	46	231
Columbus, OH	98	42	92	11	83	99	63	76	43	67	46
Corpus Christi, TX	47	81	48	11	84	34	50	74	60	54	138
Corvallis, OR	19	26	28	70	19	84	52	31	97	47	208
Cumberland, MD-WV	38	84	2	71	2	42	35	14	28	35	326
Dallas-Plano-Irving, TX	96	42	98	16	99	87	46	89	38	68	43
Dalton, GA	11	82	25	50	10	8	12	22	52	30	357
Danville, IL	10	99	1	26	24	8	26	7	18	24	374
Danville, VA	22	98	0	83	14	32	16	2	75	38	301
Davenport-Moline, IA-IL	54	67	46	14	96	49	38	30	19	46	230
Dayton, OH	78	60	58	39	92	93	66	34	51	63	74
Decatur, AL	20	96	16	76	4	17	20	68	16	37	312
Decatur, IL	49	96	13	10	50	16	54	15	7	34	332
Deltona-Daytona Beach, FL	64	25	24	19	51	69	31	89	73	50	185
Denver-Aurora, CO	98	26	99	58	93	84	71	90	33	72	19
Des Moines, IA	57	44	74	71	88	67	44	71	3	58	111
Detroit-Livonia-Dearborn, MI	73	59	33	3	95	57	18	61	48	50	186
Dothan, AL	3	95	15	65	27	2	84	8	75	41	270
Dover, DE	29	41	29	47	34	63	10	82	74	45	236
Dubuque, IA	31	53	21	84	58	42	78	26	5	44	248
Duluth, MN-WI	32	52	28	73	66	57	91	91	16	56	123
Durham, NC	96	42	91	7	79	95	99	60	49	69	36
Eau Claire, WI	39	50	24	90	55	87	97	31	39	57	120
Edison, NJ	76	6	93	93	7	88	61	92	84	67	50
El Centro, CA	2	29	21	20	15	2	0	53	88	26	371
El Paso, TX	41	79	69	60	87	52	11	17	85	56	127
Elizabethtown, KY	8	74	37	59	7	10	22	2	36	28	364
Elkhart-Goshen, IN	35	60	39	43	29	20	14	4	4	27	367
Elmira, NY	54	89	1	86	53	11	78	17	46	48	194
Erie, PA	52	78	22	86	69	79	51	74	12	58	108
Essex County, MA	91	10	63	75	12	65	26	25	53	47	216
Eugene-Springfield, OR	74	31	48	42	79	70	43	66	97	61	93
Evansville, IN-KY	58	81	42	68	79	81	82	75	55	69	34
Fairbanks, AK	29	32	33	31	73	40	34	9	66	39	296

Metro Area	🎭	🏠	🗑	👁	📻	💡	⚕	🏛	⛳	Mean Score	Rank
Metro Area Average	*50*	*50*	*50*	*50*	*50*	*50*	*50*	*50*	*50*	*50*	–
Fargo, ND-MN	55	63	53	**95**	72	60	**90**	13	59	62	**82**
Farmington, NM	5	80	65	56	9	11	5	11	81	36	**317**
Fayetteville, NC	16	88	60	2	46	43	29	2	57	38	**299**
Fayetteville-Springdale, AR-MO	53	51	83	84	76	56	31	47	30	57	**119**
Flagstaff, AZ	**95**	13	52	38	41	51	58	45	74	52	**162**
Flint, MI	33	61	40	15	60	42	25	28	42	39	**297**
Florence, SC	25	**93**	38	2	24	17	80	13	66	40	**286**
Florence-Muscle Shoals, AL	8	**97**	3	81	5	47	30	48	16	37	**310**
Fond du Lac, WI	17	50	13	**100**	57	75	16	38	34	44	**246**
Fort Collins-Loveland, CO	76	28	84	80	41	83	48	62	42	60	**96**
Fort Lauderdale, FL	53	10	90	39	78	60	55	16	62	51	**170**
Fort Smith, AR-OK	5	**99**	44	50	44	13	28	66	24	41	**273**
Fort Walton Beach, FL	39	24	80	74	55	15	59	53	49	50	**183**
Fort Wayne, IN	65	78	45	65	67	44	88	26	20	55	**131**
Fort Worth-Arlington, TX	72	55	**97**	31	**97**	77	15	68	38	61	**92**
Fresno, CA	8	14	72	23	71	46	30	77	89	48	**203**
Gadsden, AL	4	**97**	1	41	2	5	55	19	46	30	**358**
Gainesville, FL	70	34	35	6	63	80	**99**	72	69	59	**107**
Gainesville, GA	8	44	49	67	22	33	40	20	60	38	**298**
Gary, IN	29	51	55	54	30	45	47	63	4	42	**264**
Glens Falls, NY	40	43	3	**91**	19	15	33	49	32	36	**315**
Goldsboro, NC	7	90	2	20	11	14	6	6	44	22	**379**
Grand Forks, ND-MN	56	64	5	83	52	64	79	21	72	55	**133**
Grand Junction, CO	27	33	37	72	58	18	75	44	61	47	**210**
Grand Rapids-Wyoming, MI	72	54	87	52	81	56	40	87	9	60	**102**
Great Falls, MT	38	61	1	53	81	12	89	34	48	46	**222**
Greeley, CO	58	38	64	62	14	62	9	31	18	39	**289**
Green Bay, WI	38	41	68	**90**	75	79	49	**94**	30	63	**79**
Greensboro-High Point, NC	56	68	56	19	75	59	66	43	63	56	**124**
Greenville, NC	55	83	52	2	24	58	**93**	2	44	46	**228**
Greenville, SC	67	65	71	30	64	72	65	60	82	64	**69**
Gulfport-Biloxi, MS	25	58	69	17	52	16	47	**90**	37	46	**234**
Hagerstown-Martinsburg, MD-WV	61	31	42	74	29	19	35	43	43	42	**266**
Hanford-Corcoran, CA	1	27	48	78	12	0	1	0	**91**	29	**361**
Harrisburg-Carlisle, PA	71	49	83	88	62	71	76	54	57	68	**40**
Harrisonburg, VA	57	35	21	**99**	20	76	27	39	72	50	**184**
Hartford, CT	**99**	19	67	70	**90**	96	62	49	58	68	**42**
Hattiesburg, MS	33	87	26	34	4	45	**90**	57	31	45	**239**
Hickory-Lenoir-Morganton, NC	56	80	25	51	13	19	47	72	52	46	**226**
Hinesville-Fort Stewart, GA	13	75	43	61	6	1	0	19	80	33	**338**
Holland-Grand Haven, MI	30	45	76	**94**	36	60	2	46	13	45	**244**
Honolulu, HI	76	5	49	47	85	90	74	36	**96**	62	**84**
Hot Springs, AR	24	65	14	26	23	12	**90**	**94**	25	41	**275**
Houma-Bayou Cane, LA	3	88	27	32	1	25	30	33	47	32	**347**
Houston-Sugar Land, TX	84	49	**99**	24	**99**	63	51	**96**	39	67	**48**
Huntington-Ashland, WV-KY-OH	44	**93**	29	59	39	58	88	60	20	54	**137**
Huntsville, AL	64	65	72	48	64	83	56	66	26	60	**97**
Idaho Falls, ID	34	59	40	83	38	2	21	79	65	47	**214**
Indianapolis-Carmel, IN	80	52	**92**	33	**93**	92	90	81	13	70	**30**
Iowa City, IA	49	38	56	78	54	89	**100**	28	2	55	**134**
Ithaca, NY	72	40	18	**91**	72	91	21	53	40	55	**132**
Jackson, MI	4	58	11	56	20	24	6	65	15	29	**360**
Jackson, MS	77	71	77	6	59	35	87	35	33	53	**151**
Jackson, TN	43	84	47	6	52	37	**93**	8	26	44	**250**
Jacksonville, FL	80	28	89	12	72	46	69	**91**	74	62	**83**
Jacksonville, NC	13	74	34	68	33	1	2	26	49	33	**336**

Metro Area	🎭	🏠	🧢	🌀	📷	🏺	⚕	🏛	🏒	Mean Score	Rank
Metro Area Average	*50*	*50*	*50*	*50*	*50*	*50*	*50*	*50*	*50*	*50*	*–*
Janesville, WI	45	54	18	69	36	36	31	12	10	35	**329**
Jefferson City, MO	15	82	40	83	22	50	6	17	4	36	**321**
Johnson City, TN	49	88	39	55	57	40	97	42	35	56	**126**
Johnstown, PA	42	95	6	92	40	31	62	35	11	46	**229**
Jonesboro, AR	24	93	12	38	26	34	79	7	15	36	**314**
Joplin, MO	14	96	32	42	30	36	31	3	8	33	**342**
Kalamazoo-Portage, MI	67	56	26	40	72	65	69	78	0	53	**157**
Kankakee-Bradley, IL	26	57	16	74	9	30	39	19	29	33	**337**
Kansas City, MO-KS	84	45	88	29	96	88	65	77	8	64	**63**
Kennewick-Richland, WA	26	64	83	71	41	7	12	24	92	47	**218**
Killeen-Temple, TX	9	79	74	46	17	50	67	6	53	45	**245**
Kingsport-Bristol, TN-VA	36	91	16	74	46	21	86	61	35	52	**169**
Kingston, NY	68	18	6	92	5	35	14	44	54	37	**308**
Knoxville, TN	95	62	84	42	74	66	96	84	24	70	**31**
Kokomo, IN	12	79	38	63	28	37	40	5	9	35	**328**
La Crosse, WI-MN	30	53	20	98	69	81	96	64	23	59	**103**
Lafayette, IN	80	62	46	79	58	73	22	9	21	50	**182**
Lafayette, LA	37	71	70	31	46	81	75	56	20	54	**144**
Lake Charles, LA	10	92	36	5	33	43	61	88	28	44	**249**
Lake-Kenosha Counties, IL-WI	77	19	98	82	24	72	50	89	27	60	**101**
Lakeland, FL	34	48	53	13	22	26	19	73	60	39	**293**
Lancaster, PA	69	36	37	90	30	78	17	16	84	51	**175**
Lansing-East Lansing, MI	69	47	67	66	77	88	23	25	7	52	**163**
Laredo, TX	19	84	66	21	62	30	3	1	87	41	**274**
Las Cruces, NM	40	77	35	18	33	44	5	14	87	39	**290**
Las Vegas-Paradise, NV	65	12	99	27	94	74	19	94	87	63	**75**
Lawrence, KS	51	33	28	81	37	80	10	40	2	40	**284**
Lawton, OK	16	92	7	24	73	8	25	47	22	35	**325**
Lebanon, PA	17	41	10	92	16	20	28	8	71	34	**334**
Lewiston, ID-WA	26	40	17	68	40	6	43	40	78	40	**287**
Lewiston-Auburn, ME	11	37	10	76	3	12	67	29	48	33	**342**
Lexington-Fayette, KY	82	53	75	30	80	96	98	12	30	62	**88**
Lima, OH	20	83	6	35	27	35	88	4	43	38	**302**
Lincoln, NE	75	48	58	36	65	94	77	27	5	54	**145**
Little Rock-North Little Rock, AR	61	79	78	14	77	62	98	80	22	63	**73**
Logan, UT-ID	28	47	34	100	43	51	4	61	26	44	**251**
Longview, TX	25	73	29	30	23	16	35	15	28	31	**355**
Longview, WA	4	38	17	17	26	1	22	42	86	28	**365**
Los Angeles, CA	96	3	76	36	94	58	58	93	98	68	**41**
Louisville, KY-IN	80	56	82	29	88	71	85	79	29	67	**51**
Lubbock, TX	66	86	31	3	97	65	94	4	36	53	**148**
Lynchburg, VA	44	61	18	96	47	73	39	56	79	57	**116**
Macon, GA	78	86	24	7	23	58	85	44	56	51	**171**
Madera, CA	1	9	45	35	0	0	1	46	90	25	**372**
Madison, WI	96	25	88	82	98	100	95	72	7	74	**10**
Manchester-Nashua, NH	89	13	71	96	62	61	43	13	51	55	**130**
Mansfield, OH	57	69	9	45	34	48	16	15	21	35	**327**
McAllen-Edinburg-Mission, TX	7	100	65	15	61	39	9	21	65	42	**262**
Medford, OR	51	15	54	69	63	13	72	43	93	53	**156**
Memphis, TN-MS-AR	70	69	92	0	89	51	69	84	17	60	**99**
Merced, CA	2	10	12	22	7	5	2	51	93	23	**378**
Miami-Miami Beach, FL	86	9	79	6	85	11	86	63	67	55	**135**
Michigan City-La Porte, IN	3	57	5	62	15	14	41	18	0	24	**376**
Midland, TX	37	66	47	57	64	22	13	1	68	42	**268**
Milwaukee-Waukesha, WI	85	28	77	58	100	96	82	84	13	69	**33**
Minneapolis-St. Paul, MN-WI	88	22	95	69	99	97	75	98	17	73	**11**

582

Metro Area	🎭	🏠	🧳	👆	📷	🍵	⚕	🏛	🧹	Mean Score	Rank
Metro Area Average	*50*	*50*	*50*	*50*	*50*	*50*	*50*	*50*	*50*	*50*	*–*
Missoula, MT	61	23	51	53	84	68	89	64	84	64	67
Mobile, AL	59	86	26	4	48	68	53	52	23	46	219
Modesto, CA	3	8	66	24	20	41	18	32	94	34	333
Monroe, LA	18	98	28	12	65	49	59	65	9	45	243
Monroe, MI	14	41	41	77	6	5	1	45	27	28	363
Montgomery, AL	32	89	68	8	44	48	37	23	56	45	240
Morgantown, WV	56	83	47	81	13	57	97	27	19	53	149
Morristown, TN	6	74	19	53	6	4	7	47	28	27	369
Mount Vernon-Anacortes, WA	13	19	49	35	28	10	28	89	96	41	281
Muncie, IN	39	91	9	77	47	83	55	10	25	48	199
Muskegon-Norton Shores, MI	19	75	33	34	47	16	6	92	15	37	309
Myrtle Beach-Conway, SC	62	34	60	0	54	30	23	43	27	37	311
Napa, CA	40	2	64	89	31	41	80	30	93	52	159
Naples-Marco Island, FL	65	3	89	40	9	29	32	79	70	46	225
Nashville-Davidson, TN	94	49	93	18	78	82	89	69	14	65	58
Nassau-Suffolk, NY	71	4	69	97	68	67	83	84	85	70	29
New Haven-Milford, CT	97	14	63	58	32	80	73	71	80	63	77
New Orleans, LA	85	44	70	25	83	74	93	94	44	68	39
New York, NY-NJ	100	4	76	64	96	54	79	99	83	73	18
Newark-Union, NJ-PA	89	6	75	63	94	86	82	86	78	73	15
Niles-Benton Harbor, MI	21	57	11	50	35	21	23	62	6	31	349
Norwich-New London, CT	76	17	62	75	39	29	21	58	80	51	174
Oakland-Fremont-Hayward, CA	77	2	94	41	84	85	54	95	99	70	27
Ocala, FL	21	40	37	27	8	6	10	73	61	31	348
Ocean City, NJ	62	7	4	46	4	10	2	76	81	32	344
Odessa, TX	1	99	8	28	56	23	15	1	70	33	335
Ogden-Clearfield, UT	66	43	74	77	8	46	8	90	22	48	198
Oklahoma City, OK	91	84	67	19	78	86	67	51	23	63	78
Olympia, WA	42	25	69	60	29	39	41	38	89	48	202
Omaha-Council Bluffs, NE-IA	73	46	81	43	92	69	92	80	3	64	65
Orlando-Kissimmee, FL	81	16	95	8	87	77	68	100	67	67	49
Oshkosh-Neenah, WI	51	50	52	97	84	73	66	34	13	58	110
Owensboro, KY	24	94	22	70	21	19	42	24	34	39	292
Oxnard-Thousand Oaks, CA	35	1	81	89	29	44	24	50	98	50	180
Palm Bay-Melbourne, FL	42	22	64	27	38	47	30	85	76	48	206
Panama City-Lynn Haven, FL	0	29	51	22	48	3	48	58	63	36	318
Parkersburg-Marietta, WV-OH	46	90	8	89	19	34	49	44	31	46	235
Pascagoula, MS	16	70	11	11	2	9	11	80	37	27	368
Pensacola, FL	40	43	75	36	59	43	74	61	54	54	146
Peoria, IL	29	67	52	9	77	39	60	77	1	46	233
Philadelphia, PA	99	21	77	54	93	94	81	81	77	75	5
Phoenix-Mesa, AZ	84	14	100	16	88	80	36	73	88	64	66
Pine Bluff, AR	20	100	4	1	10	7	24	18	29	24	377
Pittsburgh, PA	87	71	76	82	91	93	83	95	64	82	1
Pittsfield, MA	83	32	9	80	31	36	54	39	60	47	211
Pocatello, ID	42	77	20	84	51	33	37	75	58	53	152
Port St. Lucie-Fort Pierce, FL	2	16	63	32	3	26	19	74	76	35	331
Portland, ME	81	18	65	90	67	75	85	72	62	68	37
Portland-Vancouver, OR-WA	97	18	94	47	93	87	68	93	87	76	4
Poughkeepsie, NY	91	11	61	93	37	63	40	80	83	62	86
Prescott, AZ	50	22	53	45	11	27	25	57	93	42	260
Providence, RI-MA	92	13	65	70	81	90	48	92	83	70	26
Provo-Orem, UT	46	34	73	86	17	65	8	74	18	47	217
Pueblo, CO	21	72	32	29	34	26	64	28	16	36	319
Punta Gorda, FL	12	22	50	75	2	2	52	75	67	40	288
Racine, WI	15	35	22	65	47	38	21	33	8	31	351

Metro Area	🎭	🏠	🧳	🌀	📷	🍵	⚕️	🏛️	🧹	Mean Score	Rank
Metro Area Average	*50*	*50*	*50*	*50*	*50*	*50*	*50*	*50*	*50*	*50*	–
Raleigh-Cary, NC	93	39	96	37	71	89	44	70	50	65	57
Rapid City, SD	67	54	32	69	61	24	92	42	26	52	166
Reading, PA	48	39	32	67	19	67	17	29	62	42	263
Redding, CA	5	20	44	55	49	9	51	69	89	43	257
Reno-Sparks, NV	81	11	89	45	98	53	70	69	92	67	45
Richmond, VA	94	30	86	59	67	97	87	85	52	73	17
Riverside-San Bernardino, CA	62	6	91	38	76	53	13	78	94	57	117
Roanoke, VA	53	46	59	87	70	32	94	51	71	63	80
Rochester, MN	31	46	79	94	69	28	94	32	2	53	154
Rochester, NY	90	63	58	78	90	97	69	98	31	75	6
Rockford, IL	60	58	59	1	38	32	60	25	11	38	304
Rockingham-Strafford, NH	79	13	90	99	15	69	22	42	59	54	141
Rocky Mount, NC	31	93	12	10	7	7	13	3	40	24	375
Rome, GA	23	86	10	29	36	38	98	24	70	46	227
Sacramento, CA	54	9	98	40	80	78	53	99	95	67	47
Saginaw, MI	48	77	35	24	76	24	57	33	43	46	224
Salem, OR	16	33	38	50	27	28	15	35	97	38	307
Salinas, CA	47	1	88	63	57	47	20	83	100	56	125
Salisbury, MD	43	33	13	21	28	90	71	67	85	50	181
Salt Lake City, UT	95	30	94	41	91	79	56	91	12	65	56
San Angelo, TX	26	87	0	33	53	14	51	3	72	38	305
San Antonio, TX	83	68	94	27	89	75	73	52	77	71	24
San Diego, CA	79	4	98	64	89	63	70	93	99	73	13
San Francisco, CA	98	0	90	60	85	82	87	97	100	78	2
San Jose-Sunnyvale, CA	90	1	93	84	80	96	74	59	98	75	8
San Luis Obispo, CA	60	4	67	79	66	56	33	48	98	57	121
Sandusky, OH	79	63	19	67	25	27	17	76	39	46	232
Santa Ana-Anaheim-Irvine, CA	84	1	98	85	60	72	69	86	94	72	22
Santa Barbara-Santa Maria, CA	63	2	62	82	86	84	54	49	99	64	62
Santa Cruz-Watsonville, CA	50	0	57	63	18	79	27	87	99	53	150
Santa Fe, NM	85	18	60	4	34	17	60	22	86	43	259
Santa Rosa-Petaluma, CA	54	2	86	73	12	61	52	63	96	55	129
Sarasota-Bradenton-Venice, FL	63	11	81	25	66	37	76	88	71	58	112
Savannah, GA	75	47	39	15	67	52	83	81	55	57	115
Scranton--Wilkes-Barre, PA	60	62	31	93	65	71	58	57	44	60	98
Seattle-Bellevue-Everett, WA	92	9	96	43	88	89	85	100	96	77	3
Sebastian-Vero Beach, FL	4	21	49	49	44	6	84	37	78	41	276
Sheboygan, WI	24	45	27	96	32	38	33	58	20	41	270
Sherman-Denison, TX	12	73	17	52	21	10	47	29	37	33	340
Shreveport-Bossier City, LA	65	90	57	4	25	29	96	40	25	48	204
Sioux City, IA-NE-SD	13	83	26	42	85	18	34	21	5	36	316
Sioux Falls, SD	71	50	78	87	51	17	99	13	1	52	165
South Bend-Mishawaka, IN-MI	78	72	41	31	83	92	26	65	1	54	140
Spartanburg, SC	7	88	31	15	70	28	43	34	81	44	247
Spokane, WA	68	37	54	23	79	82	83	67	79	64	71
Springfield, IL	59	76	42	9	95	44	94	18	6	49	188
Springfield, MA	73	29	42	23	50	91	45	47	68	52	164
Springfield, MO	66	69	61	49	94	84	80	23	7	59	104
Springfield, OH	33	77	4	18	74	23	8	22	57	35	323
St. Cloud, MN	70	37	50	98	51	58	91	25	42	58	109
St. George, UT	28	23	56	97	37	24	13	41	86	45	241
St. Joseph, MO-KS	41	82	2	61	37	21	7	6	4	29	359
St. Louis, MO-IL	89	49	79	37	97	98	74	96	17	71	25
State College, PA	67	43	36	99	54	89	8	14	8	46	223
Stockton, CA	1	6	62	14	25	30	7	48	97	32	345
Sumter, SC	12	92	3	1	18	3	3	30	66	25	373

Metro Area	🎭	🏠					⚕			Mean Score	Rank
Metro Area Average	50	50	50	50	50	50	50	50	50	50	–
Syracuse, NY	87	75	48	72	48	98	84	83	30	69	**32**
Tacoma, WA	47	23	89	20	68	40	28	78	95	54	**142**
Tallahassee, FL	74	36	72	5	91	75	29	79	72	59	**105**
Tampa-St. Petersburg, FL	81	24	91	9	61	74	72	99	65	64	**68**
Terre Haute, IN	38	90	8	11	99	53	37	35	50	47	**213**
Texarkana, TX-AR	15	99	15	33	32	9	62	10	54	37	**313**
Toledo, OH	90	60	53	18	33	93	87	92	36	62	**81**
Topeka, KS	46	70	29	8	70	56	50	33	3	41	**279**
Trenton-Ewing, NJ	75	12	57	51	16	81	78	15	75	51	**173**
Tucson, AZ	83	27	80	13	6	86	67	70	85	57	**113**
Tulsa, OK	74	85	85	25	90	35	34	87	17	59	**106**
Tuscaloosa, AL	32	72	30	13	86	66	35	37	47	46	**220**
Tyler, TX	27	64	61	32	18	21	96	28	40	43	**258**
Utica-Rome, NY	52	85	10	80	42	30	38	62	33	48	**205**
Valdosta, GA	17	89	15	55	35	49	42	38	52	43	**254**
Vallejo-Fairfield, CA	20	5	85	48	3	33	5	48	92	38	**305**
Victoria, TX	23	97	43	34	50	14	63	71	40	48	**196**
Vineland-Millville-Bridgeton, NJ	21	40	15	20	4	8	7	49	74	27	**370**
Virginia Beach-Norfolk, VA-NC	97	25	85	58	75	91	64	98	59	72	**20**
Visalia-Porterville, CA	19	24	38	25	31	4	4	45	91	31	**352**
Waco, TX	39	75	40	13	57	51	53	16	46	43	**256**
Warner Robins, GA	9	76	74	46	16	4	3	3	56	32	**346**
Warren-Troy, MI	90	31	96	87	1	76	60	97	34	64	**72**
Washington, DC-VA-MD-WV	93	5	97	60	96	100	62	98	64	75	**7**
Waterloo-Cedar Falls, IA	48	64	7	57	48	66	53	6	11	40	**285**
Wausau, WI	34	55	30	95	73	20	46	19	21	44	**252**
Weirton-Steubenville, WV-OH	45	97	3	96	10	31	17	36	25	40	**283**
Wenatchee, WA	23	35	19	61	53	3	42	85	82	45	**242**
West Palm Beach, FL	72	8	97	7	76	83	76	76	61	62	**89**
Wheeling, WV-OH	64	96	7	99	26	50	63	22	41	52	**161**
Wichita Falls, TX	6	94	2	22	43	28	49	17	24	31	**349**
Wichita, KS	41	73	59	32	82	52	59	29	11	49	**193**
Williamsport, PA	37	68	5	92	53	60	36	7	24	42	**261**
Wilmington, DE-MD-NJ	68	24	85	45	1	97	41	88	63	57	**118**
Wilmington, NC	60	31	71	5	62	54	65	52	41	49	**189**
Winchester, VA-WV	27	20	36	88	1	49	78	8	66	41	**277**
Winston-Salem, NC	66	60	78	10	21	55	94	30	58	53	**155**
Worcester, MA	69	15	66	72	15	69	61	39	48	50	**178**
Yakima, WA	6	72	29	14	49	4	20	31	95	36	**320**
York-Hanover, PA	58	36	41	97	13	41	18	10	53	41	**278**
Youngstown-Warren, OH-PA	63	85	27	49	30	68	29	53	31	48	**195**
Yuba City, CA	2	17	45	37	12	7	10	37	90	29	**362**
Yuma, AZ	13	55	39	51	44	3	1	21	88	35	**324**

Appendix A

METROPOLITAN AREAS BY STATE

Every state has at least one metro area. Massachusetts and New Jersey are the only states whose entire land area is covered by these combinations of urban and suburban counties, though Connecticut and Florida aren't far behind.

One of every five metro areas are found in California, which has 28; Texas, which has 26; and Florida with 21. Hawaii, Rhode Island, and Vermont have just one. Below is a list of metro areas grouped by state. Forty-four metro areas cover parts of two or more states. These are listed under every state in which they have a component county.

Alabama

Anniston-Oxford
Auburn-Opelika
Birmingham-Hoover
Columbus (GA-AL)
Decatur
Dothan
Florence-Muscle Shoals
Gadsden
Huntsville
Mobile
Montgomery
Tuscaloosa

Alaska

Anchorage
Fairbanks

Arizona

Flagstaff
Phoenix-Mesa-Scottsdale
Prescott
Tucson
Yuma

Arkansas

- Fayetteville-Springdale (AR-MO)
- Fort Smith (AR-OK)
- Hot Springs
- Jonesboro
- Little Rock-North Little Rock
- Memphis (TN-MS-AR)
- Pine Bluff
- Texarkana (TX-AR)

California

- Bakersfield
- Chico
- El Centro
- Fresno
- Hanford-Corcoran
- Los Angeles-Long Beach
- Madera
- Merced
- Modesto
- Napa
- Oakland-Fremont-Hayward
- Oxnard-Thousand Oaks
- Redding
- Riverside-San Bernardino

Sacramento--Arden-Arcade
Salinas
San Diego-Carlsbad
San Francisco-San Mateo
San Jose-Sunnyvale
San Luis Obispo-Paso Robles
Santa Ana-Anaheim-Irvine
Santa Barbara-Santa Maria
Santa Cruz-Watsonville
Santa Rosa-Petaluma
Stockton
Vallejo-Fairfield
Visalia-Porterville
Yuba City

Colorado

Boulder
Colorado Springs
Denver-Aurora
Fort Collins-Loveland
Grand Junction
Greeley
Pueblo

Connecticut

Bridgeport-Stamford-Norwalk
Hartford-West Hartford
New Haven-Milford
Norwich-New London

Delaware

Dover
Wilmington (DE-MD-NJ)

District of Columbia

Washington-Arlington
  (DC-VA-MD-WV)

Florida

Cape Coral-Fort Myers
Deltona-Daytona Beach
Fort Lauderdale-Pompano Beach
Fort Walton Beach-Crestview
Gainesville
Jacksonville
Lakeland
Miami-Miami Beach-Kendall
Naples-Marco Island
Ocala
Orlando-Kissimmee
Palm Bay-Melbourne-Titusville
Panama City-Lynn Haven
Pensacola-Ferry Pass-Brent
Port St. Lucie-Fort Pierce
Punta Gorda
Sarasota-Bradenton-Venice
Tallahassee
Tampa-St. Petersburg
Vero Beach
West Palm Beach-Boca Raton

Georgia

Albany
Athens-Clarke County
Atlanta-Sandy Springs
Augusta GA-SC)
Brunswick
Chattanooga (TN-GA)
Columbus (GA-AL)
Dalton
Gainesville
Hinesville-Fort Stewart
Macon

Rome
Savannah
Valdosta
Warner Robins

Hawaii

Honolulu

Idaho

Boise City-Nampa
Coeur d'Alene
Idaho Falls
Lewiston (ID-WA)
Logan (UT-ID)
Pocatello

Illinois

Bloomington-Normal
Champaign-Urbana
Chicago-Naperville-Joliet
Danville
Davenport (IA-IL)
Decatur
Kankakee-Bradley
Lake County (IL-WI)
Peoria
Rockford
Springfield (MO-IL)
St. Louis (MO-IL)

Indiana

Anderson
Bloomington
Cincinnati (OH-KY-IN)
Columbus
Elkhart-Goshen
Evansville (IN-KY)
Fort Wayne
Gary
Indianapolis
Kokomo
Lafayette
Louisville (KY-IN)
Michigan City-La Porte
Muncie
South Bend (IN-MI)
Terre Haute

Iowa

Ames
Cedar Rapids
Davenport (IA-IL)
Des Moines
Dubuque
Iowa City
Omaha-Council Bluffs (NE-IA)
Sioux City (IA-NE-SD)
Waterloo-Cedar Falls

Kansas

Kansas City (MO-KS)
Lawrence
St. Joseph (MO-KS)
Topeka
Wichita

Kentucky

Bowling Green
Cincinnati (OH-KY-IN)
Clarksville (TN-KY)
Elizabethtown
Evansville (IN-KY)

Huntington-Ashland (WV-KY-OH)
Lexington-Fayette
Louisville (KY-IN)
Owensboro

Louisiana

Alexandria
Baton Rouge
Houma-Bayou Cane
Lafayette
Lake Charles
Monroe
New Orleans-Metairie
Shreveport-Bossier City

Maine

Bangor
Lewiston-Auburn
Portland-South Portland

Maryland

Baltimore-Towson
Bethesda-Gaithersburg
Cumberland (MD-WV)
Hagerstown-Martinsburg (MD-WV)
Salisbury
Washington-Arlington
  (DC-VA-MD-WV)
Wilmington (DE-MD-NJ)

Massachusetts

Barnstable Town
Boston-Quincy
Cambridge-Newton-Framingham
Essex County
Pittsfield
Providence-New Bedford (RI-MA)
Springfield
Worcester

Michigan

Ann Arbor
Battle Creek
Bay City
Detroit-Livonia-Dearborn
Flint
Grand Rapids-Wyoming
Holland-Grand Haven
Jackson
Kalamazoo-Portage
Lansing-East Lansing
Monroe
Muskegon-Norton Shores
Niles-Benton Harbor
Saginaw-Saginaw Township North
South Bend-Mishawaka
Warren-Farmington Hills

Minnesota

Duluth (MN-WI)
Fargo (ND-MN)
Grand Forks (ND-MN)
La Crosse (WI-MN)
Minneapolis-St. Paul (MN-WI)
Rochester
St. Cloud

Mississippi

Gulfport-Biloxi
Hattiesburg
Jackson
Memphis (TN-MS-AR)

Pascagoula

Missouri

Columbia
Fayetteville-Springdale (AR-MO)
Jefferson City
Joplin
Kansas City (MO-KS)
Springfield
St. Joseph (MO-KS)
St. Louis (MO-IL)

Montana

Billings
Great Falls
Missoula

Nebraska

Lincoln
Omaha-Council Bluffs (NE-IA)
Sioux City (IA-NE-SD)

Nevada

Carson City
Las Vegas-Paradise
Reno-Sparks

New Hampshire

Manchester-Nashua
Rockingham-Strafford County

New Jersey

Allentown-Bethlehem (PA-NJ)
Atlantic City
Camden
Edison
New York-White Plains
Newark-Union (NJ-PA)
Ocean City
Trenton-Ewing
Vineland-Millville
Wilmington (DE-MD-NJ)

New Mexico

Albuquerque
Farmington
Las Cruces
Santa Fe

New York

Albany-Schenectady-Troy
Binghamton
Buffalo-Niagara Falls
Elmira
Glens Falls
Ithaca
Kingston
Nassau-Suffolk
New York-White Plains (NY-NJ)
Poughkeepsie-Newburgh
Rochester
Syracuse
Utica-Rome

North Carolina

Asheville
Burlington
Charlotte-Gastonia (NC-SC)
Durham
Fayetteville

Goldsboro
Greensboro-High Point
Greenville
Hickory-Lenoir-Morganton
Jacksonville
Raleigh-Cary
Rocky Mount
Virginia Beach-Norfolk (VA-NC)
Wilmington
Winston-Salem

North Dakota

Bismarck
Fargo (ND-MN)
Grand Forks (ND-MN)

Ohio

Akron
Canton-Massillon
Cincinnati-Middletown (OH-KY-IN)
Cleveland-Elyria-Mentor
Columbus
Dayton
Huntington-Ashland (WV-KY-OH)
Lima
Mansfield
Parkersburg-Marietta (WV-OH)
Sandusky
Springfield
Toledo
Weirton-Steubenville (WV-OH)
Wheeling (WV-OH)
Youngstown-Warren (OH-PA)

Oklahoma

Fort Smith (AR-OK)
Lawton
Oklahoma City
Tulsa

Oregon

Bend
Corvallis
Eugene-Springfield
Medford
Portland-Vancouver (OR-WA)
Salem

Pennsylvania

Allentown-Bethlehem (PA-NJ)
Altoona
Erie
Harrisburg-Carlisle
Johnstown
Lancaster
Lebanon
Newark-Union (NJ-PA)
Philadelphia
Pittsburgh
Reading
Scranton--Wilkes-Barre
State College
Williamsport
York-Hanover
Youngstown-Warren (OH-PA)

Rhode Island

Providence-New Bedford (RI-MA)

South Carolina

Anderson
Augusta GA-SC)

Charleston-North Charleston
Charlotte-Gastonia (NC-SC)
Columbia
Florence
Greenville
Myrtle Beach-Conway-North
Myrtle
Spartanburg
Sumter

South Dakota

Rapid City
Sioux City (IA-NE-SD)
Sioux Falls

Tennessee

Chattanooga (TN-GA)
Clarksville (TN-KY)
Cleveland
Jackson
Johnson City
Kingsport-Bristol-Bristol (TN-VA)
Knoxville
Memphis (TN-MS-AR)
Morristown
Nashville-Davidson

Texas

Abilene
Amarillo
Austin-Round Rock
Beaumont-Port Arthur
Brownsville-Harlingen
College Station-Bryan
Corpus Christi
Dallas-Plano-Irving
El Paso
Fort Worth-Arlington
Houston-Sugar Land-Baytown
Killeen-Temple-Fort Hood
Laredo
Longview
Lubbock
McAllen-Edinburg-Mission
Midland
Odessa
San Angelo
San Antonio
Sherman-Denison
Texarkana (TX-AR)
Tyler
Victoria
Waco
Wichita Falls

Utah

Logan (UT-ID)
Ogden-Clearfield
Provo-Orem
Salt Lake City
St. George

Vermont

Burlington-South Burlington

Virginia

Blacksburg-Christiansburg-
    Radford
Charlottesville
Danville
Harrisonburg
Kingsport-Bristol-Bristol (TN-VA)
Lynchburg

Richmond
Roanoke
Virginia Beach-Norfolk (VA-NC)
Washington-Arlington
   (DC-VA-MD-WV)
Winchester (VA-WV)

Washington

Bellingham
Bremerton-Silverdale
Kennewick-Richland-Pasco
Lewiston (ID-WA)
Longview
Mount Vernon-Anacortes
Olympia
Portland-Vancouver (OR-WA)
Seattle-Bellevue-Everett
Spokane
Tacoma

Wenatchee
Yakima

West Virginia

Charleston
Cumberland (MD-WV)
Hagerstown-Martinsburg (MD-WV)
Huntington-Ashland (WV-KY-OH)
Morgantown
Parkersburg-Marietta (WV-OH)
Washington-Arlington
   (DC-VA-MD-WV)
Weirton-Steubenville (WV-OH)
Wheeling (WV-OH)
Winchester (VA-WV)

Wisconsin

Appleton

Duluth (MN-WI)
Eau Claire
Fond du Lac
Green Bay
Janesville
La Crosse (WI-MN)
Lake-Kenosha Counties
Madison
Milwaukee-Waukesha
Minneapolis-St. Paul (MN-WI)
Oshkosh-Neenah
Racine
Sheboygan
Wausau

Wyoming

Casper
Cheyenne

Appendix B

PEOPLE

The following tables show figures for population diversity, age, education, and wealth in each metro area.

DIVERSITY

America's metropolitan area population is 63.8 percent White, 13.4 percent Black, 16.7 percent Latino, 5.5 percent Asian and Pacific Islander, and 0.6 percent Native American.

Sumter, South Carolina, and Albany, Georgia, are America's two metro areas with a Black majority according to Woods & Poole Economics estimates. Fifteen metro areas have Latino populations greater than 50 percent. Honolulu has a 67 percent Asian and Pacific Islander majority. The metro area with the highest portion of Native Americans—40 percent—is Farmington, New Mexico.

Which metro areas are the most diverse? Via the "chi-square test," a statistical technique used to compare observed data with expected data, metro areas are scored from 100 (most diverse) to 0 (least diverse) by how closely they match national diversity. West Palm Beach, Florida, and College Station, Texas are most like metropolitan America. Other metro areas close behind are Atlantic City, Bridgeport, Newark, and Denver. At the other extreme, Altoona, Pennsylvania, with a population that is 97 percent White, and Laredo, Texas, that has a 96 percent Latino population, are among the least diverse.

MEDIAN AGE

The two metro areas with the youngest populations are military posts: Jacksonville, North Carolina (home of the Marines Camp Lejeune) and Hinesville-Fort Stewart, Georgia (home of the largest Army installation east of the Mississippi, Fort Stewart). Their residents' median age—a point where half the population is younger and the other half older—is under 25. Since 1970, median age has advanced from 27.5 to 36.6 across North America. The oldest metro area, at 54, is Punta Gorda on Florida's gulf coast.

WEALTH

Most per capita income comes from what you earn on the job. The figure has increased from $4,000 in 1970 to $36,500 today. It's no surprise that price inflation has taken a similar trajectory. The metro areas with the highest figures are found among New York suburbs and the San Francisco Bay area. The poorest are smaller metro areas along the Rio Grande and in the inner South.

But there's more to per capita income than just earnings. There's also income from dividends, interest, rent, and government welfare payments. The Woods & Poole Wealth Index shown in the following pages weights income more positively for a relatively high proportion of income from dividends, interest, and rent and more negatively for a relatively high proportion of income from transfer payments. The Wealth Index average for the United States is 100, ranging from 186 in Bridgeport-Stamford-Norwalk, Connecticut, to 51 in McAllen-Edinburg-Mission, Texas.

EDUCATION ATTAINMENT INDEX

Today about 52 percent of metro area adults over the age of 25 have attended college after high school, whether for an Associates degree from a community college, a Bachelors degrees from a college or university, or an advanced degree.

It makes a big difference in lifetime earnings. Adults with a bachelor's degree will make almost twice the income that adults with just a high school diploma will earn. Advanced degree holders will do even better, more than triple the income of high school graduates only.

In the following pages, the number under the EDUCATION column on the far right compares each metro area's education attainment, defined here is the percent of adults who've had at least some college, against the metro area average of 52. The higher the index number the better. It ranges from 171 in Boulder, Colorado, all the way down to 40 for Dalton, Georgia.

Metro Area	% White	% Black	% Latino	% Asian	% Native American	Politics	Median Age (yrs)	Wealth	Education
Metro Area Average	*63.8*	*13.4*	*16.7*	*5.5*	*0.60*	*50.7 D*	*36.6*	*100*	*100*
Abilene, TX	71.7	6.7	19.8	1.4	0.47	65.3 R	34	81	73
Akron, OH	84.8	12.0	1.0	1.9	0.24	58.6 D	38	98	95
Albany, GA	47.9	49.6	1.4	0.8	0.23	57.1 D	34	74	70
Albany-Schenectady, NY	85.2	7.8	3.6	3.1	0.23	55.8 D	39	102	112
Albuquerque, NM	44.5	2.6	44.4	2.1	6.42	50.8 R	37	91	101
Alexandria, LA	67.3	29.2	1.7	1.0	0.79	71.7 R	36	82	67
Allentown, PA-NJ	84.5	3.2	9.6	2.6	0.15	53.8 R	40	97	89
Altoona, PA	97.4	1.4	0.5	0.6	0.10	67.8 R	41	79	65
Amarillo, TX	68.5	5.9	23.0	2.0	0.62	89.3 R	34	82	81
Ames, IA	89.7	1.9	1.8	6.4	0.16	51.6 R	30	90	165
Anchorage, AK	72.8	5.9	6.4	6.7	8.19	50.1 R	34	110	103
Anderson, IN	88.4	8.7	2.0	0.6	0.31	62.4 R	39	83	66
Anderson, SC	80.2	17.4	1.6	0.7	0.20	81.6 R	38	81	68
Ann Arbor, MI	74.8	13.3	2.9	8.7	0.40	64.8 D	33	116	159
Anniston-Oxford, AL	76.3	20.2	2.3	0.9	0.42	69.5 R	38	77	69
Appleton, WI	92.8	0.7	2.2	2.9	1.34	62.3 R	37	100	95
Asheville, NC	89.5	5.1	4.2	0.8	0.37	53.7 R	41	90	100
Athens-Clarke, GA	70.5	20.7	5.9	2.7	0.20	55.3 R	32	83	109
Atlanta, GA	57.6	29.4	8.2	4.4	0.23	57.5 R	34	109	111
Atlantic City, NJ	60.6	17.0	15.4	6.8	0.23	55.2 R	38	98	81
Auburn-Opelika, AL	72.7	23.5	1.6	2.0	0.21	63.4 R	31	75	101
Augusta-Richmond, GA-SC	59.5	36.0	2.5	1.7	0.31	63.9 R	36	84	83
Austin-Round Rock, TX	57.6	7.4	30.1	4.7	0.30	53.6 R	33	109	124
Bakersfield, CA	44.1	6.0	45.1	3.9	0.96	77.7 R	31	73	62
Baltimore-Towson, MD	65.2	27.9	2.5	4.0	0.30	55.1 D	38	114	107
Bangor, ME	96.8	0.5	0.7	0.9	0.97	54.3 D	40	83	90
Barnstable Town, MA	94.6	2.2	1.7	1.0	0.54	59.2 D	46	125	123
Baton Rouge, LA	61.0	35.1	2.0	1.7	0.22	63.3 R	34	85	74

Metro Area	% White	% Black	% Latino	% Asian	% Native American	Politics	Median Age (yrs)	Wealth	Education
Metro Area Average	*63.8*	*13.4*	*16.7*	*5.5*	*0.60*	*50.7 D*	*36.6*	*100*	*100*
Battle Creek, MI	82.0	11.7	3.8	1.6	0.76	57.6 R	38	84	69
Bay City, MI	92.5	1.7	4.6	0.7	0.57	59.7 D	41	86	79
Beaumont-Port Arthur, TX	61.2	25.7	10.4	2.4	0.31	51.6 D	36	82	63
Bellingham, WA	85.9	1.0	6.2	4.0	2.87	61.2 D	35	88	109
Bend, OR	93.0	0.4	4.7	1.1	0.81	63.8 R	39	95	103
Bethesda, MD	61.1	13.5	12.0	13.1	0.23	62.4 D	38	159	159
Billings, MT	90.9	0.7	4.1	0.9	3.43	65.6 R	39	94	91
Binghamton, NY	90.5	3.6	2.5	3.1	0.22	53.9 D	41	84	98
Birmingham-Hoover, AL	67.5	28.6	2.6	1.1	0.24	68.1 R	37	99	87
Bismarck, ND	95.2	0.3	0.7	0.5	3.30	58.3 R	38	91	118
Blacksburg, VA	91.9	4.2	1.4	2.3	0.19	50.4 D	32	73	106
Bloomington, IN	92.7	2.1	1.7	3.2	0.33	51.0 R	32	82	98
Bloomington-Normal, IL	86.5	7.0	3.3	3.1	0.18	57.5 R	32	107	131
Boise City-Nampa, ID	85.6	0.7	11.0	1.9	0.74	66.8 R	34	97	90
Boston-Quincy, MA	72.4	12.3	8.3	6.8	0.21	74.4 D	37	131	127
Boulder, CO	80.7	0.9	13.6	4.4	0.44	69.6 D	35	144	171
Bowling Green, KY	86.7	8.0	3.4	1.7	0.23	65.7 R	34	80	103
Bremerton, WA	82.8	3.6	5.3	6.6	1.77	59.2 D	37	105	105
Bridgeport, CT	69.5	10.6	14.8	5.0	0.14	50.1 R	39	186	134
Brownsville, TX	12.1	0.2	87.0	0.5	0.10	58.4 D	29	55	55
Brunswick, GA	72.2	23.8	3.1	0.7	0.27	81.9 R	38	93	78
Buffalo, NY	80.6	13.0	3.8	1.9	0.69	56.4 D	40	90	98
Burlington, NC	68.8	18.8	10.7	1.4	0.36	62.5 R	36	88	78
Burlington, VT	95.4	0.9	1.0	2.1	0.58	53.5 D	38	104	133
Cambridge-Newton, MA	82.2	3.9	5.4	8.4	0.14	70.3 D	38	149	146
Camden, NJ	71.9	16.5	7.6	3.9	0.23	57.1 D	38	103	100
Canton-Massillon, OH	90.4	7.5	1.0	0.8	0.31	57.1 R	40	89	68
Cape Coral-Fort Myers, FL	76.7	7.8	14.3	1.0	0.22	62.7 R	44	110	82
Carson City, NV	77.3	1.4	17.5	1.8	2.00	65.1 R	40	107	69
Casper, WY	91.9	1.2	5.2	0.6	1.15	60.0 R	38	107	87
Cedar Rapids, IA	93.6	2.9	1.5	1.7	0.24	52.3 R	37	99	93
Champaign-Urbana, IL	78.3	10.8	3.3	7.3	0.22	53.7 R	32	96	125
Charleston, WV	93.1	5.2	0.5	1.0	0.22	50.4 R	41	90	68
Charleston, SC	63.2	31.9	2.7	1.8	0.40	67.9 R	36	89	101
Charlotte, NC-SC	65.5	23.4	7.9	2.8	0.38	57.0 R	35	106	106
Charlottesville, VA	80.5	13.5	2.9	2.9	0.17	60.0 R	36	108	123
Chattanooga, TN-GA	82.2	14.3	1.8	1.3	0.31	65.0 R	38	88	80
Cheyenne, WY	82.7	3.2	11.9	1.4	0.81	56.9 R	37	103	86
Chicago-Joliet, IL	54.6	19.5	19.9	5.8	0.16	61.9 D	35	115	107
Chico, CA	78.8	1.8	12.7	4.8	2.00	56.5 R	36	80	95
Cincinnati, OH-KY-IN	84.4	11.9	1.5	2.0	0.21	63.7 R	36	104	90
Clarksville, TN-KY	71.5	21.2	4.5	2.3	0.54	67.2 R	32	81	75
Cleveland, TN	93.0	3.6	2.3	0.7	0.32	71.1 R	38	80	63
Cleveland-Elyria, OH	73.8	19.9	3.9	2.1	0.22	62.6 D	39	104	91
Coeur d'Alene, ID	94.9	0.3	2.8	0.7	1.31	67.9 R	37	81	84
College Station-Bryan, TX	64.3	12.5	19.4	3.5	0.30	59.9 R	29	75	110
Colorado Springs, CO	74.8	7.5	13.2	3.6	0.87	70.1 R	34	101	119
Columbia, MO	84.7	9.5	2.0	3.5	0.39	55.0 R	32	92	140
Columbia, SC	60.2	34.8	3.1	1.7	0.26	55.6 R	36	90	104
Columbus, GA-AL	53.4	40.8	3.7	1.7	0.40	51.9 R	34	86	84
Columbus, IN	91.8	2.0	3.2	2.8	0.20	67.5 R	38	100	81
Columbus, OH	79.1	14.5	2.4	3.6	0.31	56.7 R	35	103	105
Corpus Christi, TX	38.3	3.2	56.8	1.4	0.33	51.2 R	35	82	70
Corvallis, OR	86.0	1.1	6.0	6.0	0.85	61.6 D	34	105	147
Cumberland, MD-WV	93.6	4.9	0.8	0.5	0.14	64.4 R	40	73	65
Dallas-Plano-Irving, TX	51.6	14.8	27.8	5.4	0.43	61.5 R	33	117	104

Metro Area	% White	% Black	% Latino	% Asian	% Native American	Politics	Median Age (yrs)	Wealth	Education
Metro Area Average	*63.8*	*13.4*	*16.7*	*5.5*	*0.60*	*50.7 D*	*36.6*	*100*	*100*
Dalton, GA	74.4	2.6	21.6	1.1	0.27	85.5 R	34	82	40
Danville, IL	83.1	11.9	3.9	0.8	0.25	57.6 R	38	75	54
Danville, VA	63.8	33.7	1.8	0.5	0.16	53.6 R	42	75	60
Davenport, IA-IL	84.4	6.7	6.9	1.6	0.25	53.2 D	38	95	93
Dayton, OH	81.2	15.2	1.3	2.0	0.29	58.0 R	38	97	87
Decatur, AL	81.0	12.3	4.3	0.6	1.87	55.2 R	39	82	66
Decatur, IL	81.5	15.9	1.3	1.1	0.22	52.3 R	39	93	82
Deltona-Daytona Beach, FL	78.6	10.2	9.5	1.4	0.29	51.5 D	43	86	84
Denver-Aurora, CO	66.9	5.7	22.7	4.1	0.62	51.9 D	35	128	121
Des Moines, IA	86.8	4.2	5.5	3.2	0.23	51.1 D	36	107	109
Detroit, MI	48.7	43.2	4.8	2.8	0.39	70.6 D	36	86	74
Dothan, AL	73.3	24.1	1.7	0.6	0.40	76.8 R	39	82	70
Dover, DE	71.9	21.5	3.8	2.2	0.64	65.6 R	35	80	65
Dubuque, IA	96.3	1.1	1.4	1.0	0.16	52.1 D	39	93	89
Duluth, MN-WI	94.3	1.2	0.8	0.9	2.74	72.3 D	40	87	93
Durham, NC	58.0	28.5	9.3	3.9	0.35	68.1 D	35	104	133
Eau Claire, WI	95.5	0.5	0.9	2.5	0.52	62.5 D	36	90	100
Edison, NJ	71.3	7.4	11.3	9.8	0.14	52.4 R	39	126	116
El Centro, CA	17.0	3.3	76.9	1.8	1.11	55.8 D	32	64	54
Elizabethtown, KY	81.6	12.1	3.4	2.5	0.43	70.2 R	36	84	77
Elkhart-Goshen, IN	79.9	5.6	13.0	1.3	0.26	71.4 R	33	92	53
Elmira, NY	89.2	6.8	2.5	1.2	0.24	55.0 R	40	78	88
El Paso, TX	13.2	2.1	83.4	1.0	0.29	62.2 D	31	66	63
Erie, PA	89.5	6.9	2.5	0.9	0.17	51.2 D	38	82	84
Essex County, MA	78.4	2.6	15.1	3.7	0.18	64.2 D	39	120	118
Eugene-Springfield, OR	88.5	1.2	6.0	3.1	1.25	63.6 D	38	89	96
Evansville, IN-KY	91.8	6.0	1.2	0.9	0.19	57.5 R	38	95	76
Fairbanks, AK	76.8	7.2	5.1	2.8	8.06	50.1 R	31	96	108
Fargo, ND-MN	94.1	1.2	2.0	1.6	1.14	53.2 D	33	97	117
Farmington, NM	43.0	0.5	16.1	0.4	40.01	58.7 R	31	69	53
Fayetteville, NC	50.4	38.3	6.1	2.6	2.57	53.6 D	31	82	79
Fayetteville, AR-MO	84.1	1.5	10.8	2.1	1.52	62.2 R	34	85	84
Flagstaff, AZ	54.1	0.9	11.6	1.1	32.21	53.4 D	31	86	107
Flint, MI	74.3	21.3	2.5	1.2	0.66	65.2 D	36	83	77
Florence, SC	55.9	42.0	1.2	0.7	0.22	50.6 D	37	80	77
Florence, AL	85.3	12.5	1.4	0.4	0.36	56.3 D	40	76	67
Fond du Lac, WI	94.7	1.1	2.7	1.1	0.45	69.3 R	39	95	70
Fort Collins, CO	86.3	0.9	10.1	2.2	0.58	50.6 R	34	109	139
Fort Lauderdale, FL	47.9	25.4	23.1	3.4	0.19	62.9 D	39	105	102
Fort Smith, AR-OK	81.3	3.9	6.0	2.4	6.46	57.7 R	37	75	57
Fort Walton Beach, FL	81.2	10.1	4.7	3.4	0.60	80.2 R	37	101	108
Fort Wayne, IN	82.3	10.5	5.1	1.8	0.34	65.1 R	35	96	91
Fort Worth, TX	61.2	11.6	22.6	4.1	0.51	65.5 R	33	98	90
Fresno, CA	36.8	5.4	48.3	8.6	0.89	61.1 R	31	75	75
Gadsden, AL	81.6	15.0	2.6	0.5	0.32	65.2 R	39	74	61
Gainesville, FL	69.1	21.0	5.7	4.0	0.26	55.6 D	32	84	130
Gainesville, GA	67.1	6.6	24.3	1.7	0.26	88.7 R	33	86	69
Gary, IN	69.5	18.6	10.5	1.1	0.24	61.9 D	37	88	72
Glens Falls, NY	95.1	2.1	2.1	0.6	0.20	63.3 R	41	82	92
Goldsboro, NC	58.3	33.5	6.7	1.2	0.33	59.9 D	36	77	72
Grand Forks, ND-MN	92.0	1.3	3.1	1.3	2.24	56.0 D	34	87	110
Grand Junction, CO	86.5	0.5	11.6	0.7	0.66	64.2 R	38	88	87
Grand Rapids, MI	80.7	8.2	8.4	2.1	0.53	63.8 R	34	93	92
Great Falls, MT	88.5	1.9	3.1	1.3	5.25	62.3 R	40	89	85
Greeley, CO	64.6	0.6	33.2	1.1	0.52	59.5 R	31	82	95
Green Bay, WI	90.0	1.4	4.2	2.3	2.09	63.0 R	37	100	90

Metro Area	% White	% Black	% Latino	% Asian	% Native American	Politics	Median Age (yrs)	Wealth	Education
Metro Area Average	*63.8*	*13.4*	*16.7*	*5.5*	*0.60*	*50.7 D*	*36.6*	*100*	*100*
Greensboro, NC	66.2	24.6	6.2	2.5	0.42	55.8 R	37	93	87
Greenville, NC	58.1	35.5	5.0	1.1	0.28	64.7 D	32	82	104
Greenville, SC	75.9	17.5	4.8	1.6	0.18	72.6 R	37	89	91
Gulfport-Biloxi, MS	73.9	20.4	2.4	2.8	0.48	53.2 D	36	83	80
Hagerstown, MD-WV	90.5	6.7	1.6	0.9	0.23	66.5 R	38	84	67
Hanford-Corcoran, CA	40.4	8.0	47.2	3.4	1.09	63.2 R	32	61	58
Harrisburg-Carlisle, PA	84.3	10.0	3.1	2.5	0.17	61.6 R	40	102	98
Harrisonburg, VA	88.2	3.0	7.0	1.5	0.16	51.7 D	32	81	77
Hartford, CT	74.6	10.4	11.1	3.6	0.20	60.0 D	40	118	112
Hattiesburg, MS	70.1	27.3	1.5	0.9	0.21	55.2 R	33	74	86
Hickory-Lenoir, NC	84.5	6.8	5.4	3.0	0.22	65.1 R	38	84	70
Hinesville, GA	50.7	38.9	7.1	2.6	0.65	72.8 R	25	63	55
Holland-Grand Haven, MI	86.9	1.2	8.7	2.9	0.34	76.1 R	33	94	99
Honolulu, HI	21.7	3.8	7.0	67.3	0.21	56.9 D	38	104	105
Hot Springs, AR	86.8	8.3	3.3	0.8	0.69	54.6 R	43	88	74
Houma-Thibodaux, LA	76.3	16.6	1.8	1.0	4.26	60.9 R	35	79	53
Houston-Baytown, TX	44.2	16.1	33.5	6.0	0.27	58.0 R	33	112	92
Huntington, WV-KY-OH	95.8	2.6	0.7	0.6	0.21	55.7 D	40	75	68
Huntsville, AL	72.2	22.3	2.5	2.2	0.70	56.1 D	37	97	115
Idaho Falls, ID	88.6	0.4	9.4	0.9	0.59	79.2 R	32	82	92
Indianapolis-Carmel, IN	78.7	14.9	4.1	2.0	0.25	62.3 R	35	107	99
Iowa City, IA	88.7	3.1	2.8	5.1	0.25	53.7 D	32	102	147
Ithaca, NY	82.3	4.0	3.7	9.6	0.37	65.4 D	32	88	163
Jackson, MI	87.4	8.7	2.7	0.8	0.45	58.6 R	38	81	81
Jackson, MS	51.2	46.5	1.2	0.9	0.13	61.8 R	35	89	104
Jackson, TN	66.1	30.9	2.1	0.8	0.19	55.0 D	36	82	70
Jacksonville, FL	68.8	23.1	4.7	3.1	0.32	67.5 R	36	98	95
Jacksonville, NC	72.9	18.6	5.1	2.7	0.73	64.7 D	24	85	69
Janesville, WI	89.0	5.0	4.5	1.2	0.30	52.3 D	38	87	69
Jefferson City, MO	89.4	7.8	1.5	0.9	0.42	55.3 R	37	88	80
Johnson City, TN	94.6	2.9	1.6	0.7	0.25	71.0 R	40	74	73
Johnstown, PA	95.1	3.3	1.0	0.5	0.09	69.2 D	43	76	67
Jonesboro, AR	87.2	9.4	2.4	0.6	0.34	57.3 D	35	74	68
Joplin, MO	91.4	1.6	4.2	1.0	1.81	73.9 R	36	77	61
Kalamazoo-Portage, MI	82.8	9.7	4.7	2.1	0.61	56.2 R	35	89	104
Kankakee-Bradley, IL	76.3	16.3	6.3	0.9	0.22	57.9 R	36	85	63
Kansas City, MO-KS	77.2	13.0	6.7	2.6	0.54	50.1 D	36	105	105
Kennewick-Richland, WA	70.6	1.4	24.9	2.4	0.69	65.2 R	33	86	88
Killeen-Temple, TX	59.0	19.9	17.3	3.0	0.68	66.5 R	30	80	84
Kingsport-Bristol, TN-VA	96.5	2.0	0.8	0.5	0.20	69.2 R	42	80	64
Kingston, NY	83.5	6.3	8.0	1.8	0.30	61.7 D	40	87	94
Knoxville, TN	90.2	6.5	1.5	1.5	0.30	71.4 R	39	91	89
Kokomo, IN	89.6	6.8	2.0	1.3	0.38	66.4 R	38	91	63
La Crosse, WI-MN	93.8	1.2	1.0	3.6	0.44	56.5 D	36	94	109
Lafayette, IN	86.1	2.3	6.1	5.3	0.26	62.1 R	31	88	102
Lafayette, LA	70.1	26.5	1.7	1.4	0.27	63.4 R	34	91	81
Lake Charles, LA	73.1	24.2	1.6	0.9	0.29	52.4 R	35	81	67
Lake-Kenosha, IL-WI	71.1	7.1	16.4	5.2	0.25	53.0 R	35	145	121
Lakeland, FL	69.3	14.9	14.2	1.3	0.31	62.9 R	38	86	67
Lancaster, PA	88.1	3.0	6.8	1.9	0.13	67.5 R	38	97	78
Lansing-East Lansing, MI	81.2	9.4	5.1	3.8	0.53	51.6 R	35	92	106
Laredo, TX	3.8	0.1	95.6	0.4	0.06	59.7 D	26	56	63
Las Cruces, NM	29.6	1.5	67.1	1.0	0.82	50.9 D	32	68	80
Las Vegas-Paradise, NV	57.5	9.0	26.0	6.8	0.62	52.5 D	35	99	73
Lawrence, KS	85.0	4.5	3.9	4.0	2.67	59.5 D	30	90	144
Lawton, OK	61.0	22.2	8.0	3.3	5.47	78.2 R	32	78	62

Metro Area	% White	% Black	% Latino	% Asian	% Native American	Politics	Median Age (yrs)	Wealth	Education
Metro Area Average	*63.8*	*13.4*	*16.7*	*5.5*	*0.60*	*50.7 D*	*36.6*	*100*	*100*
Lebanon, PA	91.4	1.3	6.1	1.1	0.15	59.4 R	41	91	62
Lewiston, ID-WA	92.5	0.3	2.2	0.9	4.16	63.1 R	41	86	72
Lewiston-Auburn, ME	96.7	1.0	1.2	0.8	0.32	59.8 D	40	84	73
Lexington-Fayette, KY	82.6	10.7	4.0	2.4	0.18	50.4 D	35	102	108
Lima, OH	83.7	13.6	1.6	0.9	0.23	57.0 R	37	84	71
Lincoln, NE	88.4	3.3	3.9	3.8	0.60	54.8 R	33	100	119
Little Rock, AR	72.9	22.7	2.6	1.4	0.44	53.4 D	36	93	90
Logan, UT-ID	88.8	0.5	8.0	2.2	0.59	80.8 R	27	72	104
Longview, TX	70.8	17.9	10.2	0.6	0.48	67.3 R	37	85	64
Longview, WA	89.5	0.8	6.1	1.7	1.86	59.3 D	38	81	69
Los Angeles, CA	28.5	9.2	48.5	13.4	0.33	66.5 D	34	99	94
Louisville, KY-IN	82.2	13.6	2.4	1.5	0.23	57.6 R	37	101	82
Lubbock, TX	59.6	7.6	31.0	1.4	0.37	71.2 R	32	82	84
Lynchburg, VA	79.0	18.8	1.1	0.9	0.30	73.7 R	39	84	75
Macon, GA	54.1	43.0	1.5	1.1	0.22	53.3 D	36	89	69
Madera, CA	43.2	3.4	50.3	1.7	1.41	68.1 R	33	66	58
Madison, WI	86.7	4.5	4.0	4.5	0.33	64.8 D	35	115	136
Manchester-Nashua, NH	90.5	1.7	4.3	3.3	0.27	57.5 R	39	113	115
Mansfield, OH	87.7	10.2	1.0	0.8	0.25	56.5 R	39	81	56
McAllen-Edinburg, TX	8.7	0.3	90.2	0.6	0.08	60.3 D	28	51	50
Medford, OR	88.3	0.6	8.4	1.5	1.14	61.8 R	40	90	83
Memphis, TN-MS-AR	48.7	45.9	3.2	2.0	0.21	52.6 D	35	97	82
Merced, CA	36.4	3.6	52.9	6.5	0.65	54.0 D	30	65	57
Miami-Miami Beach, FL	16.2	19.0	63.3	1.4	0.09	50.6 D	38	86	91
Michigan City, IN	84.1	11.2	3.7	0.5	0.40	51.3 D	38	83	67
Midland, TX	57.4	6.5	34.7	1.0	0.38	82.9 R	35	112	85
Milwaukee-Waukesha, WI	72.3	16.8	7.4	3.0	0.53	51.9 R	37	110	102
Minneapolis, MN-WI	83.4	6.1	4.4	5.4	0.73	52.5 D	36	122	125
Missoula, MT	93.5	0.5	1.8	1.6	2.68	50.2 R	36	91	118
Mobile, AL	60.3	35.7	1.3	2.0	0.71	58.5 R	36	75	75
Modesto, CA	52.0	2.8	39.1	5.2	0.84	57.1 R	32	76	60
Monroe, LA	63.3	34.1	1.6	0.8	0.22	70.5 R	34	81	74
Monroe, MI	94.2	2.2	2.5	0.8	0.33	58.3 D	38	94	71
Montgomery, AL	54.8	42.5	1.4	1.1	0.30	59.5 R	35	91	89
Morgantown, WV	93.5	2.7	0.9	2.6	0.20	55.5 D	34	81	88
Morristown, TN	91.5	2.9	4.7	0.6	0.25	68.9 R	39	73	50
Mount Vernon, WA	80.7	0.6	14.7	2.2	1.93	56.5 D	38	95	90
Muncie, IN	90.1	7.2	1.3	1.1	0.29	59.0 R	34	83	71
Muskegon, MI	79.0	15.1	4.3	0.7	0.87	50.3 R	36	77	77
Myrtle Beach, SC	79.1	16.2	3.4	1.0	0.37	77.8 R	40	84	84
Napa, CA	62.9	1.7	29.7	5.1	0.64	66.0 D	39	123	108
Naples, FL	67.3	5.7	26.0	0.8	0.19	69.1 R	44	152	97
Nashville-Davidson, TN	77.4	15.4	4.7	2.3	0.29	50.1 R	36	101	93
Nassau-Suffolk, NY	70.7	9.6	13.9	5.6	0.20	53.6 D	40	135	120
Newark-Union, NJ-PA	56.5	21.9	16.0	5.5	0.16	53.8 D	38	135	116
New Haven-Milford, CT	70.5	12.3	13.0	3.9	0.23	60.0 D	38	109	104
New Orleans, LA	53.4	38.5	4.9	2.8	0.37	51.4 D	36	93	83
New York, NY-NJ	39.3	21.0	27.7	11.7	0.28	71.5 D	37	120	110
Niles-Benton Harbor, MI	77.0	16.5	4.2	1.7	0.52	61.8 R	39	87	87
Norwich-New London, CT	82.4	6.6	6.4	3.4	1.15	50.1 D	39	113	103
Oakland-Fremont, CA	44.5	11.8	21.7	21.5	0.46	72.0 D	37	129	126
Ocala, FL	78.4	12.2	8.0	1.0	0.39	60.8 R	44	81	66
Ocean City, NJ	90.0	4.9	4.1	0.8	0.16	65.8 R	44	109	90
Odessa, TX	45.1	4.4	49.3	0.7	0.47	76.9 R	32	73	47
Ogden-Clearfield, UT	85.3	1.5	10.4	2.2	0.61	75.3 R	29	88	101
Oklahoma City, OK	72.4	11.4	8.6	3.5	4.00	72.7 R	35	92	91

Metro Area	% White	% Black	% Latino	% Asian	% Native American	Politics	Median Age (yrs)	Wealth	Education
Metro Area Average	*63.8*	*13.4*	*16.7*	*5.5*	*0.60*	*50.7 D*	*36.6*	*100*	*100*
Olympia, WA	83.3	3.2	5.4	6.5	1.61	61.1 D	38	97	109
Omaha, NE-IA	81.8	8.3	7.0	2.4	0.49	62.2 R	35	107	109
Orlando-Kissimmee, FL	59.0	15.3	21.5	3.9	0.27	53.3 R	36	91	98
Oshkosh-Neenah, WI	93.4	1.3	2.3	2.5	0.52	59.8 R	37	98	94
Owensboro, KY	94.2	4.0	1.2	0.5	0.12	61.2 R	38	82	59
Oxnard, CA	52.9	1.9	38.1	6.6	0.50	54.9 R	36	112	106
Palm Bay-Melbourne, FL	82.0	9.4	6.1	2.2	0.36	61.4 R	44	92	102
Panama City, FL	83.2	11.3	2.4	2.2	0.79	61.2 R	39	84	72
Parkersburg, WV-OH	97.4	1.1	0.5	0.7	0.27	55.5 D	41	80	68
Pascagoula, MS	74.6	20.8	2.3	2.0	0.33	51.1 R	36	74	76
Pensacola, FL	75.8	18.3	2.3	2.7	0.98	72.2 R	37	83	90
Peoria, IL	86.4	9.7	2.0	1.5	0.26	62.0 R	38	98	87
Philadelphia, PA	67.0	22.2	5.5	5.2	0.19	61.1 D	38	116	106
Phoenix-Scottsdale, AZ	61.3	3.7	30.4	2.7	1.99	63.7 R	33	94	95
Pine Bluff, AR	50.1	47.5	1.4	0.8	0.26	62.1 D	37	68	53
Pittsburgh, PA	89.0	8.4	0.8	1.6	0.12	54.9 D	42	103	98
Pittsfield, MA	93.4	2.4	2.4	1.5	0.16	85.7 D	43	106	112
Pocatello, ID	87.6	0.6	7.4	1.4	3.06	60.5 R	32	76	100
Portland, ME	96.2	1.0	1.0	1.5	0.26	58.6 D	41	103	116
Portland, OR-WA	78.9	3.2	10.3	6.7	0.89	60.8 D	36	104	108
Port St. Lucie, FL	75.4	12.3	11.0	1.1	0.30	60.2 R	45	111	83
Poughkeepsie-Newburgh, NY	73.0	10.1	13.6	3.0	0.27	56.7 R	37	97	104
Prescott, AZ	85.8	0.4	11.7	0.7	1.51	63.1 R	46	80	86
Providence, RI-MA	82.9	4.7	9.0	2.9	0.40	68.9 D	38	96	95
Provo-Orem, UT	88.3	0.5	8.4	2.1	0.60	80.4 R	25	72	125
Pueblo, CO	56.4	1.8	40.3	0.8	0.72	58.3 D	36	76	85
Punta Gorda, FL	89.8	4.7	4.3	1.1	0.18	59.3 R	54	97	67
Racine, WI	77.9	11.3	9.3	1.0	0.38	57.9 R	38	97	79
Raleigh-Cary, NC	67.6	19.9	8.3	3.9	0.34	51.0 D	34	108	136
Rapid City, SD	87.4	1.6	2.8	1.3	6.84	62.0 R	36	95	101
Reading, PA	82.0	3.9	12.6	1.4	0.14	50.5 R	38	95	76
Redding, CA	86.0	1.1	7.5	2.5	2.92	70.3 R	40	85	79
Reno-Sparks, NV	70.3	1.7	21.3	5.1	1.60	59.8 R	36	126	93
Richmond, VA	63.1	30.9	3.1	2.5	0.40	65.1 R	37	105	99
Riverside-San Bernardino, CA	41.6	8.0	44.4	5.3	0.72	61.2 R	32	79	72
Roanoke, VA	84.2	12.8	1.5	1.3	0.18	71.2 R	41	97	86
Rochester, MN	89.8	2.8	2.7	4.5	0.26	59.1 R	37	109	127
Rochester, NY	79.3	12.0	5.8	2.6	0.28	52.3 R	39	97	115
Rockford, IL	76.7	10.3	10.6	2.1	0.28	59.1 R	37	89	72
Rockingham-Strafford, NH	95.7	0.8	1.4	1.9	0.22	55.6 R	40	114	117
Rocky Mount, NC	50.5	44.4	4.2	0.5	0.40	61.9 D	38	80	63
Rome, GA	77.8	13.8	6.9	1.4	0.25	68.8 R	36	83	55
Sacramento, CA	60.8	7.9	18.4	12.1	0.91	52.4 R	35	101	107
Saginaw, MI	70.8	20.3	7.3	1.2	0.41	51.4 D	38	81	72
St. Cloud, MN	95.0	1.2	1.6	1.8	0.33	54.5 R	33	91	86
St. George, UT	91.6	0.3	5.6	1.1	1.44	73.6 R	30	73	87
St. Joseph, MO-KS	91.4	5.1	2.4	0.6	0.52	61.0 R	38	79	63
St. Louis, MO-IL	77.1	18.7	1.9	2.1	0.25	53.3 D	37	106	96
Salem, OR	74.8	1.1	20.1	2.5	1.48	51.4 R	34	84	80
Salinas, CA	36.5	3.4	53.1	6.5	0.46	62.7 D	33	106	86
Salisbury, MD	68.5	27.3	2.2	1.8	0.24	66.4 R	37	81	80
Salt Lake City, UT	78.1	1.3	15.1	4.7	0.83	52.4 R	30	98	101
San Angelo, TX	60.3	3.5	34.7	1.0	0.44	75.8 R	35	87	74
San Antonio, TX	38.4	5.7	53.7	1.8	0.31	57.6 R	34	89	85
San Diego, CA	52.0	5.8	30.7	10.8	0.64	53.7 R	35	113	115
Sandusky, OH	87.1	9.5	2.6	0.6	0.26	58.7 D	42	98	66

Metro Area	% White	% Black	% Latino	% Asian	% Native American	Politics	Median Age (yrs)	Wealth	Education
Metro Area Average	*63.8*	*13.4*	*16.7*	*5.5*	*0.60*	*50.7 D*	*36.6*	*100*	*100*
San Francisco, CA	50.5	4.7	17.8	26.7	0.26	78.8 D	41	183	150
San Jose-Sunnyvale, CA	40.7	2.4	25.9	30.7	0.34	67.7 D	37	149	140
San Luis Obispo, CA	75.4	2.1	18.6	3.1	0.74	58.6 R	39	105	109
Santa Ana-Anaheim, CA	46.7	1.7	34.4	16.9	0.35	62.7 R	36	126	117
Santa Barbara, CA	53.8	2.2	38.8	4.6	0.62	55.5 D	35	117	107
Santa Cruz, CA	64.5	1.1	29.5	4.2	0.61	75.3 D	37	126	125
Santa Fe, NM	45.0	0.6	50.5	1.2	2.65	75.9 D	41	111	124
Santa Rosa-Petaluma, CA	70.7	1.7	22.3	4.5	0.90	69.6 D	39	121	107
Sarasota-Bradenton, FL	82.3	6.6	9.7	1.2	0.20	54.6 R	47	130	95
Savannah, GA	61.0	34.5	2.3	1.9	0.29	59.5 R	34	93	92
Scranton--Wilkes-Barre, PA	95.3	1.8	1.8	0.9	0.11	58.8 R	42	88	77
Seattle-Bellevue, WA	73.1	5.4	7.1	13.4	1.08	64.3 D	38	131	131
Sebastian-Vero Beach, FL	81.4	8.7	8.8	0.9	0.20	65.5 R	47	140	87
Sheboygan, WI	89.5	1.2	4.1	4.9	0.37	61.5 R	39	100	82
Sherman-Denison, TX	83.3	5.7	8.6	0.8	1.54	70.5 R	37	76	80
Shreveport, LA	56.4	39.7	2.3	1.2	0.41	56.7 R	36	86	69
Sioux City, IA-NE-SD	80.0	2.1	12.7	3.3	1.85	53.3 R	35	91	76
Sioux Falls, SD	92.5	2.0	2.2	1.4	1.82	52.4 R	35	106	106
South Bend, IN-MI	80.3	11.6	5.8	1.8	0.50	52.6 R	36	93	83
Spartanburg, SC	71.9	21.5	4.3	2.1	0.23	67.3 R	37	82	71
Spokane, WA	90.0	2.2	3.5	2.6	1.63	56.6 R	36	87	103
Springfield, IL	86.0	10.8	1.4	1.6	0.23	64.5 R	38	104	100
Springfield, MA	77.4	6.1	14.0	2.3	0.22	80.5 D	38	92	100
Springfield, MO	94.2	2.1	1.9	1.1	0.71	65.1 R	36	85	76
Springfield, OH	87.8	9.5	1.5	0.9	0.35	57.2 R	39	84	69
State College, PA	91.2	2.4	1.5	4.7	0.15	70.8 R	31	87	124
Stockton, CA	41.9	7.8	35.7	13.8	0.70	55.7 R	32	77	72
Sumter, SC	46.4	50.2	1.9	1.3	0.27	57.3 D	35	71	72
Syracuse, NY	85.4	8.4	2.9	2.4	0.82	63.7 R	38	90	102
Tacoma, WA	74.3	8.9	7.4	7.8	1.56	55.9 D	35	94	93
Tallahassee, FL	60.0	33.8	4.1	1.9	0.27	64.8 D	33	88	122
Tampa-St. Petersburg, FL	71.9	11.3	13.7	2.8	0.30	57.8 R	41	97	90
Terre Haute, IN	92.4	4.9	1.1	1.3	0.31	51.8 R	36	78	75
Texarkana, TX-AR	70.6	24.5	3.7	0.6	0.64	61.1 R	37	79	56
Toledo, OH	80.4	12.9	4.9	1.5	0.27	58.0 D	36	93	84
Topeka, KS	82.3	7.8	7.3	1.1	1.49	57.0 R	38	93	82
Trenton-Ewing, NJ	59.1	20.3	12.4	7.9	0.17	59.1 D	37	126	119
Tucson, AZ	57.4	2.9	34.1	2.6	2.97	50.3 D	36	87	105
Tulsa, OK	74.0	9.6	6.4	1.8	8.19	63.3 R	36	98	92
Tuscaloosa, AL	60.5	36.7	1.5	1.0	0.21	54.5 R	34	82	81
Tyler, TX	66.0	18.2	14.6	0.8	0.35	71.4 R	36	93	84
Utica-Rome, NY	89.1	5.3	3.7	1.6	0.24	61.9 R	40	79	90
Valdosta, GA	61.9	33.2	3.4	1.1	0.42	61.1 R	32	76	82
Vallejo-Fairfield, CA	46.2	16.0	21.5	15.7	0.66	61.6 D	35	94	92
Victoria, TX	50.5	5.2	42.7	1.3	0.24	80.0 R	36	87	60
Vineland, NJ	53.2	21.0	23.7	1.2	0.84	55.8 R	37	80	60
Virginia Beach, VA-NC	60.1	32.6	3.5	3.4	0.43	53.2 R	35	94	95
Visalia-Porterville, CA	37.5	1.5	56.9	3.1	0.90	70.4 R	30	68	56
Waco, TX	62.3	15.0	21.0	1.3	0.34	50.8 R	32	80	79
Warner Robins, GA	68.1	26.0	3.4	2.2	0.39	66.6 R	35	87	85
Warren-Troy, MI	84.9	7.8	2.5	4.4	0.37	53.9 R	39	128	107
Washington, DC-VA-MD-WV	50.8	29.7	11.3	7.9	0.31	69.4 D	36	134	136
Waterloo-Cedar Falls, IA	89.3	7.1	2.0	1.4	0.15	51.9 R	37	88	94
Wausau, WI	92.2	0.4	1.0	6.0	0.38	67.4 D	39	97	87
Weirton, WV-OH	94.2	4.4	0.7	0.5	0.18	68.3 D	44	77	55
Wenatchee, WA	75.9	0.2	22.1	0.8	0.93	66.5 R	38	87	88

Metro Area	% White	% Black	% Latino	% Asian	% Native American	Politics	Median Age (yrs)	Wealth	Education
Metro Area Average	*63.8*	*13.4*	*16.7*	*5.5*	*0.60*	*50.7 D*	*36.6*	*100*	*100*
West Palm Beach, FL	63.5	16.6	17.6	2.2	0.17	52.9 D	42	146	102
Wheeling, WV-OH	95.4	3.4	0.5	0.6	0.13	60.5 D	43	83	67
Wichita, KS	78.0	8.0	9.3	3.6	1.08	65.5 R	35	96	87
Wichita Falls, TX	75.6	8.9	12.6	2.0	0.90	83.9 R	34	88	71
Williamsport, PA	93.6	4.8	0.7	0.6	0.23	81.4 R	41	82	72
Wilmington, DE-MD-NJ	72.0	18.6	6.0	3.2	0.22	54.7 R	37	110	99
Wilmington, NC	79.6	16.0	3.2	0.8	0.47	55.9 D	39	90	103
Winchester, VA-WV	90.3	4.5	4.0	1.0	0.21	69.4 R	38	92	72
Winston-Salem, NC	69.7	20.1	8.8	1.1	0.25	55.8 R	37	97	89
Worcester, MA	83.6	3.4	8.5	4.3	0.22	70.5 D	38	102	112
Yakima, WA	52.0	0.9	41.6	1.1	4.31	58.8 R	32	76	59
York-Hanover, PA	90.8	4.1	3.8	1.2	0.18	78.8 R	40	94	73
Youngstown, OH-PA	85.9	11.3	1.9	0.7	0.19	68.0 D	41	82	64
Yuba City, CA	59.1	2.7	24.8	11.4	1.96	69.1 R	33	76	72
Yuma, AZ	40.9	1.4	54.4	1.0	2.26	54.2 R	35	62	53

Source: Figures for race and Latino origin, median age in years, and the Wealth Index are forecasts for 2007 from Woods & Poole Economics, Washington, DC. Politics data are from Election Data Services, Washington, DC

Appendix C

METROPOLITAN AREA PLACE FINDER

Listed are cities, towns, and unincorporated places with more than 2,500 people within a metropolitan area's boundaries. In instances where an area has just one place over 2,500 persons, the largest places are listed.

The names of the 600 Principal Cities are **Bolded**. Principal cities are officially-defined as the largest incorporated place in the metro area, plus up to two additional places if more than 50,000 persons work in them.

The names of incorporated areas are shown in Plain Text. They have official boundaries and have met legal requirements of their respective states for incorporation as municipalities.

The names of unincorporated areas are shown in *Italics*. These 2,072 entries are populated places identified in the 2000 Census as having local recognition but no legal boundaries.

Bedroom communities—1,856 locations where a third or more of their residents work in other communities—are identified by an asterisk (*).

Whenever metro areas cross state lines, the postal abbreviation for each state or province follows the place name.

ABILENE, TX

Abilene	**114,757**
Clyde	3,673
Merkel	2,592
Stamford	3,213

AKRON, OH

Akron	**210,795**
Aurora	14,353
Barberton	27,192
Brimfield	*3,248*
Cuyahoga Falls	50,494
Fairlawn	7,202
Green	23,463
Hudson	23,084
Kent	28,135
Lakemore	2,649
Macedonia	10,314
Mogadore	3,966
Munroe Falls*	5,300
New Franklin	14,960
Northfield	3,722
Norton	11,552
*Portage Lakes**	*9,870*
Ravenna	11,510
Reminderville	2,512
Richfield	3,553
Silver Lake	3,159

Stow* 34,404
Streetsboro 14,210
Tallmadge 17,408
Twinsburg 17,380
Windham 2,749

ALBANY, GA

Albany.........................**75,394**
Dawson.........................4,859
Leesburg......................2,777
Putney........................2,998
Sylvester.....................5,924

ALBANY-SCHENECTADY-TROY, NY

Albany.........................**93,523**
Ballston Spa 5,574
Cobleskill 4,706
Cohoes* 15,085
Colonie........................8,236
Delmar.........................8,292
East Glenville.............6,064
East Greenbush...............4,085
Green Island 2,572
Hampton Manor................2,525
Hoosick Falls 3,350
Mechanicville 4,997
Menands.......................3,825
Milton 2,692
Niskayuna....................4,892
Ravena 3,323
Rensselaer 7,859
Rotterdam...................20,536
Saratoga Springs...........28,036
Schenectady **61,280**
Scotia* 7,958
South Glens Falls 3,445
Troy **48,310**
Voorheesville 2,782
Watervliet*....................9,889
Westmere.....................7,188
Wynantskill 3,018

ALBUQUERQUE, NM

Albuquerque **494,236**
Belen 7,121
Bernalillo....................6,938
Bosque Farms 3,969
Corrales*.....................7,638
Los Chaves...................5,033
Los Lunas 11,338
Los Ranchos de Albuquerque*........
.................................5,396
Meadow Lake 4,491
North Valley 11,923
Peralta 3,750
Placitas 3,452
Rio Rancho...................66,599
Santo Domingo Pueblo 2,550
South Valley 39,060
Valencia....................4,500

ALEXANDRIA, LA

Alexandria........................**45,693**
Ball...........................3,684
Colfax 1,676
Glenmora 1,558
Lecompte 1,338
Pineville 14,083

ALLENTOWN-BETHLEHEM-EASTON, PA-NJ

Allentown, PA **106,992**
Ancient Oaks, PA 3,161
Bangor borough, PA 5,305
Bath borough, PA 2,768
Beatyestown, NJ 3,223
Belvidere, NJ 2,732
Bethlehem, PA...................**72,895**
Catasauqua borough*, PA.....6,553
Coopersburg borough, PA.....2,570
Coplay borough, PA 3,371
Eastlawn Gardens, PA 2,832
Easton, PA......................**26,267**
Emmaus borough, PA...........11,351
Fountain Hill borough, PA.....4,595
Fullerton, PA 14,268
Hackettstown, NJ 9,375
Hellertown borough*, PA 5,615
Hokendauqua, PA..............3,411
Jim Thorpe borough, PA........4,892
Lansford borough, PA..........4,210
Lehighton borough, PA.........5,523
Macungie borough, PA..........3,111
*Middletown *, PA* 7,378
Nazareth borough, PA..........6,023
Nesquehoning borough, PA ..3,356
North Catasauqua borough, PA .....
.................................2,863
Northampton borough*, PA ...9,699
Palmer Heights, PA 3,612
Palmerton borough, PA.........5,279
Pen Argyl borough, PA.........3,670
Phillipsburg, NJ..............14,920
Slatington borough, PA.........4,413
Summit Hill borough, PA 3,010
Washington borough, NJ.......6,876
Weatherly borough, PA 2,621
Wilson borough, PA.............7,753
Wind Gap borough, PA..........2,827

ALTOONA, PA

Altoona **47,176**
Bellwood borough.................1,916
Hollidaysburg borough 5,519
Martinsburg borough 2,157
Roaring Spring borough 2,309
Tyrone borough 5,324

AMARILLO, TX

Amarillo **183,021**
Canyon* 13,353
Claude 1,328
Panhandle 2,609
White Deer.....................1,071

AMES, IA

Ames...........................**52,263**
Huxley........................2,347
Nevada* 6,129
Roland 1,242
Slater 1,421
Story City...................3,141

ANCHORAGE, AK

Anchorage......................**275,043**
Big Lake.....................2,635
Butte 2,561
Gateway.....................2,952
Meadow Lakes 4,819
Palmer 6,920
Tanaina.....................4,993
Wasilla 8,471

ANDERSON, IN

Alexandria* 5,868
Anderson......................**57,500**
Chesterfield 2,789
Elwood* 9,160
Pendleton 3,859

ANDERSON, SC

Anderson......................**25,899**
Belton 4,568
Centerville..................5,181
Homeland Park................6,337
Honea Path 3,517
Northlake 3,659
Pendleton 3,050
Piedmont 4,684
Powderville..................5,362
Williamston 3,878

ANN ARBOR, MI

Ann Arbor......................**113,271**
Chelsea 4,801
Dexter 3,198
Milan 3,396
Saline........................8,826
*Whitmore Lake**................6,574
Ypsilanti 21,832

ANNISTON-OXFORD, AL

Alexandria...................3,692
Anniston......................**23,741**
Jacksonville 8,862
Oxford........................**17,360**
Piedmont 4,968
*Saks**.......................10,698
Weaver........................2,555

APPLETON, WI

Appleton......................**69,411**
Brillion 2,910
Chilton 3,617
Combined Locks................3,000
Hortonville 2,630
Kaukauna 14,656

Kimberly 6,230
Little Chute 10,870
New Holstein 3,200
Seymour 3,432

ASHEVILLE, NC

Asheville.............................**72,231**
Black Mountain 7,650
Canton 4,002
East Flat Rock 4,151
Etowah 2,766
Flat Rock 2,750
Fletcher....................................4,522
Hendersonville 11,396
Lake Junaluska......................2,675
Mills River 5,979
*Royal Pines** 5,334
Swannanoa..............................4,132
Waynesville 9,386
Weaverville 2,508
Woodfin 3,277

ATHENS-CLARKE COUNTY, GA

Athens-Clarke County 103,238
Bogart....................................**1,094**
Comer.......................................1,156
Watkinsville..............................2,535
Winterville 1,059

ATLANTA-SANDY SPRINGS-MARIETTA, GA

Acworth* 18,428
Adairsville 3,090
Alpharetta..............................40,128
Atlanta **470,688**
Auburn*...................................7,134
Austell.....................................6,566
Avondale Estates...................2,623
Barnesville 5,808
*Belvedere Park** 18,945
Bonanza 2,904
Bremen 5,350
Buford 10,698
Canton 17,685
Carrollton...............................21,837
Cartersville 17,653
Chamblee 9,763
Clarkston*...............................7,078
College Park..........................20,181
Conley 6,188
Conyers 12,205
Covington 13,856
Cumming 5,802
Dacula 4,425
Dallas.......................................8,667
Decatur 17,884
Doraville 9,872
Douglasville 27,568
Druid Hills 12,741
Duluth 24,482
Dunwoody.............................32,808
East Point* 40,680
Euharlee 3,859
Experiment 3,233

Fair Oaks*..............................8,443
Fairburn 8,564
Fayetteville............................14,363
Forest Park 22,201
*Gresham Park**......................9,215
Griffin.....................................23,286
Hampton 4,743
Hapeville 6,085
Holly Springs 5,328
*Irondale**.................................7,727
Jackson 4,358
Jasper 2,837
Jonesboro................................3,922
Kennesaw 30,522
Lake City 2,776
Lakeview Estates 2,637
Lawrenceville 28,393
Lilburn 11,416
Locust Grove 3,434
Loganville 8,881
*Mableton**.............................29,733
Manchester..............................3,626
Marietta **61,261**
McDonough 15,523
Monroe 12,329
Monticello 2,565
Morrow.....................................5,283
*Mountain Park**.....................11,753
Newnan 24,654
Norcross 9,887
*North Atlanta**.......................38,579
North Decatur......................15,270
North Druid Hills 18,852
Palmetto 4,676
*Panthersville**........................11,791
Peachtree City 34,524
Powder Springs*...................14,507
*Redan**..................................33,841
Riverdale 15,475
Roswell 85,920
***Sandy Springs**.................**85,781**
Scottdale 9,803
Senoia 2,719
Smyrna 47,643
Snellville 19,238
Social Circle 4,053
Statham 2,555
Stockbridge 13,140
Stone Mountain 7,080
Sugar Hill* 15,696
Suwanee 12,553
Tallapoosa 3,031
Temple 3,910
Tucker..................................26,532
Tyrone 5,789
Union City 15,382
Villa Rica 9,897
Vinings 9,677
Winder 12,451
Woodstock 19,602

ATLANTIC CITY, NJ

Absecon 7,989
Atlantic City **40,368**
Brigantine* 12,861

Buena borough......................3,848
Egg Harbor City 4,497
Hammonton 13,585
Linwood 7,398
Margate City*..........................8,666
Northfield 8,025
Pleasantville 19,032
Pomona 4,019
Somers Point 11,701
Ventnor City* 12,737

AUBURN-OPELIKA, AL

Auburn...............................**49,928**
Opelika **23,804**
*Smiths** 21,756
Smiths Station 4,477

AUGUSTA-RICHMOND COUNTY, GA-SC

Aiken, SC...............................27,490
Augusta-Richmond County, GA.
....**190,782**
Belvedere, SC 5,631
Burnettown, SC 2,784
Clearwater, SC 4,199
Edgefield, SC...........................4,520
Evans *, GA............................17,727
Gloverville, SC 2,805
Grovetown*, GA........................7,483
Hephzibah, GA 4,210
Martinez *, GA.......................27,749
North Augusta*, SC 19,467
Thomson, GA 6,866
Waynesboro, GA 5,999

AUSTIN-ROUND ROCK, TX

*Anderson Mill**......................8,953
Austin **690,252**
Bastrop 7,297
*Brushy Creek** 15,371
Buda 3,948
Camp Swift 4,731
Cedar Park* 48,139
Elgin..8,689
Georgetown..........................39,015
Hutto 7,401
*Jollyville**..............................15,813
Kyle 17,770
Lago Vista 5,573
Lakeway* 8,852
Leander*.................................17,851
Lockhart.................................13,567
Lost Creek 4,729
Luling 5,386
Pflugerville* 27,531
Round Rock **86,316**
San Marcos...........................46,098
*Shady Hollow** 5,140
Smithville 4,370
Taylor 15,014
*Wells Branch**.......................11,271
West Lake Hills......................3,021
Wimberley...............................2,712
*Windemere**...........................6,868

BAKERSFIELD, CA

Arvin*	14,724
Bakersfield	**295,536**
Bear Valley Springs	4,232
California City*	11,790
Delano	45,531
Ford City	3,512
Golden Hills*	7,434
Lake Isabella	3,315
Lamont*	13,296
McFarland	11,875
Mojave	3,836
Oildale*	27,885
Ridgecrest	25,974
Rosamond*	14,349
Rosedale*	8,445
Shafter	14,569
Taft	9,106
Tehachapi	11,752
Wasco	23,874

BALTIMORE-TOWSON, MD

Aberdeen	14,305
Annapolis	36,300
Arbutus	20,116
Arnold*	23,422
Baltimore	**635,815**
Bel Air	10,014
Bowleys Quarters*	6,314
Brooklyn Park*	10,938
Cape St. Claire*	8,022
Carney*	28,264
Catonsville	39,820
Centreville	2,660
Chester	3,723
Cockeysville	19,388
Columbia	88,254
Crofton*	20,091
Deale*	4,796
Dundalk*	62,306
Edgemere	9,248
Eldersburg*	27,741
Elkridge*	22,042
Ellicott City*	56,397
Essex*	39,078
Fallston*	8,427
Ferndale*	16,056
Garrison	7,969
Glen Burnie	38,922
Green Haven*	17,415
Hampstead*	5,451
Hampton	5,004
Havre de Grace	11,884
Hillsmere Shores	2,977
Jarrettsville	2,756
Jessup	7,865
Joppatowne*	11,391
Kingsville	4,214
Lake Shore*	13,065
Linthicum	7,539
Lochearn*	25,269
Londontowne*	7,595
Manchester	3,557
Maryland City*	6,814

Mayo	3,153
Mays Chapel*	11,427
Middle River*	23,958
Milford Mill	26,527
Mount Airy	4,065
North Laurel*	20,468
Odenton*	20,534
Overlea*	12,148
Owings Mills	20,193
Parkville*	31,118
Parole	14,031
Pasadena*	12,093
Perry Hall*	28,705
Pikesville	29,123
Pleasant Hills	2,851
Pumphrey	5,317
Randallstown*	30,870
Reisterstown*	22,438
Riva	3,966
Riverside	6,128
Riviera Beach*	12,695
Rosedale	19,199
Rossville	11,515
Selby-on-the-Bay	3,674
Severn*	35,076
Severna Park*	28,507
Shady Side*	5,559
South Gate*	28,672
Stevensville*	5,880
Sykesville	4,440
Taneytown	5,453
Towson	**51,793**
Westminster	17,761
White Marsh	8,485
Woodlawn	36,079

BANGOR, ME

Bangor	31,074
Bangor	**31,074**
Brewer	9,138
Carmel	2,508
Corinth	2,631
Dexter	3,789
Glenburn	4,380
Hampden	6,773
Hampden	4,126
Hermon	4,921
Holden	2,940
Lincoln	5,258
Lincoln	2,933
Milford	3,013
Millinocket	5,034
Newport	3,104
Old Town	7,792
Orono	9,463
Orono	8,253
Orrington	3,627

BARNSTABLE TOWN, MA

Barnstable Town	**47,826**
Bourne	19,356
Brewster	10,242
Buzzards Bay	3,549
Chatham	6,832

Dennis	15,891
Dennis Port	3,612
East Dennis	3,299
East Falmouth*	6,615
East Harwich	4,744
East Sandwich	3,720
Eastham	5,551
Falmouth	33,644
Forestdale	3,992
Harwich	12,675
Mashpee	14,280
North Falmouth	3,355
Orleans	6,458
Pocasset	2,671
Provincetown	3,426
Sagamore	3,544
Sandwich	20,726
South Dennis	3,679
South Yarmouth*	11,603
Wellfleet	2,822
West Dennis	2,570
West Yarmouth*	6,460
Yarmouth	24,621
Yarmouth Port	5,395

BATON ROUGE, LA

Baker*	13,250
Baton Rouge	**222,064**
Brownfields	5,222
Denham Springs	10,206
Donaldsonville	7,535
Gardere*	8,992
Gonzales	8,499
Inniswold	4,944
Jackson	3,774
Merrydale*	10,427
Monticello	4,763
New Roads	4,790
Oak Hills Place*	7,996
Old Jefferson*	5,631
Plaquemine	6,717
Port Allen	5,062
Shenandoah*	17,070
St. Gabriel	5,471
Village St. George*	6,993
Walker	5,751
Westminster	2,515
Zachary	12,258

BATTLE CREEK, MI

Albion	9,348
Battle Creek	**53,202**
Brownlee Park	2,588
Marshall	7,363
Springfield	5,203

BAY CITY, MI

Auburn	2,057
Bay City	**34,879**
Essexville	3,590
Pinconning	1,349

BEAUMONT-PORT ARTHUR, TX

Beaumont	**111,799**

Bridge City 8,800
Central Gardens 4,106
Groves* 15,006
Lumberton* 9,637
Mauriceville 2,743
Nederland 16,751
Orange.............................. 18,052
Port Arthur **56,684**
Port Neches* 13,131
Silsbee..............................6,722
Vidor 11,290
West Orange 3,993

BELLINGHAM, WA

Bellingham **74,547**
Birch Bay 4,961
Blaine.............................4,330
Ferndale 9,977
Lynden 10,697
Sudden Valley..................... 4,165

BEND, OR

Bend..............................**67,152**
Deschutes River Woods 4,631
La Pine 5,799
Redmond 19,771

BETHESDA-GAITHERSBURG-FREDERICK, MD

*Adelphi** 14,998
*Aspen Hill** 50,228
*Ballenger Creek** 13,518
Bethesda **55,277**
*Braddock Heights** 4,627
Brookmont 3,202
Brunswick 5,242
*Burtonsville** 7,305
Calverton 12,610
Chevy Chase 2,776
Clover Hill 3,260
*Cloverly** 7,835
Colesville* 19,810
Damascus* 11,430
*Darnestown** 6,378
*Fairland** 21,738
Forest Glen........................7,344
Frederick **57,907**
Friendship Village................. 4,512
Gaithersburg...................**57,698**
*Germantown** 55,419
*Green Valley** 12,262
Hillandale.........................3,054
*Kemp Mill** 9,956
*Langley Park** 16,214
Middletown 2,860
*Montgomery Village**........... 38,051
Mount Airy 4,310
North Bethesda 38,610
*North Kensington** 8,940
*North Potomac** 23,044
*Olney** 31,438
Poolesville* 5,498
*Potomac** 44,822
*Redland** 16,998

Rockville 57,402
Rossmoor 7,569
Silver Spring 76,540
South Kensington* 7,887
Takoma Park* 18,540
Thurmont 6,036
*Travilah** 7,442
Walkersville* 5,593
*White Oak** 20,973

BILLINGS, MT

Billings **98,721**
Laurel..............................6,342
Lockwood 4,306
Red Lodge 2,401

BINGHAMTON, NY

Binghamton **45,492**
Endicott............................ 12,639
*Endwell** 11,706
Johnson City...................... 14,955
Owego 3,794
Waverly 4,493

BIRMINGHAM-HOOVER, AL

Adamsville 4,845
Alabaster* 27,517
Bessemer 28,641
Birmingham **231,483**
Brent 4,129
Brighton 3,416
*Cahaba Heights** 5,203
Calera 6,707
Center Point* 15,368
Centreville.........................2,507
Chalkville 3,829
Chelsea 3,635
Clanton 8,336
*Clay** 4,947
Columbiana 3,664
Fairfield........................... 11,696
*Forestdale** 10,509
Fultondale* 6,853
Gardendale* 12,830
*Grayson Valley** 5,447
Helena* 13,237
Homewood 23,963
Hoover **67,469**
Hueytown* 15,192
Irondale............................9,531
Jasper 14,088
*Lake Purdy** 5,799
Leeds 11,053
Meadowbrook 4,697
Midfield 5,319
Montevallo 5,092
*Moody** 10,764
Mount Olive 3,957
Mountain Brook 20,821
Oneonta 6,537
Pelham 19,450
Pell City 11,010
Pinson 5,033
Pleasant Grove* 10,312

Springville 3,054
Sumiton 2,582
Tarrant 6,691
Trussville..........................16,760
Vestavia Hills 31,022
Warrior..............................3,037

BISMARCK, ND

Bismarck **57,377**
Mandan* 17,225
Lincoln 2,297

BLACKSBURG–CHRISTIANS-BURG–RADFORD, VA

Blacksburg......................**39,130**
Christiansburg.................**17,926**
Pearisburg 2,768
Pulaski 9,088
Radford........................**14,575**

BLOOMINGTON, IN

Bloomfield..........................2,542
Bloomington **69,017**
Ellettsville* 5,294
Jasonville 2,508
Linton 5,808
Spencer 2,549

BLOOMINGTON-NORMAL, IL

Bloomington **69,749**
Le Roy 3,391
Normal **49,927**
Heyworth 2,470
Lexington 1,866
Chenoa 1,805
Hudson 1,664
Gridley 1,398
Danvers 1,132

BOISE CITY-NAMPA, ID

Boise City.......................**193,161**
Caldwell............................34,433
Eagle* 17,338
Emmett 6,124
Garden City 11,424
Homedale 2,577
Kuna* 10,153
Meridian 52,240
Middleton 4,409
Nampa..........................**71,713**
Star 2,767

BOSTON-QUINCY, MA

Abington 16,351
Avon..............................4,340
Bellingham........................ 15,784
Boston **559,034**
Braintree 33,681
Bridgewater 25,720
Brockton 94,632
Brookline..........................55,590
Canton 21,571

CAMBRIDGE-NEWTON-FRAMINGHAM, MA

Acton	20,562
Arlington	41,224
Ashby	2,930
Ashland	15,551
Ayer	7,228
Bedford	12,462
Belmont	23,371
Billerica	39,963
Boxborough	5,062
Burlington	23,299
Cambridge	**100,135**
Carlisle	4,829
Chelmsford	33,759
Cochituate*	*6,768*
Concord	16,833
Dracut	28,892
Dunstable	3,154
Everett	36,837
Framingham	**65,060**
Groton	10,437
Holliston	13,847
Hopkinton	14,112
Hudson	18,943
Lexington	30,266
Lincoln	7,931
Littleton	8,589
Littleton Common	*2,816*
Lowell	103,111
Malden	55,871
Marlborough	37,444
Maynard	10,230
Medford	53,523
Melrose	26,365
Natick	31,943
Newton	**83,158**
North Reading	13,949
Pepperell	11,408
Pinehurst	*6,941*
Reading	23,164
Sherborn	4,223
Shirley	7,612
Somerville	74,963
Stoneham	21,582
Stow	6,179
Sudbury	17,066
Tewksbury	29,043
Townsend	9,285
Tyngsborough	11,338
Wakefield	24,575
Waltham	59,556
Watertown	32,303
Wayland	13,002
West Concord	*5,632*
Westford	21,461
Weston	11,581
Wilmington	21,472
Winchester	21,181
Woburn	37,147

CAMDEN, NJ

Ashland	*8,375*
Audubon borough*	9,047
Barrington borough*	7,050
Beckett	*4,726*
Bellmawr borough	11,159
Berlin borough	7,844
Beverly	2,670
Blackwood	*4,692*
Bordentown	3,989
Browns Mills*	*11,257*
Burlington	9,791
Camden	**80,010**
Clayton borough*	7,447
Clementon borough	4,944
Collingswood borough*	14,083
Country Lake Estates	*4,012*
Echelon	*10,440*
Gibbstown	*3,758*
Glassboro borough	19,290
Glendora	*4,907*
Gloucester City*	11,582
Golden Triangle	*3,511*
Greentree	*11,536*
Haddon Heights borough*	7,427
Haddonfield borough	11,591
Lawnside borough	2,778
Leisuretowne	*2,535*
Lindenwold borough*	17,265
Magnolia borough	4,389
Marlton	*10,260*
Medford Lakes borough	4,185
Merchantville borough	3,820
Mount Ephraim borough	4,467
National Park borough	3,223
Oak Valley	*3,747*
Oaklyn borough	4,116
Palmyra borough*	7,641
Paulsboro borough	6,096
Pemberton Heights	*2,512*
Pennsauken	35,737
Pine Hill borough*	11,305
Pitman borough*	9,251
Ramblewood	*6,003*
Riverton borough	2,739
Runnemede borough*	8,520
Somerdale borough*	5,155
Springdale	*14,409*
Stratford borough	7,184
Turnersville	*3,867*
Westville borough	4,466
Williamstown*	*11,812*
Woodbury	10,435
Woodbury Heights borough	3,022
Woodlynne borough	2,745

CANTON-MASSILLON, OH

Alliance	22,742
Canal Fulton	5,054
Canton	**79,478**
Carrollton	3,297
Greentown	*3,154*
Louisville*	9,367
Massillon	**32,150**
Minerva	3,970
North Canton	16,780
Perry Heights*	*8,900*
Uniontown	*2,802*

CAPE CORAL-FORT MYERS, FL

Bonita Springs	37,992
Buckingham	*3,742*
Cape Coral*	**140,010**
Cypress Lake	*12,072*
Estero*	*9,503*
Fort Myers Beach	6,834
Fort Myers Shores*	*5,793*
Fort Myers	**58,428**
Gateway	*2,943*
Iona*	*11,756*
Lehigh Acres*	33,430
Lochmoor Waterway Estates	3,858
McGregor*	*7,136*
North Fort Myers*	40,214
Pine Manor	3,785
San Carlos Park*	16,317
Sanibel	6,072
St. James City	*4,105*
Suncoast Estates	*4,867*
Tice	*4,538*
Villas	*11,346*
Whiskey Creek	*4,806*

CARSON CITY, NV

Carson City	**56,062**

CASPER, WY

Bar Nunn	1,292
Casper	**51,738**
Evansville	2,328
Mills	2,898

CEDAR RAPIDS, IA

Anamosa	5,616
Belle Plaine	2,919
Cedar Rapids	**123,119**
Hiawatha	6,596
Marion*	30,233
Monticello	3,701
Mount Vernon	4,051
Vinton	5,219

CHAMPAIGN-URBANA, IL

Champaign	**71,568**
Gibson	3,281
Lake of the Woods	*3,026*
Mahomet	5,714
Monticello	5,275
Paxton	4,534
Rantoul	12,483
Savoy	4,839
St. Joseph	3,629
Tolono	2,776
Urbana	**38,463**

CHARLESTON, WV

Charleston	**51,176**
Cross Lanes*	*10,353*
Culloden	*2,940*
Dunbar	7,740
Hurricane	5,968

Madison 2,634
Nitro 6,750
Pinch................................ 2,811
Sissonville...........................4,399
South Charleston 12,700
St. Albans 11,105
Teays Valley* 12,704

CHARLESTON-NORTH CHARLESTON, SC

Charleston...................... **106,712**
Goose Creek 32,516
Hanahan*............................. 13,818
Hollywood..........................4,307
Isle of Palms 4,579
Ladson*............................... 13,264
Moncks Corner 6,525
Mount Pleasant................. 57,932
North Charleston.............. **86,313**
Summerville.......................37,714

CHARLOTTE-GASTONIA-CONCORD, NC-SC

Belmont, NC 8,779
Bessemer City, NC 5,319
Charlotte, NC **610,949**
Cherryville, NC 5,455
Clover, SC..........................4,251
Concord, NC **61,092**
Cornelius, NC 18,870
Cramerton, NC 3,005
Dallas, NC 3,411
Davidson, NC 8,544
Fairview, NC 4,493
Fort Mill, SC 8,257
Gastonia, NC...................... **68,964**
Harrisburg, NC 5,145
Huntersville*, NC 36,377
Indian Trail, NC................. 16,473
Kannapolis, NC.................. 30,089
Lake Park, NC 2,562
Lake Wylie, SC 3,061
Lowell, NC 2,671
Marshville, NC 2,820
Matthews, NC 25,306
Midland, NC 2,834
Mint Hill*, NC 17,871
Monroe, NC 29,987
Mount Holly, NC 9,676
Newport, SC 4,033
Pineville, NC 3,650
Polkton, NC 2,514
Rock Hill, SC......................59,554
South Gastonia *, NC 5,433
Stallings, NC......................3,854
Stanley, NC........................3,094
Tega Cay, SC......................4,372
Unionville*, NC 6,477
Wadesboro, NC 5,263
Waxhaw, NC 3,207
Weddington*, NC 8,465
Wesley Chapel, NC 3,378
Wingate, NC 2,866
York, SC 7,233

CHARLOTTESVILLE, VA

Charlottesville **40,437**
Crozet 2,820
Lake Monticello* 6,852

CHATTANOOGA, TN-GA

Chattanooga Valley, GA 4,065
Chattanooga, TN **154,762**
Collegedale, TN.................7,215
Dunlap, TN 4,681
East Brainerd *, TN...............14,132
East Ridge*, TN.................. 19,821
Fairview *, GA 6,601
Fort Oglethorpe, GA 8,964
Harrison *, TN 7,630
Jasper, TN 3,082
La Fayette, GA 6,753
Lakeview, GA 4,820
Middle Valley *, TN 11,854
Ooltewah *, TN 5,681
Red Bank*, TN....................11,726
Ringgold, GA 2,793
Rossville, GA 3,416
Signal Mountain*, TN...........7,146
Soddy-Daisy*, TN 11,985
South Pittsburg, TN.............3,123

CHEYENNE, WY

Cheyenne **55,731**
Pine Bluffs 1,162
Ranchettes*..........................4,869
South Greeley.......................4,201

CHICAGO-NAPERVILLE-JOLIET, IL

Addison............................. 36,811
Algonquin* 29,022
Alsip................................. 19,072
Arlington Heights 74,619
Aurora...............................168,181
Barrington 5,593
Barrington Hills 3,701
Bartlett*............................. 38,479
Batavia.............................. 27,172
Beecher 2,769
Bellwood*..........................19,517
Bensenville 20,514
Berkeley............................5,006
Berwyn* 51,409
Bloomingdale.................... 21,924
Blue Island........................22,788
Bolingbrook* 68,365
Boulder Hill* 8,169
Braidwood..........................6,320
Bridgeview 14,933
Broadview 7,856
Brookfield* 18,462
Buffalo Grove 13,946
Burbank*.............................27,634
Burnham 4,080
Burr Ridge 10,949
Calumet City*......................37,795
Calumet Park* 8,124

Carol Stream 40,040
Carpentersville* 37,204
Cary*................................... 19,115
Channahon*........................ 12,218
Chicago Heights 31,373
Chicago Ridge 13,668
Chicago **2,842,518**
Cicero*................................82,741
Clarendon Hills* 8,397
Coal City 5,170
Cortland 3,135
Country Club Hills* 16,534
Countryside 5,831
Crest Hill*...........................19,438
Crestwood 11,207
Crete* 8,772
Crystal Lake 40,922
Crystal Lawns......................2,933
Darien*................................22,730
DeKalb...............................42,085
Des Plaines 56,551
Dixmoor 3,813
Dolton*...............................24,504
Downers Grove....................49,094
East Dundee 3,138
Elburn 4,236
Elgin...................................98,645
Elk Grove Village.............34,025
Elmhurst 44,976
Elmwood Park* 24,499
Evanston.............................75,236
Evergreen Park.................. 19,876
Fairmont 2,563
Flossmoor* 9,390
Ford Heights 3,294
Forest Park 15,197
Fox River Grove* 4,890
Frankfort 15,819
Frankfort Square*................. 7,766
Franklin Park 18,490
Geneva 23,424
Genoa................................. 4,671
Gilberts 4,869
Glen Ellyn 27,193
Glencoe 8,979
Glendale Heights* 32,465
Glenview............................45,989
Glenwood* 8,663
Goodings Grove* 17,084
Hampshire 4,077
Hanover Park* 37,229
Harvard...............................9,104
Harvey 28,771
Harwood Heights.................. 8,188
Hazel Crest* 14,415
Hickory Hills* 13,542
Hillside...............................7,771
Hinsdale............................. 17,898
Hoffman Estates.................52,046
Homer Glen 24,736
Hometown 4,241
Homewood 18,917
Huntley 17,674
Indian Head Park..................3,656
Ingalls Park...........................3,082

Inverness*	7,343
Island Lake*	5,151
Itasca	8,444
Johnsburg*	6,277
Joliet	**136,208**
Justice*	12,692
La Grange	15,482
La Grange Park*	12,726
Lake in the Hills*	28,786
Lakemoor	3,321
Lakewood	3,502
Lansing	27,324
Lemont	15,146
Lincolnwood	12,026
Lisle	23,376
Lockport*	22,161
Lombard	42,816
Lynwood*	7,655
Lyons*	10,466
Manhattan	5,169
Marengo	7,381
Markham	12,304
Matteson	15,675
Maywood	25,777
McHenry	24,863
Melrose Park	22,512
Midlothian*	13,949
Minooka	8,403
Mokena*	17,396
Monee	4,629
Montgomery	11,959
Morris	12,939
Morton Grove	22,202
Mount Prospect*	54,482
Naperville	**141,579**
New Lenox*	23,197
Niles	29,330
Norridge	14,054
North Aurora*	14,394
North Riverside	6,382
Northbrook	34,190
Northfield	5,543
Northlake	11,358
Oak Brook	8,835
Oak Forest*	28,116
Oak Lawn	53,991
Oak Park*	50,757
Olympia Fields	4,673
Orland Hills*	7,273
Orland Park	55,461
Oswego*	23,330
Palatine*	67,232
Palos Heights	12,561
Palos Hills*	17,258
Palos Park	4,757
Park Forest*	23,036
Park Ridge	36,983
Peotone	3,981
Pistakee Highlands	3,812
Plainfield	28,162
Plano*	7,338
Posen	4,929
Preston Heights	2,527
Prospect Heights*	16,387
Richton Park*	12,998

River Forest	11,289
River Grove	10,216
Riverdale*	14,588
Riverside*	8,485
Robbins	6,375
Rolling Meadows	23,909
Romeoville	36,396
Roselle*	23,240
Rosemont	4,037
Sandwich	7,018
Sauk Village*	10,486
Schaumburg	72,805
Schiller Park	11,597
Shorewood*	12,114
Skokie	64,678
Sleepy Hollow	3,695
South Barrington	3,935
South Chicago Heights	3,873
South Elgin*	20,758
South Holland	21,552
Spring Grove	5,303
St. Charles	32,332
Steger*	10,409
Stickney	5,899
Stone Park	4,905
Streamwood*	37,312
Sugar Grove	8,416
Summit	10,348
Sycamore	14,831
Tinley Park*	57,477
University Park	8,102
Villa Park	22,616
Warrenville	13,217
West Chicago	26,554
West Dundee	7,875
Westchester	16,177
Western Springs*	12,530
Westmont	24,863
Wheaton	54,700
Wheeling	36,636
Willow Springs	6,011
Willowbrook	8,893
Wilmette*	26,922
Wilmington	5,957
Winfield	9,844
Winnetka	12,452
Wonder Lake	2,751
*Wonder Lake**	7,463
Wood Dale	13,419
Woodridge*	34,058
Woodstock	21,985
Worth*	10,652
Yorkville	10,791

CHICO, CA

Chico	**71,427**
Durham	5,220
Gridley	5,588
*Magalia**	10,569
Oroville	13,468
Palermo	5,720
Paradise	26,517
South Oroville	7,695
Thermalito	6,045

CINCINNATI-MIDDLETOWN, OH-KY-IN

Alexandria*, KY	7,996
Amberley, OH	3,276
Amelia, OH	3,481
Aurora, IN	4,064
Beckett Ridge *, OH	8,663
Bellevue*, KY	6,022
Bethel, OH	2,590
Blue Ash, OH	11,747
Bright *, IN	5,405
Brookville, IN	2,933
Burlington *, KY	10,779
Carlisle*, OH	5,362
Cherry Grove, OH	4,555
Cheviot*, OH	8,235
Cincinnati, OH	**308,728**
Claryville, KY	2,588
Cleves, OH	2,574
Cold Spring, KY	5,255
Covedale *, OH	6,360
Covington, KY	42,811
Crescent Springs, KY	3,975
Crestview Hills, KY	3,362
Crittenden, KY	2,571
Day Heights, OH	2,823
Dayton*, KY	5,556
Deer Park*, OH	5,615
Dent *, OH	7,612
Dillonvale, OH	3,716
Dry Run *, OH	6,553
Edgewood, KY	8,913
Elsmere*, KY	7,948
Erlanger, KY	16,852
Evendale, OH	2,880
Fairfield, OH	42,294
Finneytown *, OH	13,492
Florence, KY	26,349
Forest Park, OH	18,069
Forestville, OH	10,978
Fort Mitchell, KY	7,605
Fort Thomas*, KY	15,592
Fort Wright*, KY	5,438
Franklin, OH	12,410
Fruit Hill, OH	3,945
Georgetown, OH	3,720
Golf Manor, OH	3,682
Greendale, IN	4,357
Greenhills, OH	3,758
Groesbeck *, OH	7,202
Hamilton, OH	61,943
Harrison, OH	7,821
Hidden Valley, IN	4,417
Highland Heights*, KY	5,791
Independence*, KY	19,065
Kenwood, OH	7,423
Lakeside Park, KY	2,687
Landen *, OH	12,766
Lawrenceburg, IN	4,750
Lebanon, OH	19,978
Lincoln Heights, OH	3,817
Lockland, OH	3,393
Loveland*, OH	11,219
Ludlow, KY	4,647
Madeira*, OH	8,330

Cusseta-Chattahochee County, GA
.... 9,805
Ladonia, AL 3,229
Phenix City, AL 27,183

COLUMBUS, IN

Columbus **39,380**
Hope 2,185

COLUMBUS, OH

Ashville 3,252
Baltimore 2,919
Bexley* 12,322
*Blacklick Estates** 9,518
Buckeye Lake 3,060
Canal Winchester 5,652
Circleville 13,559
Columbus **730,657**
Delaware 31,322
Dublin 34,964
Gahanna 33,077
Grandview Heights 6,273
Granville 5,281
Grove City 30,892
Groveport 4,753
Heath 8,888
Hilliard 26,656
*Huber Ridge** 4,883
Johnstown 3,883
Lake Darby 3,727
Lancaster 36,063
Lincoln Village 9,482
London 9,396
Marysville 17,483
Mount Gilead 3,547
New Albany 5,827
Newark 47,301
Obetz 4,079
Pataskala* 12,624
Pickerington* 15,878
Plain City 3,462
Powell* 10,504
Reynoldsburg* 33,059
Sunbury 3,225
Upper Arlington* 31,550
West Jefferson 4,287
Westerville 34,722
Whitehall 18,052
Worthington 13,202

CORPUS CHRISTI, TX

Aransas Pass 8,877
Bishop 3,204
Corpus Christi **283,365**
Ingleside 9,531
Mathis 5,462
Port Aransas 3,667
Portland* 16,219
Robstown 12,484
Rockport 9,041
Sinton 5,509
Taft, TX 3,429

CORVALLIS, OR

Albany 5,672
Corvallis **49,553**
Philomath 4,213

CUMBERLAND, MD-WV

Cumberland, MD **20,915**
Frostburg, MD 7,958
Keyser, WV 5,410
La Vale, MD 4,613

DALLAS-PLANO-IRVING, TX

Addison 13,667
Allen* 69,222
Argyle 2,969
Balch Springs* 19,475
Carrollton 118,870
Cedar Hill* 41,582
Celina 3,716
Cockrell Hill 4,289
Commerce 8,971
Coppell 38,704
Corinth* 17,980
Crandall 3,475
Dallas **1,213,825**
Denton 104,153
DeSoto* 44,653
Double Oak 2,864
Duncanville* 35,150
Ennis 18,735
Fairview 5,201
Farmers Branch 26,487
Farmersville 3,357
Fate 2,533
Flower Mound* 63,524
Forney 10,579
Frisco* 70,793
Garland* 216,346
Glenn Heights* 9,324
Grand Prairie 112,124
Greenville 25,637
Heath 6,418
Hickory Creek 3,044
Highland Park 8,793
Highland Village* 15,105
Hutchins 2,941
Irving **193,649**
Justin 2,938
Kaufman 7,872
Krum 3,368
Lake Dallas* 7,000
Lancaster 32,233
Lewisville 90,348
Little Elm 18,012
Lucas 3,971
McKinney 96,581
Mesquite* 129,902
Midlothian 13,188
Murphy 11,026
Ovilla 3,780
Parker 2,513
Pilot Point 4,042
Plano **250,096**
Princeton 4,115

Prosper 4,207
Red Oak 7,171
Richardson 99,187
Roanoke 3,518
Rockwall 29,354
Rowlett* 53,664
Royse City 5,589
Sachse* 17,009
Sanger 6,354
Seagoville* 11,112
Sunnyvale 3,817
Terrell 17,665
The Colony* 37,972
Trophy Club* 7,333
University Park 23,806
Waxahachie 25,454
Wilmer 3,571
Wylie* 29,061

DALTON, GA

Chatsworth 3,924
Dalton **32,140**
Tunnel Hill 1,072
Varnell......................................1,261

DANVILLE, IL

Danville **32,920**
Georgetown 3,516
Hoopeston 5,753
Tilton 2,847
Westville 3,058

DANVILLE, VA

Chatham 1,298
Danville **46,143**
Gretna 1,222
Hurt 1,245

DAVENPORT-MOLINE-ROCK ISLAND, IA-IL

Aledo, IL 3,535
Bettendorf, IA 31,890
Coal Valley, IL 3,904
Colona*, IL 5,275
Davenport, IA **98,845**
East Moline, IL 21,250
Eldridge, IA 4,484
Galva, IL 2,705
Geneseo, IL 6,524
Kewanee, IL 12,655
Le Claire, IA 3,123
Milan, IL 5,237
Moline, IL **42,892**
Rock Island, IL **38,702**
Silvis, IL 7,489

DAYTON, OH

Beavercreek 39,655
Bellbrook* 6,960
Brookville 5,317
Cedarville 4,037
Centerville 23,162
Clayton* 13,194

Covington 2,575
Dayton **158,873**
Eaton 8,242
Englewood............................. 12,727
Fairborn 31,650
Fort McKinley 3,989
Germantown............................5,157
Huber Heights* 38,089
Kettering 55,481
Miamisburg 19,796
Moraine................................. 6,702
New Lebanon 4,208
Northridge............................. 8,487
Oakwood* 8,749
Piqua 20,883
Riverside* 22,733
*Shiloh** 11,272
Tipp City 9,357
Trotwood* 26,608
Troy....................................... 22,343
Union* 5,920
Vandalia 14,298
West Carrollton City 13,198
West Milton 4,684
Xenia..................................... 23,600
Yellow Springs...................... 3,665

DECATUR, AL

Decatur............................**54,727**
Falkville..................................1,177
Hartselle 13,080
Moulton................................. 3,276
Priceville 2,233
Town Creek 1,209
Trinity.................................... 1,842

DECATUR, IL

Decatur............................**77,836**
Forsyth.................................. 2,762
Harristown 1,259
Long Creek 1,319
Macon.................................... 1,151
Maroa 1,563
Mount Zion............................ 5,032
Warrensburg 1,209

DELTONA-DAYTONA BEACH-ORMOND BEACH, FL

Daytona Beach Shores 4,817
Daytona Beach **64,421**
De Bary*.................................16,413
De Land 24,375
Deltona* 82,788
Edgewater*............................. 21,132
Holly Hill............................... 12,630
Lake Helen 2,816
New Smyrna Beach.............. 22,356
Orange City 7,862
Ormond Beach **38,613**
*Ormond-By-The-Sea** 8,430
Pierson 2,604
Ponce Inlet............................ 3,202
Port Orange* 53,746

South Daytona...................... 13,733
West De Land 3,424

DENVER-AURORA, CO

Acres Green 3,205
*Applewood** 7,123
Arvada*.................................. 103,966
Aurora* **297,235**
Bennett 2,536
*Berkley** 10,743
Brighton 27,374
Broomfield 43,478
*Castle Pines** 5,958
Castle Rock 35,745
Castlewood........................... 25,567
Centennial 98,243
Cherry Hills Village.............. 6,138
*Columbine** 24,095
Commerce City...................... 34,189
Denver **557,917**
Derby 6,423
Edgewater* 5,211
Englewood............................. 32,350
Evergreen 9,216
Federal Heights*....................11,706
Genesee 3,699
Glendale 4,771
Golden 17,366
Greenwood Village 12,817
*Highlands Ranch** 70,931
*Ken Caryl** 30,887
Lakewood 140,671
Littleton 40,396
Lone Tree 8,554
Northglenn* 32,684
Parker*................................... 38,428
Ponderosa Park....................3,112
Roxborough Park* 4,446
Sheridan 5,483
Sherrelwood........................ 17,657
*Southglenn** 43,520
*Stonegate** 6,284
*The Pinery** 7,253
Thornton* 105,178
Twin Lakes........................... 6,301
*Welby** 12,973
Westminster* 105,084
Wheat Ridge......................... 31,242

DES MOINES-WEST DES MOINES, IA

Adel 4,046
Altoona* 12,938
Ankeny.................................. 36,681
Carlisle.................................. 3,544
Clive 13,851
Des Moines **194,163**
Grimes*.................................. 6,037
Indianola 13,944
Johnston 12,931
Norwalk* 7,877
Perry* 8,865
Pleasant Hill* 6,229
Polk City 2,940

Saylorville 3,238
Urbandale............................. 34,696
Waukee* 9,213
West Des Moines............. **52,768**
Windsor Heights*.................. 4,607
Winterset 4,877

DETROIT-LIVONIA-DEARBORN, MI

Allen Park 28,083
Belleville 3,853
*Canton**................................ 76,366
Dearborn Heights*.............. 56,176
Dearborn **94,090**
Detroit............................. **886,671**
Ecorse 10,757
Flat Rock 9,560
Garden City* 28,960
Gibraltar................................ 5,191
*Grosse Ile** 10,894
Grosse Pointe 5,426
Grosse Pointe Farms........... 9,325
Grosse Pointe Park* 11,905
Grosse Pointe Shores 2,630
Grosse Pointe Woods* 16,317
Hamtramck*........................... 21,994
Harper Woods* 13,621
Highland Park 15,430
Inkster* 28,870
Lincoln Park* 38,237
Livonia **97,977**
Melvindale 10,612
Northville 3,068
Plymouth............................... 9,100
*Redford** 51,622
River Rouge* 9,202
Riverview* 12,744
Rockwood..............................3,411
Romulus 23,853
Southgate 29,572
Taylor.................................... 64,962
Trenton..................................19,311
Wayne.................................... 18,589
Westland* 85,623
Woodhaven............................ 13,354
Wyandotte............................. 26,940

DOTHAN, AL

Abbeville................................2,963
Dothan **61,851**
Geneva 4,379
Headland 3,714

DOVER, DE

Dover **34,288**
Harrington............................. 3,236
Highland Acres 3,379
Milford................................... 3,098
Smyrna 7,356

DUBUQUE, IA

Asbury, IA 3,384
Cascade 1,662

Dubuque, IA **57,798**
Dyersville, IA 3,928
Epworth 1,580
Farley 1,363

DULUTH, MN-WI

Arnold, MN 3,032
Chisholm, MN 4,701
Cloquet, MN 11,476
Duluth, MN 84,896
Ely, MN 3,633
Eveleth, MN 3,661
Hermantown, MN 8,861
Hibbing, MN 16,509
Moose Lake, MN 2,551
Mountain Iron, MN 2,945
Proctor, MN 2,779
Superior, WI 26,779
Virginia, MN 8,666

DURHAM, NC

Carrboro* 16,425
Chapel Hill 49,543
Durham 204,843
Hillsborough 5,382
Roxboro 8,755
Siler City 8,079

EAU CLAIRE, WI

Altoona* 6,448
Bloomer 3,280
Chippewa Falls 13,374
Eau Claire 62,570
Lake Hallie 4,479
Stanley 3,304

EDISON, NJ

Asbury Park* 16,624
Atlantic Highlands borough ... 4,625
Avenel 17,552
Beach Haven West 4,444
Beachwood borough* 10,738
Belmar borough 5,962
Bernardsville borough 7,612
Bound Brook borough* 10,168
Bradley Beach borough 4,782
Brielle borough 4,878
Brownville 2,660
Carteret borough 21,460
Clearbrook Park 3,053
Cliffwood Beach 3,538
*Colonia** 17,811
Concordia 3,658
Crestwood Village 8,392
Dayton 6,235
Dunellen borough* 6,994
East Brunswick 46,756
*East Freehold** 4,936
Eatontown borough 14,088
Edison **97,687**
Fair Haven borough* 5,899
Fairview 3,942
*Fords** 15,032

Forked River 4,914
Freehold borough 11,439
*Heathcote** 4,755
Highland Park borough* 14,268
Highlands borough* 4,998
Iselin 16,698
Jamesburg borough 6,521
Keansburg borough* 10,619
*Kendall Park** 9,006
Keyport borough* 7,505
Lakehurst borough 2,683
Lakewood 36,065
*Laurence Harbor** 6,227
Lavallette borough 2,747
Leisure Village 4,443
Leonardo 2,823
Lincroft 6,255
Little Silver borough 6,137
Long Branch* 32,091
*Madison Park** 6,929
Manasquan borough 6,201
Manville borough* 10,404
Matawan borough* 8,819
Metuchen borough 13,383
Middlesex borough 13,938
Milltown borough* 7,130
Monmouth Beach borough ... 3,593
Monmouth Junction 2,721
*Morganville** 11,255
*Mystic Island** 8,694
Neptune City borough 5,176
New Brunswick 50,156
New Egypt 2,519
North Middletown 3,165
North Plainfield borough* 21,608
Oakhurst 4,152
*Ocean Acres** 13,155
Ocean Grove 4,256
Oceanport borough 5,780
*Old Bridge** 22,833
Perth Amboy* 48,797
Point Pleasant Beach borough 5,397
Point Pleasant borough* 19,861
Port Monmouth 3,742
Port Reading 3,829
*Princeton Meadows** 13,436
*Ramtown** 5,932
Raritan borough 6,391
Red Bank borough 11,876
Rossmoor 3,129
Rumson borough* 7,233
Sayreville borough* 43,017
Seaside Heights borough 3,220
Sewaren 2,780
Shark River Hills 3,878
Shrewsbury borough 3,742
Society Hill 3,804
*Somerset** 23,040
Somerville borough 12,478
South Amboy* 7,975
South Bound Brook borough . 4,505
South Plainfield borough 23,064
South River borough* 16,060
South Toms River borough 3,698

Spotswood borough* 8,237
Spring Lake borough 3,506
Spring Lake Heights borough 5,135
*Strathmore** 6,740
Tinton Falls borough 17,274
Toms River 86,327
Tuckerton borough 3,780
Union Beach borough* 6,659
Wanamassa 4,551
Watchung borough 6,170
West Belmar 2,606
*West Freehold** 12,498
West Long Branch borough ... 8,286
Woodbridge 18,309
*Yorketown** 6,712

EL CENTRO, CA

Brawley 22,433
Calexico 36,005
Calipatria 7,725
El Centro 39,636
Heber 2,988
Holtville 5,470
Imperial* 9,707

ELIZABETHTOWN, KY

Elizabethtown 23,450
Hodgenville 2,788
Radcliff* 21,471
Vine Grove 3,983

ELKHART-GOSHEN, IN

*Dunlap** 5,887
Elkhart 52,270
Goshen 31,269
Middlebury 3,150
Nappanee 6,634
Simonton Lake 4,053

ELMIRA, NY

Elmira Heights 4,011
Elmira 29,928
Horseheads 6,366
*Southport** 7,396
West Elmira 5,136

EL PASO, TX

Anthony 4,072
Canutillo 5,129
El Paso 598,590
Fabens 8,043
Horizon City 8,695
*San Elizario** 11,046
Socorro* 29,685
Sparks 2,974
Westway 3,829

ERIE, PA

Corry 6,548
Edinboro borough 6,737
Erie 102,612

Girard borough 3,017
Lake City borough 2,981
Lawrence Park 4,048
North East borough 4,331
Union City borough............... 3,364
Wesleyville borough 3,443

ESSEX COUNTY, MA

Amesbury* 16,643
Andover 33,042
Beverly 39,876
Boxford 8,177
Danvers 26,045
Essex 3,346
Georgetown 8,041
Gloucester 30,713
Groveland 6,608
Hamilton 8,349
Haverhill.............................. 60,242
Ipswich................................ 13,302
Lawrence.............................. 71,314
Lynn 88,792
Lynnfield 11,546
Manchester-by-the-Sea........ 5,335
Marblehead* 20,297
Merrimac 6,360
Methuen............................... 44,609
Middleton 9,273
Nahant 3,591
Newbury 7,002
Newburyport......................... 17,414
North Andover 27,155
Peabody 51,239
Rockport* 7,763
Rowley 5,845
Salem 41,756
Salisbury................................ 8,284
Saugus* 26,915
Swampscott* 14,288
Topsfield 6,183
Topsfield 2,826
Wenham 4,650
West Newbury 4,306

EUGENE-SPRINGFIELD, OR

Cottage Grove 8,724
Creswell................................. 4,632
Eugene............................. **144,515**
Florence..................................7,841
Junction City.......................... 5,369
Oakridge.................................3,147
Springfield **55,641**
Veneta 3,477

EVANSVILLE, IN-KY

Boonville, IN 6,782
Chandler, IN........................... 3,065
Evansville, IN 115,918
Henderson, KY 27,666
Highland, IN 4,107
Melody Hill, IN 3,066
Mount Vernon, IN 7,238
Newburgh, IN 3,298
Oakland City, IN 2,596

Princeton, IN........................ 8,652
Providence, KY......................3,549

FAIRBANKS, AK

College 11,402
Fairbanks........................ **31,324**
North Pole 1,778

FARGO, ND-MN

Dilworth, MN........................ 3,452
Fargo, ND **90,672**
Moorhead, MN...................... 34,081
West Fargo*, ND................... 19,487

FARMINGTON, NM

Aztec 7,084
Bloomfield............................ 7,442
Farmington...................... **43,161**
Kirtland 6,190
Shiprock............................... 8,156

FAYETTEVILLE, NC

Fayetteville **129,928**
Hope Mills* 12,782
Raeford................................ 3,594
Spring Lake* 8,197

FAYETTEVILLE-SPRINGDALE-ROGERS, AR-MO

Bella Vista *, AR 16,582
Bentonville, AR.................... 29,538
Centerton, AR....................... 5,477
Farmington, AR 4,376
Fayetteville, AR................**66,655**
Gentry, AR............................ 2,613
Johnson, AR.......................... 2,746
Little Flock, AR...................... 2,781
Lowell, AR 7,042
Pea Ridge, AR.......................3,344
Prairie Grove, AR 2,996
Rogers, AR........................**48,353**
Siloam Springs, AR 13,604
Springdale, AR **60,096**

FLAGSTAFF, AZ

Flagstaff **57,391**
Kachina Village......................2,664
Page 6,794
Sedona 3,213
Tuba City 8,225
Williams 3,094

FLINT, MI

Beecher............................... 12,793
Burton 30,916
Clio 2,619
Davison.................................. 5,372
Fenton................................... 11,901
Flint.................................. **118,551**
Flushing*................................8,110
Grand Blanc.......................... 7,898
*Lake Fenton** 4,876

Linden................................... 3,452
Mount Morris 3,321
Swartz Creek........................ 5,341

FLORENCE, SC

Darlington 6,525
Florence **31,269**
Hartsville.............................. 7,414
Lake City................................6,690
North Hartsville.................... 3,136

FLORENCE-MUSCLE SHOALS, AL

Florence **36,480**
Muscle Shoals **12,523**
Sheffield 9,228
Tuscumbia 8,170

FOND DU LAC, WI

Fond du Lac **42,435**
North Fond du Lac................ 5,024
Ripon 7,268
Waupun 3,267

FORT COLLINS-LOVELAND, CO

Berthoud* 4,887
Estes Park 5,812
Fort Collins **128,026**
Laporte 2,691
Loveland............................**59,563**
Wellington 3,469

FORT LAUDERDALE-POMPANO BEACH-DEERFIELD BEACH, FL

Broadview Park.................... 6,798
Broward Estates 3,416
Carver Ranches 4,299
Coconut Creek* 49,017
Cooper City* 30,022
Coral Springs* 128,804
Dania Beach 28,782
Davie 84,204
Deerfield Beach................**76,348**
Fort Lauderdale.............. **167,380**
Hallandale Beach 37,083
Hollywood 145,629
Kendall Green.......................3,084
Lake Forest...........................4,994
Lauderdale Lakes*.............. 31,826
Lauderdale-by-the-Sea 5,990
Lauderhill*............................59,621
Lighthouse Point* 11,262
Margate* 56,002
Melrose Park........................ 7,114
Miami Gardens 2,706
Miramar*............................. 106,623
*North Andrews Gardens** 9,656
North Lauderdale* 42,262
Oakland Park........................31,713
Parkland* 22,145
Pembroke Park.................... 5,487
Pembroke Pines*............... 150,380
Pine Island Ridge 5,199

Plantation.............................85,989
Pompano Beach Highlands.6,505
Pompano Beach 104,179
Rock Island............................3,076
Southwest Ranches 7,388
Sunrise 90,589
Tamarac*...............................59,923
Terra Mar..............................2,631
Weston*.................................65,679
Wilton Manors*......................12,858

FORT SMITH, AR-OK

Alma, AR 4,734
Barling, AR 4,318
Charleston, AR 3,025
Fort Smith, AR 82,481
Greenwood*, AR.....................7,914
Heavener, OK 3,246
Muldrow, OK 3,168
Ozark, AR 3,586
Pocola, OK 4,373
Poteau, OK 8,152
Roland, OK 3,110
Sallisaw, OK 8,621
Van Buren, AR......................21,249

FORT WALTON BEACH-
CRESTVIEW-DESTIN, FL

Crestview 17,707
Destin 12,423
Fort Walton Beach 19,817
Lake Lorraine........................7,106
Mary Esther 4,086
Niceville 12,582
Ocean City............................5,594
Valparaiso.............................6,365
Wright..................................21,697

FORT WAYNE, IN

Bluffton 9,460
Columbia City 8,024
Fort Wayne 223,341
Leo-Cedarville......................2,902
New Haven 13,676
Ossian 2,908
Tri-Lakes..............................3,925

FORT WORTH-ARLINGTON, TX

Aledo 2,524
Alvarado 3,977
Arlington 362,805
Azle.......................................10,350
Bedford*................................48,390
Benbrook*.............................21,922
*Briar**....................................5,350
Bridgeport.............................5,659
Burleson 29,613
Cleburne 29,184
Colleyville*............................22,394
Crowley*................................9,691
Decatur..................................6,031
Eagle Mountain*.....................6,599
Edgecliff Village....................2,523

Euless*.................................51,226
Everman 5,733
Forest Hill*........................... 13,227
Fort Worth 623,074
Grand Prairie 32,213
Grapevine.............................47,374
Haltom City 39,875
Hurst 37,967
Joshua 5,500
Keene 5,952
Keller*...................................35,706
Kennedale 6,547
Lake Worth 4,681
Mansfield*.............................37,627
North Richland Hills*............ 61,115
Rendon*.................................9,022
Reno 2,864
Richland Hills........................8,047
River Oaks*...........................6,910
Saginaw*...............................17,701
Sansom Park 4,121
Southlake 24,244
Springtown............................2,639
Watauga*...............................23,548
Weatherford.........................23,315
Westworth Village 2,870
White Settlement 15,736
Willow Park...........................3,463

FRESNO, CA

Clovis*..................................86,527
Coalinga* 17,350
Firebaugh 7,001
Fowler 4,713
Fresno............................461,116
Huron 7,187
Kerman 11,223
Kingsburg*............................11,148
Mendota............................... 8,942
Orange Cove 9,578
Parlier*................................. 13,025
Reedley 22,368
San Joaquin 3,579
Sanger 22,041
Selma 22,261
Squaw Valley........................2,691

GADSDEN, AL

Attalla 6,474
Gadsden 37,405
Glencoe................................5,254
Hokes Bluff 4,317
Rainbow City 8,880
Southside*............................7,691

GAINESVILLE, FL

Alachua.................................7,557
Gainesville 108,184
High Springs.........................4,157
Newberry 3,804

GAINESVILLE, GA

Flowery Branch 2,087

Gainesville 32,444
Lula.......................................1,752
Oakwood 3,408

GARY, IN

Cedar Lake*.......................... 9,901
Chesterton 12,032
Crown Point 22,697
De Motte 3,785
Dyer*.....................................15,071
East Chicago 30,946
Gary 98,715
Griffith*................................ 16,666
Hammond 79,217
Hebron 3,570
Highland 23,172
Hobart...................................27,768
Lake Station* 13,565
Lakes of the Four Seasons*.. 7,291
Lowell....................................8,039
Merrillville 31,525
Munster 22,347
Portage 35,687
Porter 5,217
Rensselaer 6,234
Roselawn..............................3,933
Schererville*........................ 28,394
South Haven*..........................5,619
St. John*............................... 10,783
Valparaiso............................29,102
Whiting 4,893
Winfield.................................3,523

GLENS FALLS, NY

Fort Edward 3,120
Glens Falls 14,108
Granville 2,623
Hudson Falls*.......................6,864
Warrensburg.........................3,208
West Glens Falls*.................6,721
Whitehall...............................2,648

GOLDSBORO, NC

Brogden...............................2,907
Elroy 3,896
Goldsboro 38,670
Mar-Mac 3,004
Mount Olive 4,410

GRAND FORKS, ND-MN

Crookston, MN......................7,929
East Grand Forks, MN..........7,734
Grand Forks, ND..............49,792

GRAND JUNCTION, CO

Clifton*.................................. 17,345
Fruita* 6,878
Fruitvale* 6,936
Grand Junction..................45,299
Orchard Mesa*......................6,456
Palisade................................2,683
Redlands*...............................8,043

GRAND RAPIDS-WYOMING, MI

Belding	5,895
Byron Center	3,777
Cedar Springs	3,234
Comstock Park*	10,674
Cutlerville*	15,114
East Grand Rapids*	10,384
Forest Hills	20,942
Fremont	4,256
Grand Rapids	**193,780**
Grandville	16,711
Hastings	7,166
Ionia	12,336
Kentwood	46,491
Lowell	4,140
Middleville	2,790
Northview	14,730
Portland	3,822
Rockford	5,062
Sparta	4,046
Walker	23,420
Wyoming	**70,122**

GREAT FALLS, MT

Great Falls	**56,338**

GREELEY, CO

Dacono	3,529
Eaton	3,932
Erie*	4,906
Evans*	17,470
Firestone	6,410
Fort Lupton	7,121
Frederick	6,620
Greeley	**87,596**
Johnstown	6,672
Lochbuie	3,588
Mead	2,663
Milliken	5,593
Platteville	2,598
Windsor*	13,839

GREEN BAY, WI

Algoma	3,197
Allouez*	14,875
Ashwaubenon	16,911
Bellevue	14,467
De Pere	23,375
Green Bay	**101,203**
Hobart	5,795
Howard	15,911
Kewaunee	2,877
Oconto	4,564
Oconto Falls	2,729
Pulaski	3,479
Suamico	10,221

GREENSBORO-HIGH POINT, NC

Archdale	9,428
Asheboro	23,639
Eden	15,679
Forest Oaks	3,241
Greensboro	231,962
High Point	**93,601**
Jamestown	2,997
Liberty	2,712
Oak Ridge	4,196
Pleasant Garden	4,911
Randleman	3,653
Reidsville	14,778
Stokesdale	3,524
Summerfield*	7,228
Trinity*	6,915
Wentworth	2,777

GREENVILLE, NC

Ayden	4,798
Farmville	4,546
Greenville	**69,517**
Winterville	4,688

GREENVILLE, SC

Arial	2,607
Berea*	14,158
Central	4,039
Clemson	12,311
Clinton	9,071
Dunean	4,158
Easley	18,851
Five Forks*	8,064
Fountain Inn	6,729
Gantt	13,962
Greenville	**56,676**
Greer	13,564
Laurens	9,824
Liberty	3,004
Mauldin	19,343
Parker*	10,760
Pickens	2,974
Piedmont	4,684
Sans Souci*	7,836
Simpsonville*	15,135
Taylors*	20,125
Travelers Rest	4,237
Wade Hampton*	20,458
Welcome*	6,390

GULFPORT-BILOXI, MS

Bay St. Louis	8,317
Biloxi	**50,209**
Diamondhead	5,912
D'Iberville*	7,900
Gulfport	**72,464**
Long Beach*	17,283
Pass Christian	6,851
Waveland	7,227
Wiggins	4,463

HAGERSTOWN-MARTINSBURG, MD-WV

Boonsboro, MD	2,982
Hagerstown, MD	**38,326**
Halfway *, MD	10,065
Martinsburg, WV	**15,996**
Robinwood, MD	4,731
Smithsburg, MD	2,859

HANFORD-CORCORAN, CA

Armona	3,239
Avenal	16,631
Corcoran	**22,456**
Hanford	**47,485**
Lemoore*	22,699

HARRISBURG-CARLISLE, PA

Boiling Springs	2,769
Camp Hill borough	7,424
Carlisle borough	**18,108**
Colonial Park	13,259
Enola*	5,627
Harrisburg	**47,472**
Hershey	12,771
Highspire borough	2,625
Hummelstown borough	4,402
Lawnton	3,787
Lemoyne borough	3,952
Linglestown*	6,414
Lower Allen*	6,619
Mechanicsburg borough	8,818
Middletown borough*	8,944
New Cumberland borough*	7,127
Paxtonia	5,254
Penbrook borough	2,926
Progress*	9,647
Rutherford	3,859
Schlusser*	4,750
Shippensburg borough	4,465
Steelton borough	5,667
Wormleysburg borough	2,651

HARRISONBURG, VA

Bridgewater	5,413
Broadway	2,460
Dayton	1,345
Elkton	2,606
Grottoes	2,164
Harrisonburg	**40,438**
Timberville	1,703

HARTFORD-WEST HARTFORD-EAST HARTFORD, CT

Andover	3,209
Avon	17,209
Berlin	19,590
Bloomfield	20,581
Blue Hills	3,020
Bolton	5,170
Bristol*	61,353
Broad Brook	3,469
Burlington	9,097
Canton	9,932
Chester	3,832
Clinton	13,612
Collinsville	2,686
Columbia	5,336
Coventry	12,190
Coventry Lake	2,914
Cromwell	13,594

Deep River......................4,714
Durham.............................7,266
Durham...........................2,773
East Granby......................5,058
East Haddam....................8,808
East Hampton.................12,194
East Hartford **49,173**
East Windsor 10,447
Ellington.........................14,217
Enfield.............................45,441
Essex................................6,783
Farmington 24,941
Glastonbury.....................33,089
Granby 11,088
Haddam 7,635
Hartford 124,397
Hartford **124,397**
Hazardville......................4,900
Hebron..............................9,198
Kensington.......................8,541
Killingworth......................6,403
Lake Pocotopaug...............3,169
Manchester......................55,572
Mansfield.........................24,558
Marlborough 6,267
Middlefield 4,281
Middletown......................47,438
New Britain 71,254
Newington.......................29,676
Old Saybrook...................10,512
Plainville.........................17,382
Portland............................9,543
*Rockville**........................7,708
Rocky Hill........................18,760
*Sherwood Manor**.............5,689
Simsbury.........................23,656
Somers 10,877
South Windsor................25,985
Southington.....................42,077
*Southwood Acres**............8,067
Stafford...........................11,857
Storrs............................10,996
Suffield 14,704
*Thompsonville**.................8,125
Tolland 14,571
Vernon............................29,491
Weatogue 2,805
West Hartford **61,173**
Westbrook.........................6,599
Wethersfield 26,220
Willington 6,216
Windsor...........................28,778
Windsor Locks.................12,411

HATTIESBURG, MS

Hattiesburg **47,176**
Lumberton 2,448
Petal*...............................10,088
Purvis................................2,445
Richton 1,008
Sumrall 1,163
*West Hattiesburg**.................6,305

HICKORY-LENOIR-MORGANTON, NC

Bethlehem 3,713
Cajah's Mountain.............2,634
Conover 7,093
Gamewell..........................3,866
Granite Falls 4,573
Hickory **40,232**
Hudson 3,061
Icard..............................2,734
Lenoir............................**17,912**
Long View 4,840
Maiden..............................3,263
Morganton.......................**17,041**
Mountain View 3,768
Newton 13,016
Salem 2,923
Sawmills*.........................4,931
*St. Stephens**..................9,439
Valdese............................4,530

HINESVILLE-FORT STEWART, GA

Hinesville........................**28,615**
Ludowici...........................1,558
Midway 1,008
Walthourville....................3,631

HOLLAND-GRAND HAVEN, MI

Allendale..........................11,555
Beechwood......................2,963
Coopersville.....................4,222
Ferrysburg 2,993
Grand Haven **10,586**
Holland **27,026**
Hudsonville 7,052
*Jenison**.........................17,211
Zeeland............................5,532

HONOLULU, HI

*Ahuimanu**.......................8,506
*Aiea** 9,019
*Ewa Beach**....................14,650
*Ewa Gentry** 4,939
Ewa Villages 4,741
Halawa..........................13,891
Hauula 3,651
Heeia..............................4,944
Honolulu **377,379**
Kahaluu 2,935
*Kailua** 36,513
*Kaneohe**........................34,970
Laie................................4,585
Maili 5,943
*Makaha**..........................7,753
*Makakilo City**.................13,156
Maunawili.......................4,869
*Mililani Town**..................28,608
*Nanakuli**........................10,814
*Pearl City**.......................30,976
Pupukea.........................4,250
*Village Park**....................9,625
Wahiawa 16,151

Waialua...........................3,761
*Waianae** 10,506
*Waimalu**.........................29,371
Waimanalo Beach 4,271
Waimanalo.......................3,664
*Waipahu**.........................33,108
*Waipio Acres**....................5,298
*Waipio**...........................11,672
Whitmore Village 4,057

HOT SPRINGS, AR

Hot Springs Village...............8,397
Hot Springs **37,847**
Piney...............................3,988
Rockwell.........................3,024

HOUMA-BAYOU CANE-THIBODAUX, LA

Bayou Cane.....................**17,046**
Chackbay.........................4,018
Chauvin 3,229
Cut Off.............................5,635
Galliano 7,356
Gray................................4,958
Houma **32,105**
Larose.............................7,306
Lockport............................2,596
*Raceland**.......................10,224
*Schriever**........................5,880
Thibodaux **14,408**

HOUSTON-SUGAR LAND-BAYTOWN, TX

Aldine............................13,979
Alvin................................22,171
Angleton 18,761
*Atascocita**......................35,757
*Bacliff**.............................6,962
Barrett............................2,872
Baytown **68,371**
Bellaire 17,206
Bellville 4,303
Bolivar Peninsula.............3,853
Brazoria 2,897
Brookshire 3,601
Bunker Hill Village 3,710
*Channelview**...................29,685
*Cinco Ranch**...................11,196
Cleveland..........................8,032
*Cloverleaf**......................23,508
Clute 10,731
Conroe............................47,042
Dayton 6,622
Deer Park........................28,993
*Dickinson**......................17,898
El Lago 2,963
Four Corners 2,954
Freeport..........................12,605
*Fresno**...........................6,603
*Friendswood**..................33,094
Galena Park.....................10,221
Galveston **57,466**
*Greatwood** 6,640

Hempstead 6,546
*Highlands** 7,089
Hitchcock.................................7,193
Houston **2,016,582**
Humble 14,803
Hunters Creek Village 4,445
Jacinto City* 9,945
Jersey Village 7,087
Katy 13,255
La Marque* 13,860
La Porte...................................33,136
Lake Jackson* 27,386
League City* 61,490
Liberty......................................8,433
Manvel 3,287
Meadows Place 6,442
*Mission Bend** 30,831
Missouri City* 69,941
Mont Belvieu............................2,525
Nassau Bay 4,056
Needville...................................3,288
*New Territory** 13,861
Oak Ridge North 3,306
Pasadena 143,852
Pearland* 56,790
*Pecan Grove** 13,551
Pinehurst 4,266
Piney Point Village....................3,421
Prairie View 4,658
Richmond 13,262
Richwood...................................3,267
Roman Forest............................2,950
Rosenberg.................................30,322
San Leon 4,365
Santa Fe* 10,498
Seabrook 10,907
Sealy..6,038
South Houston...........................16,219
*Spring** 36,385
Spring Valley..............................3,599
Stafford......................................19,227
Sugar Land.........................**75,754**
Sweeny.......................................3,622
Taylor Lake Village 3,547
Texas City..................................44,274
The Woodlands 55,649
Tomball 9,938
Webster 8,852
West Columbia 4,240
West University Place* 14,886
Willis...4,172
Winnie...2,914

HUNTINGTON-ASHLAND, WV-KY-OH

Ashland, KY **21,510**
Barboursville, WV..................3,185
Burlington, OH.....................2,794
Culloden, WV 2,940
Flatwoods*, KY 7,621
Huntington, WV **49,198**
Ironton, OH.............................11,417
Kenova, WV.............................3,391
Pea Ridge *, WV..................6,363
Russell, KY 3,597

South Point, OH......................3,922
Westwood, KY 4,888

HUNTSVILLE, AL

Athens 20,972
Harvest 3,054
Hazel Green 3,805
Huntsville **166,313**
Madison.................................35,893
Meridianville 4,117
*Moores Mill** 5,178
New Hope...............................2,671

IDAHO FALLS, ID

Ammon* 10,925
Idaho Falls......................**52,338**
Rigby 3,245

INDIANAPOLIS-CARMEL, IN

Avon.......................................8,918
Beech Grove...........................14,069
Brownsburg* 18,290
Carmel **59,243**
Cicero 4,368
Cumberland*...........................5,319
Danville...................................7,425
Edinburgh 4,193
Fishers....................................57,220
Fortville..................................3,626
Franklin...................................21,747
Greencastle 10,065
Greenfield 16,654
Greenwood 42,236
Indianapolis **784,118**
Lawrence 40,959
Lebanon..................................14,633
Martinsville 11,657
Mooresville 11,111
New Whiteland 4,431
Noblesville..............................38,825
Plainfield.................................23,532
Shelbyville 18,063
Sheridan..................................2,661
Speedway................................12,408
Westfield..................................12,322
Whiteland 4,271
Zionsville.................................11,853

IOWA CITY, IA

Coralville.................................17,811
Iowa City...........................**62,887**
North Liberty* 8,808
Washington.............................7,207

ITHACA, NY

Cayuga Heights......................3,699
Ithaca **29,766**
Lansing 3,417
South Hill 6,003

JACKSON, MI

Brooklyn..................................1,363

Concord 1,112
Grass Lake.............................1,171
Jackson............................**34,879**
Michigan Center 4,641
Vandercook Lake.................4,809

JACKSON, MS

Brandon 19,390
*Byram** 7,386
Canton 12,507
Clinton 26,017
Crystal Springs......................5,913
Florence.................................3,063
Flowood 6,762
Hazlehurst 4,372
Jackson **177,977**
Madison* 16,737
Magee.....................................4,294
Mendenhall.............................2,544
Pearl.......................................23,111
Richland.................................7,051
Ridgeland 21,236

JACKSON, TN

Henderson 6,061
Jackson............................**62,099**
Three Way 1,342

JACKSONVILLE, FL

Atlantic Beach* 13,436
Butler Beach........................4,436
Fernandina Beach 11,264
*Fruit Cove** 16,077
Green Cove Springs.............6,085
Hilliard...................................2,913
Jacksonville Beach..............21,770
Jacksonville **782,623**
*Lakeside** 30,927
Macclenny 5,186
*Middleburg** 10,338
Neptune Beach......................7,018
Orange Park 9,205
*Palm Valley** 19,860
Sawgrass.............................4,942
St. Augustine 12,263
St. Augustine Beach* 5,753
St. Augustine Shores..........4,922
Villano Beach 2,533
*Yulee** 8,392

JACKSONVILLE, NC

*Half Moon** 6,645
Jacksonville **62,628**
*Piney Green** 11,658
Swansboro..............................1,338

JANESVILLE, WI

Beloit......................................35,621
Clinton 3,124
Edgerton 5,034
Evansville...............................4,658
Janesville **61,962**
Milton* 5,464

JEFFERSON CITY, MO

California	4,137
Fulton	12,101
Holts Summit	3,384
Jefferson City	**39,062**
Tipton	3,142

JOHNSON CITY, TN

Central	2,717
Elizabethton	13,944
Erwin	5,786
Johnson City	**58,434**
Jonesborough	4,550
Oak Grove	4,072
Pine Crest	2,872
Spurgeon	3,460
Unicoi	3,481

JOHNSTOWN, PA

Belmont	2,846
Ebensburg borough	2,938
Elim	4,175
Johnstown	**22,539**
Nanty-Glo borough	2,903
Northern Cambria borough	4,022
Portage borough	2,686
Westmont borough	5,234

JONESBORO, AR

Harrisburg	2,165
Jonesboro	**59,358**
Lake	2,002
Lepanto	2,079
Marked Tree	2,720
Trumann	6,922

JOPLIN, MO

Carl Junction*	6,483
Carthage	13,096
Joplin	**47,183**
Neosho	11,130
Webb City	10,764

KALAMAZOO-PORTAGE, MI

Eastwood*	6,265
Kalamazoo	**72,700**
Mattawan	2,838
Paw Paw	3,328
Portage	**45,277**
South Haven	5,148
Westwood*	9,122

KANKAKEE-BRADLEY, IL

Bourbonnais*	16,875
Bradley	**13,812**
Kankakee	**26,642**
Manteno	7,955
Momence	3,066

KANSAS CITY, MO-KS

Basehor, KS	3,287
Belton*, MO	24,140
Blue Springs*, MO	53,099
Bonner Springs, KS	6,942
Buckner, MO	2,724
Butler, MO	4,249
Cameron, MO	4,570
De Soto, KS	5,170
Edwardsville, KS	4,503
Excelsior Springs, MO	11,472
Fairway, KS	3,840
Gardner*, KS	14,317
Gladstone*, MO	27,306
Grain Valley*, MO	8,644
Grandview, MO	24,549
Greenwood, MO	4,512
Harrisonville, MO	9,790
Higginsville, MO	4,660
Independence*, MO	110,208
Kansas City, KS	**144,210**
Kansas City, MO	**444,965**
Kearney, MO	7,399
Lansing*, KS	10,214
Leavenworth, KS	35,213
Leawood, KS	30,145
Lee's Summit, MO	80,338
Lenexa, KS	43,434
Lexington, MO	4,632
Liberty, MO	29,042
Louisburg, KS	3,313
Merriam, KS	10,769
Mission, KS	9,751
Mission Hills, KS	3,523
North Kansas City, MO	5,388
Oak Grove, MO	6,763
Odessa, MO	4,841
Olathe, KS	111,334
Osawatomie, KS	4,616
Ottawa, KS	12,597
Overland Park, KS	**164,811**
Paola, KS	5,292
Parkville, MO	5,116
Peculiar, MO	3,832
Platte City, MO	4,907
Pleasant Hill*, MO	6,747
Pleasant Valley, MO	3,445
Prairie Village*, KS	21,454
Raymore*, MO	15,530
Raytown*, MO	28,923
Richmond, MO	6,075
Riverside, MO	2,964
Roeland Park*, KS	6,975
Shawnee*, KS	57,628
Smithville*, MO	7,118
Spring Hill, KS	4,494
Sugar Creek, MO	3,598
Tonganoxie, KS	3,774

KENNEWICK-RICHLAND-PASCO, WA

Benton City	2,971
Connell	2,980
Finley	5,770
Highland	3,388
Kennewick	**60,997**
Pasco	**46,494**
Prosser	5,140
Richland	**44,317**
West Pasco	4,629
West Richland*	9,907

KILLEEN-TEMPLE-FORT HOOD, TX

Belton	15,530
Copperas Cove*	30,643
Gatesville	15,651
Harker Heights*	21,337
Killeen*	**100,233**
Lampasas	7,465
Morgan's Point Resort	4,061
Temple	**55,447**

KINGSPORT-BRISTOL-BRISTOL, TN-VA

Abingdon, VA	7,925
Bloomingdale *, TN	10,350
Blountville, TN	2,959
Bristol, VA	**17,335**
Bristol, TN	**24,994**
Church Hill, TN	6,370
Colonial Heights *, TN	7,067
Kingsport, TN	**44,130**
Mount Carmel, TN	5,270
Rogersville, TN	4,283
Spurgeon, TN	3,460
Walnut Hill, TN	2,756

KINGSTON, NY

Ellenville	3,954
Highland	5,060
Hurley	3,561
Kingston	**23,067**
New Paltz	6,765
Port Ewen	3,650
Saugerties	3,930

KNOXVILLE, TN

Alcoa	8,388
Clinton	9,381
Eagleton Village	4,883
Farragut*	19,054
Knoxville	**180,130**
Lenoir City	7,675
Loudon	4,745
Maryville	25,851
Oak Ridge	24,323
Seymour*	8,850

KOKOMO, IN

Greentown	2,459
Indian Heights	3,274
Kokomo	**46,178**
Russiaville	1,186
Tipton	5,254

LA CROSSE, WI-MN

Caledonia, MN	2,939
French Island *, WI	4,410
Holmen*, WI	7,446

La Crescent, MN 5,088
La Crosse, WI..................**50,287**
Onalaska, WI.....................15,701
West Salem, WI..................4,709

LAFAYETTE, IN

Delphi 2,980
Lafayette..........................**60,459**
West Lafayette* 28,599

LAFAYETTE, LA

Breaux Bridge.......................7,902
Broussard 6,754
Carencro 6,097
Lafayette..........................**112,030**
Scott 8,120
St. Martinville 6,947
Youngsville 5,289

LAKE CHARLES, LA

Carlyss..............................4,049
DeQuincy 3,234
Iowa 2,591
Lake Charles.....................**70,555**
*Moss Bluff**........................10,535
*Prien**..............................7,215
Sulphur 19,608
Vinton 3,173
Westlake............................4,565

LAKE COUNTY-KENOSHA COUNTY, IL-WI

Antioch, IL 12,353
Barrington, IL 4,586
Beach Park*, IL...................12,486
Buffalo Grove, IL 29,169
Camp Lake, WI 3,255
Deer Park, IL 3,232
Deerfield, IL 19,142
Fox Lake Hills, IL 2,561
Fox Lake*, IL 10,207
Gages Lake *, IL 10,415
Grandwood Park, IL 4,521
Grayslake*, IL 21,099
Green Oaks, IL 3,914
Gurnee, IL..........................30,772
Hainesville, IL 3,765
Hawthorn Woods*, IL............7,176
Highland Park, IL..................31,380
Highwood, IL.......................5,468
Island Lake*, IL 3,268
Kenosha, WI 95,240
Kildeer, IL 4,004
Lake Barrington, IL 5,033
Lake Bluff, IL.......................6,251
Lake Forest, IL.....................21,123
Lake Villa, IL........................8,492
Lake Zurich, IL.....................20,045
Libertyville, IL 21,760
Lincolnshire, IL 6,841
Lindenhurst*, IL 14,403
Long Grove*, IL....................7,833
Long Lake, IL 3,356

Mundelein*, IL 32,774
North Barrington, IL...............3,207
North Chicago, IL 33,376
Paddock Lake, WI 3,150
Park City*, IL.......................6,775
Pleasant Prairie, WI 18,551
Riverwoods, IL 4,100
Round Lake, IL 14,803
Round Lake Beach*, IL.........28,253
Round Lake Park, IL..............6,224
Silver Lake, WI 2,513
Twin Lakes, WI 5,513
Venetian Village, IL...............3,082
Vernon Hills, IL 23,957
Wadsworth, IL 3,651
Wauconda, IL 10,903
Waukegan, IL......................91,396
Winthrop Harbor*, IL 7,090
Zion*, IL 24,303

LAKELAND, FL

Auburndale 12,381
Bartow 16,278
Combee Settlement..............5,436
Crystal Lake 5,341
*Cypress Gardens**.................8,844
Dundee 3,064
Fort Meade 5,742
Frostproof 2,950
Fussels Corner 5,313
Gibsonia 4,507
Haines City 16,371
*Inwood**............................6,925
*Jan Phyl Village**.................5,633
Kathleen 3,280
Lake Alfred 3,930
Lake Wales 12,964
*Lakeland Highlands**............12,557
Lakeland...........................**88,713**
*Medulla**...........................6,637
Mulberry 3,233
Wahneta 4,731
Willow Oak........................4,917
Winston............................9,024
Winter Haven......................29,501

LANCASTER, PA

Akron borough.....................4,009
Columbia borough*..............10,092
Denver borough...................3,646
East Petersburg borough* 4,346
Elizabethtown borough........11,892
Ephrata borough.................13,092
Lancaster.........................**54,757**
Lititz borough......................9,008
Manheim borough 4,659
Marietta borough 2,603
Maytown 2,604
Millersville borough...............7,583
Mount Joy borough..............6,944
Mountville borough 2,746
New Holland borough 5,140
Reamstown.......................3,498
Rothsville 3,017

Strasburg borough................2,745
Willow Street 7,258

LANSING-EAST LANSING, MI

Charlotte 9,069
DeWitt* 4,441
East Lansing......................**46,419**
Eaton Rapids 5,266
Grand Ledge* 7,768
*Haslett**............................11,283
*Holt**...............................11,315
Lansing...........................**115,518**
Mason..............................7,985
Okemos 22,805
St. Johns............................7,436
Waverly............................16,194
Williamston 3,790

LAREDO, TX

El Cenizo 3,640
Laredo **208,754**
Rio Bravo...........................5,724

LAS CRUCES, NM

Anthony 7,904
Chaparral...........................6,117
Las Cruces........................**82,671**
Santa Teresa 2,607
Sunland Park*.....................14,089
University Park 2,732
Vado 3,003

LAS VEGAS-PARADISE, NV

Boulder City........................15,177
Enterprise 14,676
Henderson*........................232,146
Las Vegas.........................**545,147**
Laughlin 7,076
Mesquite 13,523
Moapa Valley 5,784
North Las Vegas...............176,635
Paradise **186,070**
*Spring Valley**......................117,390
*Sunrise Manor**...................156,120
*Whitney**.............................18,273
Winchester..........................26,958

LAWRENCE, KS

Baldwin City...........................3,746
Eudora 5,284
Lawrence..........................**81,816**

LAWTON, OK

Cache 2,406
Elgin................................1,278
Fletcher 1,038
Lawton............................**90,234**

LEBANON, PA

Annville 4,518
Avon................................2,856
Cornwall borough 3,447

Lebanon 23,986
Myerstown borough 3,106
Palmyra borough* 6,957

LEWISTON, ID-WA

Clarkston, WA.....................7,304
Lewiston, ID 31,081

LEWISTON-AUBURN, ME

Auburn.............................23,602
Durham 3,984
Greene 4,404
Lewiston............................36,050
Lisbon 9,444
Lisbon Falls 4,420
Livermore Falls 3,235
Mechanic Falls....................3,238
Minot 2,835
Poland 5,312
Sabattus 4,670
Turner 5,469

LEXINGTON-FAYETTE, KY

Georgetown 19,988
Lexington-Fayette 268,080
Nicholasville 23,897
Paris 9,334
Versailles 7,728
Wilmore 5,826
Winchester........................16,494

LIMA, OH

Bluffton 3,825
Delphos 3,877
Fort Shawnee 3,790
Lima.............................38,608

LINCOLN, NE

Lincoln............................239,213
Seward 6,776
Waverly 2,693

LITTLE ROCK-NORTH LITTLE ROCK, AR

Benton 25,673
Bryant*...........................13,185
Cabot*............................21,039
Conway 51,999
East End.........................5,623
England 3,028
Gibson 4,678
Gravel Ridge....................3,232
Greenbrier 3,615
Haskell 3,016
Hot Springs Village 8,397
Jacksonville 30,367
Little Rock 184,564
Lonoke 4,552
Maumelle 14,318
North Little Rock 58,803
Salem 2,789
Shannon Hills 2,651
Sheridan 4,349
Sherwood*........................23,149
Vilonia 2,719

Ward 3,271

LOGAN, UT-ID

Hyde Park, UT 2,858
Hyrum*, UT 6,061
Logan, UT 47,357
Nibley, UT 2,907
North Logan, UT 6,730
Preston, ID 5,019
Providence, UT 5,516
Smithfield*, UT 7,589
Wellsville, UT 2,575

LONGVIEW, TX

Gilmer 5,141
Gladewater 6,295
Henderson 11,496
Kilgore 11,858
Longview..........................73,941
White Oak.........................6,130

LONGVIEW, WA

Kelso 11,854
Longview Heights 3,513
Longview..........................36,137
West Longview 2,882
Woodland 4,233

LOS ANGELES-LONG BEACH-GLENDALE, CA

Agoura Hills 22,765
Alhambra*.........................87,410
Alondra Park.....................8,622
Altadena.........................42,610
Arcadia 56,153
Artesia 16,672
Avalon 3,334
Avocado Heights 15,148
Azusa.............................47,120
Baldwin Park* 78,861
Bell Gardens* 45,135
Bell*..............................37,521
Bellflower* 74,570
Beverly Hills 35,078
Burbank 104,108
Calabasas 21,908
Carson 93,955
Cerritos 52,561
Charter Oak 9,027
Citrus...........................10,581
Claremont 35,182
Commerce 13,455
Compton 95,659
Covina 47,850
Cudahy*..........................25,004
Culver City 39,603
Del Aire 9,012
Diamond Bar* 57,975
Downey...........................109,718
Duarte* 22,194
East Compton 9,286
East La Mirada 9,538
East Los Angeles 124,283

East Pasadena...................6,045
East San Gabriel................14,512
El Monte 122,513
El Segundo 16,517
Gardena...........................59,891
Glendale 200,065
Glendora*.........................50,540
Hacienda Heights...............53,122
Hawaiian Gardens*...............15,398
Hawthorne*........................85,697
Hermosa Beach..................19,500
Huntington Park 62,491
Inglewood*........................114,467
La Canada Flintridge 20,998
La Habra Heights 5,970
La Mirada.........................49,640
La Puente*........................41,762
La Verne........................33,185
Ladera Heights..................6,568
Lake Los Angeles...............11,523
Lakewood*........................80,467
Lancaster.........................134,032
Lawndale*.........................32,193
Lennox..........................22,950
Lomita*...........................20,515
Long Beach....................474,014
Los Angeles.................3,844,829
Lynwood*.........................71,208
Malibu 13,208
Manhattan Beach 36,481
Marina del Rey 8,176
Mayflower Village 5,081
Maywood*........................28,600
Monrovia 37,954
Montebello........................63,290
Monterey Park 62,065
North El Monte 3,703
Norwalk*..........................105,834
Palmdale* 134,570
Palos Verdes Estates*.........13,812
Paramount........................56,540
Pasadena 143,731
Pico Rivera*.......................64,679
Pomona 153,787
Quartz Hill......................9,890
Rancho Palos Verdes* 41,949
Redondo Beach..................66,824
Rolling Hills Estates..............8,105
Rosemead........................55,119
Rowland Heights................48,553
San Dimas 35,850
San Fernando 24,207
San Gabriel.......................41,056
San Marino 13,165
Santa Clarita* 168,253
Santa Fe Springs.................17,058
Santa Monica 87,800
Sierra Madre....................10,988
Signal Hill........................10,851
South El Monte 21,666
South Gate* 98,897
South Pasadena*................24,889
South San Gabriel...............7,595
South San Jose Hills........20,218
South Whittier..................55,193

Temple City* 37,363
Torrance 142,384
Valinda* 21,776
Vincent* 15,097
Walnut Park*........................16,180
Walnut* 31,424
West Athens*........................9,101
West Carson* 21,138
West Compton 5,435
West Covina* 108,185
West Hollywood 36,732
West Puente Valley*...........22,589
Westlake Village 8,585
Westmont* 31,623
Whittier 84,473
Willowbrook 34,138

LOUISVILLE-JEFFERSON COUNTY, KY-IN

Anchorage, KY 2,529
Bardstown, KY 10,984
Brooks, KY 2,678
Buckner, KY 4,000
Charlestown*, IN................... 8,052
Clarksville, IN 21,060
Corydon, IN 2,787
Douglass Hills*, KY...............5,597
Georgetown, IN 2,682
Graymoor-Devondale, KY 2,937
Hillview*, KY 7,349
Hurstbourne, KY 3,939
Indian Hills, KY 2,977
Jeffersontown, KY 26,100
Jeffersonville, IN................. 28,621
La Grange, KY......................6,046
Louisville/Jefferson County, KY
....**556,429**
Lyndon, KY 10,248
Middletown, KY 6,072
Mount Washington*, KY 8,624
New Albany, IN 36,772
Oak Park *, IN.......................5,379
Pioneer Village, KY 2,631
Prospect, KY 4,877
Salem, IN 6,453
Sellersburg, IN......................6,028
Shelbyville, KY 10,730
Shepherdsville, KY 8,874
Shively, KY 15,212
St. Matthews, KY................. 17,309
Windy Hills, KY.....................2,504

LUBBOCK, TX

Lubbock **209,737**
Slaton 5,727
Wolfforth 2,942

LYNCHBURG, VA

Altavista...............................3,385
Bedford 6,211
Forest* 8,006
Lynchburg.........................**66,973**
Madison Heights.................. 11,584
Timberlake* 10,683

MACON, GA

Forsyth.................................4,259
Macon................................**94,316**

MADERA, CA

Chowchilla 16,525
Madera Acres*......................7,741
Madera..............................**52,147**
Oakhurst...............................2,868
Parksdale..............................2,688
Yosemite Lakes 4,160

MADISON, WI

Columbus 5,060
Cottage Grove 5,271
Cross Plains 3,418
DeForest* 8,438
Dodgeville 4,840
Fitchburg* 22,040
Lake Wisconsin 3,493
Lodi 3,030
Madison...........................**221,551**
Marshall...............................3,561
McFarland* 7,383
Middleton 15,816
Monona.................................7,716
Mount Horeb* 6,188
Oregon* 8,493
Portage 10,035
Poynette 2,563
Stoughton 12,646
Sun Prairie 25,392
Verona 10,166
Waunakee 10,360
Windsor 2,533

MANCHESTER-NASHUA, NH

Amherst 11,614
Antrim 2,583
Bedford 20,732
Brookline..............................4,709
East Merrimack 3,784
Goffstown 17,687
Hillsborough 5,402
Hollis 7,740
Hudson 24,568
Hudson*................................7,814
Litchfield 8,277
Manchester **109,691**
Merrimack............................ 26,652
Milford 14,862
Milford..................................8,293
Nashua **87,321**
New Boston 4,880
New Ipswich 5,018
Pelham.................................12,474
Peterborough 6,073
Peterborough 2,944
Pinardville*...........................5,779
Weare 8,730
Wilton...................................3,884

MANSFIELD, OH

Lexington 4,224

Mansfield...........................**50,615**
Ontario.................................5,350
Shelby..................................9,471

MCALLEN-EDINBURG-MISSION, TX

Alamo 15,976
Alton 7,057
Doffing 4,256
Donna 15,846
Edcouch.............................. 4,426
Edinburg...........................**62,735**
Elsa......................................6,458
Hidalgo 10,889
La Homa* 10,433
La Joya 4,486
Llano Grande.......................3,333
Lopezville.............................4,476
McAllen.............................**123,622**
Mercedes.............................14,185
Mila Doce 4,907
Mission **60,146**
Nurillo 5,056
Palmhurst 4,991
Palmview 4,421
Pharr.................................**58,986**
Progreso 5,082
San Carlos...........................2,650
San Juan* 30,773
Scissors...............................2,805
South Alamo 3,101
Sullivan City 4,346
Weslaco 31,442
West Sharyland 2,947

MEDFORD, OR

Ashland............................... 20,829
Central Point* 15,672
Eagle Point 7,496
Medford **70,147**
Phoenix................................4,375
Talent.................................. 6,018
White City 5,466

MEMPHIS, TN-MS-AR

Arlington, TN 3,534
Atoka, TN............................. 5,676
Bartlett*, TN......................... 43,263
Collierville, TN 37,564
Covington, TN...................... 9,018
Earle, AR 2,895
Germantown*, TN 37,480
Hernando, MS 9,890
Holly Springs, MS................. 8,014
Horn Lake*, MS 22,151
Lakeland*, TN...................... 7,388
Lynchburg, MS......................2,959
Marion*, AR 9,792
Memphis, TN....................**672,277**
Millington, TN....................... 10,306
Munford, TN..........................5,652
Olive Branch, MS 27,964
Senatobia, MS......................6,869
Somerville, TN......................2,907

Southaven*, MS 38,840
West Memphis, AR 28,181

MERCED, CA

Atwater* 27,107
Delhi* 8,022
Dos Palos 5,036
Gustine 5,324
Livingston 12,585
Los Banos* 33,506
Merced **73,767**
Planada 4,369
Winton* 8,832

MIAMI-MIAMI BEACH-
KENDALL, FL

Aventura 29,391
Bal Harbour 3,272
Bay Harbor Islands 5,093
Biscayne Park 3,128
Brownsville 14,393
Coral Gables 42,871
Coral Terrace* 24,380
Country Club* 36,310
Country Walk* 10,653
Cutler* 17,390
Cutler Ridge* 24,781
Doral 21,895
East Perrine 7,079
Florida City 8,913
Fountainbleau* 59,549
Gladeview 14,468
Glenvar Heights 16,243
Golden Glades* 32,623
Goulds 7,453
Hialeah 220,485
Hialeah Gardens* 19,930
Homestead 44,494
Ives Estates* 17,586
Kendale Lakes* 56,901
Kendall **75,226**
Key Biscayne 10,158
Lakes by the Bay* 9,055
Leisure City* 22,152
Miami Beach **87,925**
Miami Gardens 99,438
Miami Lakes 22,321
Miami Shores 10,040
Miami Springs* 13,170
Miami **386,417**
Naranja 4,034
North Bay Village* 7,615
North Miami Beach 39,442
North Miami* 57,654
Ojus* 16,642
Olympia Heights* 13,452
Opa-locka 15,763
Palmetto Bay 23,590
Palmetto Estates* 13,675
Pinecrest* 19,204
Pinewood* 16,523
Princeton* 10,090
Richmond Heights* 8,479
South Miami 11,147

South Miami Heights* 33,522
Sunny Isles Beach* 15,315
Sunset 17,150
Surfside 4,710
Sweetwater 13,741
Tamiami* 54,788
The Crossings* 23,557
The Hammocks* 47,379
Three Lakes 6,955
University Park* 26,538
West Little River* 32,498
West Miami 5,829
West Perrine* 8,600
Westchester* 30,271
Westview 9,692
Westwood Lakes* 12,005

MICHIGAN CITY-LA PORTE, IN

La Porte **21,092**
Michigan City **32,205**
Westville 5,219

MIDLAND, TX

Midland **99,069**

MILWAUKEE-WAUKESHA-
WEST ALLIS, WI

Bayside 4,215
Brookfield 39,656
Brown Deer 11,611
Cedarburg 11,298
Cudahy 18,316
Delafield 6,767
Elm Grove 6,182
Fox Point* 6,741
Franklin* 33,263
Germantown 19,245
Glendale 12,880
Grafton 11,625
Greendale* 13,860
Greenfield* 35,753
Hales Corners 7,535
Hartford 12,878
Hartland 8,672
Jackson 6,036
Kewaskum 3,605
Menomonee Falls 34,125
Mequon 23,820
Merton 2,643
Milwaukee **578,887**
Mukwonago 6,668
Muskego* 22,872
New Berlin 38,547
Oak Creek 32,312
Oconomowoc 13,711
Okauchee Lake 3,916
Pewaukee 8,918
Port Washington 10,892
Saukville 4,184
Shorewood* 13,192
Slinger 4,358
South Milwaukee* 20,849
St. Francis* 9,382
Sussex 9,812

Thiensville 3,123
Wales 2,610
Waukesha **67,658**
Wauwatosa 45,014
West Allis **58,798**
West Bend 29,549
West Milwaukee 4,012
Whitefish Bay* 13,508

MINNEAPOLIS-ST. PAUL-
BLOOMINGTON, MN-WI

Afton, MN 2,861
Albertville, MN 5,733
Andover*, MN 29,745
Annandale, MN 2,996
Anoka, MN 17,608
Apple Valley*, MN 49,856
Arden Hills, MN 9,780
Baldwin, WI 3,509
Bayport, MN 3,249
Becker, MN 3,868
Belle Plaine, MN 4,546
Big Lake*, MN 8,804
Blaine*, MN 54,084
Bloomington, MN **81,164**
Brooklyn Center, MN 27,551
Brooklyn Park*, MN 68,550
Buffalo, MN 13,290
Burnsville, MN 59,159
Cambridge, MN 7,198
Centerville, MN 3,765
Champlin*, MN 23,302
Chanhassen, MN 23,229
Chaska, MN 22,820
Chisago City, MN 3,071
Circle Pines*, MN 5,356
Cokato, MN 2,700
Columbia Heights*, MN 18,110
Coon Rapids*, MN 62,417
Corcoran*, MN 5,683
Cottage Grove*, MN 32,553
Crystal*, MN 21,645
Dayton*, MN 4,622
Deephaven, MN 3,721
Delano, MN 4,551
Eagan, MN **63,665**
East Bethel*, MN 12,013
Eden Prairie, MN **60,649**
Edina, MN 45,567
Elk River, MN 21,329
Ellsworth, WI 3,060
Falcon Heights, MN 5,469
Farmington*, MN 17,740
Forest Lake, MN 17,353
Fridley, MN 26,515
Golden Valley, MN 20,003
Grant, MN 4,073
Greenfield, MN 2,901
Ham Lake*, MN 14,774
Hastings, MN 20,910
Hopkins, MN 16,825
Hudson, WI 11,367
Hugo*, MN 9,683
Independence, MN 3,528
Inver Grove Heights*, MN 33,182

Appendix C

NAPLES-MARCO ISLAND, FL

Golden Gate*........................20,951
Immokalee 19,763
Lely 3,857
Marco Island 16,109
Marco Island 14,879
Naples Manor 5,186
Naples Park*.........................6,741
Naples................................21,709
Pelican Bay...........................5,686

NASHVILLE-DAVIDSON-- MURFREESBORO, TN

Ashland City 4,550
Belle Meade..........................3,100
Brentwood 32,426
Centerville 4,002
Coopertown 3,221
Dickson 12,873
Fairview*...............................7,190
Forest Hills 5,168
Franklin 53,311
Gallatin 26,720
Goodlettsville 15,320
Green Hill* 7,068
Greenbrier*...........................6,054
Hartsville-Trousdale..............7,677
Hendersonville* 44,876
Kingston Springs 2,870
La Vergne 25,885
Lafayette...............................4,177
Lebanon..............................23,043
Millersville*...........................6,114
Mount Juliet* 18,099
Murfreesboro....................86,793
Nashville-Davidson..........549,110
Nolensville 2,571
Oak Hill.................................4,747
Pleasant View.......................3,453
Portland 10,342
Smyrna 33,497
Spring Hill 10,646
Springfield 15,916
White House*.........................8,723
Woodbury 2,524

NASSAU-SUFFOLK, NY

Albertson 5,200
Amityville 9,477
Babylon...............................12,659
Baldwin*..............................23,455
Baldwin Harbor* 8,147
Bay Shore............................23,852
Bayport*................................8,662
Bayville*................................7,123
Baywood*..............................7,571
Bellmore*.............................16,441
Bethpage 16,543
Blue Point 4,407
Bohemia 9,871
Brentwood*..........................53,917
Brightwaters 3,251
Brookhaven 3,570
Brookville..............................3,439

Calverton 5,704
Carle Place 5,247
Cedarhurst............................6,082
Center Moriches 6,655
Centereach*.........................27,285
Centerport*............................5,446
Central Islip* 31,950
Cold Spring Harbor 4,975
Commack 36,367
Copiague*............................21,922
Coram* 34,923
Cutchogue 2,849
Deer Park 28,316
Dix Hills* 26,024
East Farmingdale 5,400
East Hills* 6,745
East Islip*.............................14,078
East Massapequa* 19,565
East Meadow 37,461
East Moriches 4,550
East Northport*....................20,845
East Norwich 2,675
East Patchogue*..................20,824
East Quogue..........................4,265
East Rockaway* 10,263
East Shoreham* 5,809
East Williston 2,514
Elmont*...............................32,657
Elwood* 10,916
Farmingdale.........................8,668
Farmingville*........................16,458
Flanders................................3,646
Floral Park*..........................15,737
Flower Hill 4,485
Fort Salonga* 9,634
Franklin Square*..................29,342
Freeport*.............................43,519
Garden City 21,697
Garden City Park...................7,554
Garden City South.................3,974
Glen Cove............................26,633
Glen Head 4,625
Glenwood Landing 3,541
Gordon Heights 3,094
Great Neck 9,605
Great Neck Estates 2,738
Great Neck Plaza 6,929
Greenlawn*..........................13,286
Halesite................................2,582
Hampton Bays*....................12,236
Hauppauge 20,100
Hempstead 52,829
Herricks 4,076
Hewlett.................................7,060
Hicksville.............................41,260
Holbrook*............................27,512
Holtsville 17,006
Huntington 18,403
Huntington Station* 29,910
Inwood 9,325
Island Park............................4,741
Islandia 3,125
Islip*....................................20,575
Islip Terrace*.........................5,641
Jericho 13,045

Kings Park*..........................16,146
Kings Point 5,257
Lake Grove 10,670
Lake Ronkonkoma* 19,701
Lake Success 2,824
Lakeview...............................5,607
Lawrence...............................6,501
Levittown*............................53,067
Lido Beach............................2,825
Lindenhurst* 28,248
Lloyd Harbor 3,702
Locust Valley 3,521
Long Beach*.........................35,336
Lynbrook*.............................19,640
Malverne*..............................8,832
Manhasset 8,362
Manhasset Hills 3,661
Manorhaven*.........................6,328
Manorville*...........................11,131
Massapequa*........................22,652
Massapequa Park* 17,270
Mastic Beach*......................11,543
Mastic*................................15,436
Mattituck 4,198
Medford*.............................21,985
Melville................................14,533
Merrick*...............................22,764
Middle Island*........................9,702
Miller Place*.........................10,580
Mineola 18,978
Montauk................................3,851
Mount Sinai*..........................8,734
Munsey Park..........................2,594
Muttontown 3,516
Nesconset*...........................11,992
New Cassel 13,298
New Hyde Park 9,472
North Amityville*..................16,572
North Babylon*.....................17,877
North Bay Shore* 14,992
North Bellmore*....................20,079
North Bellport*........................9,007
North Great River 3,929
North Hills 4,437
North Lindenhurst*...............11,767
North Massapequa*..............19,152
North Merrick*......................11,844
North New Hyde Park..........14,542
North Patchogue 7,825
North Sea 4,493
North Valley Stream*...........15,789
North Wantagh*....................12,156
Northport 7,587
Northwest Harbor.................3,059
Noyack..................................2,696
Oakdale*................................8,075
Oceanside*...........................32,733
Old Bethpage 5,400
Old Westbury.........................5,035
Oyster Bay 6,826
Patchogue 11,901
Plainedge*.............................9,195
Plainview 25,637
Port Jefferson........................7,935
Port Jefferson Station 7,527

Port Washington 15,215
Port Washington North 3,294
Ridge* 13,380
Riverhead 10,513
Riverside 2,875
Rockville Centre 24,237
Rocky Point* 10,185
Ronkonkoma 20,029
Roosevelt* 15,854
Roslyn 2,879
Roslyn Heights* 6,295
Salisbury* 12,341
Sands Point 2,838
Sayville* 16,735
Sea Cliff* 4,996
Seaford* 15,791
Searingtown 5,034
Selden* 21,861
Shirley* 25,395
Smithtown* 26,901
Sound Beach* 9,807
South Farmingdale* 15,061
South Hempstead 3,188
South Huntington 9,465
South Valley Stream* 5,638
Southampton 4,109
Southold 5,465
Springs* 4,950
St. James* 13,268
Stony Brook 13,727
Syosset 18,544
Terryville* 10,589
Thomaston 2,580
Uniondale 23,011
University Gardens 4,138
Valley Stream* 35,799
Wading River* 6,668
Wantagh* 18,971
West Babylon* 43,452
West Bay Shore 4,775
West Hempstead* 18,713
West Hills* 5,607
West Islip* 28,907
West Sayville 5,003
Westbury 14,691
Westhampton 2,869
Wheatley Heights 5,013
Williston Park* 7,113
Woodbury 9,010
Woodmere* 16,447
Wyandanch 10,546
Yaphank 5,025

NEWARK-UNION, NJ-PA

Belleville *, NJ 35,928
Berkeley Heights, NJ 13,407
Bloomfield *, NJ 47,683
Boonton, NJ 8,555
Budd Lake *, NJ 8,100
Butler borough*, NJ 8,091
Caldwell borough, NJ 7,489
Cedar Grove, NJ 12,300
Chatham borough, NJ 8,439
Clark, NJ 14,597
Clinton, NJ 2,621

Cranford, NJ 22,578
Dover, NJ 18,441
East Orange*, NJ 68,190
Elizabeth, NJ 125,809
Fairfield, NJ 7,063
Fanwood borough*, NJ 7,228
Flemington borough, NJ 4,171
Florham Park borough, NJ .. 12,626
Franklin borough, NJ 5,233
Garwood borough, NJ 4,145
Glen Ridge borough*, NJ 7,020
Hamburg borough, NJ 3,567
High Bridge borough, NJ 3,770
Highland Lake *, NJ 5,051
Hillside *, NJ 21,747
Hopatcong borough*, NJ 16,001
Irvington *, NJ 60,695
Kenilworth borough, NJ 7,743
Kinnelon borough*, NJ 9,631
Lake Mohawk *, NJ 9,755
Lambertville, NJ 3,840
Lincoln Park borough*, NJ .. 10,899
Linden, NJ 40,014
Livingston, NJ 27,391
Madison borough, NJ 15,918
Maplewood *, NJ 23,868
Matamoras borough, PA 2,591
Mendham borough, NJ 5,172
Millburn, NJ 19,765
Montclair *, NJ 38,977
Morris Plains borough, NJ 5,629
Morristown, NJ 18,851
Mount Arlington borough*, NJ ....
.... 5,332
Mountain Lakes borough, NJ ....
.... 4,336
Mountainside borough, NJ 6,635
Netcong borough, NJ 3,294
New Providence borough, NJ ....
.... 11,905
Newark, NJ 280,666
Newton, NJ 8,416
North Caldwell borough*, NJ . 7,284
Nutley, NJ 27,362
Ogdensburg borough, NJ 2,631
Orange *, NJ 32,868
Plainfield*, NJ 47,642
Rahway, NJ 27,563
Riverdale borough, NJ 2,635
Rockaway borough, NJ 6,419
Roseland borough, NJ 5,402
Roselle borough*, NJ 21,265
Roselle Park borough*, NJ ... 13,189
Scotch Plains *, NJ 22,732
South Orange, NJ 16,964
Springfield, NJ 14,429
Stanhope borough, NJ 3,701
Summit, NJ 21,200
Union, NJ 54,405
Verona *, NJ 13,533
West Caldwell, NJ 11,233
West Orange *, NJ 44,943
Westfield*, NJ 29,918
Wharton borough*, NJ 6,222
White Meadow Lake *, NJ 9,052

NEW HAVEN-MILFORD, CT

Ansonia* 18,744
Beacon Falls 5,596
Bethany 5,473
Branford 29,089
Cheshire 29,097
Derby 12,536
East Haven* 28,755
Guilford 22,307
Hamden 58,180
Heritage Village 3,435
Madison 18,812
Meriden 59,653
Middlebury 6,974
Milford 53,045
Naugatuck* 31,864
New Haven 124,791
New Haven 124,791
North Branford 14,398
North Haven 23,908
Orange 13,970
Oxford 11,709
Prospect 9,234
Seymour 16,144
Southbury 19,677
Wallingford 44,736
Waterbury 107,902
West Haven* 52,923
Wolcott 16,228
Woodbridge 9,264

NEW ORLEANS-METAIRIE-KENNER, LA

Arabi* 8,093
Avondale 5,441
Belle Chasse 9,848
Bridge City* 8,323
Chalmette 32,069
Covington 9,347
Destrehan* 11,260
Eden Isle* 6,261
Edgard 2,637
Elmwood 4,270
Estelle* 15,880
Garyville 2,775
Gretna 17,161
Hahnville 2,792
Harahan 9,716
Harvey 22,226
Jefferson 11,843
Kenner 69,911
Lacombe* 7,518
Laplace* 27,684
Luling 11,512
Mandeville 11,632
Marrero* 36,165
Meraux* 10,192
Metairie 146,136
New Orleans 454,863
Norco 3,579
Port Sulphur 3,115
Poydras 3,886
Reserve 9,111
River Ridge* 14,588

Slidell 26,840
St. Rose.........................6,540
*Terrytown**.....................25,430
*Timberlane**.....................11,405
*Violet**..........................8,555
*Waggaman**.......................9,435
Westwego*.......................10,489
*Woodmere**......................13,058

NEW YORK-WHITE PLAINS-WAYNE, NY-NJ

Airmont*, NY 8,600
Allendale borough, NJ 6,754
Ardsley, NY 4,815
Armonk, NY 3,461
Bardonia, NY 4,367
Bayonne*, NJ 59,987
Blauvelt, NY 5,207
Bloomingdale borough*, NJ...7,654
Bogota borough*, NJ 8,150
Briarcliff Manor, NY 7,938
Bronxville, NY 6,455
Carlstadt borough, NJ 6,018
Chappaqua, NY 9,468
Chestnut Ridge*, NY 7,843
Cliffside Park borough*, NJ .23,035
Clifton, NJ 79,922
Closter borough, NJ 8,669
Congers *, NY 8,303
Cresskill borough*, NJ 8,449
Croton-on-Hudson, NY 7,803
Demarest borough, NJ 5,005
Dobbs Ferry, NY 11,070
Dumont borough*, NJ 17,474
East Rutherford borough, NJ ....
.....................................8,960
Eastchester *, NY 18,564
Edgewater borough, NJ.........9,646
Elmsford, NY 4,727
Elmwood Park borough, NJ. 18,905
Emerson borough*, NJ 7,334
Englewood, NJ 26,207
Englewood Cliffs borough, NJ.......
.....................................5,738
Fair Lawn borough, NJ 31,408
Fairview borough*, NJ 13,565
Fairview, NY 2,887
Fort Lee borough, NJ 37,175
Franklin Lakes borough, NJ..........
.....................................11,302
Garfield*, NJ 29,772
Glen Rock borough*, NJ 11,457
Greenville *, NY 8,648
Guttenberg*, NJ 10,885
Hackensack, NJ................43,735
Haledon borough*, NJ 8,398
Harrington Park borough, NJ ....
.....................................4,906
Harrison, NJ 14,060
Harrison, NY 25,827
Hartsdale *, NY 9,830
Hasbrouck Heights borough*, NJ ...
.....................................11,643
Hastings-on-Hudson*, NY 7,702

Haverstraw*, NY 10,487
Haworth borough, NJ 3,414
Hawthorne borough*, NJ 18,268
Hawthorne, NY 5,083
Heritage Hills, NY 3,683
Hillcrest *, NY 7,106
Hillsdale borough*, NJ 10,089
Hoboken*, NJ...................39,900
Ho-Ho-Kus borough, NJ.......4,090
Irvington, NY 6,615
Jersey City, NJ 239,614
Kaser, NY 3,564
Kearny, NJ 38,771
Lake Carmel *, NY 8,663
Lake Mohegan *, NY 5,979
Larchmont, NY 6,487
Leonia borough*, NJ 8,853
Little Falls, NJ 10,855
Little Ferry borough*, NJ 10,775
Lodi borough*, NJ 24,310
Lyndhurst, NJ 19,383
Mahopac *, NY 8,478
Mamaroneck, NY 18,350
Maywood borough, NJ 9,442
Midland Park borough, NJ.....6,952
Monsey, NY 14,504
Montebello, NY 3,680
Montvale borough, NJ 7,306
Moonachie borough, NJ 2,812
Mount Ivy *, NY 6,536
Mount Kisco, NY 10,331
Mount Vernon*, NY 67,924
Nanuet, NY 16,707
New City *, NY 34,038
New Hempstead, NY 4,822
New Milford borough*, NJ.... 16,318
New Rochelle*, NY 72,967
New Square, NY 6,332
New York, NY **8,143,197**
North Arlington borough*, NJ ....
.....................................15,179
North Haledon borough*, NJ ....
.....................................9,073
Northvale borough, NJ 4,564
Norwood borough, NJ 6,249
Nyack, NY 6,676
Oakland borough, NJ 13,645
Old Tappan borough, NJ 5,903
Oradell borough, NJ 8,005
Orangeburg, NY 3,388
Ossining*, NY 23,547
Palisades Park borough*, NJ........
.....................................18,857
Paramus borough, NJ.........26,545
Park Ridge borough, NJ 8,959
Passaic*, NJ 68,338
Paterson*, NJ..................149,843
Pearl River, NY 15,553
Peekskill*, NY 24,044
Pelham, NY 6,364
Pelham Manor, NY 5,395
Piermont, NY 2,598
Pleasantville, NY 7,130
Pomona, NY 2,945

Pompton Lakes borough*, NJ.........
.....................................11,313
Port Chester*, NY 27,886
Prospect Park borough, NJ ...5,760
Putnam Lake, NY 3,855
Ramsey borough, NJ...........14,558
Ridgefield borough, NJ........11,014
Ridgefield Park, NJ 12,746
Ridgewood, NJ 24,790
Ringwood borough*, NJ 12,809
River Edge borough, NJ 10,911
River Vale *, NJ 9,449
Rochelle Park, NJ 5,528
Rutherford borough, NJ 17,967
Rye, NY 14,992
Rye Brook, NY 9,471
Saddle Brook, NJ 13,155
Saddle River borough, NJ 3,766
Scarsdale*, NY 17,763
Secaucus, NJ 15,623
Sleepy Hollow*, NY 9,977
Sloatsburg, NY 3,092
South Nyack, NY 3,493
Spring Valley*, NY 25,355
Stony Point *, NY 11,744
Suffern*, NY 10,897
Tappan *, NY 6,757
Tarrytown, NY 11,346
Teaneck *, NJ 39,260
Tenafly borough*, NJ 14,362
Thiells *, NY 4,758
Thornwood, NY 5,980
Totowa borough, NJ 10,592
Tuckahoe*, NY 6,256
Union City*, NJ 65,128
Upper Saddle River borough, NJ ...
.....................................8,509
Valhalla, NY 5,379
Valley Cottage *, NY 9,269
Viola, NY 5,931
Waldwick borough*, NJ 9,650
Wallington borough*, NJ.......11,491
Wanaque borough*, NJ 10,616
***Wayne*, NJ** **54,069**
Wesley Hills, NY 5,051
West Haverstraw*, NY 10,259
West Milford *, NJ 26,410
West New York*, NJ 46,667
West Nyack, NY 3,282
West Paterson borough, NJ ....
.....................................11,245
Westwood borough, NJ 10,994
White Plains, NY **56,733**
Woodcliff Lake borough, NJ ..5,887
Wood-Ridge borough*, NJ 7,634
Wyckoff, NJ 16,508
Yonkers*, NY 196,425
Yorktown Heights, NY 7,972

NILES-BENTON HARBOR, MI

Benton Harbor **10,749**
Benton Heights.................5,458
Buchanan 4,531
*Fair Plain**.......................7,828
Niles **11,728**

Paw Paw Lake 3,944
St. Joseph.............................8,675

NORWICH-NEW LONDON, CT

Colchester 15,389
East Lyme........................... 18,459
Griswold............................. 11,254
Groton................................. 41,366
Jewett City borough.............. 3,001
Lebanon............................... 7,334
Ledyard...............................15,172
Lisbon 4,234
Long Hill..............................3,534
Montville 19,612
Mystic 4,001
New London......................**26,174**
Niantic.................................3,085
North Stonington 5,218
Norwich **36,598**
Old Lyme 7,488
Old Mystic...........................3,205
Pawcatuck 5,474
Preston 4,867
Salem 4,094
Sprague 2,992
Stonington 18,336
Voluntown 2,631
Waterford............................ 18,940

OAKLAND-FREMONT-HAYWARD, CA

Alameda*............................. 70,576
*Alamo** 15,626
Albany* 15,994
Antioch* 100,631
*Ashland** 20,793
Bay Point*........................... 21,534
Berkeley.............................. 100,744
Brentwood*.......................... 43,794
*Castro Valley** 57,292
*Cherryland** 13,837
Clayton* 11,142
Concord 123,252
Crockett 3,194
Danville*.............................. 41,852
*Discovery Bay** 8,981
Dublin 39,328
East Richmond Heights........ 3,357
El Cerrito* 22,868
*El Sobrante** 12,260
Emeryville............................ 8,528
*Fairview** 9,470
Fremont **200,468**
Hayward **140,293**
Hercules*............................. 24,109
*Kensington** 4,936
Lafayette............................. 24,767
Livermore............................. 78,409
Martinez.............................. 35,916
Moraga 16,869
Newark 41,956
Oakland **395,274**
Oakley* 27,177
Orinda* 18,259

Pacheco............................... 3,562
Piedmont*............................ 10,559
Pinole* 19,061
Pittsburg*............................ 62,547
Pleasant Hill........................ 33,153
Pleasanton........................... 65,950
Richmond 102,186
*Rodeo**...............................8,717
Rollingwood.........................2,900
San Leandro.........................78,178
*San Lorenzo** 21,898
San Pablo*........................... 31,004
San Ramon........................... 49,999
Tara Hills............................ 5,332
Union City*...........................69,176
Vine Hill.............................3,260
Waldon................................ 5,133
Walnut Creek 64,196

OCALA, FL

Belleview 3,856
Dunnellon 1,971
Ocala..............................**49,745**
Silver Springs Shores............6,690

OCEAN CITY, NJ

Cape May 3,760
Cape May Court House......... 4,704
North Cape May 3,618
North Wildwood.................... 4,778
Ocean City* **15,330**
Sea Isle City 2,968
*Villas**................................9,064
Wildwood 5,291
Wildwood Crest borough 3,872
Woodbine borough 2,569

ODESSA, TX

Odessa **92,361**
*West Odessa**.......................17,799

OGDEN-CLEARFIELD, UT

Bountiful*............................. 41,085
Centerville*.......................... 14,898
Clearfield..........................**27,413**
Clinton*................................17,735
Farmington 14,357
Farr West 4,581
Fruit Heights 4,764
Harrisville............................5,020
Hooper................................. 4,306
Kaysville*............................. 22,510
Layton* 61,782
Morgan 2,932
North Ogden* 16,542
North Salt Lake.................... 10,538
Ogden **78,309**
Plain City 4,320
Pleasant View* 6,151
Riverdale 7,934
Roy* 35,229
South Ogden* 15,195
South Weber 5,593

Sunset 4,947
Syracuse* 17,938
Washington Terrace* 8,352
West Bountiful 4,896
West Haven 5,558
West Point*.......................... 7,650
Woods Cross*....................... 8,019

OKLAHOMA CITY, OK

Bethany* 19,786
Blanchard 3,678
Chandler.............................. 2,859
Chickasha............................ 16,849
Choctaw* 10,529
Del City*............................. 21,945
Edmond*.............................. 74,881
El Reno 16,097
Guthrie................................ 10,800
Harrah................................. 4,939
Jones 2,611
Midwest City*.......................54,890
Moore*................................47,697
Mustang* 15,887
Newcastle*...........................6,303
Nichols Hills 3,997
Noble*................................. 5,518
Norman................................101,719
Oklahoma City **531,253**
Piedmont 4,667
Purcell................................. 5,858
Slaughterville....................... 3,839
Spencer............................... 3,840
Stroud 2,746
The Village* 9,827
Tuttle.................................. 5,365
Warr Acres........................... 9,475
Yukon* 22,032

OLYMPIA, WA

Lacey...................................33,368
North Yelm...........................2,793
Olympia **44,114**
Tumwater 13,331
Yelm................................... 4,543

OMAHA-COUNCIL BLUFFS, NE-IA

Bellevue*, NE 47,334
Blair, NE 7,765
Carter Lake, IA 3,404
Chalco *, NE 10,736
Council Bluffs, IA **59,568**
Elkhorn*, NE 8,192
Glenwood, IA........................ 5,650
Gretna, NE 4,860
La Vista*, NE 15,692
Missouri Valley, IA 2,932
Omaha, NE **414,521**
Papillion*, NE 20,431
Plattsmouth*, NE 7,023
Ralston*, NE 6,193
Wahoo, NE...........................4,063

ORLANDO-KISSIMMEE, FL

Altamonte Springs 41,057
Apopka 34,728
Azalea Park 11,073
Bay Hill 5,177
Belle Isle 6,431
Bithlo.................................4,626
Campbell 2,677
Casselberry 24,298
Celebration 2,736
Clermont 11,617
Conway 14,394
Doctor Phillips 9,548
Eustis 17,683
Fairview Shores................13,898
Fern Park 8,318
Forest City 12,612
Fruitland Park 3,578
Geneva 2,601
Goldenrod 12,871
Groveland 5,205
Heathrow 4,068
Holden Heights...................3,856
Hunters Creek 9,369
Kissimmee **59,364**
Lady Lake 13,244
Lake Butler 7,062
Lake Mary 14,638
Leesburg 19,086
Lockhart...........................12,944
Longwood 13,580
Maitland 14,125
Mascotte 4,647
Meadow Woods 11,286
Minneola 8,665
Mount Dora 11,474
Mount Plymouth 2,814
Oak Ridge 22,349
Ocoee 29,849
Orlando...........................**213,223**
Orlovista 6,047
Oviedo 29,848
Pine Castle 8,803
Pine Hills 41,764
Sanford 47,257
Sky Lake 5,651
South Apopka.....................5,800
Southchase.........................4,633
St. Cloud 22,508
Tavares 11,621
Umatilla..............................2,647
Union Park 10,191
Wedgefield.........................2,700
Wekiwa Springs 23,169
Williamsburg 6,736
Winter Garden 25,500
Winter Park.......................28,179
Winter Springs..................32,583
Yeehaw Junction 21,778
Zellwood 2,540

OSHKOSH-NEENAH, WI

Menasha 15,451
Neenah **24,596**

Omro.................................3,282
Oshkosh **63,485**

OWENSBORO, KY

Lewisport 1,655
Livermore............................1,469
Owensboro.......................**55,459**

OXNARD-THOUSAND OAKS-VENTURA, CA

Camarillo **61,576**
Casa Conejo.......................3,180
Channel Islands Beach 3,142
El Rio 6,193
Fillmore............................14,895
Meiners Oaks 3,750
Mira Monte 7,177
Moorpark*..........................35,844
Oak View 4,199
Ojai 7,945
Oxnard* **183,628**
Port Hueneme 22,032
San Buenaventura (Ventura).......
.... **104,017**
Santa Paula*......................28,478
Simi Valley*.......................118,687
Thousand Oaks **124,359**

PALM BAY-MELBOURNE-TITUSVILLE, FL

Cape Canaveral...................10,523
Cocoa 16,898
Cocoa Beach......................12,435
Indialantic 3,076
Indian Harbour Beach* 8,441
June Park 4,367
Malabar...............................2,772
Melbourne Beach 3,314
Melbourne **76,646**
Merritt Island 36,090
Micco................................9,498
Mims 9,147
Palm Bay* **92,833**
Port St. John 12,112
Rockledge..........................24,245
Satellite Beach* 9,811
Sharpes 3,415
South Patrick Shores 8,913
Titusville...........................**43,767**
West Melbourne 15,054

PANAMA CITY-LYNN HAVEN, FL

Callaway*...........................14,437
Cedar Grove 5,226
Laguna Beach 2,909
Lower Grand Lagoon............4,082
Lynn Haven **15,677**
Panama City Beach.............11,477
Panama City......................**37,188**
Parker 4,672
Pretty Bayou 3,519
Springfield*..........................9,043
Upper Grand Lagoon..........10,889

PARKERSBURG-MARIETTA-VIENNA, WV-OH

Belpre, OH...........................6,560
Blennerhassett, WV 3,225
Devola, OH 2,771
Marietta, OH **14,270**
Parkersburg, WV **32,020**
Vienna, WV 10,770
Williamstown, WV.................2,955

PASCAGOULA, MS

Escatawpa..........................3,566
Gautier* 16,846
Gulf Hills...........................5,900
Gulf Park Estates................4,272
Hickory Hills.......................3,046
Latimer...............................4,288
Lucedale 2,890
Moss Point.........................15,125
Ocean Springs....................17,783
Pascagoula **25,173**
St. Martin 6,676
Vancleave 4,910

PENSACOLA-FERRY PASS-BRENT, FL

Bellview 21,201
Brent............................**22,257**
Ensley 18,752
Ferry Pass.....................**27,176**
Gonzalez 11,365
Goulding 4,484
Gulf Breeze 6,455
Milton.................................8,131
Myrtle Grove 17,211
Pace 7,393
Pensacola.........................**54,055**
Warrington 15,207
West Pensacola 21,939

PEORIA, IL

Bartonville............................6,146
Chillicothe*...........................5,781
Creve Coeur*........................5,261
East Peoria.........................22,536
El Paso 2,746
Eureka 5,084
Germantown Hills 2,943
Henry 2,530
Marquette Heights.................2,826
Metamora 3,067
Morton 15,761
Pekin.................................33,331
Peoria Heights*....................6,298
Peoria...............................112,685
Washington* 12,759
West Peoria 4,710

PHILADELPHIA, PA

Aldan borough 4,294
Ambler borough* 6,349
Ardmore 12,616
Audubon............................6,549

Blue Bell	6,395
Boothwyn*	5,206
Bridgeport borough	4,402
Bristol borough	9,810
Brookhaven borough*	7,849
Broomall	11,046
Bryn Mawr	4,382
Chalfont borough	4,198
Chester	37,058
Chesterbrook	4,625
Churchville	4,469
Clifton Heights borough*	6,626
Coatesville*	11,495
Collegeville borough	5,055
Collingdale borough*	8,501
Conshohocken borough	7,711
Croydon*	9,993
Darby borough	10,046
Downingtown borough	7,858
Doylestown borough	8,225
Drexel Hill*	29,364
Eagleville	4,458
East Greenville borough	3,085
East Lansdowne borough	2,517
East Norriton	13,211
Exton	4,267
Fairless Hills	8,365
Flourtown	4,669
Folcroft borough	6,906
Folsom*	8,072
Fort Washington	3,680
Gilbertsville	4,242
Glenolden borough*	7,309
Glenside*	7,914
Harleysville	8,795
Hatboro borough	7,288
Hatfield borough	2,872
Horsham	14,779
Jenkintown borough	4,404
Kennett Square borough	5,292
King of Prussia	18,511
Kulpsville*	8,005
Lansdale borough	15,913
Lansdowne borough*	10,789
Levittown*	53,966
Lima	3,225
Linwood	3,374
Malvern borough	3,100
Maple Glen*	7,042
Media borough	5,451
Montgomeryville	12,031
Morrisville borough*	9,810
Morton borough	2,665
Narberth borough	4,154
Newtown Grant	3,887
Norristown borough	30,689
North Wales borough	3,299
Norwood borough*	5,852
Oreland*	5,509
Oxford borough	4,682
Paoli	5,425
Parkesburg borough	3,445
Penn Wynne	5,382
Pennsburg borough	3,371
Perkasie borough*	8,736

Philadelphia	**1,463,281**
Phoenixville borough*	15,420
Plymouth Meeting	5,593
Pottsgrove	3,266
Pottstown borough	21,551
Prospect Park borough*	6,449
Quakertown borough	8,823
Radnor Township	30,878
Richboro*	6,678
Ridley Park borough*	7,062
Rockledge borough	2,537
Royersford borough	4,330
Sanatoga*	7,734
Sellersville borough*	4,496
Sharon Hill borough	5,357
Skippack	2,889
Souderton borough*	6,691
Spring City borough	3,284
Spring House	3,290
Springfield	23,677
Stowe	3,585
Swarthmore borough	6,146
Telford borough	4,633
Thorndale	3,561
Trappe borough	3,422
Trooper*	6,061
Upland borough	2,910
Village Shires	4,137
Warminster Heights	4,191
West Chester borough	18,047
West Goshen	8,472
West Grove borough	2,640
West Norriton	14,901
Willow Grove	16,234
Woodbourne	3,512
Woodlyn*	10,036
Woodside	2,575
Wyncote	3,046
Wyndmoor	5,601
Yardley borough	2,542
Yeadon borough*	11,506

PHOENIX-MESA-SCOTTSDALE, AZ

Apache Junction*	32,297
Arizona City	4,385
Avondale*	66,706
Buckeye	9,619
Carefree	3,706
Casa Grande	32,855
Cave Creek	4,884
Chandler*	234,939
Coolidge	8,154
El Mirage*	22,171
Eloy	10,855
Florence	17,053
Fountain Hills*	23,217
Gilbert*	173,989
Glendale*	239,435
Gold Camp	6,029
Goodyear	43,941
Guadalupe	5,258
Kearny	2,765
Litchfield Park	4,523
Mesa	**442,780**

New River*	10,740
Oracle	3,563
Paradise Valley	14,558
Peoria*	137,935
Phoenix	**1,461,575**
Queen Creek	16,628
San Manuel	4,375
Scottsdale	**226,013**
Sun City	38,309
Sun Lakes	11,936
Superior	3,158
Surprise	74,411
Tempe	161,143
Tolleson	5,974
Wickenburg	6,224
Youngtown	4,021

PINE BLUFF, AR

Gould	1,210
Pine Bluff	**52,693**
Rison	1,340
Star	2,321
White Hall	5,114

PITTSBURGH, PA

Aliquippa	11,105
Ambridge borough	7,329
Arnold	5,401
Aspinwall borough	2,789
Avalon borough	4,962
Baden borough	4,172
Baldwin borough*	18,842
Beaver borough	4,550
Beaver Falls	9,402
Bellevue borough*	8,231
Bethel Park borough	32,313
Brackenridge borough	3,322
Braddock borough	2,744
Brentwood borough*	9,811
Bridgeville borough	5,022
Brownsville borough	2,690
Butler	14,521
California borough	5,072
Canonsburg borough	8,810
Carnegie borough	8,149
Castle Shannon borough*	8,269
Centerville borough	3,294
Charleroi borough	4,696
Churchill borough	3,350
Clairton	8,081
Connellsville	8,644
Coraopolis borough	5,754
Crafton borough*	6,289
Derry borough	2,869
Donora borough	5,420
Dormont borough*	8,696
Duquesne	6,875
East Uniontown	2,760
Economy borough*	9,291
Edgewood borough	3,098
Etna borough	3,671
Fernway*	12,188
Ford City borough	3,258
Forest Hills borough	6,424

Fox Chapel borough 5,238
Fox Run 3,044
Franklin Park borough* 11,765
Gastonville 3,002
Glassport borough 4,675
Green Tree borough 4,453
Greensburg 15,569
Homestead borough 3,535
Ingram borough 3,478
Irwin borough 4,187
Jeannette 10,196
Jefferson Hills borough 9,642
Kittanning borough 4,454
Latrobe 8,654
Liberty borough 2,509
Lower Burrell* 12,444
Manor borough 2,792
Masontown borough 3,469
McGovern 2,538
McKees Rocks borough 6,201
McKeesport 22,701
McMurray 4,726
Meadowood 2,912
Meridian 3,794
Midland borough 2,969
Millvale borough 3,772
Monaca borough 5,973
Monessen* 8,307
Monongahela 4,562
*Mount Lebanon** 33,017
Mount Oliver borough 3,772
Mount Pleasant borough 4,531
Munhall borough* 11,513
Municipality of Monroeville
borough 28,175
Municipality of Murrysville
borough 19,441
New Brighton borough* 6,275
New Kensington 14,085
North Braddock borough 5,996
North Versailles 11,125
Oakmont borough 6,587
Ohioville borough 3,686
Oliver 2,925
*Penn Hills** 46,809
Pitcairn borough 3,449
Pittsburgh **316,718**
Pleasant Hills borough 7,940
Plum borough* 26,452
Port Vue borough 3,965
Rochester borough 3,804
Scottdale borough 4,567
Sewickley borough 3,674
Sharpsburg borough 3,366
Slippery Rock borough 3,210
Springdale borough 3,597
Swissvale borough* 9,043
Tarentum borough 4,677
Thompsonville 3,592
Trafford borough 3,106
Turtle Creek borough* 5,704
Uniontown 11,935
Upper St. Clair 20,053
Vandergrift borough 5,190
Verona borough 2,931

Washington 15,136
West Mifflin borough 21,236
West Newton borough 2,948
West View borough* 6,863
White Oak borough* 8,185
Whitehall borough* 13,744
Wilkinsburg borough* 18,008
Wolfdale 2,873
Youngwood borough 3,171
Zelienople borough 4,010

PITTSFIELD, MA

Adams 8,455
Cheshire 3,357
Dalton 6,700
Great Barrington 7,441
Lanesborough 2,953
Lee 5,885
Lenox 5,156
North Adams 14,010
Pittsfield **43,860**
Sheffield 3,366
Williamstown 8,238

POCATELLO, ID

American Falls 4,162
Chubbuck* 10,707
Fort Hall 3,193
Pocatello **53,372**

PORTLAND-SOUTH PORTLAND-BIDDEFORD, ME

Alfred 2,818
Arundel 4,031
Bath 9,257
Berwick 7,348
Biddeford **22,072**
Bowdoin 2,918
Bowdoinham 2,794
Bridgton 5,216
Brunswick 21,820
Buxton 8,163
Cape Elizabeth 8,922
Cape Neddick 2,997
Casco 3,649
Cumberland 7,656
Eliot 6,413
Falmouth 10,601
Freeport 8,066
Gorham 15,300
Gray 7,376
Harpswell 5,242
Hollis 4,556
Kennebunk 11,510
Kennebunkport 4,033
Kittery 10,453
Lebanon 5,561
Limerick 2,544
Limington 3,678
Lyman 4,173
Naples 3,561
New Gloucester 5,291
North Berwick 4,802
North Windham 4,568

North Yarmouth 3,485
Old Orchard Beach 9,350
Portland **63,889**
Raymond 4,578
Richmond 3,425
Saco 18,230
Sanford 21,734
Scarborough 18,897
Shapleigh 2,509
South Berwick 7,304
South Eliot 3,445
South Portland **23,742**
South Sanford 4,173
Springvale 3,488
Standish 9,915
Topsham 9,939
Waterboro 7,233
Wells 10,088
Westbrook 16,108
Windham 16,371
Woolwich 2,956
Yarmouth 8,257
York 13,490
York Harbor 3,321

PORTLAND-VANCOUVER-BEAVERTON, OR-WA

Aloha *, OR 41,741
Barberton, WA 4,617
Battle Ground, WA 13,237
Beaverton, OR **85,775**
Camas, WA 16,671
Canby, OR 14,989
Cedar Hills, OR 8,949
Cedar Mill *, OR 12,597
Clackamas, OR 5,177
Cornelius*, OR 10,820
Damascus, OR 9,454
Dundee, OR 2,977
Fairview*, OR 9,327
Felida *, WA 5,683
Five Corners *, WA 12,207
Forest Grove, OR 19,689
Gladstone*, OR 12,117
Gresham*, OR 96,072
Happy Valley, OR 8,282
Hillsboro, OR **84,533**
Hockinson, WA 5,136
Jennings Lodge *, OR 7,036
Lafayette, OR 2,898
Lake Oswego, OR 36,502
Lake Shore *, WA 6,670
McMinnville, OR 29,646
Metzger, OR 3,354
Mill Plain *, WA 7,400
Milwaukie, OR 20,810
Minnehaha *, WA 7,689
Molalla, OR 6,737
Mount Hood Village, OR 3,306
Mount Vista *, WA 5,770
Newberg, OR 20,681
Oak Grove *, OR 12,808
Oak Hills *, OR 9,050
Orchards *, WA 17,852
Oregon City, OR 30,221

Portland, OR 533,427
Raleigh Hills *, OR.................5,865
Ridgefield, WA 2,869
Rockcreek *, OR....................9,404
Salmon Creek *, WA...........16,767
Sandy, OR 7,871
Scappoose, OR 5,913
Sheridan, OR.........................5,570
Sherwood*, OR....................15,398
St. Helens, OR 11,874
Sunnyside, OR 6,791
Tigard, OR 47,968
Troutdale*, OR....................14,898
Tualatin, OR 25,881
Vancouver, WA 157,493
Venersborg, WA 3,274
Walnut Grove *, WA...............7,164
Washougal*, WA 10,732
West Linn*, OR....................25,094
West Slope *, OR..................6,442
Wilsonville, OR 16,075
Wood Village, OR 2,888

PORT ST. LUCIE-FORT PIERCE, FL

Fort Pierce....................38,552
Hobe Sound*.......................11,376
Indian River Estates 5,793
Indiantown 5,588
Jensen Beach......................11,100
Lakewood Park* 10,458
North River Shores.................3,101
Palm City*...........................20,097
Port Salerno*......................10,141
Port St. Lucie*................131,692
Stuart................................15,764
White City 4,221

POUGHKEEPSIE-NEWBURGH-MIDDLETOWN, NY

Arlington 12,481
Balmville 3,339
Beacon*..............................14,836
Brinckerhoff 2,734
Chester 3,604
Cornwall-on-Hudson 3,110
Crown Heights 2,992
Fairview 5,421
Firthcliffe 4,970
Florida..................................2,781
Gardnertown.........................4,533
Goshen 5,437
Greenwood Lake 3,461
Haviland...............................3,710
Highland Falls.......................3,761
Highland Mills 3,468
Hopewell Junction 2,610
Kiryas Joel..........................18,300
Maybrook...............................4,068
Mechanicstown......................6,061
Middletown.......................26,067
Monroe 8,127
Montgomery 4,238
Myers Corner*........................5,546

New Windsor*.........................9,077
Newburgh.........................28,548
Orange Lake*.........................6,085
Port Jervis 9,202
Poughkeepsie..................30,355
Red Oaks Mill 4,930
Rhinebeck.............................3,126
Scotchtown*..........................8,954
Spackenkill 4,756
Vails Gate 3,319
Walden*................................6,755
Wappingers Falls 5,085
Warwick 6,571
Washingtonville*....................6,236

PRESCOTT, AZ

Big Park.................................5,245
Black Canyon City 2,697
Camp Verde..........................10,155
Chino Valley 9,710
Clarkdale 3,753
Cornville................................3,335
Cottonwood 10,894
Dewey-Humboldt....................3,613
Lake Montezuma 3,344
Paulden 3,420
Prescott Valley* 33,068
Prescott............................40,360
Sedona 8,007
Williamson 3,776

PROVIDENCE-NEW BEDFORD-FALL RIVER, RI-MA

Acushnet, MA 10,544
Attleboro, MA......................43,382
Barrington *, RI 16,819
Berkley, MA 6,375
Bliss Corner, MA...................5,466
Bristol *, RI.........................22,469
Burrillville, RI 16,563
Central Falls*, RI..................19,159
Charlestown, RI......................8,269
Coventry, RI........................35,080
Cranston, RI 81,614
Cumberland, RI 34,360
Cumberland Hill *, RI 7,738
Dartmouth, MA 31,389
Dighton, MA...........................6,665
East Greenwich, RI 13,616
East Providence, RI.............49,515
Easton, MA 23,028
Exeter, RI 6,298
Fairhaven, MA 16,222
Fall River, MA 91,802
Foster, RI 4,505
Freetown, MA 8,979
Glocester, RI.........................10,603
Greenville *, RI 8,626
Hopkinton, RI.........................8,121
Jamestown, RI 5,611
Johnston, RI 29,163
Kingston, RI............................5,446
Lincoln, RI 22,106
Little Compton, RI..................3,587

Mansfield, MA.......................22,977
Middletown, RI 16,737
Narragansett, RI 16,906
New Bedford, MA 93,102
Newport, RI 25,340
North Attleborough, MA 28,133
North Kingstown, RI 27,093
North Providence *, RI.........32,411
North Seekonk, MA 2,598
North Smithfield, RI 11,191
North Westport, MA...............4,533
Norton, MA 19,169
Ocean Grove, MA 3,012
Pascoag, RI 4,742
Pawtucket, RI 73,742
Portsmouth, RI 17,129
Providence, RI 176,862
Raynham, MA 13,498
Rehoboth, MA 11,256
Richmond, RI 7,769
Scituate, RI 10,971
Seekonk, MA 13,668
Smith Mills, MA......................4,432
Smithfield, RI 21,806
Somerset *, MA 18,234
South Kingstown, RI.............29,327
Swansea, MA 16,250
Taunton, MA 56,251
Tiverton*, RI.........................15,336
Valley Falls *, RI 11,599
Warren, RI 11,328
Warwick, RI 87,233
West Greenwich, RI...............5,677
West Warwick*, RI...............29,984
Westerly, RI 23,635
Westport, MA 15,071
Woonsocket, RI 44,328

PROVO-OREM, UT

Alpine* 9,063
American Fork 21,372
Cedar Hills 7,790
Eagle Mountain 10,343
Highland* 13,350
Lehi*...................................31,730
Lindon 9,679
Mapleton 5,972
Nephi 5,045
Orem 89,713
Payson..................................16,442
Pleasant Grove* 29,376
Provo................................113,459
Salem 4,725
Santaquin 6,901
Saratoga Springs...................6,502
Spanish Fork 26,606
Springville............................25,309

PUEBLO, CO

Pueblo West*........................16,899
Pueblo............................103,495

PUNTA GORDA, FL

Charlotte Harbor....................3,647

Cleveland.............................3,268
Englewood........................ 16,196
Harbour Heights 2,873
Port Charlotte.................... 46,451
Punta Gorda...................... **17,111**
Rotonda 6,574

RACINE, WI

Burlington 11,130
Mount Pleasant...................25,999
Racine.............................**79,392**
Sturtevant 6,190
Union Grove 4,614
Waterford 4,828
Wind Lake* 5,202

RALEIGH-CARY, NC

Apex* 28,551
Benson 3,282
Cary **106,324**
Clayton 12,943
Fuquay-Varina 12,200
Garner 22,364
Holly Springs* 15,228
Knightdale* 6,319
Louisburg...........................3,356
Morrisville 12,186
Raleigh **340,952**
Selma 6,646
Smithfield...........................11,970
Wake Forest* 20,126
Wendell 4,516
Zebulon 4,218

RAPID CITY, SD

Box Elder 2,992
Colonial Pine Hills 2,561
Rapid City.........................**62,167**
Sturgis 6,260

READING, PA

Amity Gardens.....................3,370
Birdsboro borough* 5,191
Boyertown borough 3,946
Fleetwood borough................4,006
Hamburg borough 4,183
Kenhorst borough 2,652
Kutztown borough 4,926
Laureldale borough 3,752
Lorane 2,994
Mohnton borough 3,071
Mount Penn borough 2,994
Reading 80,855
Reiffton 2,888
Shillington borough 5,031
Sinking Spring borough 3,443
West Reading borough 4,005
West Wyomissing 3,016
Whitfield.............................2,952
Womelsdorf borough 2,766
Wyomissing borough...........10,434

REDDING, CA

Anderson 10,528

Burney 3,217
Cottonwood 2,960
Redding **89,641**
Shasta Lake* 10,233

RENO-SPARKS, NV

Cold Springs......................3,834
Reno..............................**203,550**
Sparks...........................**82,051**
Sun Valley* 19,461

RICHMOND, VA

Ashland.............................6,996
Bellwood 5,974
Bensley 5,435
Bon Air.............................. 16,213
Chamberlayne 4,380
Chester* 17,890
Chesterfield Court House......3,558
Colonial Heights 17,567
Dumbarton 6,674
East Highland Park* 12,488
Ettrick 5,627
Glen Allen* 12,562
Highland Springs*................15,137
Hopewell...........................22,690
Lakeside 11,157
Laurel............................... 14,875
Mechanicsville 30,464
Montrose............................7,018
Petersburg 32,604
Richmond........................ **193,777**
Tuckahoe*..........................43,242
West Point 3,013
Wyndham*..........................6,176

RIVERSIDE-SAN BERNARDINO-ONTARIO, CA

Adelanto 24,360
Apple Valley* 65,156
Banning 29,308
Barstow.............................23,737
Beaumont 20,530
Bermuda Dunes*...................6,229
Big Bear City* 5,779
Big Bear Lake 6,158
Bloomington*......................19,318
Blythe............................... 22,130
Calimesa* 7,491
Canyon Lake* 11,287
Cathedral City* 51,713
Cherry Valley 5,891
Chino Hills* 75,722
Chino **77,578**
Coachella* 32,432
Colton **51,350**
Corona 149,387
Crestline* 10,218
Desert Hot Springs*.............20,492
East Hemet* 14,823
El Cerrito 4,590
Fontana 163,860
Glen Avon 14,853
Grand Terrace* 12,342

Hemet............................68,063
Hesperia* 77,984
Highgrove 3,445
Highland* 50,892
Home Gardens*....................9,461
Homeland 3,710
Indian Wells 4,933
Indio.................................70,542
Joshua Tree.......................4,207
La Quinta 38,232
Lake Arrowhead 8,934
Lake Elsinore*....................39,258
Lakeland Village 5,626
Lenwood 3,222
Loma Linda 20,901
Mecca 5,402
Mentone* 7,803
Mira Loma* 17,617
Montclair 35,474
Moreno Valley* 178,367
Mountain View Acres............2,521
Murrieta Hot Springs 2,948
Murrieta* 82,778
Muscoy 8,919
Needles 5,348
Norco................................26,960
Nuevo 4,135
Ontario...........................**172,679**
Palm Desert.......................47,058
Palm Springs 47,082
Pedley* 11,207
Perris 45,671
Rancho Cucamonga* 169,353
Rancho Mirage 16,514
Redlands **69,995**
Rialto* 99,513
Riverside **290,086**
Romoland 2,764
Rubidoux*.......................... 29,180
Running Springs.................5,125
San Antonio Heights............. 3,122
San Bernardino **198,550**
San Jacinto* 30,253
Sedco Hills 3,078
Sun City*...........................17,773
Sunnyslope........................4,437
Temecula 85,799
Thousand Palms...................5,120
Twentynine Palms* 28,409
Upland*..............................73,589
Valle Vista* 10,488
Victorville..........................91,264
Wildomar*.......................... 14,064
Woodcrest*.........................8,342
Wrightwood 3,837
Yucaipa* 49,100
Yucca Valley 19,696

ROANOKE, VA

Blue Ridge 3,188
Cave Spring........................24,941
Cloverdale 2,986
Hollins...............................14,309
Roanoke **92,631**
Rocky Mount 4,568

Bethalto*, IL 9,660
Black Jack*, MO 6,920
Breckenridge Hills, MO.........4,608
Breese, IL 4,202
Brentwood, MO 7,365
Bridgeton, MO 15,259
Byrnes Mill, MO 2,746
Cahokia*, IL 15,608
Carlinville, IL 5,768
Carlyle, IL 3,377
Caseyville, IL 4,297
Castle Point, MO 4,559
Centralia, IL 2,594
Centreville, IL 5,837
Chesterfield, MO 47,020
Clarkson Valley, MO 2,602
Clayton, MO 16,061
Collinsville*, IL 25,487
Columbia*, IL 8,902
Concord *, MO 16,689
Crestwood, MO 11,691
Creve Coeur, MO 16,975
Crystal City, MO 4,508
Dardenne Prairie, MO 6,984
De Soto, MO 6,552
Dellwood*, MO 5,027
Des Peres, MO 8,619
Dupo, IL 3,957
East Alton, IL 6,609
East St. Louis, IL 29,843
Edwardsville, IL 24,047
Ellisville, MO 9,353
Eureka, MO 8,957
Fairview Heights, IL 16,471
Fenton, MO 4,376
Ferguson*, MO 21,458
Festus, MO 10,905
Florissant*, MO 51,812
Freeburg, IL 4,092
Frontenac, MO 3,517
Gillespie, IL 3,278
Glasgow Village, MO 5,234
Glen Carbon*, IL 11,932
Glendale*, MO 5,595
Godfrey*, IL 16,996
Granite City, IL 30,796
Gray Summit, MO 2,640
Green Park, MO 2,657
Greenville, IL 7,067
Hazelwood, MO 25,535
Herculaneum, MO 3,172
High Ridge, MO 4,236
Highland, IL 9,200
Imperial, MO 4,373
Jennings*, MO 14,926
Jerseyville, IL 8,187
Kirkwood, MO 27,038
Ladue, MO 8,269
Lake St. Louis*, MO 13,281
Lebanon, IL 3,749
Lemay *, MO 17,215
Madison, IL 4,558
Manchester*, MO 18,970
Maplewood, MO 8,808
Maryland Heights, MO 26,544

Maryville, IL 6,629
Mascoutah*, IL 5,824
Mehlville *, MO 28,822
Millstadt, IL 3,067
Moline Acres, MO 2,579
Murphy *, MO 9,048
New Baden, IL 3,048
Normandy, MO 5,032
Northwoods, MO 4,435
Oakville *, MO 35,309
O'Fallon*, MO 69,694
Olivette, MO 7,455
Overland, MO 16,082
Pacific, MO 7,098
Pagedale, MO 3,486
Pevely, MO 4,208
Pine Lawn, MO 4,092
Pontoon Beach*, IL 6,046
Potosi, MO 2,709
Richmond Heights, MO 9,309
Riverview, MO 2,995
Rock Hill, MO 4,700
Rosewood Heights, IL 4,262
Sappington, MO 7,287
Shiloh*, IL 10,367
Shrewsbury, MO 6,393
Smithton, IL 2,870
Spanish Lake *, MO 21,337
St. Ann*, MO 13,092
St. Charles, MO 62,304
St. Clair, MO 4,405
St. John*, MO 6,558
St. Louis, MO 344,362
St. Peters, MO 54,209
Staunton, IL 5,109
Sullivan, MO 5,177
Sunset Hills, MO 8,374
Swansea, IL 12,274
Town and Country, MO 10,807
Trenton, IL 2,651
Troy*, MO 9,862
Union, MO 8,897
University City*, MO 37,170
Valley Park*, MO 6,405
Virden, IL 3,364
Warrenton, MO 6,612
Washington, MO 14,136
Washington Park, IL 5,740
Waterloo, IL 9,225
Webster Groves, MO 22,896
Weldon Spring, MO 5,361
Wentzville, MO 17,988
Wildwood*, MO 34,831
Wood River, IL 10,985
Woodson Terrace, MO 4,111

SALEM, OR

Aumsville 3,202
Dallas....................................14,001
Four Corners* 13,922
Hayesville* 18,222
Hubbard 2,545
Independence........................8,193
Jefferson................................2,607
Keizer* 34,644

Monmouth* 8,987
Mount Angel 3,355
Salem...............................148,751
Silverton 8,233
Stayton 7,184
Woodburn 21,736

SALINAS, CA

Aromas 2,797
Carmel Valley Village*...........4,700
Carmel-by-the-Sea................3,994
Castroville..............................6,724
Del Monte Forest 4,531
Gonzales 8,498
Greenfield* 13,330
King City 11,004
Las Lomas 3,078
Marina* 19,006
Monterey...............................29,217
Pacific Grove* 15,091
Pajaro 3,384
Prunedale*...........................16,432
Salinas..............................146,431
Seaside* 34,214
Soledad 27,210

SALISBURY, MD

Crisfield 2,808
Fruitland................................3,953
Princess Anne 2,800
Salisbury 26,295

SALT LAKE CITY, UT

Bluffdale 6,569
Canyon Rim* 10,428
Cottonwood Heights*...........27,569
Draper...................................34,133
East Millcreek* 21,385
Grantsville* 7,494
Herriman 11,226
Holladay................................19,319
Kearns* 33,659
Little Cottonwood Creek Valley*.....
....7,221
Magna* 22,770
Midvale 27,170
Millcreek 30,377
Mount Olympus*....................7,103
Murray 44,555
Oquirrh* 10,390
Park City 8,065
Riverton*..............................32,089
Salt Lake City..................178,097
Sandy*..................................89,664
South Jordan*.......................40,209
South Salt Lake 21,411
Summit Park* 6,597
Taylorsville*..........................58,009
Tooele*.................................28,369
West Jordan* 91,444
West Valley City...................113,300
White City*.............................5,988

Appendix C

SAN ANGELO, TX

Grape Creek 3,138
San Angelo......................**88,014**

SAN ANTONIO, TX

Alamo Heights 7,113
Balcones Heights 2,991
Boerne 8,054
Bulverde 4,446
*Canyon Lake** 16,870
Castle Hills...........................4,172
Castroville.............................2,936
Cibolo 7,804
Converse** 12,650
Devine 4,409
Fair Oaks Ranch...................5,715
Floresville 7,024
Garden Ridge 2,538
Helotes 6,187
Hollywood Park 3,210
Hondo 8,779
Jourdanton 4,235
Kirby** 8,612
Lakehills.............................4,668
Leon Valley 9,650
Live Oak** 10,942
Lytle 2,646
McQueeney 2,527
New Braunfels 47,168
Pleasanton...........................9,375
Poteet 3,626
Redwood 3,586
San Antonio **1,256,509**
Scenic Oaks 3,279
Schertz** 26,668
Seguin 24,230
Terrell Hills 5,108
*Timberwood Park** 5,889
Universal City 16,653
Windcrest.............................5,090

SAN DIEGO-CARLSBAD-SAN MARCOS, CA

*Alpine** 13,143
*Bonita** 12,401
Bonsall...............................3,401
Borrego Springs 2,535
*Bostonia** 15,169
Carlsbad 90,773
*Chula Vista** 210,497
Coronado 26,424
Crest 2,716
Del Mar 4,378
El Cajon 92,487
Encinitas** 59,525
Escondido............................134,085
*Fallbrook** 29,100
Granite Hills.......................3,246
Harbison Canyon................3,645
Hidden Meadows................3,463
Imperial Beach** 26,374
*Jamul** 5,920
La Mesa...............................53,081
*La Presa** 32,721

Lake San Marcos 4,138
*Lakeside** 19,560
Lemon Grove** 24,124
National City **61,419**
Oceanside** 166,108
Poway 48,476
Ramona 15,691
*Rancho San Diego** 20,155
*San Diego Country Estates** ..9,262
San Diego....................**1,255,540**
San Marcos **73,487**
Santee** 52,306
Solana Beach 12,716
*Spring Valley** 26,663
*Valley Center** 7,323
Vista.....................................90,402
*Winter Gardens** 19,771

SANDUSKY, OH

Huron** 7,581
Sandusky **26,666**
Vermilion** 4,819

SAN FRANCISCO-SAN MATEO-REDWOOD CITY, CA

Atherton...............................7,177
Belmont** 24,522
Brisbane 3,556
Broadmoor 4,026
Burlingame 27,380
Corte Madera 9,120
Daly City** 100,339
East Palo Alto** 32,242
*El Granada** 5,724
Emerald Lake Hills 3,899
*Fairfax** 7,106
Foster City 28,756
Half Moon Bay 12,203
*Hillsborough** 10,615
Kentfield............................6,351
Larkspur...............................11,724
Menlo Park 29,661
Mill Valley 13,286
*Millbrae** 20,342
Montara 2,950
*North Fair Oaks** 15,440
Novato..................................50,335
*Pacifica** 37,092
Portola Valley 4,417
Redwood City **73,114**
San Anselmo** 12,018
San Bruno** 39,752
San Carlos...........................26,821
San Francisco.................**739,426**
San Mateo **91,081**
San Rafael...........................55,716
Santa Venetia 4,298
Sausalito..............................7,184
South San Francisco 60,735
*Strawberry** 5,302
Tiburon** 8,671
West Menlo Park 3,629
Woodside..............................5,463

SAN JOSE-SUNNYVALE-SANTA CLARA, CA

*Alum Rock** 13,479
Aromas 2,797
*Burbank** 5,239
Cambrian Park 3,258
Campbell 37,042
Cupertino.........................52,171
*East Foothills** 8,133
Gilroy 45,718
Hollister** 35,941
Los Altos 27,096
Los Altos Hills** 8,164
Los Gatos 28,029
Loyola 3,478
Milpitas..........................**63,383**
Monte Sereno 3,462
Morgan Hill 34,852
Mountain View **69,276**
Palo Alto..........................**56,982**
Ridgemark 2,741
San Jose.........................**912,332**
San Martin 4,230
Santa Clara....................**105,402**
Saratoga** 29,663
Stanford 13,315
Sunnyvale **128,902**

SAN LUIS OBISPO-PASO ROBLES, CA

Arroyo Grande......................16,315
Atascadero............................27,130
Cambria 6,232
Cayucos.............................2,943
El Paso de Robles (Paso Robles)
..................................**27,477**
Grover Beach 12,887
Morro Bay 10,208
*Nipomo** 12,626
*Oceano** 7,260
Pismo Beach 8,419
San Luis Obispo...............**43,509**
Templeton...........................4,687

SANTA ANA-ANAHEIM-IRVINE, CA

Aliso Viejo** 41,541
Anaheim **331,804**
Brea.....................................38,465
Buena Park...........................79,174
Costa Mesa 109,830
*Coto de Caza** 13,057
Cypress 47,383
Dana Point** 35,867
*Foothill Ranch** 10,899
Fountain Valley 55,942
Fullerton...............................132,787
Garden Grove** 166,075
Huntington Beach**............. 194,457
Irvine...............................186,852
La Habra** 59,326
La Palma 15,805
Laguna Beach 24,127
Laguna Hills 32,198

636

Laguna Niguel* 64,664
Laguna Woods 18,293
Lake Forest* 76,412
Las Flores* 5,625
Los Alamitos 11,657
Mission Viejo* 94,982
Newport Beach 79,834
Orange 134,950
Placentia* 49,795
Portola Hills* 6,391
Rancho Santa Margarita* 50,682
Rossmoor* 10,298
San Clemente* 60,235
San Joaquin Hills 2,959
San Juan Capistrano 34,673
Santa Ana 340,368
Seal Beach 24,295
Stanton* 37,661
Tustin 69,096
Tustin Foothills* 24,044
Villa Park* 6,026
Westminster* 89,523
Yorba Linda* 64,476

SANTA BARBARA-SANTA MARIA, CA

Buellton 4,293
Carpinteria 13,549
Goleta 29,367
Guadalupe 6,346
Isla Vista 18,344
Lompoc* 39,985
Mission Canyon 2,610
Mission Hills 3,142
Montecito 10,000
Orcutt* 28,830
Santa Barbara 85,899
Santa Maria 84,346
Santa Ynez 4,584
Solvang 5,141
Vandenberg Village* 5,802

SANTA CRUZ-WATSONVILLE, CA

Aptos 9,396
Boulder Creek 4,081
Capitola 9,553
Day Valley 3,587
Freedom 6,000
Interlaken* 7,328
Live Oak 16,628
Opal Cliffs* 6,458
Rio del Mar* 9,198
Santa Cruz 54,760
Scotts Valley 11,154
Soquel 5,081
Twin Lakes* 5,533
Watsonville 47,927

SANTA FE, NM

Chimayo 2,924
Eldorado at Santa Fe* 5,799
Espanola 2,754
La Cienega 3,007

Santa Fe 70,631
SANTA ROSA-PETALUMA, CA
Boyes Hot Springs* 6,665
Cloverdale* 8,016
Cotati* 7,138
El Verano 3,954
Healdsburg 11,051
Petaluma 54,846
Rohnert Park* 41,101
Roseland* 6,369
Santa Rosa 153,158
Sebastopol 7,598
Sonoma 9,885
Windsor* 24,968

SARASOTA-BRADENTON-VENICE, FL

Bayshore Gardens* 17,350
Bee Ridge 8,744
Bradenton 53,917
Cortez 4,491
Desoto Lakes 3,198
Ellenton 3,142
Englewood 16,196
Fruitville 12,741
Gulf Gate Estates 11,647
Holmes Beach 5,100
Kensington Park 3,720
Lake Sarasota 4,458
Laurel* 8,393
Longboat Key 7,583
Memphis* 7,264
Nokomis 3,334
North Port* 42,253
North Sarasota* 6,738
Osprey 4,143
Palmetto 13,510
Plantation 4,168
Ridge Wood Heights* 5,028
Samoset 3,440
Sarasota Springs* 15,875
Sarasota 53,711
Siesta Key* 7,150
South Bradenton 21,587
South Gate Ridge* 5,655
South Sarasota 5,314
South Venice* 13,539
Southgate* 7,455
The Meadows 4,423
Vamo 5,285
Venice Gardens* 7,466
Venice 20,974
Warm Mineral Springs 4,811
West Bradenton 4,444
West Samoset 5,507
Whitfield 2,984

SAVANNAH, GA

Bloomingdale 2,677
Garden City 9,550
Georgetown* 10,599
Isle of Hope 2,605
Montgomery 4,134
Pembroke 2,503

Pooler 10,019
Port Wentworth 3,238
Richmond Hill 9,187
Rincon 6,349
Savannah 128,453
Skidaway Island 6,914
Tybee Island 3,614
Whitemarsh Island* 5,824
Wilmington Island* 14,213

SCRANTON–WILKES-BARRE, PA

Archbald borough 6,290
Ashley borough 2,726
Avoca borough 2,712
Back Mountain* 26,690
Blakely borough 6,817
Carbondale 9,348
Clarks Summit borough 5,010
Dallas borough 2,508
Dickson City borough 5,967
Dunmore borough 13,968
Dupont borough 2,626
Duryea borough 4,414
Edwardsville borough 4,741
Exeter borough 6,007
Forty Fort borough 4,331
Freeland borough 3,455
Harveys Lake borough 2,868
Hazleton 22,125
Jessup borough 4,579
Kingston borough 13,176
Larksville borough 4,519
Luzerne borough 2,805
Moosic borough 5,738
Mountain Top* 15,269
Nanticoke* 10,382
Old Forge borough* 8,558
Olyphant borough 4,900
Pittston 7,689
Plymouth borough* 6,161
Scranton 73,120
Swoyersville borough 4,930
Taylor borough 6,227
Throop borough 3,949
West Hazleton borough 3,375
West Pittston borough 4,870
West Wyoming borough 2,722
Wilkes-Barre 41,337
Wyoming borough 3,053

SEATTLE-BELLEVUE-EVERETT, WA

Alderwood Manor* 15,329
Algona 2,644
Arlington 15,277
Arlington Heights 2,510
Auburn 45,753
Bellevue 117,137
Black Diamond 3,929
Bothell 30,916
Brier* 6,344
Burien* 30,737
Cathcart 3,015

SPRINGFIELD, MO

Battlefield	3,612
Bolivar	10,179
Buffalo	3,006
Marshfield	6,763
Nixa*	15,925
Ozark	15,265
Republic*	10,637
Springfield	**150,298**
Willard	3,330

SPRINGFIELD, OH

Enon	2,581
New Carlisle*	5,639
Northridge*	6,853
Park Layne	4,519
Springfield	**63,302**

STATE COLLEGE, PA

Bellefonte borough	6,161
Boalsburg	3,578
Park Forest Village*	8,830
Philipsburg borough	2,942
State College borough	**38,720**

STOCKTON, CA

August	7,808
Country Club*	9,462
Escalon	7,171
French Camp	4,109
Garden Acres*	9,747
Kennedy	3,275
Lathrop	13,116
Lincoln Village	4,216
Lockeford	3,179
Lodi	62,133
Manteca*	62,651
Morada	3,726
Ripon*	13,658
Stockton	**286,926**
Tracy*	79,964

SUMTER, SC

Lakewood	2,603
Mayesville	1,042
South Sumter	3,365
Sumter	**39,679**

SYRACUSE, NY

Baldwinsville	7,149
Brewerton	3,453
Canastota	4,429
Cazenovia	2,698
Chittenango	4,901
East Syracuse	3,076
Fairmount*	10,795
Fayetteville	4,171
Fulton	11,525
Galeville	4,476
Hamilton	3,550
Lakeland	2,852
Lyncourt	4,268
Manlius	4,695
Mattydale*	6,367
Minoa	3,255
North Syracuse	6,726
Oneida	10,923
Oswego	17,705
Skaneateles	2,589
Solvay	6,606
Syracuse	**141,683**
Village Green	3,945
Westvale	5,166

TACOMA, WA

Artondale*	8,630
Bonney Lake*	14,611
Buckley	4,473
DuPont	5,374
Edgewood*	9,718
Elk Plain*	15,697
Fife	5,567
Fircrest*	6,086
Fox Island	2,803
Frederickson*	5,758
Gig Harbor	6,620
Graham*	8,739
Lakewood	57,671
Midland	7,414
Milton*	5,587
Orting	4,789
Parkland*	24,053
Prairie Ridge*	11,688
Puyallup	35,861
South Hill*	31,623
Spanaway*	21,588
Steilacoom*	6,140
Summit*	8,041
Sumner	9,298
Tacoma	**195,898**
University Place*	30,425
Waller*	9,200

TALLAHASSEE, FL

Chattahoochee	3,720
Monticello	2,546
Quincy	6,993
Tallahassee	**158,500**
Woodville	3,006

TAMPA-ST. PETERSBURG-CLEARWATER, FL

Apollo Beach*	7,444
Bay Pines	3,065
Bayonet Point*	23,577
Beacon Square*	7,263
Belleair	4,170
Bloomingdale*	19,839
Boyette*	5,895
Brandon*	77,895
Brookridge	3,279
Brooksville	7,637
Cheval*	7,602
Citrus Park*	20,226
Clearwater	**108,687**
Dade City	6,823
Dover	2,798
Dunedin	36,690
East Lake*	29,394
Elfers*	13,161
Feather Sound	3,597
Gibsonton*	8,752
Gulfport*	12,661
Harbor Bluffs	2,807
Holiday*	21,904
Hudson	12,765
Indian Rocks Beach*	5,265
Jasmine Estates*	18,213
Kenneth City	4,419
Keystone*	14,627
Lake Magdalene*	28,755
Land O' Lakes*	20,971
Largo	**74,473**
Lutz*	17,081
Madeira Beach	4,464
Mango*	8,842
New Port Richey	16,928
Odessa	3,173
Oldsmar	13,552
Palm Harbor*	59,248
Pebble Creek	4,824
Pinellas Park	47,352
Plant City	31,450
Port Richey	3,333
Ridge Manor	4,108
Riverview*	12,035
Ruskin	8,321
Safety Harbor*	17,517
Seffner*	5,467
Seminole	18,505
Shady Hills*	7,798
South Highpoint	8,839
South Pasadena	5,715
Spring Hill*	69,078
St. Pete Beach	10,173
St. Petersburg	**249,079**
Tampa	**325,989**
Tarpon Springs	22,651
Temple Terrace	21,978
Thonotosassa*	6,091
Tierra Verde	3,574
Timber Pines	5,840
Town 'n' Country	72,523
Treasure Island*	7,542
Trinity	4,279
Valrico*	6,582
Wesley Chapel*	5,691
Westchase*	11,116
Wimauma	4,246
Zephyrhills	12,258

TERRE HAUTE, IN

Brazil	8,214
Clinton	4,906
North Terre Haute	4,606
Sullivan	4,537
Terre Haute	**56,893**

TEXARKANA, TX-TEXARKANA, AR

Hooks, TX	2,924

New Boston, TX 4,624
Texarkana, AR.................30,006
Texarkana, TX 35,746
Wake Village*, TX.................5,226

TOLEDO, OH

Archbold 4,505
Bowling Green..................29,793
Delta 2,927
Maumee.......................14,285
North Baltimore 3,343
Northwood 5,499
Oak Harbor 2,816
Oregon..........................19,175
Ottawa Hills 4,608
Perrysburg.....................16,980
Port Clinton 6,336
Rossford* 6,387
Swanton........................3,557
Sylvania 19,069
Toledo 301,285
Walbridge 3,096
Waterville......................5,189
Wauseon 7,311
Whitehouse.....................3,303

TOPEKA, KS

Holton 3,400
Osage City......................2,987
Topeka 121,946

TRENTON-EWING, NJ

Ewing **35,707**
Hightstown borough 5,293
Lawrenceville..................4,081
Pennington borough 2,696
Princeton borough 13,495
Trenton 84,639
Twin Rivers...................7,422
White Horse 9,373

TUCSON, AZ

Ajo 3,705
Avra Valley....................5,038
Casas Adobes...................54,011
Catalina.......................7,025
Catalina Foothills.............53,794
Drexel Heights.................23,849
Flowing Wells..................15,050
Green Valley 17,283
Marana..........................26,098
Oro Valley.....................38,438
Picture Rocks..................8,139
Sahuarita 9,007
Sells.........................2,799
South Tucson....................5,562
Summit 3,702
Tanque Verde...................16,195
Three Points 5,273
Tortolita......................3,740
Tucson Estates.................9,755
Tucson.......................515,526

TULSA, OK

Bixby* 18,600
Bristow.........................4,397
Broken Arrow* 86,228
Catoosa........................6,440
Claremore 17,161
Cleveland 3,247
Collinsville 4,325
Coweta*........................8,352
Drumright.......................2,815
Glenpool*......................8,960
Henryetta.......................6,110
Hominy 3,733
Jenks* 13,095
Mannford 2,758
Oakhurst 2,731
Okmulgee 12,854
Owasso* 23,771
Pawhuska 3,533
Sand Springs.....................17,667
Sapulpa 20,619
Skiatook 6,290
Tulsa 382,457
Turley 3,231
Verdigris 2,765
Wagoner 7,877

TUSCALOOSA, AL

Greensboro 2,616
Holt 4,103
Northport 21,216
Tuscaloosa.....................81,358

TYLER, TX

Hideaway.......................2,808
Lindale 4,030
Tyler 91,936
Whitehouse* 7,122

UTICA-ROME, NY

Herkimer......................7,264
Ilion 8,330
Little Falls 5,026
Mohawk 2,569
New York Mills 3,146
Rome........................34,344
Sherrill 3,164
Utica........................59,336
Whitesboro 3,854
Yorkville 2,613

VALDOSTA, GA

Lakeland 2,769
Quitman 4,520
Valdosta.......................45,205

VALLEJO-FAIRFIELD, CA

Benicia 26,489
Dixon* 17,330
Fairfield 104,476
Rio Vista 7,077
Suisun City* 26,762

Vacaville*.......................92,985
Vallejo*.........................**117,483**

VICTORIA, TX

Bloomington 2,562
Goliad 2,006
Port Lavaca 11,696
Seadrift 1,390
Victoria 61,790

VINELAND-MILLVILLE-BRIDGETON, NJ

Bridgeton **23,959**
Laurel Lake.........................2,929
Millville **27,886**
Vineland **58,164**

VIRGINIA BEACH-NORFOLK-NEWPORT NEWS, VA-NC

Chesapeake, VA................218,968
Gloucester Point *, VA...........9,429
Hampton, VA................. 145,579
Newport News, VA........... 179,899
Norfolk, VA.................231,954
Poquoson*, VA...................11,811
Portsmouth, VA 100,169
Smithfield, VA....................6,840
Suffolk*, VA.......................78,994
Virginia Beach, VA 438,415
Williamsburg, VA 11,751

VISALIA-PORTERVILLE, CA

Cutler.........................4,491
Dinuba 19,308
Earlimart 6,583
East Porterville 6,730
Exeter........................9,974
Farmersville...................9,918
Ivanhoe......................4,474
Lindsay 10,767
Orosi 7,318
Pixley 2,586
Porterville.........................44,959
Richgrove 2,723
Strathmore.....................2,584
Terra Bella 3,466
Tulare..........................50,127
Visalia **108,669**
Woodlake.......................7,215

WACO, TX

Bellmead* 9,555
Hewitt* 12,987
Lacy-Lakeview* 5,804
Mart 2,530
McGregor 4,831
Robinson* 9,062
Waco.........................120,465
West...........................2,711
Woodway* 8,689

WARNER ROBINS, GA

Centerville 6,624

Perry 10,972
Warner Robins **57,750**

WARREN-TROY-FARMINGTON HILLS, MI

Algonac 4,598
Almont 2,874
Auburn Hills 21,011
Berkley* 15,089
Beverly Hills* 10,086
Birmingham 19,081
Bloomfield Hills 3,851
Brighton 7,139
Center Line 8,308
Clawson* 12,337
Clinton 95,648
Eastpointe* 33,180
Farmington 10,035
Farmington Hills **80,223**
Ferndale 21,460
Fowlerville 3,132
Franklin 2,958
Fraser 15,095
Harrison 24,461
Hazel Park* 18,391
Holly 6,375
Howell 9,757
Huntington Woods* 5,928
Imlay City 3,850
Keego Harbor 2,791
Lake Orion 2,756
Lapeer 9,370
Lathrup Village 4,157
Madison Heights 30,251
Marine City 4,475
Marysville 10,042
Milford 6,587
Mount Clemens 17,053
New Baltimore 11,165
New Haven 4,708
Northville 3,243
Novi **53,115**
Oak Park* 31,194
Oxford 3,564
Pearl Beach 3,224
Pleasant Ridge 2,501
Pontiac 67,331
Port Huron 31,501
Richmond 5,607
Rochester 11,209
Rochester Hills 69,995
Romeo 3,815
Roseville 47,708
Royal Oak 58,299
Shelby 65,159
South Lyon* 11,040
Southfield 76,818
St. Clair 5,933
St. Clair Shores* 61,561
Sterling Heights 128,034
Troy **81,168**
Utica 4,913
Walled Lake 6,919
Warren **135,311**
Waterford 73,150

Whitmore Lake* 6,574
Wixom 13,384
Wolverine Lake* 4,269

WASHINGTON-ARLINGTON-ALEXANDRIA, DC-VA-MD-WV

Accokeek *, MD 7,349
Adelphi *, MD 14,998
Alexandria, VA **135,337**
Annandale, VA 54,994
Aquia Harbour *, VA 7,856
Arlington, VA **195,965**
Bailey's Crossroads, VA 23,166
Belle Haven *, VA 6,269
Beltsville, MD 15,690
Bennsville *, MD 7,325
Berryville, VA 3,157
Berwyn Heights, MD 3,068
Bladensburg *, MD 7,918
Bowie *, MD 53,878
Brentwood, MD 2,937
Bryans Road, MD 4,912
Bull Run *, VA 11,337
Burke *, VA 57,737
Calverton, MD 12,610
Camp Springs *, MD 17,968
Capitol Heights, MD 4,313
Centreville *, VA 48,661
Chantilly, VA 41,041
Charles Town, WV 3,704
Chesapeake Beach, MD 3,463
Cheverly *, MD 6,668
Chillum *, MD 34,252
Clinton *, MD 26,064
College Park, MD 25,171
Coral Hills *, MD 10,720
Corporation of Ranson, WV .. 3,793
Dale City *, VA 55,971
District Heights *, MD 6,296
Dumfries, VA 4,816
Dunn Loring *, VA 7,861
East Riverdale *, MD 14,961
Fairfax, VA 21,963
Falls Church, VA 10,781
Falmouth, VA 3,624
Forest Heights, MD 2,679
Forestville, MD 12,707
Fort Hunt *, VA 12,923
Fort Washington *, MD 23,845
Franconia *, VA 31,907
Fredericksburg, VA 20,732
Friendly *, MD 10,938
Front Royal, VA 14,499
Gainesville, VA 4,382
Glenarden, MD 6,380
Glenn Dale *, MD 12,609
Goddard, MD 5,554
Great Falls *, VA 8,549
Greenbelt, MD 22,242
Groveton *, VA 21,296
Herndon, VA 21,965
Hillandale, MD 3,054
Hillcrest Heights *, MD 16,359
Huntington *, VA 8,325
Hyattsville, MD 16,677

Hybla Valley *, VA 16,721
Idylwood *, VA 16,005
Indian Head, MD 3,642
Jefferson *, VA 27,422
Kettering *, MD 11,008
La Plata, MD 8,442
Lake Arbor, MD 8,533
Lake Barcroft *, VA 8,906
Lake Ridge *, VA 30,404
Langley Park *, MD 16,214
Largo *, MD 8,408
Laurel, MD 22,125
Leesburg, VA 36,269
Lincolnia *, VA 15,788
Linton Hall *, VA 8,620
Loch Lomond, VA 3,411
Lorton *, VA 17,786
Manassas, VA 37,569
Manassas Park*, VA 11,622
Mantua *, VA 7,485
Marlow Heights, MD 6,059
Marlton *, MD 7,798
McLean, VA 38,929
Merrifield, VA 11,170
Mitchellville, MD 9,611
Montclair *, VA 15,728
Mount Rainier*, MD 8,751
Mount Vernon *, VA 28,582
New Carrollton*, MD 12,818
Newington, VA 19,784
North Springfield, VA 9,173
Oakton *, VA 29,348
Pimmit Hills *, VA 6,152
Purcellville, VA 4,680
Reston, VA 56,407
*Riverdale Park**, MD 6,630
Rosaryville *, MD 12,322
Rose Hill *, VA 15,058
Seat Pleasant, MD 5,063
Seven Corners *, VA 8,701
South Laurel *, MD 20,479
Spotsylvania Courthouse, VA 3,833
Springdale, MD 2,645
Springfield, VA 30,417
St. Charles *, MD 33,379
Sudley *, VA 7,719
Temple Hills *, MD 7,792
Triangle *, VA 5,500
Tysons Corner, VA 18,540
Vienna, VA 14,842
Waldorf, MD 22,312
Walker Mill *, MD 11,104
Warrenton, VA 8,635
Washington, DC **550,521**
West Gate *, VA 7,493
West Laurel, MD 4,083
West Springfield *, VA 28,378
Wolf Trap *, VA 14,001
Woodbridge, VA 31,941
Woodlawn *, MD 6,251
Woodmore *, MD 6,077
Yorkshire *, VA 6,732

WATERLOO-CEDAR FALLS, IA

Cedar Falls	**36,471**
Evansdale	4,585
Grundy Center	2,583
Waterloo	**66,483**
Waverly	9,298

WAUSAU, WI

Evergreen	3,611
Kronenwetter	6,228
Mosinee	3,996
Rib Mountain	6,059
Rothschild	5,096
Wausau	**37,292**
Weston*	12,921

WEIRTON-STEUBENVILLE, WV-OH

Follansbee, WV	2,971
Hooverson Heights, WV	2,909
Mingo Junction, OH	3,426
Steubenville, OH	**19,314**
Toronto, OH	5,402
Weirton, WV	**19,544**
Wellsburg, WV	2,727
Wintersville, OH	3,889

WENATCHEE, WA

Cashmere	2,985
Chelan	3,684
East Wenatchee	8,819
East Wenatchee Bench *	13,658
Sunnyslope	2,521
Wenatchee	**29,374**

WEST PALM BEACH-BOCA RATON-BOYNTON BEACH, FL

Belle Glade	15,423
Boca Del Mar *	21,832
Boca Pointe	3,302
Boca Raton	**86,632**
Boynton Beach	**66,885**
Century Village	7,616
Delray Beach	64,757
Golden Lakes	6,694
Greenacres*	32,525
Hamptons at Boca Raton *	11,306
Highland Beach	4,123
Hypoluxo	2,612
Juno Beach	3,395
Jupiter	47,909
Kings Point	12,207
Lake Clarke Shores	3,460
Lake Park	9,039
Lake Worth*	36,342
Lakeside Green	3,311
Lantana	10,498
Mission Bay	2,926
North Palm Beach	12,633
Pahokee	6,554
Palm Beach	9,852
Palm Beach Gardens	48,989
Palm Springs*	15,267

Riviera Beach	33,772
Royal Palm Beach*	30,886
Royal Palm Estates	3,583
Sandalfoot Cove *	16,582
Seminole Manor	2,546
South Bay	4,059
Tequesta	5,989
Villages of Oriole	4,758
Wellington*	53,583
West Palm Beach	**97,498**
Whisper Walk	5,135

WHEELING, WV-OH

Barnesville, OH	4,149
Bellaire, OH	4,738
Bethlehem, WV	2,547
Martins Ferry, OH	6,860
Moundsville, WV	9,567
Shadyside, OH	3,562
St. Clairsville, OH	5,075
Wheeling, WV	**29,639**

WICHITA, KS

Andover	9,114
Augusta*	8,608
Bel Aire*	6,557
Derby*	20,543
El Dorado	12,659
Goddard	3,337
Haysville*	9,817
Hesston	3,631
Mulvane	5,628
Newton	18,229
Park City*	7,173
Rose Hill	3,896
Valley Center	5,508
Wellington	8,098
Wichita	**354,865**

WICHITA FALLS, TX

Burkburnett*	10,378
Electra	2,938
Henrietta	3,325
Iowa Park*	6,175
Wichita Falls	**99,846**

WILLIAMSPORT, PA

Garden View	2,679
Montoursville borough	4,628
Muncy borough	2,533
South Williamsport borough*	6,189
Williamsport	**30,112**

WILMINGTON, DE-MD-NJ

Bear *, DE	17,593
Brookside *, DE	14,806
Carneys Point *, NJ	6,914
Claymont *, DE	9,220
Edgemoor, DE	5,992
Elkton, MD	14,466
Elsmere*, DE	5,722
Glasgow *, DE	12,840
Hockessin *, DE	12,902

Middletown, DE	9,121
New Castle, DE	4,836
Newark, DE	30,060
North East, MD	2,817
North Star *, DE	8,277
Penns Grove borough, NJ	4,824
Pennsville, NJ	11,657
Perryville, MD	3,770
Pike Creek *, DE	19,751
Salem, NJ	5,812
Wilmington Manor *, DE	8,262
Wilmington, DE	**72,786**
Woodstown borough, NJ	3,312

WILMINGTON, NC

Bayshore	2,512
Boiling Spring Lakes	4,107
Burgaw	3,756
Carolina Beach*	5,388
Kings Grant *	7,738
Leland	4,440
Masonboro *	11,812
Murraysville *	7,279
Myrtle Grove *	7,125
Oak Island*	7,679
Ogden *	5,481
Seagate	4,590
Silver Lake *	5,788
Southport	2,725
Wilmington	**95,476**
Wrightsboro	4,496
Wrightsville Beach	2,567

WINCHESTER, VA-WV

Middletown, VA	1,098
Romney, WV	1,975
Stephens, VA	1,247
Winchester, VA	**25,119**

WINSTON-SALEM, NC

Clemmons	16,430
Kernersville	21,360
King	6,353
Lewisville*	9,547
Mocksville	4,464
Rural Hall	2,577
Walkertown	4,294
Winston-Salem	**193,755**
Yadkinville	2,867

WORCESTER, MA

Ashburnham	5,981
Athol	11,697
Auburn	16,400
Barre	5,380
Berlin	2,689
Blackstone	9,057
Bolton	4,435
Boylston	4,259
Brookfield	3,096
Charlton	12,475
Clinton	13,995
Clinton	7,884

Cordaville............................2,515
Douglas 7,885
Dudley 10,812
Fitchburg.............................40,045
Gardner...............................20,908
Grafton 16,890
Hardwick.............................2,655
Harvard...............................6,074
Holden 16,592
Hopedale.............................6,243
Hubbardston.........................4,352
Lancaster.............................6,845
Leicester.............................10,967
Leominster...........................41,804
Lunenburg............................10,024
Mendon...............................5,754
Milford.................................27,519
Millbury...............................13,459
Millville................................2,943
North Brookfield 4,814
Northborough.......................14,675
Northbridge 14,216
Oxford.................................13,718
Oxford*...............................5,899
Paxton 4,558
Princeton 3,523
Rutland 7,446
Shrewsbury..........................33,174
Southborough.......................9,559
Southbridge.........................17,234
Spencer 12,092
Sterling 7,770
Sturbridge............................8,860
Sutton 8,989
Templeton 7,491
Upton 6,397
Uxbridge 12,409
Warren 5,045
Webster 16,851
West Boylston.......................7,699
West Brookfield 3,895
Westborough 18,732
Westminster.........................7,370

Whitinsville 6,340
Winchendon..........................10,104
Worcester 175,898

YAKIMA, WA

Ahtanum 4,181
Gleed 2,947
Grandview 8,908
Granger 2,836
Selah 6,875
Sunnyside 14,426
Terrace Heights*....................6,447
Toppenish 9,207
Union Gap 5,707
Wapato 4,619
West Valley* 10,433
White Swan 3,033
Yakima 81,214
Zillah 2,599

YORK-HANOVER, PA

Dallastown borough..............4,080
East York 8,782
Grantley 3,580
Hallam borough 2,513
Hanover borough 14,990
New Freedom borough.........3,889
Parkville*..............................6,593
Red Lion borough.................6,084
Shiloh..................................10,192
Shrewsbury borough 3,525
Spry*...................................4,903
Valley Green 3,550
Valley View 2,743
Weigelstown*........................10,117
West York borough...............4,230
York..................................40,418

YOUNGSTOWN-WARREN-BOARDMAN, OH-PA

Austintown *, OH 31,627
Boardman, OH 37,215

Campbell*, OH......................8,888
Canfield, OH.........................7,153
Churchill*, OH 2,601
Cortland*, OH 6,640
Farrell, PA............................5,999
Girard*, OH 10,490
Greenville borough, PA 6,355
Grove City borough, PA.........7,764
Hermitage, PA 16,571
Howland Center, OH..............6,481
Hubbard*, OH 8,006
Lordstown, OH......................3,636
Masury, OH 2,618
McDonald, OH.......................3,357
Mineral Ridge, OH.................3,900
Newton Falls, OH 4,833
Niles, OH 20,016
Poland, OH 2,750
Sebring, OH 4,706
Sharon, PA 15,504
Sharpsville borough, PA........4,281
Struthers*, OH 11,240
Warren, OH......................45,796
West Hill, OH 2,523
Youngstown, OH...............82,837

YUBA CITY, CA

Linda*..................................13,474
Live Oak 7,128
Marysville 12,131
Olivehurst*............................11,061
South Yuba City* 12,651
Sutter...................................2,885
Tierra Buena.........................4,587
Wheatland 3,638
Yuba City 58,628

YUMA, AZ

Fortuna Foothills* 20,478
San Luis* 21,646
Somerton.............................10,071
Yuma...................................84,688

Index

P–Y

Notes

Notes

Notes

Notes

Notes

Notes

Notes

Notes

Notes

Notes